Story & Art by
Rumiko Takahashi

INUYASHA

Volume 14
VIZBIG Edition

Story and Art by RUMIKO TAKAHASHI

English Adaptation/Gerard Jones
Translation/Mari Morimoto
Transcription/David Smith
Touch-up Art & Lettering/Steve Dutro, Leonard Clark, Primary Graphix
VIZ Media Series Design/Yuki Ameda
VIZBIG Edition Design/Sam Elzway
VIZ Media Series Editors (VIZ Media/Action Edition)/
Shaenon K. Garrity & Annette Roman
VIZBIG Edition Editor/Annette Roman

The stories, characters and incidents mentioned in
this publication are entirely fictional.

Printed in China

Published by VIZ Media, LLC
P.O. Box 77010
San Francisco, CA 94107

10 9 8 7 6 5 4 3 2 1
First printing, February 2013

InuYasha

Volume 40
One Soul

Volume 41
The Invincible Blade

Volume 42
Meido Zangetsuha

Story & Art by
Rumiko Takahashi

Shonen Sunday Manga / VIZBIG Edition

CONTENTS

Volume 42: Meido Zangetsuha

CAST OF CHARACTERS

Kagome
A modern-day Japanese schoolgirl who is the rein-carnation of Kikyo, the priestess who imprisoned Inuyasha for fifty years with her enchanted arrow. As Kikyo's reincarnation, Kagome has the power to see the Shikon Jewel shards.

Inuyasha
A half-human, half-demon hybrid, Inuyasha has doglike ears and demonic strength. He assists Kagome in her search for the shards of the Shikon Jewel, mostly because a charmed necklace allows Kagome to restrain him with a single word.

Naraku
This enigmatic demon is responsible for both Miroku's curse and for turning Kikyo and Inuyasha against each other.

Kanna
Kanna is Naraku's first incarnation and the one he trusts the most. Her demonic mirror steals souls and the powers of those it reflects.

Totosai
The fire-breathing old blacksmith who forged Inuyasha's blade Tetsusaiga and Sesshomaru's blade Tenseiga.

Kohaku
Naraku controlled Kohaku with a Shikon shard, then resurrected him after he was killed and used him as a puppet. Kohaku has regained his memories and is trying to redeem himself.

Miroku

An easygoing Buddhist priest of questionable morals. Miroku bears a curse passed down from his grandfather and is searching for the demon Naraku, who first inflicted the curse.

Kikyo

A village priestess who was the original protector of the Shikon Jewel. She died fifty years ago.

Sango

A proud Demon Slayer from the village where the first Shikon Jewel was born. Her clan and family lost, she fights on against the demonic Naraku along with Inuyasha.

Shippo

A young orphan fox demon. The mischievous Shippo enjoys goading Inuyasha and playing tricks with his shape-shifting abilities.

The Infant

Naraku's heart is safely housed inside the body of the Infant that he created. The Infant enables Naraku to avoid being influenced by the heart's feelings and to survive even if his primary body is killed.

Sesshomaru

Inuyasha's half brother by the same demon father, Sesshomaru is a pureblood demon who covets the sword left to Inuyasha by their father.

InuYasha

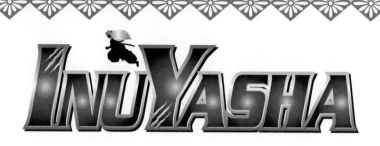

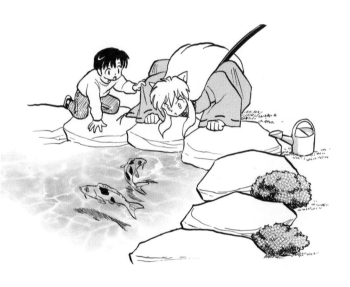

Volume 40
One Soul

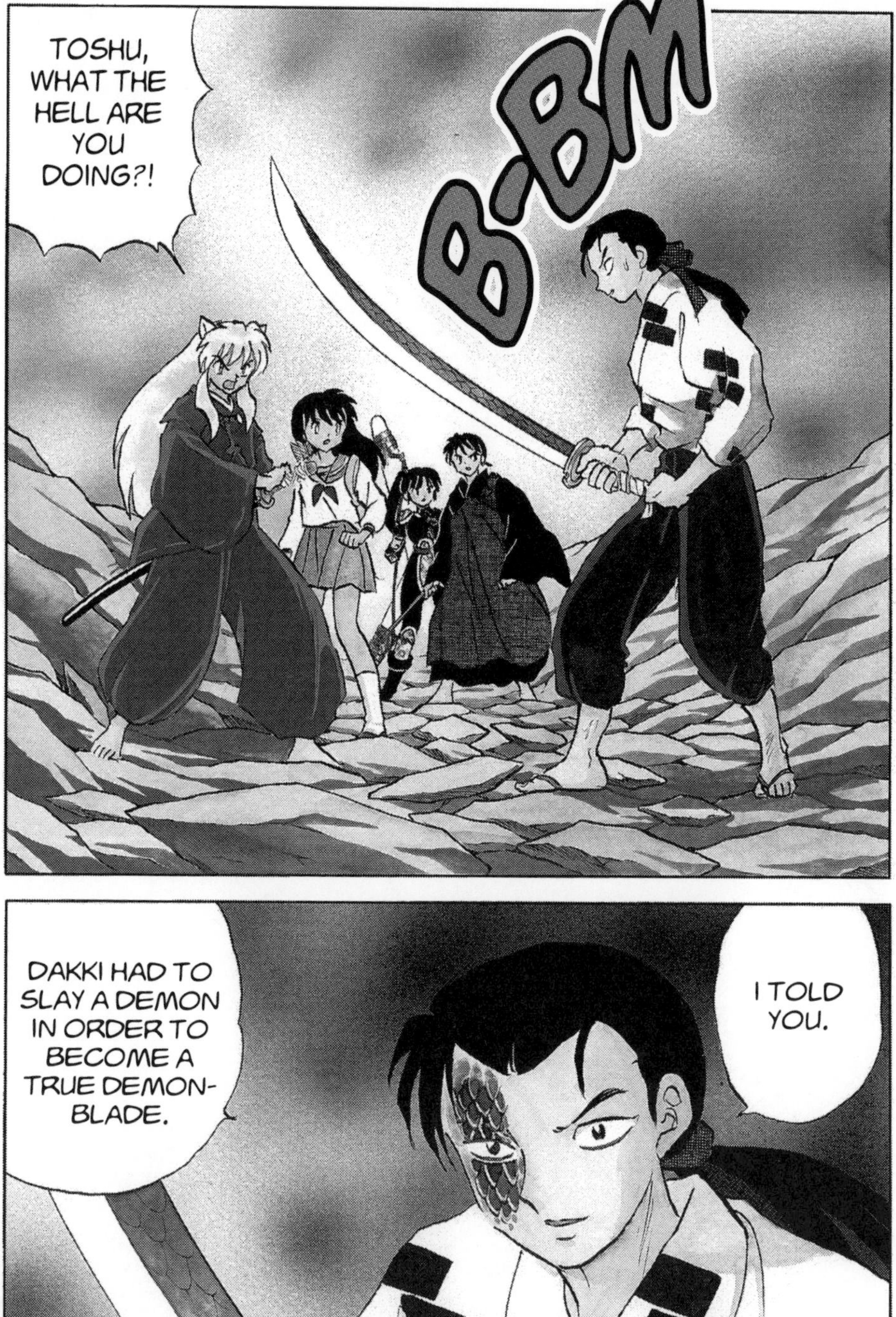
B-BM
TOSHU, WHAT THE HELL ARE YOU DOING?!
I TOLD YOU.
DAKKI HAD TO SLAY A DEMON IN ORDER TO BECOME A TRUE DEMON-BLADE.

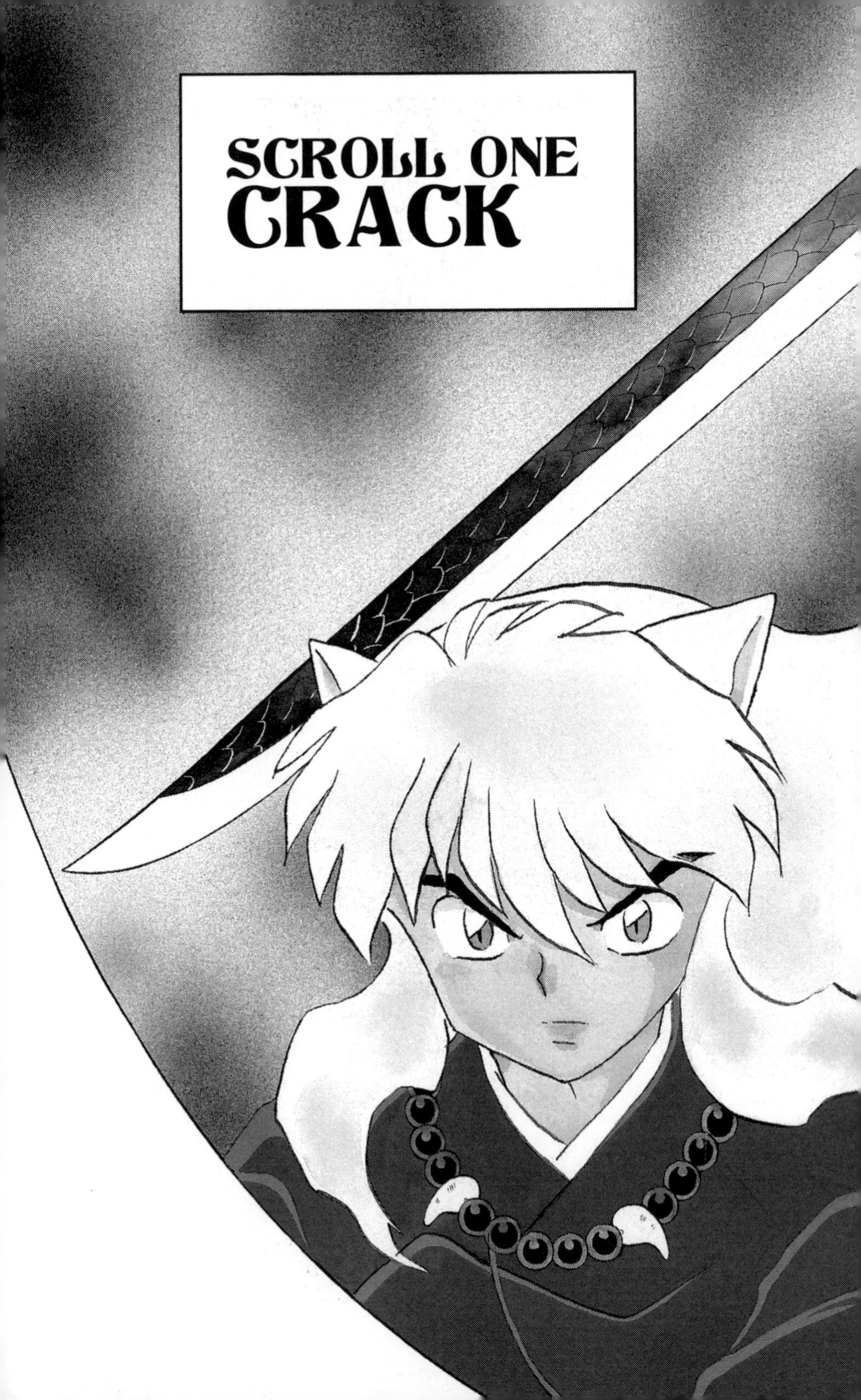
SCROLL ONE
CRACK

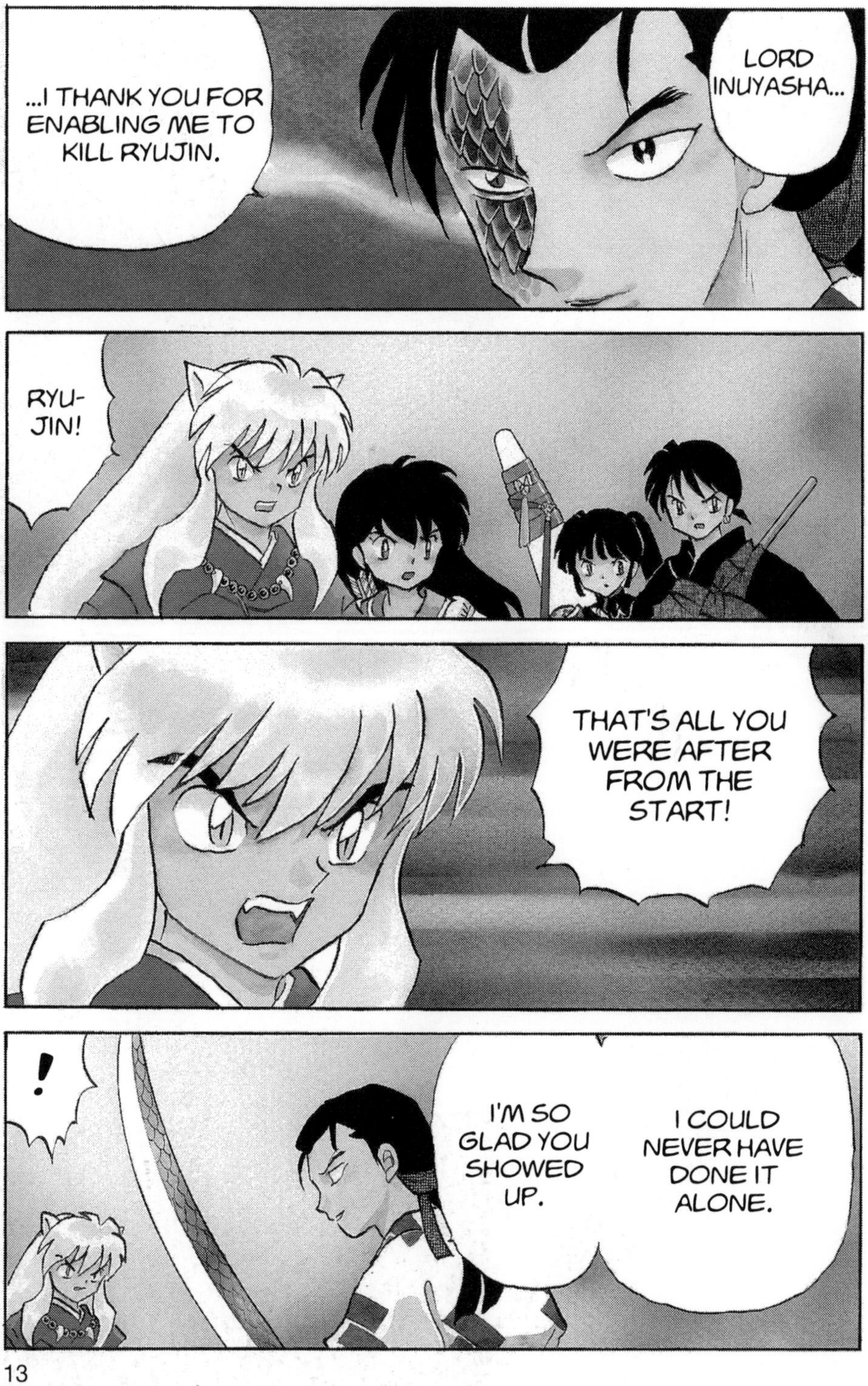
LORD INUYASHA...
...I THANK YOU FOR ENABLING ME TO KILL RYUJIN.
RYU-JIN!
THAT'S ALL YOU WERE AFTER FROM THE START!
I COULD NEVER HAVE DONE IT ALONE.
I'M SO GLAD YOU SHOWED UP.
!

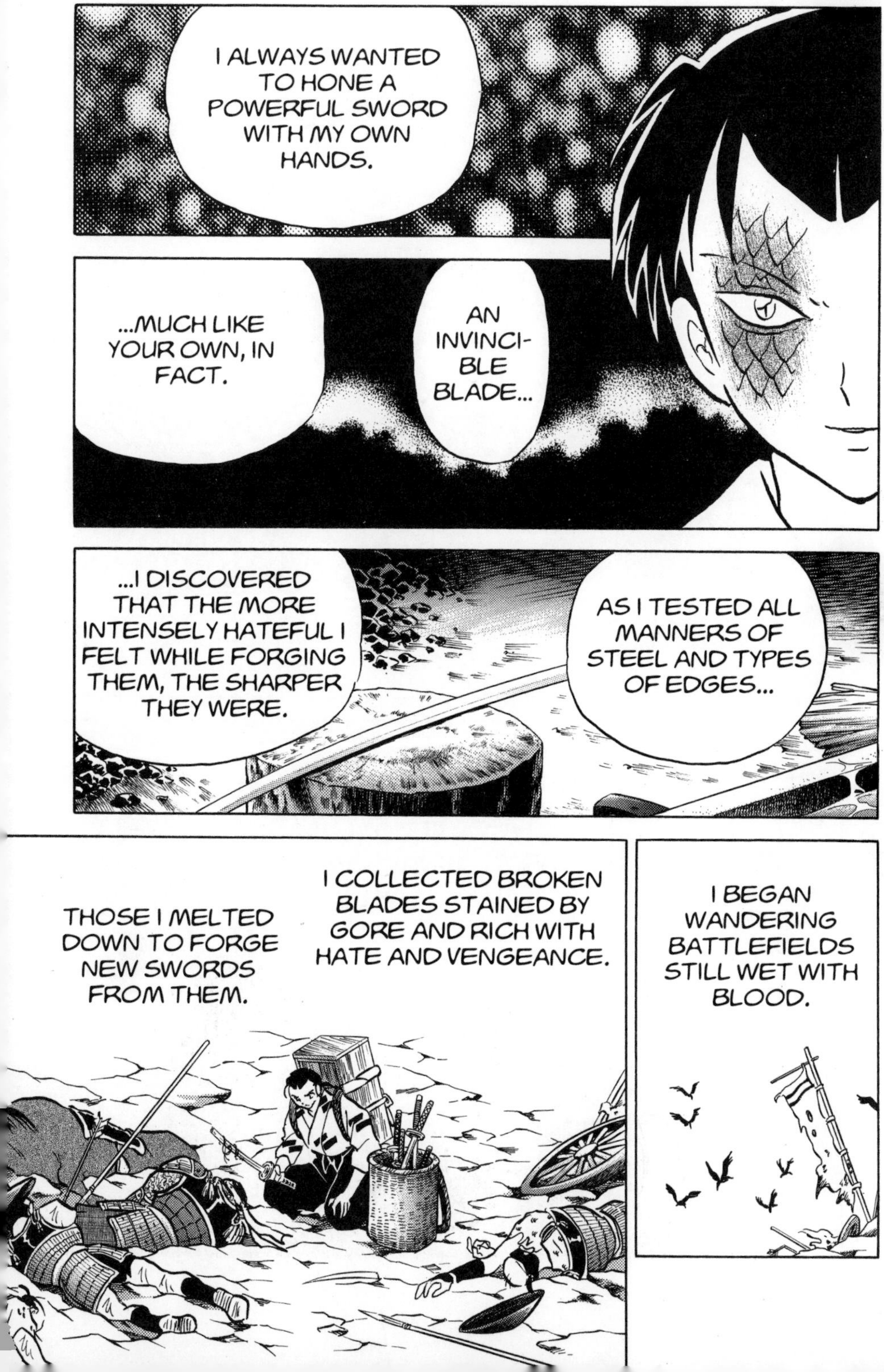
I ALWAYS WANTED TO HONE A POWERFUL SWORD WITH MY OWN HANDS.
AN INVINCI-BLE BLADE...
...MUCH LIKE YOUR OWN, IN FACT.
AS I TESTED ALL MANNERS OF STEEL AND TYPES OF EDGES...
...I DISCOVERED THAT THE MORE INTENSELY HATEFUL I FELT WHILE FORGING THEM, THE SHARPER THEY WERE.
I BEGAN WANDERING BATTLEFIELDS STILL WET WITH BLOOD.
I COLLECTED BROKEN BLADES STAINED BY GORE AND RICH WITH HATE AND VENGEANCE.
THOSE I MELTED DOWN TO FORGE NEW SWORDS FROM THEM.

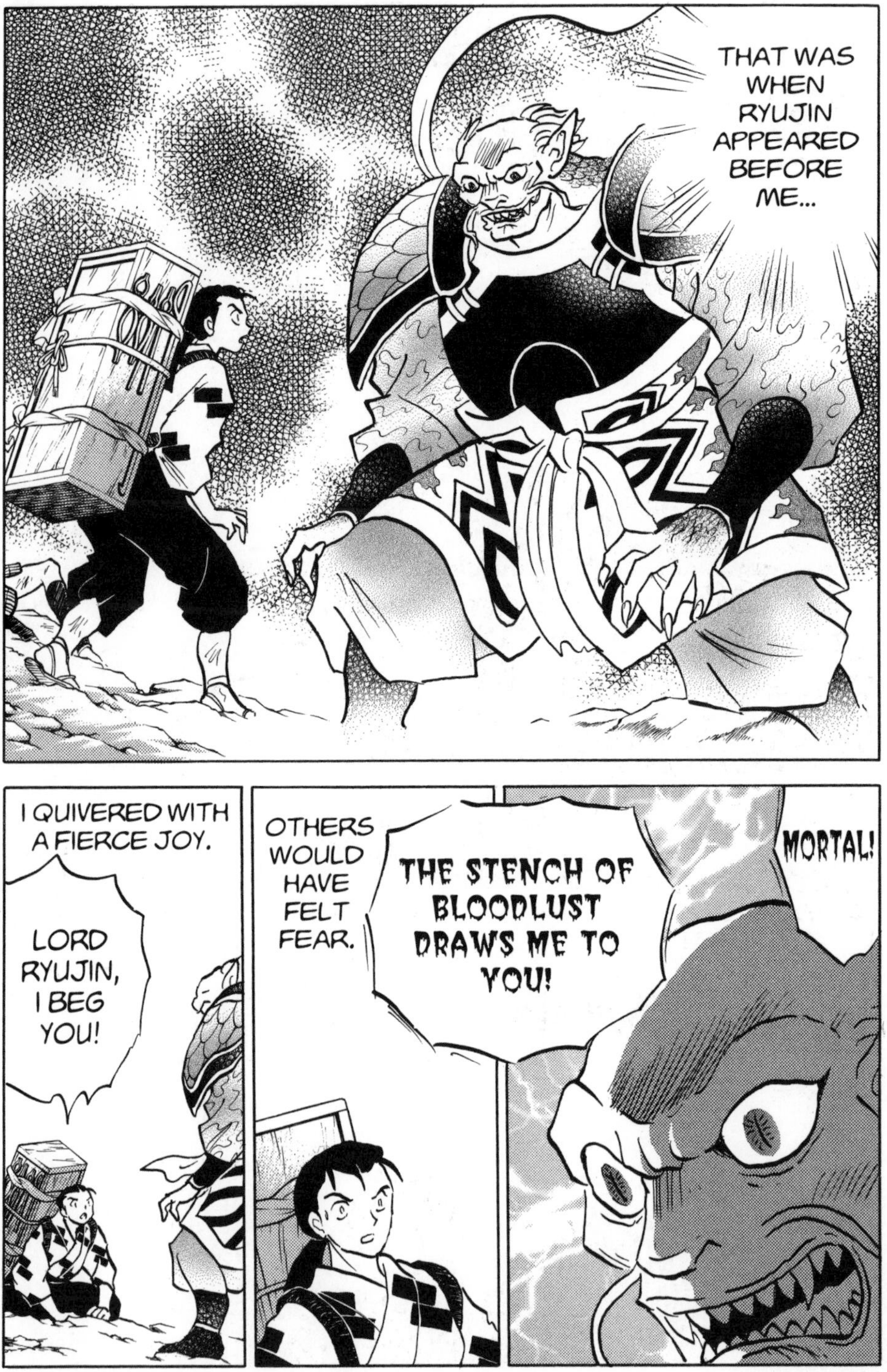
THAT WAS WHEN RYUJIN APPEARED BEFORE ME...
MORTAL!
THE STENCH OF BLOODLUST DRAWS ME TO YOU!
OTHERS WOULD HAVE FELT FEAR.
I QUIVERED WITH A FIERCE JOY.
LORD RYUJIN, I BEG YOU!

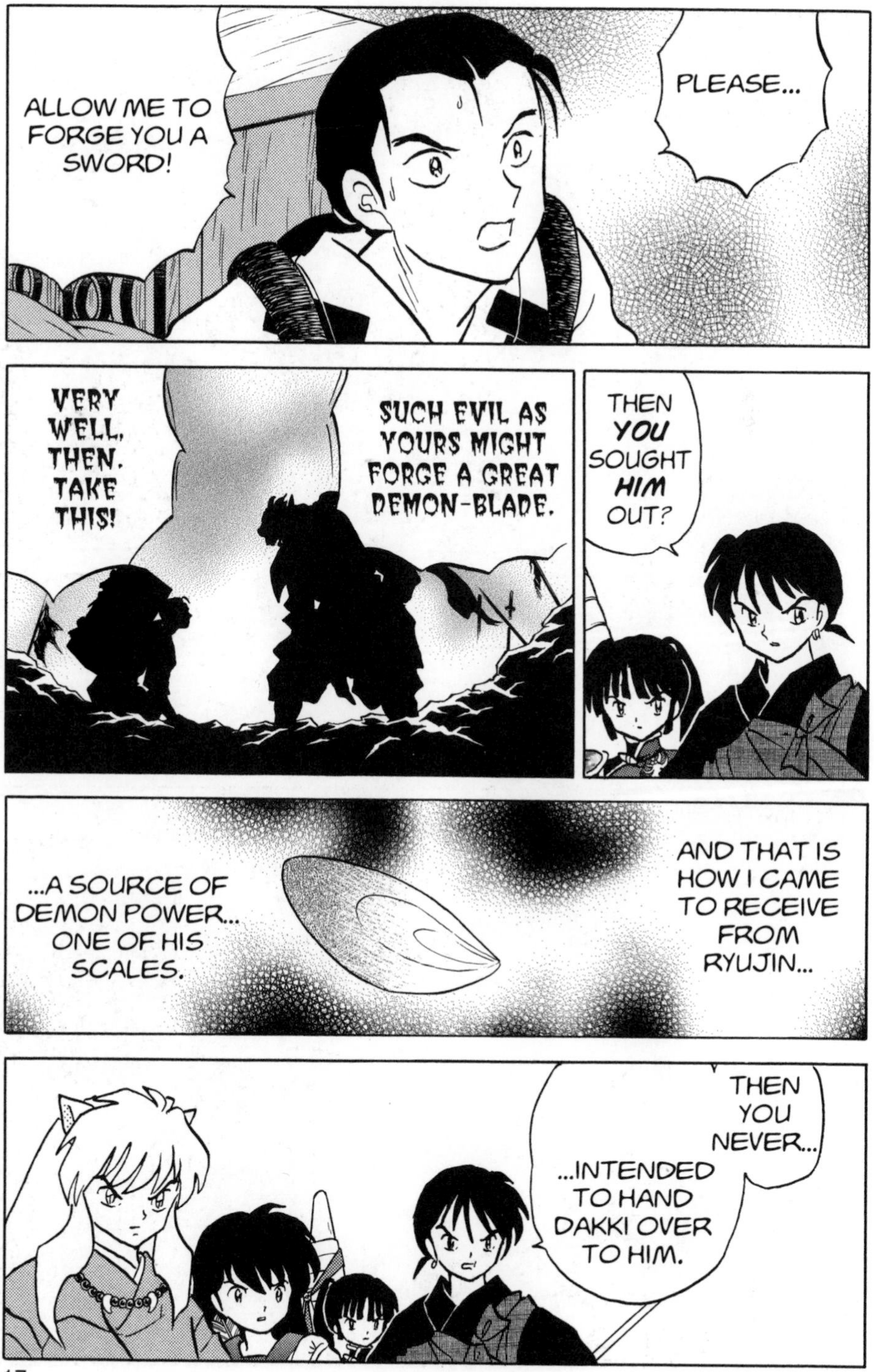
PLEASE...
ALLOW ME TO FORGE YOU A SWORD!
THEN YOU SOUGHT HIM OUT?
SUCH EVIL AS YOURS MIGHT FORGE A GREAT DEMON-BLADE.
VERY WELL, THEN. TAKE THIS!
AND THAT IS HOW I CAME TO RECEIVE FROM RYUJIN...
...A SOURCE OF DEMON POWER... ONE OF HIS SCALES.
THEN YOU NEVER...
...INTENDED TO HAND DAKKI OVER TO HIM.

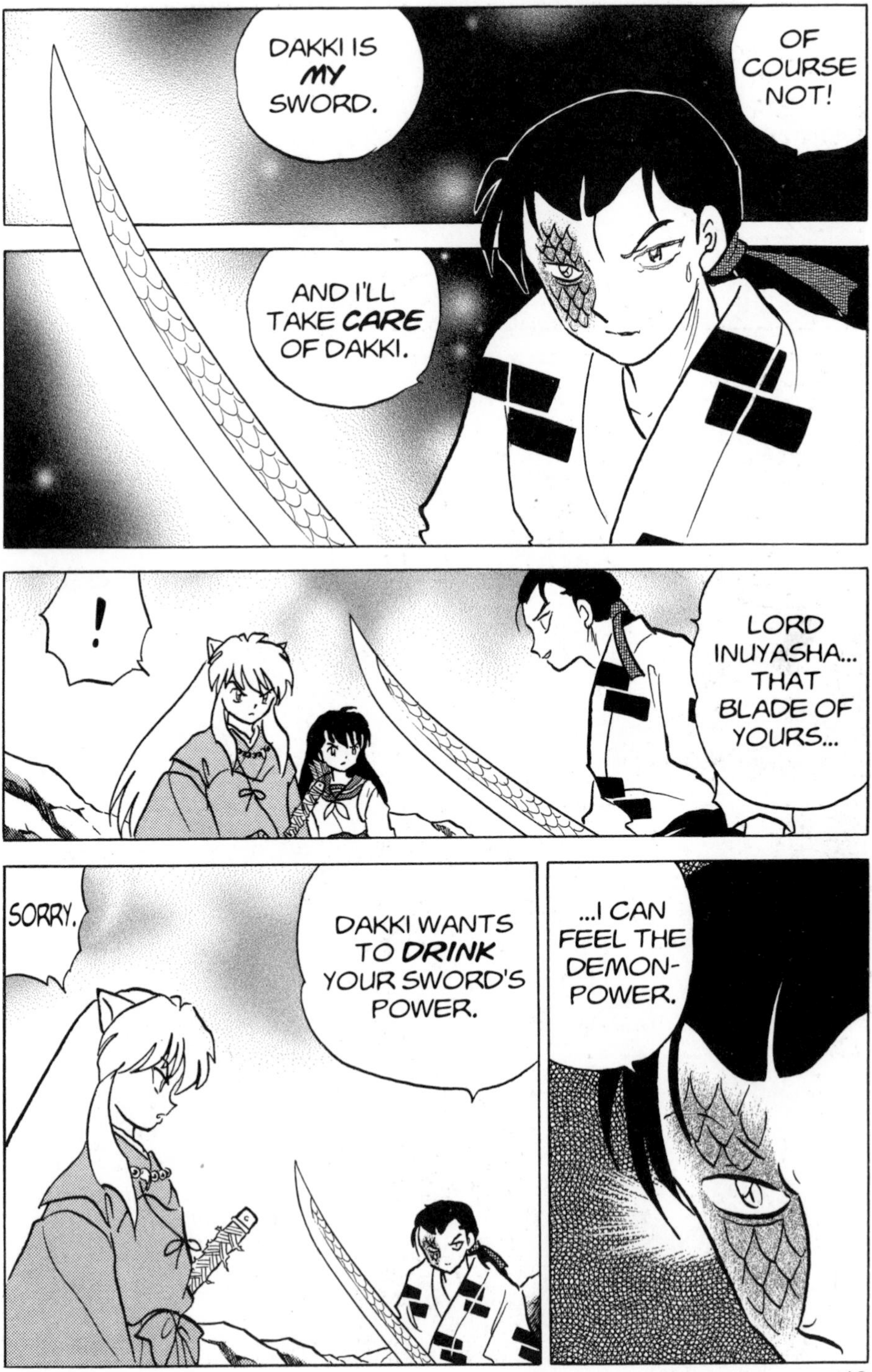
OF COURSE NOT!
DAKKI IS MY SWORD.
AND I'LL TAKE CARE OF DAKKI.
LORD INUYASHA... THAT BLADE OF YOURS...
!
...I CAN FEEL THE DEMON-POWER.
DAKKI WANTS TO DRINK YOUR SWORD'S POWER.
SORRY.

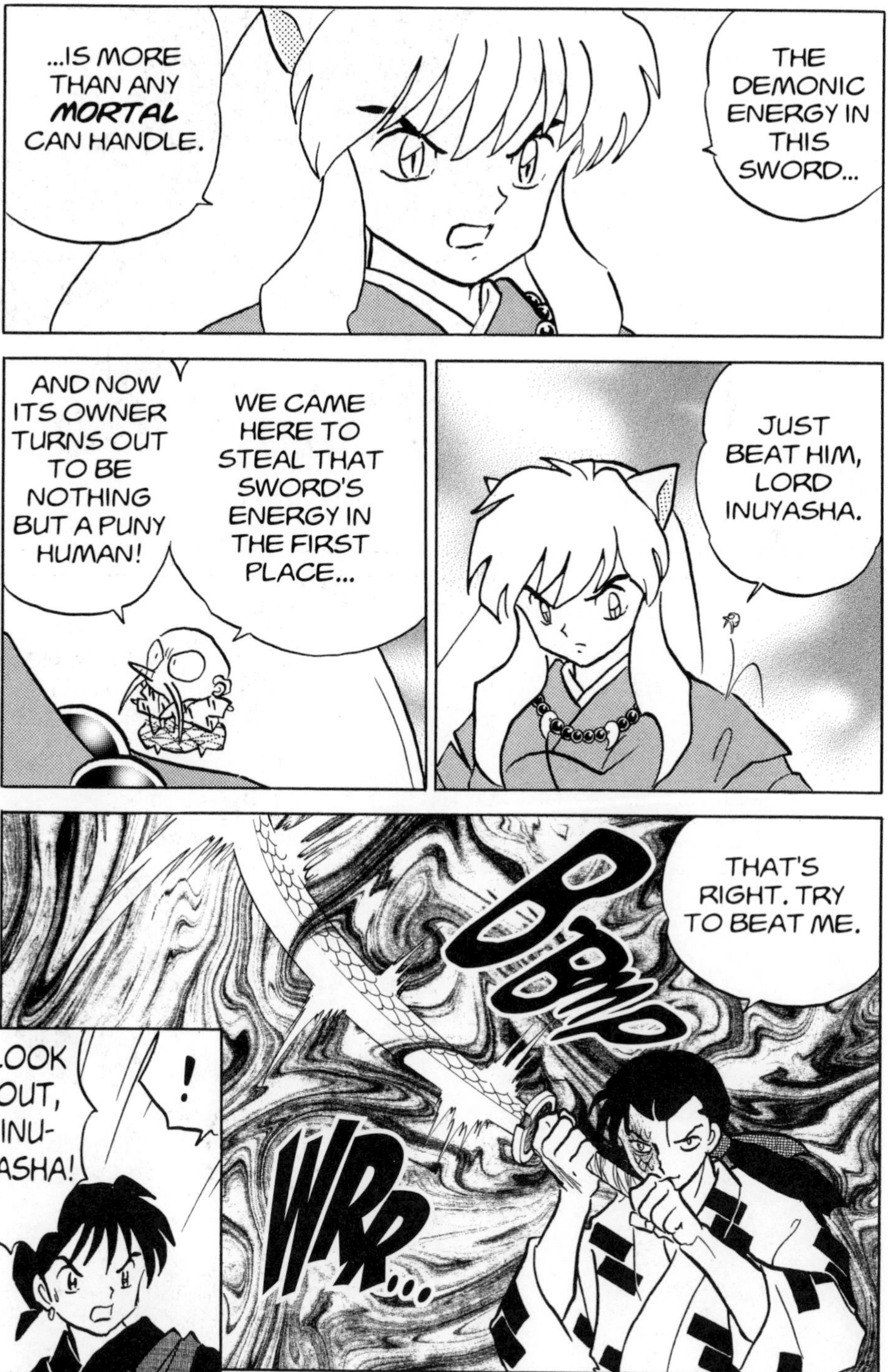
THE DEMONIC ENERGY IN THIS SWORD...
...IS MORE THAN ANY *MORTAL* CAN HANDLE.
JUST BEAT HIM, LORD INUYASHA.
WE CAME HERE TO STEAL THAT SWORD'S ENERGY IN THE FIRST PLACE...
AND NOW ITS OWNER TURNS OUT TO BE NOTHING BUT A PUNY HUMAN!
THAT'S RIGHT. TRY TO BEAT ME.
WRR...
!
LOOK OUT, INU-YASHA!

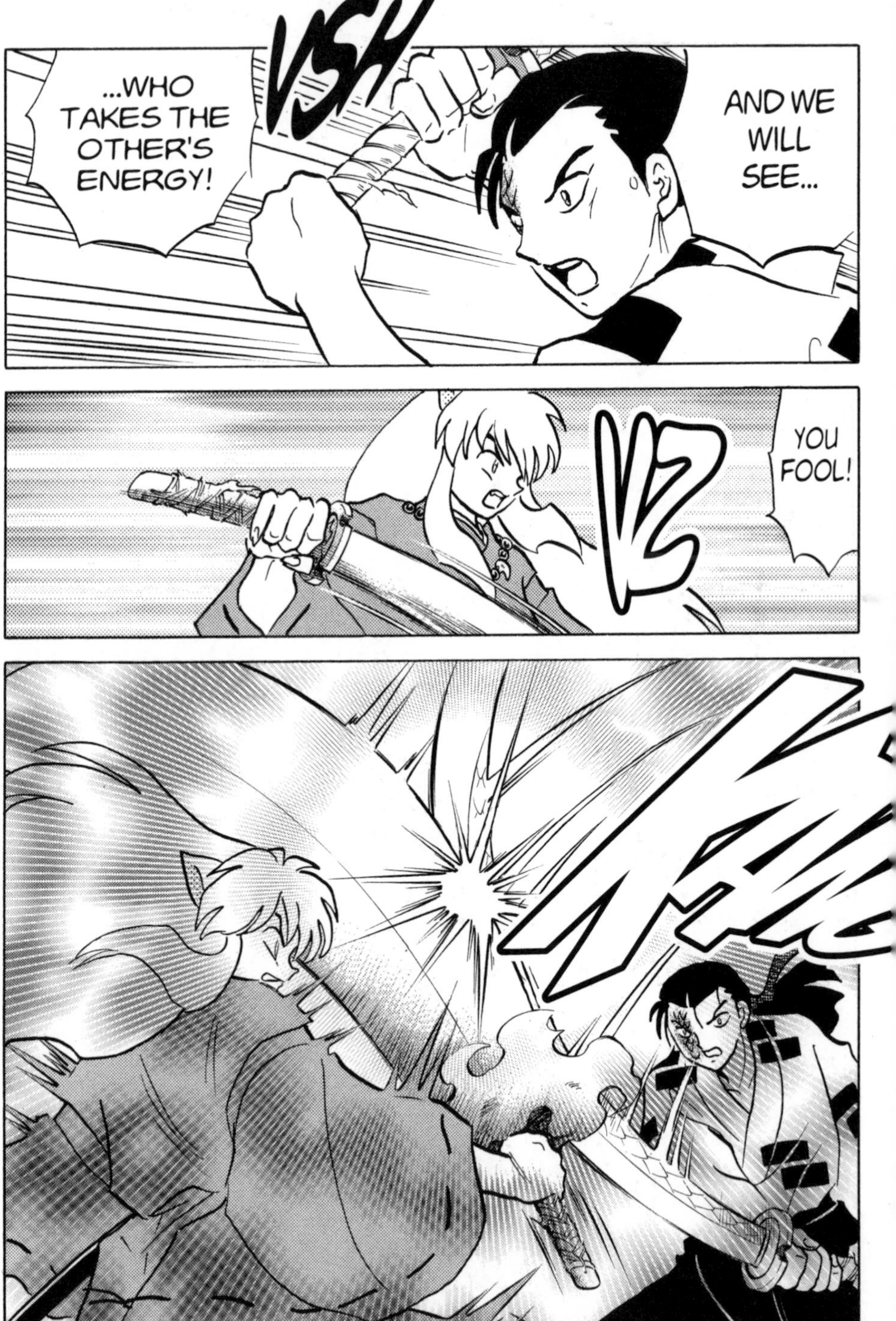
AND WE WILL SEE...
VSH
...WHO TAKES THE OTHER'S ENERGY!
YOU FOOL!

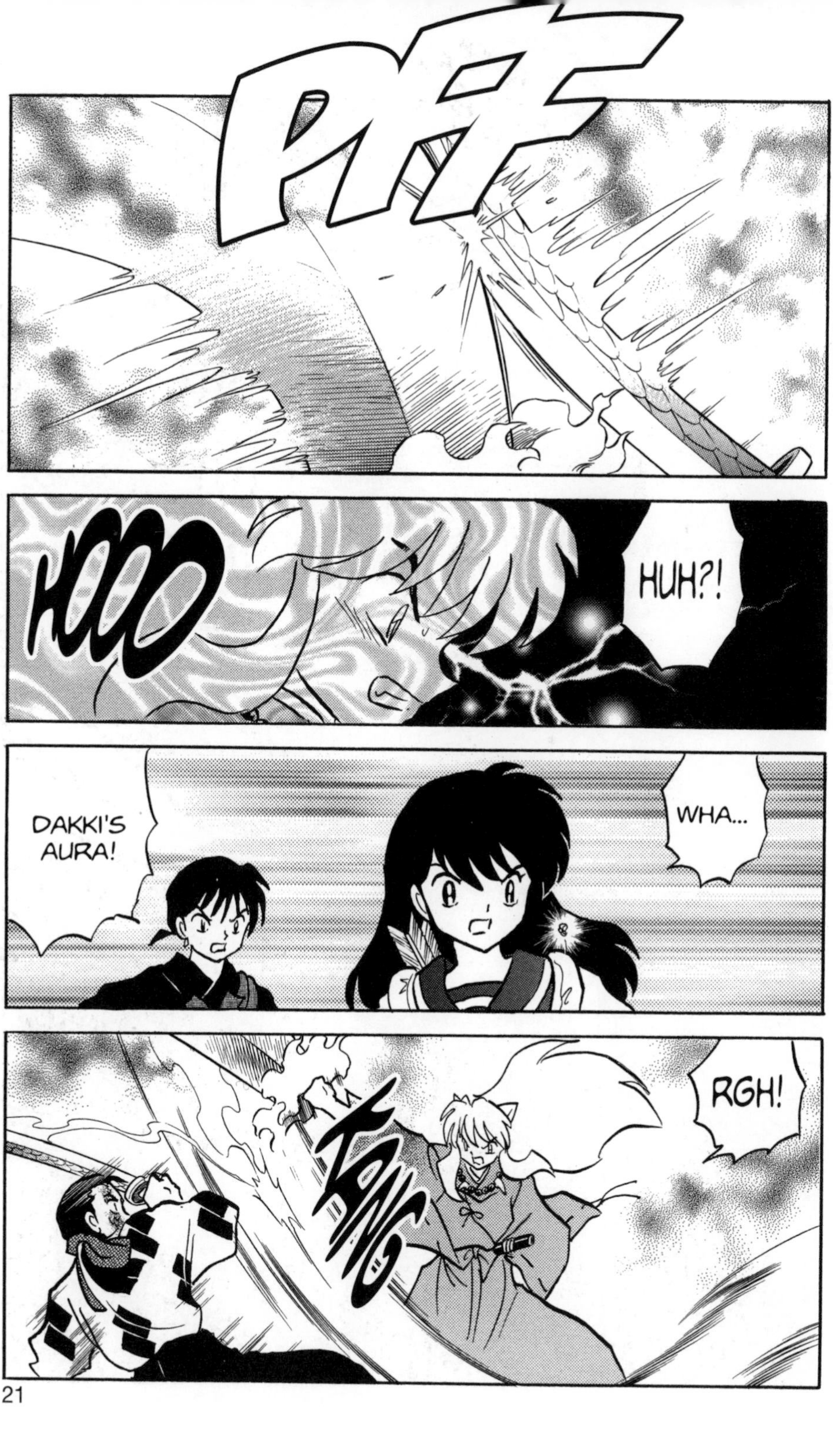
PFFF
HUH?!
HOOO
WHA...
DAKKI'S AURA!
RGH!
KANG

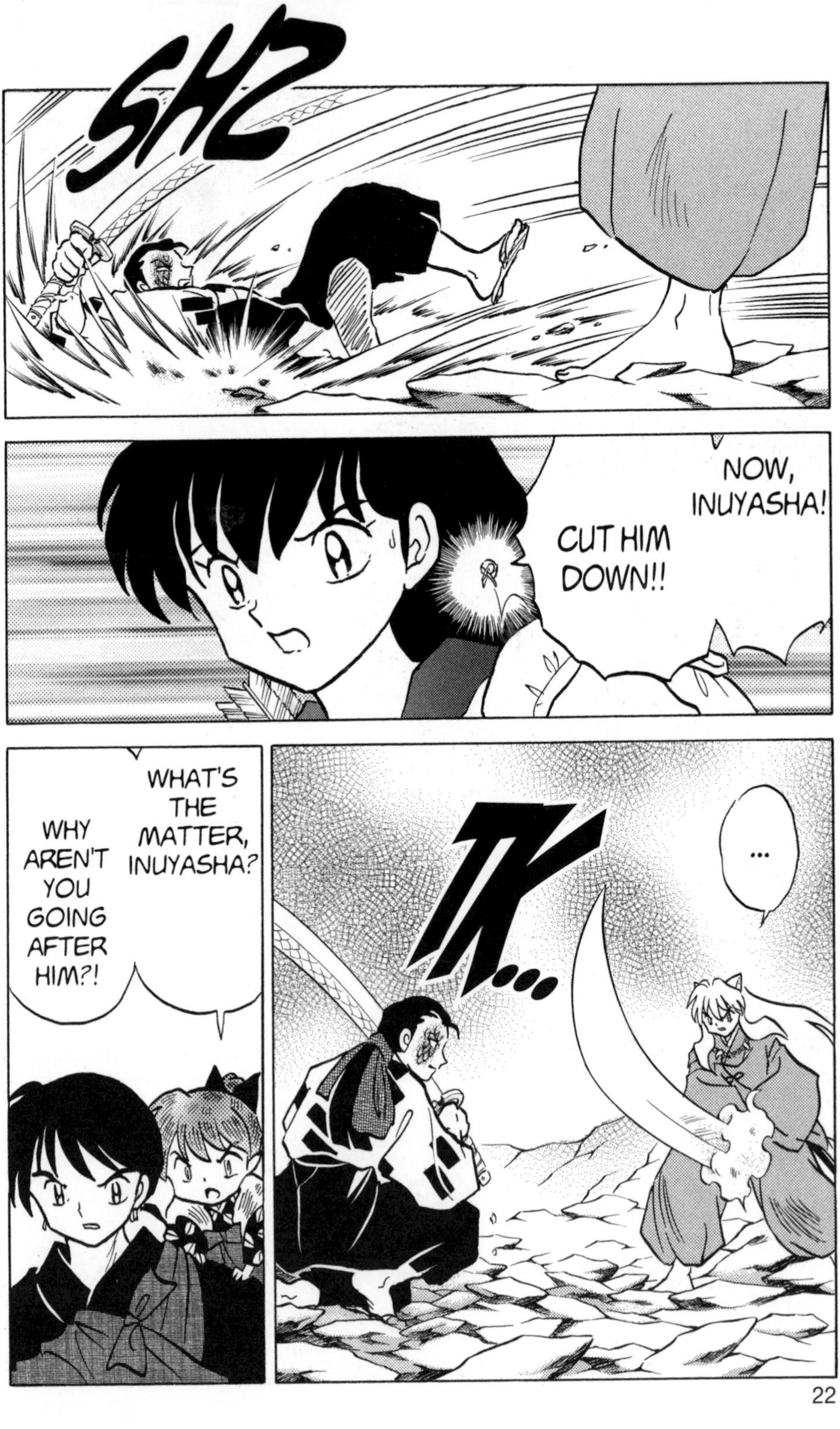
SHZ
NOW, INUYASHA!
CUT HIM DOWN!!
...
TK...
WHAT'S THE MATTER, INUYASHA?
WHY AREN'T YOU GOING AFTER HIM?!

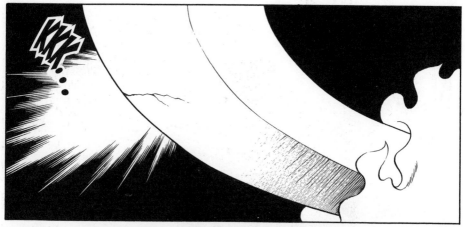

A CRACK IN TETSU-SAIGA!

OH...!

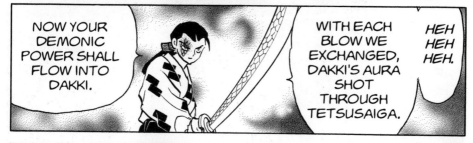

NOW YOUR DEMONIC POWER SHALL FLOW INTO DAKKI.

WITH EACH BLOW WE EXCHANGED, DAKKI'S AURA SHOT THROUGH TETSUSAIGA.

HEH HEH HEH.

WITH EACH BLOW, EH...?

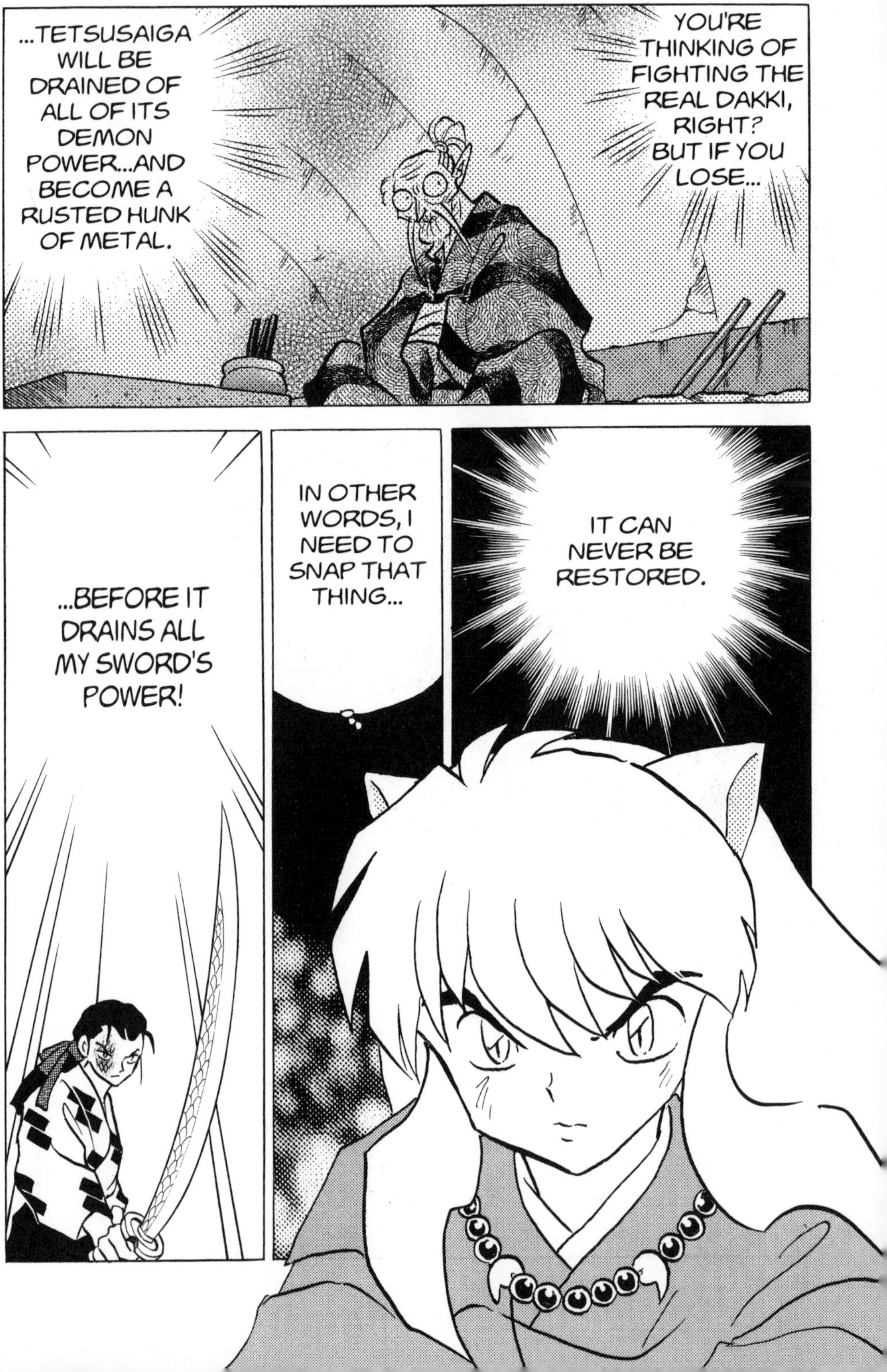
YOU'RE THINKING OF FIGHTING THE REAL DAKKI, RIGHT? BUT IF YOU LOSE...
...TETSUSAIGA WILL BE DRAINED OF ALL OF ITS DEMON POWER...AND BECOME A RUSTED HUNK OF METAL.
IT CAN NEVER BE RESTORED.
IN OTHER WORDS, I NEED TO SNAP THAT THING...
...BEFORE IT DRAINS ALL MY SWORD'S POWER!

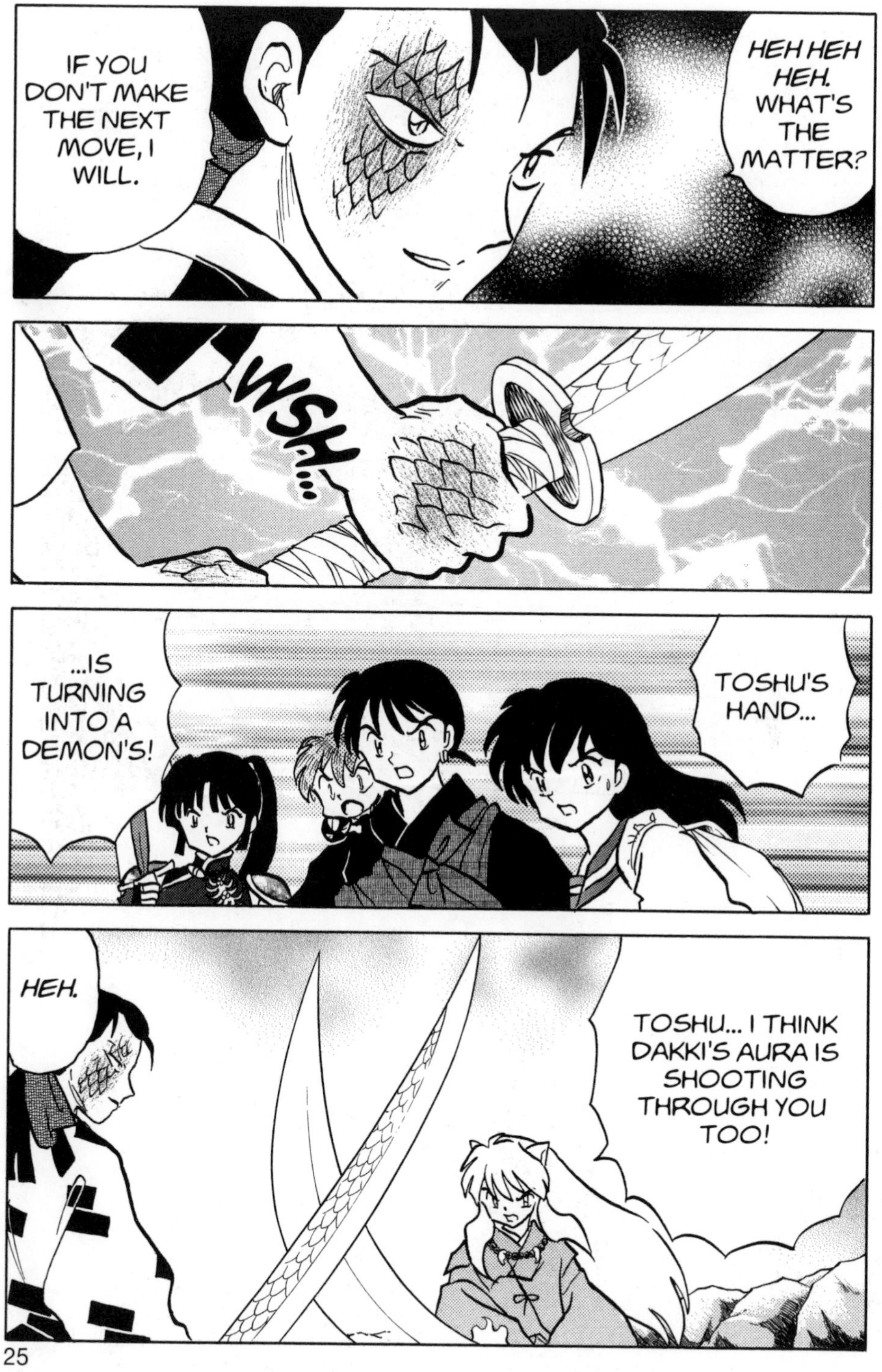
HEH HEH HEH. WHAT'S THE MATTER?
IF YOU DON'T MAKE THE NEXT MOVE, I WILL.
WSH...
TOSHU'S HAND...
...IS TURNING INTO A DEMON'S!
TOSHU... I THINK DAKKI'S AURA IS SHOOTING THROUGH YOU TOO!
HEH.

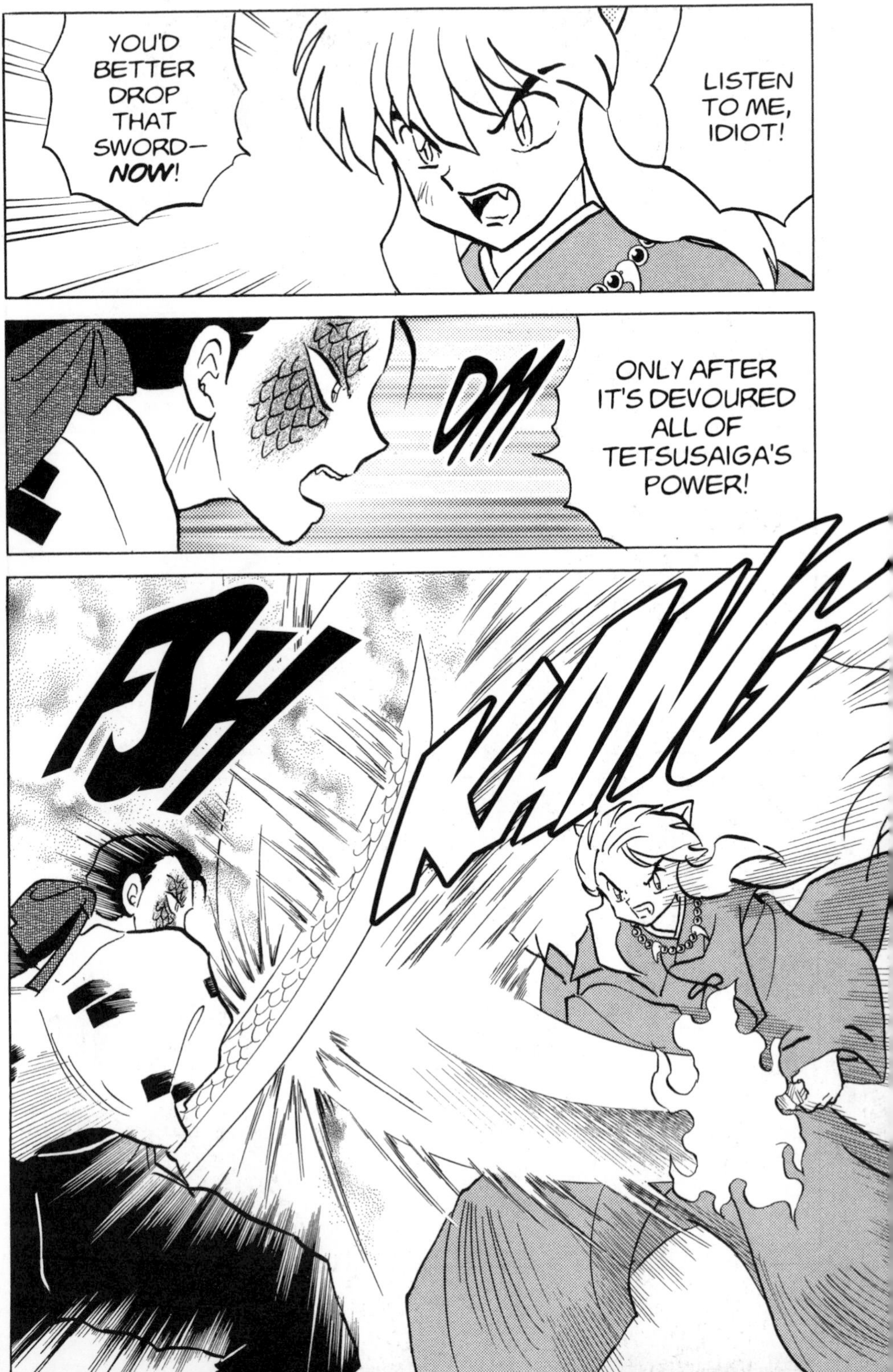
LISTEN TO ME, IDIOT!
YOU'D BETTER DROP THAT SWORD—*NOW*!
ONLY AFTER IT'S DEVOURED ALL OF TETSUSAIGA'S POWER!
DM
FSH

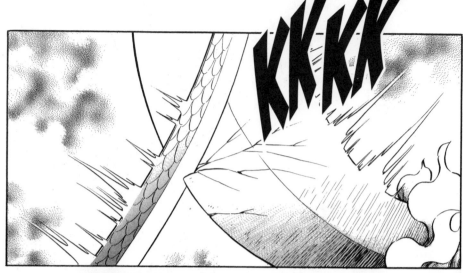

AGH...

AHHH...
THE
POWER
FLOWING
INTO ME...

KK.

M-MORE
CRACKS
...!

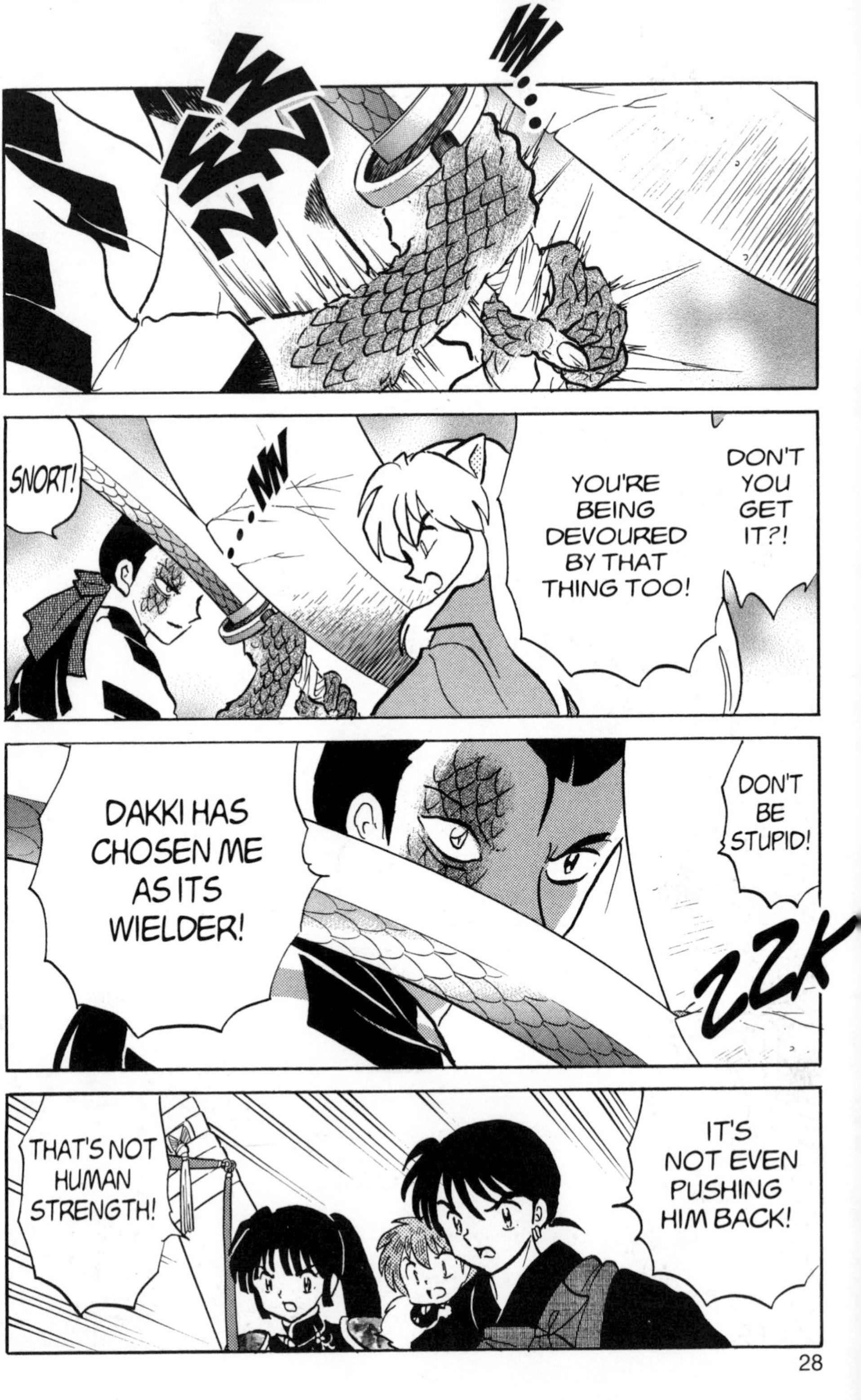
MN...
DON'T YOU GET IT?!
YOU'RE BEING DEVOURED BY THAT THING TOO!
...MN
SNORT!
DON'T BE STUPID!
ZZK
DAKKI HAS CHOSEN ME AS ITS WIELDER!
IT'S NOT EVEN PUSHING HIM BACK!
THAT'S NOT HUMAN STRENGTH!

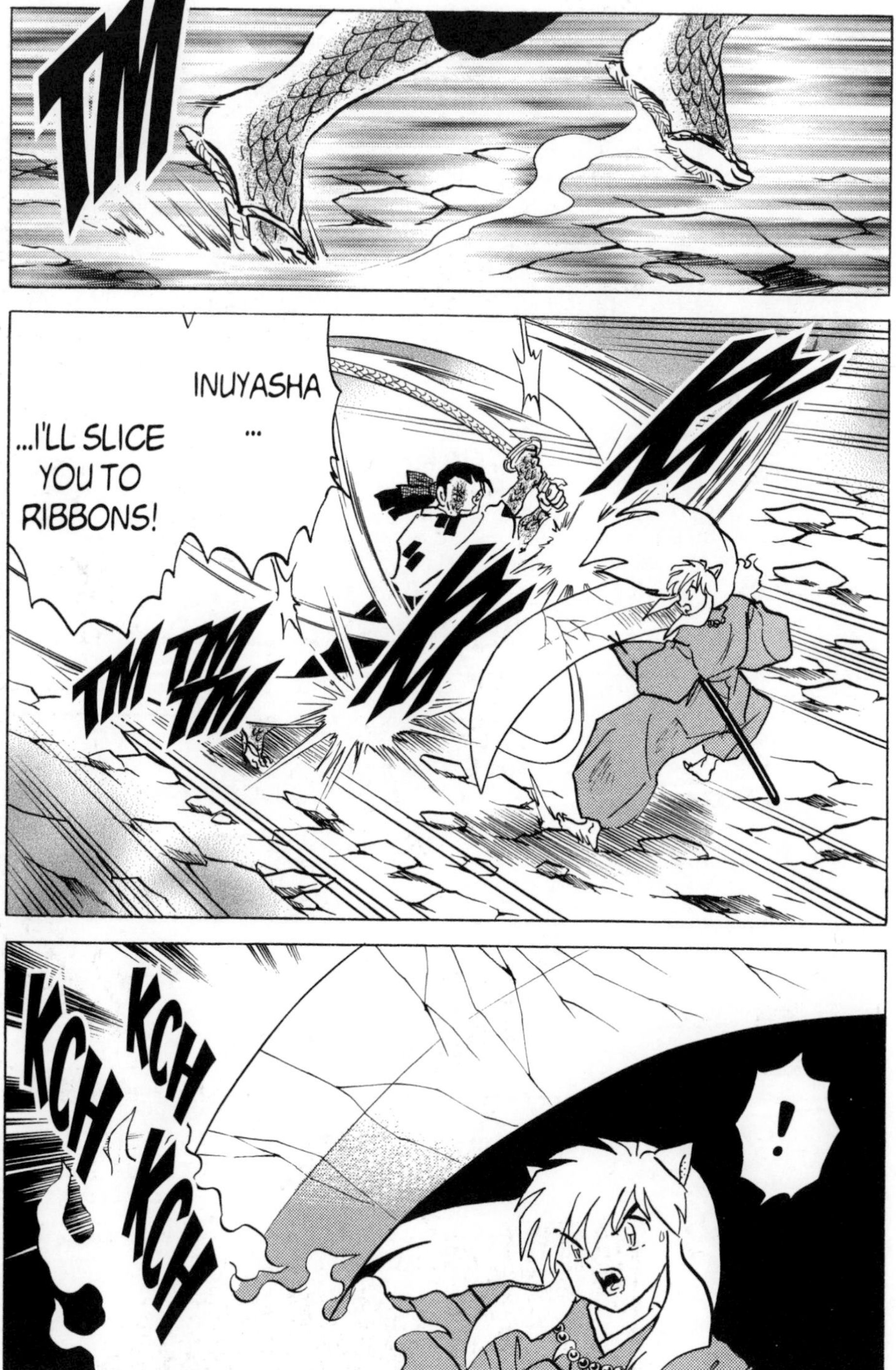
TM
INUYASHA...
...I'LL SLICE YOU TO RIBBONS!
TM TM TM
!
KCH KCH
KCH KCH

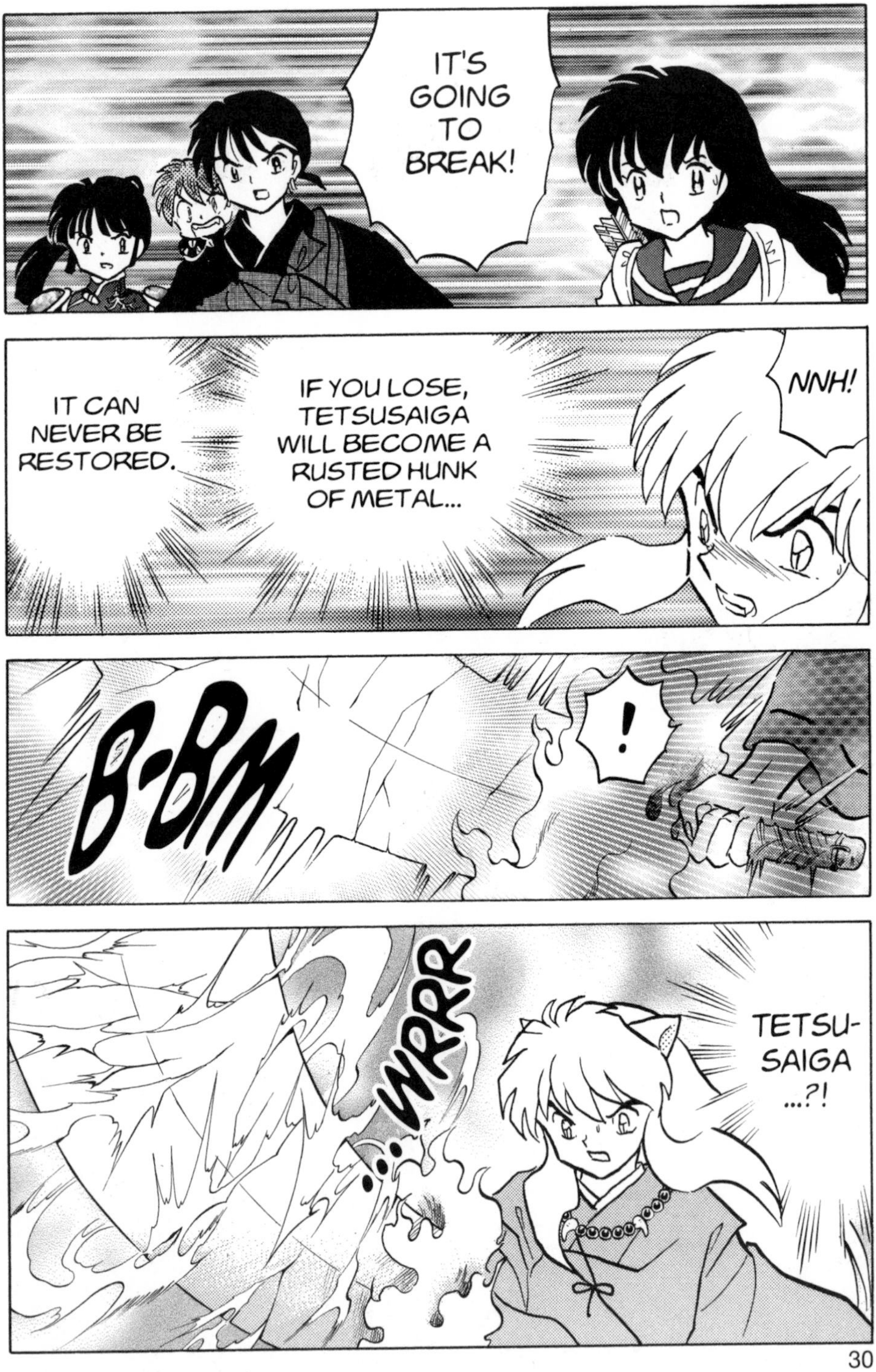
IT'S GOING TO BREAK!
NNH!
IF YOU LOSE, TETSUSAIGA WILL BECOME A RUSTED HUNK OF METAL...
IT CAN NEVER BE RESTORED.
!
B-BM
TETSU-SAIGA ...?!
WRRR

SCROLL TWO
RESIGNATION

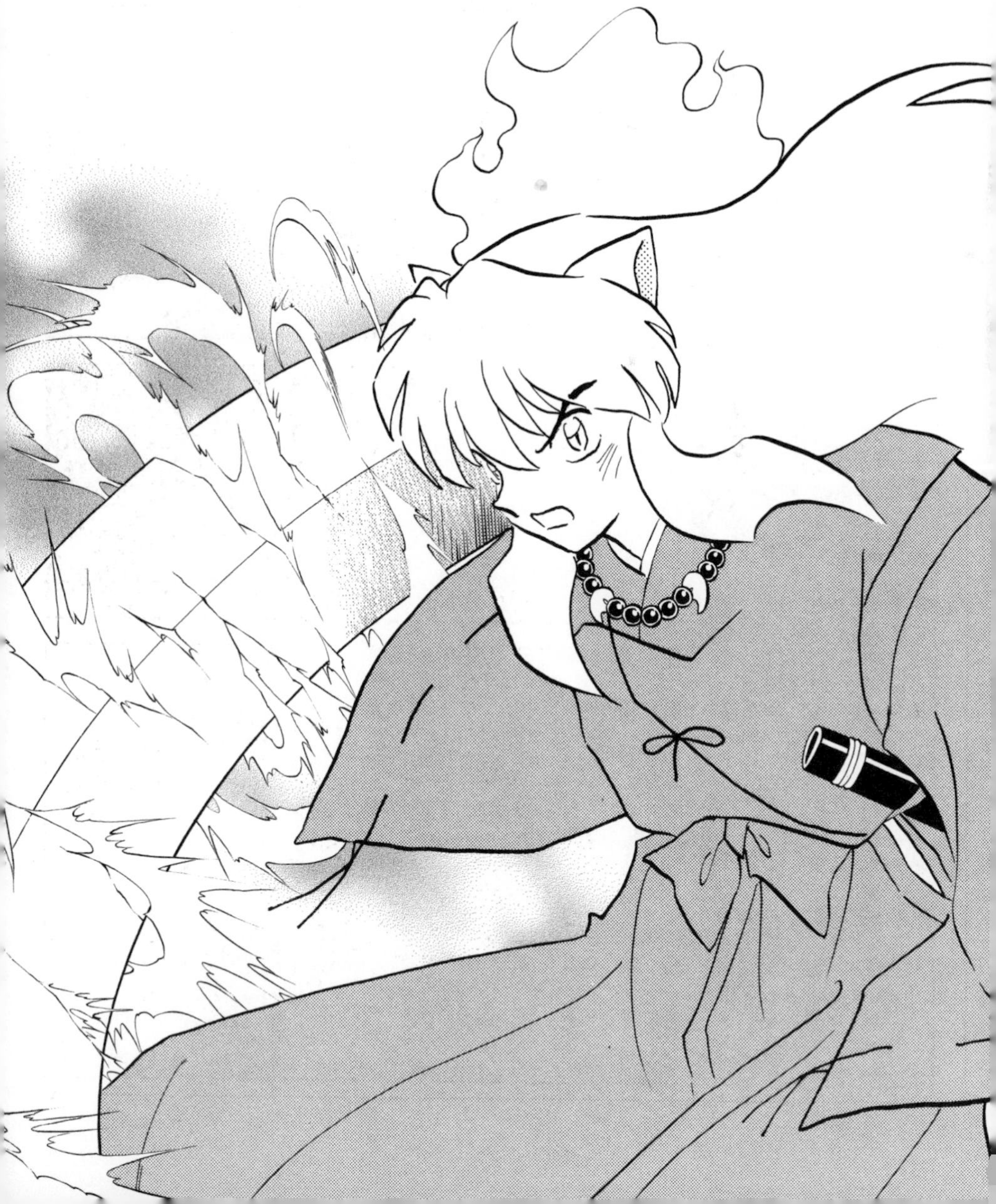

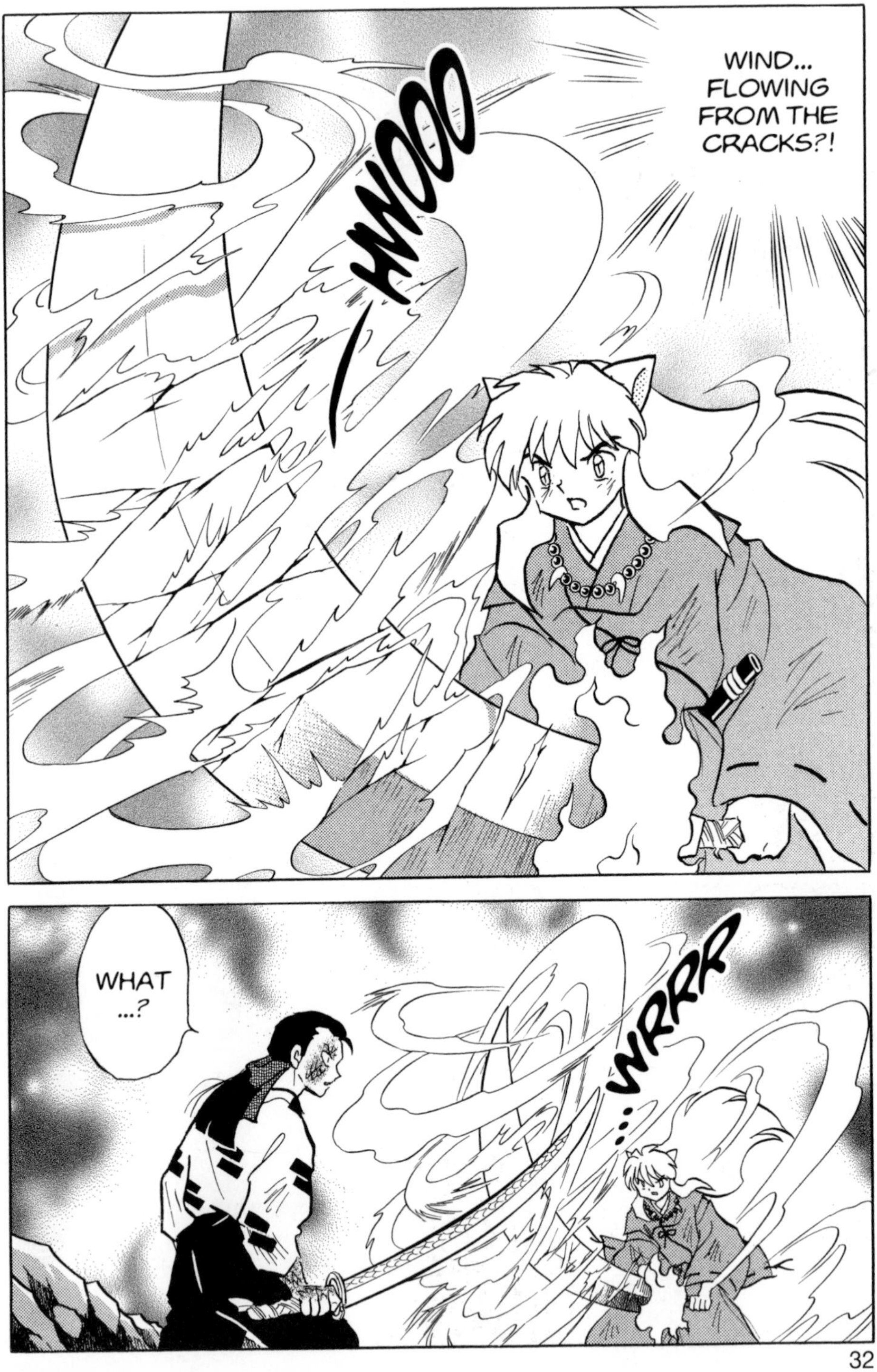
WIND... FLOWING FROM THE CRACKS?!
HWOOO
WRRR...
WHAT ...?

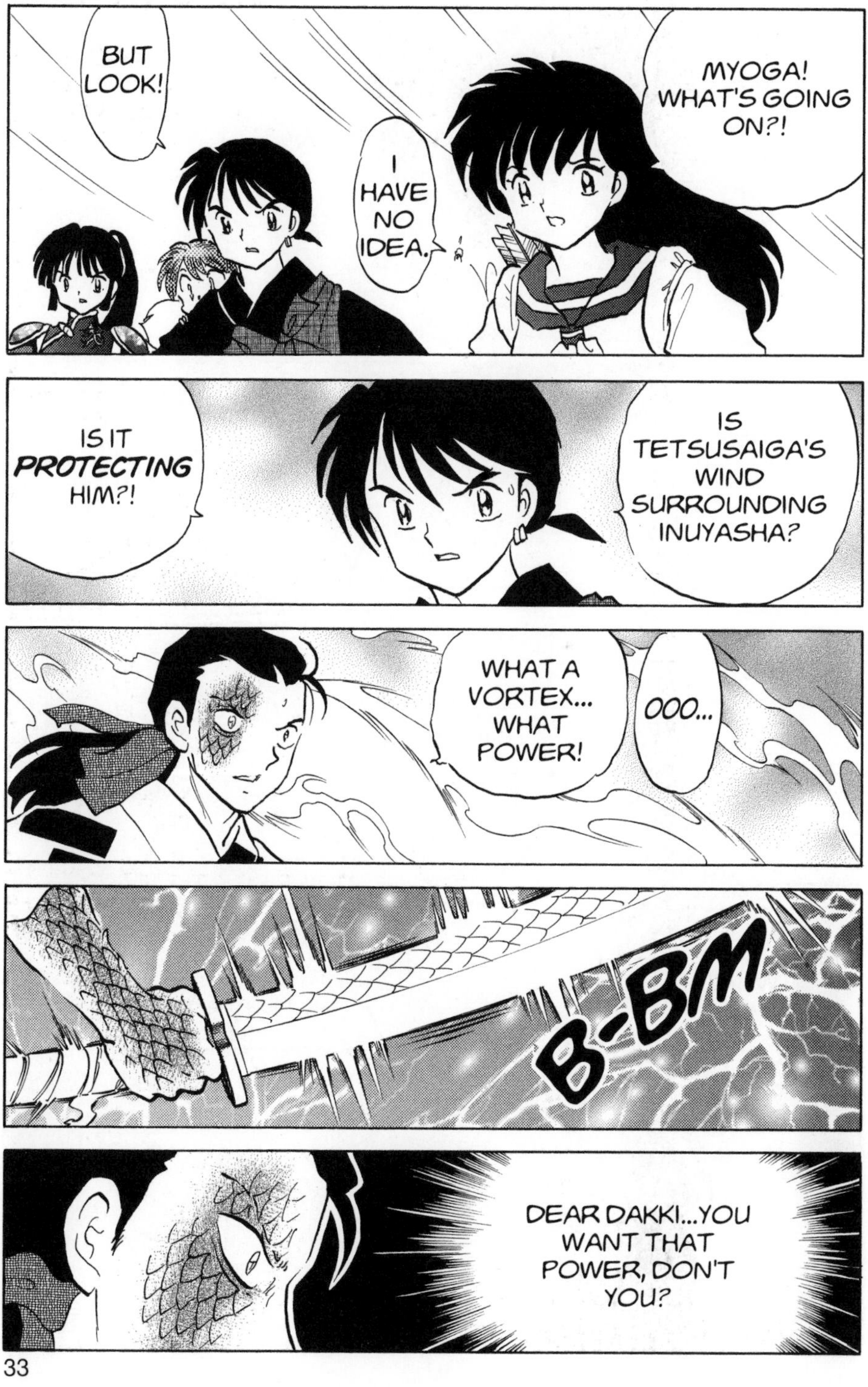
MYOGA! WHAT'S GOING ON?!
I HAVE NO IDEA.
BUT LOOK!
IS TETSUSAIGA'S WIND SURROUNDING INUYASHA?
IS IT *PROTECTING* HIM?!
OOO...
WHAT A VORTEX... WHAT POWER!
B-BM
DEAR DAKKI...YOU WANT THAT POWER, DON'T YOU?

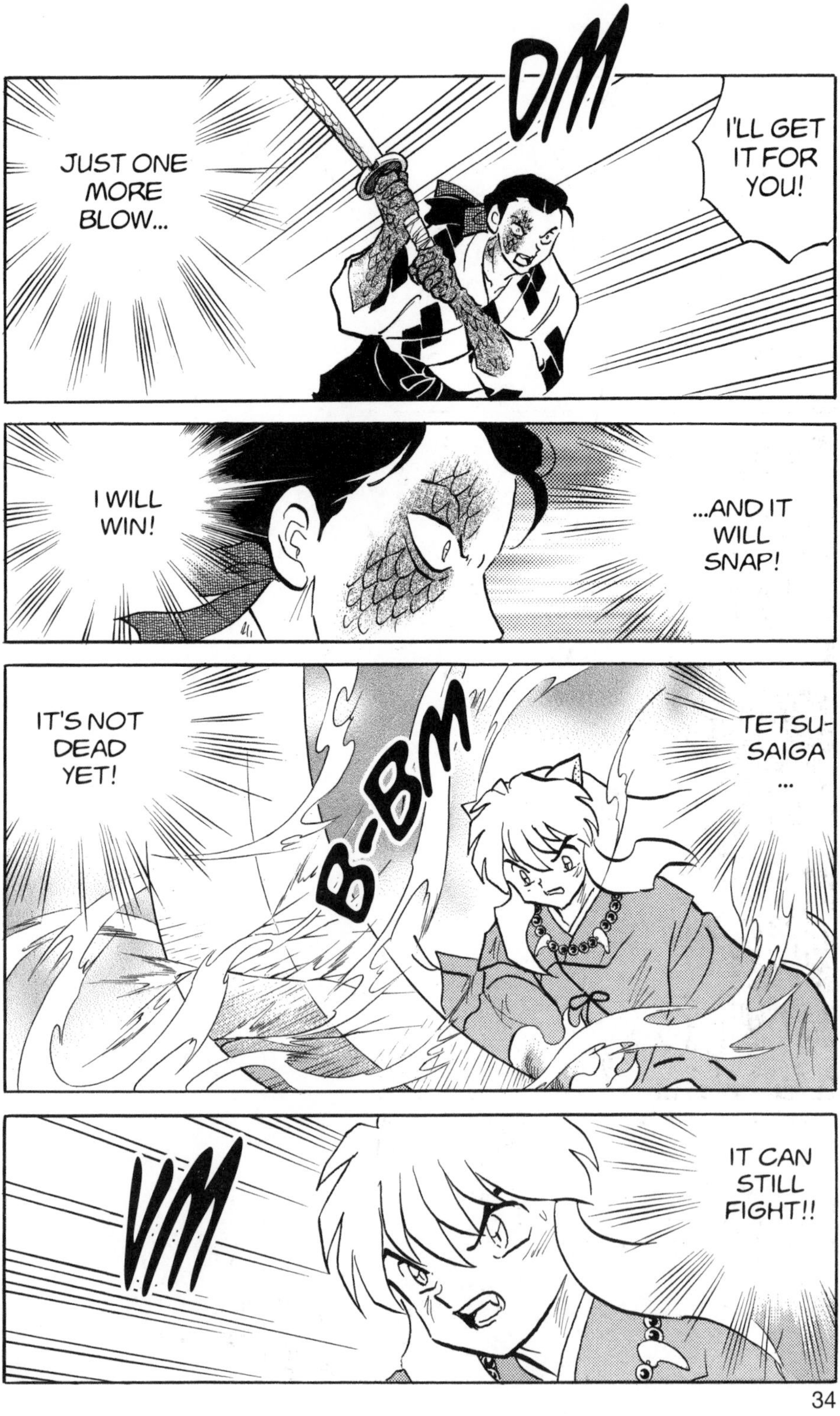
I'LL GET IT FOR YOU!
DM
JUST ONE MORE BLOW...
...AND IT WILL SNAP!
I WILL WIN!
TETSU-SAIGA ...
B-BM
IT'S NOT DEAD YET!
IT CAN STILL FIGHT!!
VM

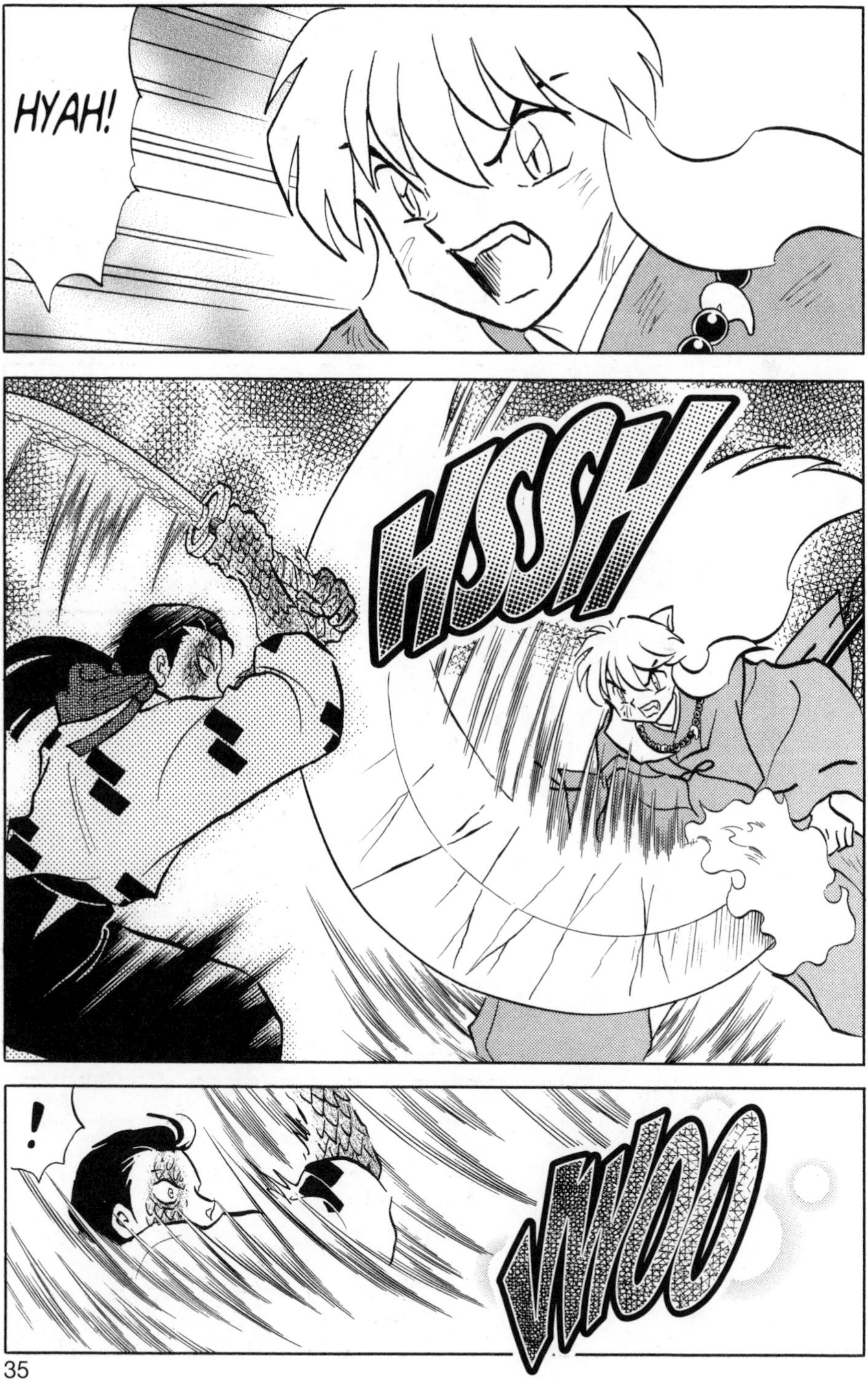
HYAH!
HSSH
!
WHOO

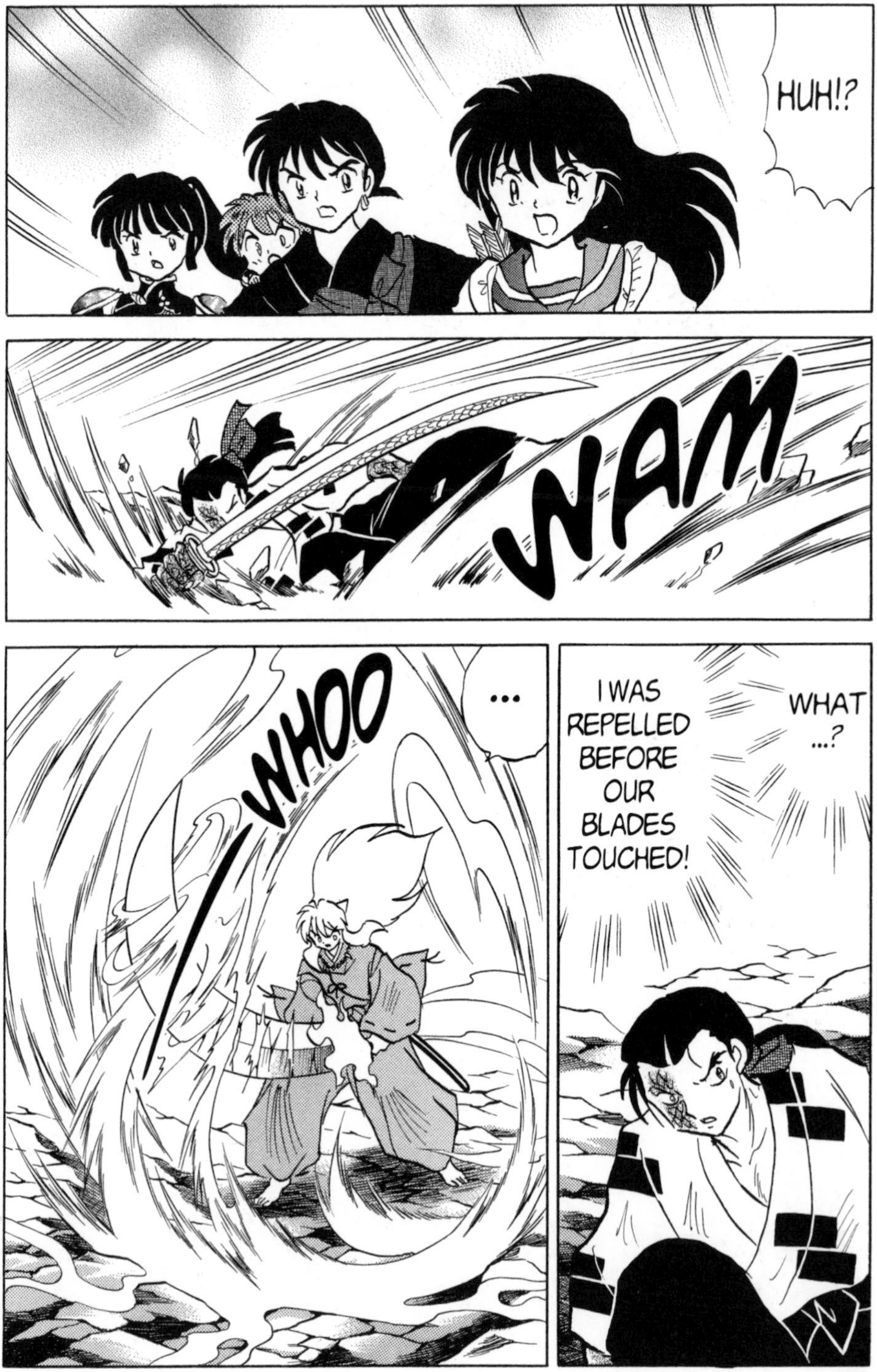
HUH!?
WAM
WHAT ...?
I WAS REPELLED BEFORE OUR BLADES TOUCHED!
...
WHOO

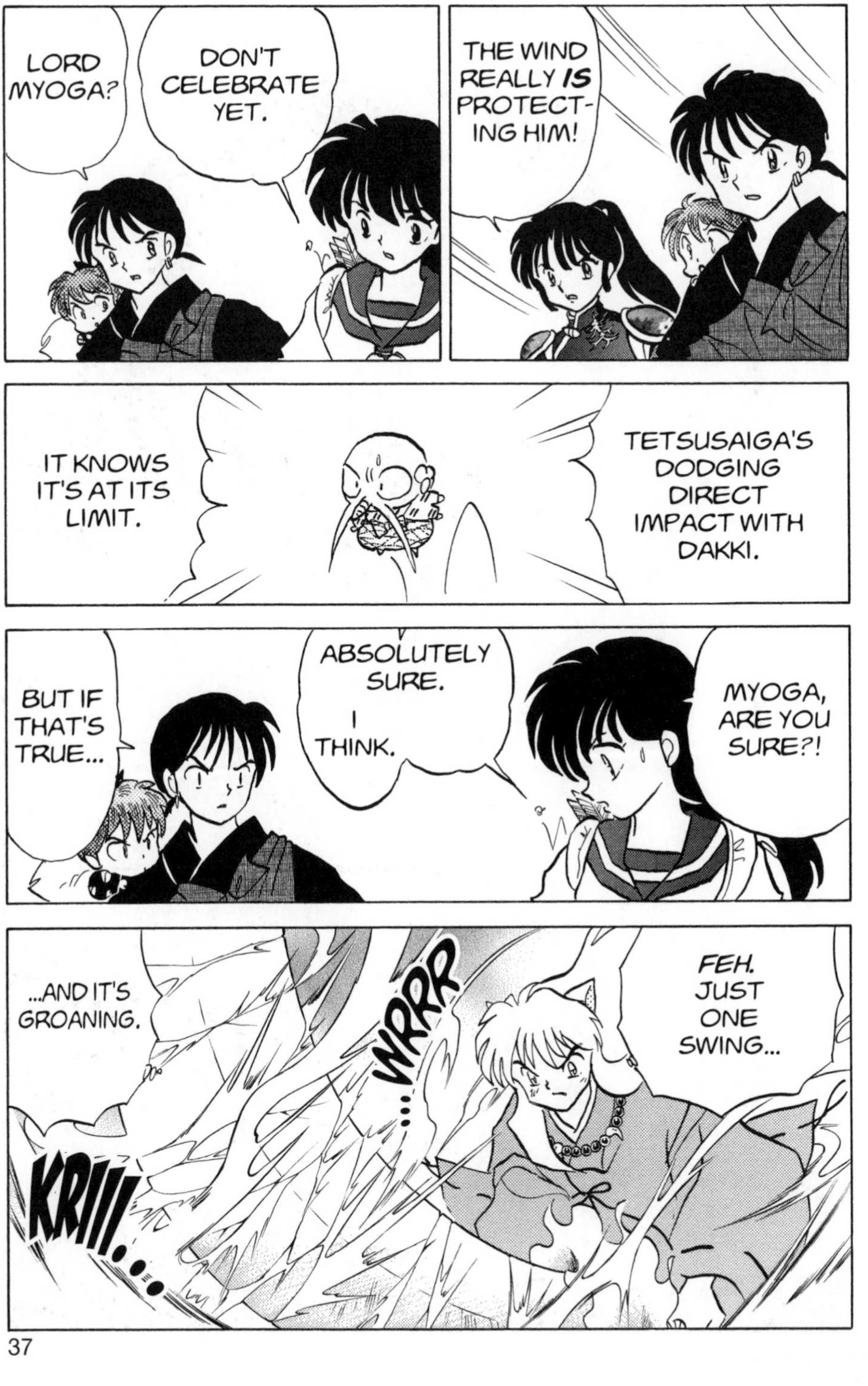
THE WIND REALLY IS PROTECTING HIM!
DON'T CELEBRATE YET.
LORD MYOGA?
TETSUSAIGA'S DODGING DIRECT IMPACT WITH DAKKI.
IT KNOWS IT'S AT ITS LIMIT.
MYOGA, ARE YOU SURE?!
ABSOLUTELY SURE.
I THINK.
BUT IF THAT'S TRUE...
FEH. JUST ONE SWING...
WRRR...
...AND IT'S GROANING.
KRIII...

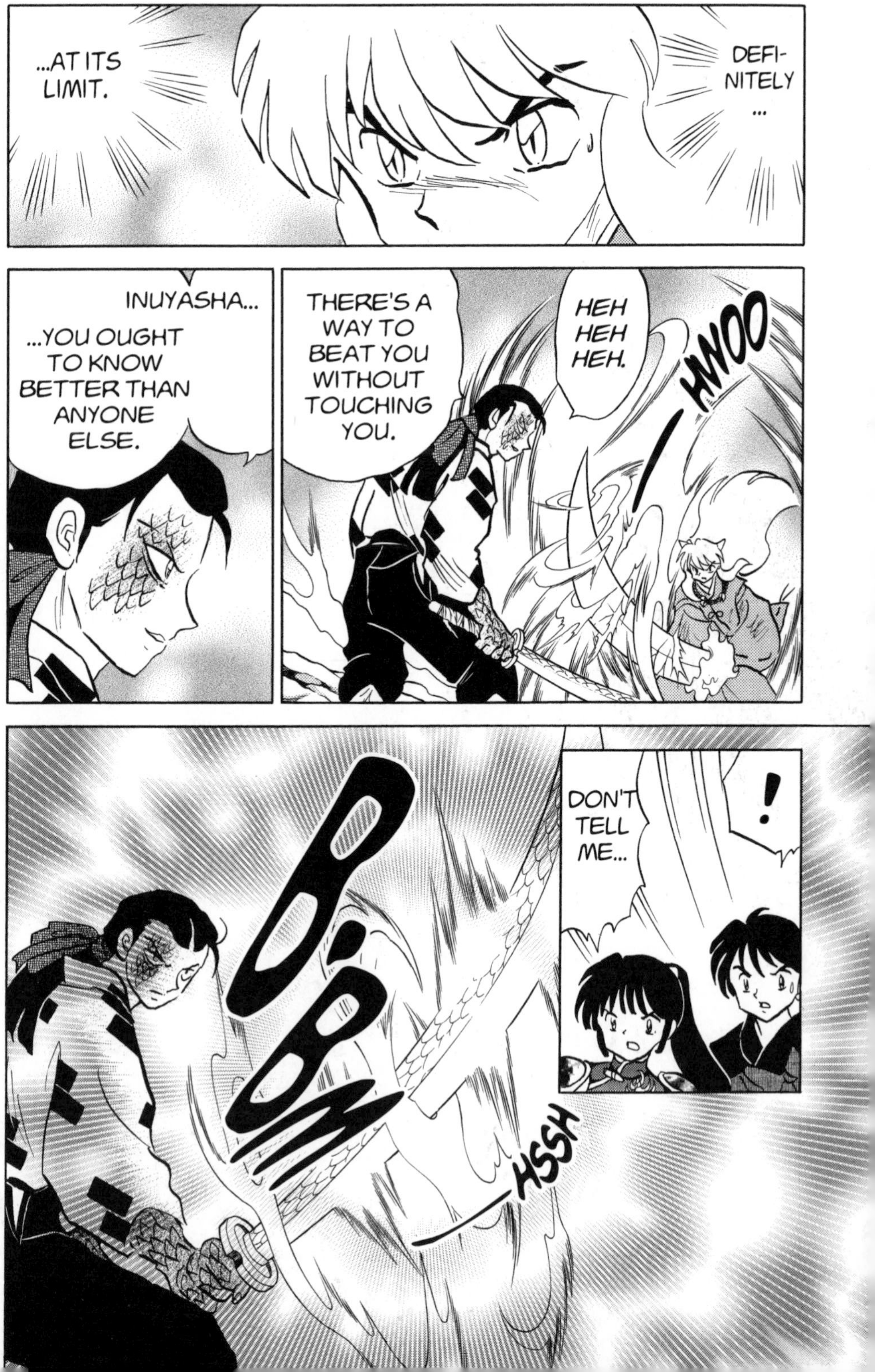

DEFI-NITELY ...
...AT ITS LIMIT.
HWOO
HEH HEH HEH.
THERE'S A WAY TO BEAT YOU WITHOUT TOUCHING YOU.
INUYASHA...
...YOU OUGHT TO KNOW BETTER THAN ANYONE ELSE.
!
DON'T TELL ME...
BOOM
HSSH

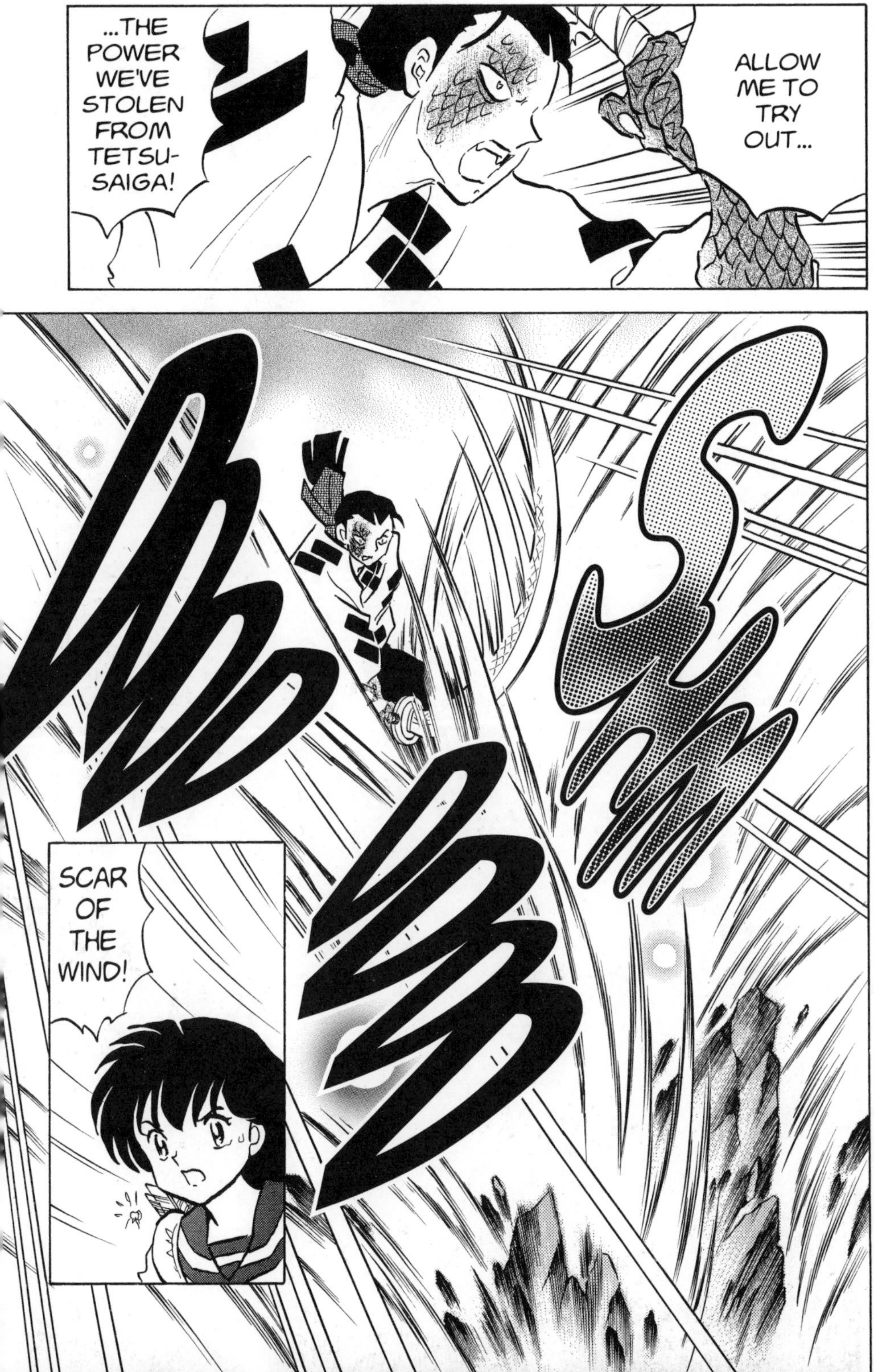
ALLOW ME TO TRY OUT...
...THE POWER WE'VE STOLEN FROM TETSU-SAIGA!
SCAR OF THE WIND!

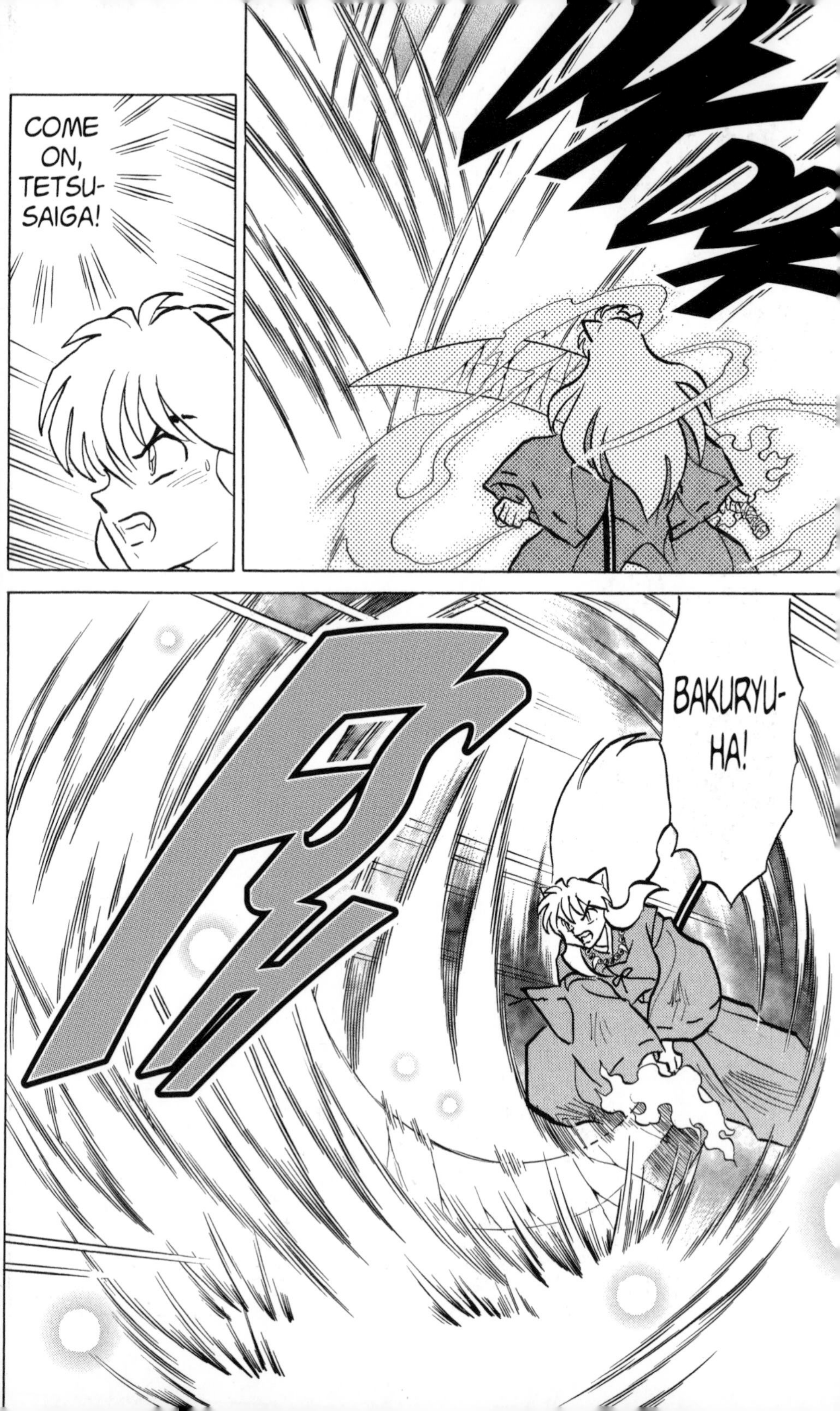
COME ON, TETSU-SAIGA!
BAKURYU-HA!

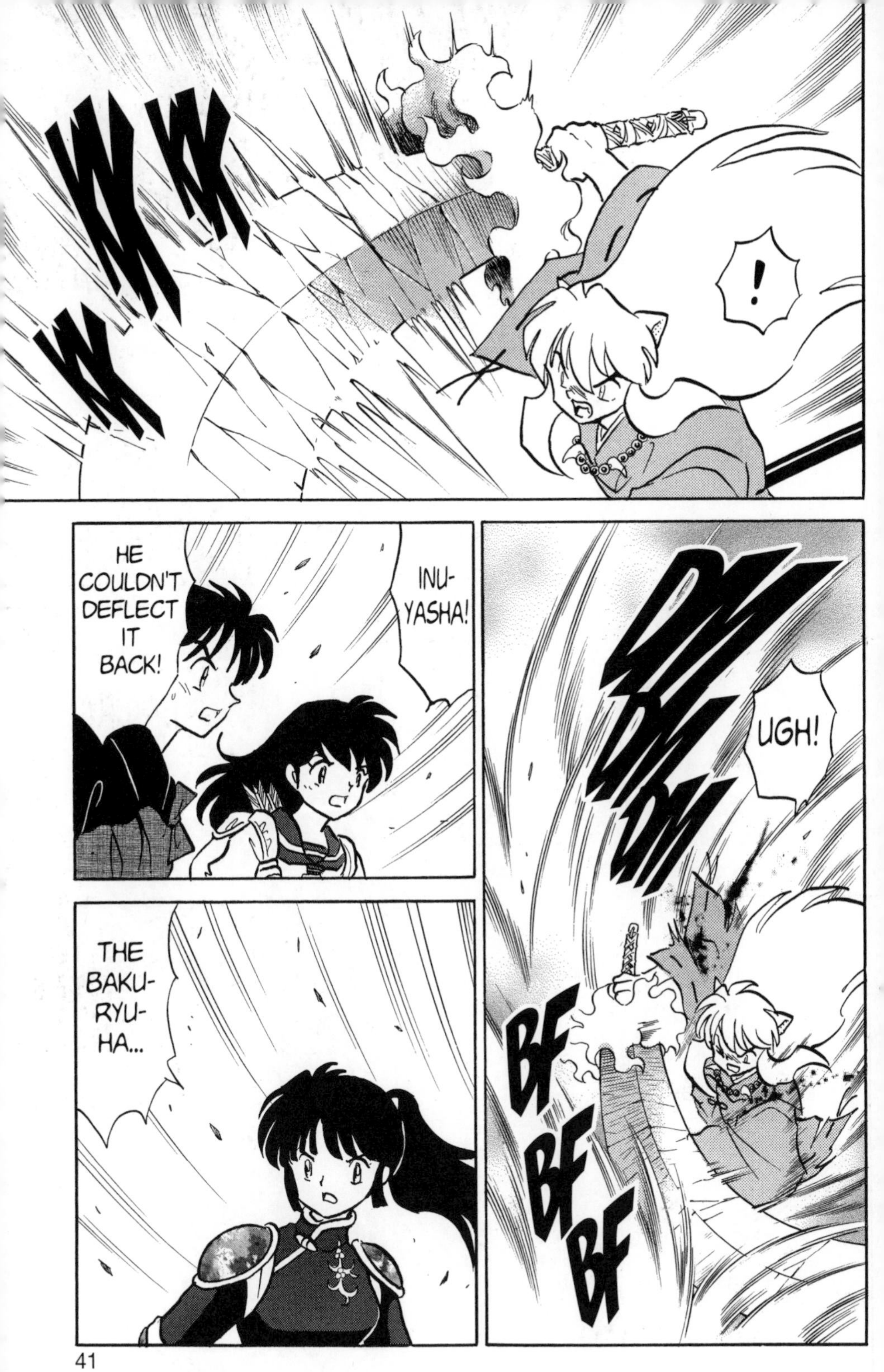
!
UGH!
BF
BF
BF
BF
INU-YASHA!
HE COULDN'T DEFLECT IT BACK!
THE BAKU-RYU-HA...

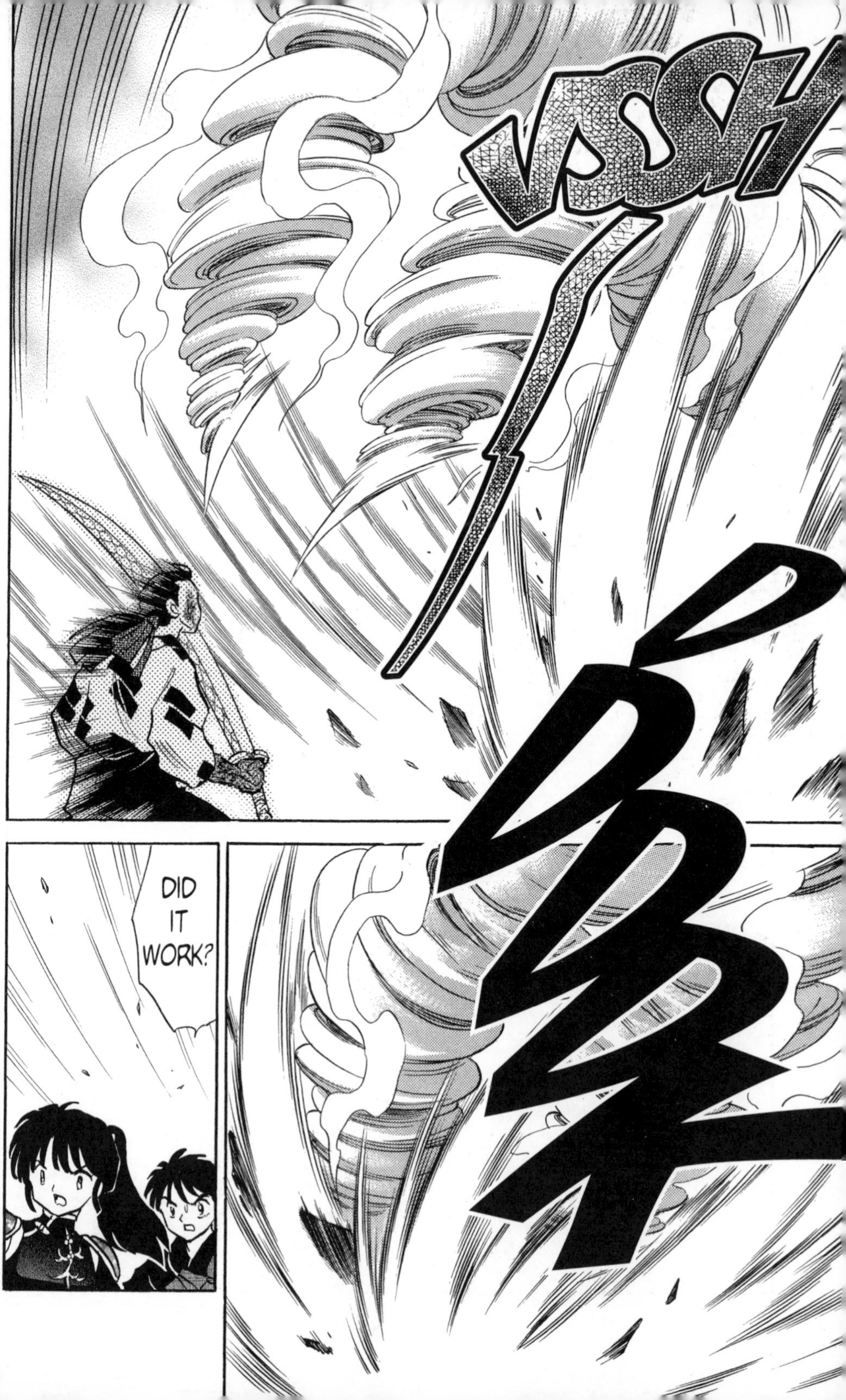
VSCH
DID IT WORK?

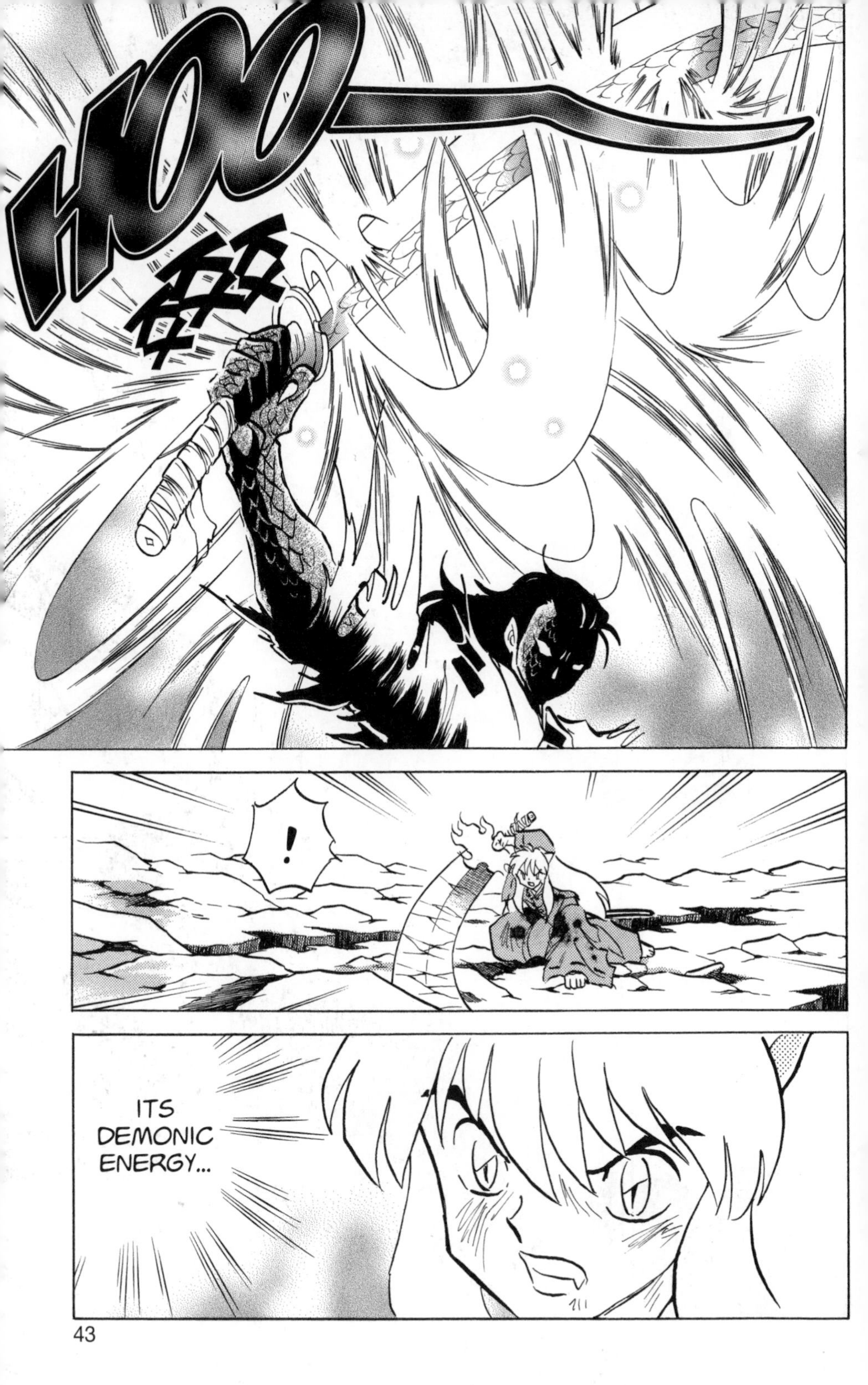
HOOO—
!
ITS DEMONIC ENERGY...

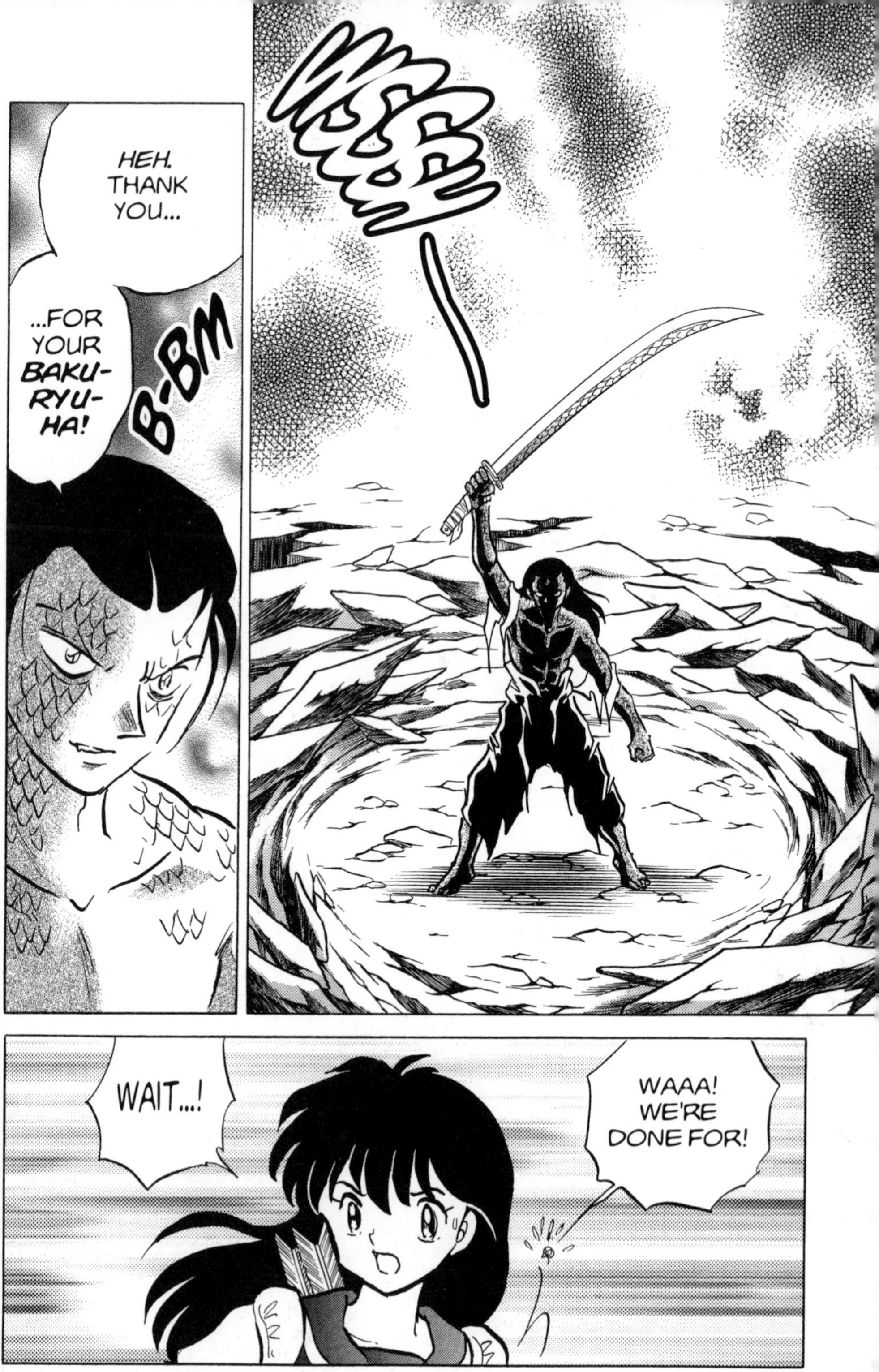
HEH. THANK YOU...
...FOR YOUR BAKU-RYU-HA!
B-BM
WAAA! WE'RE DONE FOR!
WAIT...!

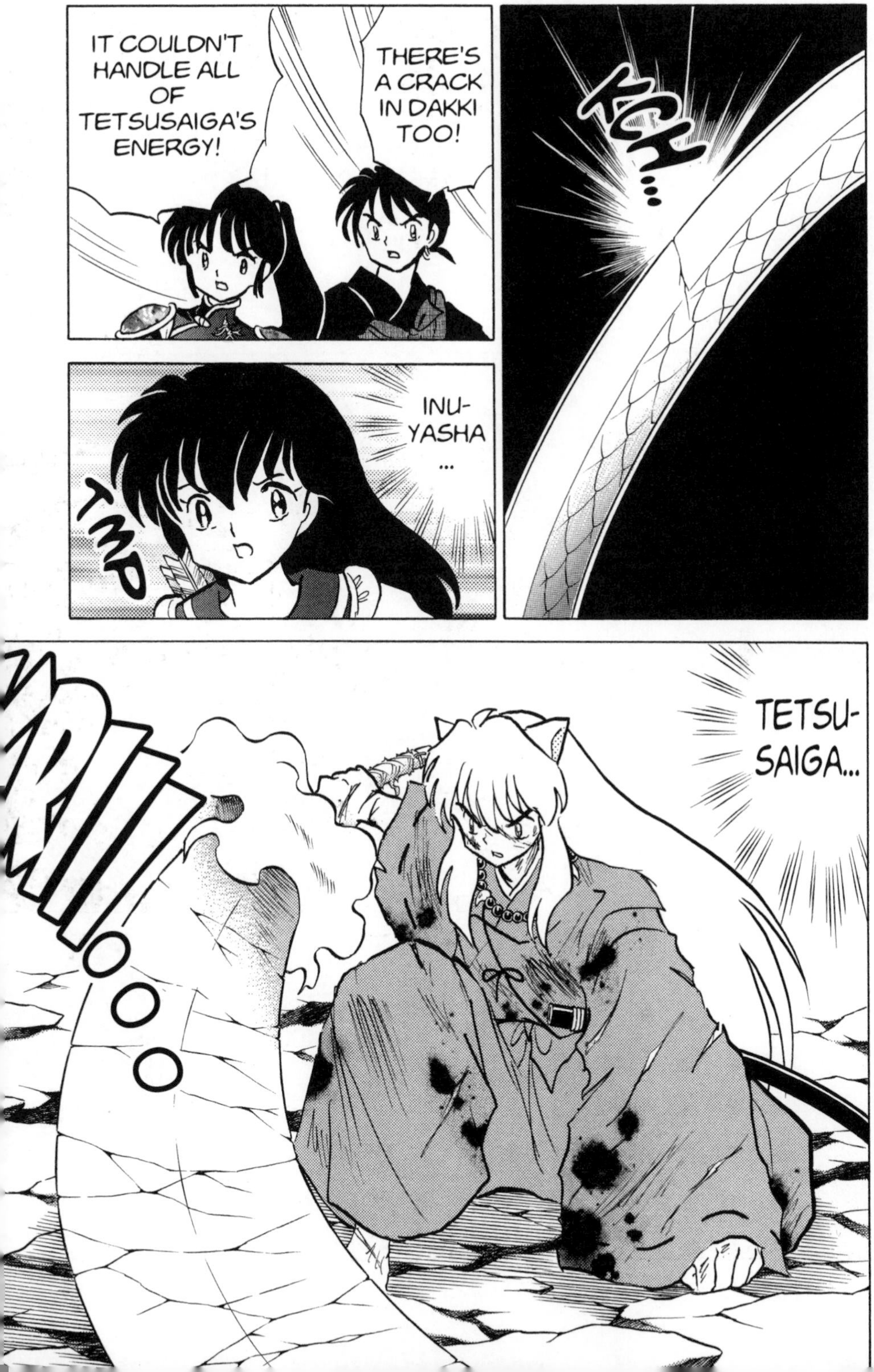
KCH...
THERE'S A CRACK IN DAKKI TOO!
IT COULDN'T HANDLE ALL OF TETSUSAIGA'S ENERGY!
INU-YASHA ...
TMP
TETSU-SAIGA...
RIIIOOO

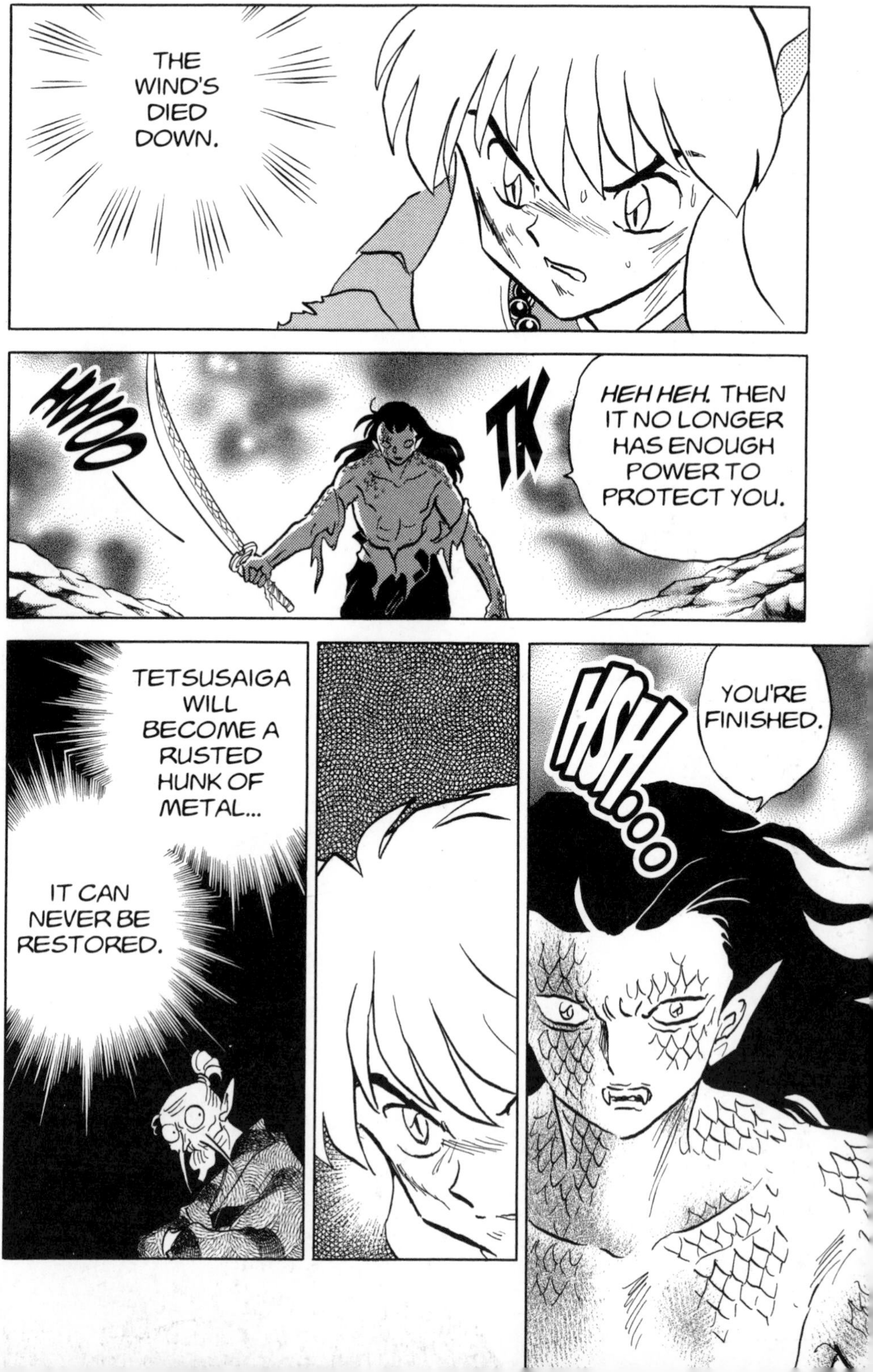
THE WIND'S DIED DOWN.
HEH HEH. THEN IT NO LONGER HAS ENOUGH POWER TO PROTECT YOU.
TK
HWOO
YOU'RE FINISHED.
HSH...OOO
TETSUSAIGA WILL BECOME A RUSTED HUNK OF METAL...
IT CAN NEVER BE RESTORED.

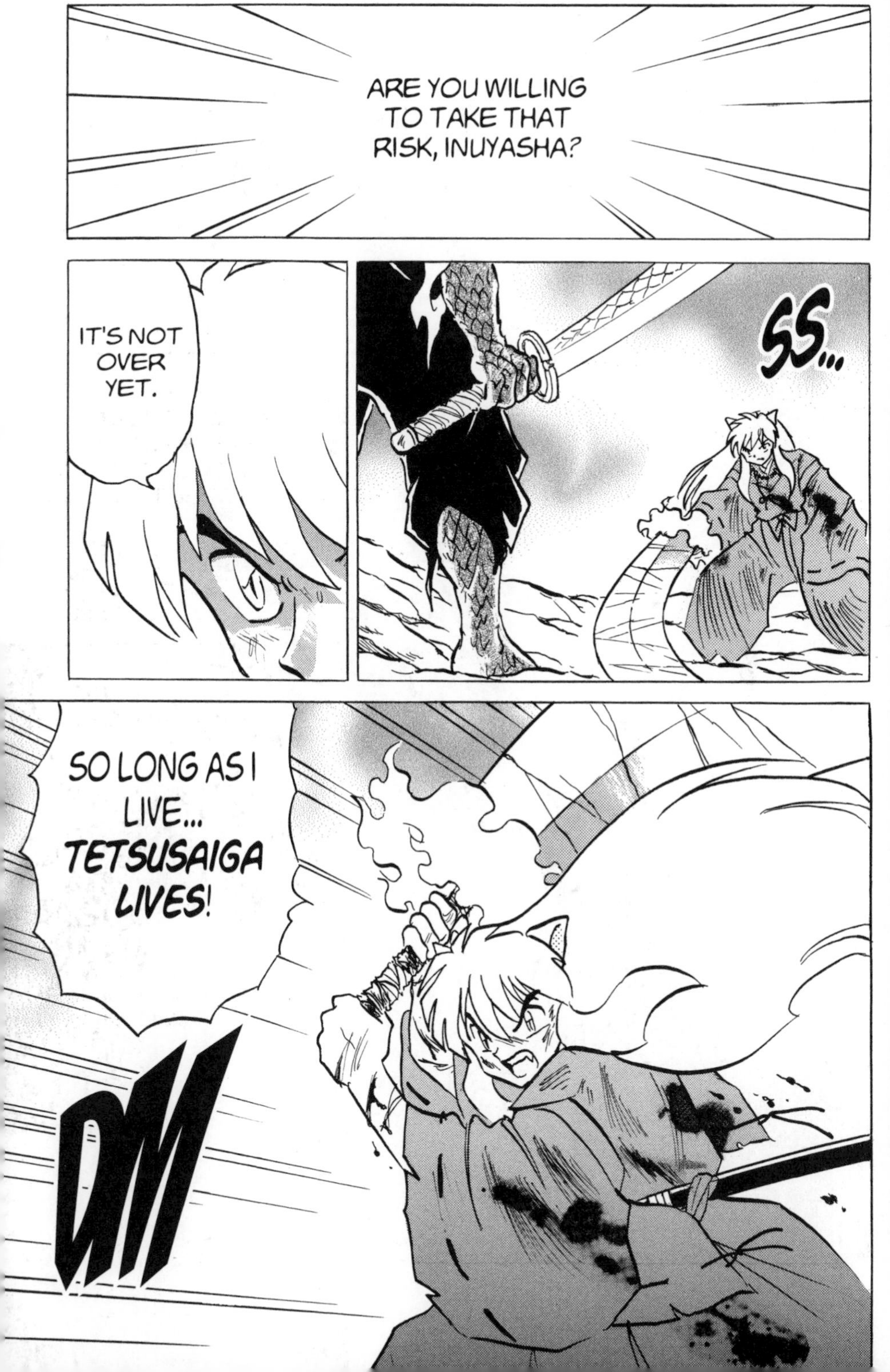
ARE YOU WILLING TO TAKE THAT RISK, INUYASHA?
SS...
IT'S NOT OVER YET.
SO LONG AS I LIVE... **TETSUSAIGA LIVES!**
DM

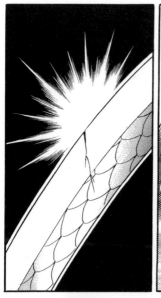

TETSUSAIGA!

I WON'T WASTE...

VM

FOOL!

KRASH

...THE CHANCE YOU GAVE ME!

SCROLL THREE
ONE SOUL

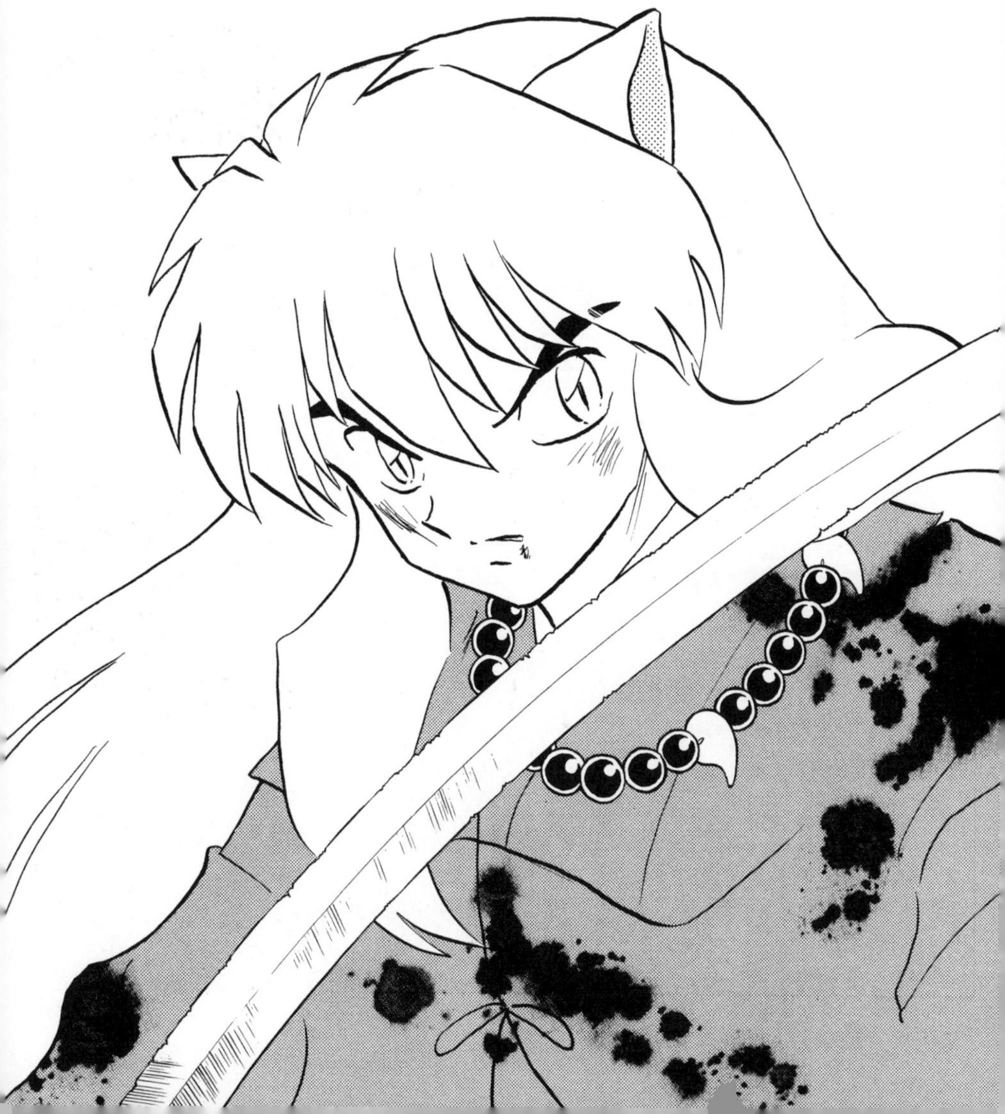

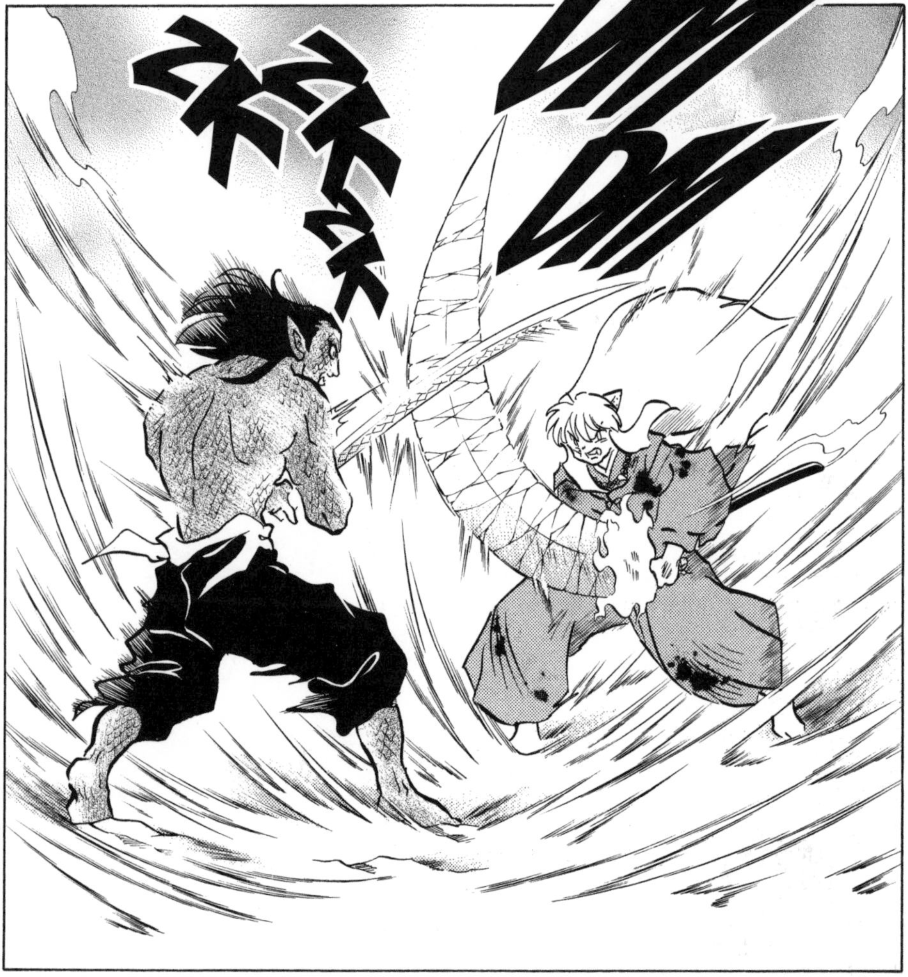
DM DM

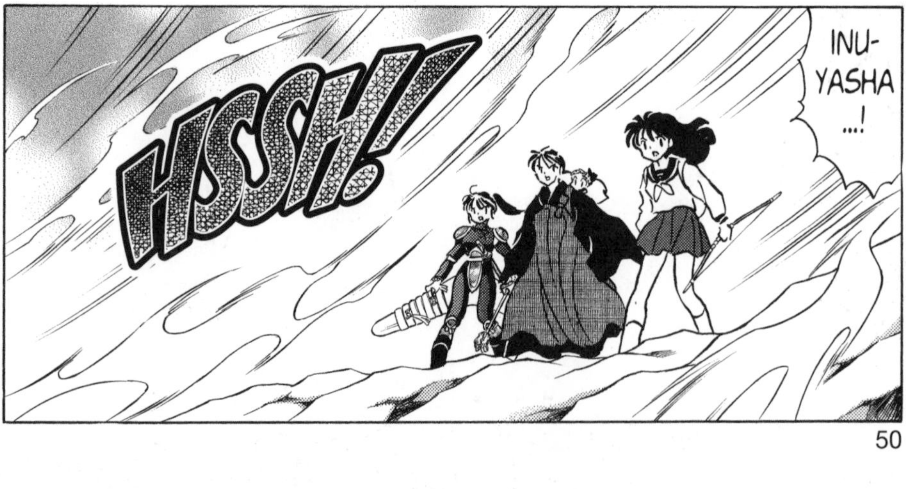
INU-YASHA ...!
HSSH!

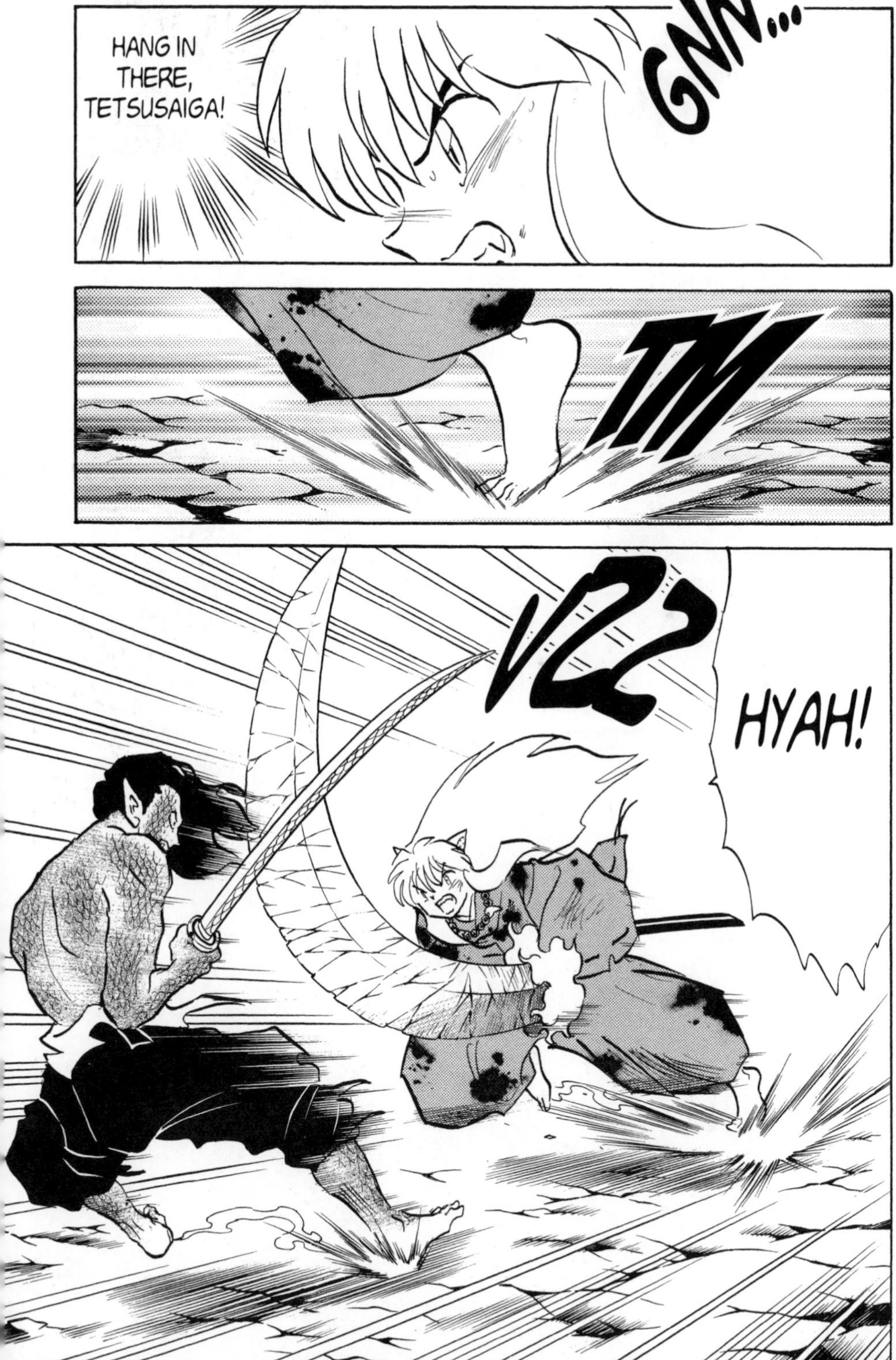
GNN...
HANG IN THERE, TETSUSAIGA!
TM
VZZ
HYAH!

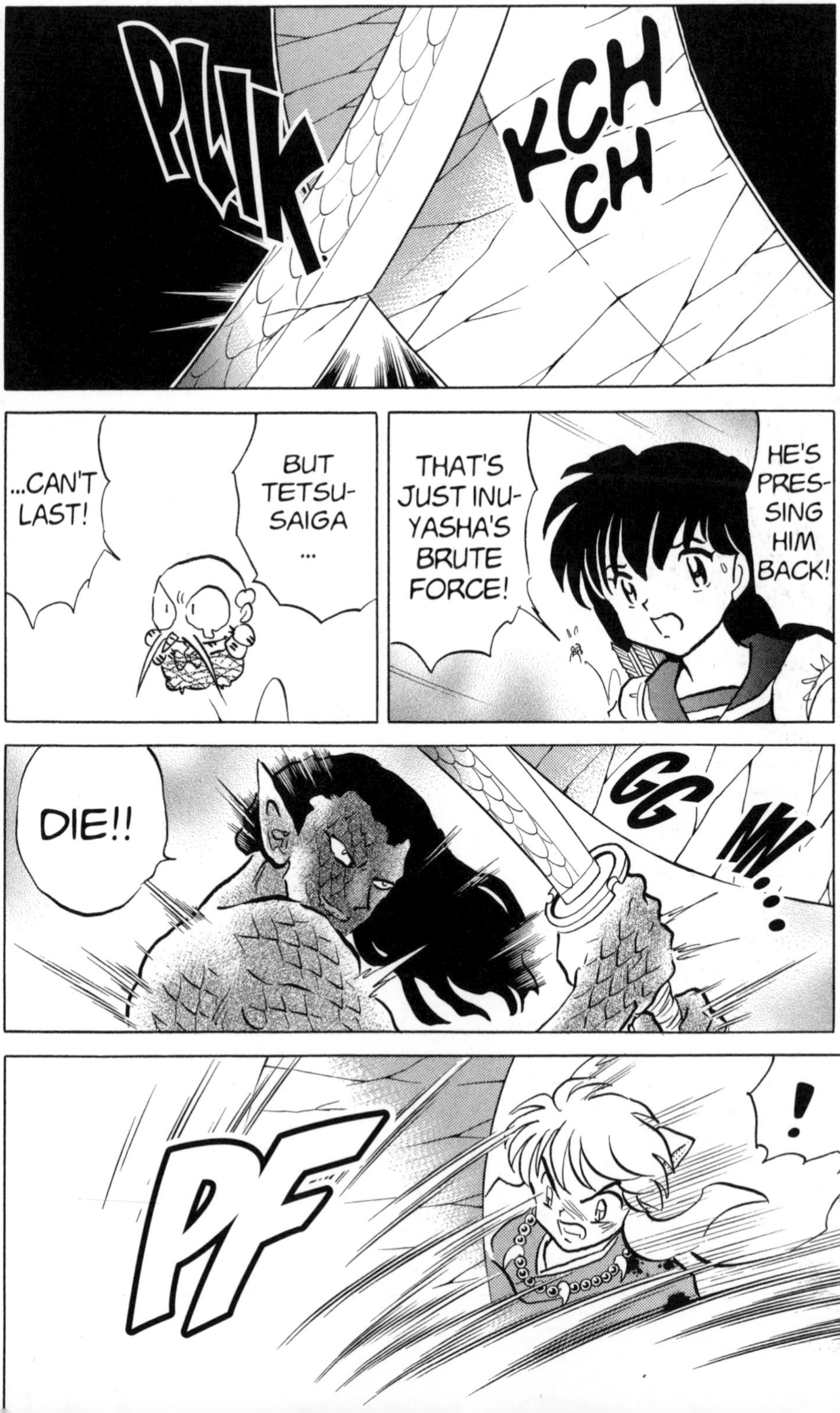
KCH CH
PLIK
HE'S PRES-SING HIM BACK!
THAT'S JUST INU-YASHA'S BRUTE FORCE!
BUT TETSU-SAIGA ...
...CAN'T LAST!
GG MN...
DIE!!
!
PF

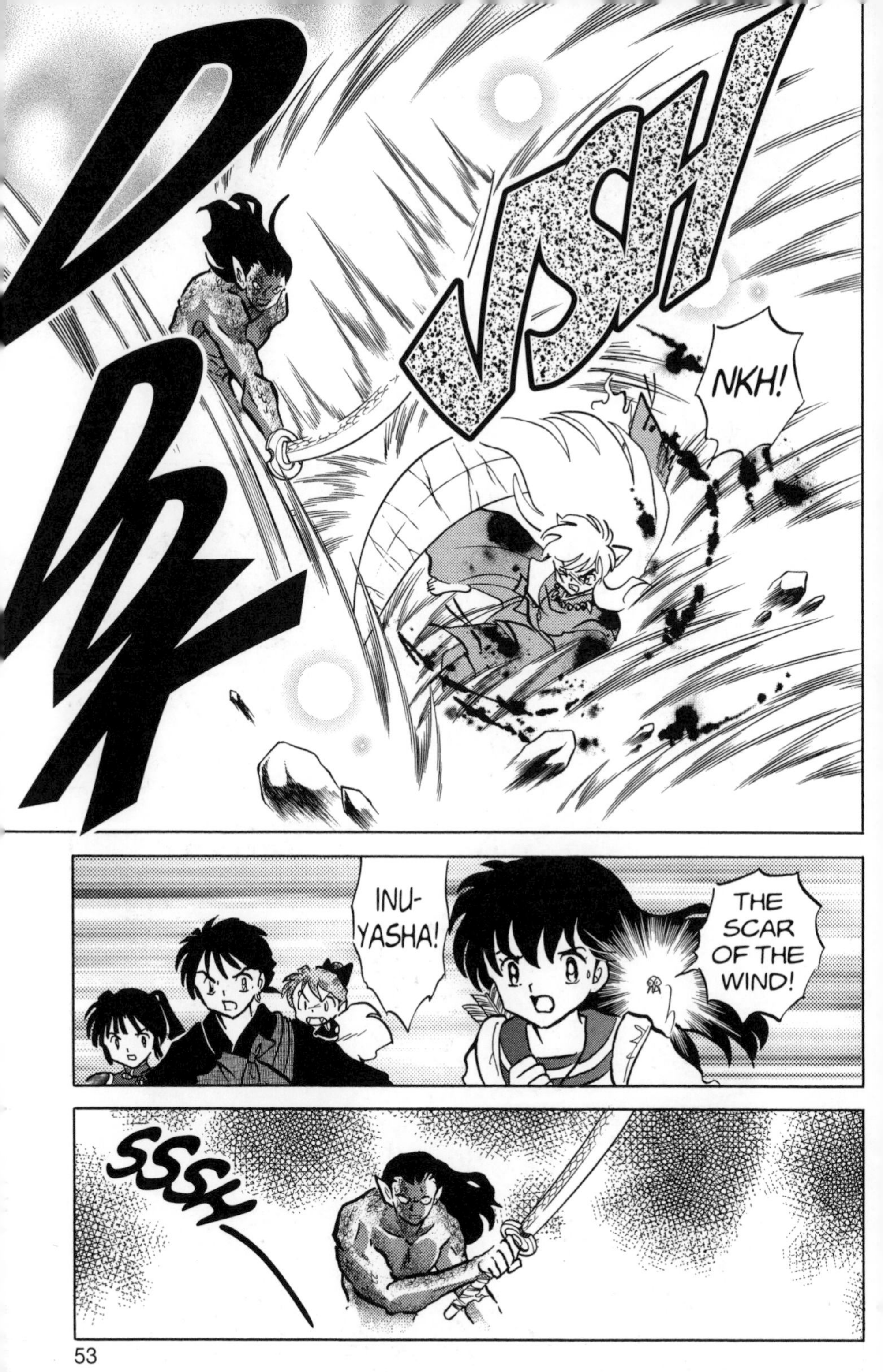
VSH
NKH!
THE SCAR OF THE WIND!
INU-YASHA!
SSSH

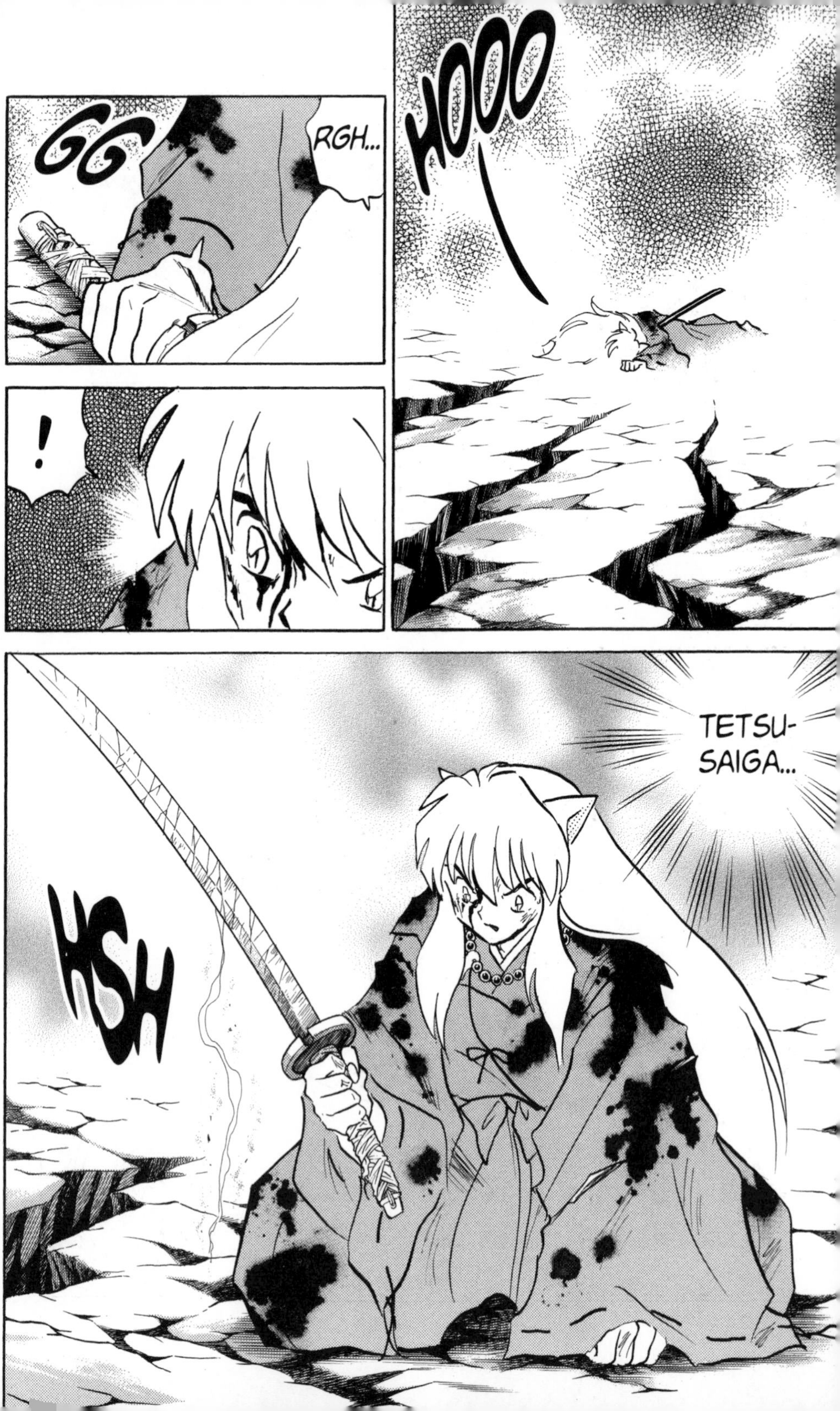
HOOO
GG
RGH...
!
TETSU-SAIGA...
HSH

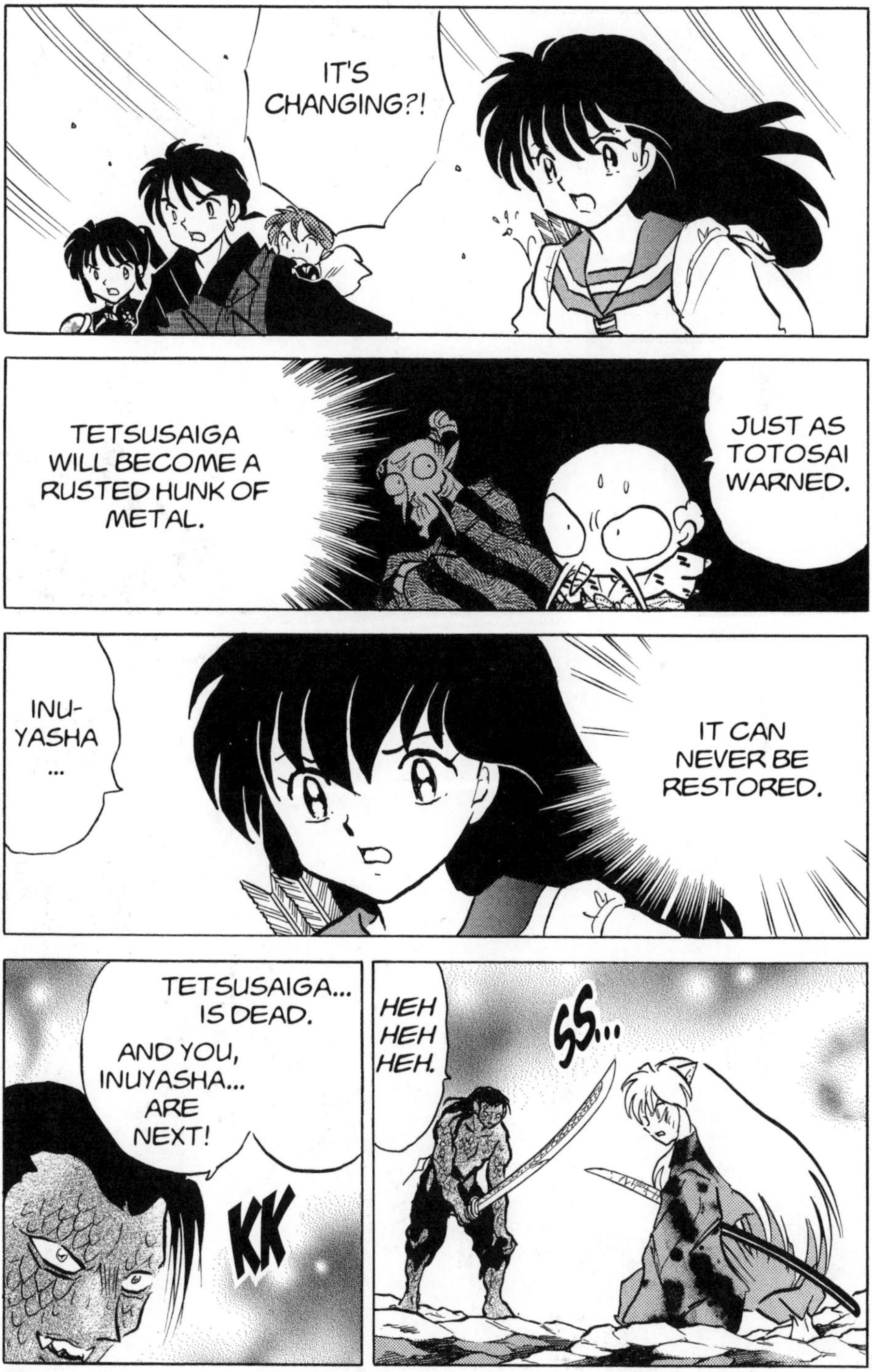
IT'S CHANGING?!
JUST AS TOTOSAI WARNED.
TETSUSAIGA WILL BECOME A RUSTED HUNK OF METAL.
IT CAN NEVER BE RESTORED.
INU-YASHA ...
HEH HEH HEH.
SS...
TETSUSAIGA... IS DEAD.
AND YOU, INUYASHA... ARE NEXT!
KK

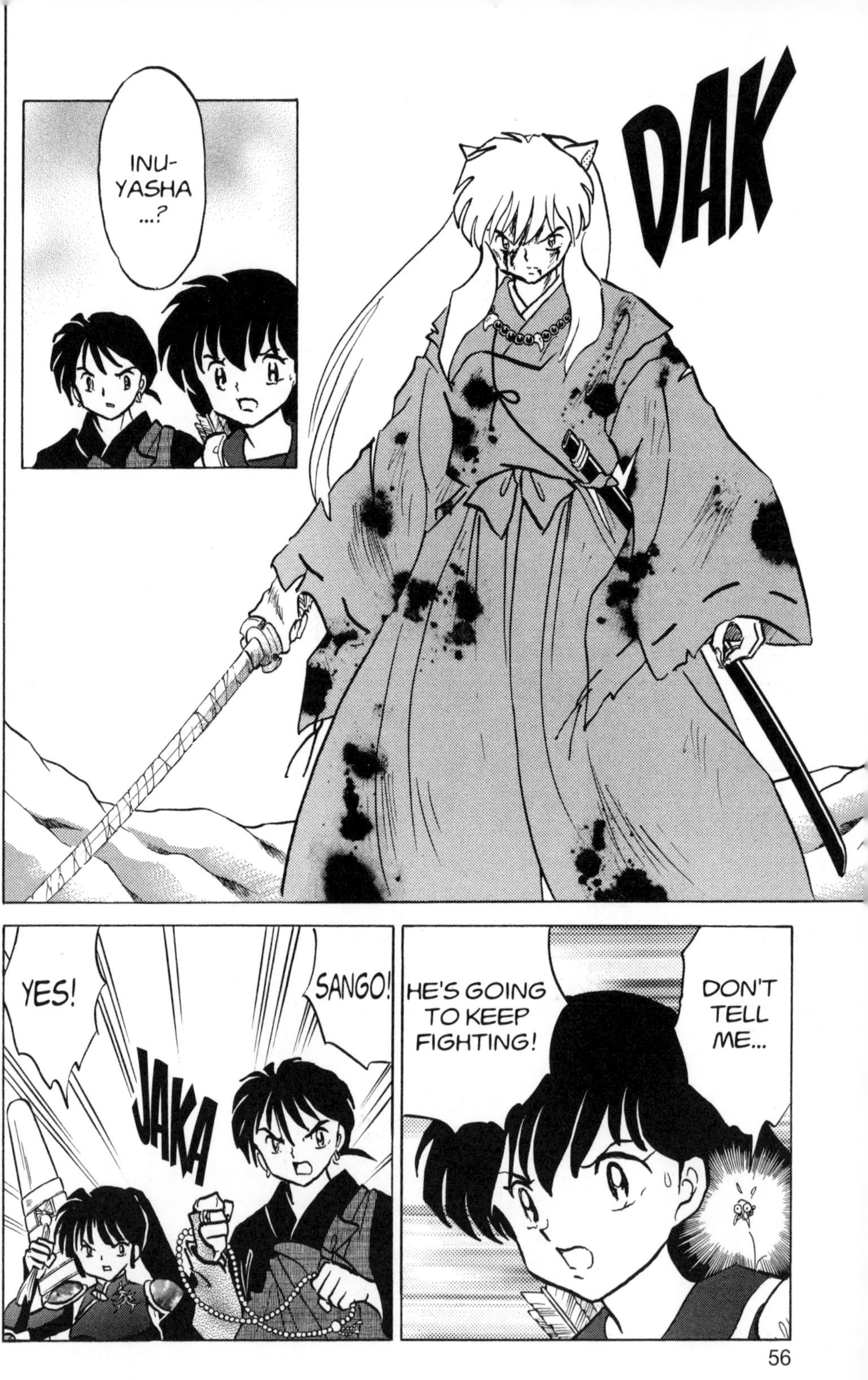
DAK
INU-YASHA ...?
DON'T TELL ME...
HE'S GOING TO KEEP FIGHTING!
SANGO!
JAKA
YES!

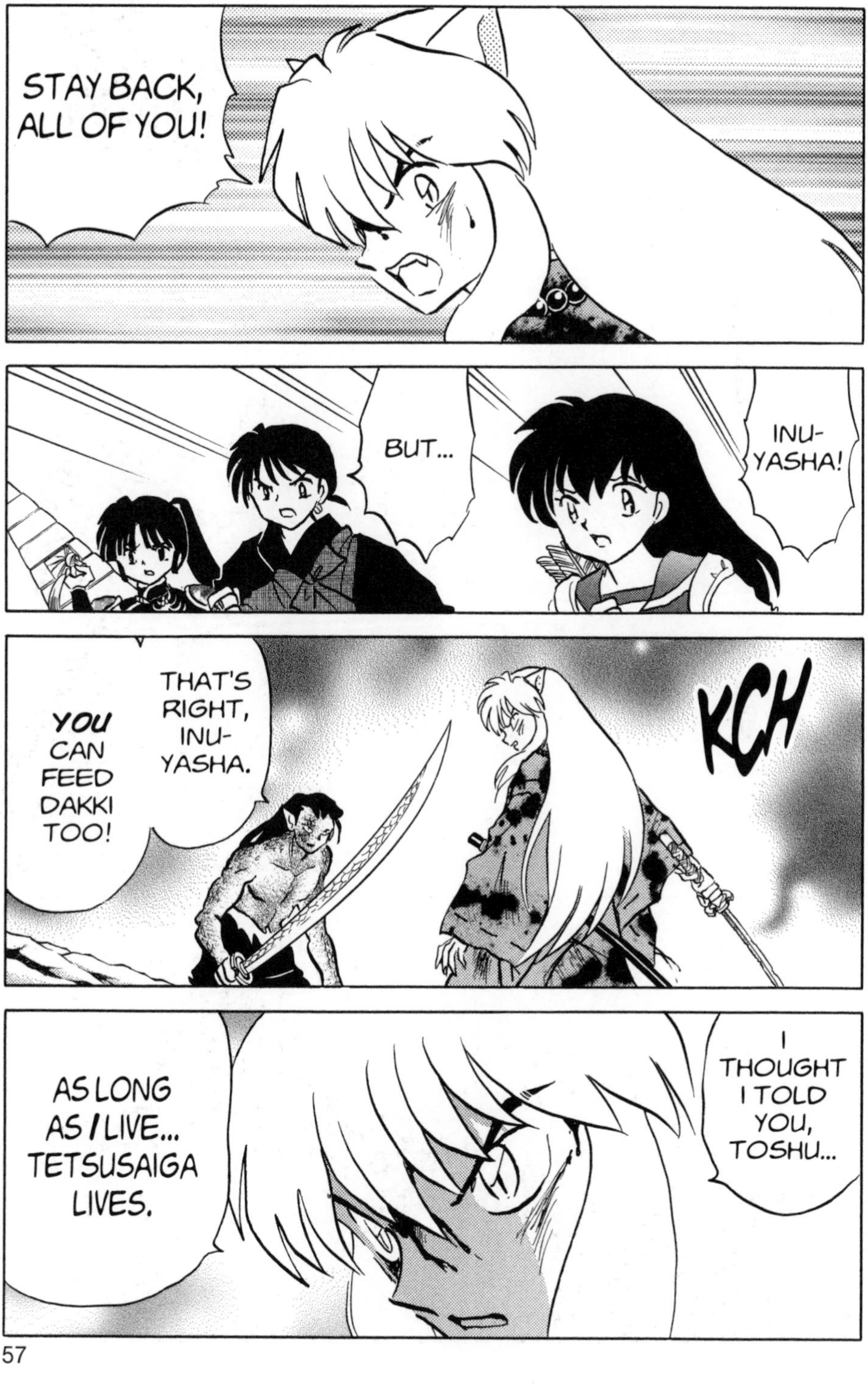
STAY BACK, ALL OF YOU!
INU-YASHA!
BUT...
KCH
THAT'S RIGHT, INU-YASHA.
YOU CAN FEED DAKKI TOO!
I THOUGHT I TOLD YOU, TOSHU...
AS LONG AS I LIVE... TETSUSAIGA LIVES.

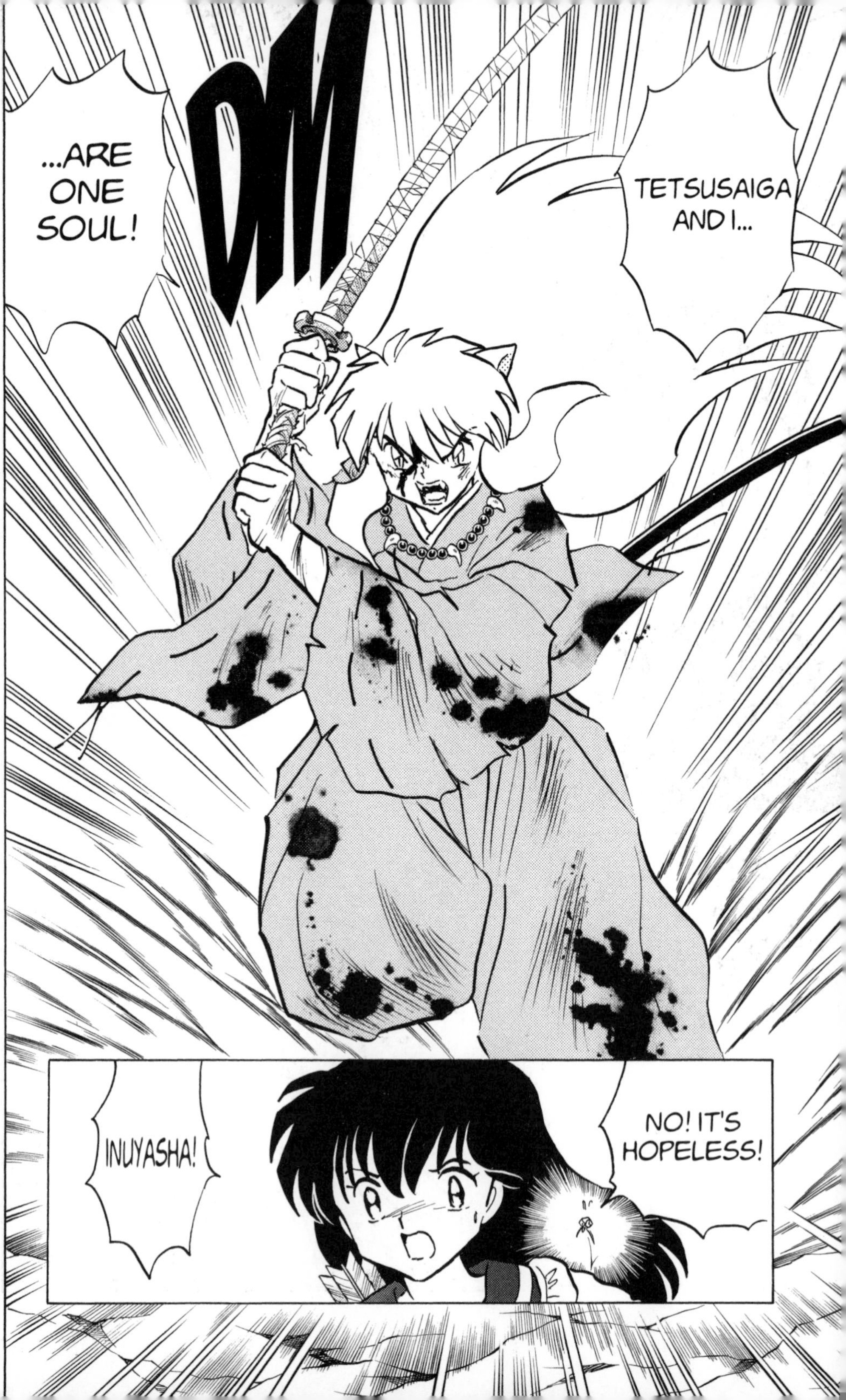
TETSUSAIGA AND I...
DM
...ARE ONE SOUL!
NO! IT'S HOPELESS!
INUYASHA!

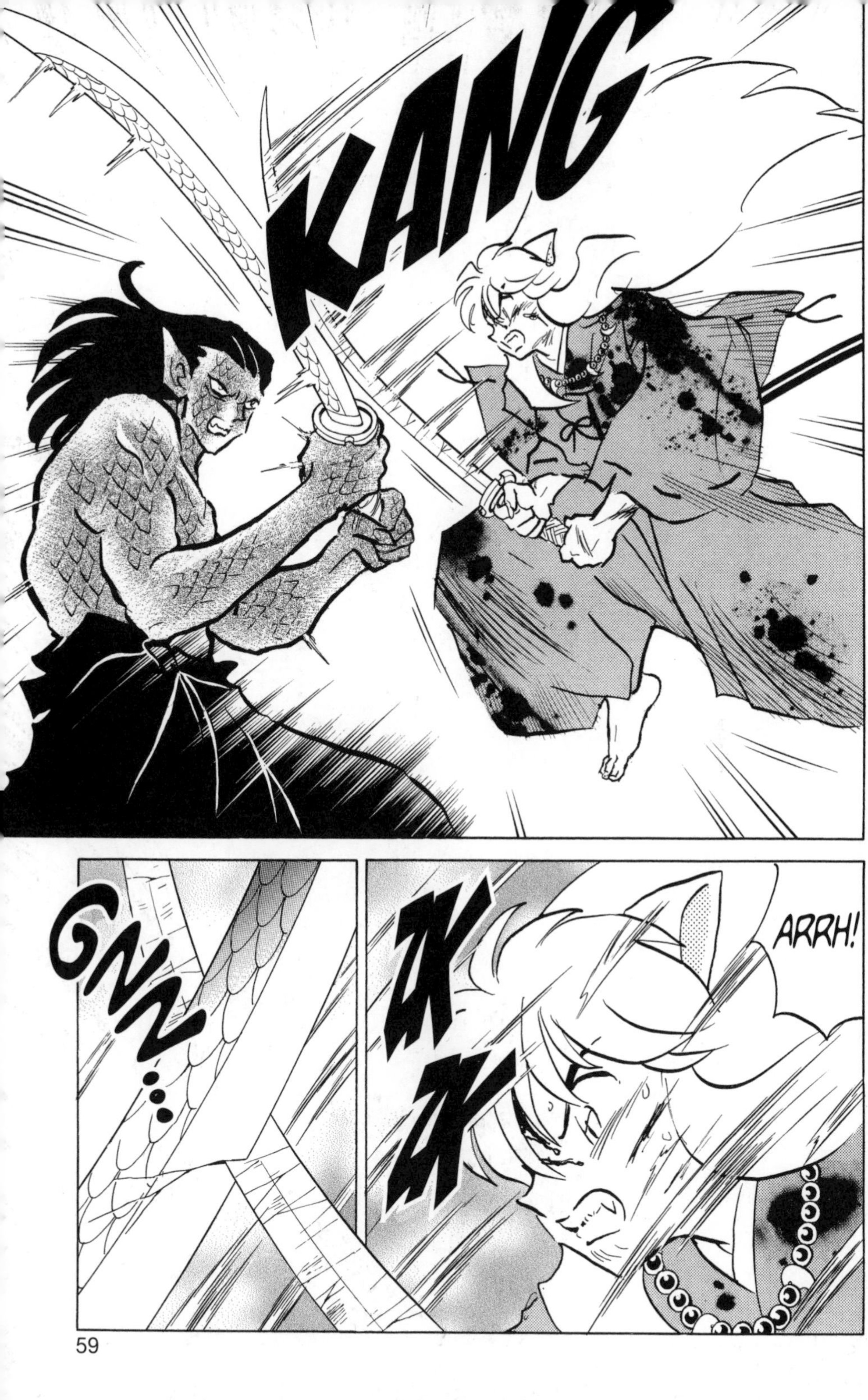
KANG
ARRH!
GNN...

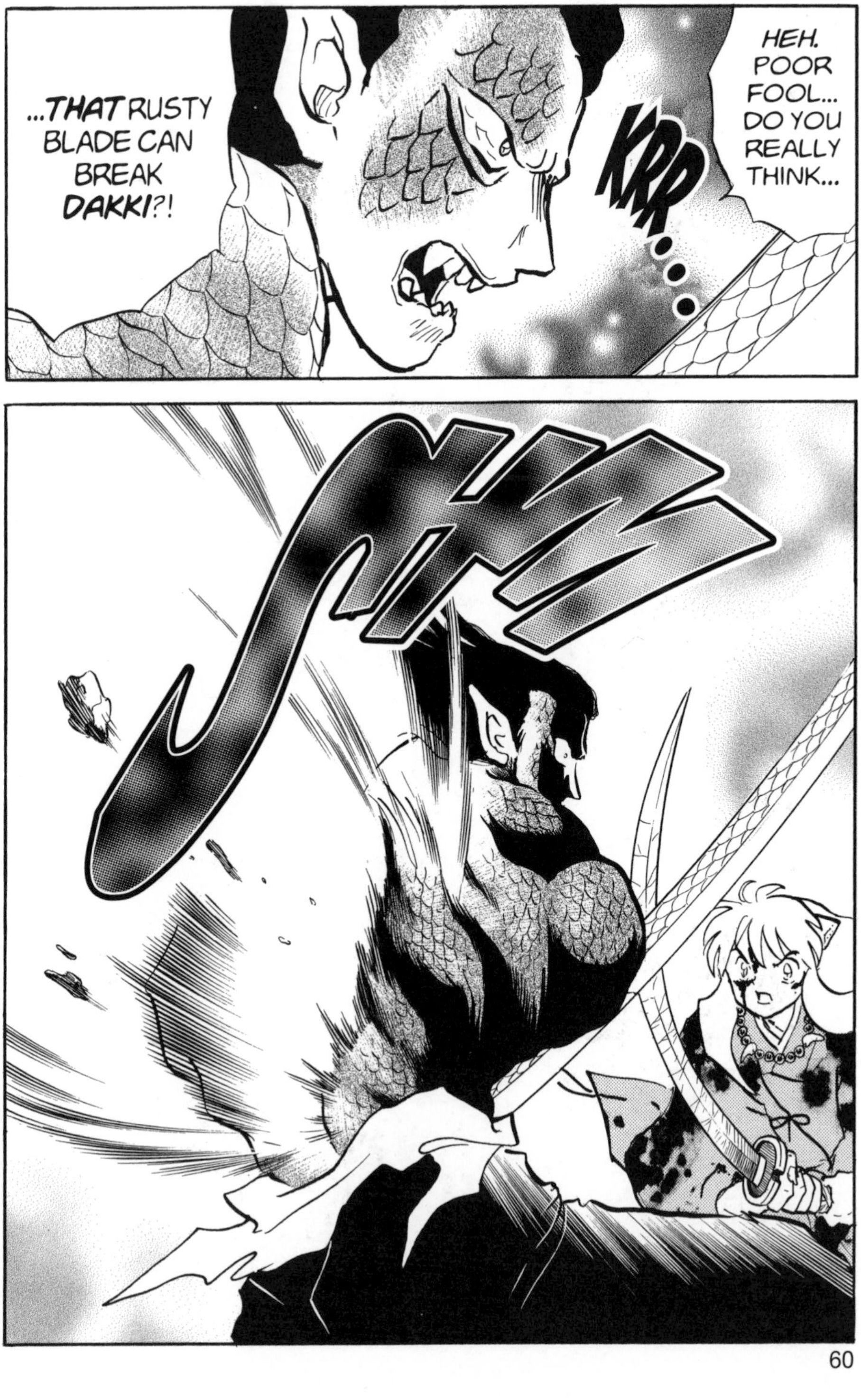
HEH. POOR FOOL... DO YOU REALLY THINK...
KRR...
...THAT RUSTY BLADE CAN BREAK DAKKI?!

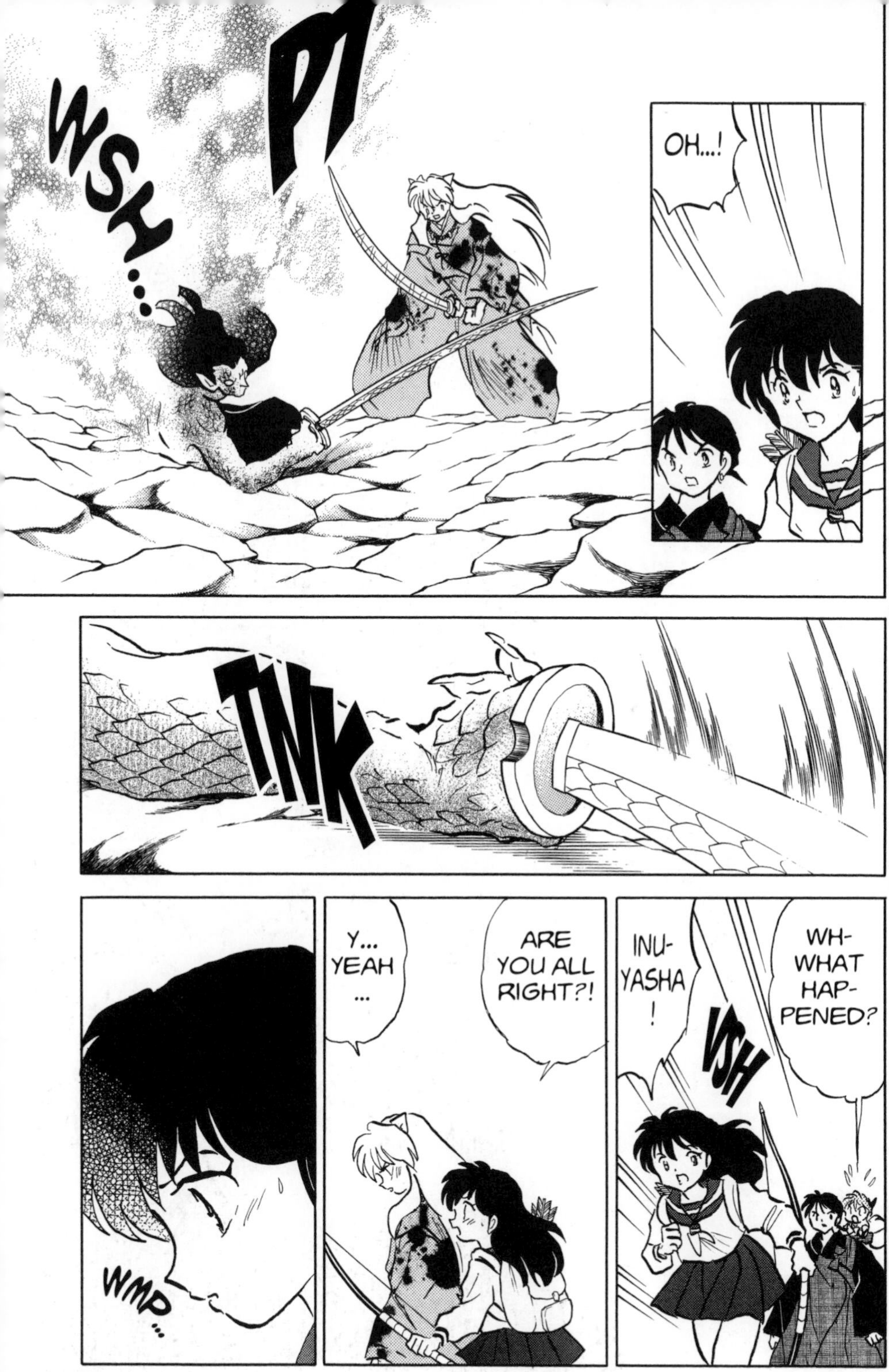

OH...!
WSH...
TINK
WH-WHAT HAP-PENED?
VSH
INU-YASHA!
ARE YOU ALL RIGHT?!
Y... YEAH ...
WMP...

TETSUSAIGA...
...DIDN'T CHANGE!
LOOK AT THIS, INU-YASHA.
DAKKI'S FUSED WITH TOSHU'S HAND.
IT'S... LIKE THEY MELDED TO-GETHER.
I SUSPECT...
...DAKKI, FEARING ITS OWN DESTRUC-TION...
...SIPHONED ALL OF INUYASHA'S ATTACKS...
...INTO TOSHU'S BODY... AND HAD HIM TAKE THE DAMAGE.
PK PK

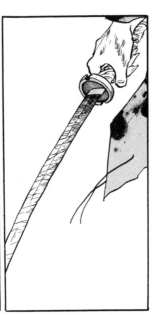

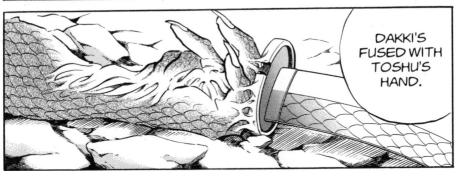

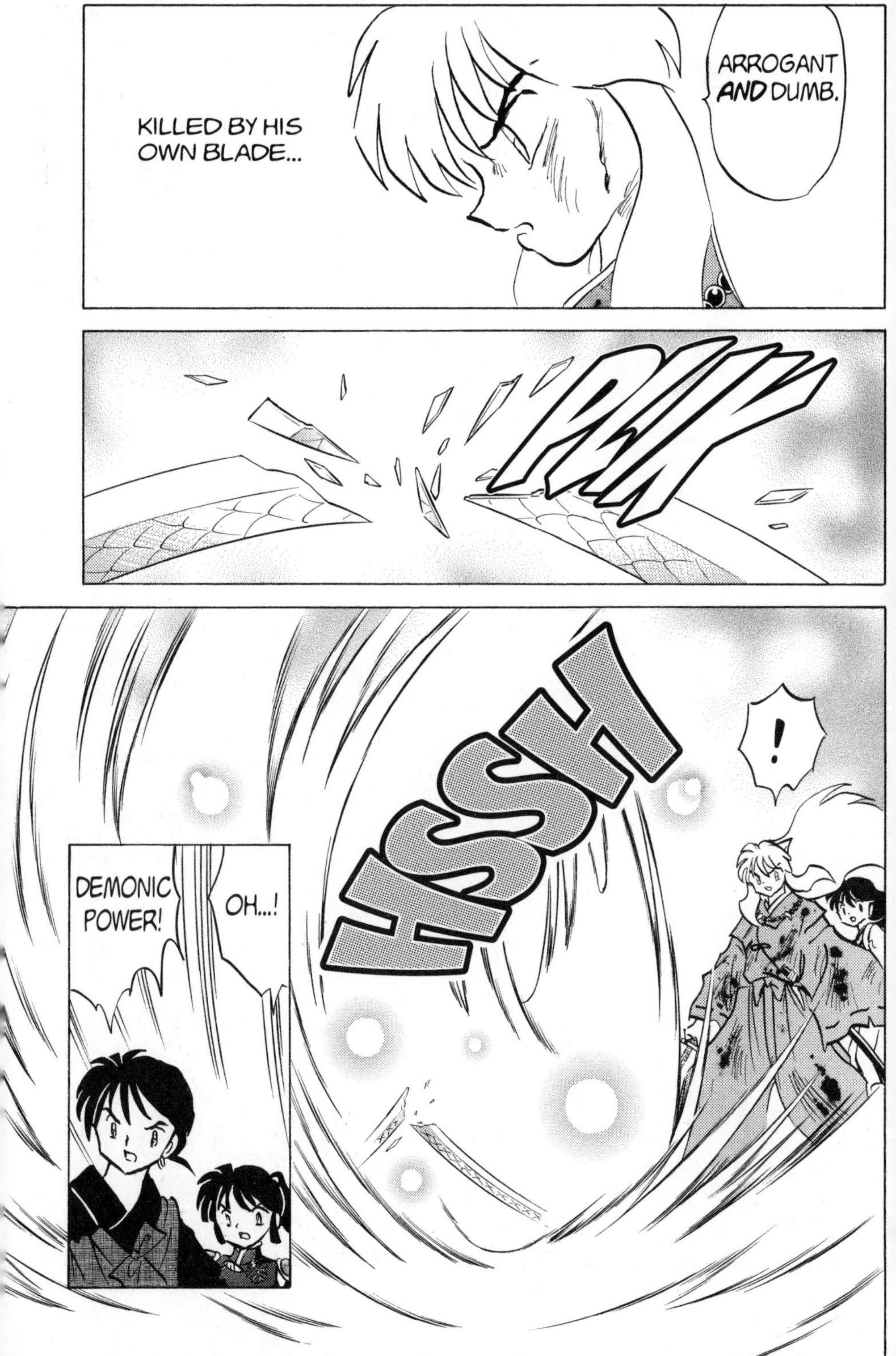
ARROGANT AND DUMB.
KILLED BY HIS OWN BLADE...
!
HISSH
OH...!
DEMONIC POWER!

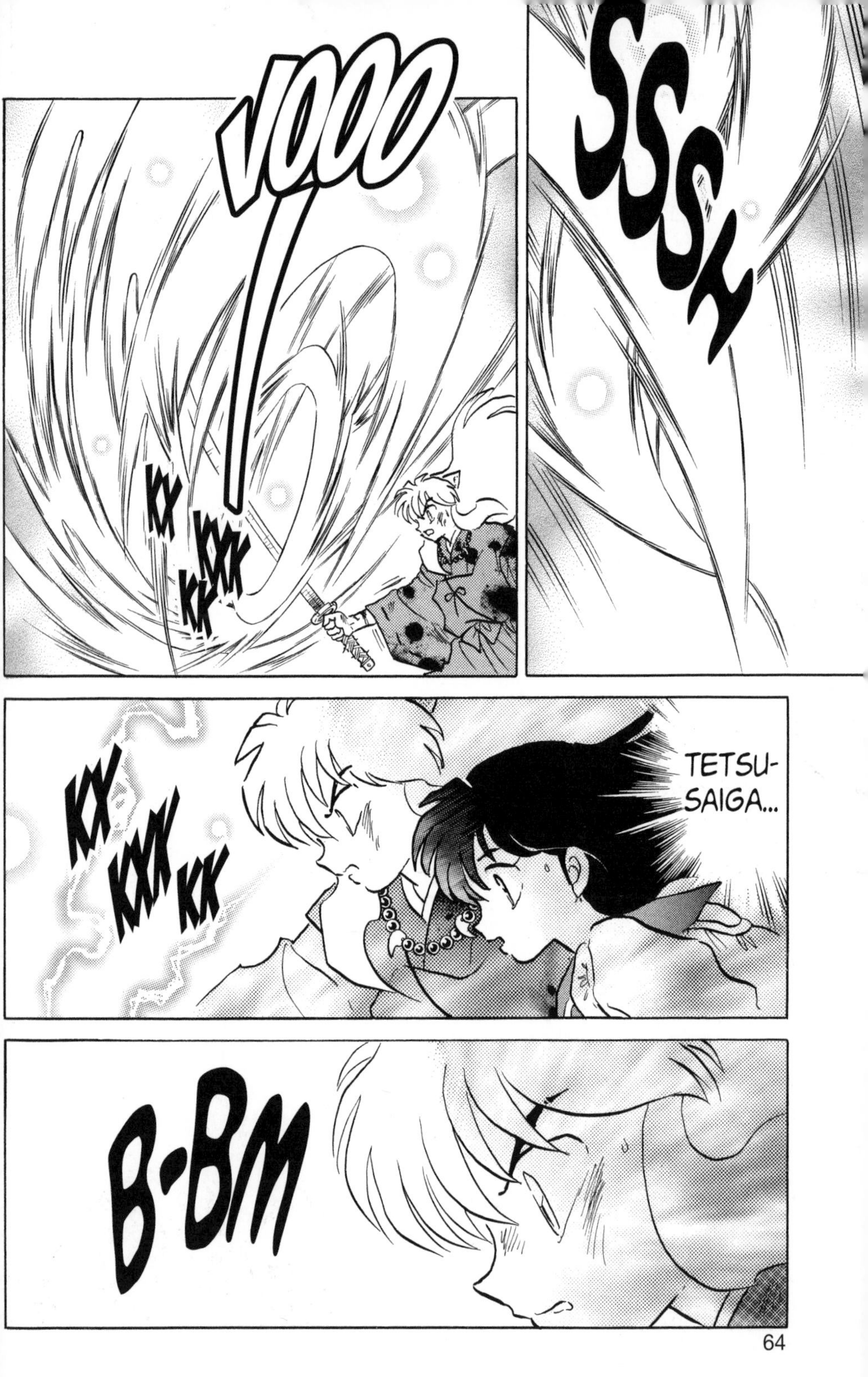
SSSH
VOOO
KKKKK KK
TETSU-
SAIGA...
KKKKK KK
B-BM

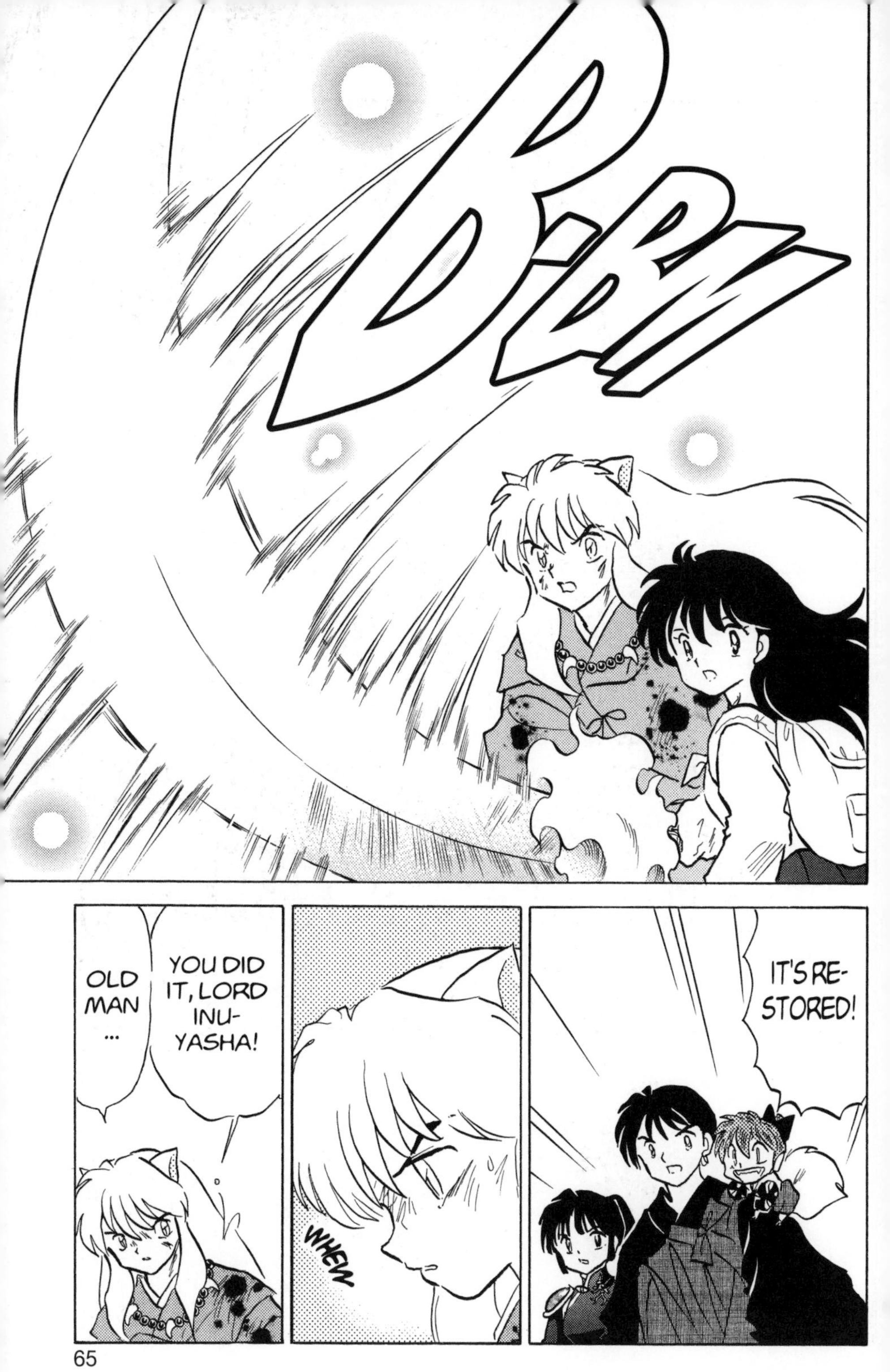
IT'S RE-STORED!
WHEW
YOU DID IT, LORD INU-YASHA!
OLD MAN ...

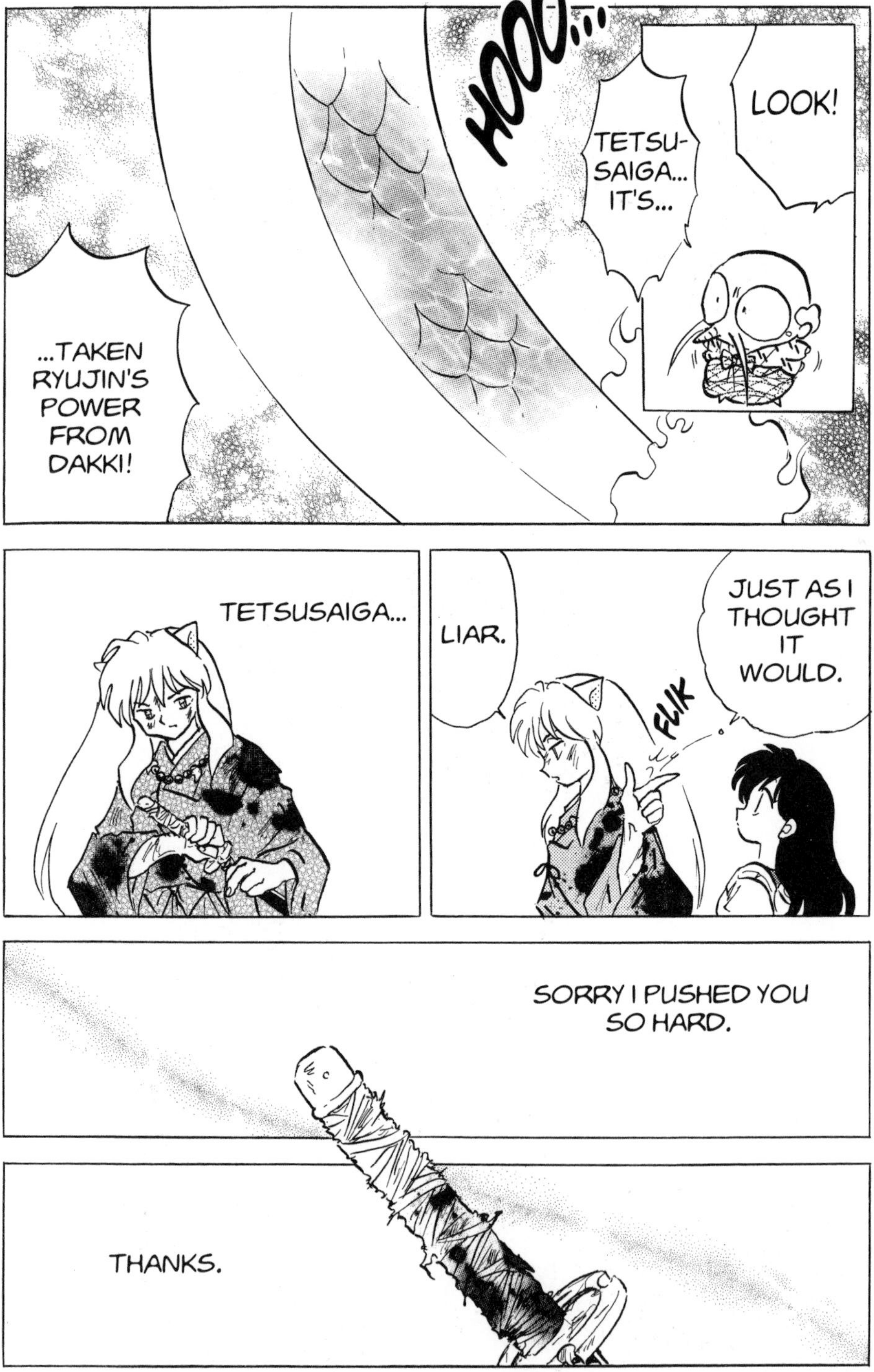
LOOK!
TETSU-SAIGA... IT'S...
HOOO...
...TAKEN RYUJIN'S POWER FROM DAKKI!
JUST AS I THOUGHT IT WOULD.
FLIK
LIAR.
TETSUSAIGA...
SORRY I PUSHED YOU SO HARD.
THANKS.

SCROLL FOUR
A PEACEFUL MEAL

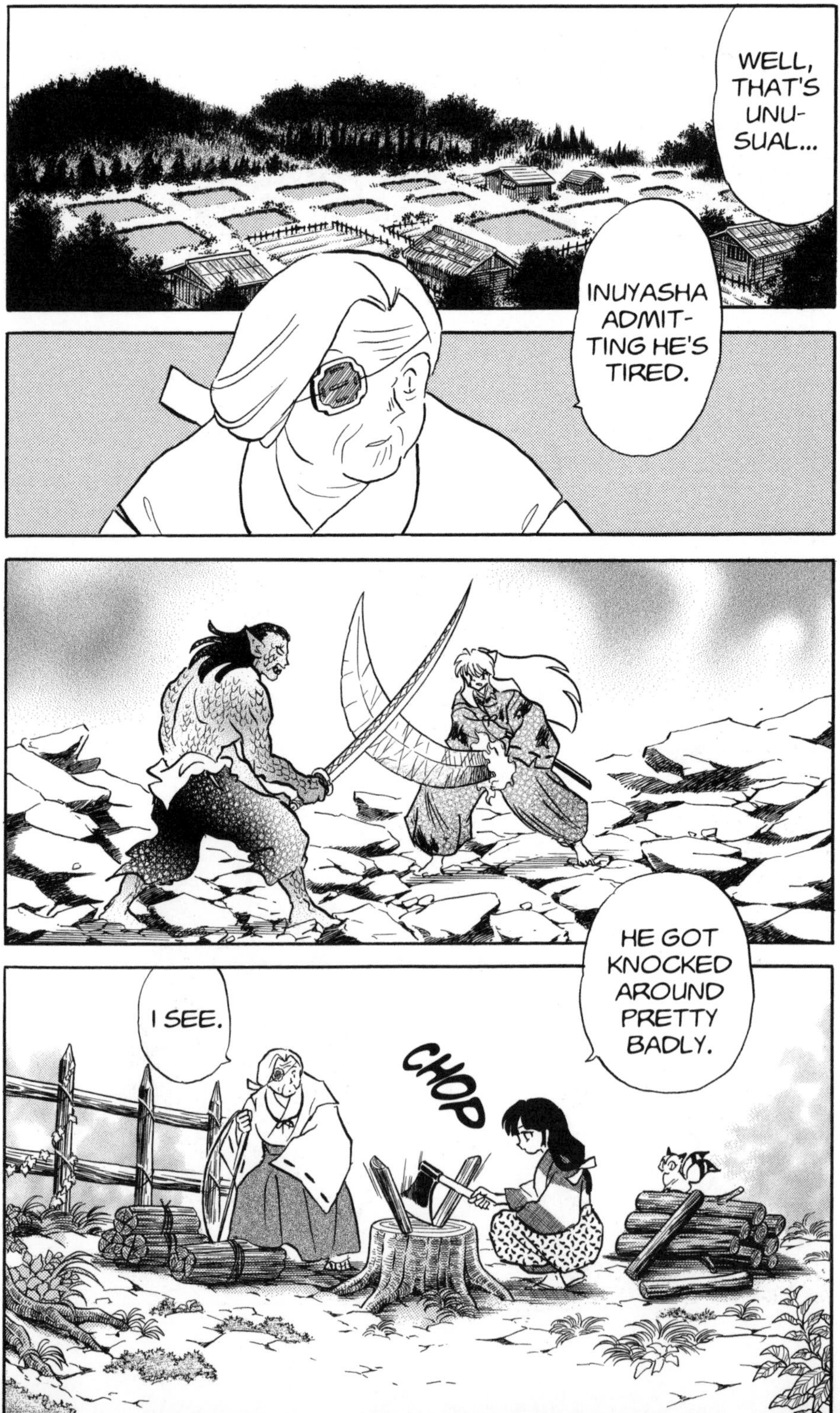
WELL, THAT'S UNUSUAL...
INUYASHA ADMITTING HE'S TIRED.
HE GOT KNOCKED AROUND PRETTY BADLY.
CHOP
I SEE.

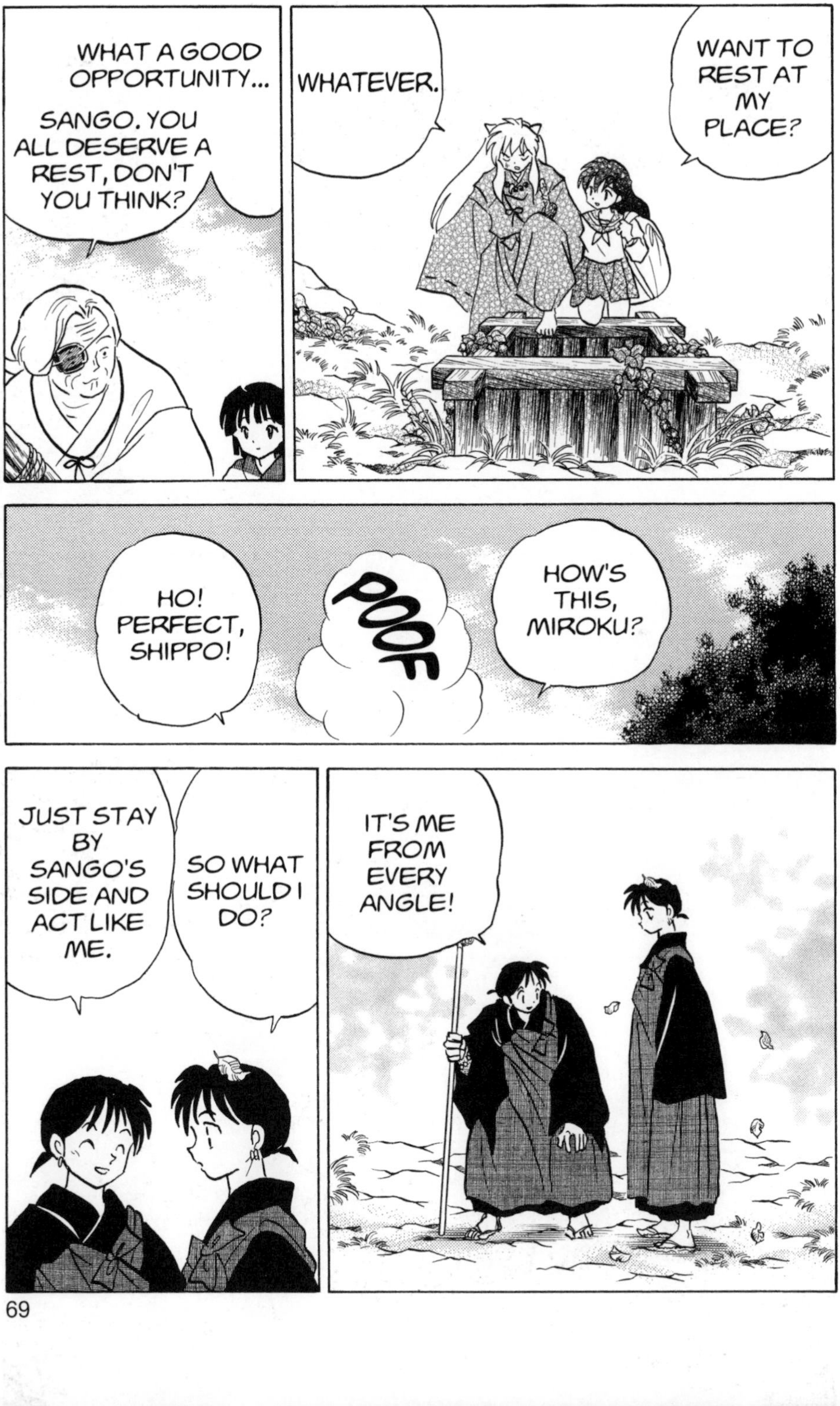
WANT TO REST AT MY PLACE?
WHATEVER.
WHAT A GOOD OPPORTUNITY...
SANGO. YOU ALL DESERVE A REST, DON'T YOU THINK?
HOW'S THIS, MIROKU?
POOF
HO! PERFECT, SHIPPO!
IT'S ME FROM EVERY ANGLE!
SO WHAT SHOULD I DO?
JUST STAY BY SANGO'S SIDE AND ACT LIKE ME.

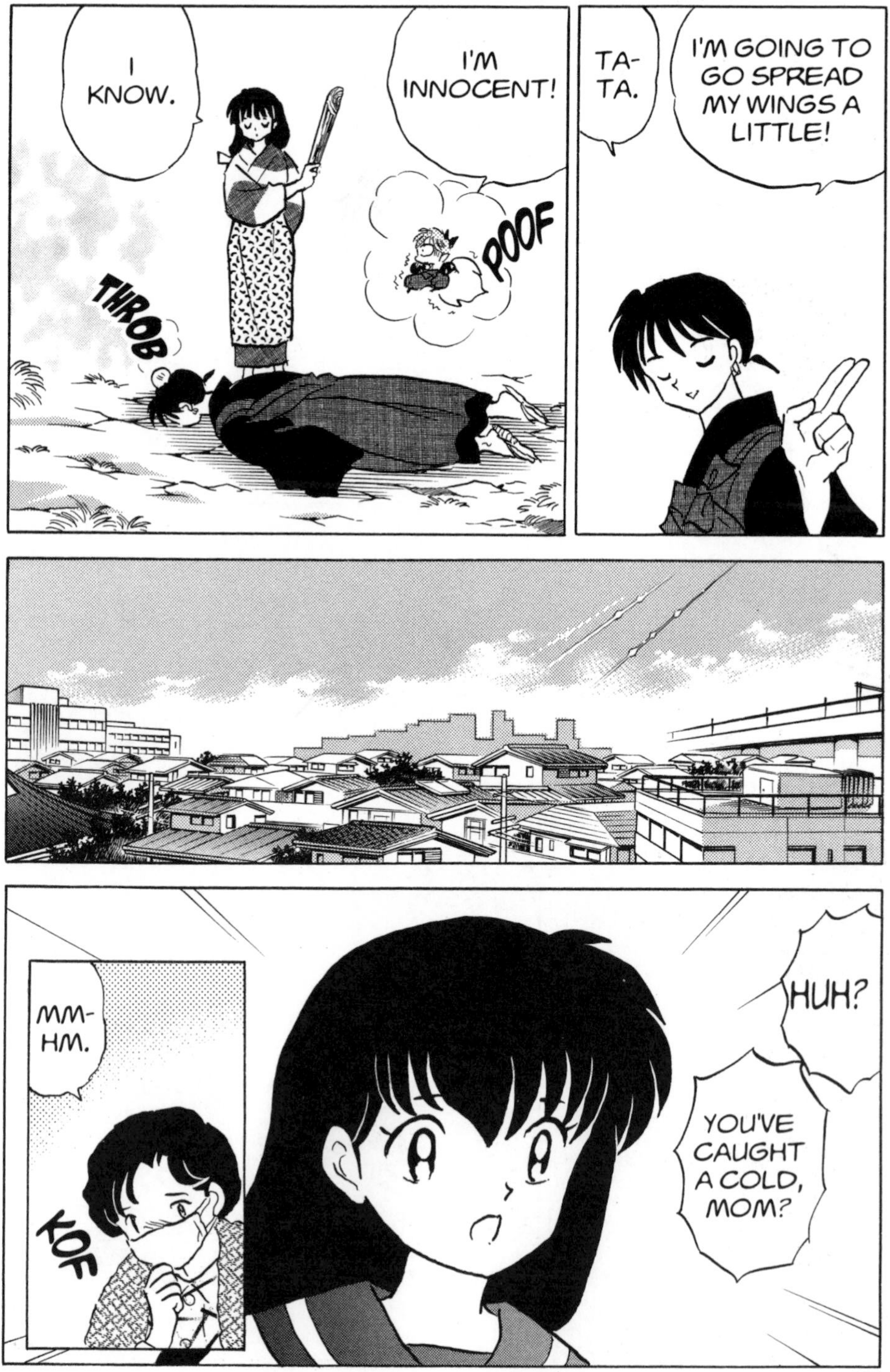
I'M GOING TO GO SPREAD MY WINGS A LITTLE!
TA-TA.
I'M INNOCENT!
POOF
I KNOW.
THROB
HUH?
YOU'VE CAUGHT A COLD, MOM?
MM-HM.
KOF

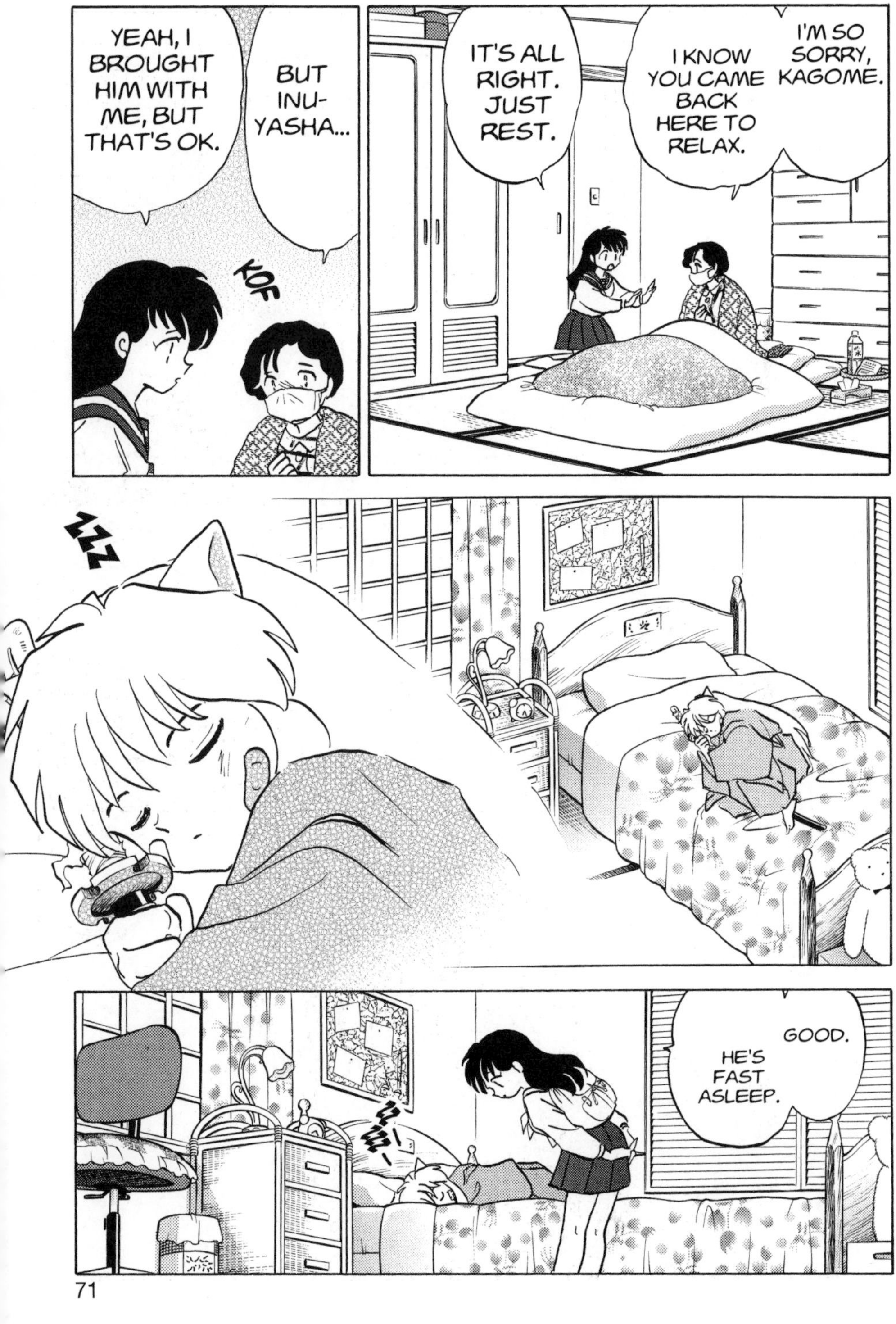
I'M SO SORRY, KAGOME.
I KNOW YOU CAME BACK HERE TO RELAX.
IT'S ALL RIGHT. JUST REST.
BUT INU-YASHA...
YEAH, I BROUGHT HIM WITH ME, BUT THAT'S OK.
KOF
ZZZ
GOOD.
HE'S FAST ASLEEP.

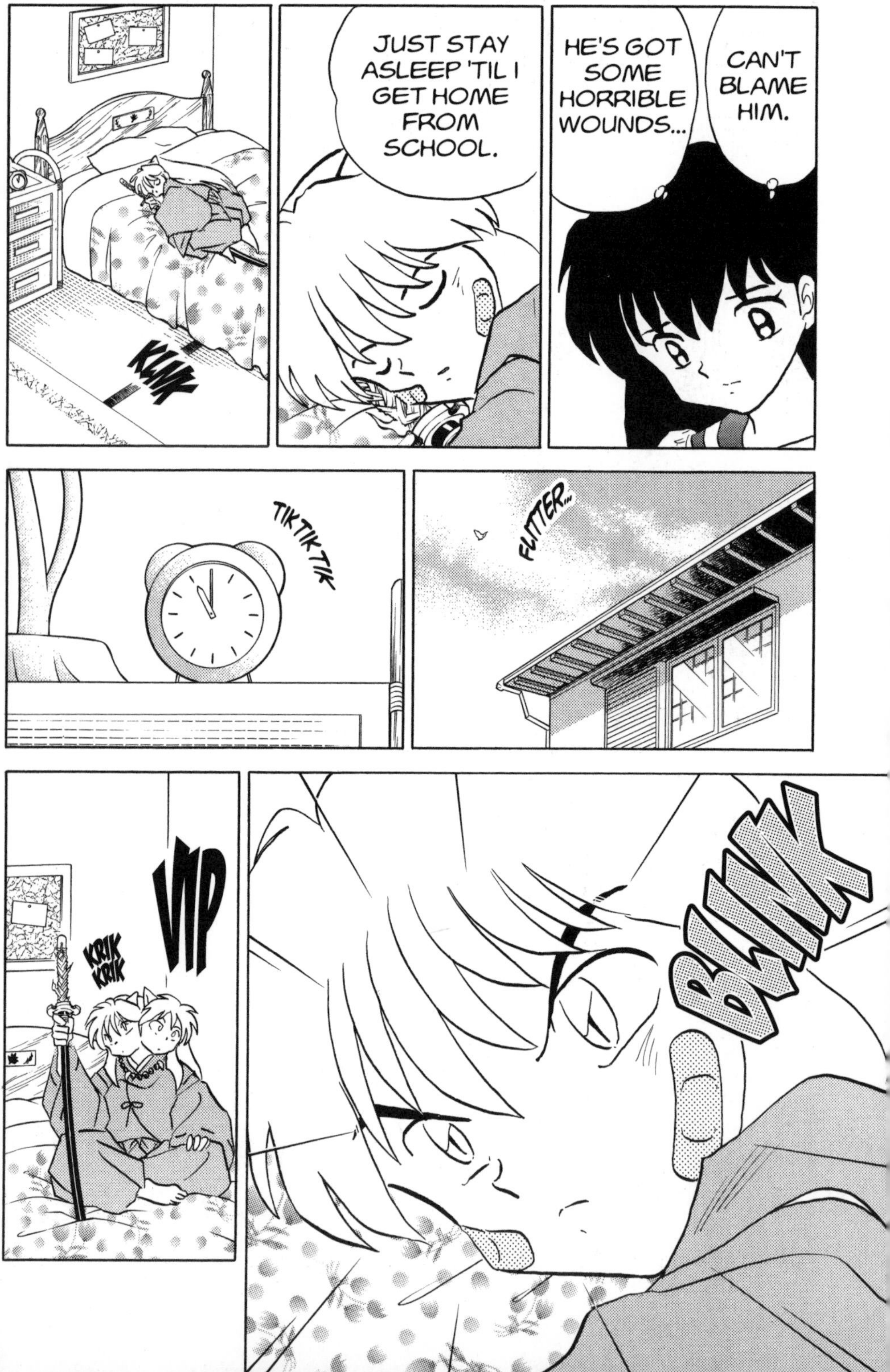
CAN'T BLAME HIM.
HE'S GOT SOME HORRIBLE WOUNDS...
JUST STAY ASLEEP 'TIL I GET HOME FROM SCHOOL.
KLINK
FLUTTER...
TIKTIKTIK
BLINK
VIP
KRIK KRIK

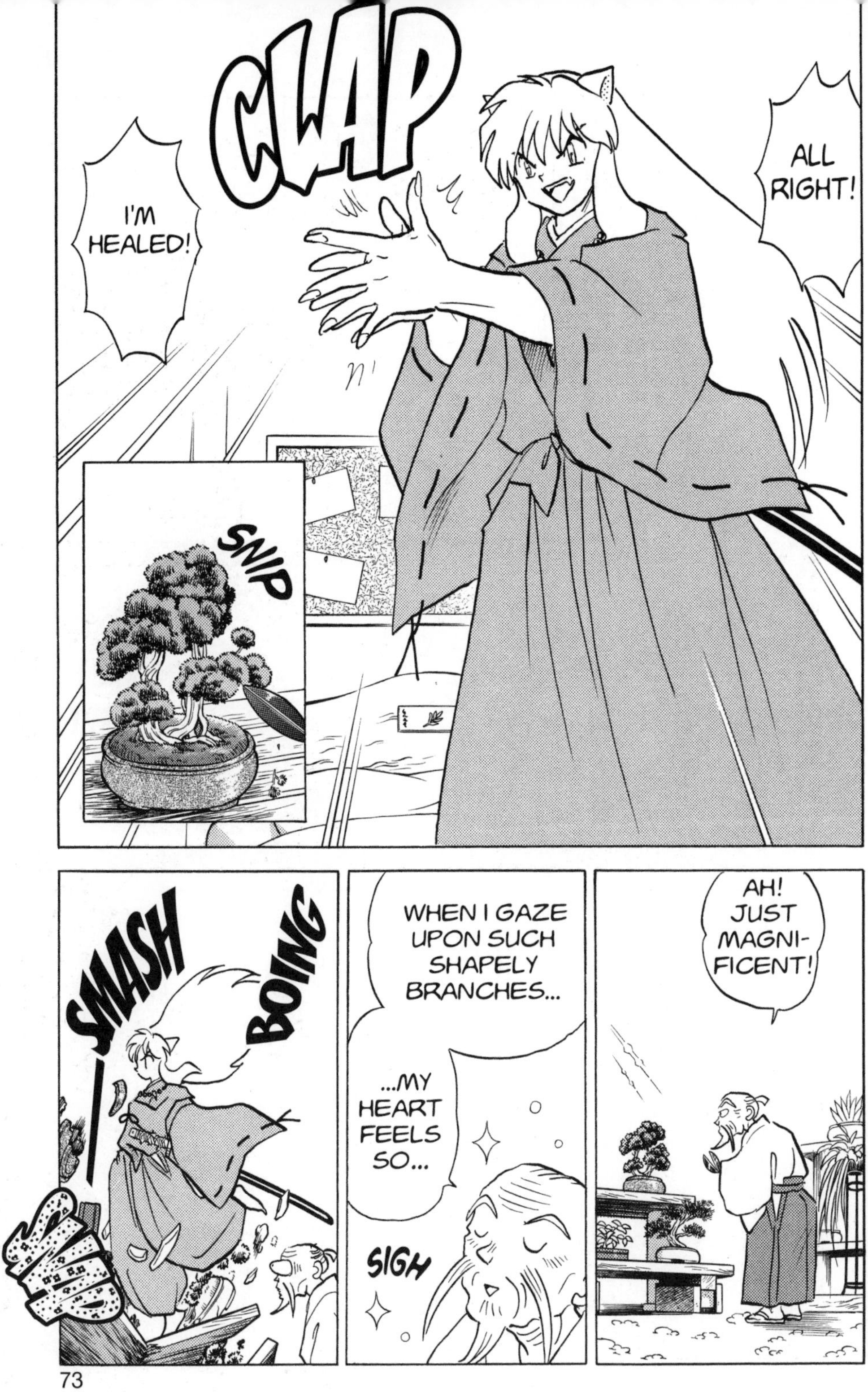
CLAP
ALL RIGHT!
I'M HEALED!
SNIP
AH! JUST MAGNI- FICENT!
WHEN I GAZE UPON SUCH SHAPELY BRANCHES...
...MY HEART FEELS SO...
SIGH
BOING
SMASH

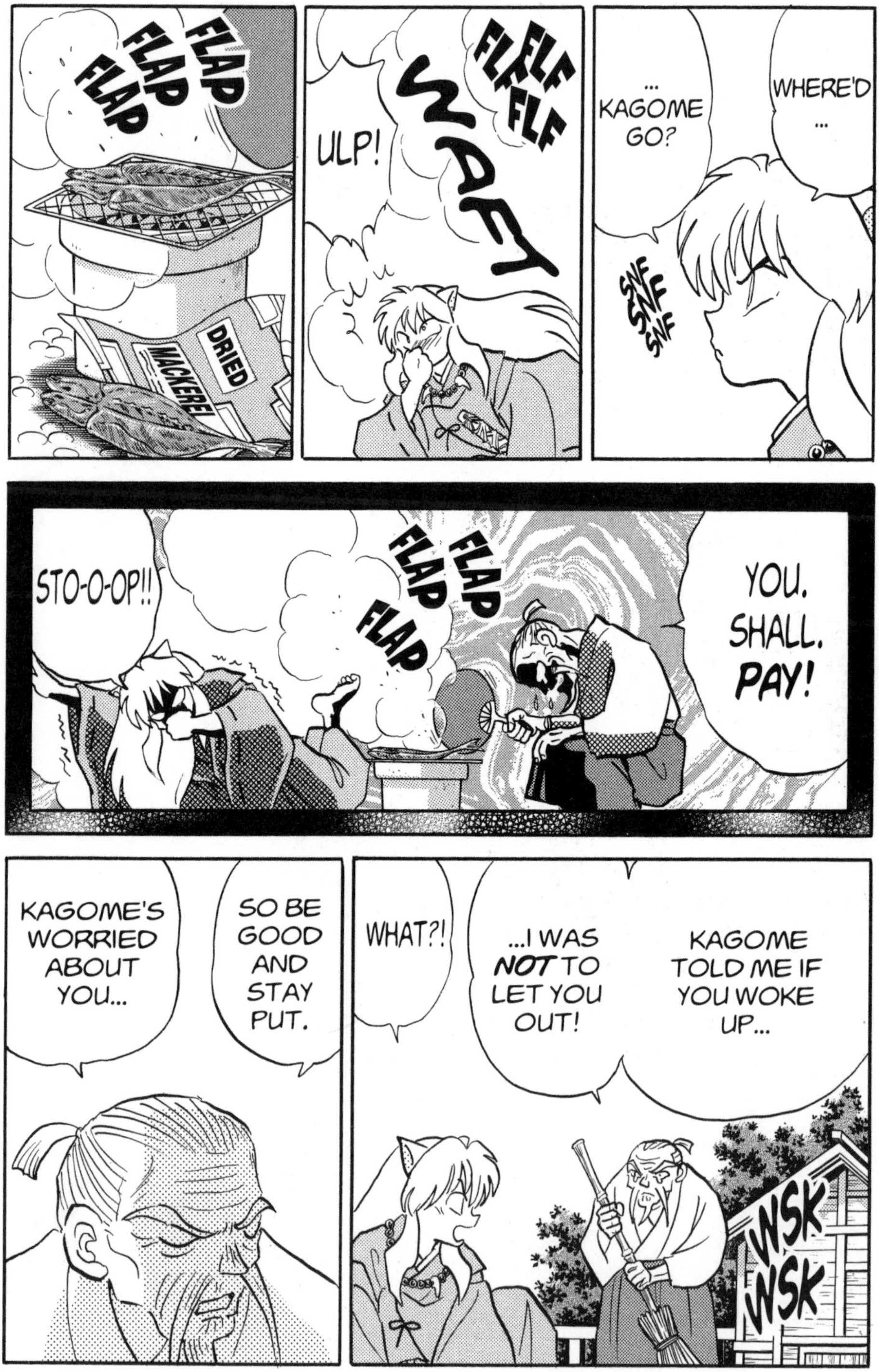
WHERE'D ...
... KAGOME GO?
SNF SNF SNF SNF
FLF FLF FLF
WAFT
ULP!
FLAP FLAP FLAP
DRIED MACKEREL
YOU. SHALL. PAY!
FLAP FLAP FLAP
STO-O-OP!!
KAGOME TOLD ME IF YOU WOKE UP...
...I WAS *NOT* TO LET YOU OUT!
WHAT?!
WSK WSK
SO BE GOOD AND STAY PUT.
KAGOME'S WORRIED ABOUT YOU...

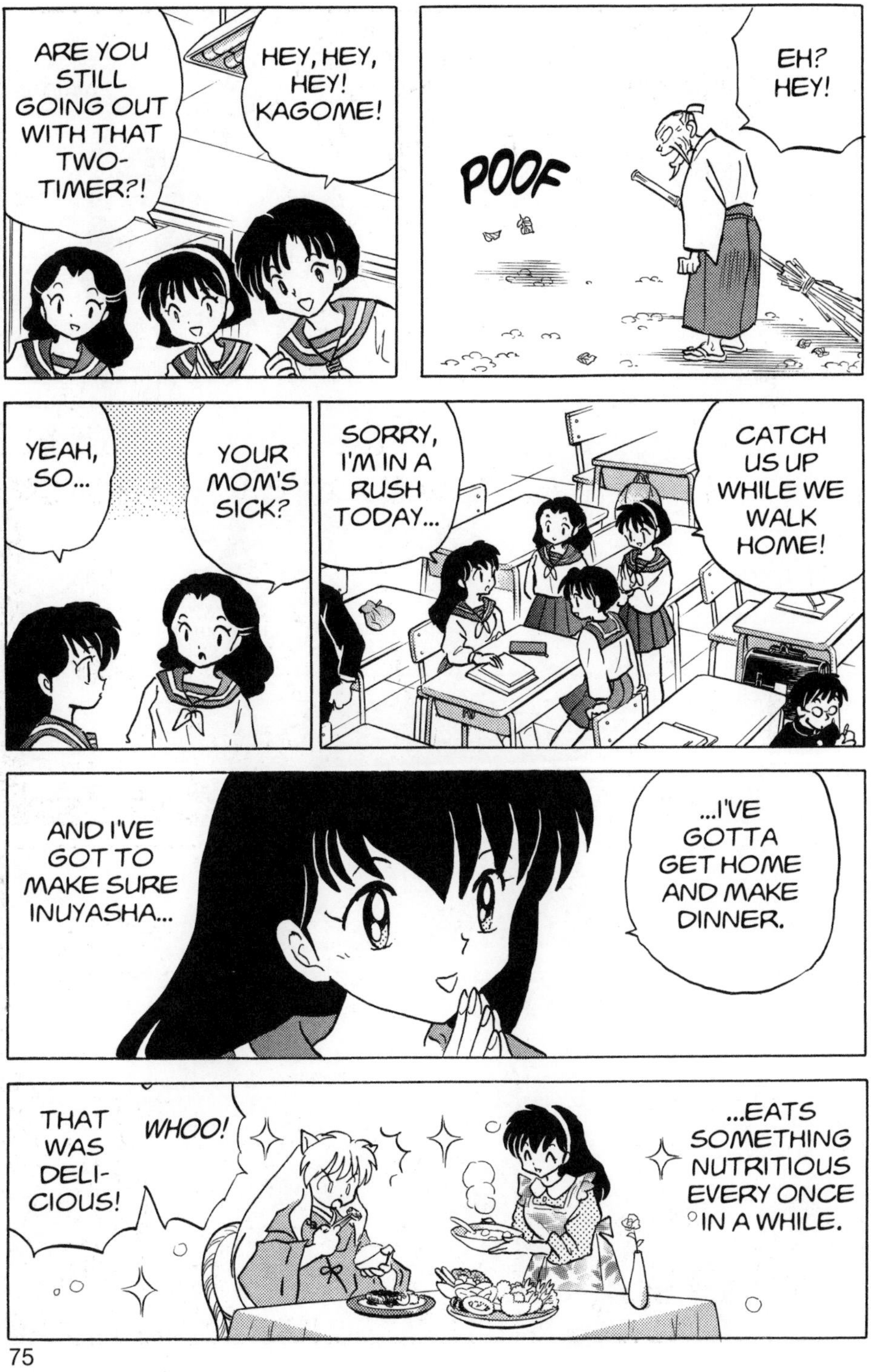
EH? HEY!
POOF
HEY, HEY, HEY! KAGOME!
ARE YOU STILL GOING OUT WITH THAT TWO-TIMER?!
CATCH US UP WHILE WE WALK HOME!
SORRY, I'M IN A RUSH TODAY...
YOUR MOM'S SICK?
YEAH, SO...
...I'VE GOTTA GET HOME AND MAKE DINNER.
AND I'VE GOT TO MAKE SURE INUYASHA...
...EATS SOMETHING NUTRITIOUS EVERY ONCE IN A WHILE.
WHOO!
THAT WAS DELI-CIOUS!

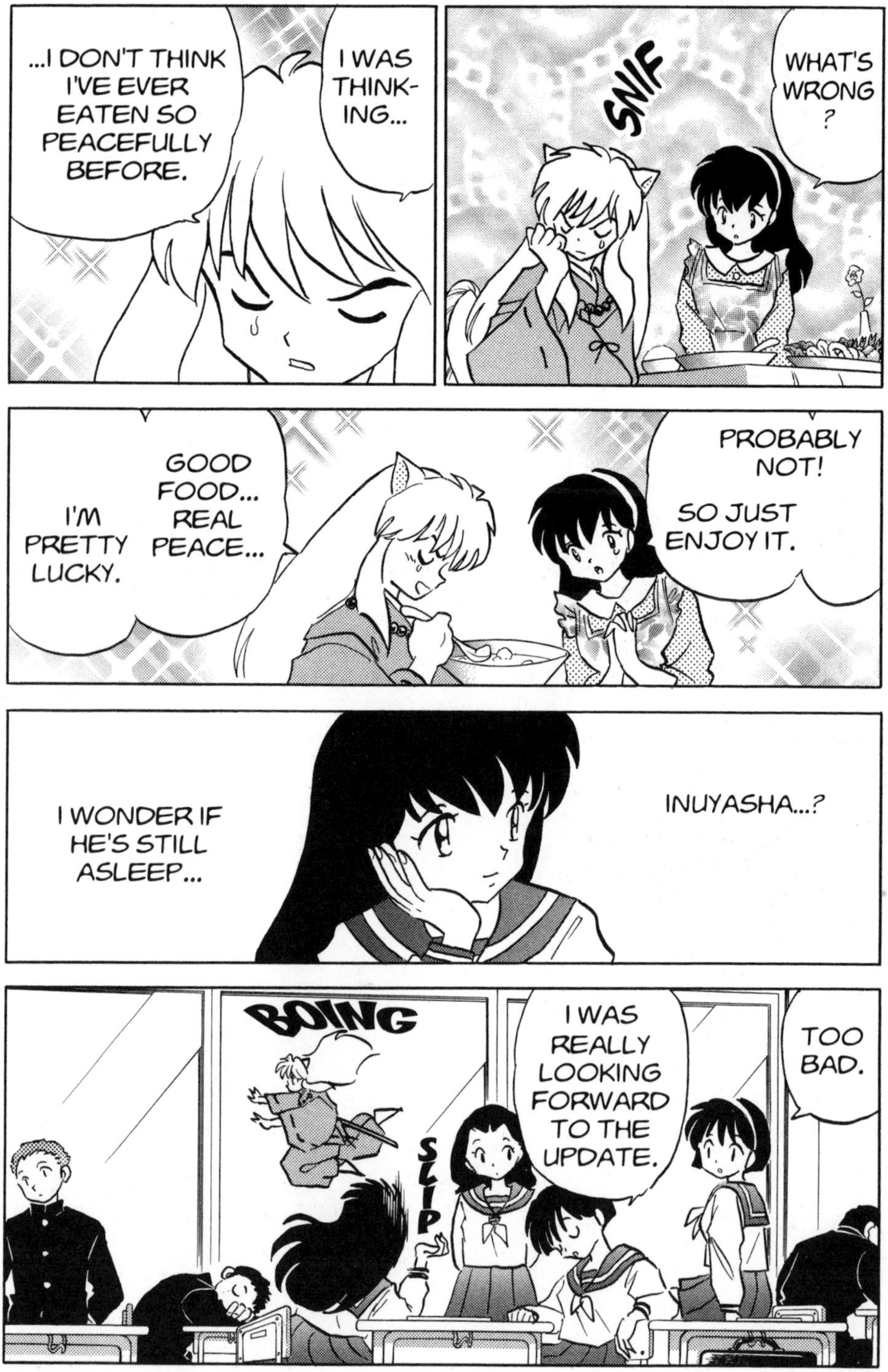
WHAT'S WRONG?
SNIF
I WAS THINKING...
...I DON'T THINK I'VE EVER EATEN SO PEACEFULLY BEFORE.
PROBABLY NOT!
SO JUST ENJOY IT.
GOOD FOOD... REAL PEACE...
I'M PRETTY LUCKY.
INUYASHA...?
I WONDER IF HE'S STILL ASLEEP...
TOO BAD.
I WAS REALLY LOOKING FORWARD TO THE UPDATE.
BOING
SLIP

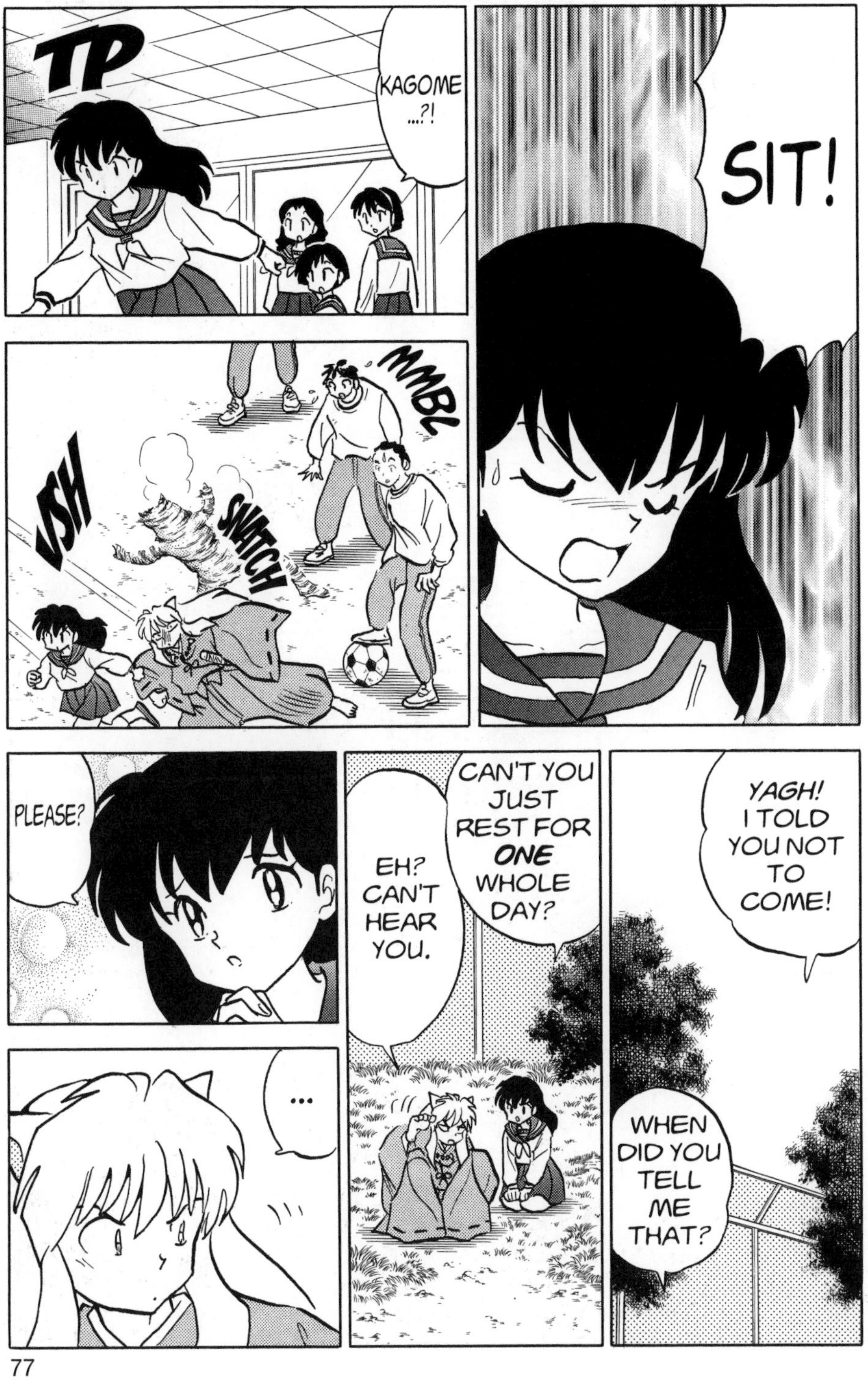
SIT!
TP
KAGOME ...?!
MMBL
SNATCH
VSH
YAGH! I TOLD YOU NOT TO COME!
WHEN DID YOU TELL ME THAT?
CAN'T YOU JUST REST FOR *ONE* WHOLE DAY?
EH? CAN'T HEAR YOU.
PLEASE?
...

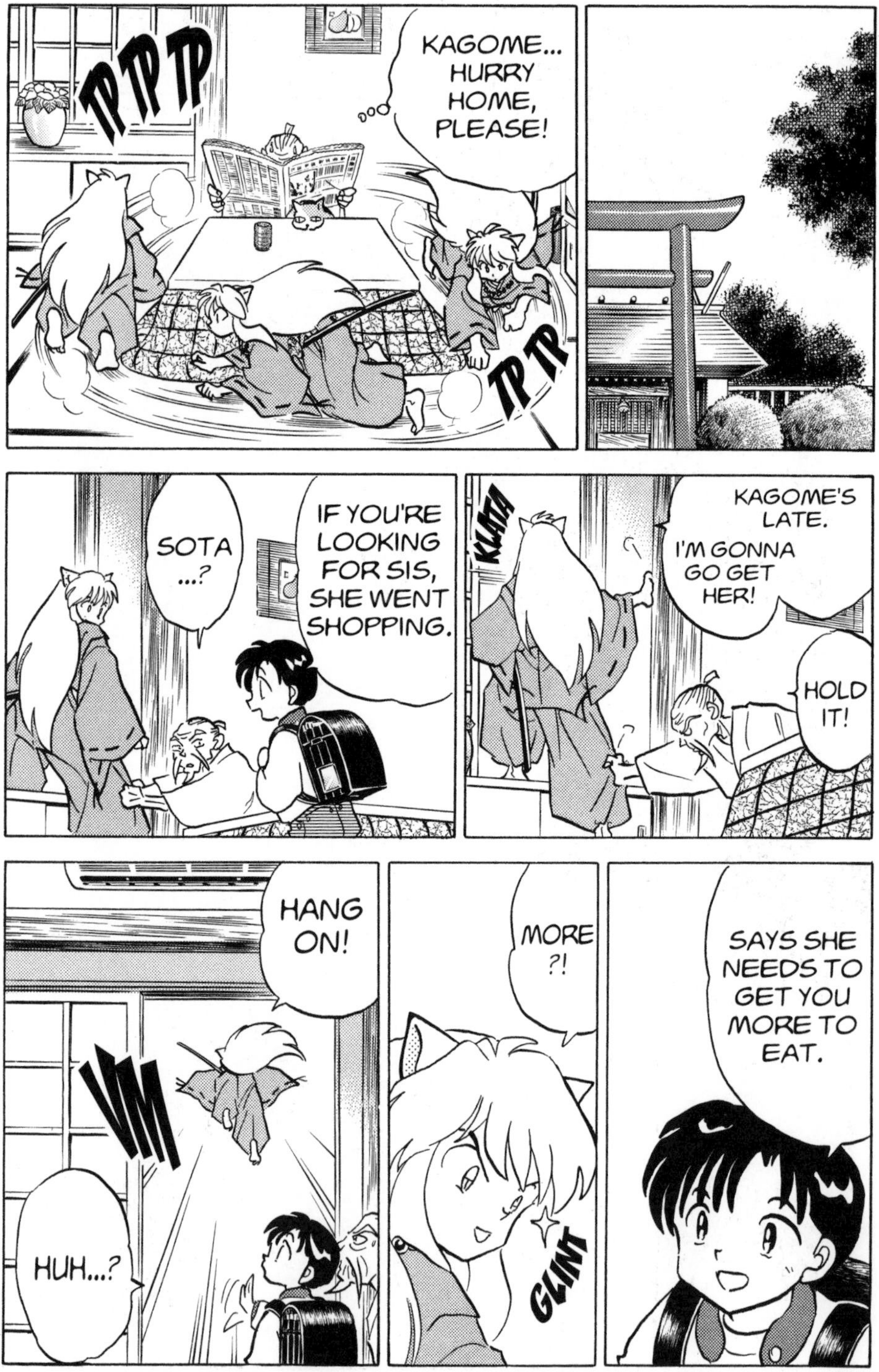
KAGOME... HURRY HOME, PLEASE!
TP TP TP
TP TP
KAGOME'S LATE. I'M GONNA GO GET HER!
KLATA
HOLD IT!
IF YOU'RE LOOKING FOR SIS, SHE WENT SHOPPING.
SOTA ...?
SAYS SHE NEEDS TO GET YOU MORE TO EAT.
MORE ?!
GLINT
HANG ON!
VM
HUH...?

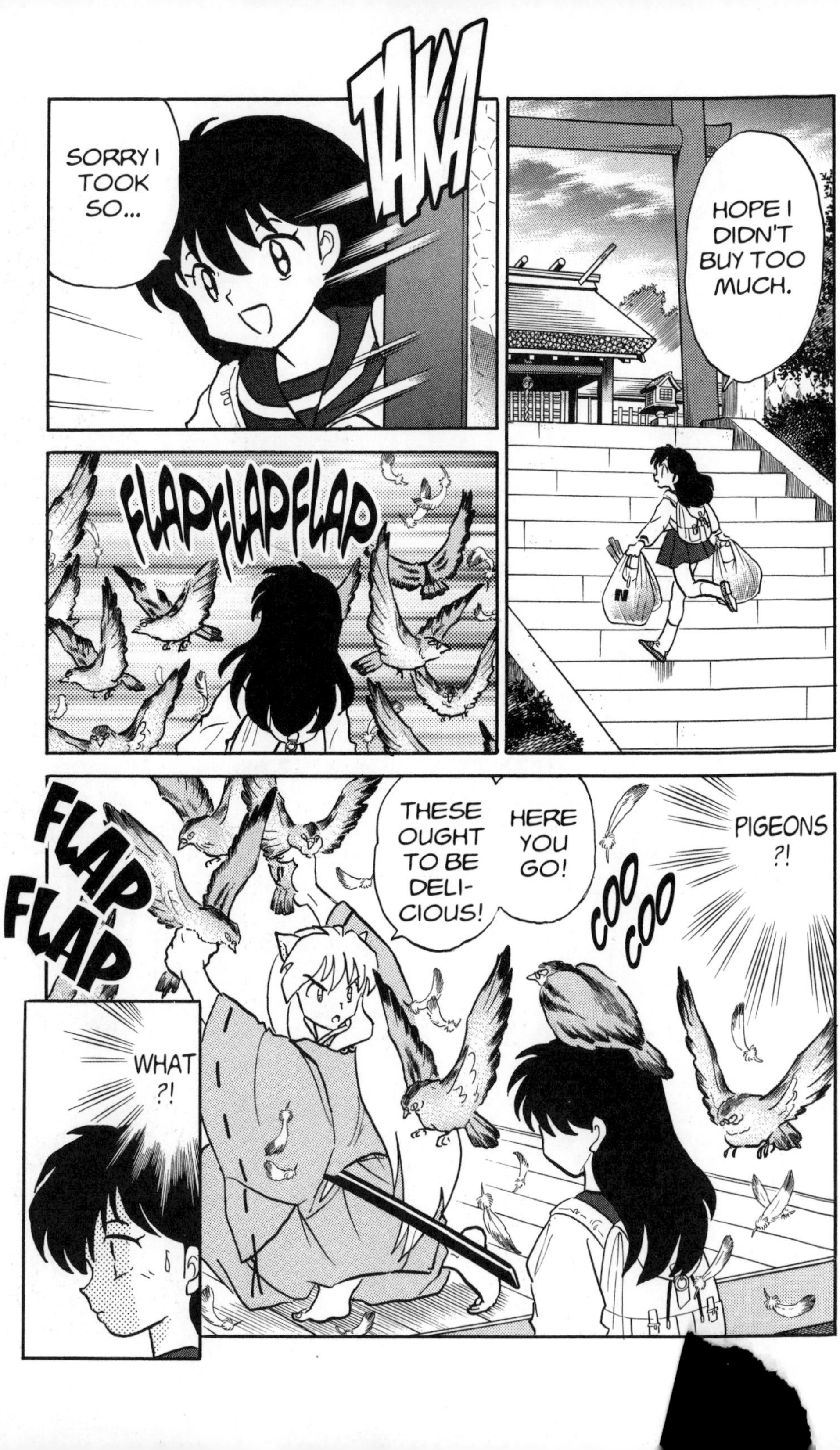
HOPE I DIDN'T BUY TOO MUCH.
TAKA
SORRY I TOOK SO...
FLAPFLAPFLAP
PIGEONS ?!
COO COO
HERE YOU GO!
THESE OUGHT TO BE DELI-CIOUS!
FLAP FLAP
WHAT ?!

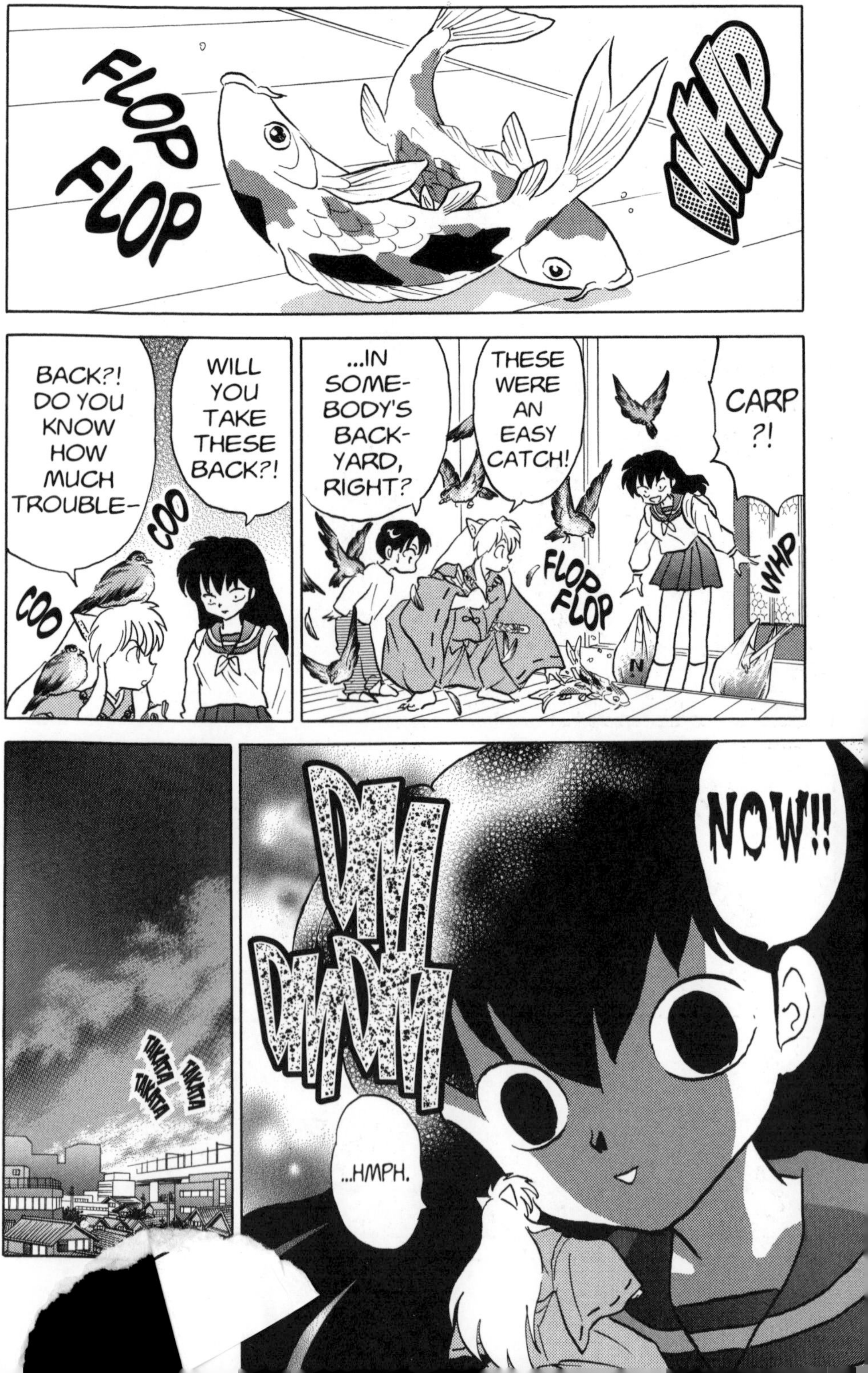
WHP
FLOP FLOP
CARP?!
WHP
FLOP FLOP
THESE WERE AN EASY CATCH!
...IN SOME-BODY'S BACK-YARD, RIGHT?
WILL YOU TAKE THESE BACK?!
COO
BACK?! DO YOU KNOW HOW MUCH TROUBLE-
COO
NOW!!
DM DMDM
...HMPH.
TAKATA TAKATA TAKATA

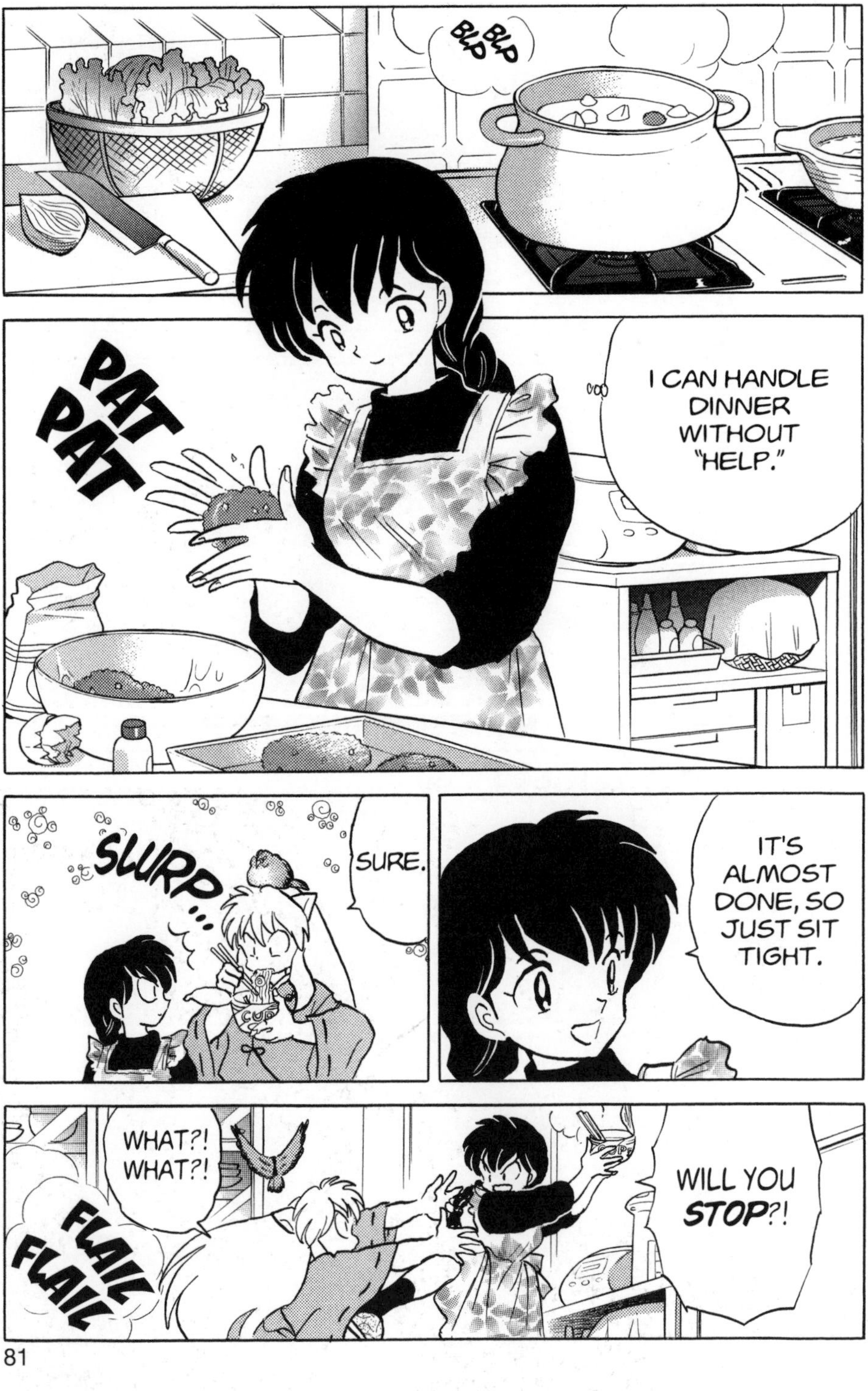
BLP BLP
I CAN HANDLE DINNER WITHOUT "HELP."
PAT PAT
IT'S ALMOST DONE, SO JUST SIT TIGHT.
SURE.
SLURP...
WILL YOU STOP?!
WHAT?! WHAT?!
FLAIL FLAIL

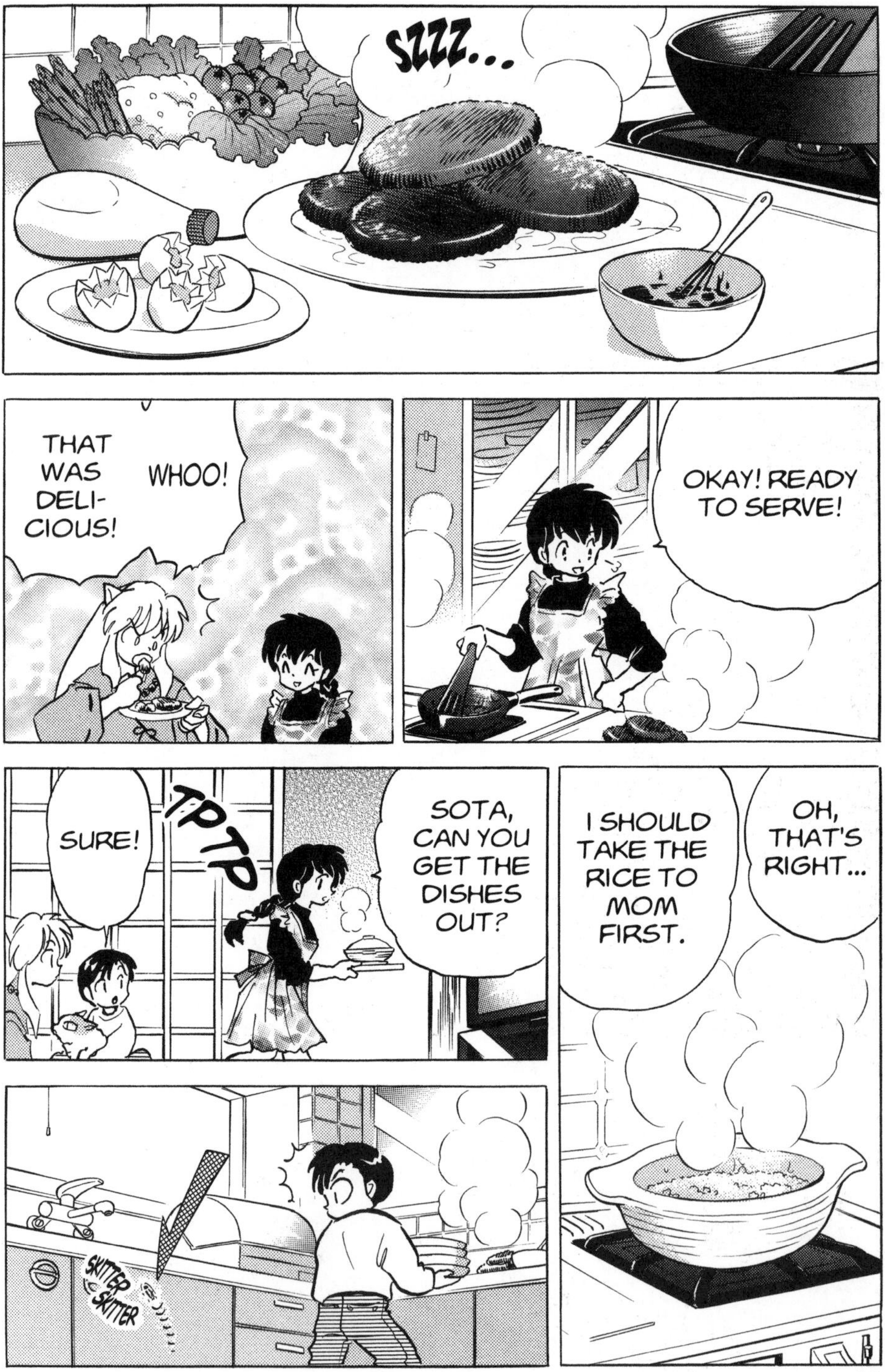
SZZZ...
OKAY! READY TO SERVE!
WHOO!
THAT WAS DELI-CIOUS!
OH, THAT'S RIGHT...
I SHOULD TAKE THE RICE TO MOM FIRST.
SOTA, CAN YOU GET THE DISHES OUT?
TP TP
SURE!
SKITTER SKITTER

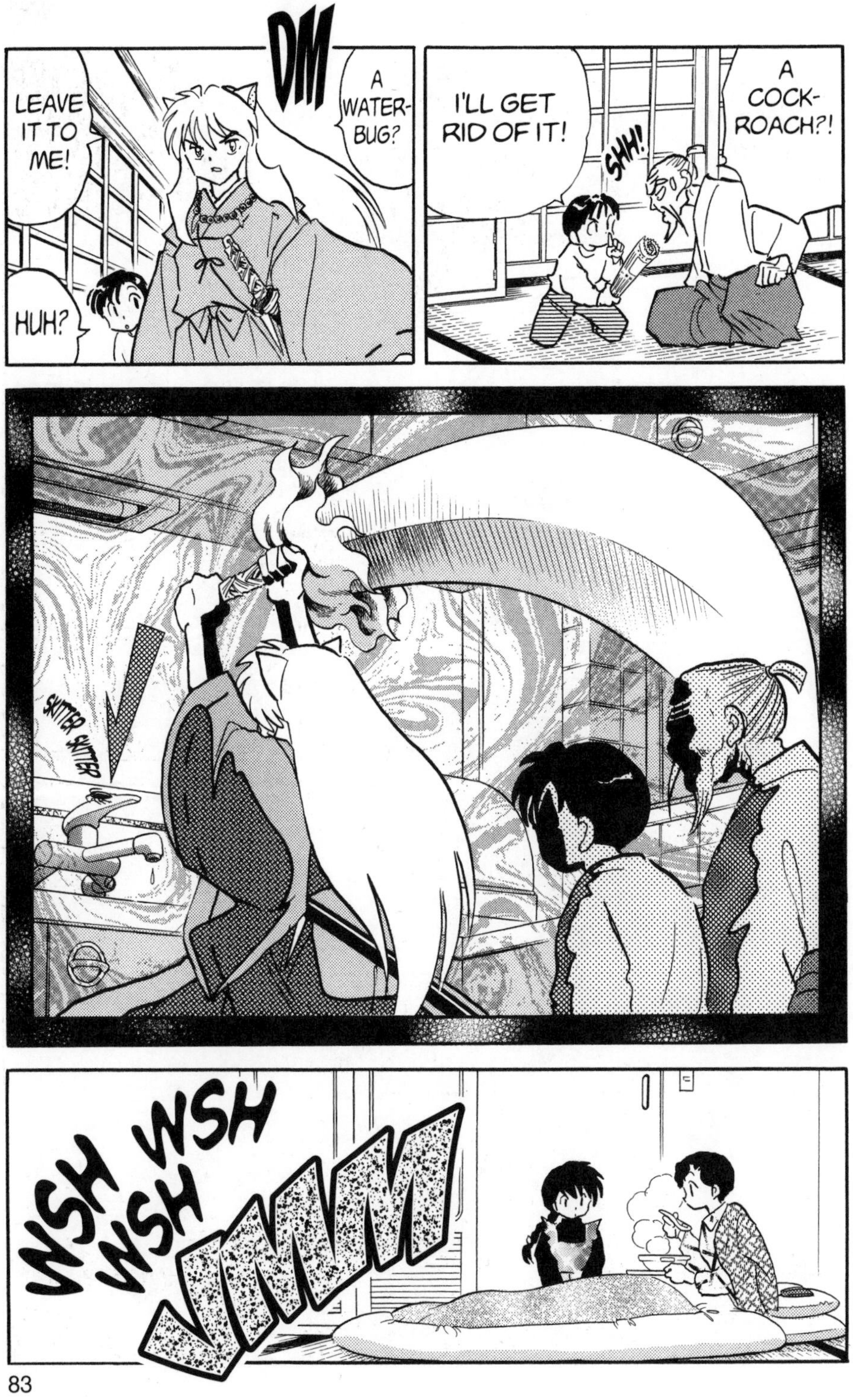
A COCK-ROACH?!
SHH!
I'LL GET RID OF IT!
A WATER-BUG?
DM
LEAVE IT TO ME!
HUH?
SKITTER SKITTER
VMMM
WSH WSH
WSH

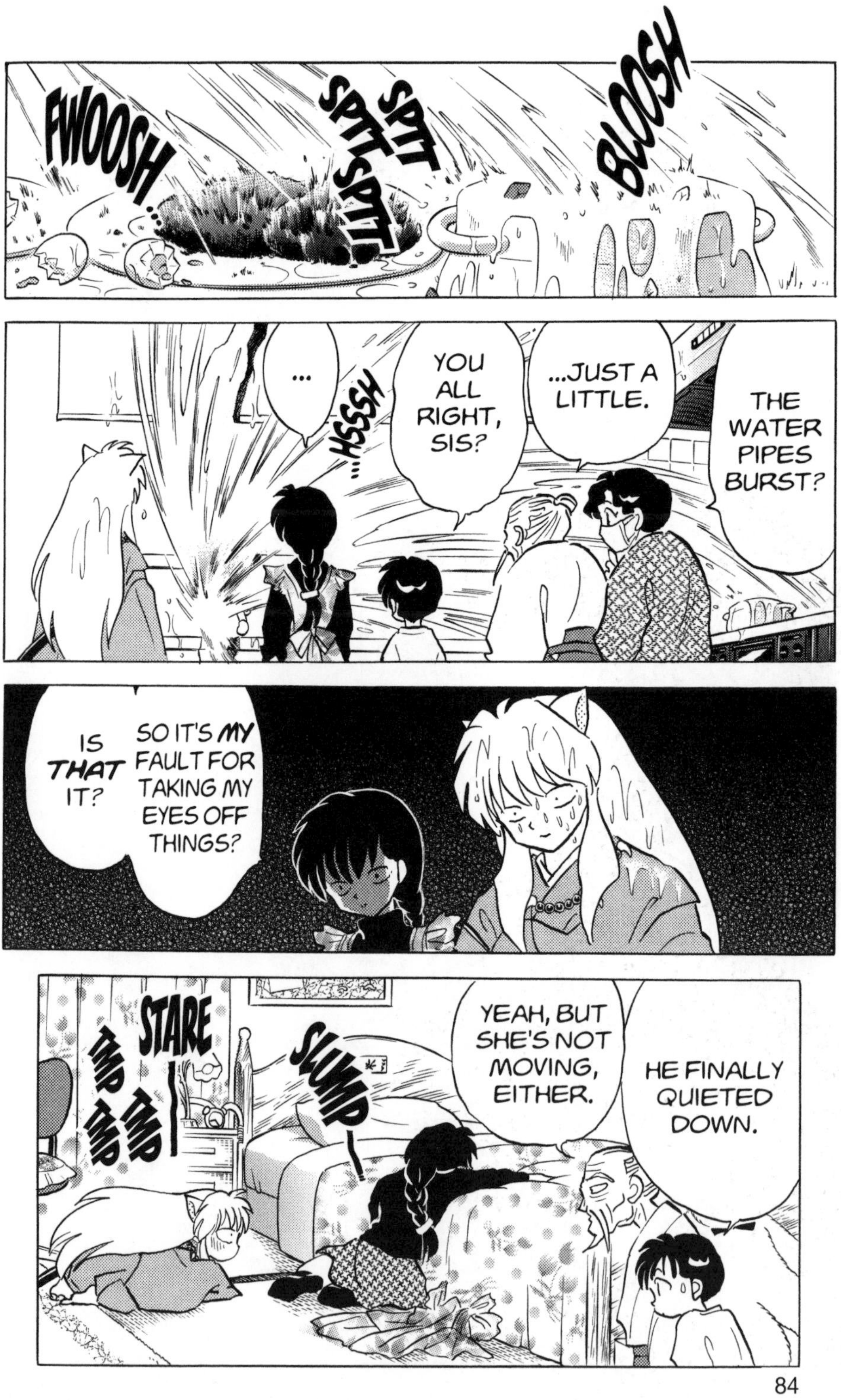
BLOOSH
SPTT SPTT SPTT
FWOOSH...
THE WATER PIPES BURST?
...JUST A LITTLE.
YOU ALL RIGHT, SIS?
HSSSH...
...
SO IT'S MY FAULT FOR TAKING MY EYES OFF THINGS?
IS THAT IT?
HE FINALLY QUIETED DOWN.
YEAH, BUT SHE'S NOT MOVING, EITHER.
SLUMP—
STARE—
TMP TMP
TMP TMP

SCROLL FIVE
THE NUNNERY

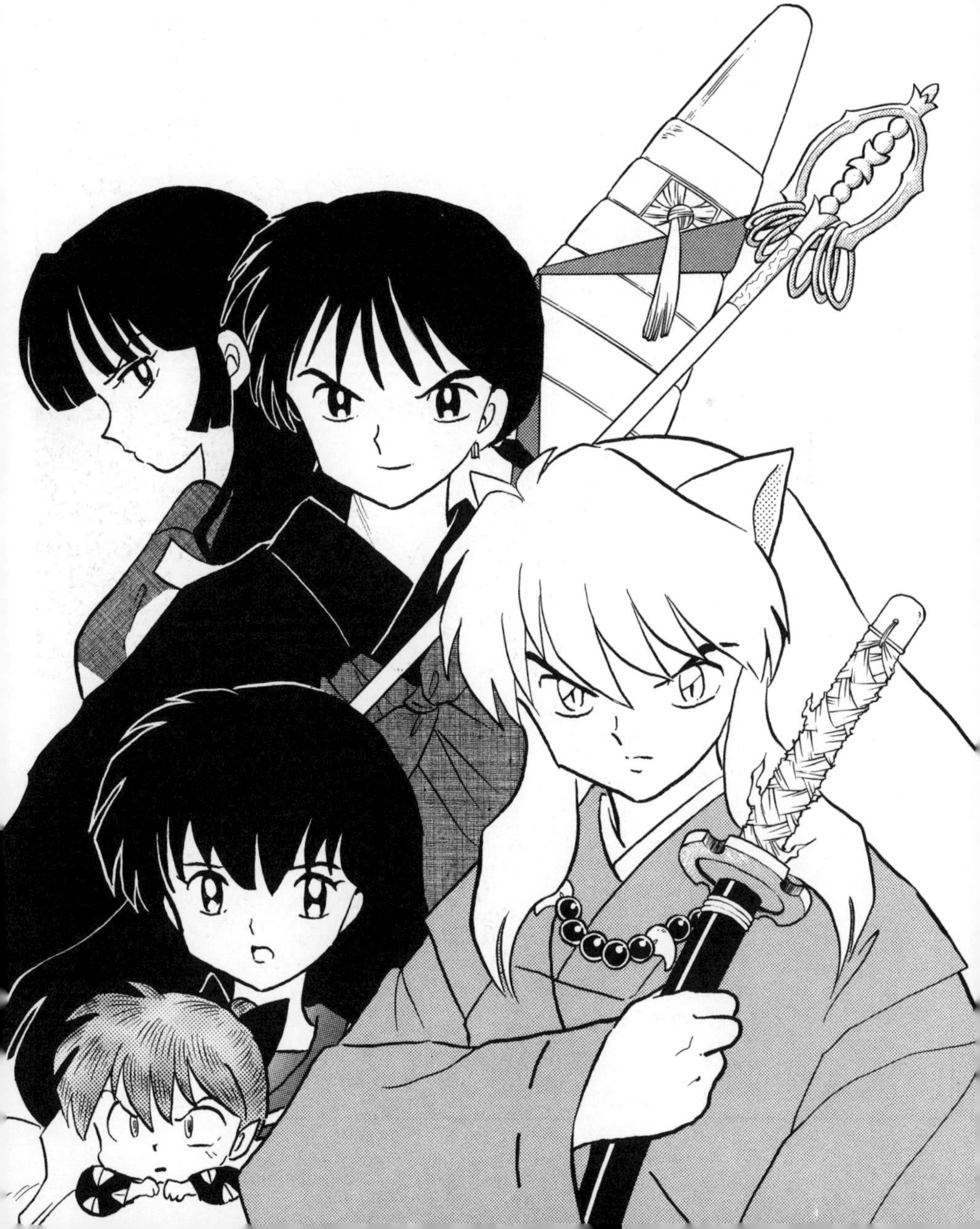

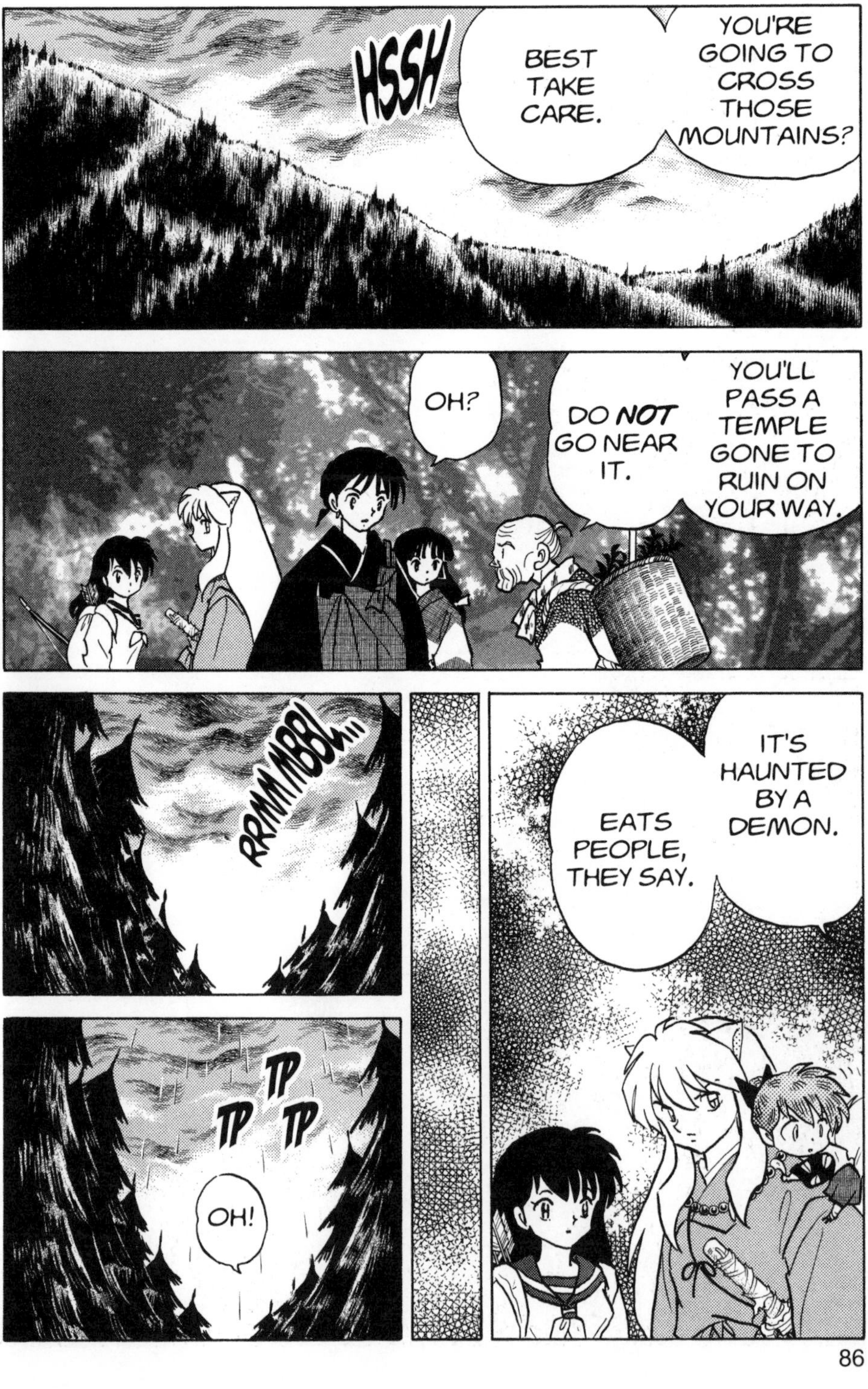
YOU'RE GOING TO CROSS THOSE MOUNTAINS?
BEST TAKE CARE.
HSSH
YOU'LL PASS A TEMPLE GONE TO RUIN ON YOUR WAY.
DO **NOT** GO NEAR IT.
OH?
IT'S HAUNTED BY A DEMON.
EATS PEOPLE, THEY SAY.
RRMMMBBL...
TP TP TP
OH!

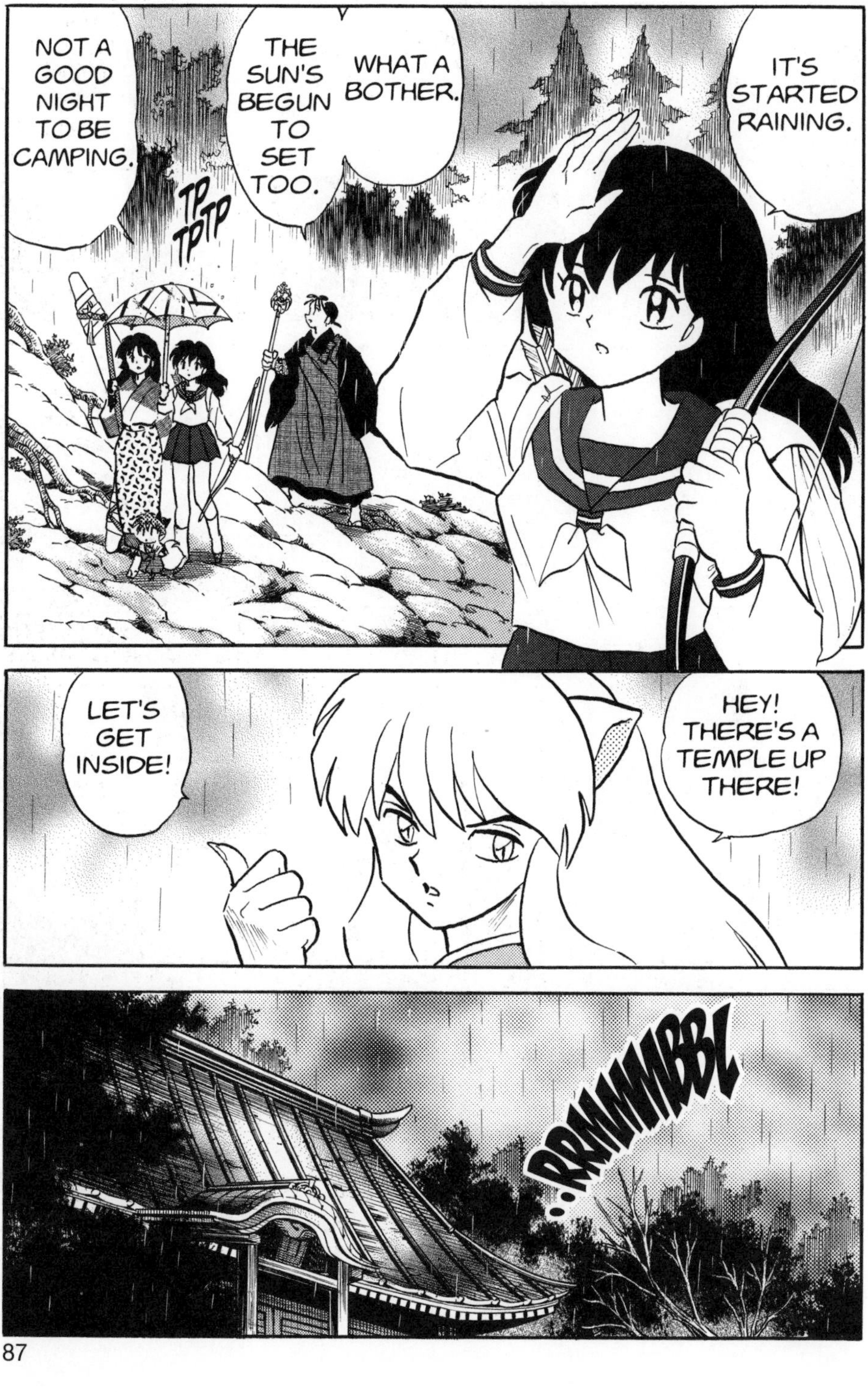
IT'S STARTED RAINING.
WHAT A BOTHER.
THE SUN'S BEGUN TO SET TOO.
NOT A GOOD NIGHT TO BE CAMPING.
TP TPTP
HEY! THERE'S A TEMPLE UP THERE!
LET'S GET INSIDE!
..RRMMMBBL

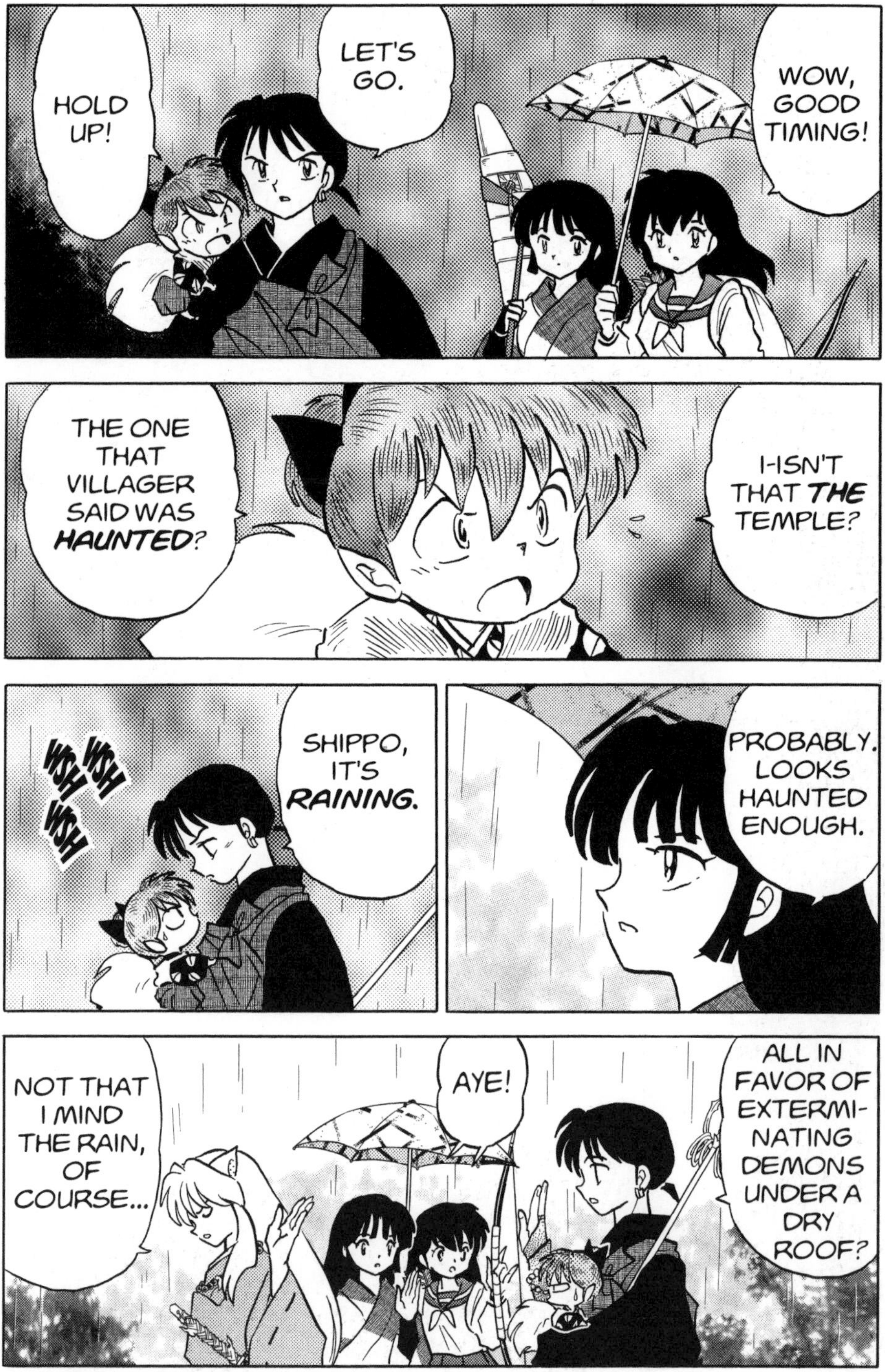
WOW, GOOD TIMING!
LET'S GO.
HOLD UP!
I-ISN'T THAT **THE** TEMPLE?
THE ONE THAT VILLAGER SAID WAS **HAUNTED**?
PROBABLY. LOOKS HAUNTED ENOUGH.
SHIPPO, IT'S **RAINING.**
VSH VSH VSH
ALL IN FAVOR OF EXTERMI-NATING DEMONS UNDER A DRY ROOF?
AYE!
NOT THAT I MIND THE RAIN, OF COURSE...

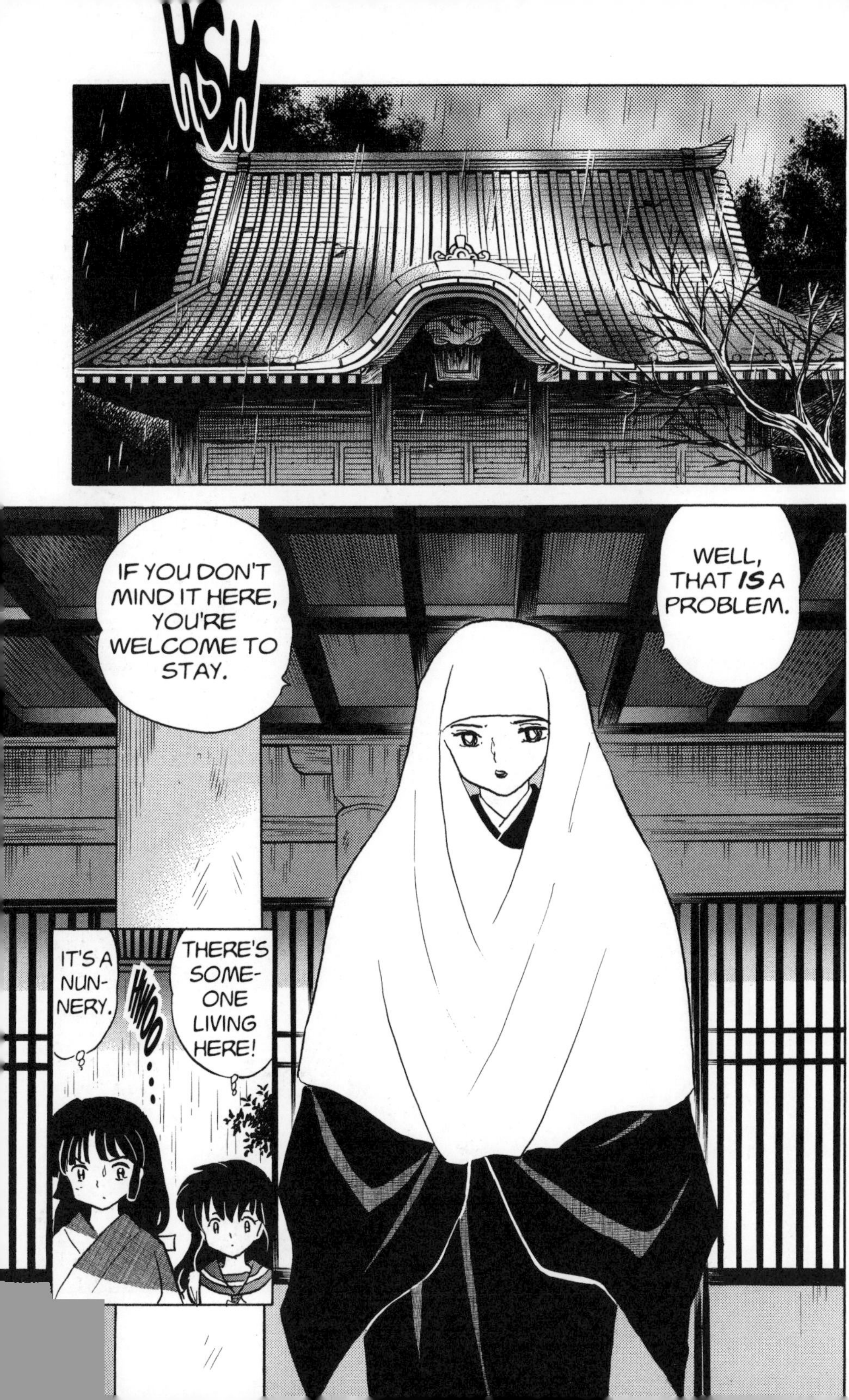
HSH
WELL, THAT IS A PROBLEM.
IF YOU DON'T MIND IT HERE, YOU'RE WELCOME TO STAY.
THERE'S SOME-ONE LIVING HERE!
HWOO...
IT'S A NUN-NERY.

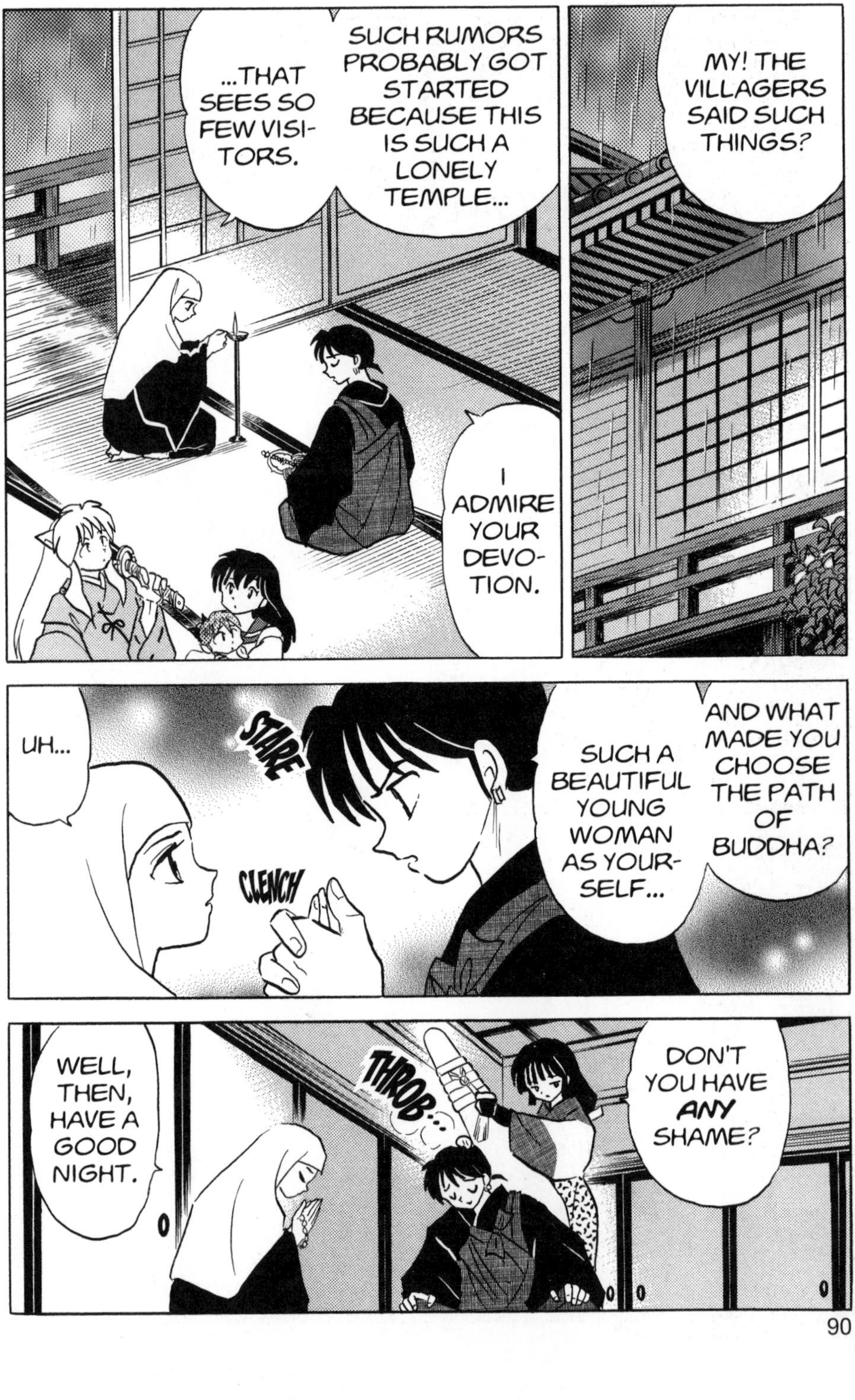
MY! THE VILLAGERS SAID SUCH THINGS?
SUCH RUMORS PROBABLY GOT STARTED BECAUSE THIS IS SUCH A LONELY TEMPLE...
...THAT SEES SO FEW VISI-TORS.
I ADMIRE YOUR DEVO-TION.
AND WHAT MADE YOU CHOOSE THE PATH OF BUDDHA?
SUCH A BEAUTIFUL YOUNG WOMAN AS YOUR-SELF...
STARE
CLENCH
UH...
DON'T YOU HAVE *ANY* SHAME?
THROB...
WELL, THEN, HAVE A GOOD NIGHT.

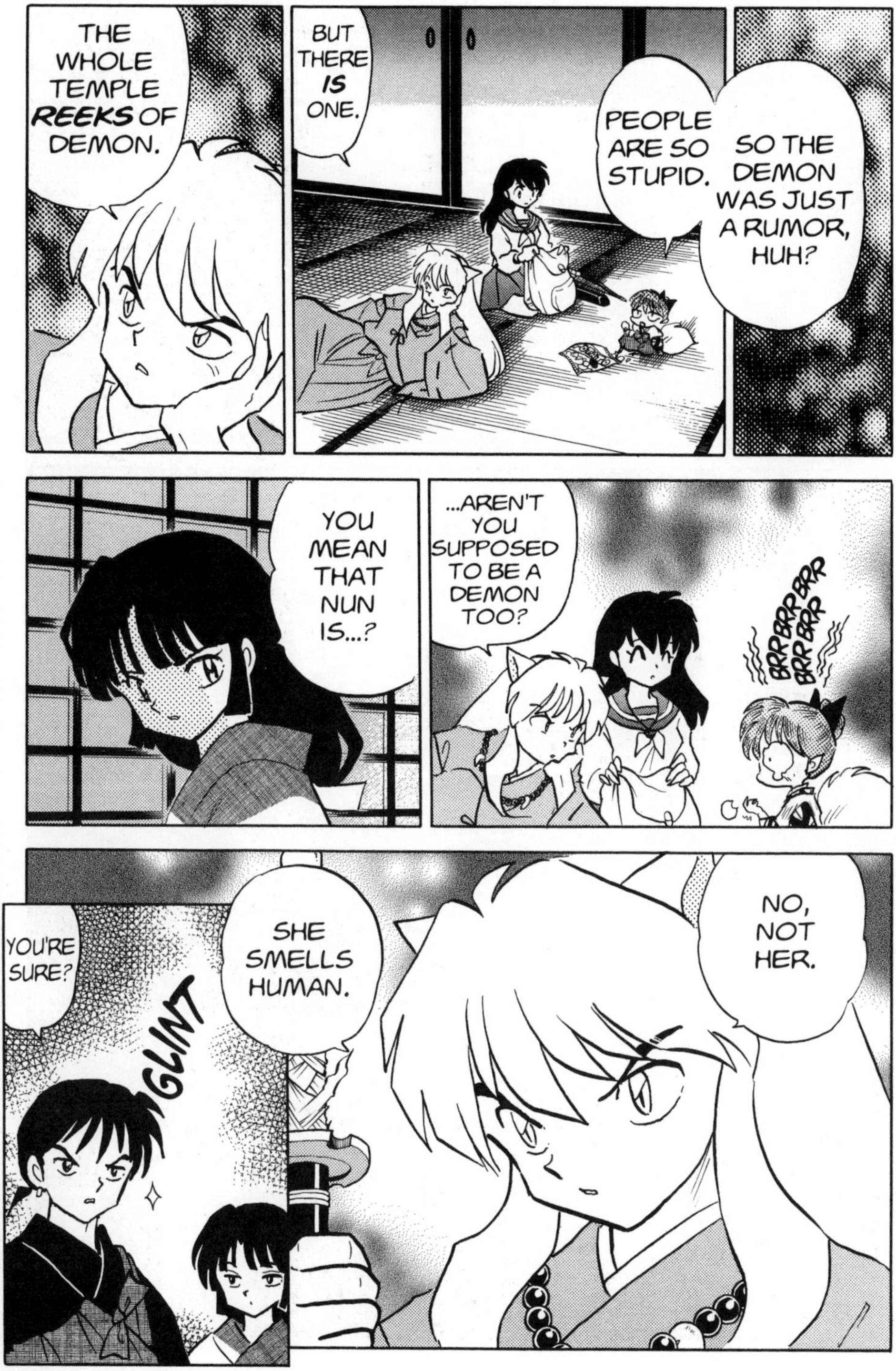
SO THE DEMON WAS JUST A RUMOR, HUH?
PEOPLE ARE SO STUPID.
BUT THERE IS ONE.
THE WHOLE TEMPLE REEKS OF DEMON.
...AREN'T YOU SUPPOSED TO BE A DEMON TOO?
BRRBRRBRR BRRBRR
YOU MEAN THAT NUN IS...?
NO, NOT HER.
SHE SMELLS HUMAN.
YOU'RE SURE?
GLINT

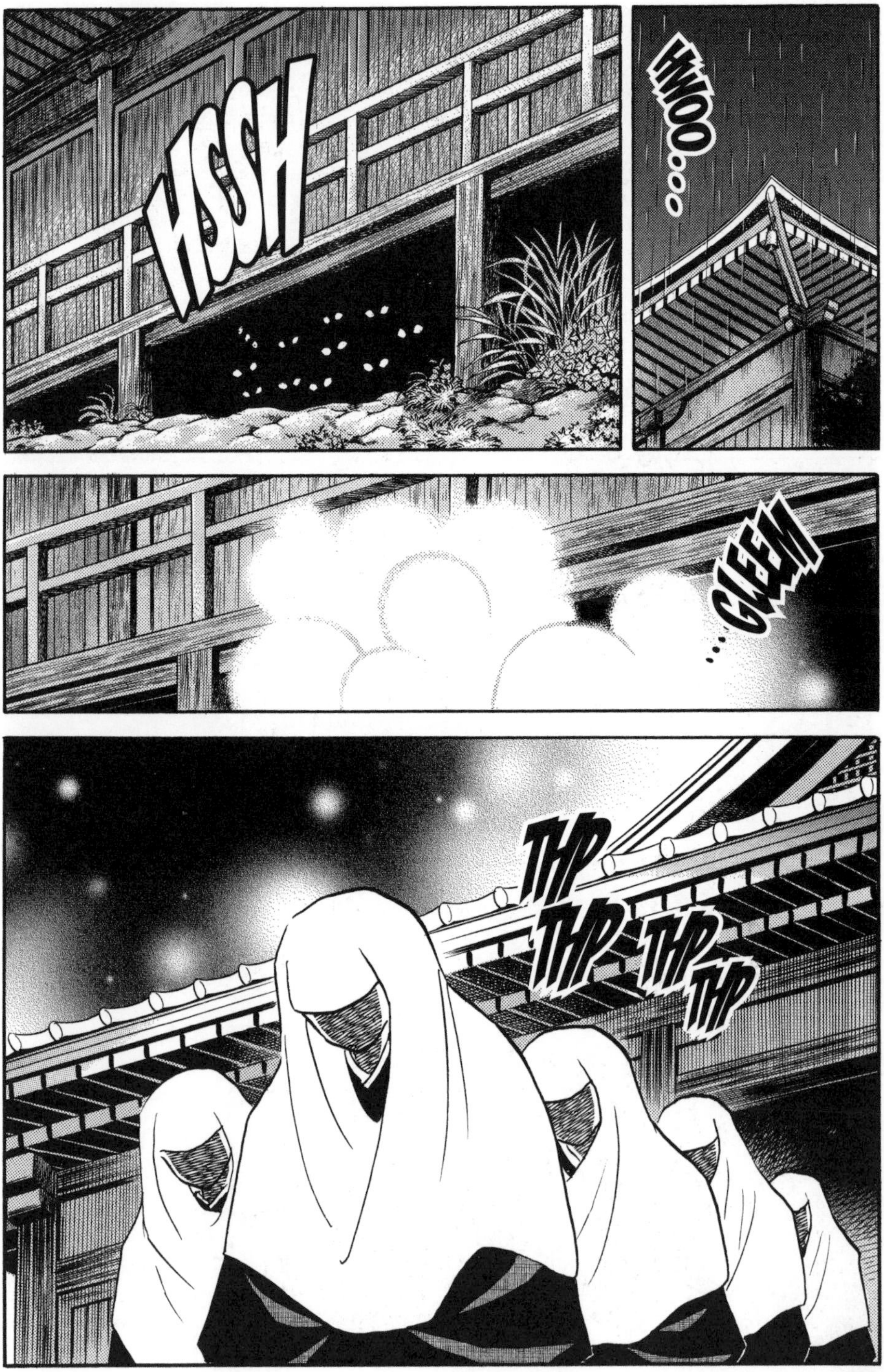
HWOO...
HSSH
...GLEEM
THP THP THP THP

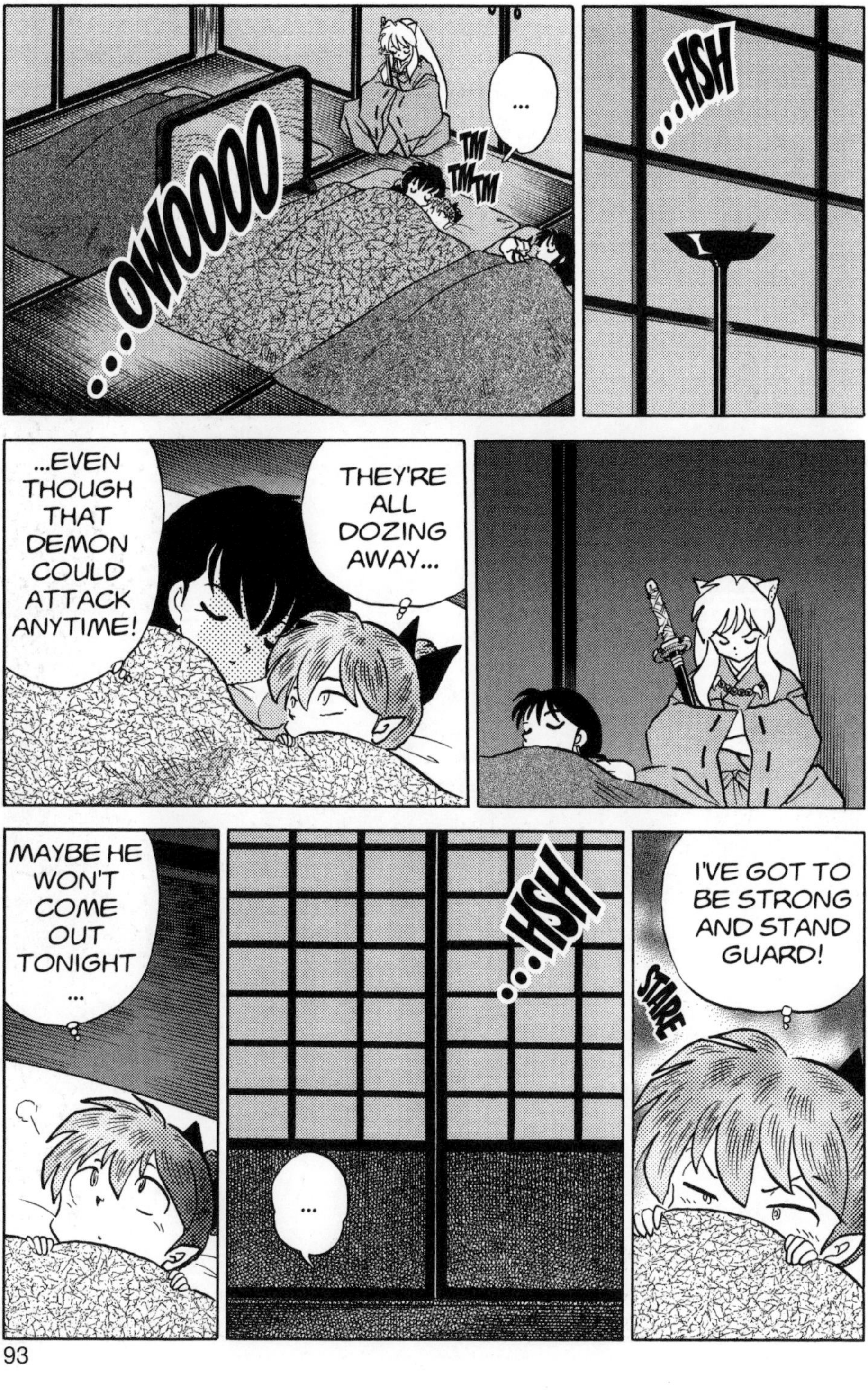
...HSH
...
TM TM TM TM
...OWOOOO
THEY'RE ALL DOZING AWAY...
...EVEN THOUGH THAT DEMON COULD ATTACK ANYTIME!
I'VE GOT TO BE STRONG AND STAND GUARD!
STARE
...HSH
...
MAYBE HE WON'T COME OUT TONIGHT ...

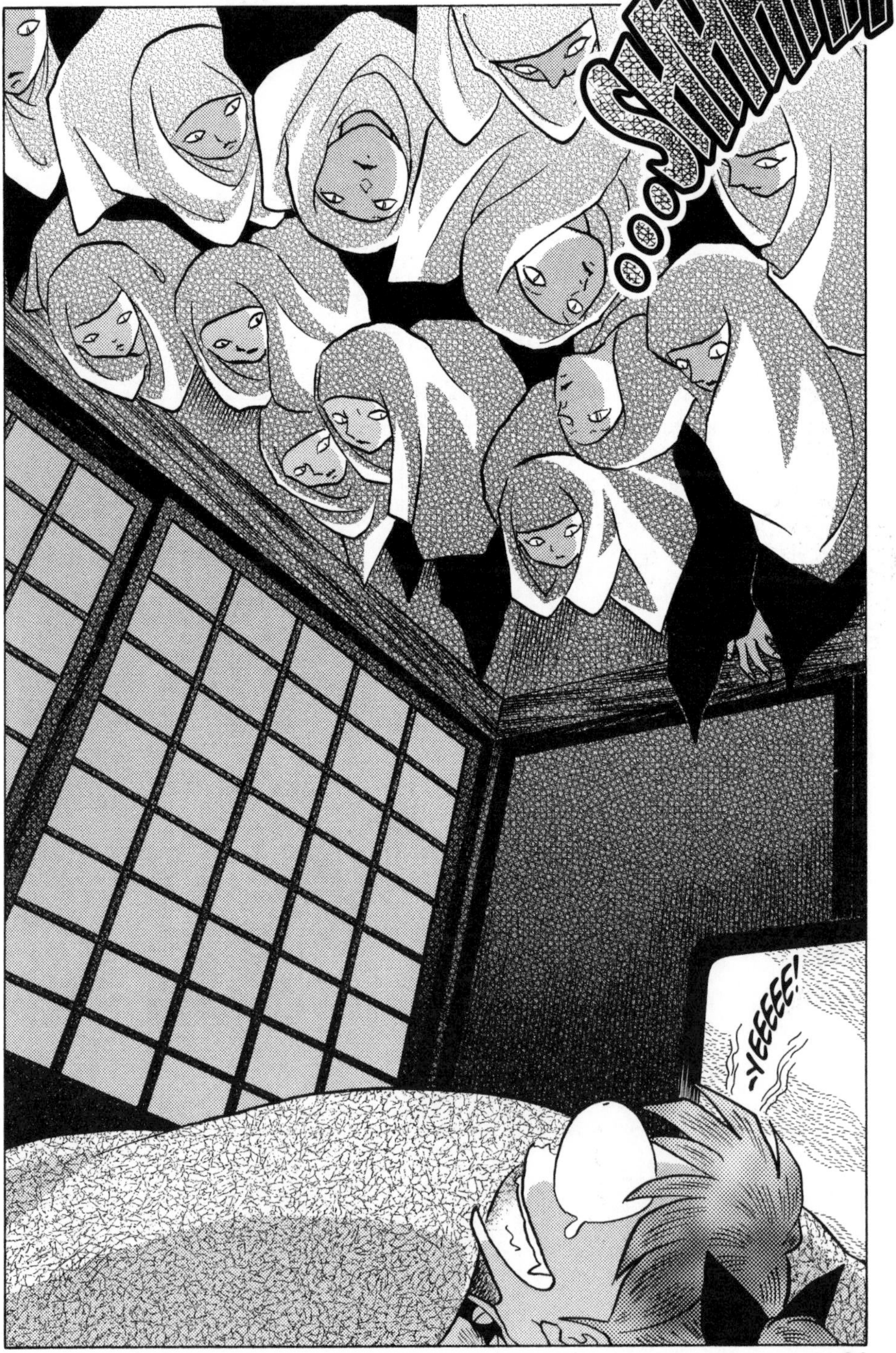
...SHHHHH!
-YEEEEE!

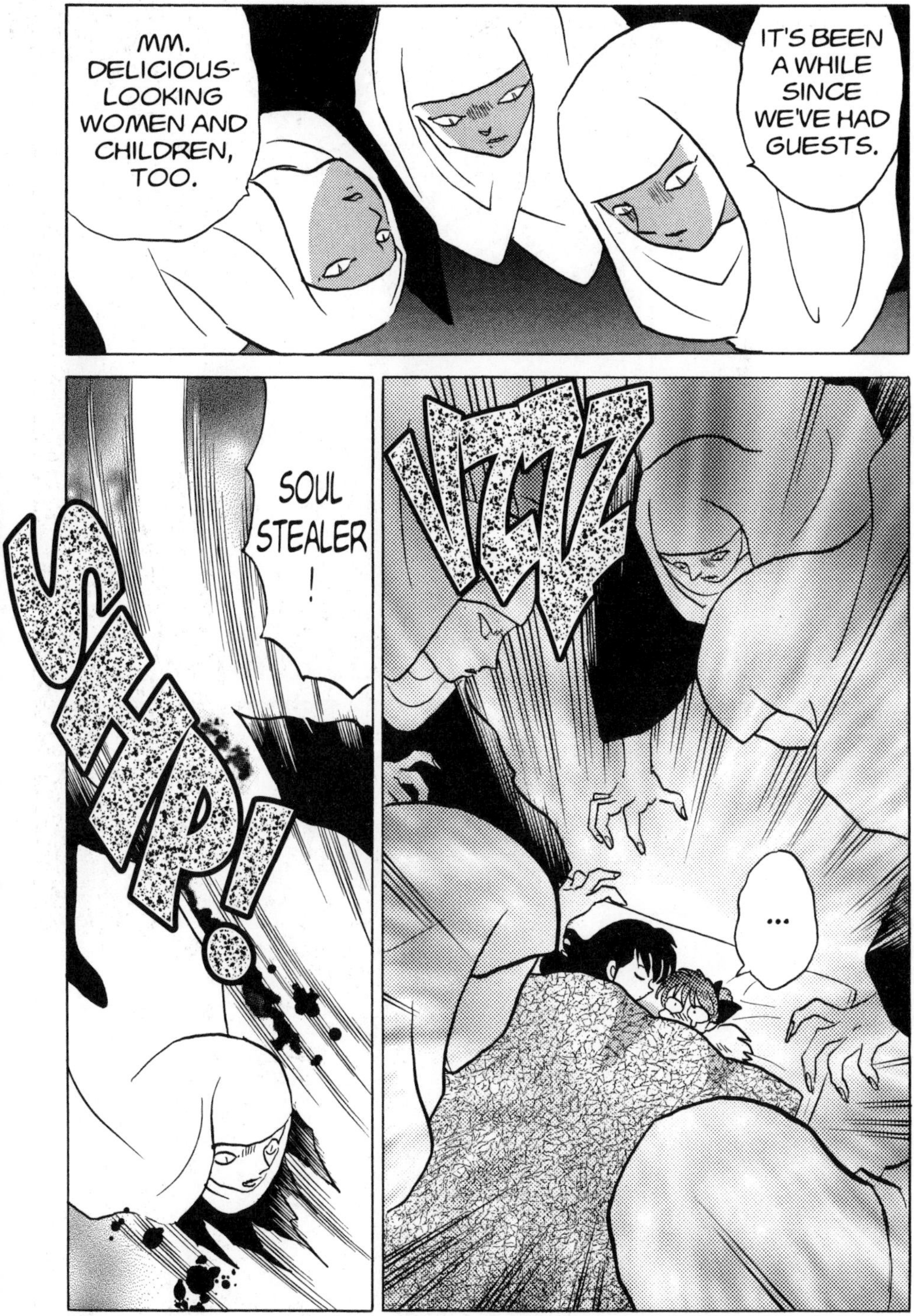
IT'S BEEN A WHILE SINCE WE'VE HAD GUESTS.
MM. DELICIOUS-LOOKING WOMEN AND CHILDREN, TOO.
VZZZ
...
SOUL STEALER!
SHP!

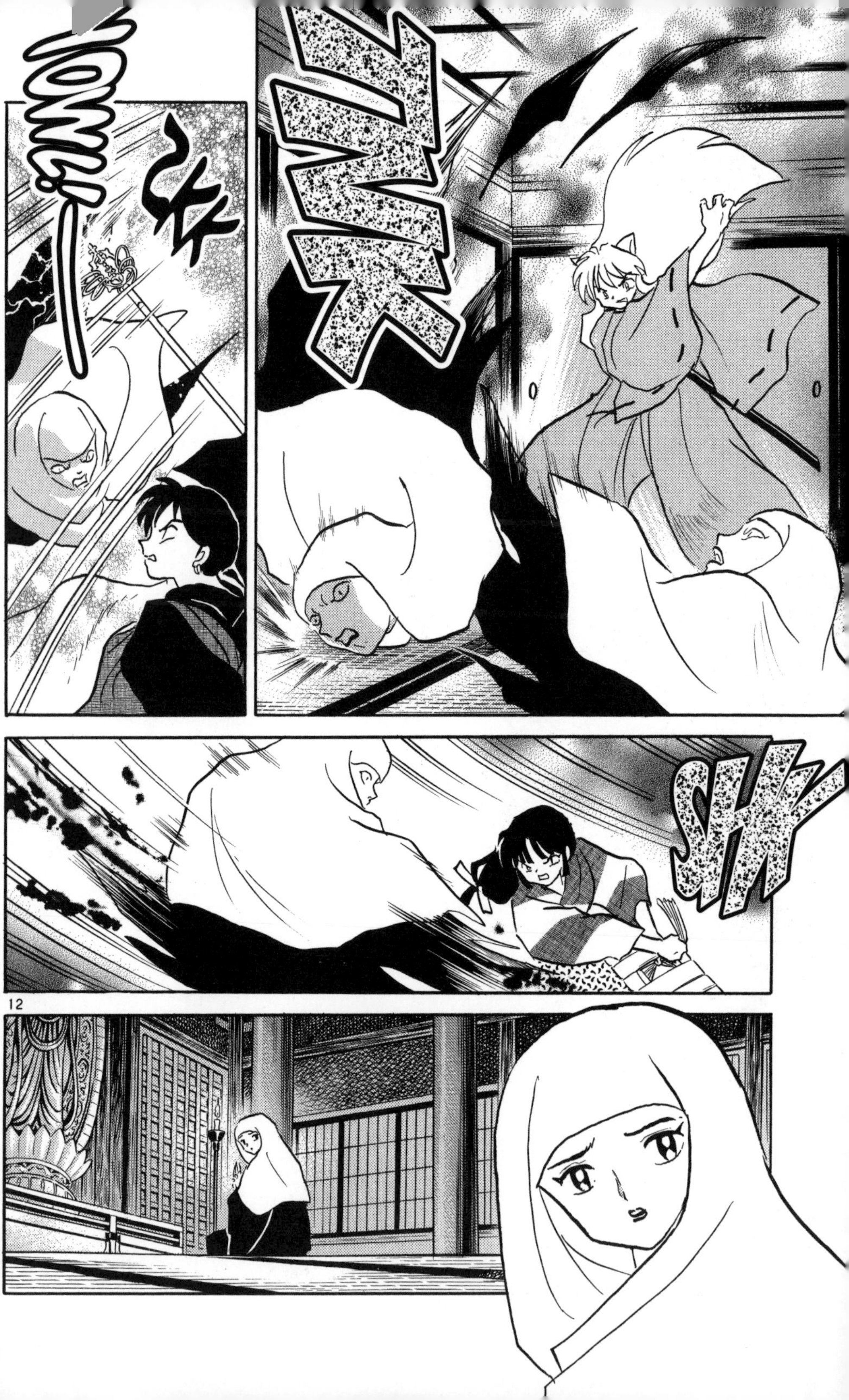
YOWL!
SHK
12

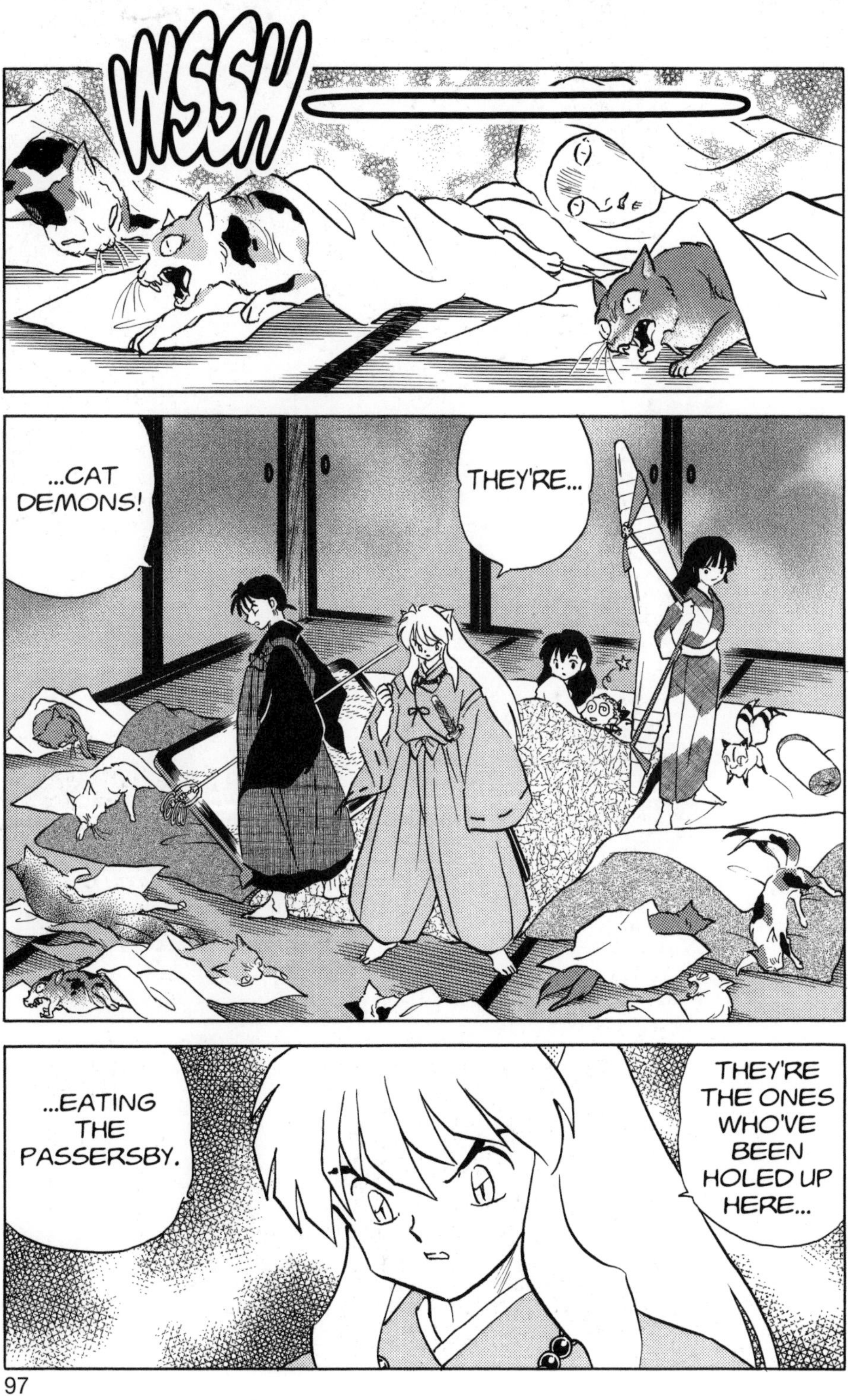
WSSH
THEY'RE...
...CAT DEMONS!
THEY'RE THE ONES WHO'VE BEEN HOLED UP HERE...
...EATING THE PASSERSBY.

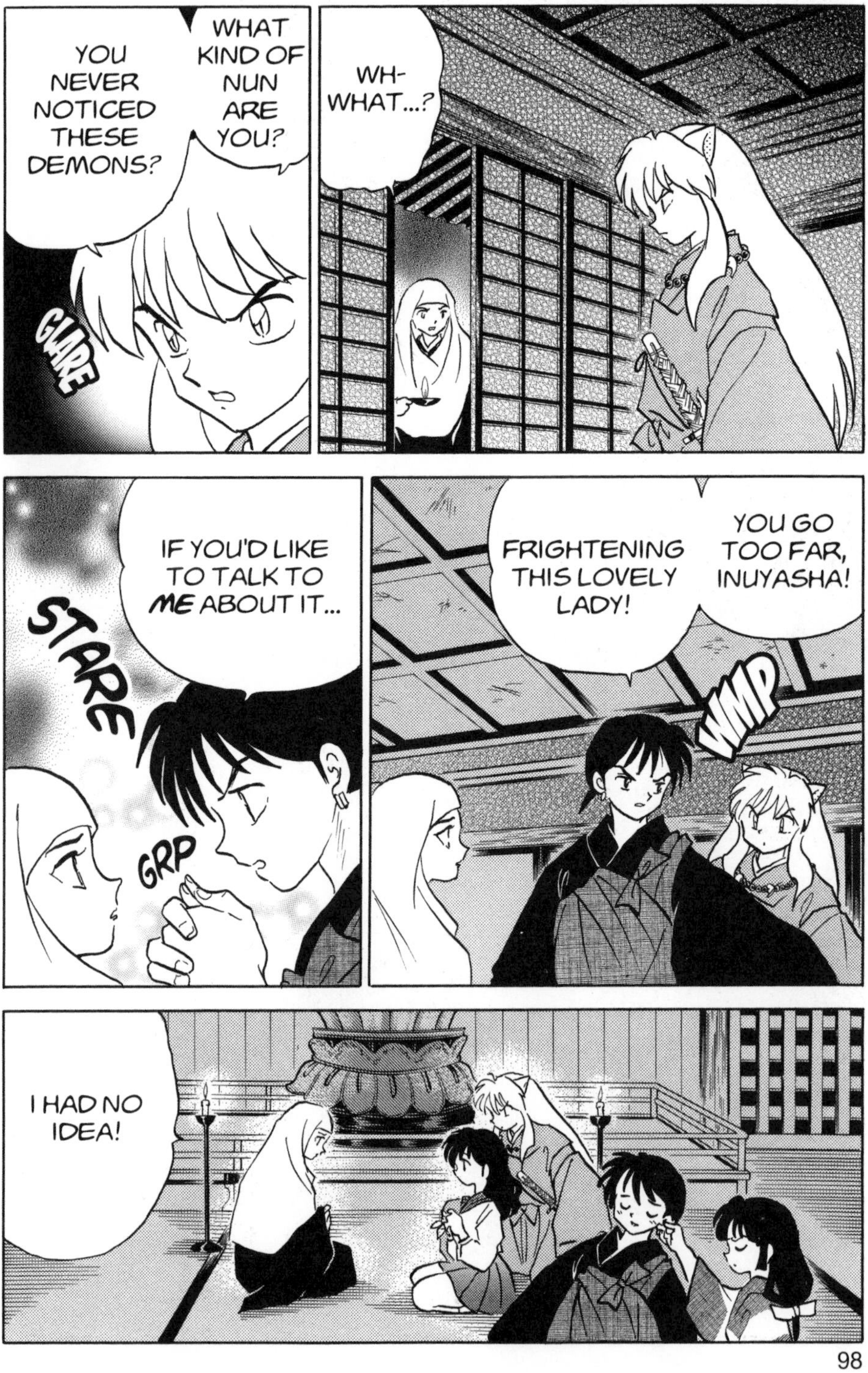
WH-WHAT...?
WHAT KIND OF NUN ARE YOU?
YOU NEVER NOTICED THESE DEMONS?
GLARE
YOU GO TOO FAR, INUYASHA!
FRIGHTENING THIS LOVELY LADY!
WMP
IF YOU'D LIKE TO TALK TO *ME* ABOUT IT...
STARE
GRP
I HAD NO IDEA!

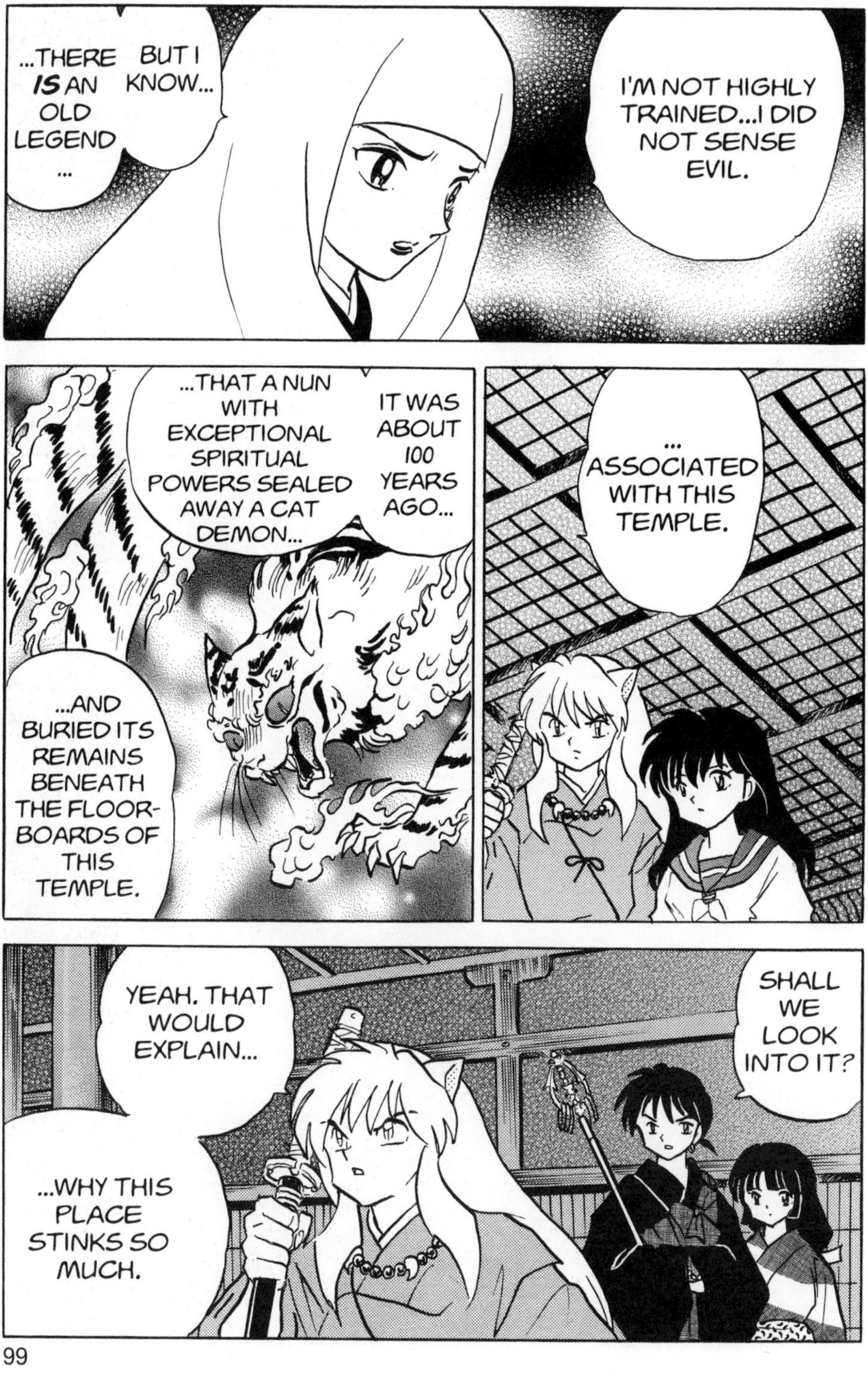
I'M NOT HIGHLY TRAINED...I DID NOT SENSE EVIL.
BUT I KNOW...
...THERE *IS* AN OLD LEGEND ...
... ASSOCIATED WITH THIS TEMPLE.
IT WAS ABOUT 100 YEARS AGO...
...THAT A NUN WITH EXCEPTIONAL SPIRITUAL POWERS SEALED AWAY A CAT DEMON...
...AND BURIED ITS REMAINS BENEATH THE FLOOR-BOARDS OF THIS TEMPLE.
SHALL WE LOOK INTO IT?
YEAH. THAT WOULD EXPLAIN...
...WHY THIS PLACE STINKS SO MUCH.

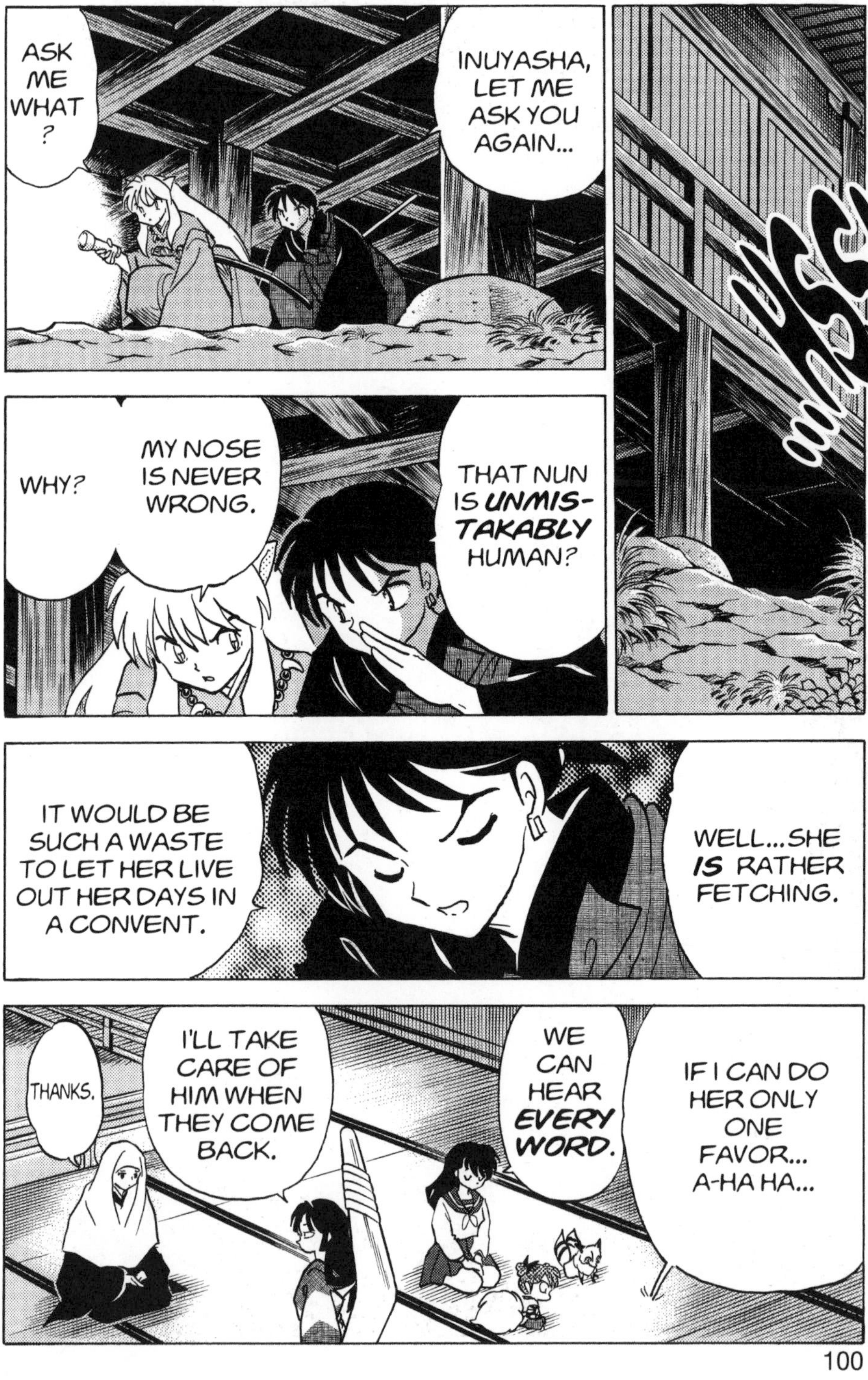
INUYASHA, LET ME ASK YOU AGAIN...
ASK ME WHAT?
THAT NUN IS **UNMIS-TAKABLY** HUMAN?
MY NOSE IS NEVER WRONG.
WHY?
WELL...SHE **IS** RATHER FETCHING.
IT WOULD BE SUCH A WASTE TO LET HER LIVE OUT HER DAYS IN A CONVENT.
IF I CAN DO HER ONLY ONE FAVOR... A-HA HA...
WE CAN HEAR **EVERY WORD**.
I'LL TAKE CARE OF HIM WHEN THEY COME BACK.
THANKS.

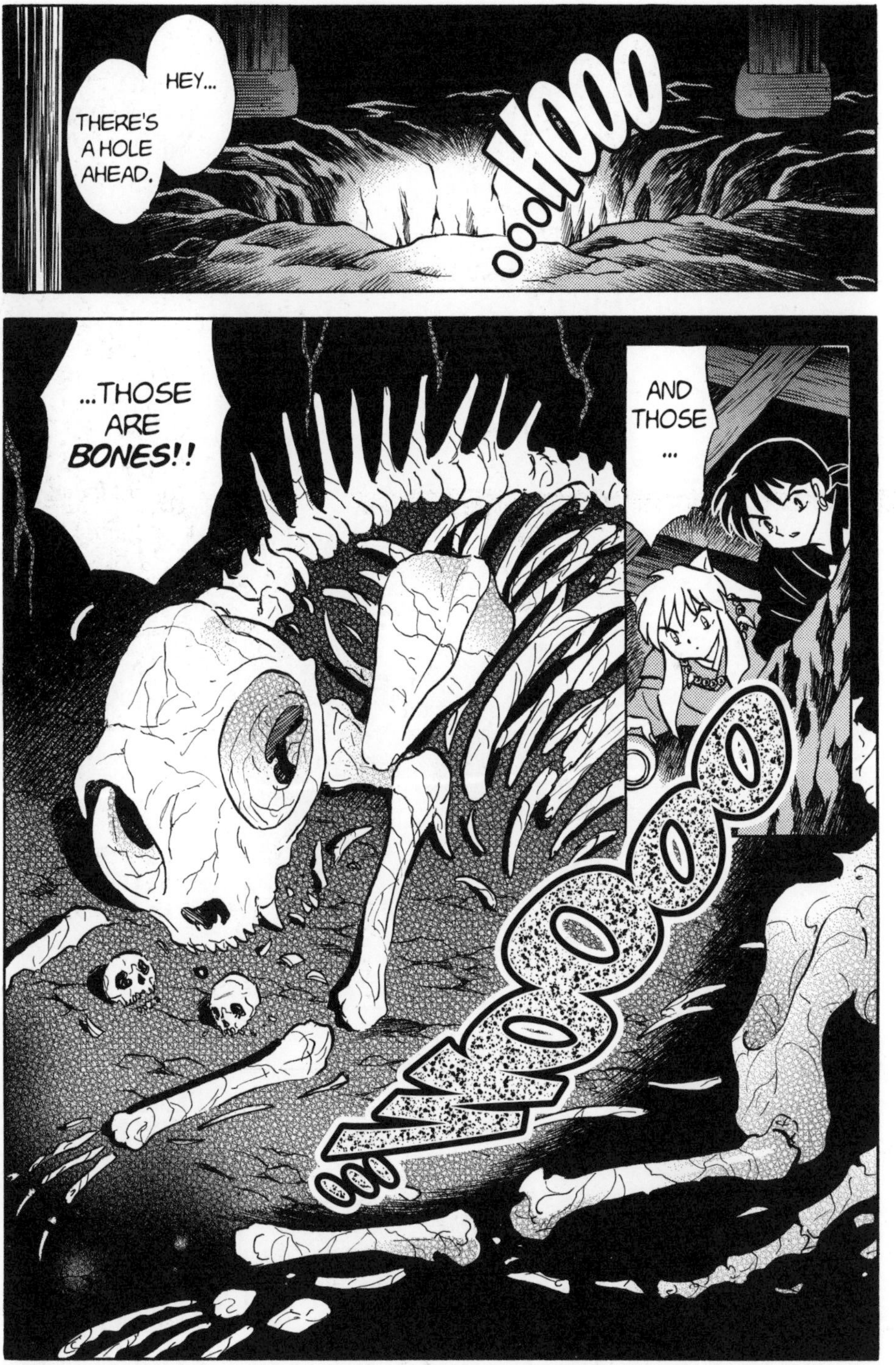
HEY...
THERE'S A HOLE AHEAD.
OOOHOOO
AND THOSE ...
...THOSE ARE **BONES!!**
WOOOOOOO

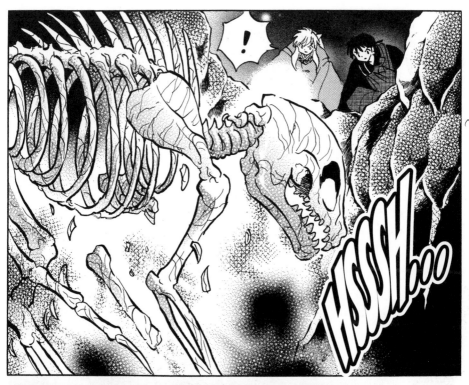

HSSSSH...

INUYASHA AND LORD MIROKU SURE ARE TAKING THEIR TIME...

SHOOO...

SCROLL SIX
CAT DEMON

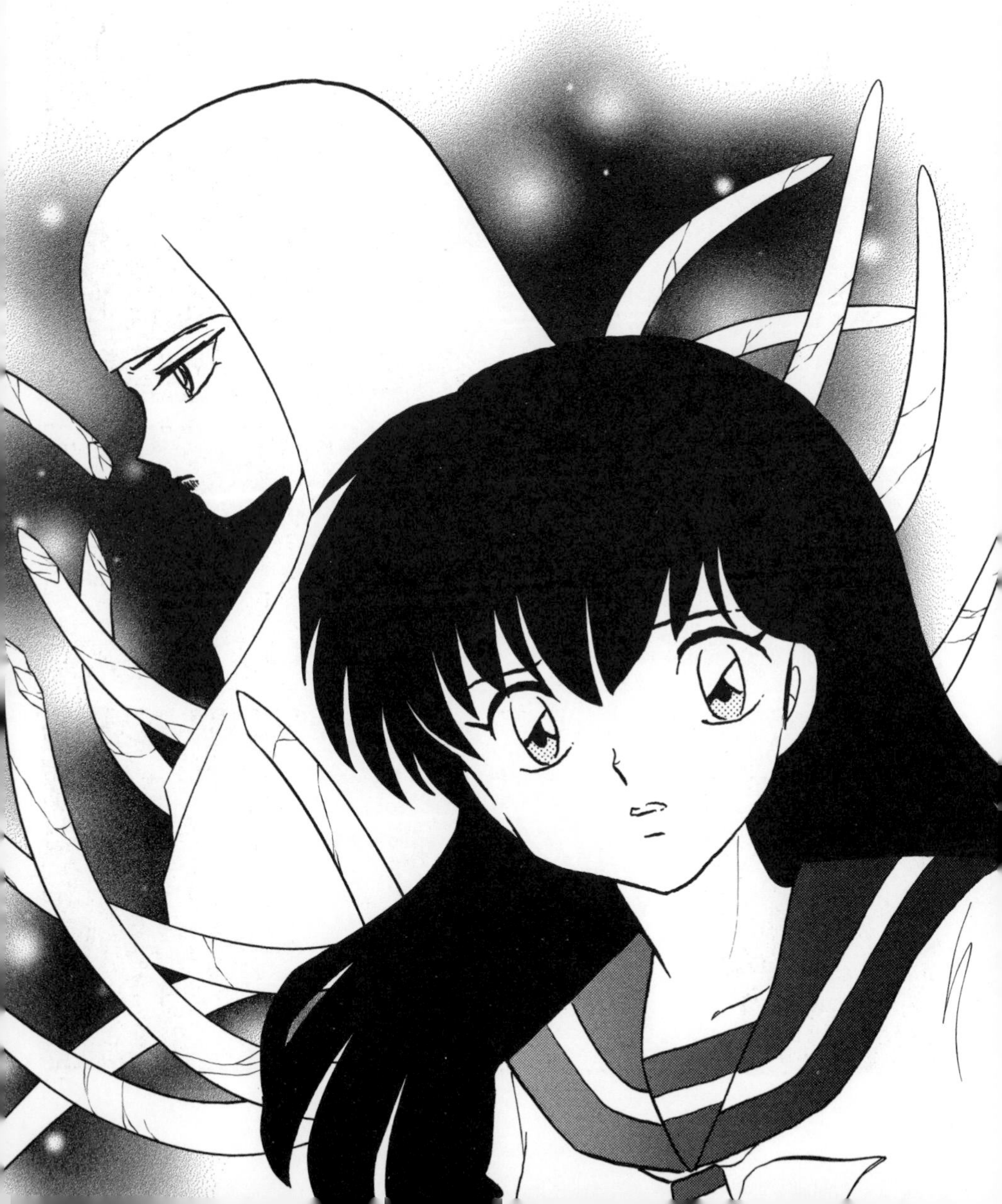

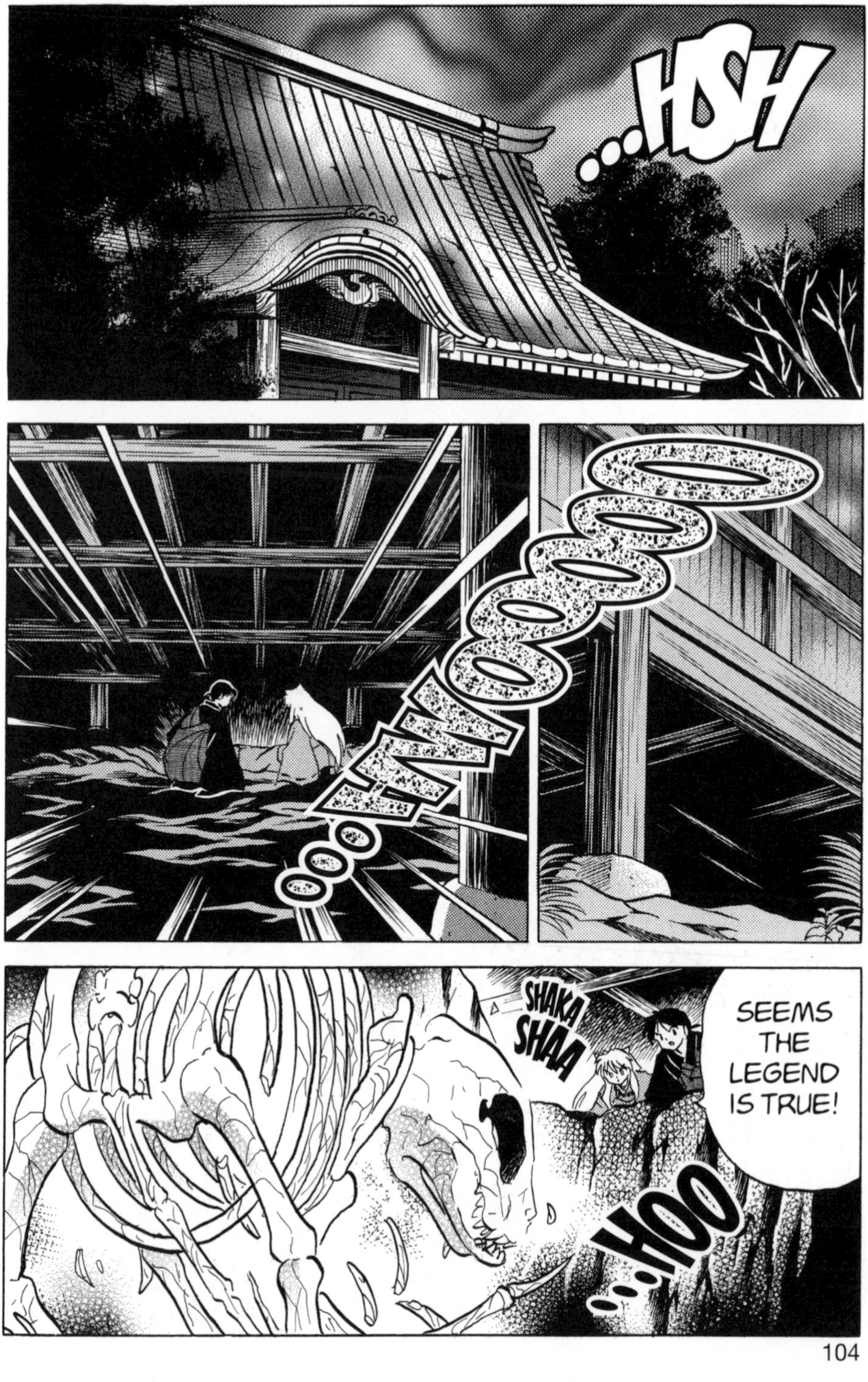
...HSH
...OOOWOOOOOO
SEEMS THE LEGEND IS TRUE!
SHAKA SHAA
...HOO

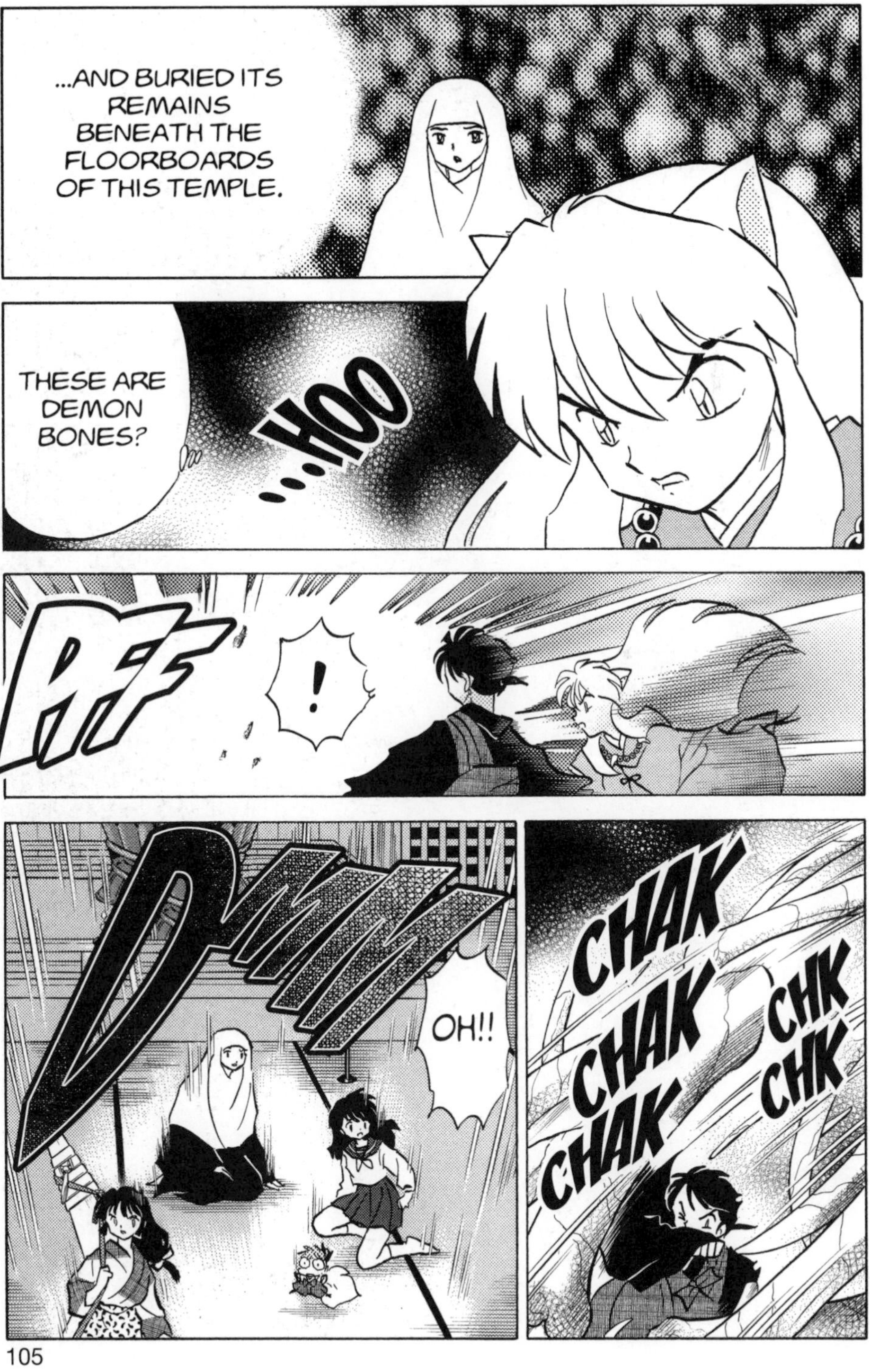

...AND BURIED ITS REMAINS BENEATH THE FLOORBOARDS OF THIS TEMPLE.
...HOO
THESE ARE DEMON BONES?
!
PFF
CHK CHK
CHAK CHAK CHAK
OH!!
DMMM

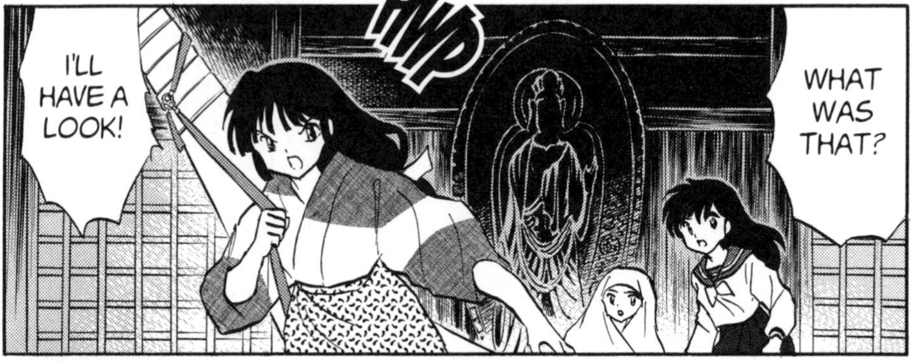
WHAT WAS THAT?
HWP
I'LL HAVE A LOOK!
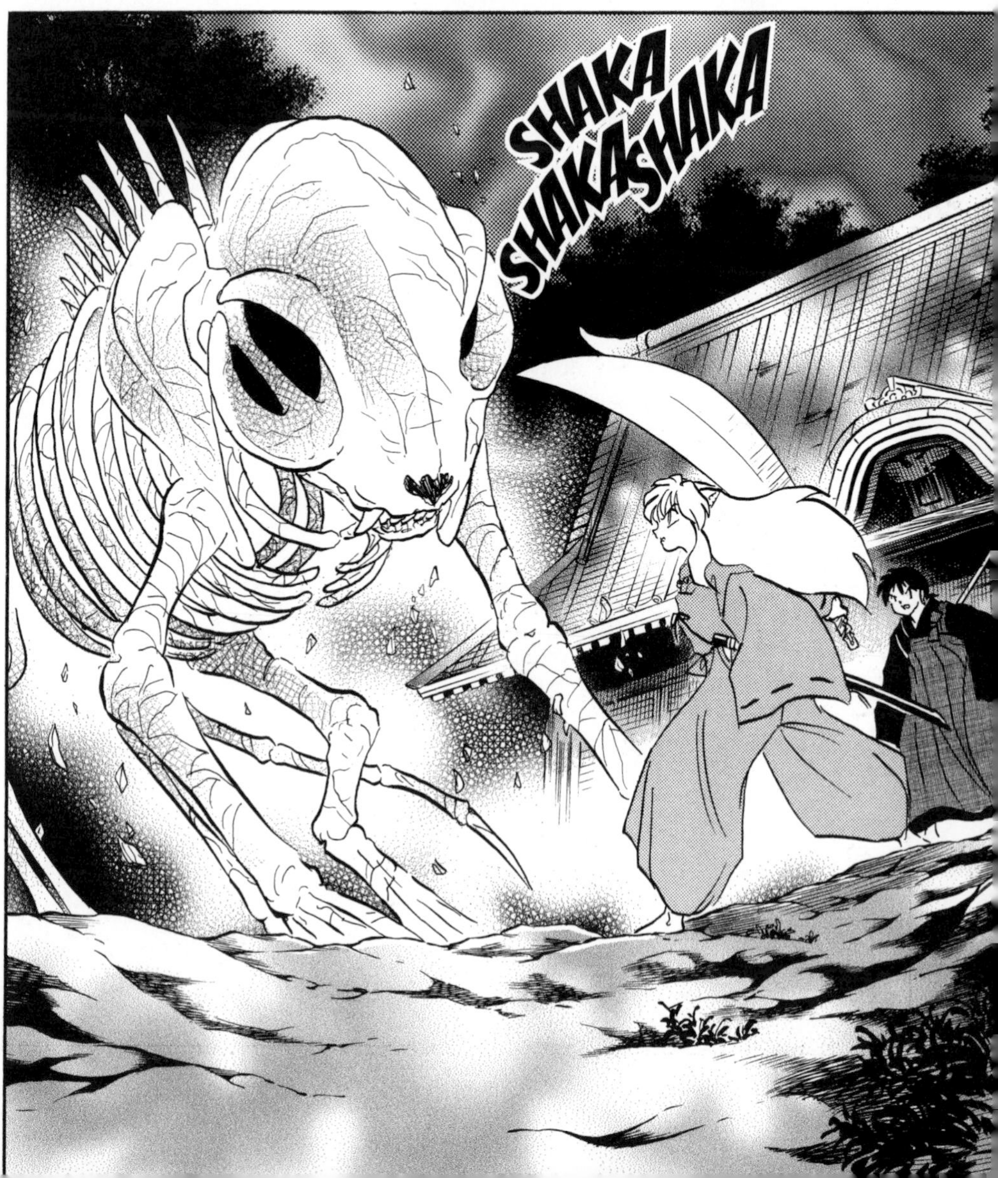
SHAKA SHAKASHAKA

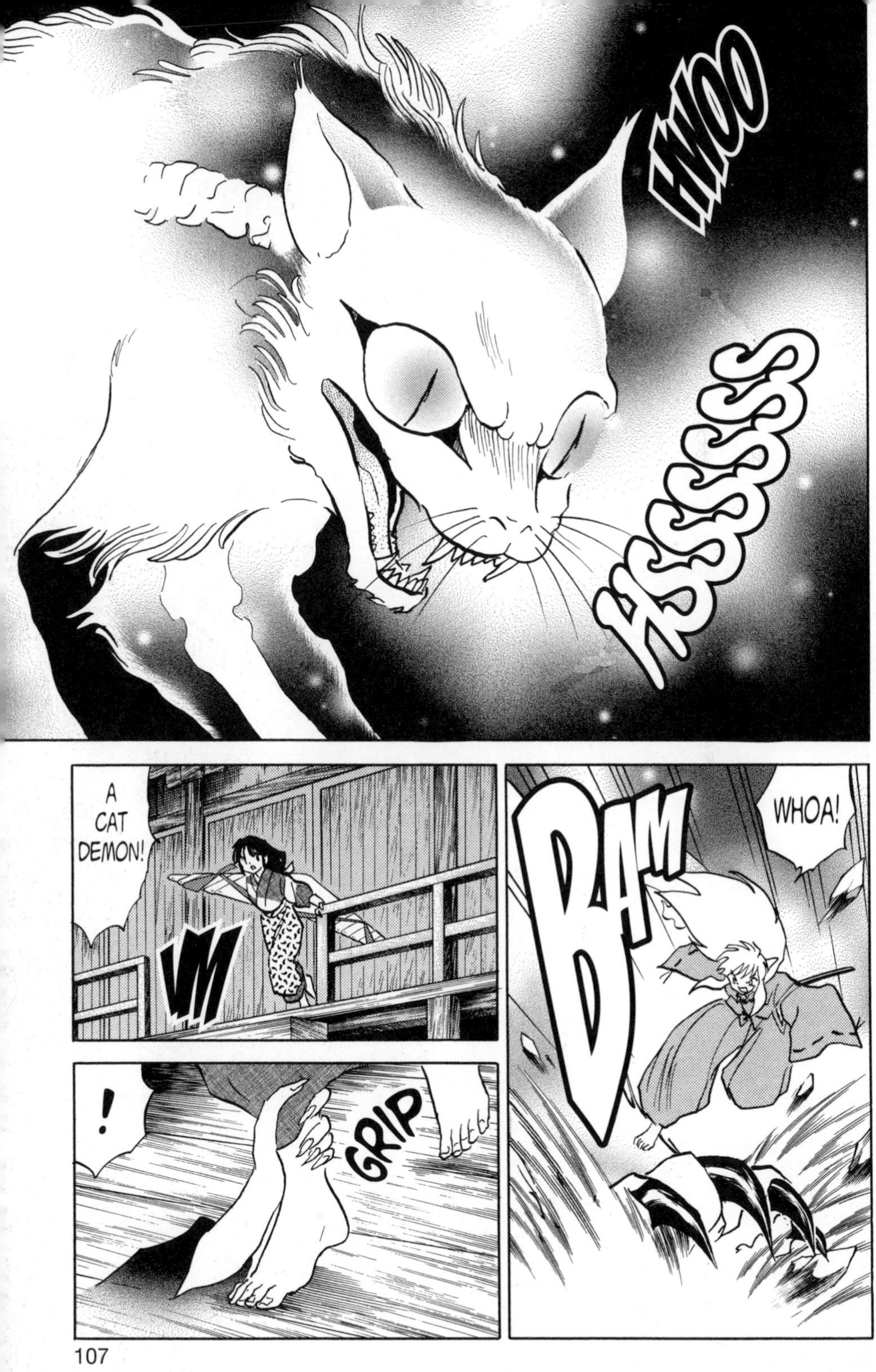
HWOO
HSSSSSS
BAM
WHOA!
A CAT DEMON!
VM
!
GRIP

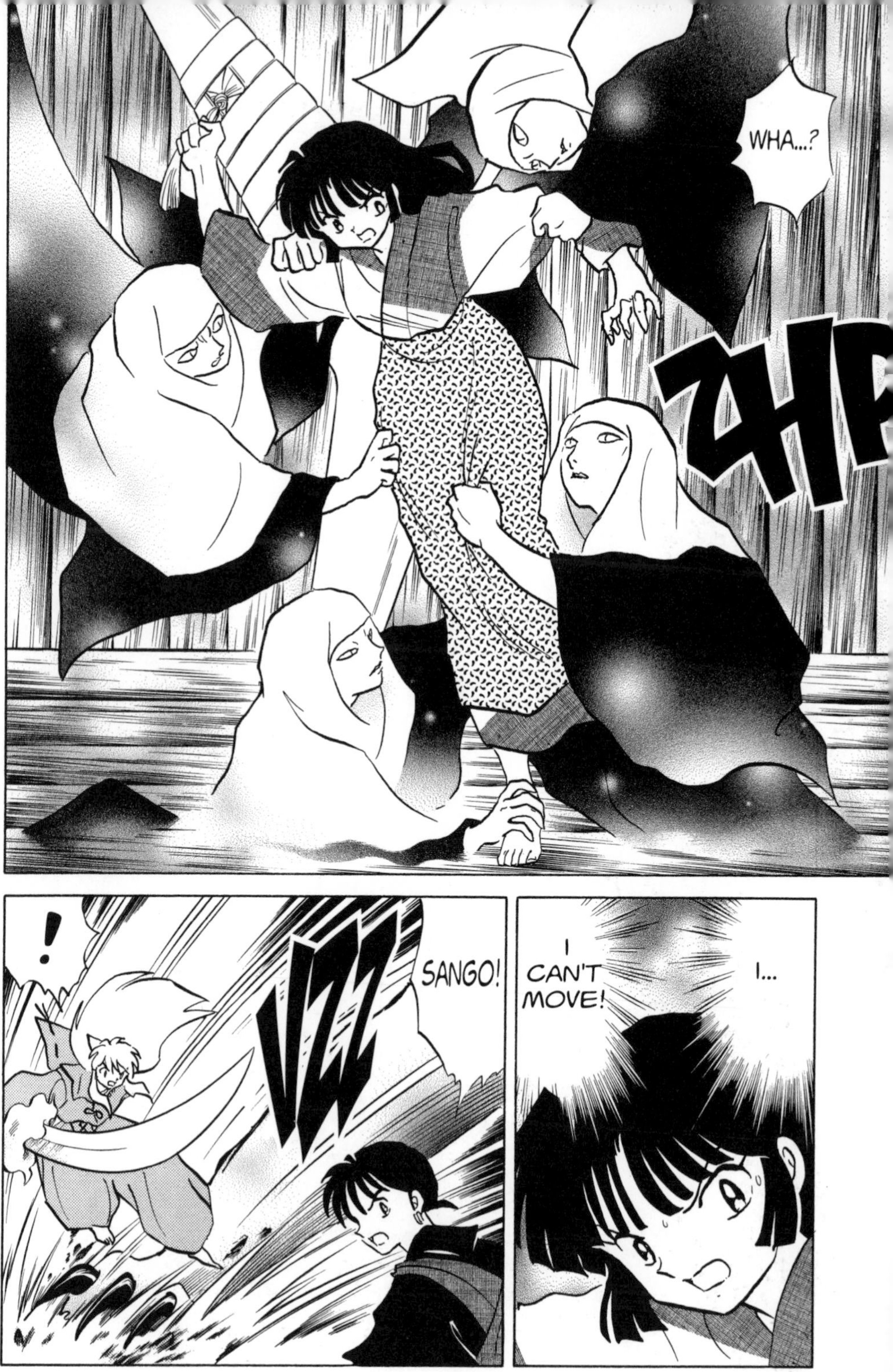
WHA...?
ZHP
I...
I CAN'T MOVE!
SANGO!
VZZ
!

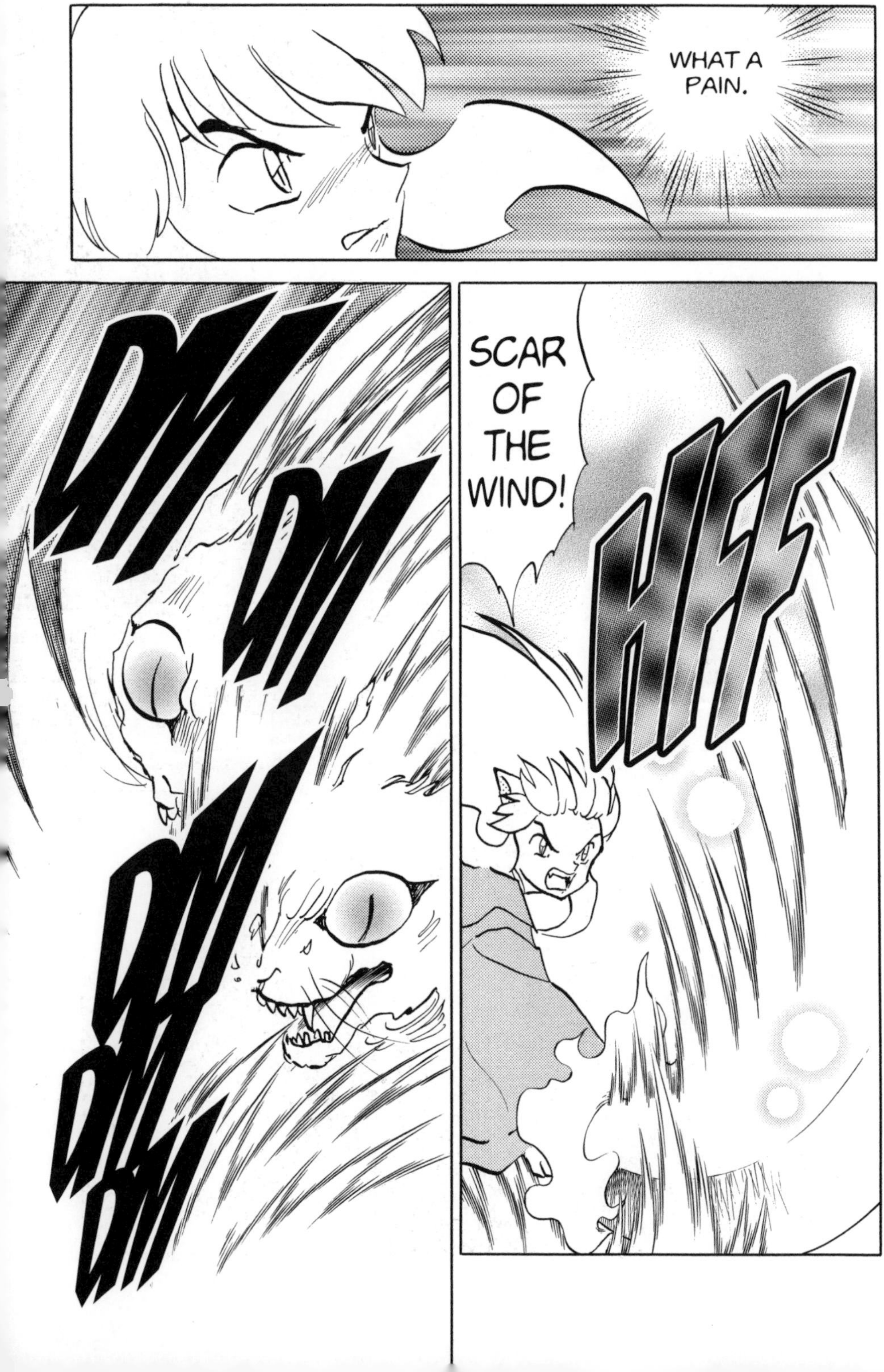
WHAT A PAIN.
SCAR OF THE WIND!

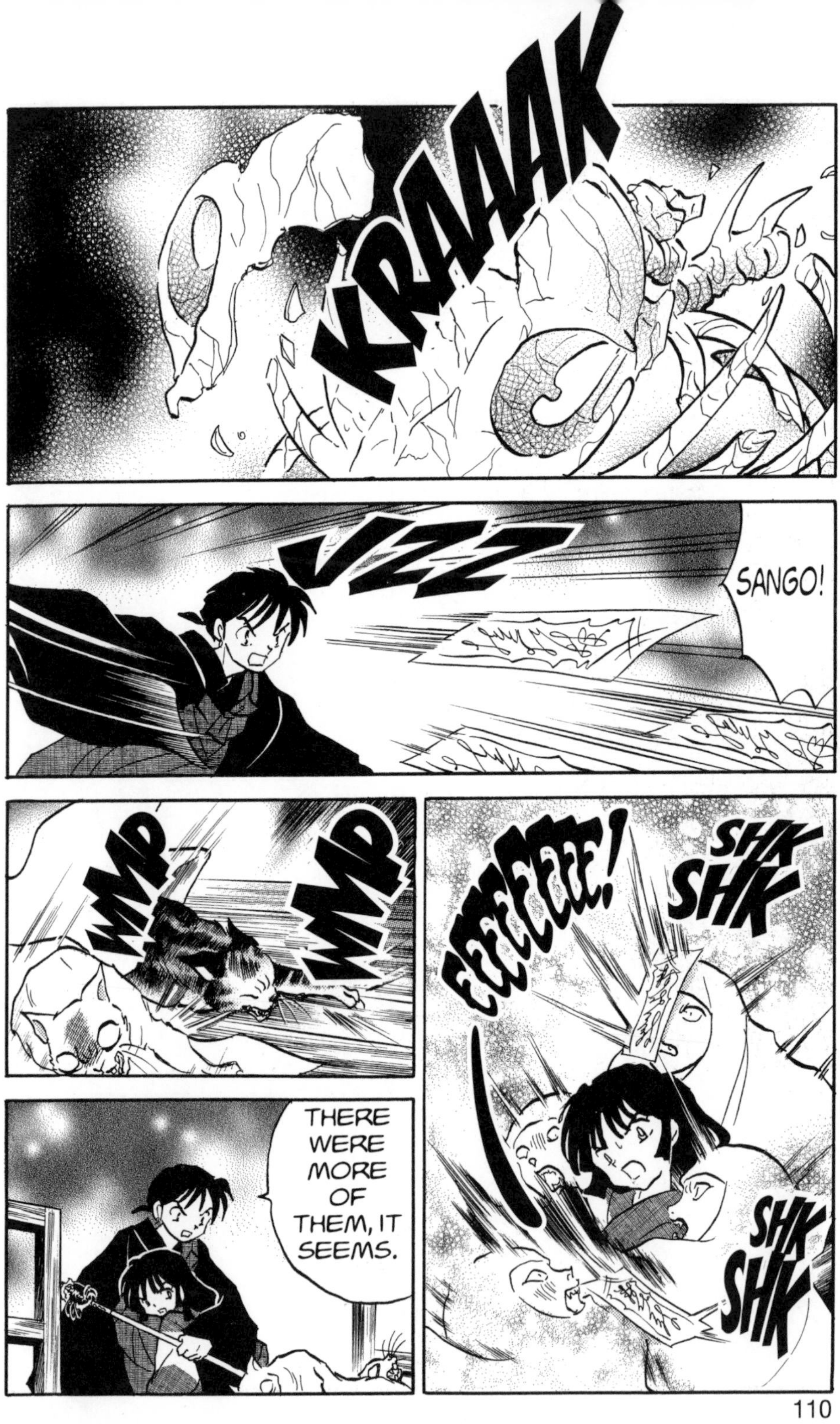
KRAAAK
SANGO!
VZZZ
EEEEEEEE!
SHK SHK
SHK SHK
WMP
WMP
THERE WERE MORE OF THEM, IT SEEMS.

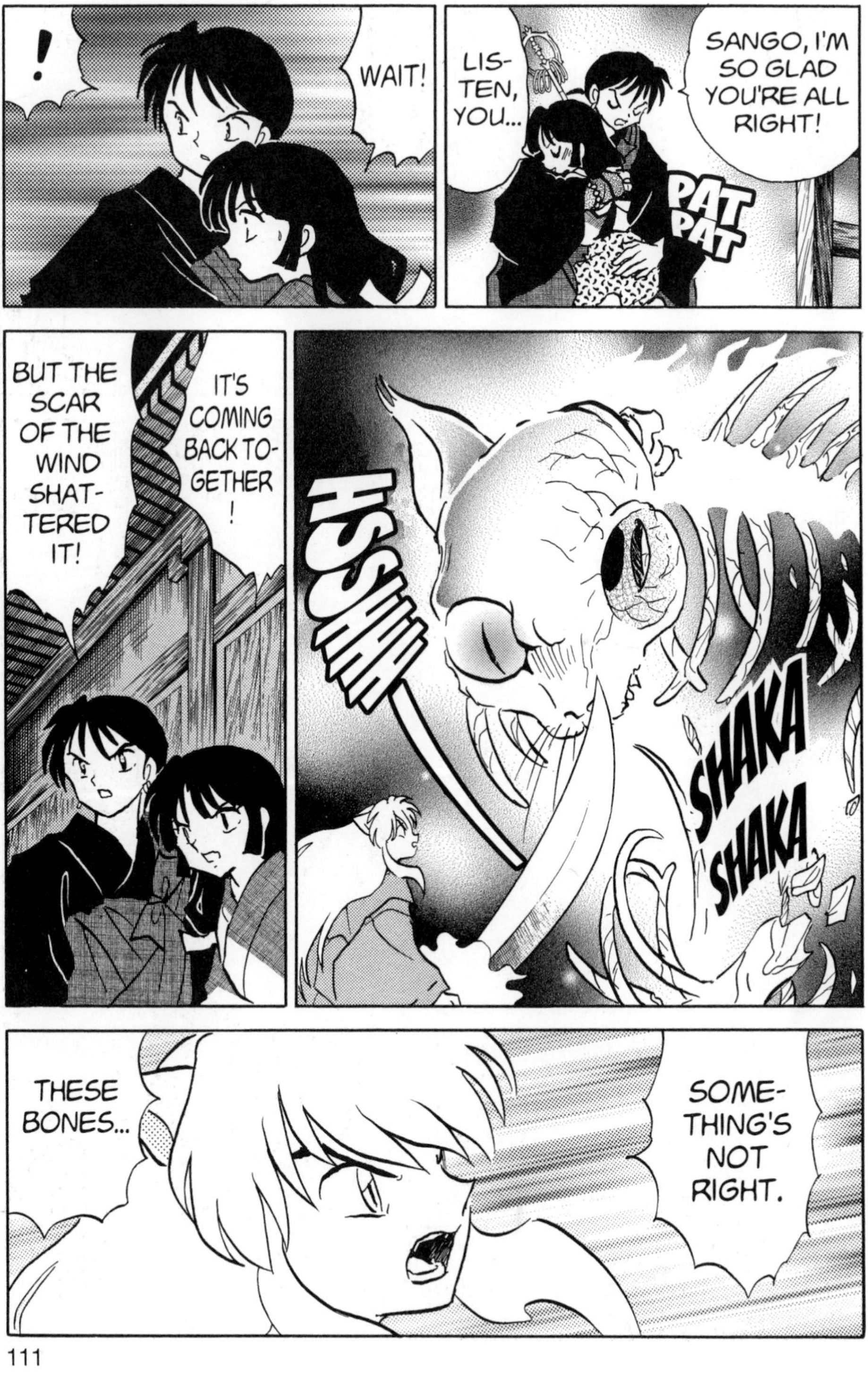
SANGO, I'M SO GLAD YOU'RE ALL RIGHT!
LIS-TEN, YOU...
PAT PAT
!
WAIT!
HSSHHH
SHAKA SHAKA
IT'S COMING BACK TO-GETHER!
BUT THE SCAR OF THE WIND SHAT-TERED IT!
SOME-THING'S NOT RIGHT.
THESE BONES...

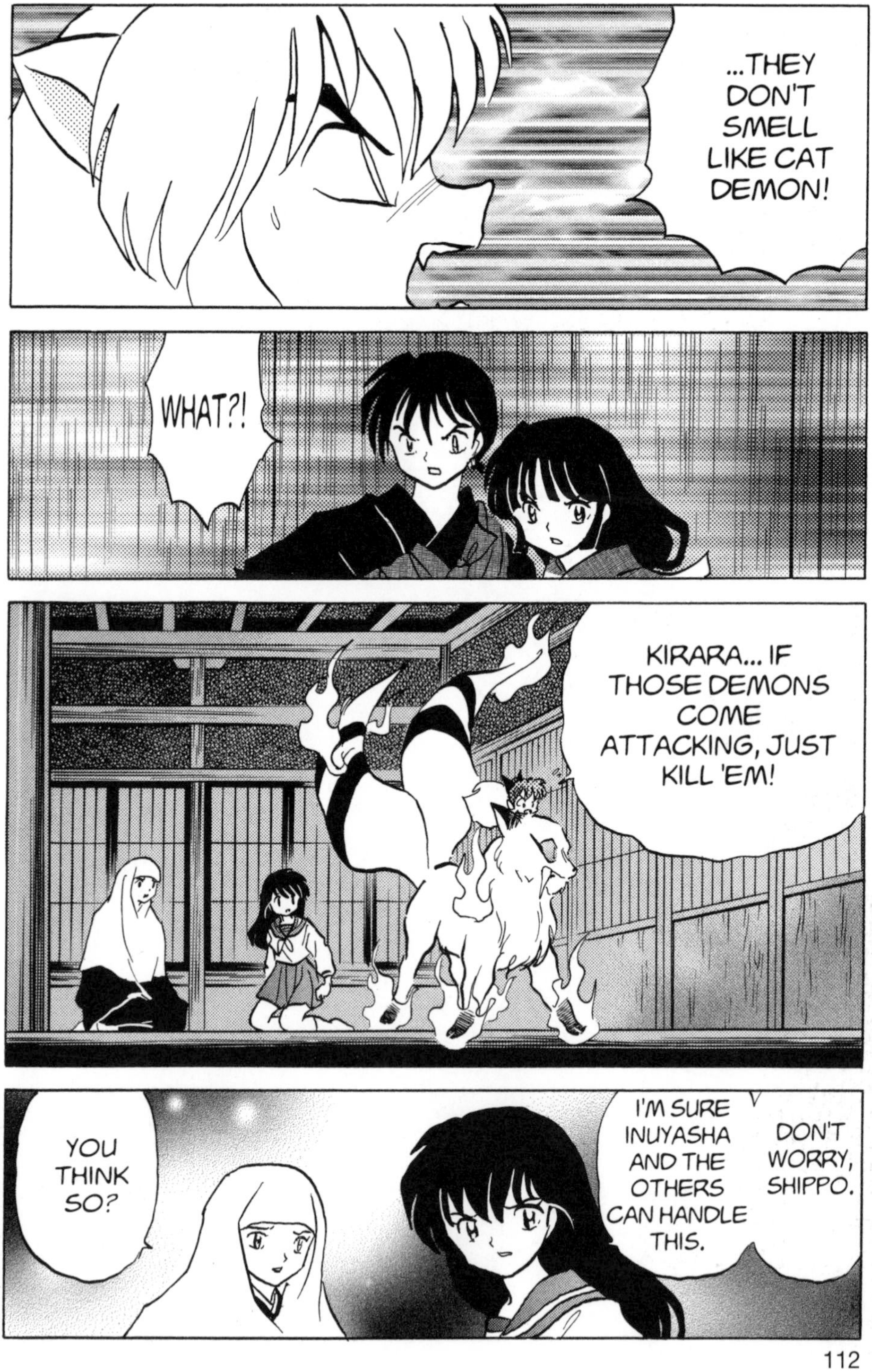
...THEY DON'T SMELL LIKE CAT DEMON!
WHAT?!
KIRARA... IF THOSE DEMONS COME ATTACKING, JUST KILL 'EM!
DON'T WORRY, SHIPPO.
I'M SURE INUYASHA AND THE OTHERS CAN HANDLE THIS.
YOU THINK SO?

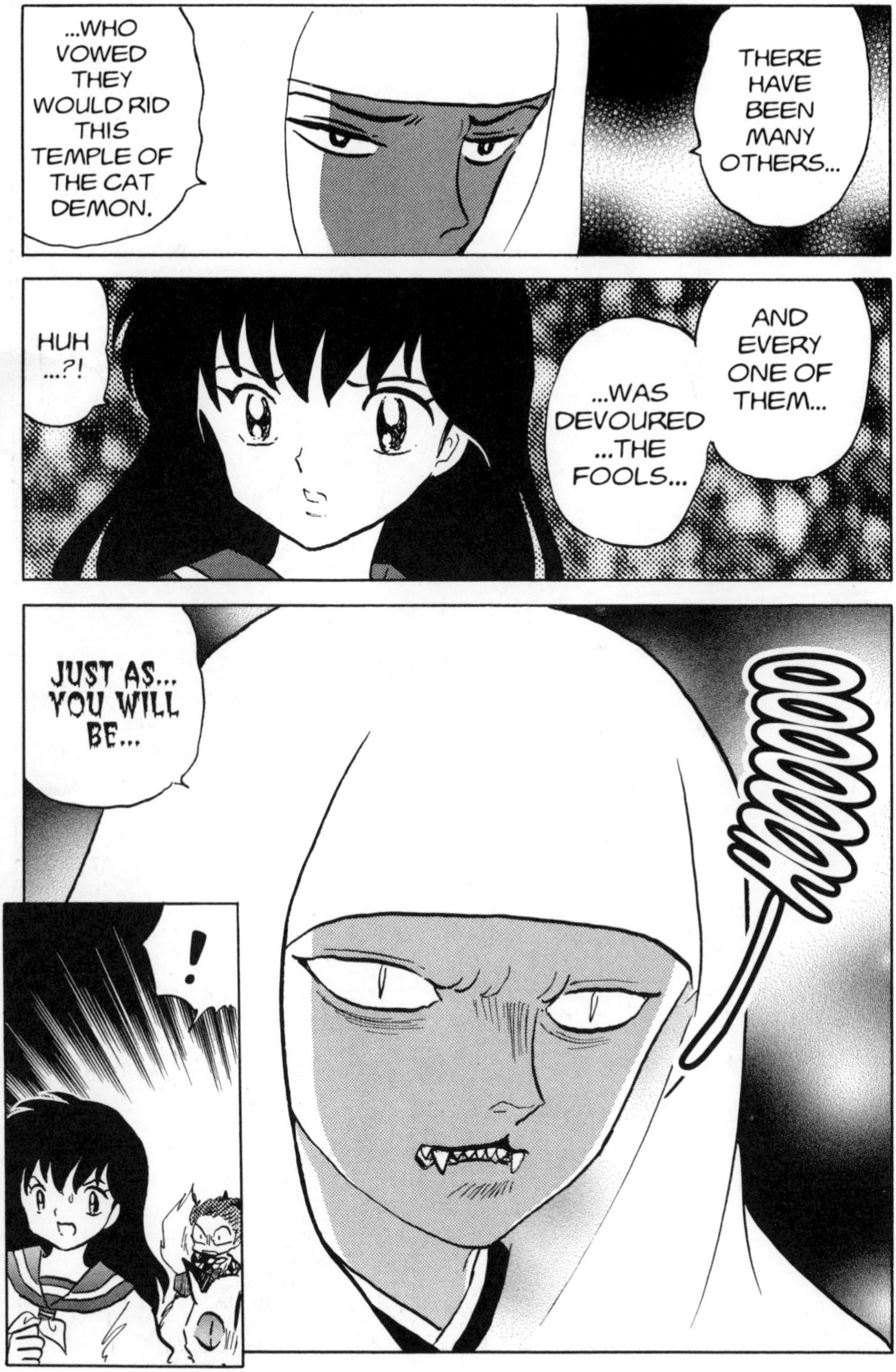
THERE HAVE BEEN MANY OTHERS...
...WHO VOWED THEY WOULD RID THIS TEMPLE OF THE CAT DEMON.
AND EVERY ONE OF THEM...
...WAS DEVOURED ...THE FOOLS...
HUH ...?!
JUST AS... YOU WILL BE...
!

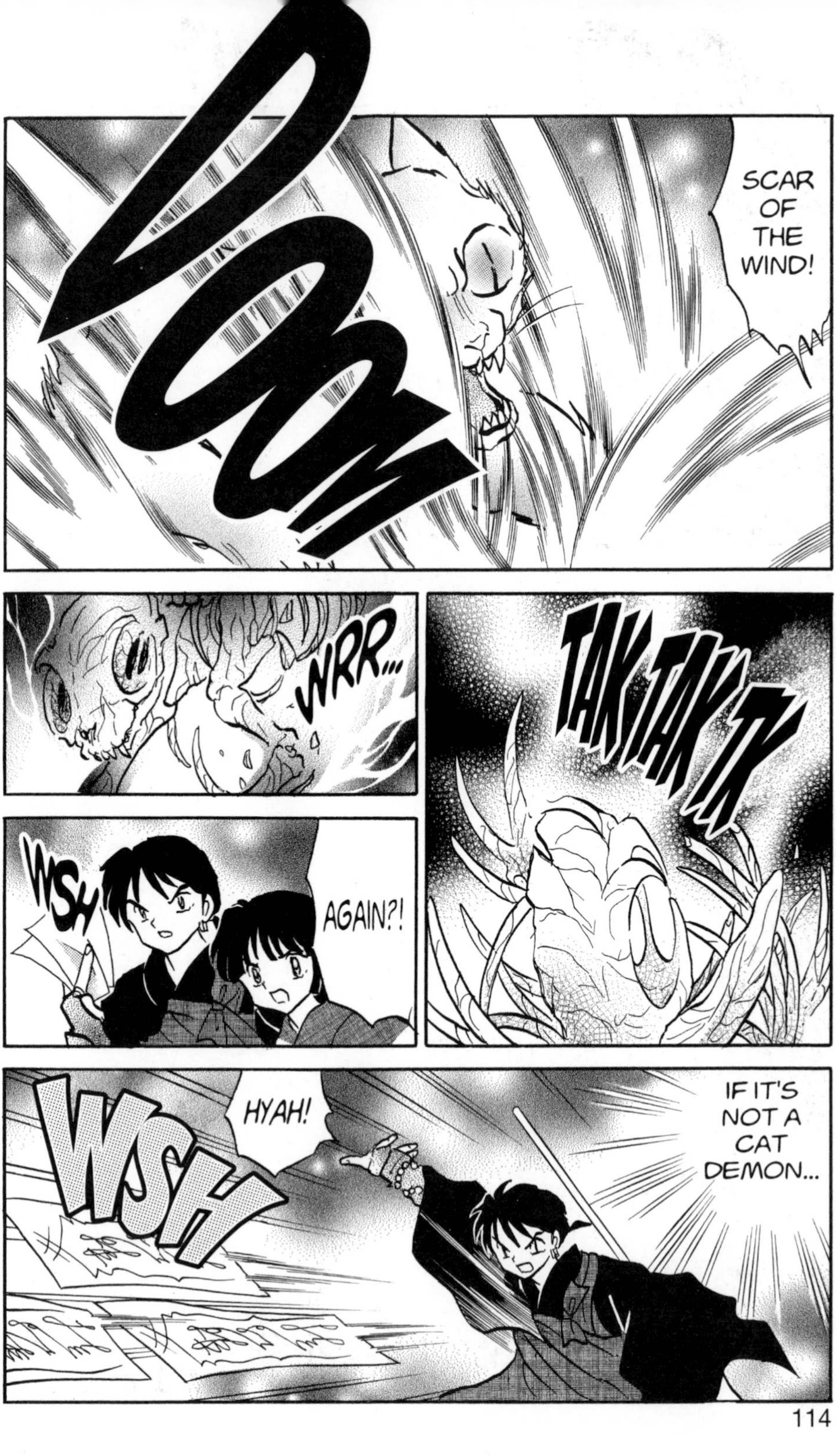
SCAR OF THE WIND!
DOOM
TAK TAK TK
WRR...
AGAIN?!
WSH
IF IT'S NOT A CAT DEMON...
HYAH!
WSH

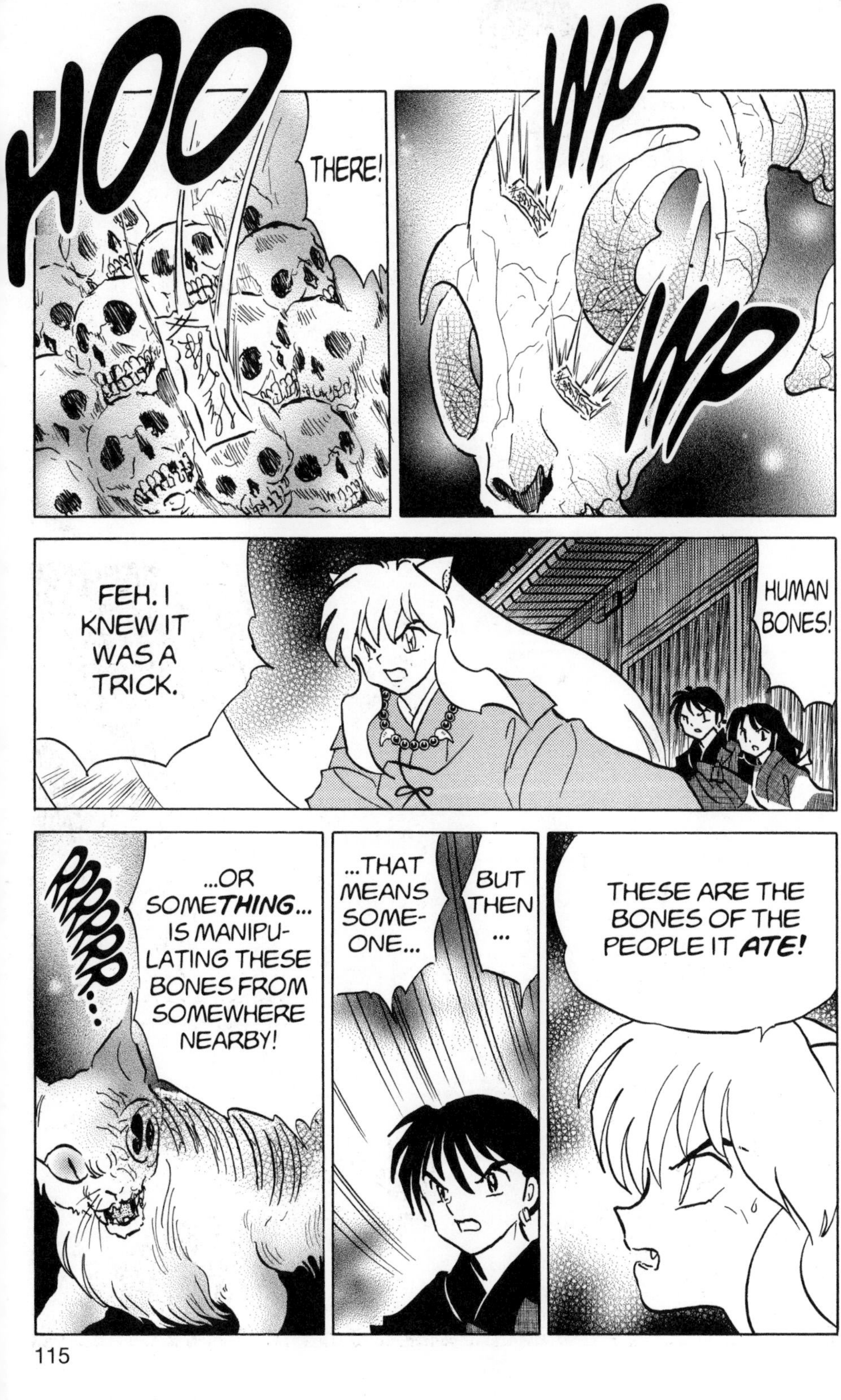
WP
WP
THERE!
HOO
HUMAN BONES!
FEH. I KNEW IT WAS A TRICK.
THESE ARE THE BONES OF THE PEOPLE IT ATE!
BUT THEN...
...THAT MEANS SOMEONE...
...OR SOMETHING... IS MANIPULATING THESE BONES FROM SOMEWHERE NEARBY!
RRRRRR...

WH-WHO ARE YOU...?!

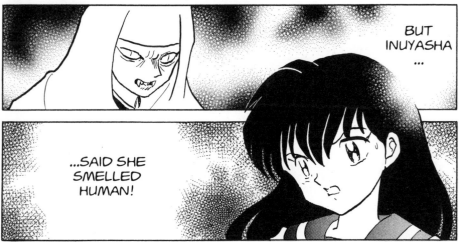

BUT INUYASHA...

...SAID SHE SMELLED HUMAN!

WAH!

ZWP

ZWP

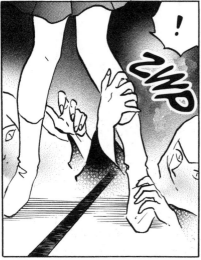

!

ZWP

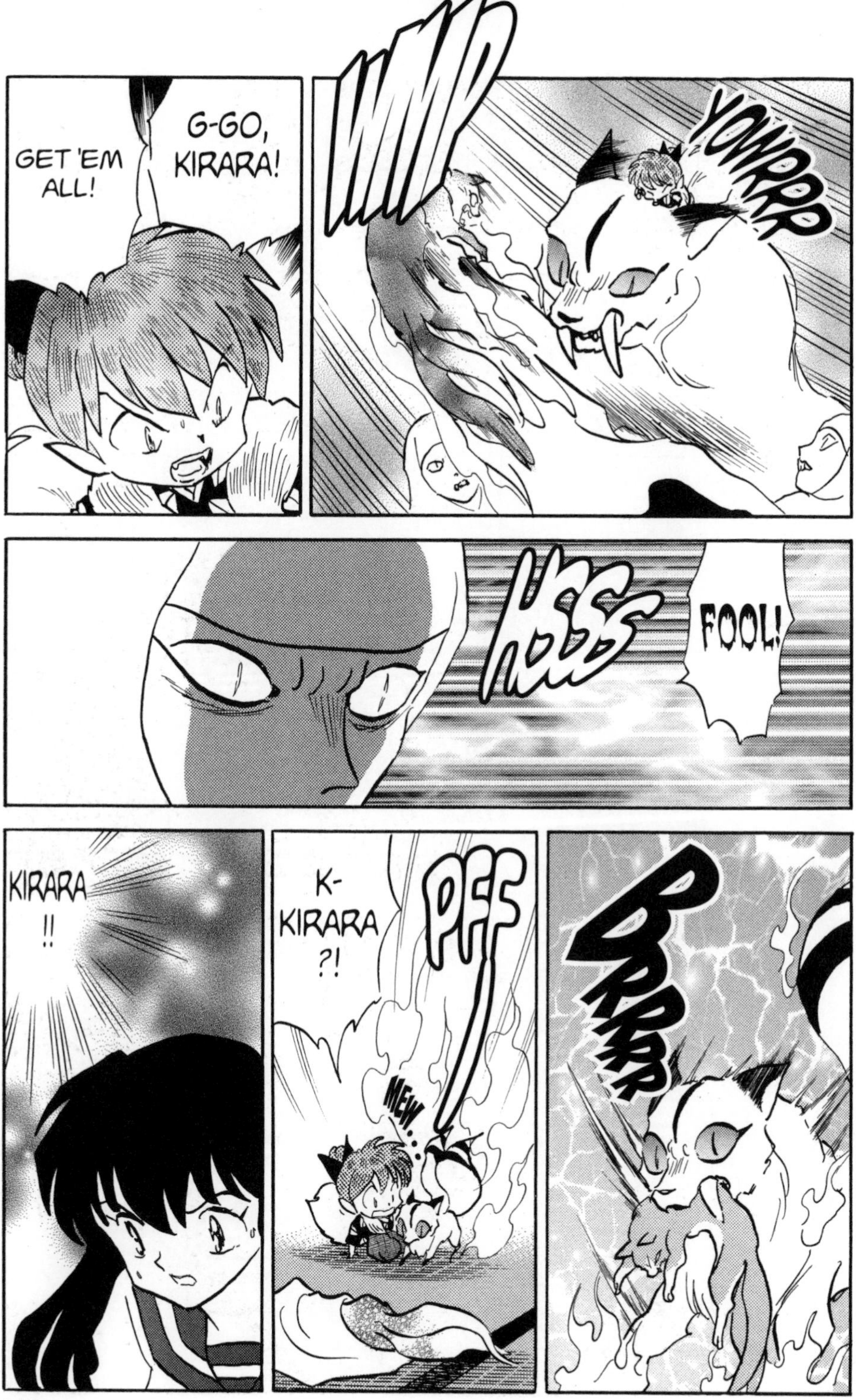
YOWRRP
G-GO, KIRARA!
GET 'EM ALL!
FOOL!
PFF
K-KIRARA ?!
MEW
KIRARA !!

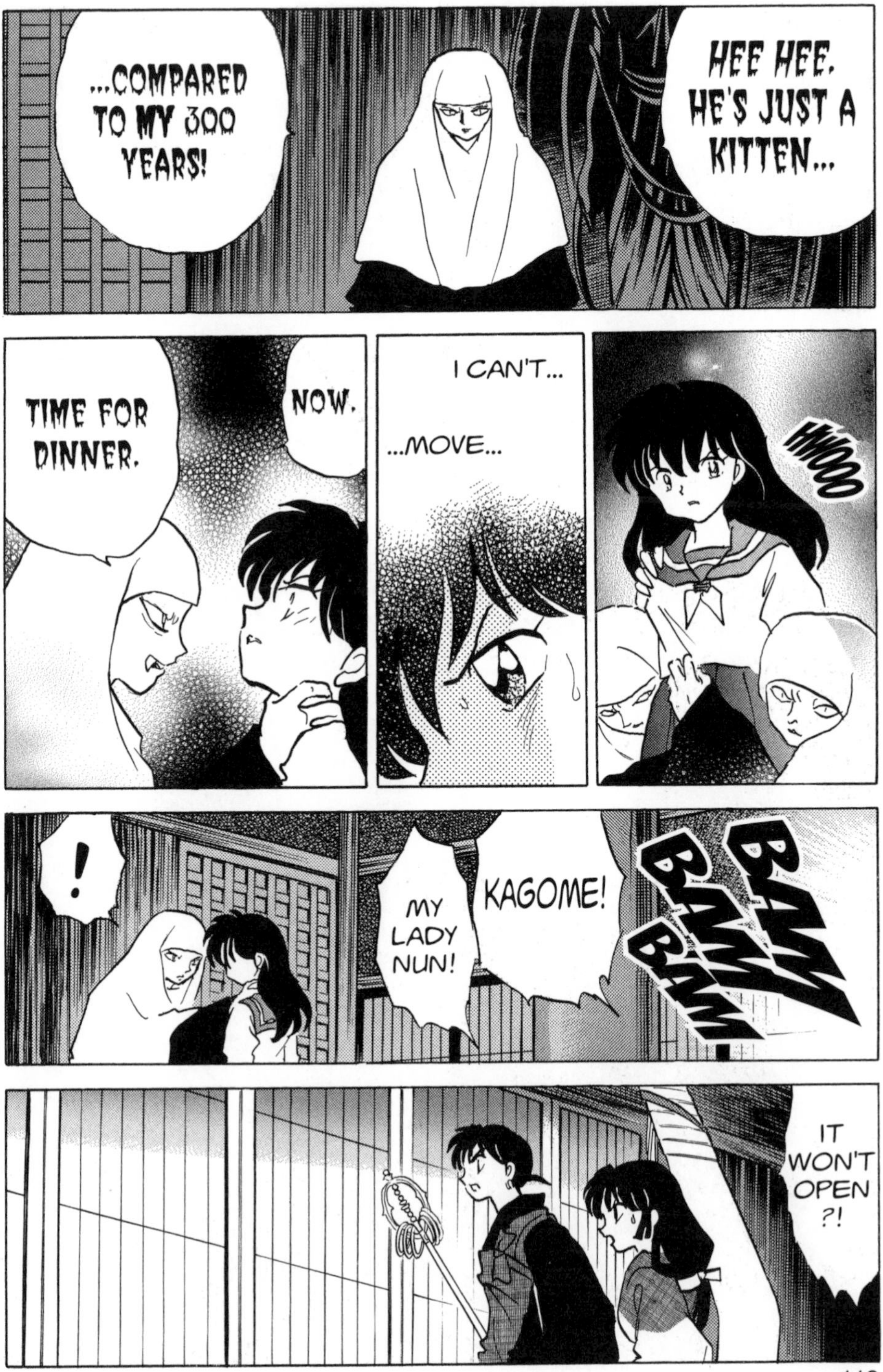
HEE HEE. HE'S JUST A KITTEN...
...COMPARED TO MY 300 YEARS!
HWOOO
I CAN'T...
...MOVE...
NOW.
TIME FOR DINNER.
BAM BAM BAM
KAGOME!
MY LADY NUN!
!
IT WON'T OPEN?!

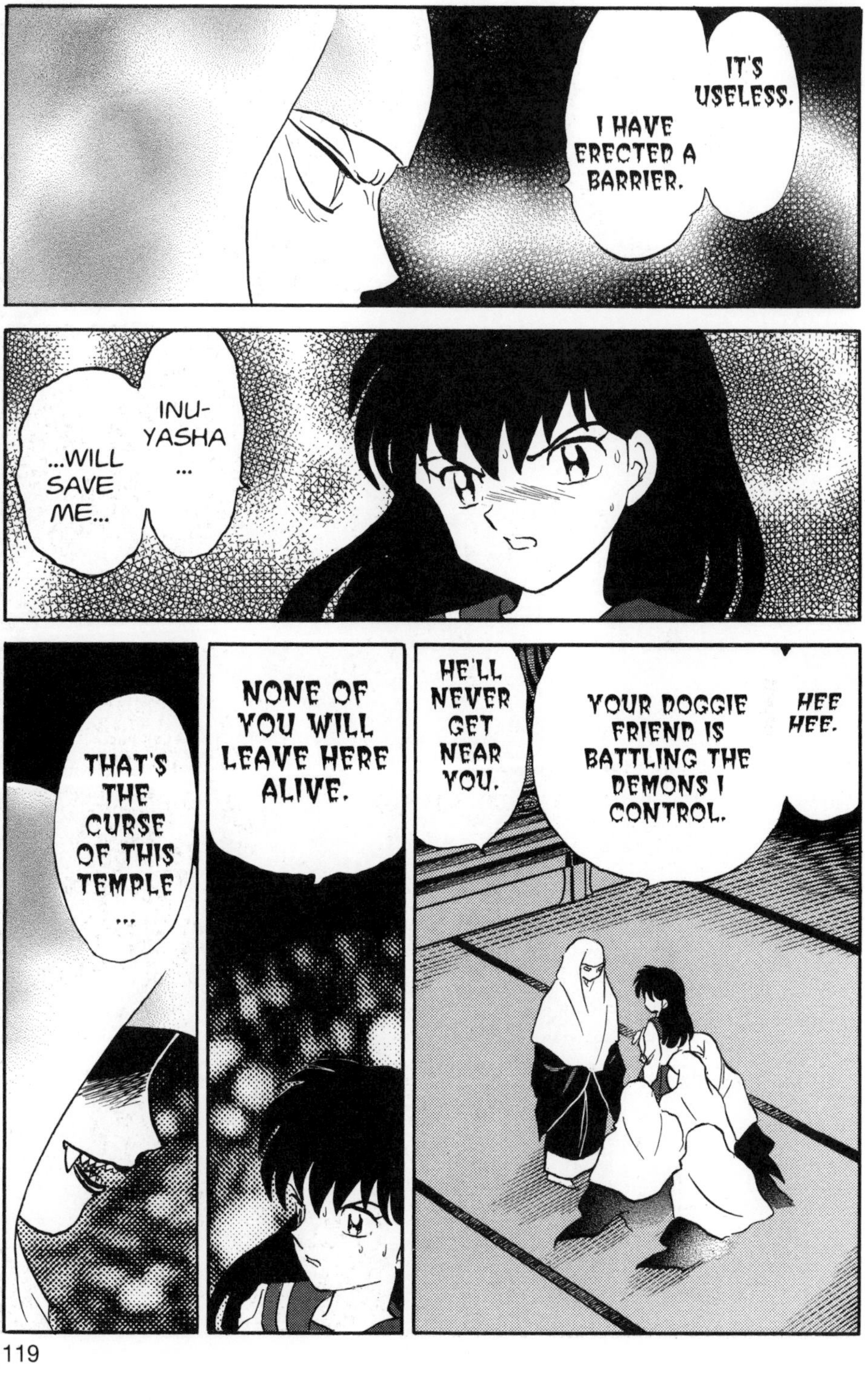
IT'S USELESS.
I HAVE ERECTED A BARRIER.
INU-YASHA...
...WILL SAVE ME...
HEE HEE.
YOUR DOGGIE FRIEND IS BATTLING THE DEMONS I CONTROL.
HE'LL NEVER GET NEAR YOU.
NONE OF YOU WILL LEAVE HERE ALIVE.
THAT'S THE CURSE OF THIS TEMPLE...

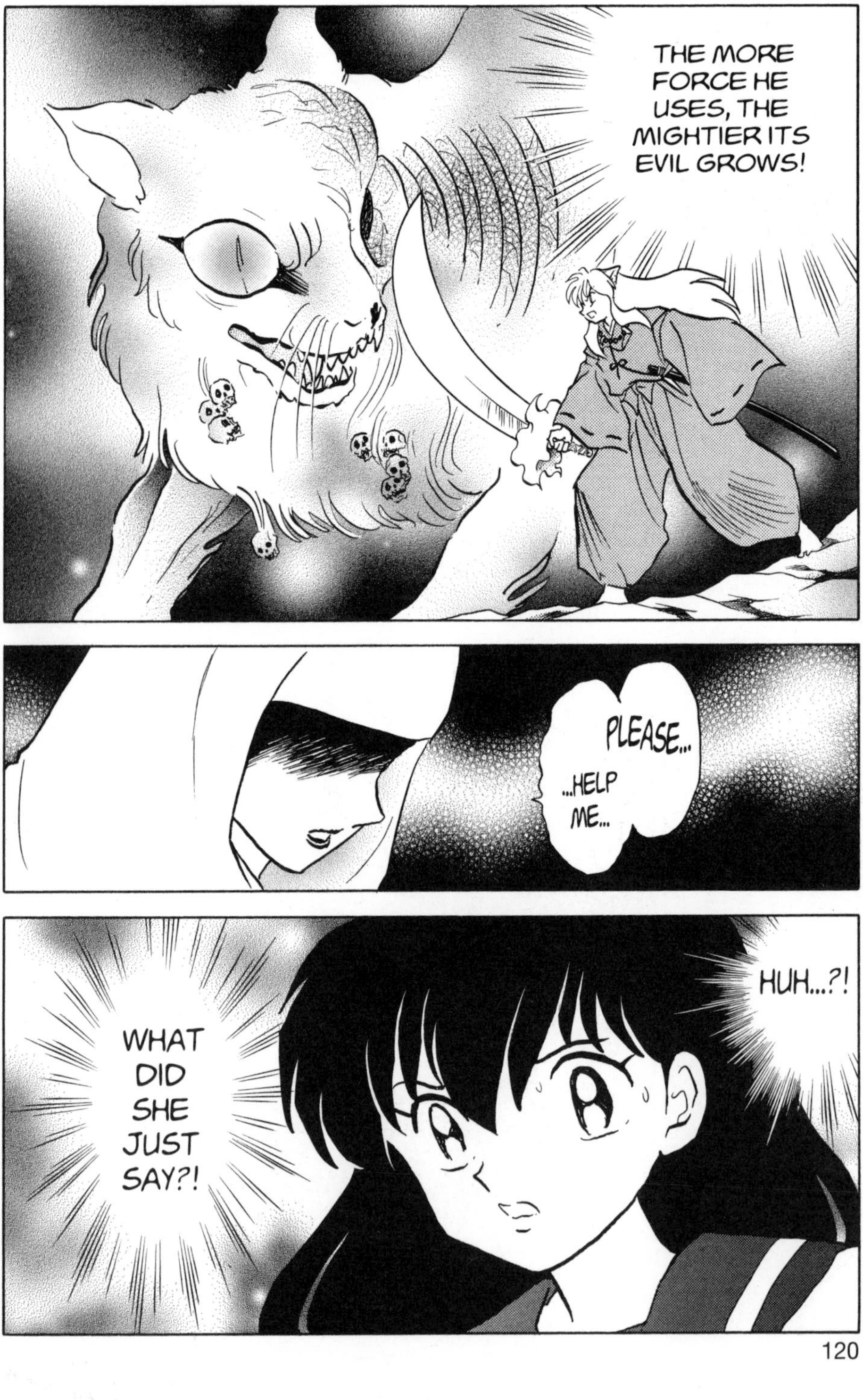
THE MORE FORCE HE USES, THE MIGHTIER ITS EVIL GROWS!
PLEASE...
...HELP ME...
HUH...?!
WHAT DID SHE JUST SAY?!

SCROLL SEVEN
THE DRAGON-SCALED TETSUSAIGA

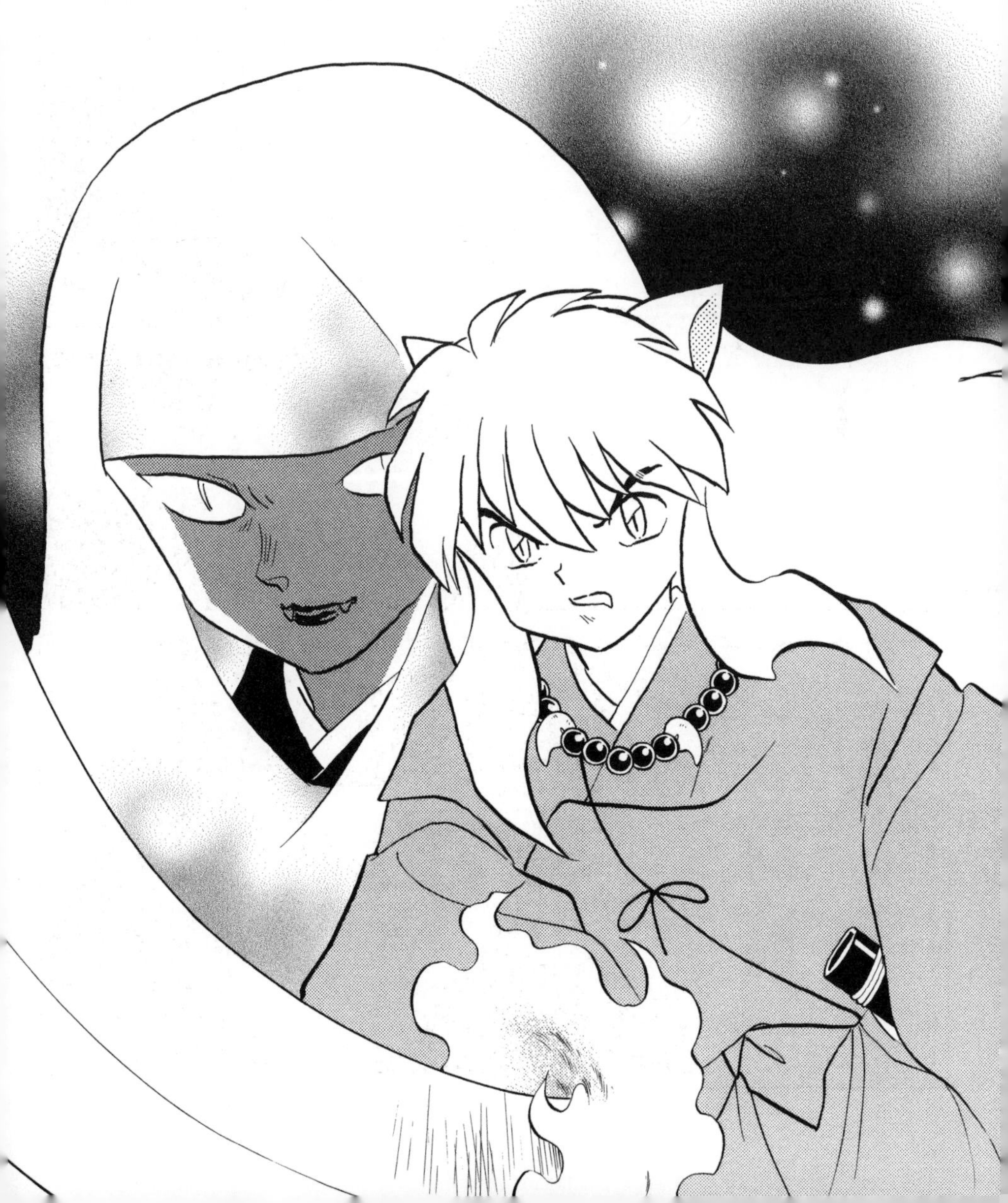

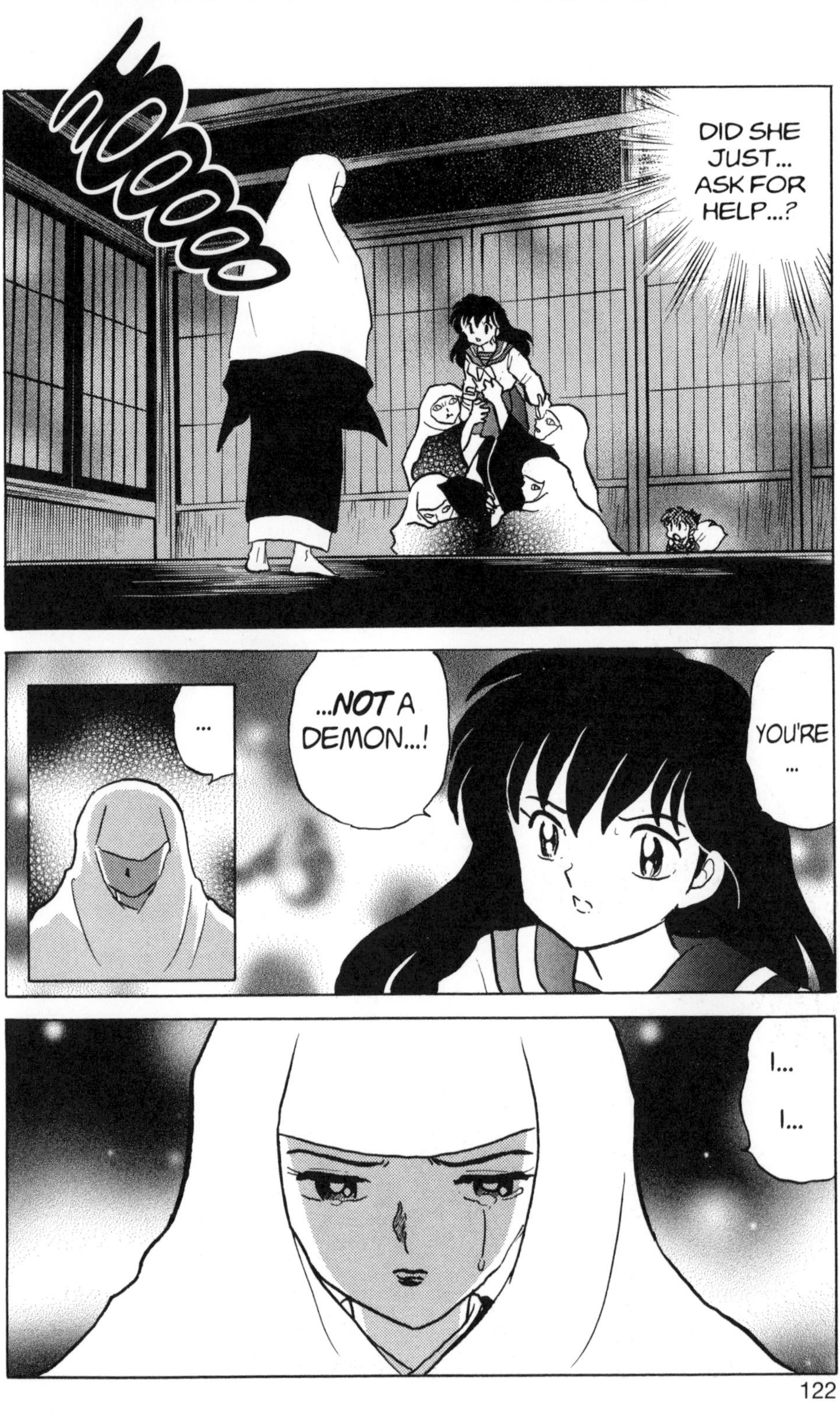
DID SHE JUST... ASK FOR HELP...?
HOOOOO
YOU'RE ...
...NOT A DEMON...!
...
I...
I...

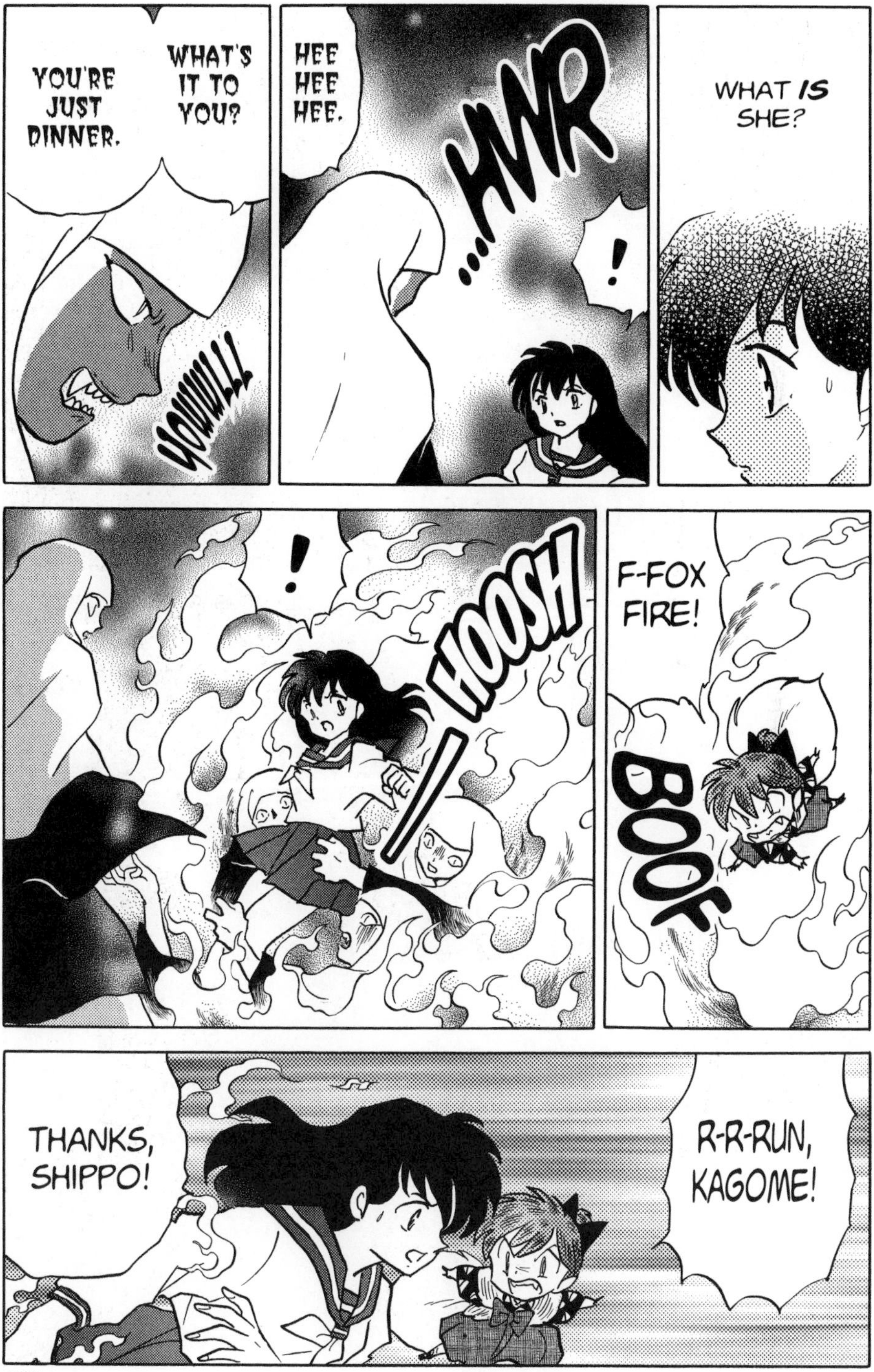
WHAT *IS* SHE?
HEE HEE HEE.
...HMR
!
WHAT'S IT TO YOU?
YOU'RE JUST DINNER.
YOWWLLL
F-FOX FIRE!
BOOF
!
HOOSH
R-R-RUN, KAGOME!
THANKS, SHIPPO!

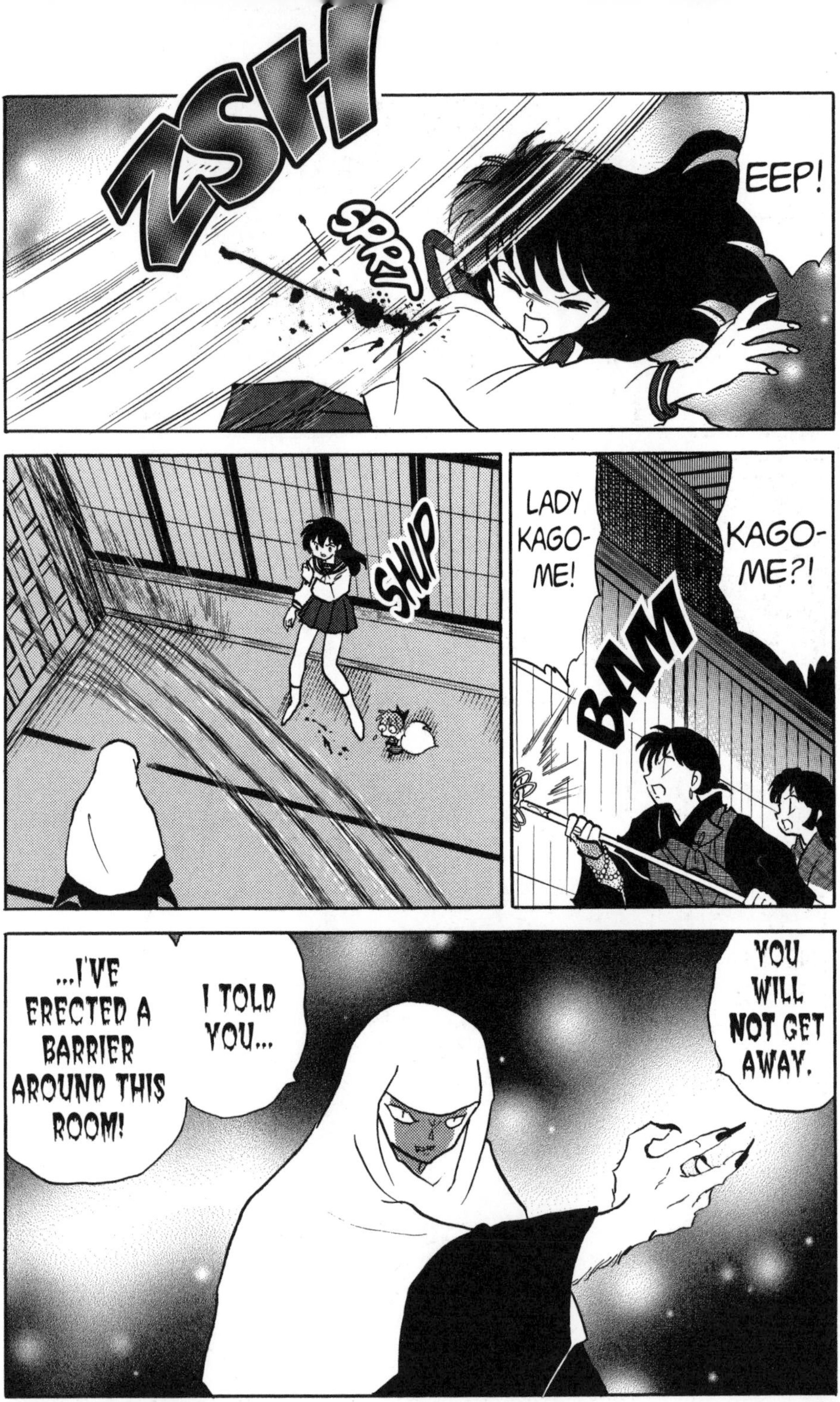
ZSH
EEP!
SPRIT
KAGO-ME?!
LADY KAGO-ME!
BAM
SHUP
YOU WILL NOT GET AWAY.
I TOLD YOU...
...I'VE ERECTED A BARRIER AROUND THIS ROOM!

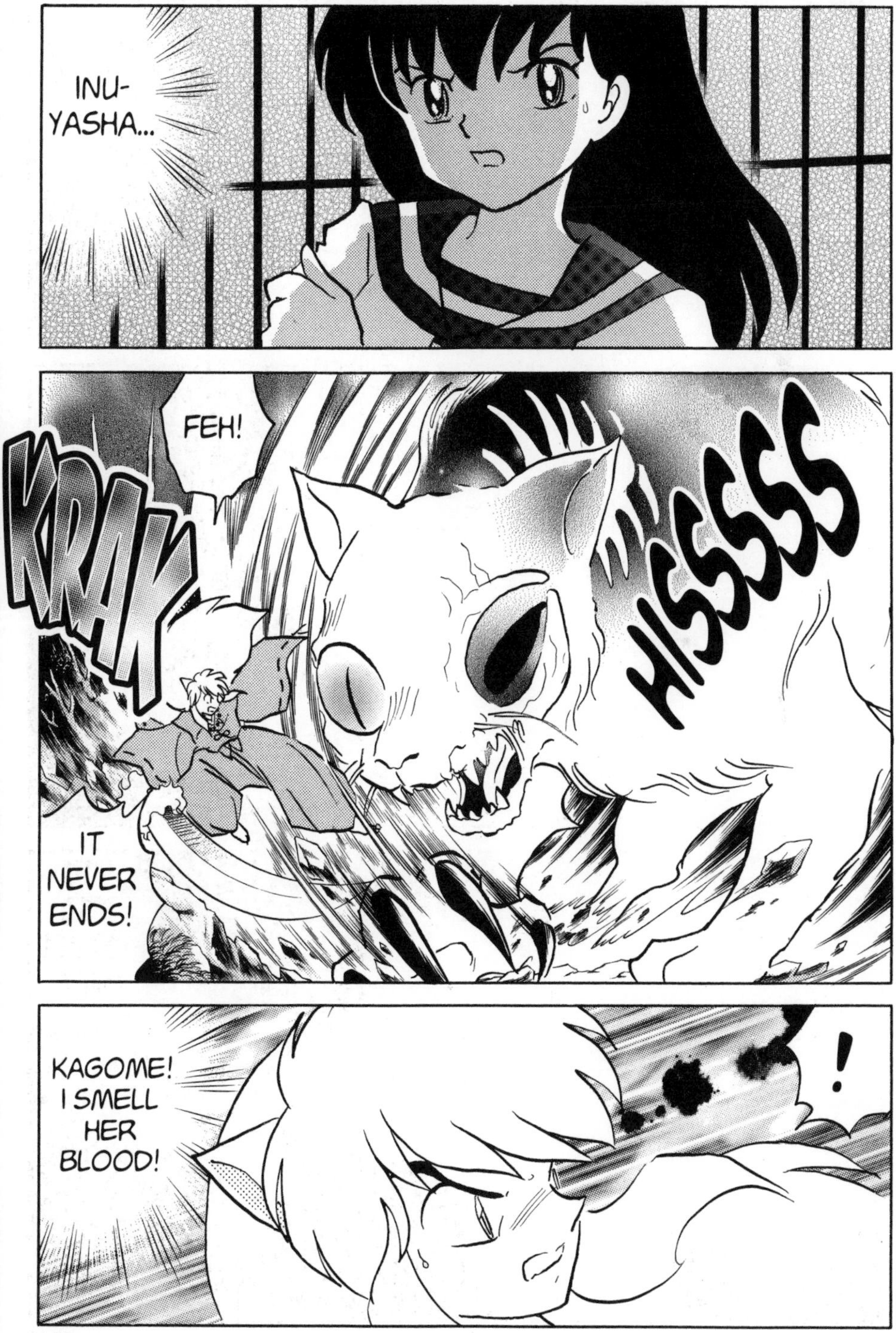
INU-YASHA...
HISSSSS
FEH!
KRAK
IT NEVER ENDS!
!
KAGOME! I SMELL HER BLOOD!

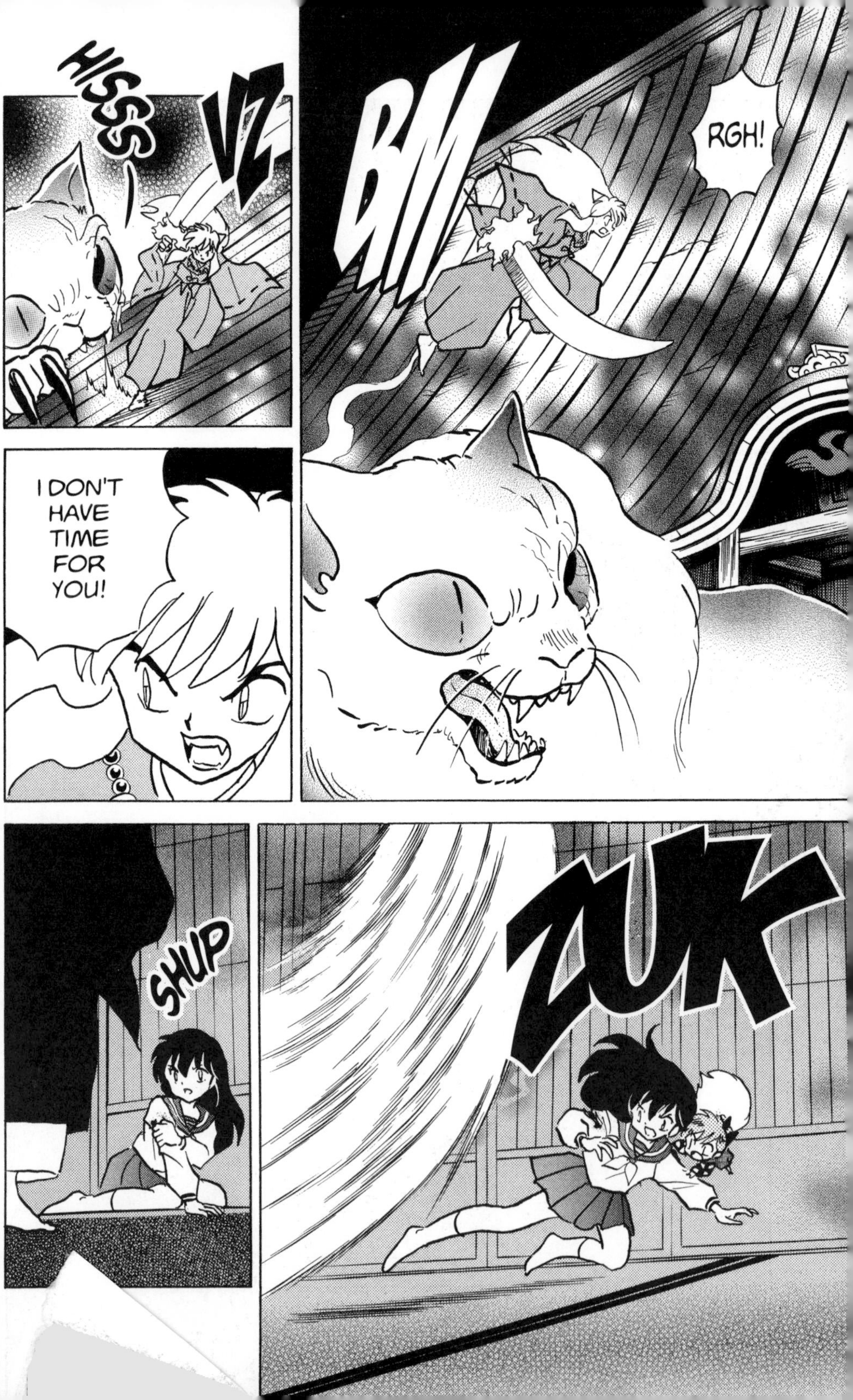
BM
RGH!
HISSS
VZ
I DON'T HAVE TIME FOR YOU!
ZUK
SHUP

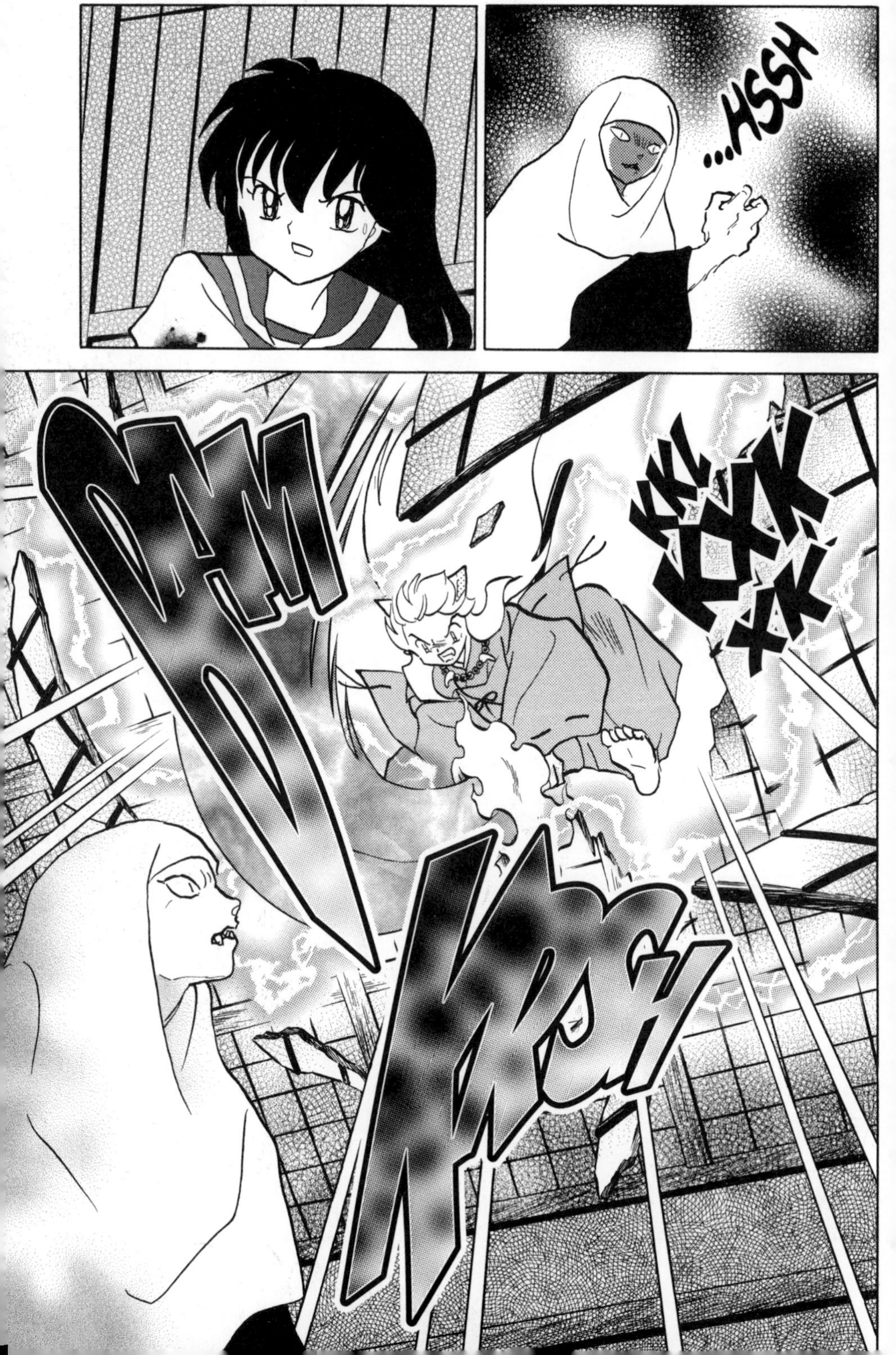
...HSSH

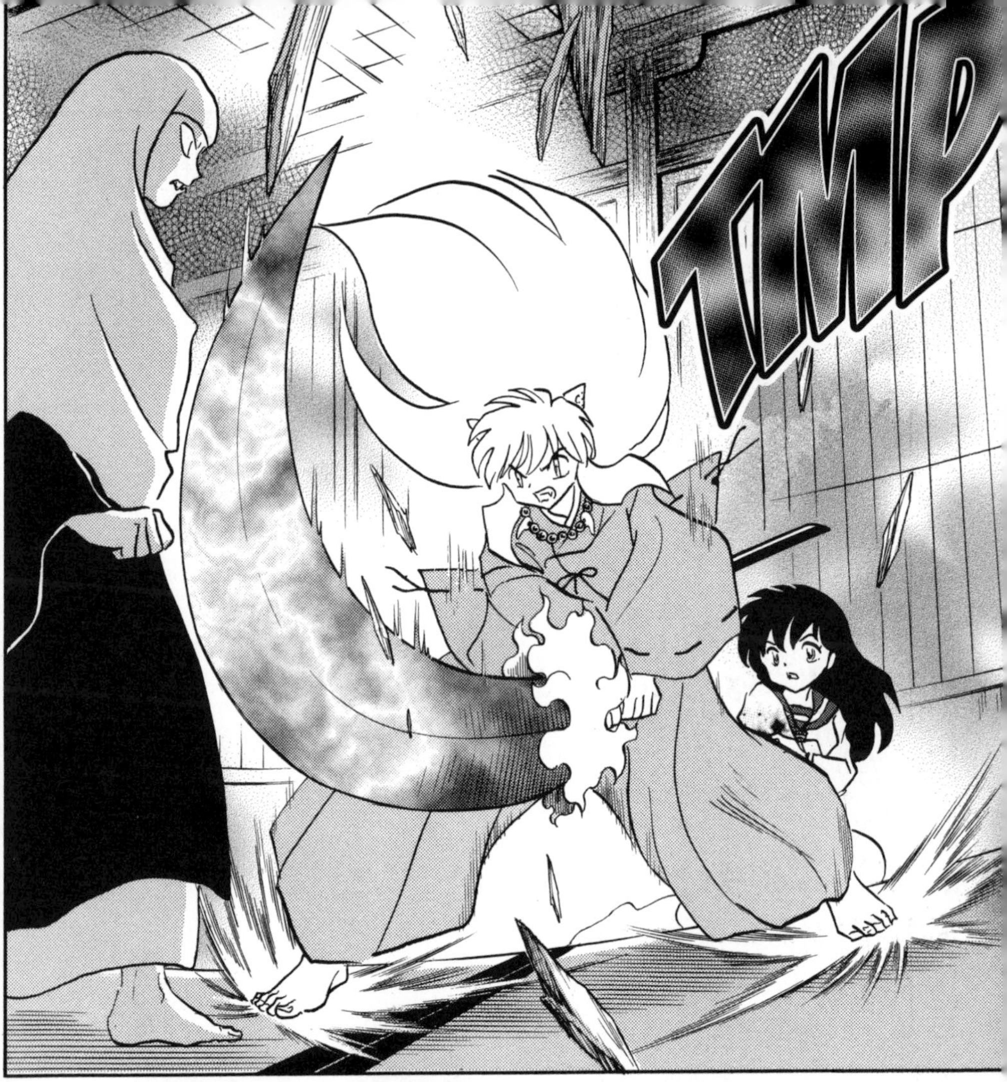
TMP

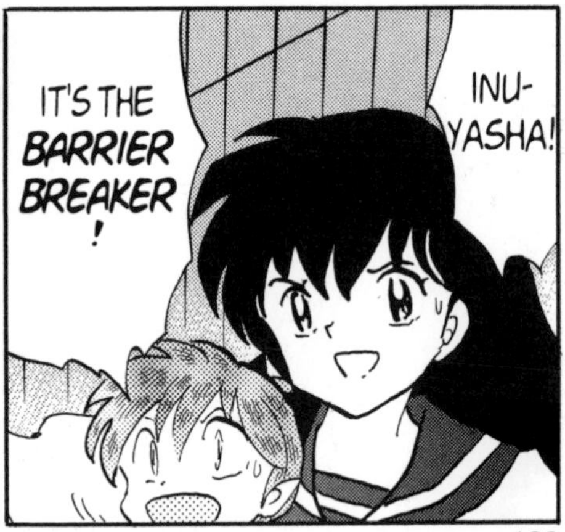
INU-
YASHA!
IT'S THE
BARRIER
BREAKER
!

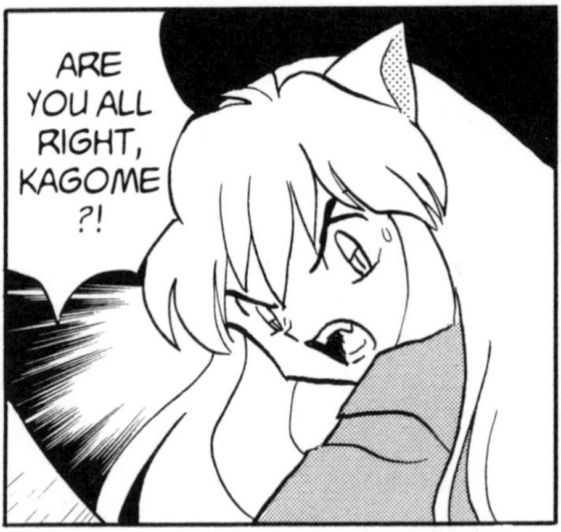
ARE
YOU ALL
RIGHT,
KAGOME
?!

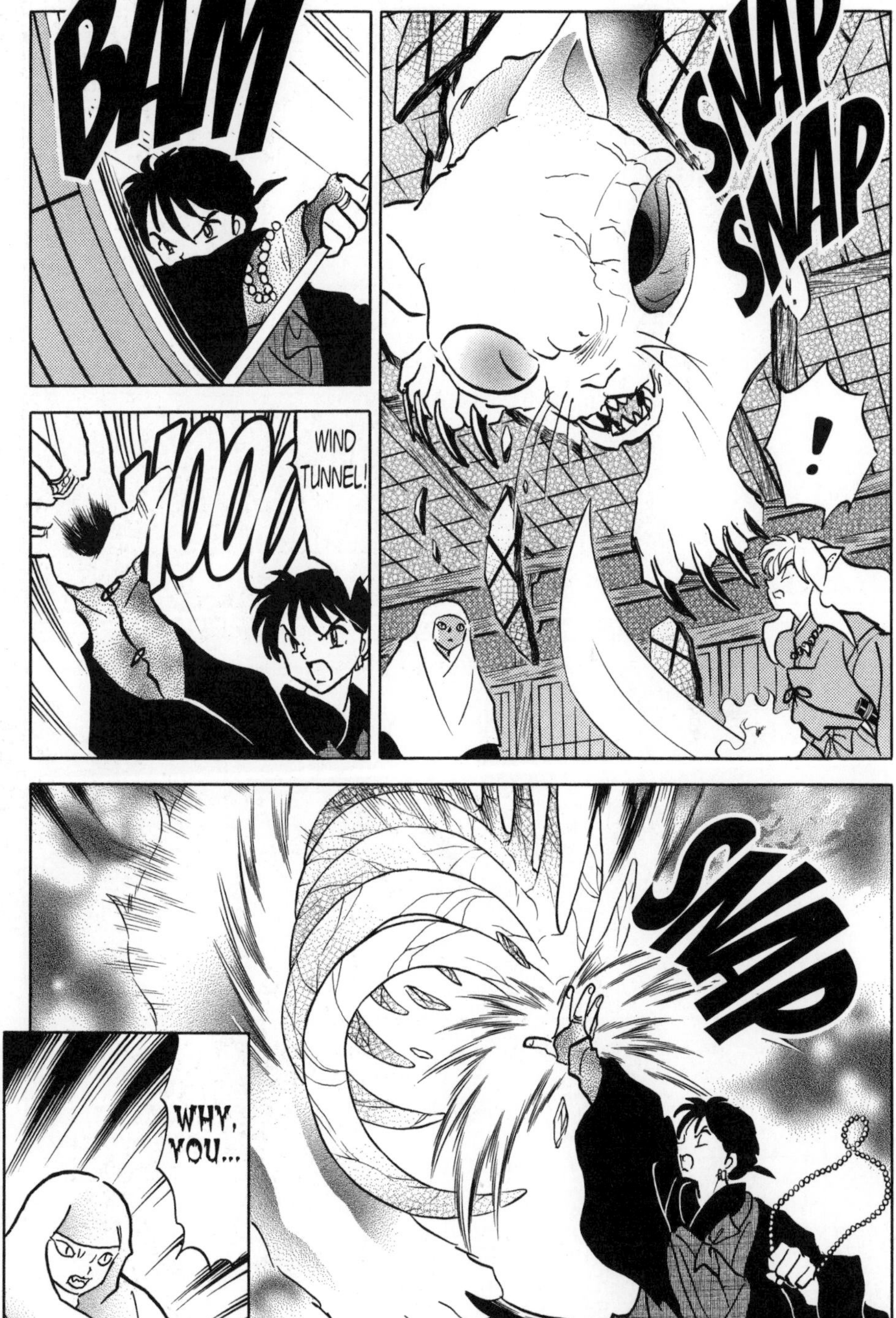
SNAP SNAP
!
BAM
WIND TUNNEL!
SNAP
WHY, YOU...

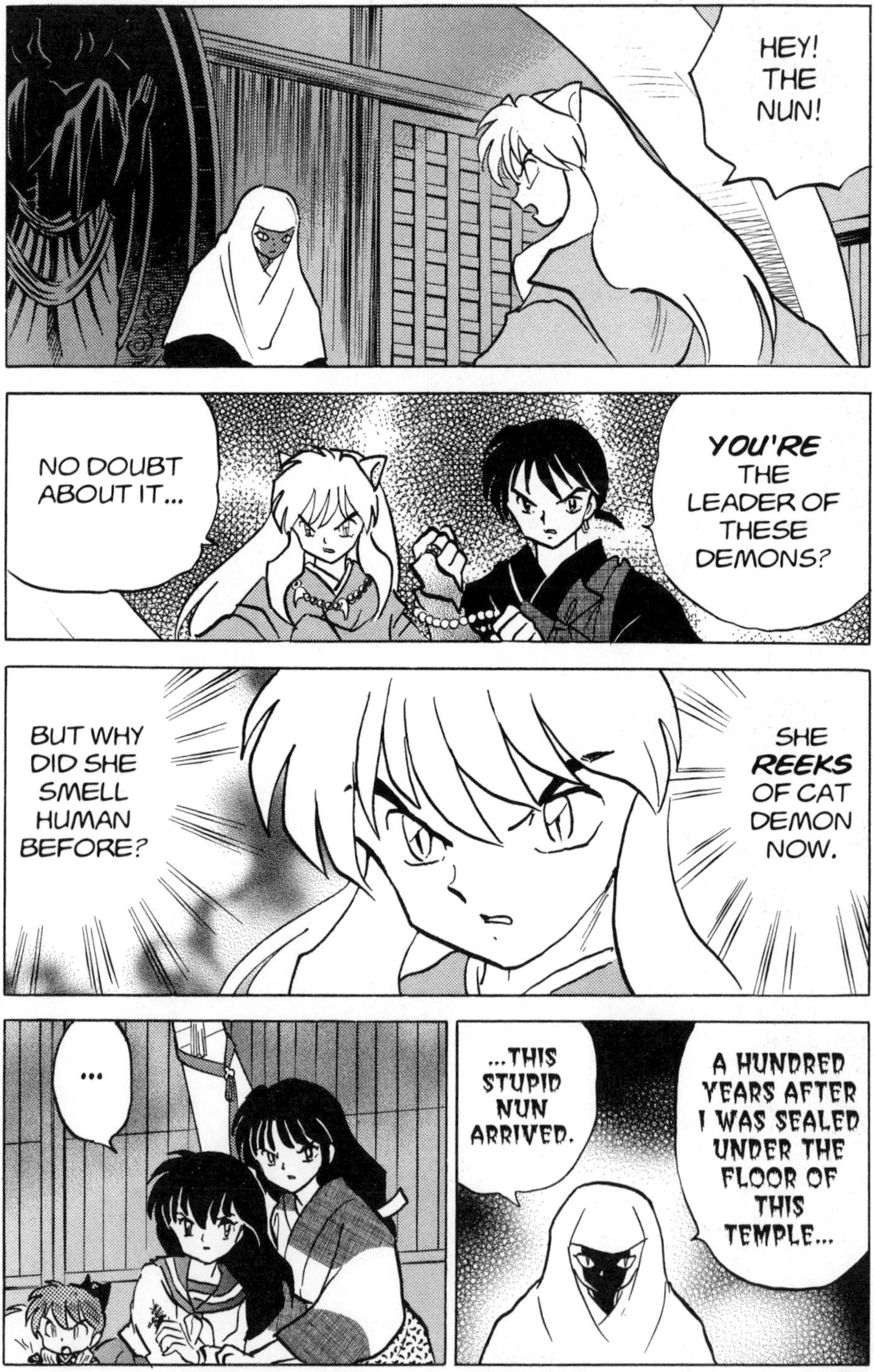
HEY! THE NUN!
YOU'RE THE LEADER OF THESE DEMONS?
NO DOUBT ABOUT IT...
SHE REEKS OF CAT DEMON NOW.
BUT WHY DID SHE SMELL HUMAN BEFORE?
A HUNDRED YEARS AFTER I WAS SEALED UNDER THE FLOOR OF THIS TEMPLE...
...THIS STUPID NUN ARRIVED.
...

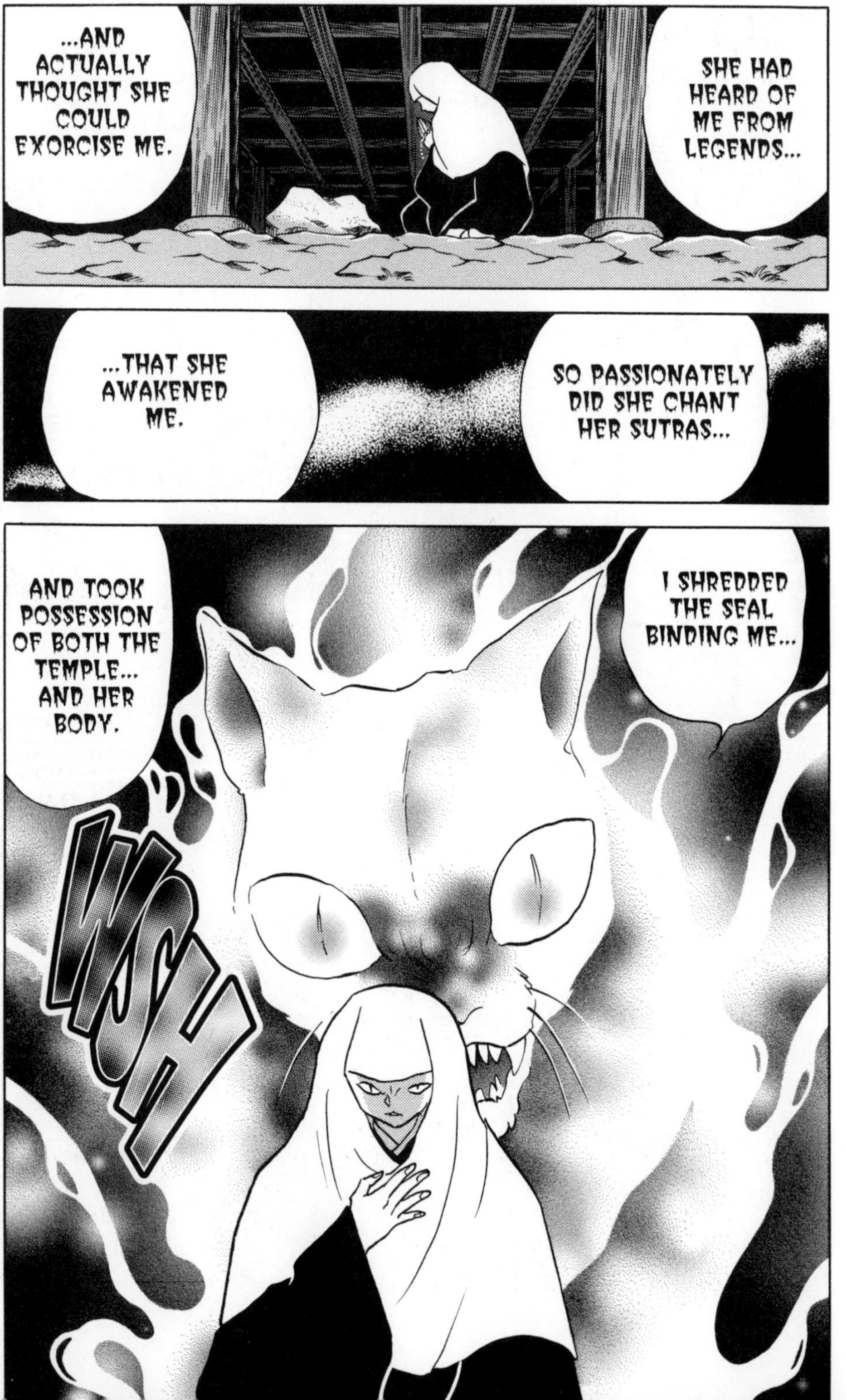
SHE HAD HEARD OF ME FROM LEGENDS...
...AND ACTUALLY THOUGHT SHE COULD EXORCISE ME.
SO PASSIONATELY DID SHE CHANT HER SUTRAS...
...THAT SHE AWAKENED ME.
I SHREDDED THE SEAL BINDING ME...
AND TOOK POSSESSION OF BOTH THE TEMPLE... AND HER BODY.
WSH

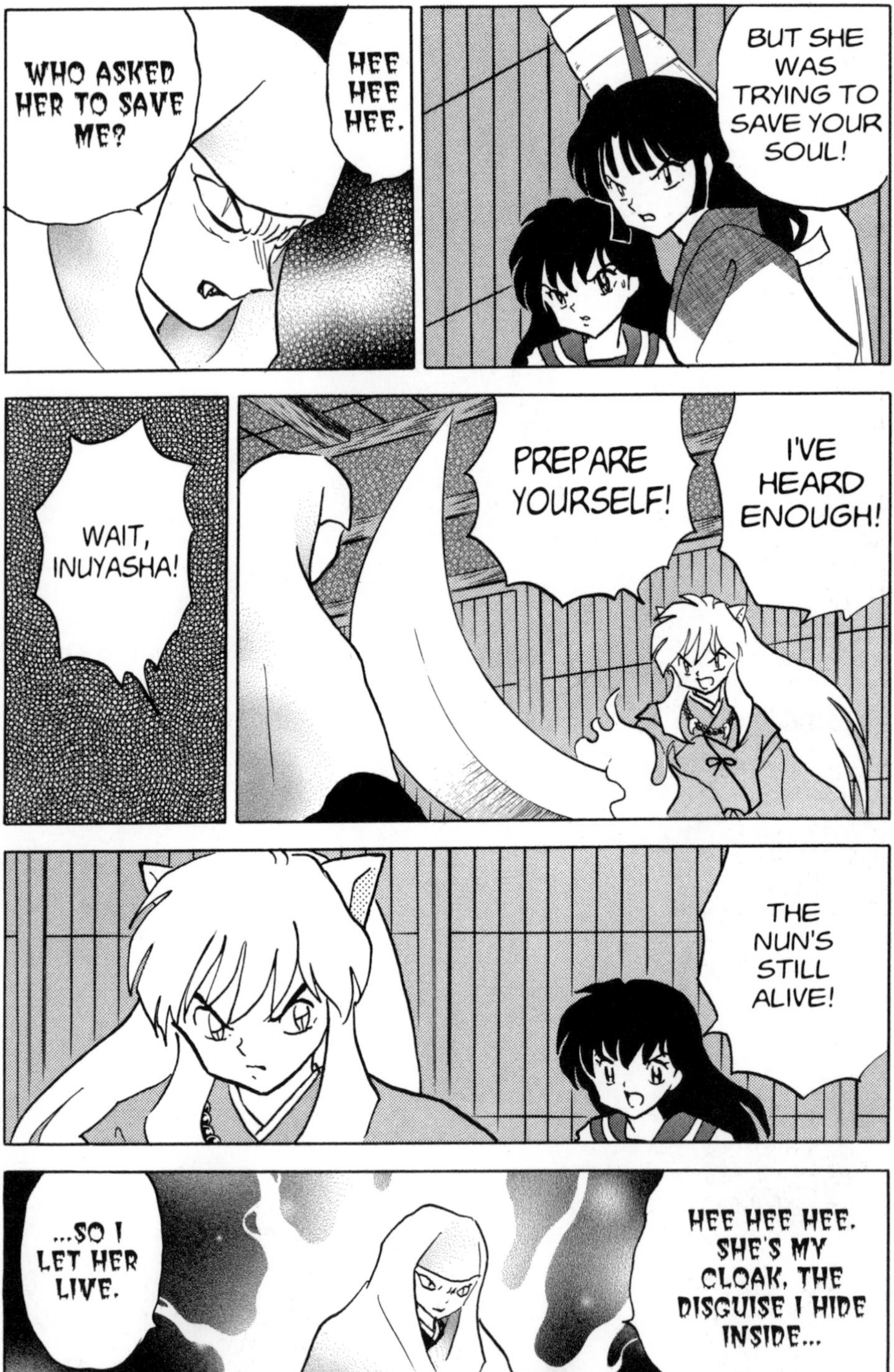
BUT SHE WAS TRYING TO SAVE YOUR SOUL!
HEE HEE HEE.
WHO ASKED HER TO SAVE ME?
I'VE HEARD ENOUGH!
PREPARE YOURSELF!
WAIT, INUYASHA!
THE NUN'S STILL ALIVE!
HEE HEE HEE. SHE'S MY CLOAK, THE DISGUISE I HIDE INSIDE...
...SO I LET HER LIVE.

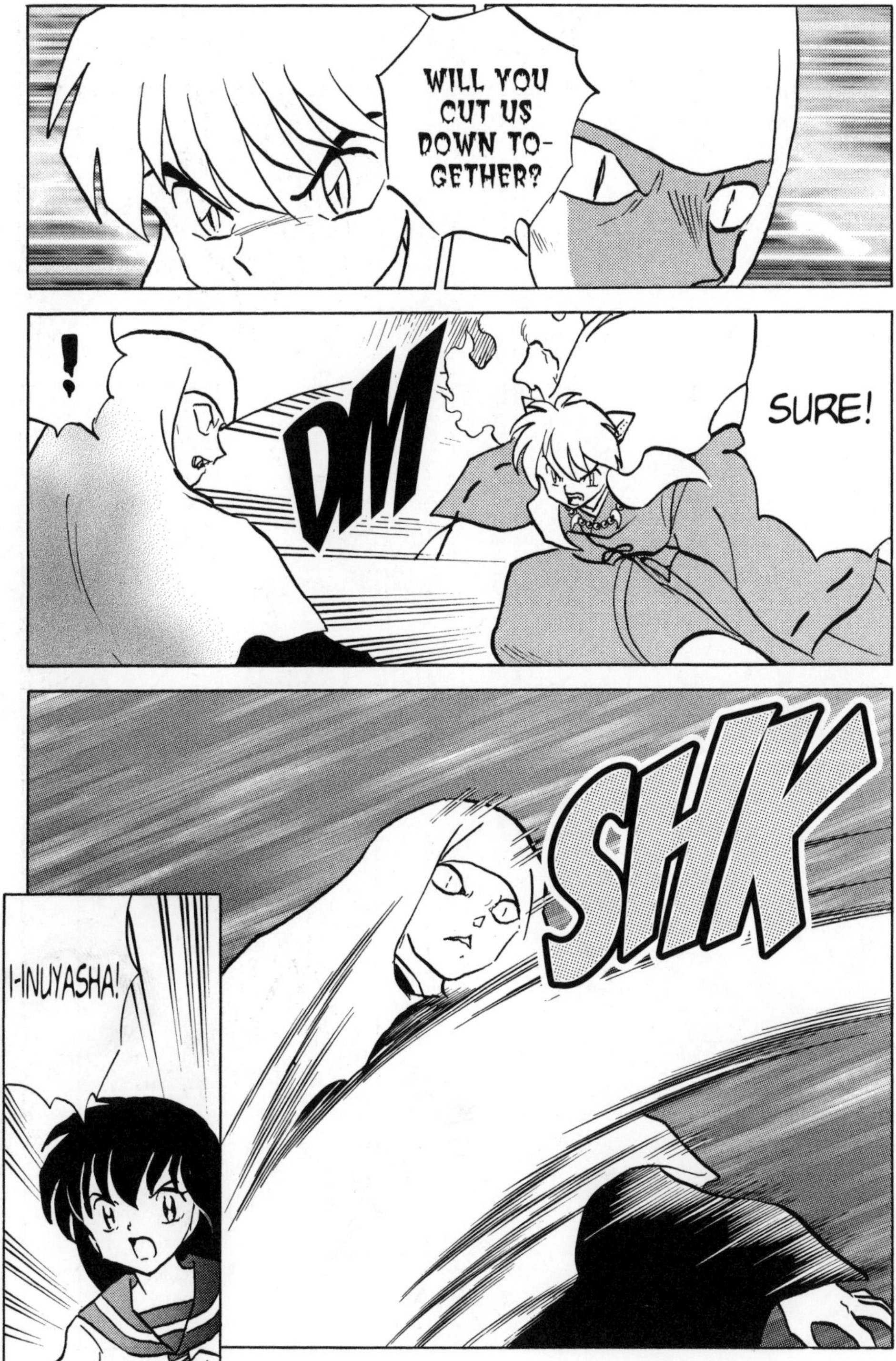
WILL YOU CUT US DOWN TO-GETHER?
SURE!
DM
!
SHK
I-INUYASHA!

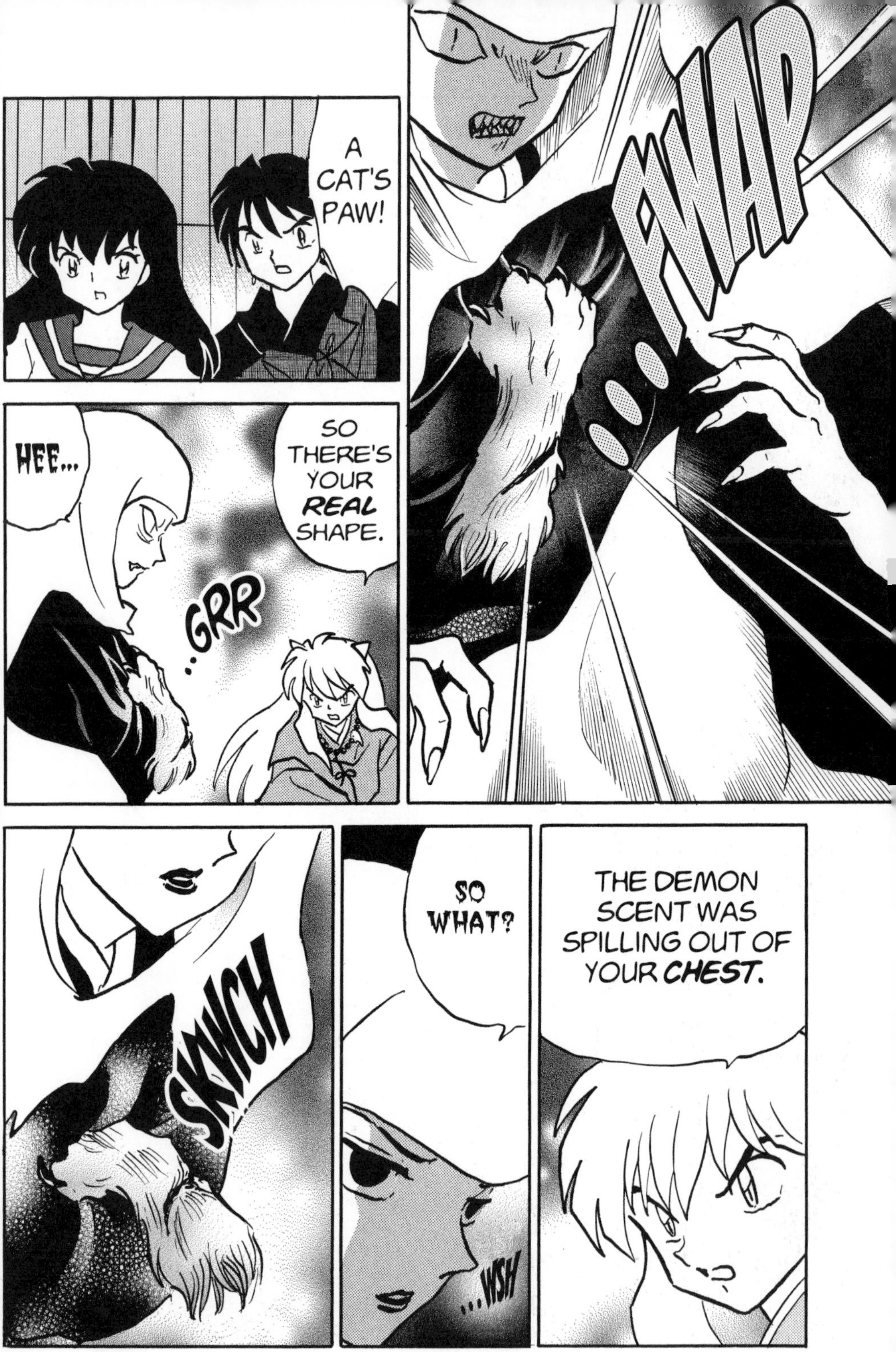
SNAP
A CAT'S PAW!
SO THERE'S YOUR REAL SHAPE.
HEE...
...GRR
THE DEMON SCENT WAS SPILLING OUT OF YOUR CHEST.
SO WHAT?
...WSH
SKWCH

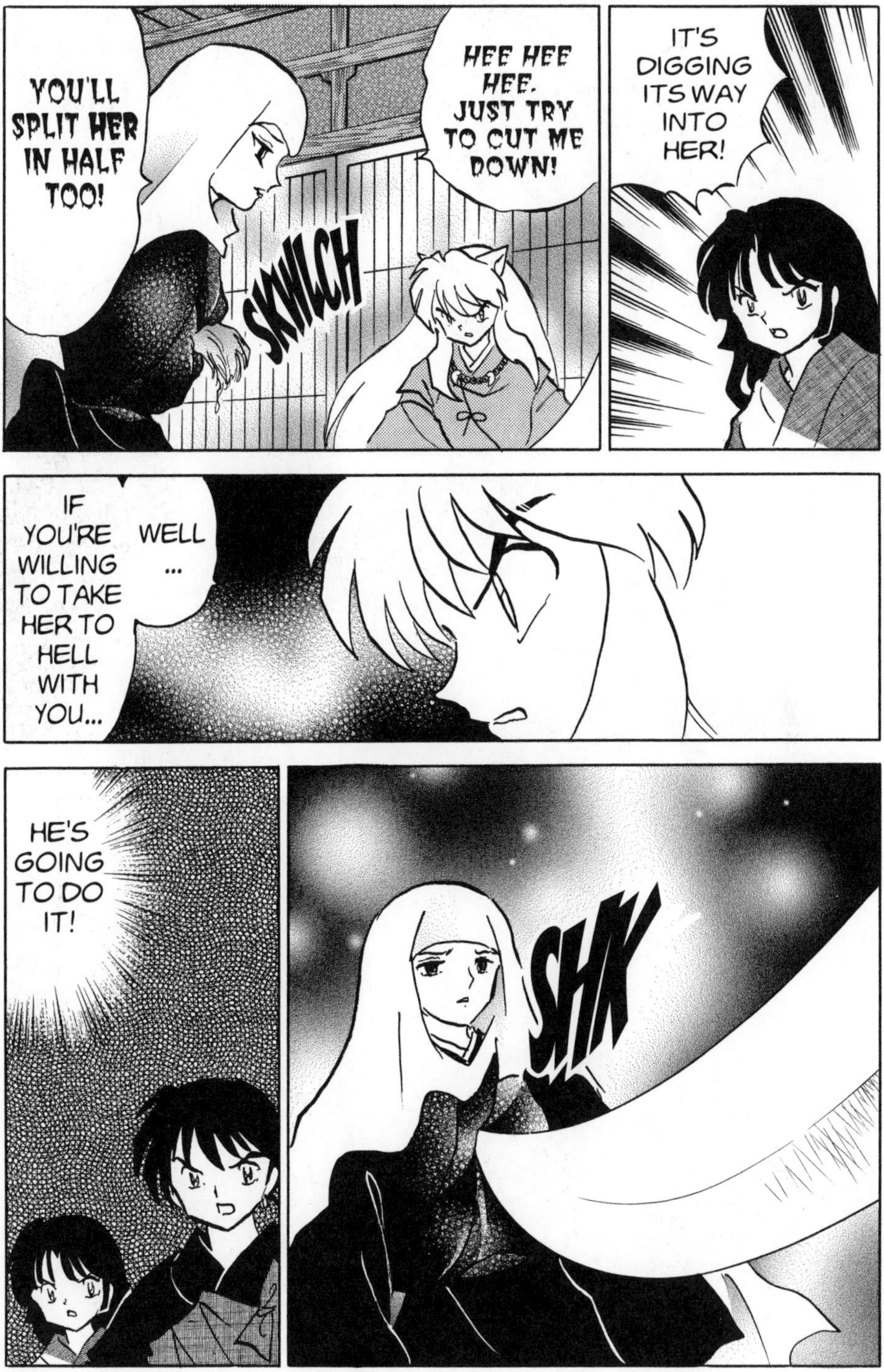
IT'S DIGGING ITS WAY INTO HER!
HEE HEE HEE. JUST TRY TO CUT ME DOWN!
YOU'LL SPLIT HER IN HALF TOO!
SKWLCH
WELL...
IF YOU'RE WILLING TO TAKE HER TO HELL WITH YOU...
SHK
HE'S GOING TO DO IT!

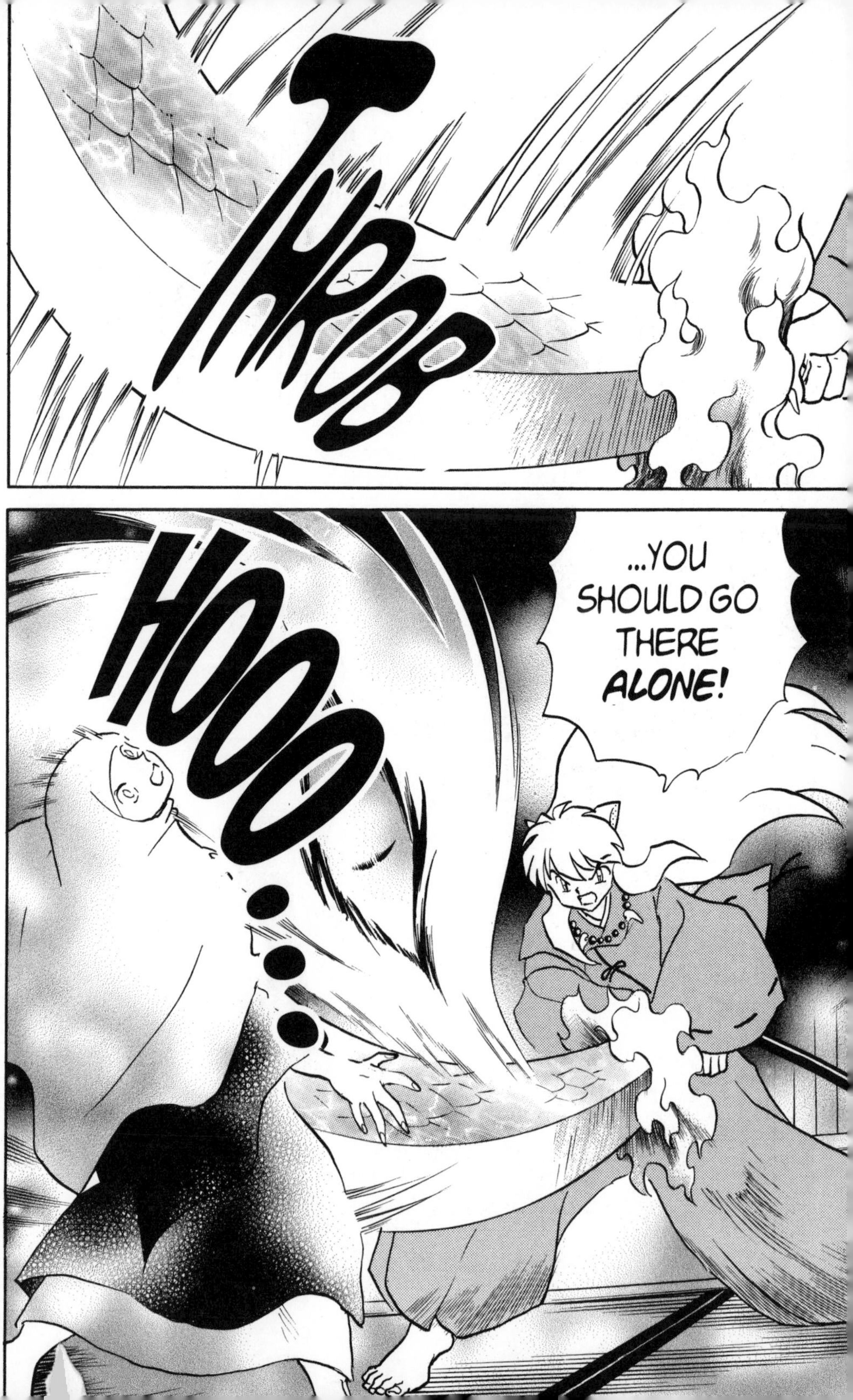
THROB
HOOO...
...YOU SHOULD GO THERE ALONE!

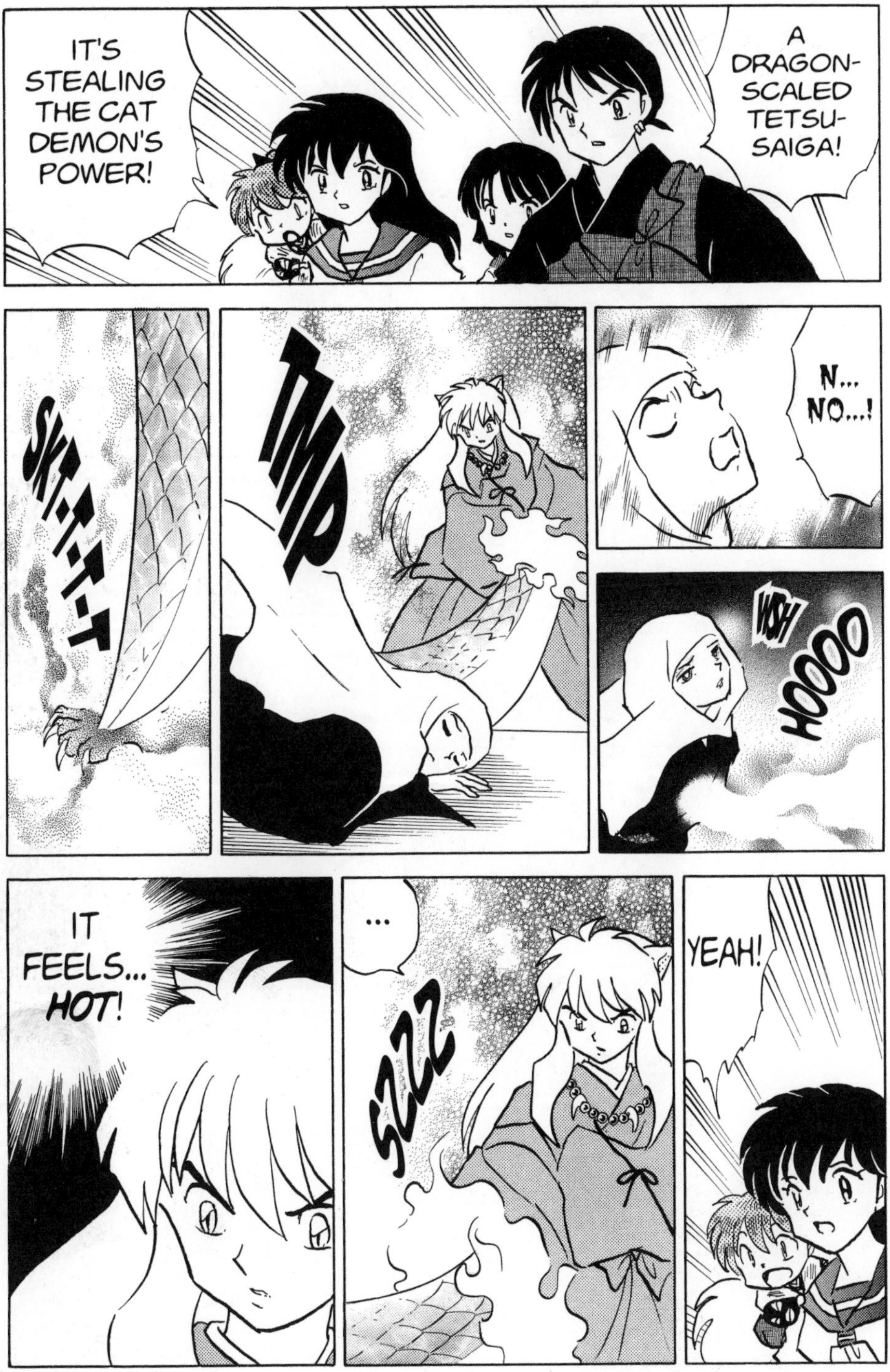
A DRAGON-SCALED TETSU-SAIGA!
IT'S STEALING THE CAT DEMON'S POWER!
N... NO...!
WSH
HOOOOO
TMP
SKT-T-T-T
YEAH!
...
SZZZ
IT FEELS... *HOT*!

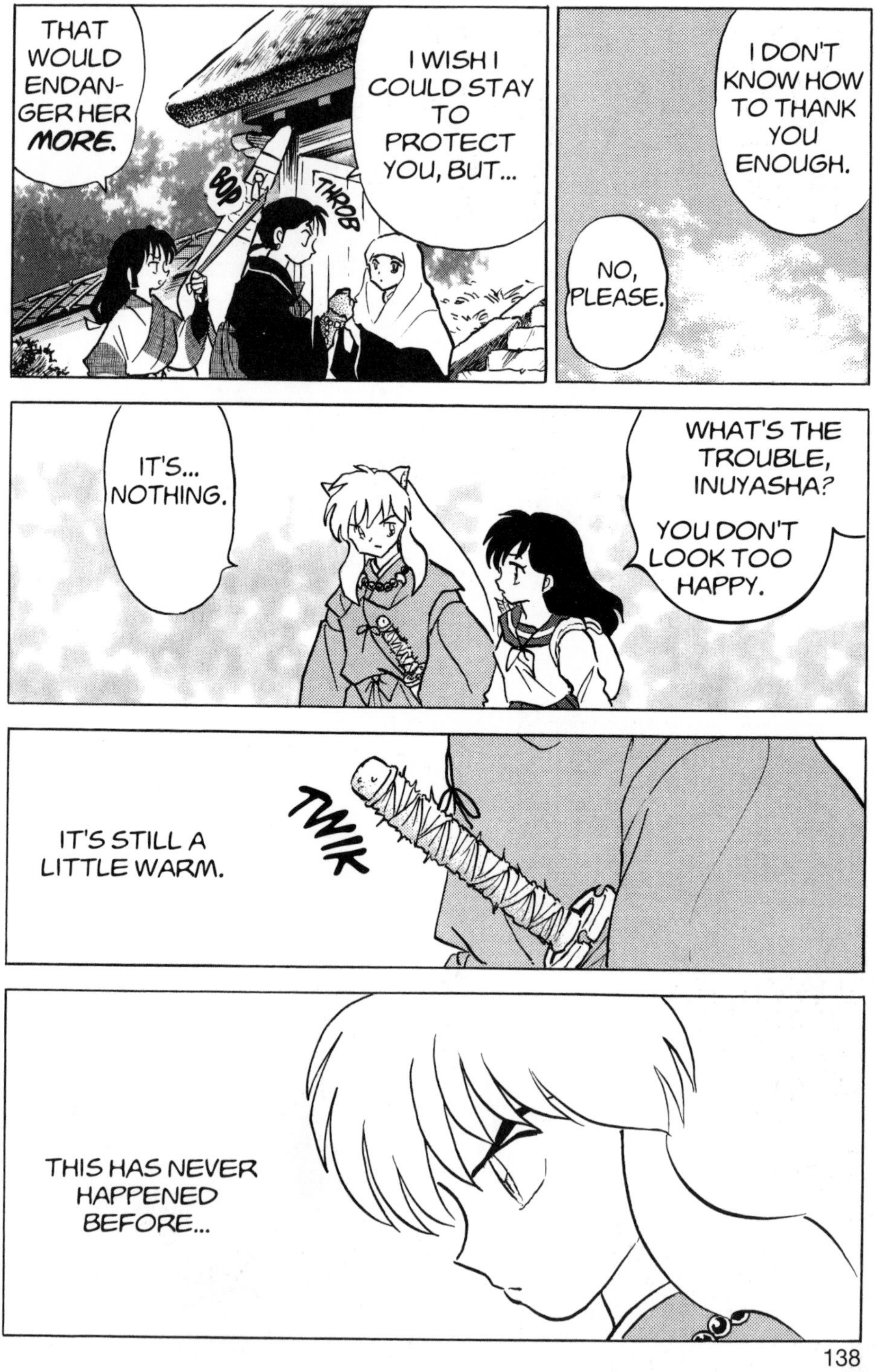
I DON'T KNOW HOW TO THANK YOU ENOUGH.
NO, PLEASE.
I WISH I COULD STAY TO PROTECT YOU, BUT...
THROB
THAT WOULD ENDANGER HER ***MORE***.
BOP
WHAT'S THE TROUBLE, INUYASHA?
YOU DON'T LOOK TOO HAPPY.
IT'S... NOTHING.
TWIK
IT'S STILL A LITTLE WARM.
THIS HAS NEVER HAPPENED BEFORE...

SCROLL EIGHT
VENOMOUS MIZUCHI

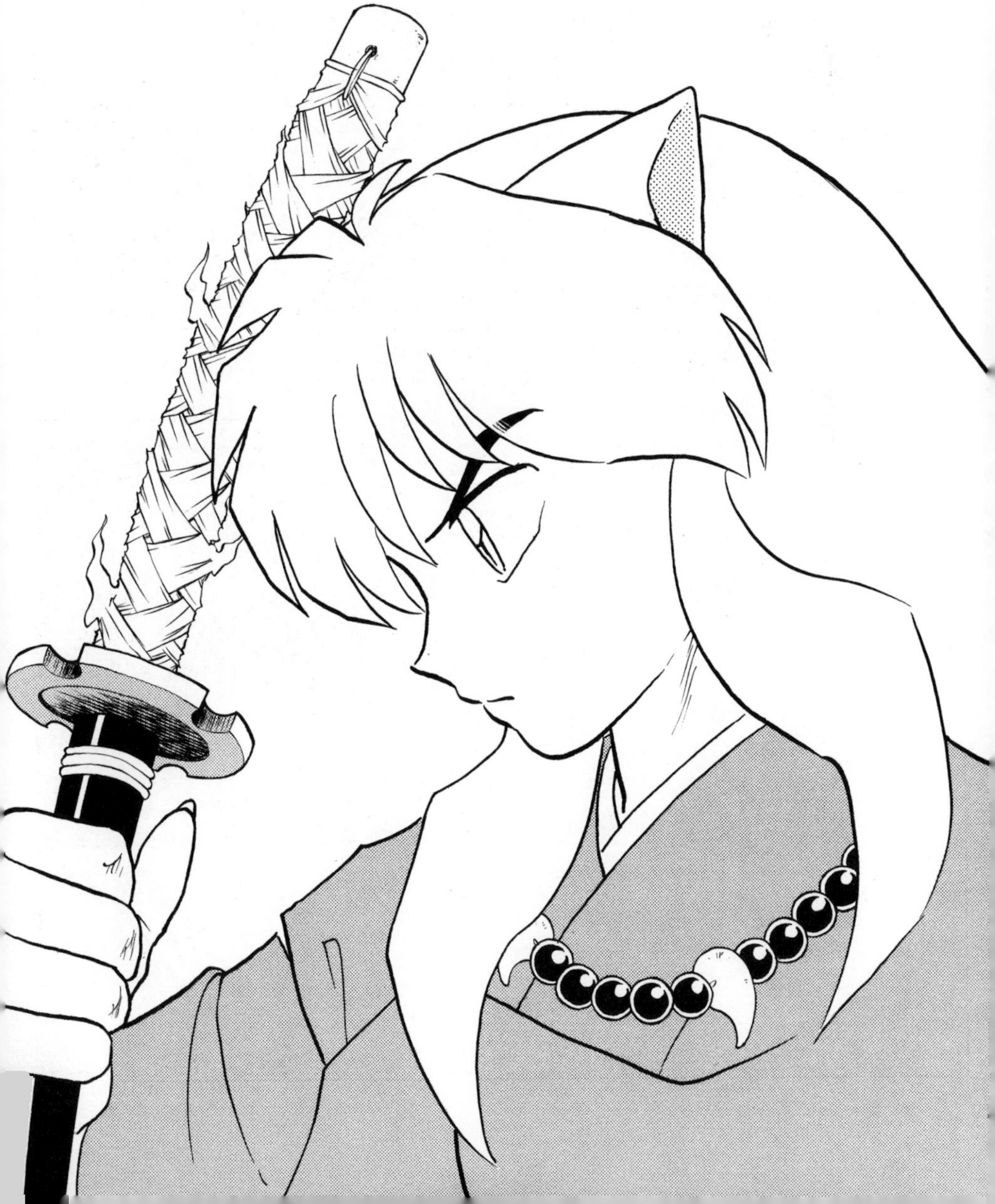

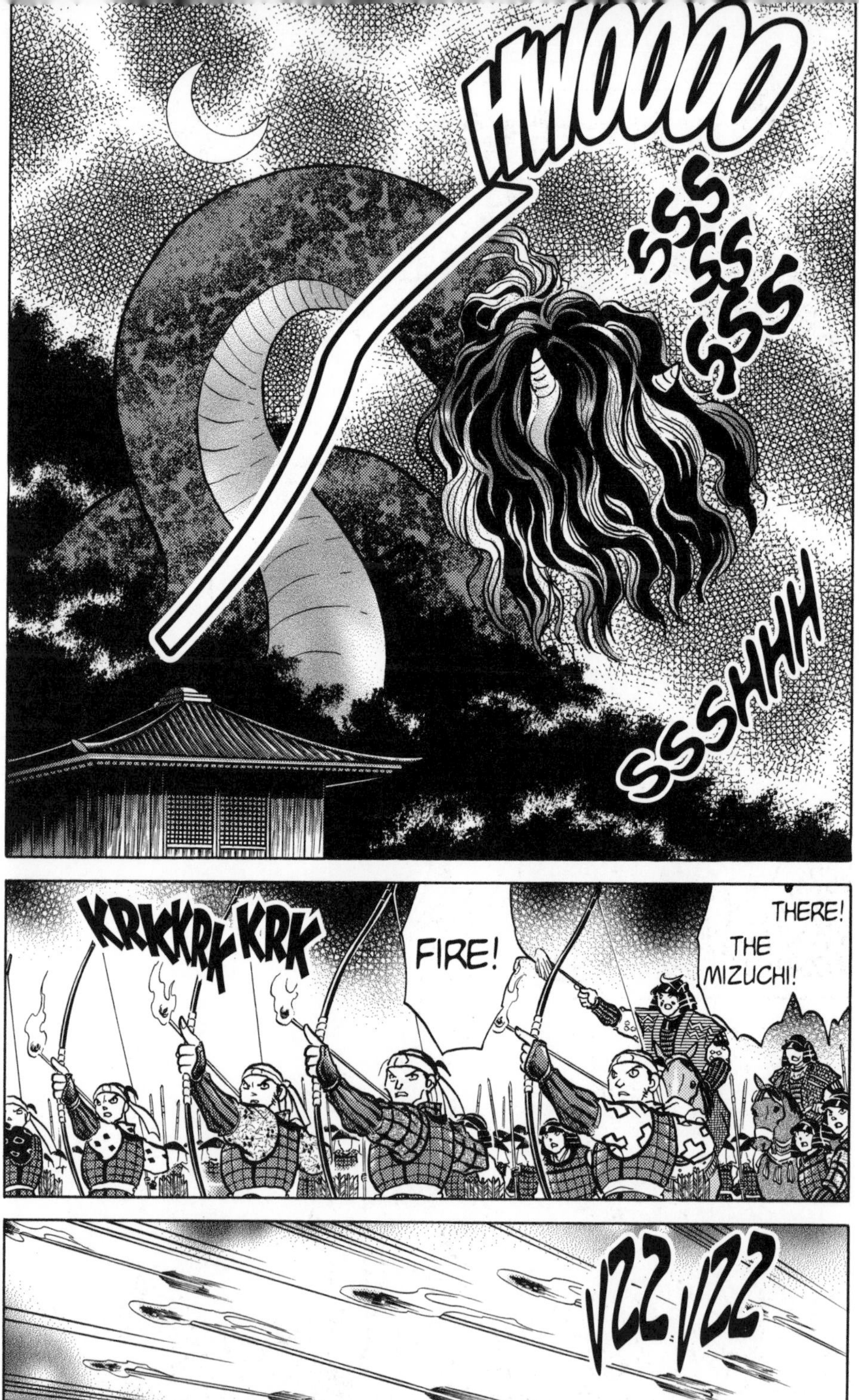
HWOOOO
SSSSSSSSS
SSSHHH
THERE! THE MIZUCHI!
FIRE!
KRKKRK KRK
VZZ VZZ

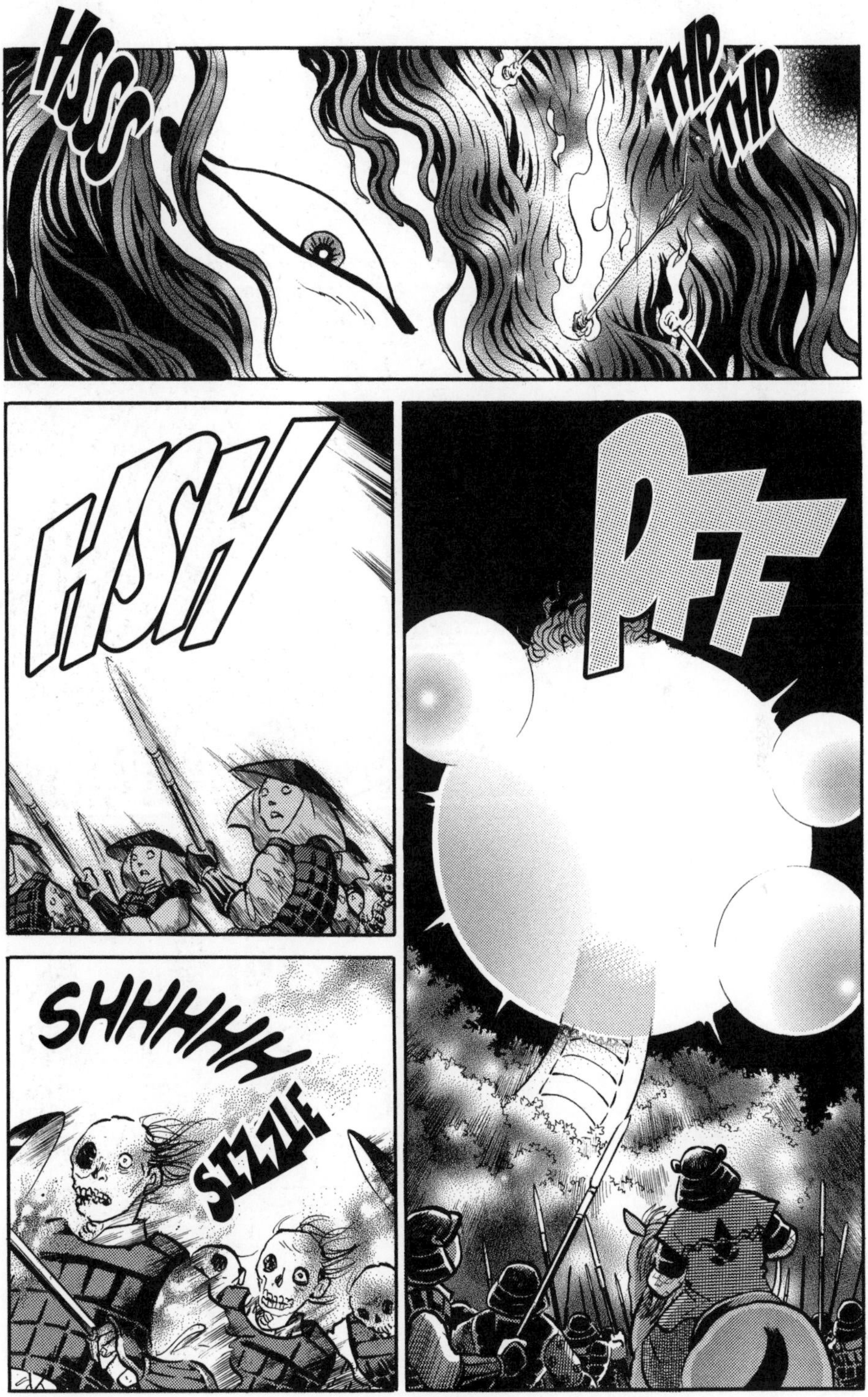
THP-THP
HSSSS
PFF
HSH
SHHHHH
SIZZLE

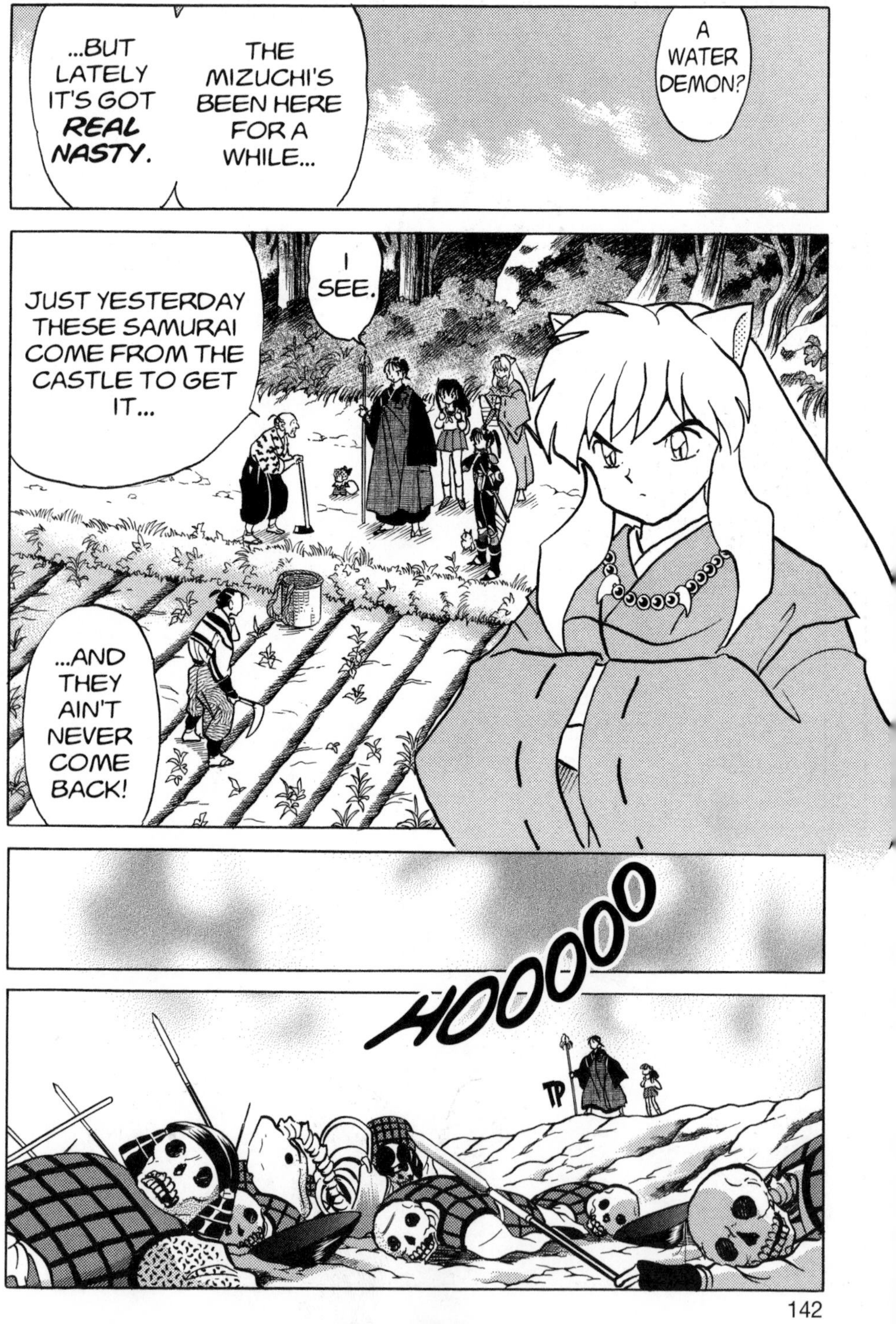
A WATER DEMON?
THE MIZUCHI'S BEEN HERE FOR A WHILE...
...BUT LATELY IT'S GOT **REAL NASTY**.
I SEE.
JUST YESTERDAY THESE SAMURAI COME FROM THE CASTLE TO GET IT...
...AND THEY AIN'T NEVER COME BACK!
HOOOOO
TP

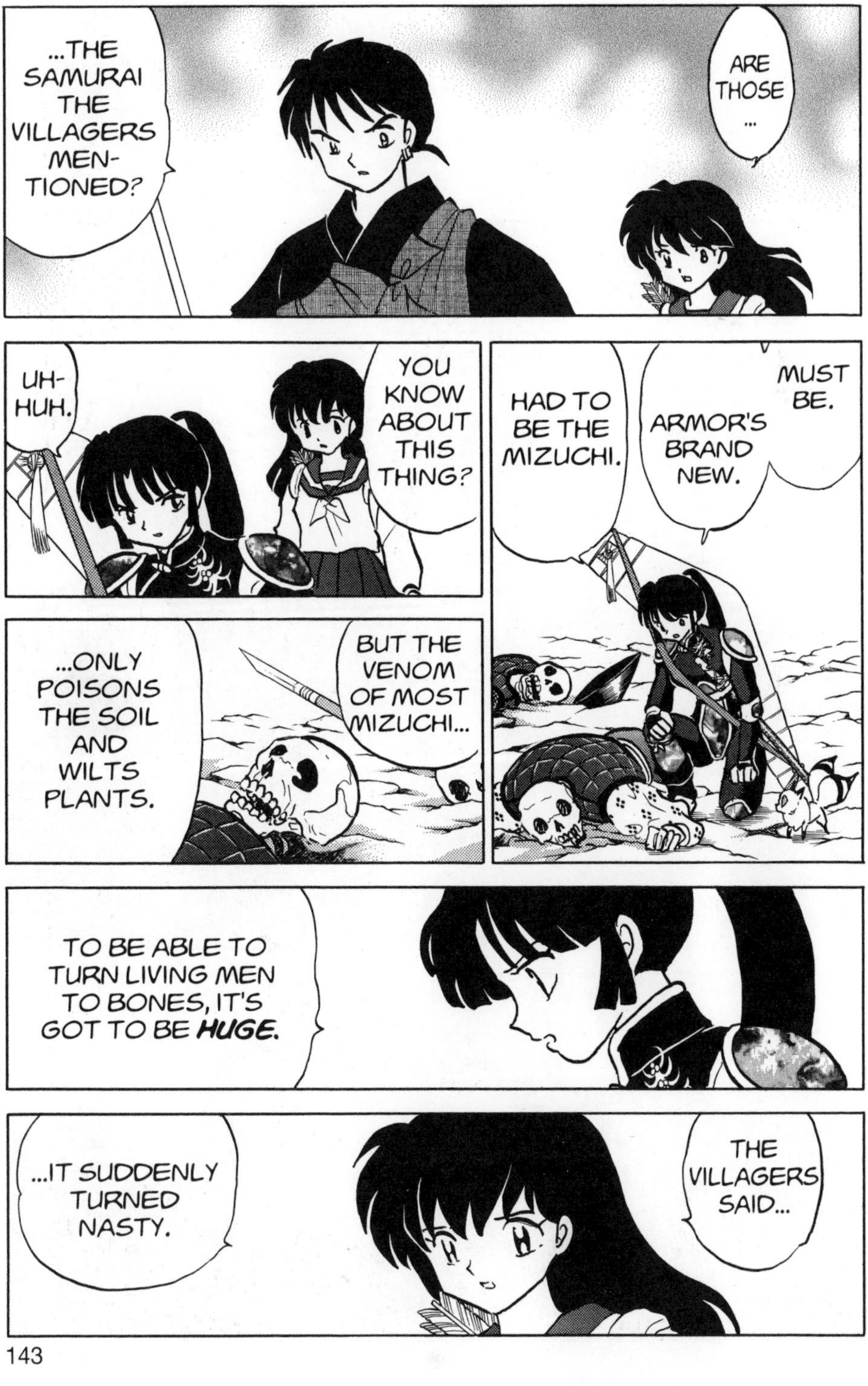
ARE THOSE ...
...THE SAMURAI THE VILLAGERS MEN-TIONED?
MUST BE.
ARMOR'S BRAND NEW.
HAD TO BE THE MIZUCHI.
YOU KNOW ABOUT THIS THING?
UH-HUH.
BUT THE VENOM OF MOST MIZUCHI...
...ONLY POISONS THE SOIL AND WILTS PLANTS.
TO BE ABLE TO TURN LIVING MEN TO BONES, IT'S GOT TO BE ***HUGE***.
THE VILLAGERS SAID...
...IT SUDDENLY TURNED NASTY.

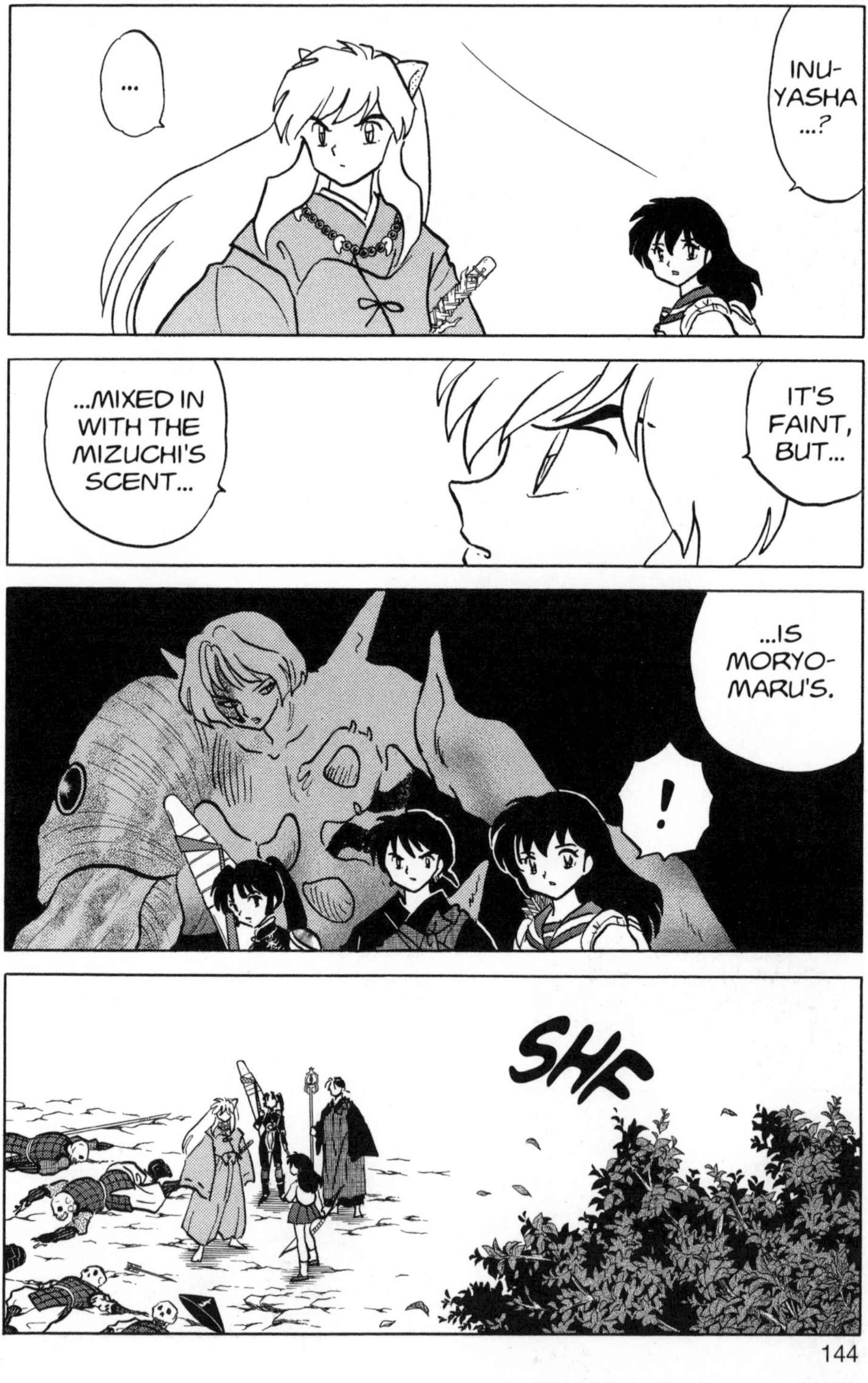
INU-YASHA ...?
...
IT'S FAINT, BUT...
...MIXED IN WITH THE MIZUCHI'S SCENT...
...IS MORYO-MARU'S.
!
SHF

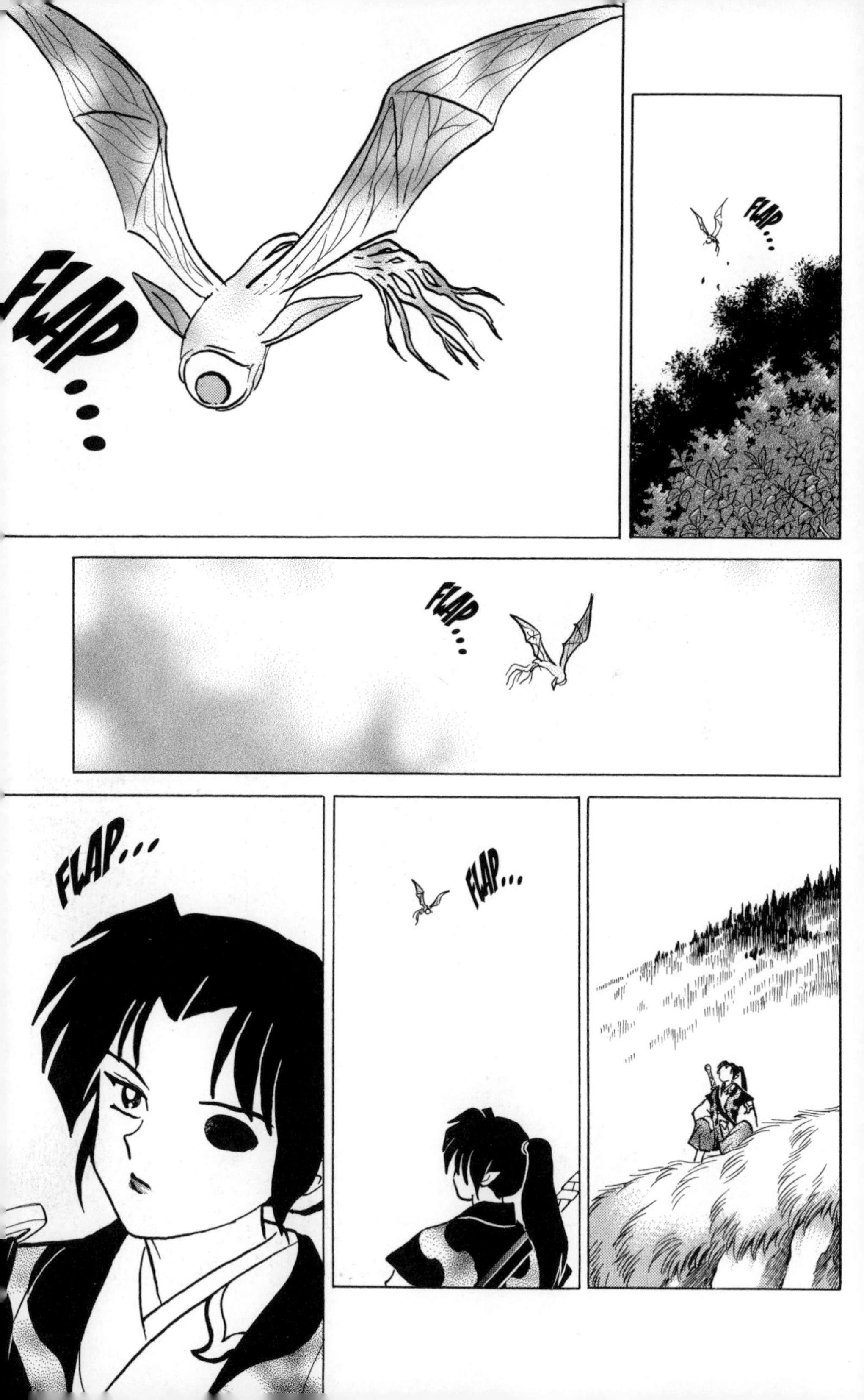
FLAP...
FLAP...
FLAP...
FLAP...
FLAP...

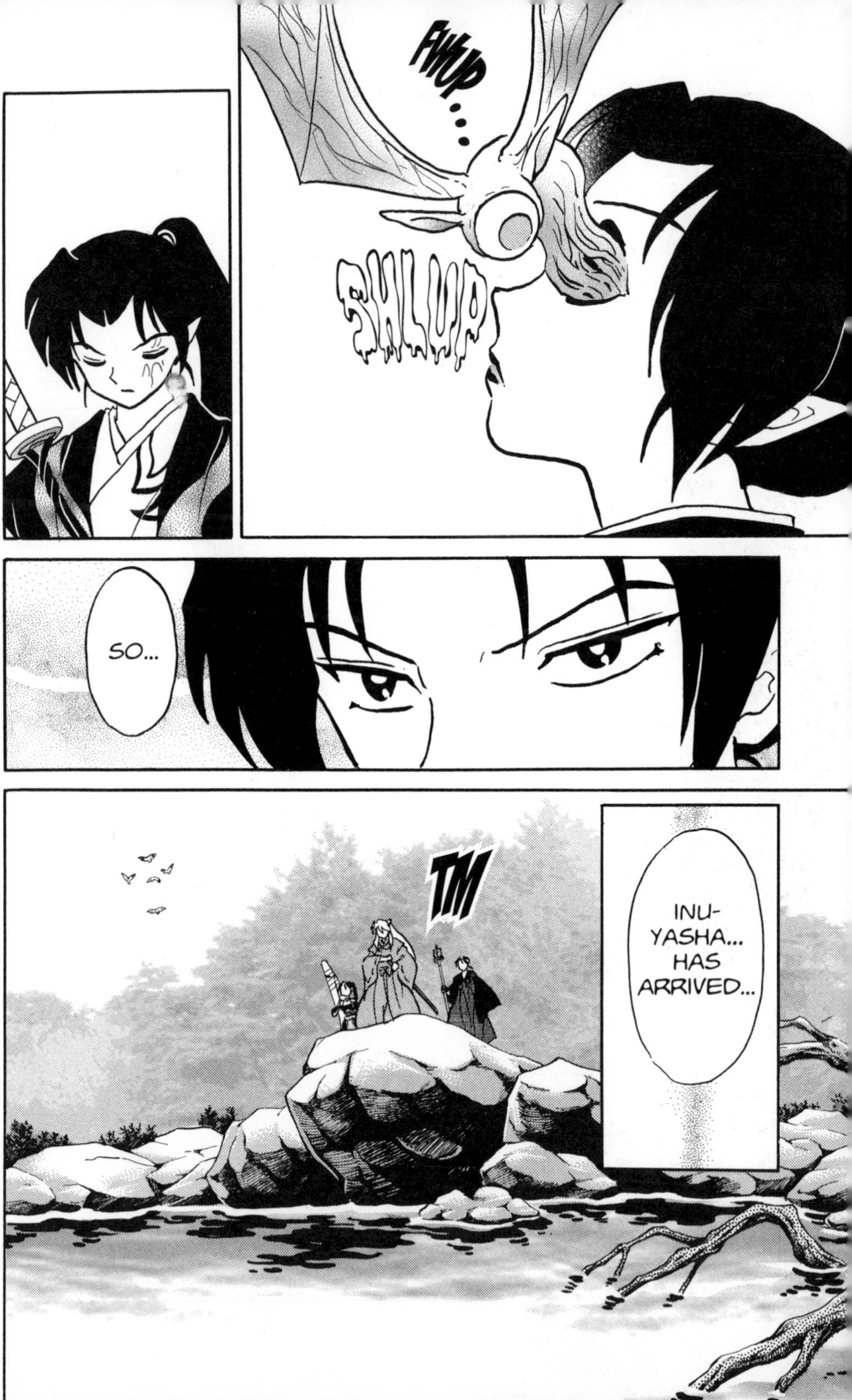
FWUP...
SHLUP
SO...
INU-YASHA... HAS ARRIVED...
TM

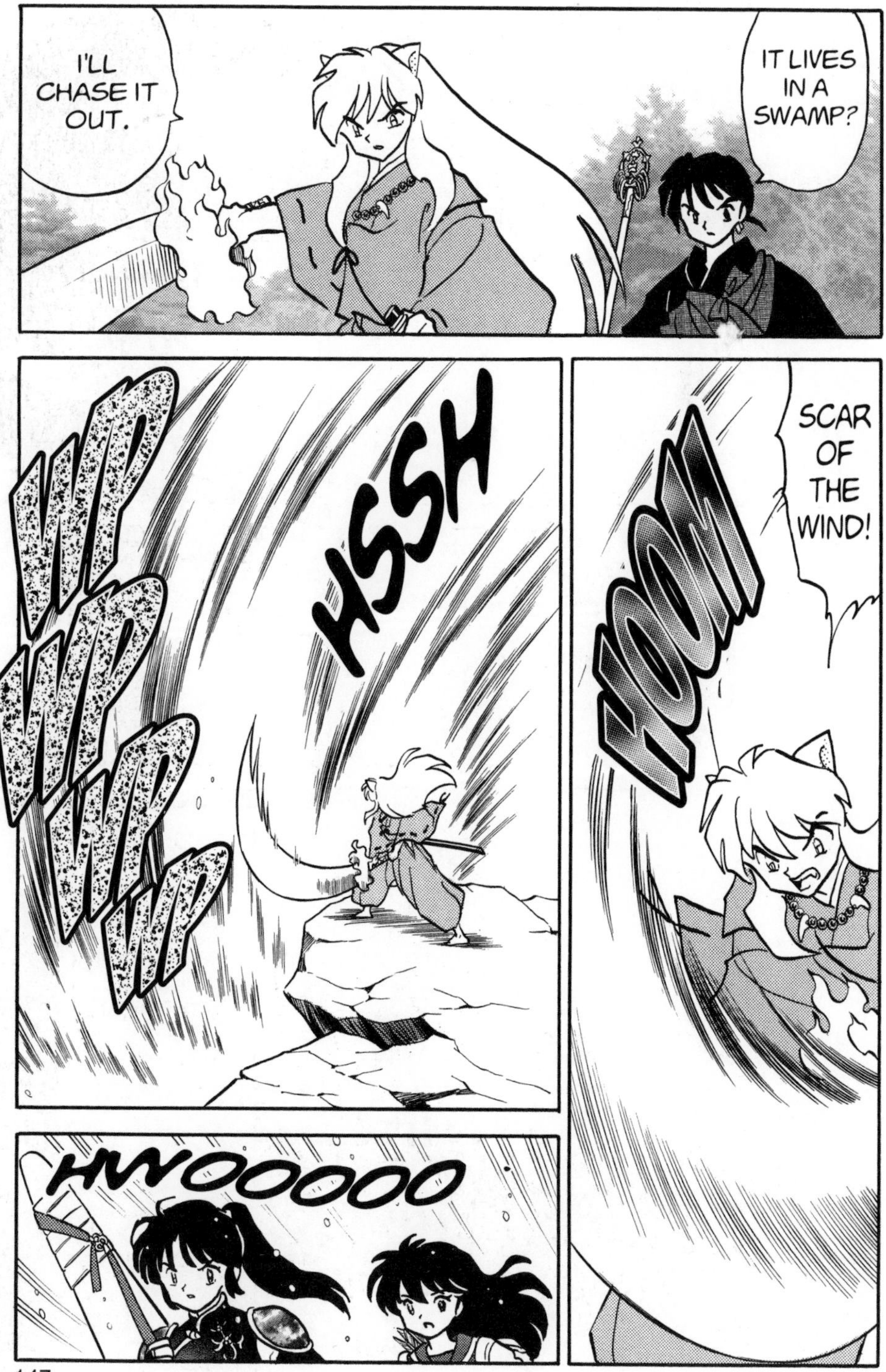
IT LIVES IN A SWAMP?
I'LL CHASE IT OUT.
SCAR OF THE WIND!
WOOM
HSSH
WP WP WP WP WP
HWOOOOOO

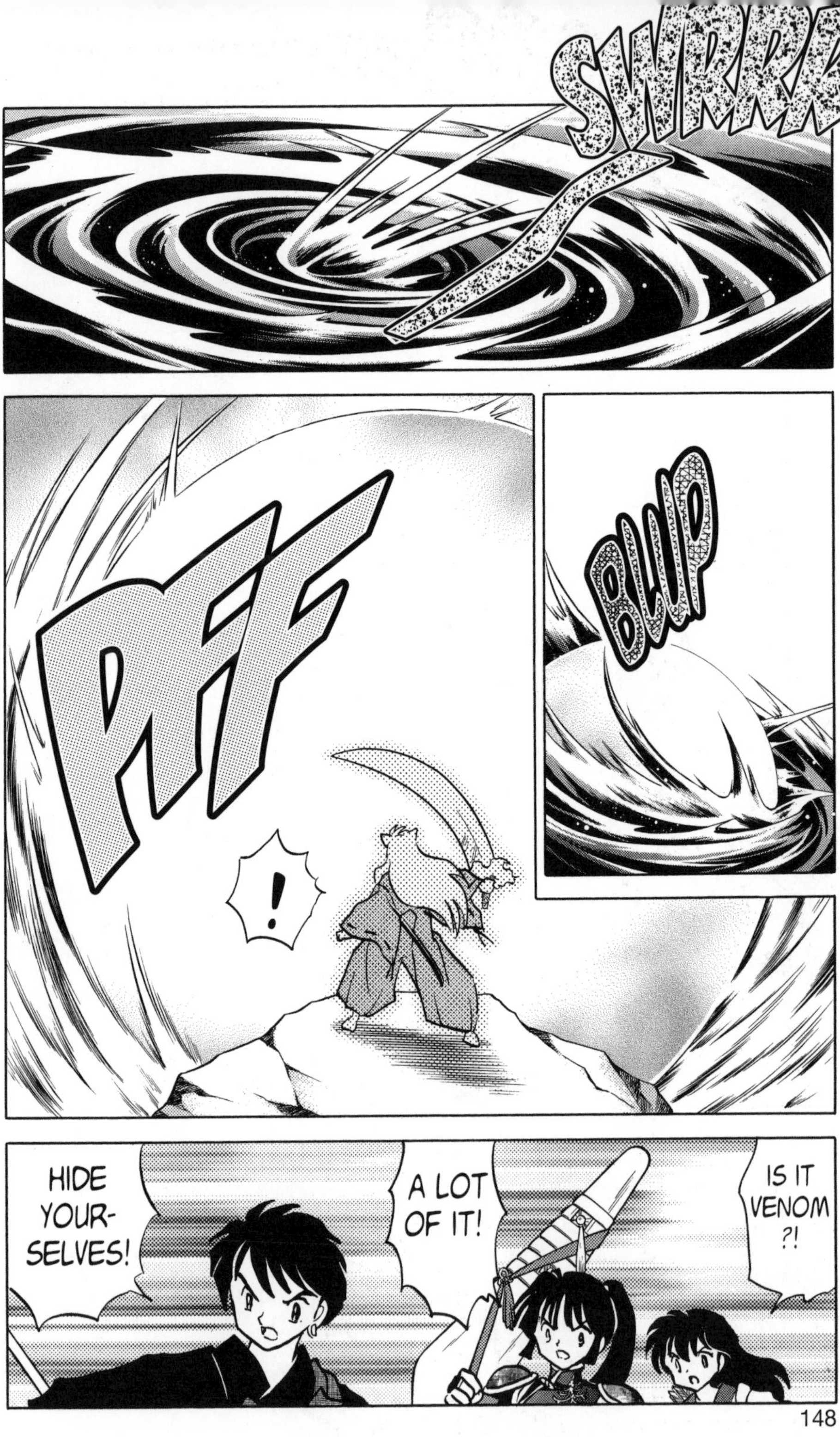
SWRRR
BLUP
PFF
!
IS IT VENOM?!
A LOT OF IT!
HIDE YOURSELVES!

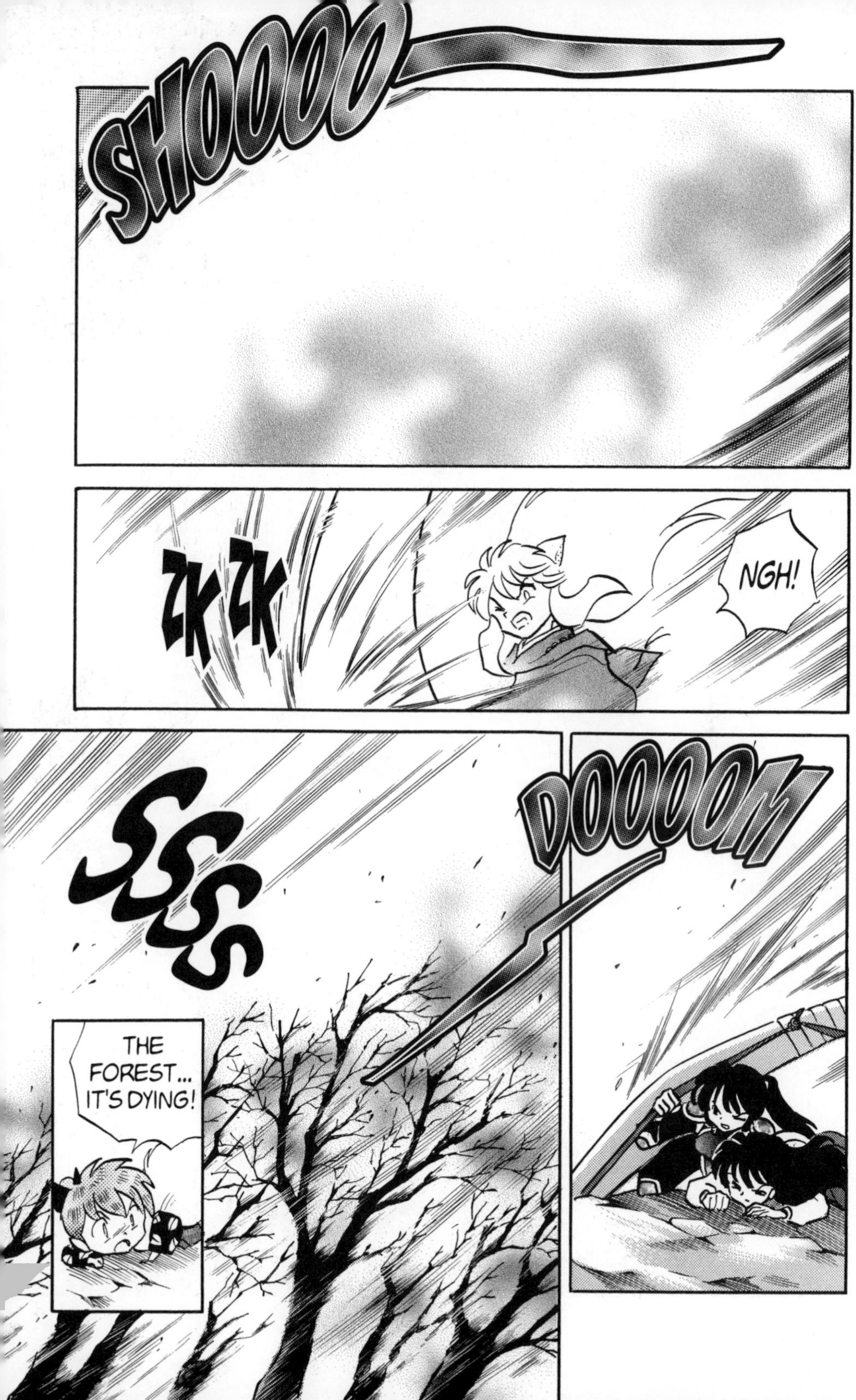
SHOOOO
NGH!
ZK ZK
DOOOOM
SSSS
THE FOREST... IT'S DYING!

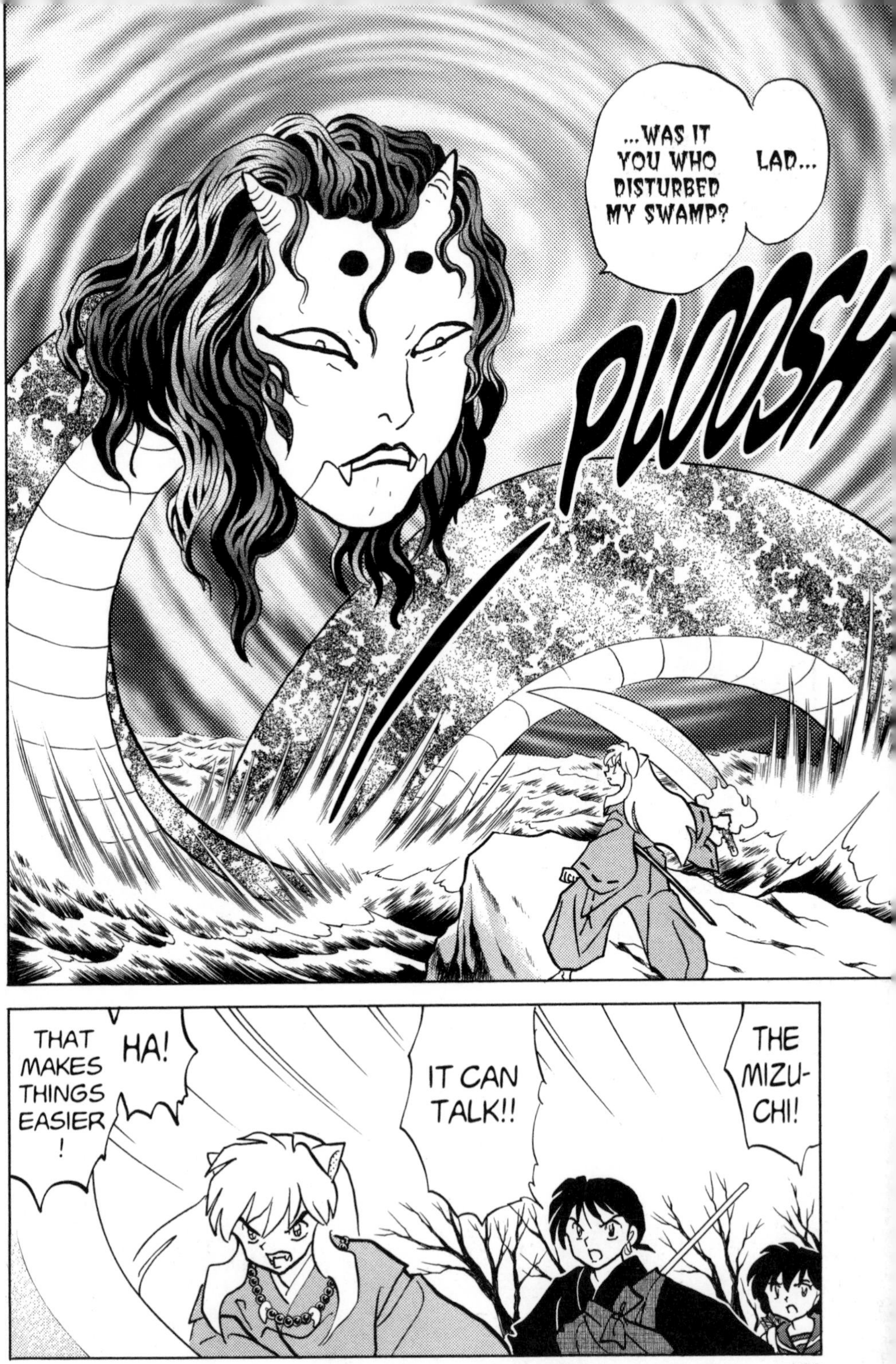
LAD...
...WAS IT YOU WHO DISTURBED MY SWAMP?
PLOOSH
THE MIZU-CHI!
IT CAN TALK!!
HA!
THAT MAKES THINGS EASIER!

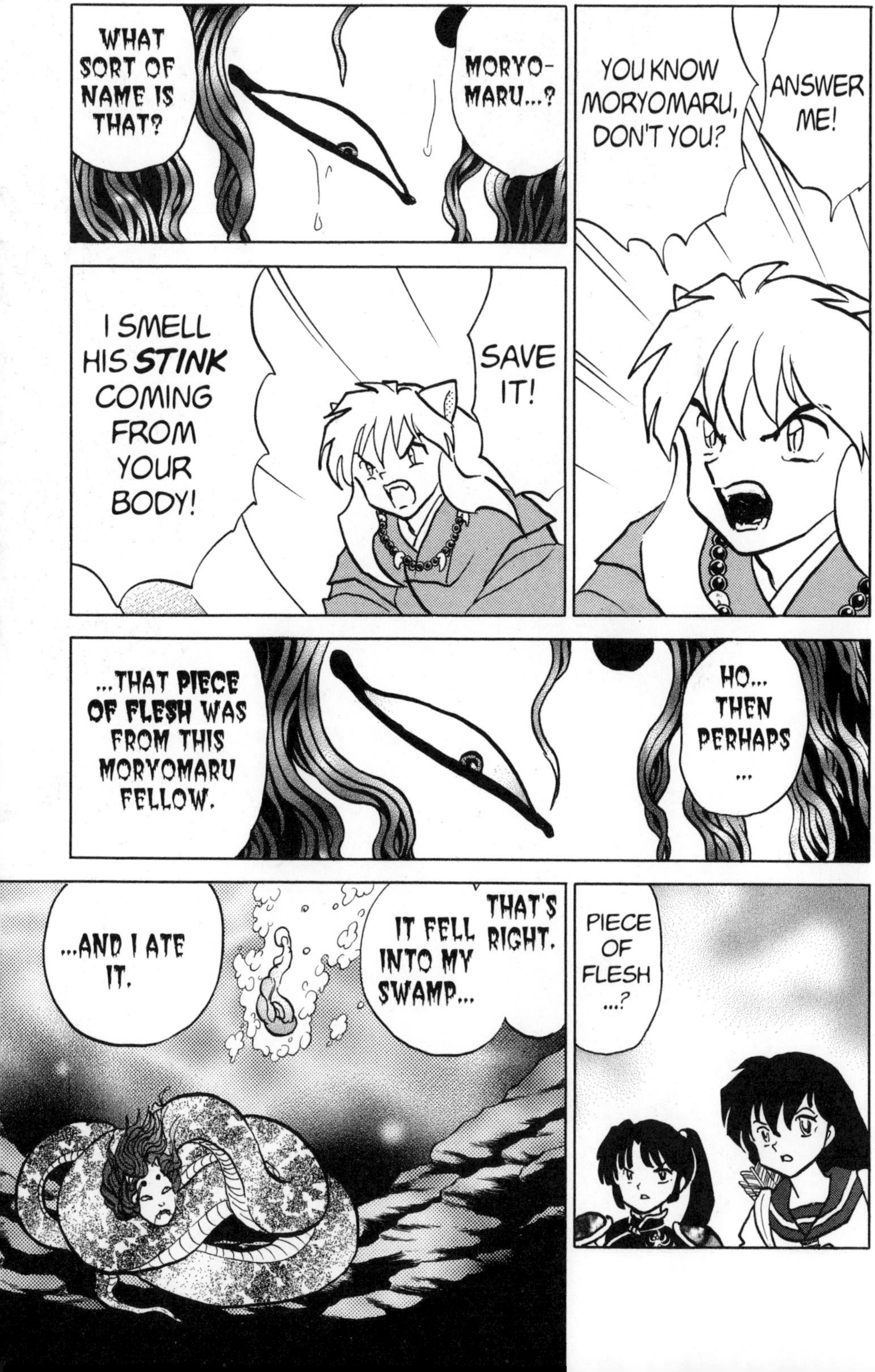
ANSWER ME!
YOU KNOW MORYOMARU, DON'T YOU?
MORYO-MARU...?
WHAT SORT OF NAME IS THAT?
SAVE IT!
I SMELL HIS **STINK** COMING FROM YOUR BODY!
HO... THEN PERHAPS ...
...THAT PIECE OF FLESH WAS FROM THIS MORYOMARU FELLOW.
PIECE OF FLESH ...?
THAT'S RIGHT.
IT FELL INTO MY SWAMP...
...AND I ATE IT.

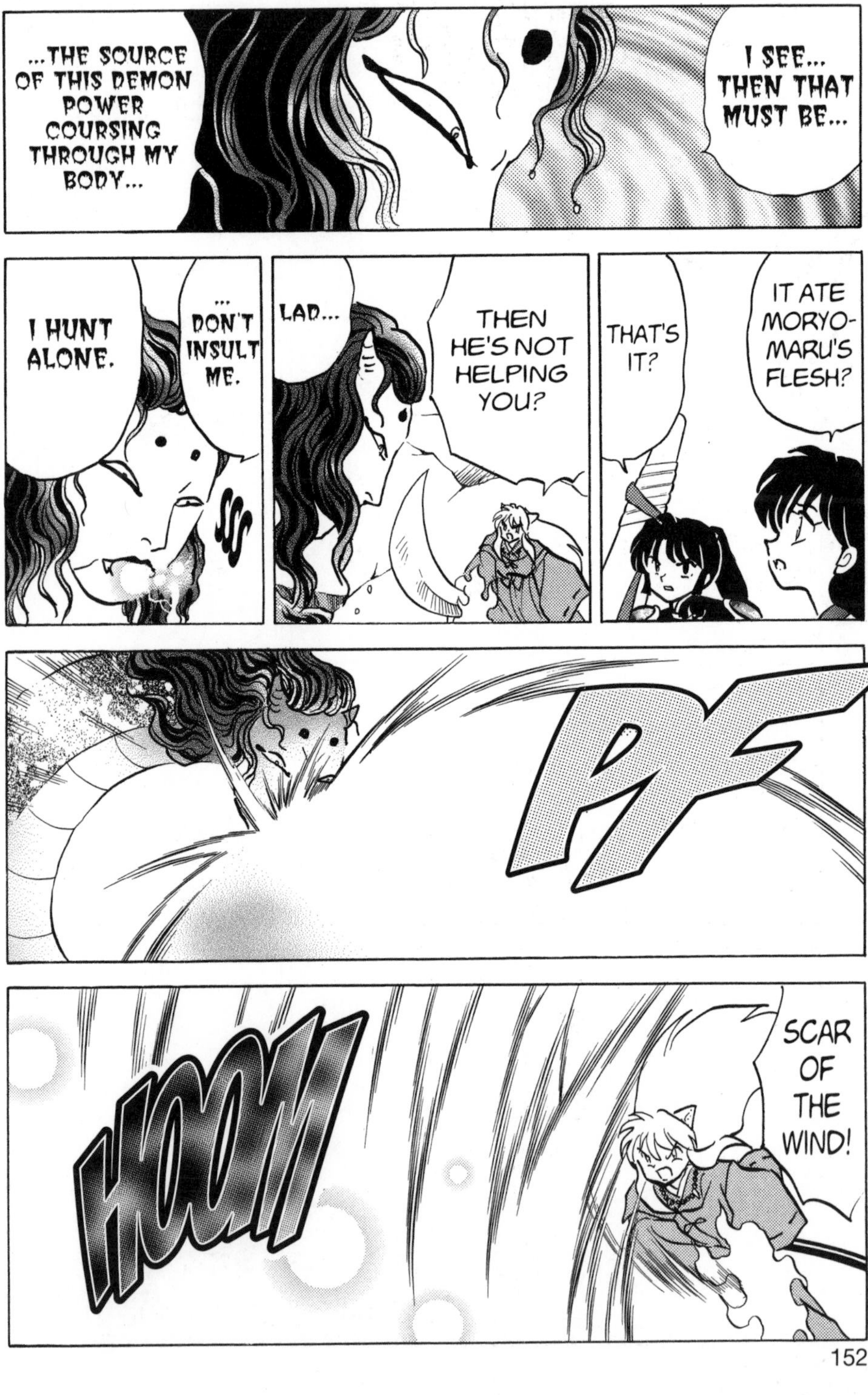
I SEE... THEN THAT MUST BE...
...THE SOURCE OF THIS DEMON POWER COURSING THROUGH MY BODY...
IT ATE MORYO-MARU'S FLESH?
THAT'S IT?
THEN HE'S NOT HELPING YOU?
LAD...
...DON'T INSULT ME.
I HUNT ALONE.
SSS
PF
SCAR OF THE WIND!
HOOM

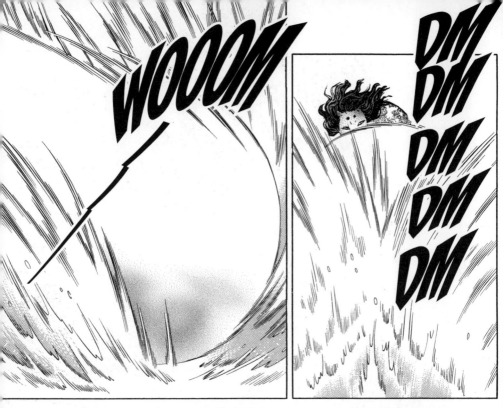

ITS VENOM JUST SHOVED THE WIND SCAR ASIDE!!

WHA...?

I NEED ...

WHAT KIND OF VENOM IS THIS?!

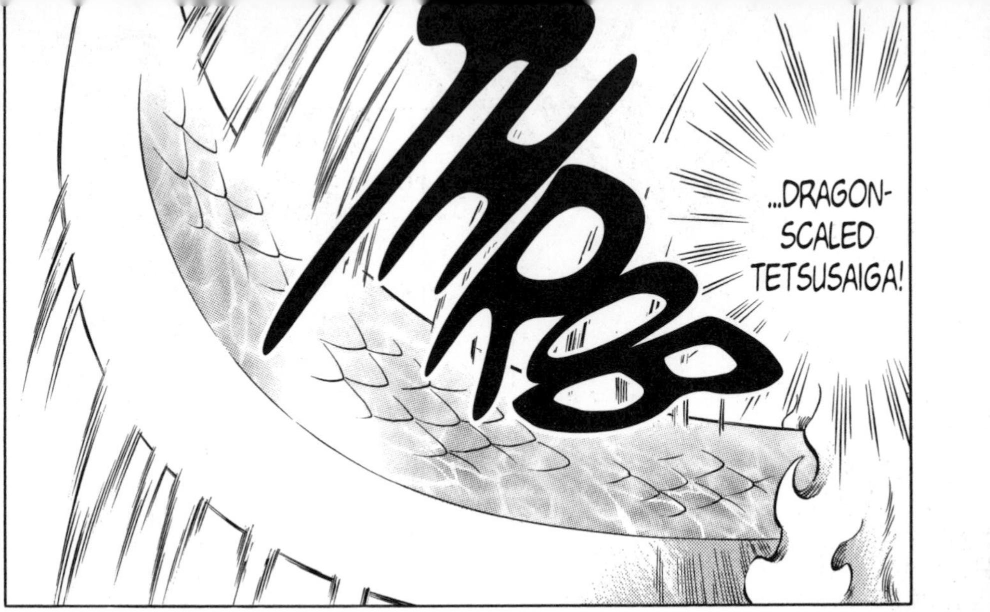
...DRAGON-
SCALED
TETSUSAIGA!

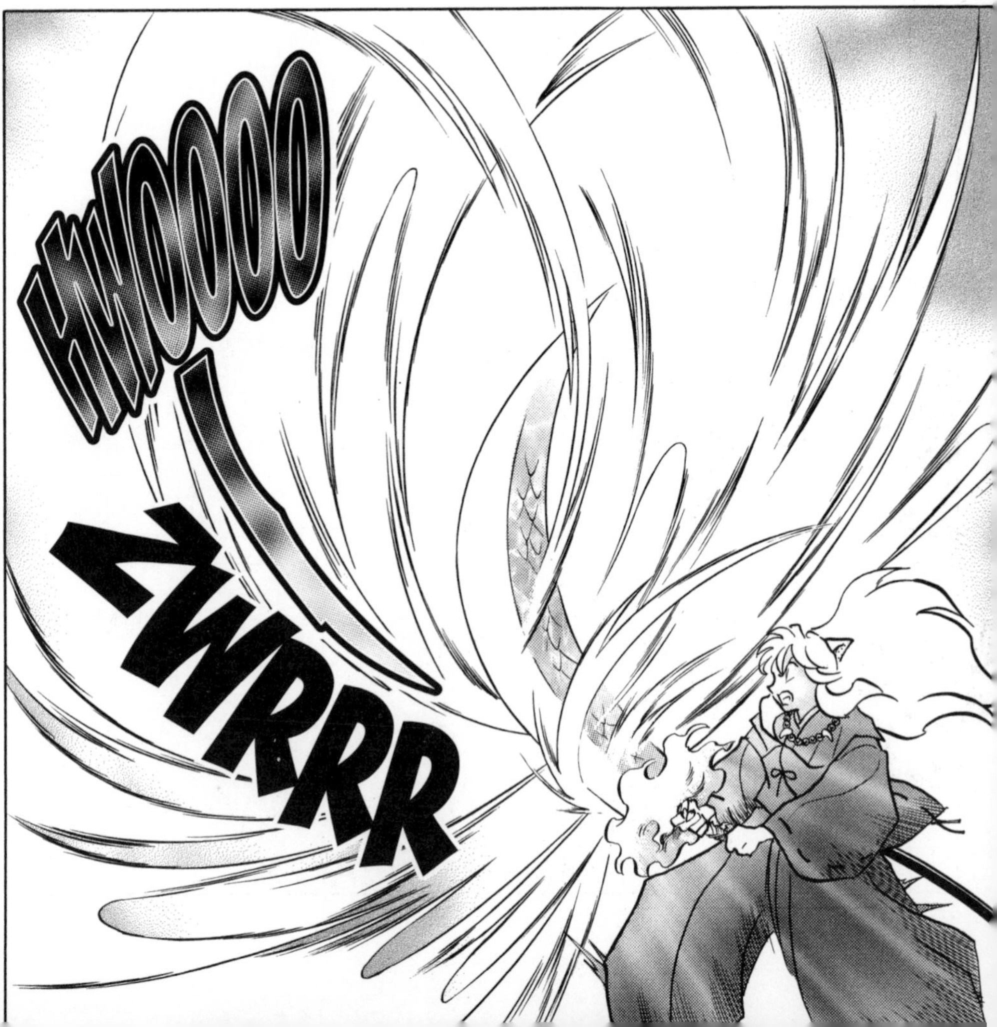
ZWRRR

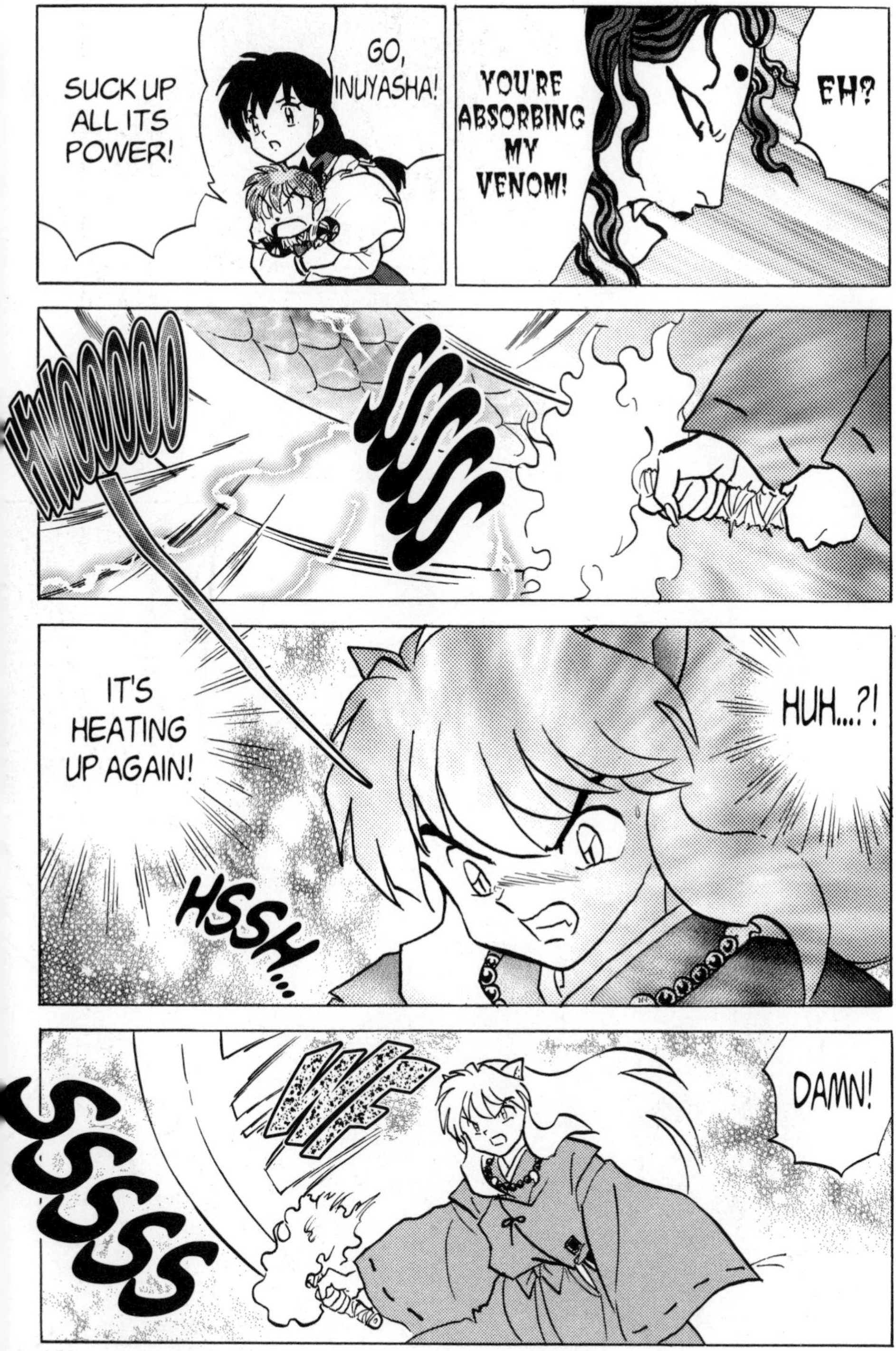
EH?
YOU'RE ABSORBING MY VENOM!
GO, INUYASHA!
SUCK UP ALL ITS POWER!
SSSS
WHOOOOO
HUH...?!
IT'S HEATING UP AGAIN!
HSSH...
DAMN!
SSSSS

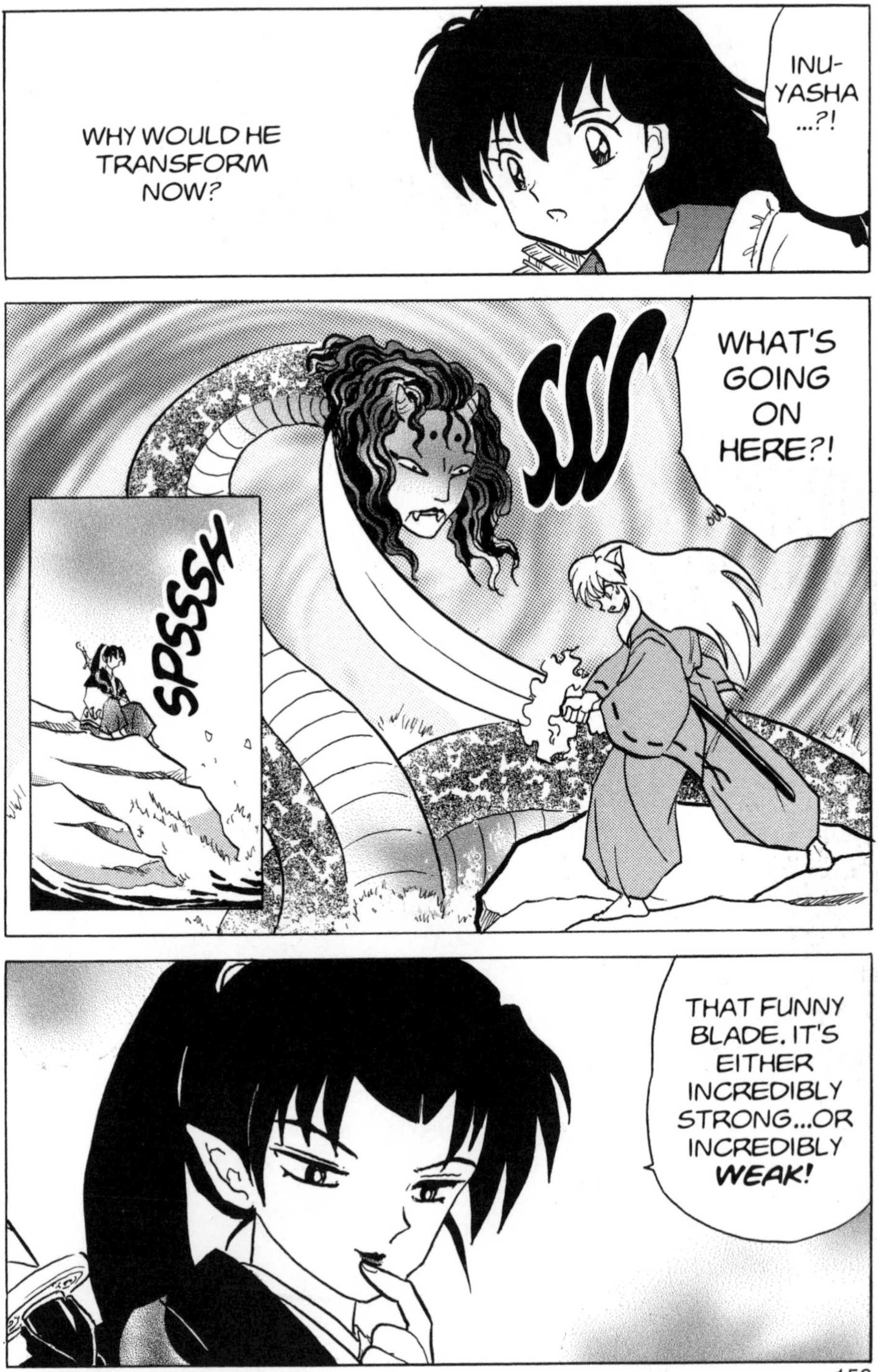
INU-YASHA ...?!
WHY WOULD HE TRANSFORM NOW?
WHAT'S GOING ON HERE?!
SSS
SPSSSH
THAT FUNNY BLADE. IT'S EITHER INCREDIBLY STRONG...OR INCREDIBLY **WEAK!**

SCROLL NINE
BYAKUYA OF THE DREAMS

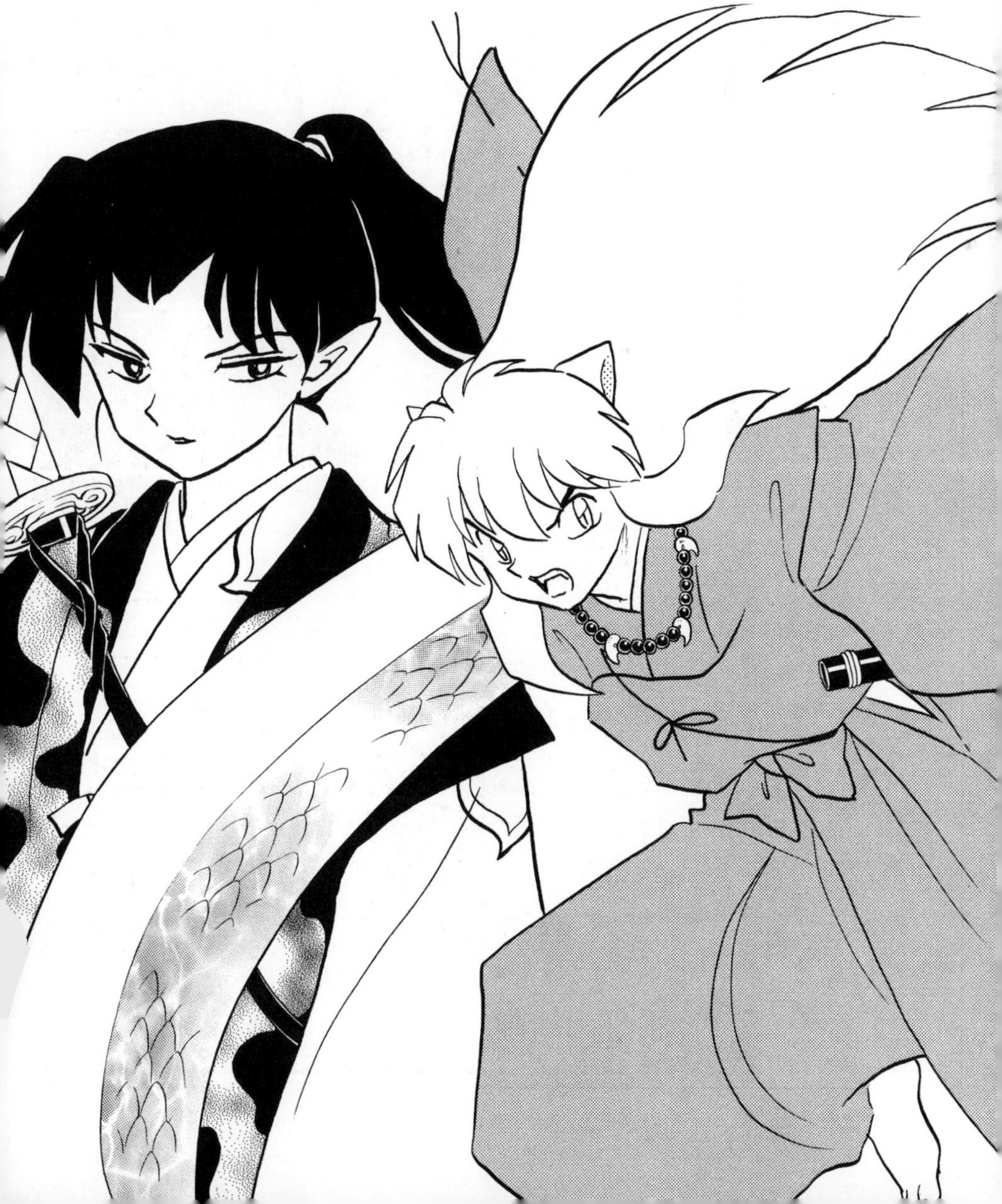

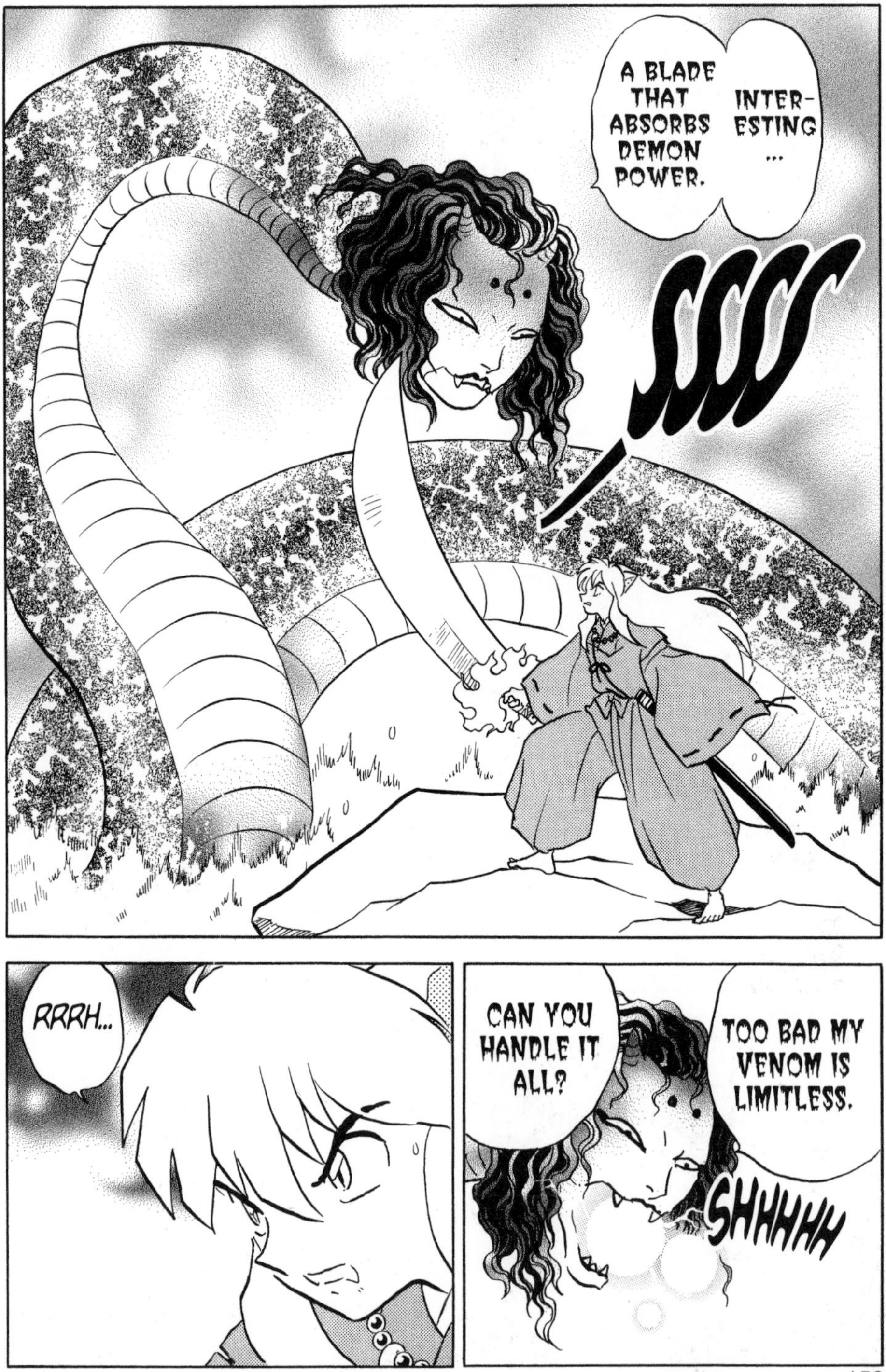
INTER-ESTING...
A BLADE THAT ABSORBS DEMON POWER.
SSSS
TOO BAD MY VENOM IS LIMITLESS.
CAN YOU HANDLE IT ALL?
SHHHHH
RRRH...

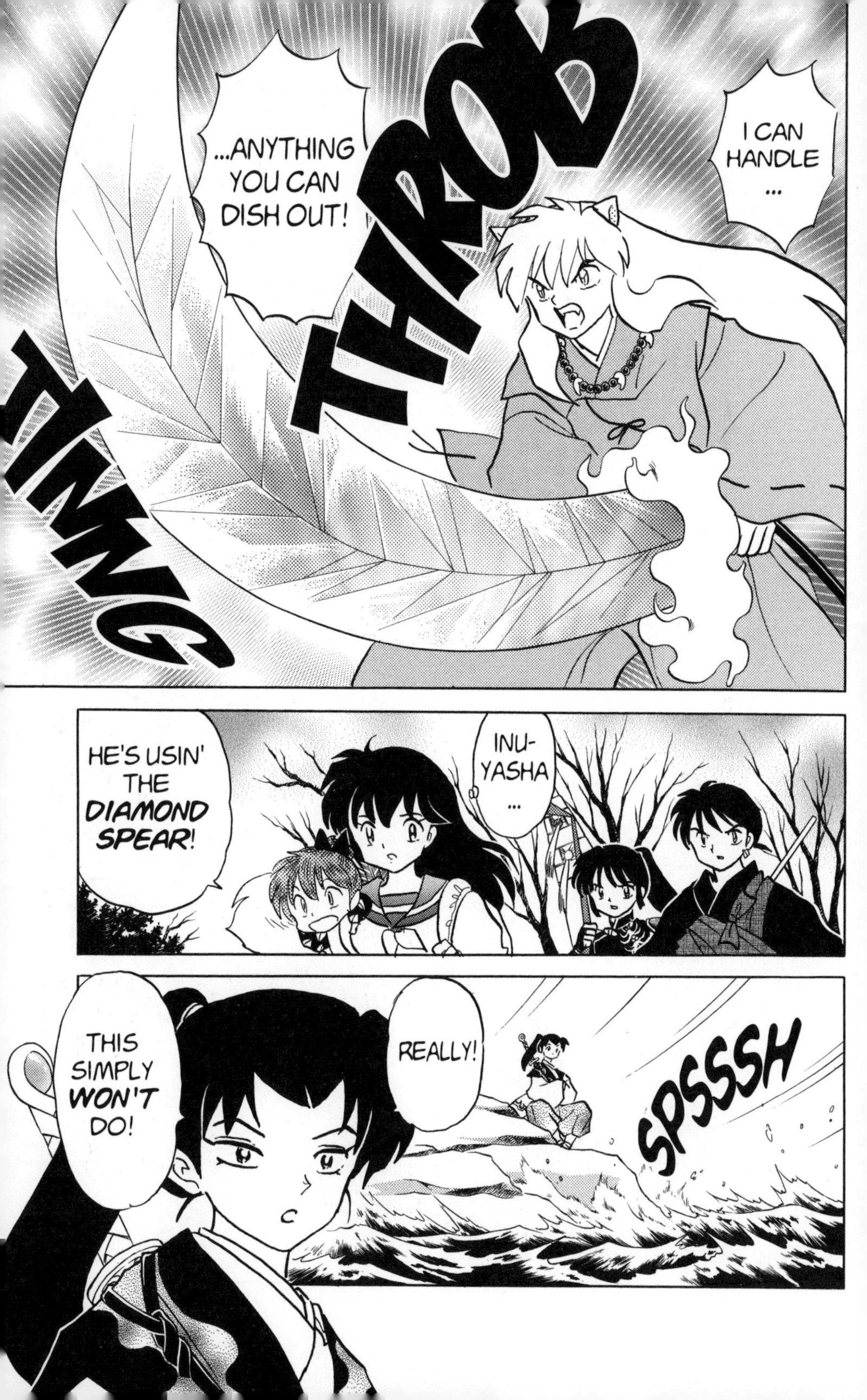
I CAN HANDLE ...
...ANYTHING YOU CAN DISH OUT!
THROB
INU-YASHA ...
HE'S USIN' THE **DIAMOND SPEAR**!
SPSSSH
REALLY!
THIS SIMPLY **WON'T** DO!

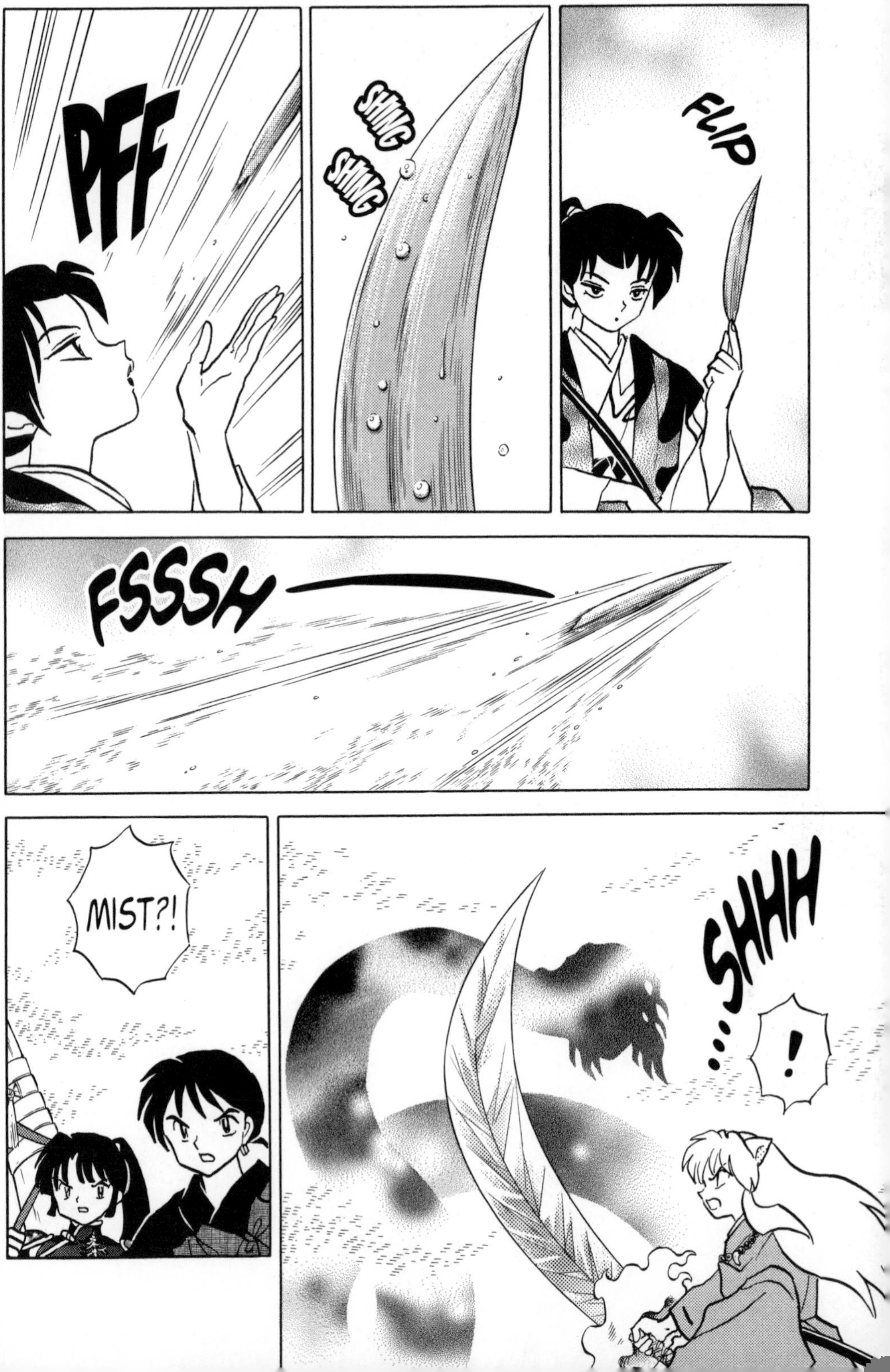
FLIP
SHING
SHING
PFF
FSSSH
SHHH
!
MIST?!

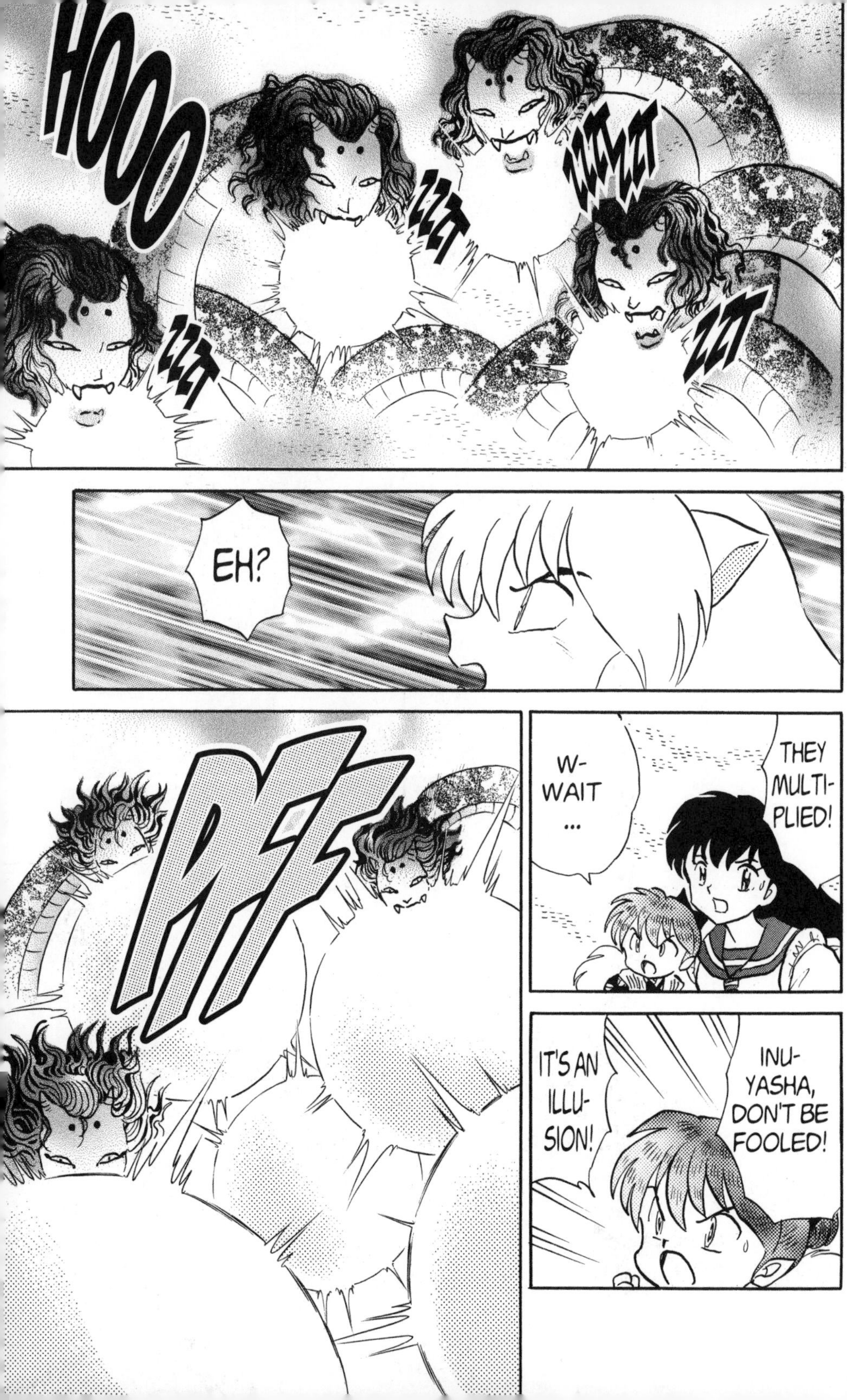
HOOO
EH?
THEY MULTI-PLIED!
W-WAIT ...
INU-YASHA, DON'T BE FOOLED!
IT'S AN ILLU-SION!

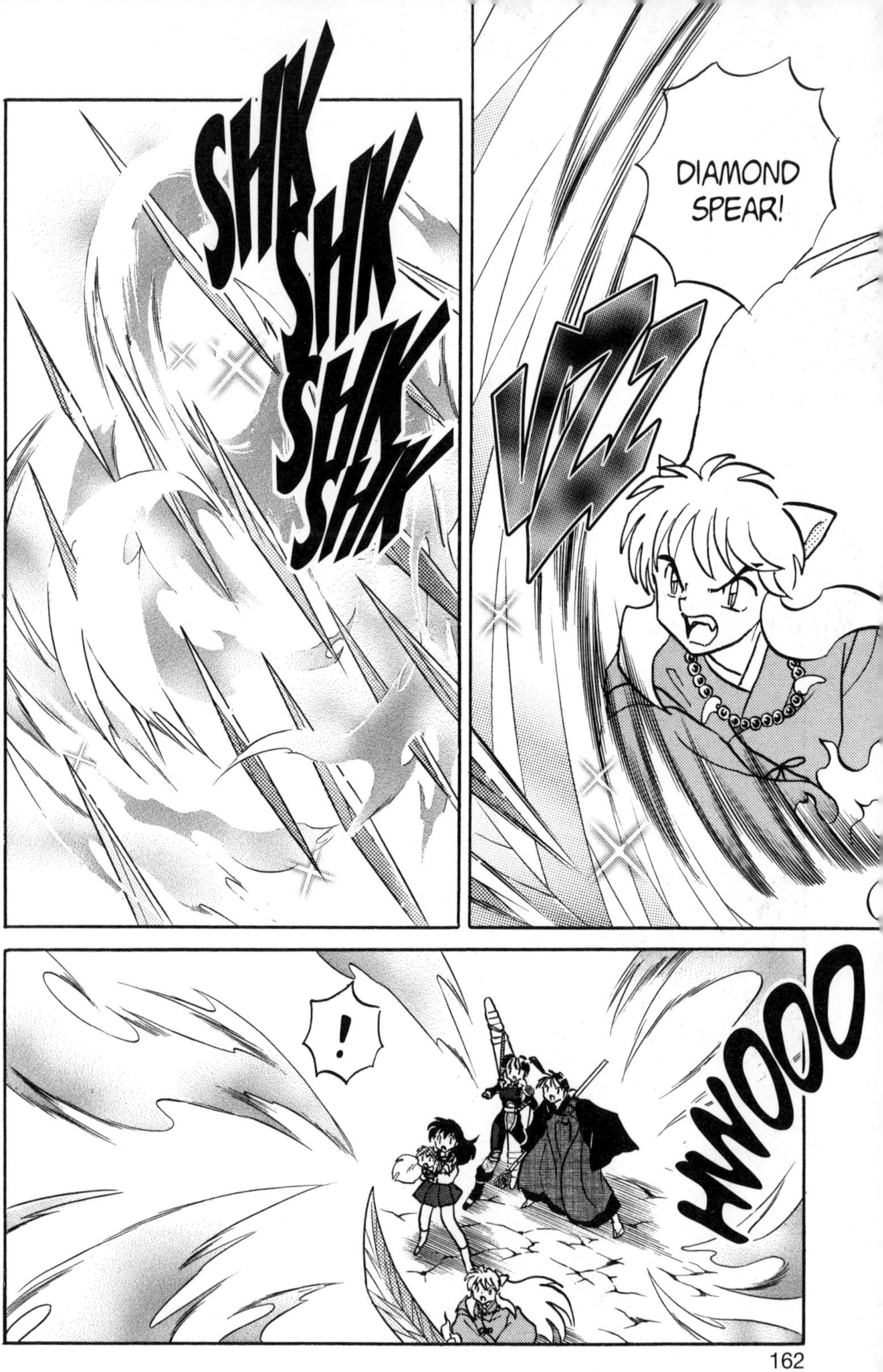
DIAMOND SPEAR!
VZZZ
SHK SHK SHK SHK
!
HWOOO

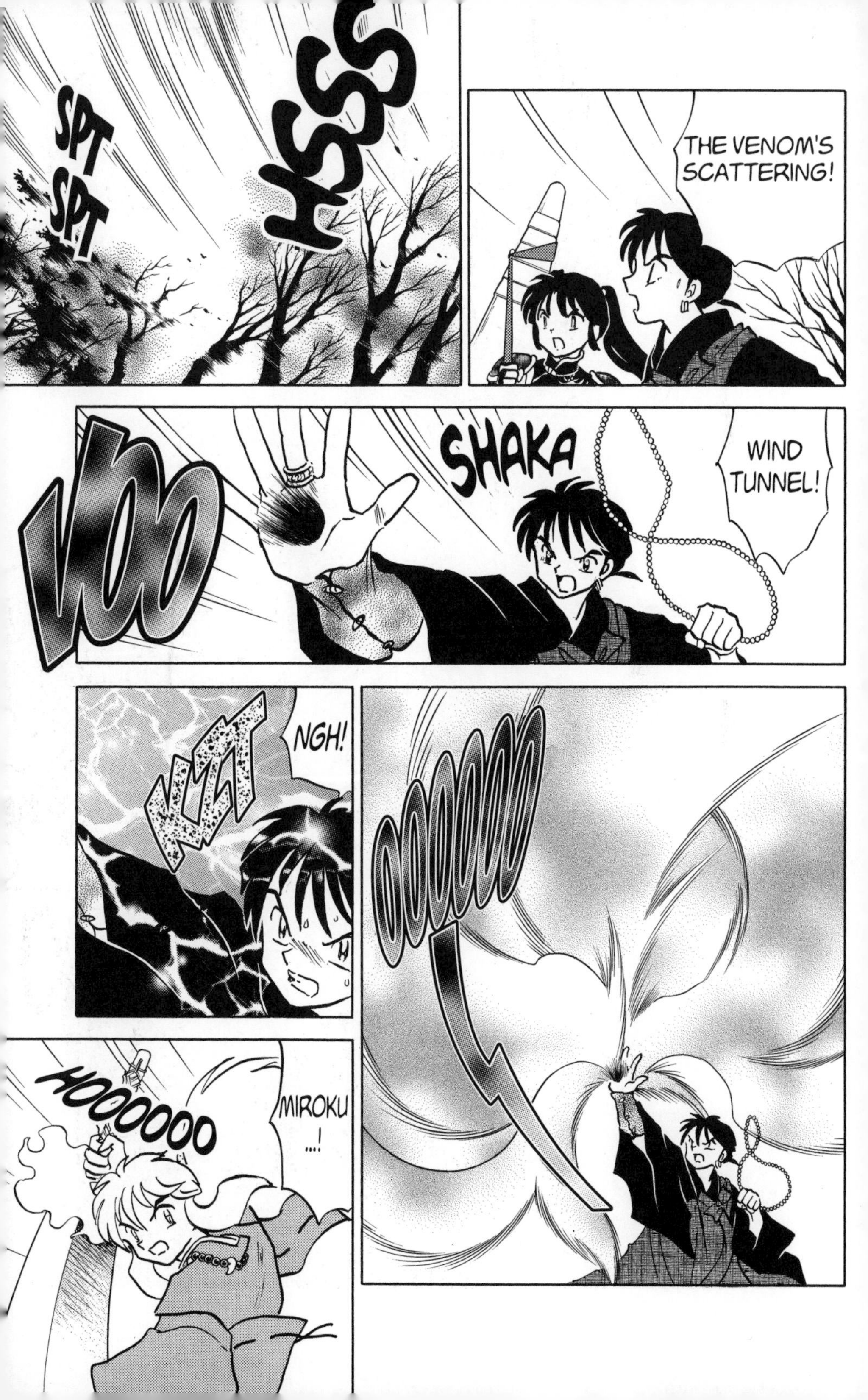
THE VENOM'S SCATTERING!
HISSS
SPT SPT
WIND TUNNEL!
SHAKA
VOOO
OOOOOOO
NGH!
MIROKU ...!
HOOOOOO

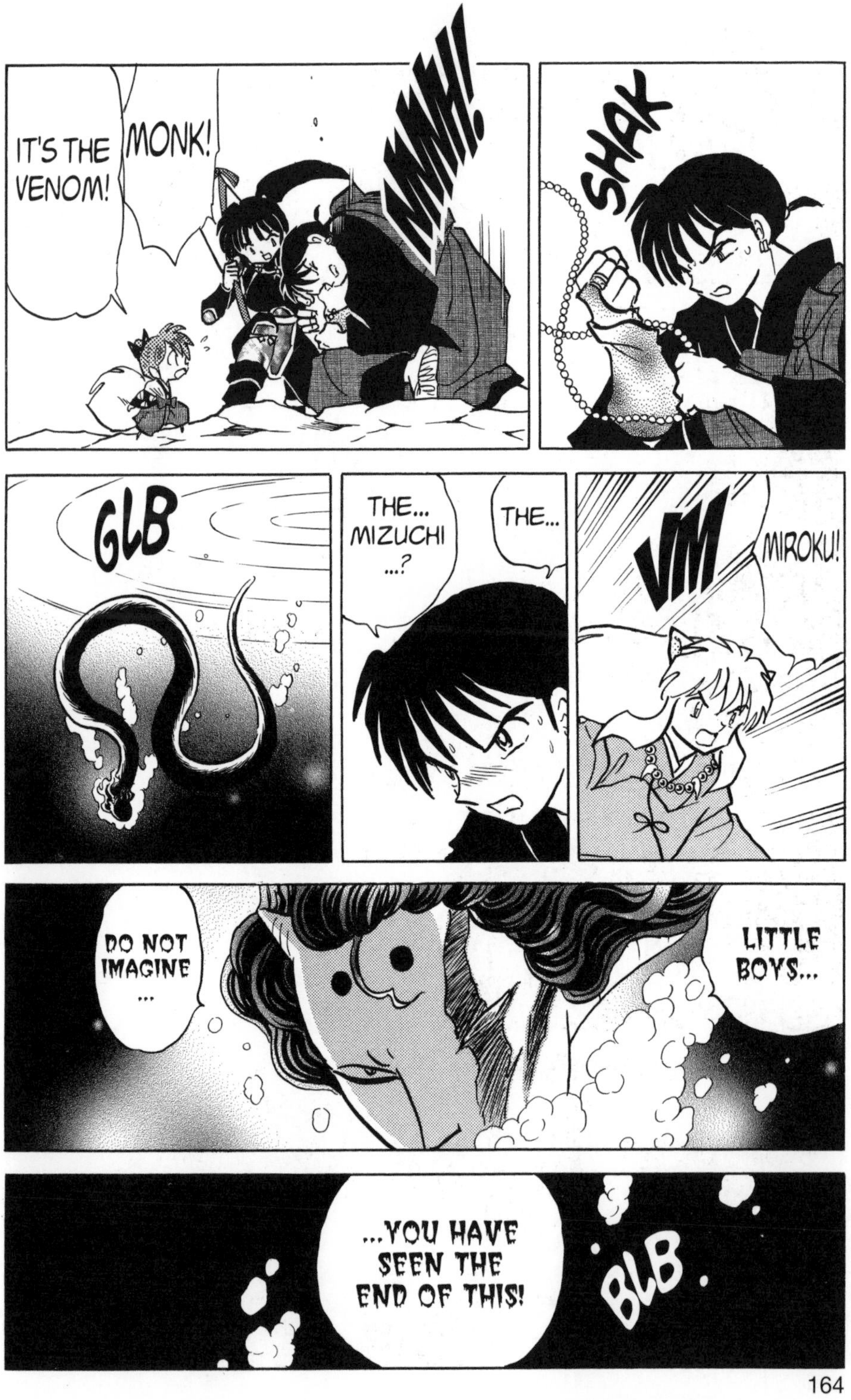
SHAK
MMMH!
MONK!
IT'S THE VENOM!
VM
MIROKU!
THE...
THE... MIZUCHI ...?
GLB
LITTLE BOYS...
DO NOT IMAGINE ...
...YOU HAVE SEEN THE END OF THIS!
BLB

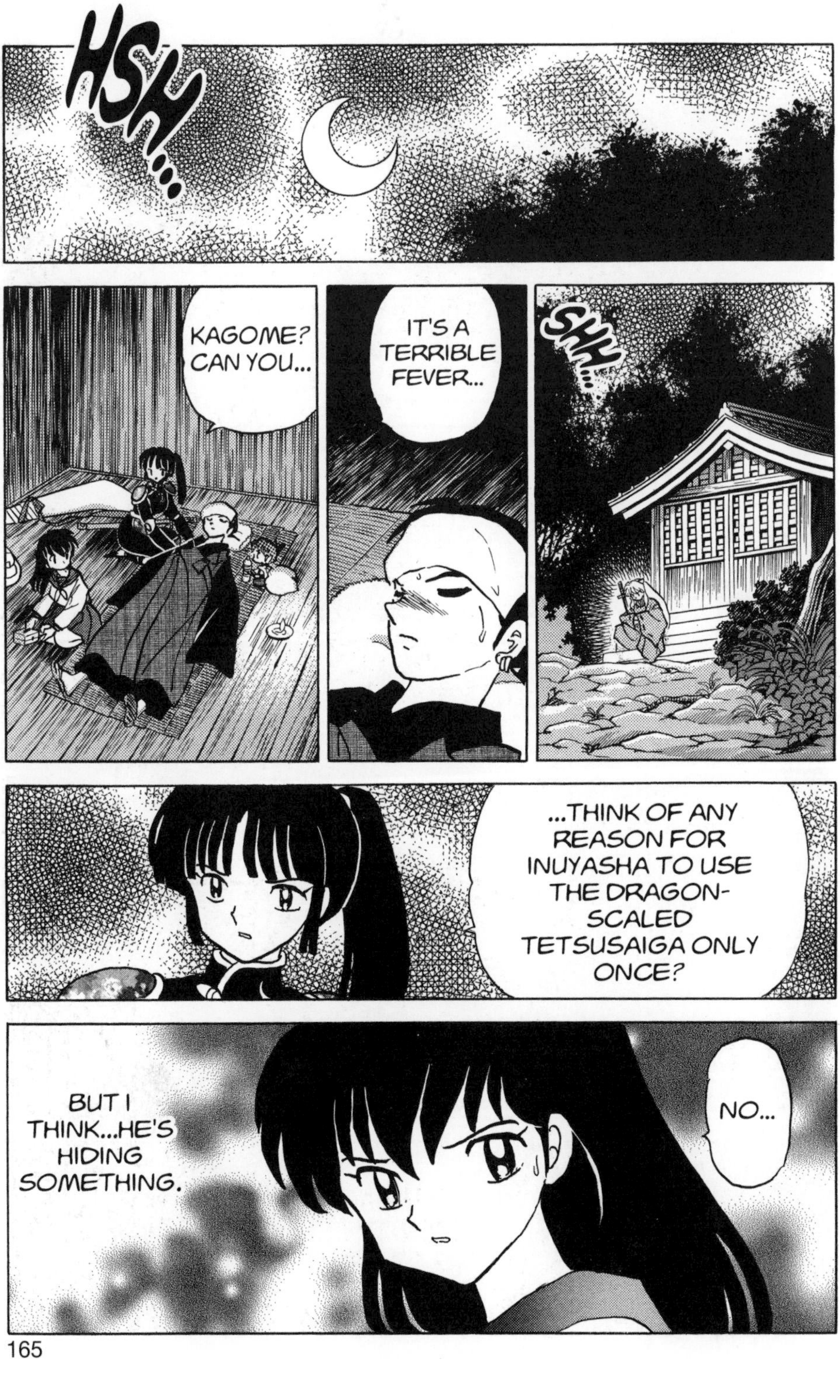
HSH...
SHH...
IT'S A TERRIBLE FEVER...
KAGOME? CAN YOU...
...THINK OF ANY REASON FOR INUYASHA TO USE THE DRAGON-SCALED TETSUSAIGA ONLY ONCE?
NO...
BUT I THINK...HE'S HIDING SOMETHING.

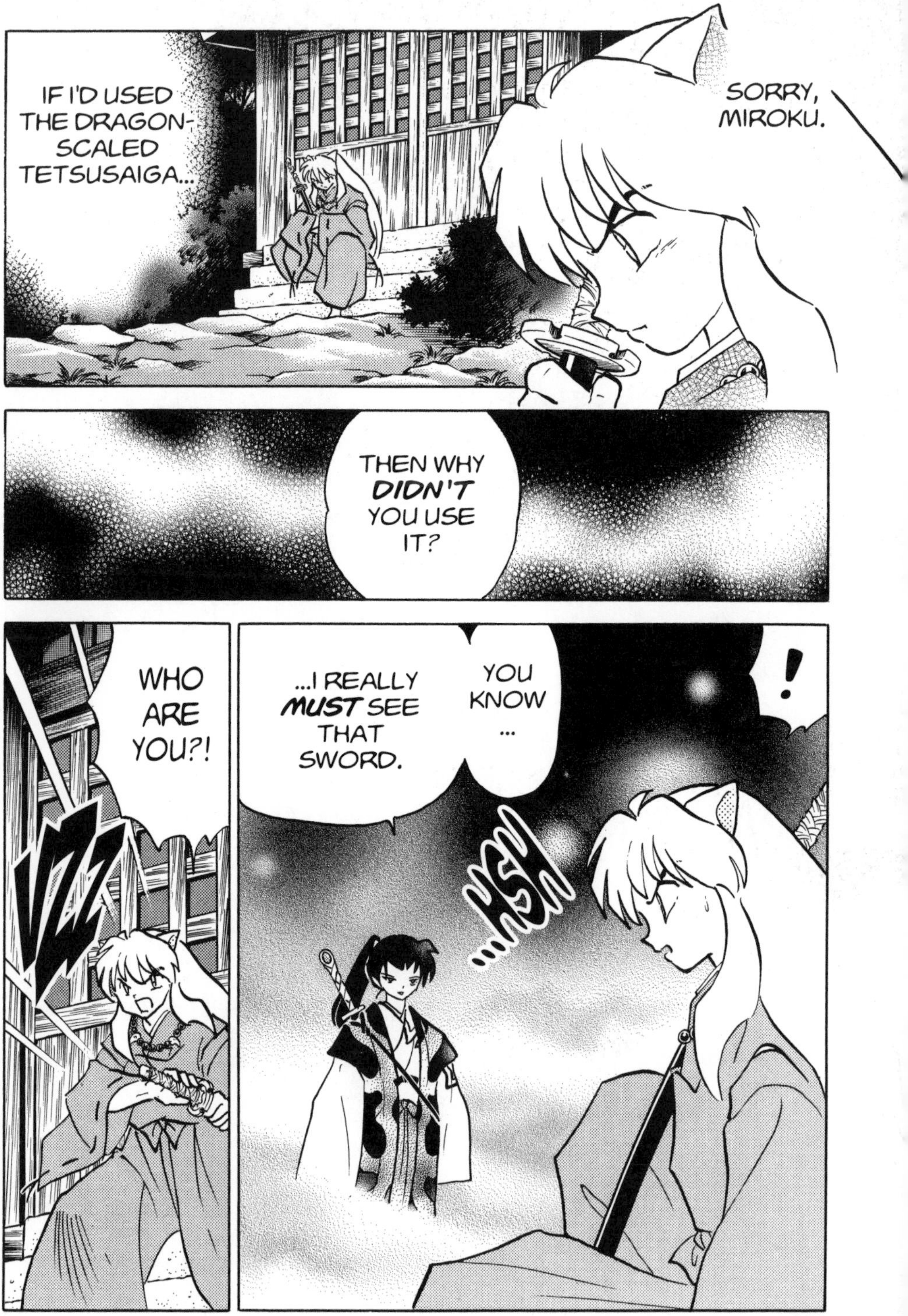
SORRY, MIROKU.
IF I'D USED THE DRAGON-SCALED TETSUSAIGA...
THEN WHY DIDN'T YOU USE IT?
!
YOU KNOW ...
...I REALLY MUST SEE THAT SWORD.
...HSH
WHO ARE YOU?!

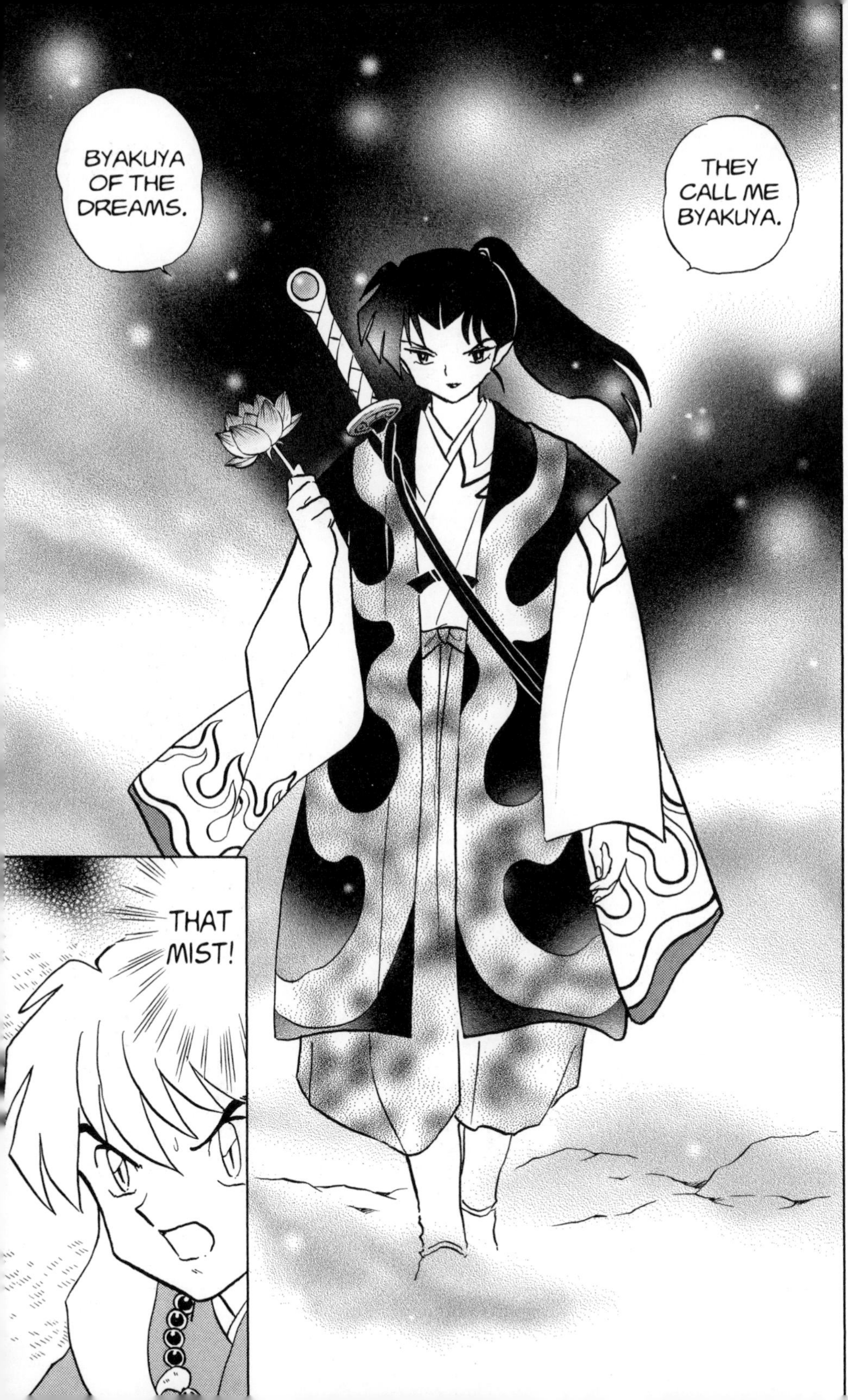
THEY CALL ME BYAKUYA.
BYAKUYA OF THE DREAMS.
THAT MIST!

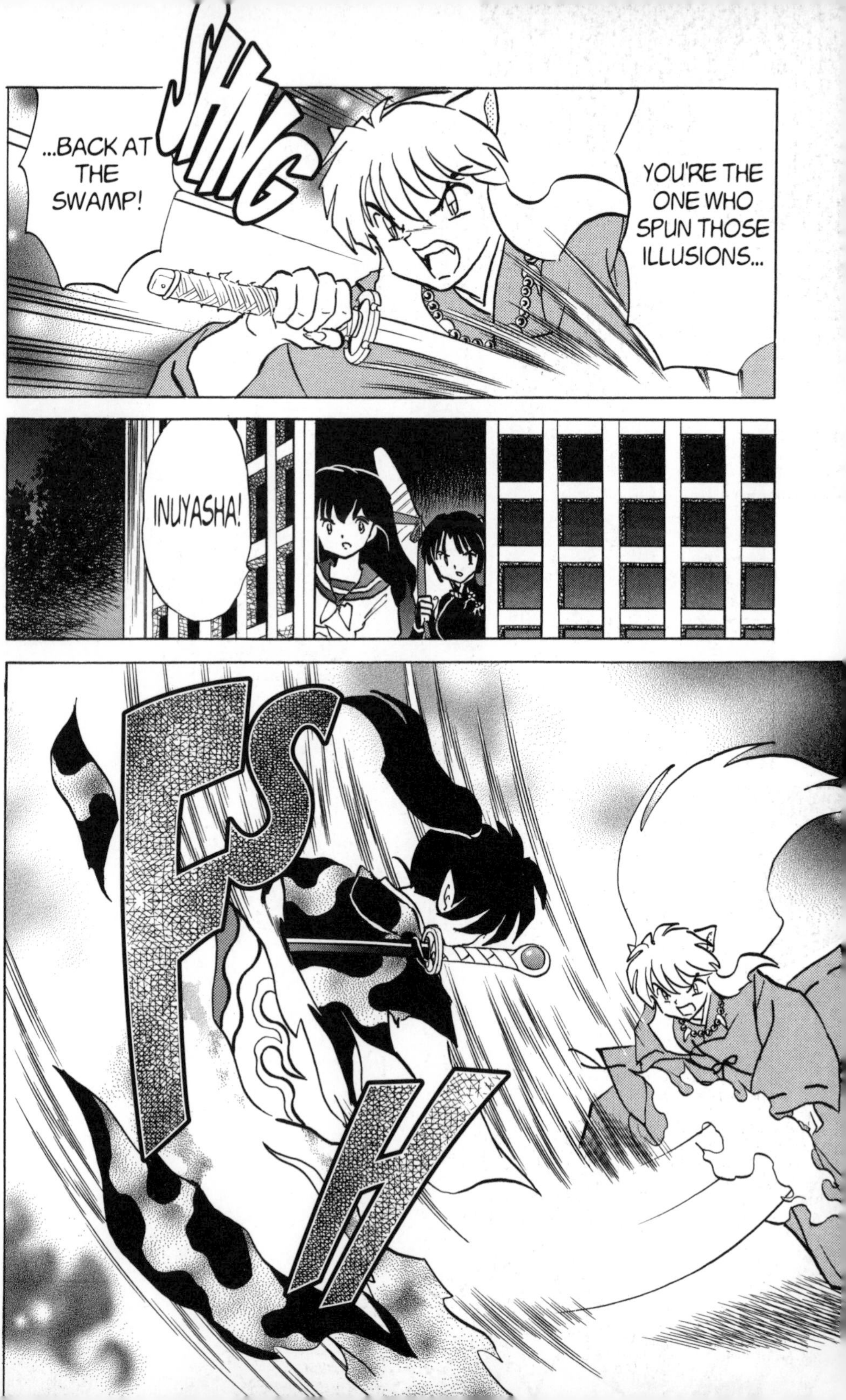
YOU'RE THE ONE WHO SPUN THOSE ILLUSIONS...
SHING
...BACK AT THE SWAMP!
INUYASHA!
FSH

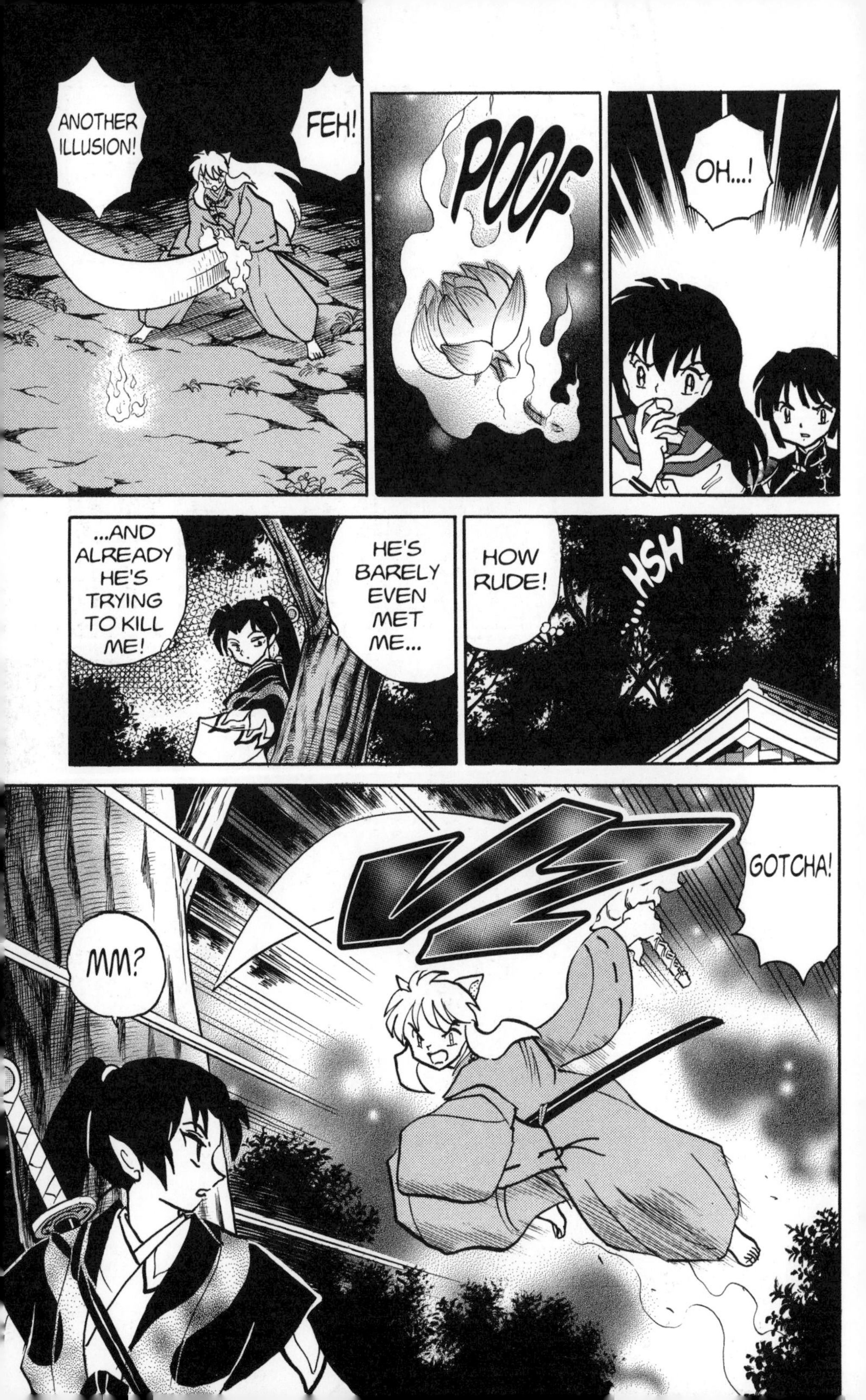
OH...!
POOF
FEH!
ANOTHER ILLUSION!
...HSH
HOW RUDE!
HE'S BARELY EVEN MET ME...
...AND ALREADY HE'S TRYING TO KILL ME!
GOTCHA!
MM?

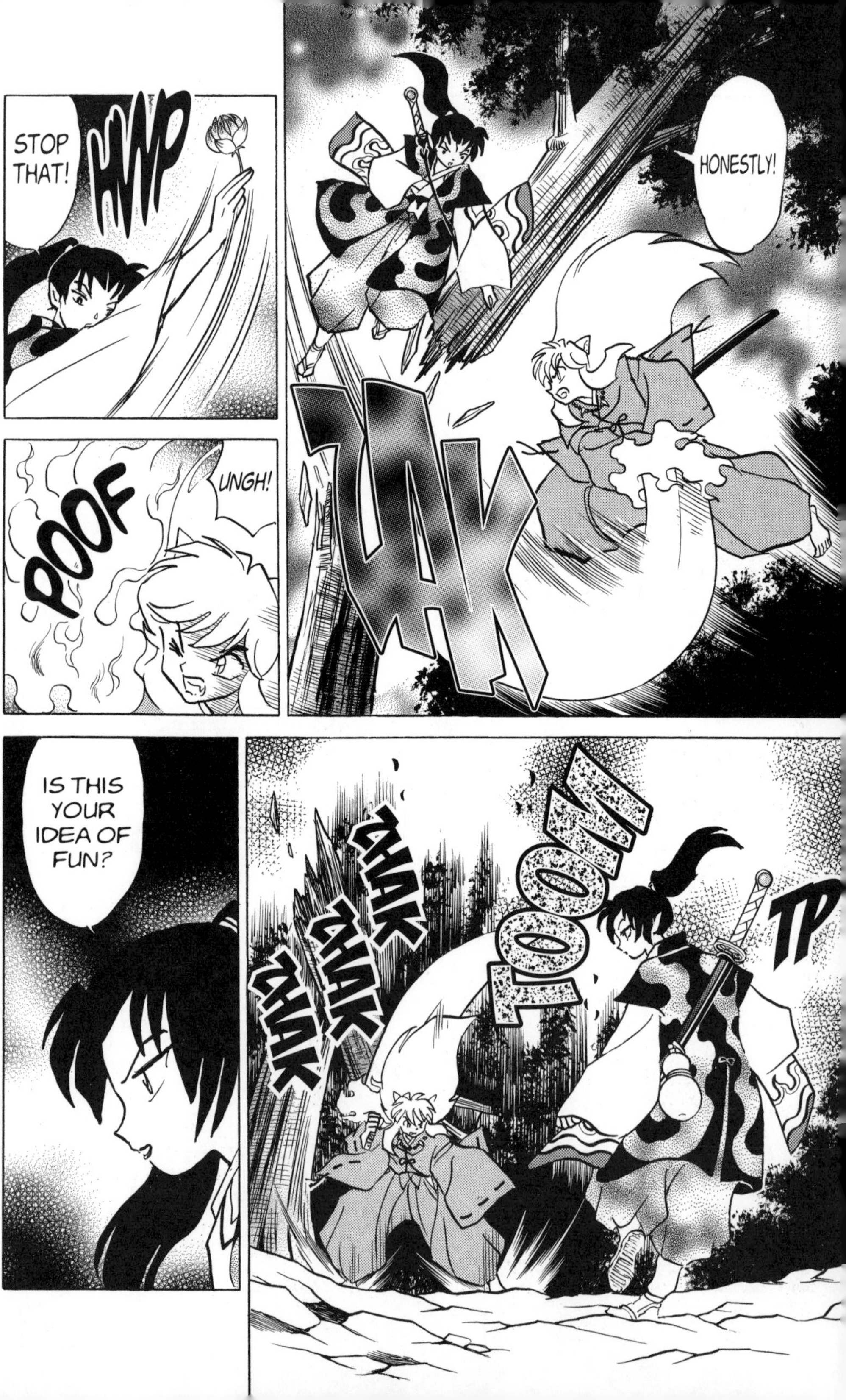
HONESTLY!
ZAK
STOP THAT!
HWP
POOF
UNGH!
TP
TOOOM
ZHAK ZHAK ZHAK
IS THIS YOUR IDEA OF FUN?

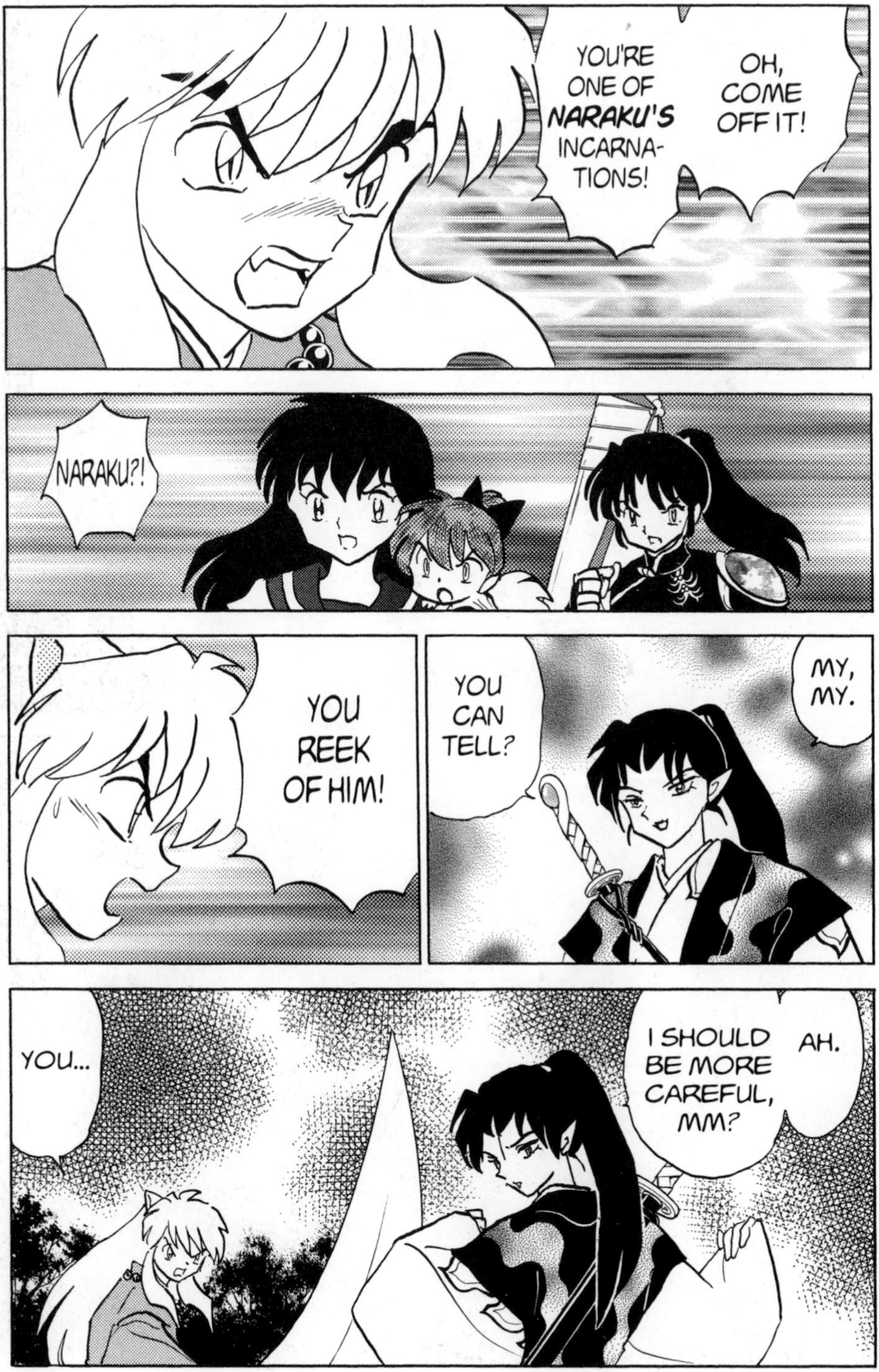
OH, COME OFF IT!
YOU'RE ONE OF NARAKU'S INCARNATIONS!
NARAKU?!
MY, MY.
YOU CAN TELL?
YOU REEK OF HIM!
AH.
I SHOULD BE MORE CAREFUL, MM?
YOU...

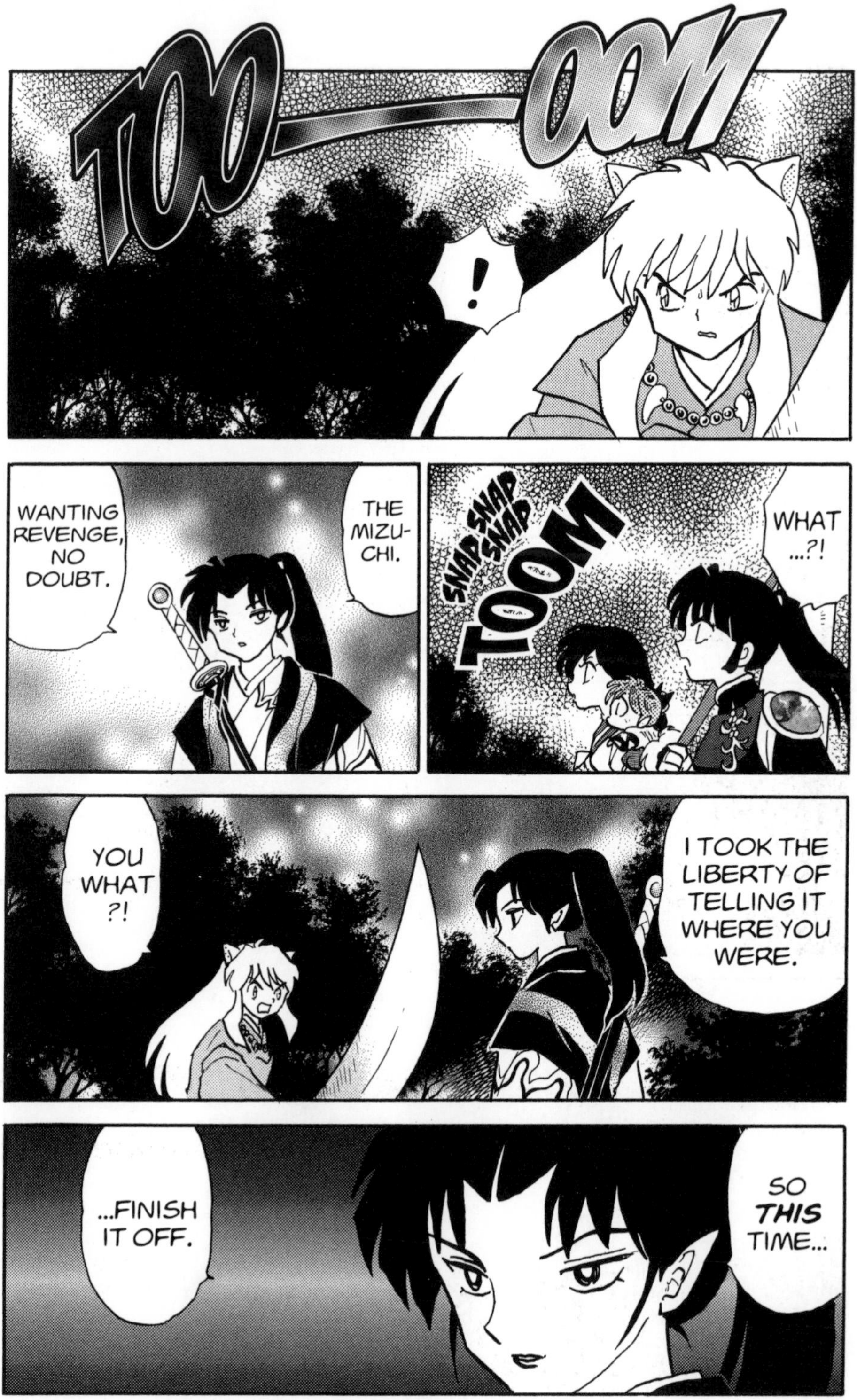
TOO—OOM
!
SNAP SNAP SNAP
TOOM
WHAT ...?!
THE MIZU-CHI.
WANTING REVENGE, NO DOUBT.
I TOOK THE LIBERTY OF TELLING IT WHERE YOU WERE.
YOU WHAT ?!
SO ***THIS*** TIME...
...FINISH IT OFF.

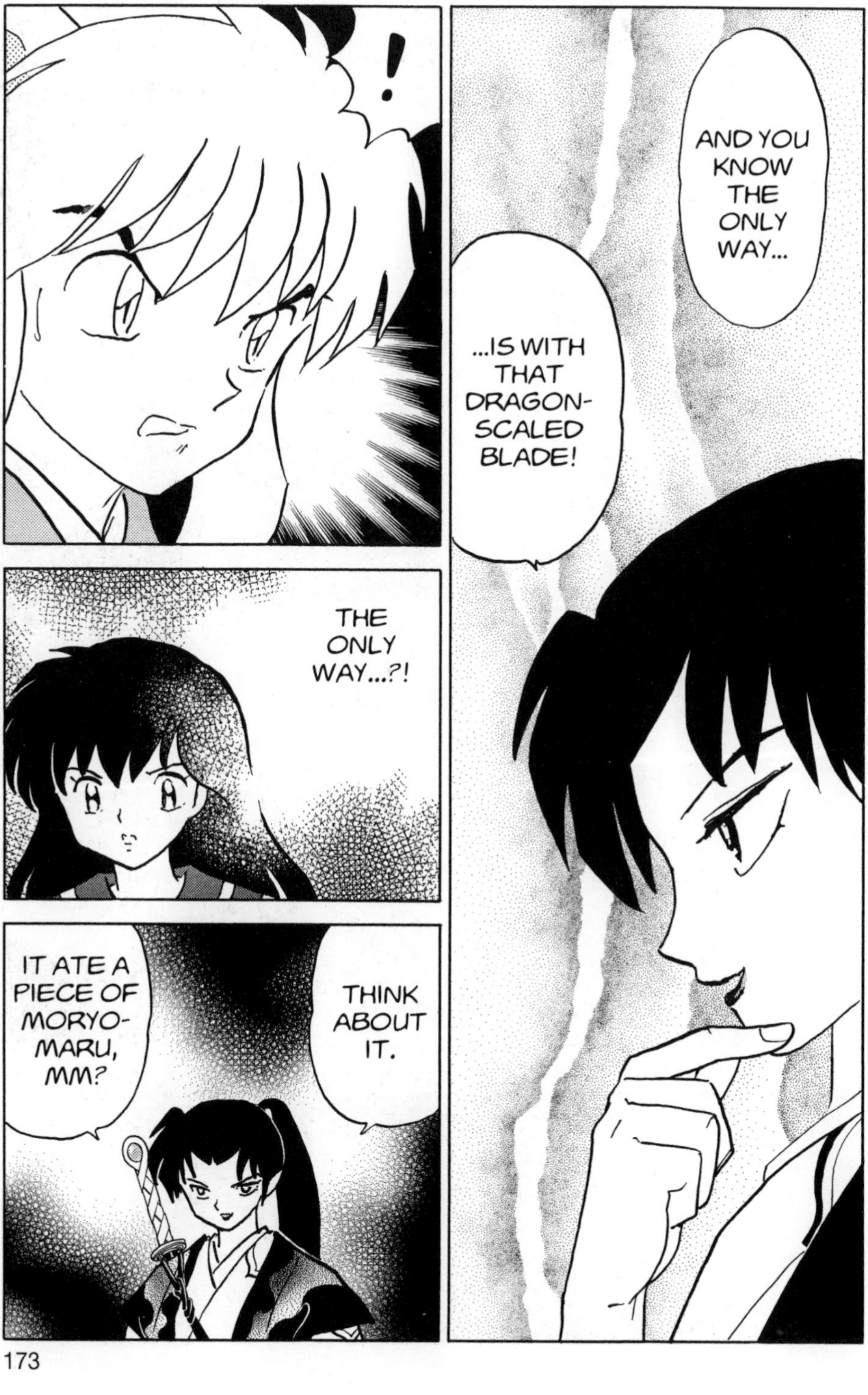
AND YOU KNOW THE ONLY WAY...
...IS WITH THAT DRAGON-SCALED BLADE!
!
THE ONLY WAY...?!
THINK ABOUT IT.
IT ATE A PIECE OF MORYO-MARU, MM?

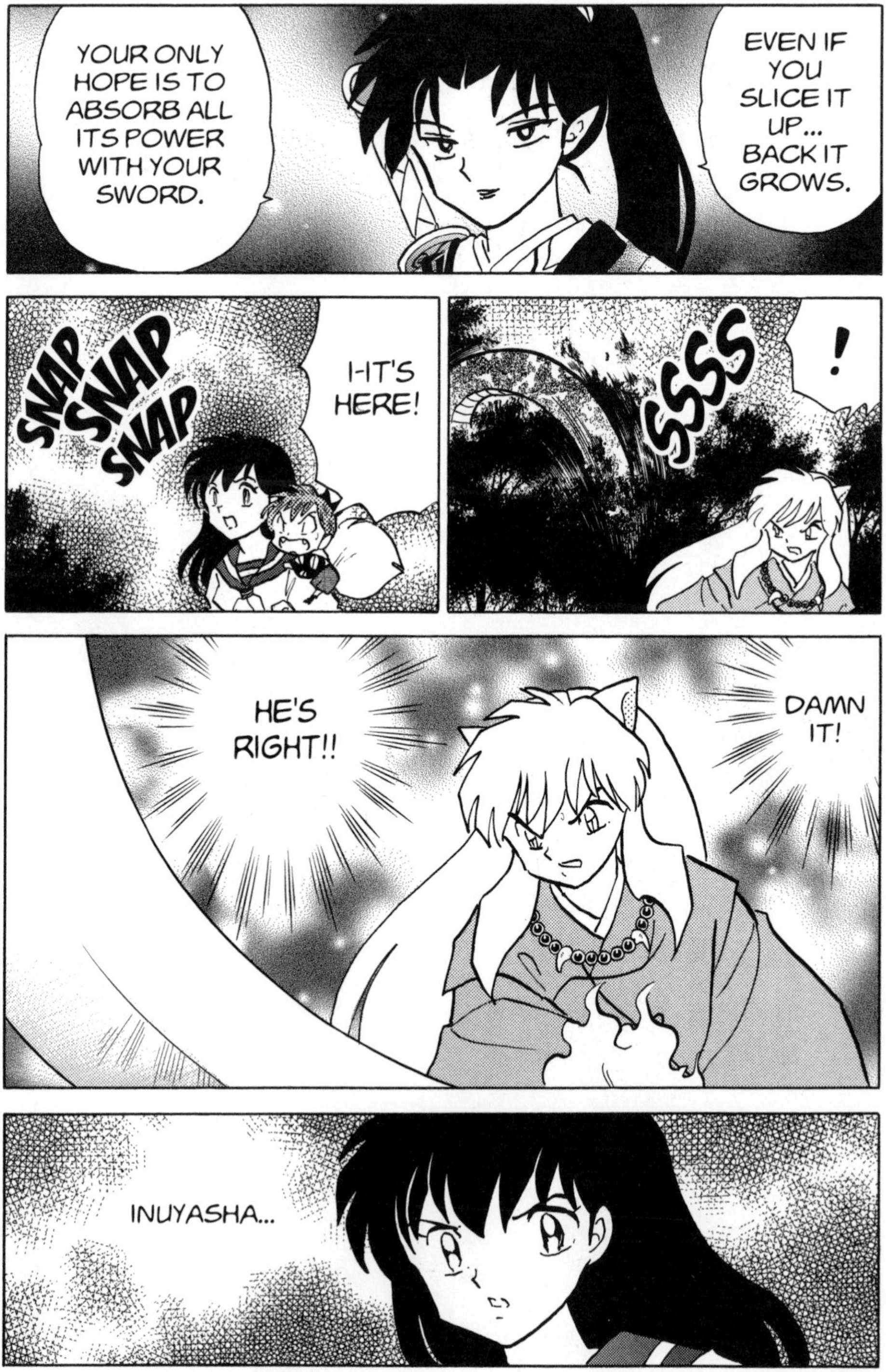
EVEN IF YOU SLICE IT UP... BACK IT GROWS.
YOUR ONLY HOPE IS TO ABSORB ALL ITS POWER WITH YOUR SWORD.
!
SSSS
I-IT'S HERE!
SNAP SNAP SNAP
DAMN IT!
HE'S RIGHT!!
INUYASHA...

SCROLL TEN
TETSUSAIGA EXPLODES

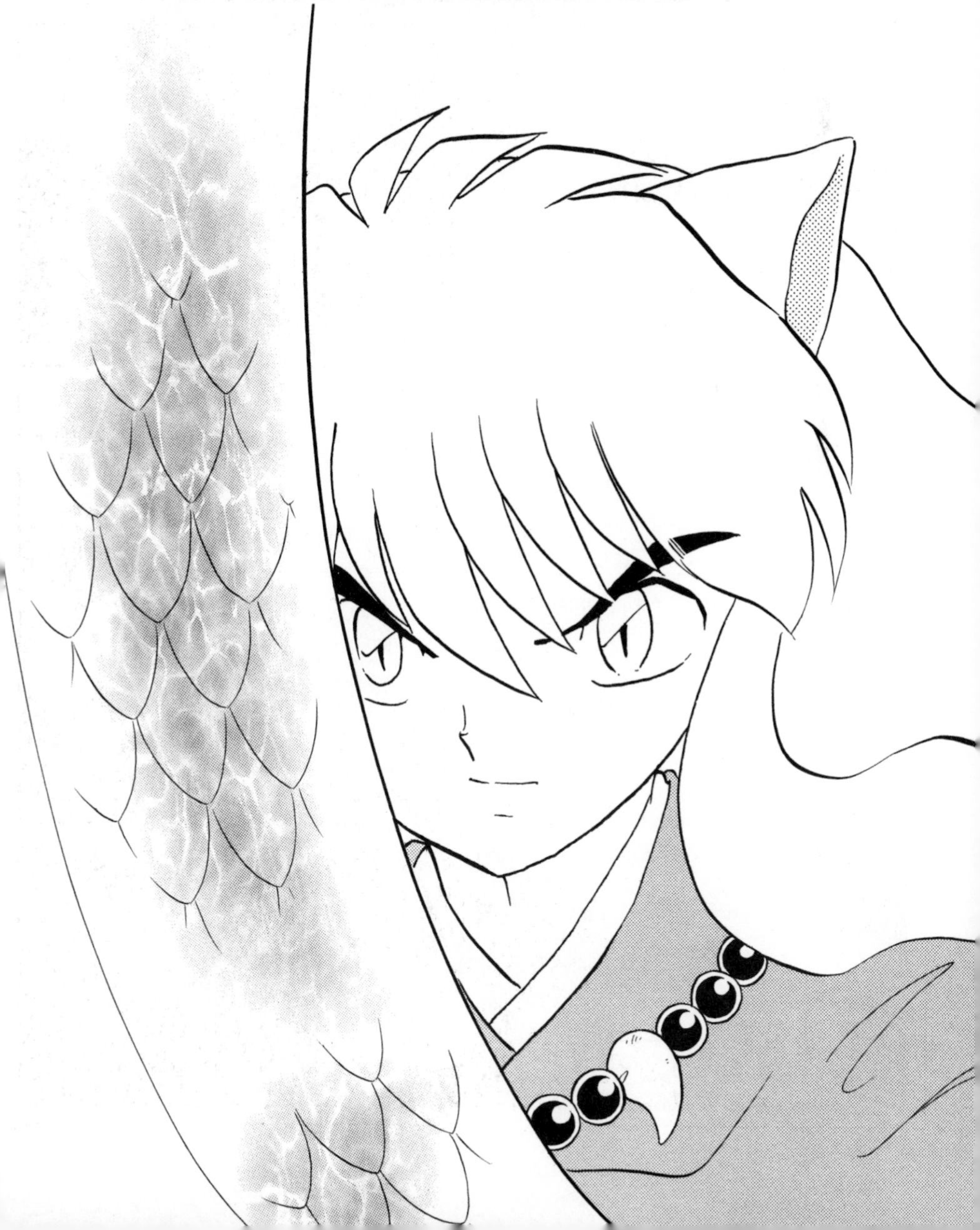

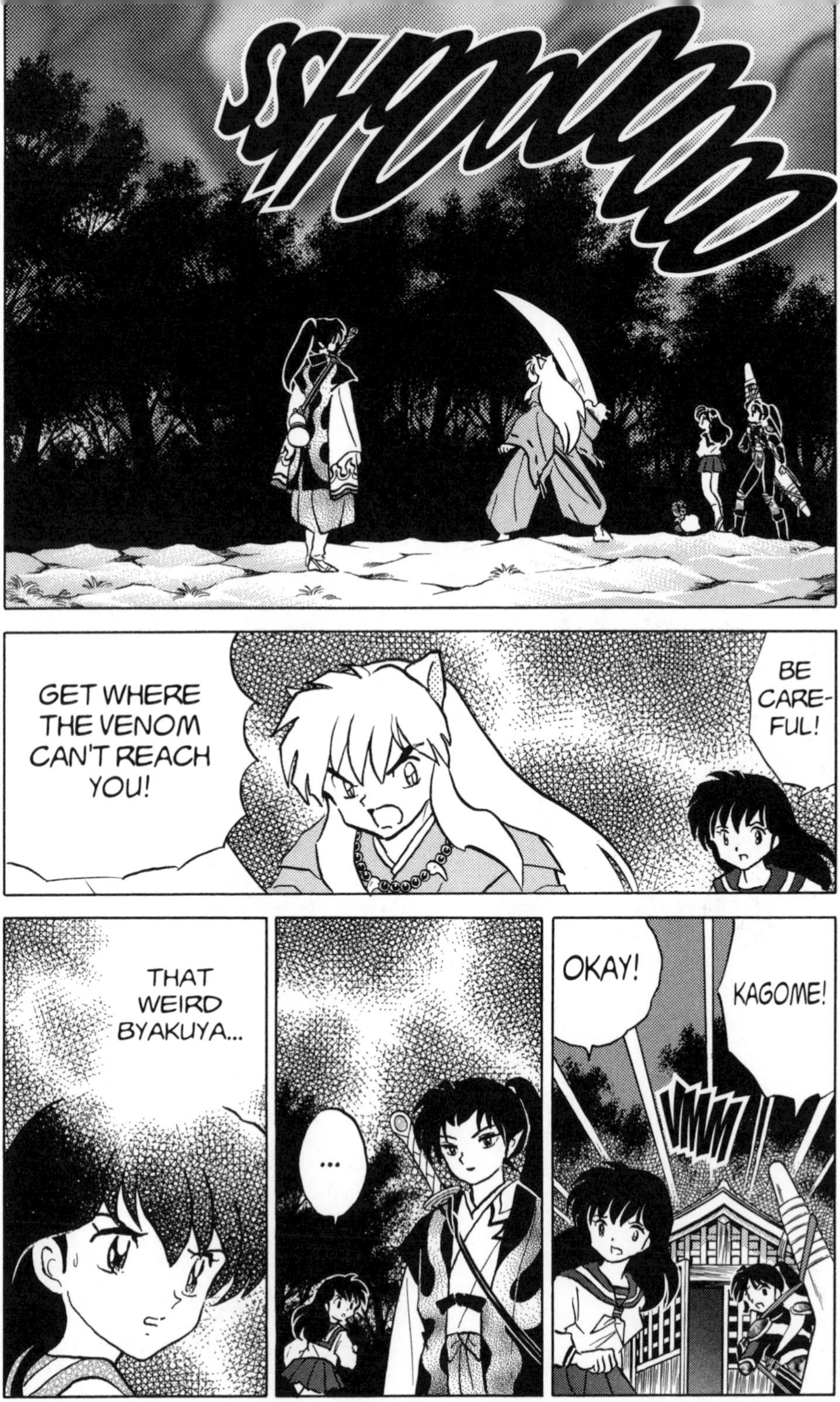
BE CARE-FUL!
GET WHERE THE VENOM CAN'T REACH YOU!
KAGOME!
OKAY!
VMMM
...
THAT WEIRD BYAKUYA...

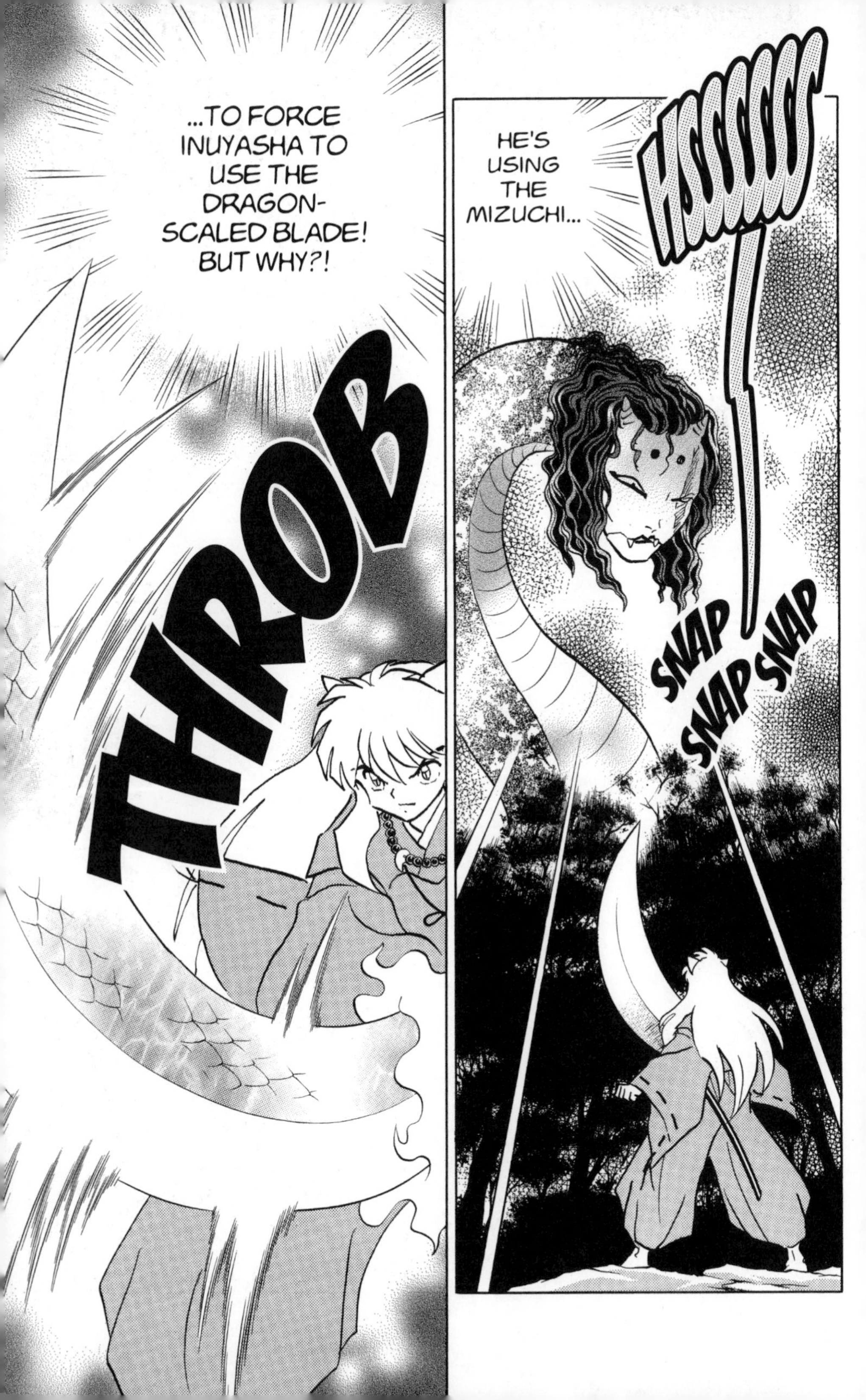
HSSSSS
HE'S USING THE MIZUCHI...
SNAP
SNAP SNAP
...TO FORCE INUYASHA TO USE THE DRAGON-SCALED BLADE! BUT WHY?!
THROB

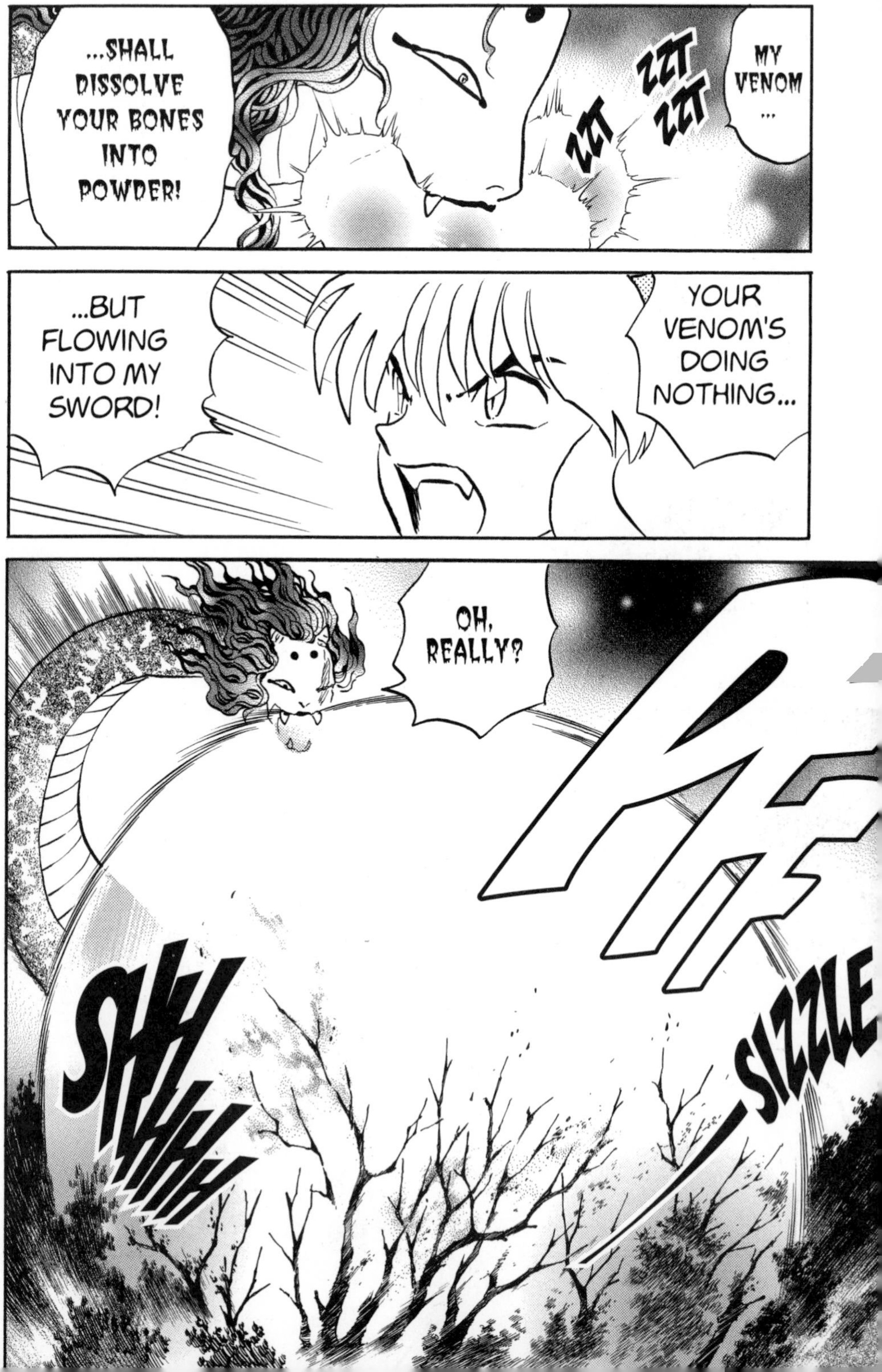
MY VENOM ...
ZZT
ZZT
ZZT
...SHALL DISSOLVE YOUR BONES INTO POWDER!
YOUR VENOM'S DOING NOTHING...
...BUT FLOWING INTO MY SWORD!
OH, REALLY?
SIZZLE

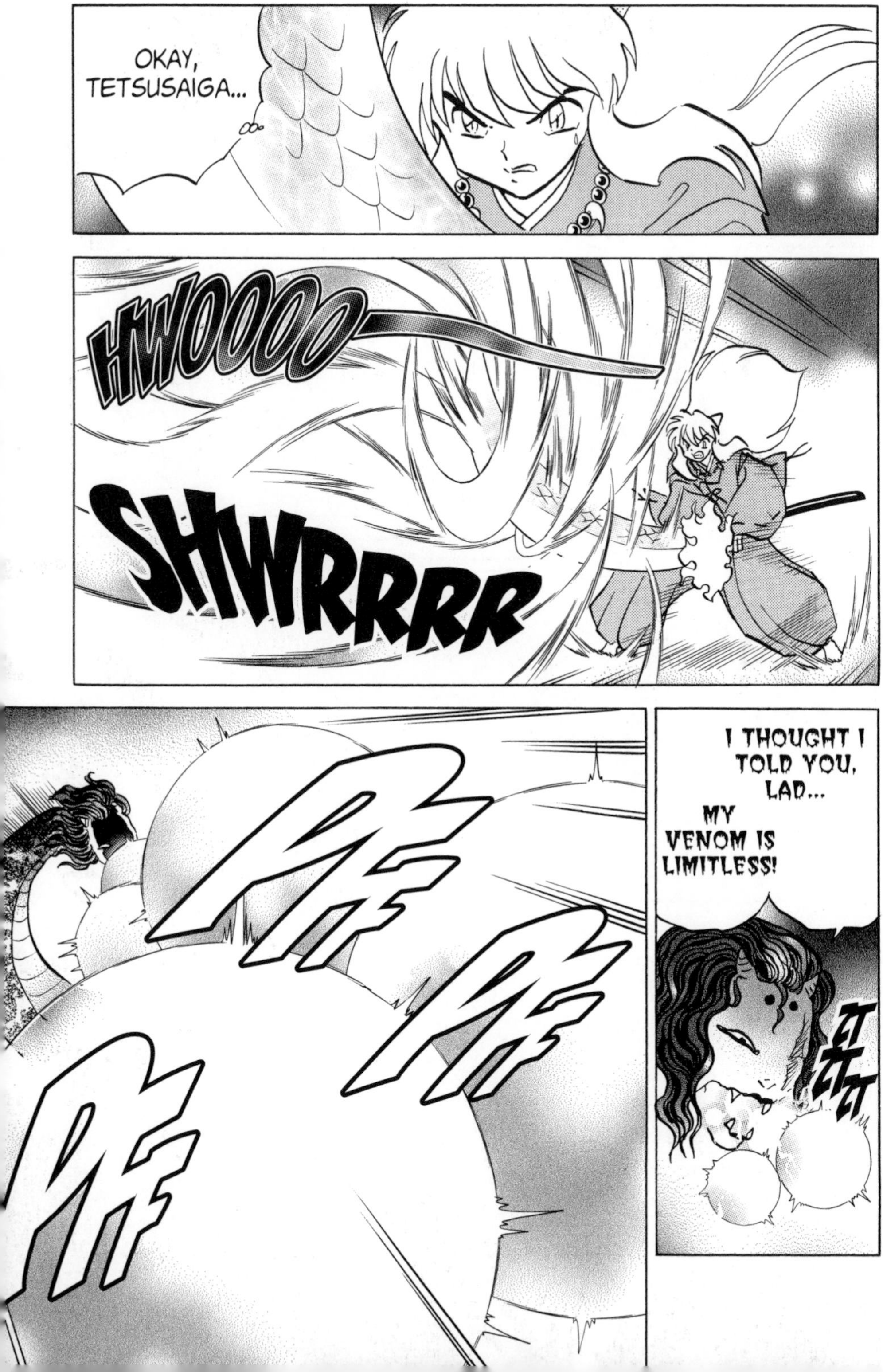
OKAY, TETSUSAIGA...
HWOOOO
SHWRRRRR
I THOUGHT I TOLD YOU, LAD...
MY VENOM IS LIMITLESS!

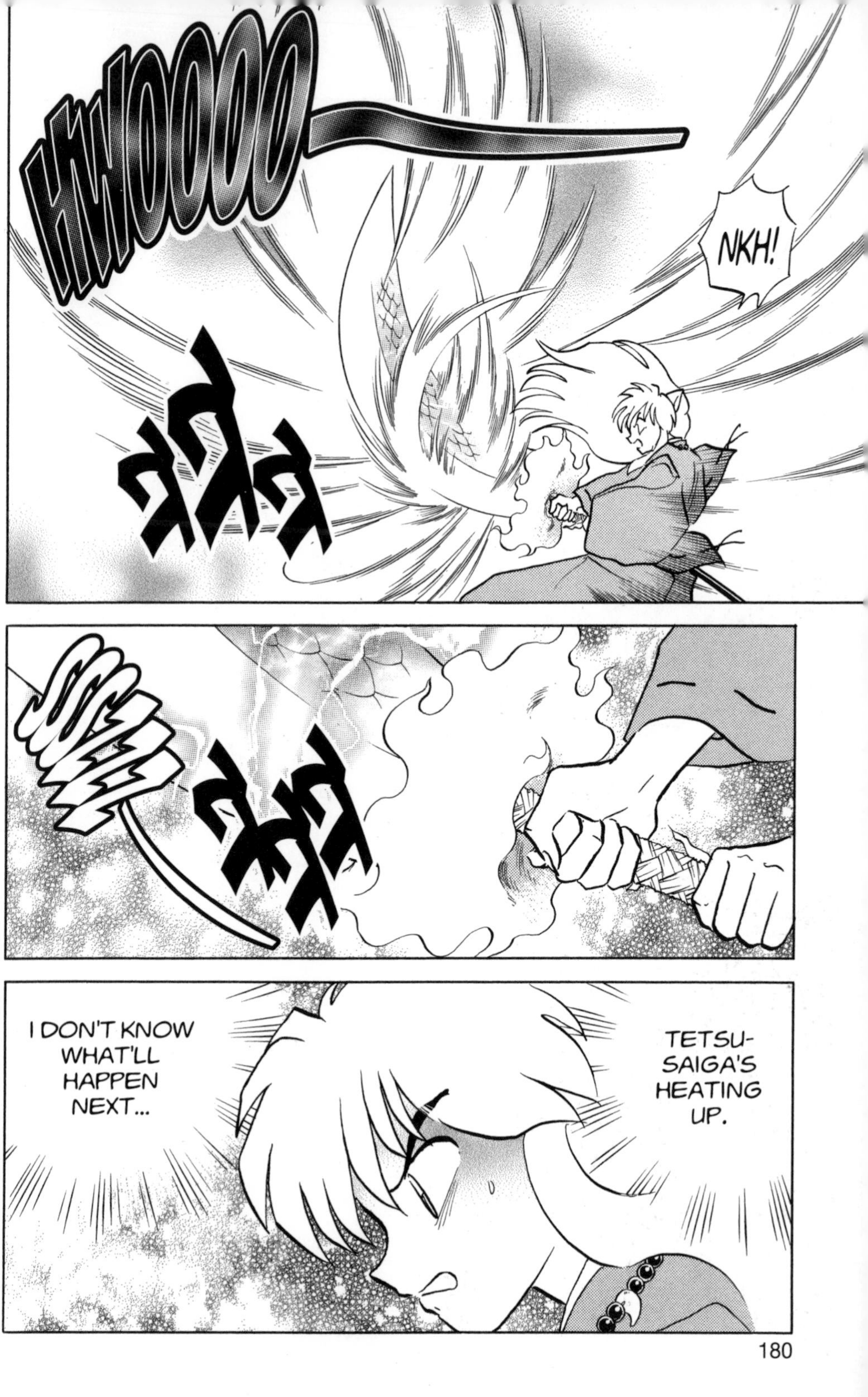
HWOOOO
NKH!
TETSU-SAIGA'S HEATING UP.
I DON'T KNOW WHAT'LL HAPPEN NEXT...

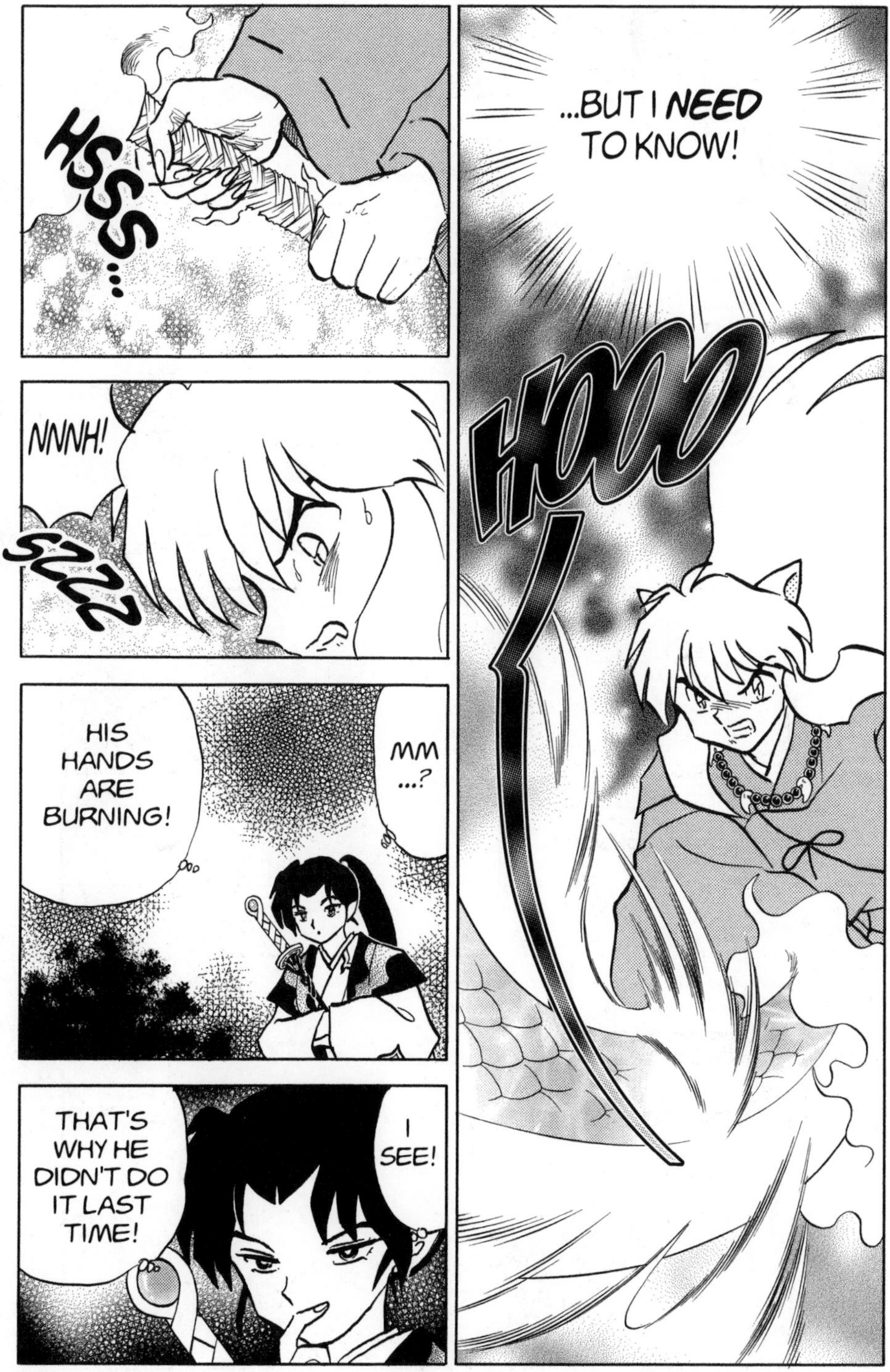
...BUT I **NEED** TO KNOW!
HOOO
HSSS...
NNNH!
SZZZ
MM ...?
HIS HANDS ARE BURNING!
I SEE!
THAT'S WHY HE DIDN'T DO IT LAST TIME!

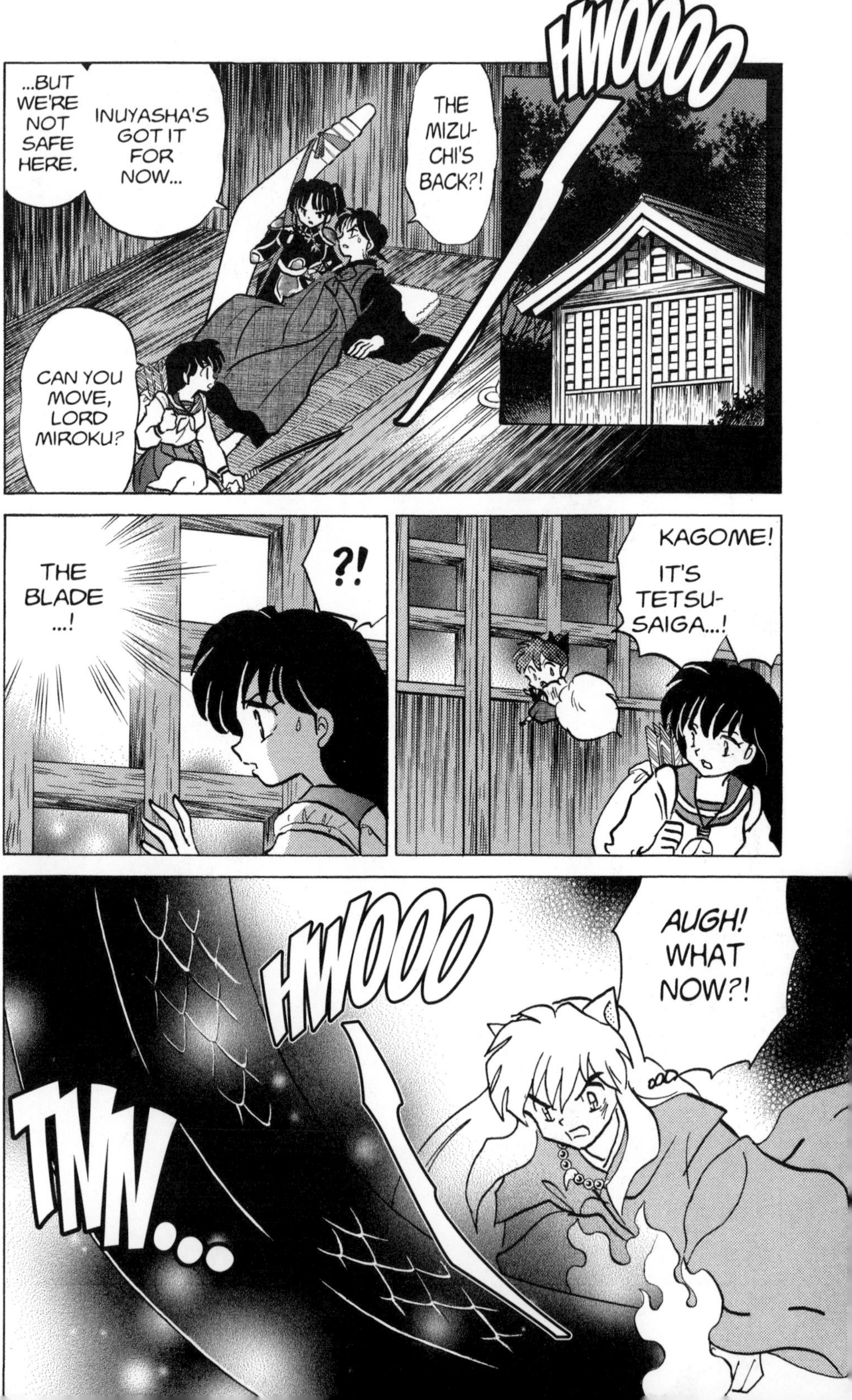
HWOOOO
THE MIZU-CHI'S BACK?!
INUYASHA'S GOT IT FOR NOW...
...BUT WE'RE NOT SAFE HERE.
CAN YOU MOVE, LORD MIROKU?
KAGOME! IT'S TETSU-SAIGA...!
?!
THE BLADE ...!
AUGH! WHAT NOW?!
HWOOO
TMN...

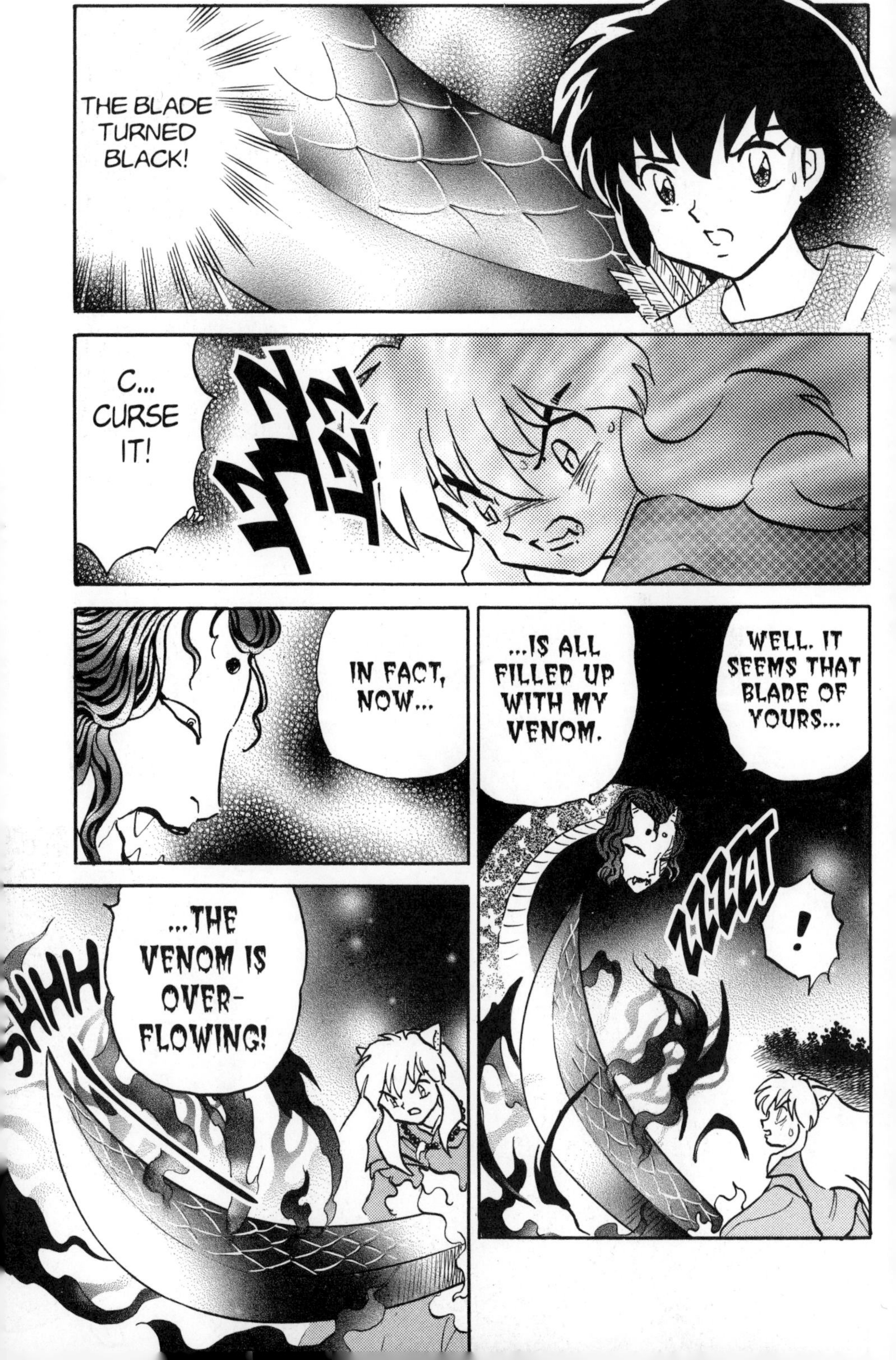
THE BLADE TURNED BLACK!
C... CURSE IT!
WELL. IT SEEMS THAT BLADE OF YOURS...
...IS ALL FILLED UP WITH MY VENOM.
!
IN FACT, NOW...
...THE VENOM IS OVER-FLOWING!
SHHH

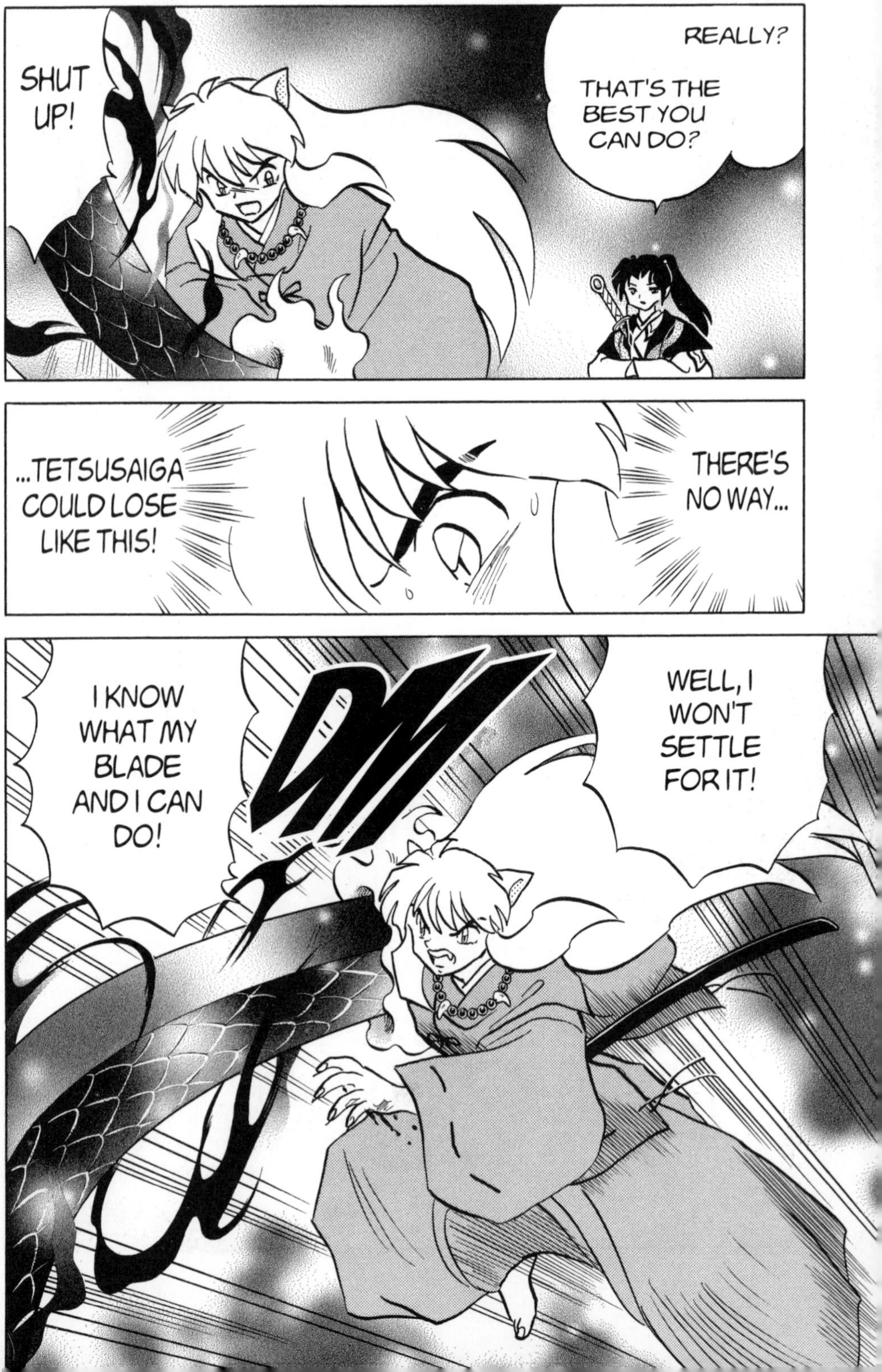
REALLY?
THAT'S THE BEST YOU CAN DO?
SHUT UP!
THERE'S NO WAY...
...TETSUSAIGA COULD LOSE LIKE THIS!
WELL, I WON'T SETTLE FOR IT!
I KNOW WHAT MY BLADE AND I CAN DO!

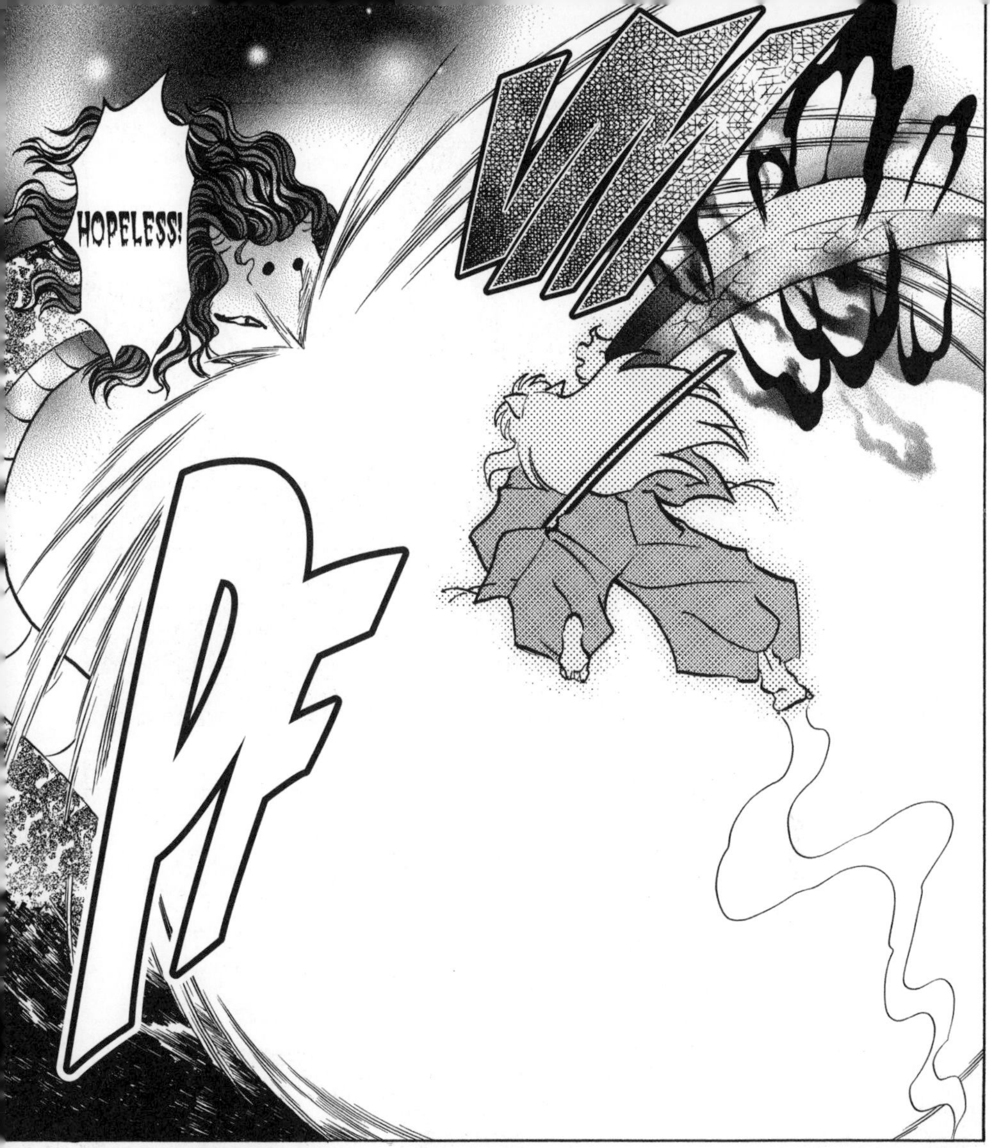
HOPELESS!
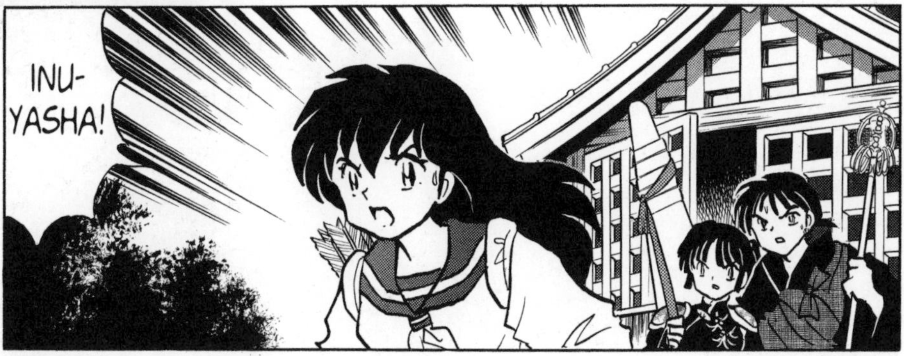
INU-
YASHA!

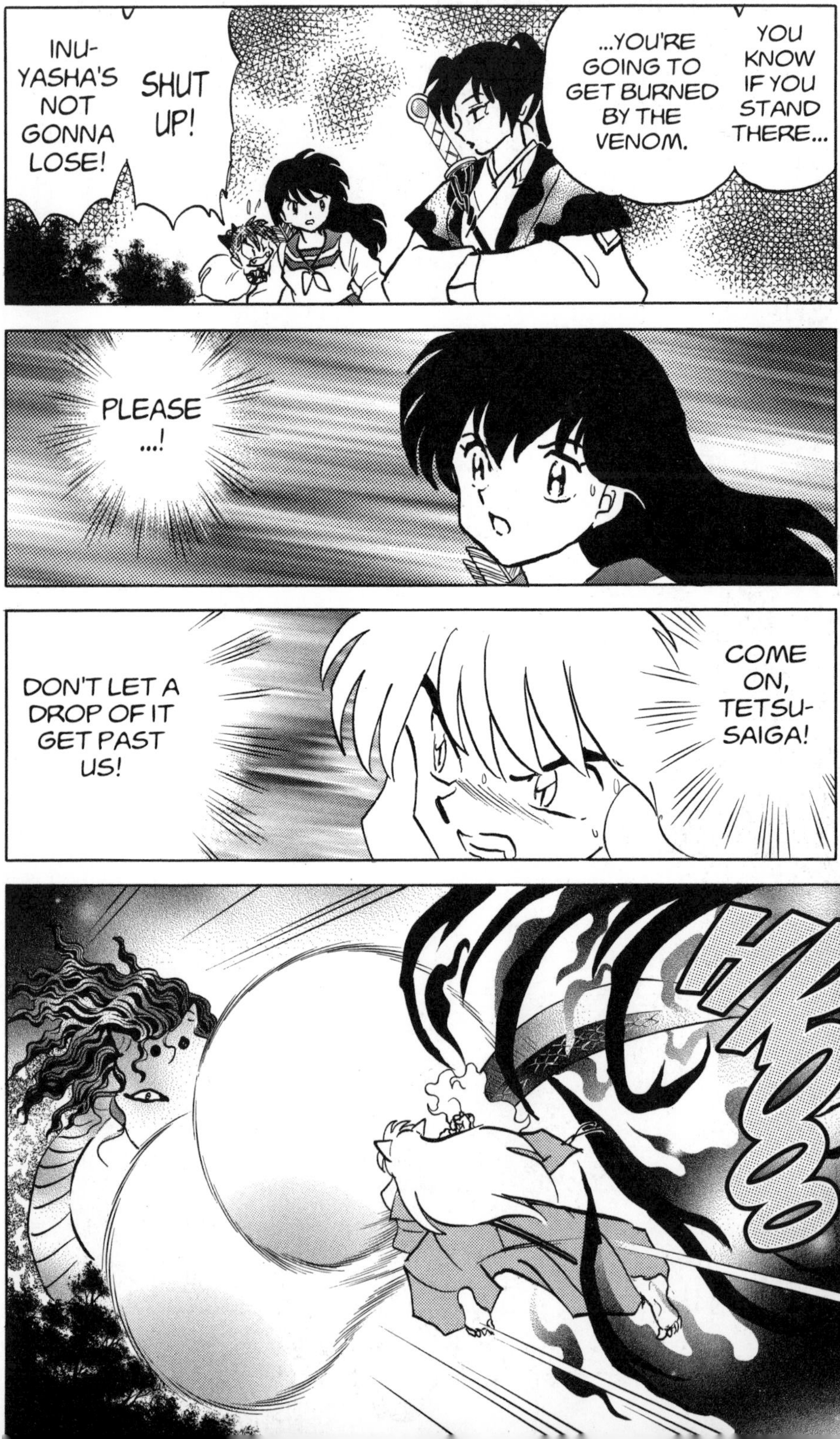
YOU KNOW IF YOU STAND THERE...
...YOU'RE GOING TO GET BURNED BY THE VENOM.
SHUT UP!
INU-YASHA'S NOT GONNA LOSE!
PLEASE ...!
COME ON, TETSU-SAIGA!
DON'T LET A DROP OF IT GET PAST US!
HROOO

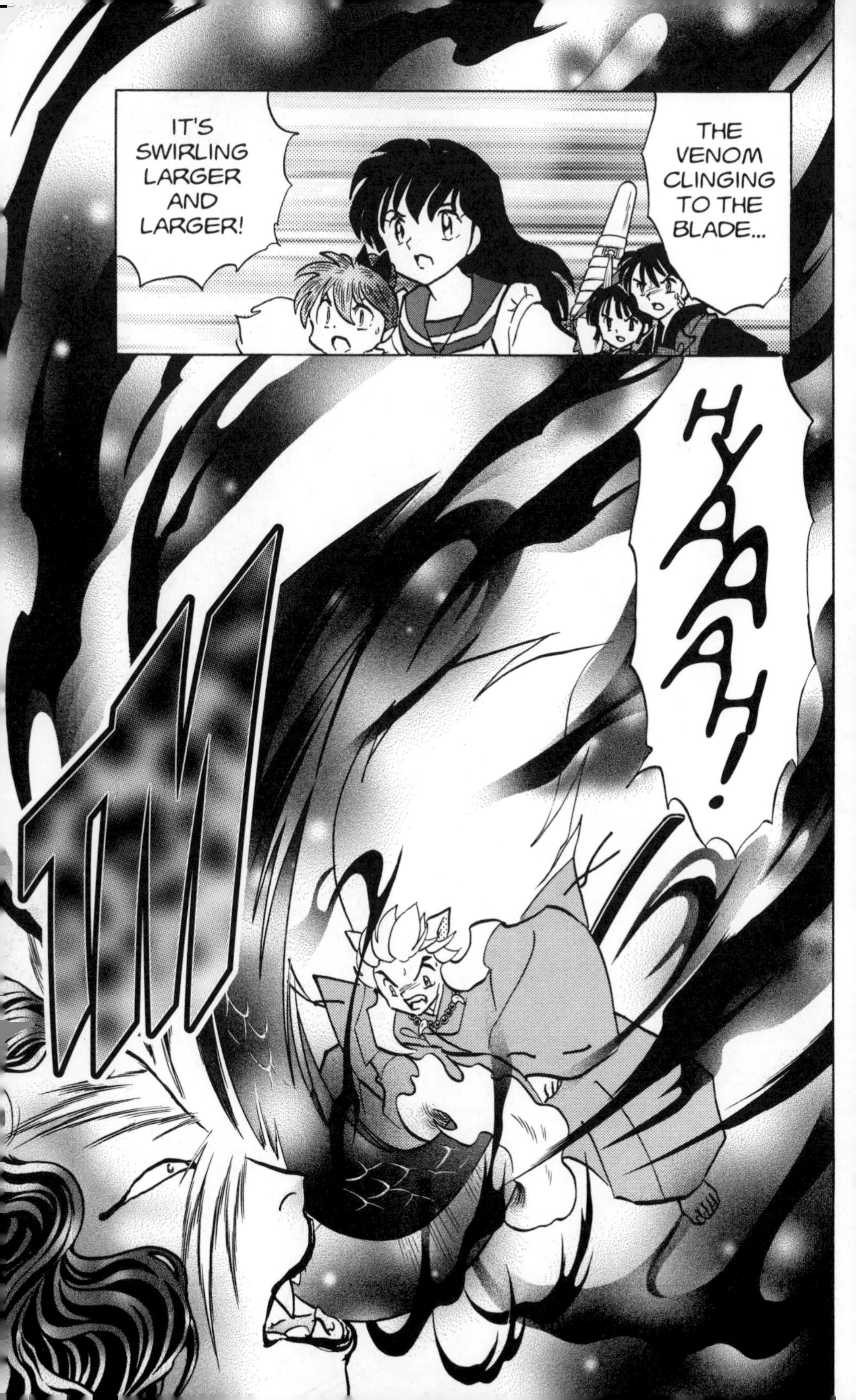
THE VENOM CLINGING TO THE BLADE...
IT'S SWIRLING LARGER AND LARGER!
HYAAAH!

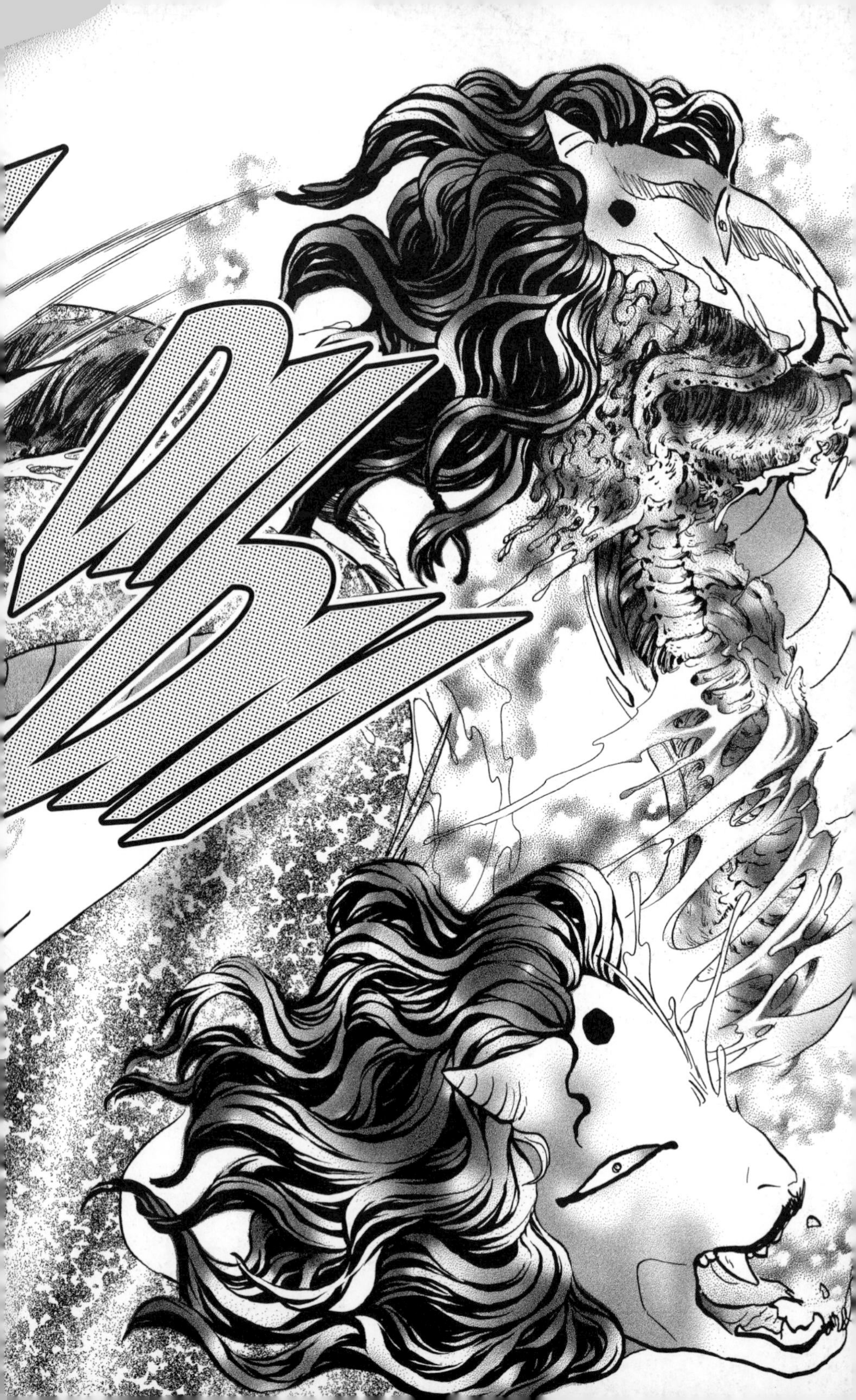

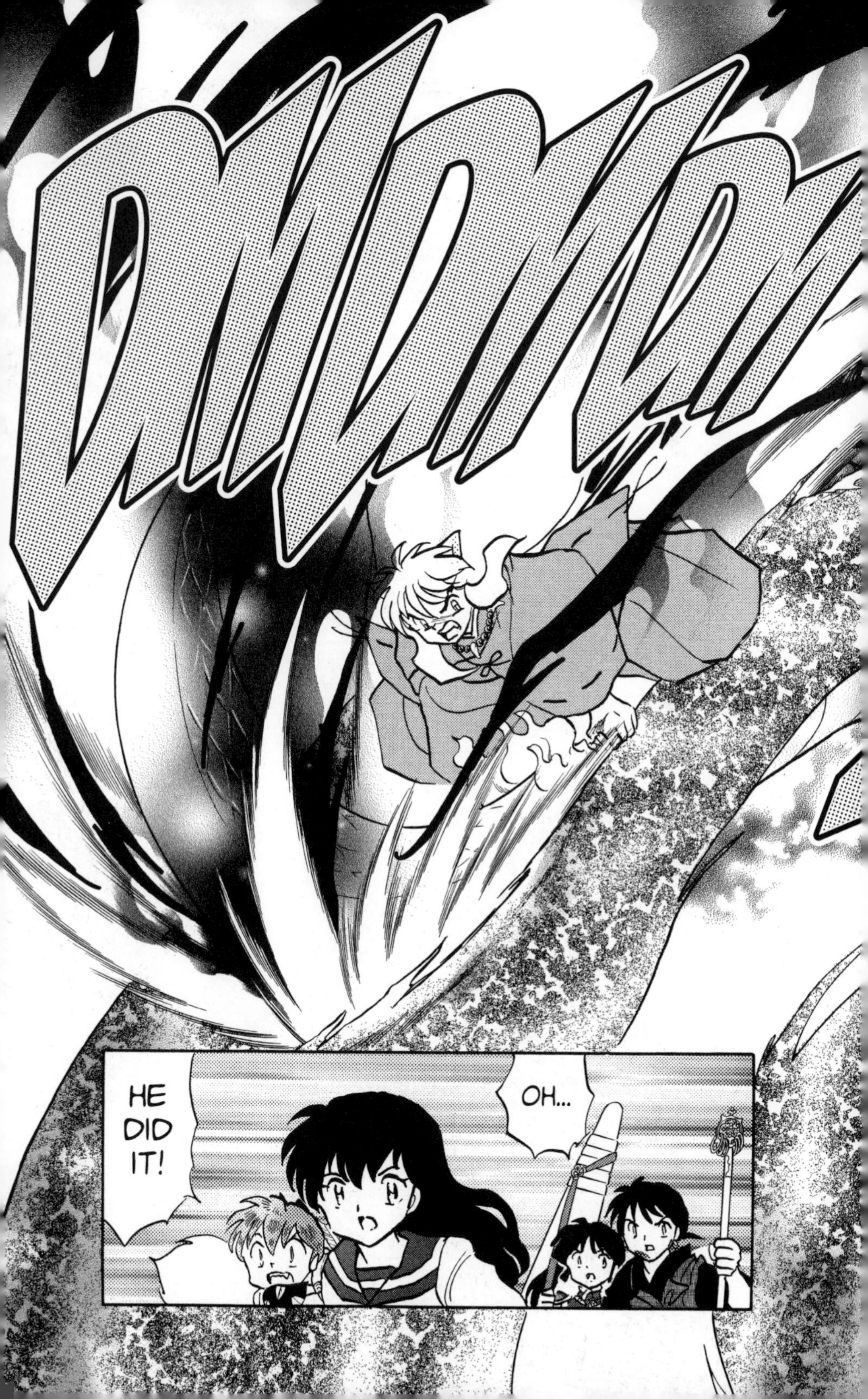
OH...
HE DID IT!

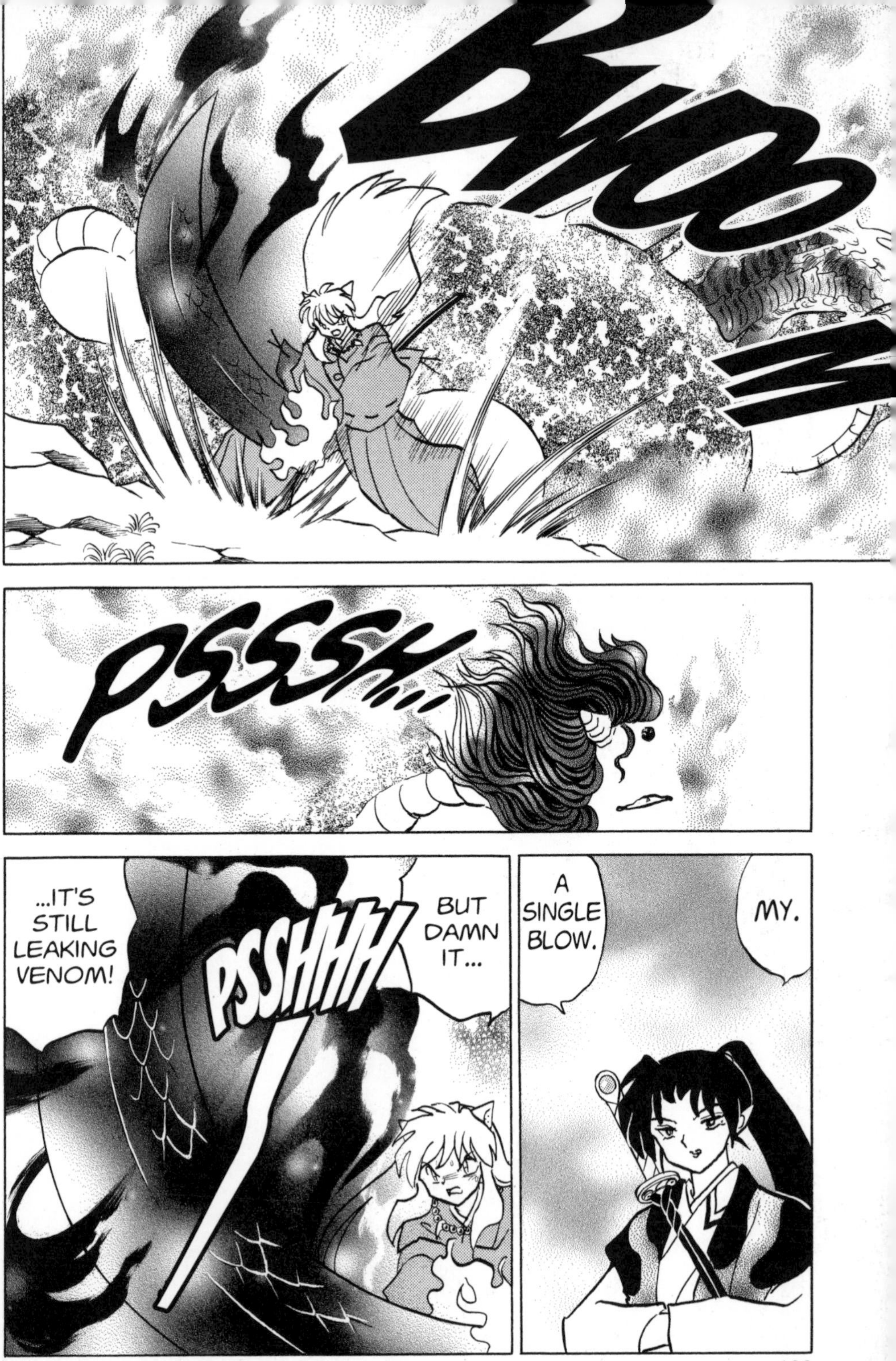
BWOOM
PSSSH...
MY.
A SINGLE BLOW.
BUT DAMN IT...
PSSHHH
...IT'S STILL LEAKING VENOM!

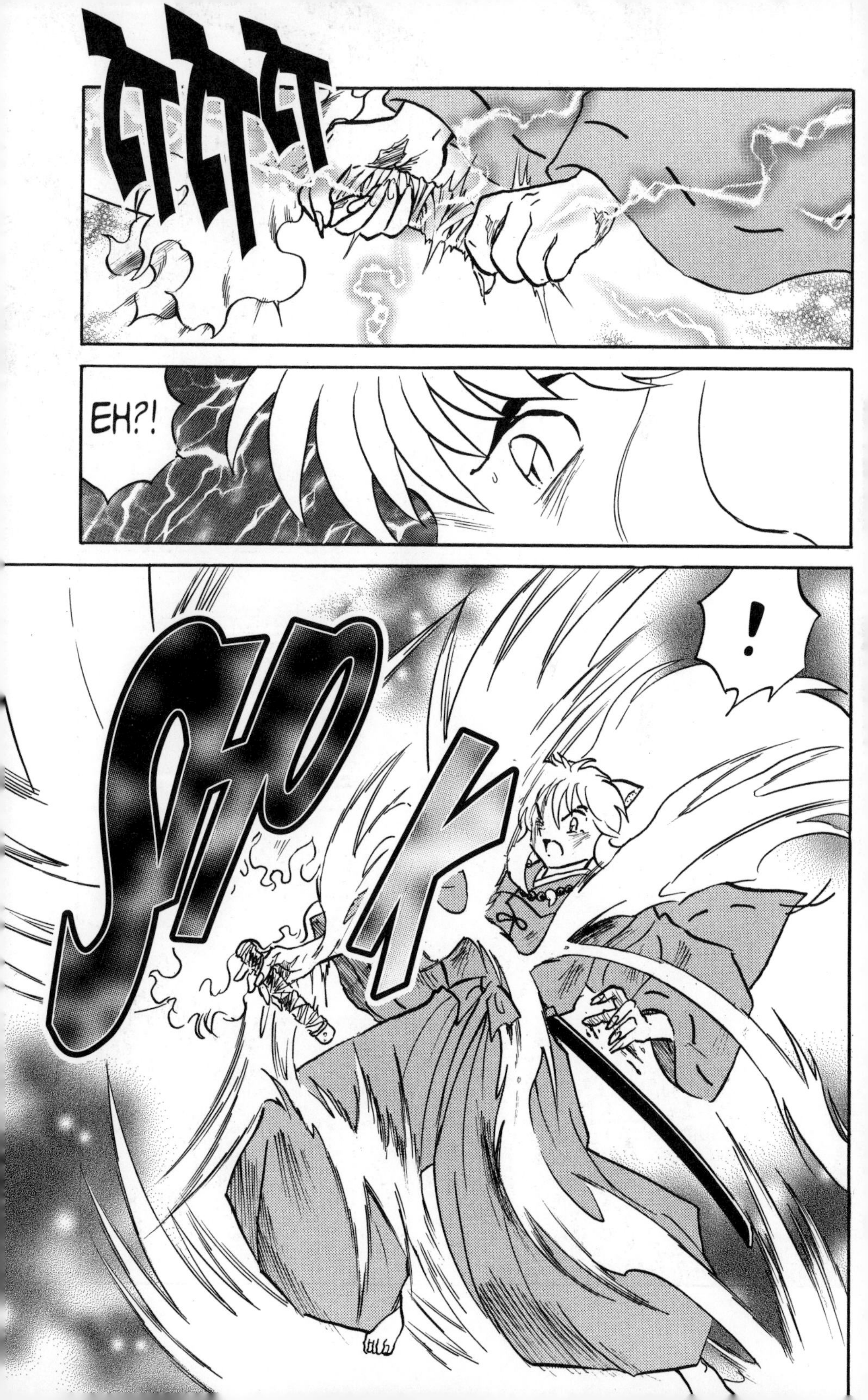
EH?!
!

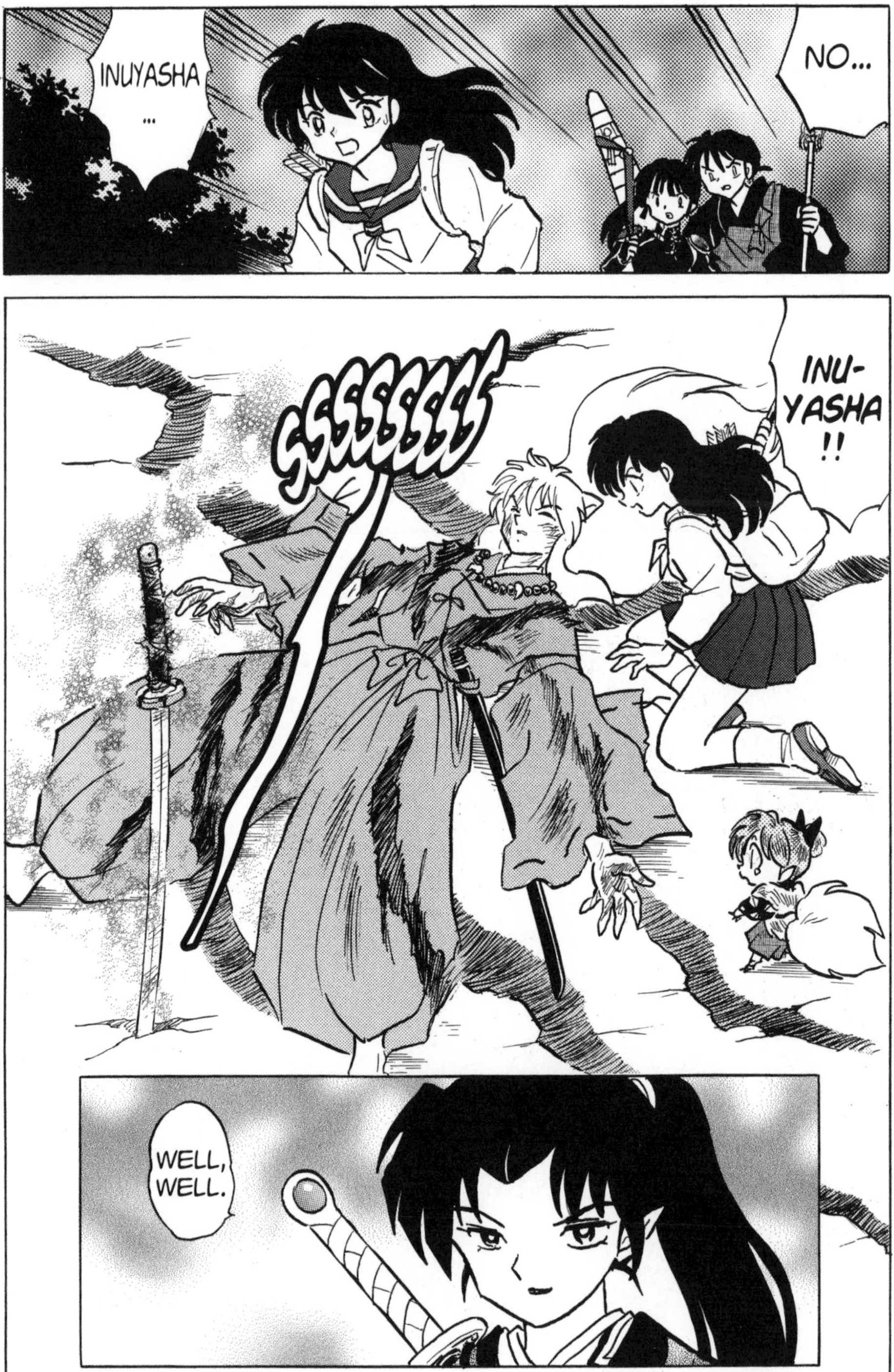
NO...
INUYASHA ...
INU-YASHA !!
SSSSSSSS
WELL, WELL.

Volume 41
The Invincible Blade

SCROLL ONE
THE INVINCIBLE BLADE

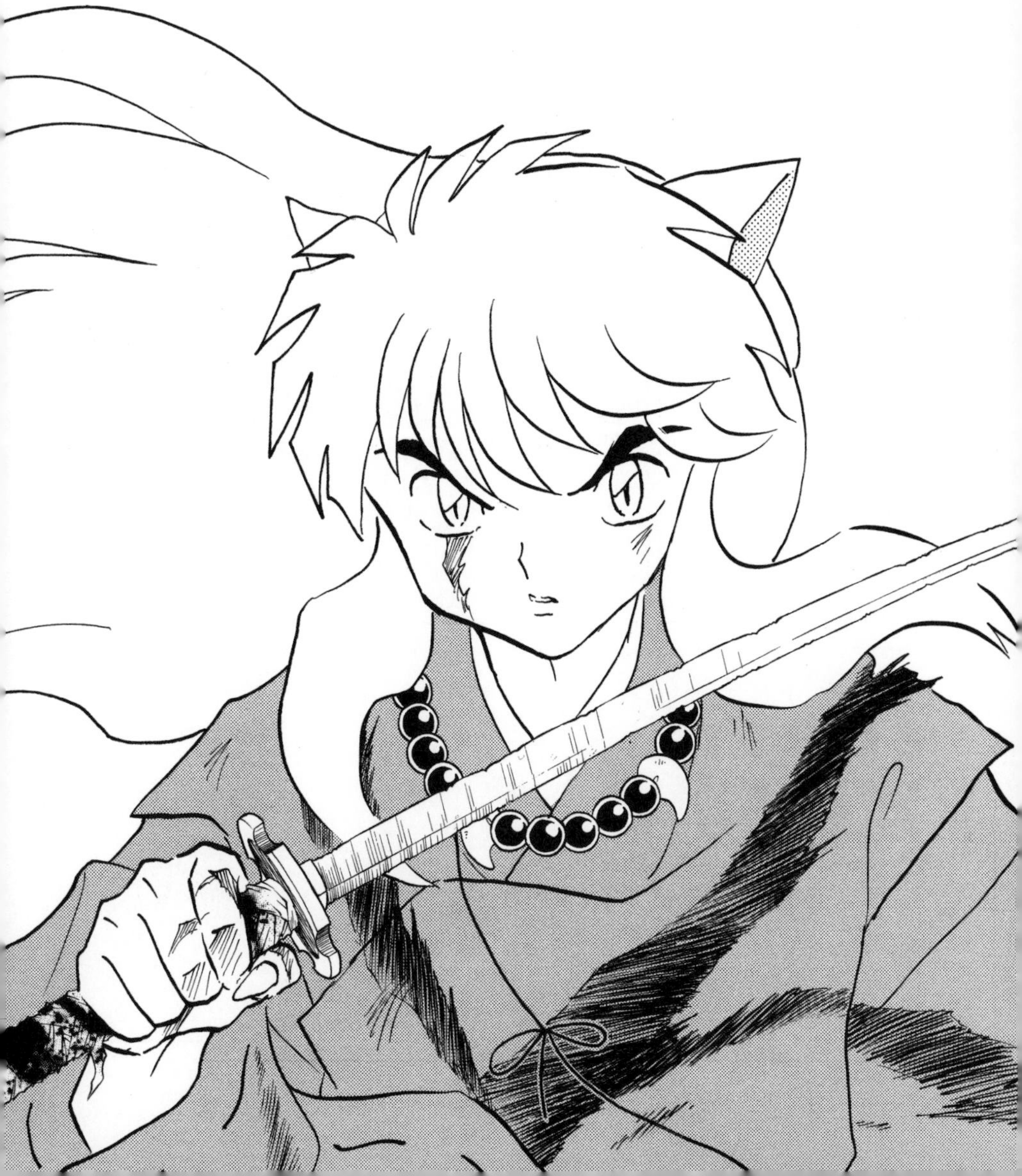

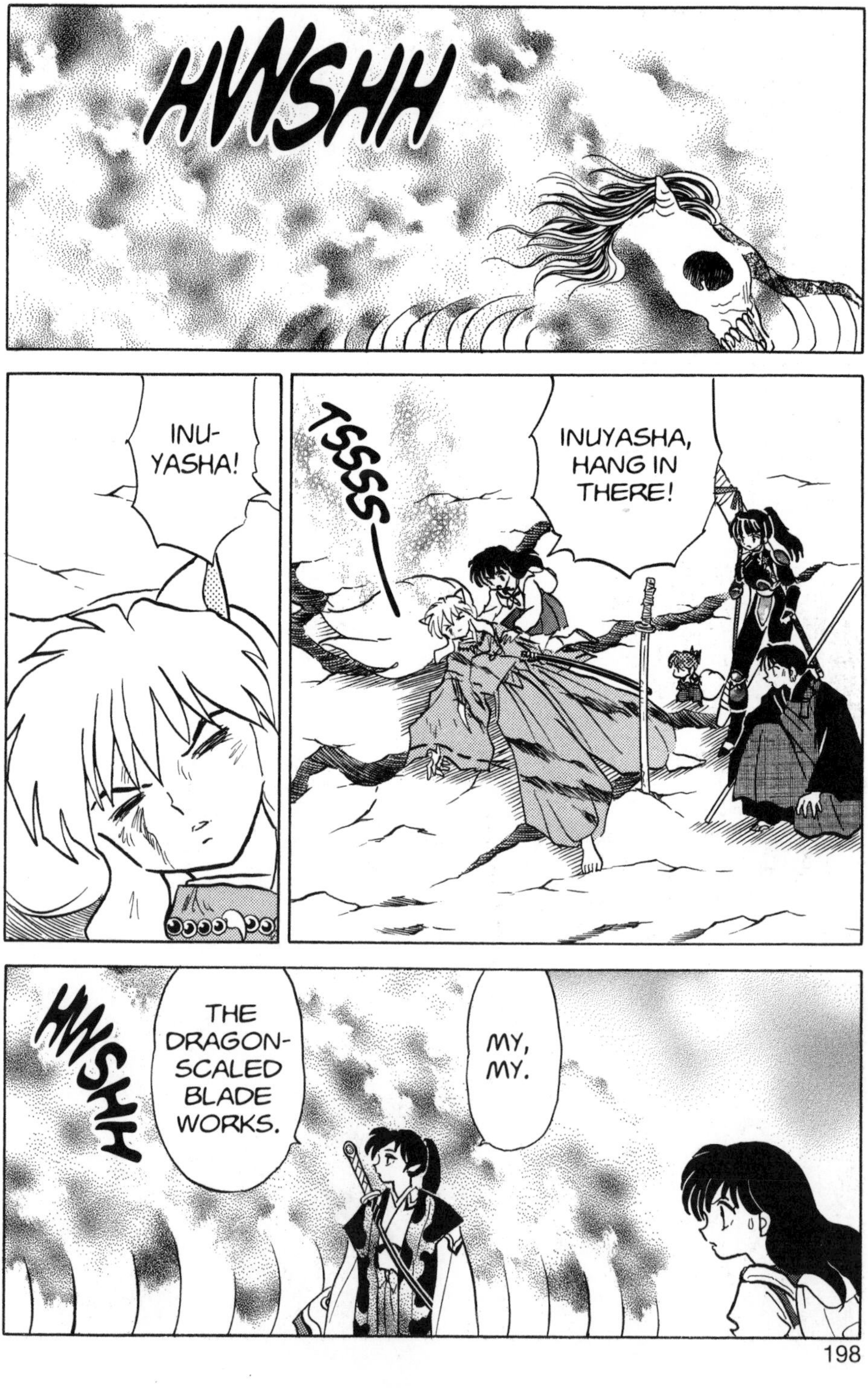
HWSHH
TSSSS—
INUYASHA, HANG IN THERE!
INU-YASHA!
MY, MY.
THE DRAGON-SCALED BLADE WORKS.
HWSHH

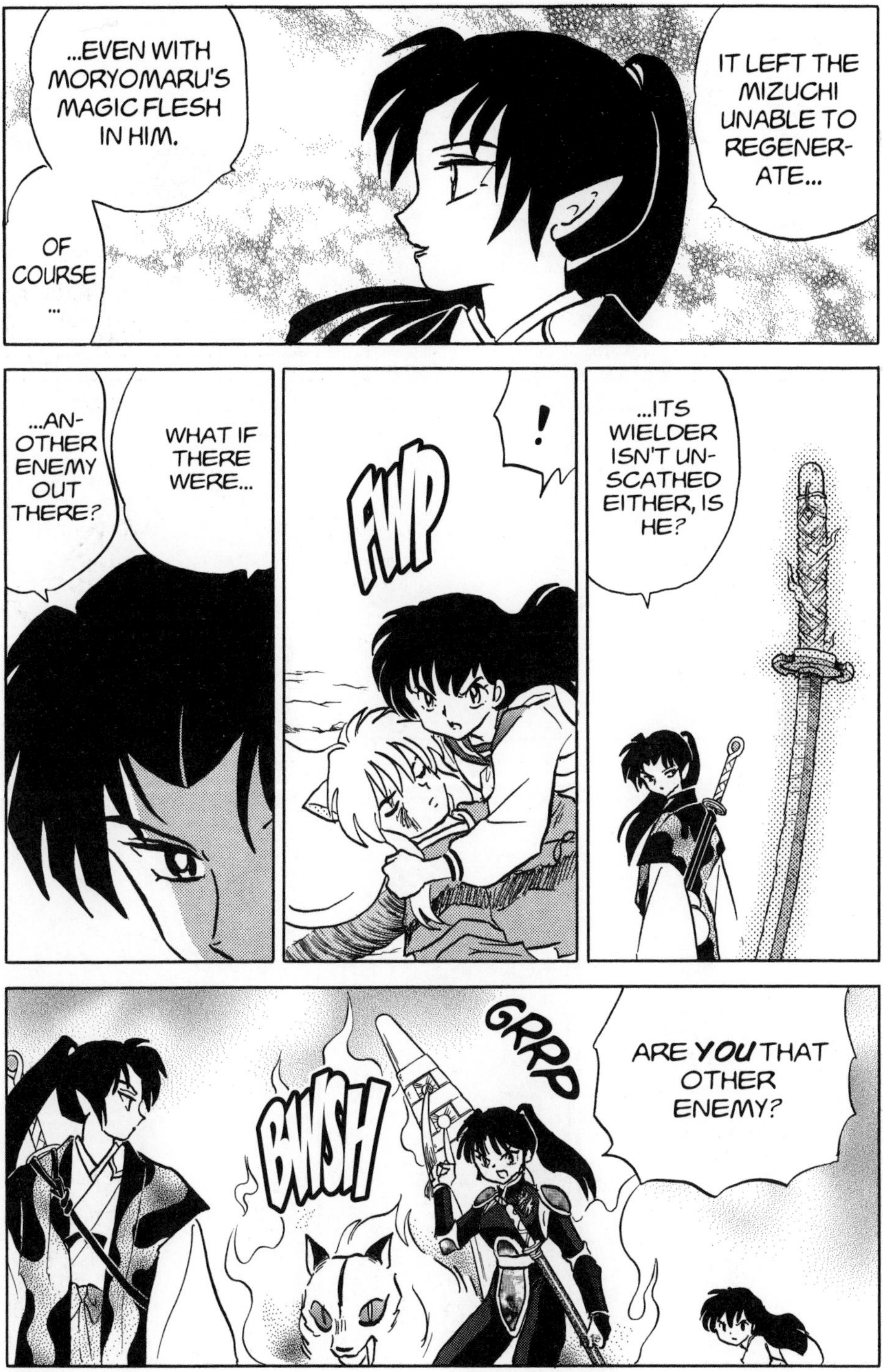
IT LEFT THE MIZUCHI UNABLE TO REGENERATE...
...EVEN WITH MORYOMARU'S MAGIC FLESH IN HIM.
OF COURSE ...
...ITS WIELDER ISN'T UNSCATHED EITHER, IS HE?
!
FWP
WHAT IF THERE WERE...
...ANOTHER ENEMY OUT THERE?
ARE **YOU** THAT OTHER ENEMY?
GRRP
BWSH

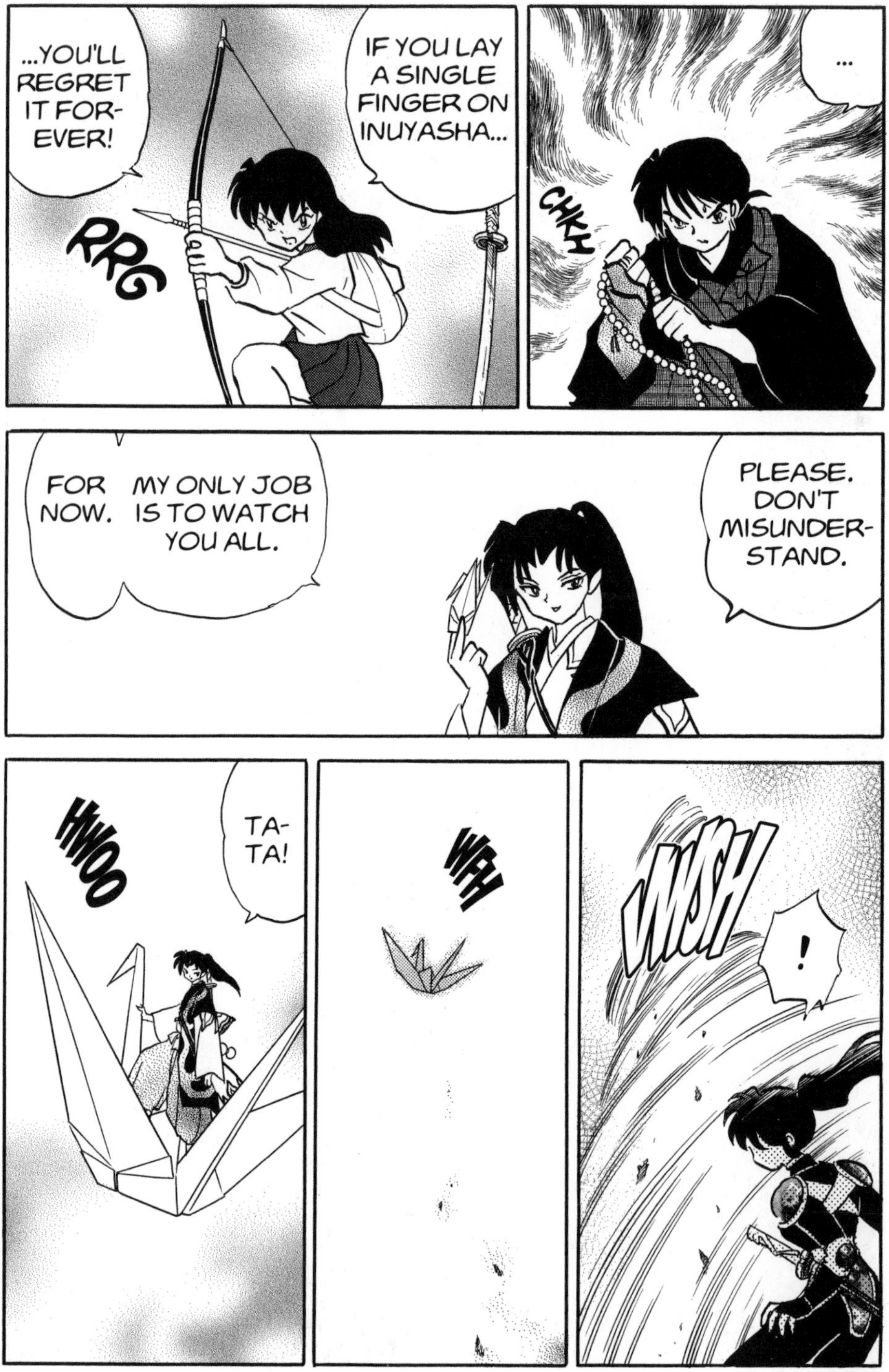
...
CHKH
IF YOU LAY A SINGLE FINGER ON INUYASHA...
...YOU'LL REGRET IT FOR-EVER!
RRG
PLEASE. DON'T MISUNDER-STAND.
MY ONLY JOB IS TO WATCH YOU ALL.
FOR NOW.
VWSH
!
WSH
TA-TA!
HWOO

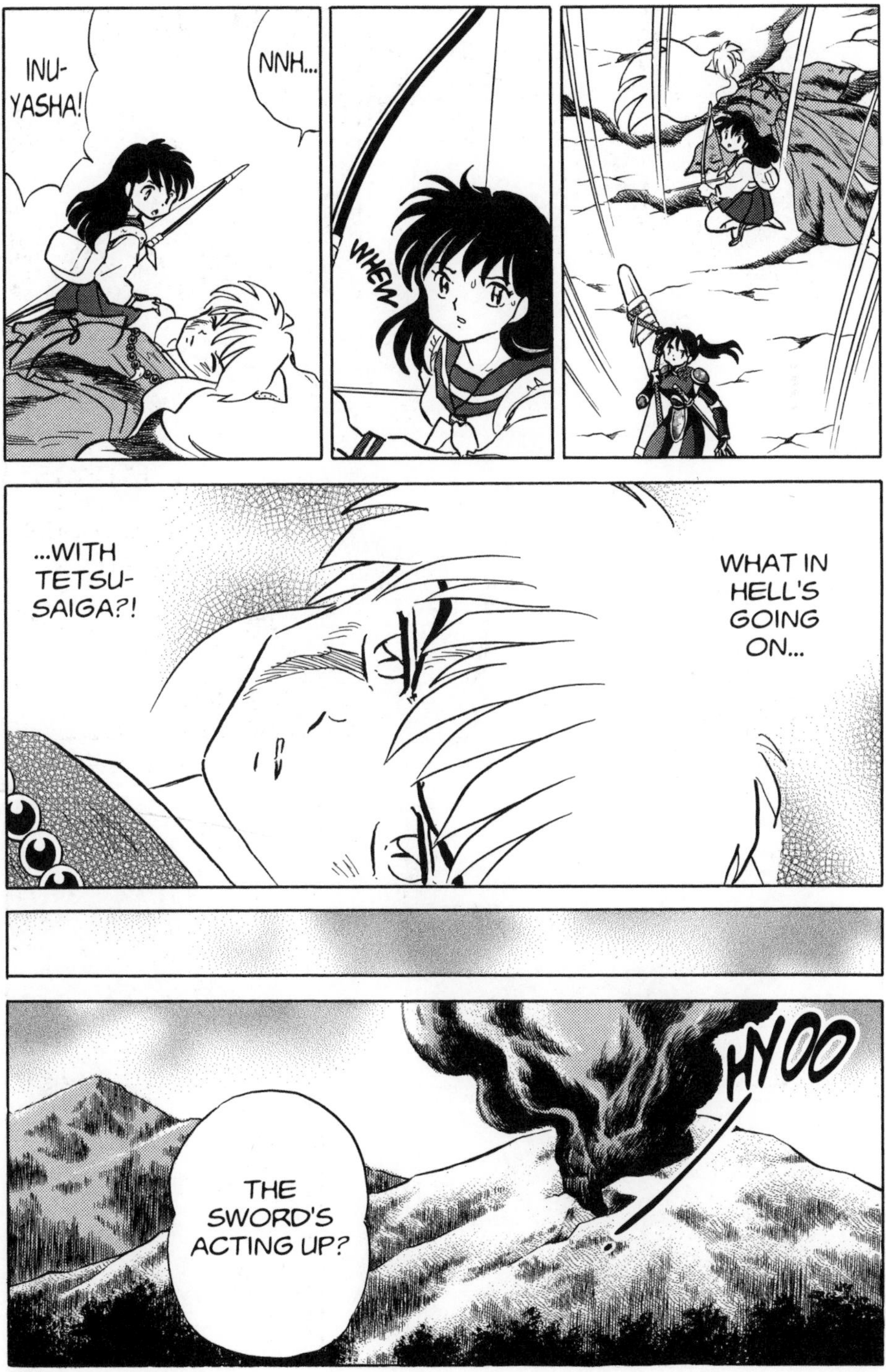
NNH...
WHEW
INU-YASHA!
WHAT IN HELL'S GOING ON...
...WITH TETSU-SAIGA?!
HYOO
THE SWORD'S ACTING UP?

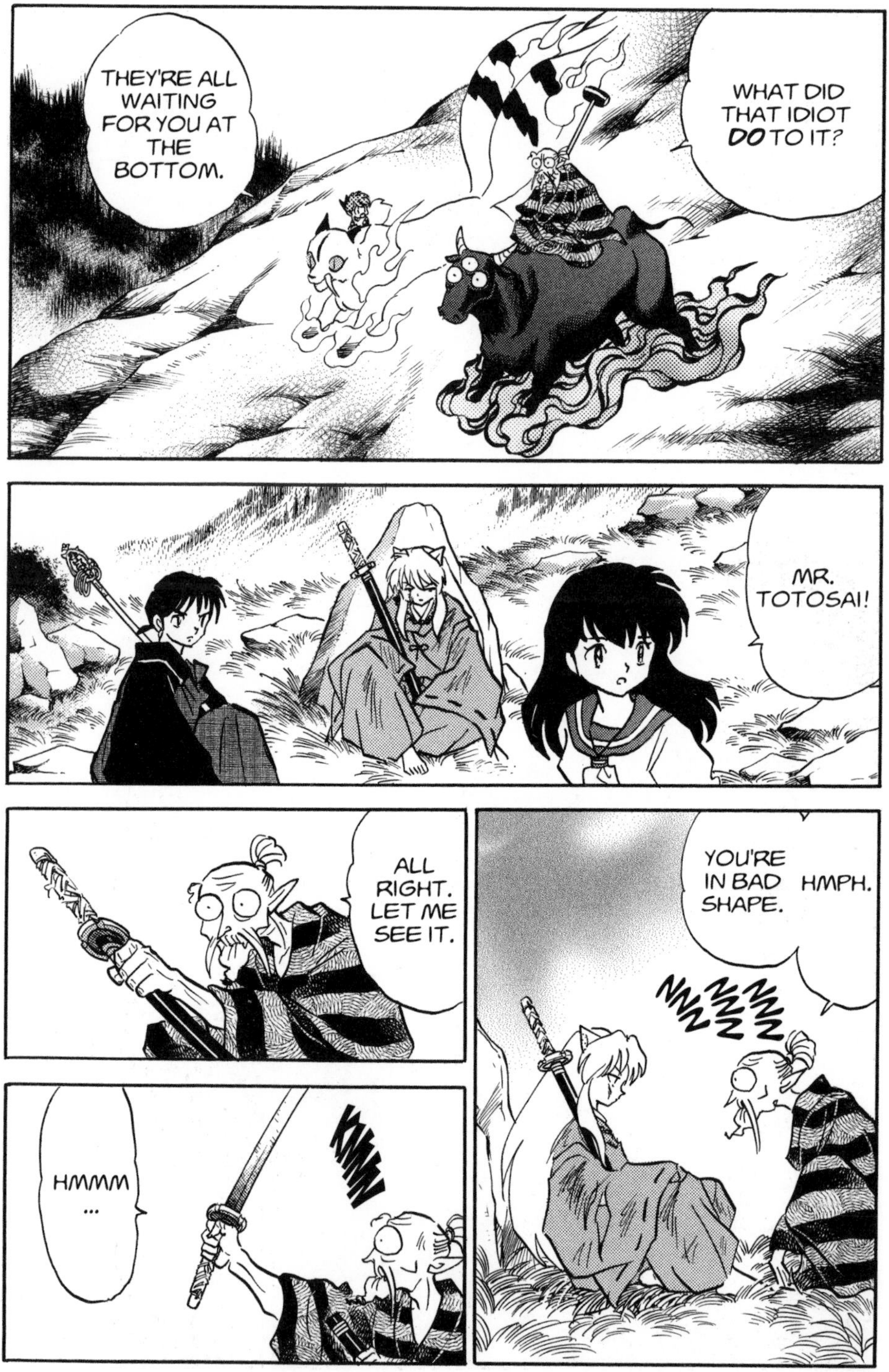
WHAT DID THAT IDIOT **DO** TO IT?
THEY'RE ALL WAITING FOR YOU AT THE BOTTOM.
MR. TOTOSAI!
HMPH.
YOU'RE IN BAD SHAPE.
ALL RIGHT. LET ME SEE IT.
HMMM ...

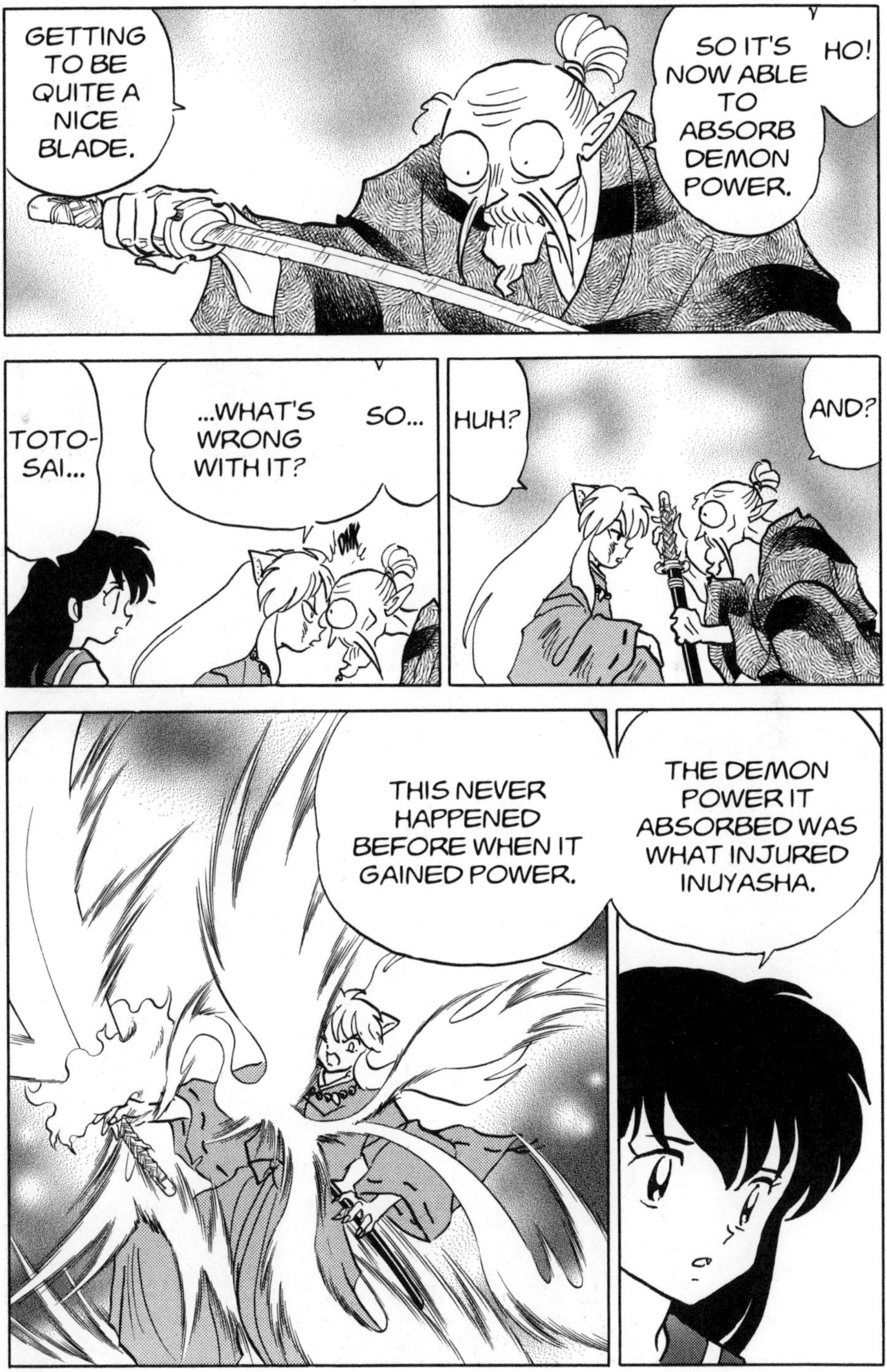
HO!
SO IT'S NOW ABLE TO ABSORB DEMON POWER.
GETTING TO BE QUITE A NICE BLADE.
AND?
HUH?
SO... ...WHAT'S WRONG WITH IT?
TOTO-SAI...
THE DEMON POWER IT ABSORBED WAS WHAT INJURED INUYASHA.
THIS NEVER HAPPENED BEFORE WHEN IT GAINED POWER.

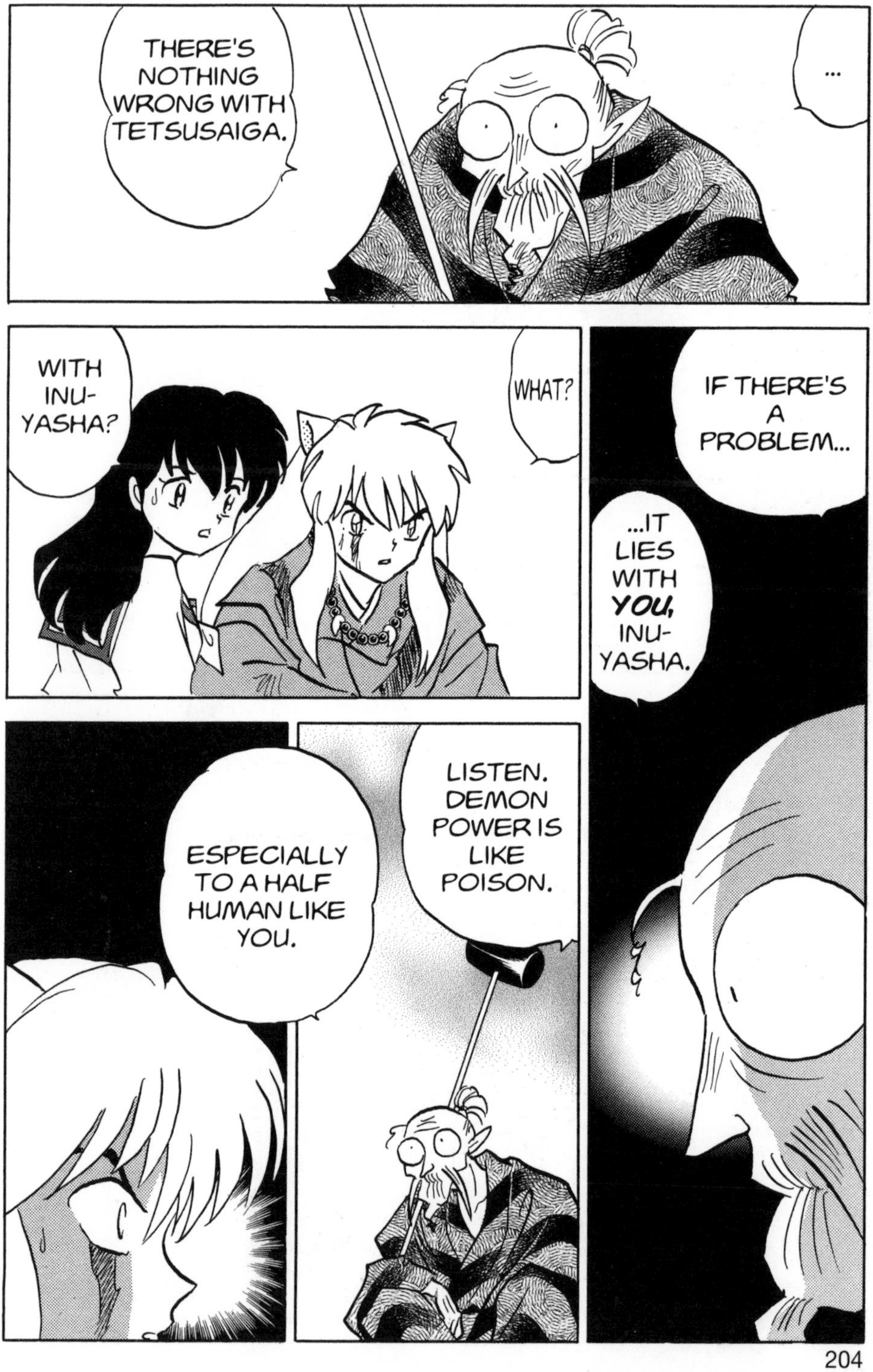
...
THERE'S NOTHING WRONG WITH TETSUSAIGA.
IF THERE'S A PROBLEM...
...IT LIES WITH **YOU,** INU-YASHA.
WHAT?
WITH INU-YASHA?
LISTEN. DEMON POWER IS LIKE POISON.
ESPECIALLY TO A HALF HUMAN LIKE YOU.

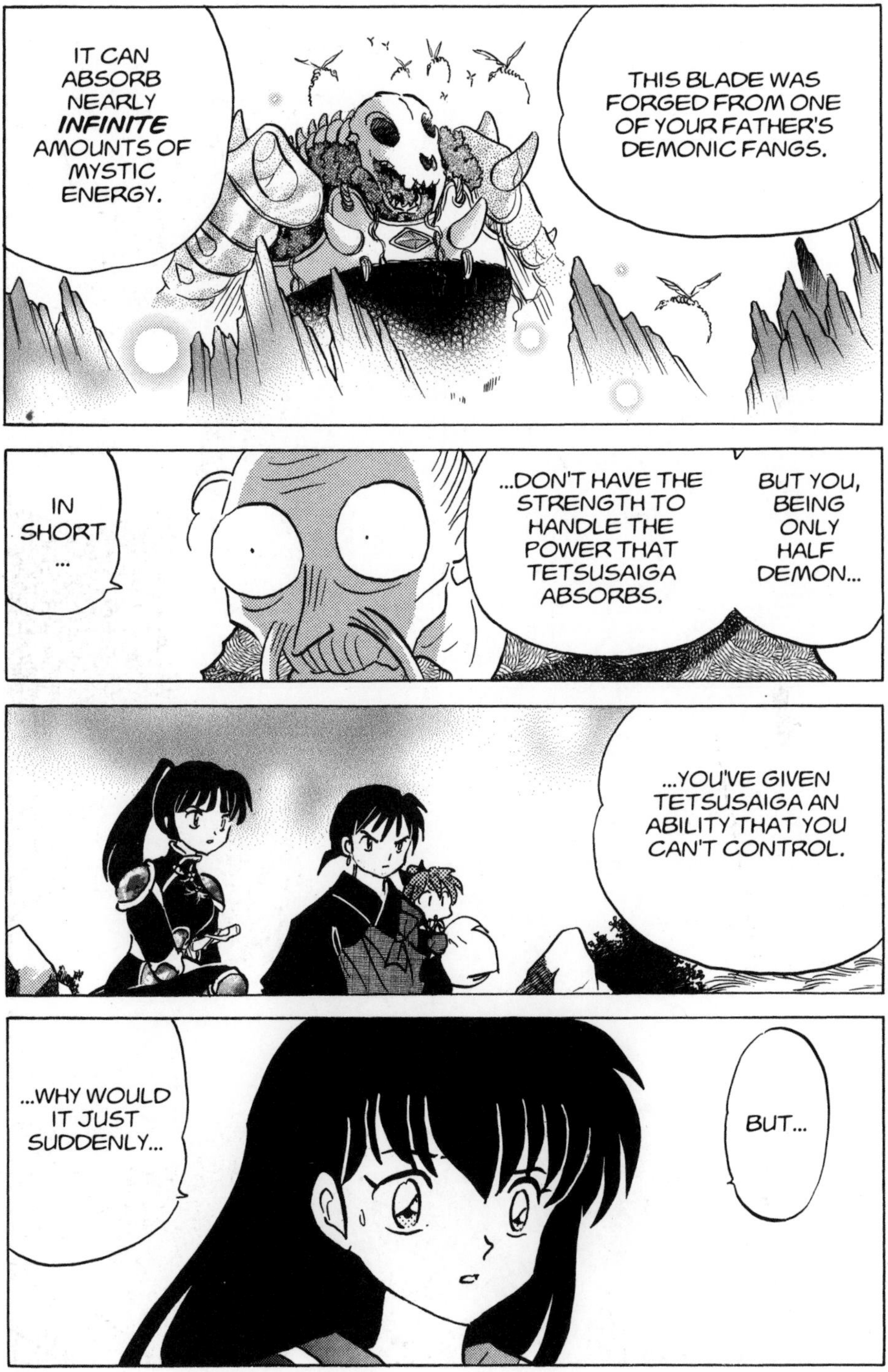
THIS BLADE WAS FORGED FROM ONE OF YOUR FATHER'S DEMONIC FANGS.
IT CAN ABSORB NEARLY ***INFINITE*** AMOUNTS OF MYSTIC ENERGY.
BUT YOU, BEING ONLY HALF DEMON...
...DON'T HAVE THE STRENGTH TO HANDLE THE POWER THAT TETSUSAIGA ABSORBS.
IN SHORT ...
...YOU'VE GIVEN TETSUSAIGA AN ABILITY THAT YOU CAN'T CONTROL.
BUT...
...WHY WOULD IT JUST SUDDENLY...

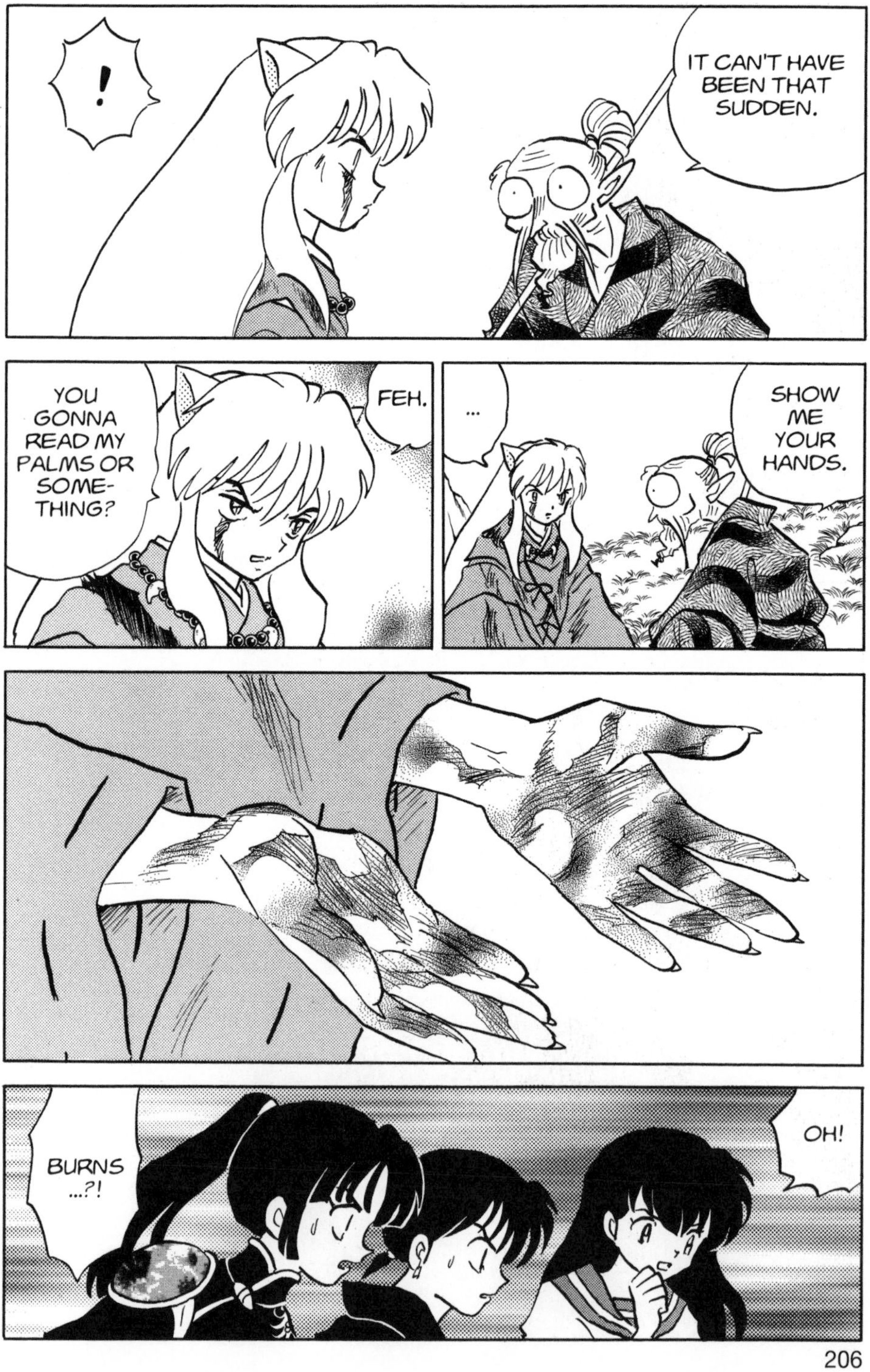
IT CAN'T HAVE BEEN THAT SUDDEN.
!
SHOW ME YOUR HANDS.
...
FEH.
YOU GONNA READ MY PALMS OR SOME-THING?
OH!
BURNS ...?!

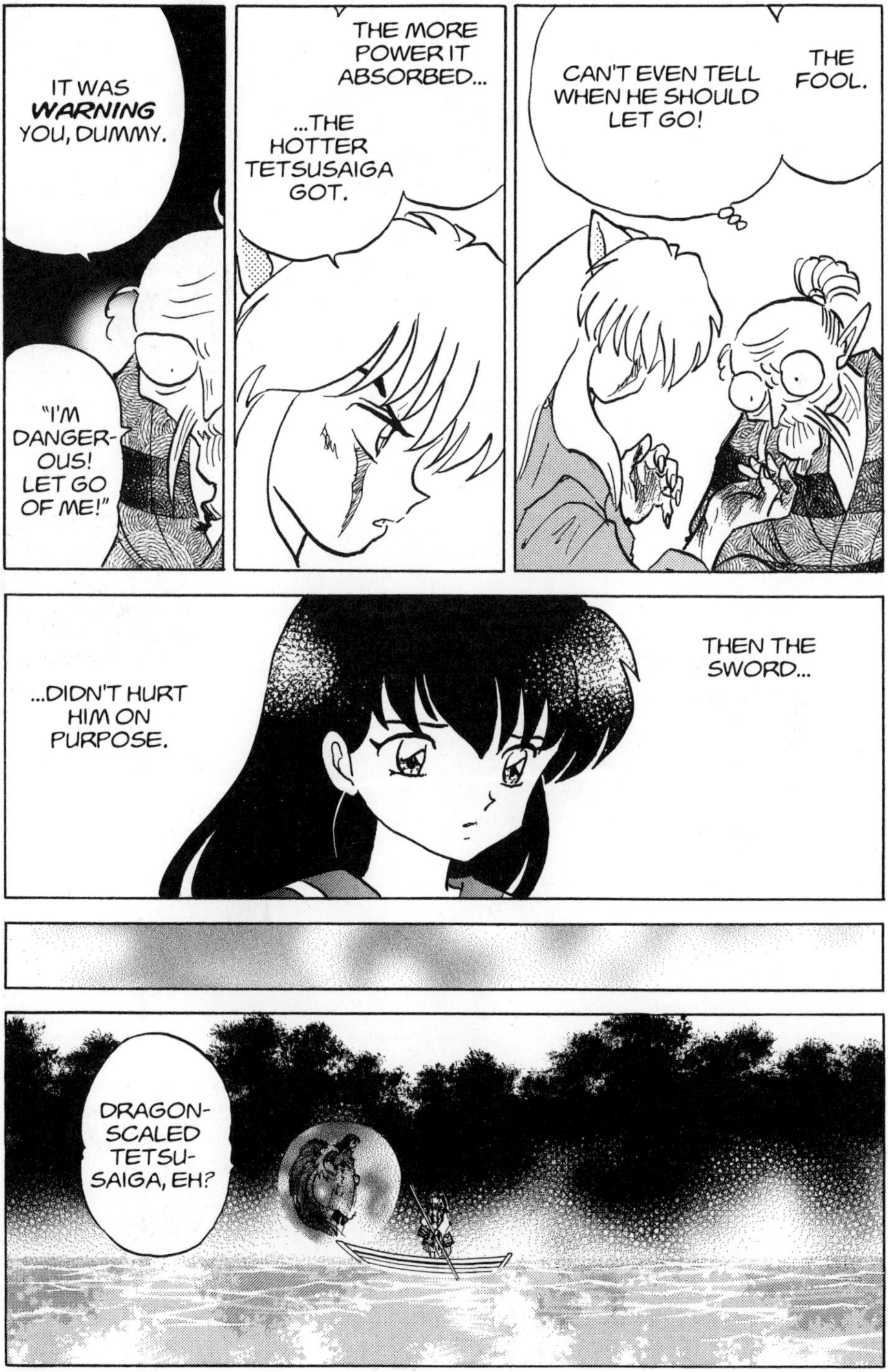
THE FOOL.
CAN'T EVEN TELL WHEN HE SHOULD LET GO!
THE MORE POWER IT ABSORBED...
...THE HOTTER TETSUSAIGA GOT.
IT WAS **WARNING** YOU, DUMMY.
"I'M DANGER-OUS! LET GO OF ME!"
THEN THE SWORD...
...DIDN'T HURT HIM ON PURPOSE.
DRAGON-SCALED TETSU-SAIGA, EH?

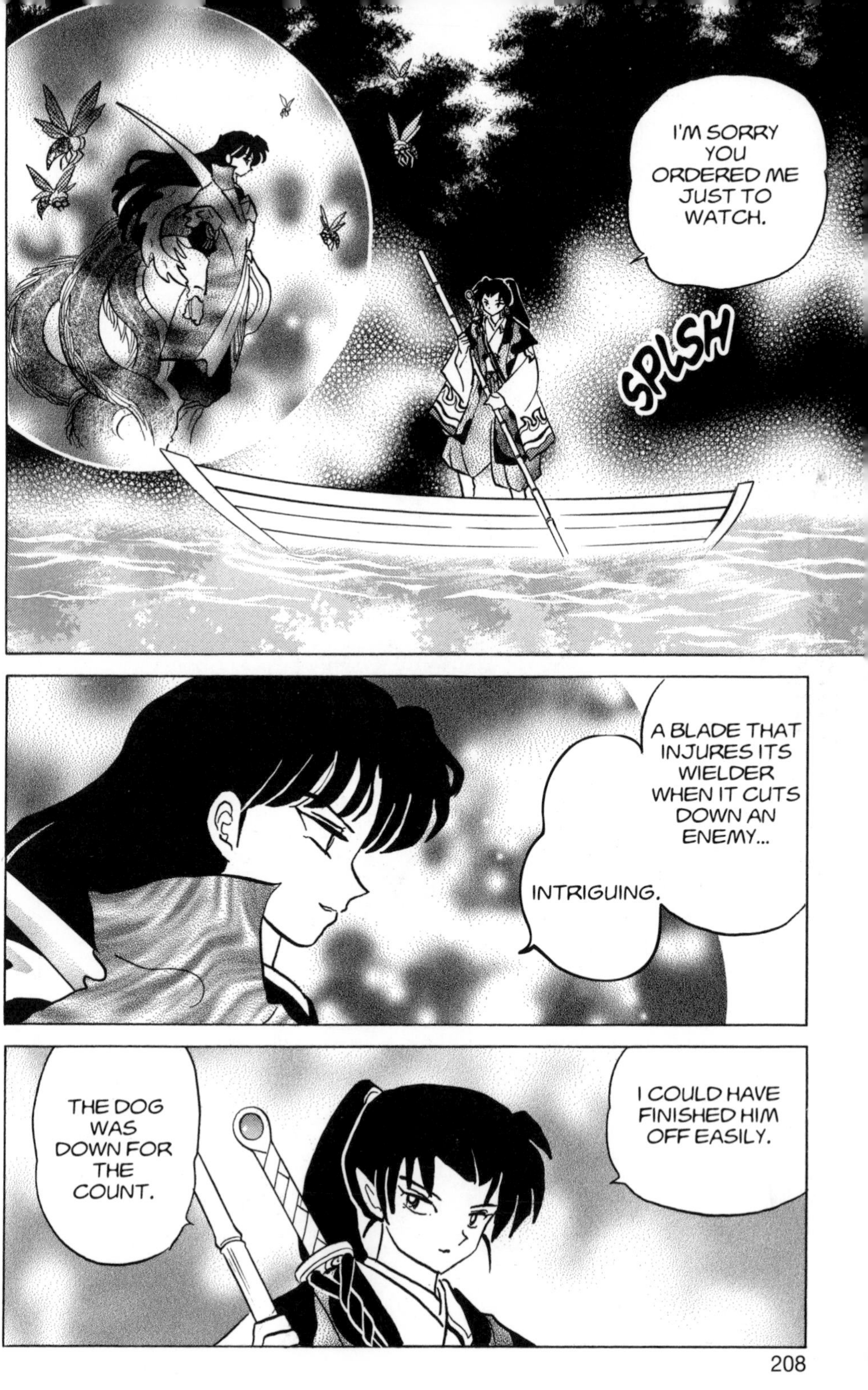
I'M SORRY YOU ORDERED ME JUST TO WATCH.
SPLSH
A BLADE THAT INJURES ITS WIELDER WHEN IT CUTS DOWN AN ENEMY...
INTRIGUING.
I COULD HAVE FINISHED HIM OFF EASILY.
THE DOG WAS DOWN FOR THE COUNT.

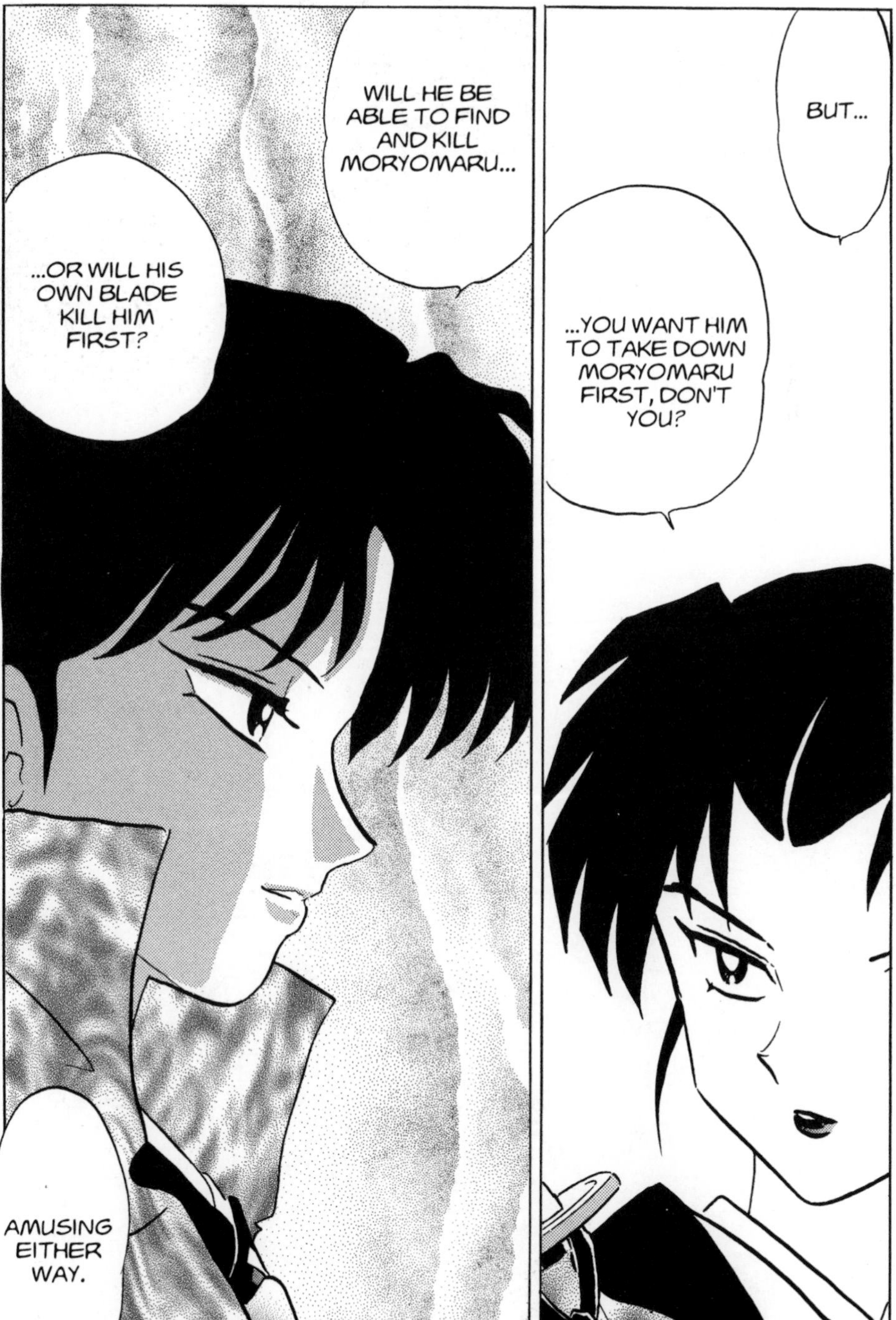
BUT...
...YOU WANT HIM TO TAKE DOWN MORYOMARU FIRST, DON'T YOU?
WILL HE BE ABLE TO FIND AND KILL MORYOMARU...
...OR WILL HIS OWN BLADE KILL HIM FIRST?
AMUSING EITHER WAY.

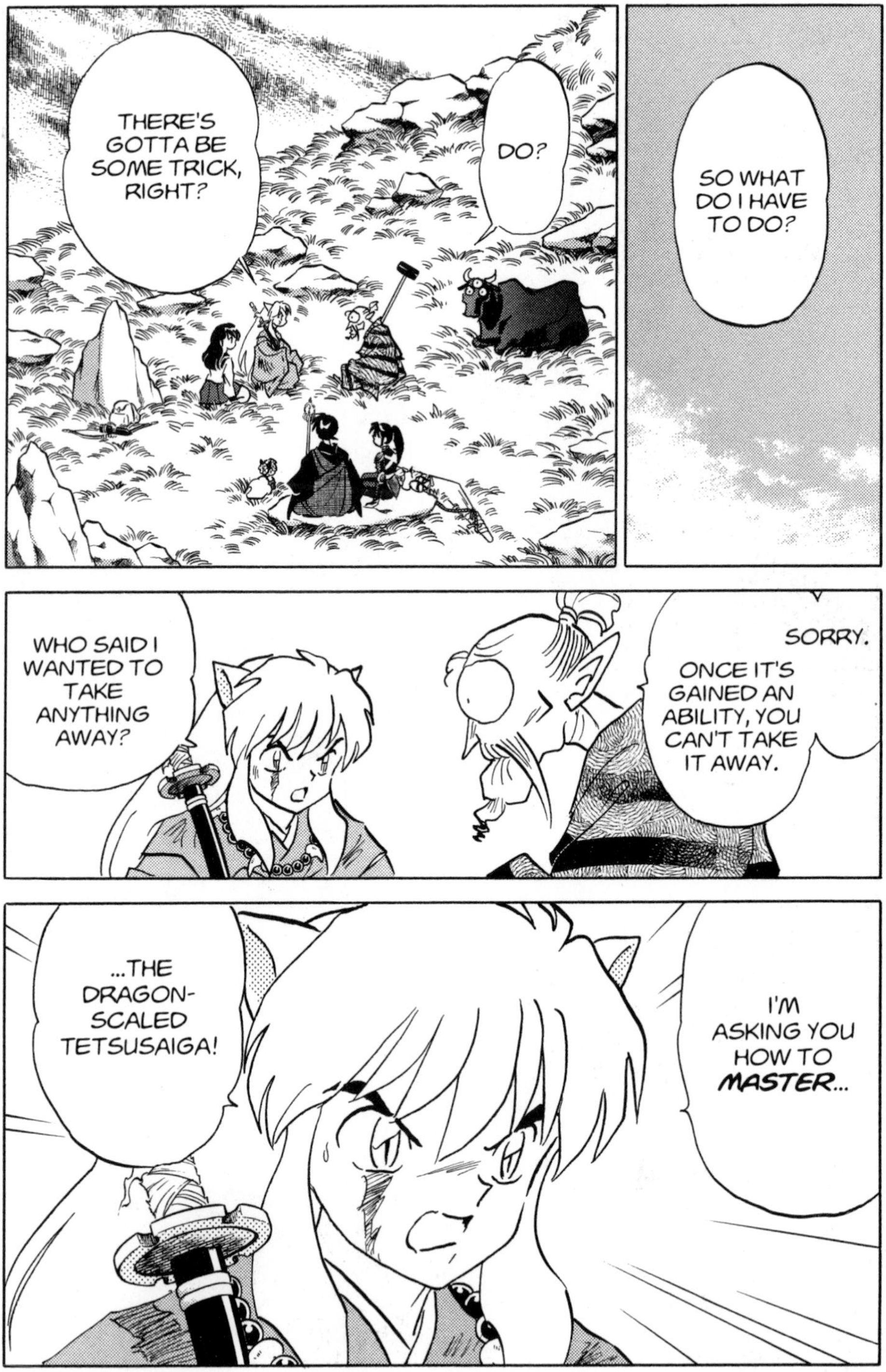
SO WHAT DO I HAVE TO DO?
DO?
THERE'S GOTTA BE SOME TRICK, RIGHT?
SORRY.
ONCE IT'S GAINED AN ABILITY, YOU CAN'T TAKE IT AWAY.
WHO SAID I WANTED TO TAKE ANYTHING AWAY?
I'M ASKING YOU HOW TO **MASTER**...
...THE DRAGON-SCALED TETSUSAIGA!

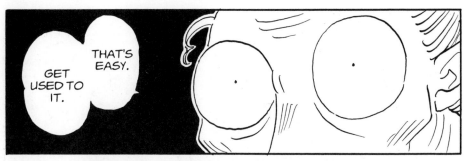

THAT'S EASY.
GET USED TO IT.
...YOU THINK I'M JOKING?
BONK...
YOU MEAN HE HAS TO KEEP USING IT?
BUT IT'S **HURTING** HIM!
THAT'S WHY HE NEEDS TO CHOOSE HIS OPPONENTS CAREFULLY.
INUYASHA, ABOUT THIS WATER DEMON...
YOU FINALLY KILLED IT BY SLICING IT UP?
YEAH, SO?

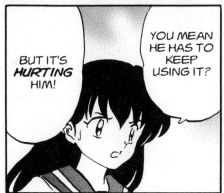

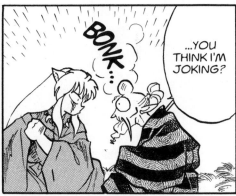

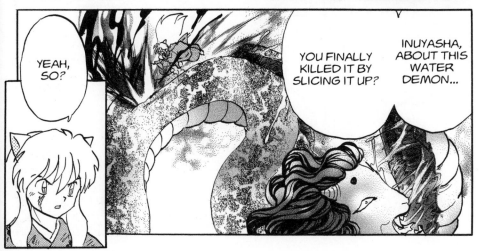

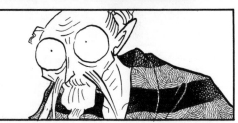

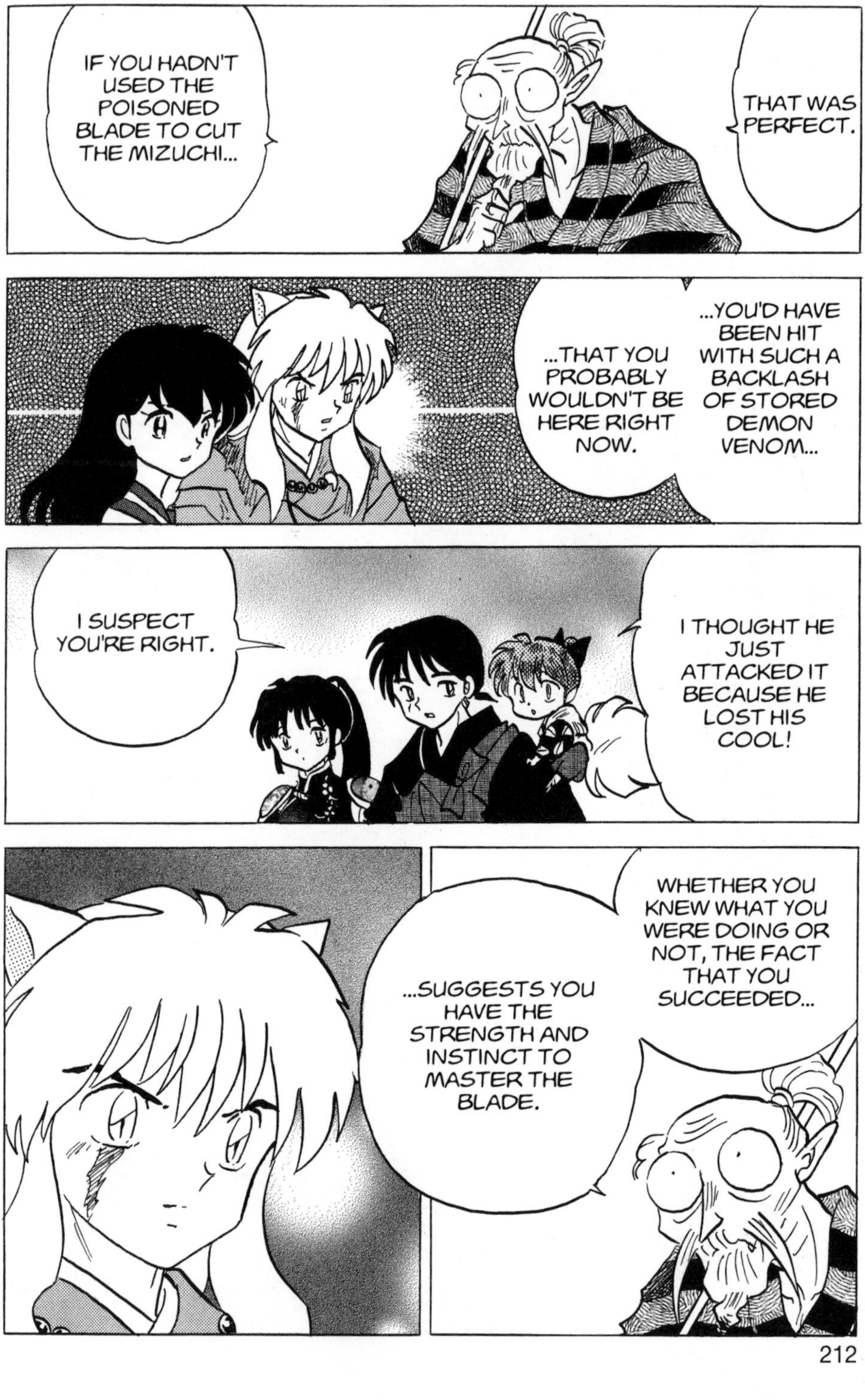
THAT WAS PERFECT.
IF YOU HADN'T USED THE POISONED BLADE TO CUT THE MIZUCHI...
...YOU'D HAVE BEEN HIT WITH SUCH A BACKLASH OF STORED DEMON VENOM...
...THAT YOU PROBABLY WOULDN'T BE HERE RIGHT NOW.
I THOUGHT HE JUST ATTACKED IT BECAUSE HE LOST HIS COOL!
I SUSPECT YOU'RE RIGHT.
WHETHER YOU KNEW WHAT YOU WERE DOING OR NOT, THE FACT THAT YOU SUCCEEDED...
...SUGGESTS YOU HAVE THE STRENGTH AND INSTINCT TO MASTER THE BLADE.

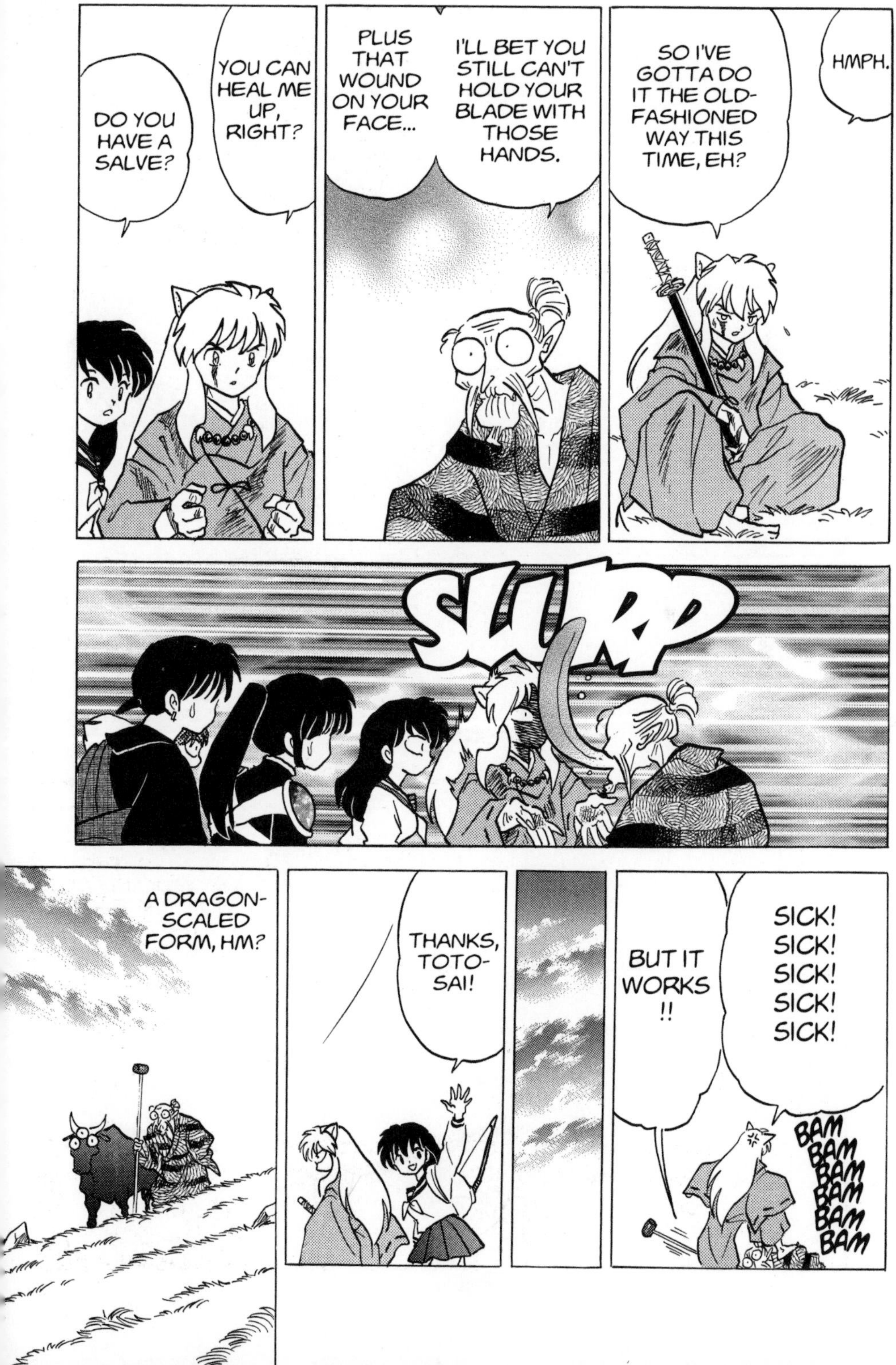
HMPH.
SO I'VE GOTTA DO IT THE OLD-FASHIONED WAY THIS TIME, EH?
I'LL BET YOU STILL CAN'T HOLD YOUR BLADE WITH THOSE HANDS.
PLUS THAT WOUND ON YOUR FACE...
YOU CAN HEAL ME UP, RIGHT?
DO YOU HAVE A SALVE?
SLURP
SICK! SICK! SICK! SICK! SICK!
BUT IT WORKS !!
BAM BAM BAM BAM BAM BAM BAM
THANKS, TOTO-SAI!
A DRAGON-SCALED FORM, HM?

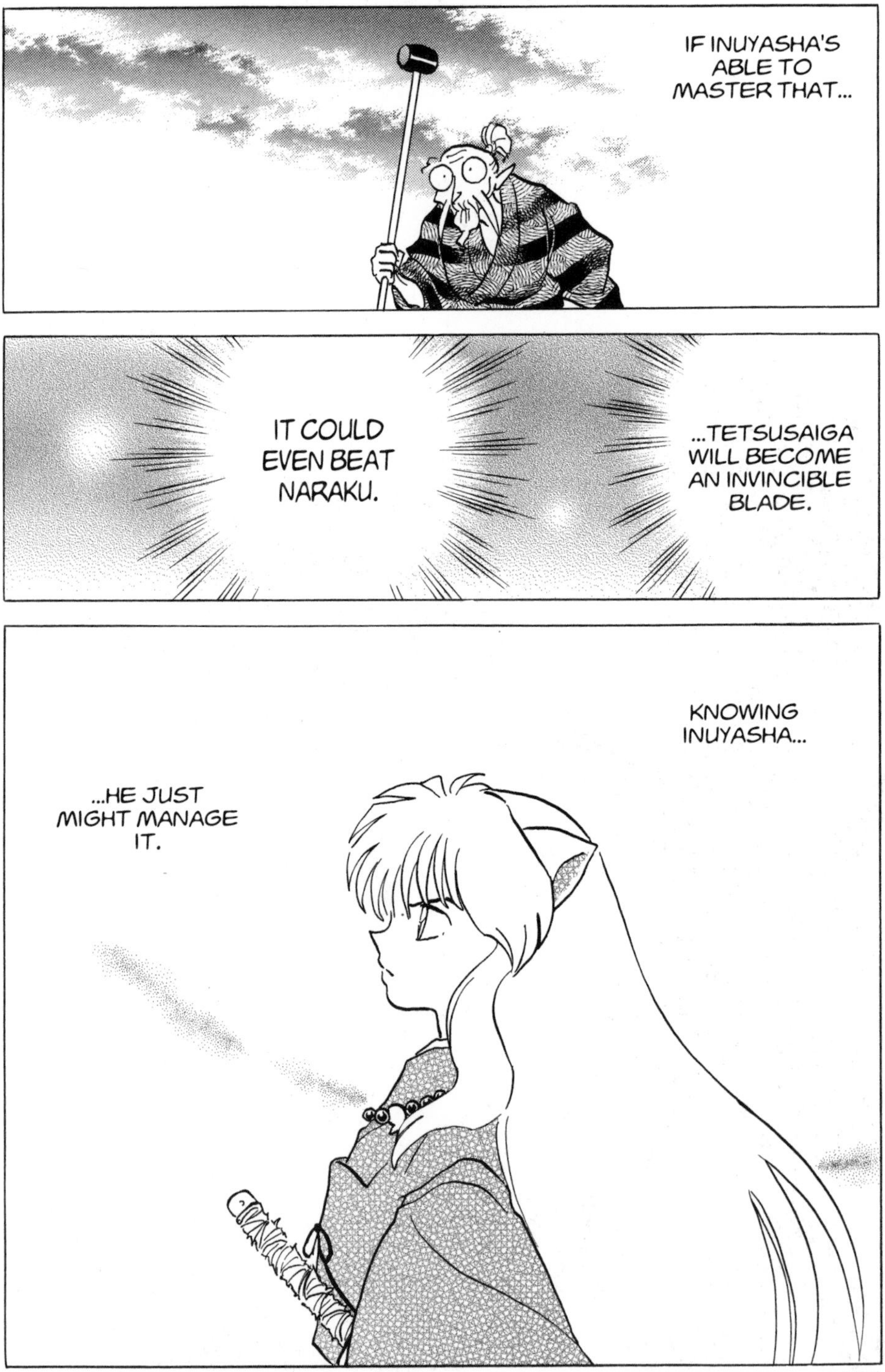
IF INUYASHA'S ABLE TO MASTER THAT...
...TETSUSAIGA WILL BECOME AN INVINCIBLE BLADE.
IT COULD EVEN BEAT NARAKU.
KNOWING INUYASHA...
...HE JUST MIGHT MANAGE IT.

SCROLL TWO
MEIOJU

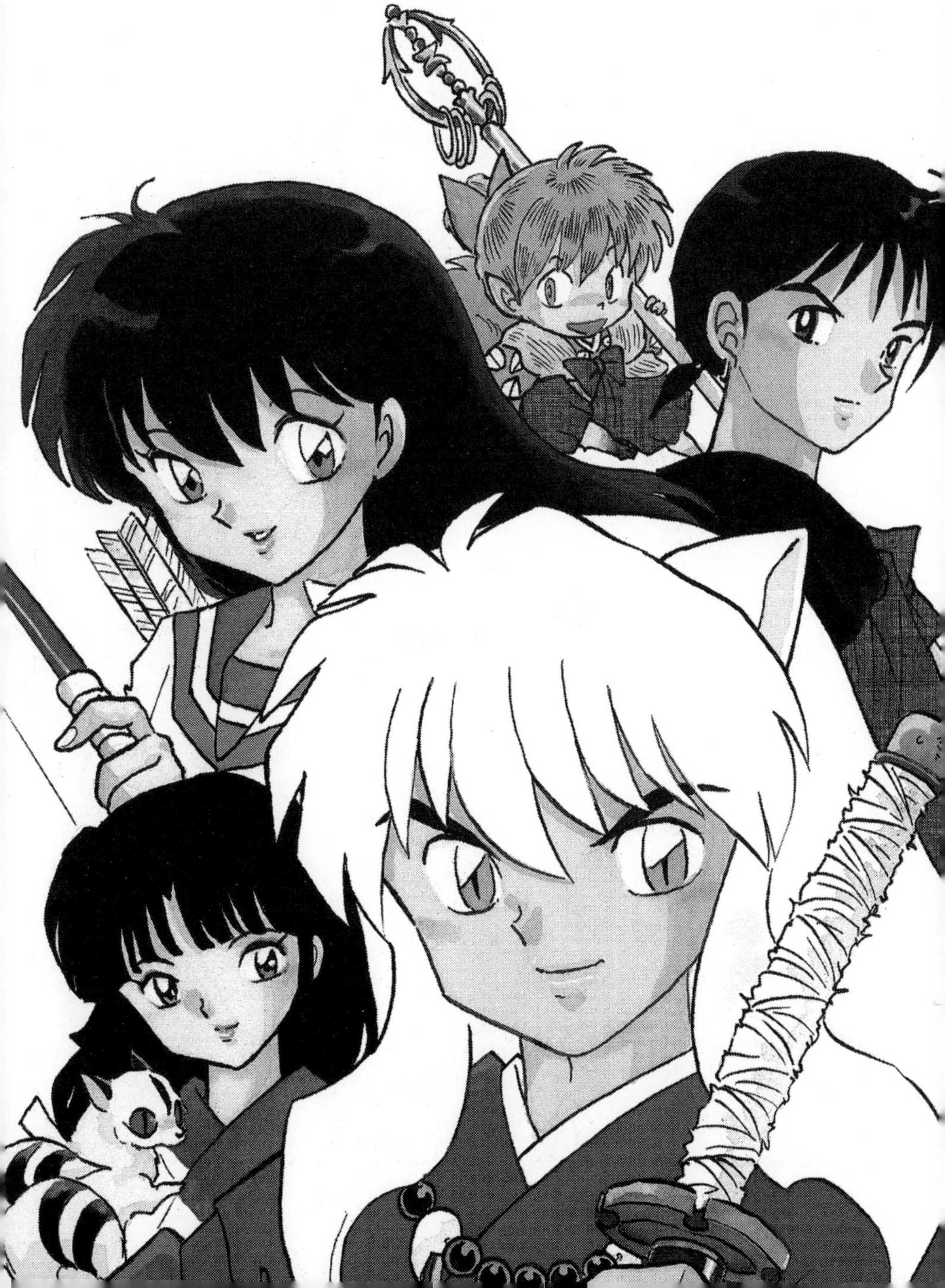

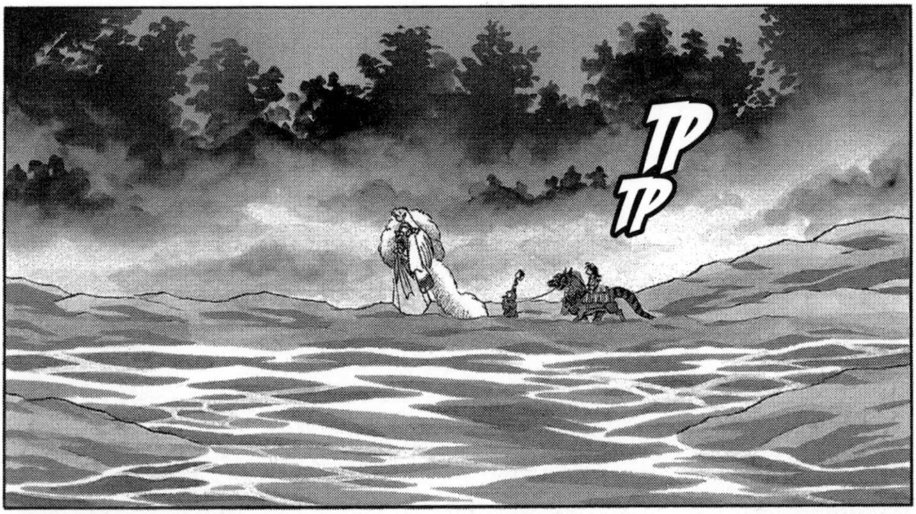
TP
TP

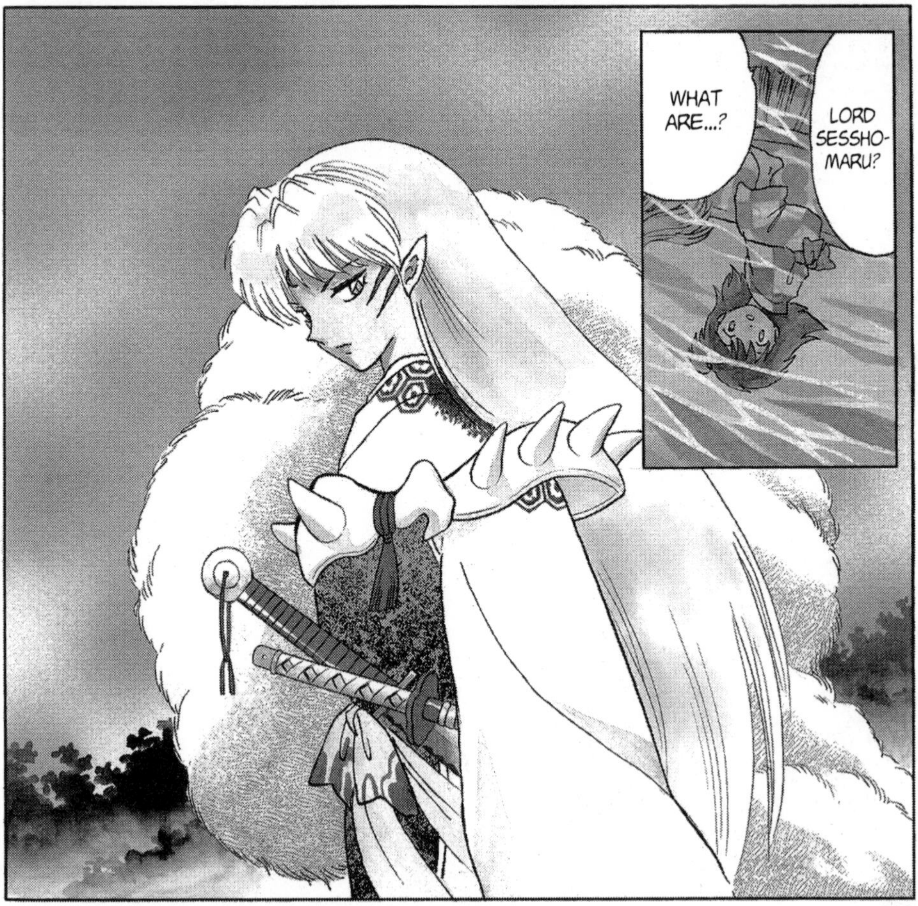
LORD SESSHO-MARU?
WHAT ARE...?

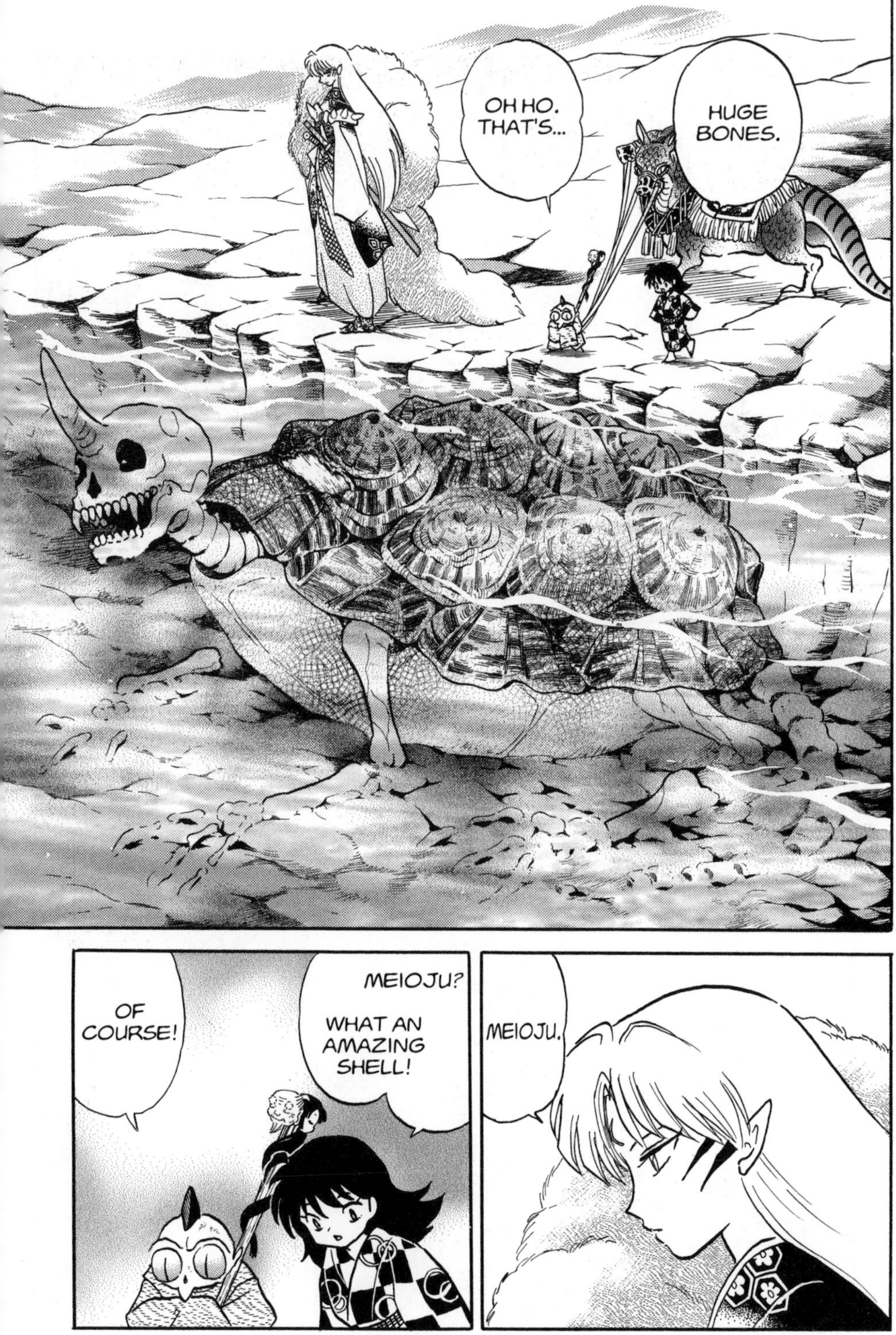
HUGE BONES.
OH HO. THAT'S...
MEIOJU.
MEIOJU?
WHAT AN AMAZING SHELL!
OF COURSE!

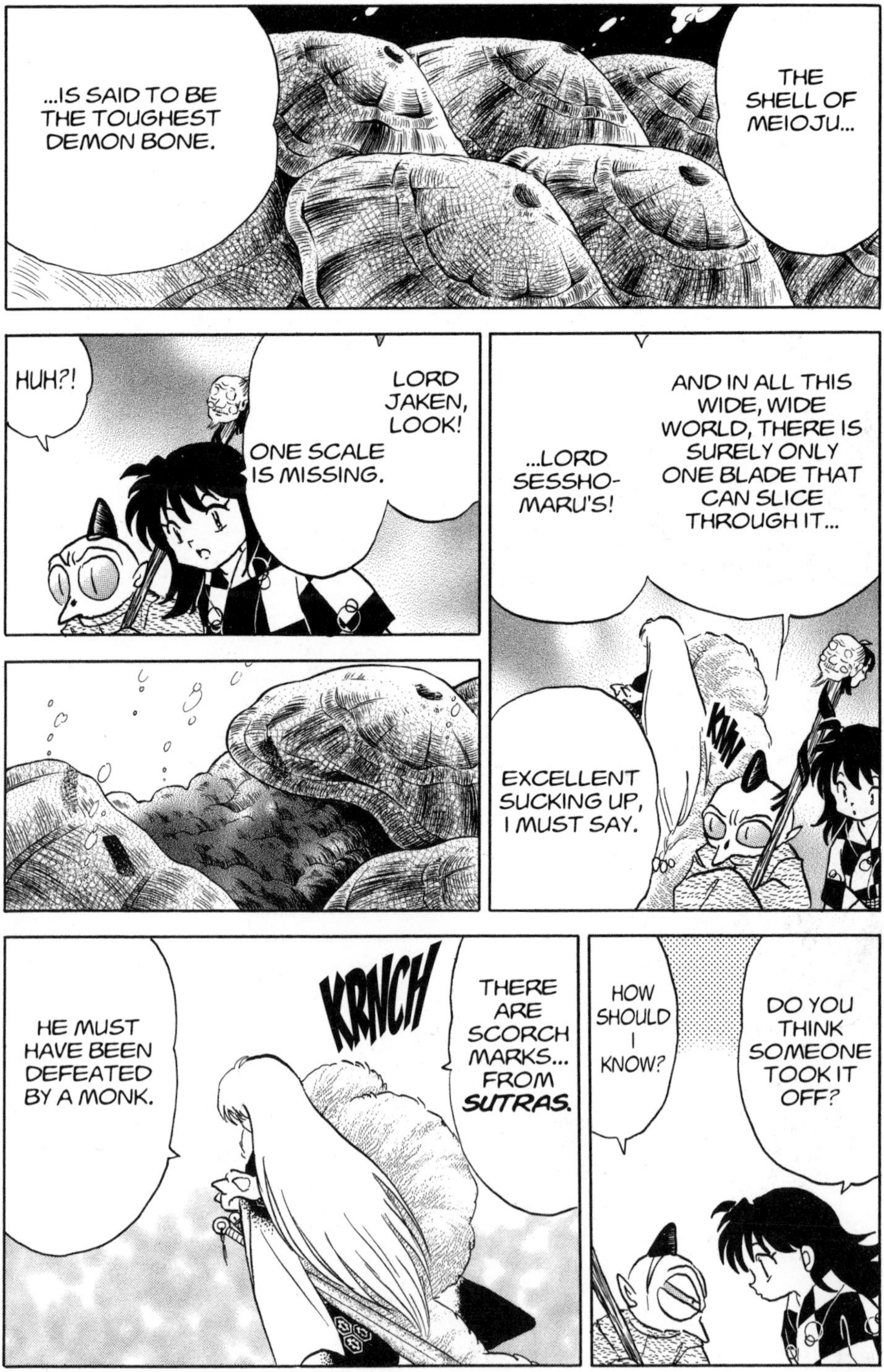
THE SHELL OF MEIOJU...
...IS SAID TO BE THE TOUGHEST DEMON BONE.
AND IN ALL THIS WIDE, WIDE WORLD, THERE IS SURELY ONLY ONE BLADE THAT CAN SLICE THROUGH IT...
...LORD SESSHOMARU'S!
EXCELLENT SUCKING UP, I MUST SAY.
LORD JAKEN, LOOK!
ONE SCALE IS MISSING.
HUH?!
DO YOU THINK SOMEONE TOOK IT OFF?
HOW SHOULD I KNOW?
THERE ARE SCORCH MARKS... FROM SUTRAS.
KRNCH
HE MUST HAVE BEEN DEFEATED BY A MONK.

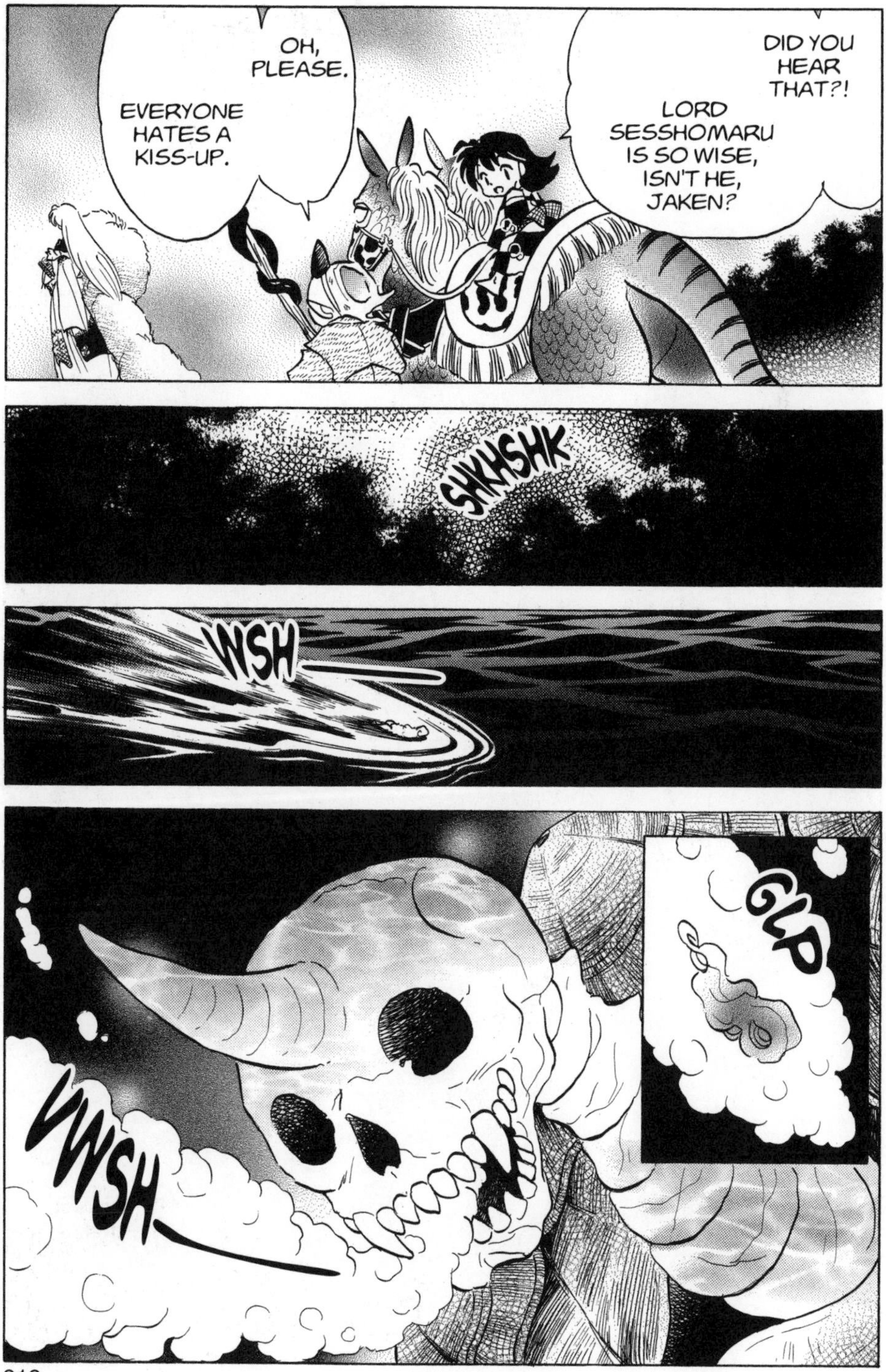
DID YOU HEAR THAT?!
LORD SESSHOMARU IS SO WISE, ISN'T HE, JAKEN?
OH, PLEASE.
EVERYONE HATES A KISS-UP.
SHKHSHK
WSH
GLP
VWSH

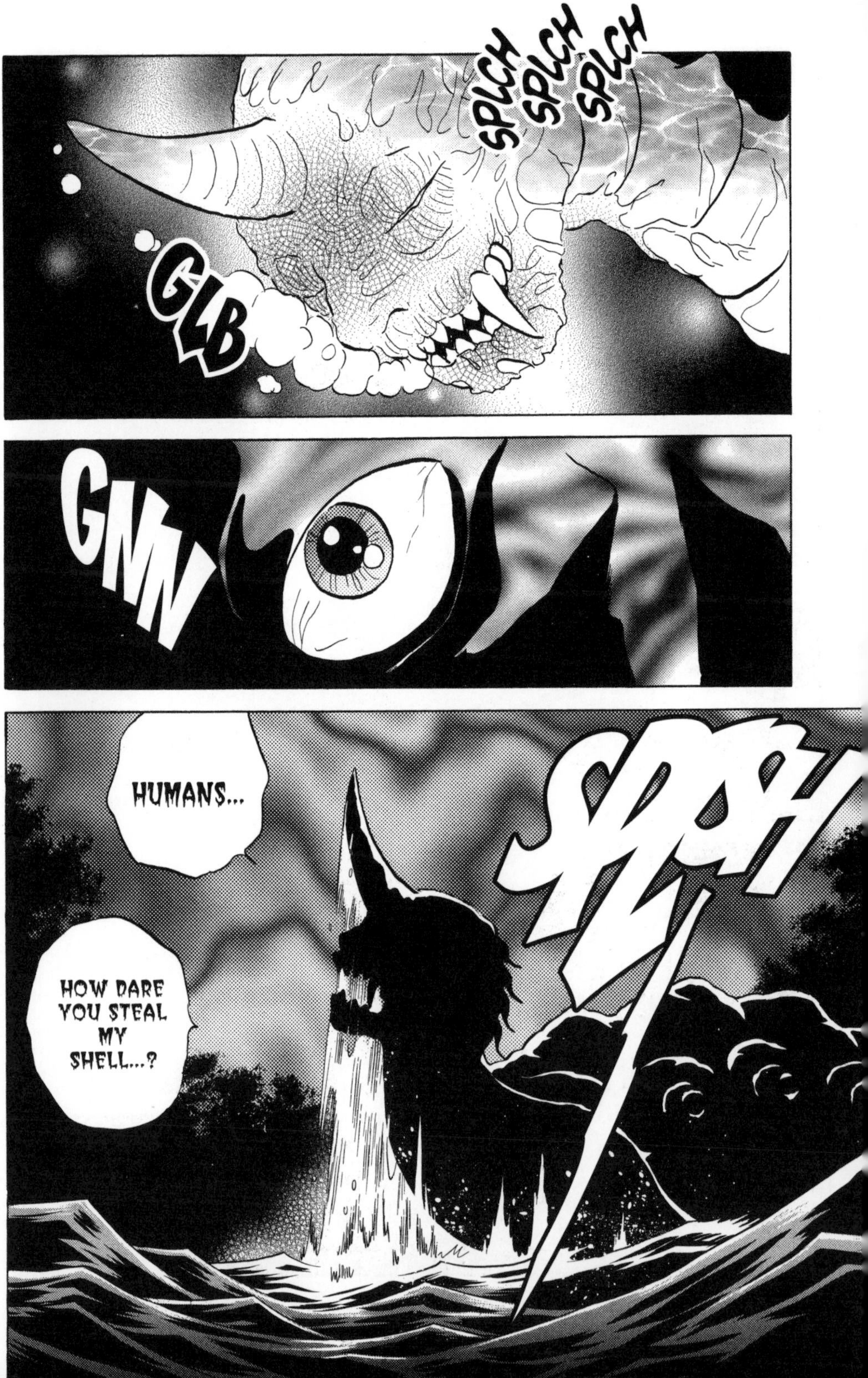
SPLCH SPLCH SPLCH
GLB
GNN
SPOSH
HUMANS...
HOW DARE YOU STEAL MY SHELL...?

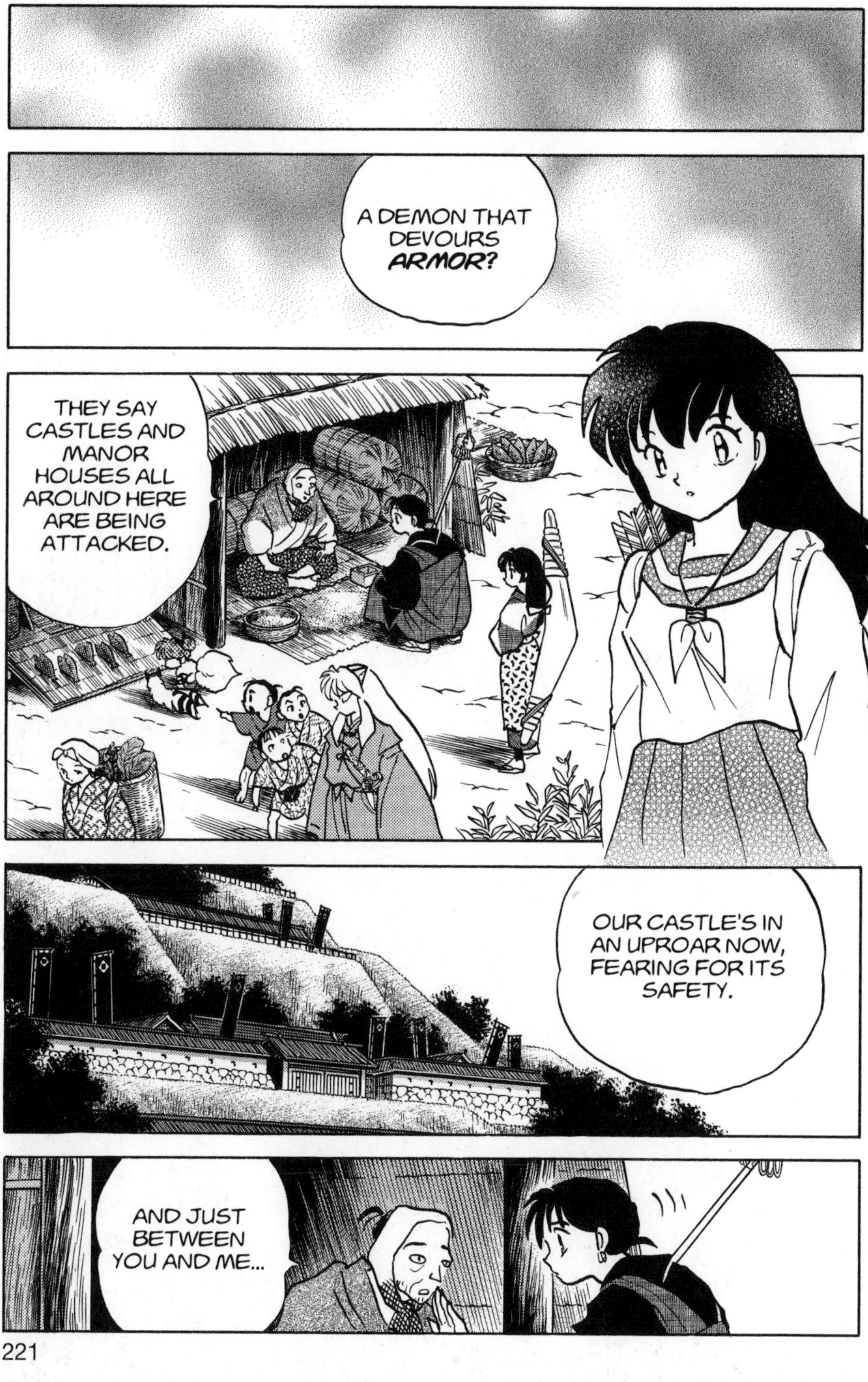
A DEMON THAT DEVOURS ARMOR?
THEY SAY CASTLES AND MANOR HOUSES ALL AROUND HERE ARE BEING ATTACKED.
OUR CASTLE'S IN AN UPROAR NOW, FEARING FOR ITS SAFETY.
AND JUST BETWEEN YOU AND ME...

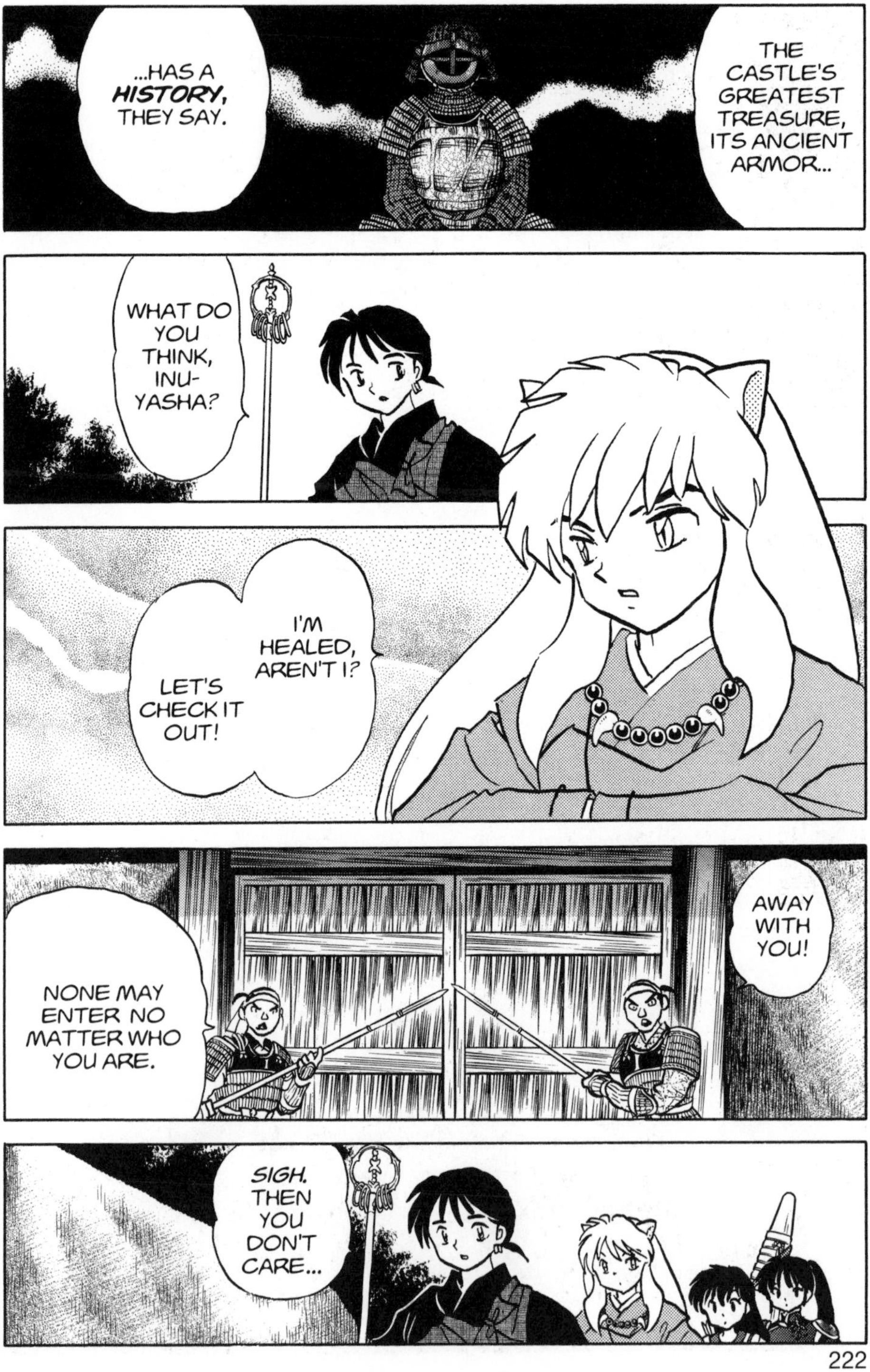
THE CASTLE'S GREATEST TREASURE, ITS ANCIENT ARMOR...
...HAS A **HISTORY,** THEY SAY.
WHAT DO YOU THINK, INU-YASHA?
I'M HEALED, AREN'T I?
LET'S CHECK IT OUT!
AWAY WITH YOU!
NONE MAY ENTER NO MATTER WHO YOU ARE.
SIGH. THEN YOU DON'T CARE...

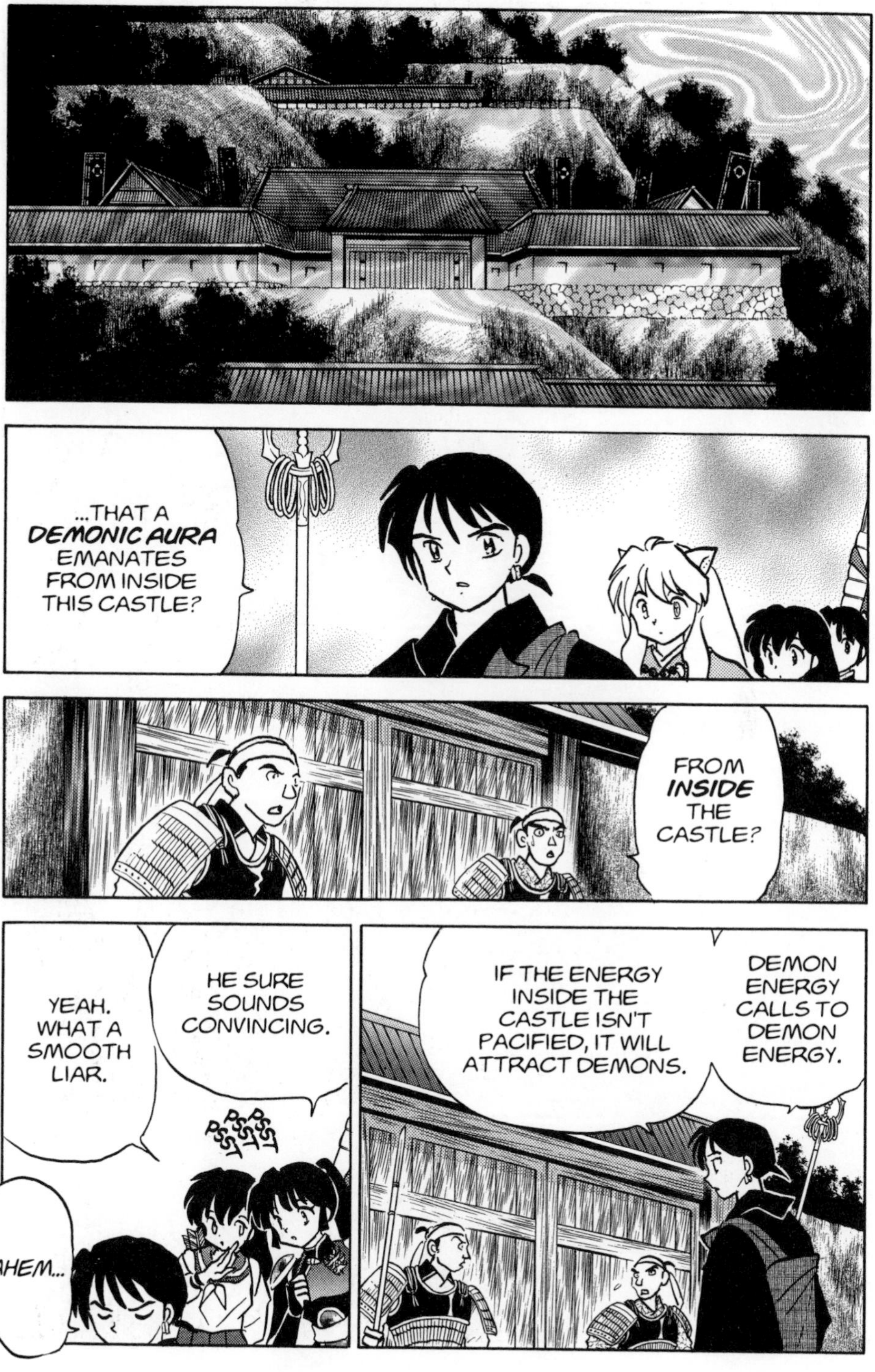
...THAT A **DEMONIC AURA** EMANATES FROM INSIDE THIS CASTLE?
FROM **INSIDE** THE CASTLE?
DEMON ENERGY CALLS TO DEMON ENERGY.
IF THE ENERGY INSIDE THE CASTLE ISN'T PACIFIED, IT WILL ATTRACT DEMONS.
HE SURE SOUNDS CONVINCING.
YEAH. WHAT A SMOOTH LIAR.
PSST PSST PSST
AHEM...

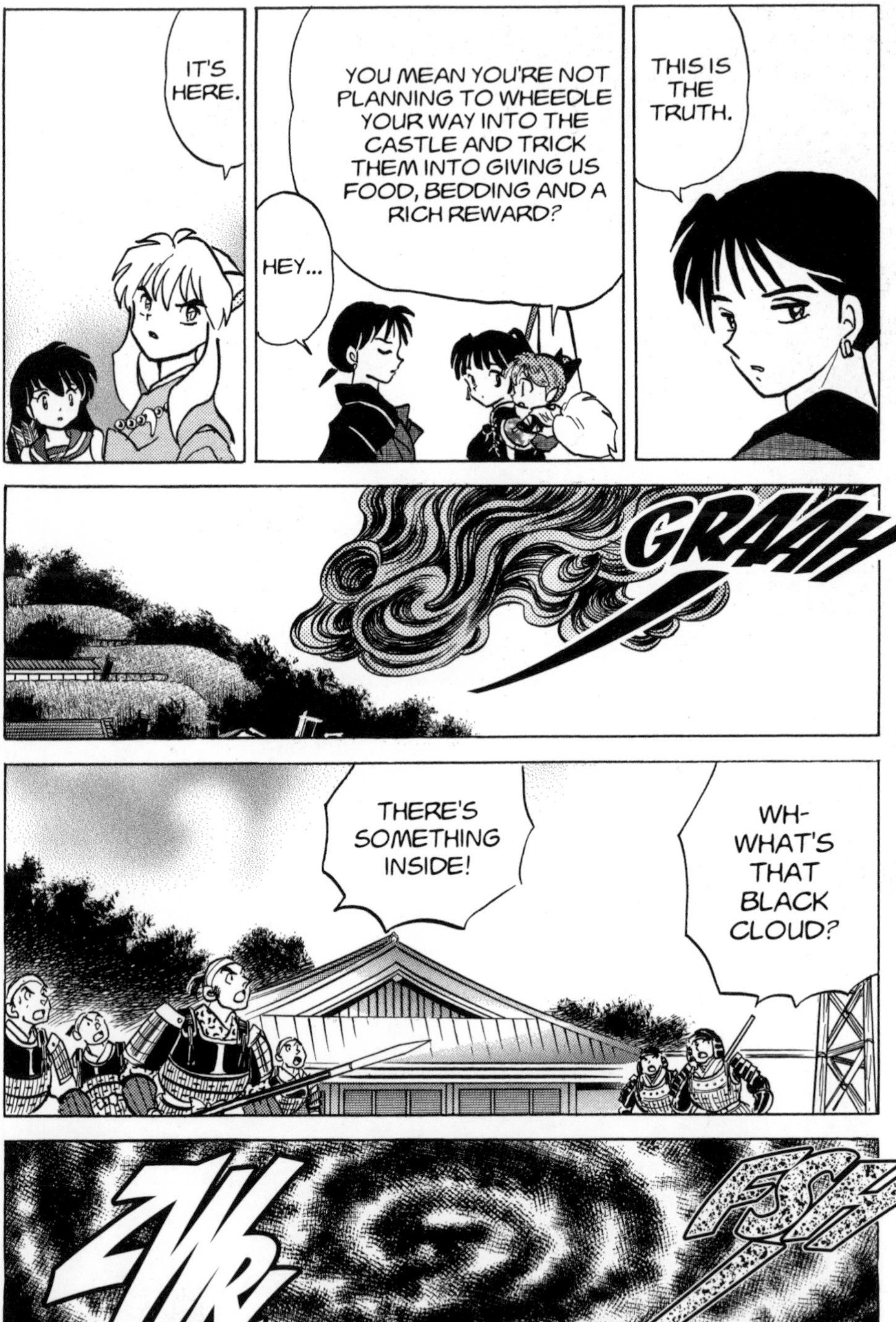
THIS IS THE TRUTH.
YOU MEAN YOU'RE NOT PLANNING TO WHEEDLE YOUR WAY INTO THE CASTLE AND TRICK THEM INTO GIVING US FOOD, BEDDING AND A RICH REWARD?
HEY...
IT'S HERE.
GRAAH
WH- WHAT'S THAT BLACK CLOUD?
THERE'S SOMETHING INSIDE!

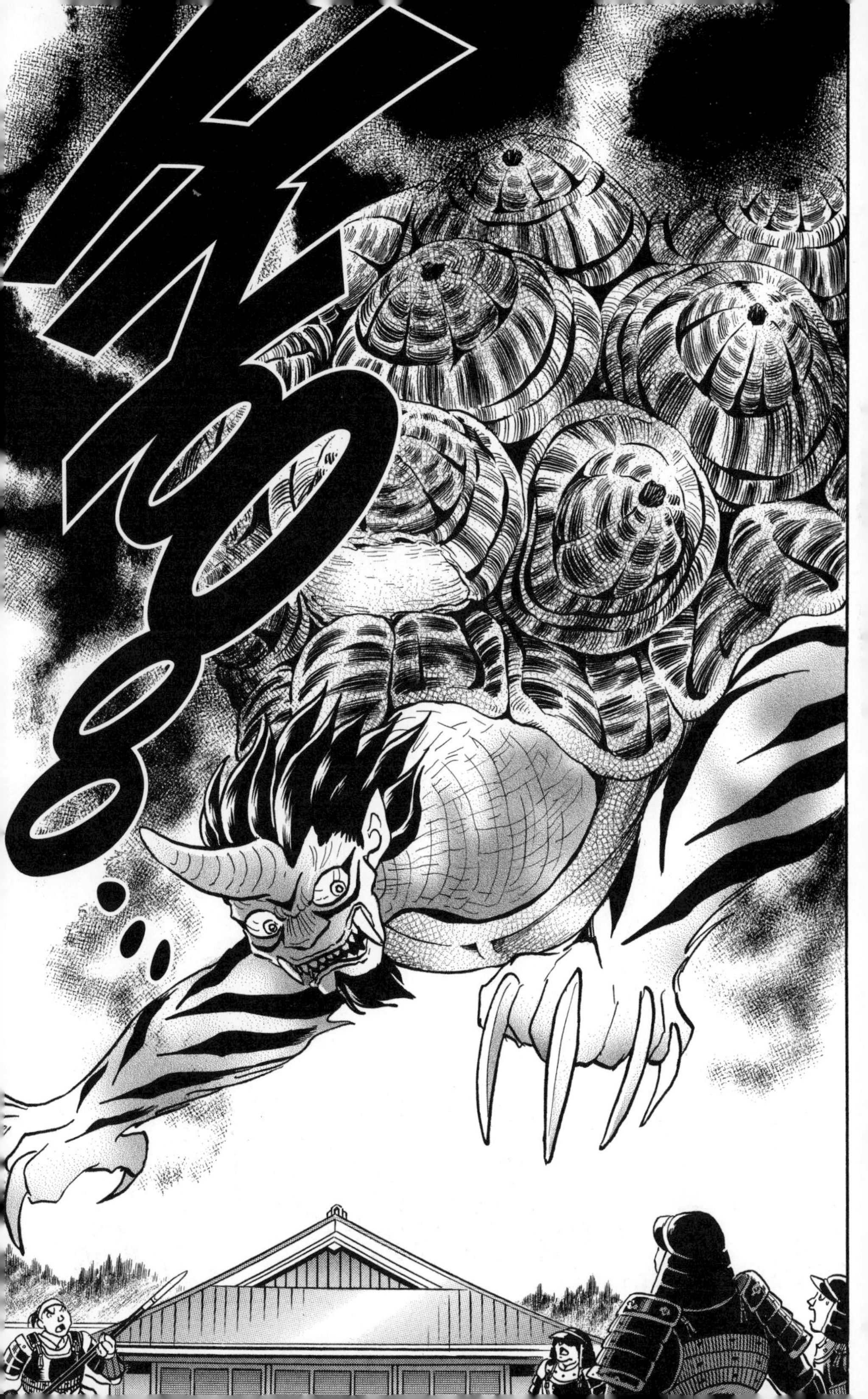

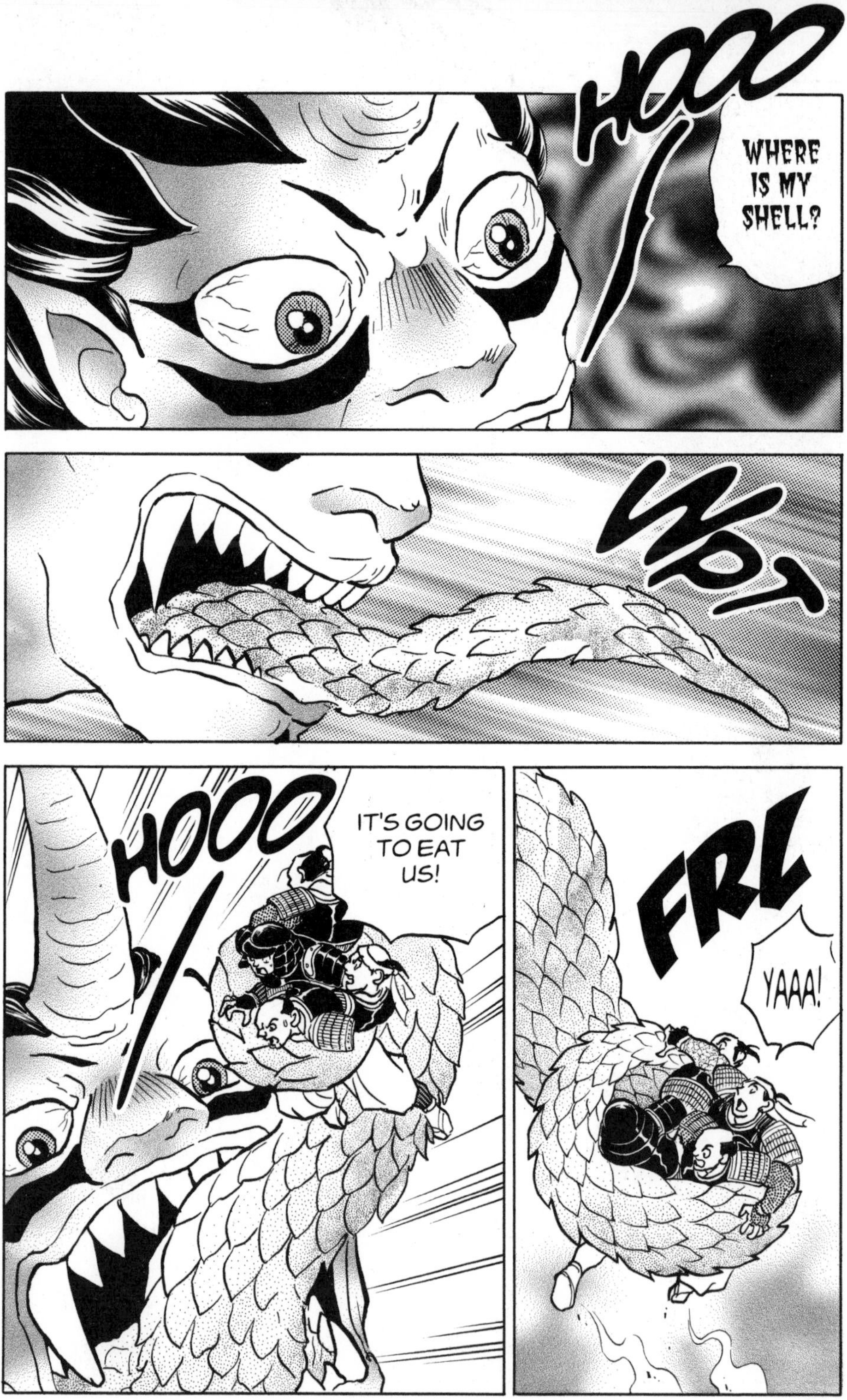
HOOO
WHERE IS MY SHELL?
WPT
FRL
YAAA!
IT'S GOING TO EAT US!
HOOO

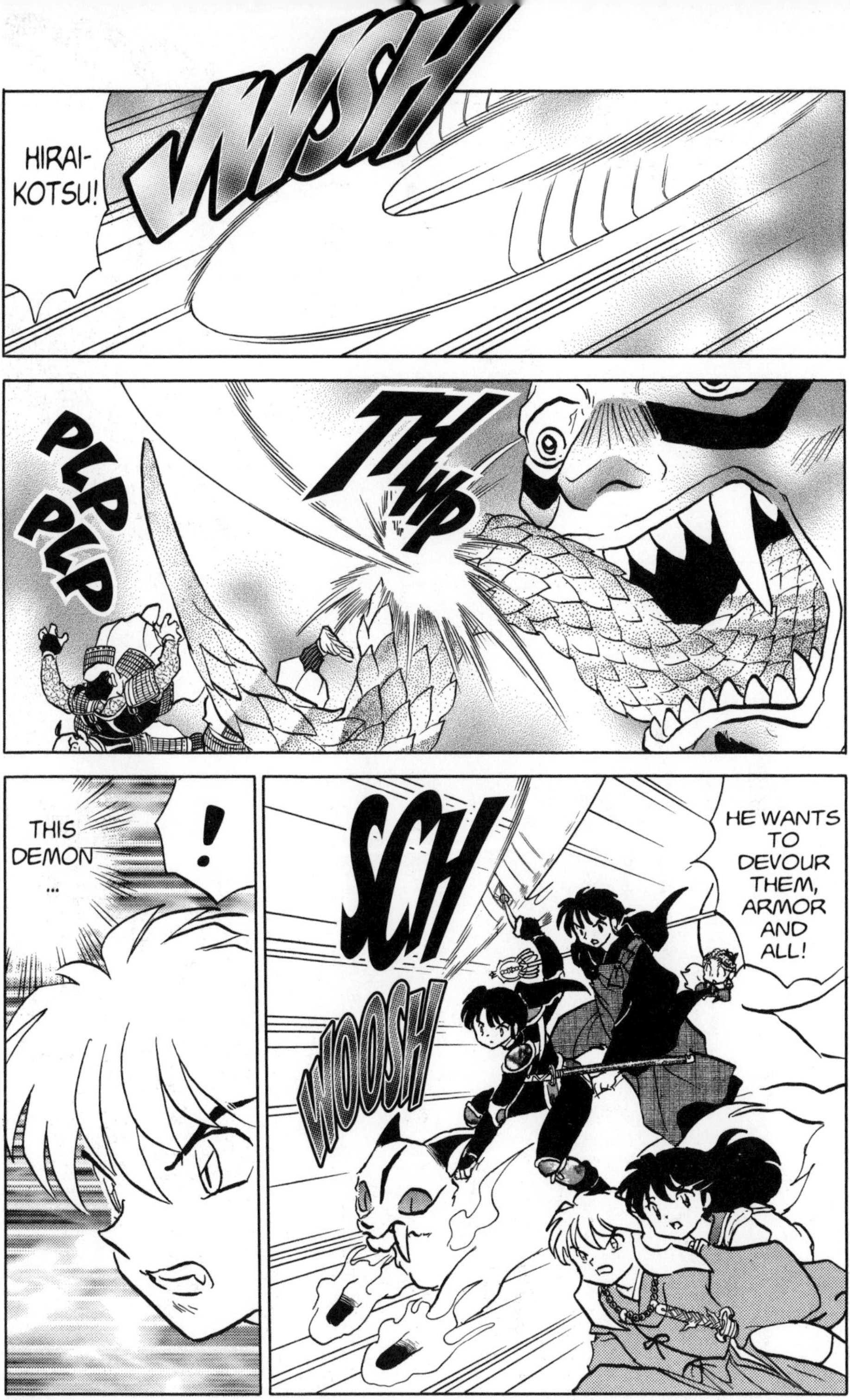
VWSH
HIRAI-KOTSU!
THWP
PLP PLP
HE WANTS TO DEVOUR THEM, ARMOR AND ALL!
SCH
WOOSH
!
THIS DEMON ...

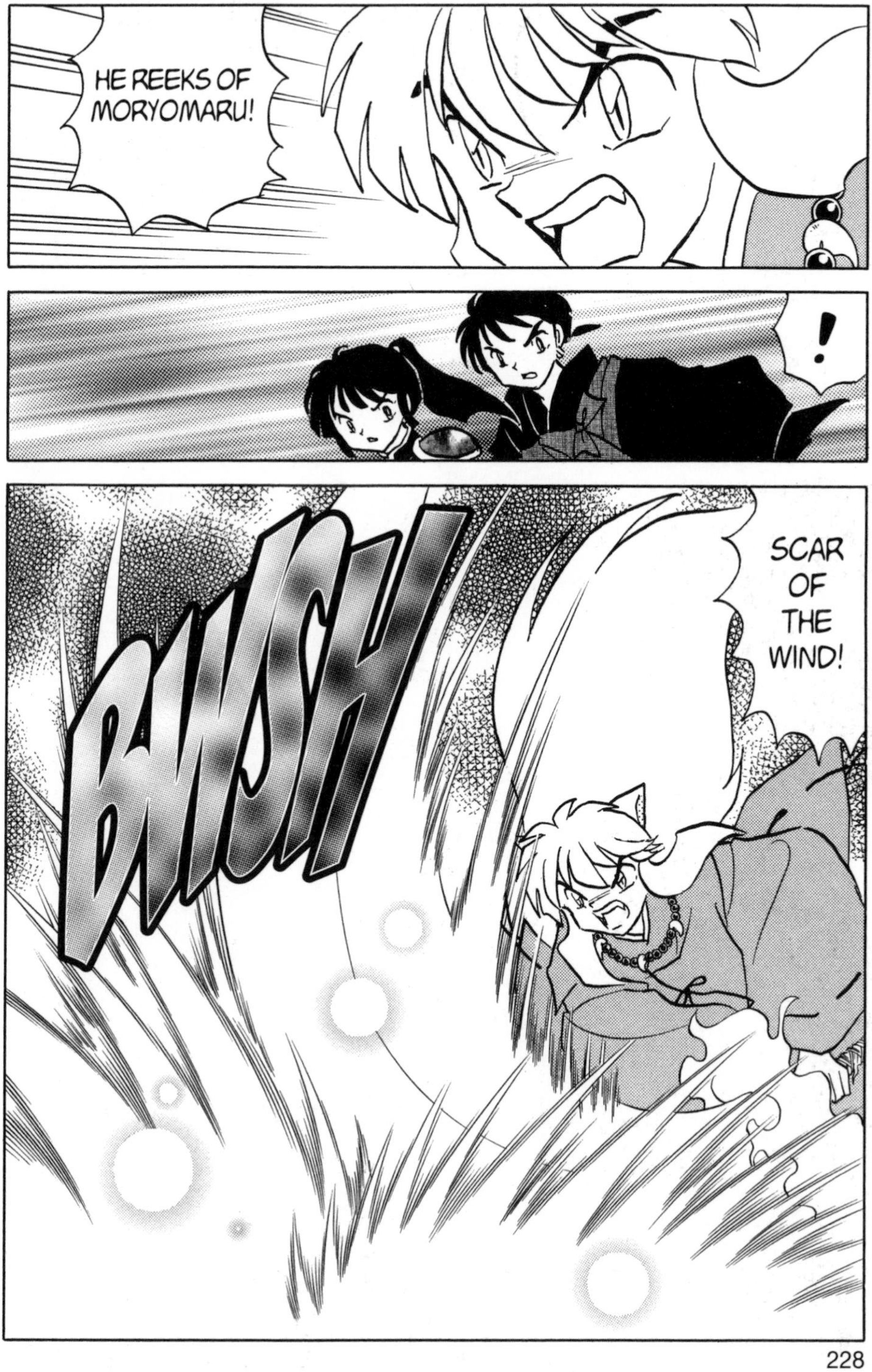
HE REEKS OF MORYOMARU!
!
SCAR OF THE WIND!
BWOSH

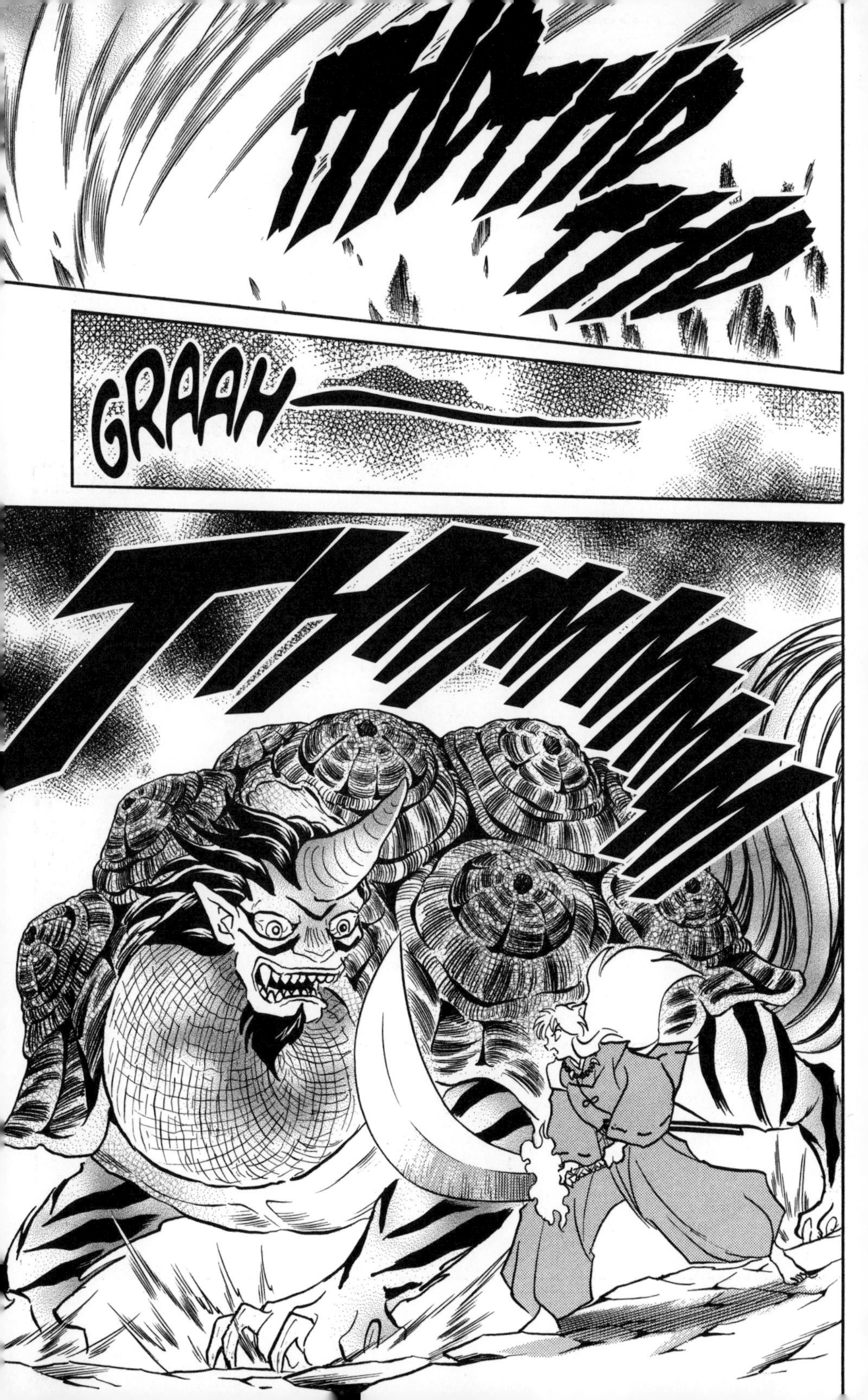
GRAAH

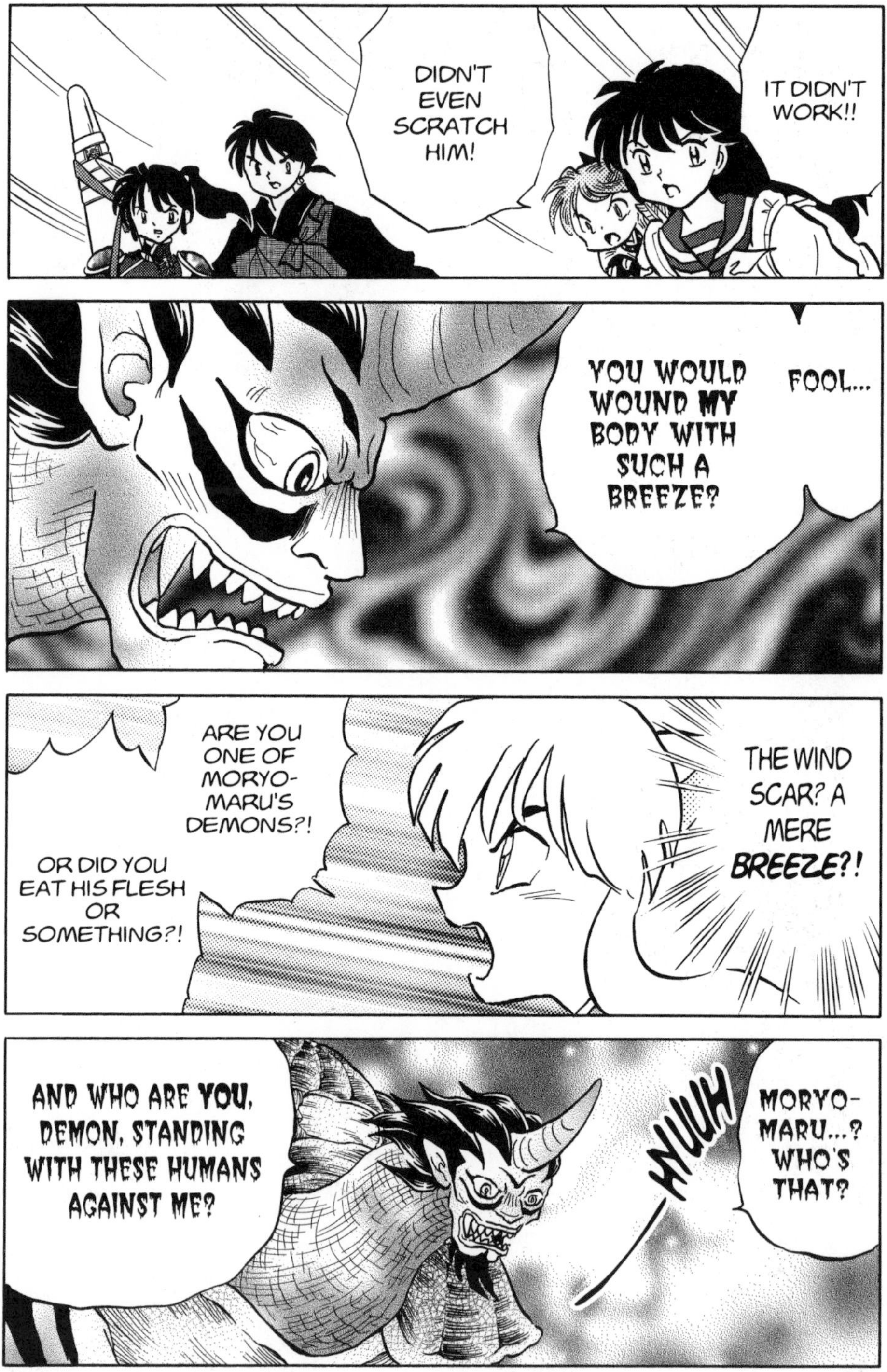
IT DIDN'T WORK!!
DIDN'T EVEN SCRATCH HIM!
FOOL...
YOU WOULD WOUND MY BODY WITH SUCH A BREEZE?
THE WIND SCAR? A MERE BREEZE?!
ARE YOU ONE OF MORYO-MARU'S DEMONS?!
OR DID YOU EAT HIS FLESH OR SOMETHING?!
MORYO-MARU...? WHO'S THAT?
HYUUH
AND WHO ARE YOU, DEMON, STANDING WITH THESE HUMANS AGAINST ME?

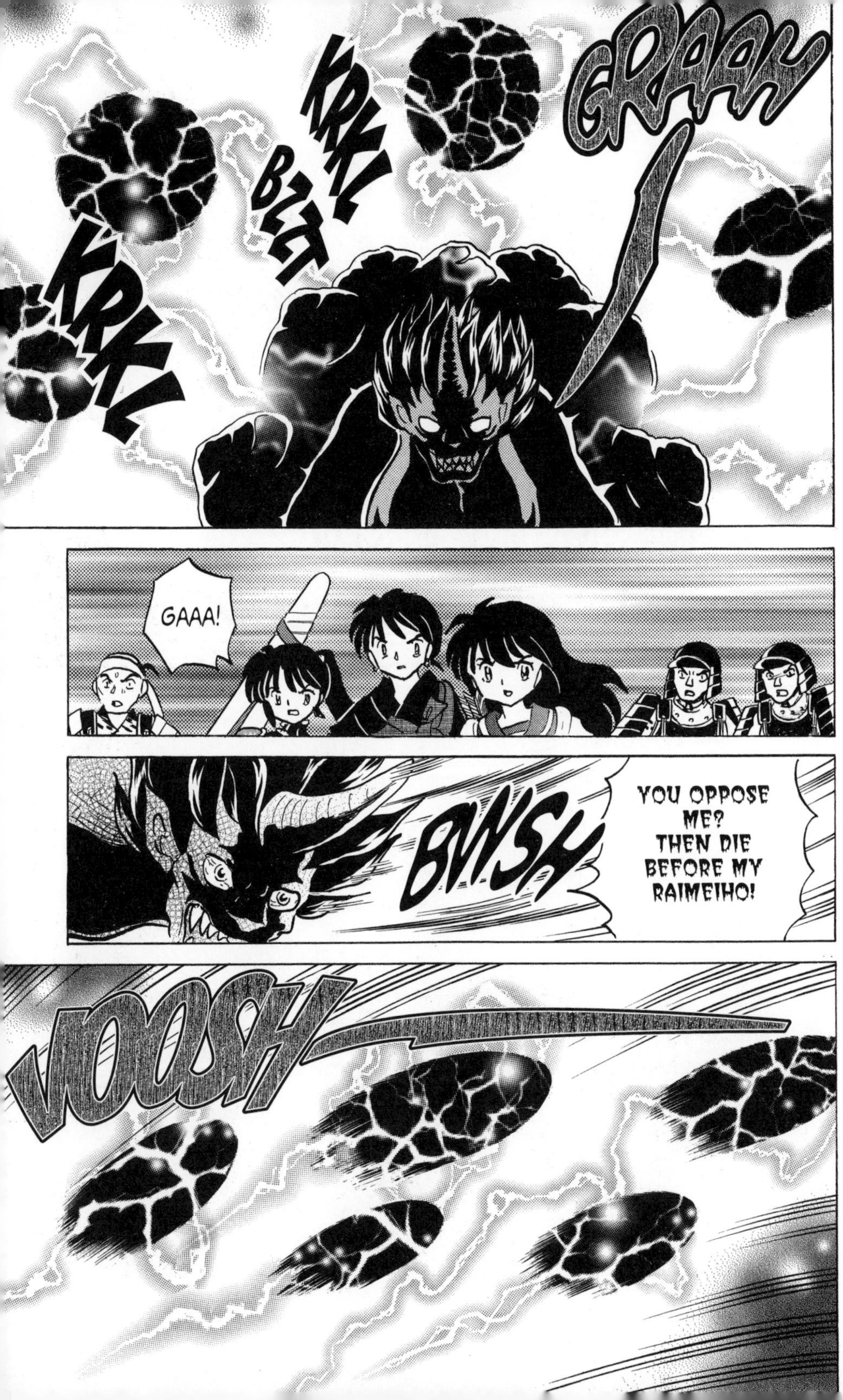
GRAAAH
KRKKL
BZZT
KRKKL
GAAA!
YOU OPPOSE ME? THEN DIE BEFORE MY RAIMEIHO!
BVVSH
VOOSH

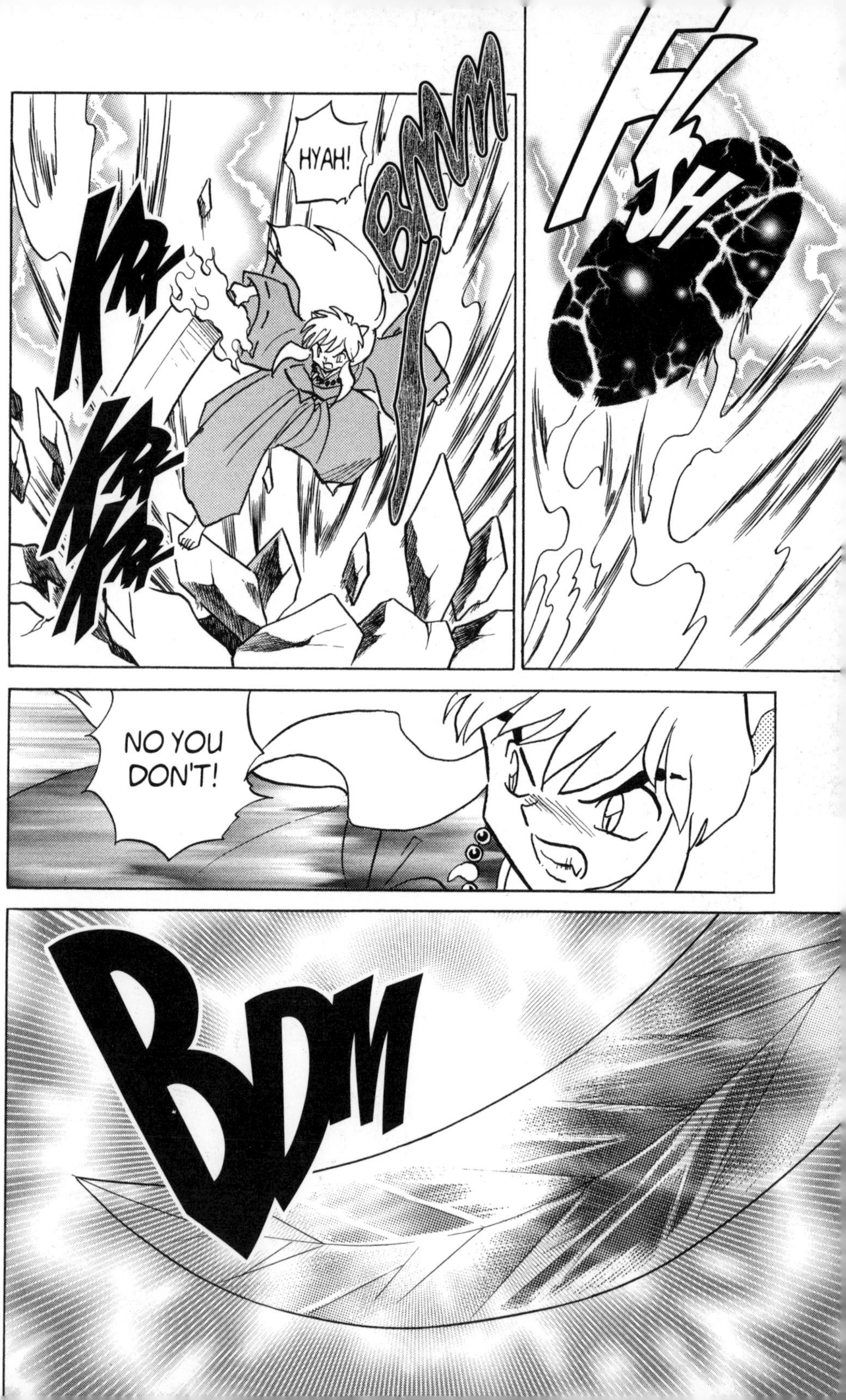
HYAH!
NO YOU DON'T!
BDM

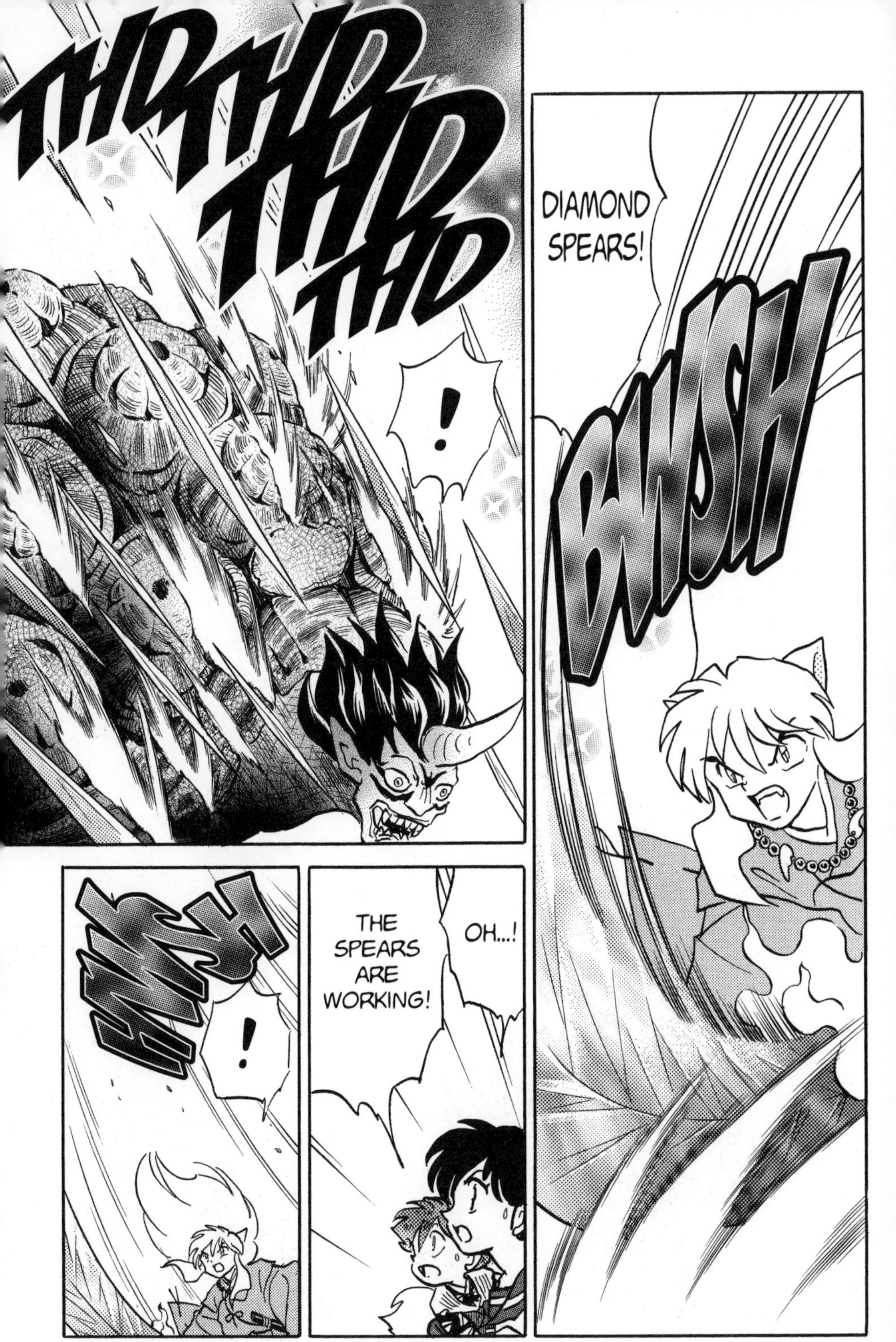
DIAMOND SPEARS!
BAMSH
THD THD THD
!
OH...!
THE SPEARS ARE WORKING!
!

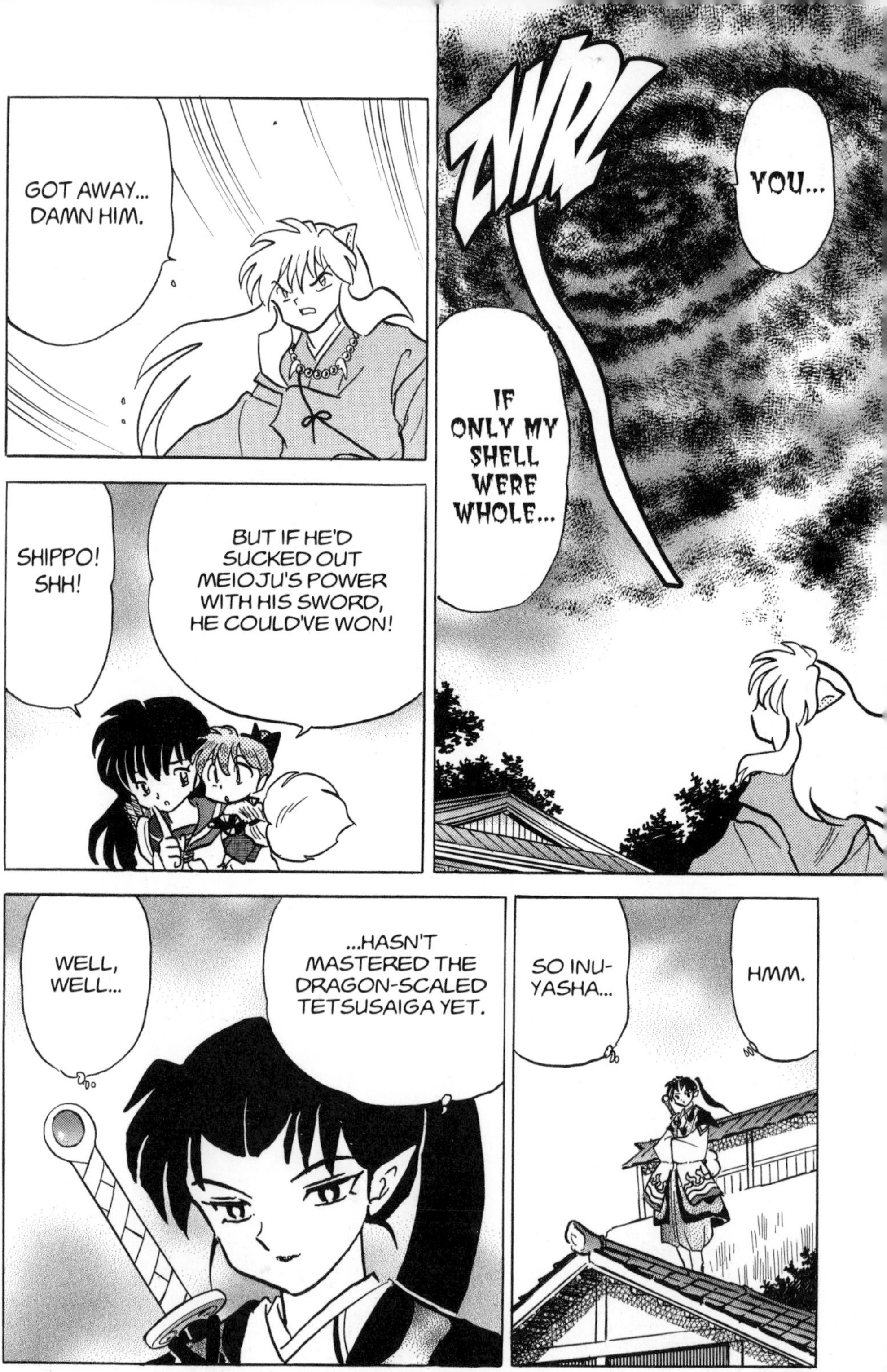
ZWRL
YOU...
IF ONLY MY SHELL WERE WHOLE...
GOT AWAY... DAMN HIM.
BUT IF HE'D SUCKED OUT MEIOJU'S POWER WITH HIS SWORD, HE COULD'VE WON!
SHIPPO! SHH!
HMM.
SO INU-YASHA...
...HASN'T MASTERED THE DRAGON-SCALED TETSUSAIGA YET.
WELL, WELL...

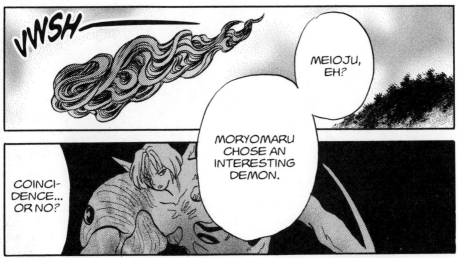

VVNSH
MEIOJU, EH?
MORYOMARU CHOSE AN INTERESTING DEMON.
COINCI-DENCE... OR NO?
FWP
HE MIGHT BE WORTH TAILING...
FWP
FWP
YOU...
YOU SAVED OUR CASTLE!
YOU'RE WEL-COME.
NOW WHAT'S THIS ABOUT ANCIENT ARMOR?

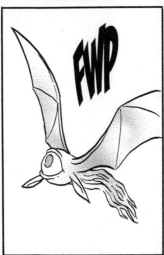

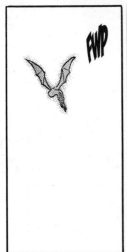

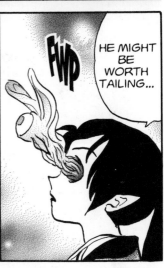

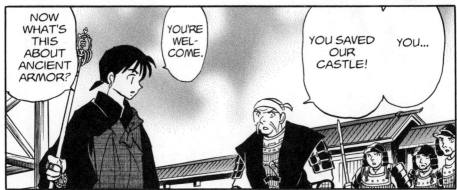

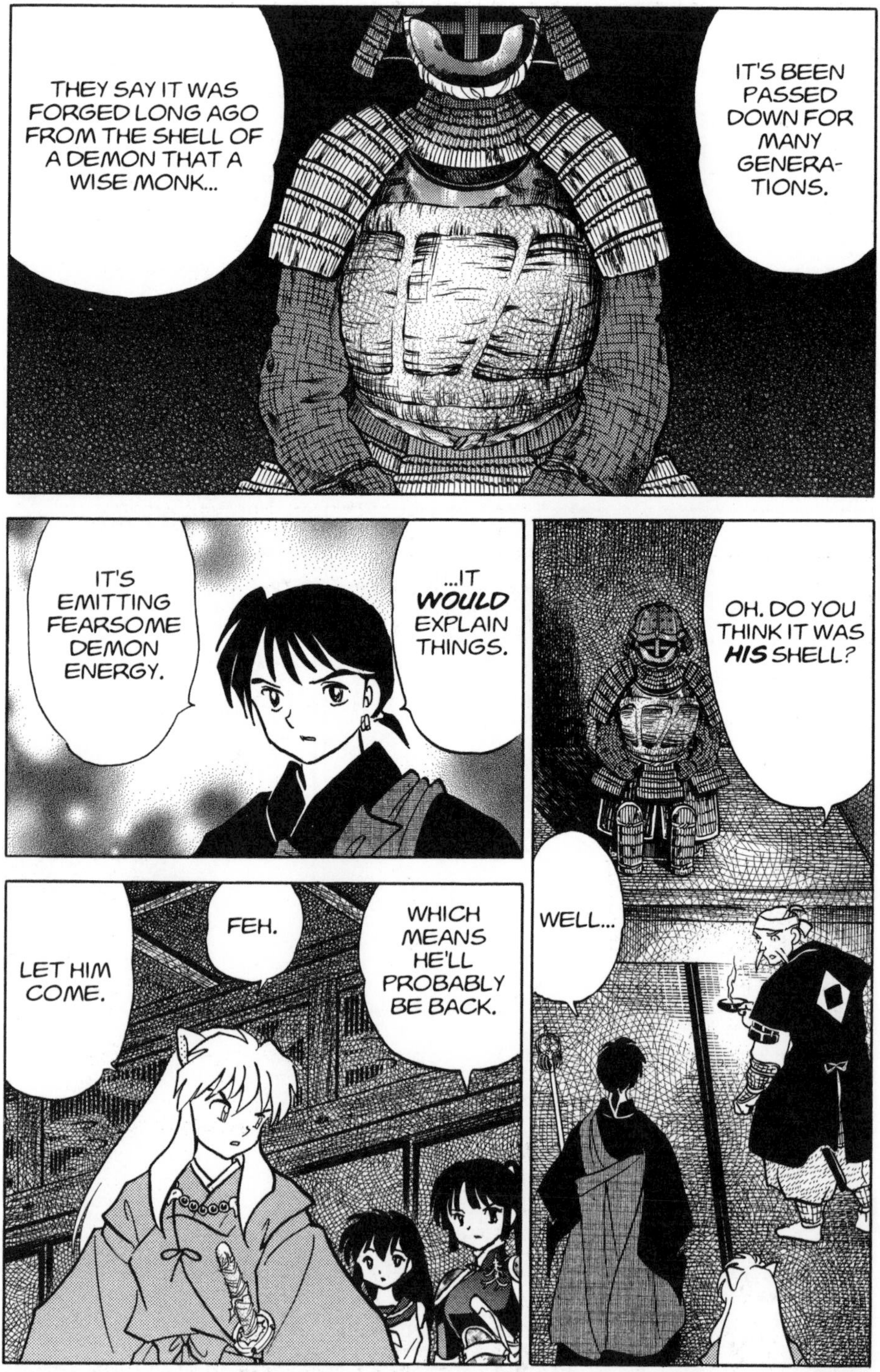
IT'S BEEN PASSED DOWN FOR MANY GENERATIONS.
THEY SAY IT WAS FORGED LONG AGO FROM THE SHELL OF A DEMON THAT A WISE MONK...
OH. DO YOU THINK IT WAS **HIS** SHELL?
WELL...
...IT **WOULD** EXPLAIN THINGS.
IT'S EMITTING FEARSOME DEMON ENERGY.
WHICH MEANS HE'LL PROBABLY BE BACK.
FEH.
LET HIM COME.

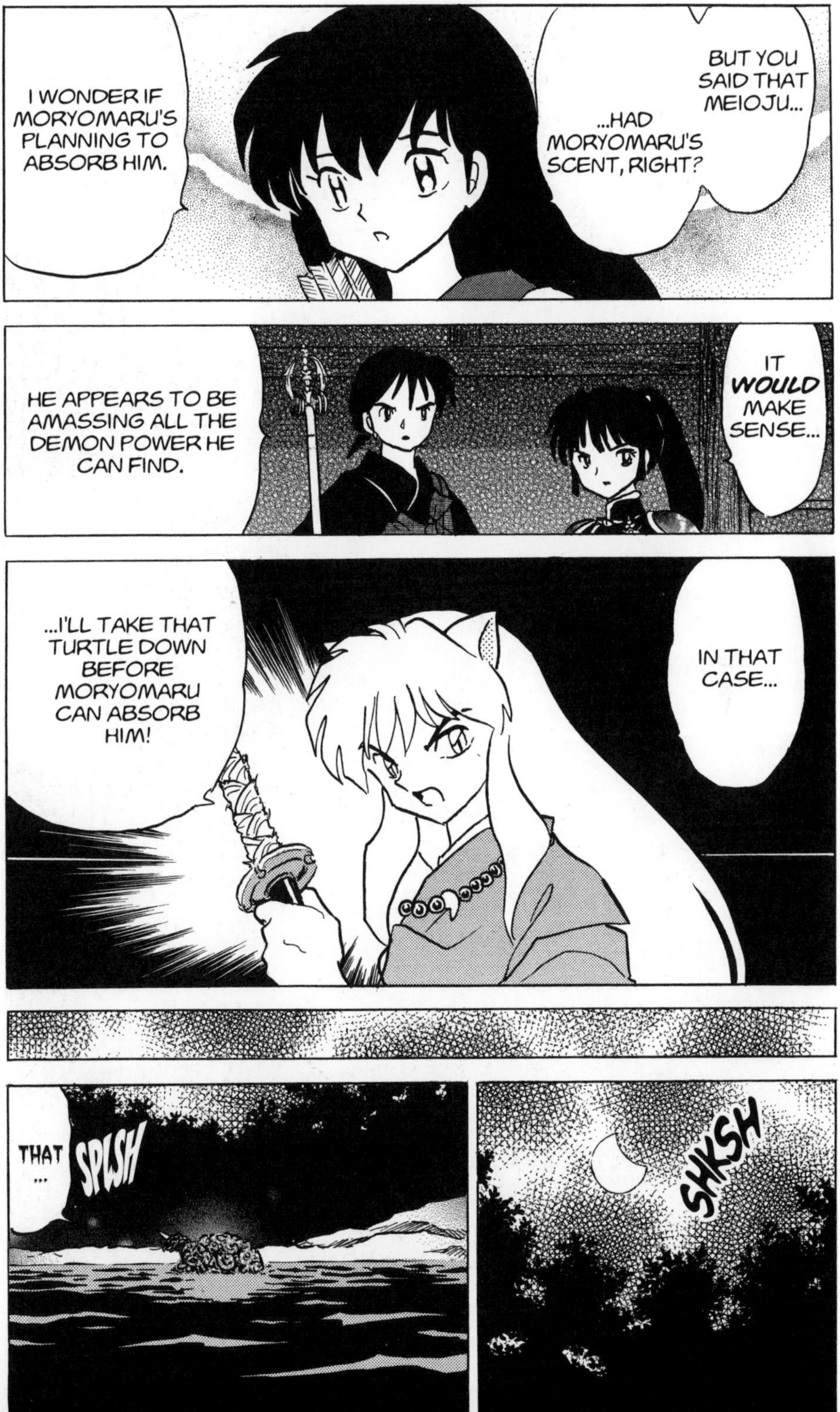
BUT YOU SAID THAT MEIOJU...
...HAD MORYOMARU'S SCENT, RIGHT?
I WONDER IF MORYOMARU'S PLANNING TO ABSORB HIM.
IT **WOULD** MAKE SENSE...
HE APPEARS TO BE AMASSING ALL THE DEMON POWER HE CAN FIND.
IN THAT CASE...
...I'LL TAKE THAT TURTLE DOWN BEFORE MORYOMARU CAN ABSORB HIM!
SHKSH
SPLSH
THAT ...

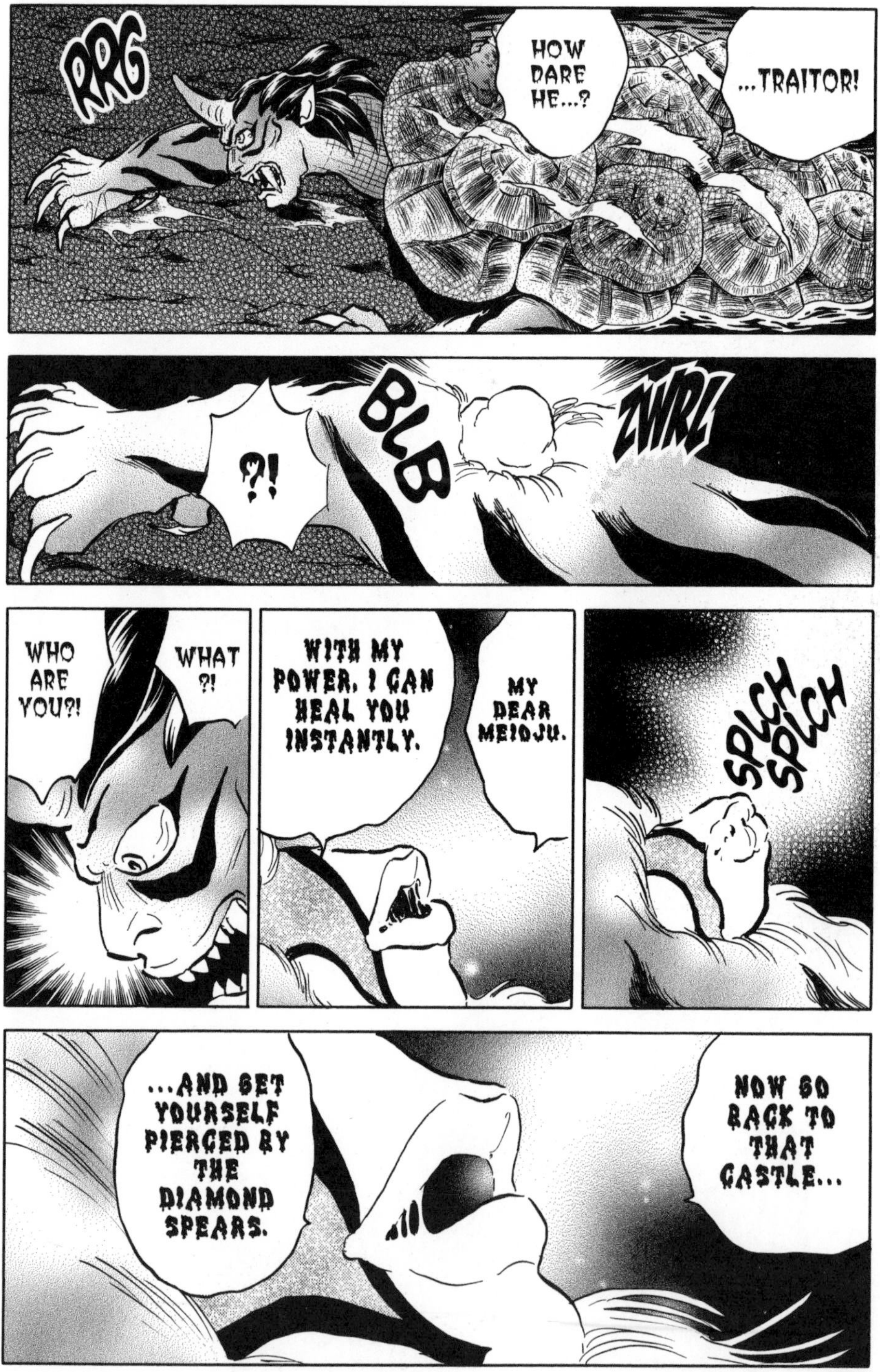
...TRAITOR!
HOW DARE HE...?
RRG
ZWRL
BLB
?!
SPLCH SPLCH
MY DEAR MEIOJU.
WITH MY POWER, I CAN HEAL YOU INSTANTLY.
WHAT?!
WHO ARE YOU?!
NOW GO BACK TO THAT CASTLE...
...AND GET YOURSELF PIERCED BY THE DIAMOND SPEARS.

SCROLL THREE
THE ARMORED SHELL

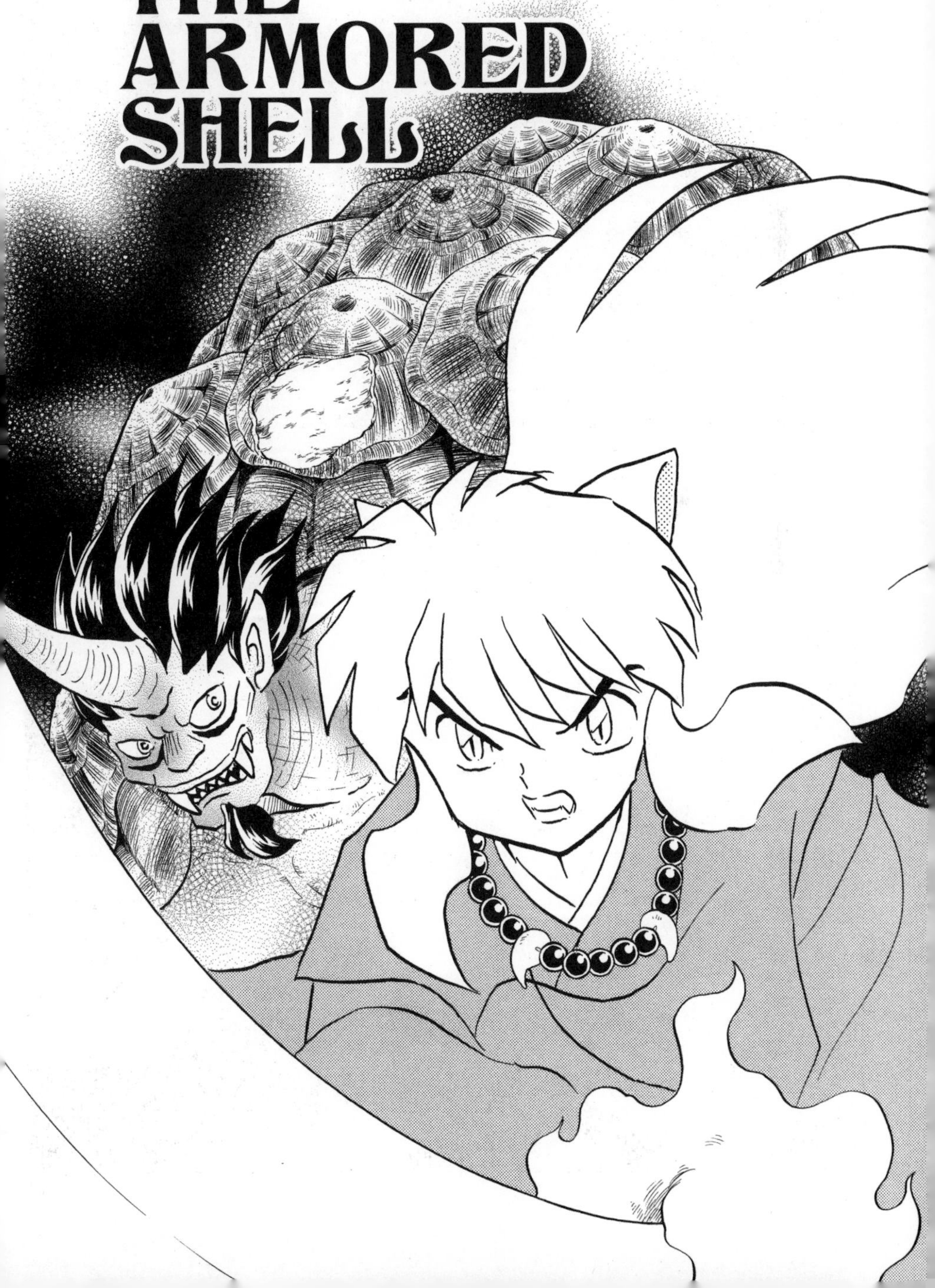

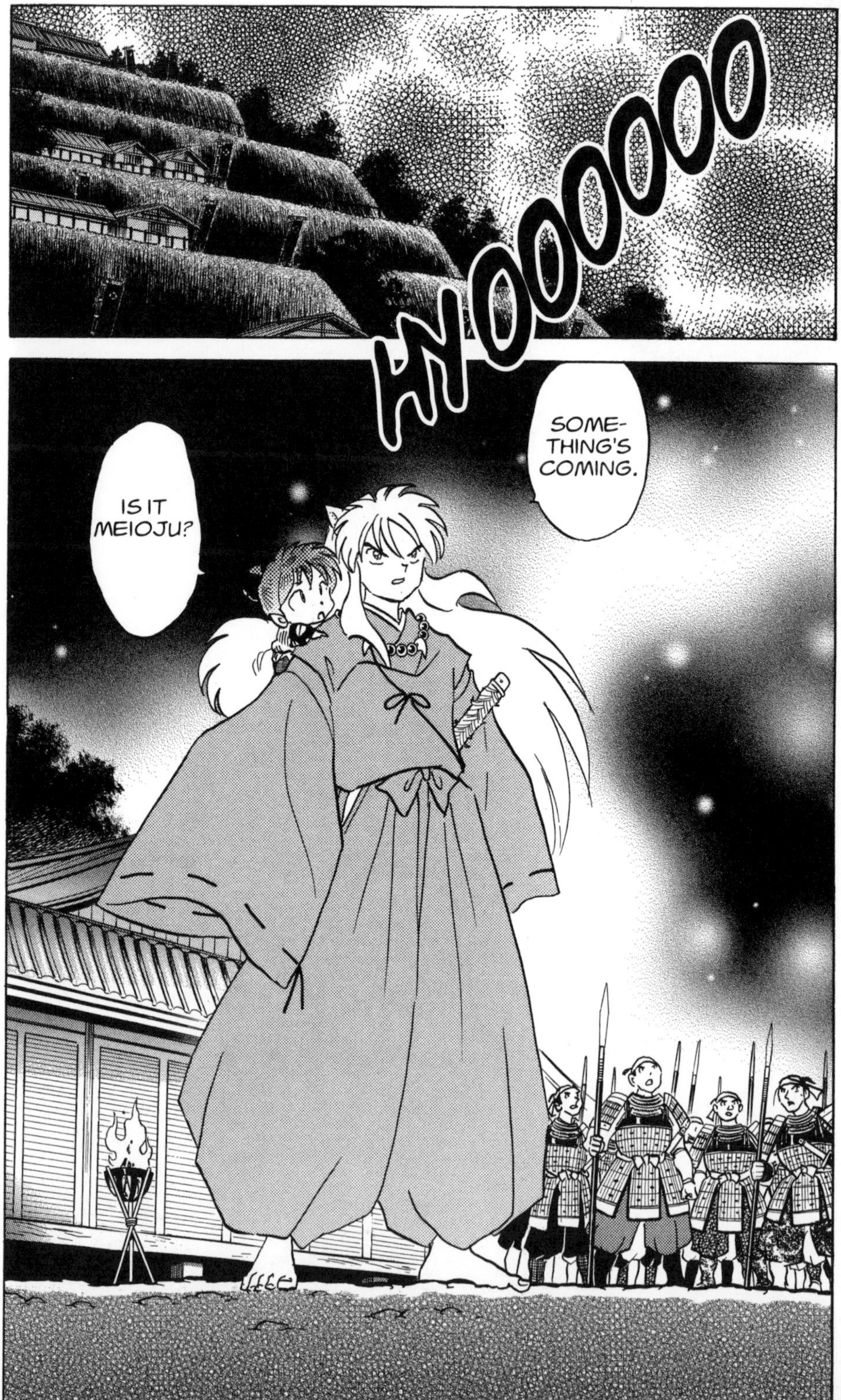
HYOOOOOO
SOME-THING'S COMING.
IS IT MEIOJU?

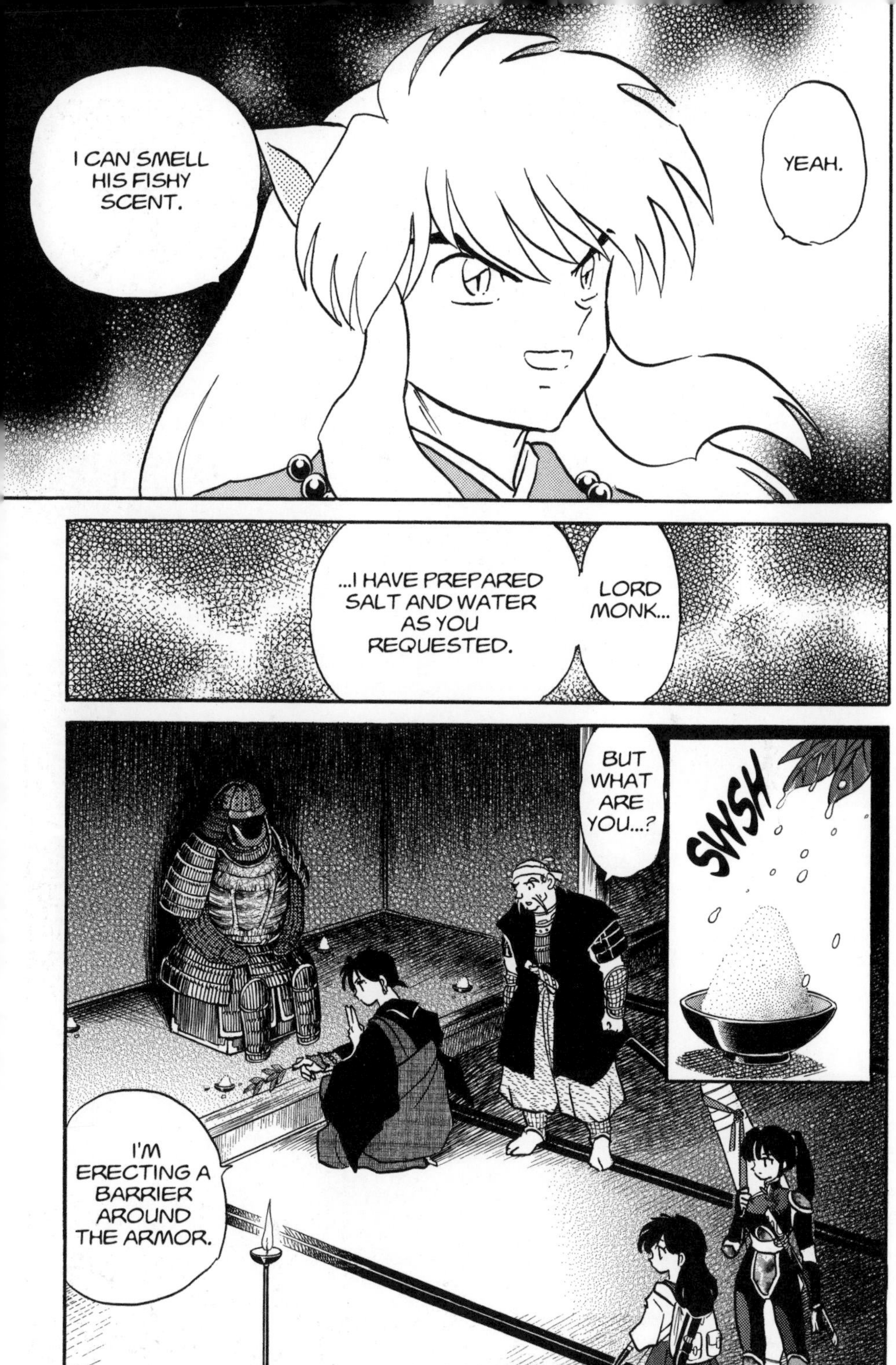
YEAH.
I CAN SMELL HIS FISHY SCENT.
LORD MONK...
...I HAVE PREPARED SALT AND WATER AS YOU REQUESTED.
SWSH
BUT WHAT ARE YOU...?
I'M ERECTING A BARRIER AROUND THE ARMOR.

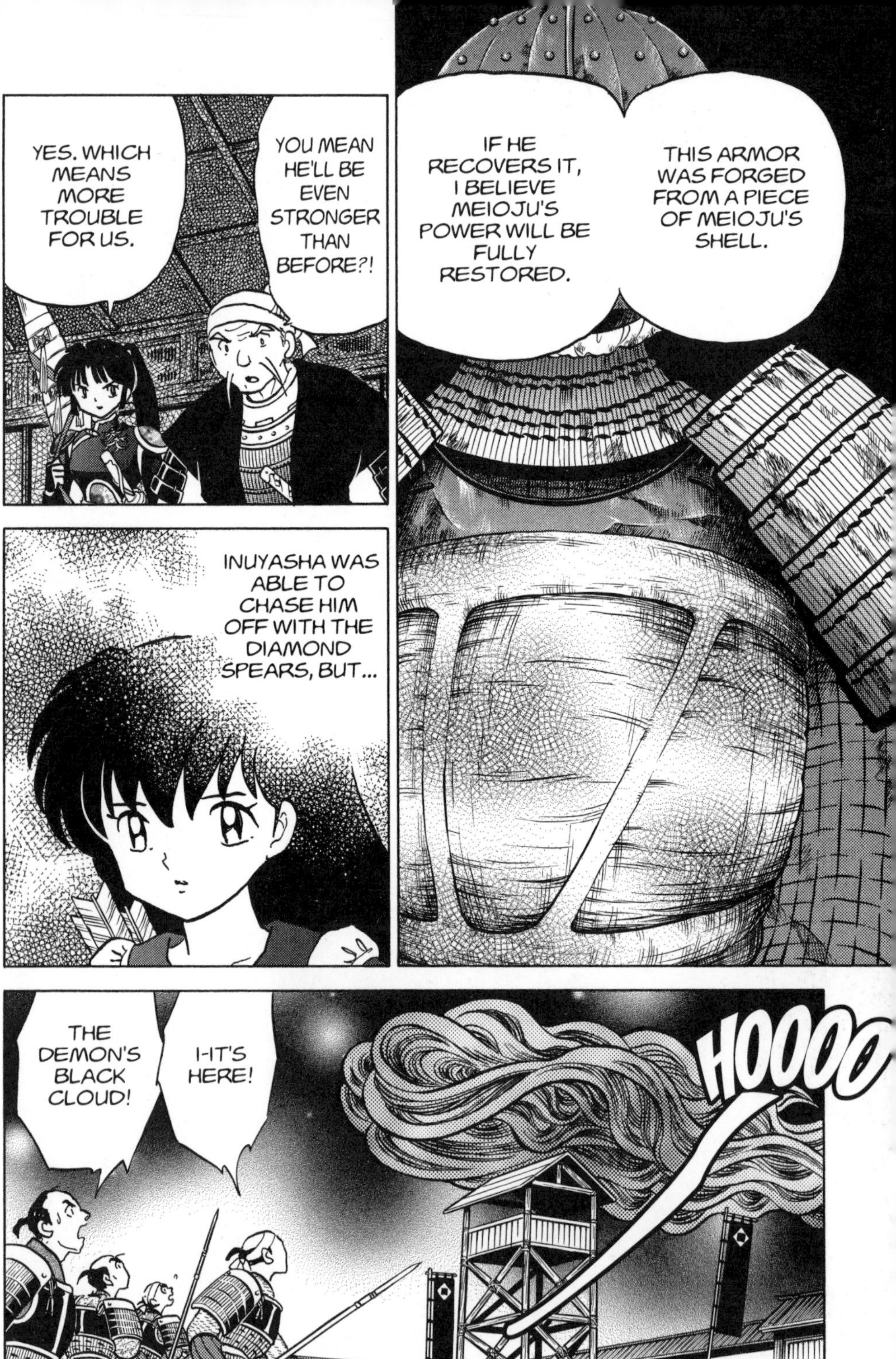
THIS ARMOR WAS FORGED FROM A PIECE OF MEIOJU'S SHELL.
IF HE RECOVERS IT, I BELIEVE MEIOJU'S POWER WILL BE FULLY RESTORED.
YOU MEAN HE'LL BE EVEN STRONGER THAN BEFORE?!
YES. WHICH MEANS MORE TROUBLE FOR US.
INUYASHA WAS ABLE TO CHASE HIM OFF WITH THE DIAMOND SPEARS, BUT...
HOOOO
I-IT'S HERE!
THE DEMON'S BLACK CLOUD!

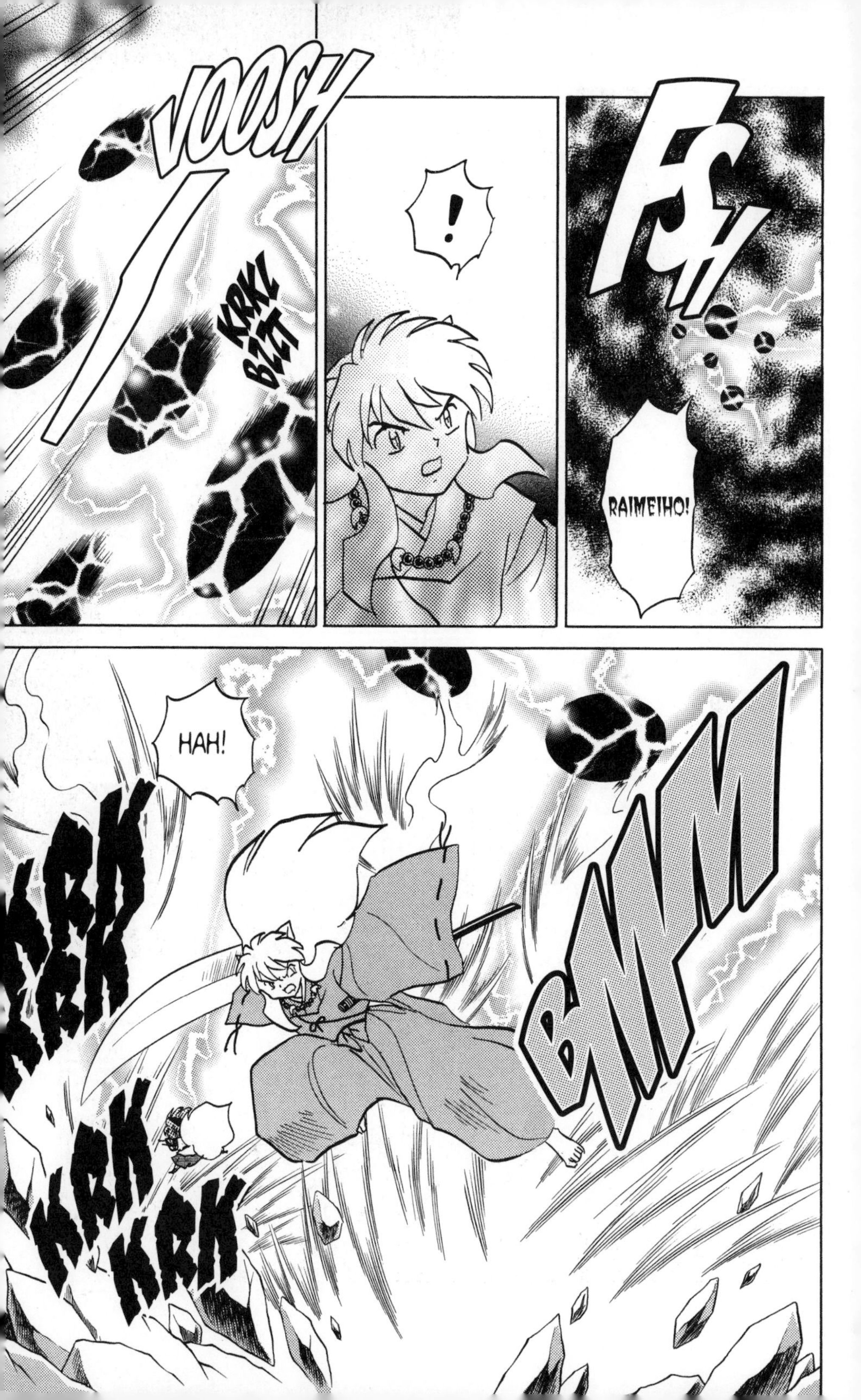
FSH
RAIMEIHO!
!
VOOSH
KRKL BZZT
BMMM
HAH!
KRK KRK
KRK KRK

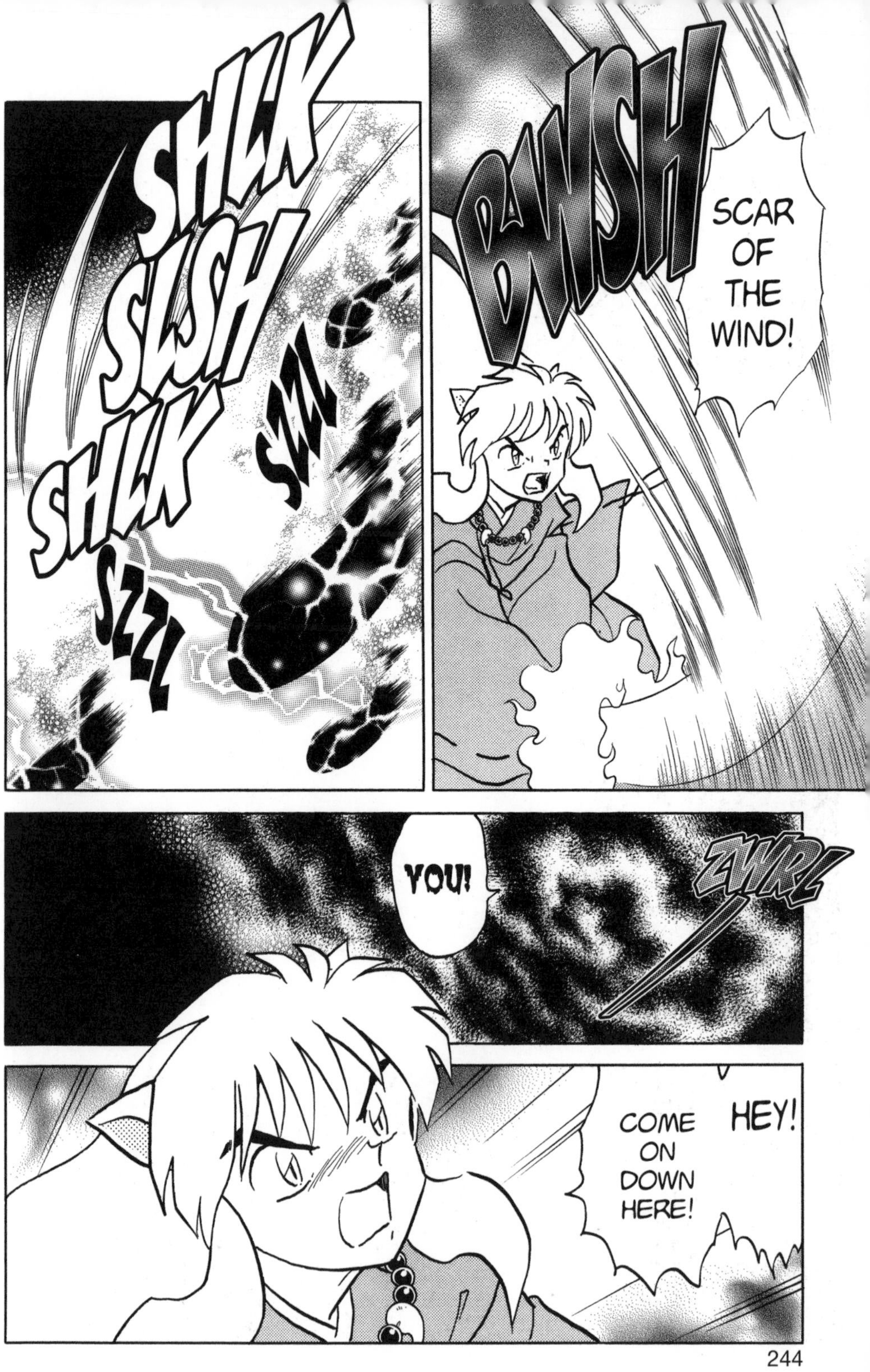
BWISH
SCAR OF THE WIND!
SHLK
SLSH
SHLK
SZZL
SZZL
ZWRL
YOU!
HEY!
COME ON DOWN HERE!

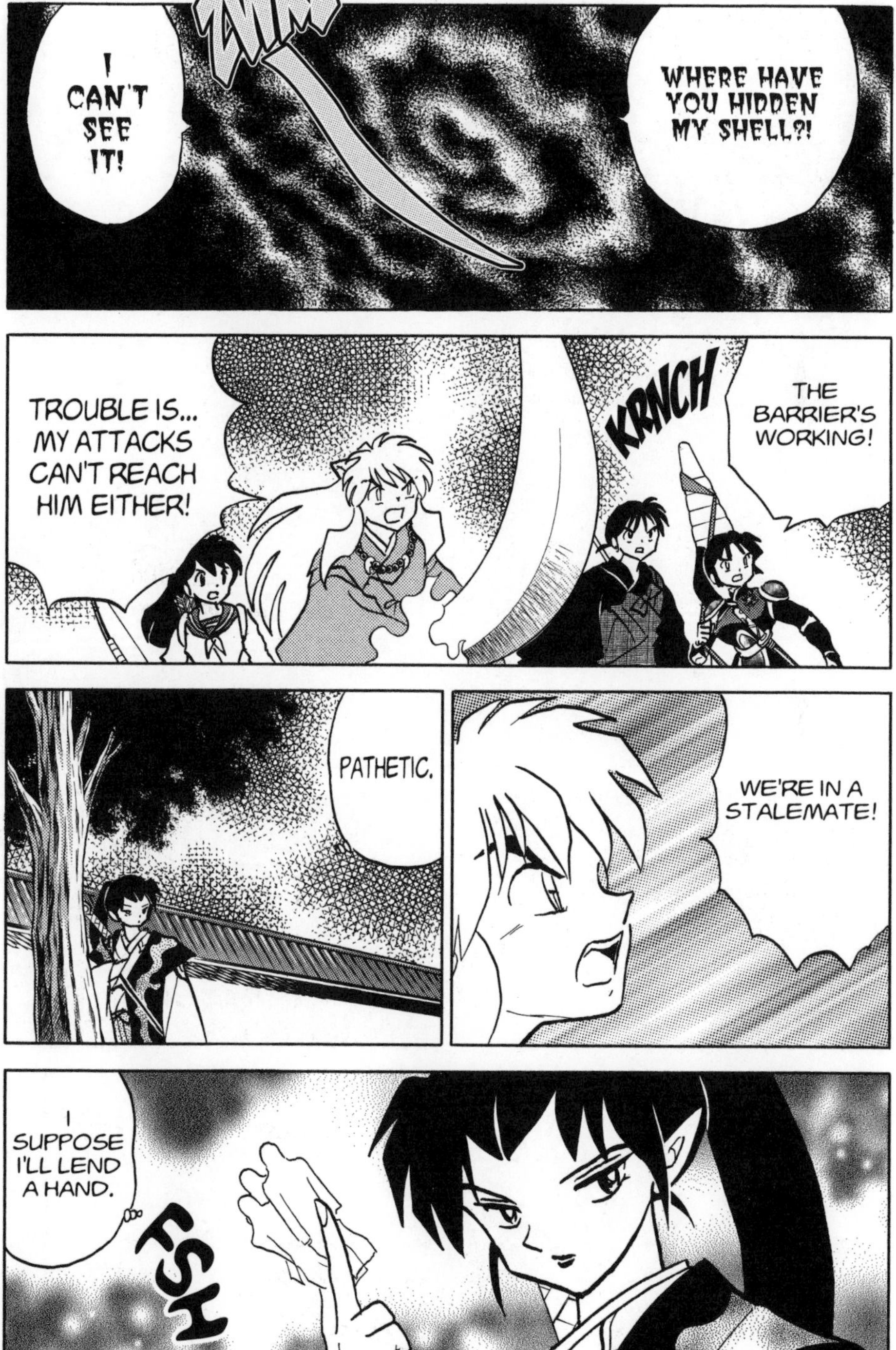
WHERE HAVE YOU HIDDEN MY SHELL?!
ZWRL
I CAN'T SEE IT!
THE BARRIER'S WORKING!
KRNCH
TROUBLE IS... MY ATTACKS CAN'T REACH HIM EITHER!
WE'RE IN A STALEMATE!
PATHETIC.
I SUPPOSE I'LL LEND A HAND.
FSH

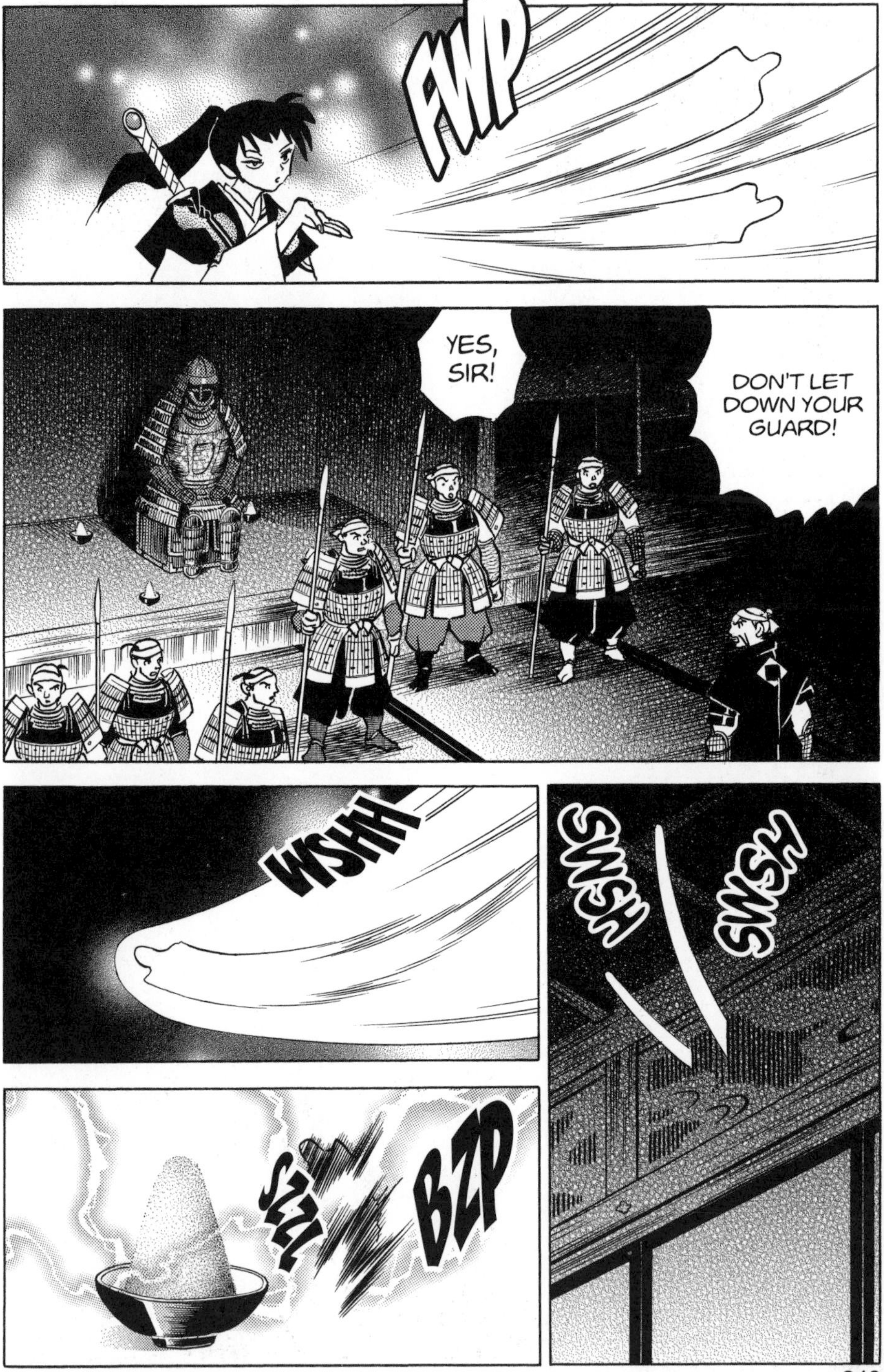
FWP
DON'T LET DOWN YOUR GUARD!
YES, SIR!
SWSH
SWSH
WSHH
BZP
SZZZ

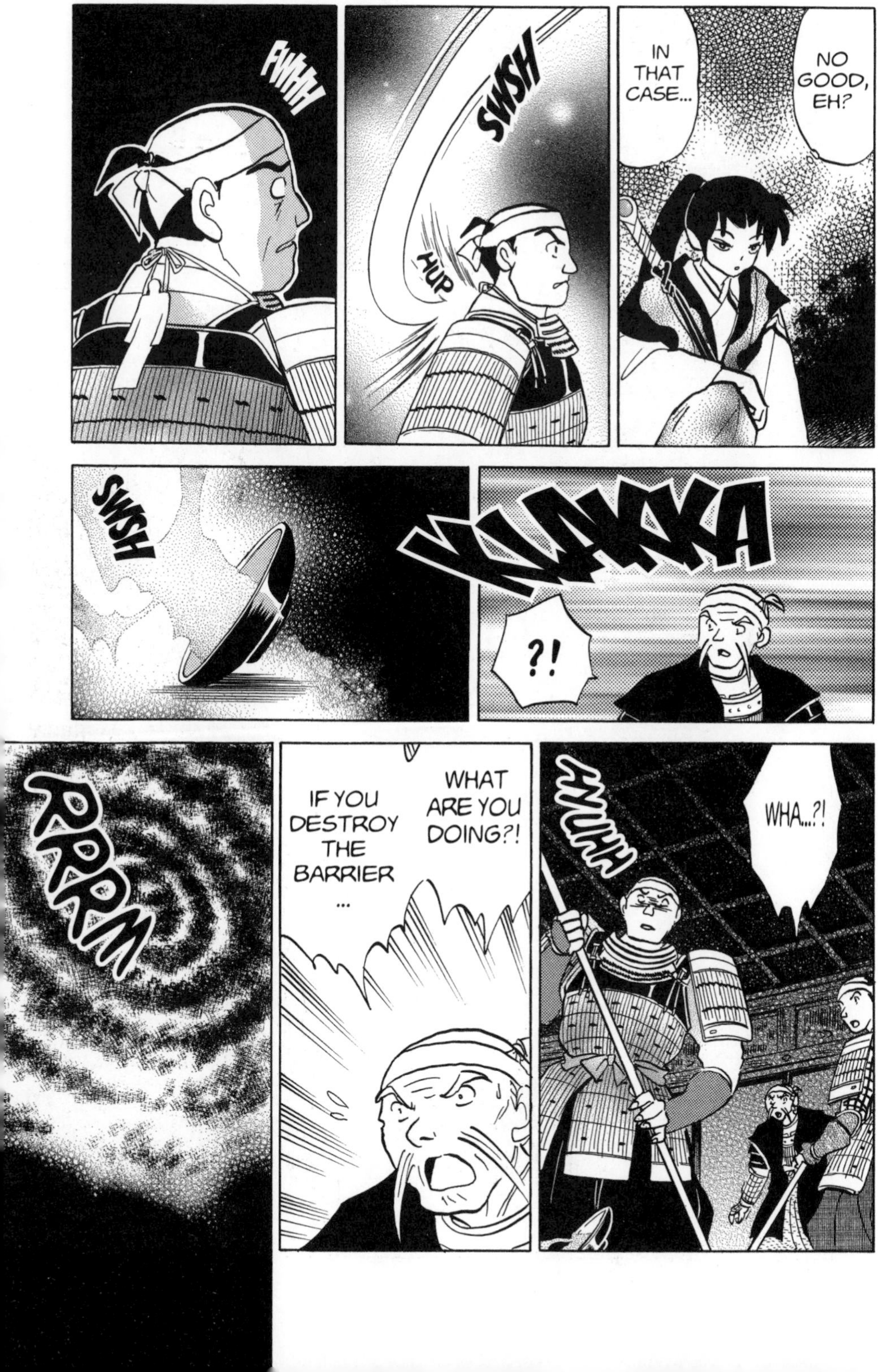
NO GOOD, EH?
IN THAT CASE...
SWSH
HUP
FWHH
WHAKKA
?!
SWSH
WHA...?!
HWUHH
WHAT ARE YOU DOING?!
IF YOU DESTROY THE BARRIER...
RRRM

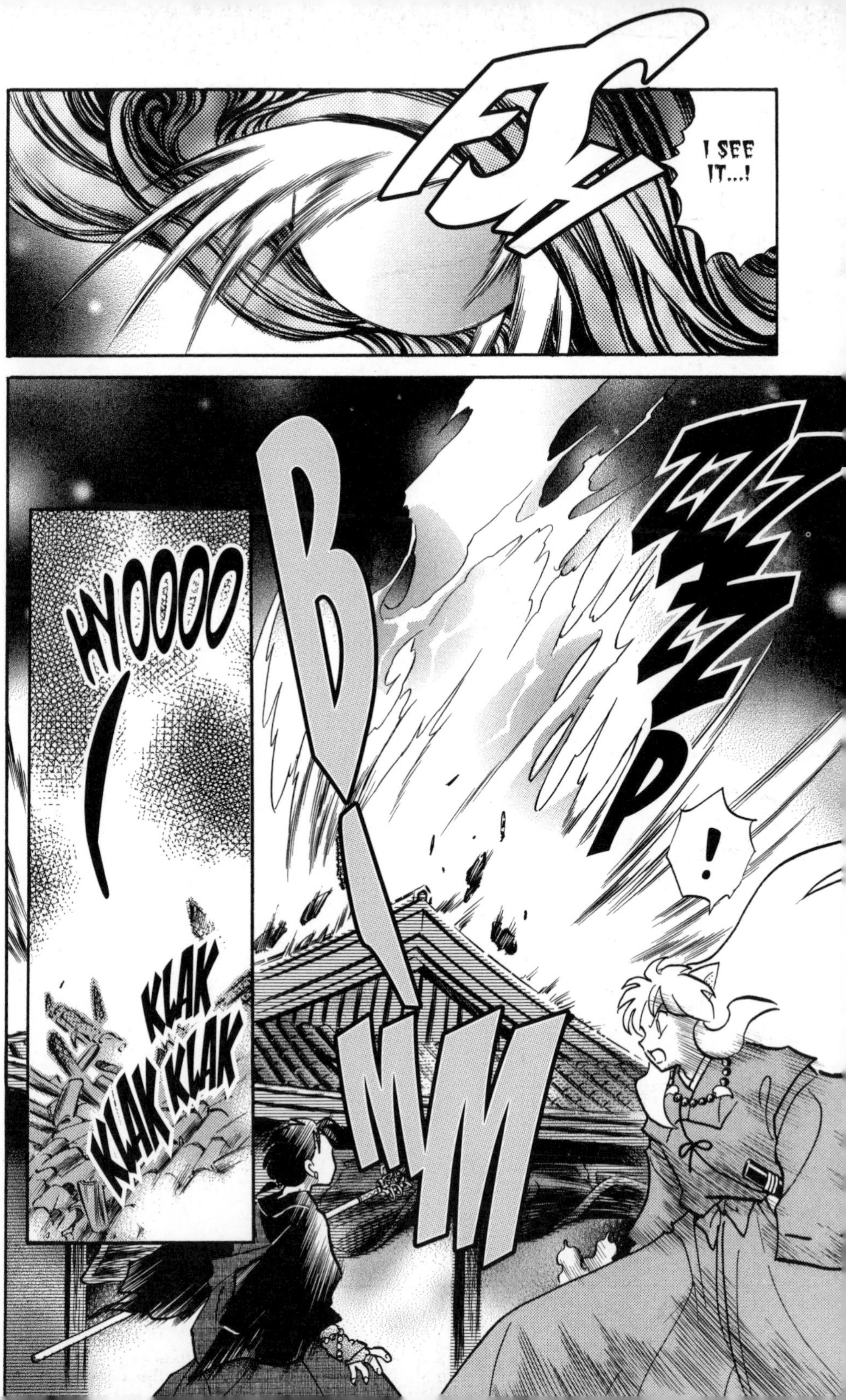
I SEE IT...!
!
HYOOOO
KLAK KLAK KLAK

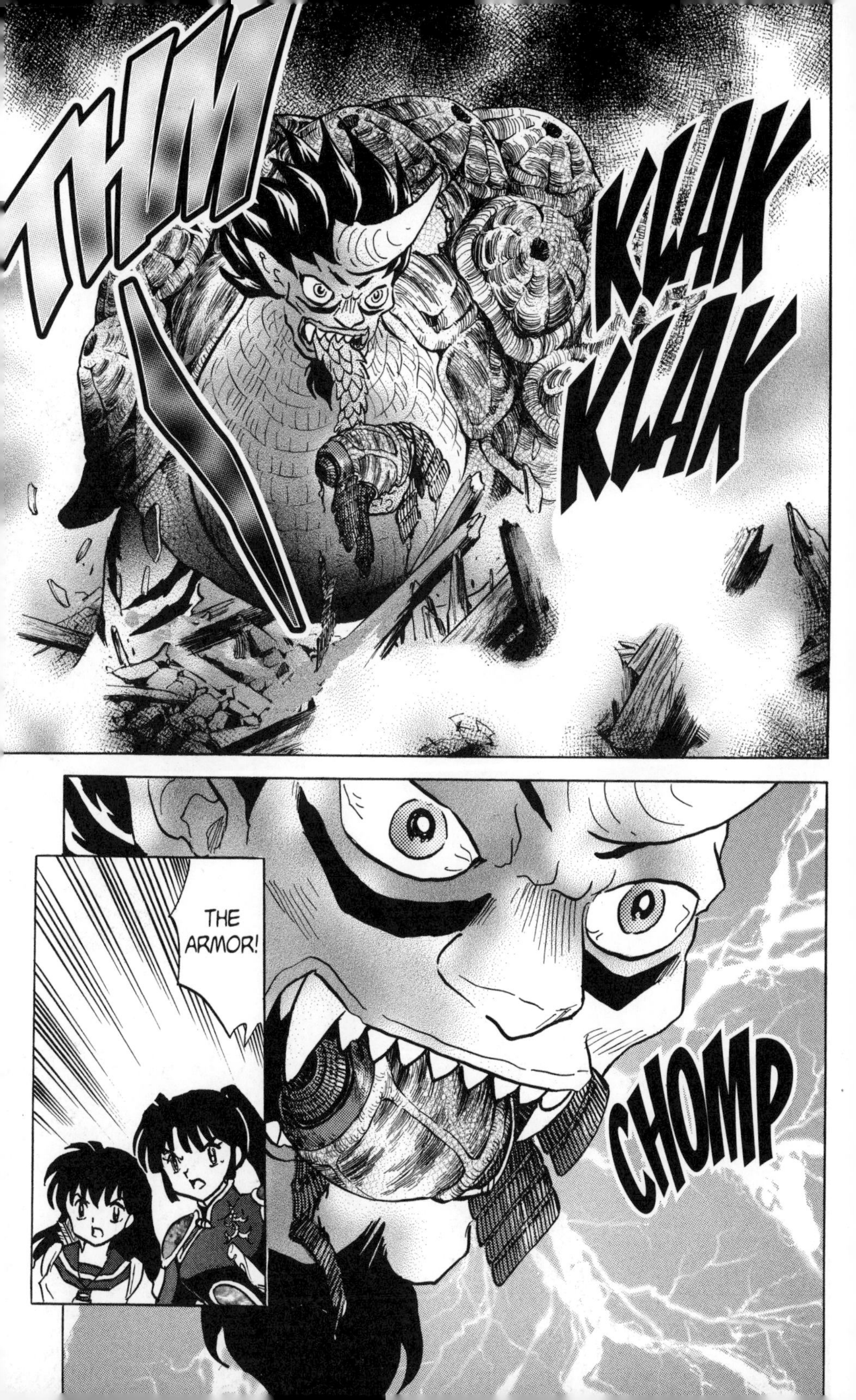
KLAK KLAK
THM
CHOMP
THE ARMOR!

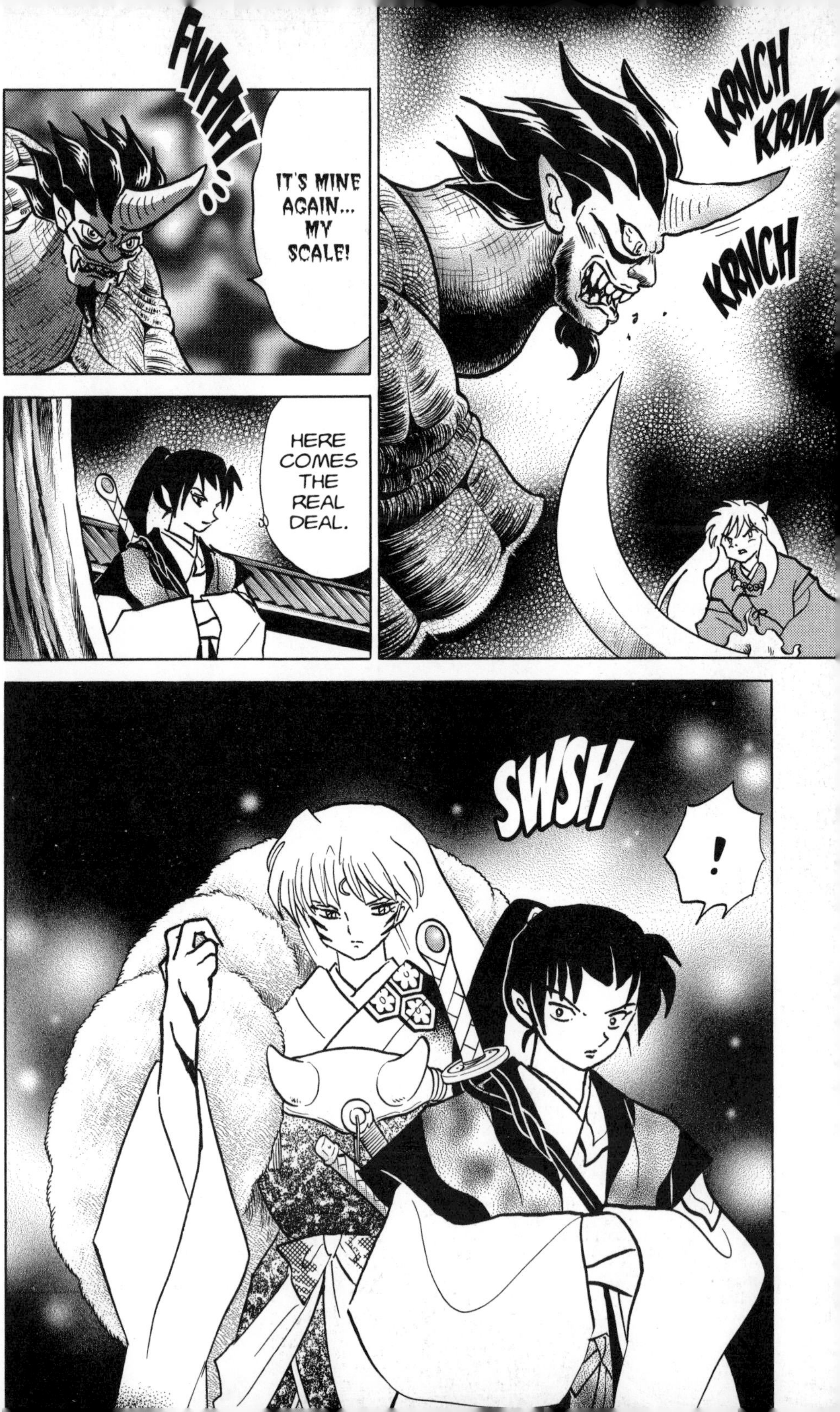
KRNCH KRNK
KRNCH
FWHH
IT'S MINE AGAIN... MY SCALE!
HERE COMES THE REAL DEAL.
SWSH
!

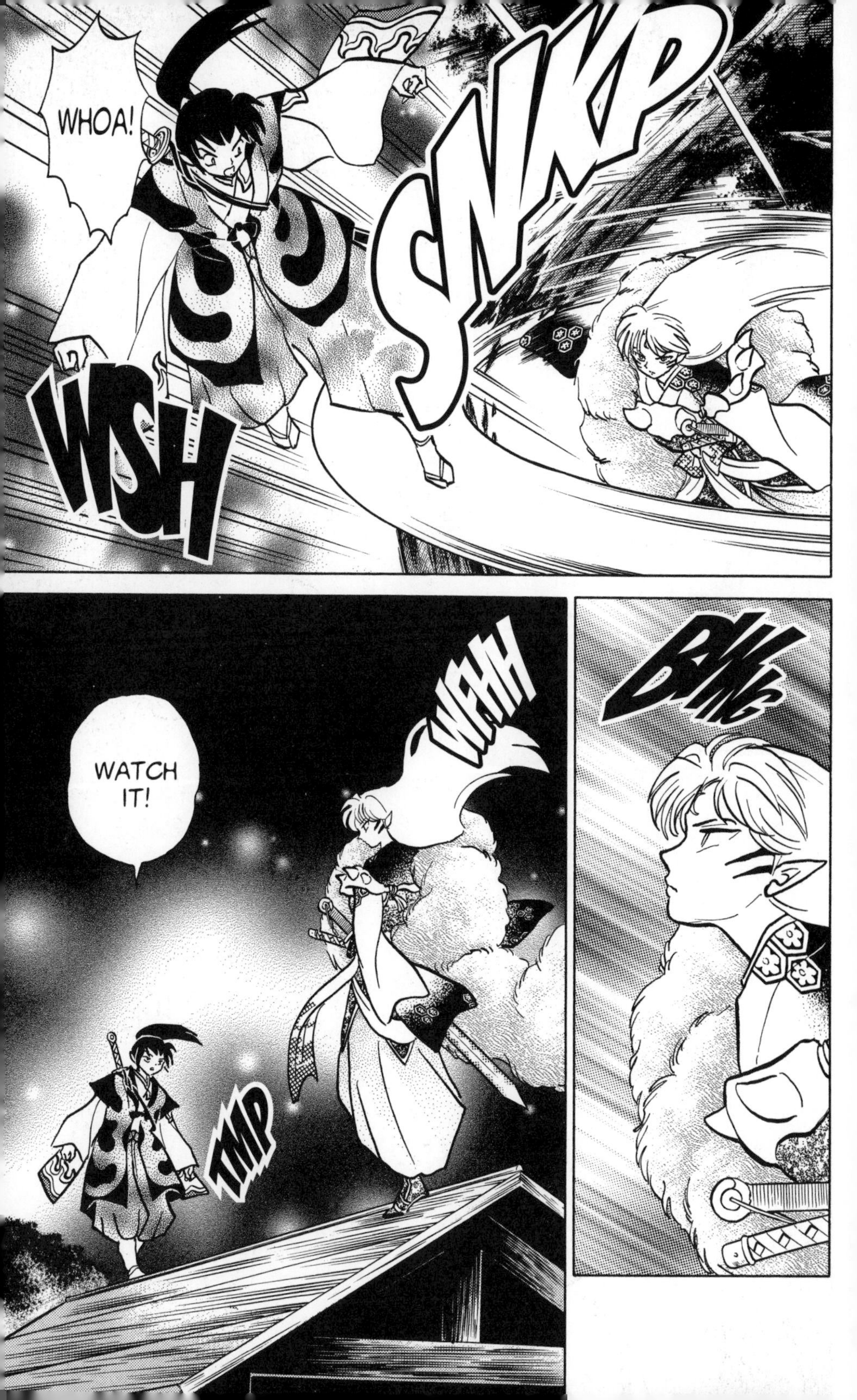
SNKP
WHOA!
WSH
BING
WHHH
WATCH IT!
TMP

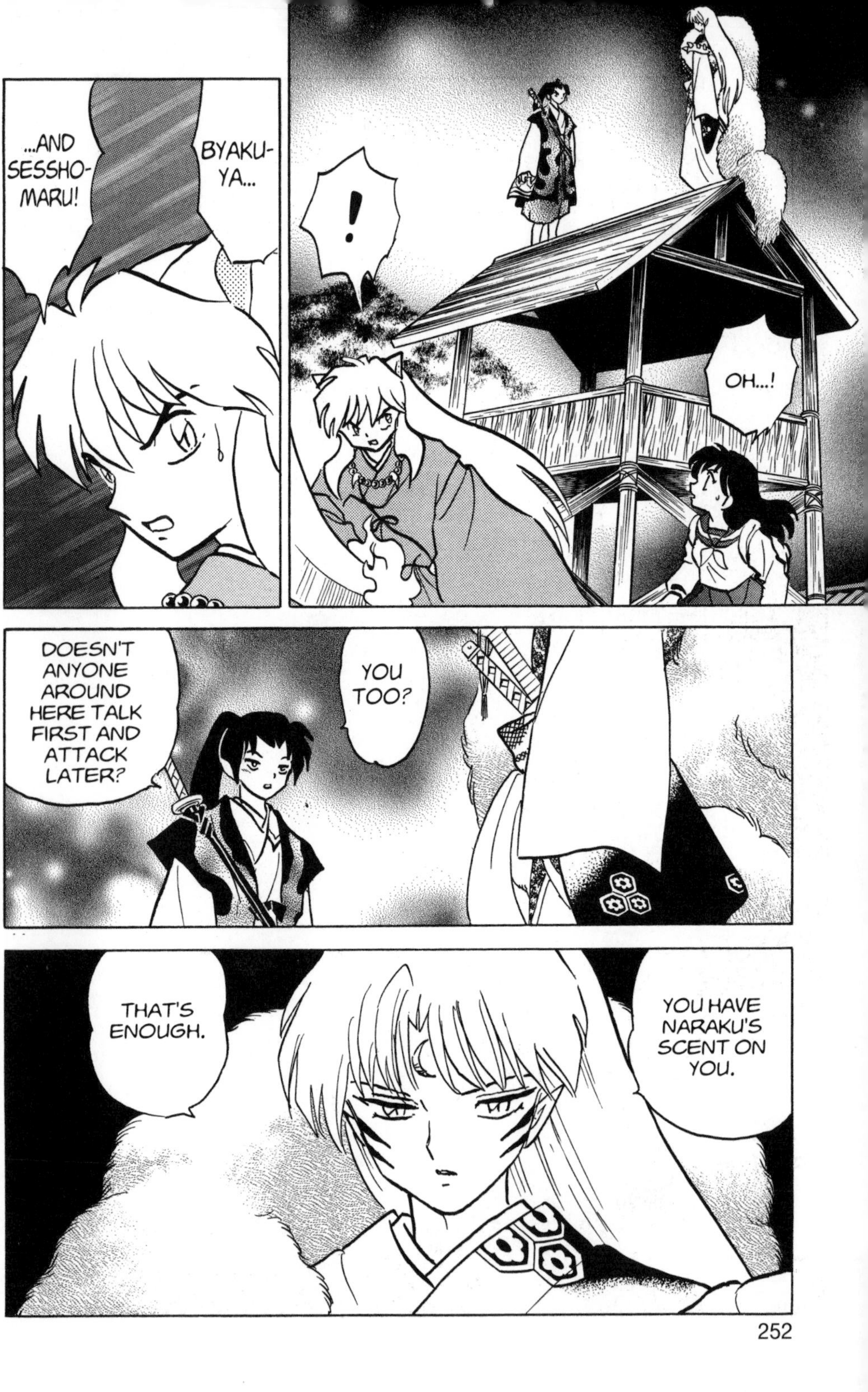
!
OH...!
BYAKU-YA...
...AND SESSHO-MARU!
YOU TOO?
DOESN'T ANYONE AROUND HERE TALK FIRST AND ATTACK LATER?
YOU HAVE NARAKU'S SCENT ON YOU.
THAT'S ENOUGH.

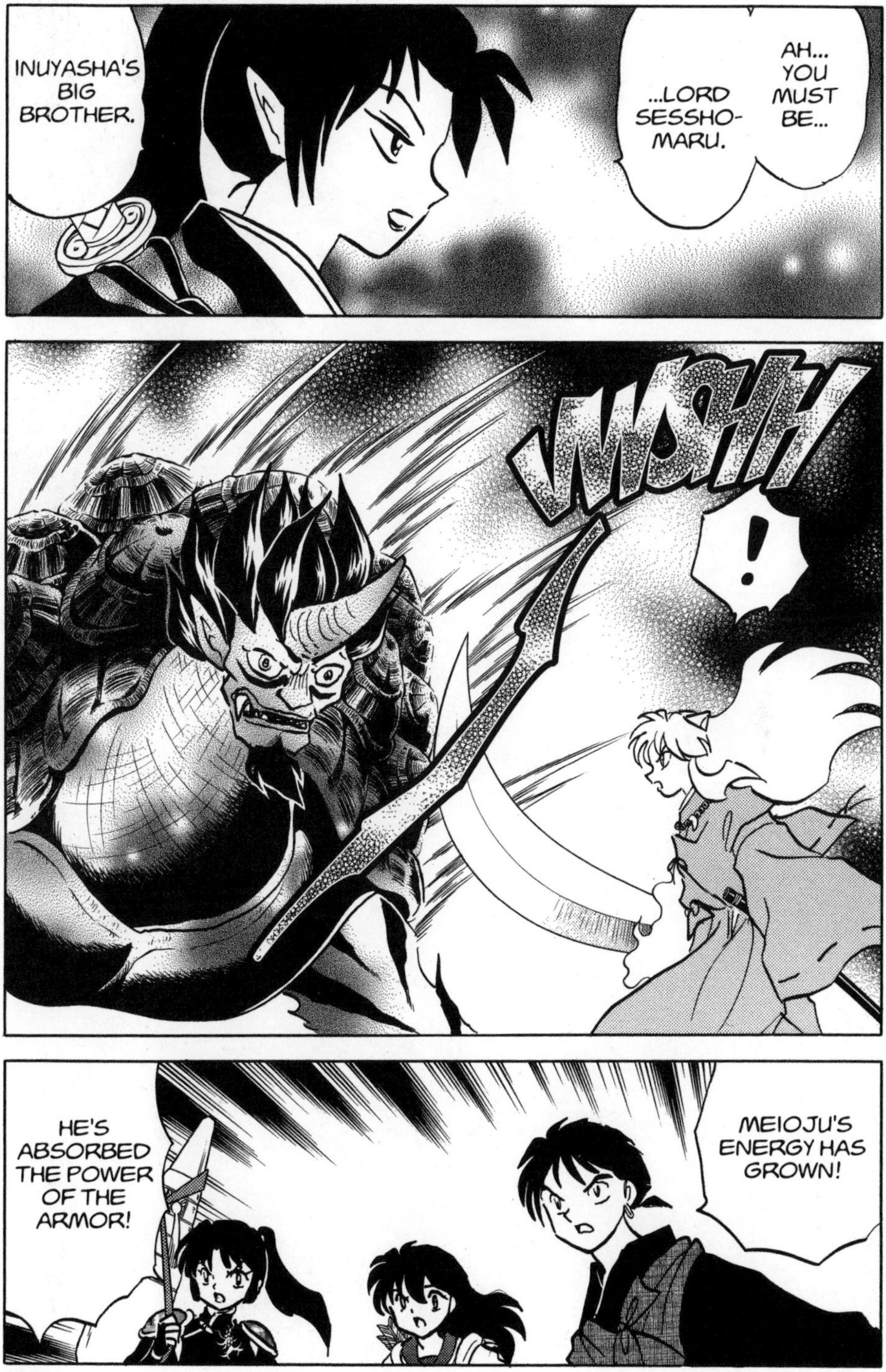
AH... YOU MUST BE...
...LORD SESSHOMARU.
INUYASHA'S BIG BROTHER.
VWSHH
!
MEIOJU'S ENERGY HAS GROWN!
HE'S ABSORBED THE POWER OF THE ARMOR!

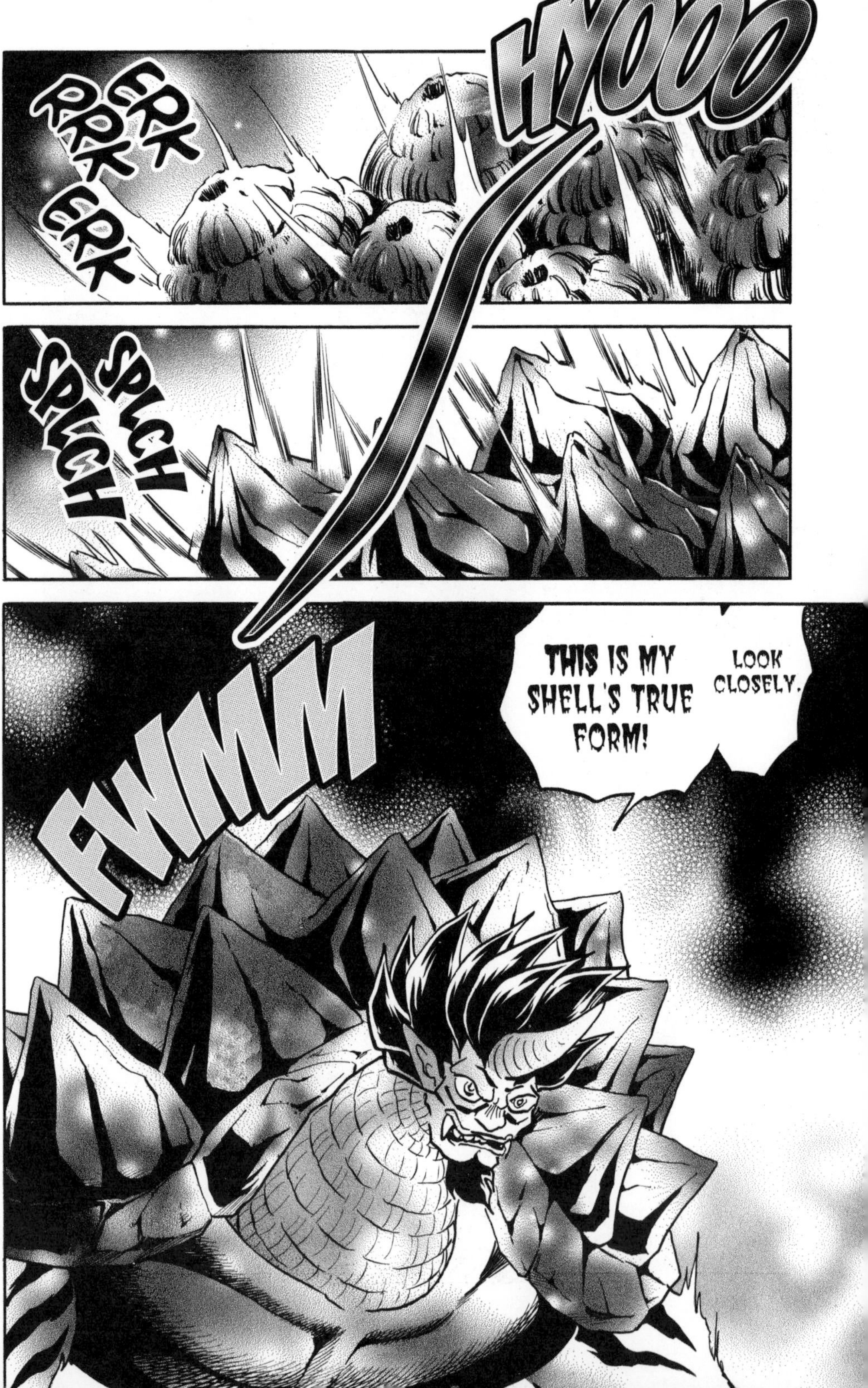
HYOOO
ERK RRK ERK
SPLCH SPLCH
LOOK CLOSELY.
THIS IS MY SHELL'S TRUE FORM!
FWMMM

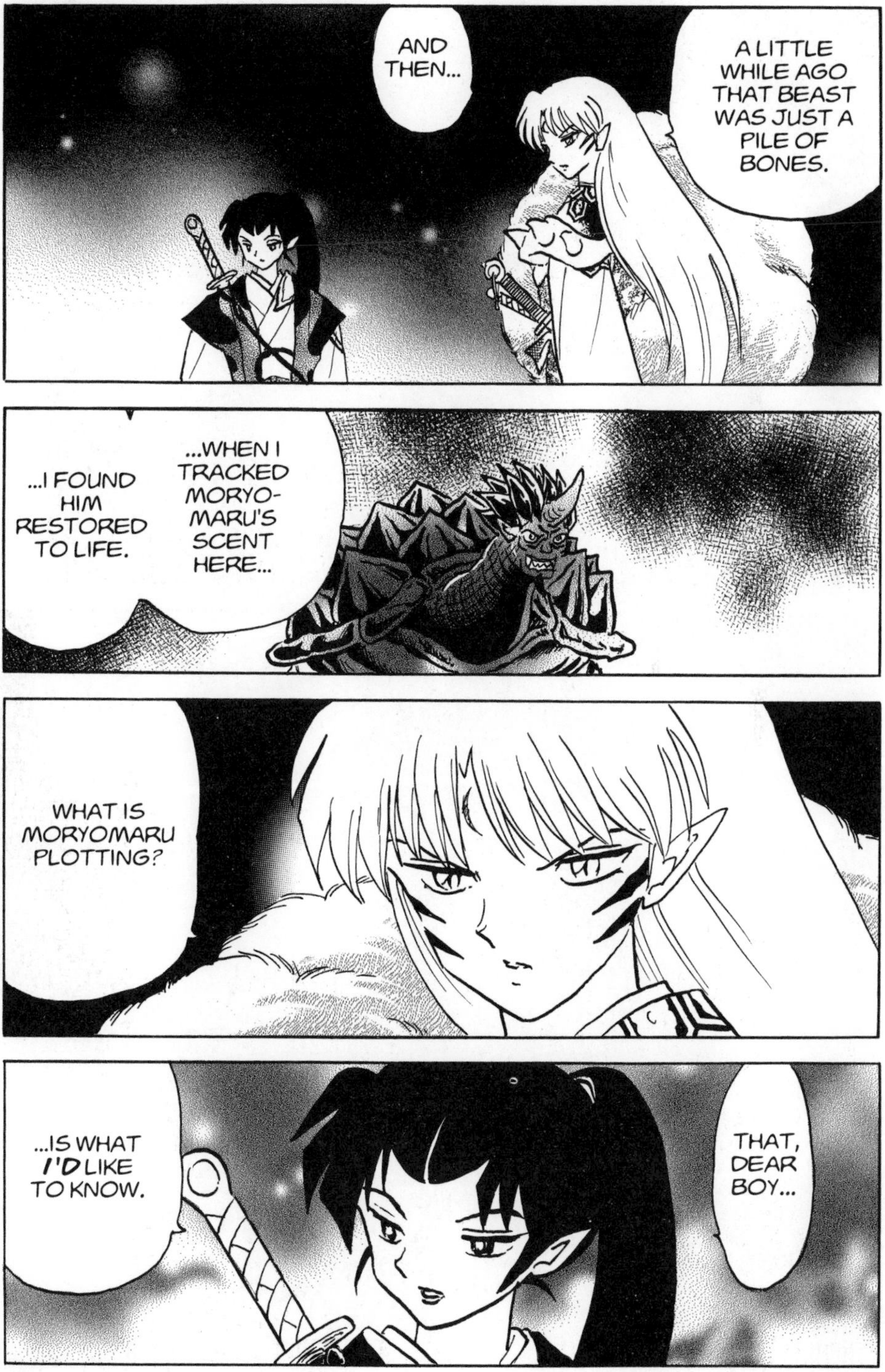
A LITTLE WHILE AGO THAT BEAST WAS JUST A PILE OF BONES.
AND THEN...
...WHEN I TRACKED MORYO-MARU'S SCENT HERE...
...I FOUND HIM RESTORED TO LIFE.
WHAT IS MORYOMARU PLOTTING?
THAT, DEAR BOY...
...IS WHAT ***I'D*** LIKE TO KNOW.

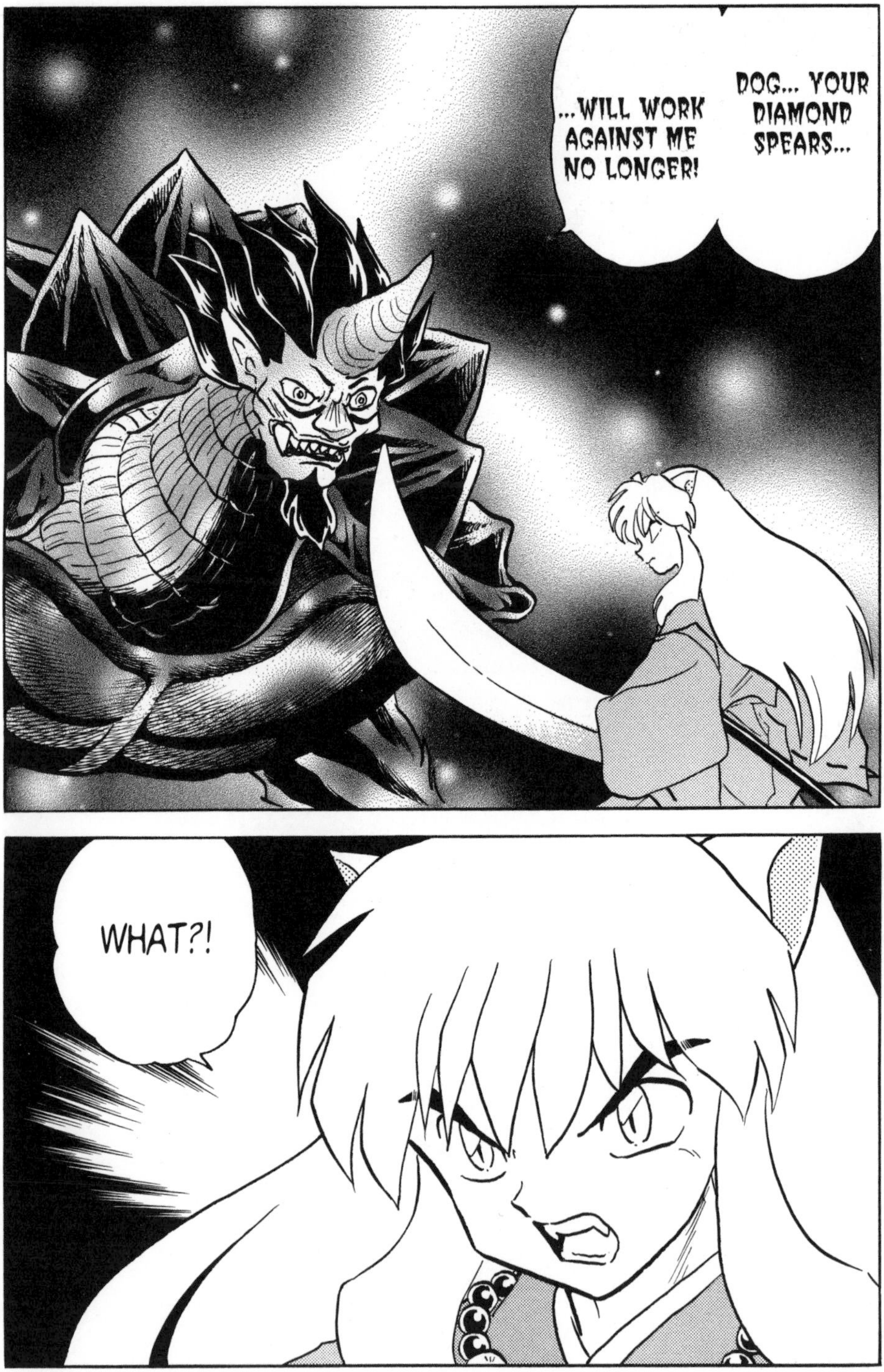
DOG... YOUR DIAMOND SPEARS...
...WILL WORK AGAINST ME NO LONGER!
WHAT?!

SCROLL FOUR
MORYOMARU'S TARGET

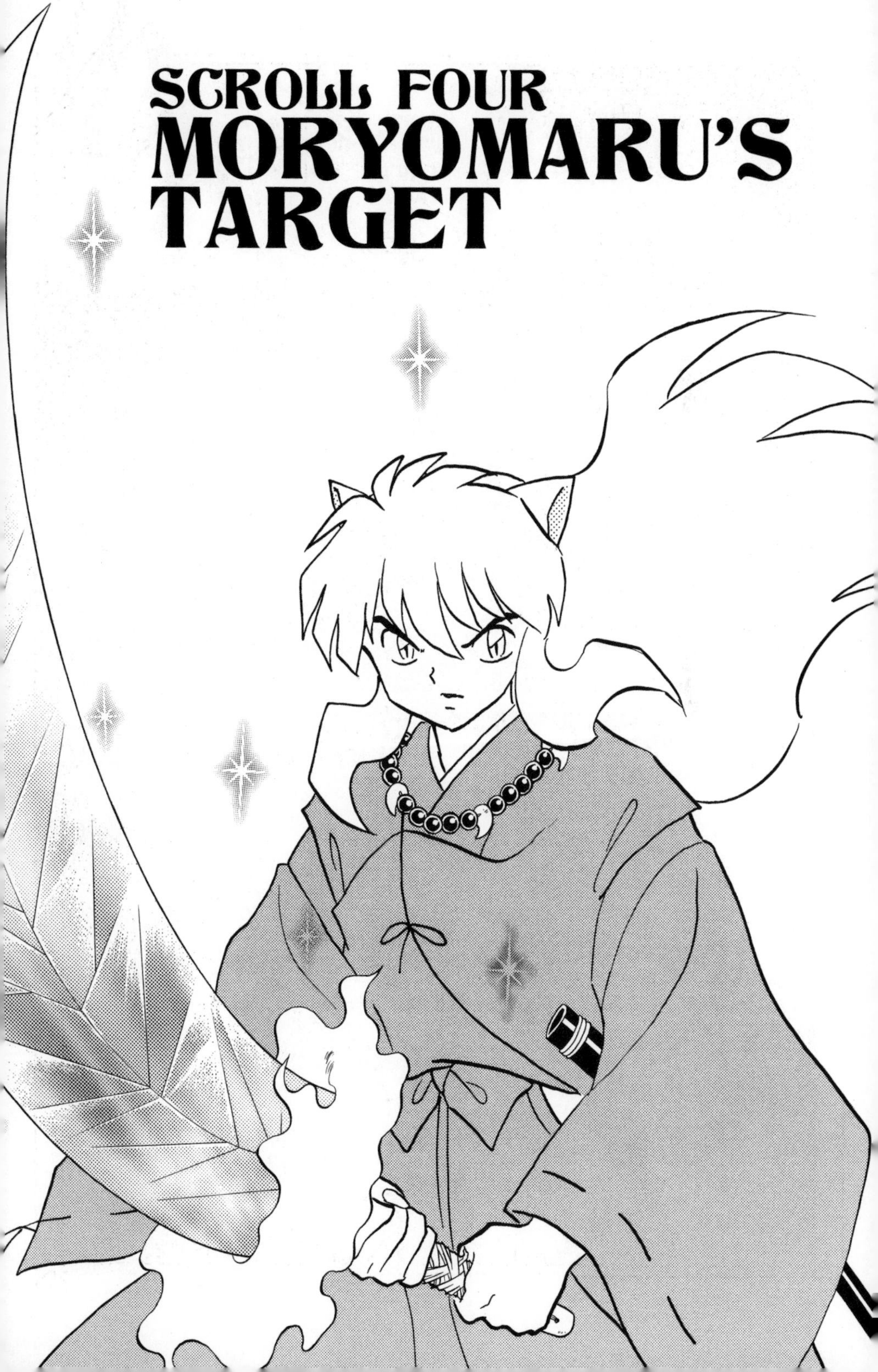

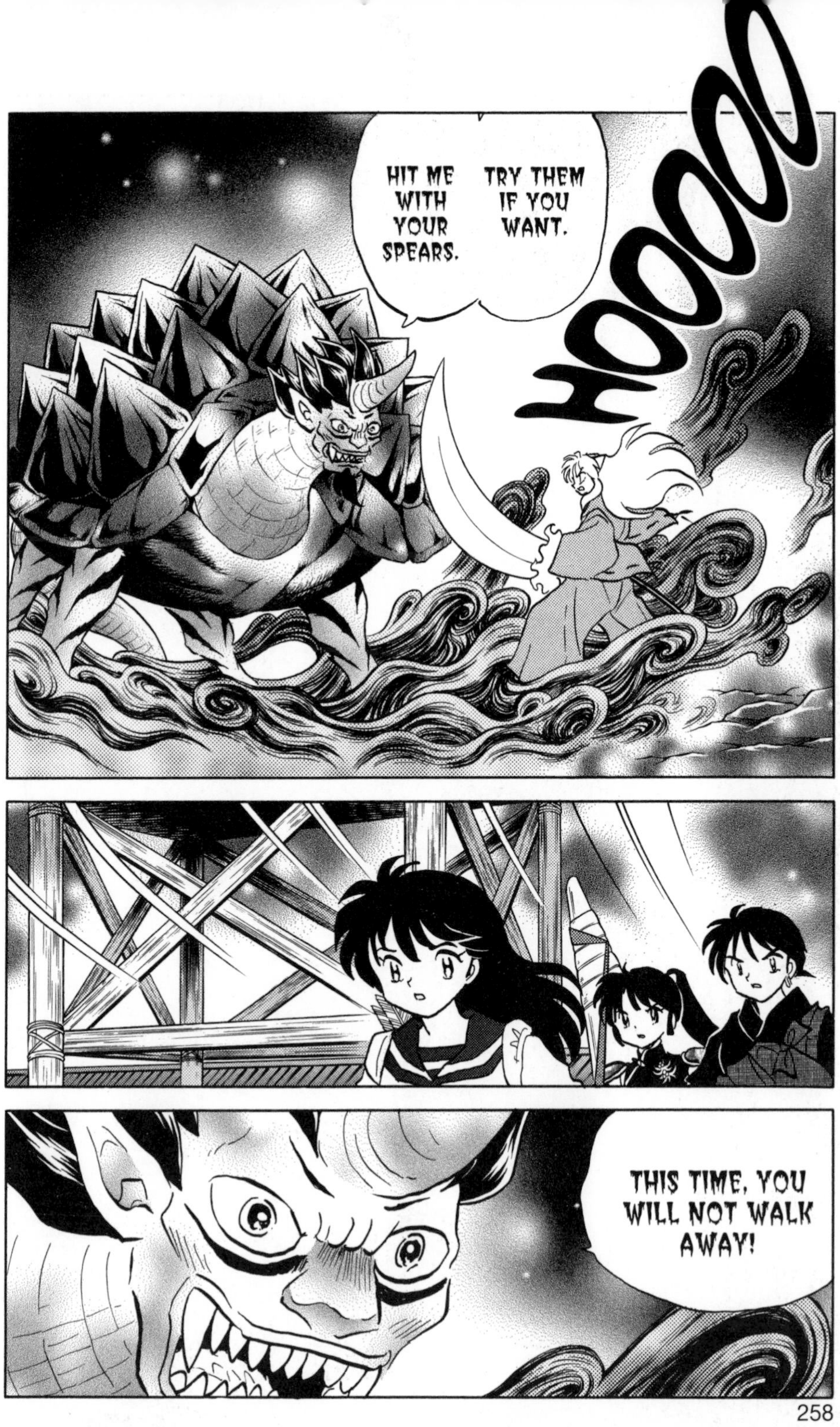
HOOOOO
HIT ME WITH YOUR SPEARS. TRY THEM IF YOU WANT.
THIS TIME, YOU WILL NOT WALK AWAY!

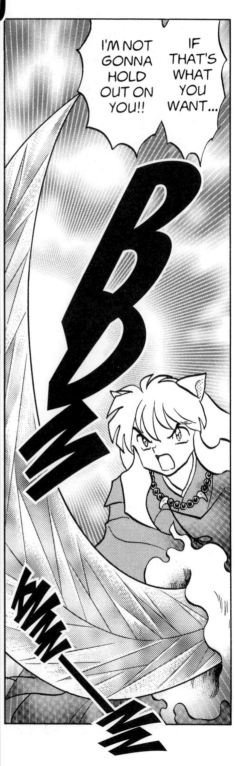

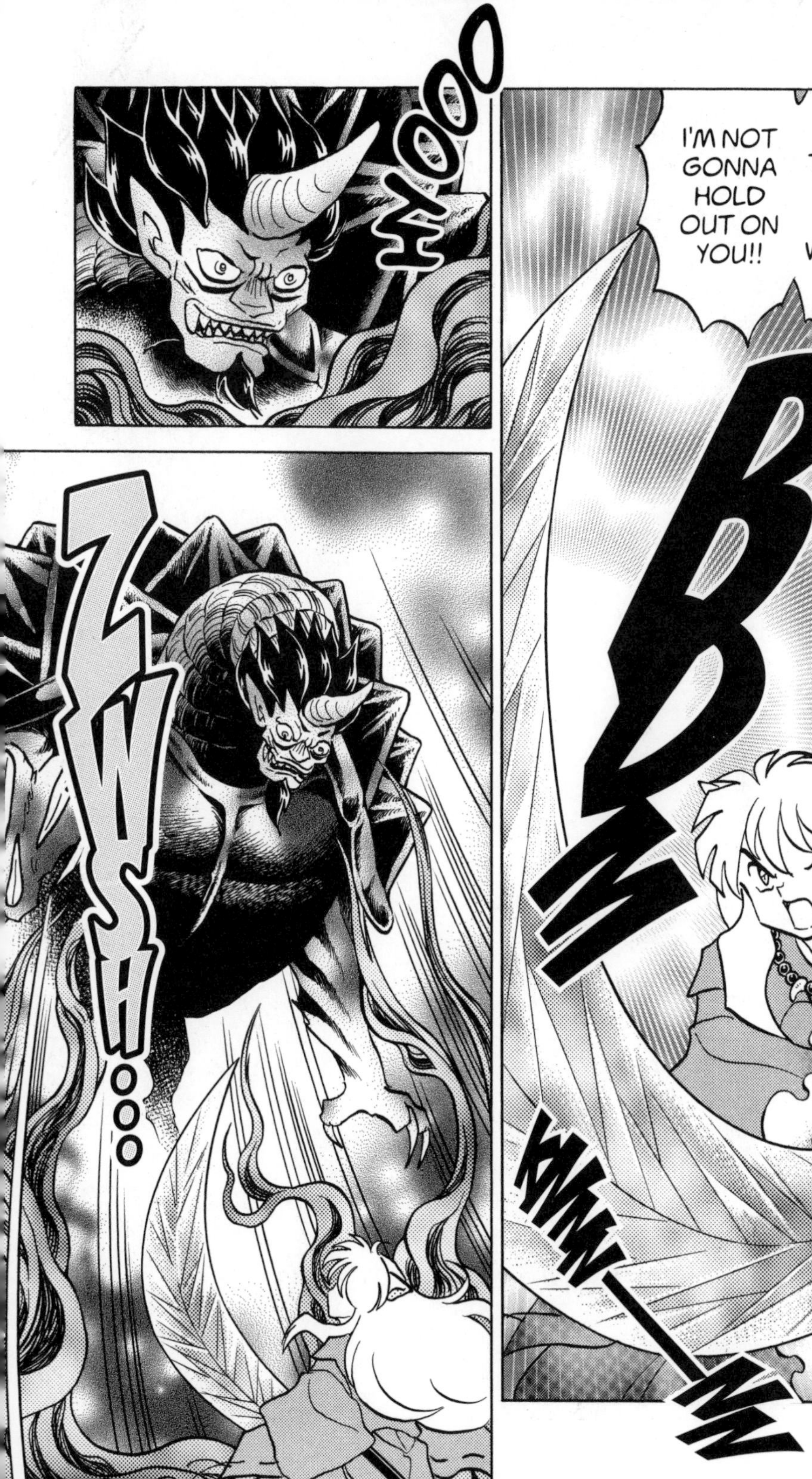
IF THAT'S WHAT YOU WANT...
I'M NOT GONNA HOLD OUT ON YOU!!
WHOOO

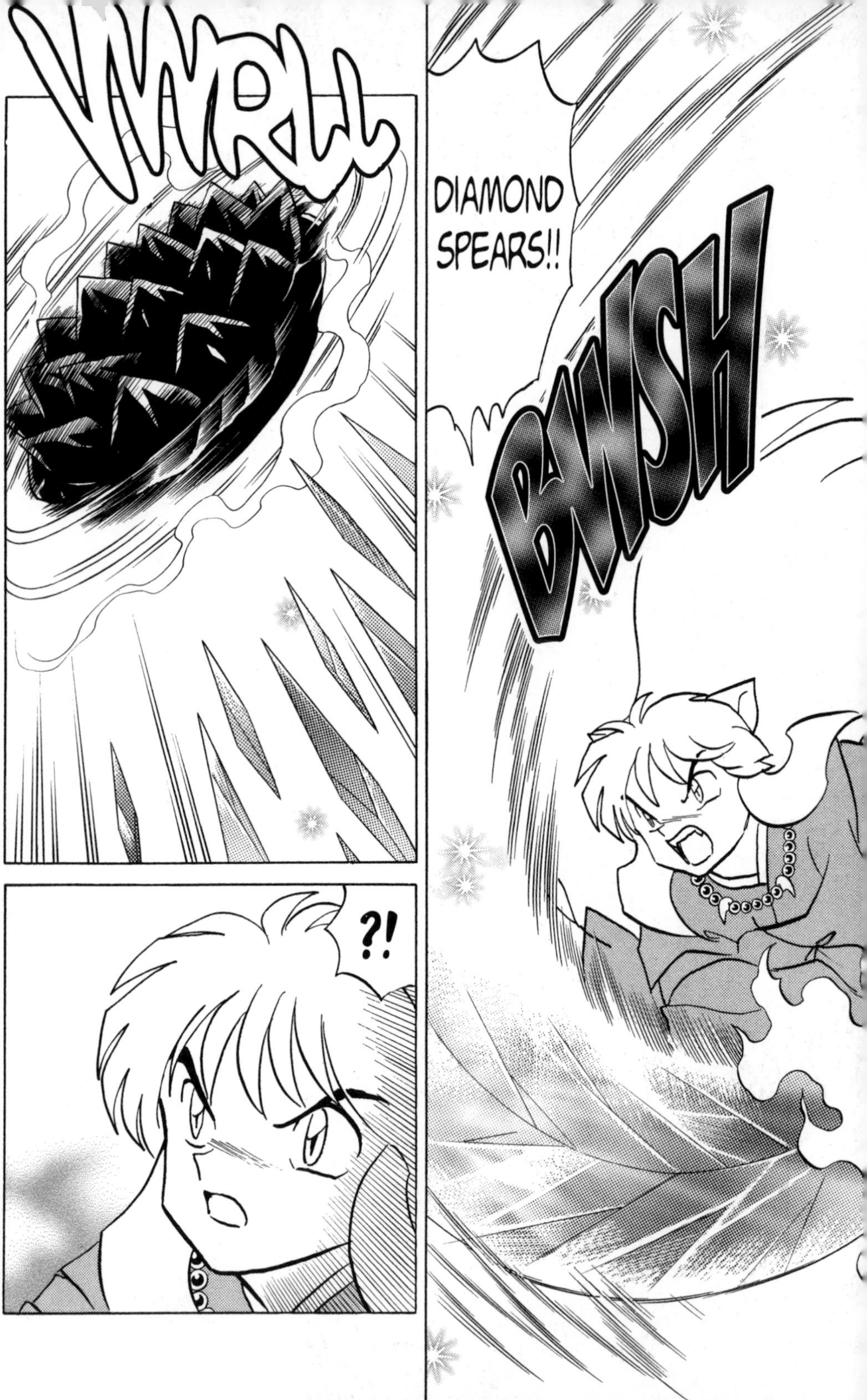
DIAMOND SPEARS!!
BWISH
VWRLL
?!

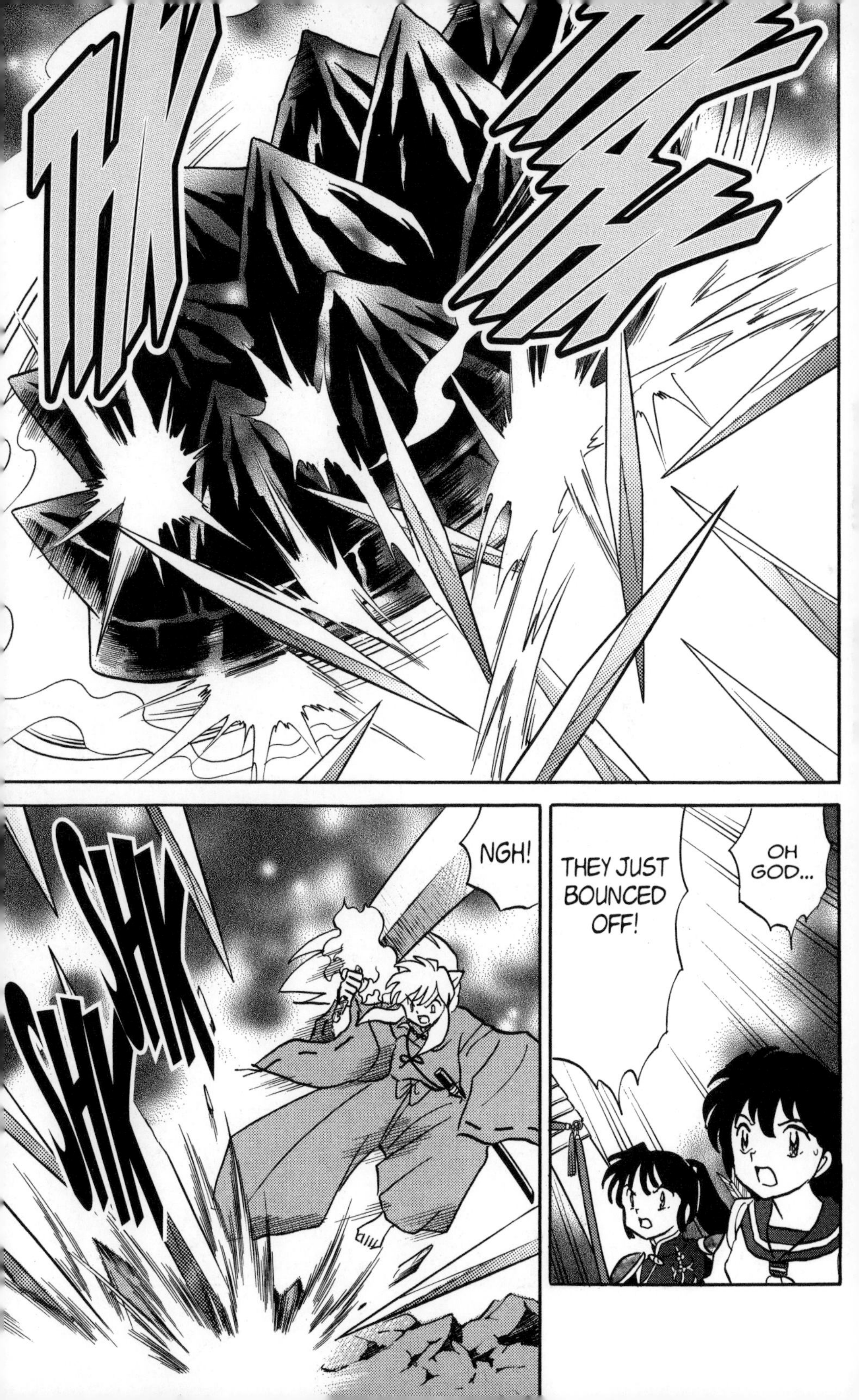
OH GOD...
THEY JUST BOUNCED OFF!
NGH!
SHK SHK

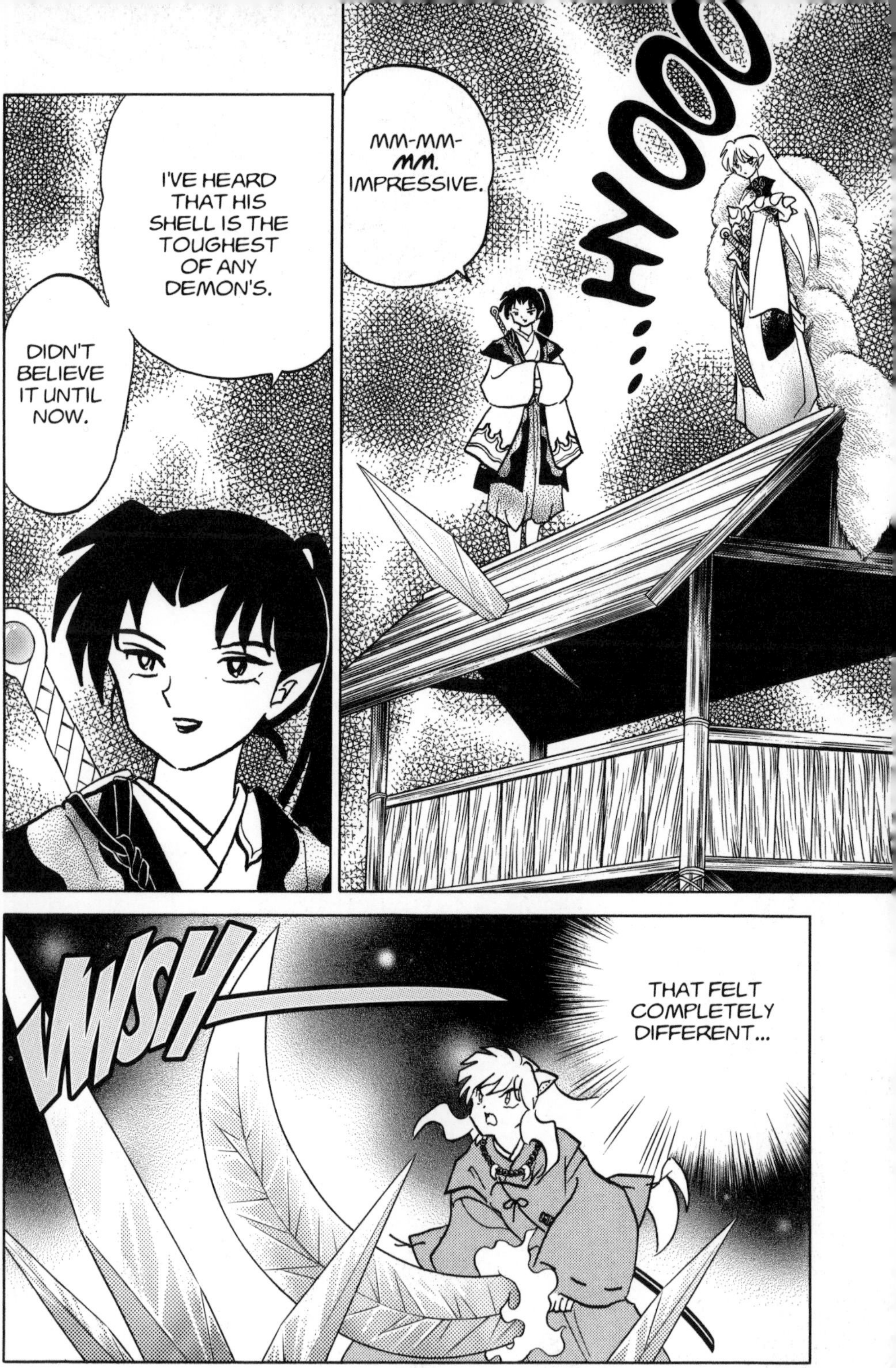
MM-MM-MM. IMPRESSIVE.
I'VE HEARD THAT HIS SHELL IS THE TOUGHEST OF ANY DEMON'S.
DIDN'T BELIEVE IT UNTIL NOW.
WSH
THAT FELT COMPLETELY DIFFERENT...

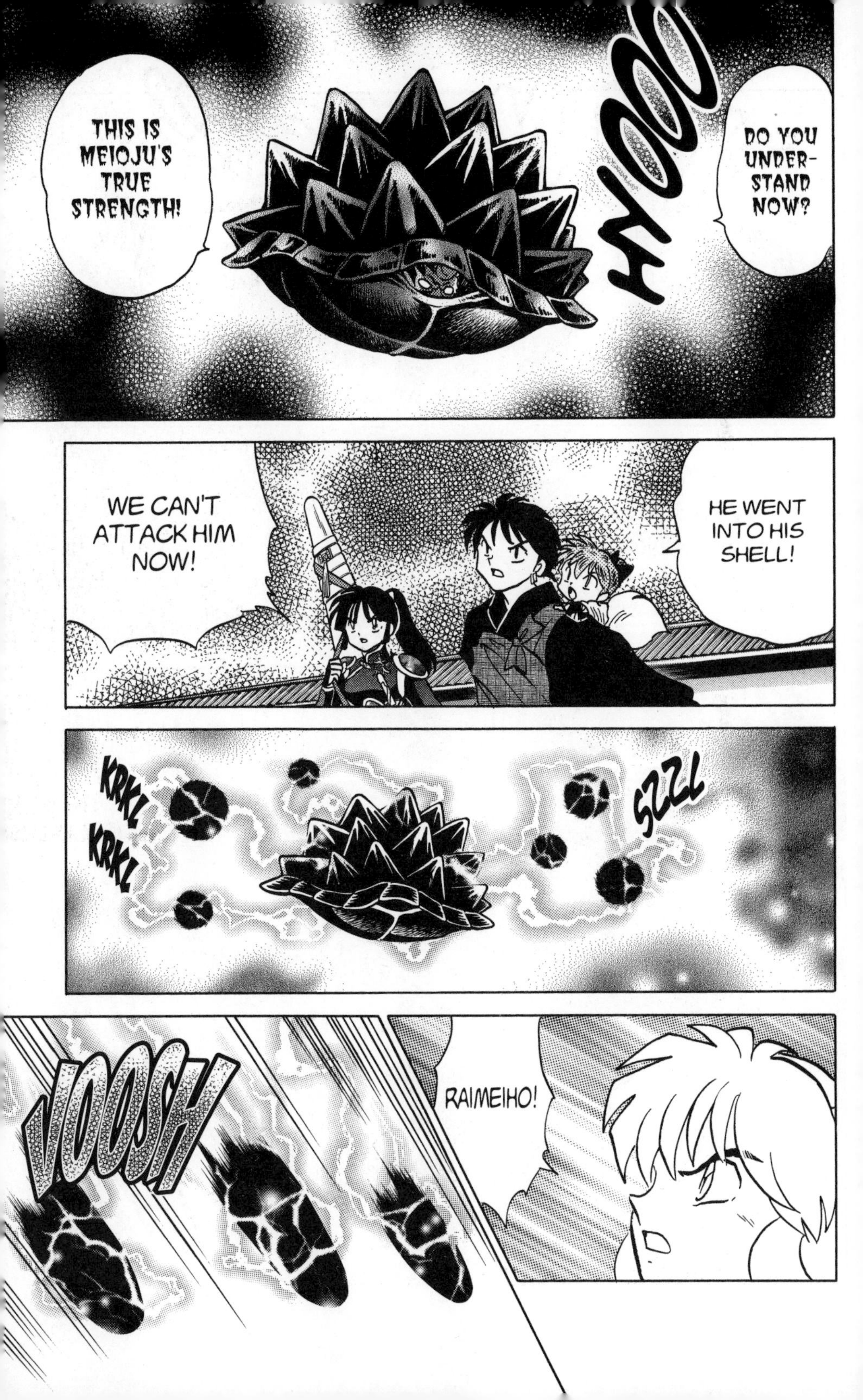
DO YOU UNDER-STAND NOW?
HYOOO
THIS IS MEIOJU'S TRUE STRENGTH!
HE WENT INTO HIS SHELL!
WE CAN'T ATTACK HIM NOW!
SZZZ
KRKL
KRKL
RAIMEIHO!
VOOSH

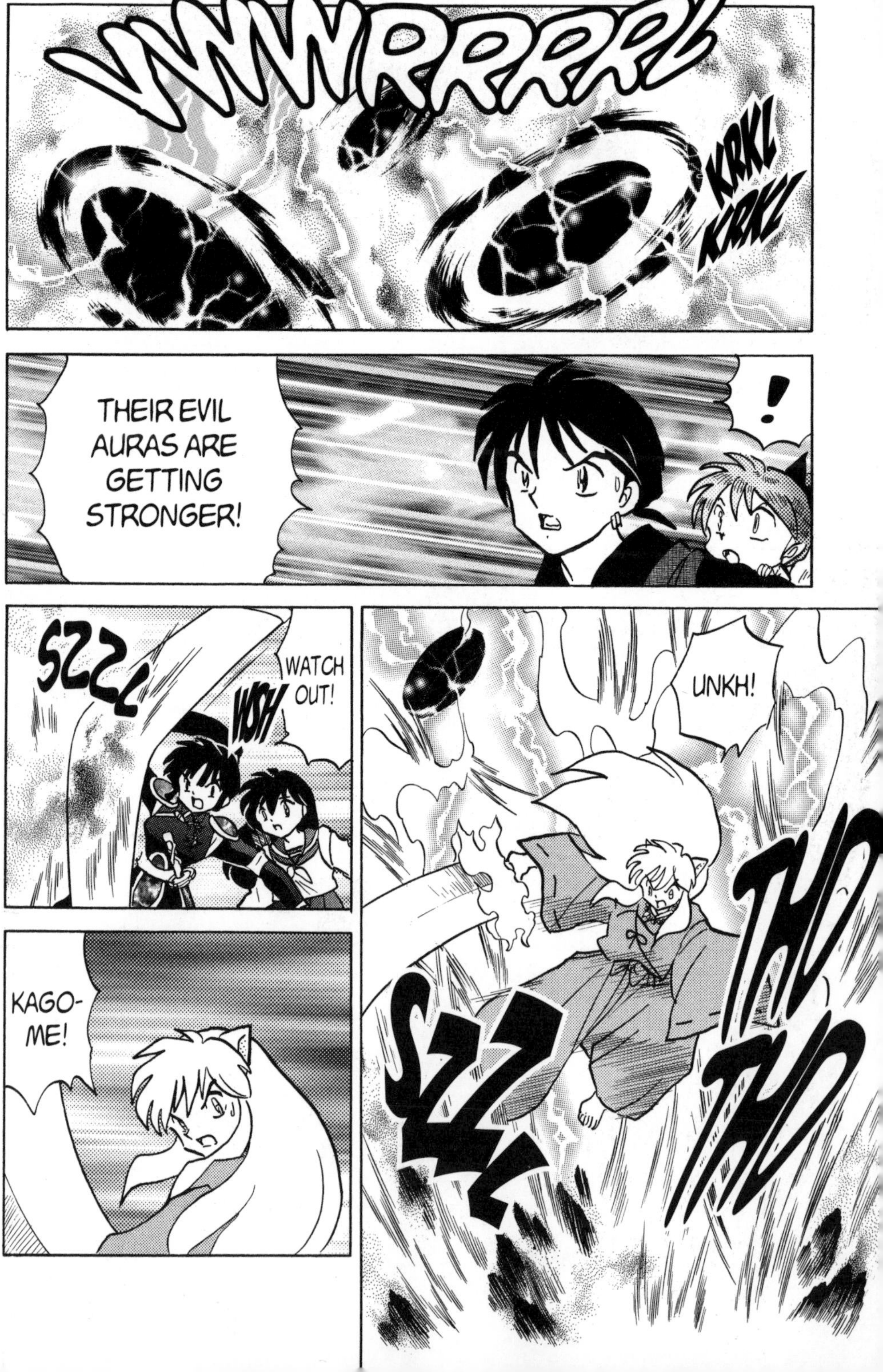
VVVVRRRRL
KRKL
KRKL
!
THEIR EVIL AURAS ARE GETTING STRONGER!
UNKH!
TH
THD
SZZZ
SZZL
WATCH OUT!
WSH
KAGO-ME!

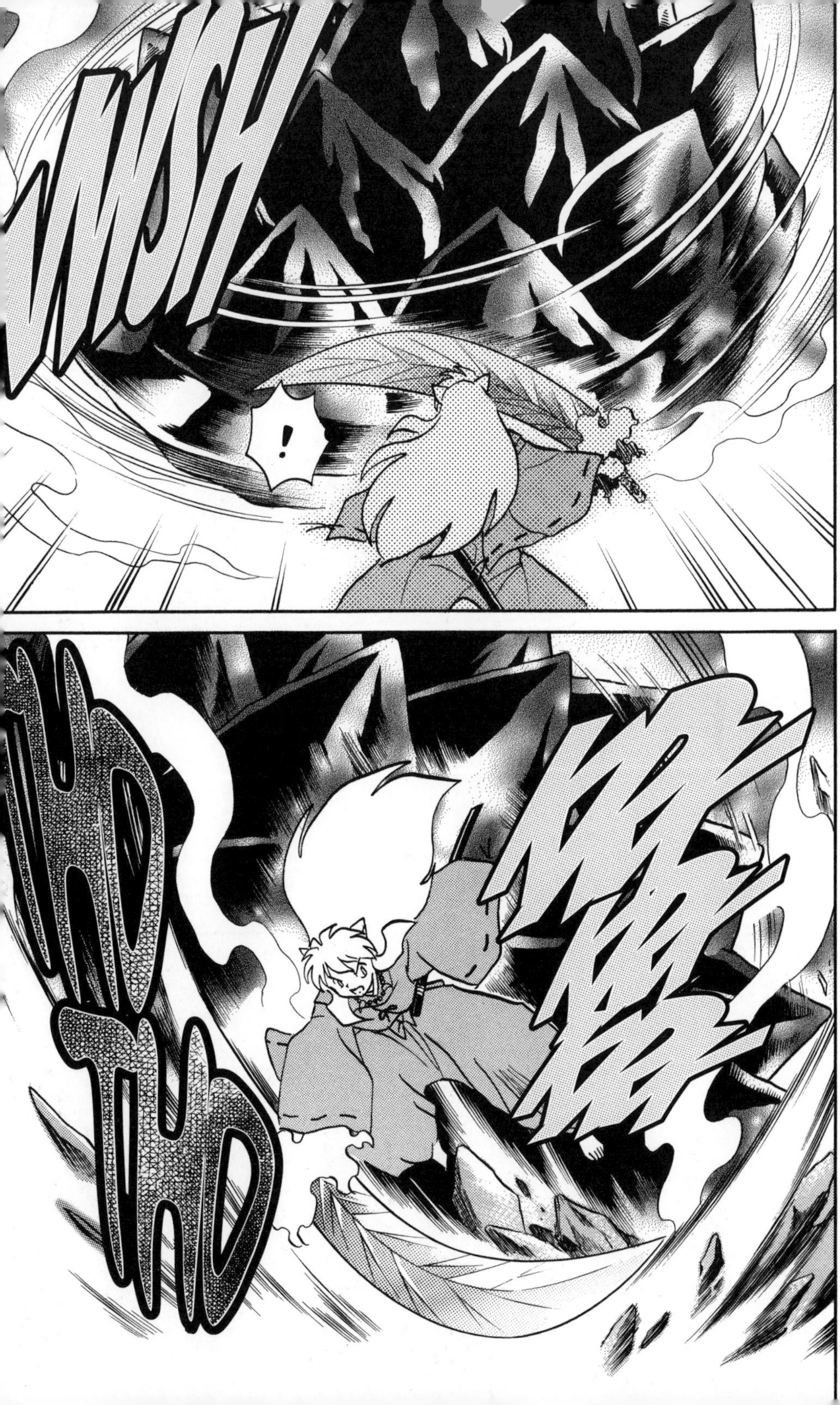
SWISH
!
THD THD

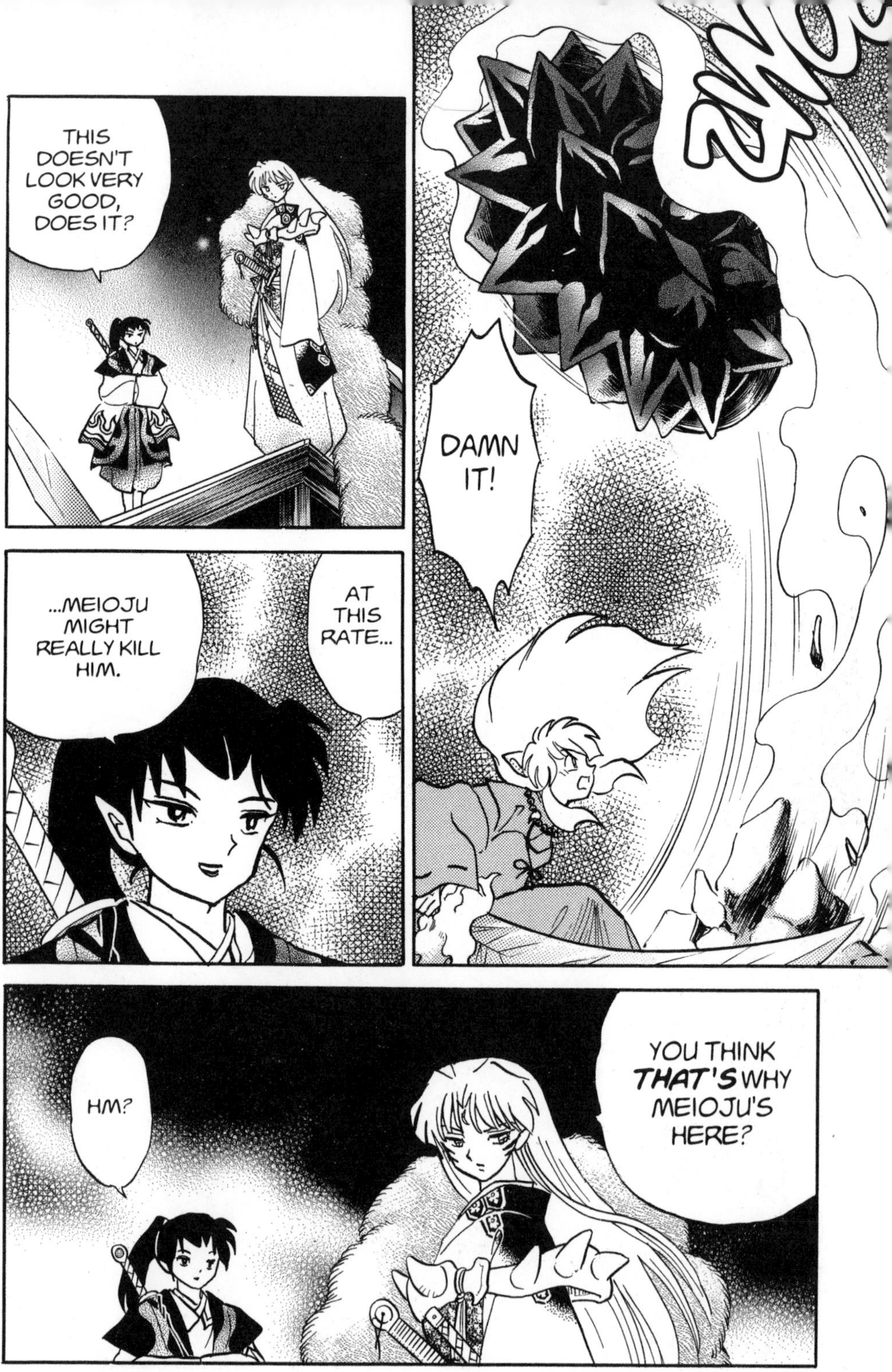
DAMN IT!
THIS DOESN'T LOOK VERY GOOD, DOES IT?
AT THIS RATE...
...MEIOJU MIGHT REALLY KILL HIM.
YOU THINK **THAT'S** WHY MEIOJU'S HERE?
HM?

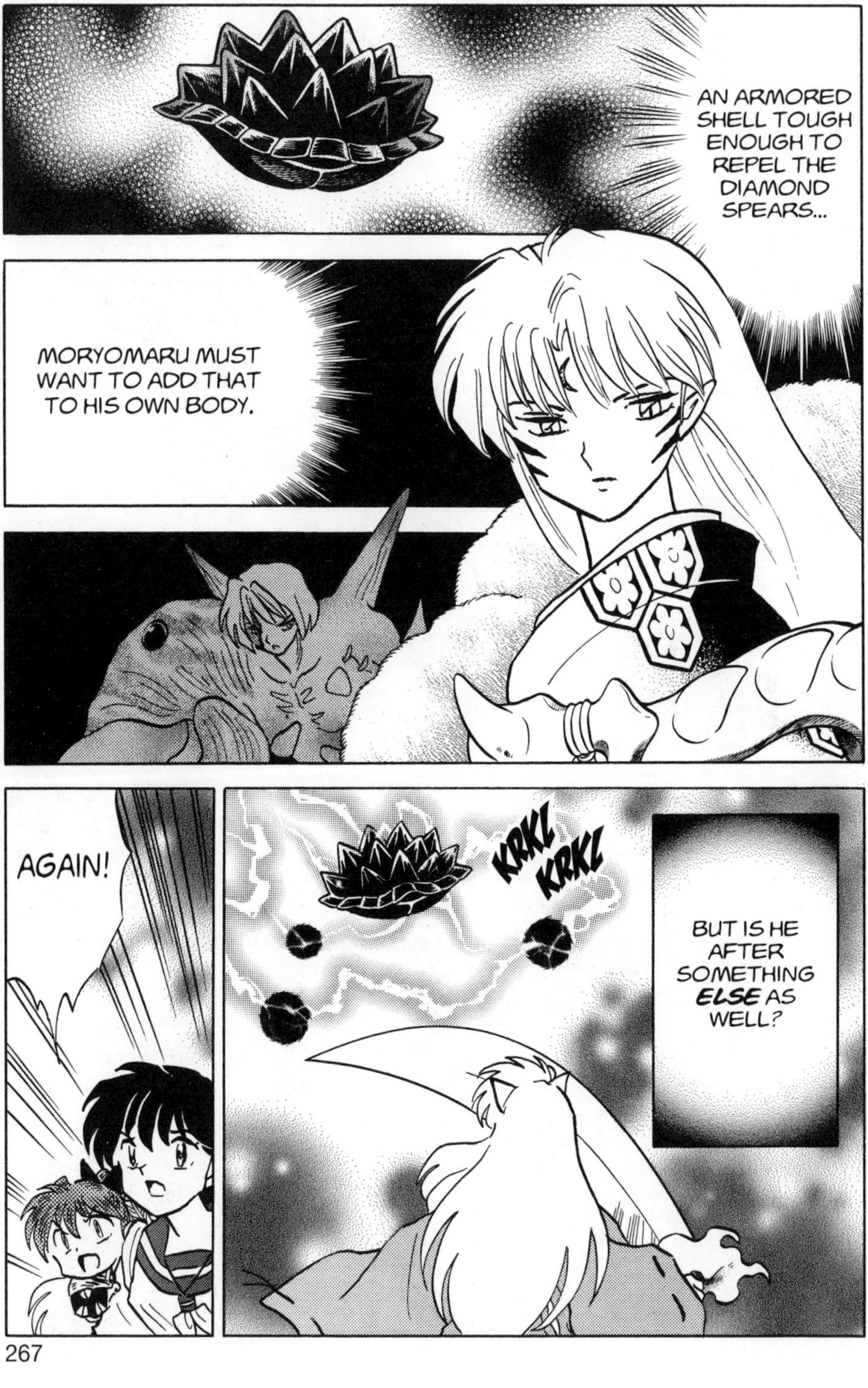
AN ARMORED SHELL TOUGH ENOUGH TO REPEL THE DIAMOND SPEARS...
MORYOMARU MUST WANT TO ADD THAT TO HIS OWN BODY.
BUT IS HE AFTER SOMETHING ***ELSE*** AS WELL?
KRKL KRKL
AGAIN!

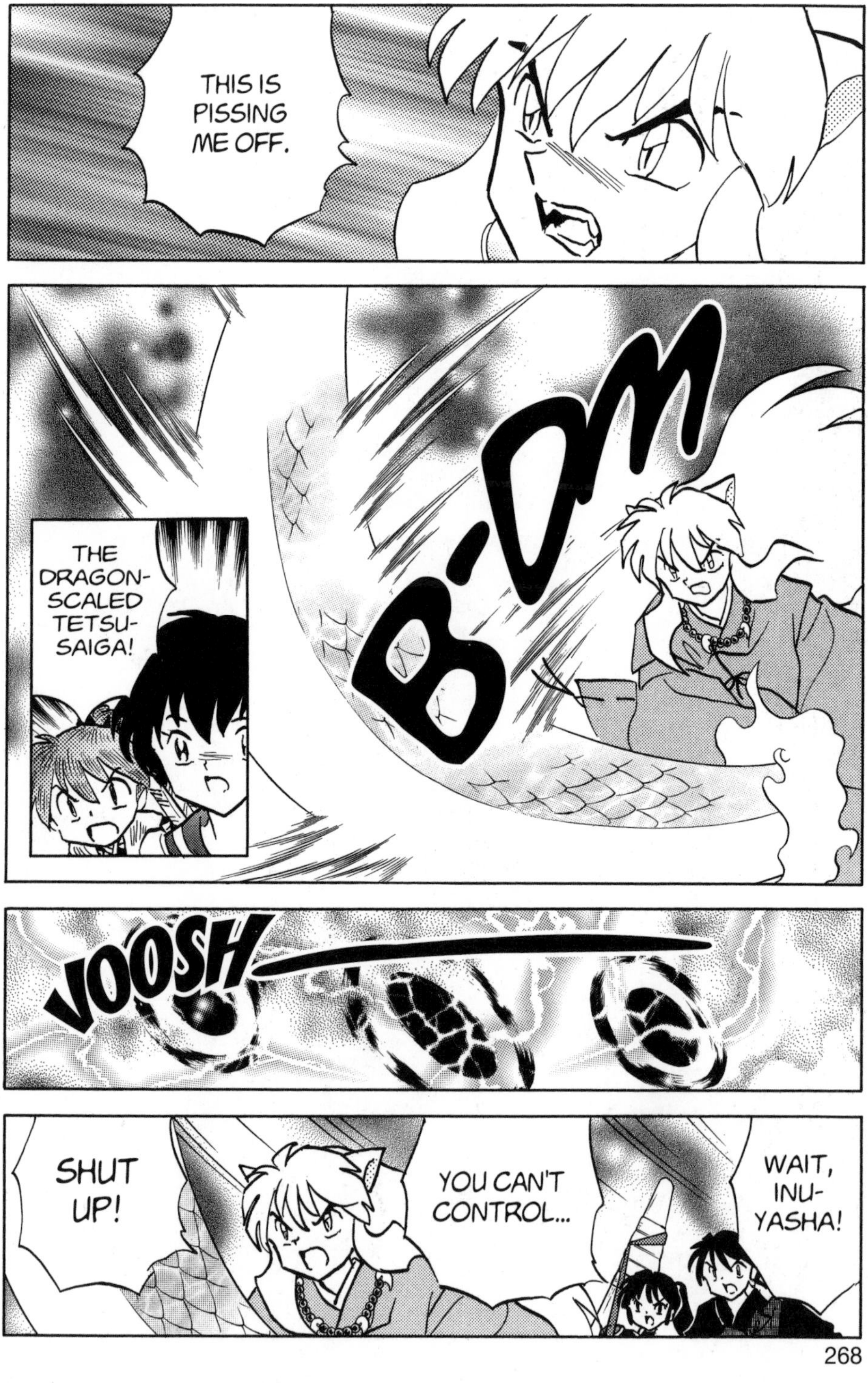
THIS IS PISSING ME OFF.
B-DM
THE DRAGON-SCALED TETSU-SAIGA!
VOOSH
WAIT, INU-YASHA!
YOU CAN'T CONTROL...
SHUT UP!

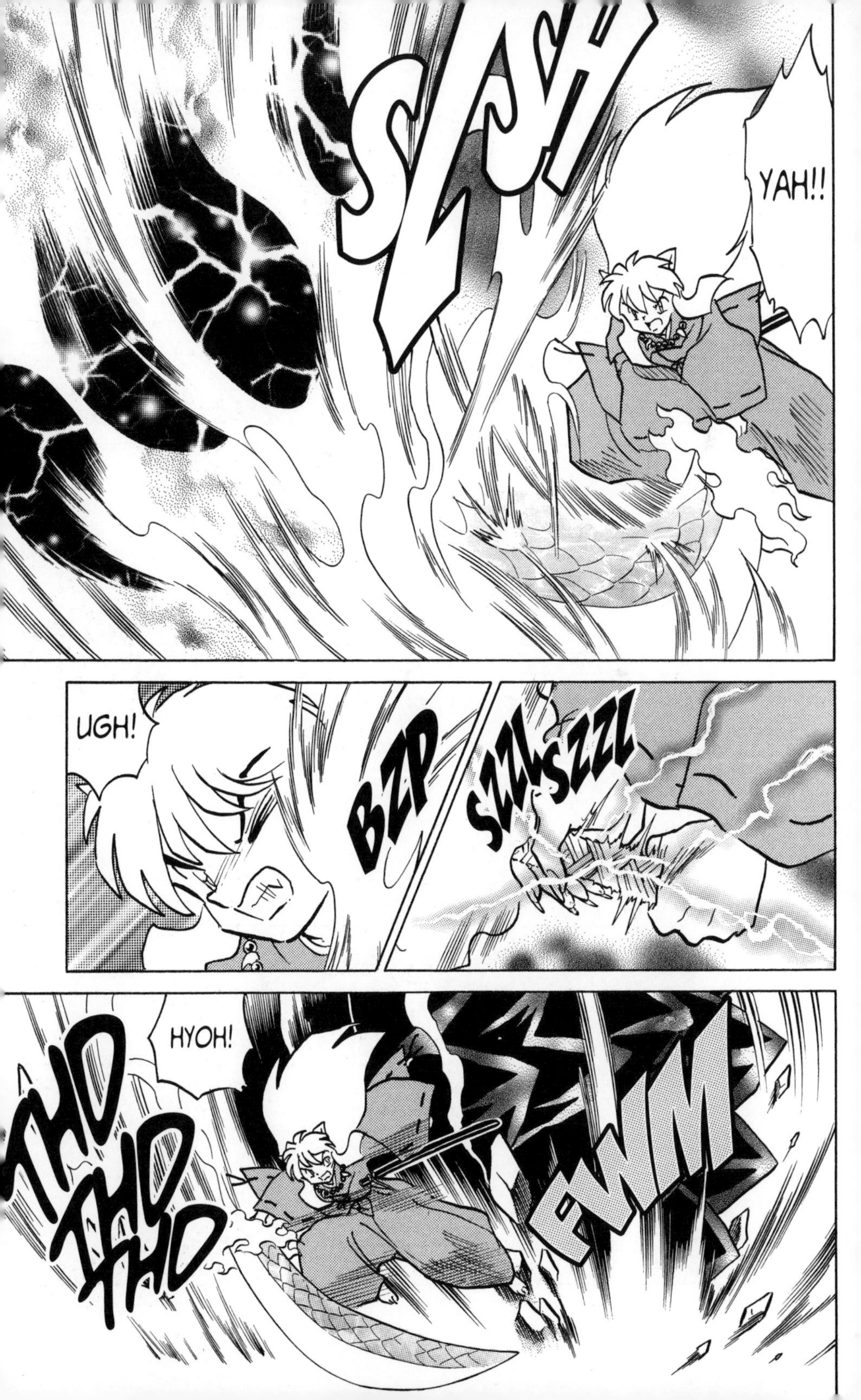
YAH!!
SLACH
SZZLSZZL
BZP
UGH!
EWM
HYOH!
THD THD THD

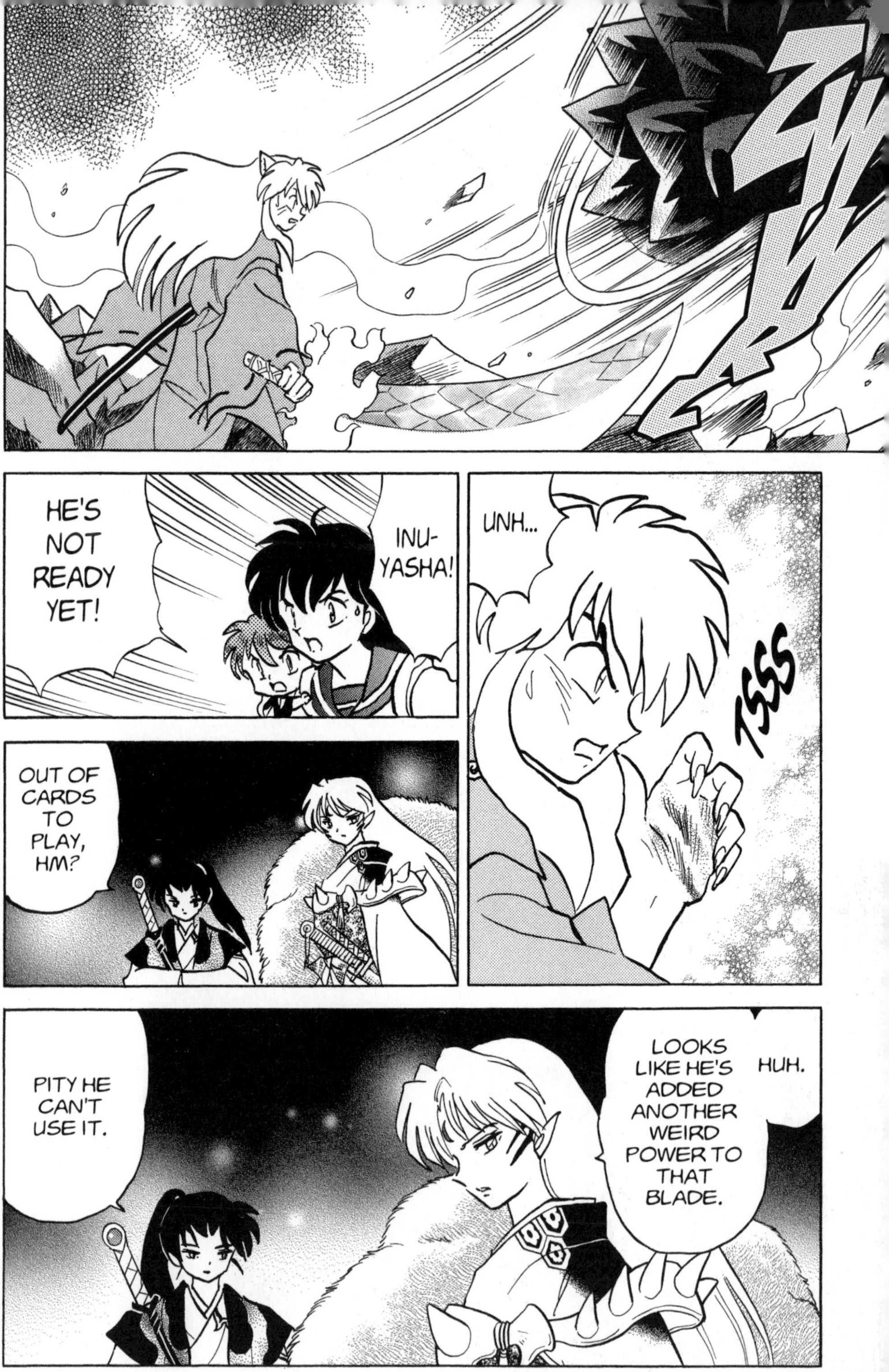
UNH...
TSSS
INU-YASHA!
HE'S NOT READY YET!
OUT OF CARDS TO PLAY, HM?
HUH.
LOOKS LIKE HE'S ADDED ANOTHER WEIRD POWER TO THAT BLADE.
PITY HE CAN'T USE IT.

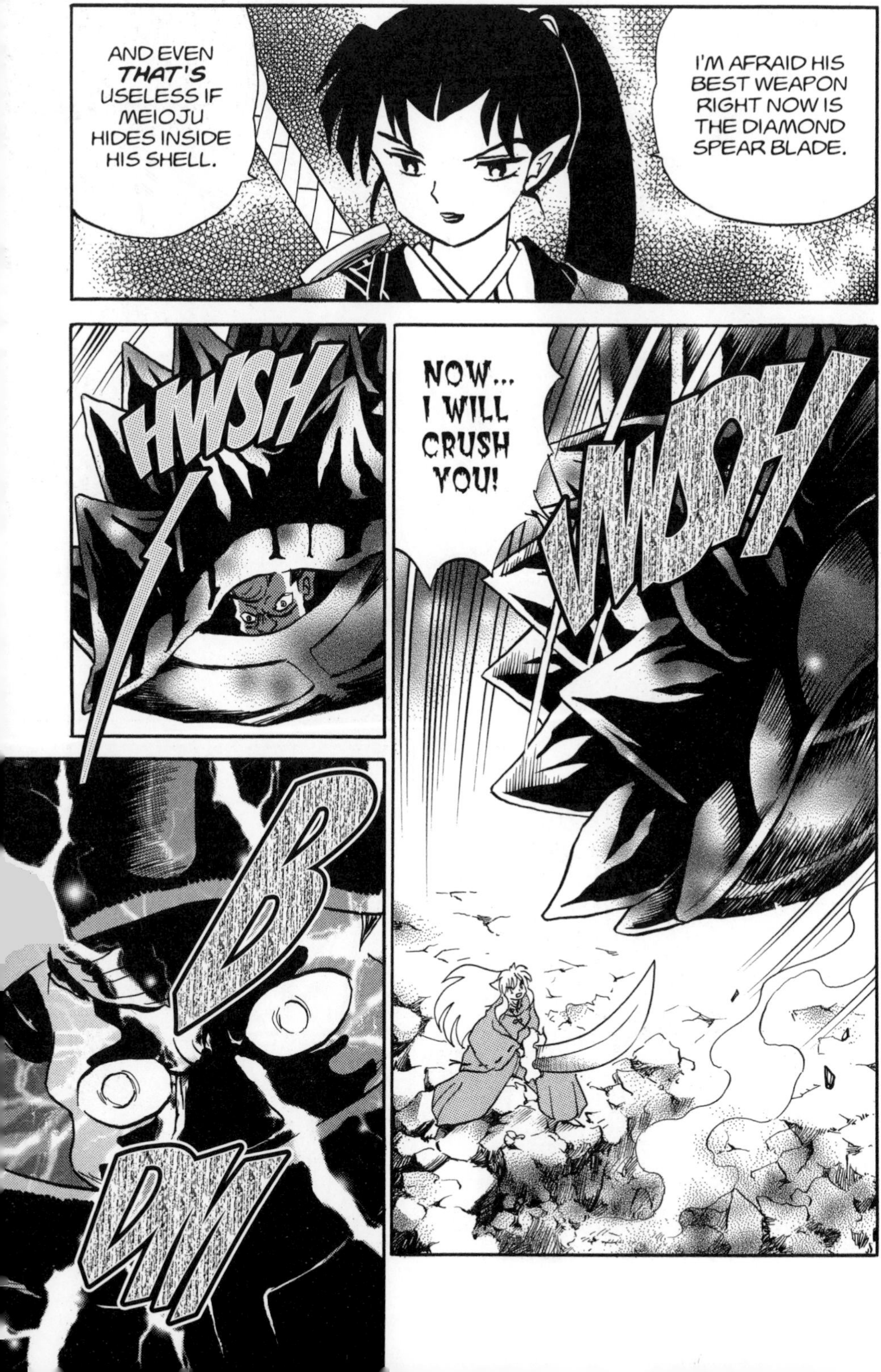
I'M AFRAID HIS BEST WEAPON RIGHT NOW IS THE DIAMOND SPEAR BLADE.
AND EVEN *THAT'S* USELESS IF MEIOJU HIDES INSIDE HIS SHELL.
NOW... I WILL CRUSH YOU!
WOOH
HWSH
BWM

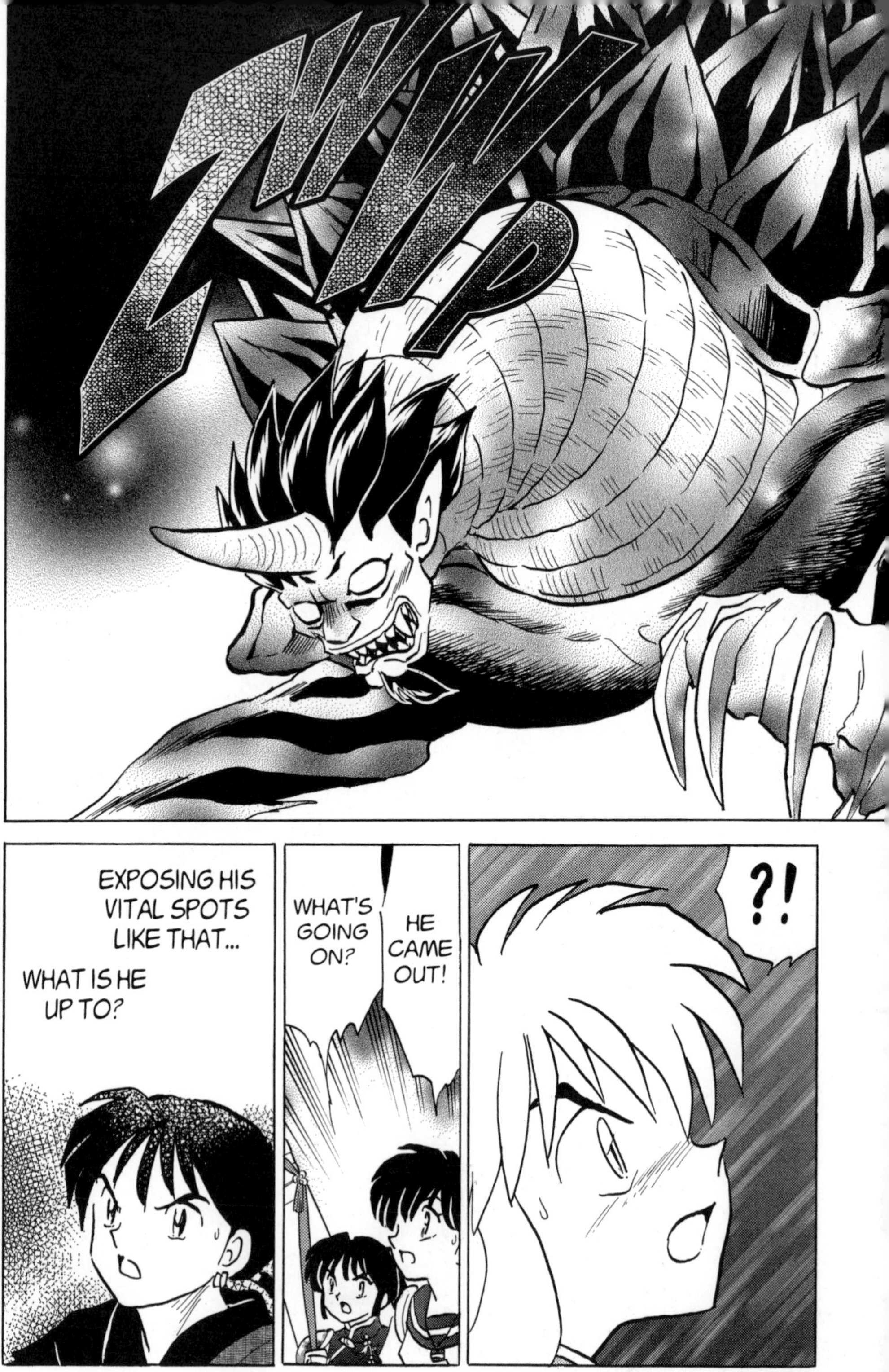
ZWIP
?!
HE CAME OUT!
WHAT'S GOING ON?
EXPOSING HIS VITAL SPOTS LIKE THAT...
WHAT IS HE UP TO?

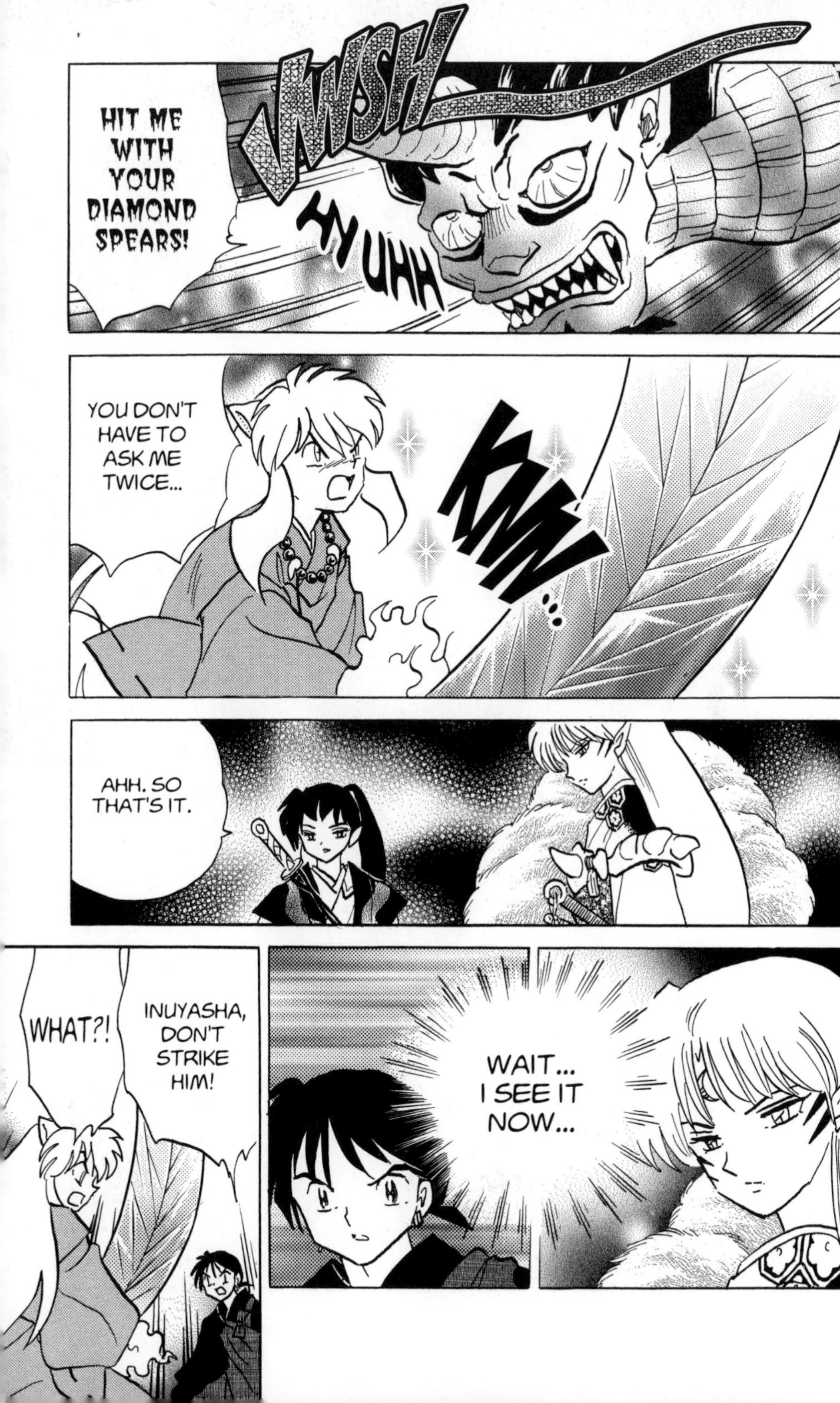
JWSH
HIT ME WITH YOUR DIAMOND SPEARS!
HN UHH
YOU DON'T HAVE TO ASK ME TWICE...
KNN...
AHH. SO THAT'S IT.
WAIT... I SEE IT NOW...
INUYASHA, DON'T STRIKE HIM!
WHAT?!

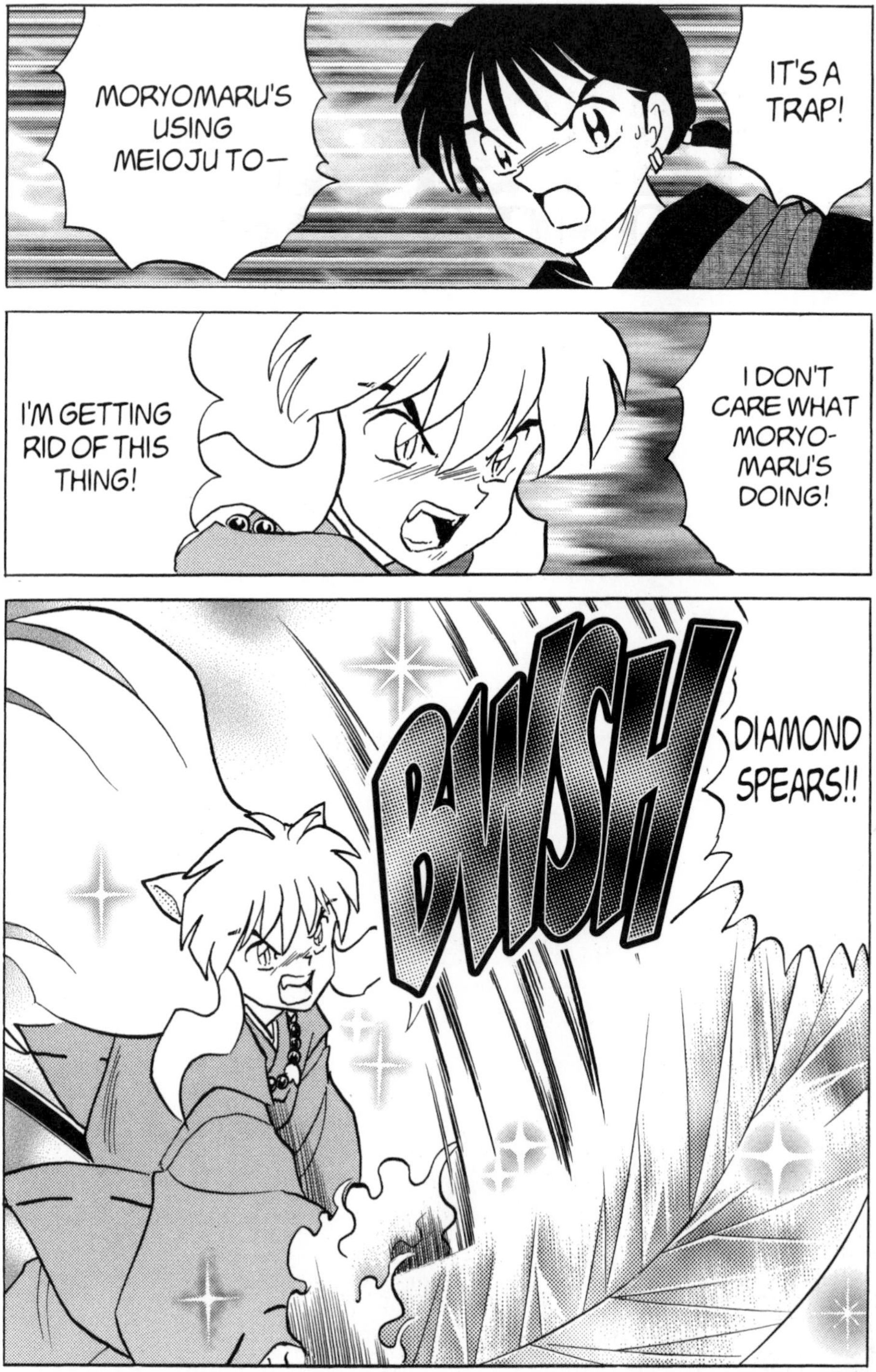
IT'S A TRAP!
MORYOMARU'S USING MEIOJU TO—
I DON'T CARE WHAT MORYO-MARU'S DOING!
I'M GETTING RID OF THIS THING!
DIAMOND SPEARS!!
BWSH

SCROLL FIVE
THE STOLEN KONGOSOHA

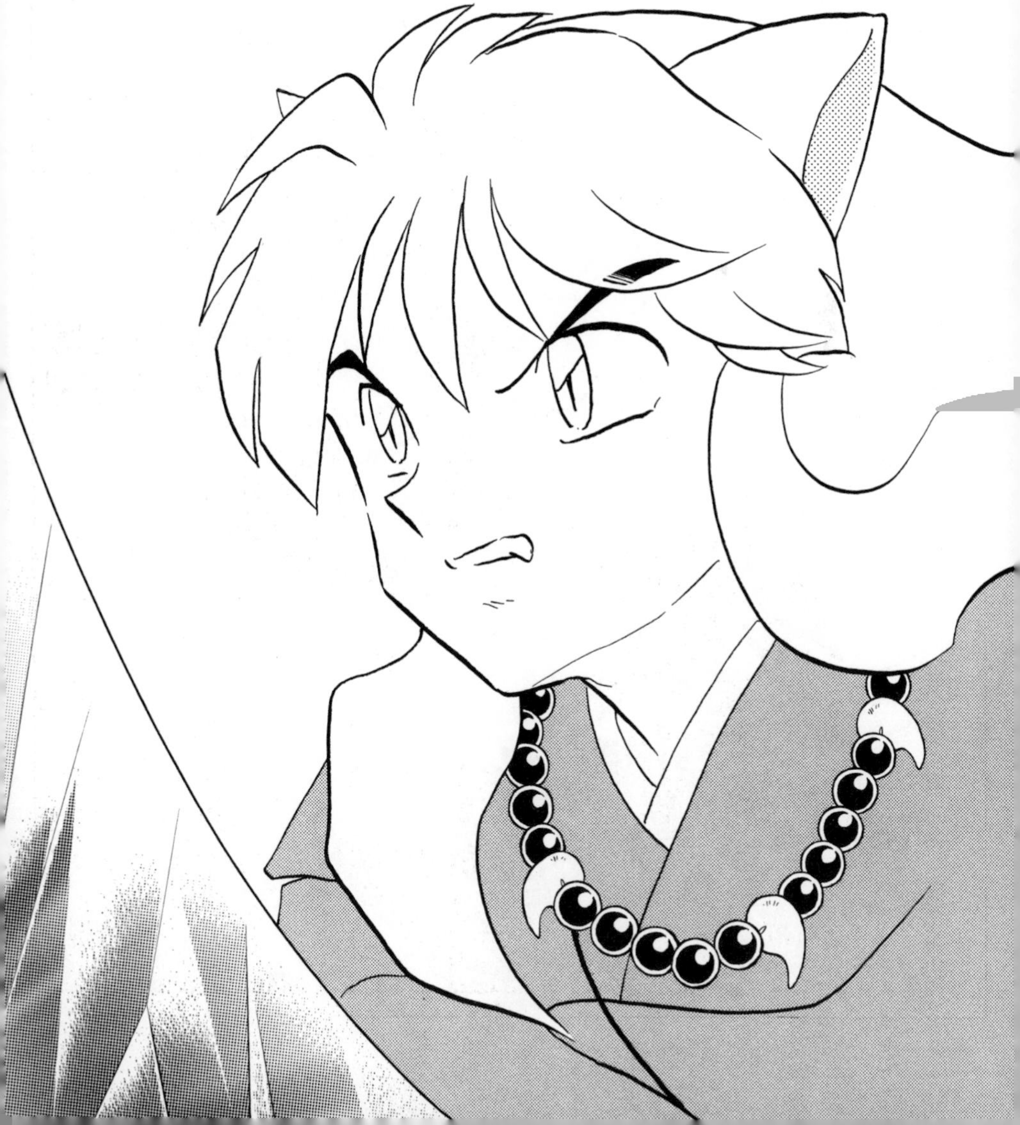

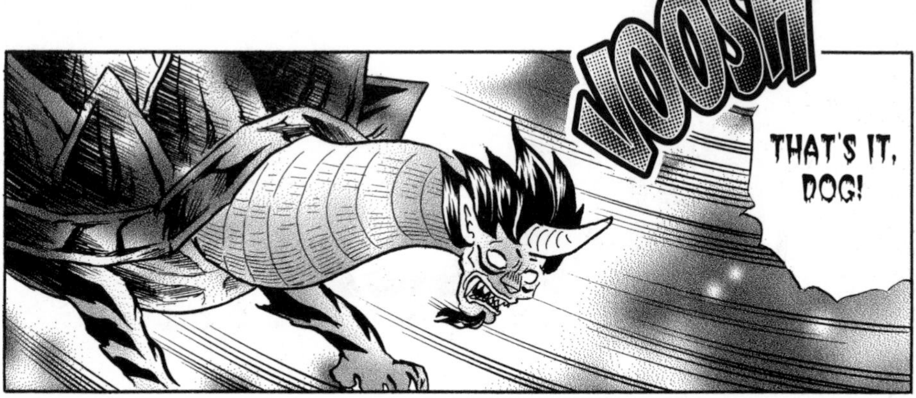
VOOSH
THAT'S IT, DOG!

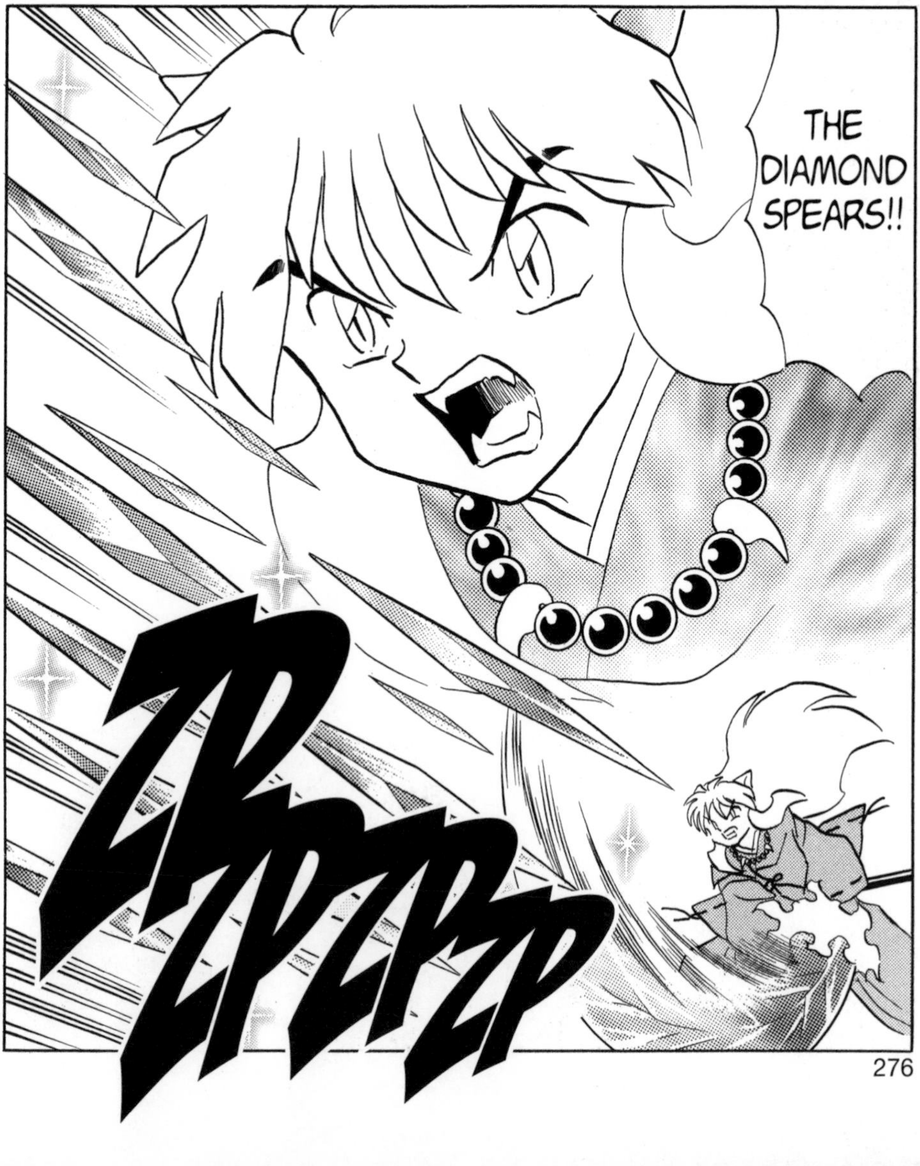
THE DIAMOND SPEARS!!
ZPZPZPZP

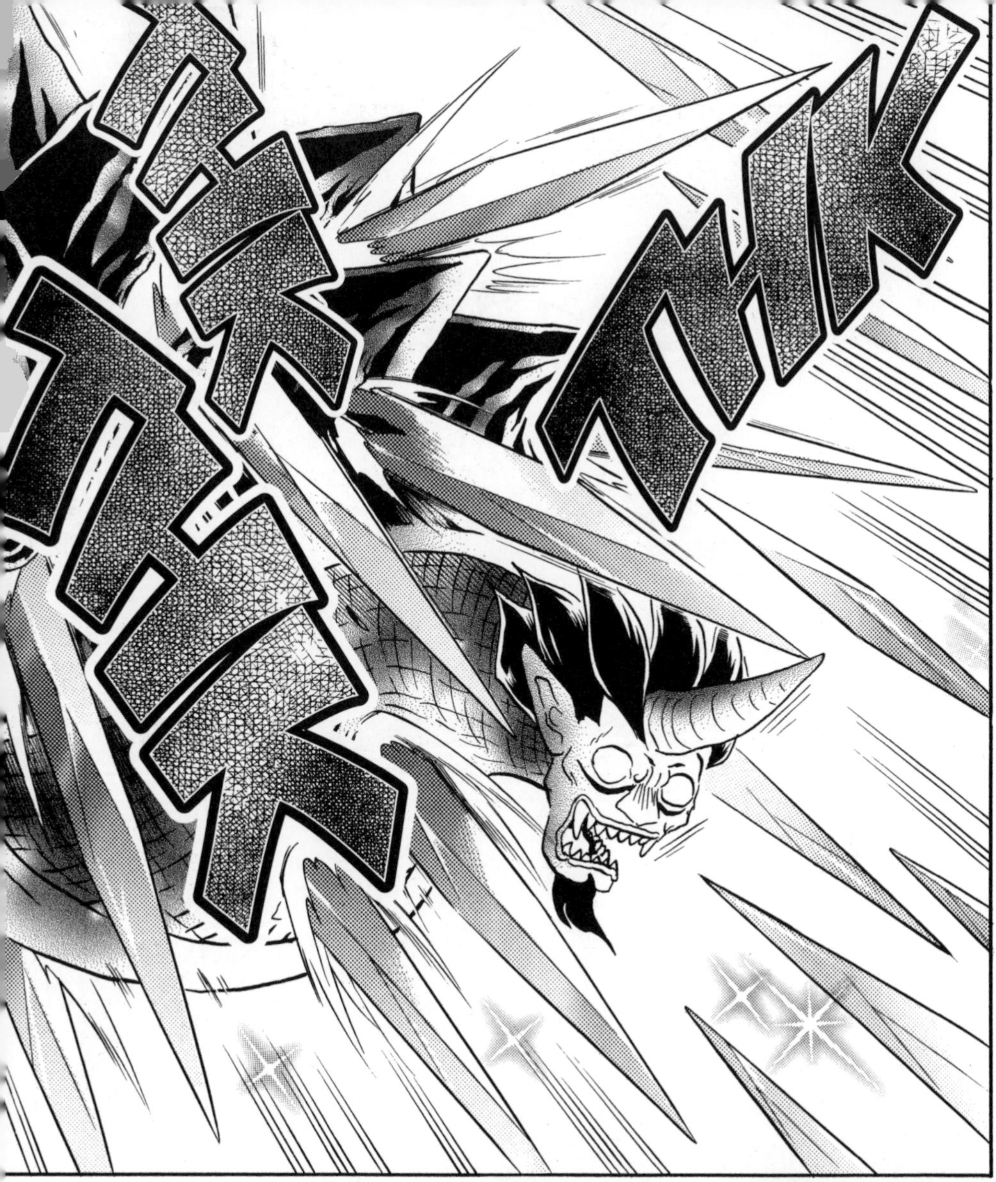

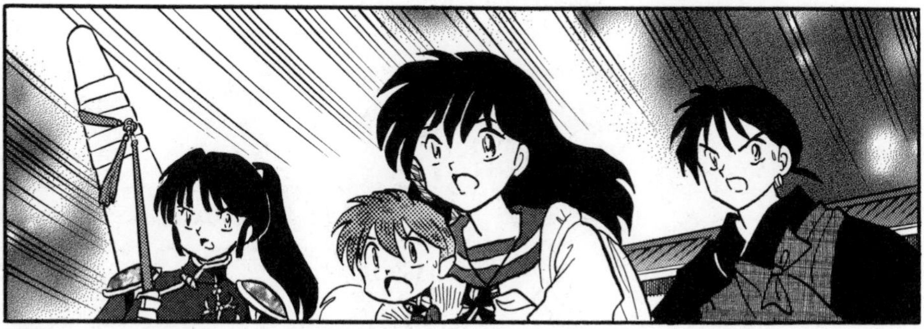

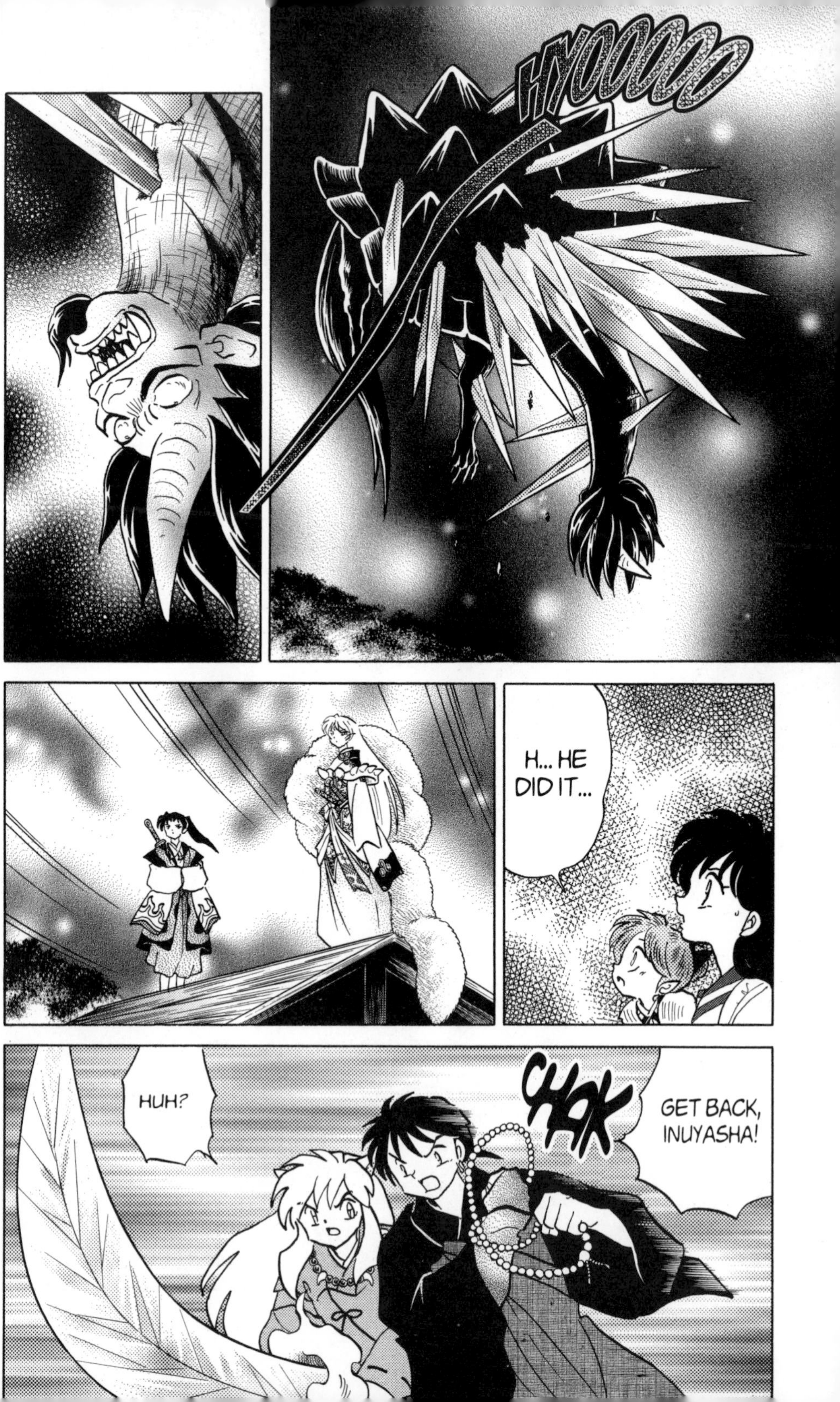
HYOOOOO
H... HE DID IT...
GET BACK, INUYASHA!
CHAK
HUH?

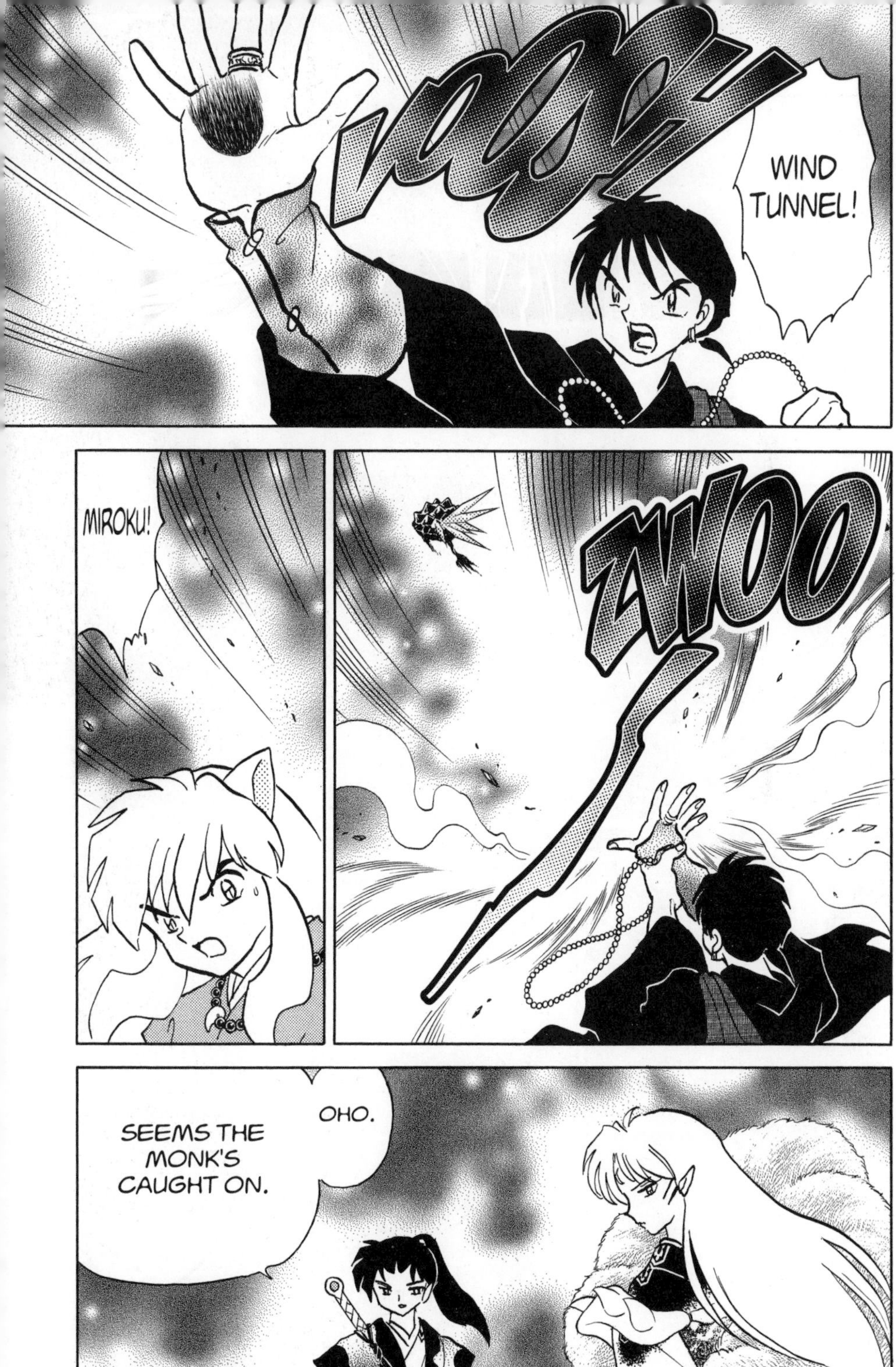
WIND TUNNEL!
ZWOO
MIROKU!
OHO.
SEEMS THE MONK'S CAUGHT ON.

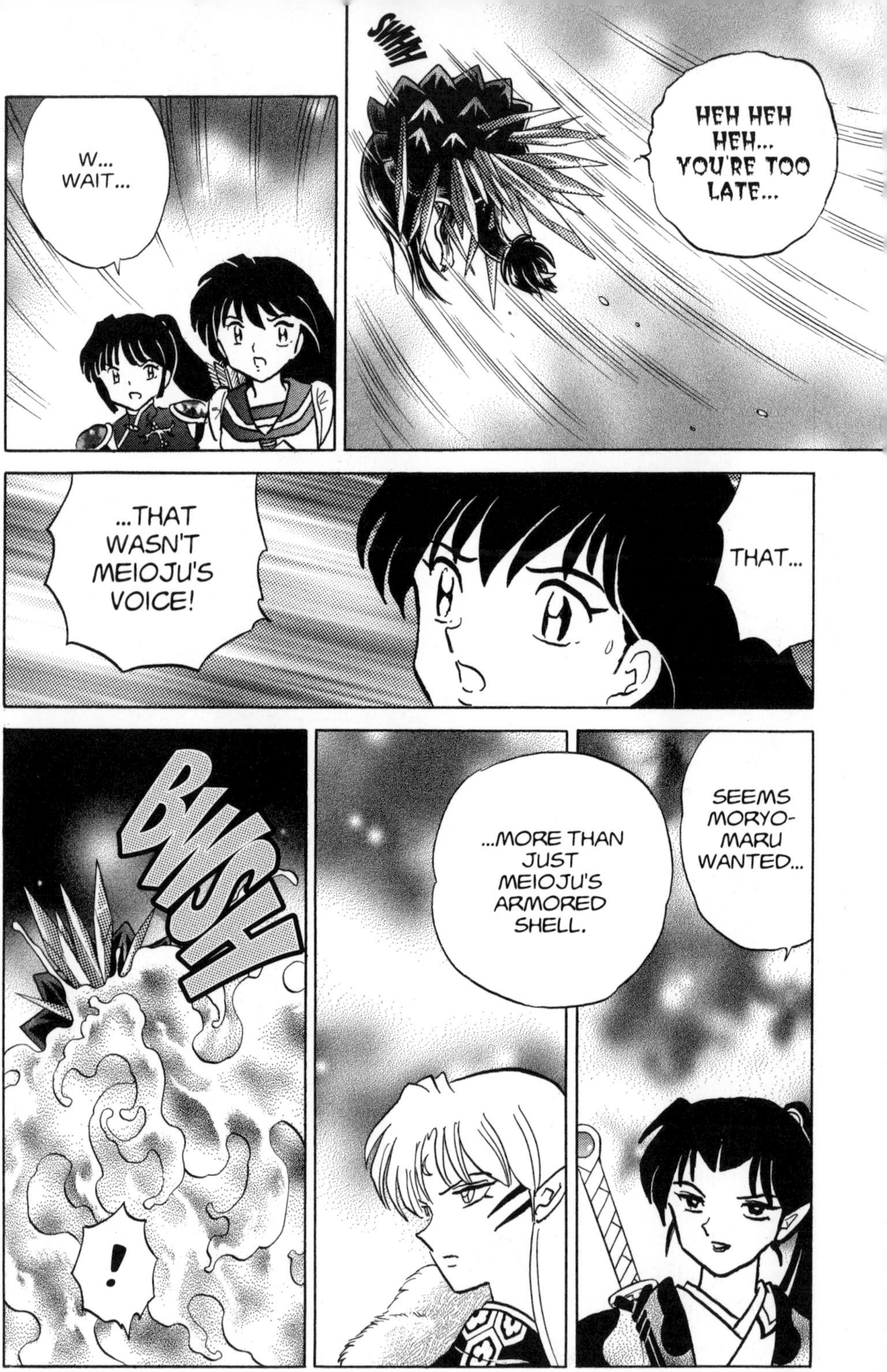
SWHH
HEH HEH HEH... YOU'RE TOO LATE...
W... WAIT...
THAT...
...THAT WASN'T MEIOJU'S VOICE!
SEEMS MORYO-MARU WANTED...
...MORE THAN JUST MEIOJU'S ARMORED SHELL.
BWSH!
!

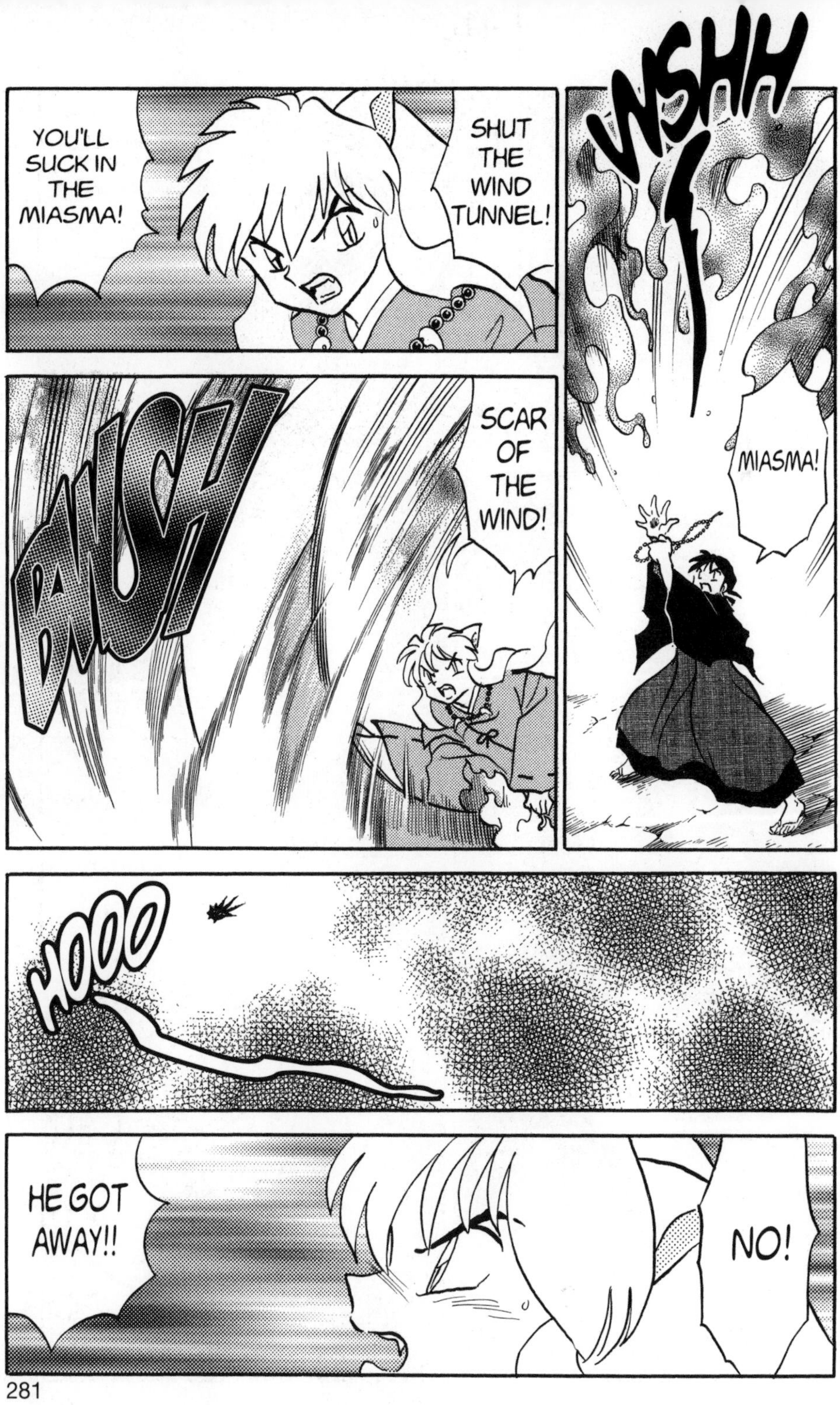
WSHH
MIASMA!
SHUT THE WIND TUNNEL!
YOU'LL SUCK IN THE MIASMA!
SCAR OF THE WIND!
BWISH
HOOO
NO!
HE GOT AWAY!!

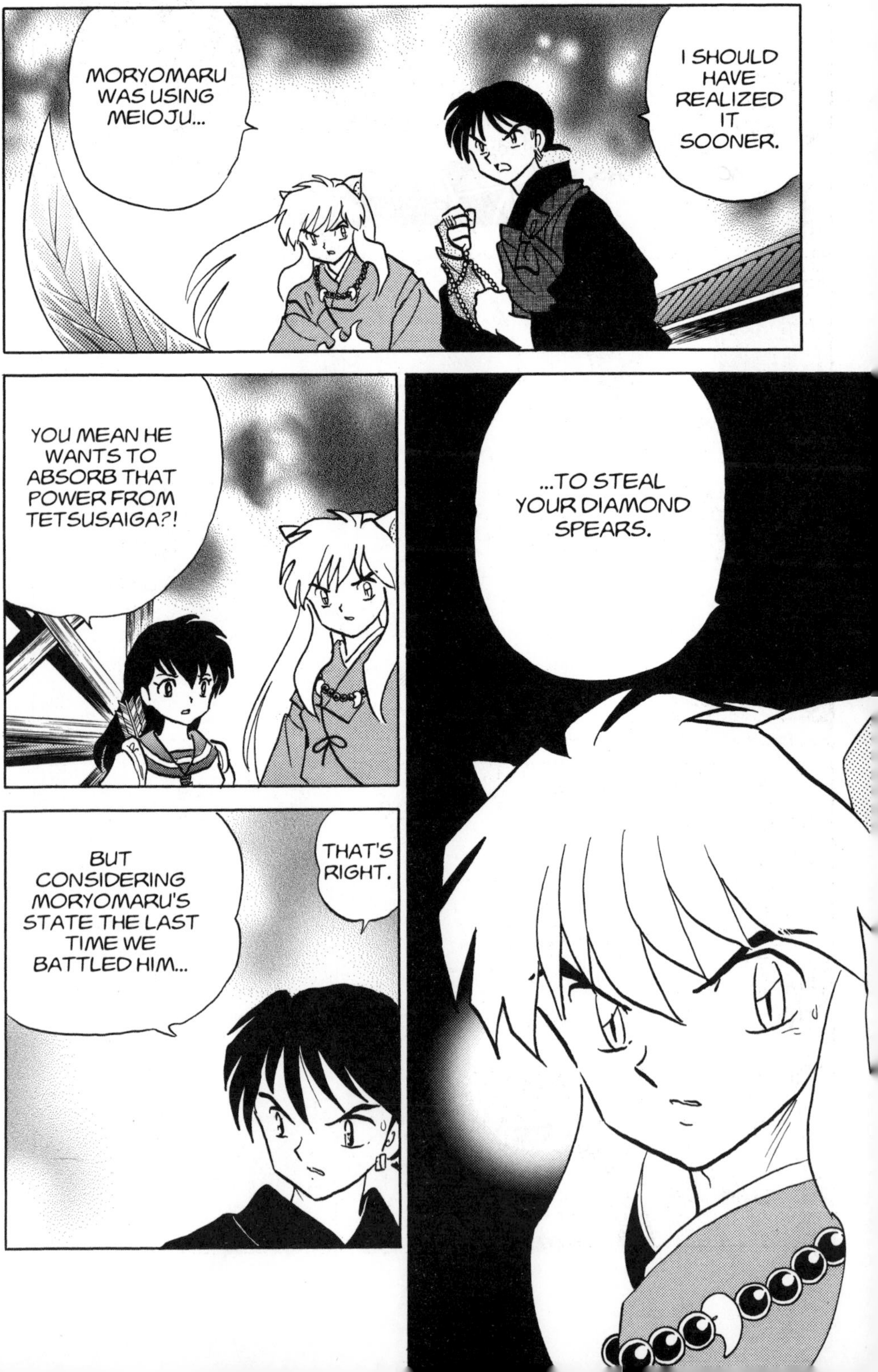
I SHOULD HAVE REALIZED IT SOONER.
MORYOMARU WAS USING MEIOJU...
...TO STEAL YOUR DIAMOND SPEARS.
YOU MEAN HE WANTS TO ABSORB THAT POWER FROM TETSUSAIGA?!
THAT'S RIGHT.
BUT CONSIDERING MORYOMARU'S STATE THE LAST TIME WE BATTLED HIM...

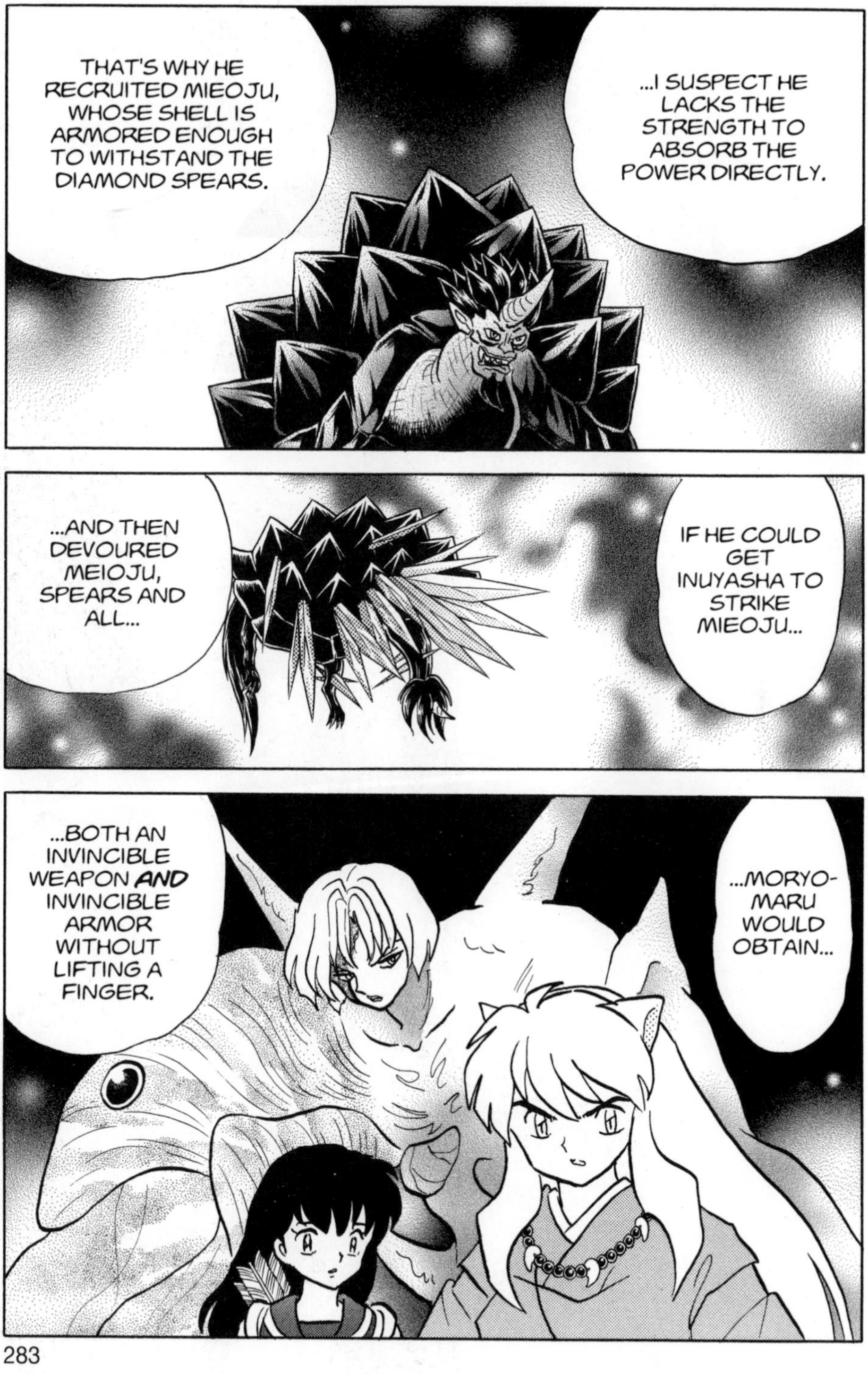
...I SUSPECT HE LACKS THE STRENGTH TO ABSORB THE POWER DIRECTLY.
THAT'S WHY HE RECRUITED MIEOJU, WHOSE SHELL IS ARMORED ENOUGH TO WITHSTAND THE DIAMOND SPEARS.
IF HE COULD GET INUYASHA TO STRIKE MIEOJU...
...AND THEN DEVOURED MEIOJU, SPEARS AND ALL...
...MORYO-MARU WOULD OBTAIN...
...BOTH AN INVINCIBLE WEAPON ***AND*** INVINCIBLE ARMOR WITHOUT LIFTING A FINGER.

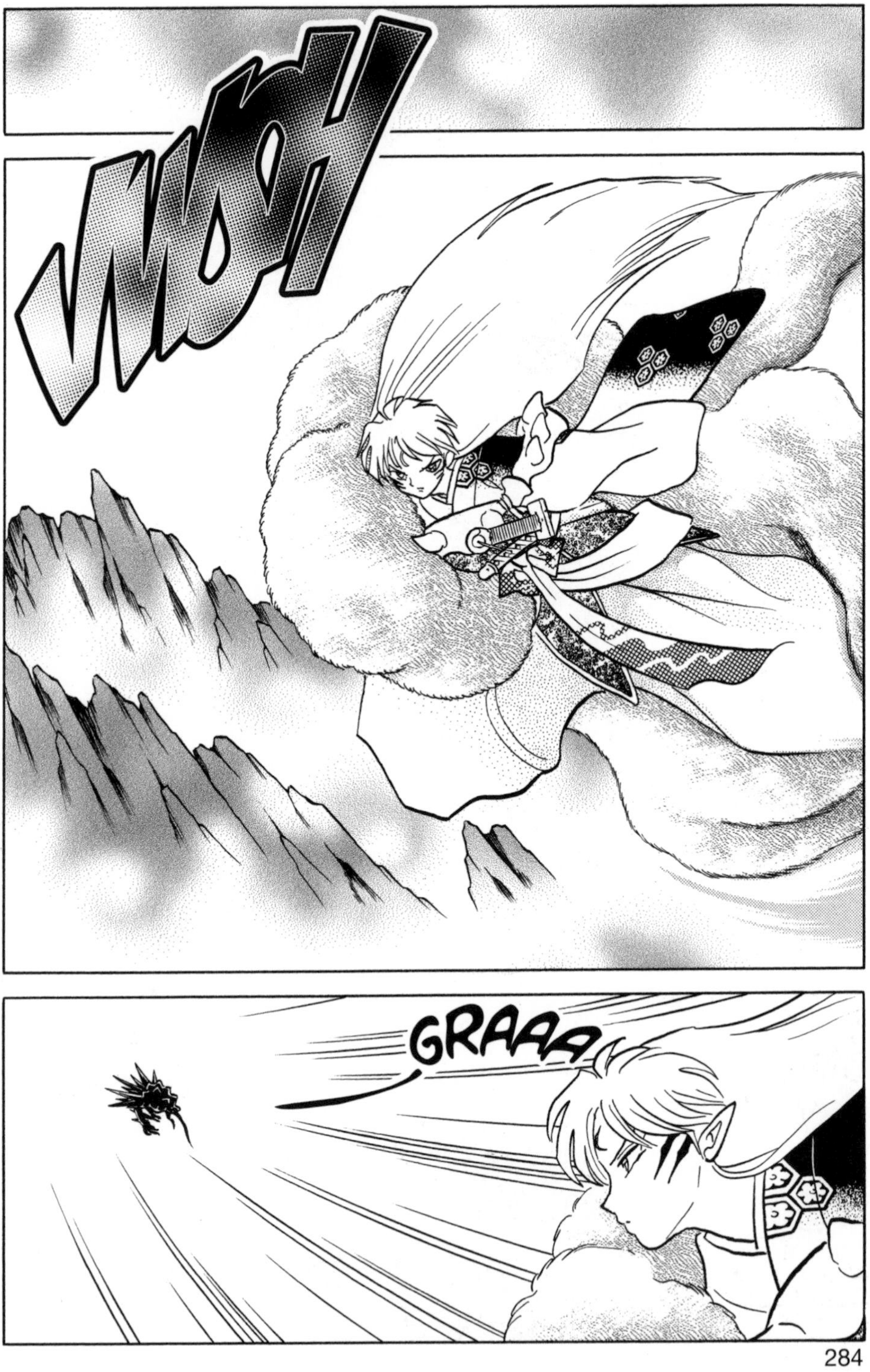
WOSH
GRAAA

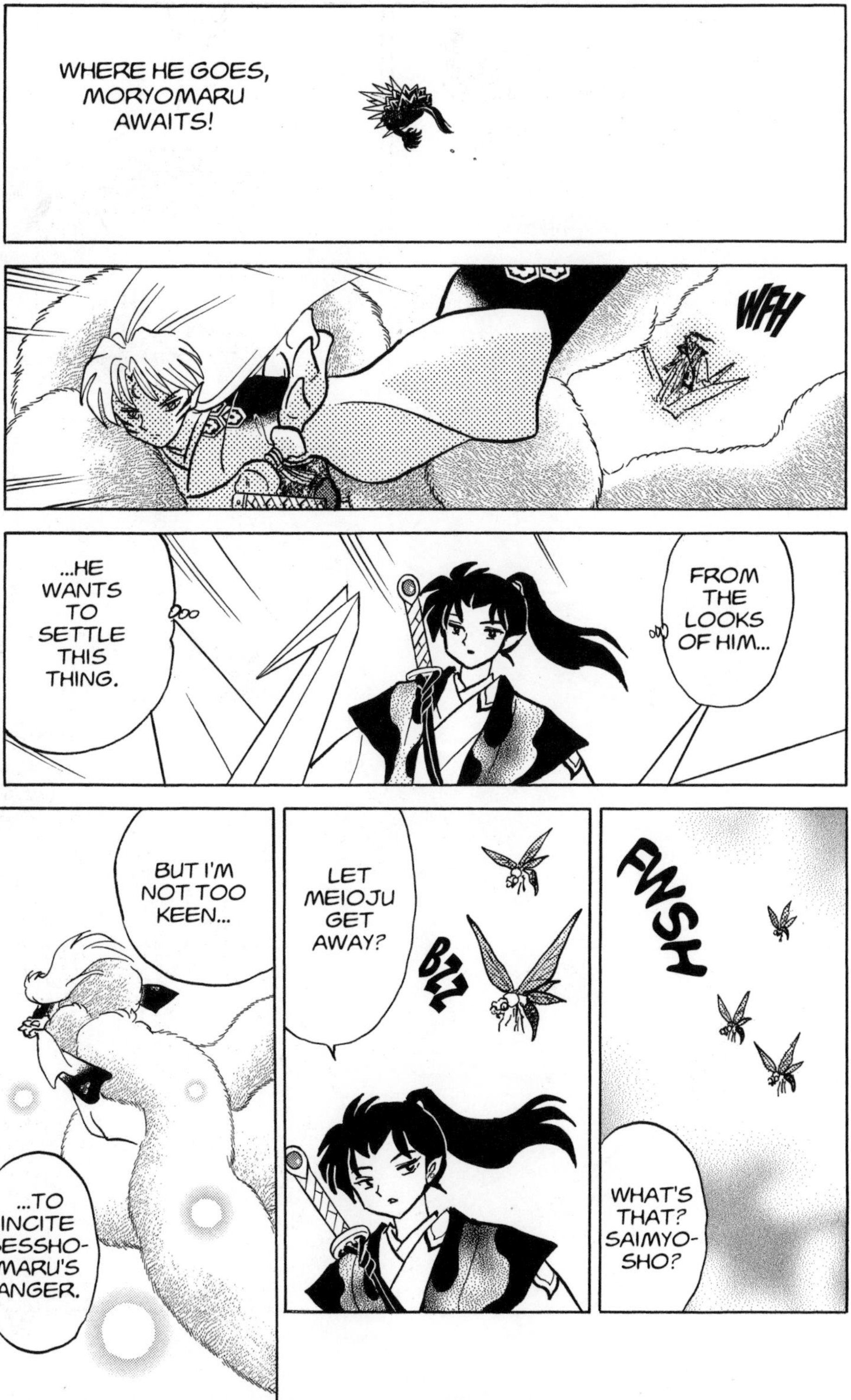
WHERE HE GOES, MORYOMARU AWAITS!
WFH
FROM THE LOOKS OF HIM...
...HE WANTS TO SETTLE THIS THING.
FWSH
WHAT'S THAT? SAIMYO-SHO?
LET MEIOJU GET AWAY?
BZZ
BUT I'M NOT TOO KEEN...
...TO INCITE SESSHO-MARU'S ANGER.

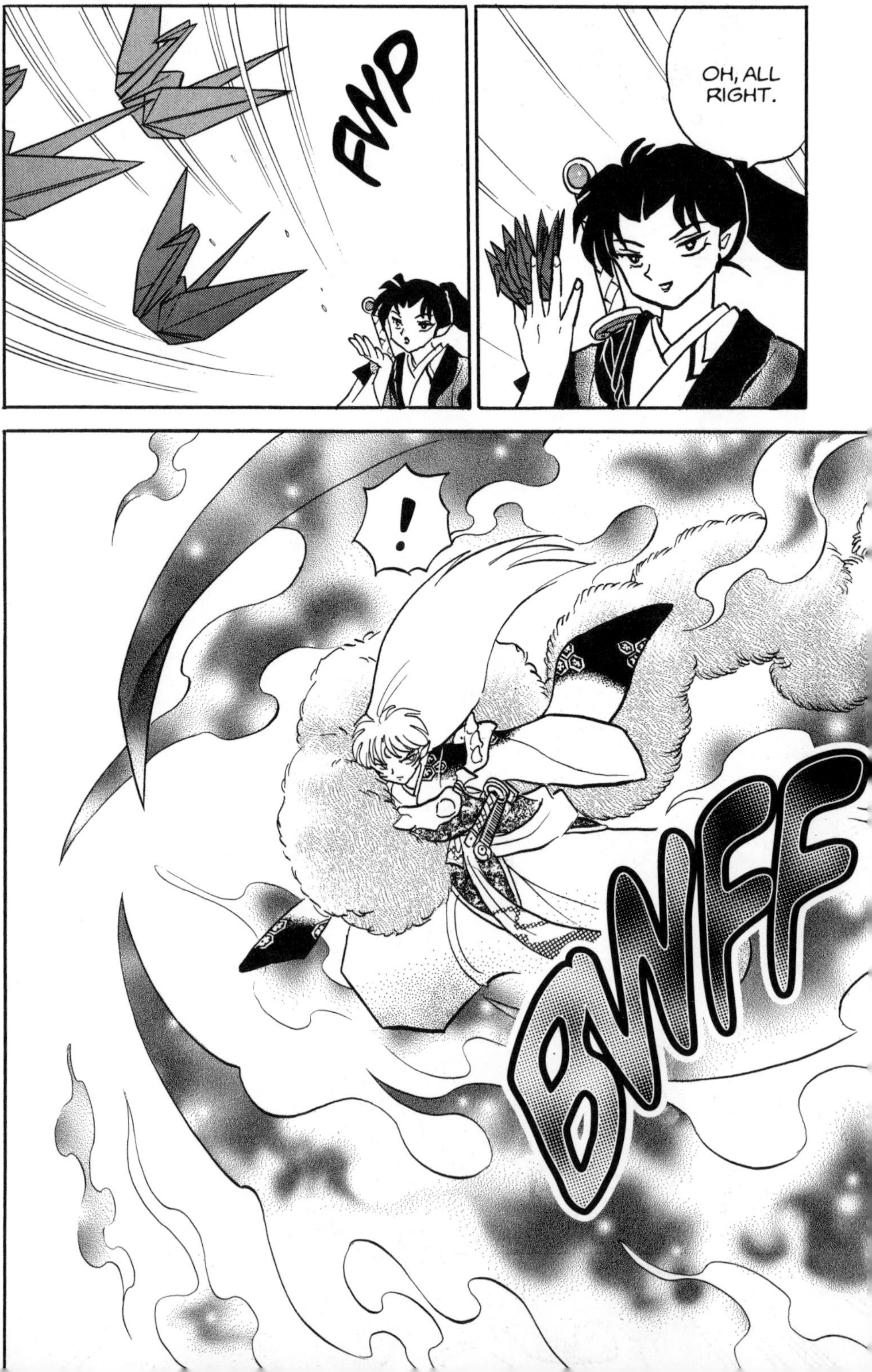
OH, ALL RIGHT.
FWP
!
BWFF

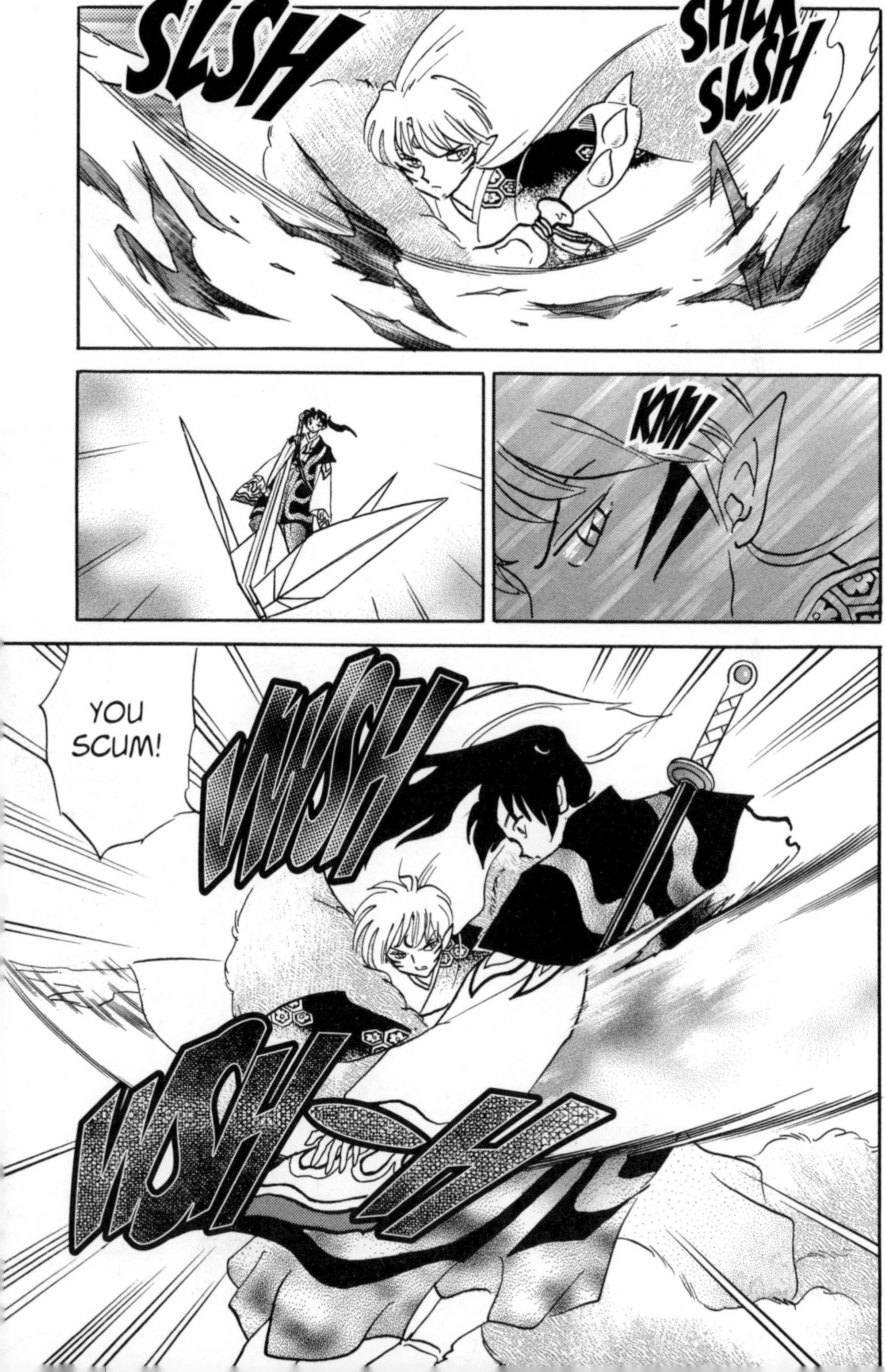
SHLK
SLSH
SLSH
KNN
YOU SCUM!
WHSH

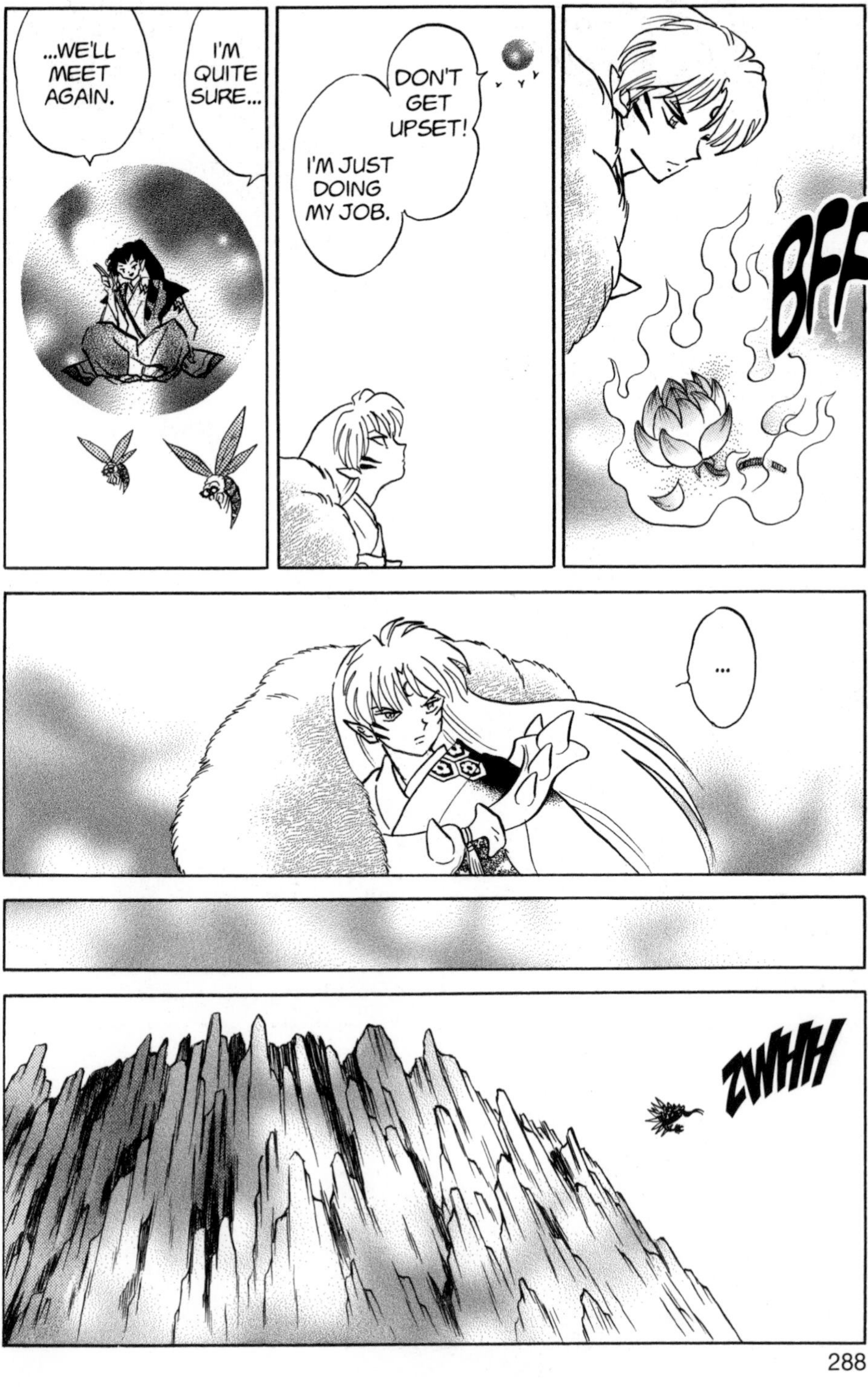
BFF
DON'T GET UPSET!
I'M JUST DOING MY JOB.
I'M QUITE SURE...
...WE'LL MEET AGAIN.
...
ZWHH

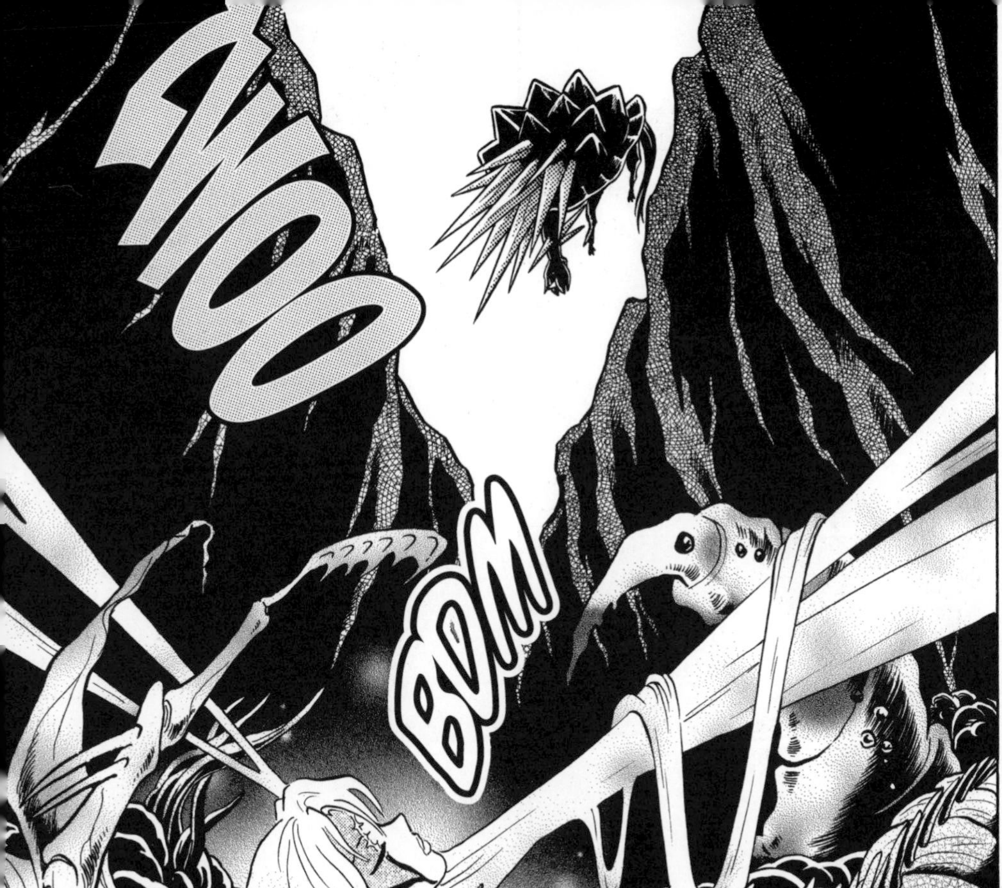
WHOO
BDM
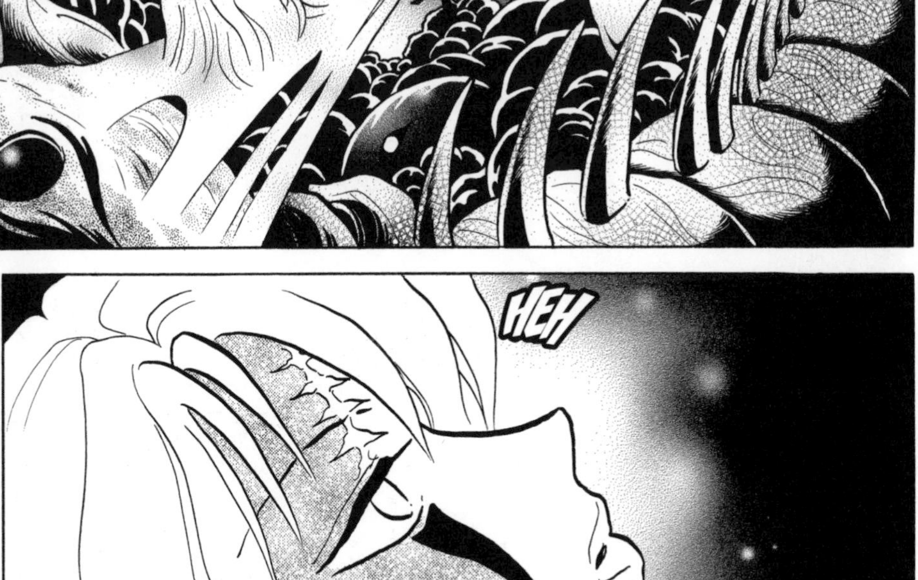
HEH

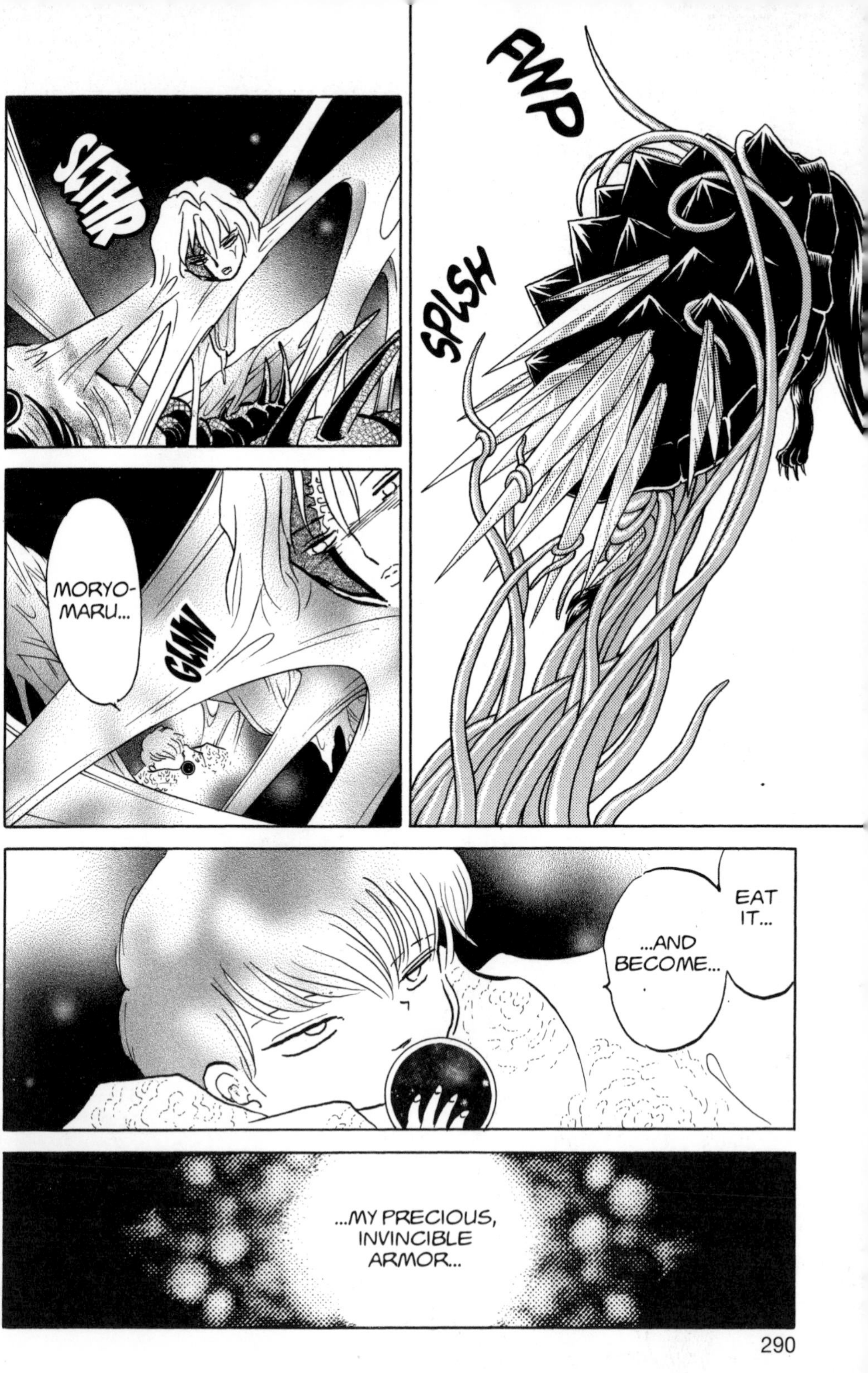
FWP
SPLSH
SKTHR
MORYO-MARU...
GLMM
EAT IT...
...AND BECOME...
...MY PRECIOUS, INVINCIBLE ARMOR...

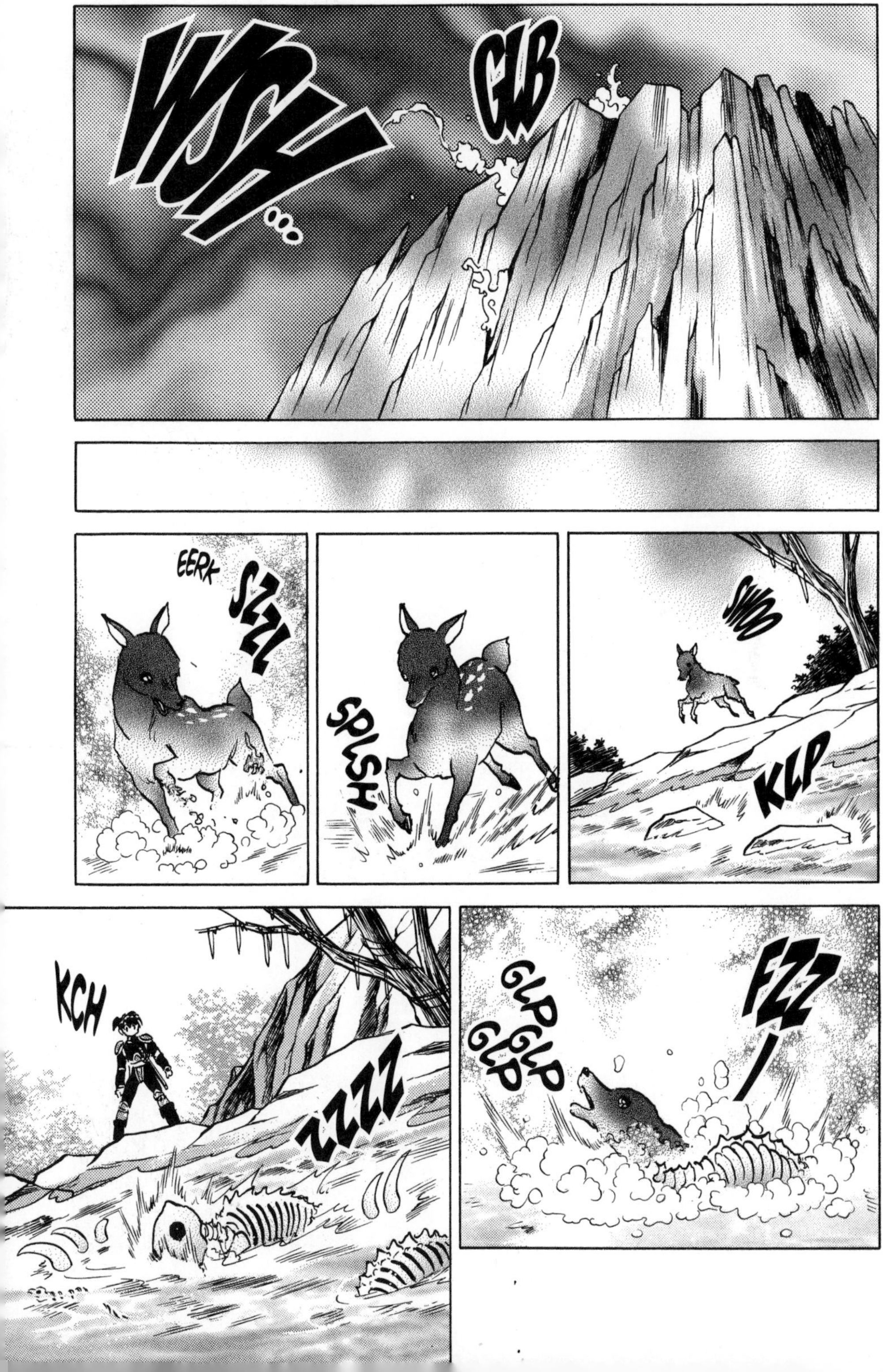
GLB
WSY...
SWOO
KLP
SPLSH
EERK
SZZL
FZZ
GLP GLP GLP
KCH
ZZZZ

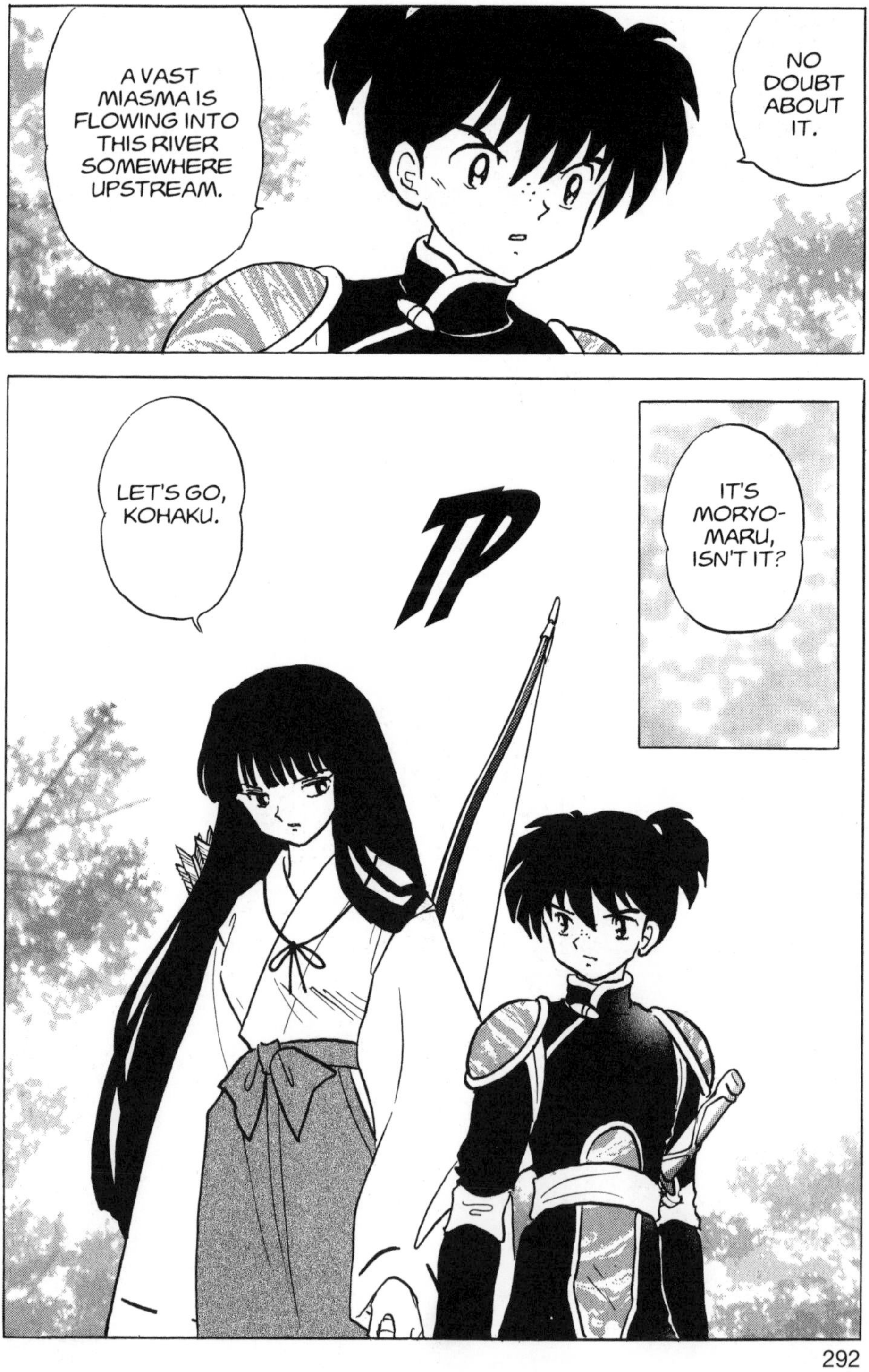
NO DOUBT ABOUT IT.
A VAST MIASMA IS FLOWING INTO THIS RIVER SOMEWHERE UPSTREAM.
IT'S MORYO-MARU, ISN'T IT?
LET'S GO, KOHAKU.

SCROLL SIX
MORYOMARU'S TRANSFORMATION

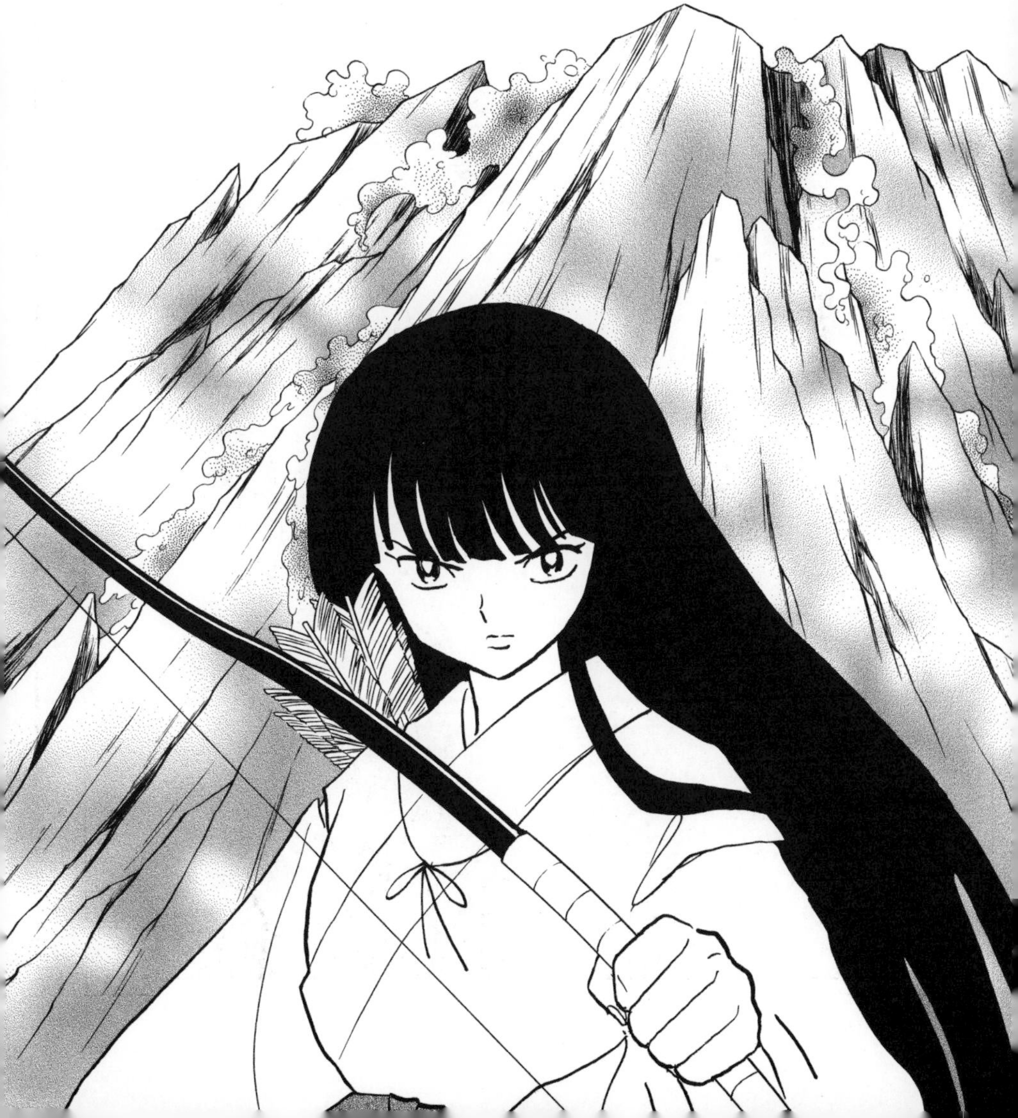

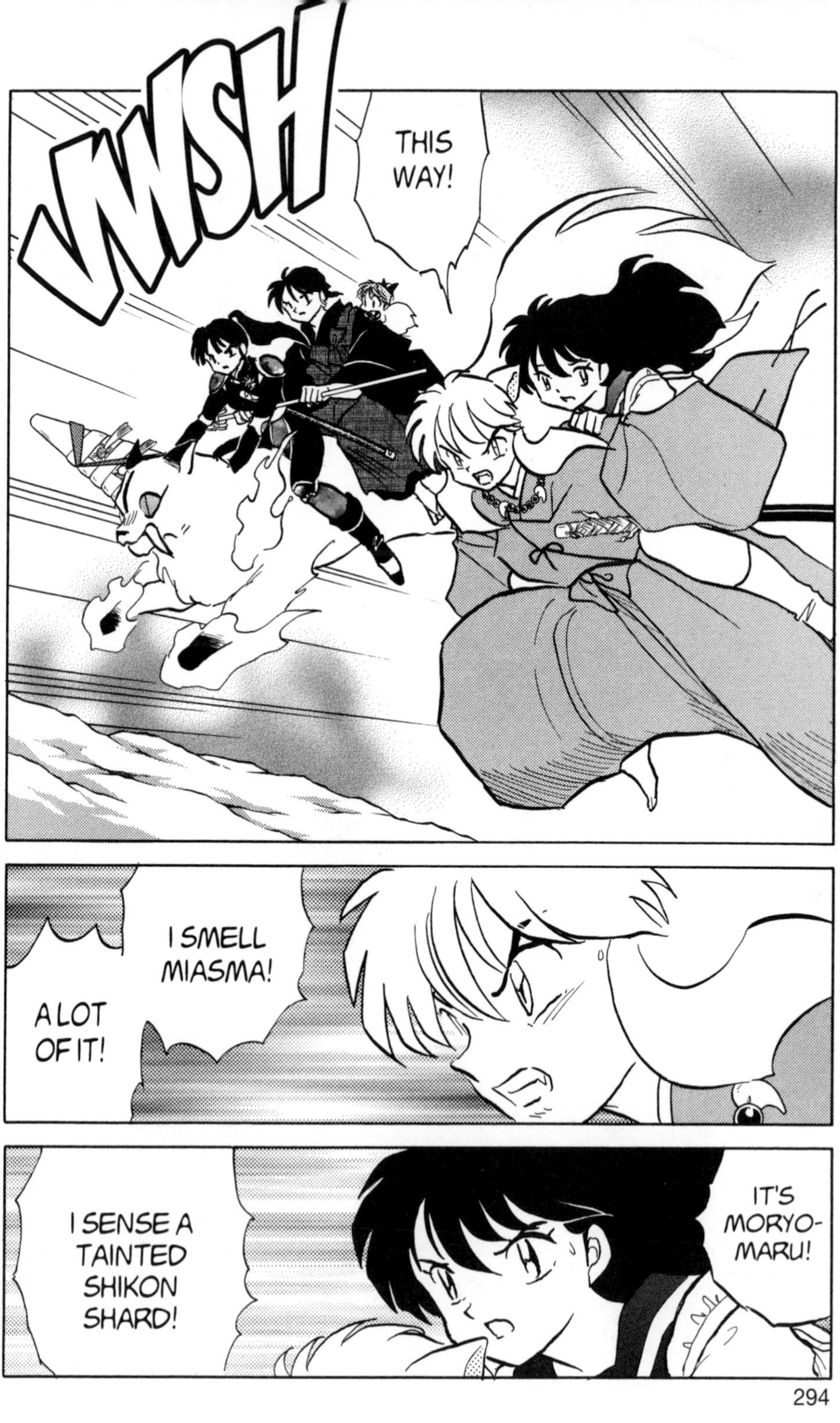
VWSH
THIS WAY!
I SMELL MIASMA!
A LOT OF IT!
IT'S MORYO-MARU!
I SENSE A TAINTED SHIKON SHARD!

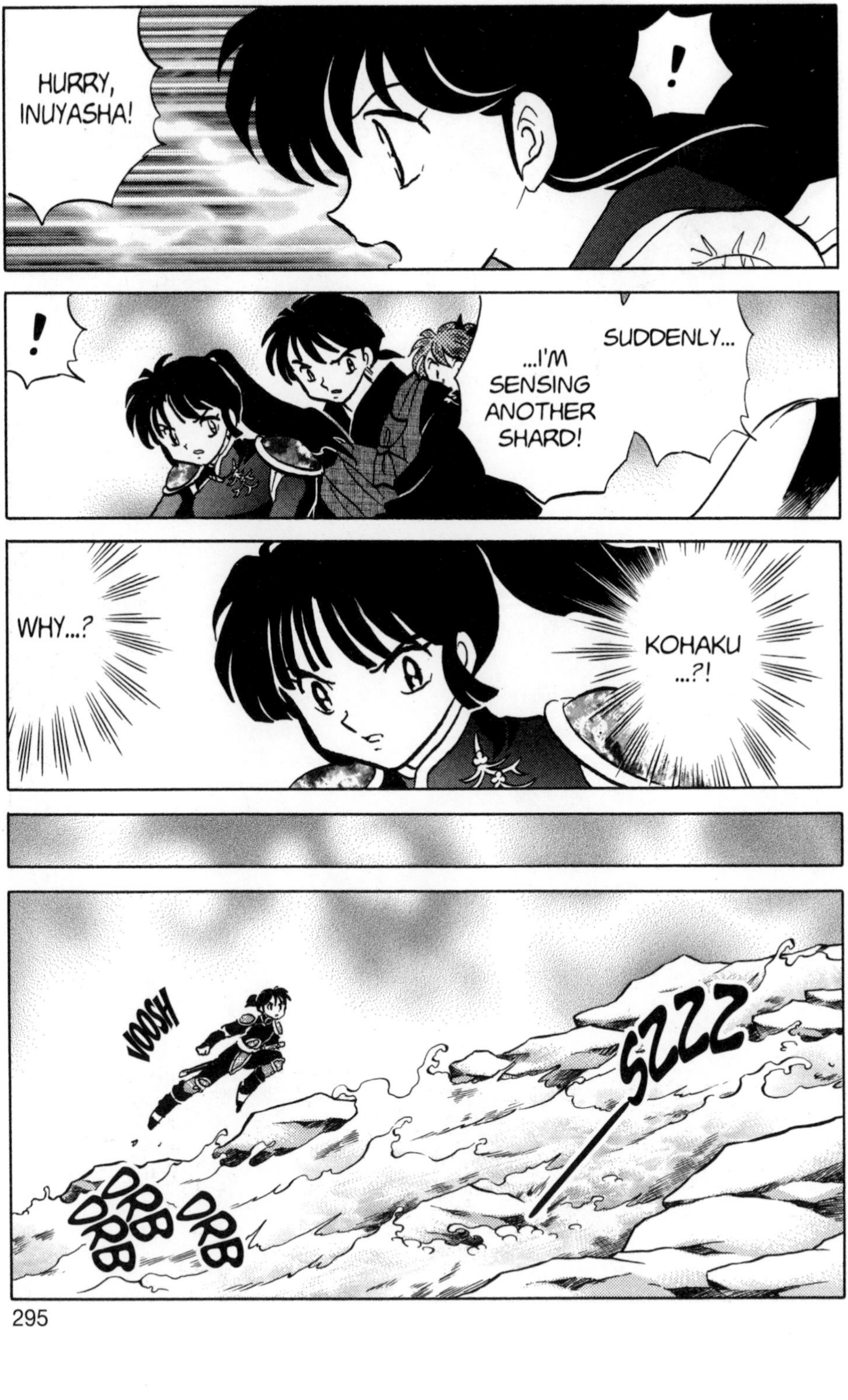
!
HURRY, INUYASHA!
SUDDENLY...
...I'M SENSING ANOTHER SHARD!
!
KOHAKU ...?!
WHY...?
SZZZ
VOOSH
DRB DRB
DRB DRB

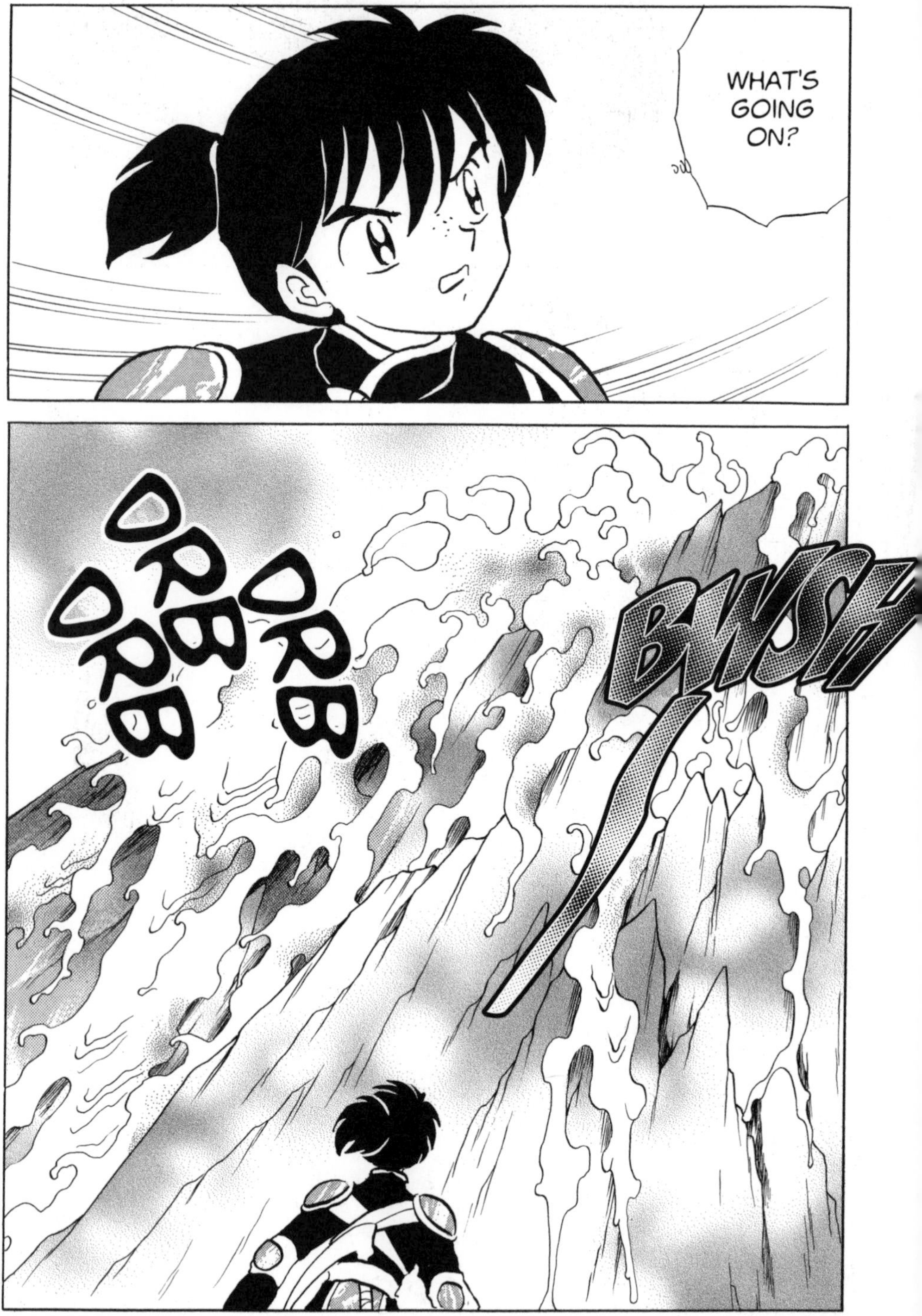
WHAT'S GOING ON?
DRB DRB DRB
BWSH

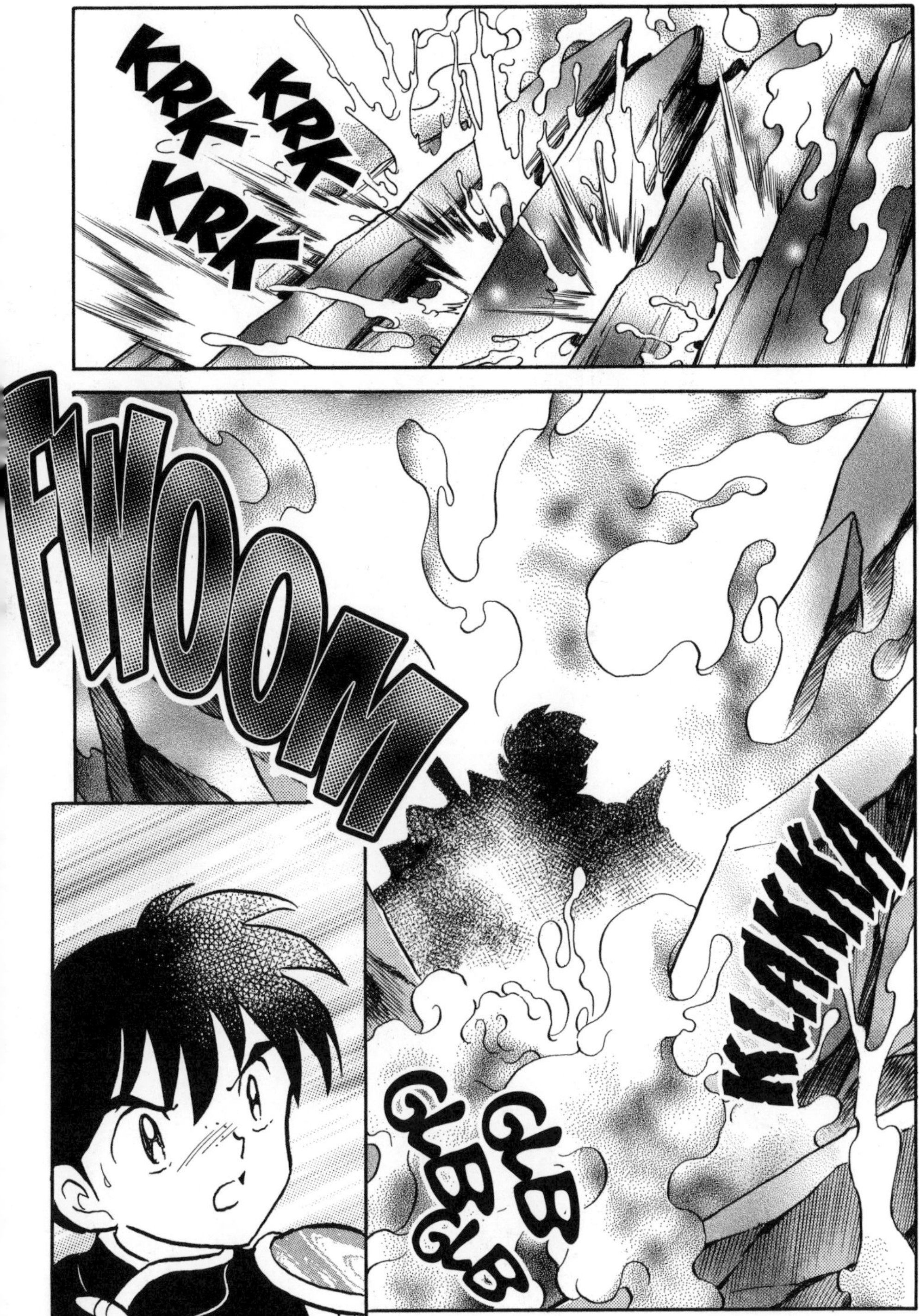
KRK KRK
KRK KRK
F'WOOM
KLAKKA
GLB
GLBGLB

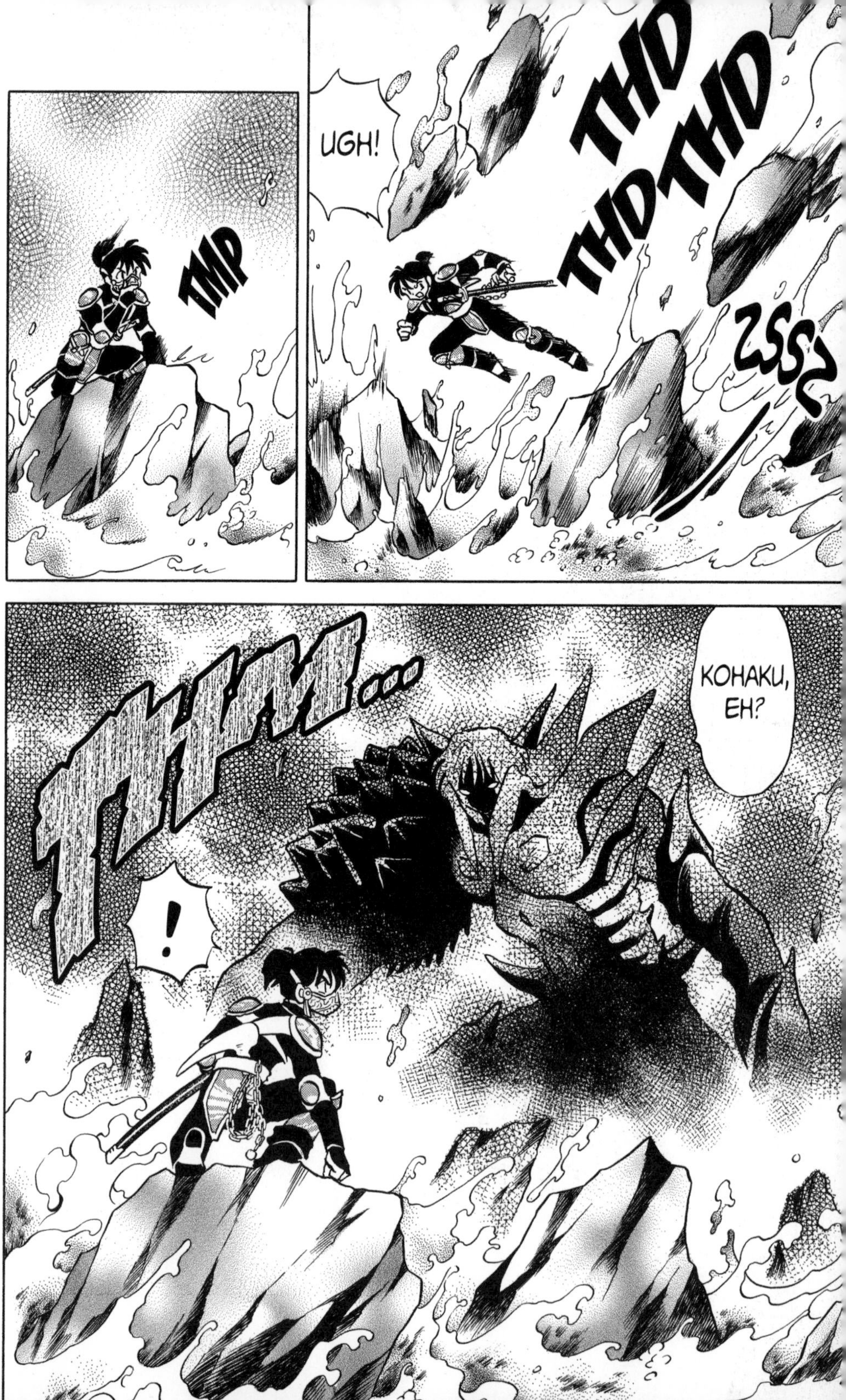
THD
THD THD
THD
UGH!
ZSSS
TMP
KOHAKU, EH?
THM...
!

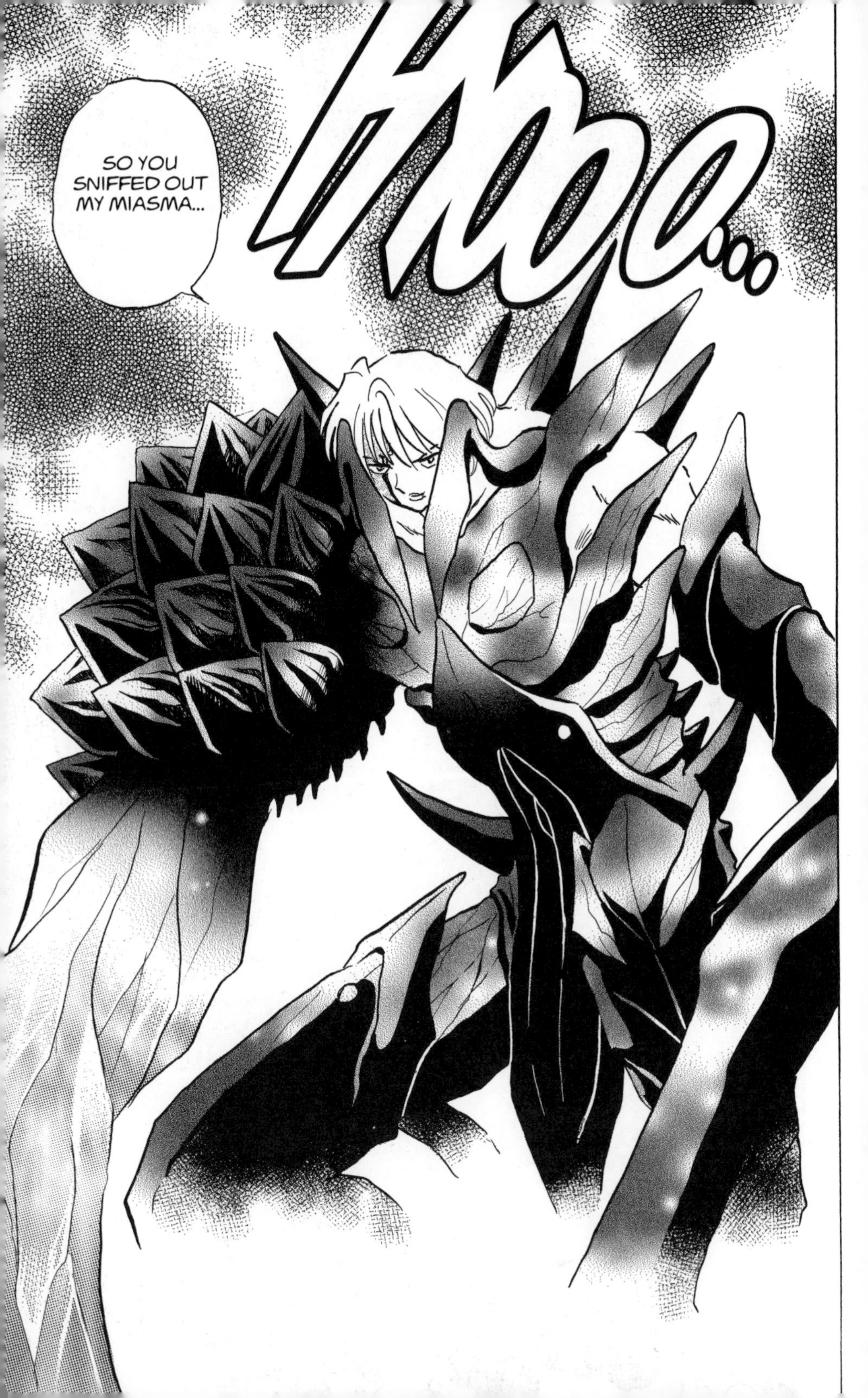

SO YOU SNIFFED OUT MY MIASMA...

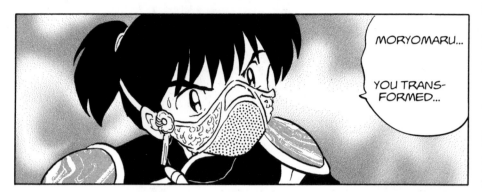

MORYOMARU...

YOU TRANS-
FORMED...

IF YOU CAME
KNOWING I
WAS HERE...

HEH
HEH
HEH.

...THAT
MEANS YOU
WON'T MIND...

...IF I
DEVOUR
YOU... YES?

ZWH

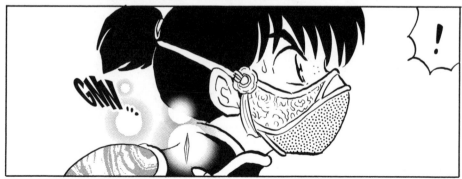

!

GMN

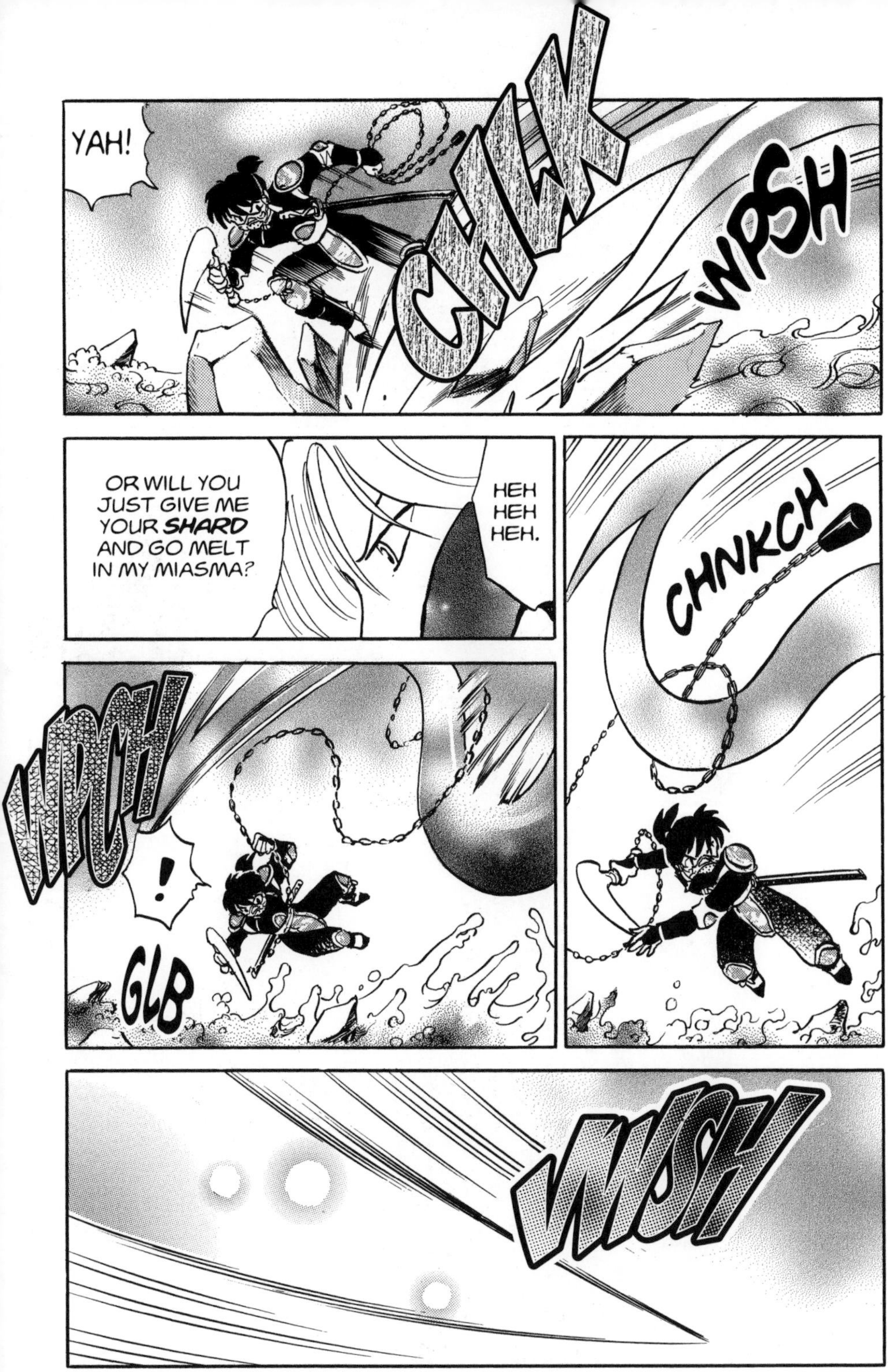
YAH!
WPSH
CHNKCH
OR WILL YOU JUST GIVE ME YOUR **SHARD** AND GO MELT IN MY MIASMA?
HEH HEH HEH.
WPCH
!
GLB

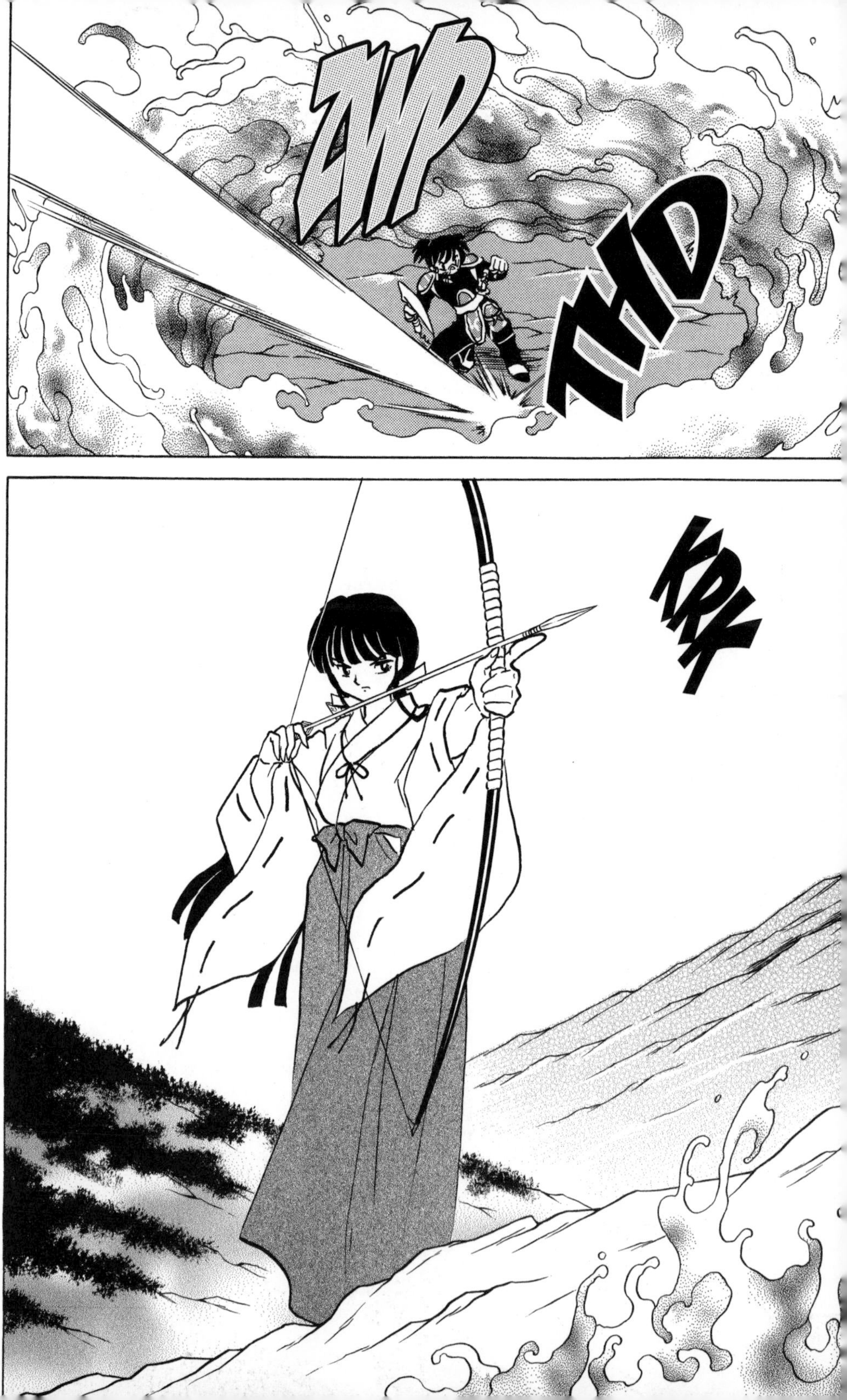
ZWIP
THD
KRK

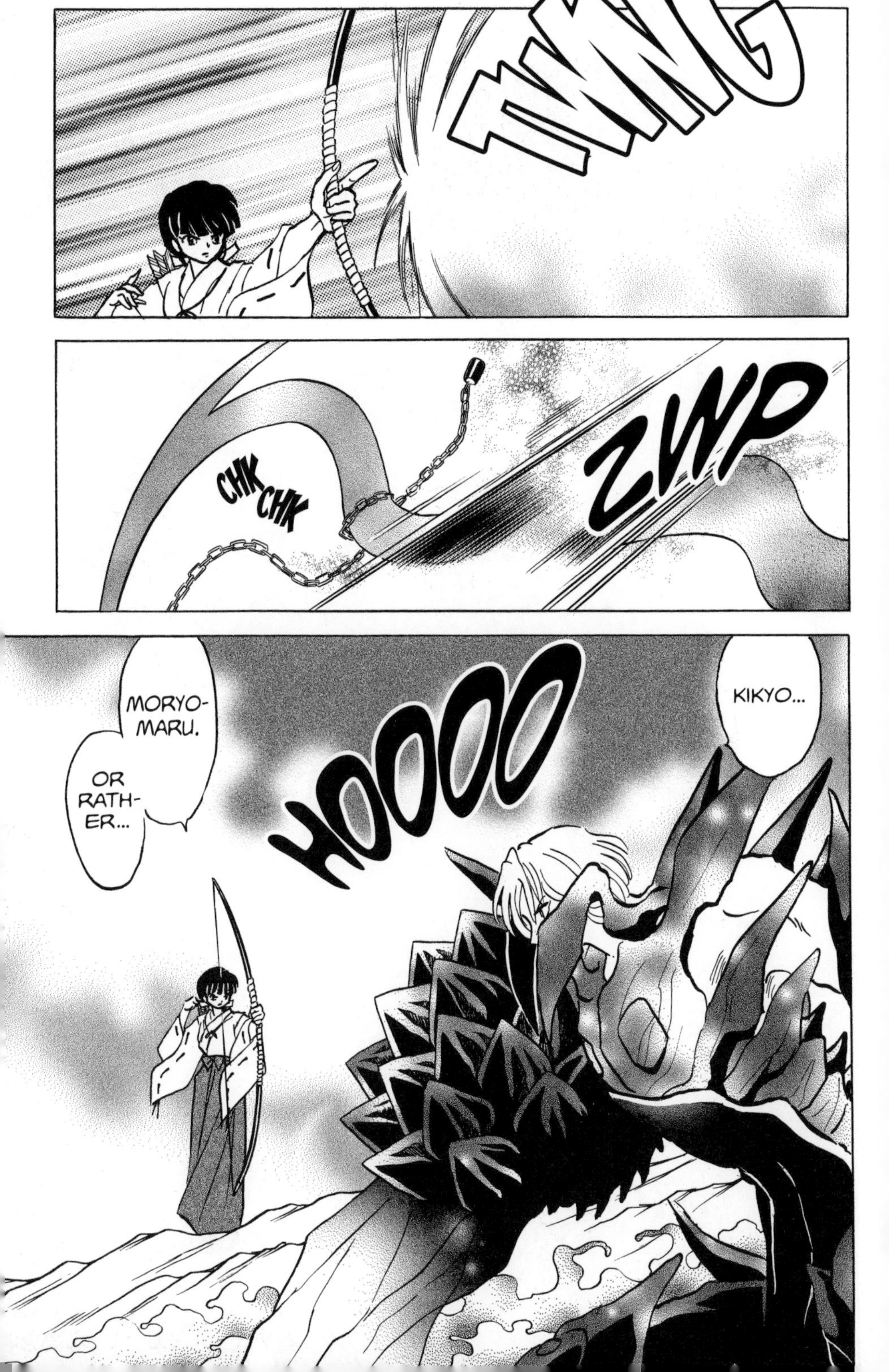
TWNG
ZWP
CHK CHK
KIKYO...
HOOOO
MORYO-MARU.
OR RATHER...

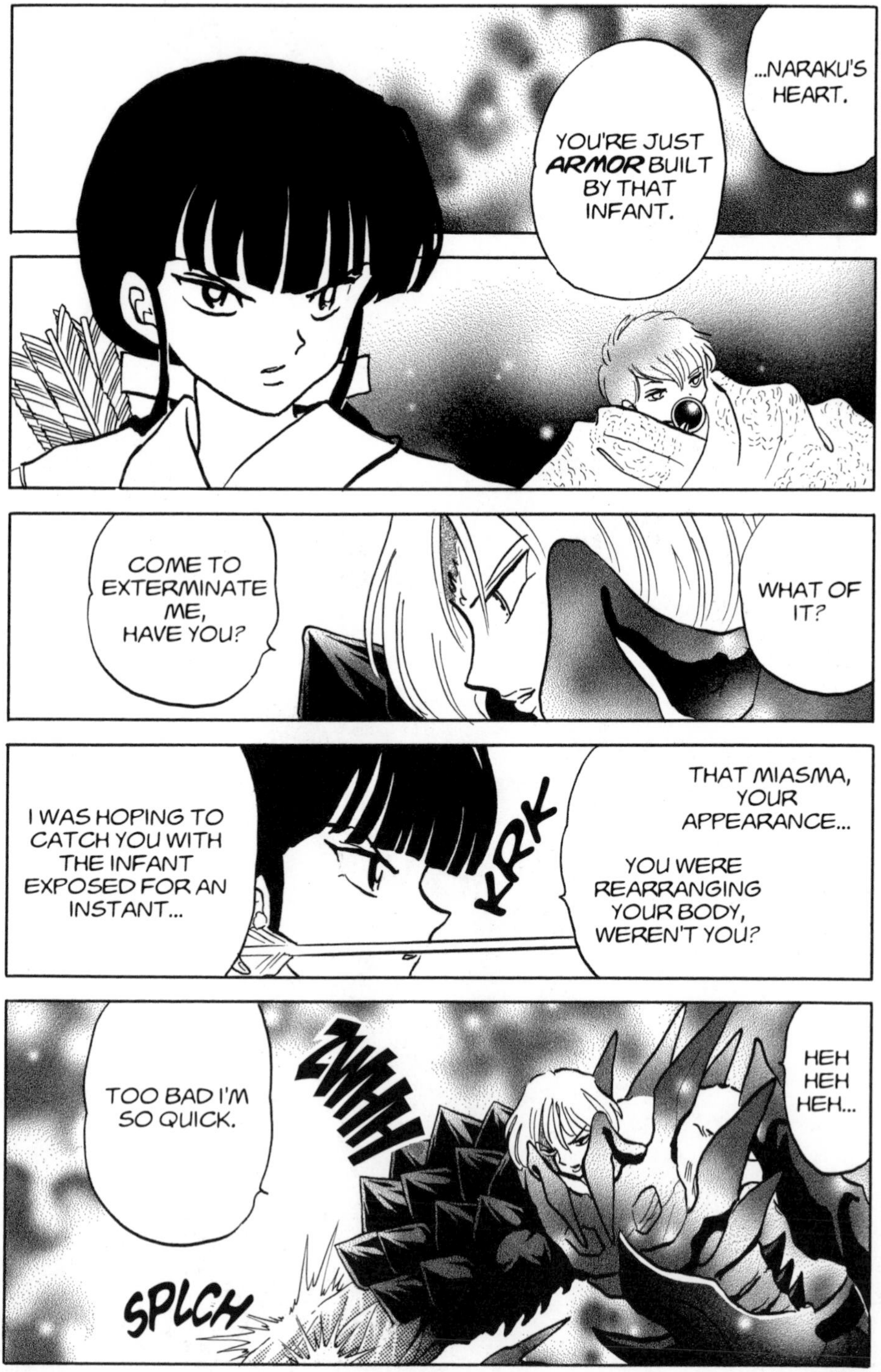
...NARAKU'S HEART.
YOU'RE JUST ARMOR BUILT BY THAT INFANT.
WHAT OF IT?
COME TO EXTERMINATE ME, HAVE YOU?
THAT MIASMA, YOUR APPEARANCE...
YOU WERE REARRANGING YOUR BODY, WEREN'T YOU?
KRK
I WAS HOPING TO CATCH YOU WITH THE INFANT EXPOSED FOR AN INSTANT...
HEH HEH HEH...
ZWHH
TOO BAD I'M SO QUICK.
SPLCH

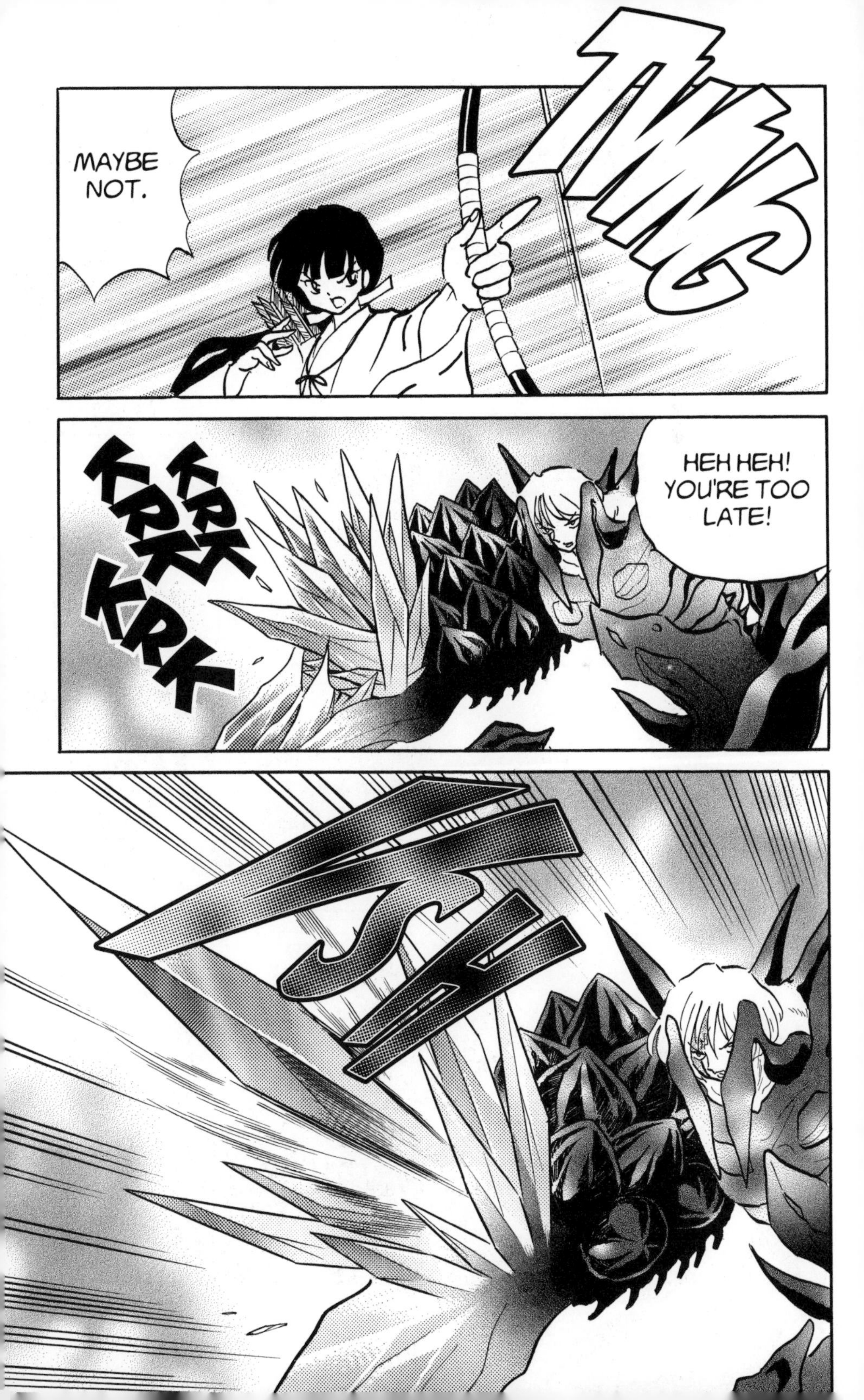

TWANG
MAYBE NOT.
HEH HEH! YOU'RE TOO LATE!
KRK KRK KRK

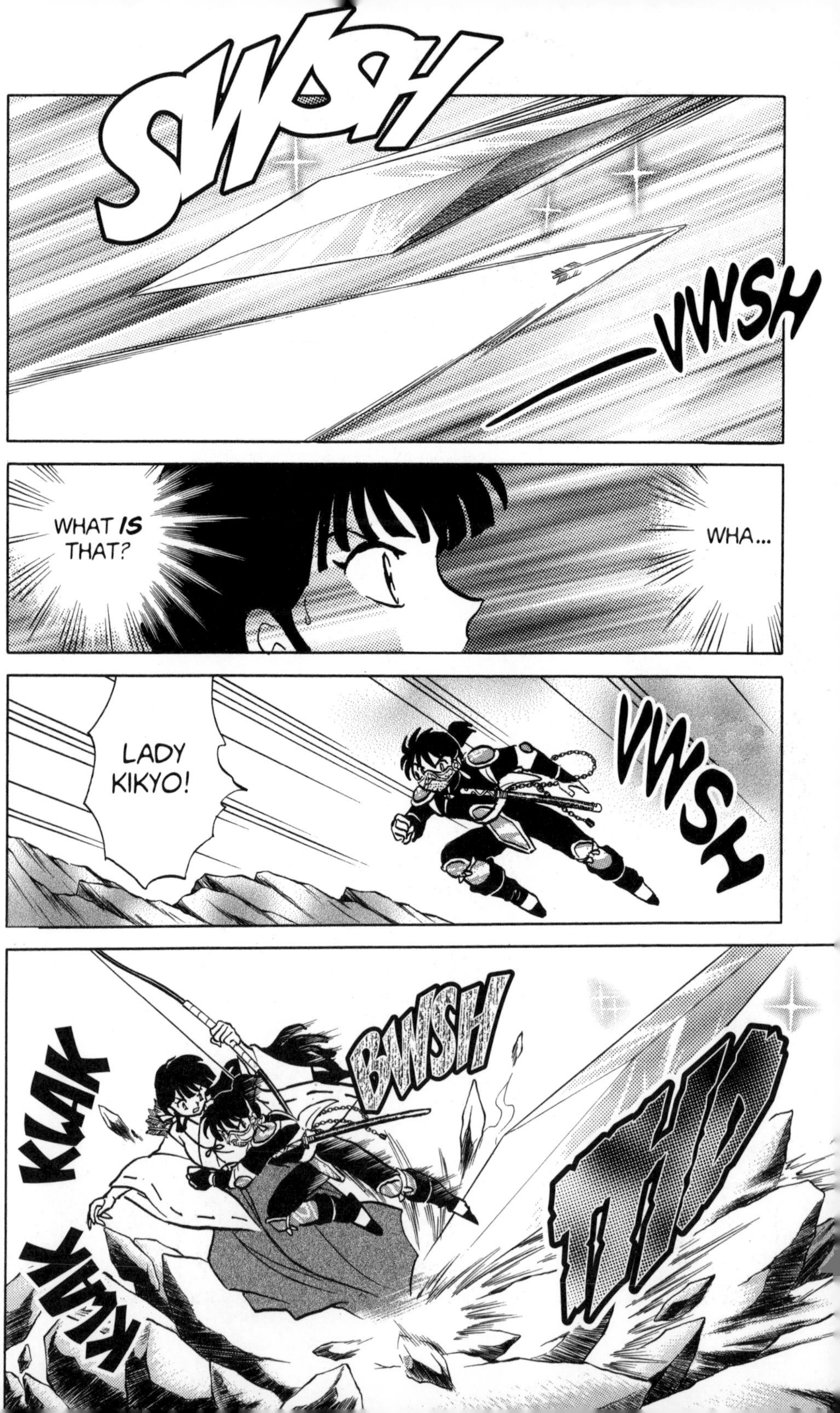
SWSH
VWSH
WHA...
WHAT *IS* THAT?
VWSH
LADY KIKYO!
BWSH
KLAK
KLAK

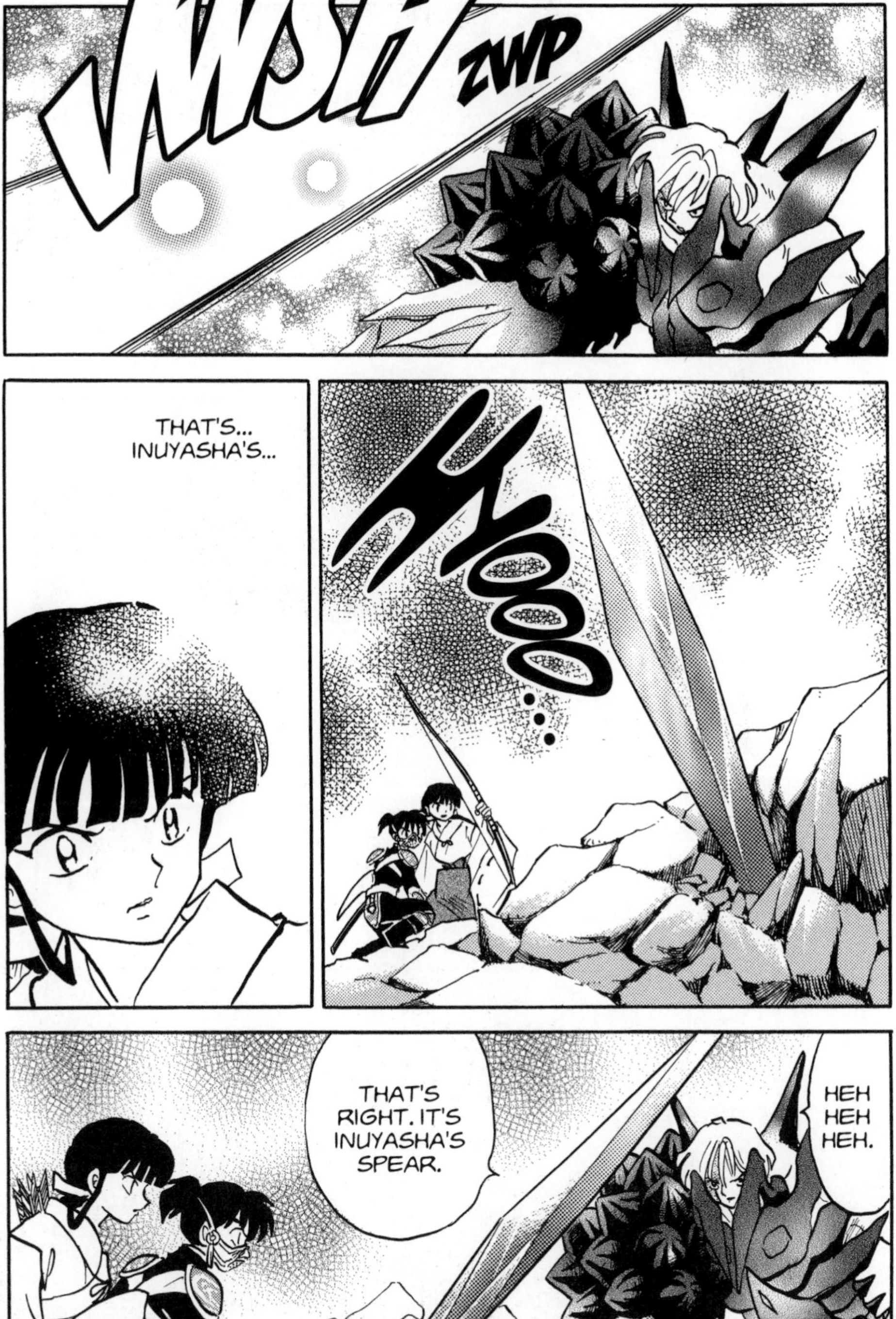
VWSH
ZWP
HYOOO...
THAT'S... INUYASHA'S...
HEH HEH HEH.
THAT'S RIGHT. IT'S INUYASHA'S SPEAR.

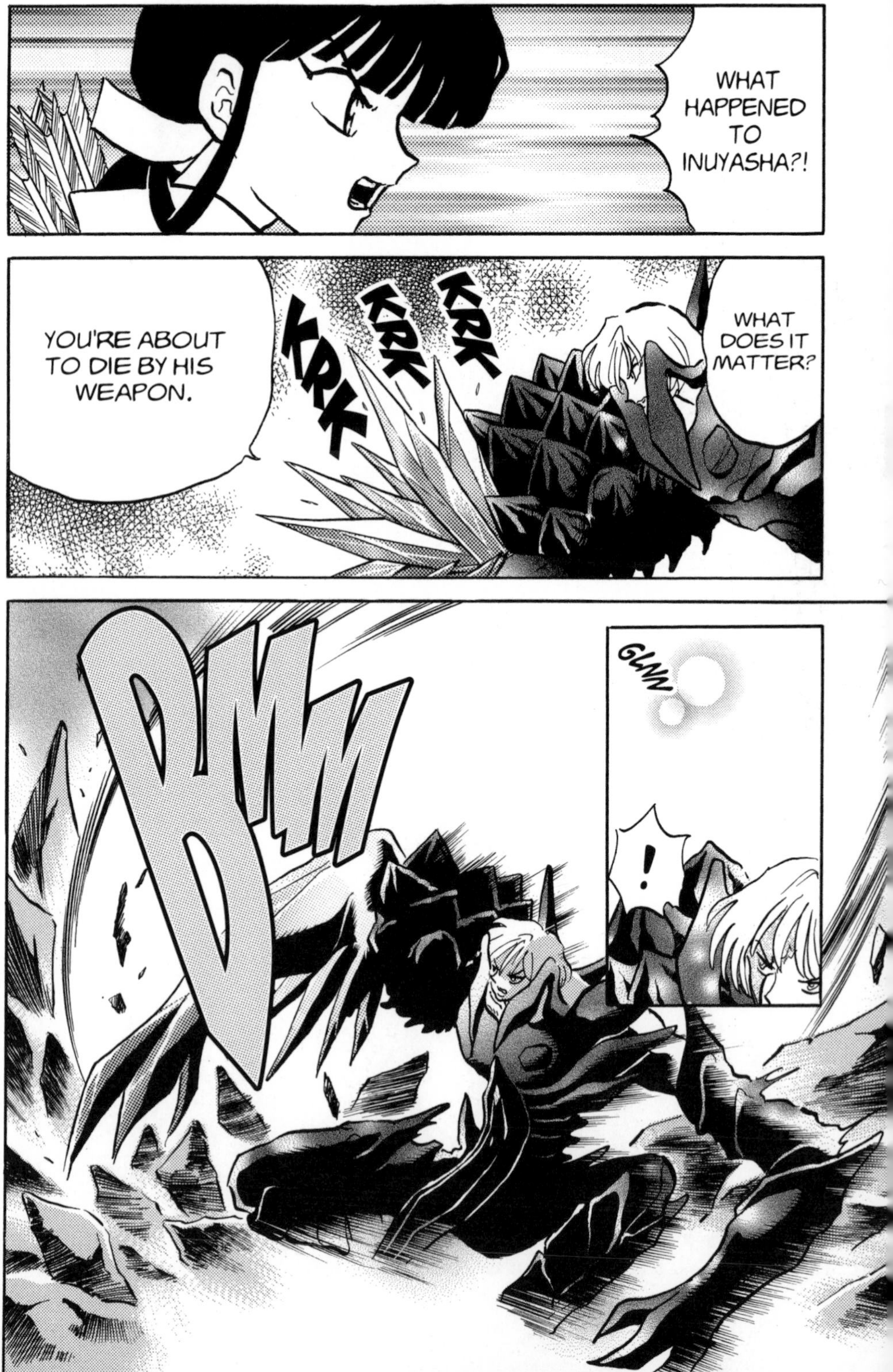
WHAT HAPPENED TO INUYASHA?!
WHAT DOES IT MATTER?
KRK KRK
KRK
YOU'RE ABOUT TO DIE BY HIS WEAPON.
GLNN
!
BMMM

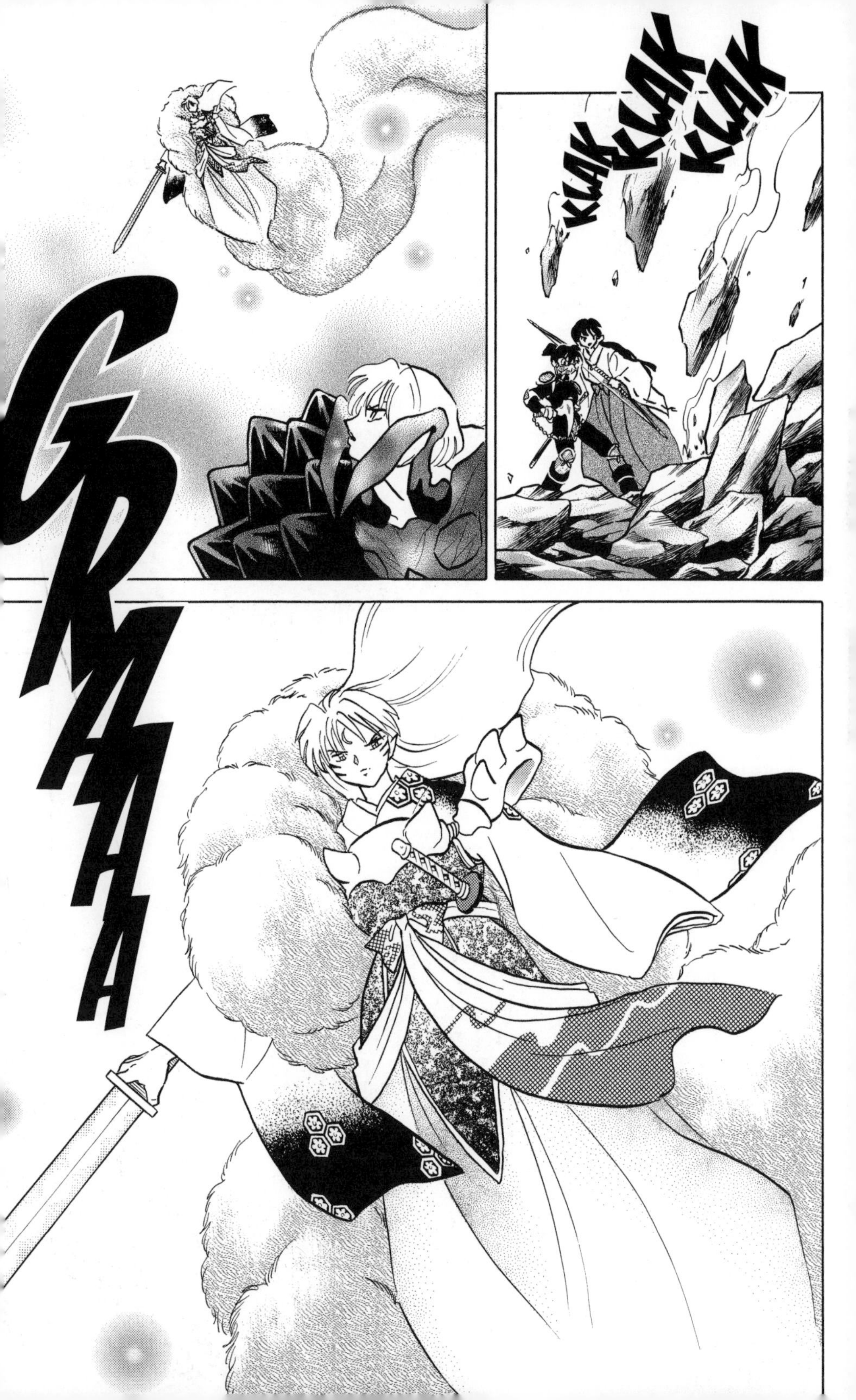
KLAK KLAK KLAK
GRMAAA

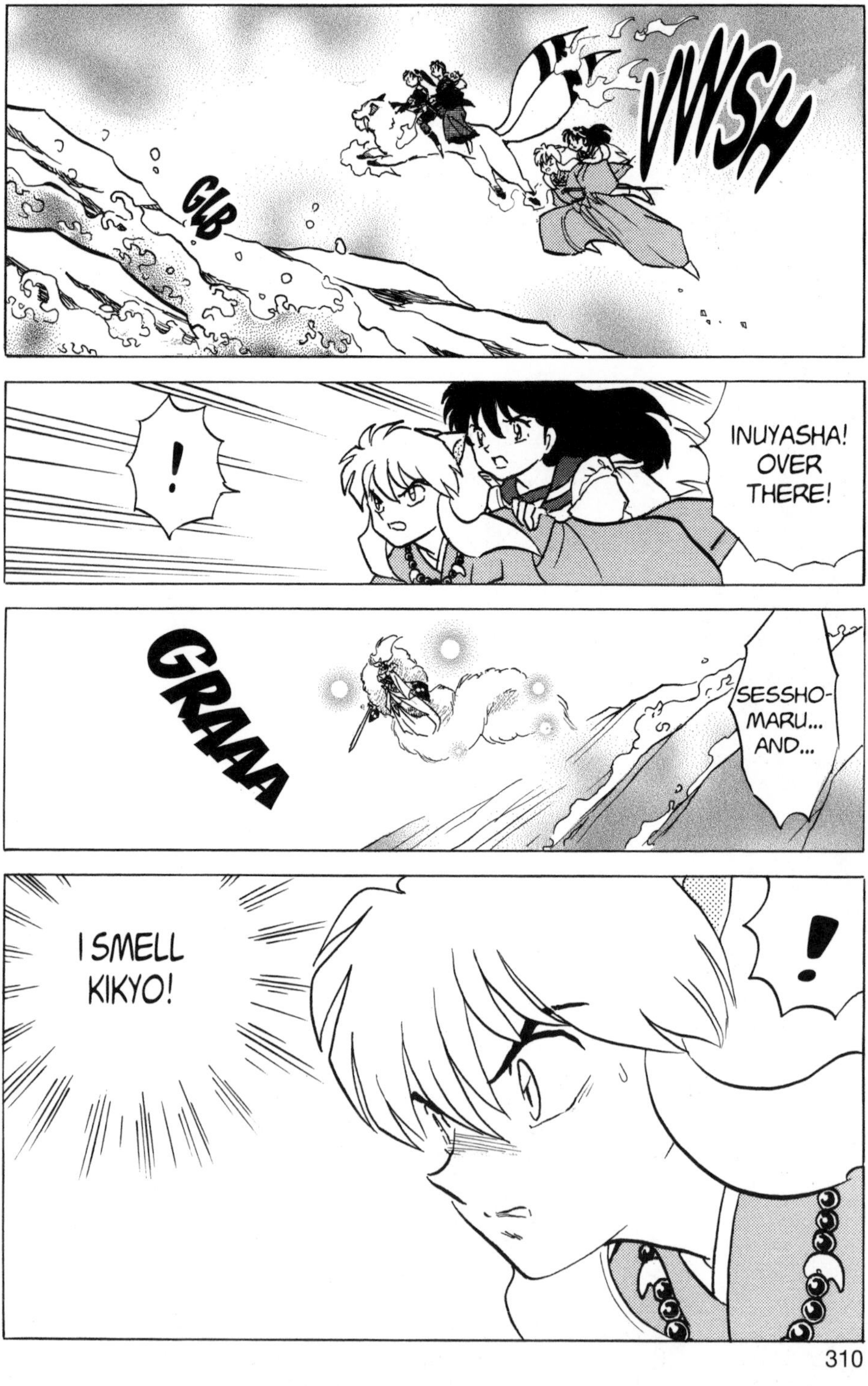
VWSH
GLB
INUYASHA! OVER THERE!
!
SESSHO-MARU... AND...
GRAAA
!
I SMELL KIKYO!

SCROLL SEVEN
RIVALRY

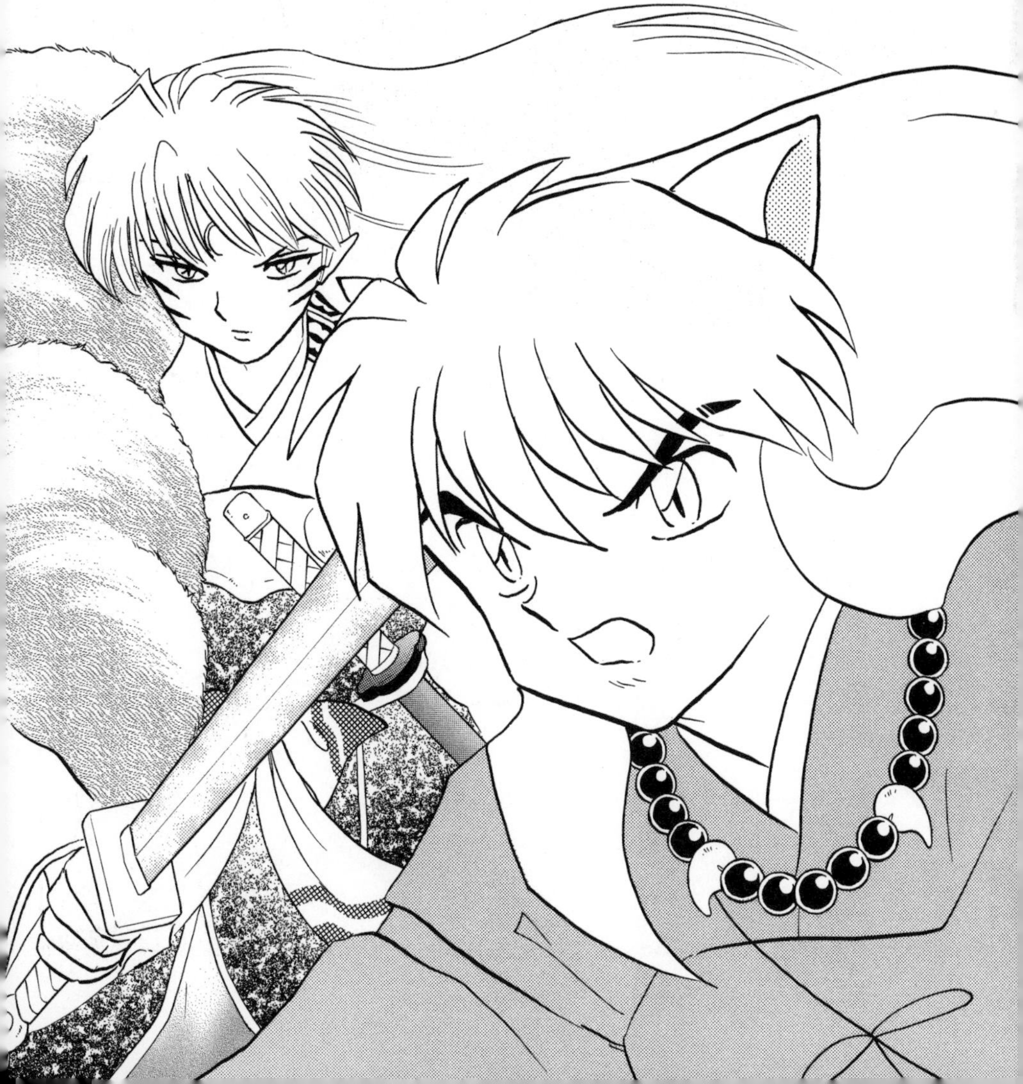

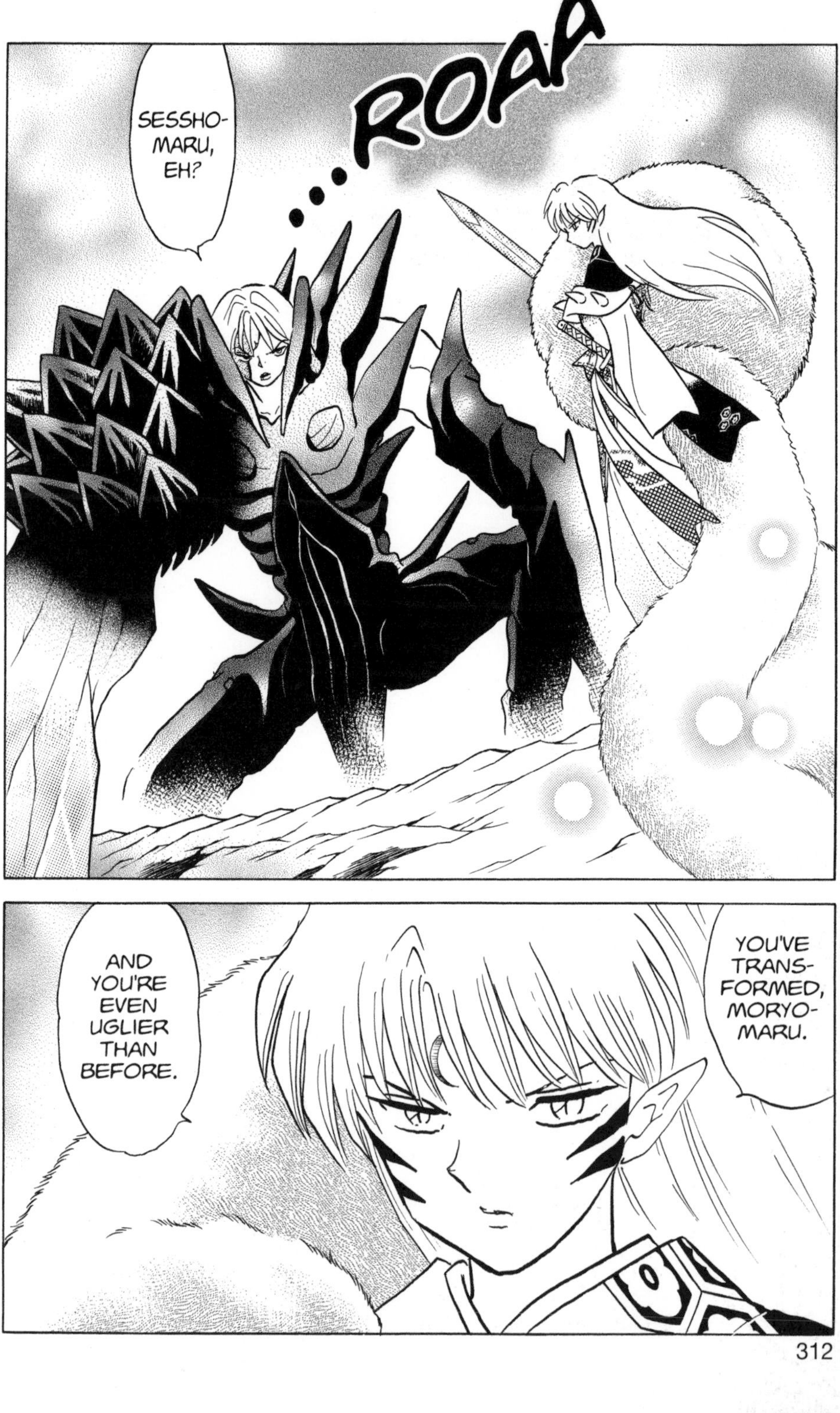
...ROAA
SESSHO-MARU, EH?
YOU'VE TRANS-FORMED, MORYO-MARU.
AND YOU'RE EVEN UGLIER THAN BEFORE.

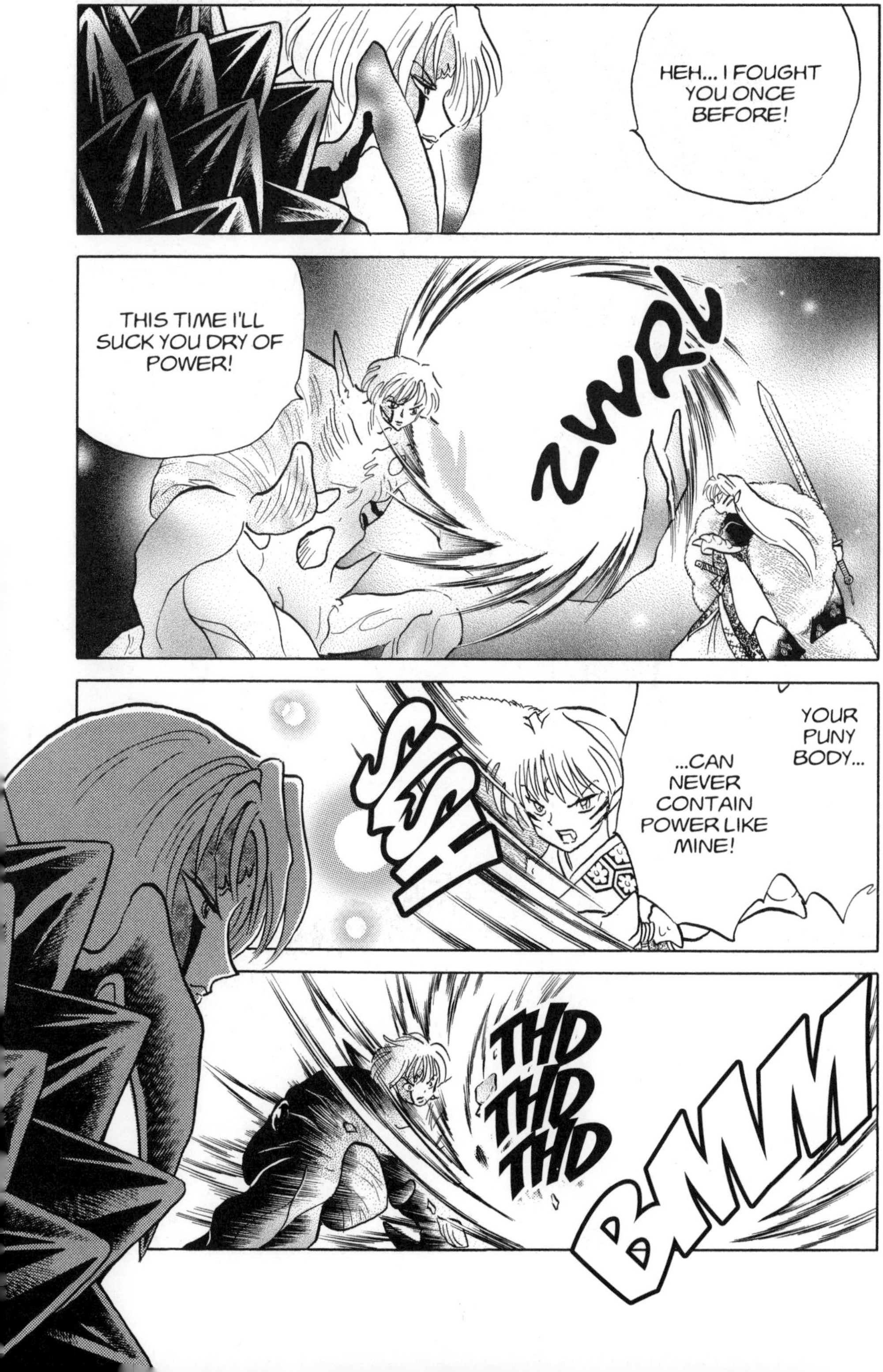
HEH... I FOUGHT YOU ONCE BEFORE!
THIS TIME I'LL SUCK YOU DRY OF POWER!
ZWRL
YOUR PUNY BODY...
...CAN NEVER CONTAIN POWER LIKE MINE!
SSSH
BMMM
THD THD THD

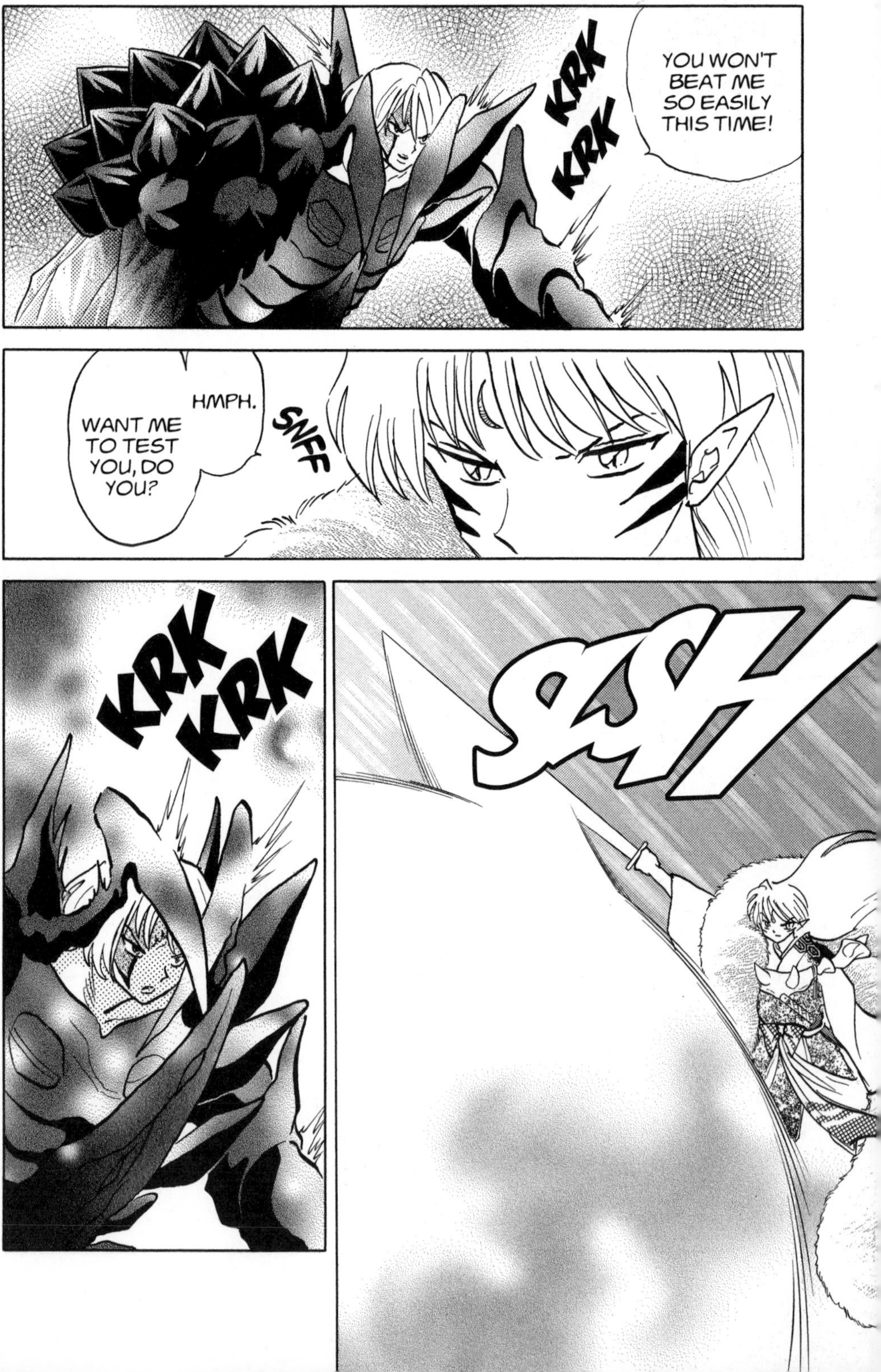
YOU WON'T BEAT ME SO EASILY THIS TIME!
KRK KRK
SNFF
HMPH. WANT ME TO TEST YOU, DO YOU?
SASH
KRK KRK

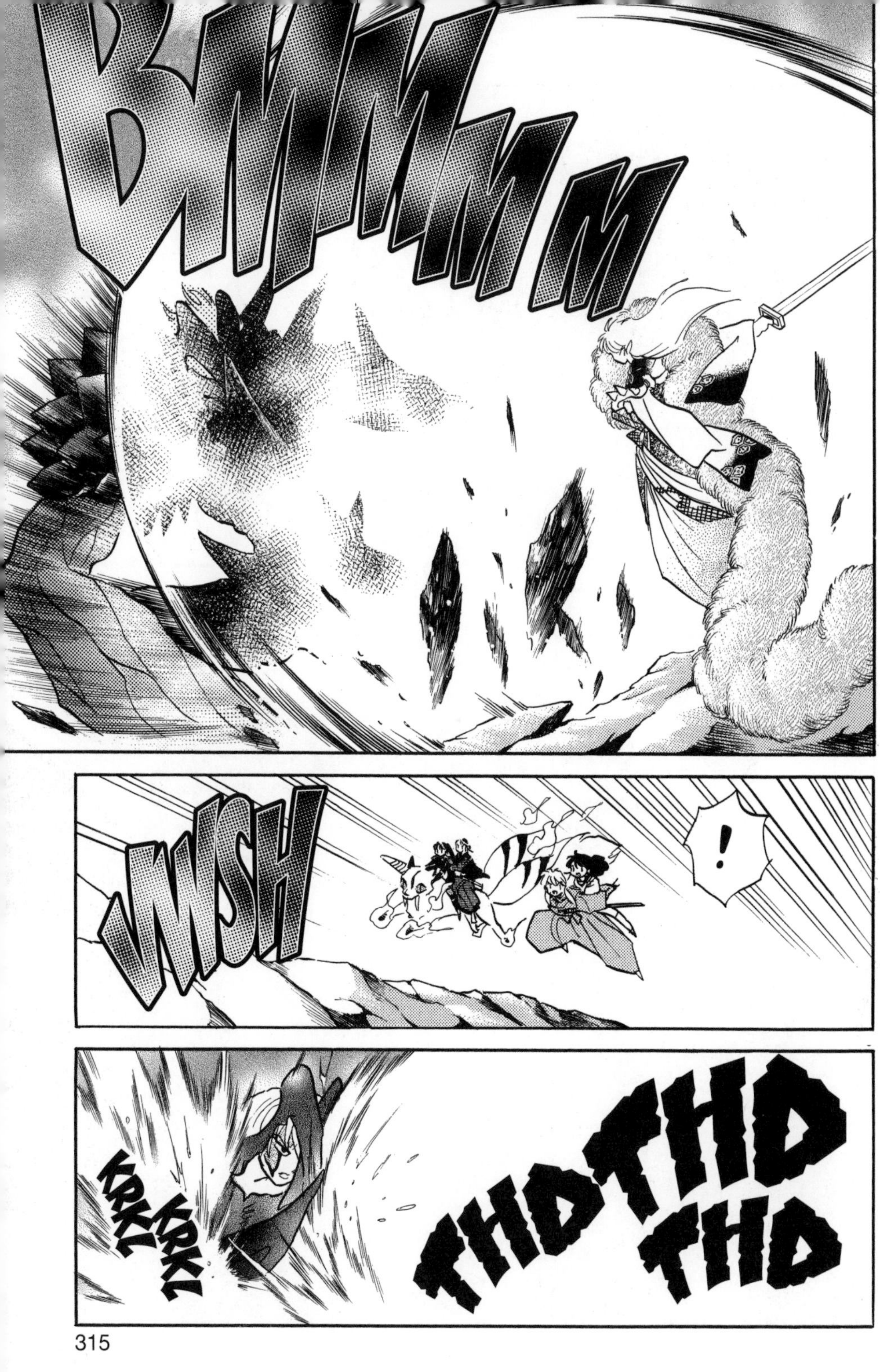
BMMMMM
!
WSH
THD THD THD
KRKL KRKL

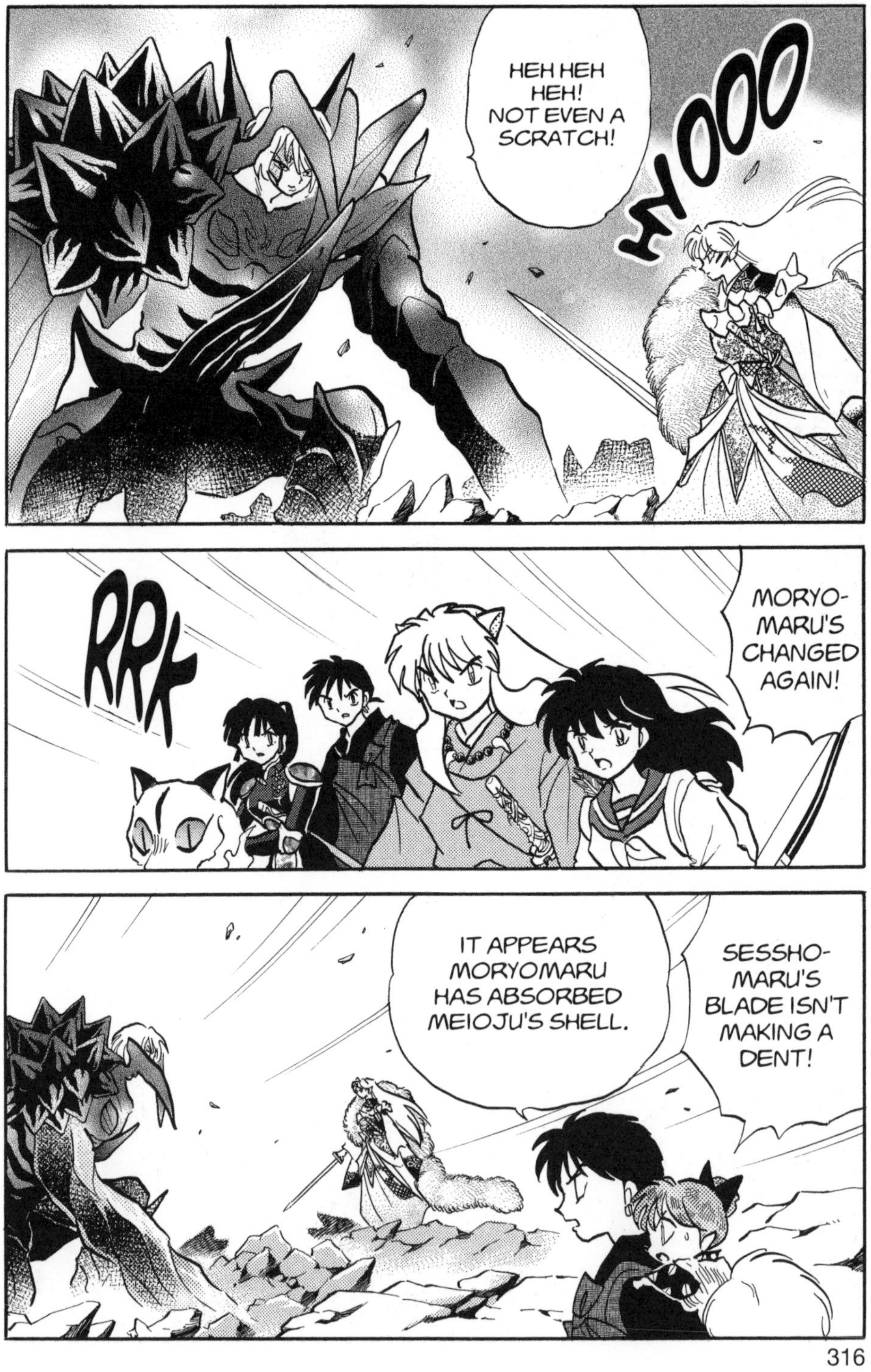
HEH HEH HEH! NOT EVEN A SCRATCH!
HYOOO
MORYO-MARU'S CHANGED AGAIN!
RRK
SESSHO-MARU'S BLADE ISN'T MAKING A DENT!
IT APPEARS MORYOMARU HAS ABSORBED MEIOJU'S SHELL.

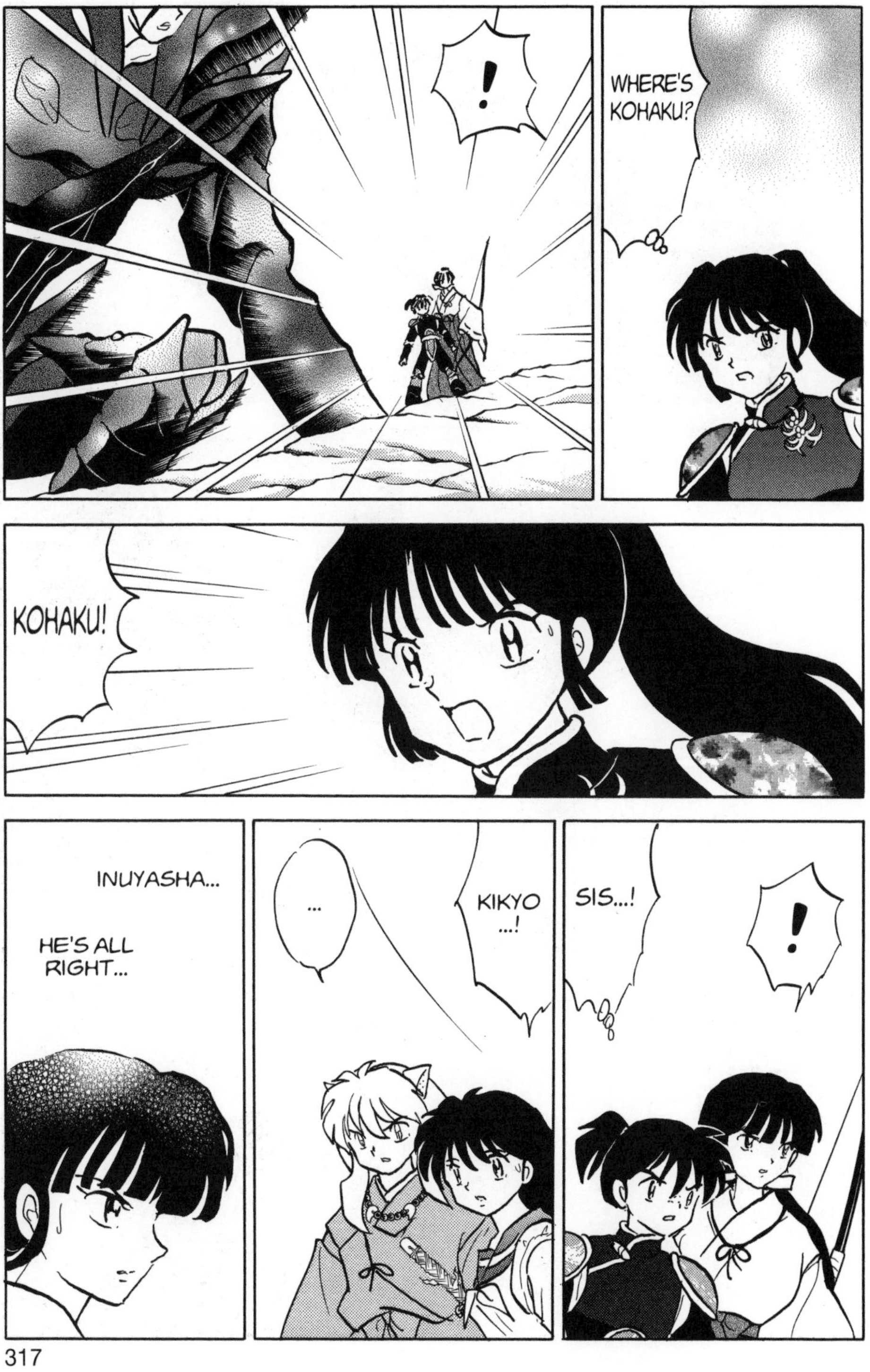
WHERE'S KOHAKU?
!
KOHAKU!
!
SIS...!
KIKYO ...!
...
INUYASHA...
HE'S ALL RIGHT...

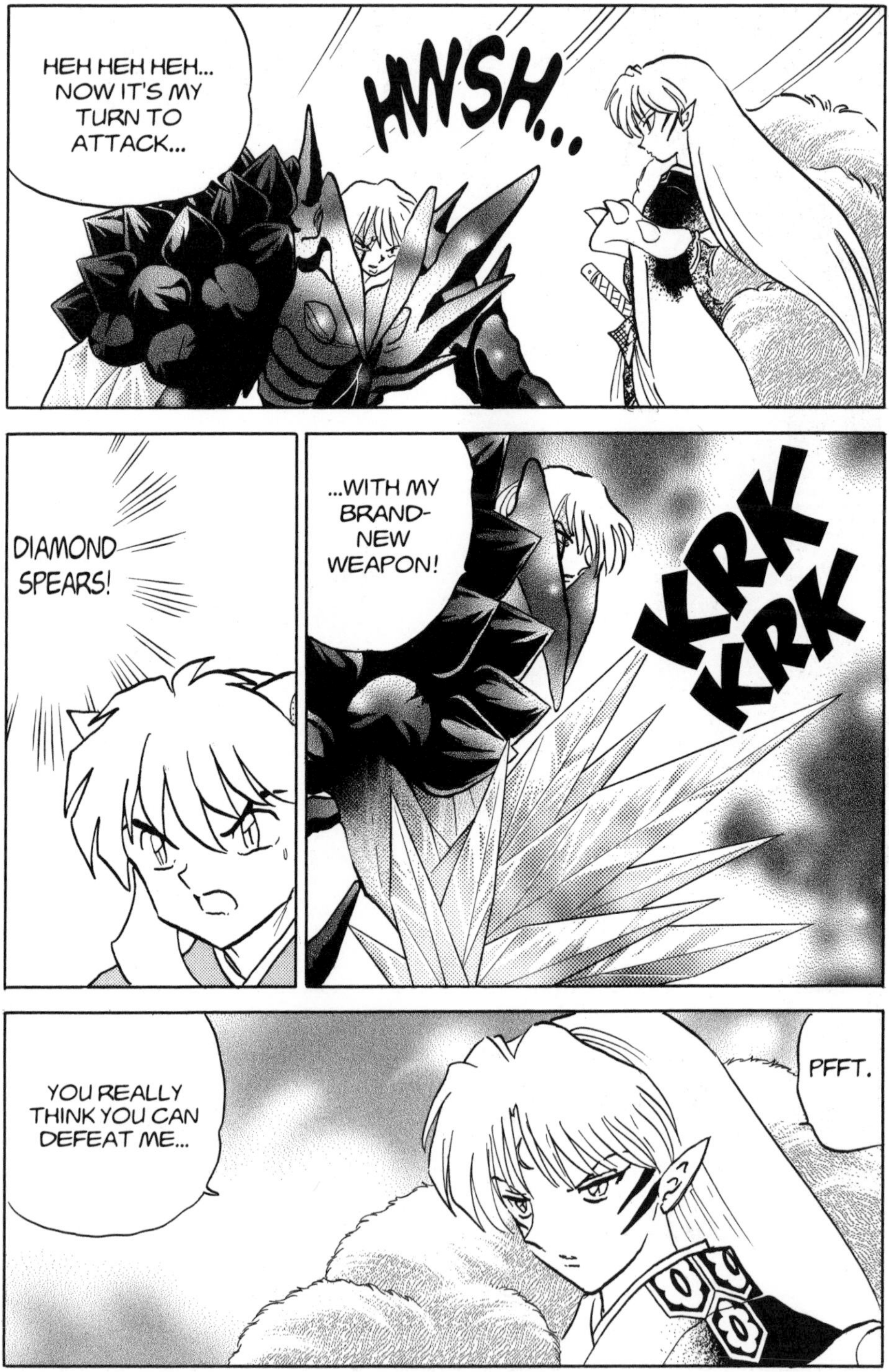
HWSH...
HEH HEH HEH... NOW IT'S MY TURN TO ATTACK...
KRK KRK
...WITH MY BRAND-NEW WEAPON!
DIAMOND SPEARS!
PFFT.
YOU REALLY THINK YOU CAN DEFEAT ME...

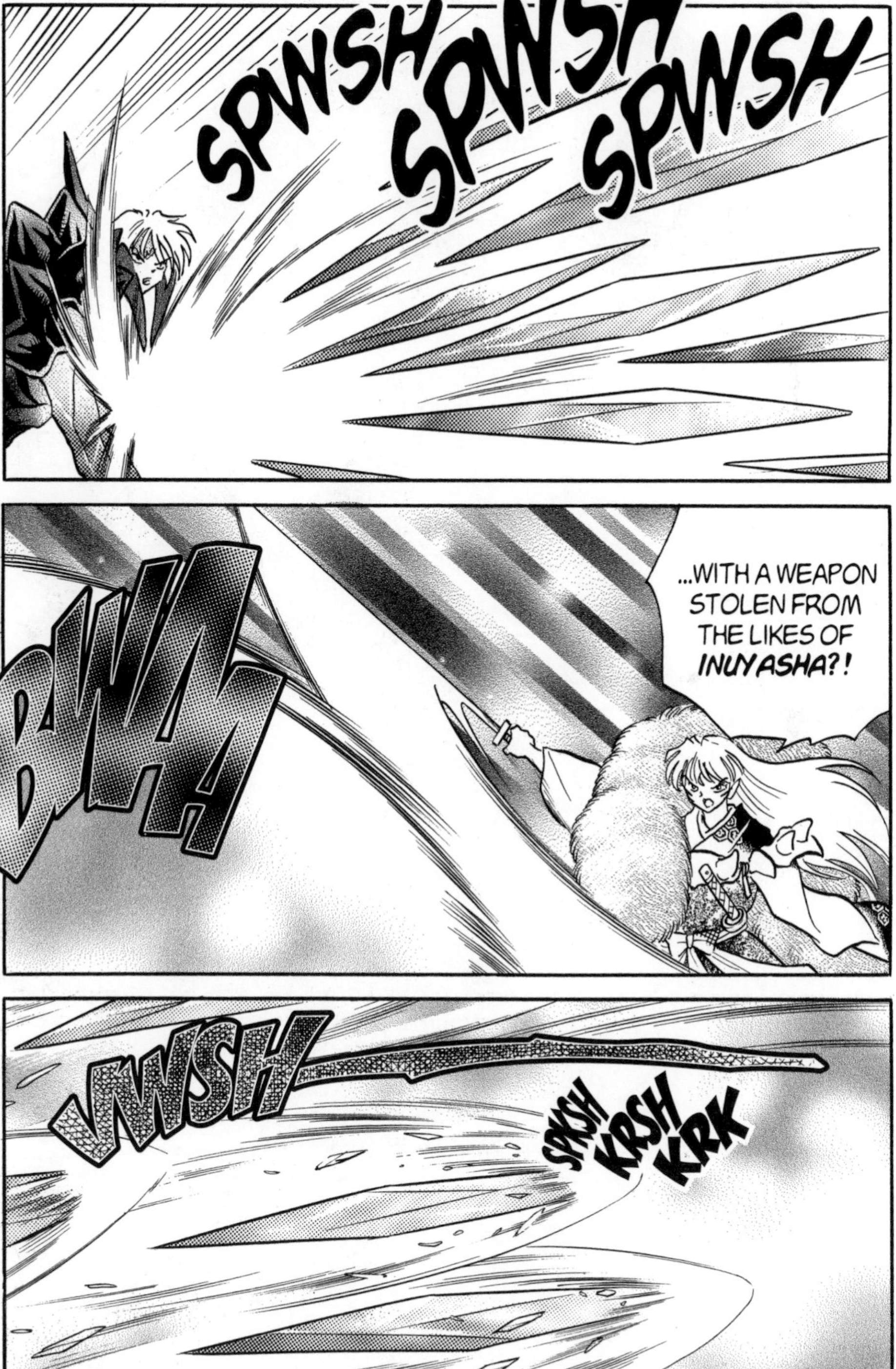
SPWSH SPWSH SPWSH
...WITH A WEAPON STOLEN FROM THE LIKES OF *INUYASHA*?!
BWAM
VWSH
SPKSH KRSH KRK

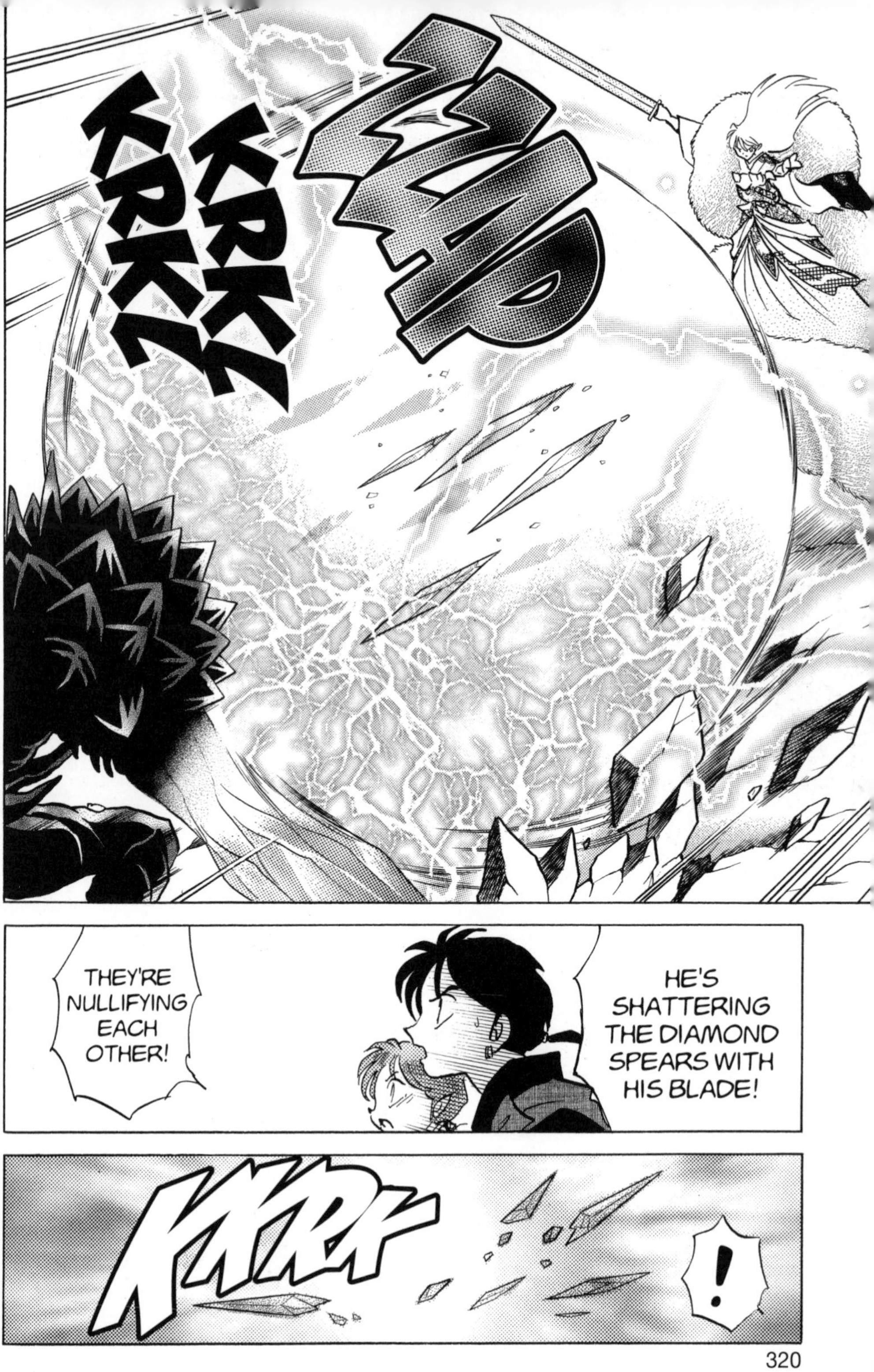
ZZAP
KRK KRKL
HE'S SHATTERING THE DIAMOND SPEARS WITH HIS BLADE!
THEY'RE NULLIFYING EACH OTHER!
KRRK
!

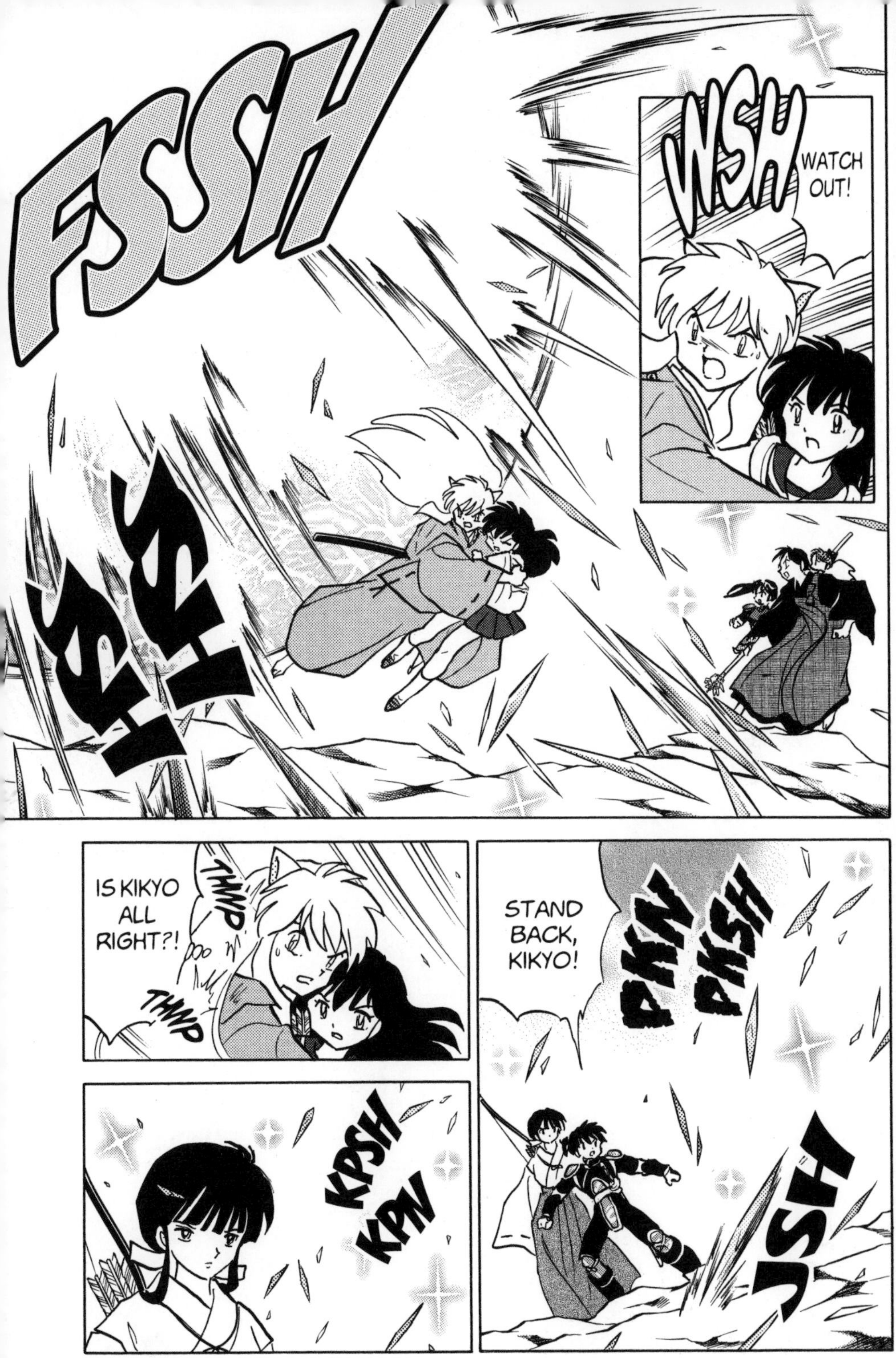
WSH
WATCH OUT!
FSSH
STAND BACK, KIKYO!
PKN
PKSH
IS KIKYO ALL RIGHT?!
THMP
THMP
KPSH
KPN

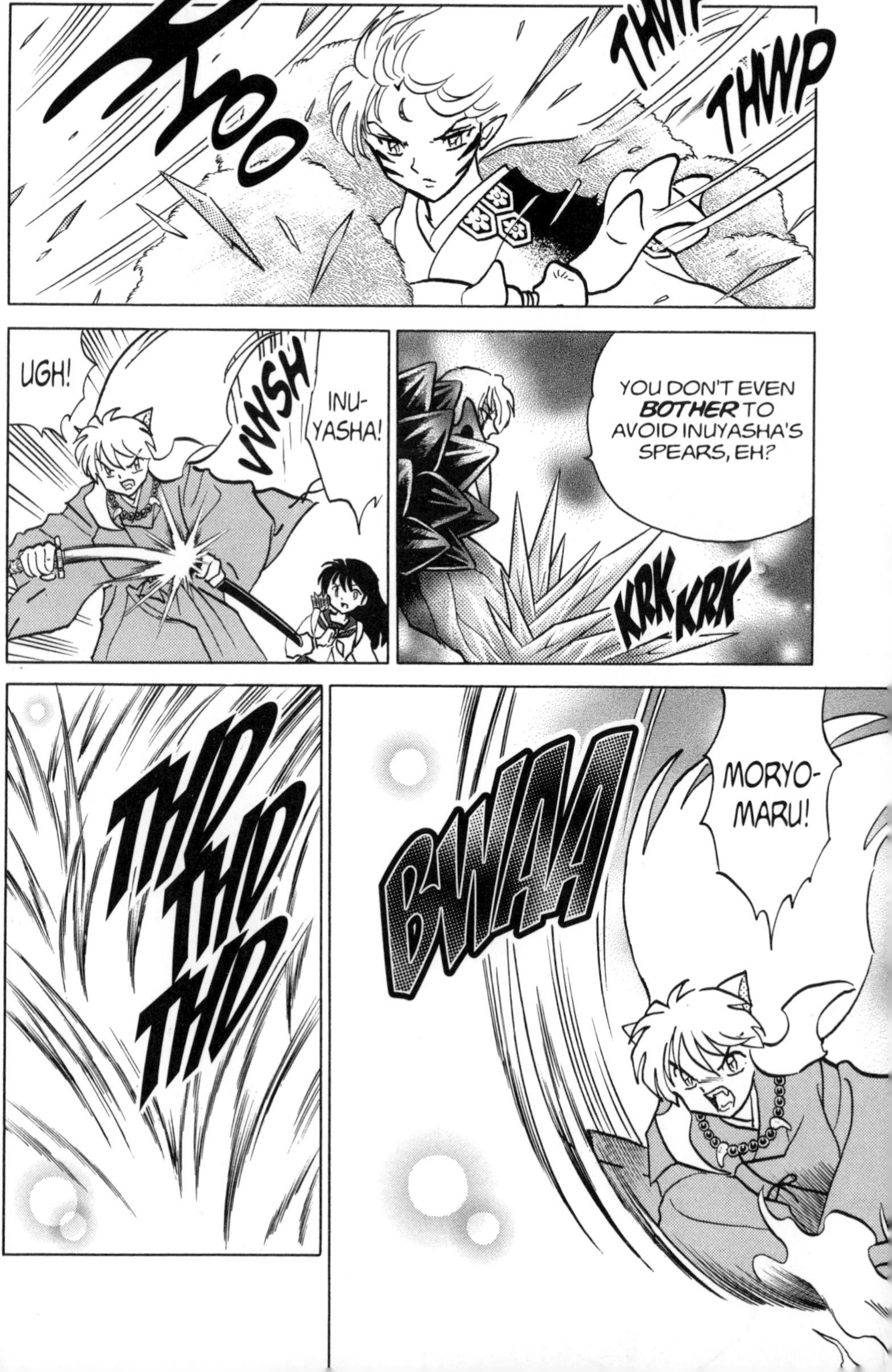
THWP
THWP
KYOO
YOU DON'T EVEN **BOTHER** TO AVOID INUYASHA'S SPEARS, EH?
KRK KRK
INU-YASHA!
VWSH
UGH!
MORYO-MARU!
BWAM
THD THD THD

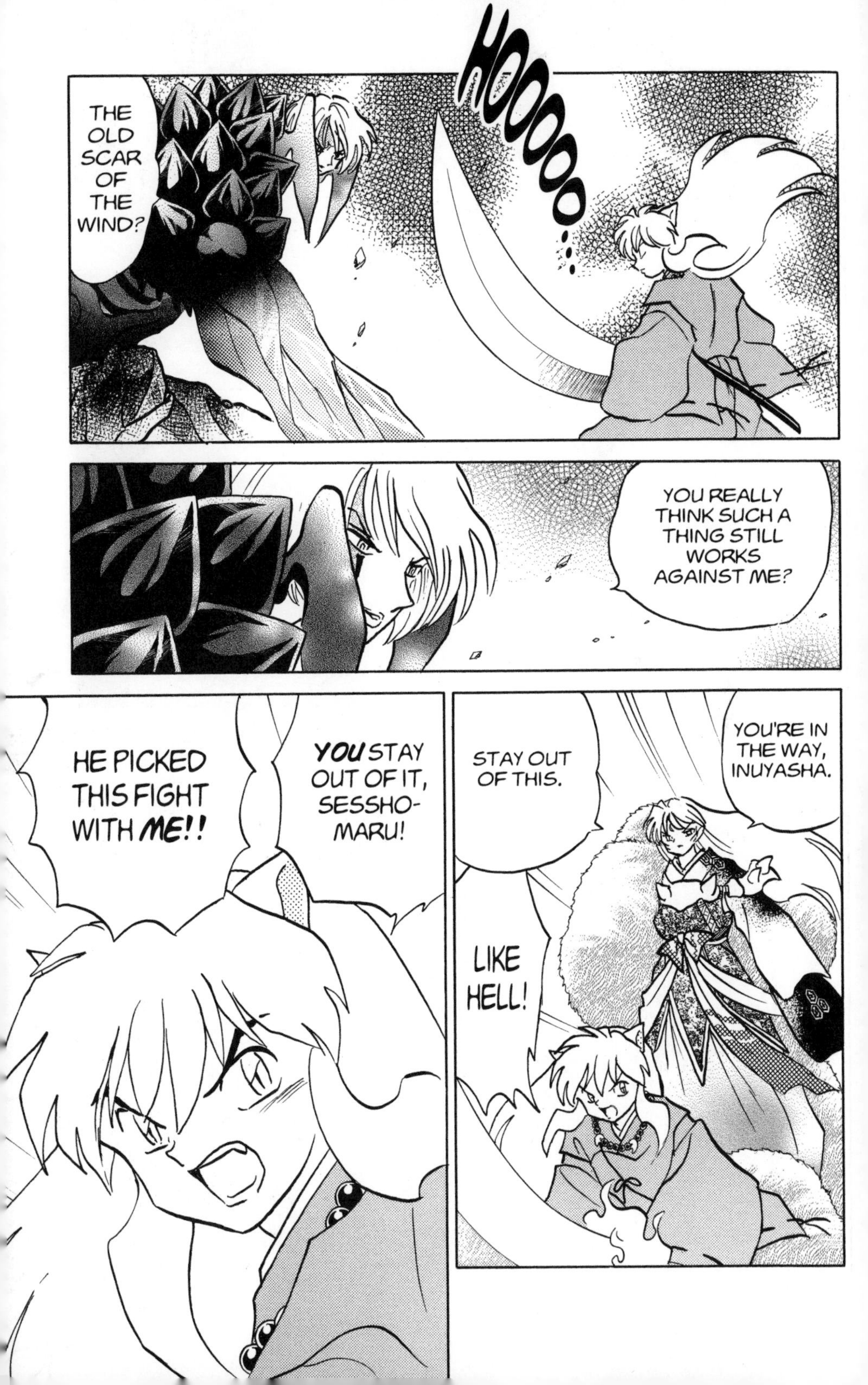
HOOOOOO...
THE OLD SCAR OF THE WIND?
YOU REALLY THINK SUCH A THING STILL WORKS AGAINST ME?
YOU'RE IN THE WAY, INUYASHA.
STAY OUT OF THIS.
LIKE HELL!
YOU STAY OUT OF IT, SESSHO-MARU!
HE PICKED THIS FIGHT WITH ME!!

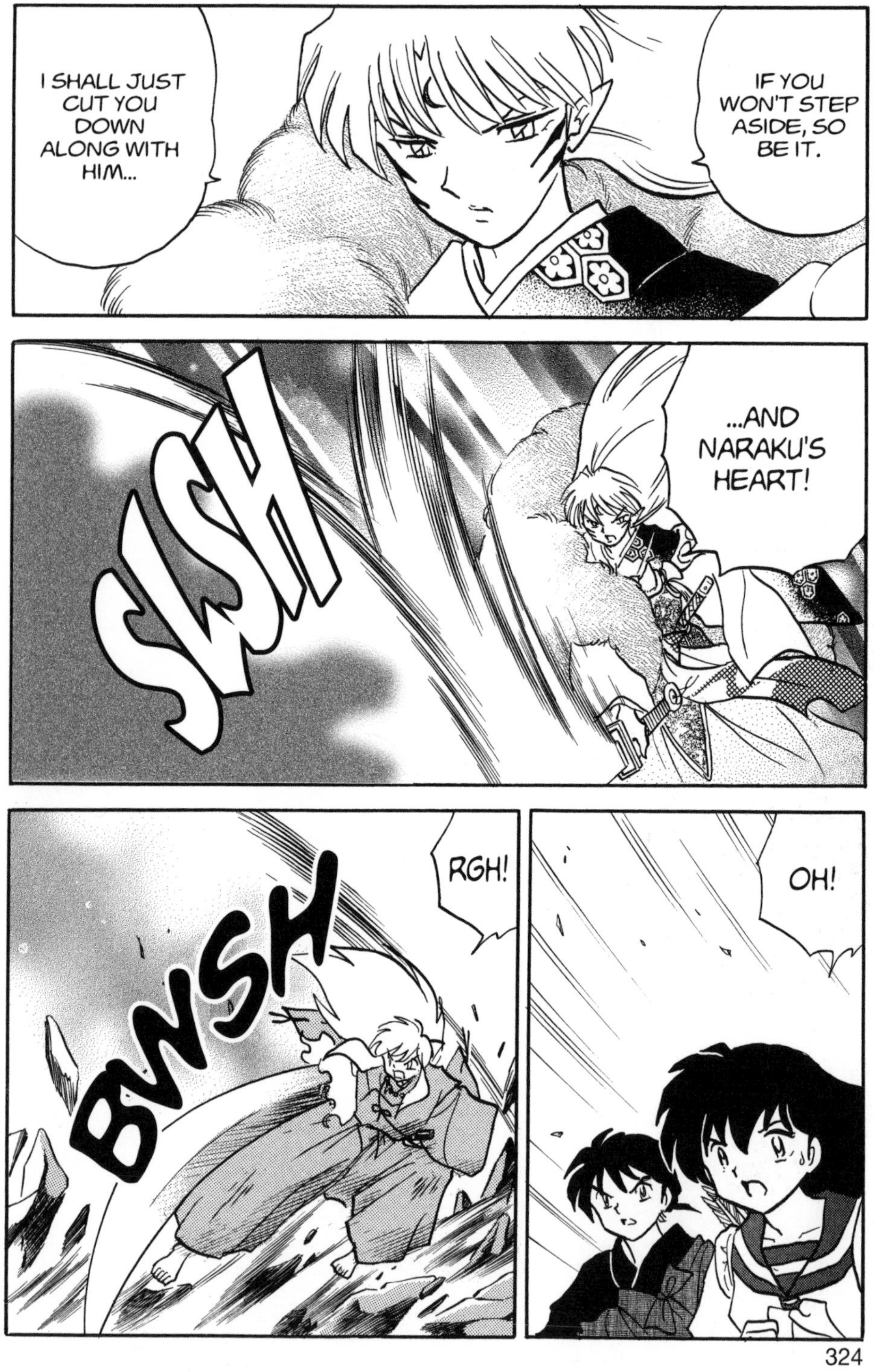
IF YOU WON'T STEP ASIDE, SO BE IT.
I SHALL JUST CUT YOU DOWN ALONG WITH HIM...
...AND NARAKU'S HEART!
SLSH
OH!
RGH!
BWSH

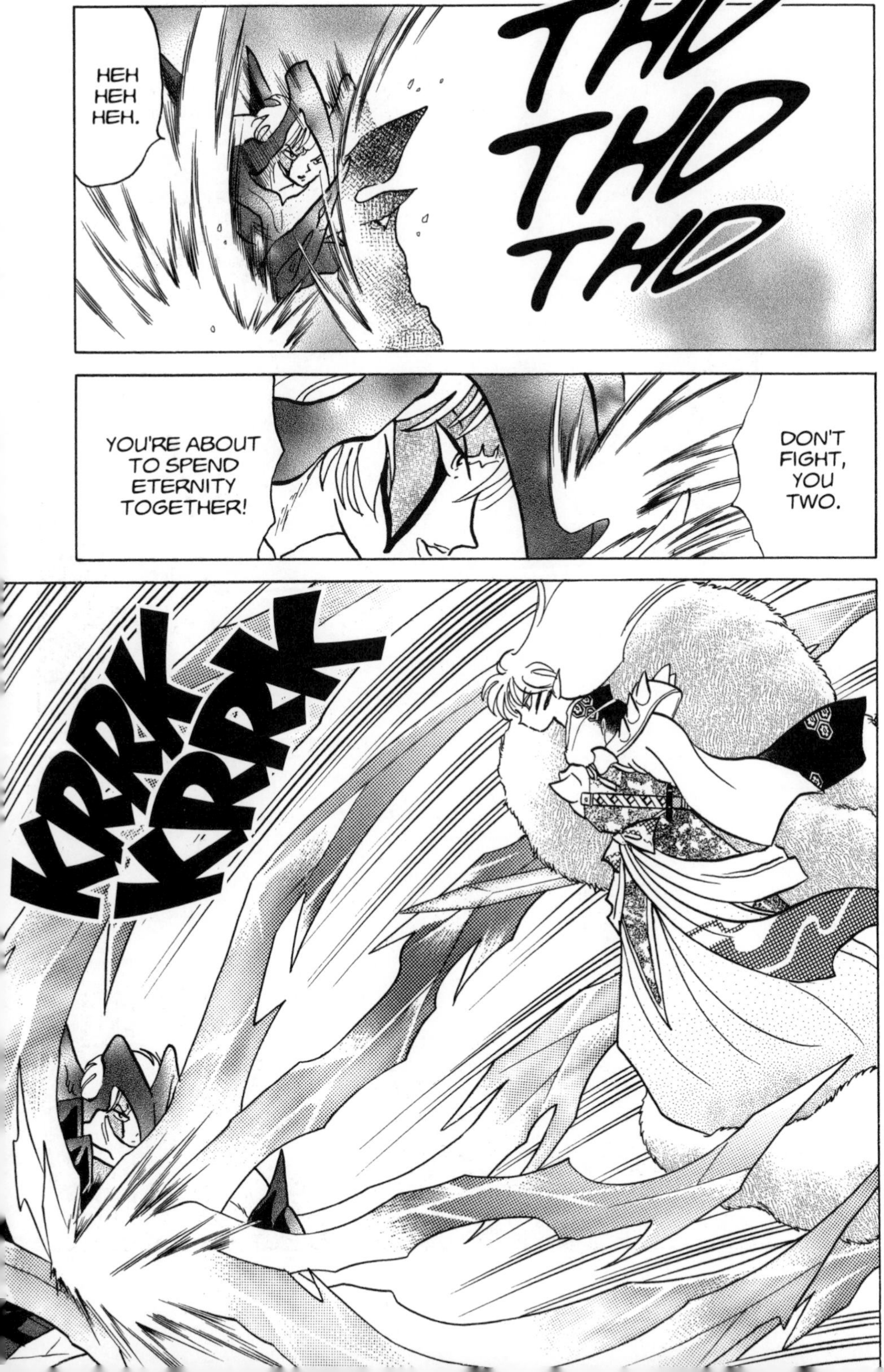
THD
THD
THD
HEH HEH HEH.
DON'T FIGHT, YOU TWO.
YOU'RE ABOUT TO SPEND ETERNITY TOGETHER!
KRRK
KRRK

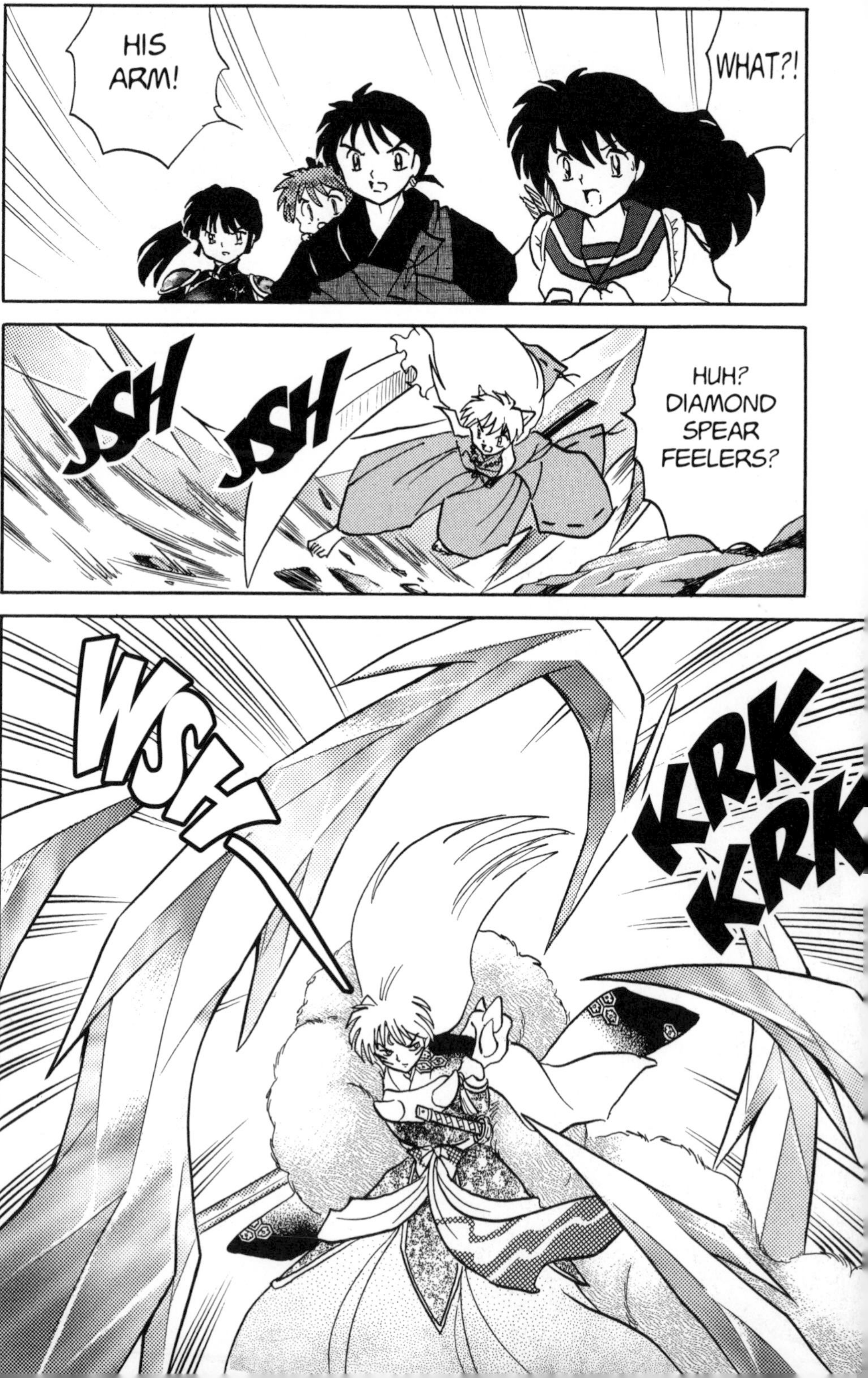
WHAT?!
HIS ARM!
HUH? DIAMOND SPEAR FEELERS?
JSH JSH
KRK KRK
WSH

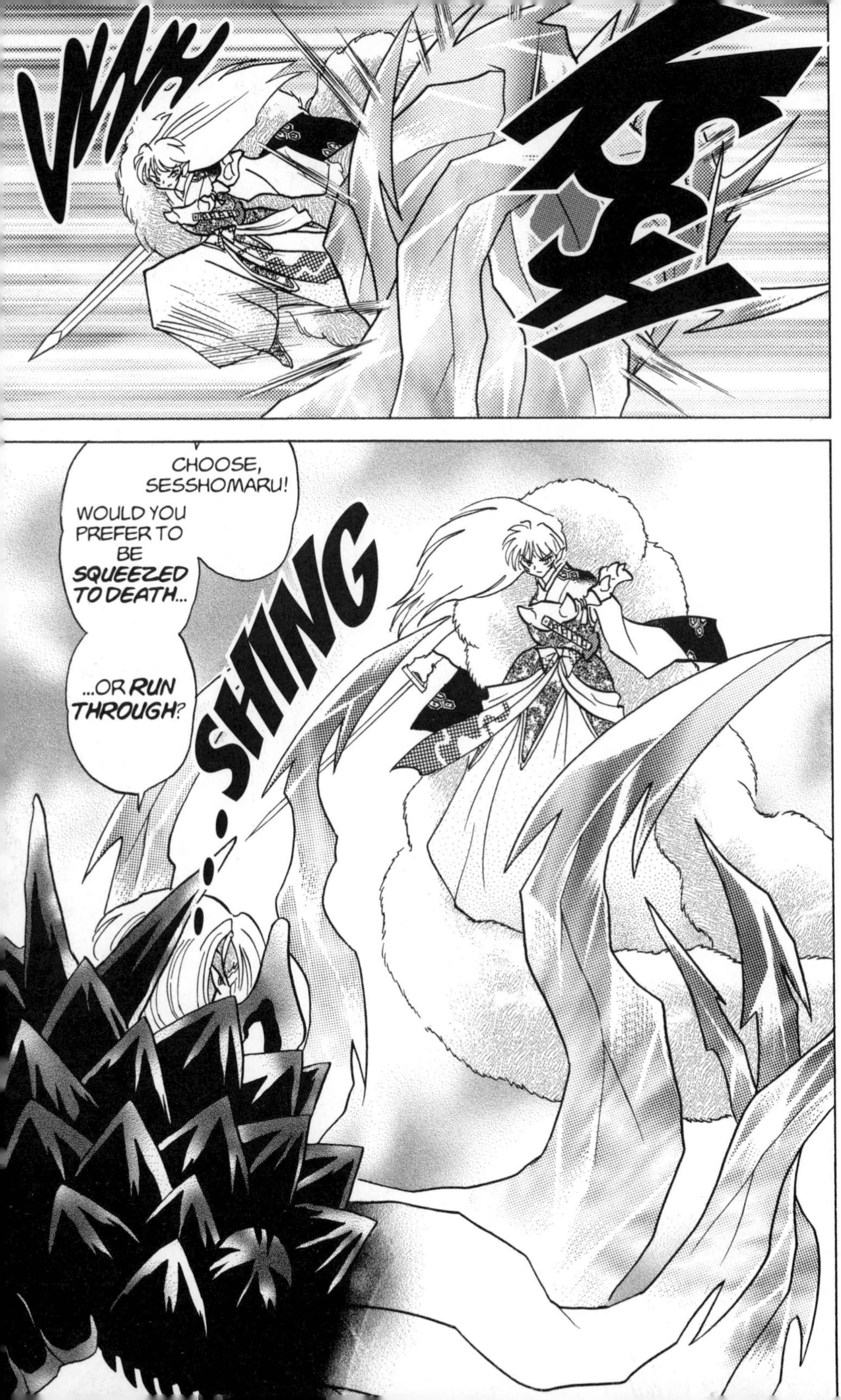
CHOOSE, SESSHOMARU!
WOULD YOU PREFER TO BE **SQUEEZED TO DEATH...**
...OR **RUN THROUGH**?
...SHING

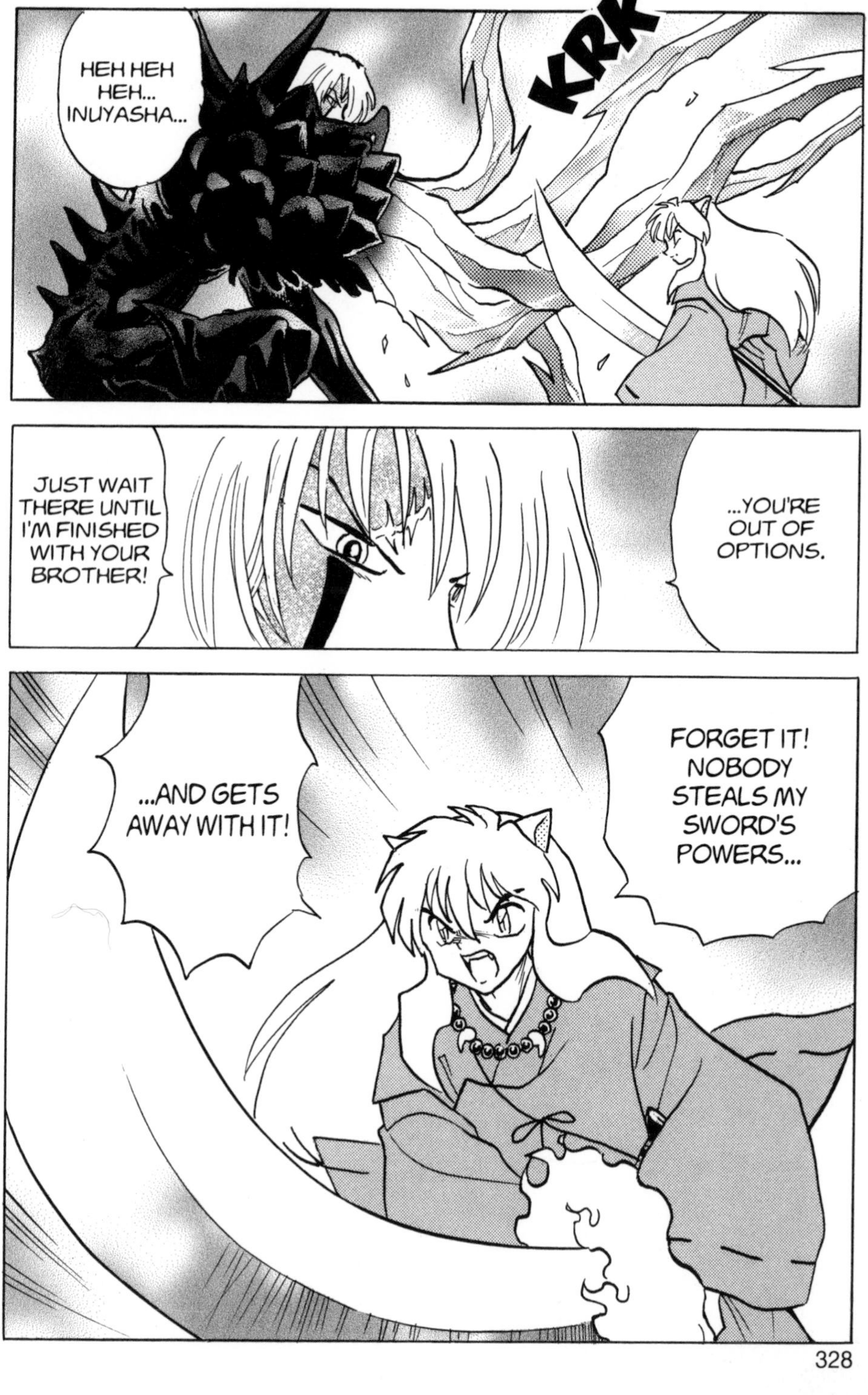
KRK
HEH HEH HEH... INUYASHA...
...YOU'RE OUT OF OPTIONS.
JUST WAIT THERE UNTIL I'M FINISHED WITH YOUR BROTHER!
FORGET IT! NOBODY STEALS MY SWORD'S POWERS...
...AND GETS AWAY WITH IT!

SCROLL EIGHT
WRATH

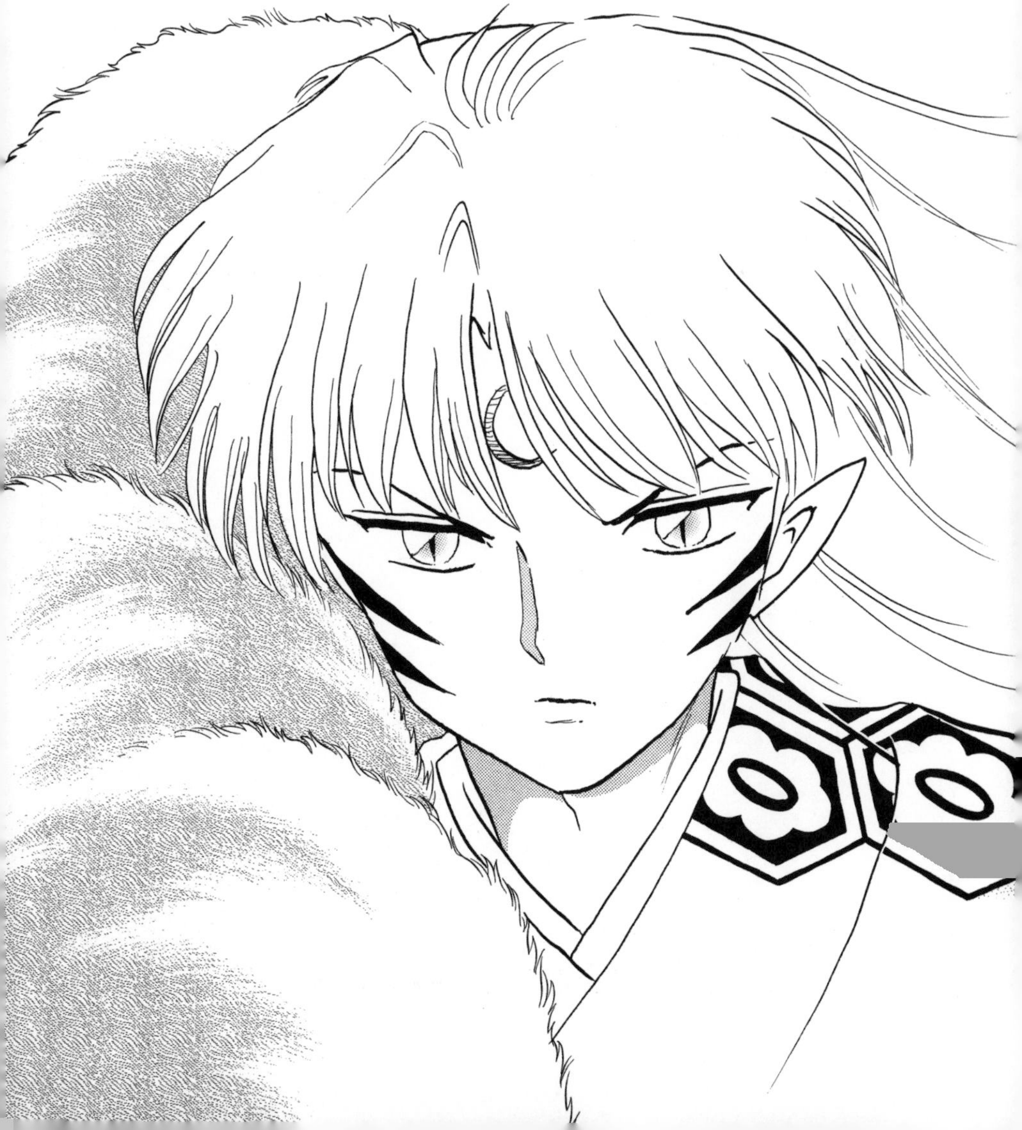

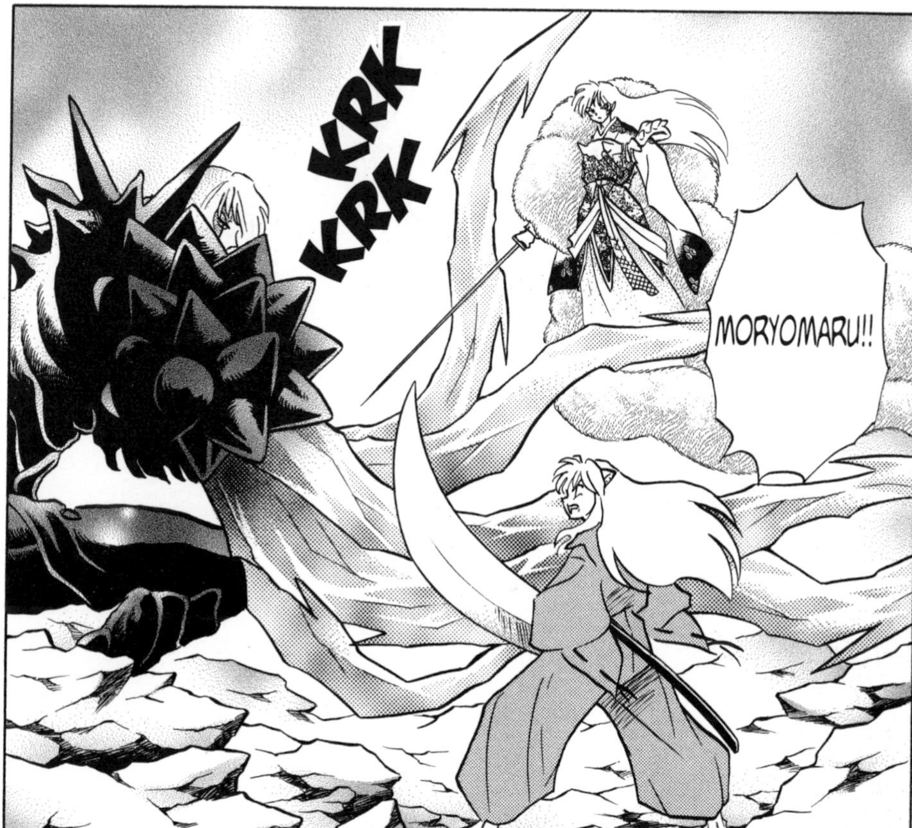
KRK KRK
MORYOMARU!!
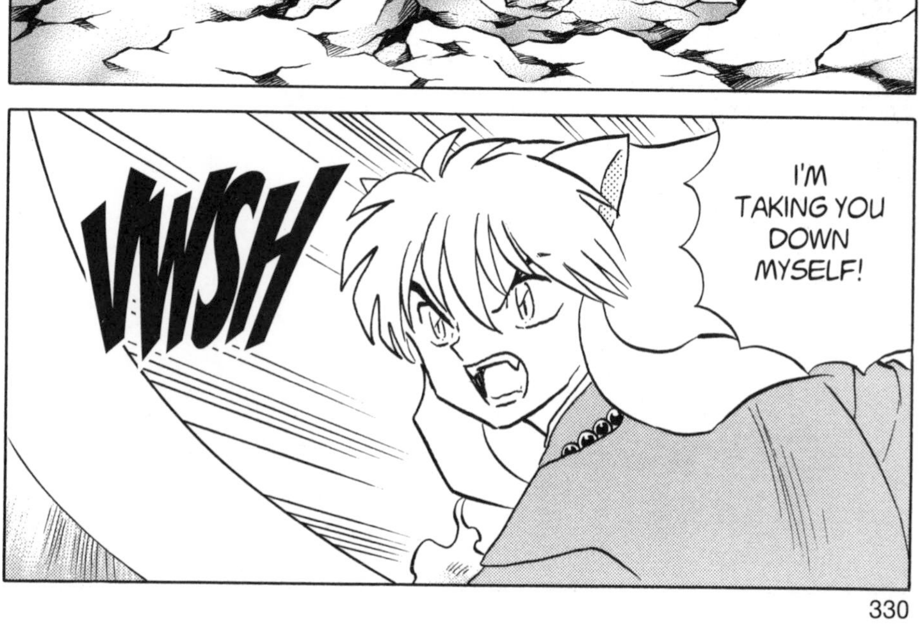
I'M TAKING YOU DOWN MYSELF!
VWSH

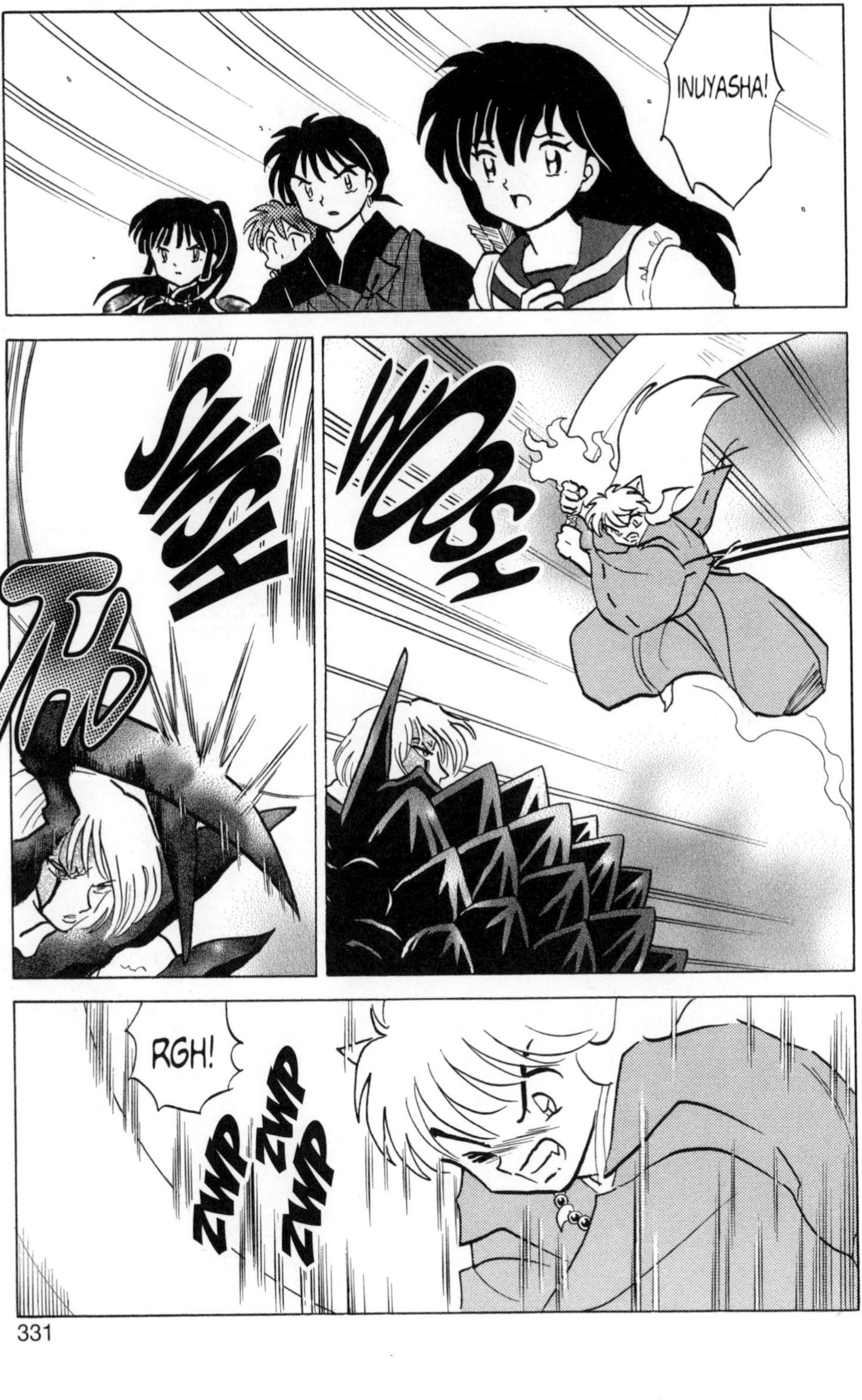
INUYASHA!
WOOSH
SWISH
THD
RGH!
ZWP
ZWP
ZWP
ZWP

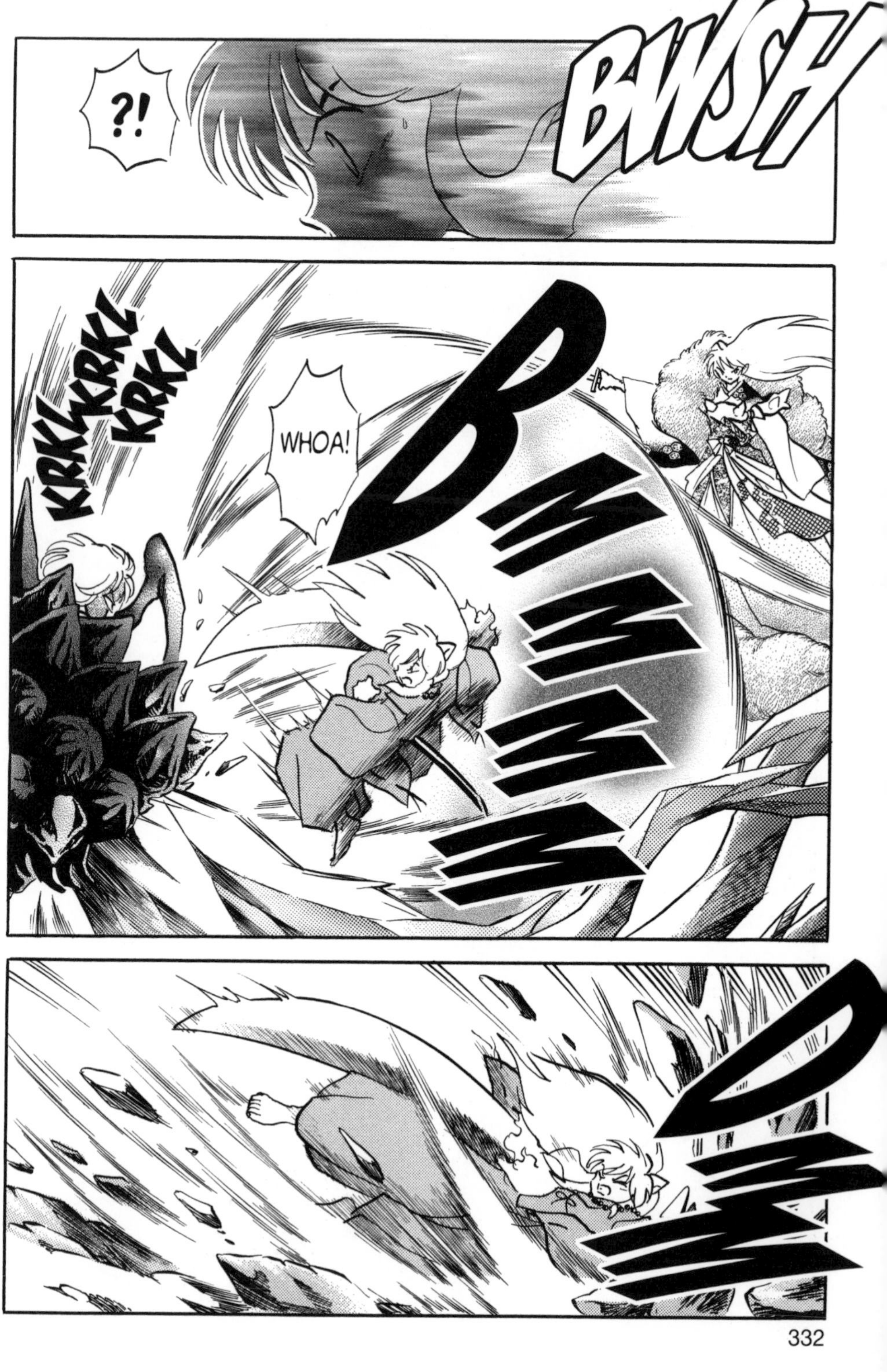
BWSH
?!
BMMMM
WHOA!
KRKL KRKL KRKL
DMM

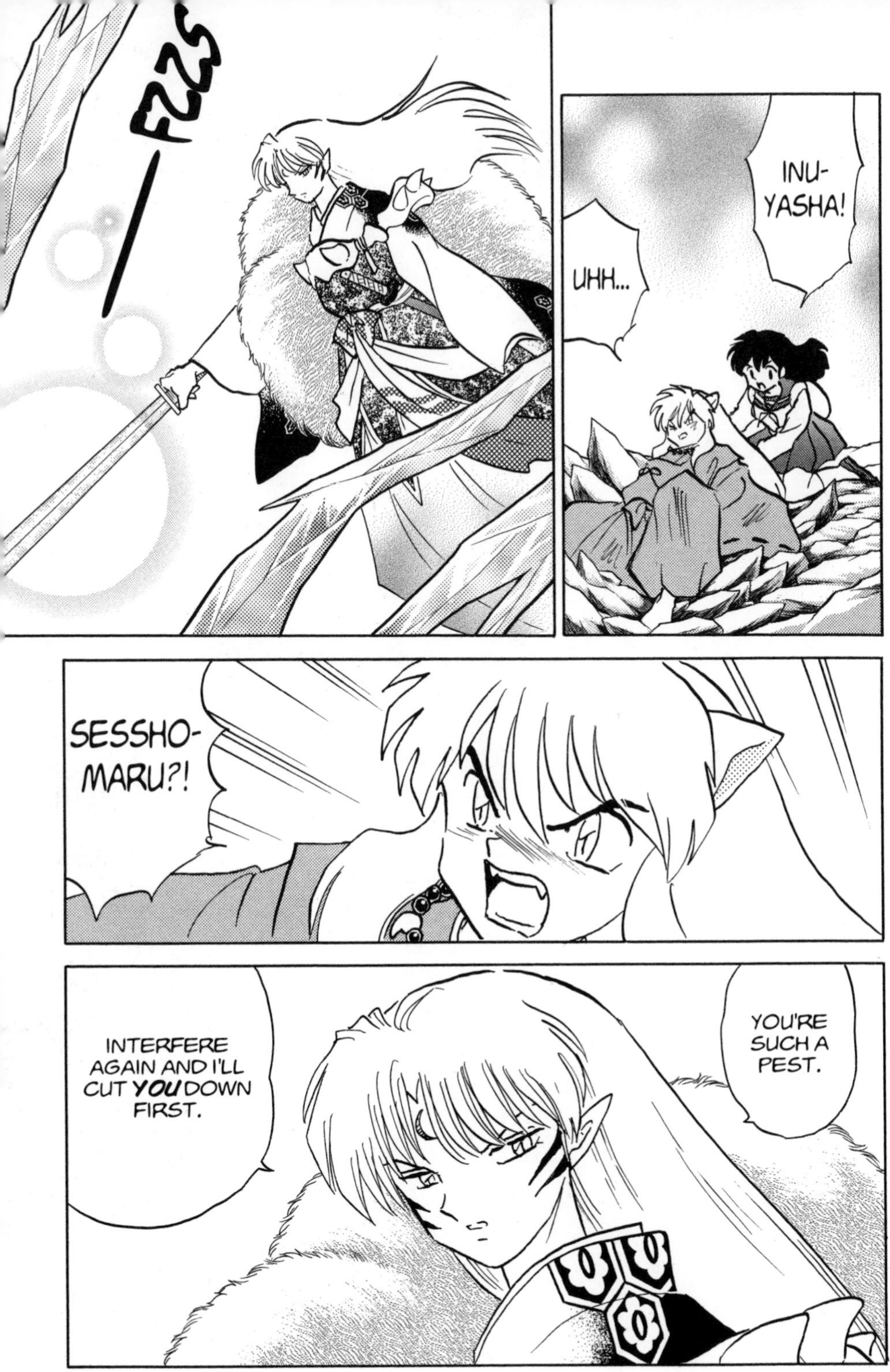
INU-YASHA!
UHH...
FZZS
SESSHO-MARU?!
YOU'RE SUCH A PEST.
INTERFERE AGAIN AND I'LL CUT *YOU* DOWN FIRST.

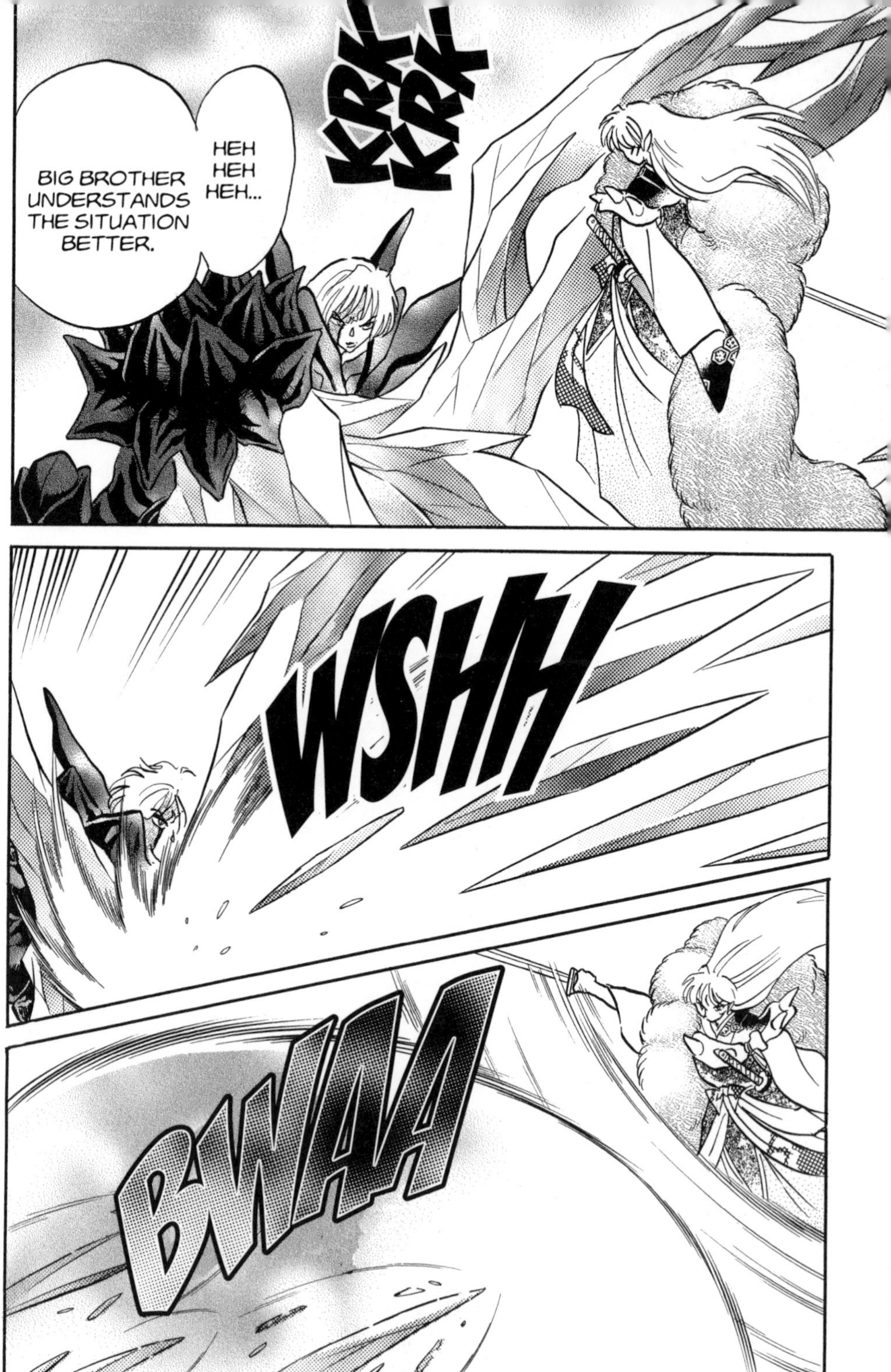
KRK KRK
HEH HEH HEH...
BIG BROTHER UNDERSTANDS THE SITUATION BETTER.
WSHH
BWAA

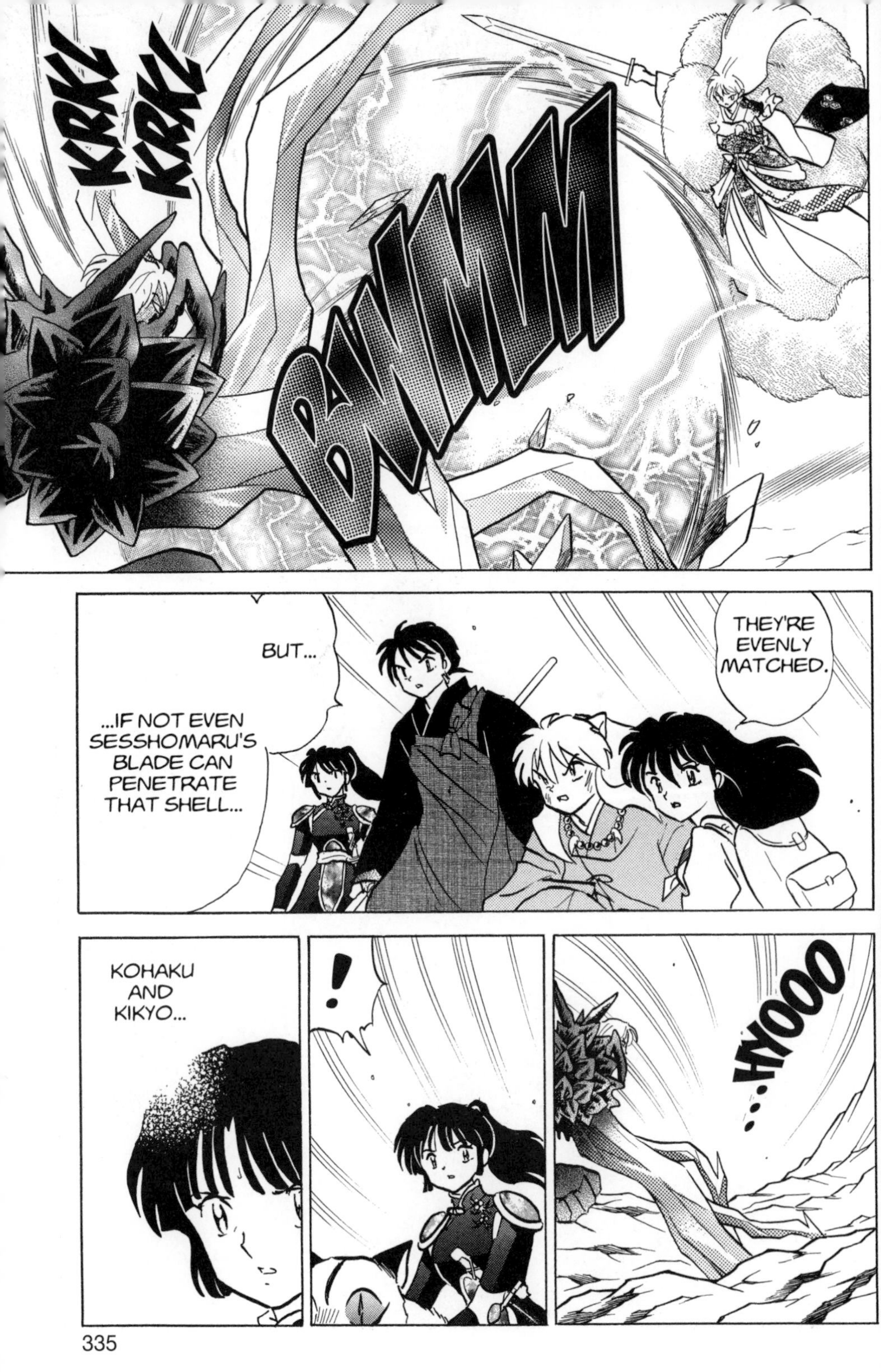
BWMMM
KRKL KRKL
THEY'RE EVENLY MATCHED.
BUT...
...IF NOT EVEN SESSHOMARU'S BLADE CAN PENETRATE THAT SHELL...
HYOOO...
!
KOHAKU AND KIKYO...

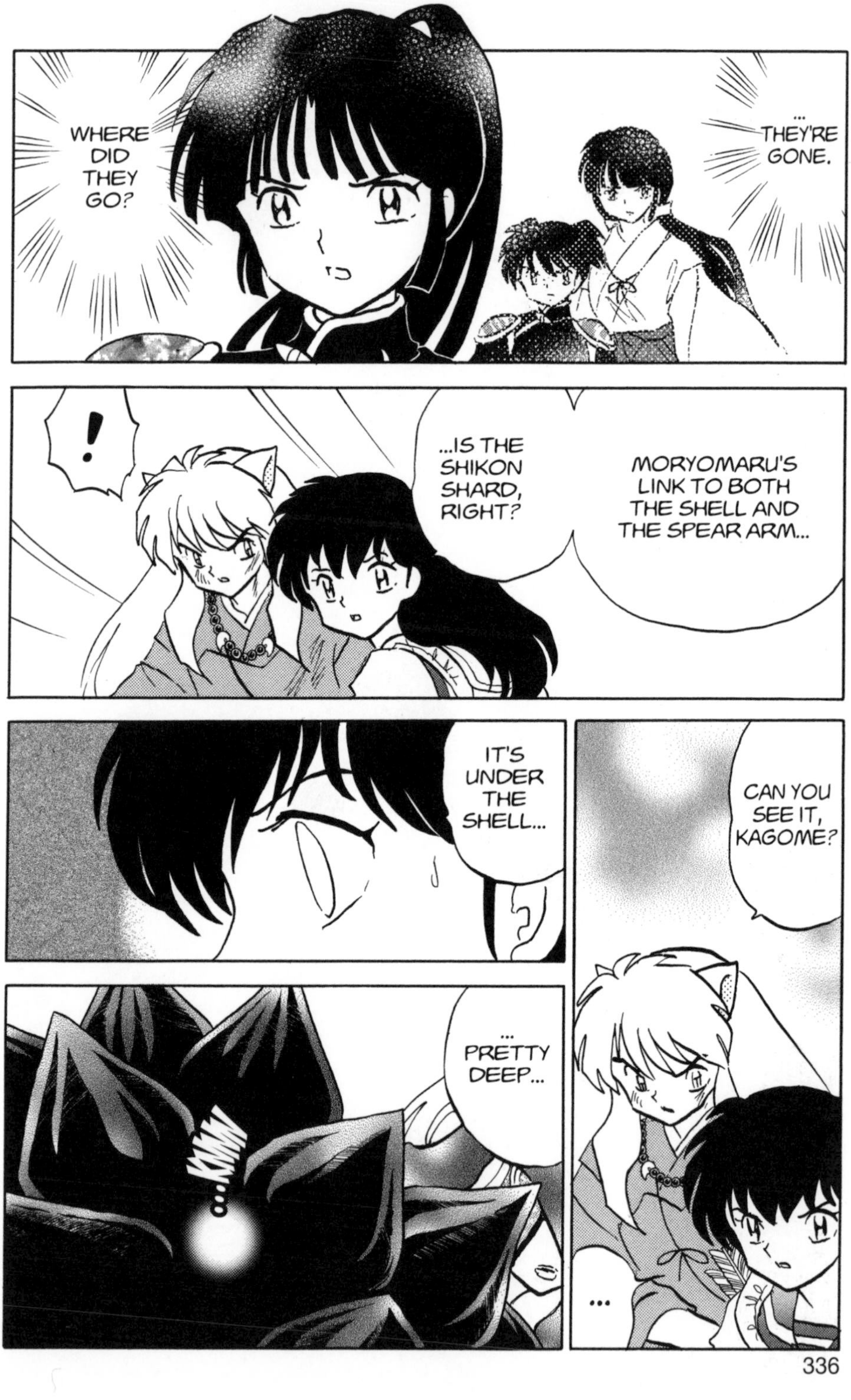
...THEY'RE GONE.
WHERE DID THEY GO?
MORYOMARU'S LINK TO BOTH THE SHELL AND THE SPEAR ARM...
...IS THE SHIKON SHARD, RIGHT?
!
CAN YOU SEE IT, KAGOME?
...
IT'S UNDER THE SHELL...
... PRETTY DEEP...

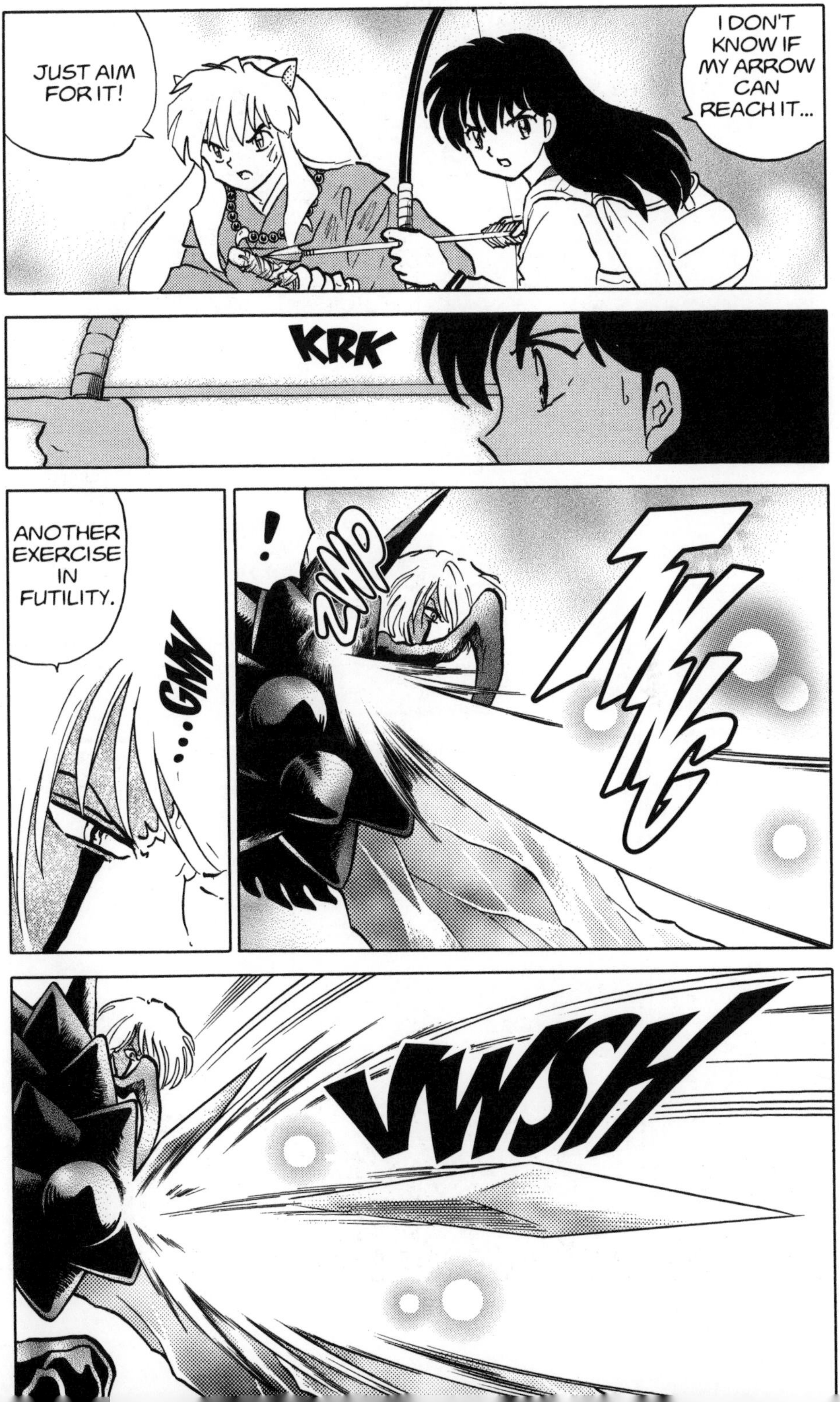
I DON'T KNOW IF MY ARROW CAN REACH IT...
JUST AIM FOR IT!
KRK
!
ZWP
TWNG
ANOTHER EXERCISE IN FUTILITY.
...GMN
VWSH

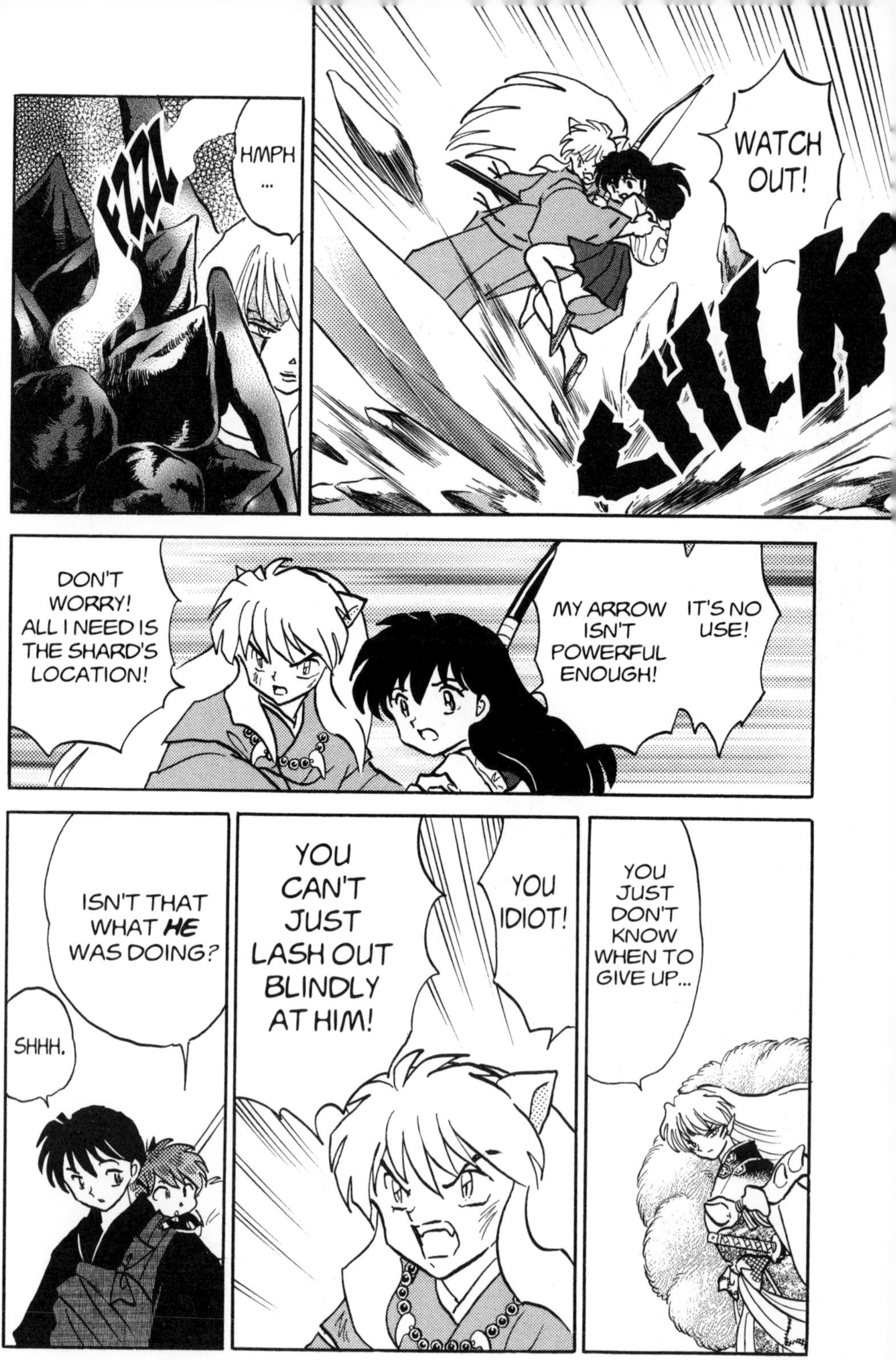
WATCH OUT!
CHLK
FZZL
HMPH ...
IT'S NO USE!
MY ARROW ISN'T POWERFUL ENOUGH!
DON'T WORRY! ALL I NEED IS THE SHARD'S LOCATION!
YOU JUST DON'T KNOW WHEN TO GIVE UP...
YOU IDIOT!
YOU CAN'T JUST LASH OUT BLINDLY AT HIM!
ISN'T THAT WHAT **HE** WAS DOING?
SHHH.

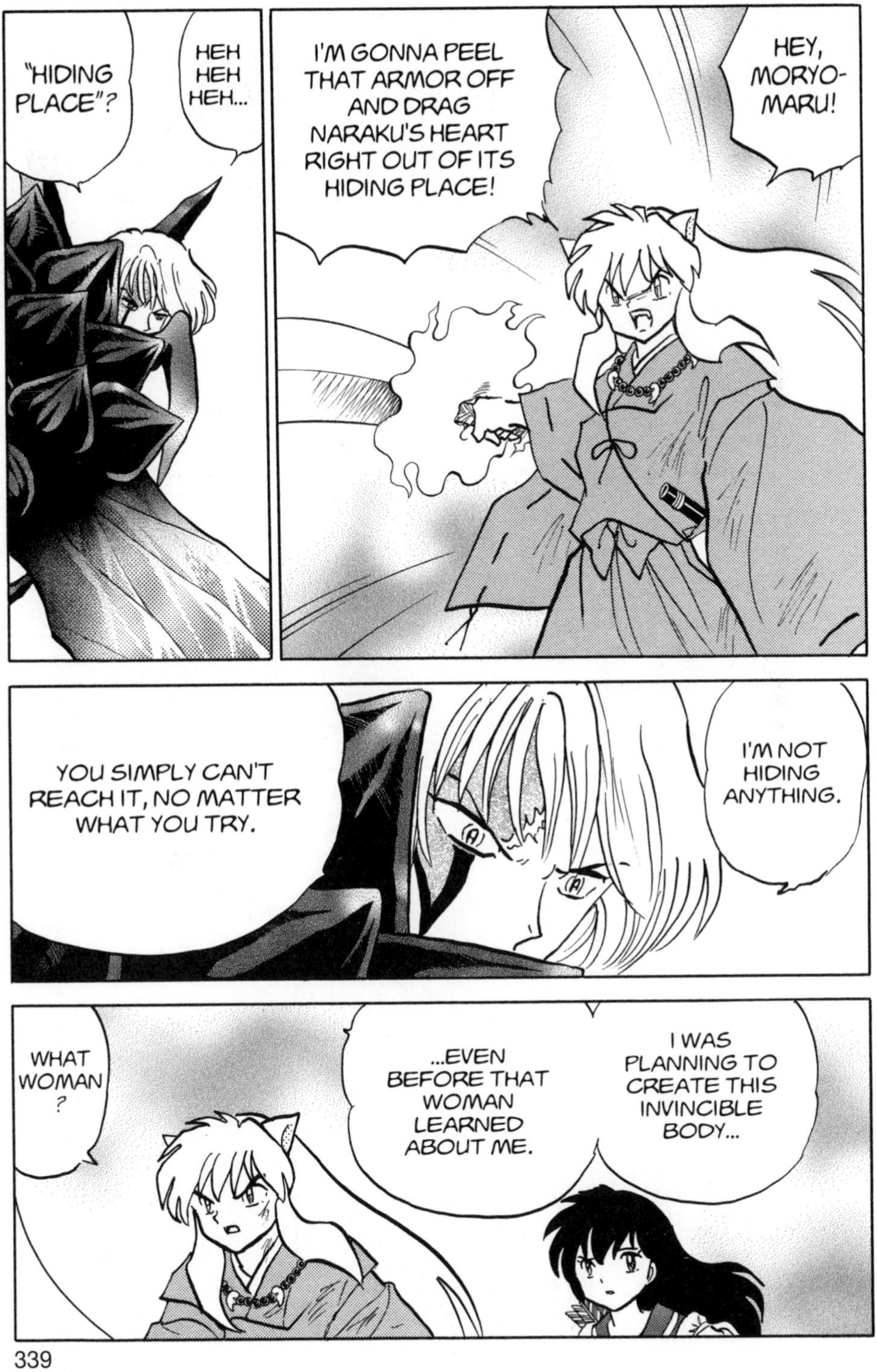
HEY, MORYO-MARU!
I'M GONNA PEEL THAT ARMOR OFF AND DRAG NARAKU'S HEART RIGHT OUT OF ITS HIDING PLACE!
HEH HEH HEH...
"HIDING PLACE"?
I'M NOT HIDING ANYTHING.
YOU SIMPLY CAN'T REACH IT, NO MATTER WHAT YOU TRY.
I WAS PLANNING TO CREATE THIS INVINCIBLE BODY...
...EVEN BEFORE THAT WOMAN LEARNED ABOUT ME.
WHAT WOMAN?

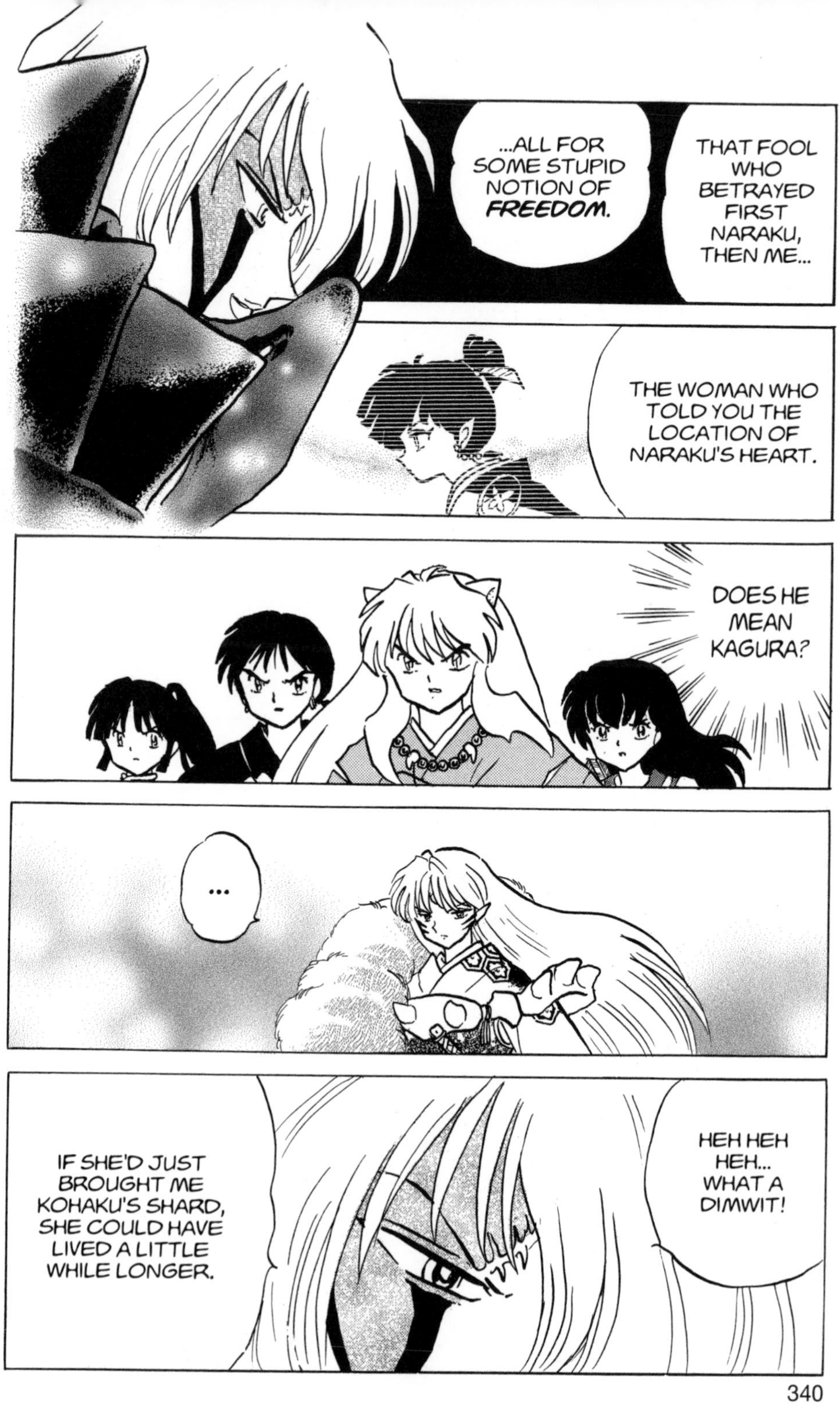
THAT FOOL WHO BETRAYED FIRST NARAKU, THEN ME...
...ALL FOR SOME STUPID NOTION OF **FREEDOM**.
THE WOMAN WHO TOLD YOU THE LOCATION OF NARAKU'S HEART.
DOES HE MEAN KAGURA?
...
HEH HEH HEH... WHAT A DIMWIT!
IF SHE'D JUST BROUGHT ME KOHAKU'S SHARD, SHE COULD HAVE LIVED A LITTLE WHILE LONGER.

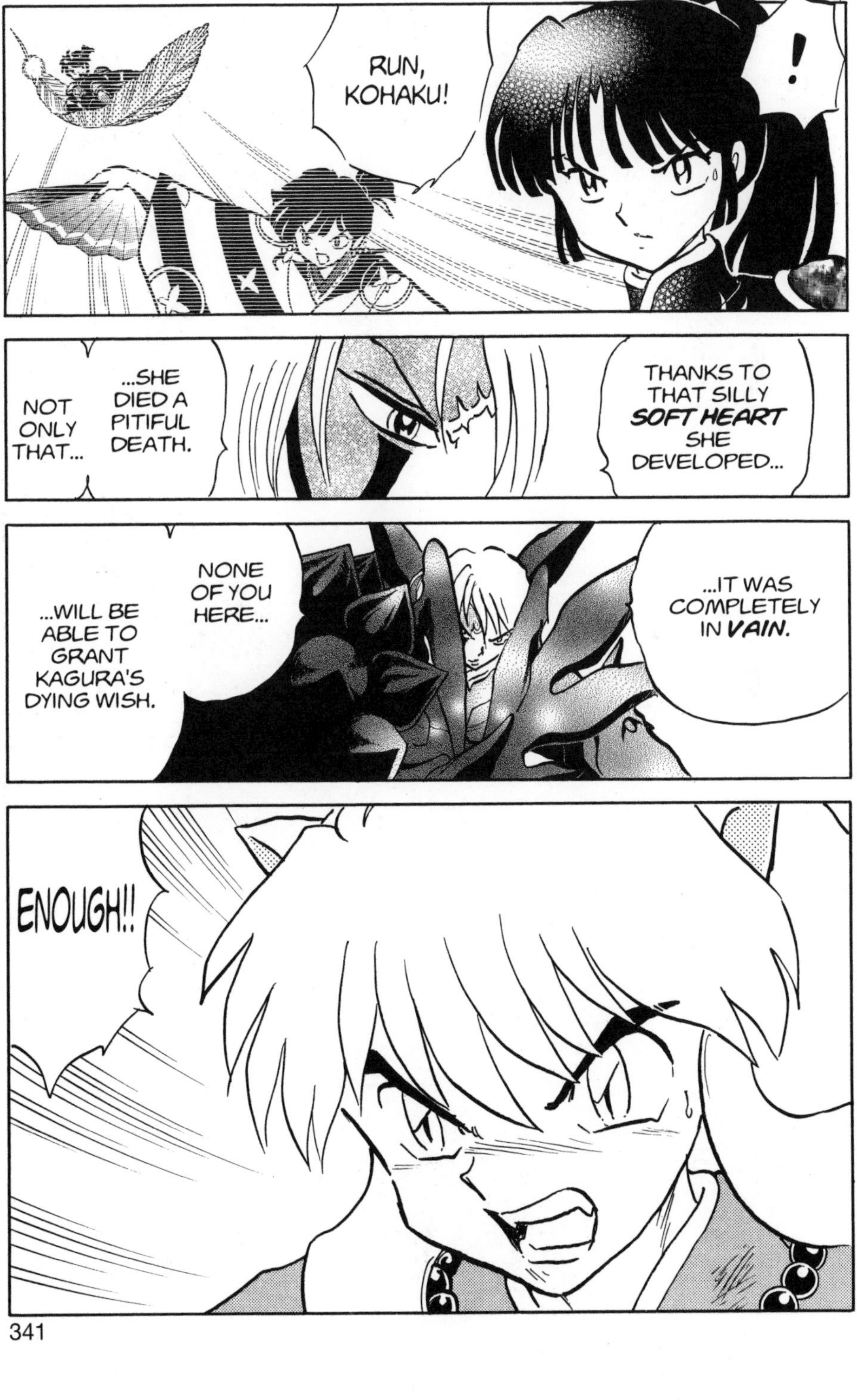
!
RUN, KOHAKU!
THANKS TO THAT SILLY SOFT HEART SHE DEVELOPED...
...SHE DIED A PITIFUL DEATH.
NOT ONLY THAT...
...IT WAS COMPLETELY IN VAIN.
NONE OF YOU HERE...
...WILL BE ABLE TO GRANT KAGURA'S DYING WISH.
ENOUGH!!

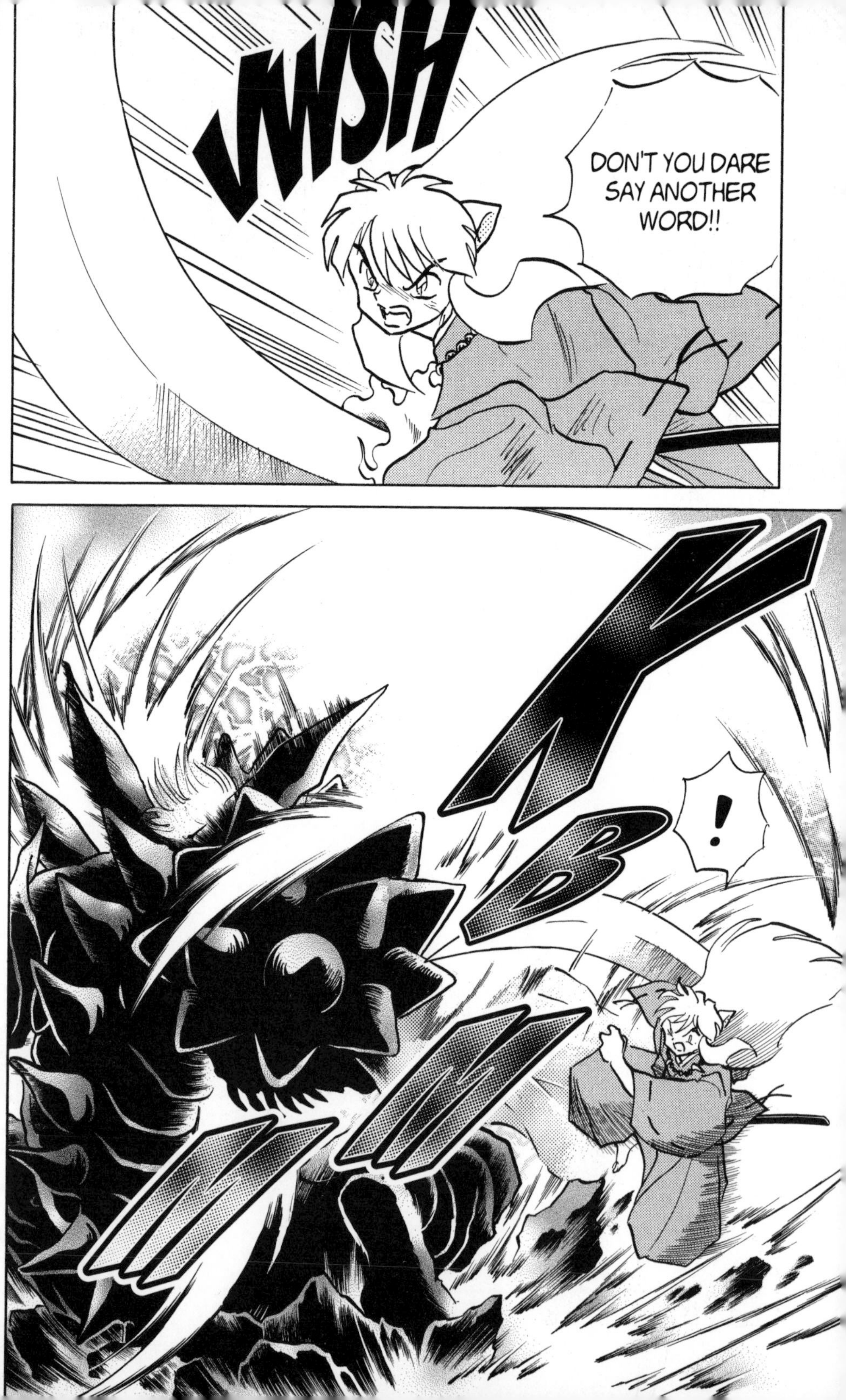
VWSH
DON'T YOU DARE SAY ANOTHER WORD!!
!

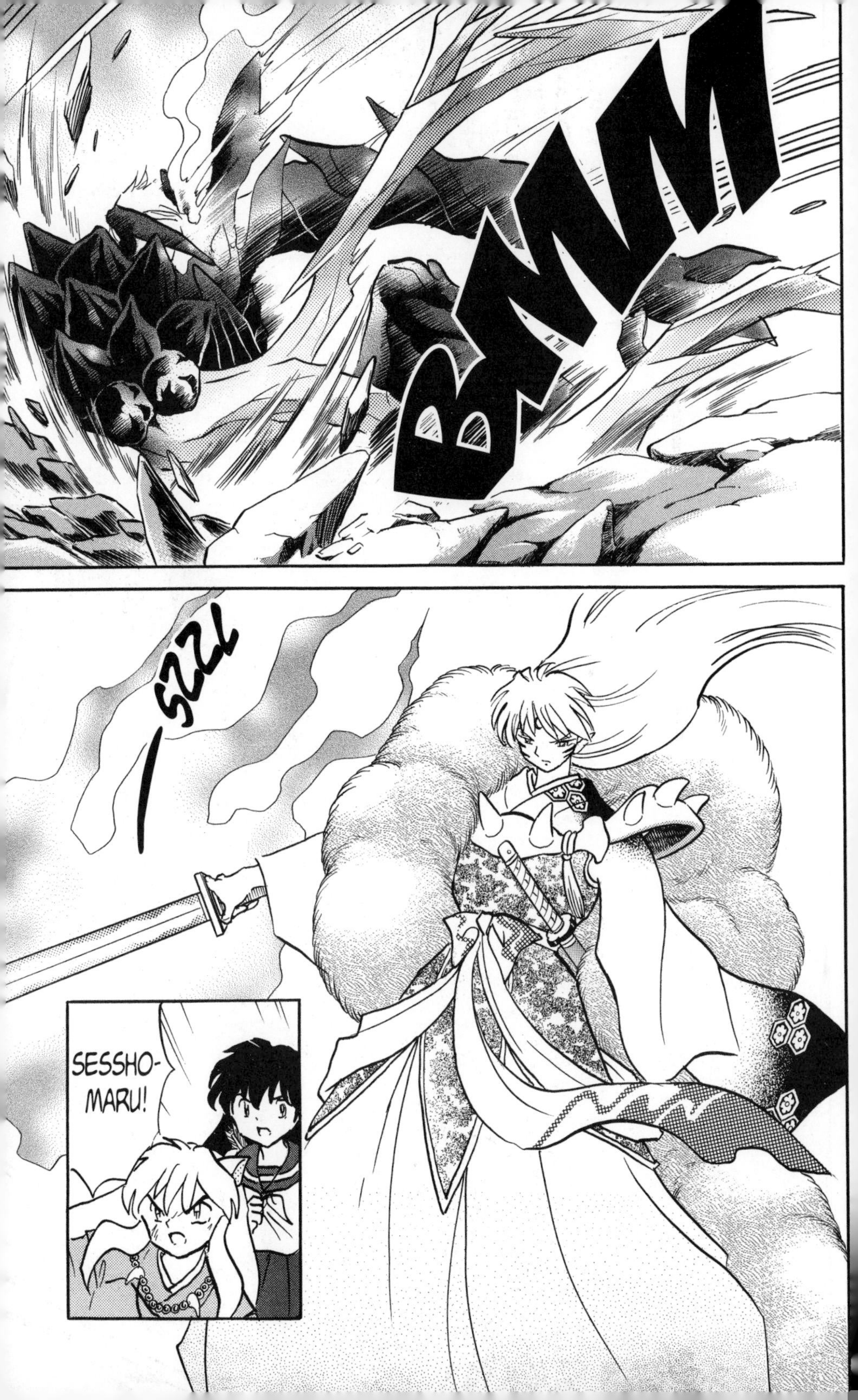
BMM
—SZZZ
SESSHO-
MARU!

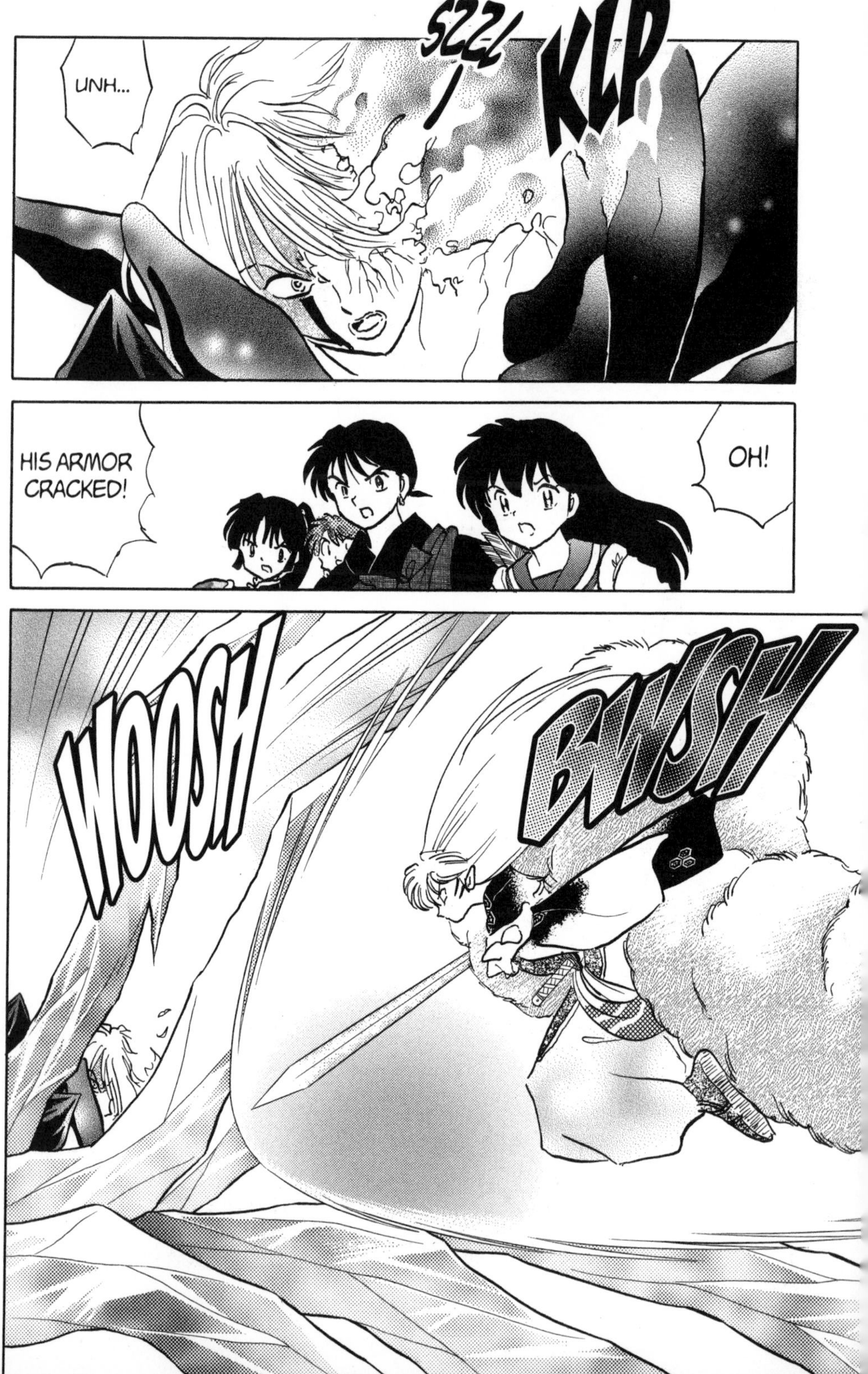

KLP
SZZZ
UNH...
OH!
HIS ARMOR CRACKED!
BWSH
WOOSH

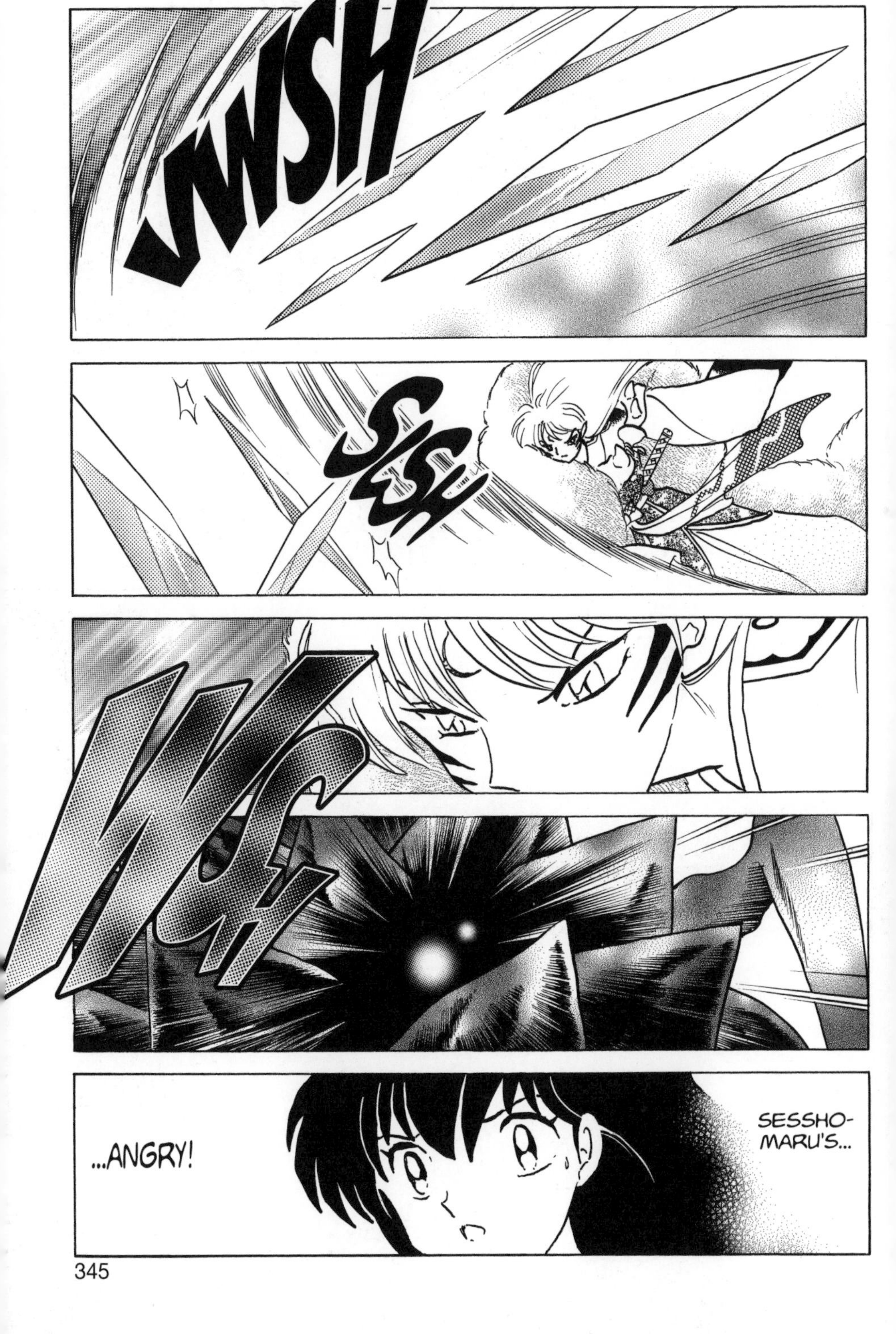
SESSHO-
MARU'S...
...ANGRY!

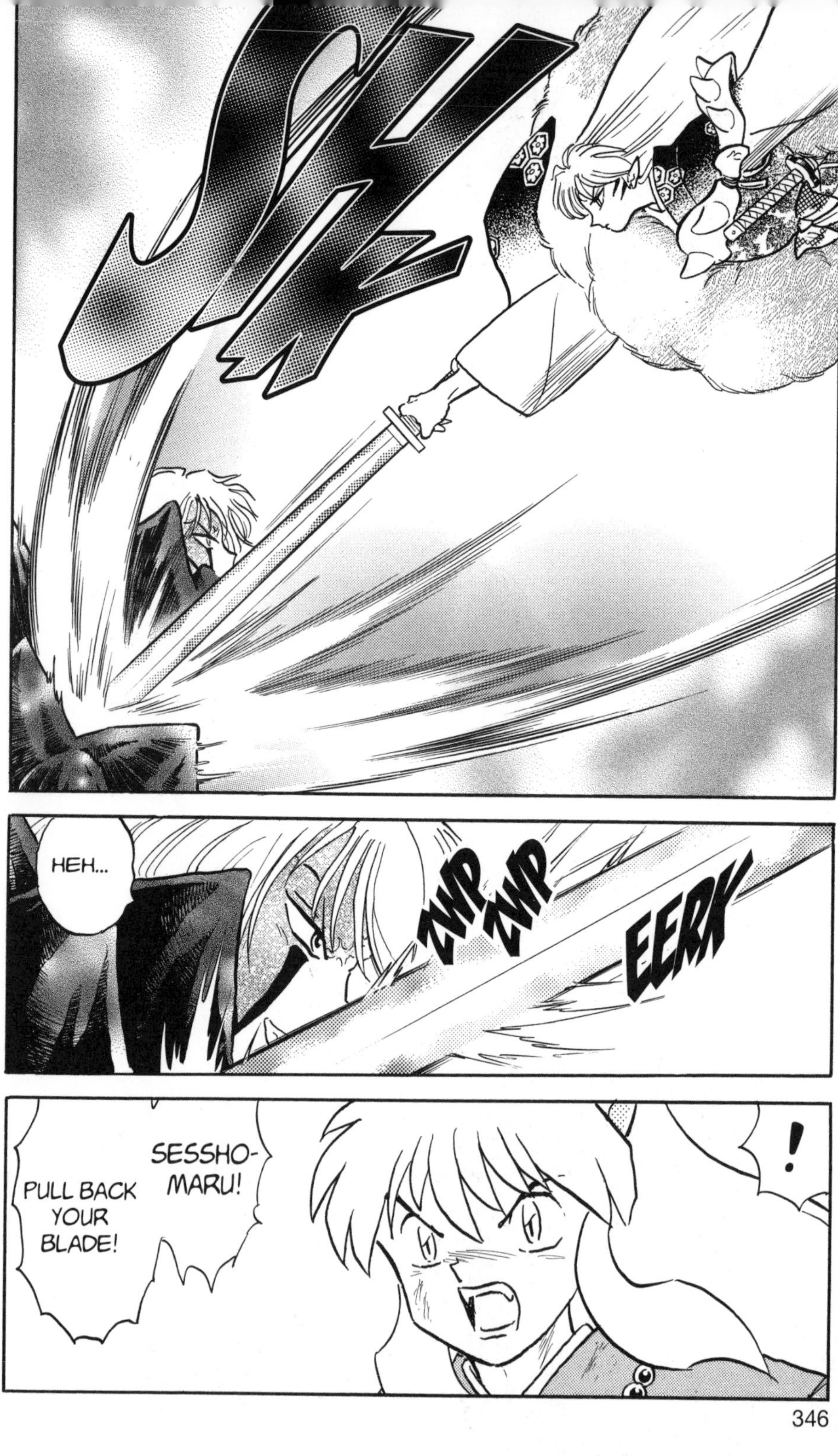
EERK
ZWP ZWP
HEH...
!
SESSHO-MARU!
PULL BACK YOUR BLADE!

SCROLL NINE
SESSHOMARU'S PERIL

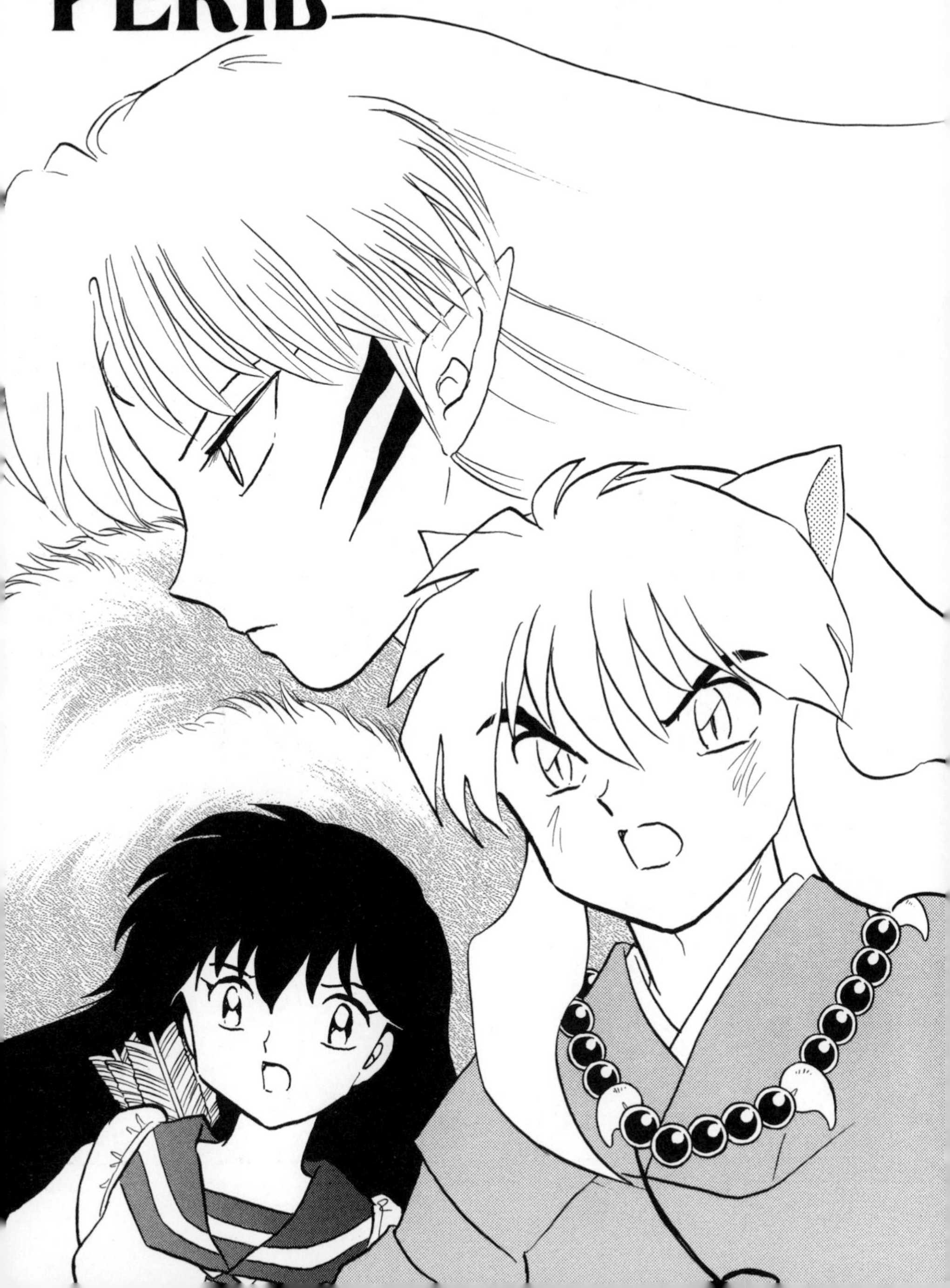

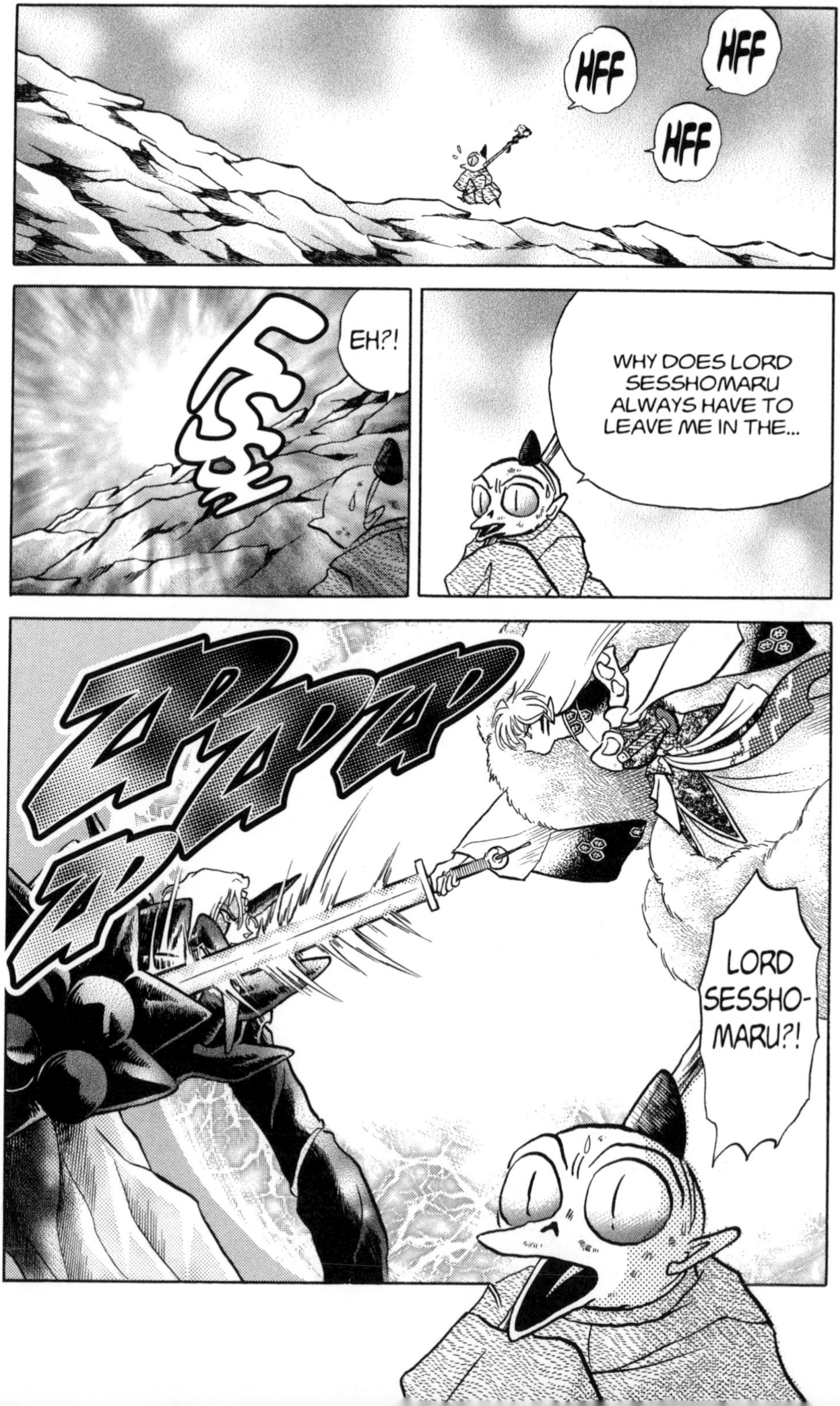
HFF
HFF
HFF
WHY DOES LORD SESSHOMARU ALWAYS HAVE TO LEAVE ME IN THE...
EH?!
LORD SESSHO-MARU?!

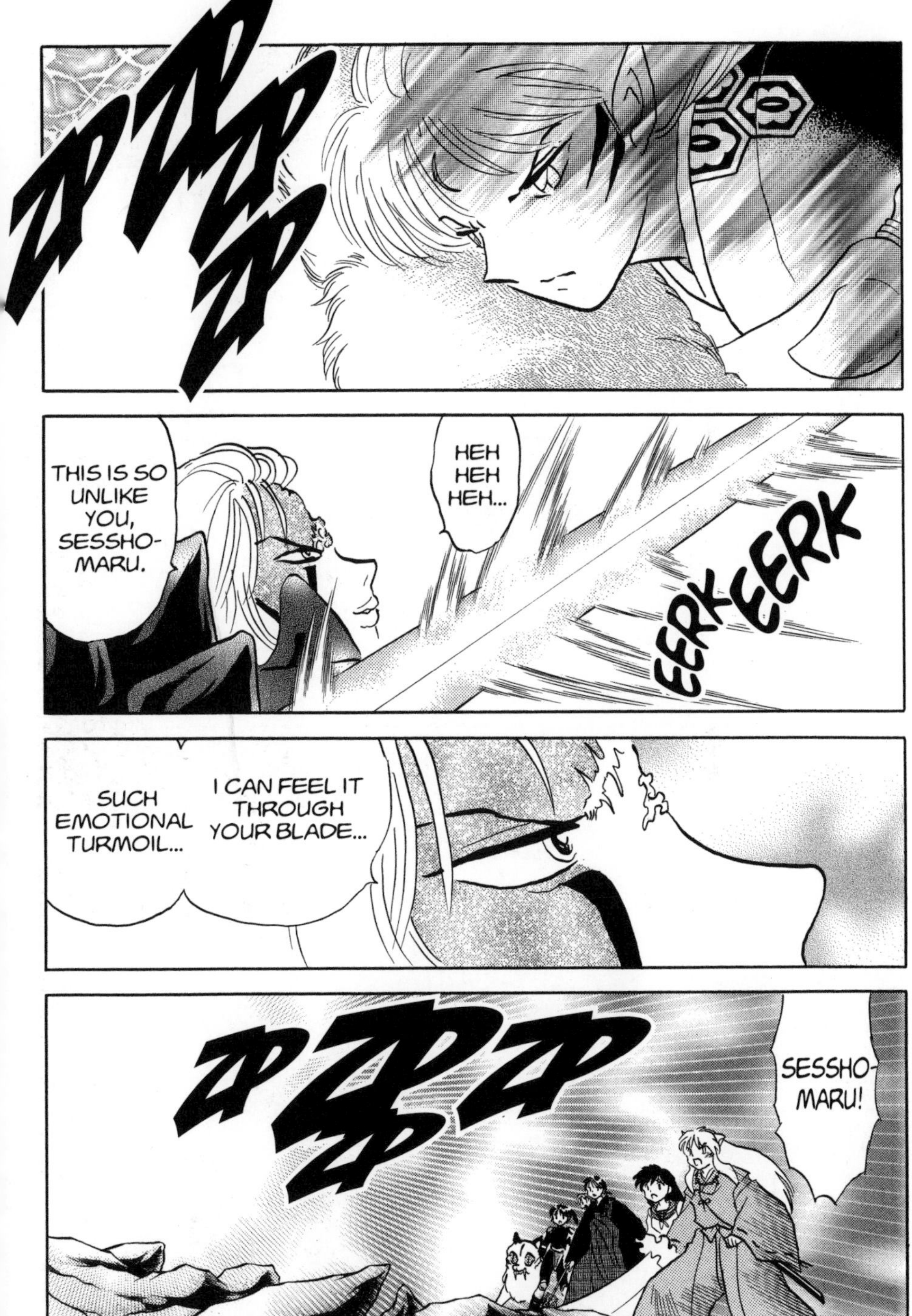
ZP ZP ZP ZP
HEH HEH HEH...
EERK EERK
THIS IS SO UNLIKE YOU, SESSHO-MARU.
I CAN FEEL IT THROUGH YOUR BLADE...
SUCH EMOTIONAL TURMOIL...
SESSHO-MARU!
ZP ZP ZP ZP

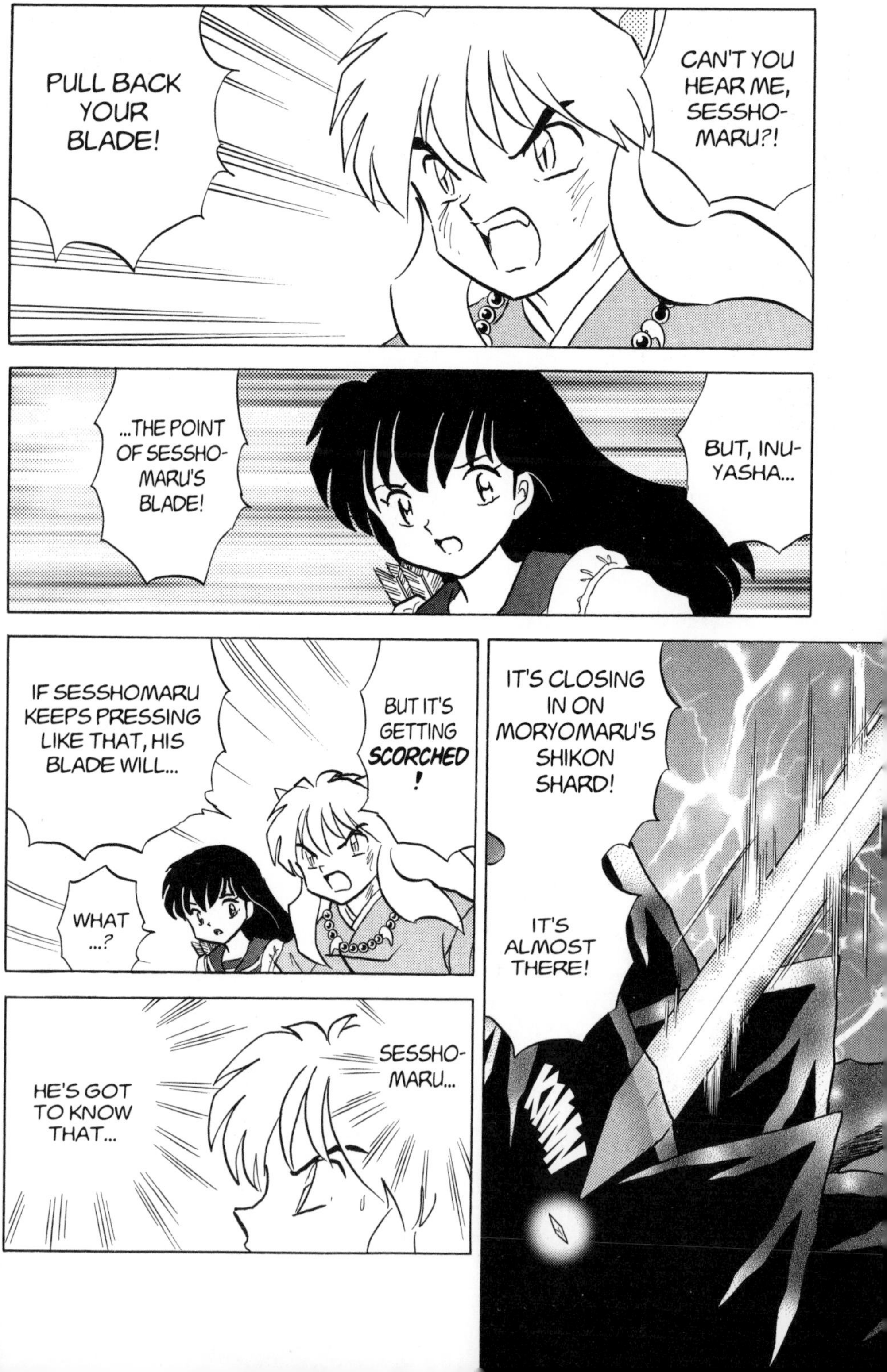
CAN'T YOU HEAR ME, SESSHOMARU?!
PULL BACK YOUR BLADE!
BUT, INUYASHA...
...THE POINT OF SESSHOMARU'S BLADE!
IT'S CLOSING IN ON MORYOMARU'S SHIKON SHARD!
IT'S ALMOST THERE!
KMM
BUT IT'S GETTING SCORCHED!
IF SESSHOMARU KEEPS PRESSING LIKE THAT, HIS BLADE WILL...
WHAT ...?
SESSHOMARU...
HE'S GOT TO KNOW THAT...

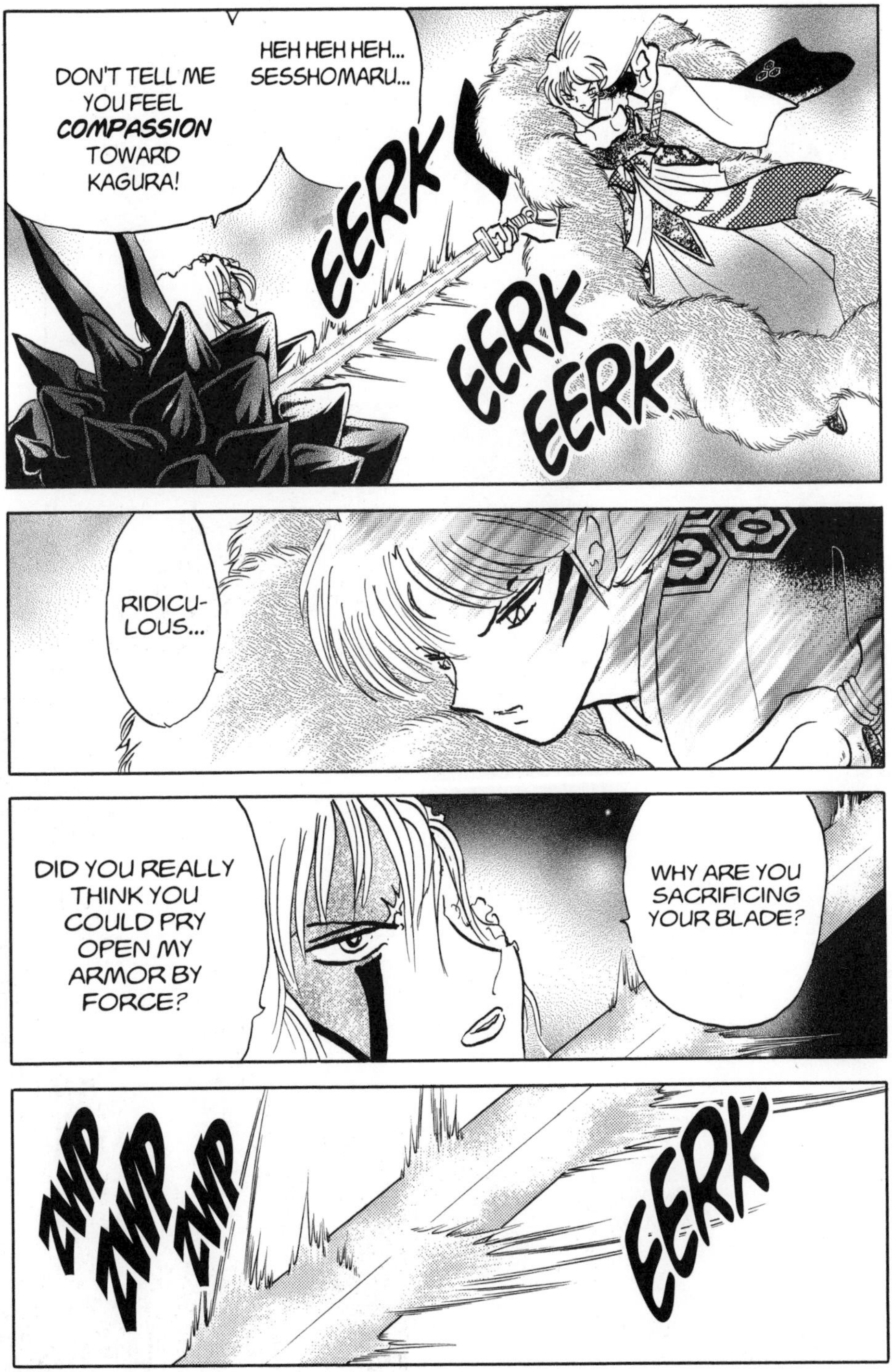
HEH HEH HEH... SESSHOMARU...
DON'T TELL ME YOU FEEL **COMPASSION** TOWARD KAGURA!
EERK
EERK
EERK
RIDICU-LOUS...
WHY ARE YOU SACRIFICING YOUR BLADE?
DID YOU REALLY THINK YOU COULD PRY OPEN MY ARMOR BY FORCE?
EERK
ZWIP
ZWIP
ZWIP

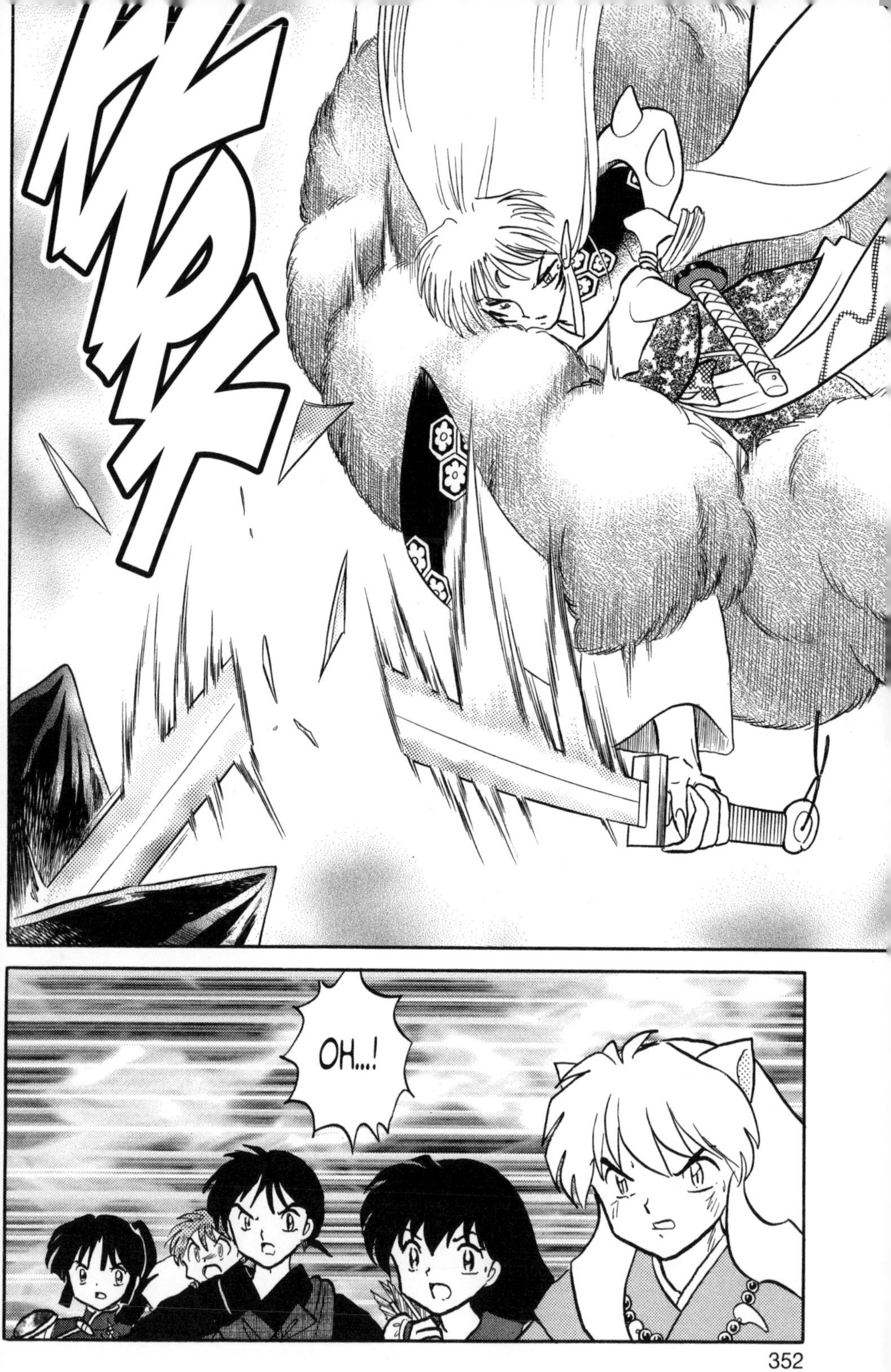
OH...!

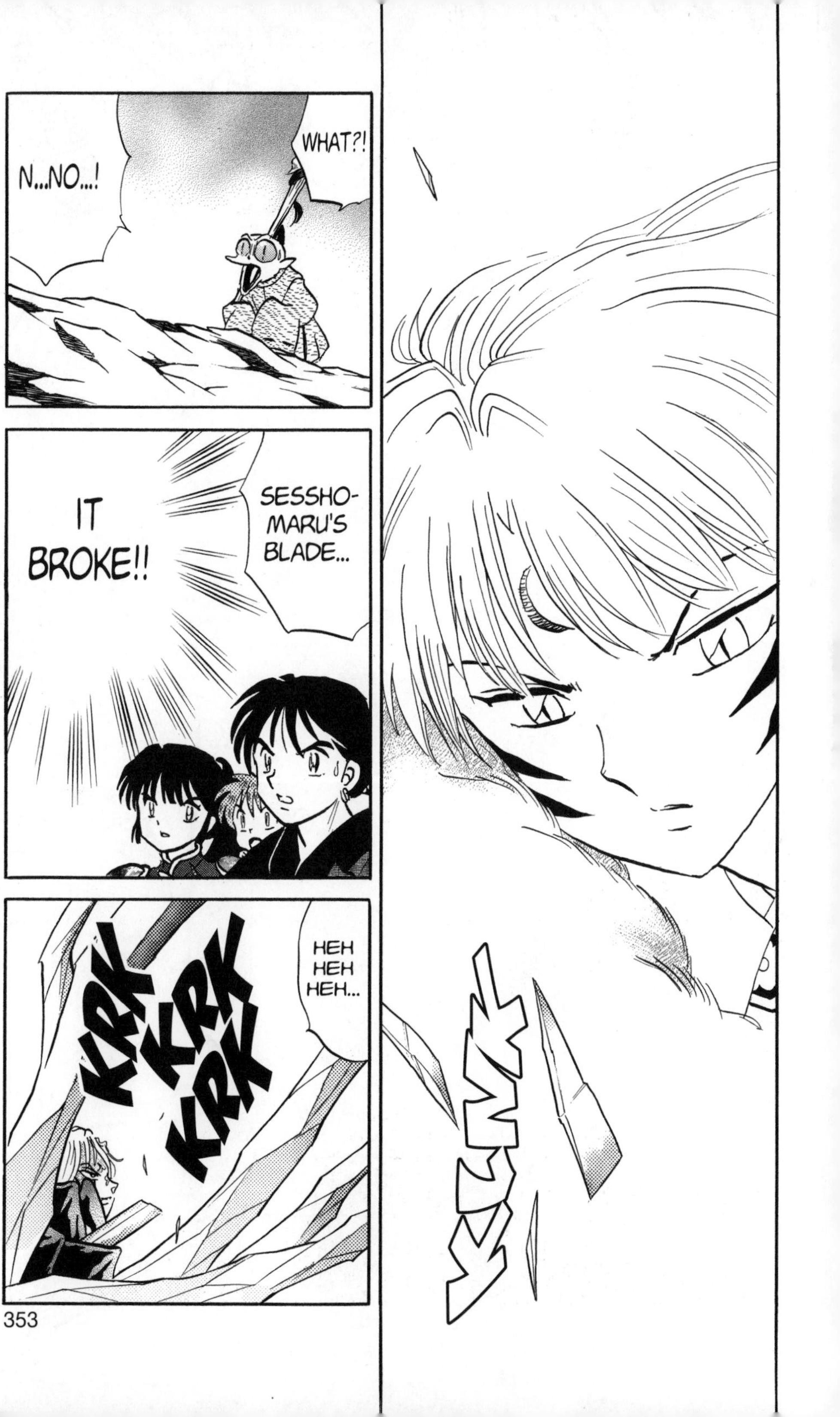
WHAT?!
N...NO...!
SESSHO-MARU'S BLADE...
IT BROKE!!
HEH HEH HEH...
KRK KRK KRK

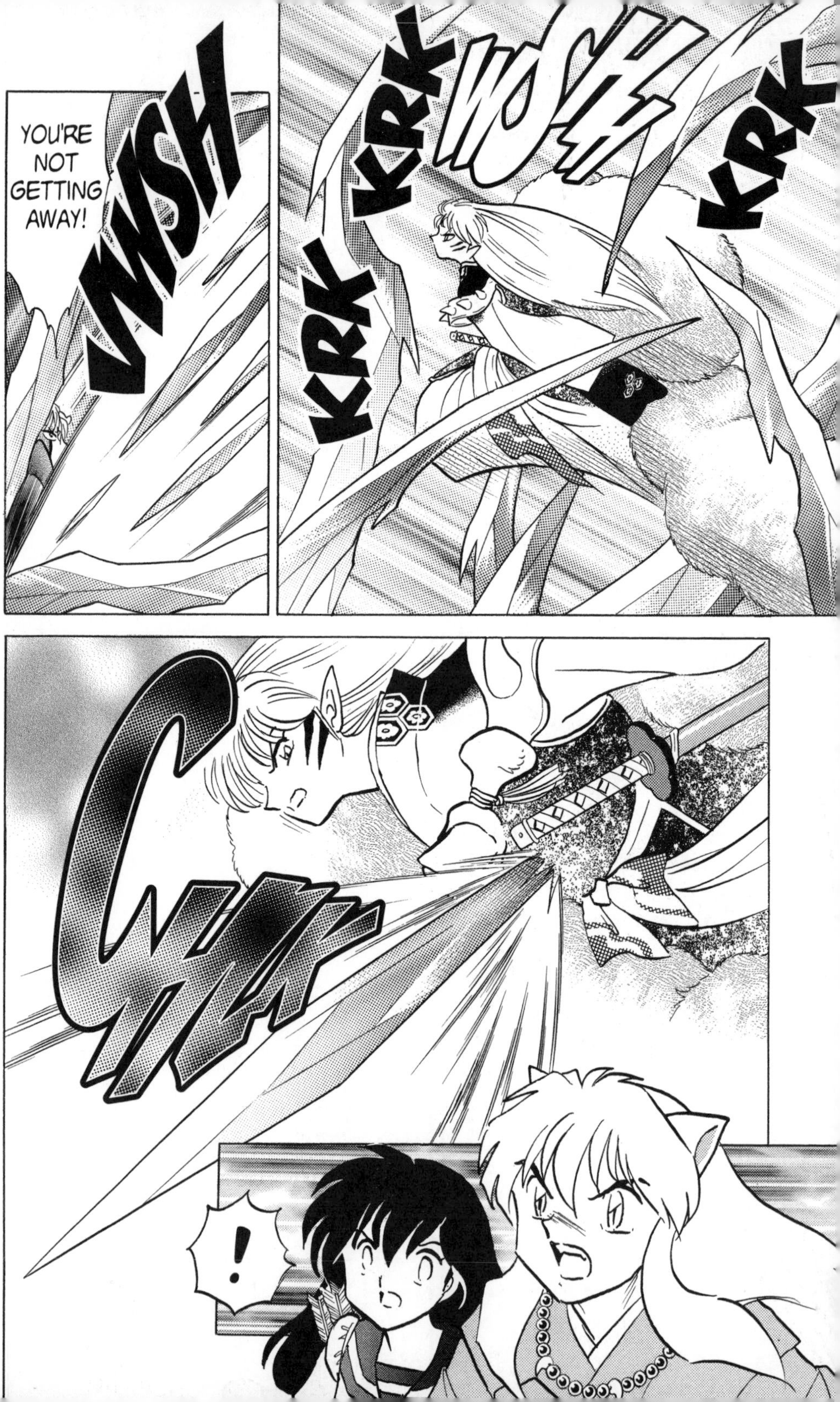
KRK
WOSH
KRK
KRK
YOU'RE NOT GETTING AWAY!
VWSH
GWAK
!

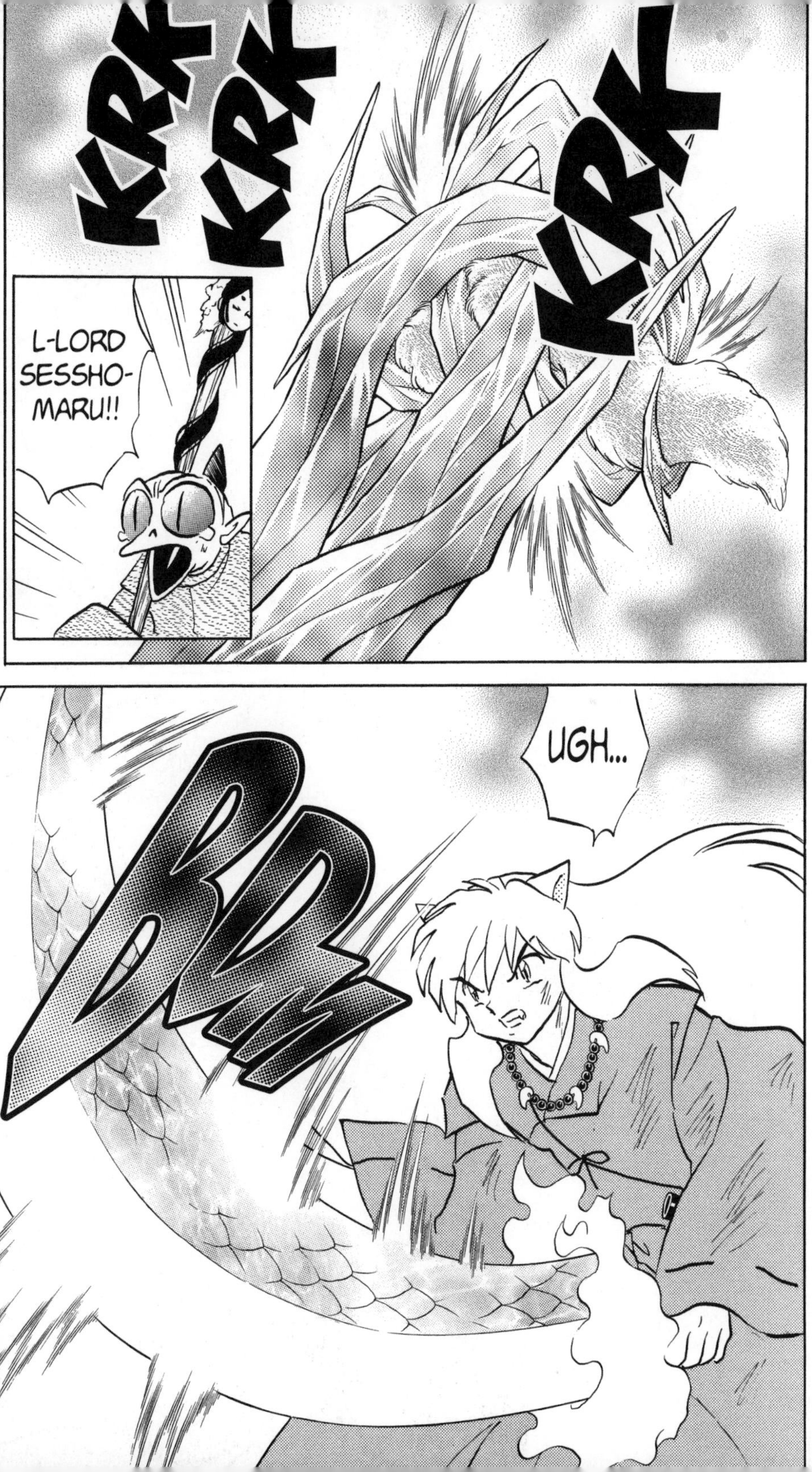
KRK
KRK
KRK
L-LORD SESSHO-MARU!!
UGH...
BRM

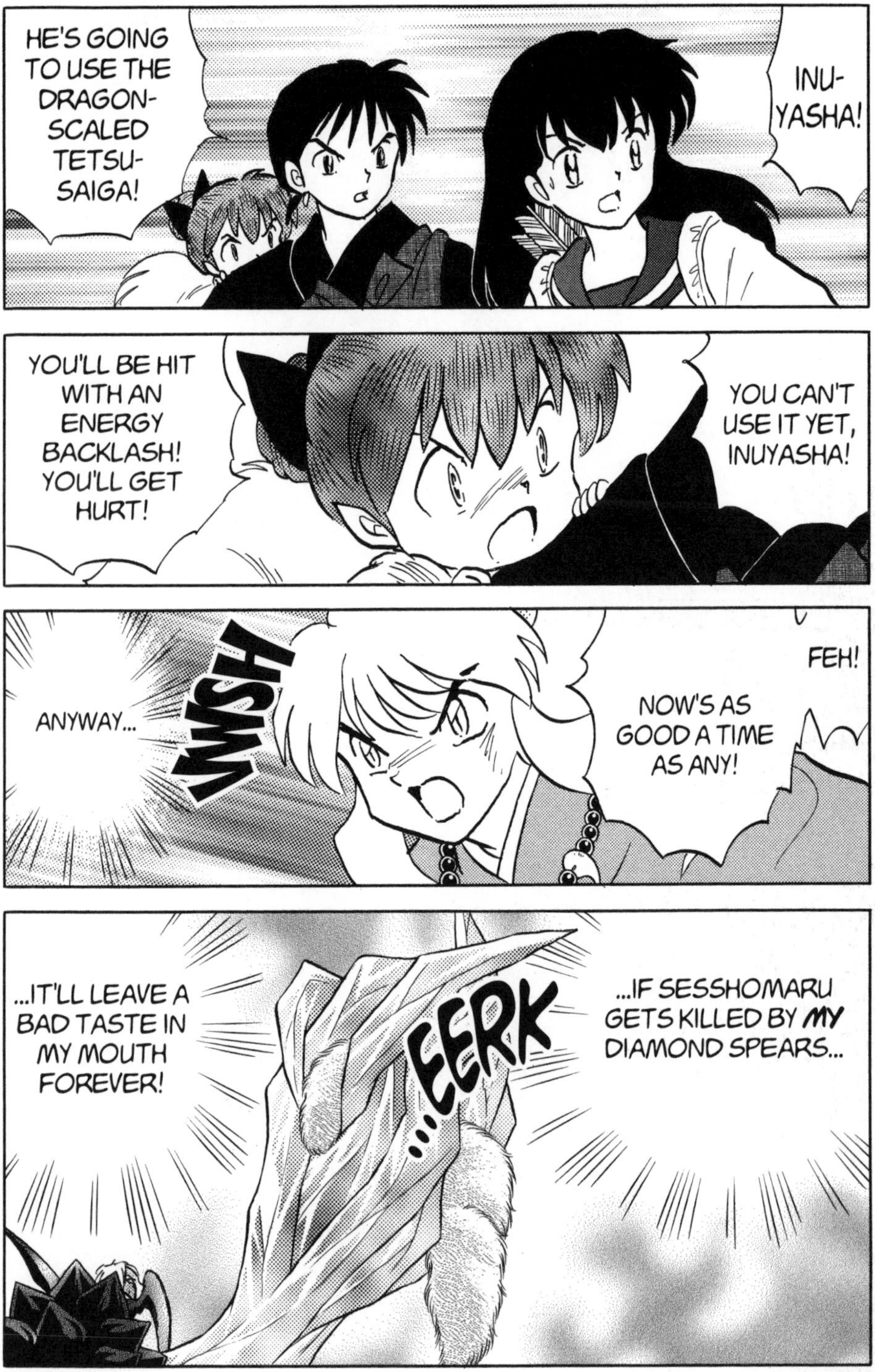
INU-YASHA!
HE'S GOING TO USE THE DRAGON-SCALED TETSU-SAIGA!
YOU CAN'T USE IT YET, INUYASHA!
YOU'LL BE HIT WITH AN ENERGY BACKLASH! YOU'LL GET HURT!
FEH!
NOW'S AS GOOD A TIME AS ANY!
WHSH
ANYWAY...
...IF SESSHOMARU GETS KILLED BY *MY* DIAMOND SPEARS...
...EERK
...IT'LL LEAVE A BAD TASTE IN MY MOUTH FOREVER!

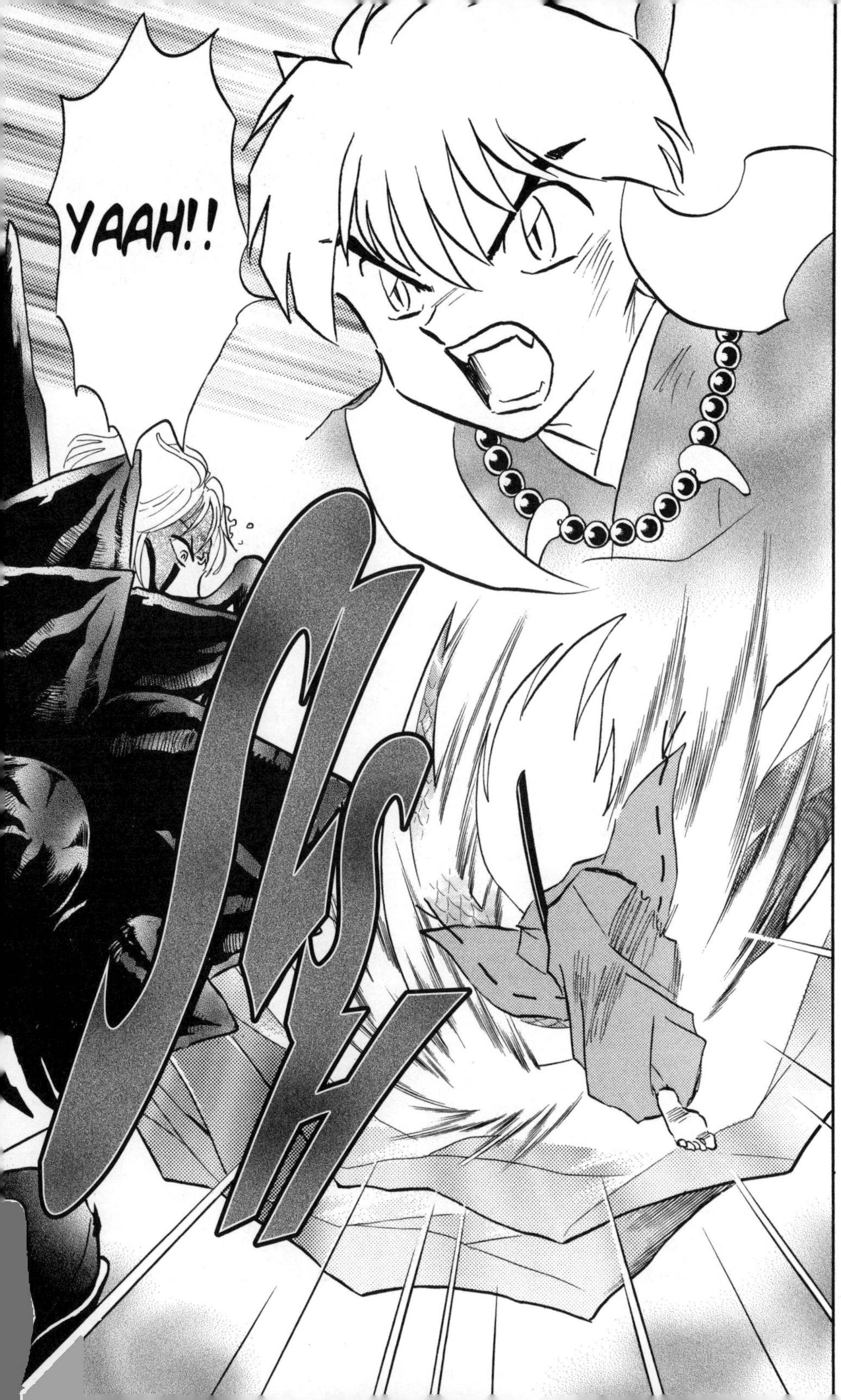
YAAH!!

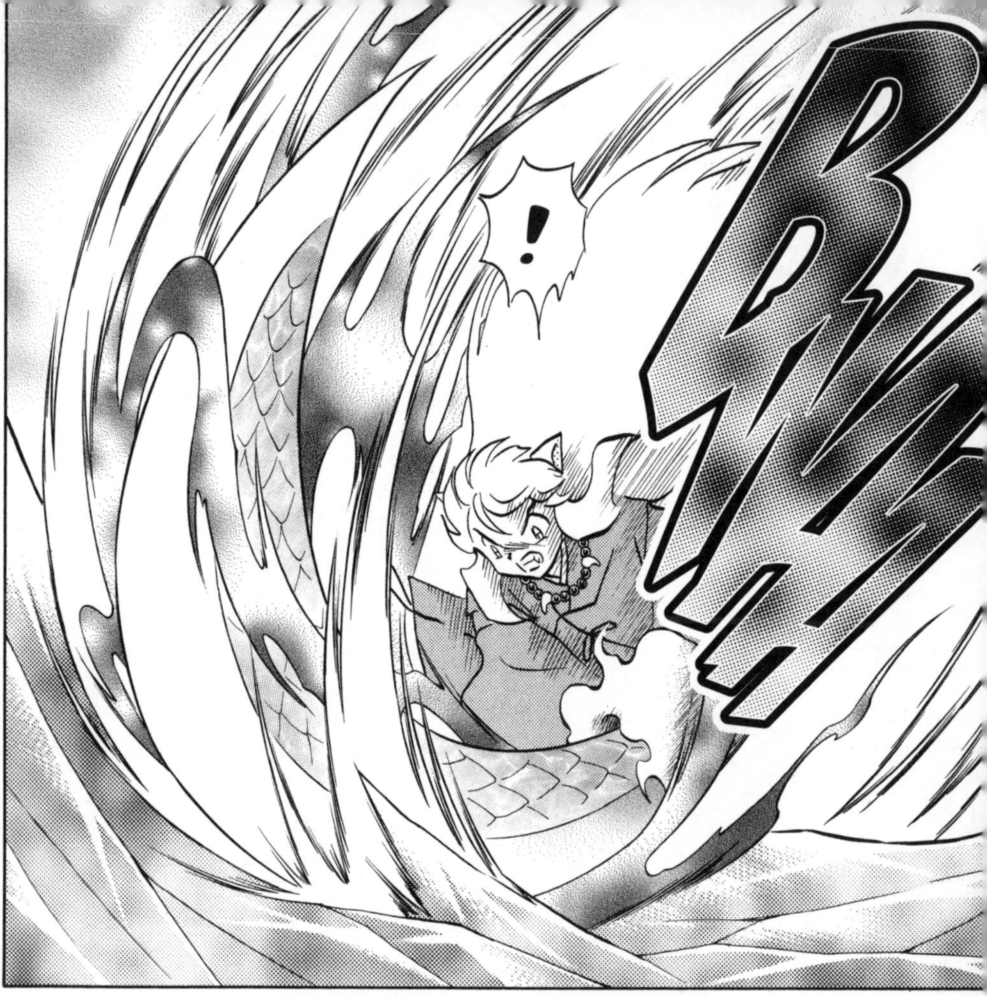
!

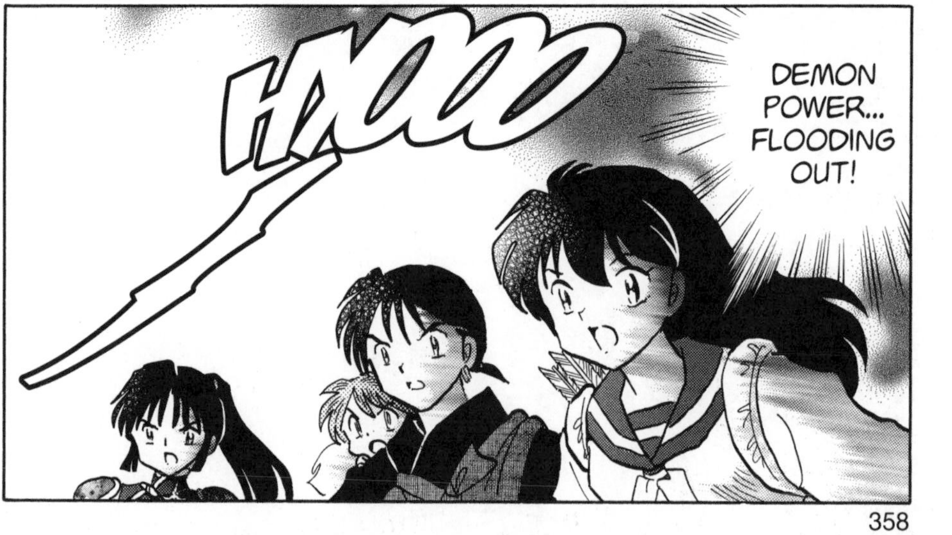
DEMON POWER... FLOODING OUT!

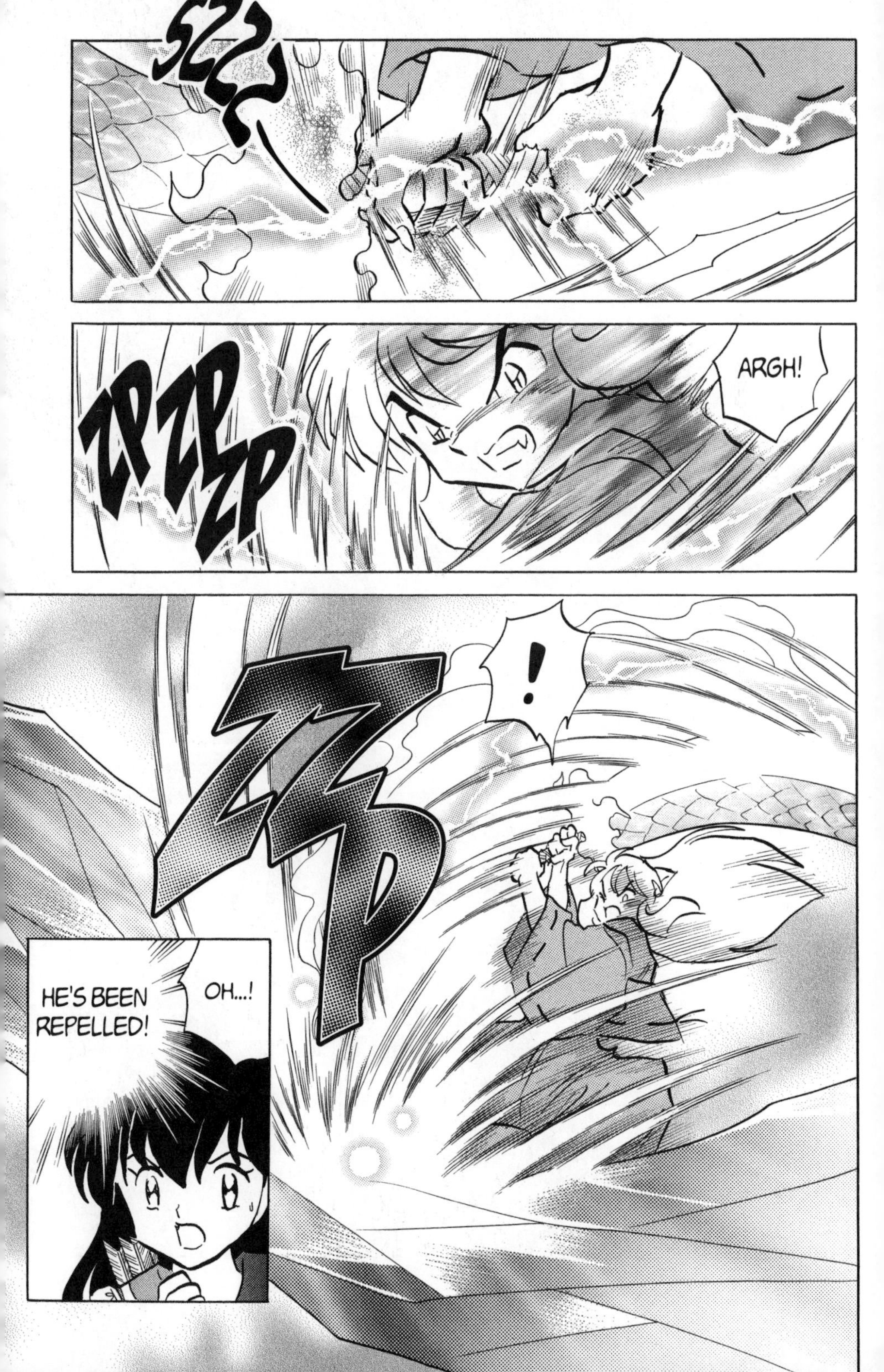
SZZZ
ARGH!
ZP ZP ZP
!
ZZP
OH...!
HE'S BEEN REPELLED!

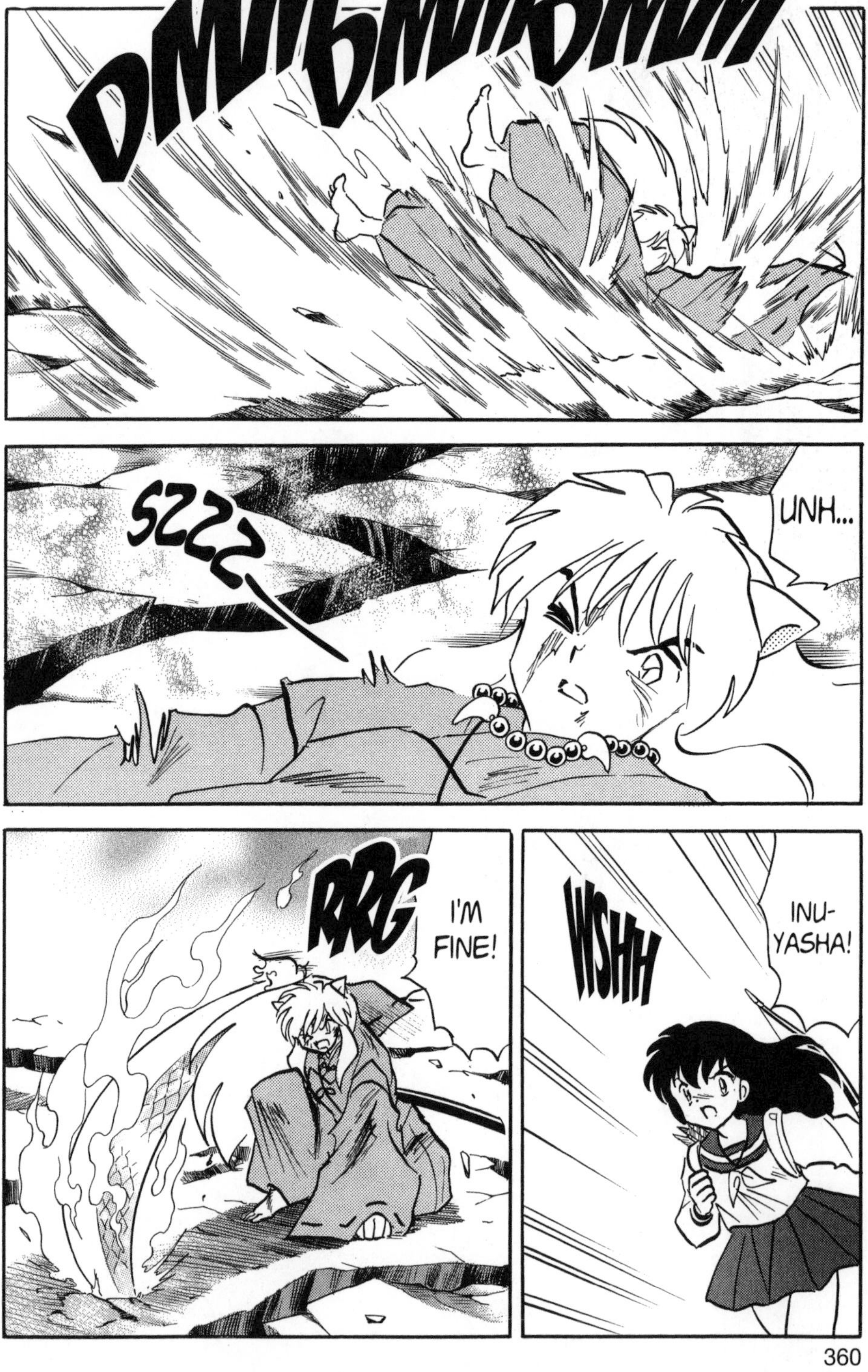
UNH...
SZZZ
INU-
YASHA!
WSHH
I'M
FINE!
RRG

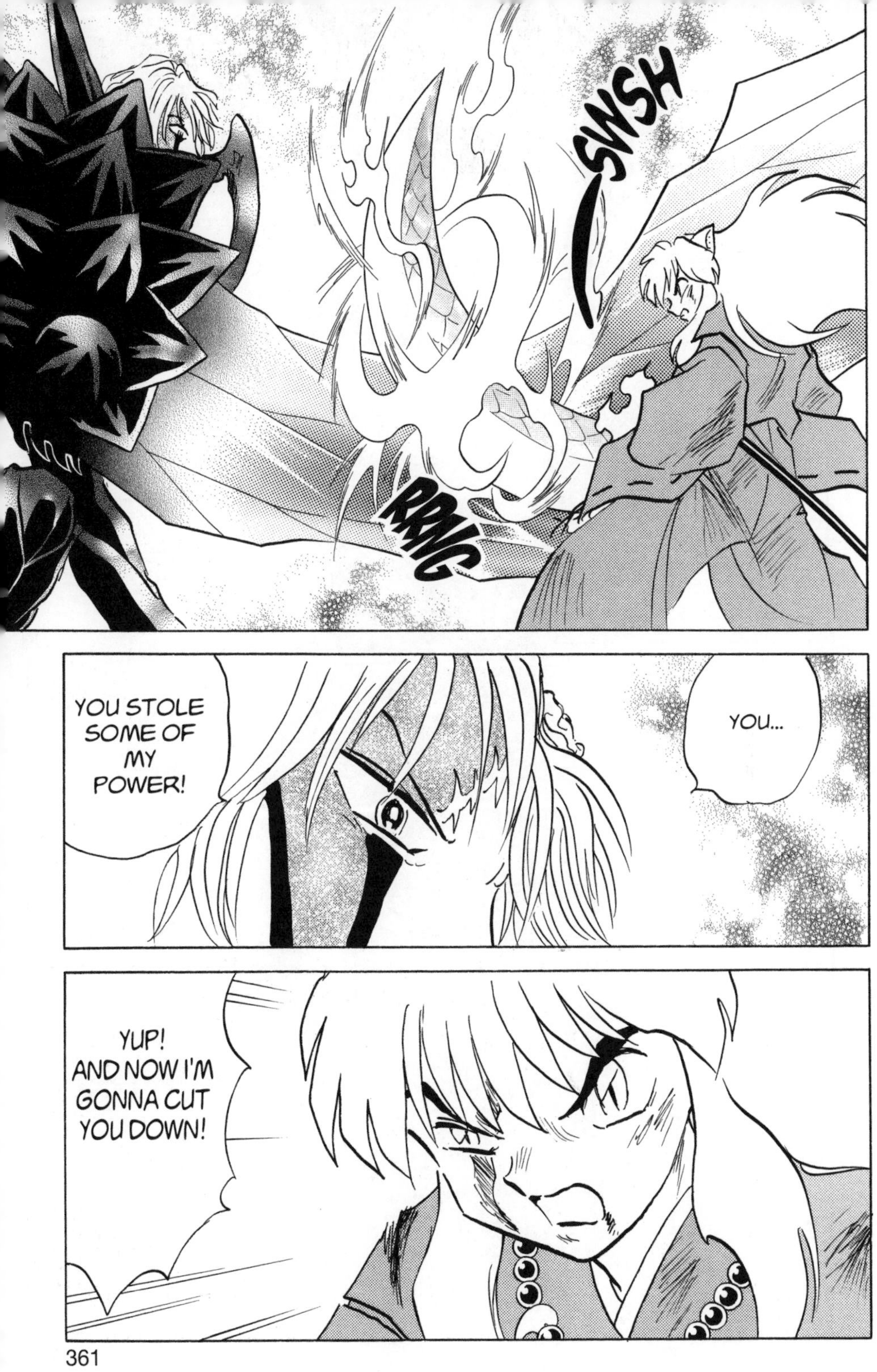
SWSH
RRING
YOU...
YOU STOLE SOME OF MY POWER!
YUP! AND NOW I'M GONNA CUT YOU DOWN!

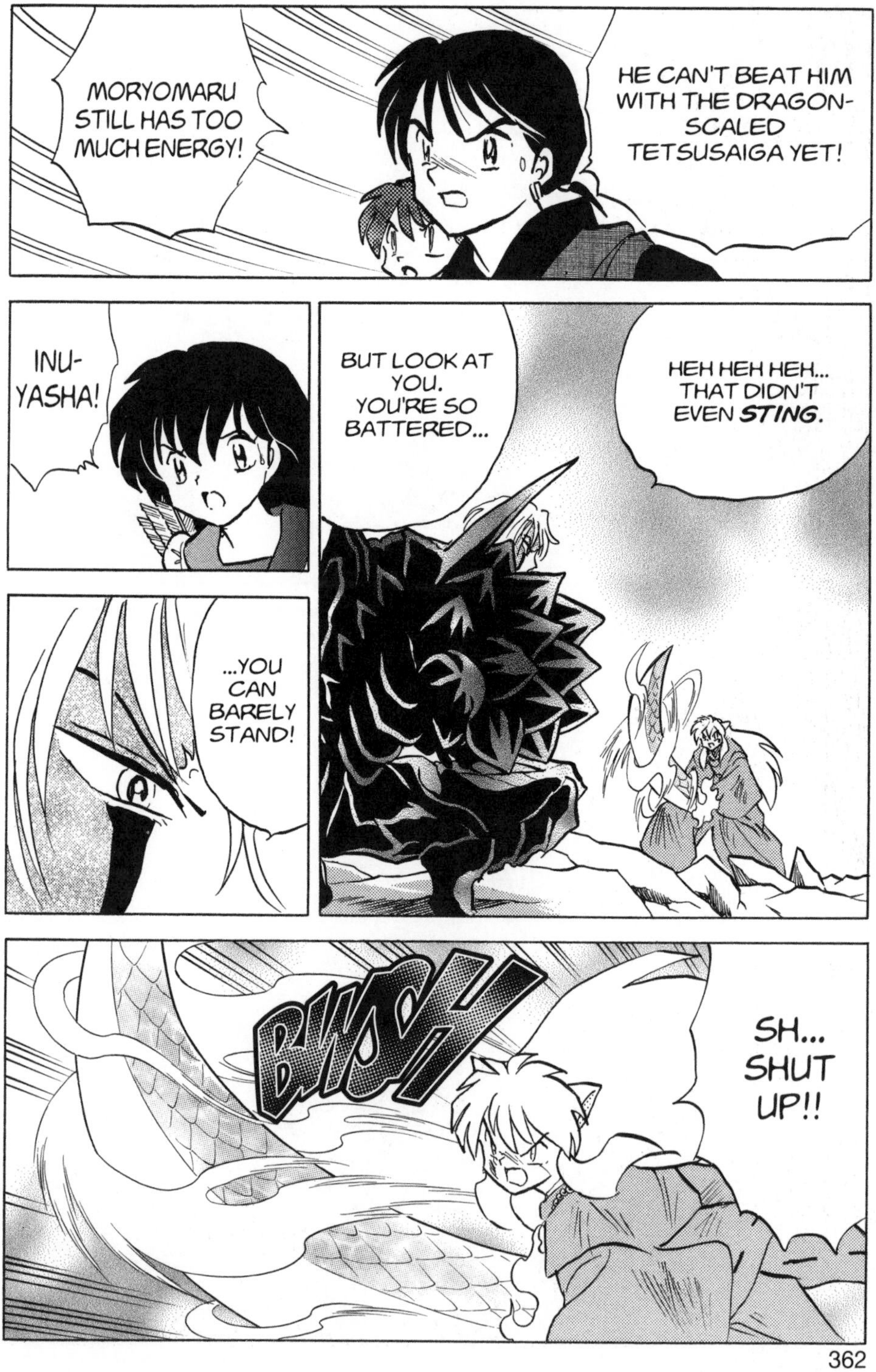
HE CAN'T BEAT HIM WITH THE DRAGON-SCALED TETSUSAIGA YET!
MORYOMARU STILL HAS TOO MUCH ENERGY!
HEH HEH HEH... THAT DIDN'T EVEN STING.
BUT LOOK AT YOU. YOU'RE SO BATTERED...
INU-YASHA!
...YOU CAN BARELY STAND!
BWOSH
SH... SHUT UP!!

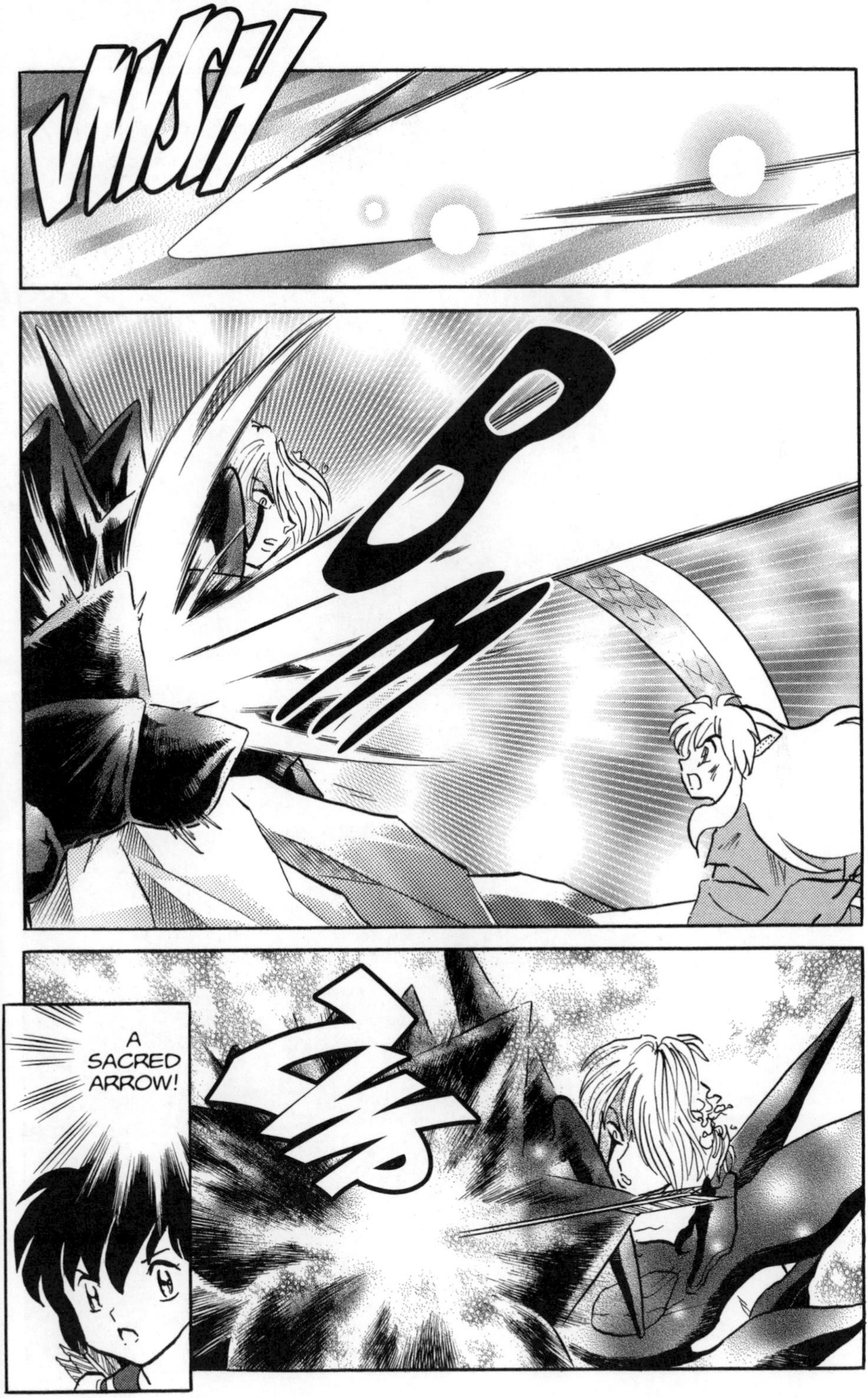
VWSH
BOM
ZWIP
A SACRED ARROW!

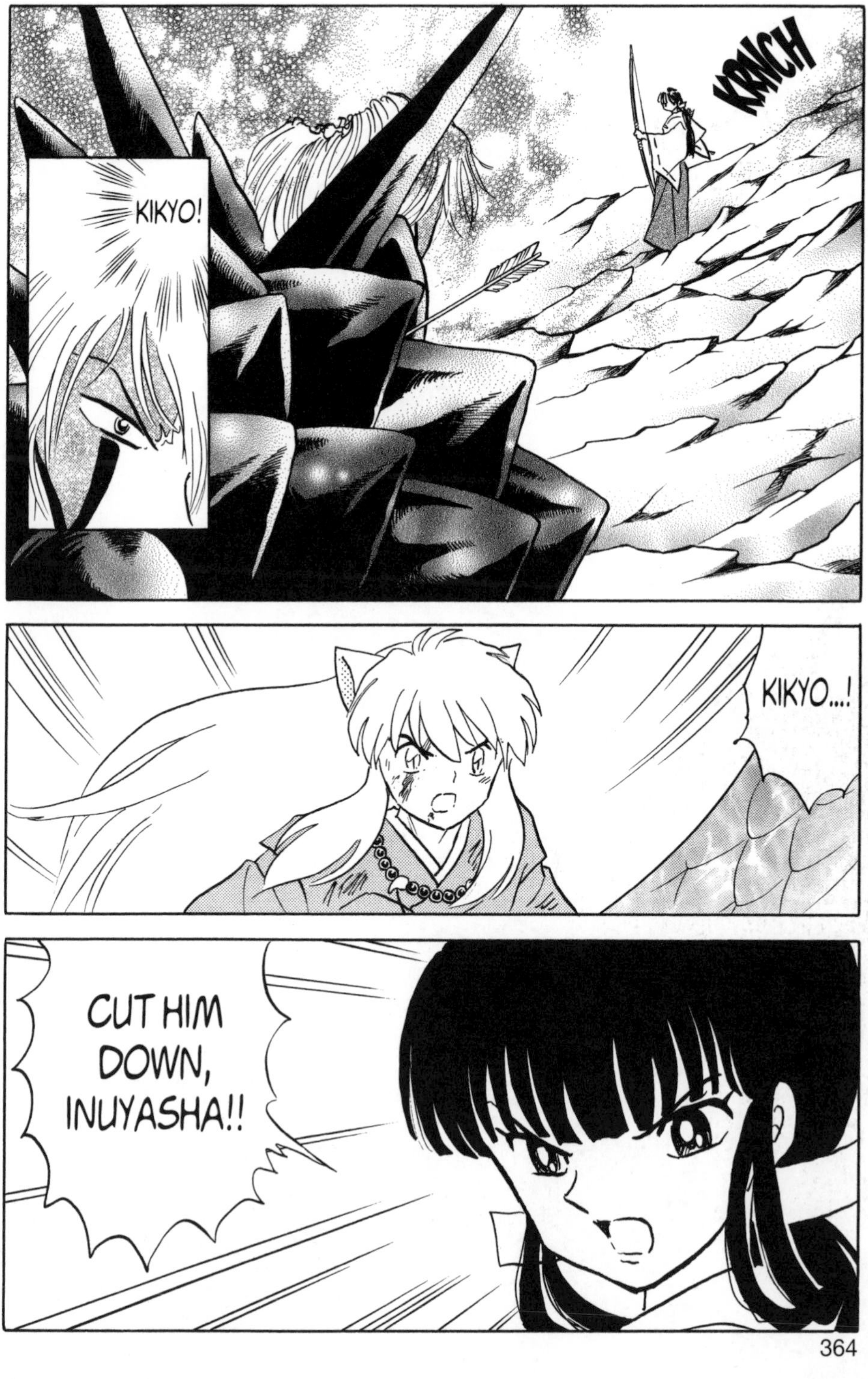
KRNCH
KIKYO!
KIKYO...!
CUT HIM DOWN, INUYASHA!!

SCROLL TEN
FLIGHT

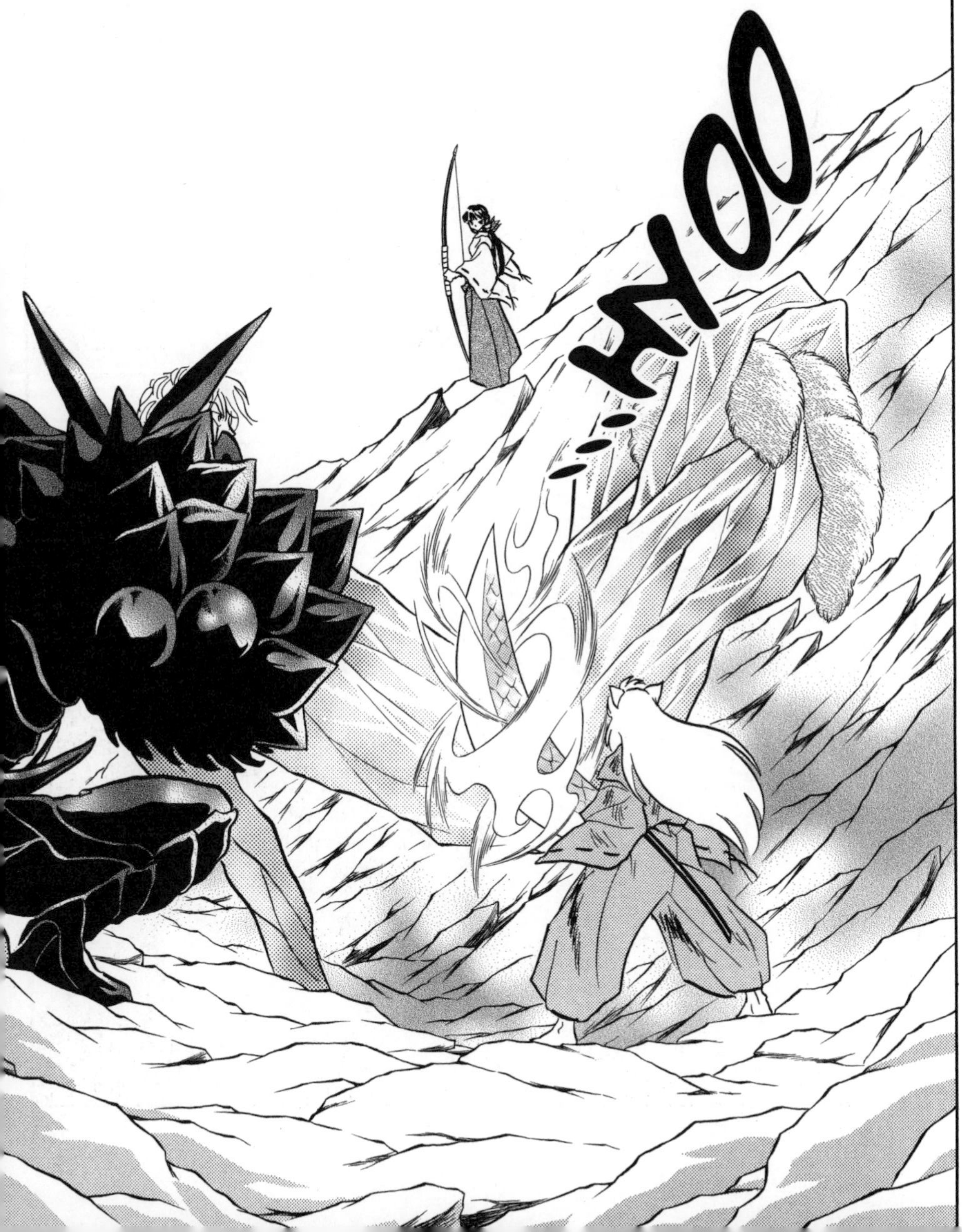
...HYOO

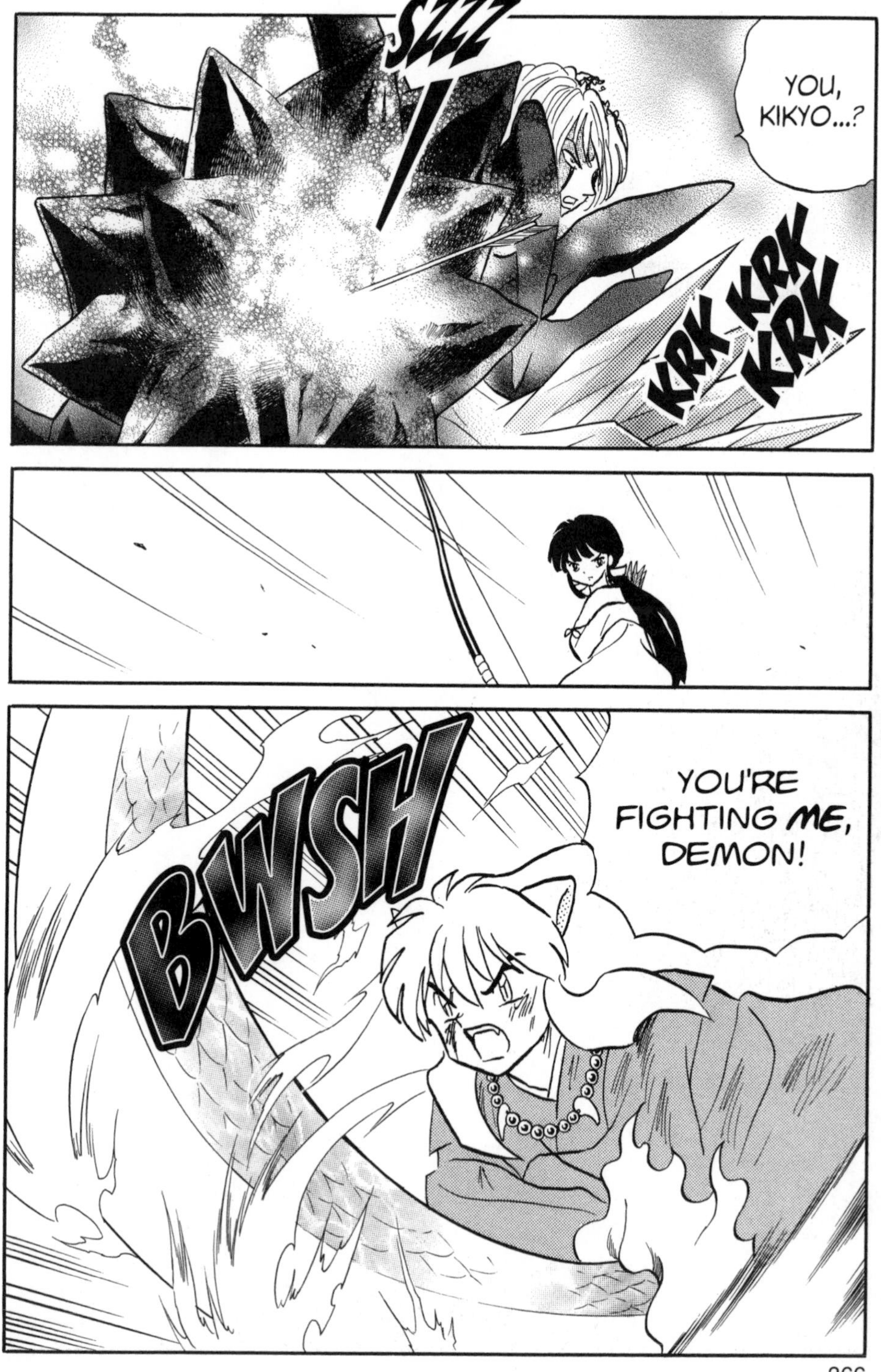
YOU, KIKYO...?
SZZZ
KRK KRK KRK
YOU'RE FIGHTING ME, DEMON!
BWSH

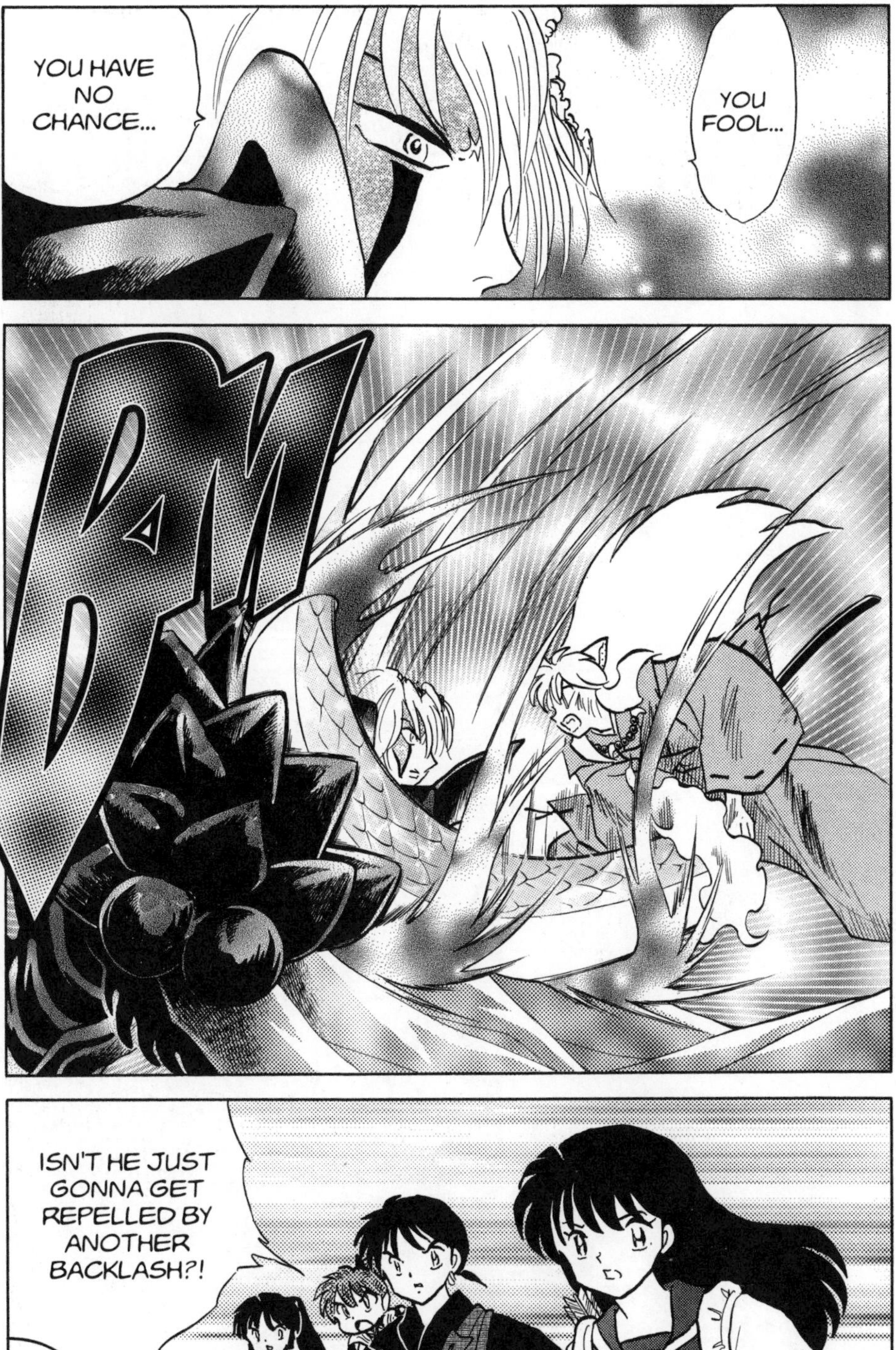
YOU FOOL...
YOU HAVE NO CHANCE...
BAM
ISN'T HE JUST GONNA GET REPELLED BY ANOTHER BACKLASH?!

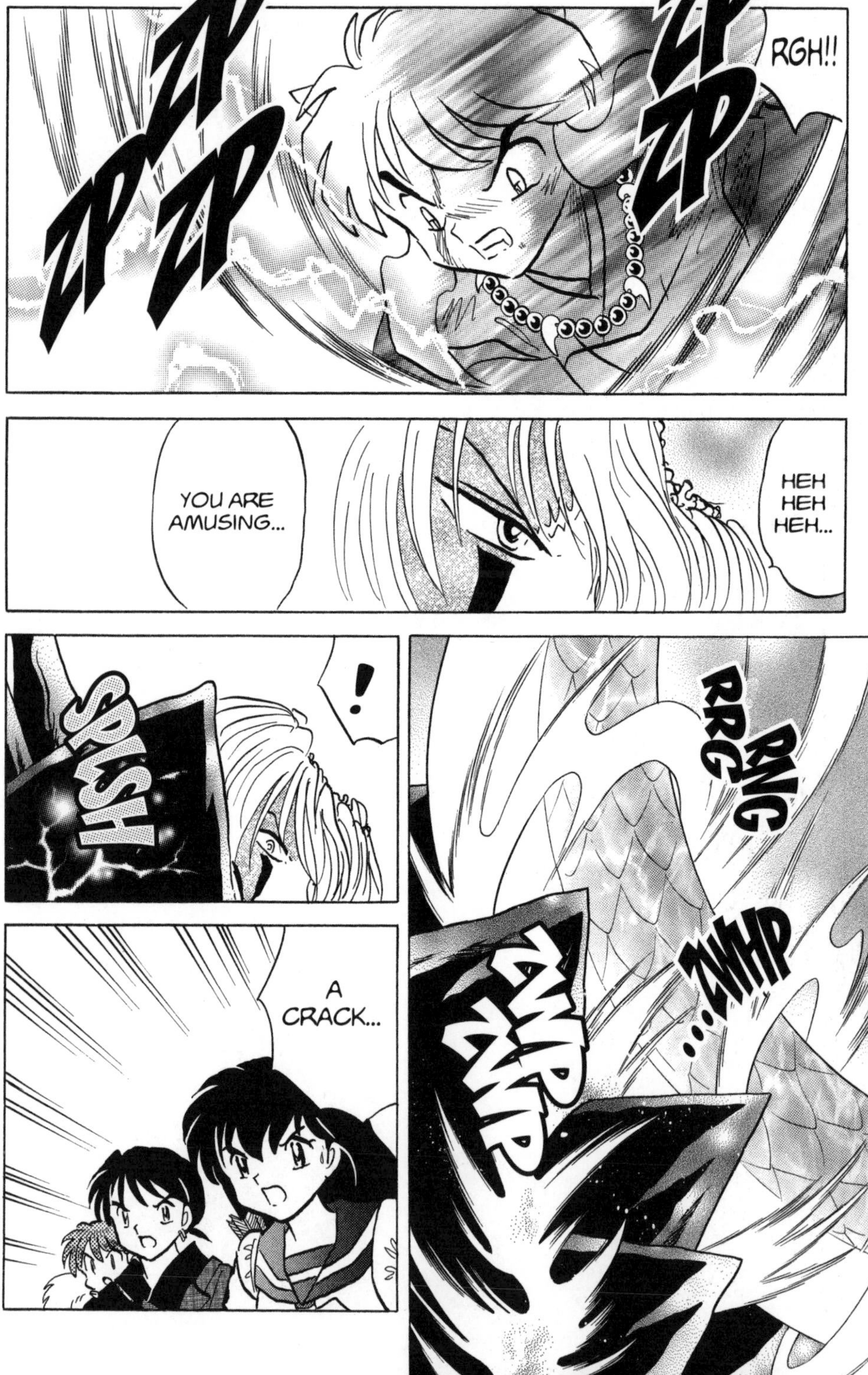
RGH!!
ZP ZP
ZP ZP
ZP ZP
HEH HEH HEH...
YOU ARE AMUSING...
RRG RNG
ZWHP...
ZWP ZWP
!
SPLSH!
A CRACK...

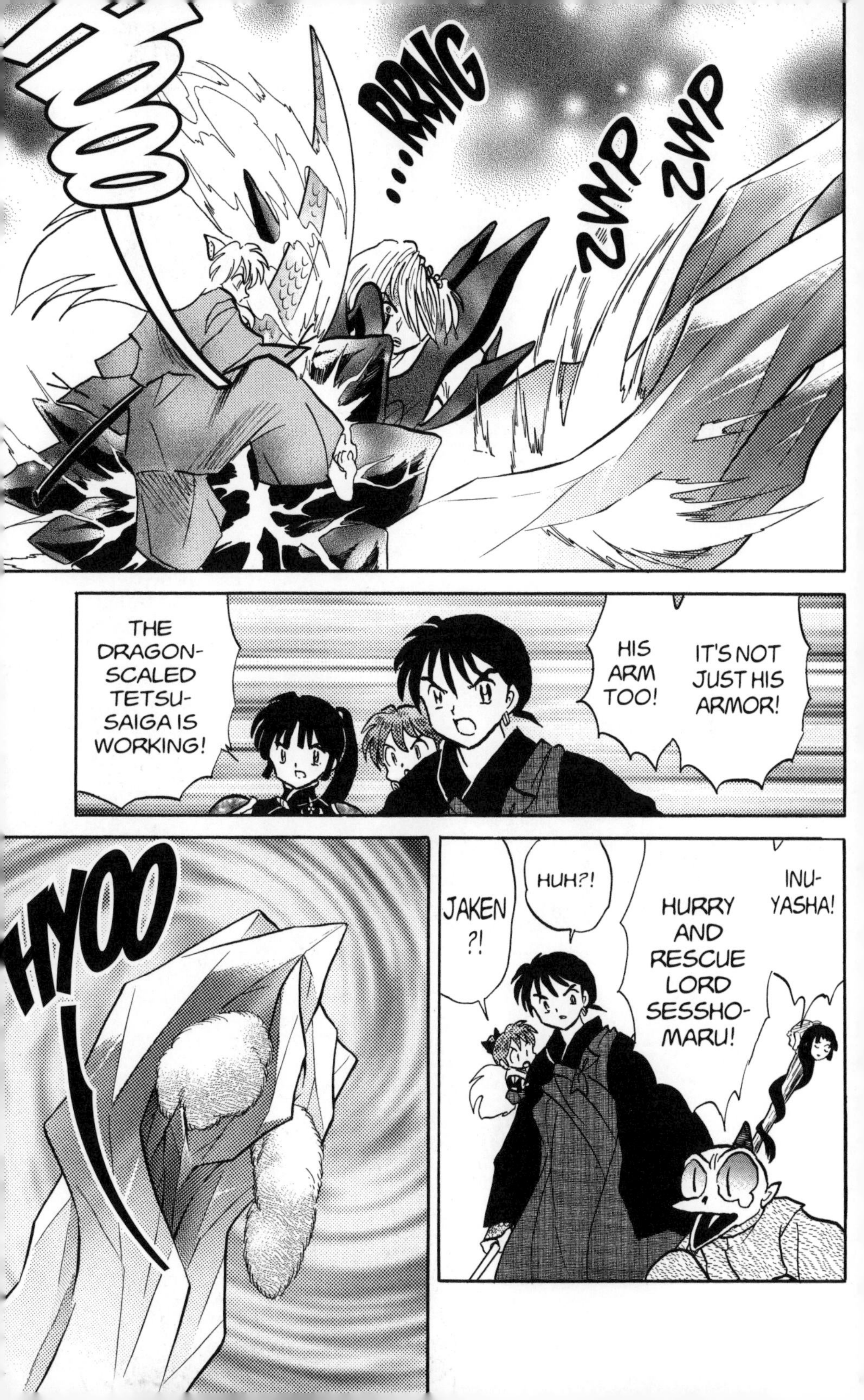
ZWP
ZWP
...RRNG
IT'S NOT JUST HIS ARMOR!
HIS ARM TOO!
THE DRAGON-SCALED TETSU-SAIGA IS WORKING!
INU-YASHA!
HURRY AND RESCUE LORD SESSHO-MARU!
HUH?!
JAKEN ?!
HYOO

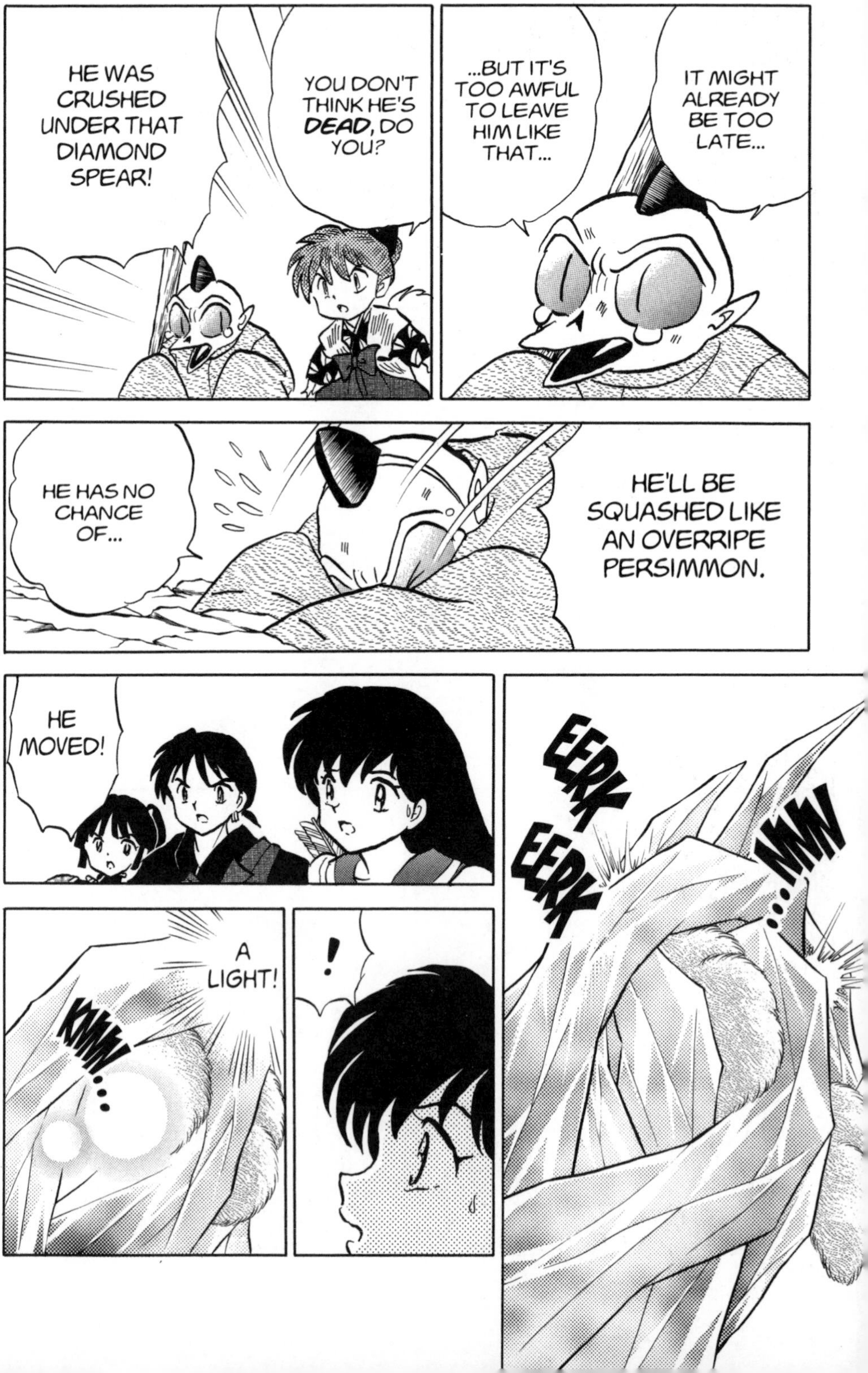
IT MIGHT ALREADY BE TOO LATE...
...BUT IT'S TOO AWFUL TO LEAVE HIM LIKE THAT...
YOU DON'T THINK HE'S DEAD, DO YOU?
HE WAS CRUSHED UNDER THAT DIAMOND SPEAR!
HE'LL BE SQUASHED LIKE AN OVERRIPE PERSIMMON.
HE HAS NO CHANCE OF...
EERK EERK
...MMV
HE MOVED!
!
A LIGHT!
KMMM...

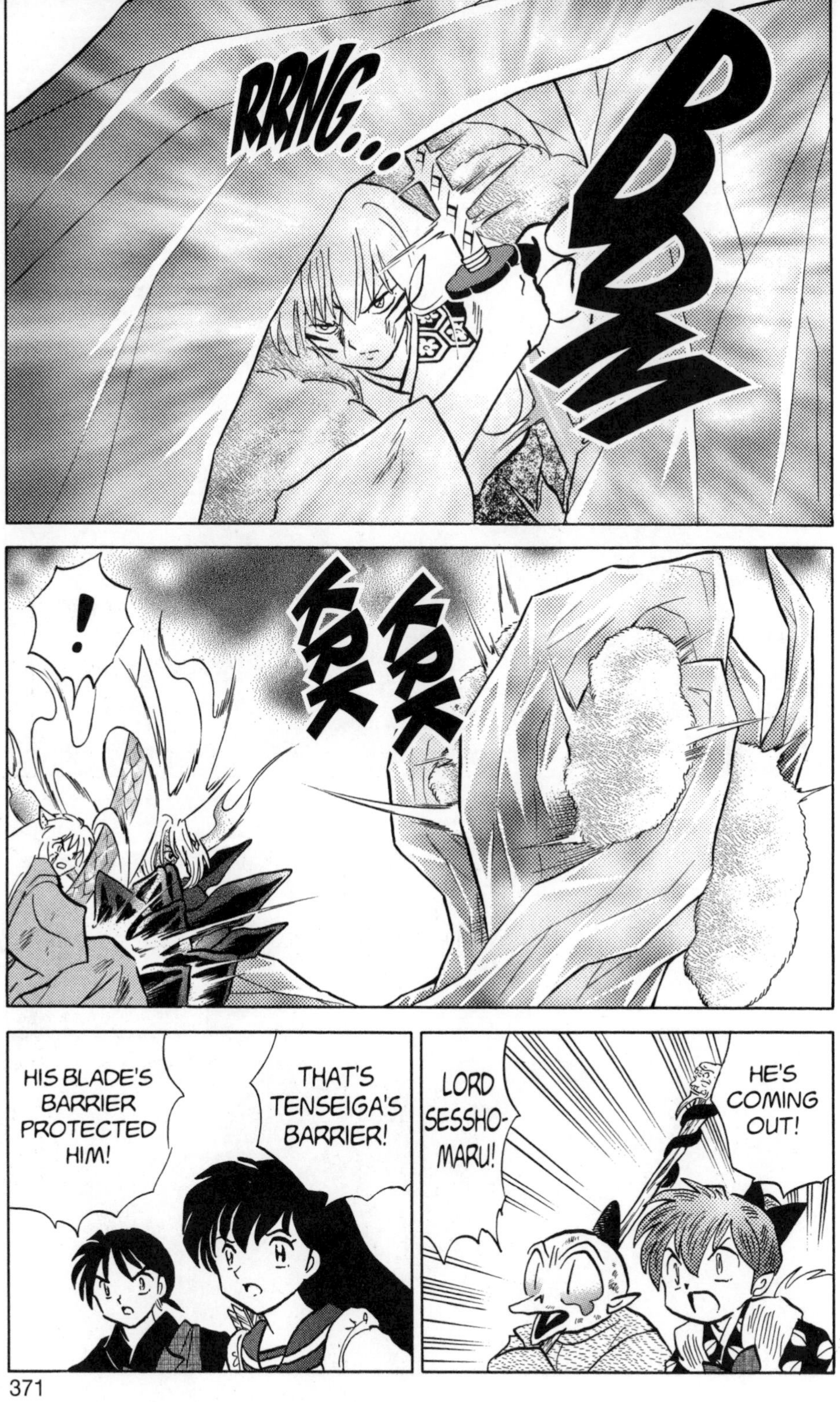
BDM
RRNG...
KRK KRK
!
HE'S COMING OUT!
LORD SESSHO-MARU!
THAT'S TENSEIGA'S BARRIER!
HIS BLADE'S BARRIER PROTECTED HIM!

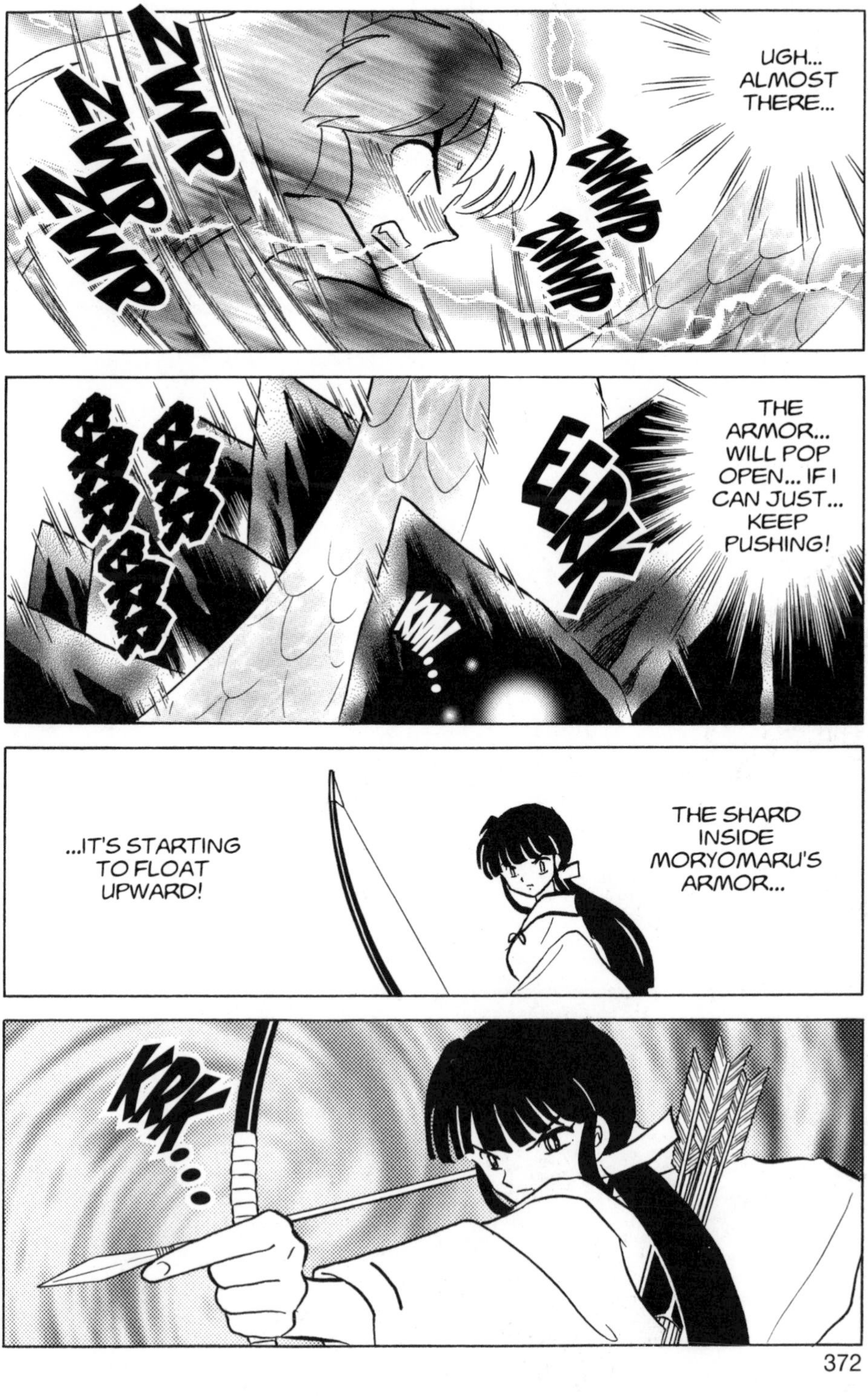
UGH... ALMOST THERE...
ZWMP ZWMP
ZWMP ZWMP ZWMP
THE ARMOR... WILL POP OPEN... IF I CAN JUST... KEEP PUSHING!
EERK
KNN...
THE SHARD INSIDE MORYOMARU'S ARMOR...
...IT'S STARTING TO FLOAT UPWARD!
KRK...

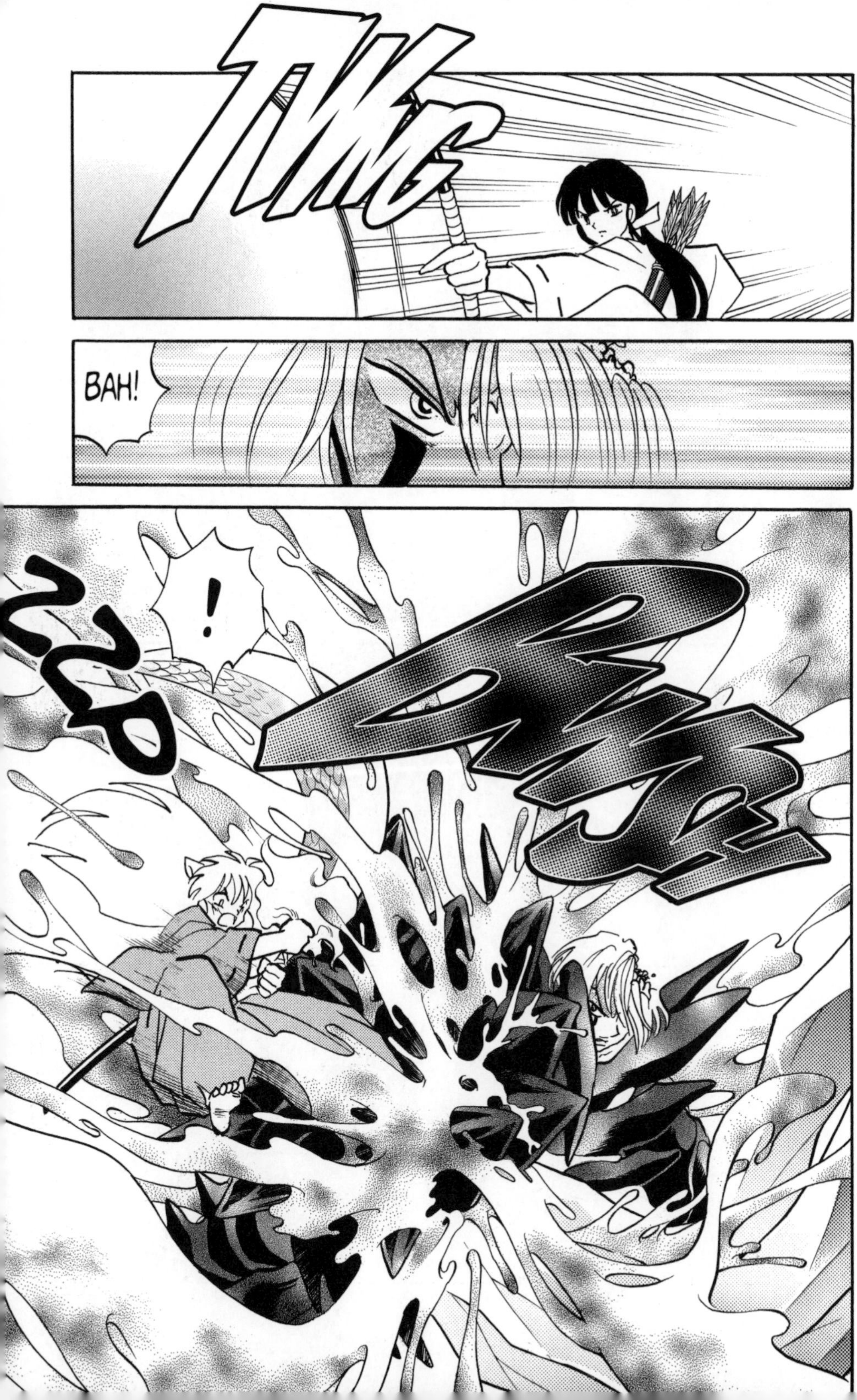
TWNG
BAH!
!

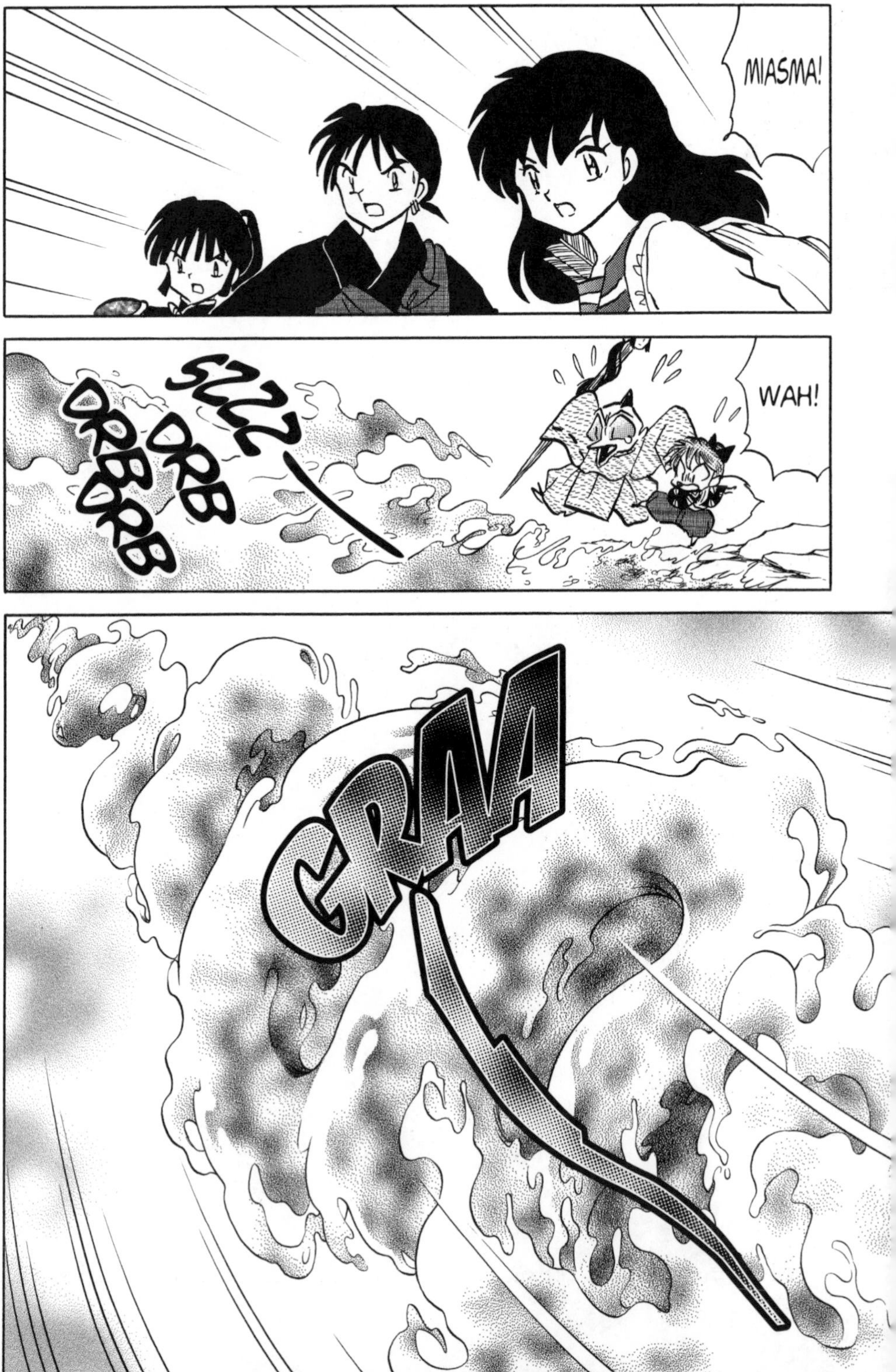
MIASMA!
WAH!
SZZZ
DRB
DRBDRB
GRAA

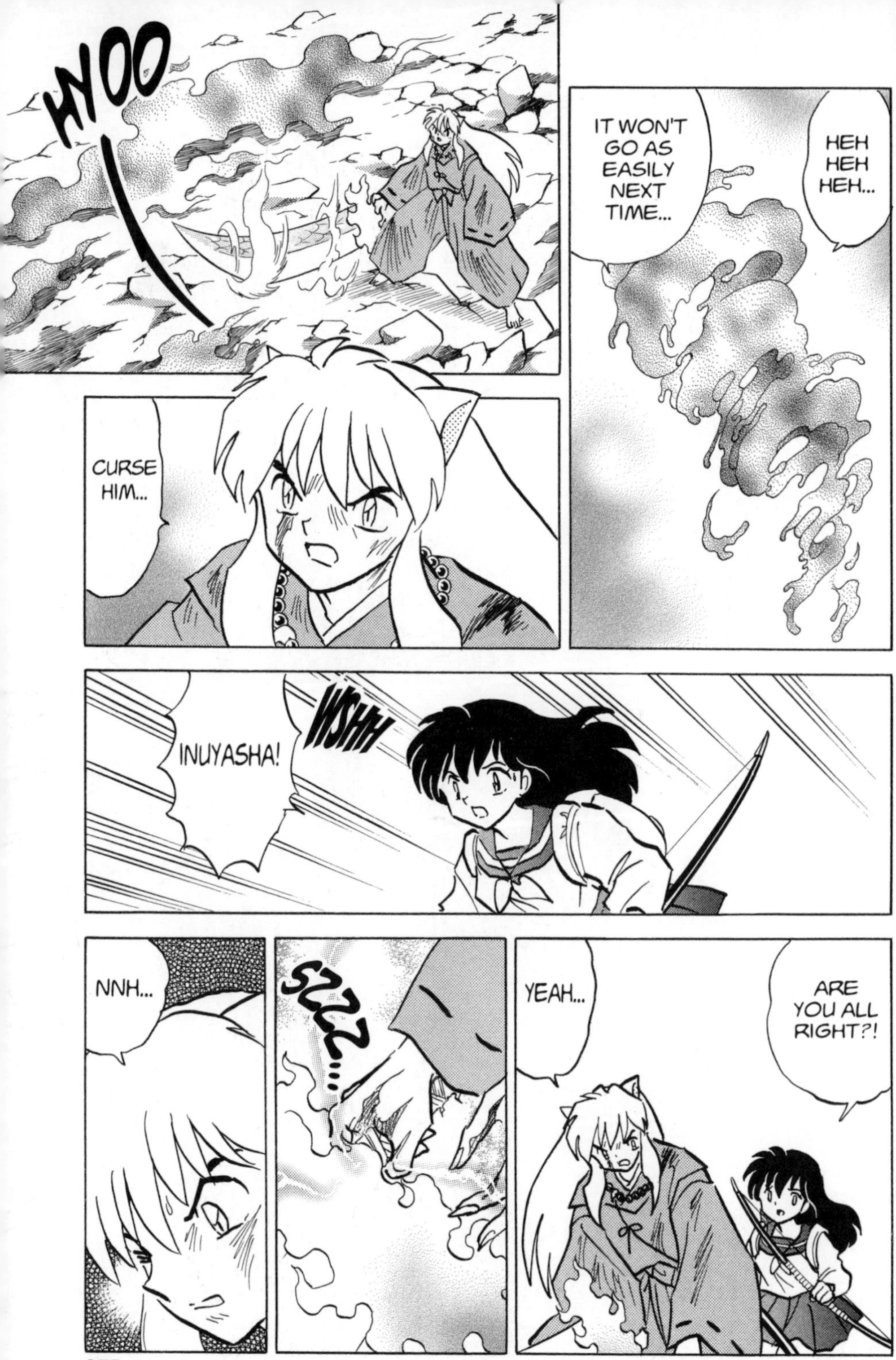
HEH HEH HEH...
IT WON'T GO AS EASILY NEXT TIME...
HYOO
CURSE HIM...
WSHH
INUYASHA!
ARE YOU ALL RIGHT?!
YEAH...
SZZZ...
NNH...

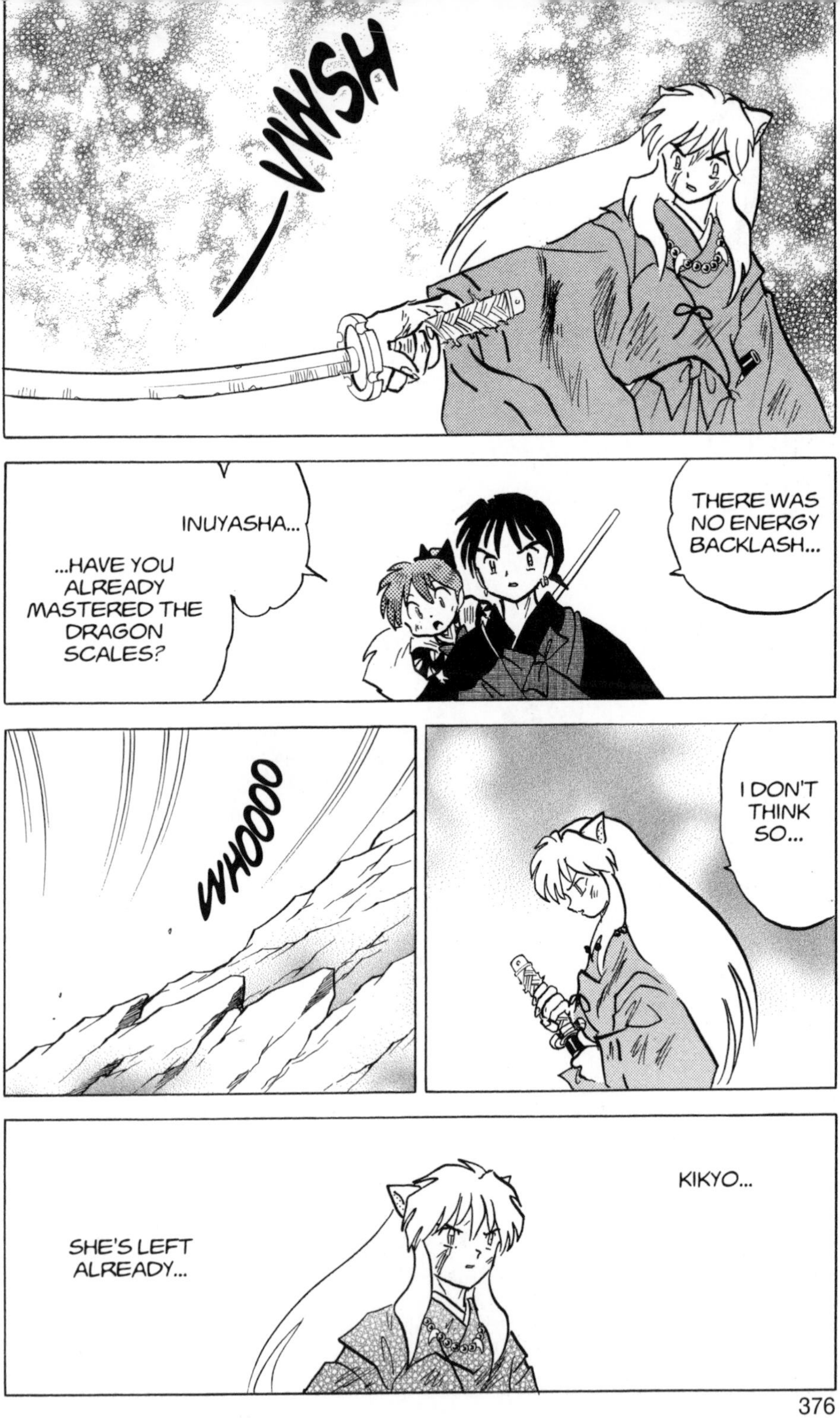
VWSH
THERE WAS NO ENERGY BACKLASH...
INUYASHA...
...HAVE YOU ALREADY MASTERED THE DRAGON SCALES?
I DON'T THINK SO...
WHOOOO
KIKYO...
SHE'S LEFT ALREADY...

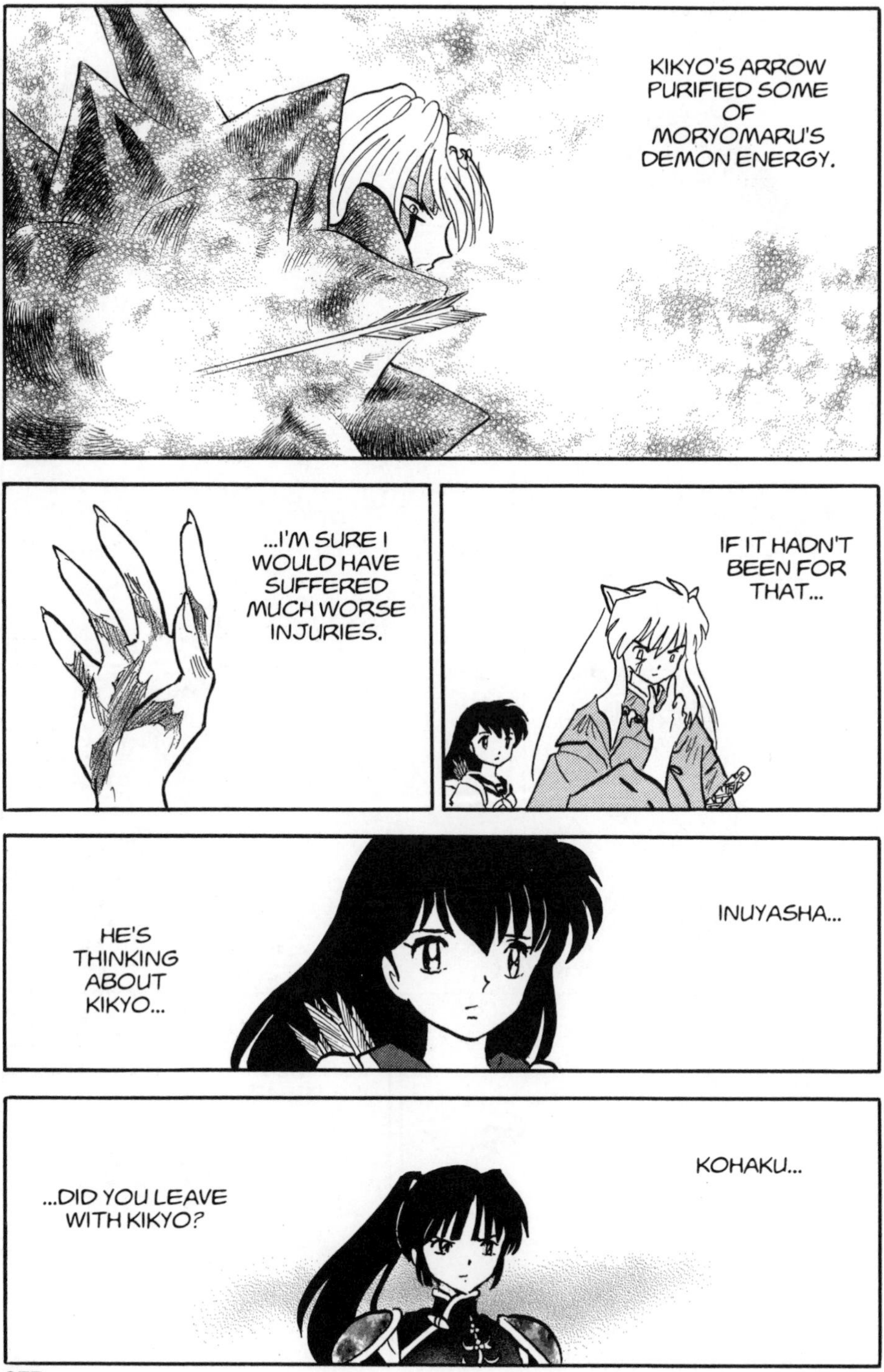
KIKYO'S ARROW PURIFIED SOME OF MORYOMARU'S DEMON ENERGY.
IF IT HADN'T BEEN FOR THAT...
...I'M SURE I WOULD HAVE SUFFERED MUCH WORSE INJURIES.
INUYASHA...
HE'S THINKING ABOUT KIKYO...
KOHAKU...
...DID YOU LEAVE WITH KIKYO?

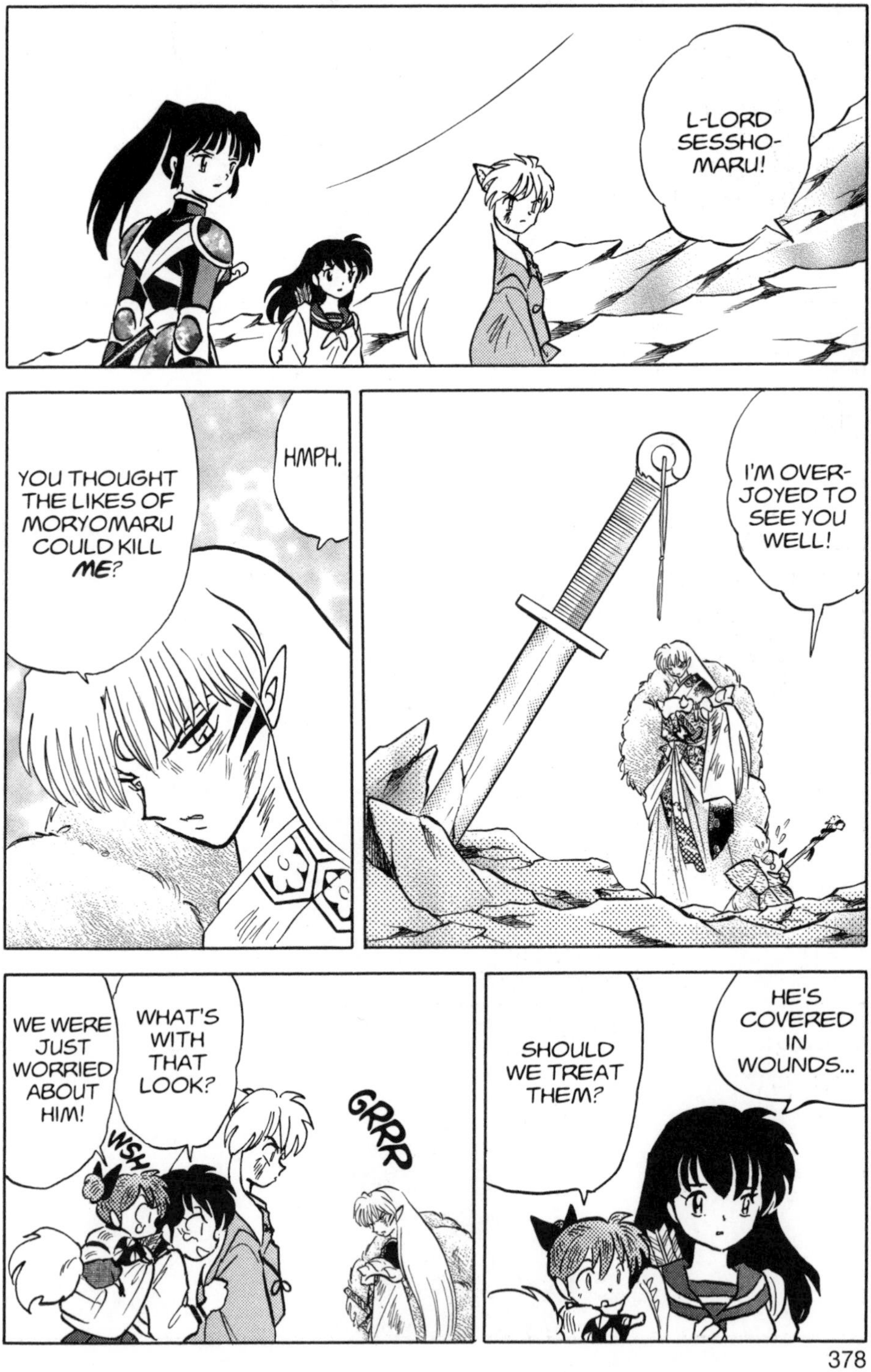
L-LORD SESSHO-MARU!
I'M OVER-JOYED TO SEE YOU WELL!
HMPH.
YOU THOUGHT THE LIKES OF MORYOMARU COULD KILL *ME*?
HE'S COVERED IN WOUNDS...
SHOULD WE TREAT THEM?
GRRR
WHAT'S WITH THAT LOOK?
WE WERE JUST WORRIED ABOUT HIM!
WSH

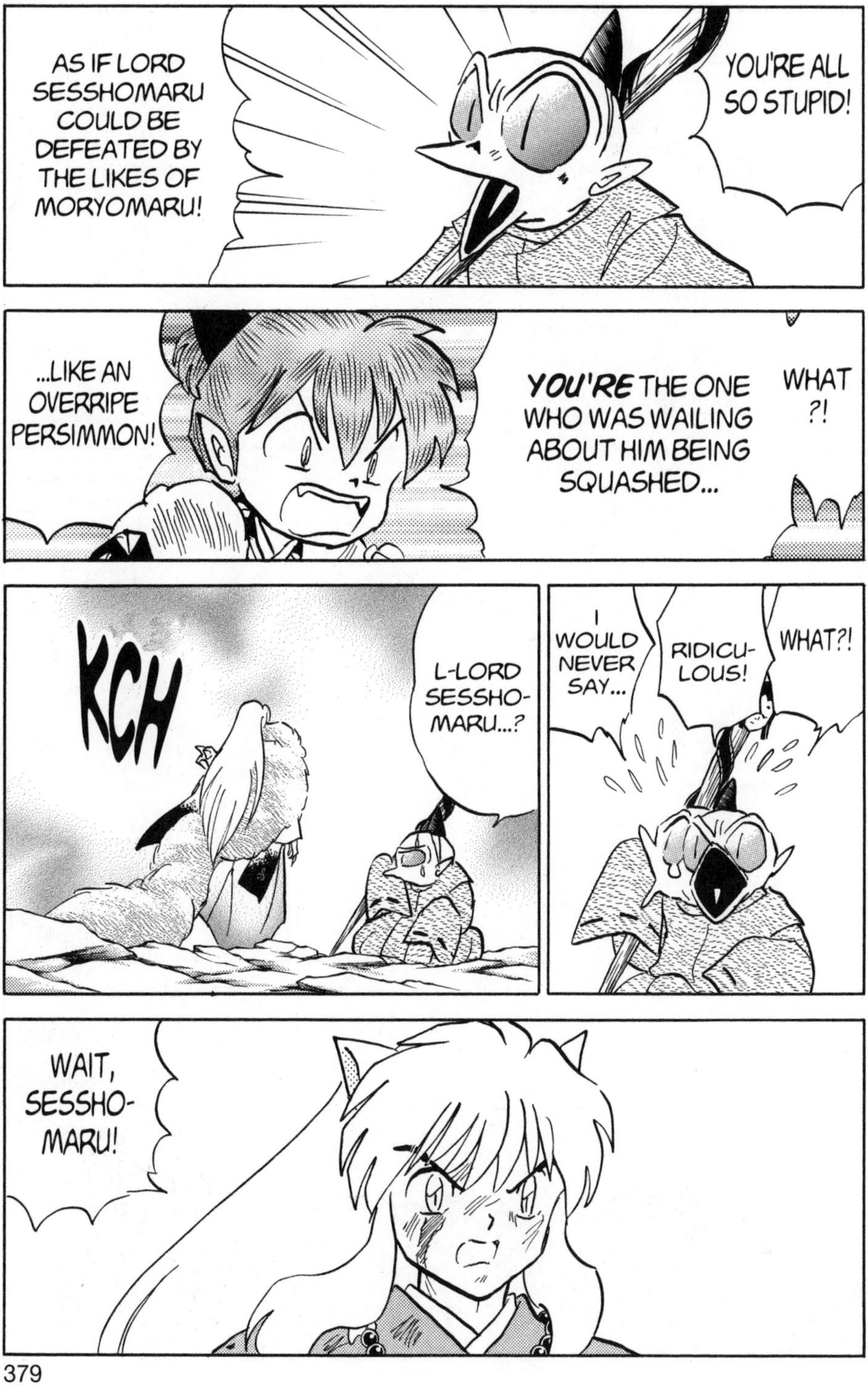
YOU'RE ALL SO STUPID!
AS IF LORD SESSHOMARU COULD BE DEFEATED BY THE LIKES OF MORYOMARU!
WHAT?!
YOU'RE THE ONE WHO WAS WAILING ABOUT HIM BEING SQUASHED...
...LIKE AN OVERRIPE PERSIMMON!
WHAT?!
RIDICU-LOUS!
I WOULD NEVER SAY...
L-LORD SESSHO-MARU...?
KCH
WAIT, SESSHO-MARU!

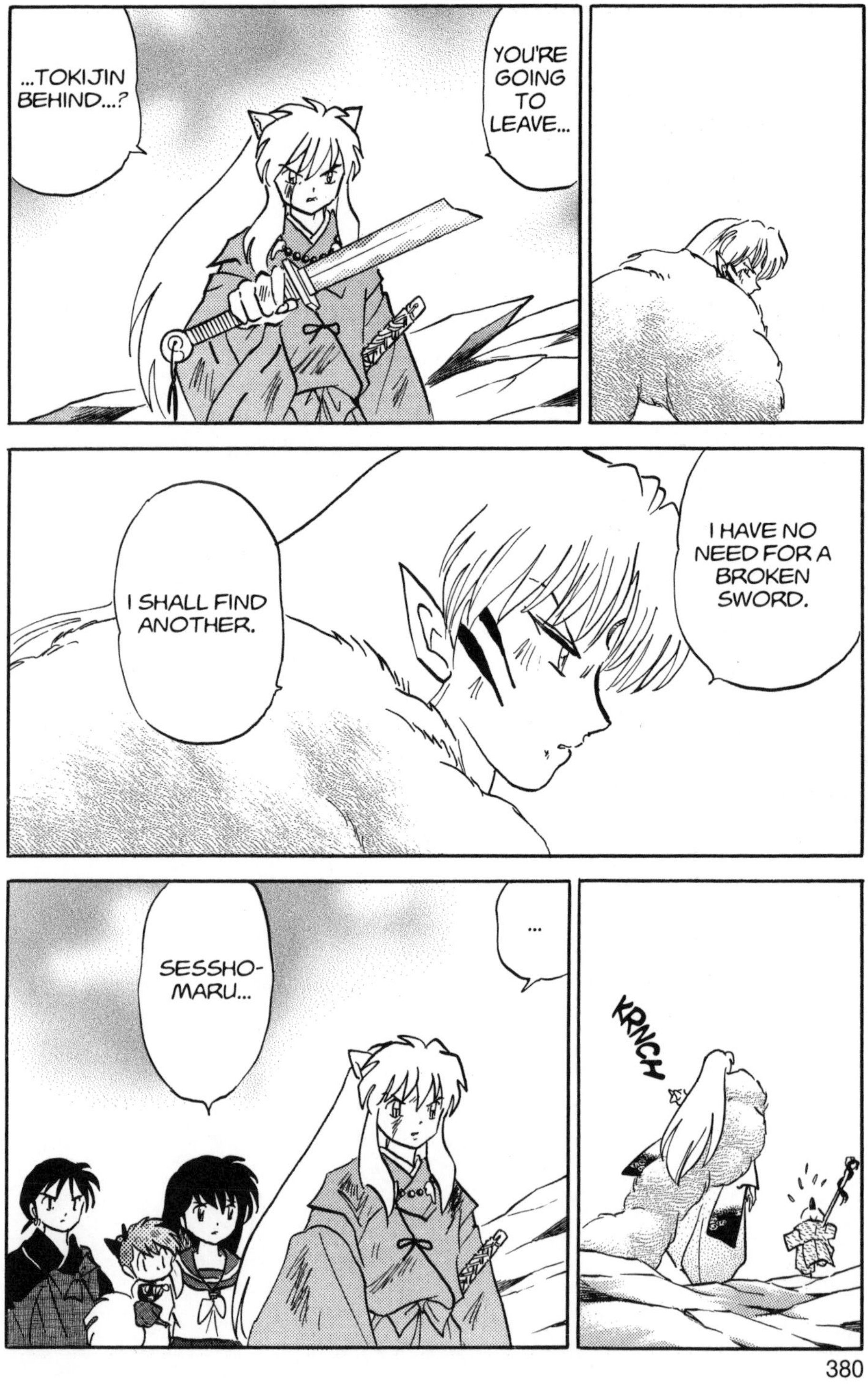
YOU'RE GOING TO LEAVE...
...TOKIJIN BEHIND...?
I HAVE NO NEED FOR A BROKEN SWORD.
I SHALL FIND ANOTHER.
KRNCH
...
SESSHO-MARU...

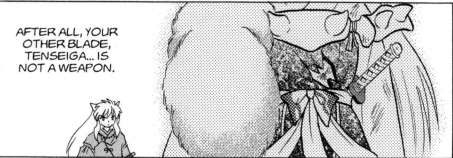

A NEW BLADE... THAT'S YOUR ONLY OPTION, HUH?

AFTER ALL, YOUR OTHER BLADE, TENSEIGA... IS NOT A WEAPON.

AN EYE-BALL!

ULP...

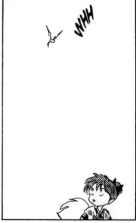

WHH

FWP

WHAT *IS* THAT THING?!

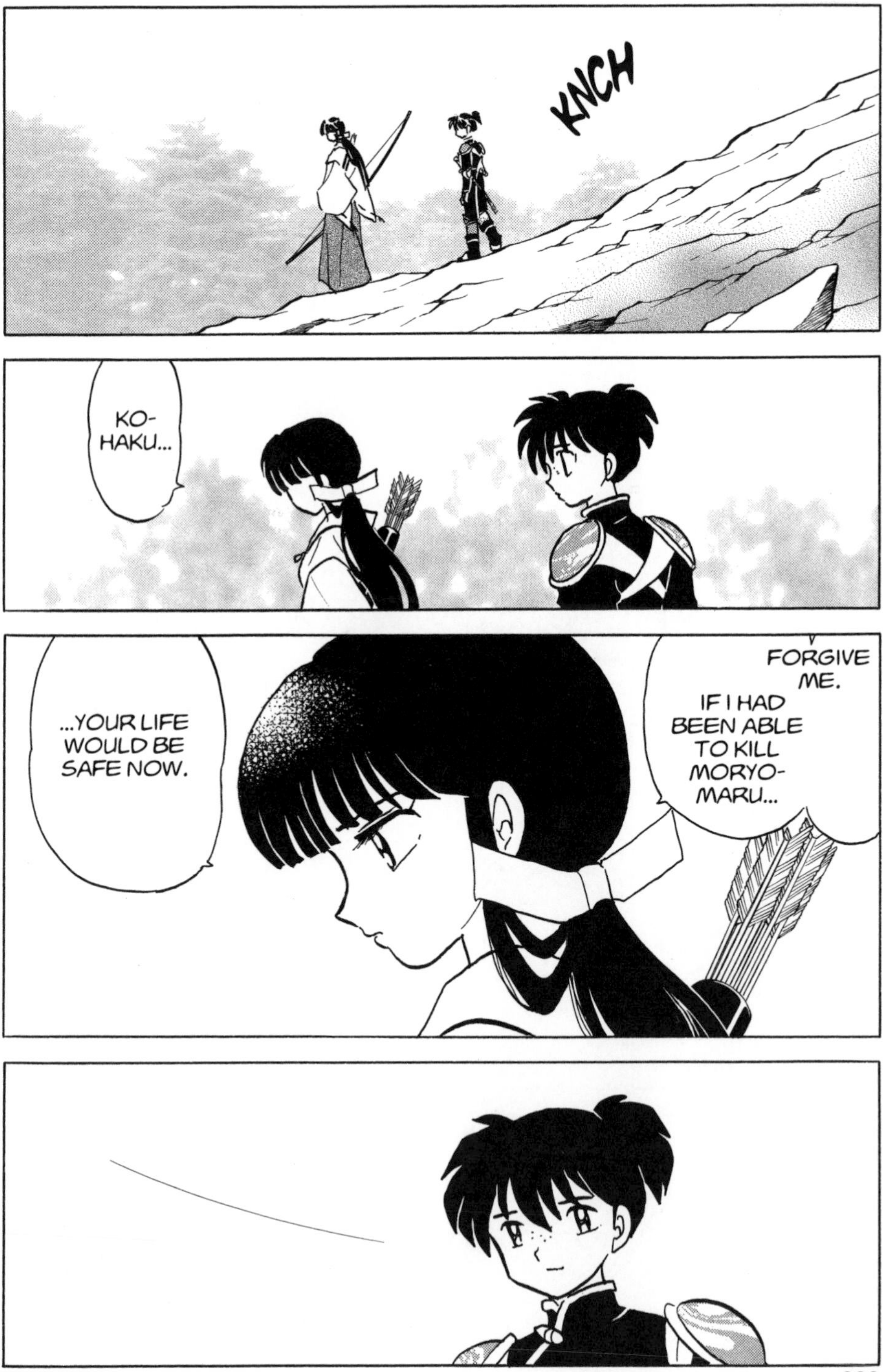
KNCH
KO-HAKU...
FORGIVE ME.
IF I HAD BEEN ABLE TO KILL MORYO-MARU...
...YOUR LIFE WOULD BE SAFE NOW.

Volume 42
Meido Zangetsuha

SCROLL ONE
DIVERGENCE

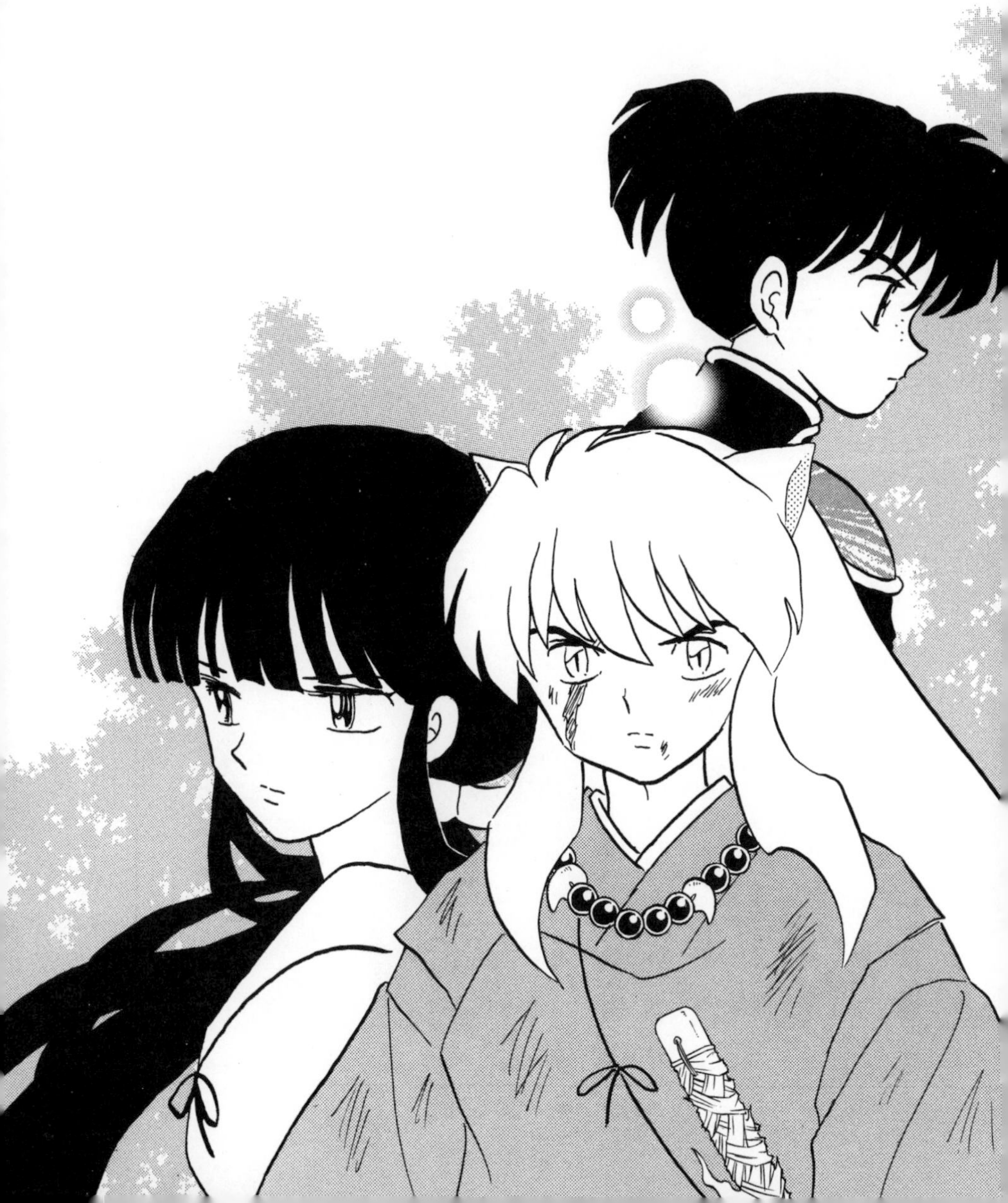

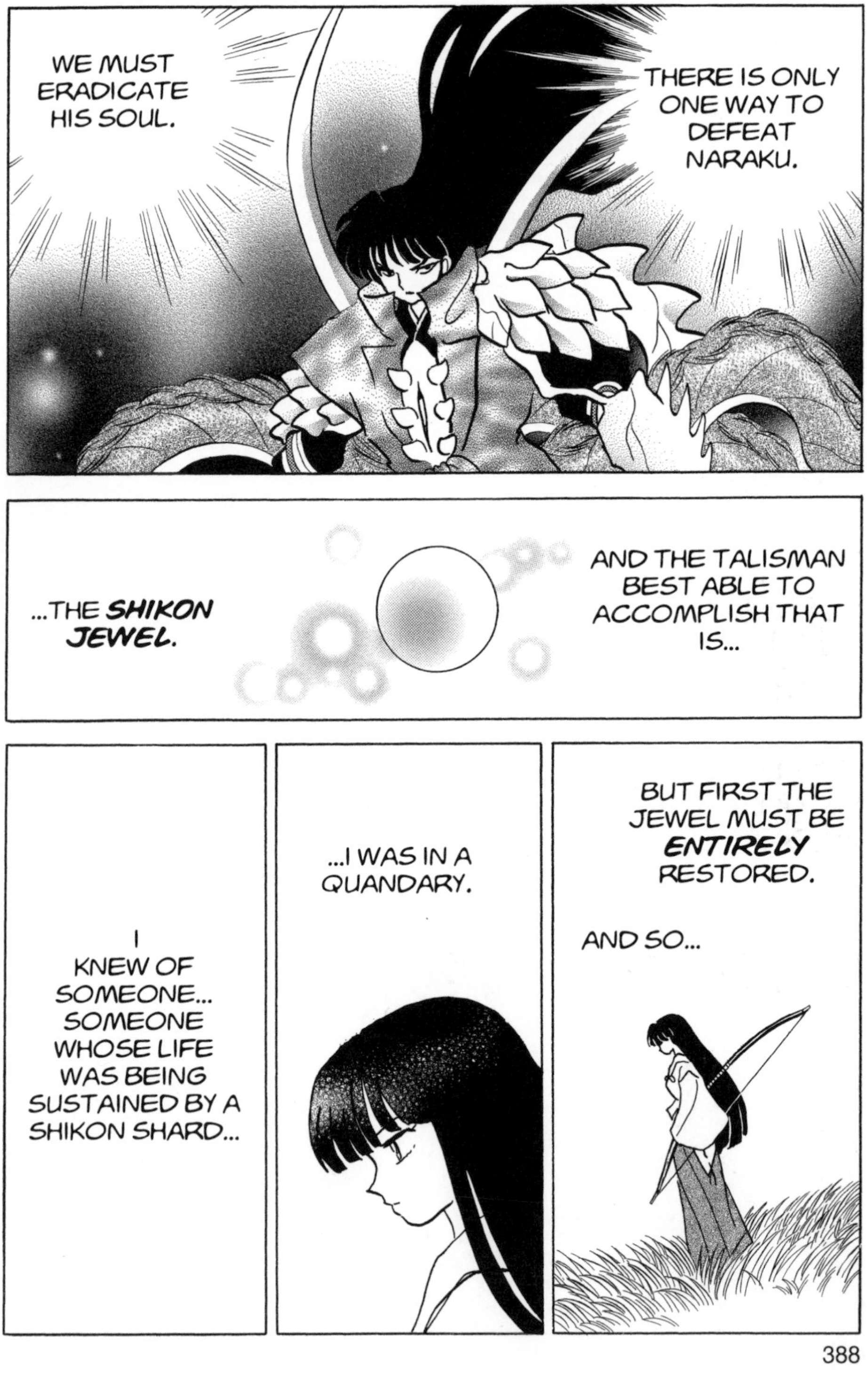
THERE IS ONLY ONE WAY TO DEFEAT NARAKU.
WE MUST ERADICATE HIS SOUL.
AND THE TALISMAN BEST ABLE TO ACCOMPLISH THAT IS...
...THE SHIKON JEWEL.
BUT FIRST THE JEWEL MUST BE ENTIRELY RESTORED.
AND SO...
...I WAS IN A QUANDARY.
I KNEW OF SOMEONE... SOMEONE WHOSE LIFE WAS BEING SUSTAINED BY A SHIKON SHARD...

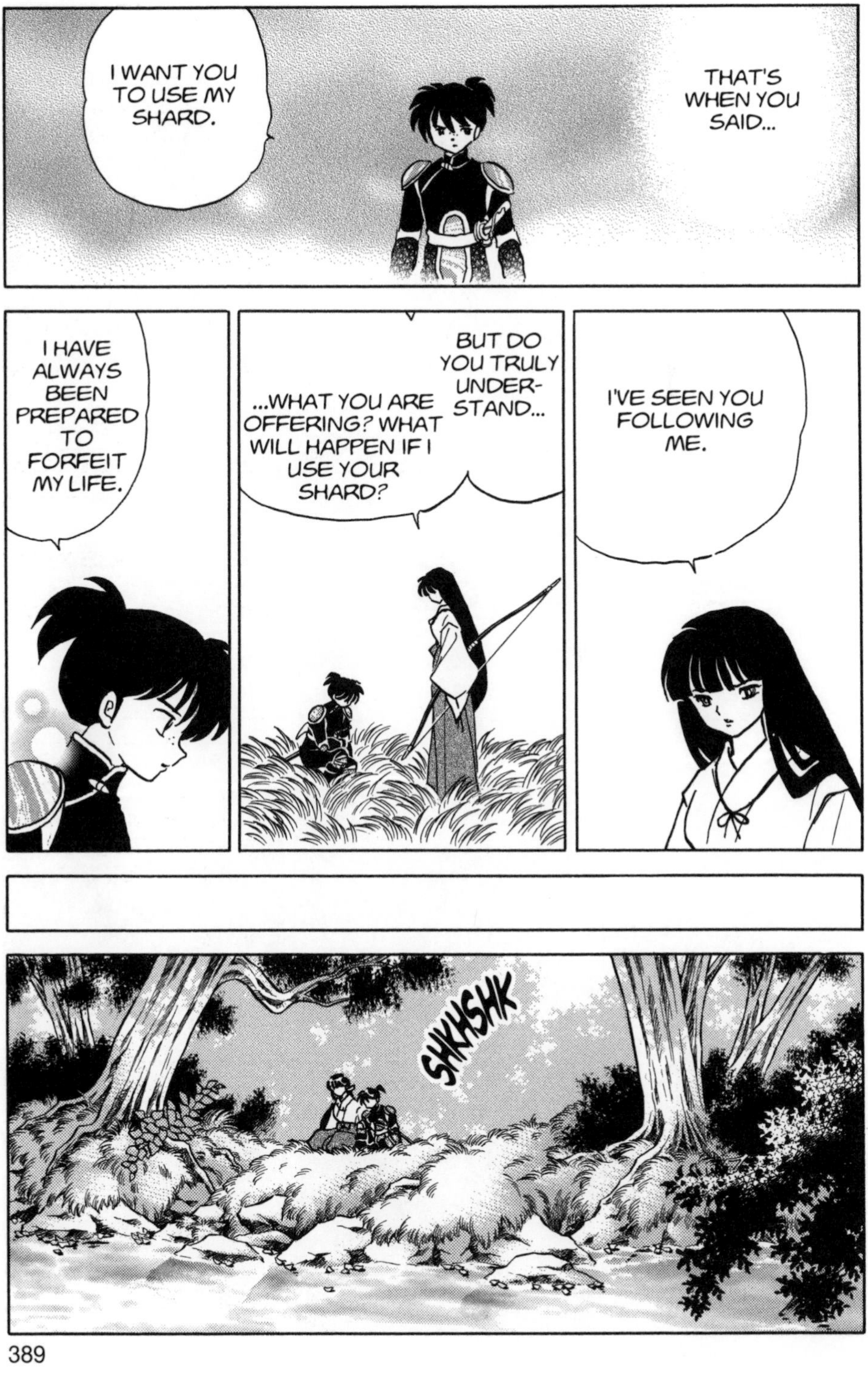
THAT'S WHEN YOU SAID...
I WANT YOU TO USE MY SHARD.
I'VE SEEN YOU FOLLOWING ME.
BUT DO YOU TRULY UNDER-STAND...
...WHAT YOU ARE OFFERING? WHAT WILL HAPPEN IF I USE YOUR SHARD?
I HAVE ALWAYS BEEN PREPARED TO FORFEIT MY LIFE.
SHKHSHK

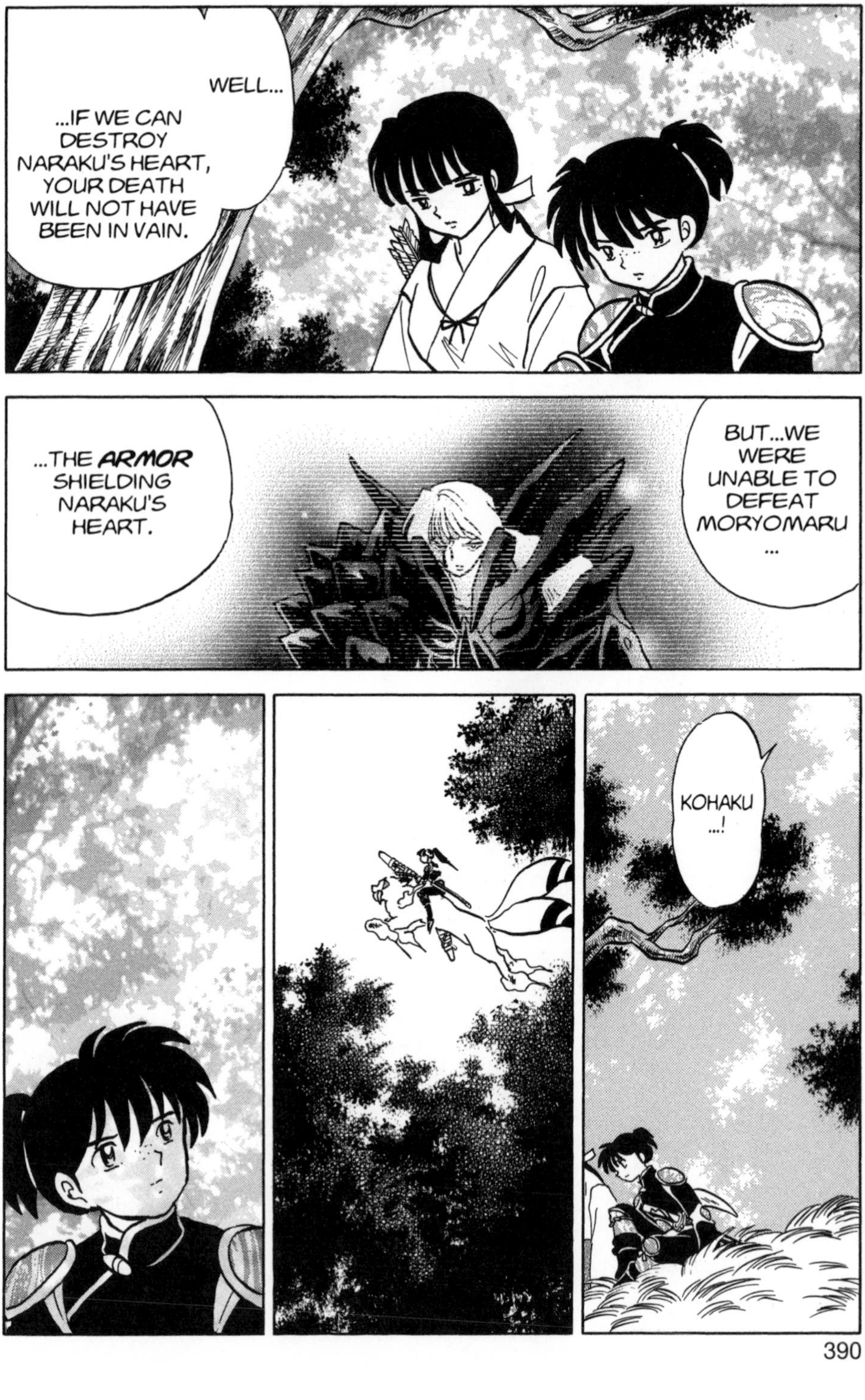
WELL...
...IF WE CAN DESTROY NARAKU'S HEART, YOUR DEATH WILL NOT HAVE BEEN IN VAIN.
BUT...WE WERE UNABLE TO DEFEAT MORYOMARU ...
...THE ARMOR SHIELDING NARAKU'S HEART.
KOHAKU ...!

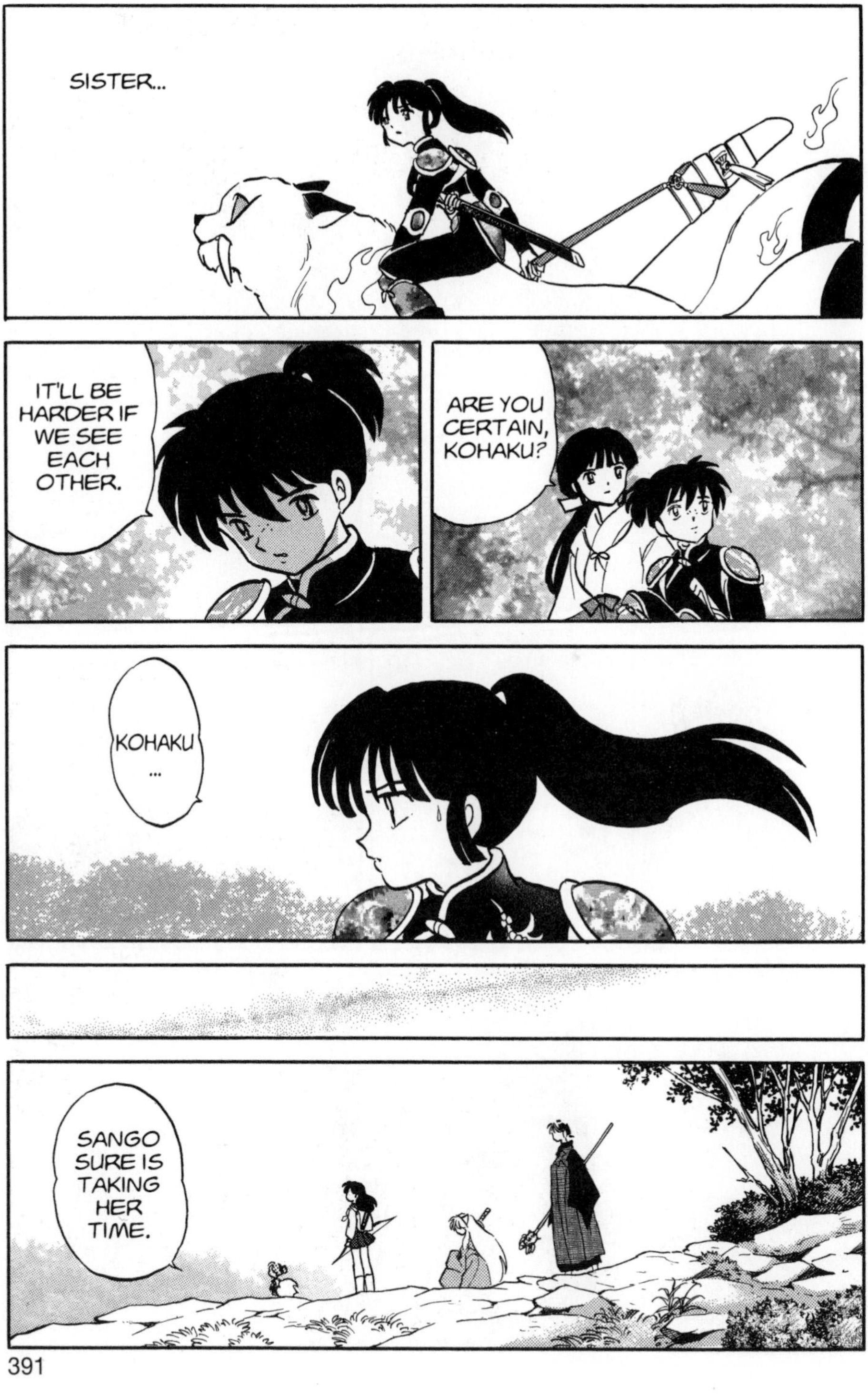
SISTER...
ARE YOU CERTAIN, KOHAKU?
IT'LL BE HARDER IF WE SEE EACH OTHER.
KOHAKU ...
SANGO SURE IS TAKING HER TIME.

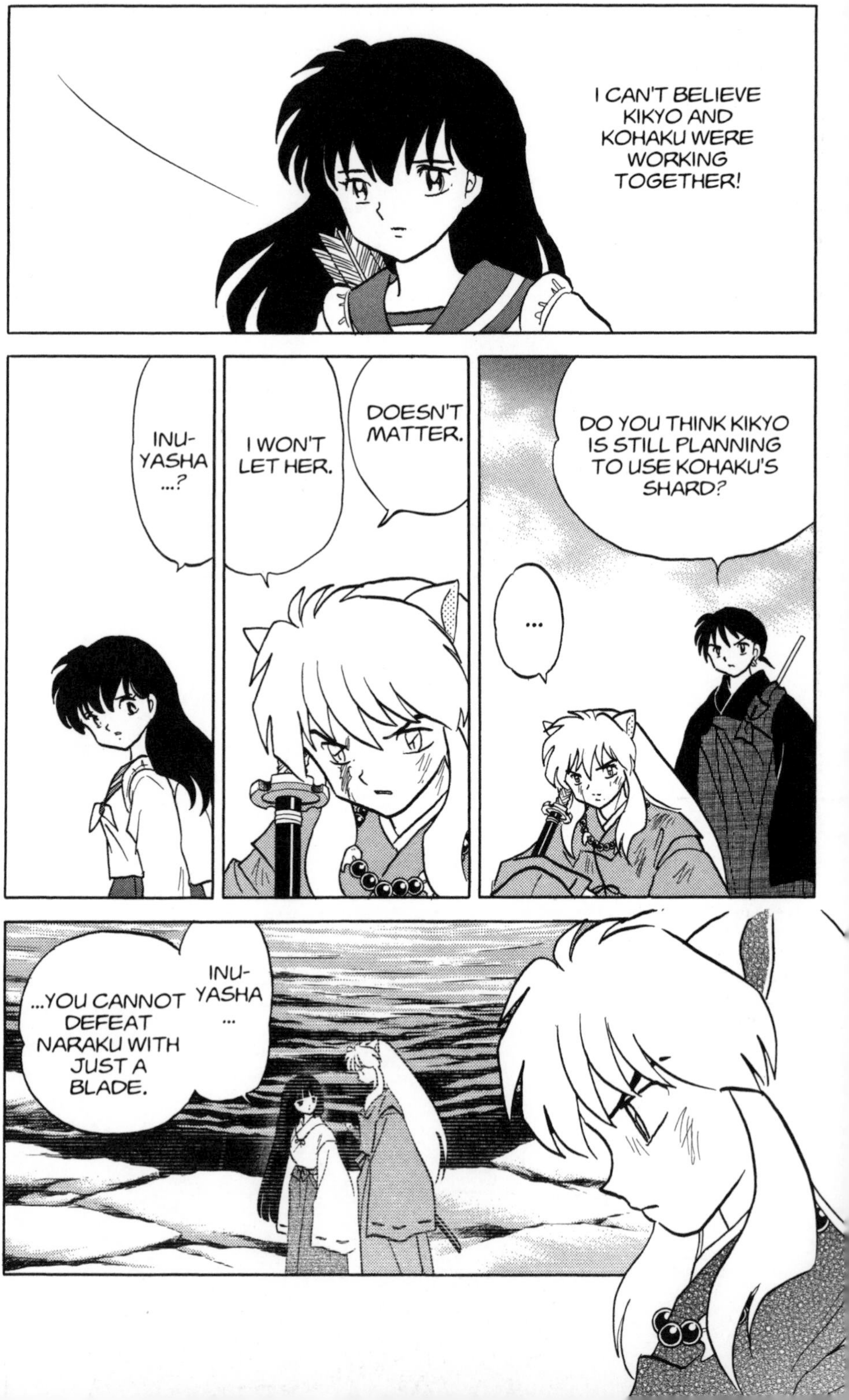
I CAN'T BELIEVE KIKYO AND KOHAKU WERE WORKING TOGETHER!
DO YOU THINK KIKYO IS STILL PLANNING TO USE KOHAKU'S SHARD?
...
DOESN'T MATTER.
I WON'T LET HER.
INU-YASHA ...?
INU-YASHA ...
...YOU CANNOT DEFEAT NARAKU WITH JUST A BLADE.

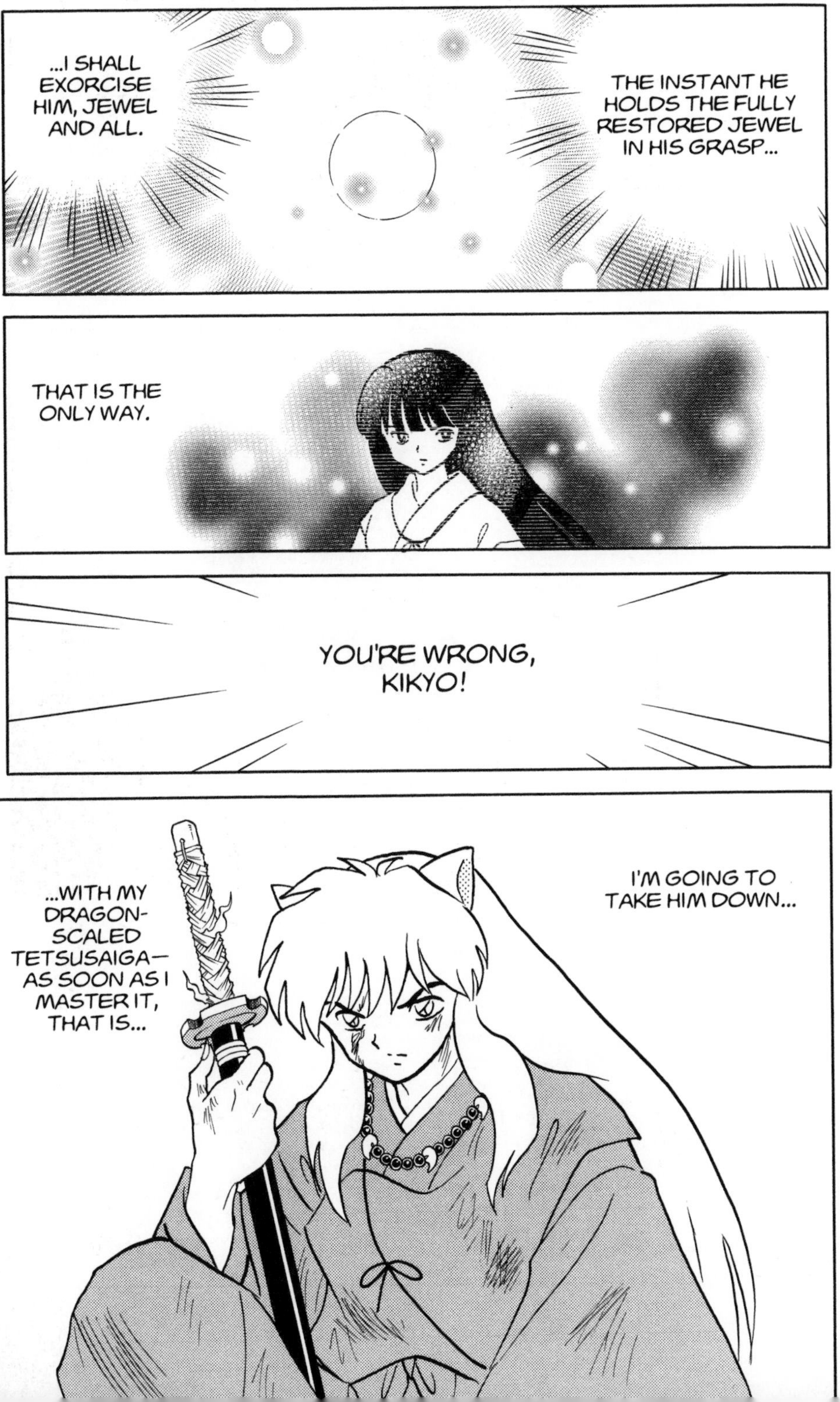
THE INSTANT HE HOLDS THE FULLY RESTORED JEWEL IN HIS GRASP...
...I SHALL EXORCISE HIM, JEWEL AND ALL.
THAT IS THE ONLY WAY.
YOU'RE WRONG, KIKYO!
I'M GOING TO TAKE HIM DOWN...
...WITH MY DRAGON-SCALED TETSUSAIGA—AS SOON AS I MASTER IT, THAT IS...

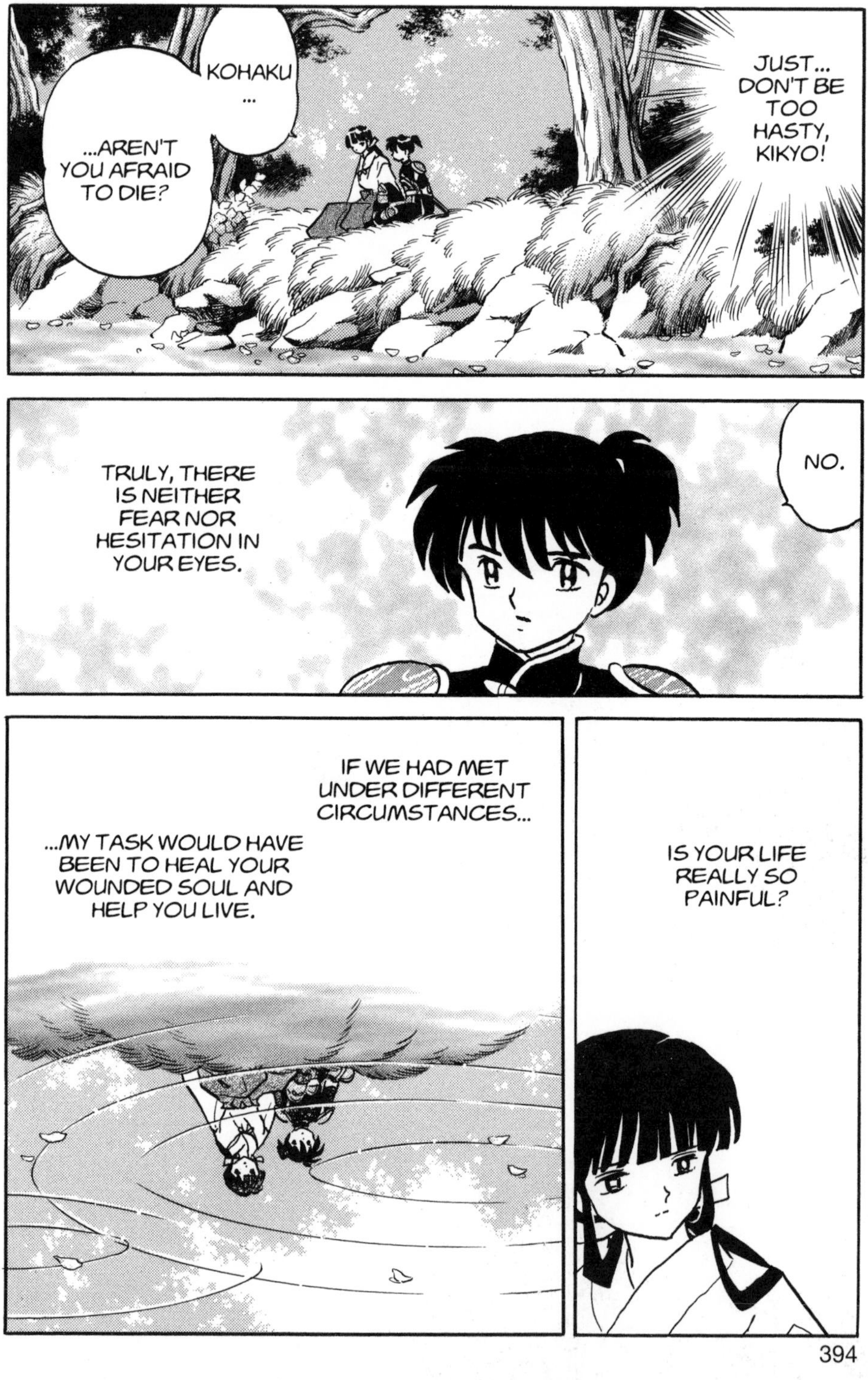
JUST... DON'T BE TOO HASTY, KIKYO!
KOHAKU ...
...AREN'T YOU AFRAID TO DIE?
NO.
TRULY, THERE IS NEITHER FEAR NOR HESITATION IN YOUR EYES.
IS YOUR LIFE REALLY SO PAINFUL?
IF WE HAD MET UNDER DIFFERENT CIRCUMSTANCES...
...MY TASK WOULD HAVE BEEN TO HEAL YOUR WOUNDED SOUL AND HELP YOU LIVE.

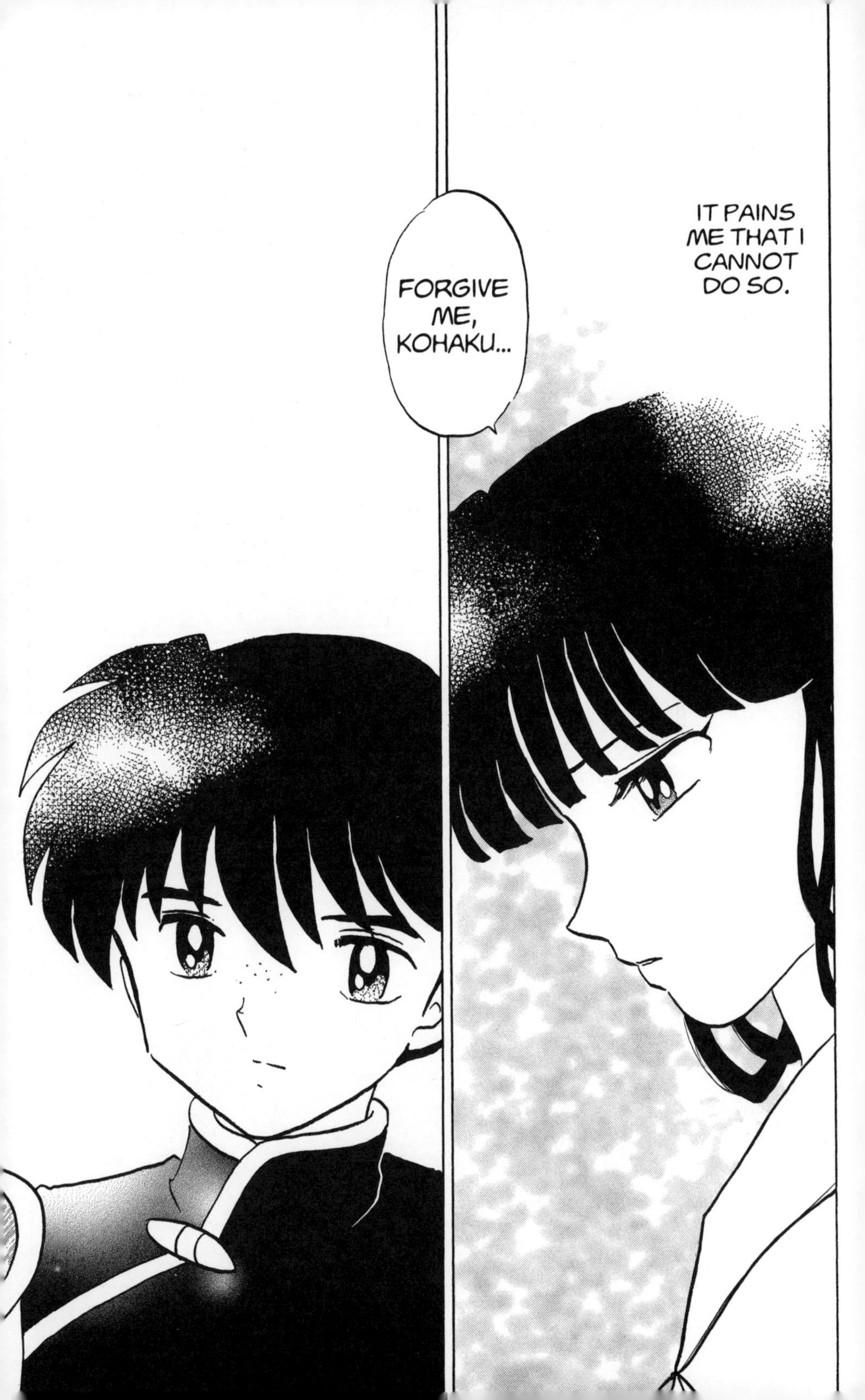
IT PAINS ME THAT I CANNOT DO SO.
FORGIVE ME, KOHAKU...

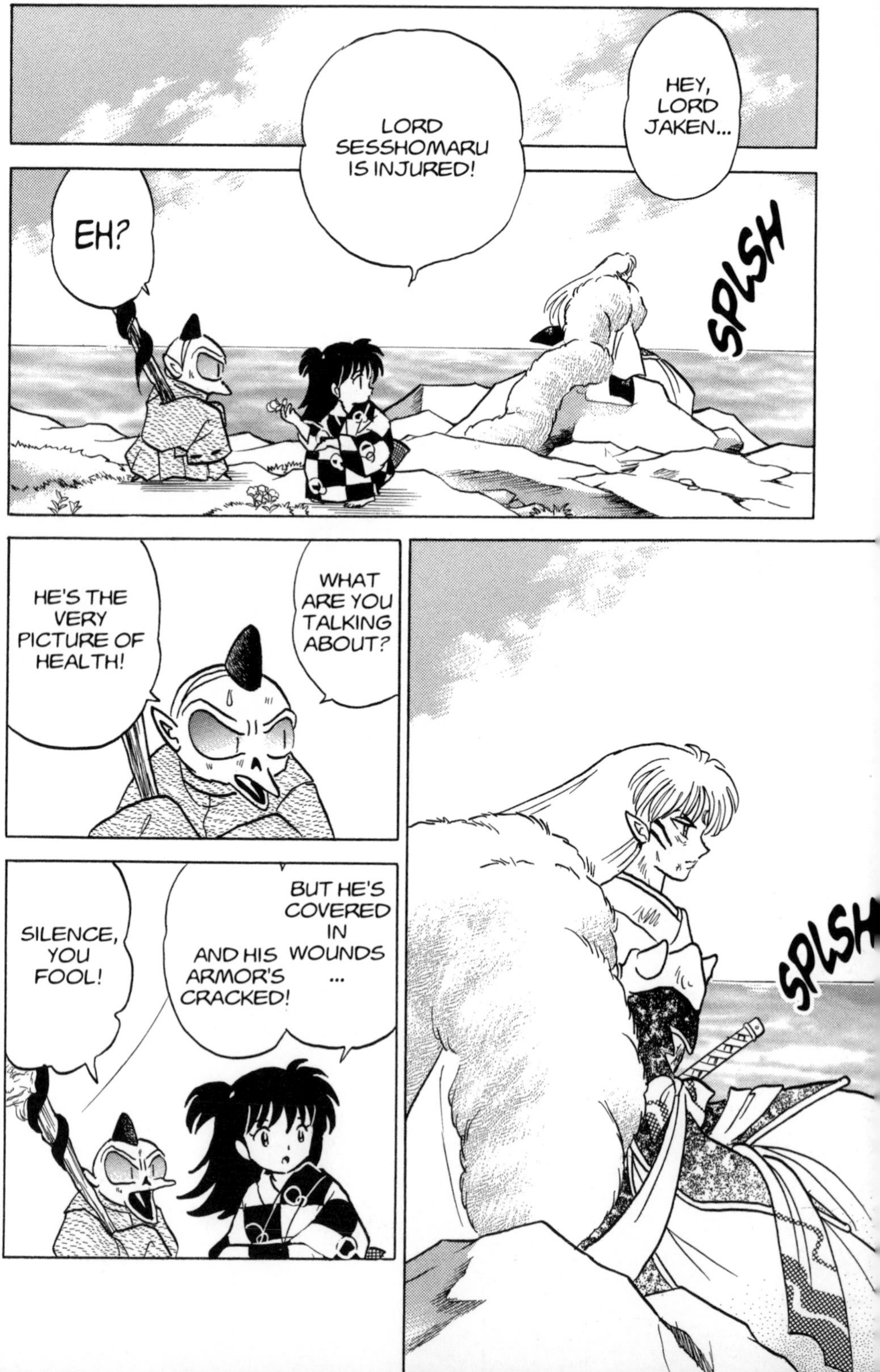
HEY, LORD JAKEN...
LORD SESSHOMARU IS INJURED!
SPLSH
EH?
SPLSH
WHAT ARE YOU TALKING ABOUT?
HE'S THE VERY PICTURE OF HEALTH!
BUT HE'S COVERED IN WOUNDS...
AND HIS ARMOR'S CRACKED!
SILENCE, YOU FOOL!

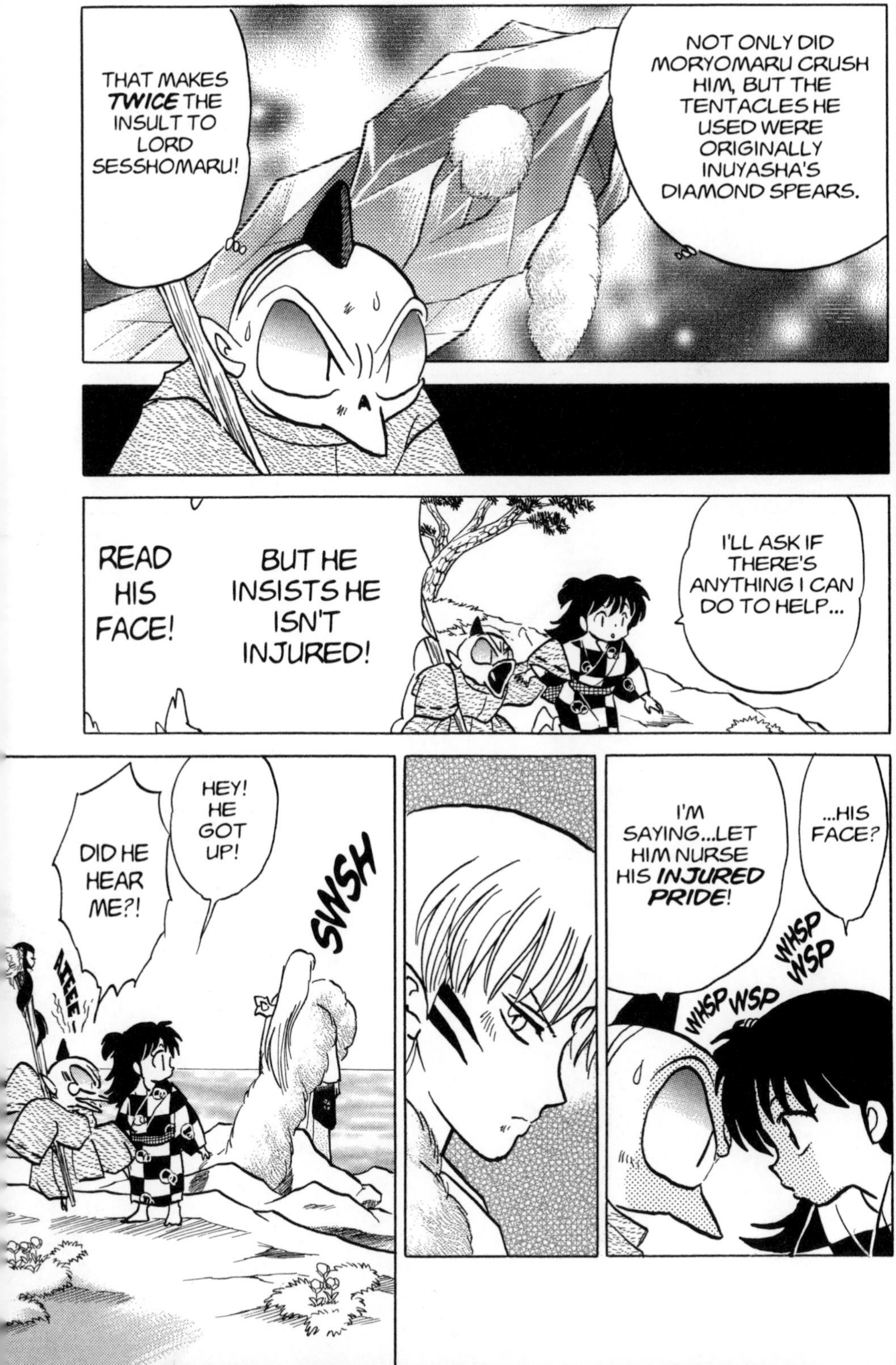
NOT ONLY DID MORYOMARU CRUSH HIM, BUT THE TENTACLES HE USED WERE ORIGINALLY INUYASHA'S DIAMOND SPEARS.
THAT MAKES **TWICE** THE INSULT TO LORD SESSHOMARU!
I'LL ASK IF THERE'S ANYTHING I CAN DO TO HELP...
BUT HE INSISTS HE ISN'T INJURED!
READ HIS FACE!
...HIS FACE?
I'M SAYING...LET HIM NURSE HIS **INJURED PRIDE**!
WHSP WSP
WHSP WSP
HEY! HE GOT UP!
DID HE HEAR ME?!
SWSH

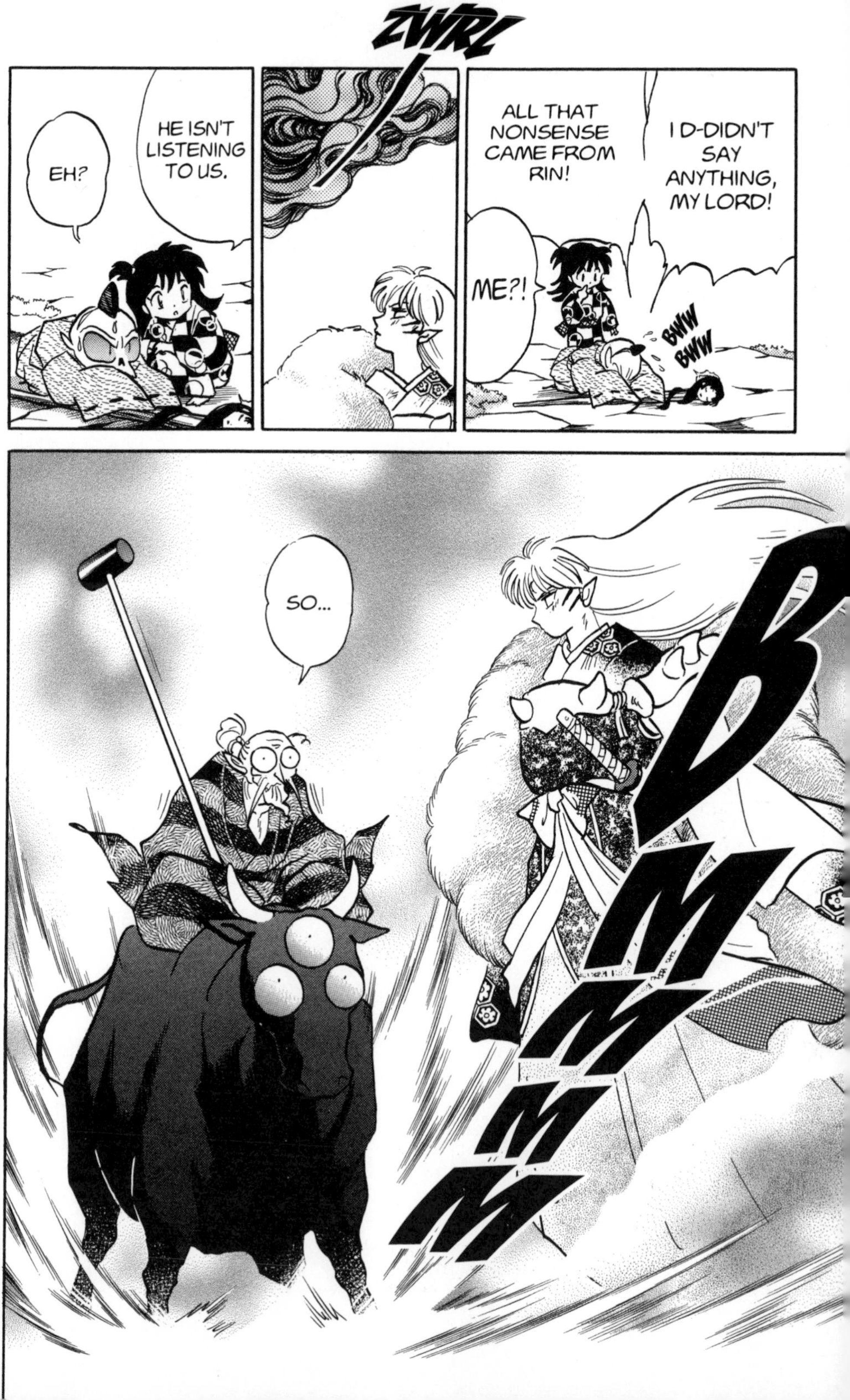
I D-DIDN'T SAY ANYTHING, MY LORD!
ALL THAT NONSENSE CAME FROM RIN!
ME?!
BWW BWW
ZWRL
HE ISN'T LISTENING TO US.
EH?
BMMMMM
SO...

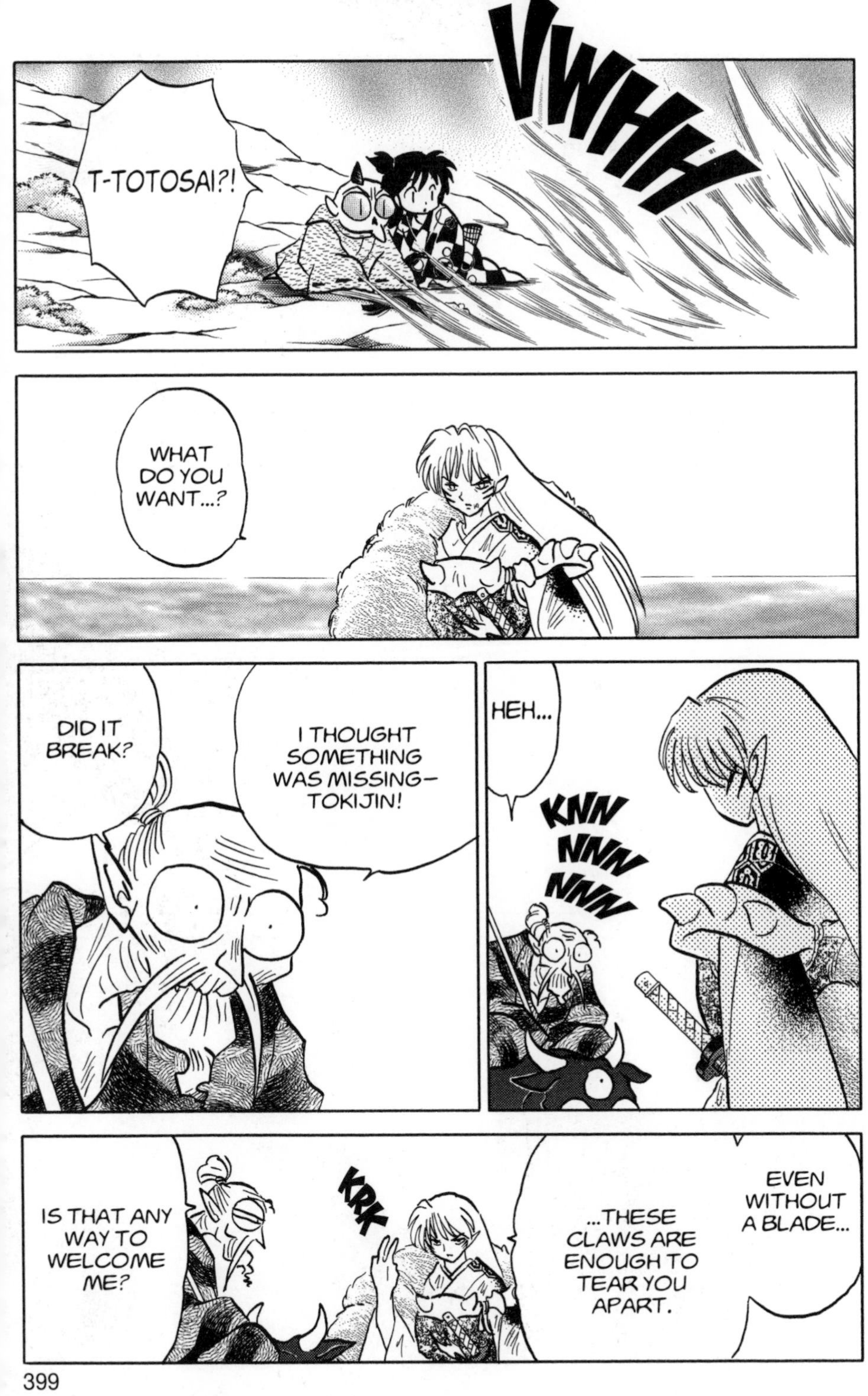
VWHH
T-TOTOSAI?!
WHAT DO YOU WANT...?
HEH...
KNNNNNNNN
I THOUGHT SOMETHING WAS MISSING—TOKIJIN!
DID IT BREAK?
EVEN WITHOUT A BLADE...
...THESE CLAWS ARE ENOUGH TO TEAR YOU APART.
KRK
IS THAT ANY WAY TO WELCOME ME?

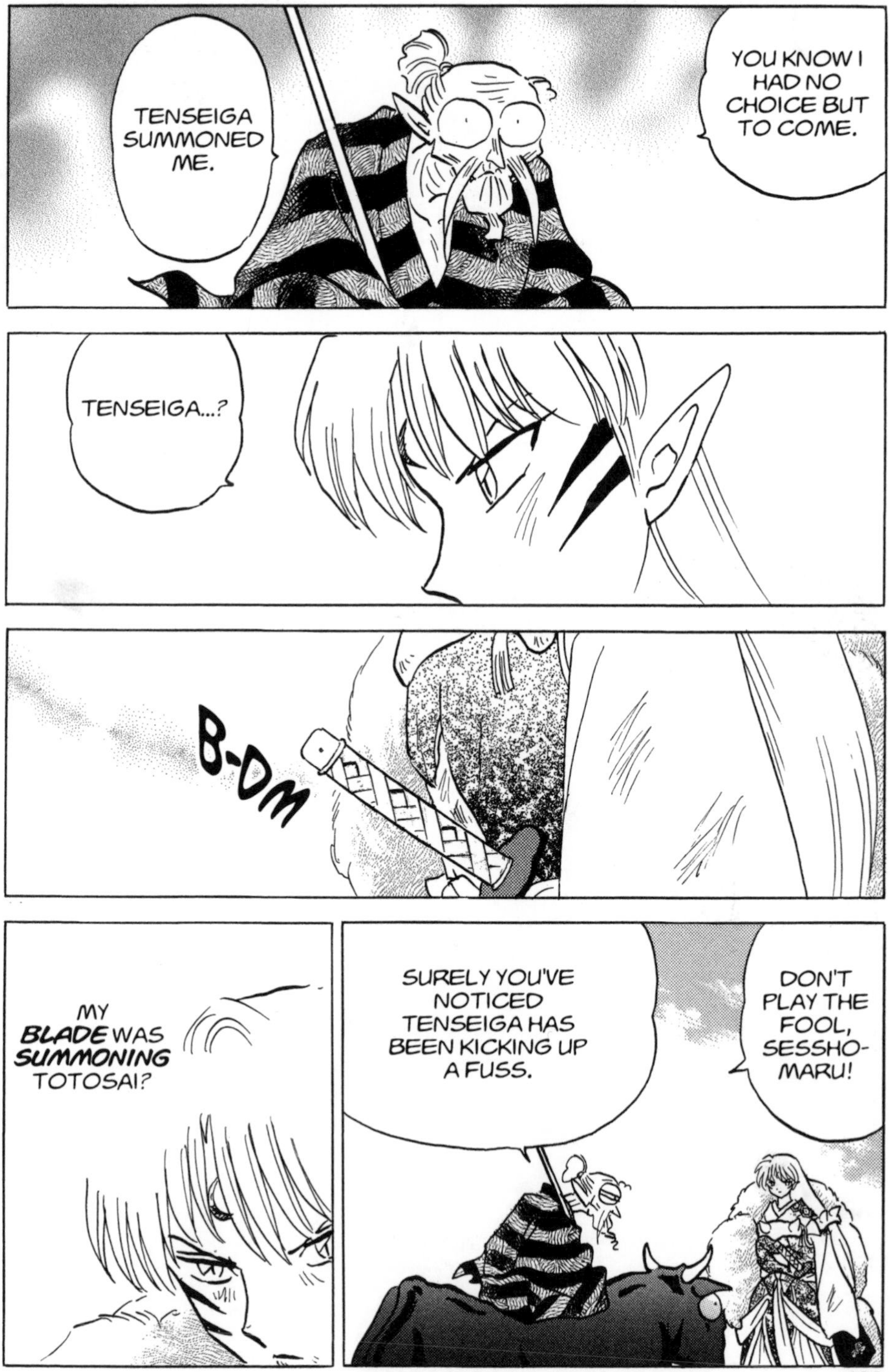
YOU KNOW I HAD NO CHOICE BUT TO COME.
TENSEIGA SUMMONED ME.
TENSEIGA...?
B-DM
DON'T PLAY THE FOOL, SESSHO-MARU!
SURELY YOU'VE NOTICED TENSEIGA HAS BEEN KICKING UP A FUSS.
MY **BLADE** WAS **SUMMONING** TOTOSAI?

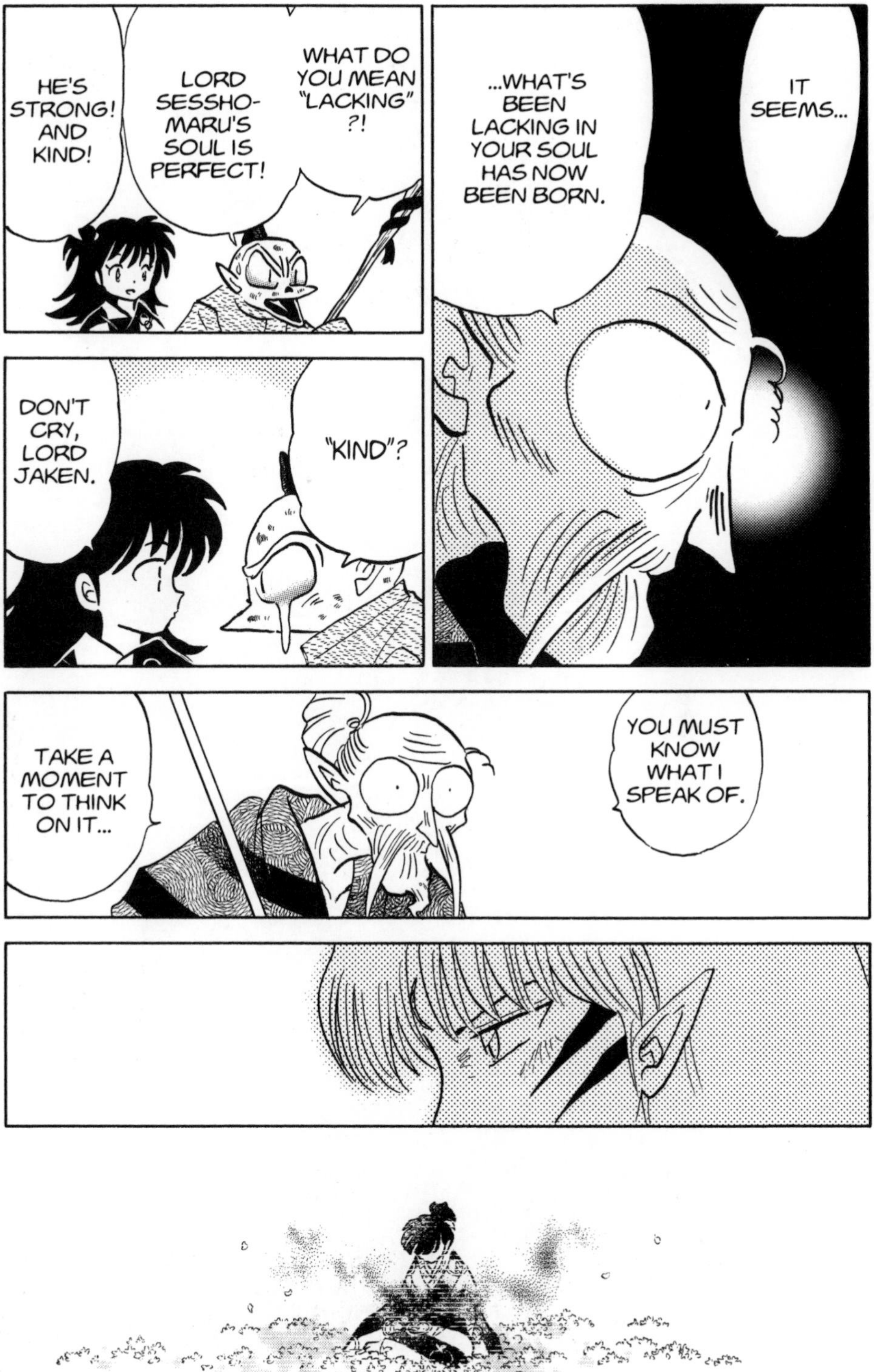
IT SEEMS...
...WHAT'S BEEN LACKING IN YOUR SOUL HAS NOW BEEN BORN.
WHAT DO YOU MEAN "LACKING"?!
LORD SESSHO-MARU'S SOUL IS PERFECT!
HE'S STRONG! AND KIND!
"KIND"?
DON'T CRY, LORD JAKEN.
YOU MUST KNOW WHAT I SPEAK OF.
TAKE A MOMENT TO THINK ON IT...

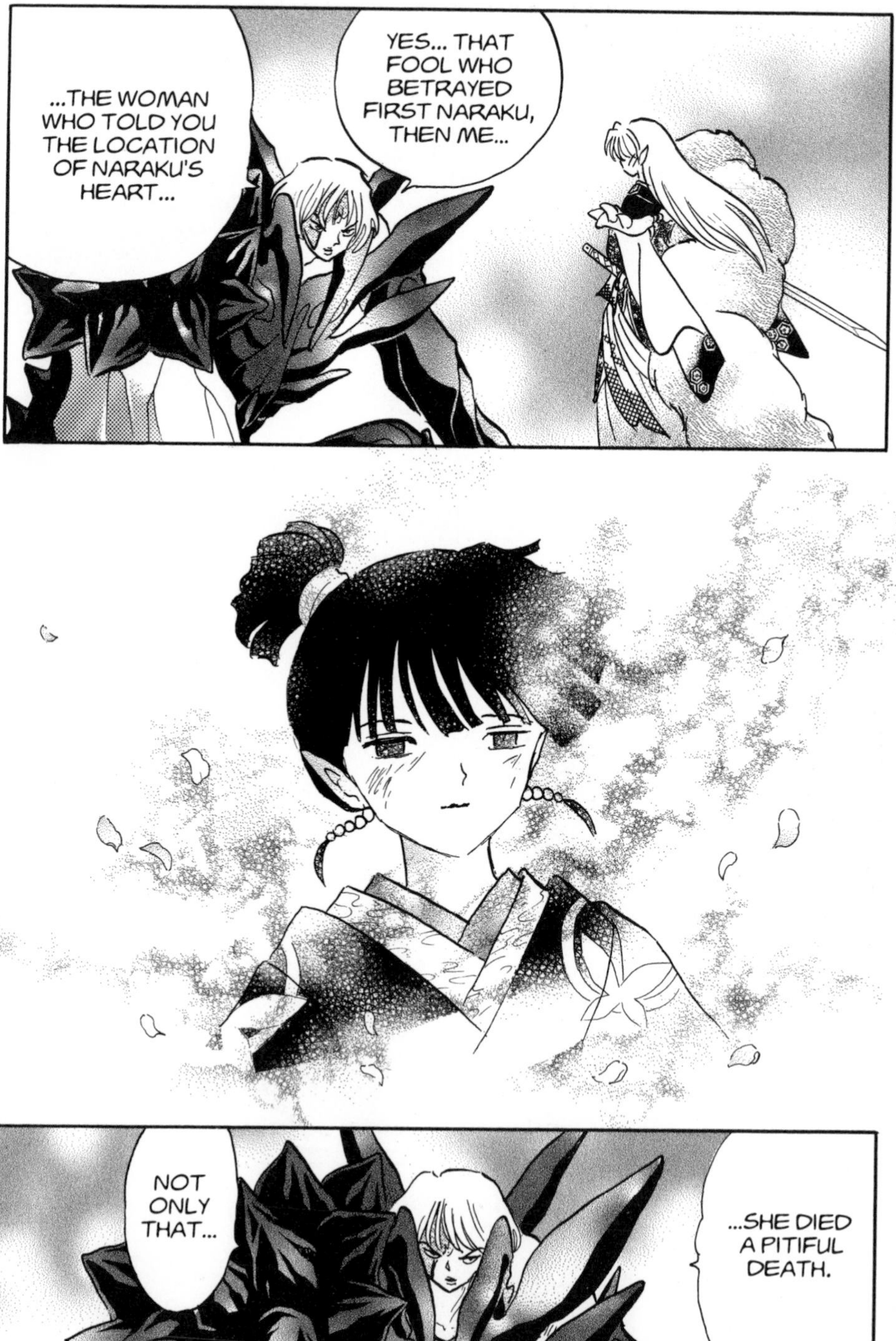
...THE WOMAN WHO TOLD YOU THE LOCATION OF NARAKU'S HEART...
YES... THAT FOOL WHO BETRAYED FIRST NARAKU, THEN ME...
NOT ONLY THAT...
...SHE DIED A PITIFUL DEATH.

...IT WAS COMPLETELY IN VAIN.

IT MUST HAVE BEEN **THEN** THAT...

WELL, I DON'T KNOW WHAT HAPPENED, BUT...

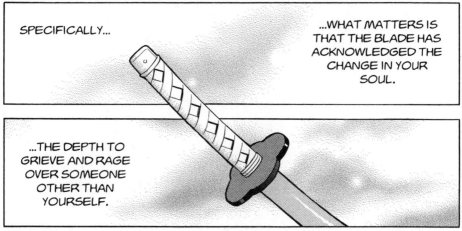

SPECIFICALLY...

...WHAT MATTERS IS THAT THE BLADE HAS ACKNOWLEDGED THE CHANGE IN YOUR SOUL.

...THE DEPTH TO GRIEVE AND RAGE OVER SOMEONE OTHER THAN YOURSELF.

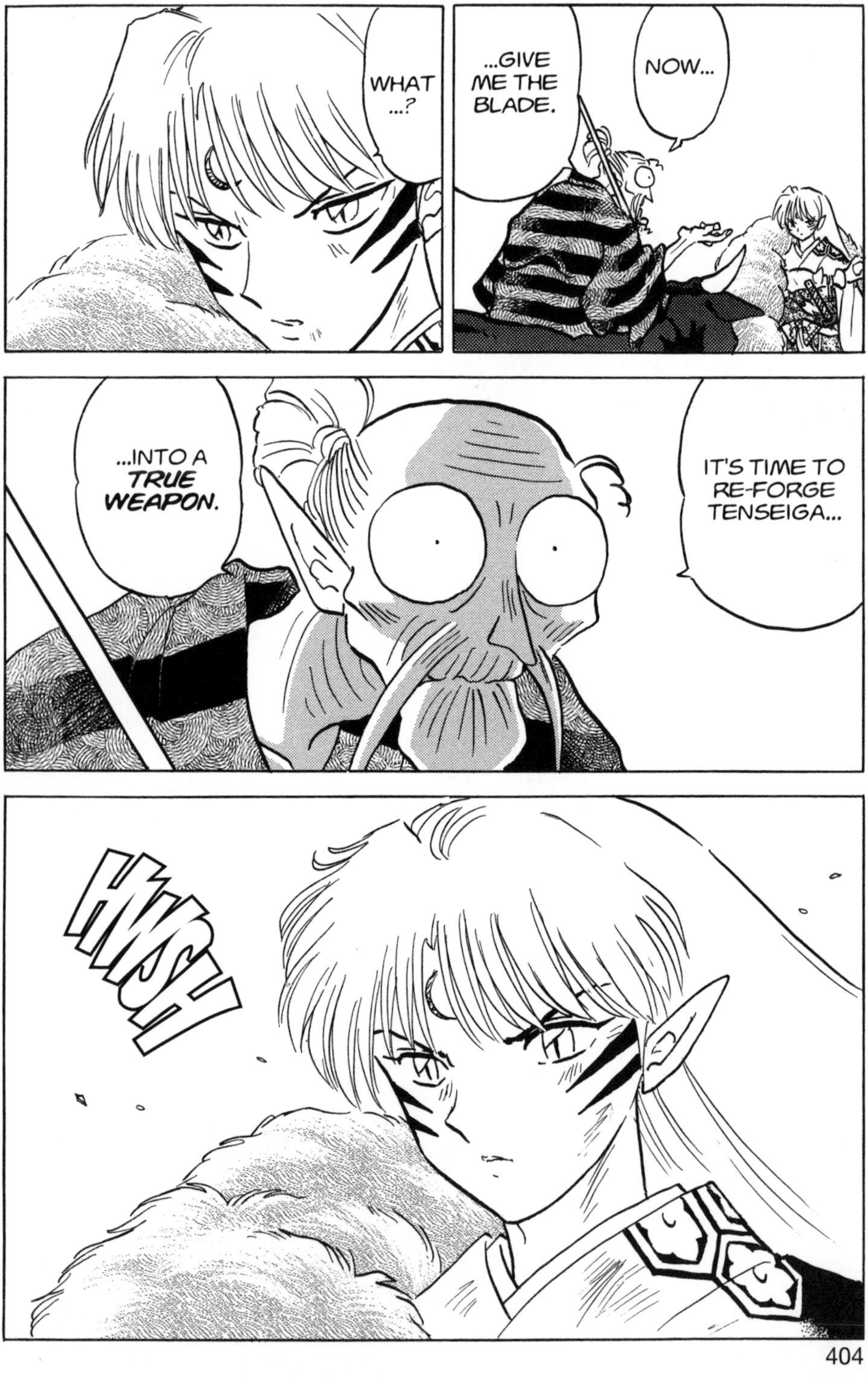
NOW...
...GIVE ME THE BLADE.
WHAT ...?
IT'S TIME TO RE-FORGE TENSEIGA...
...INTO A TRUE WEAPON.
HWSH!

SCROLL TWO

MEIDO ZANGETSUHA

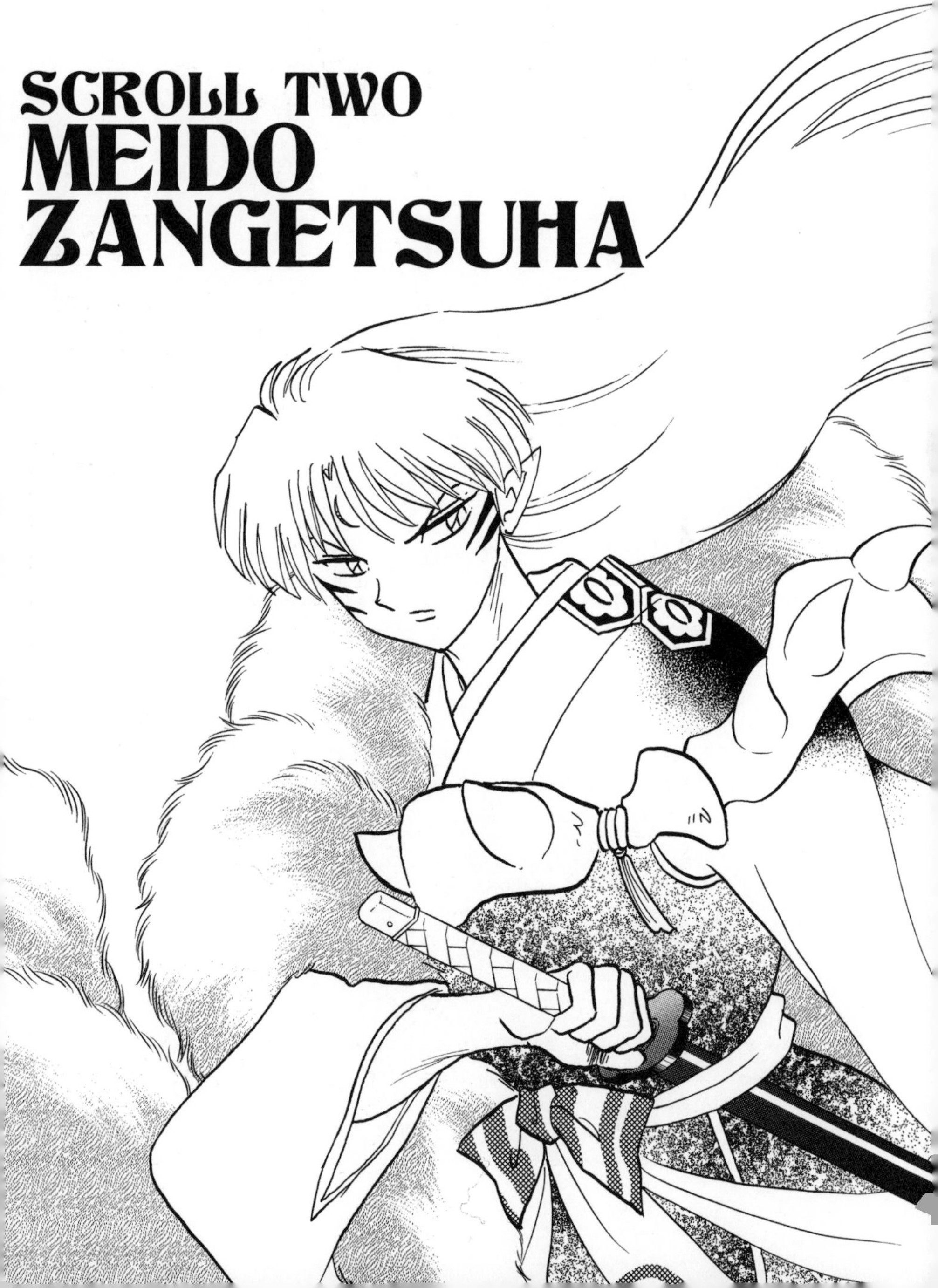

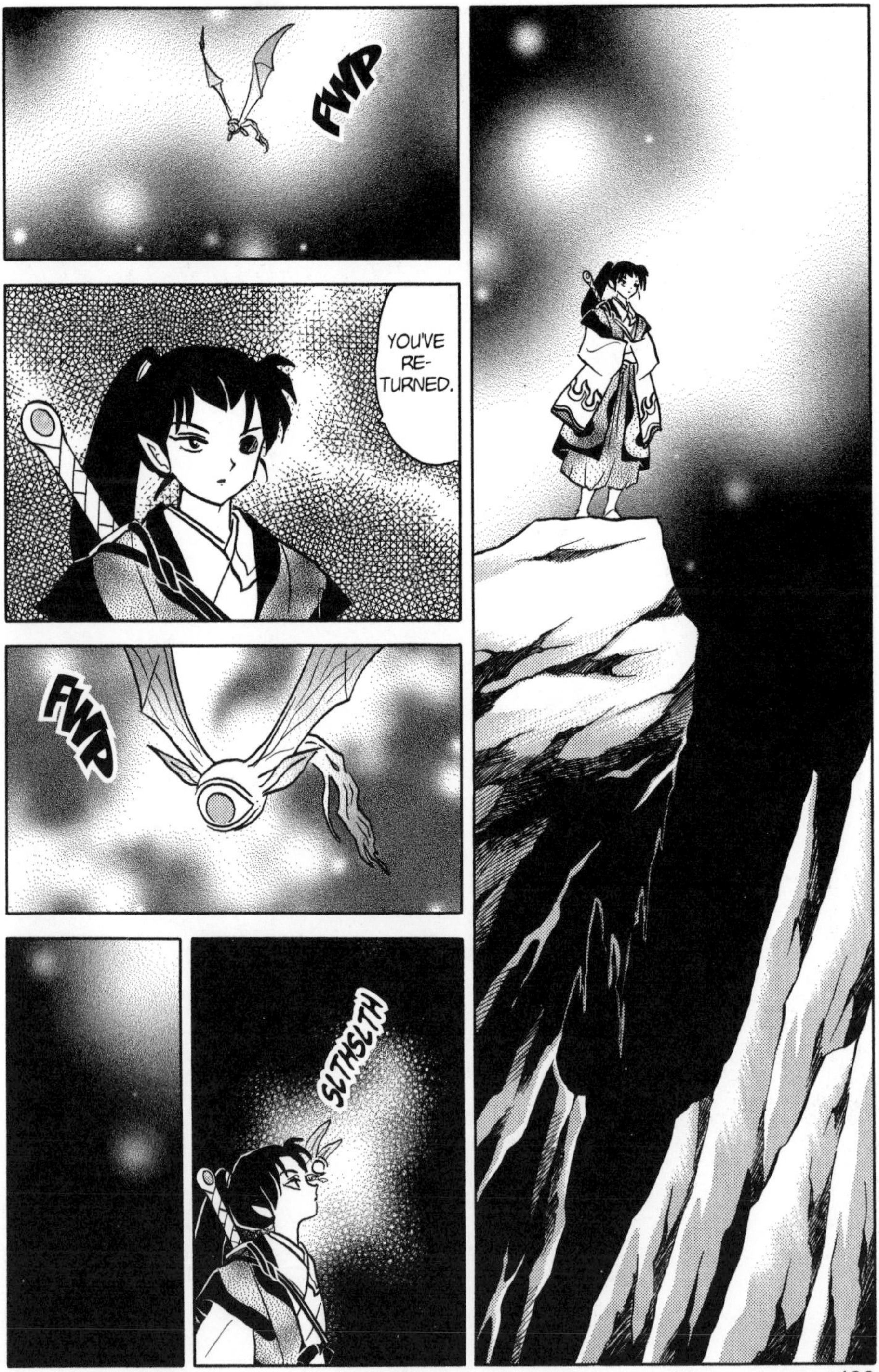
FWP
YOU'VE RETURNED.
FWP
SLTHSLTH

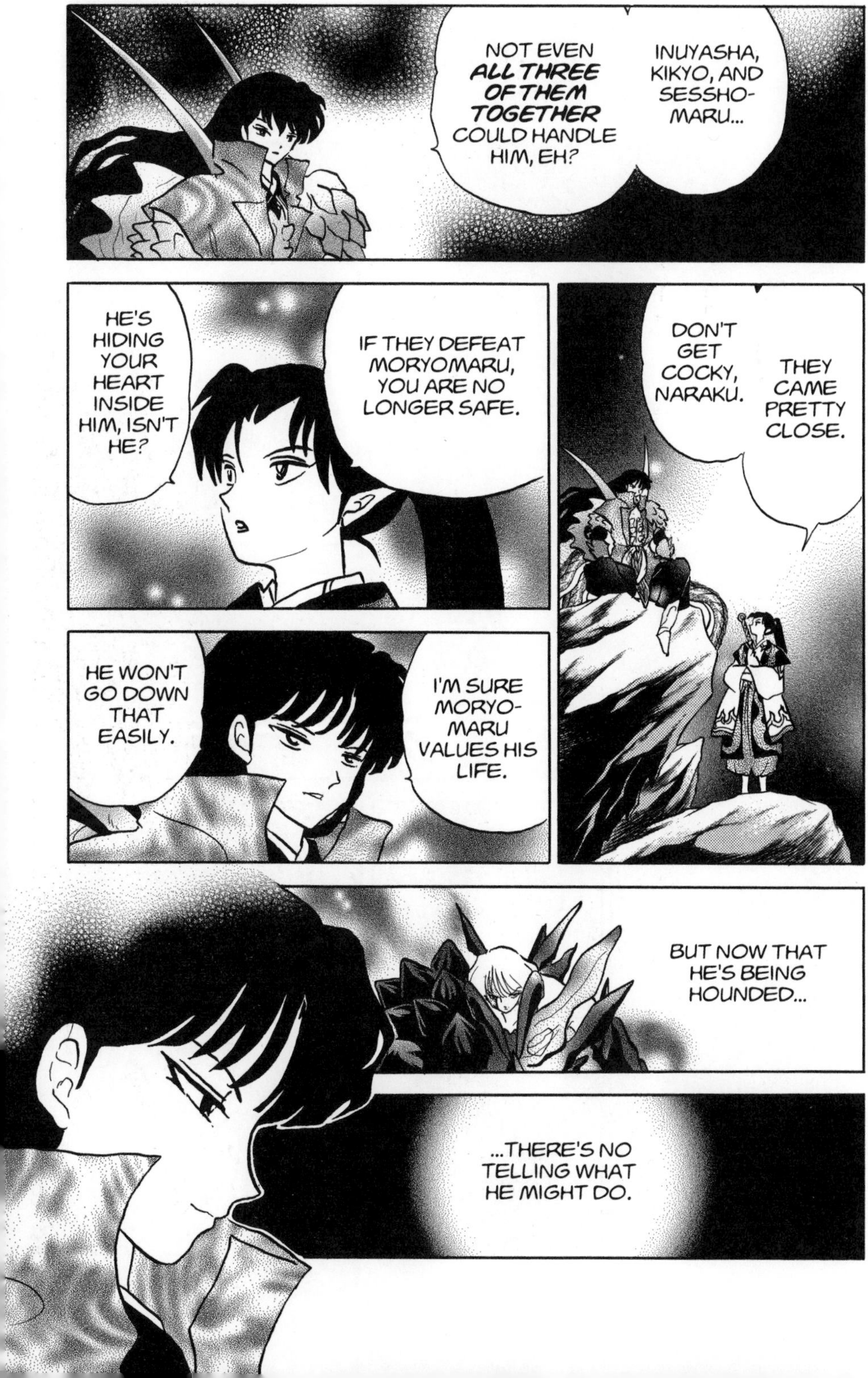
INUYASHA, KIKYO, AND SESSHOMARU...
NOT EVEN **ALL THREE OF THEM TOGETHER** COULD HANDLE HIM, EH?
THEY CAME PRETTY CLOSE.
DON'T GET COCKY, NARAKU.
IF THEY DEFEAT MORYOMARU, YOU ARE NO LONGER SAFE.
HE'S HIDING YOUR HEART INSIDE HIM, ISN'T HE?
I'M SURE MORYOMARU VALUES HIS LIFE.
HE WON'T GO DOWN THAT EASILY.
BUT NOW THAT HE'S BEING HOUNDED...
...THERE'S NO TELLING WHAT HE MIGHT DO.

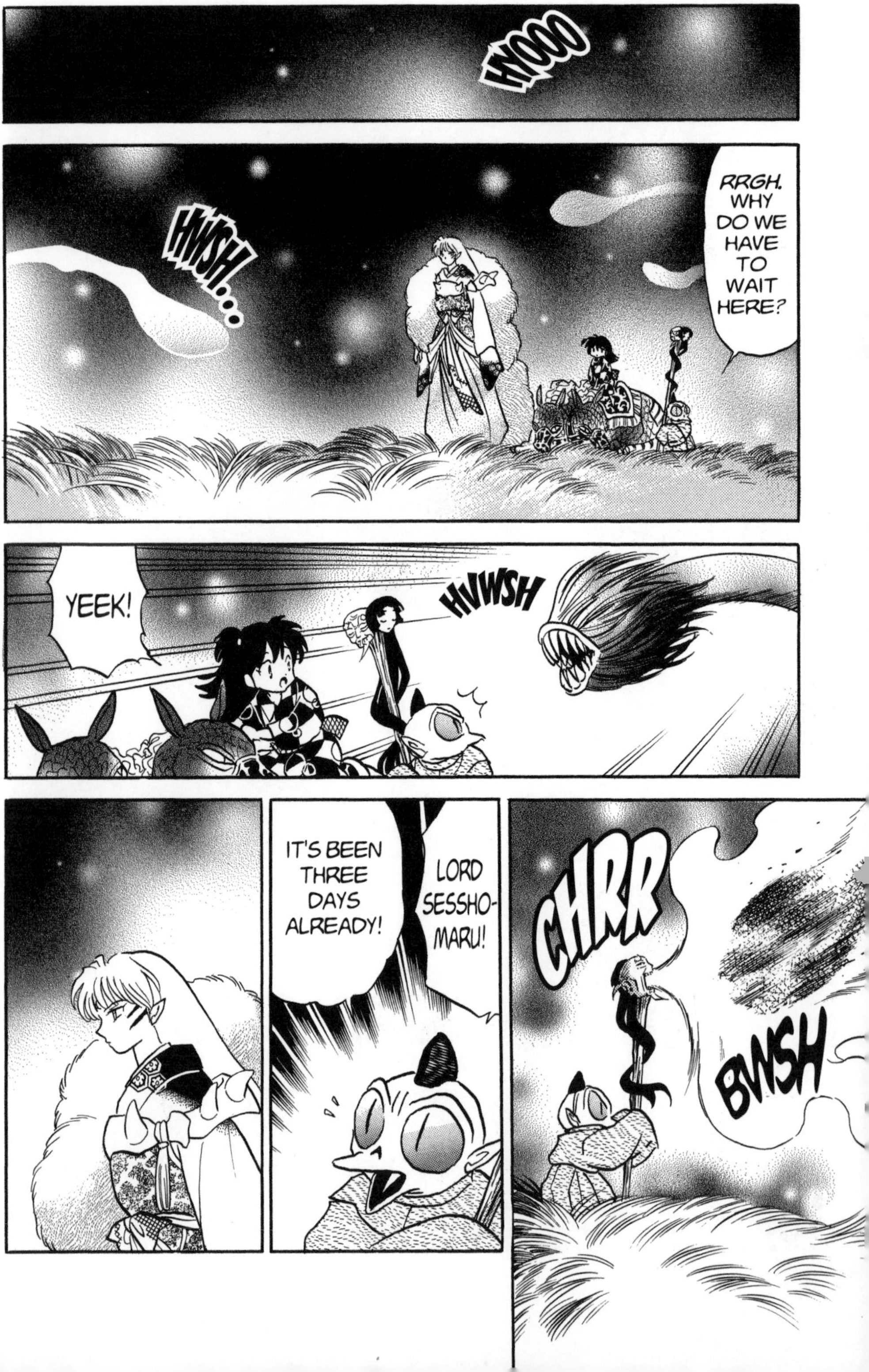
HYOOO
RRGH. WHY DO WE HAVE TO WAIT HERE?
HWSH...
HWWSH
YEEK!
CHRR
BWSH
LORD SESSHO-MARU!
IT'S BEEN THREE DAYS ALREADY!

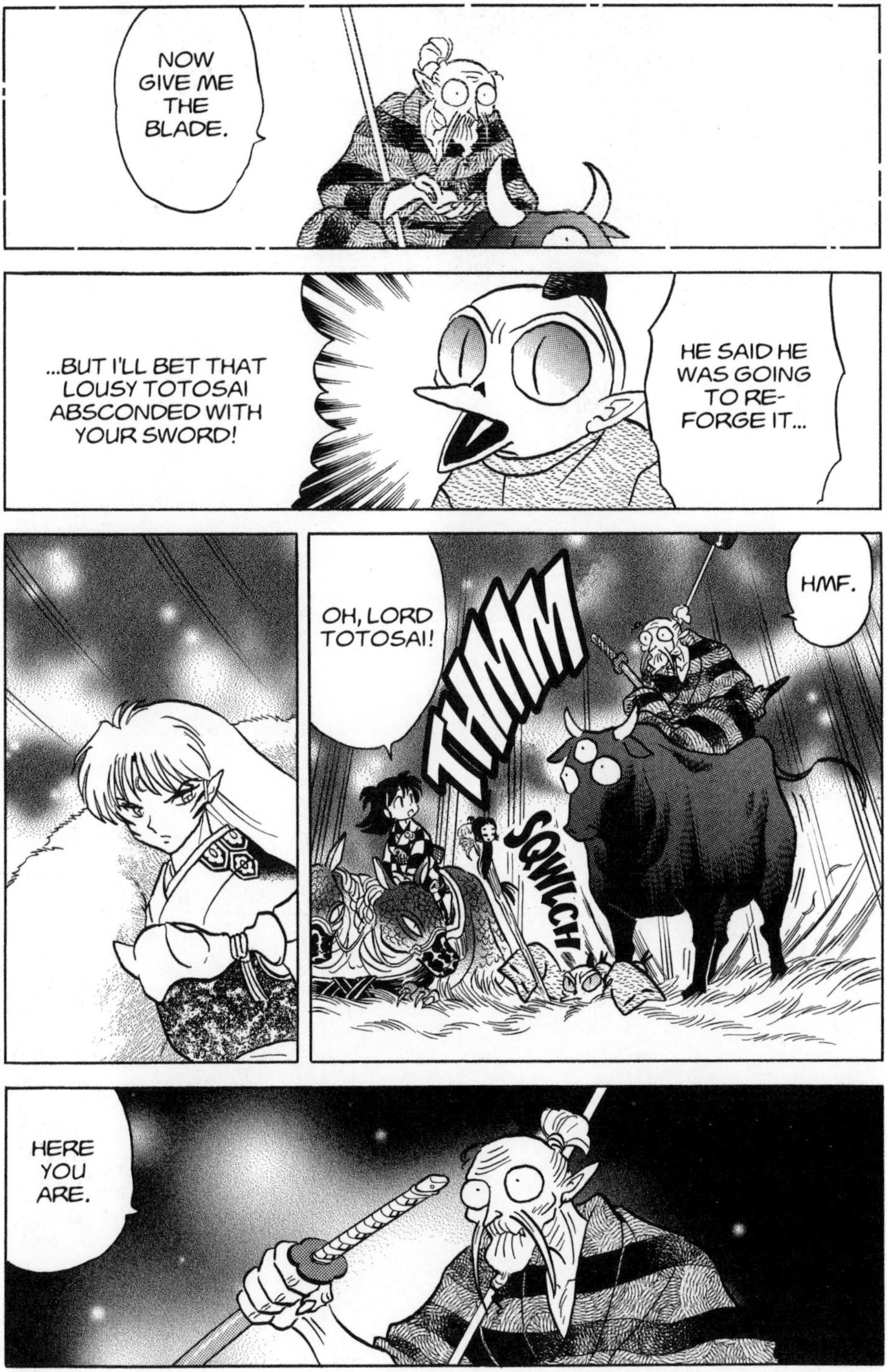
NOW GIVE ME THE BLADE.
HE SAID HE WAS GOING TO RE-FORGE IT...
...BUT I'LL BET THAT LOUSY TOTOSAI ABSCONDED WITH YOUR SWORD!
HMF.
THMM
OH, LORD TOTOSAI!
SQWLCH
HERE YOU ARE.

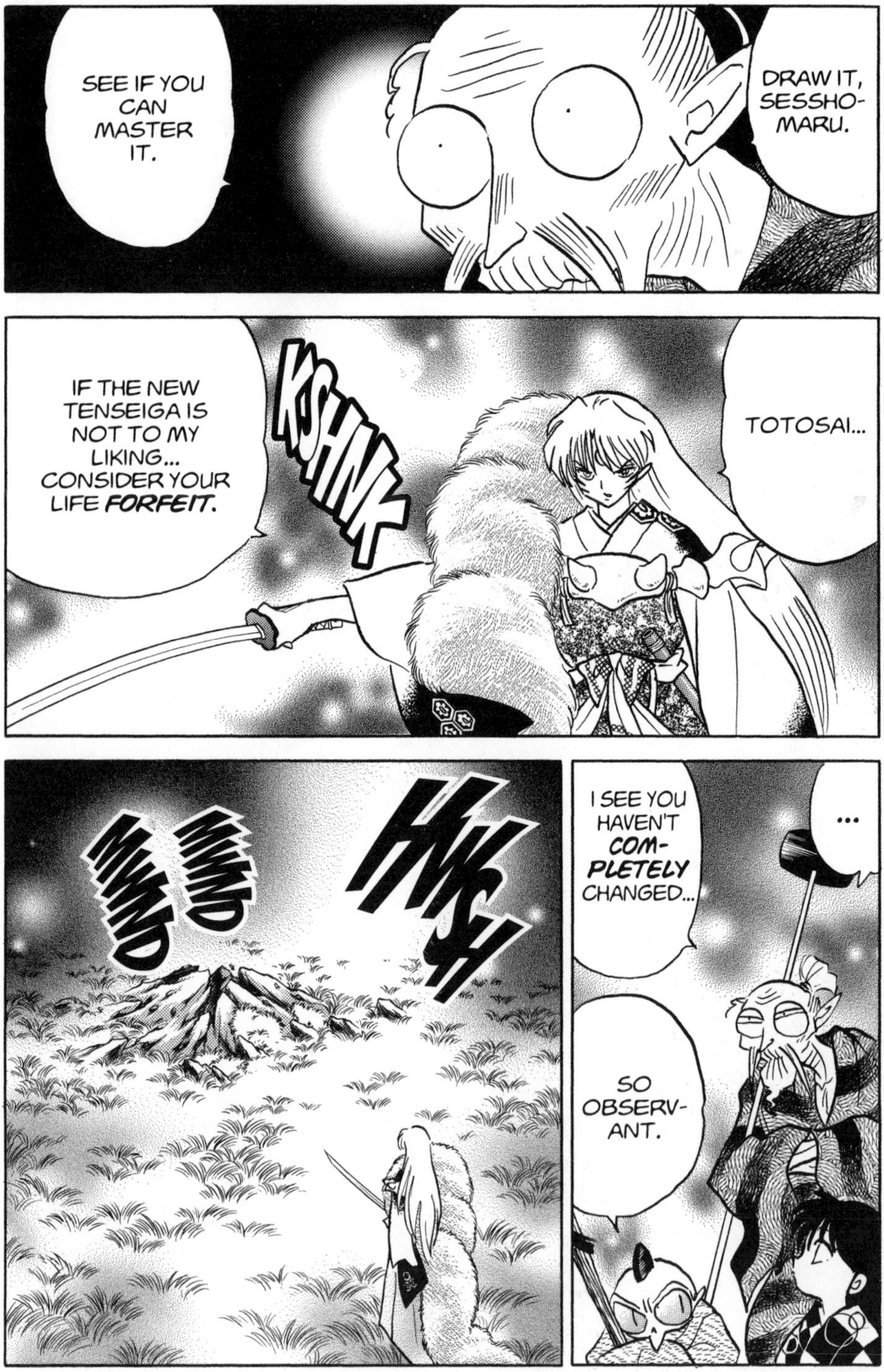
DRAW IT, SESSHO-MARU.
SEE IF YOU CAN MASTER IT.
TOTOSAI...
KSHINK
IF THE NEW TENSEIGA IS NOT TO MY LIKING... CONSIDER YOUR LIFE *FORFEIT*.
...
I SEE YOU HAVEN'T ***COM-PLETELY*** CHANGED...
SO OBSERV-ANT.
HWSH
MWWND
MWWND

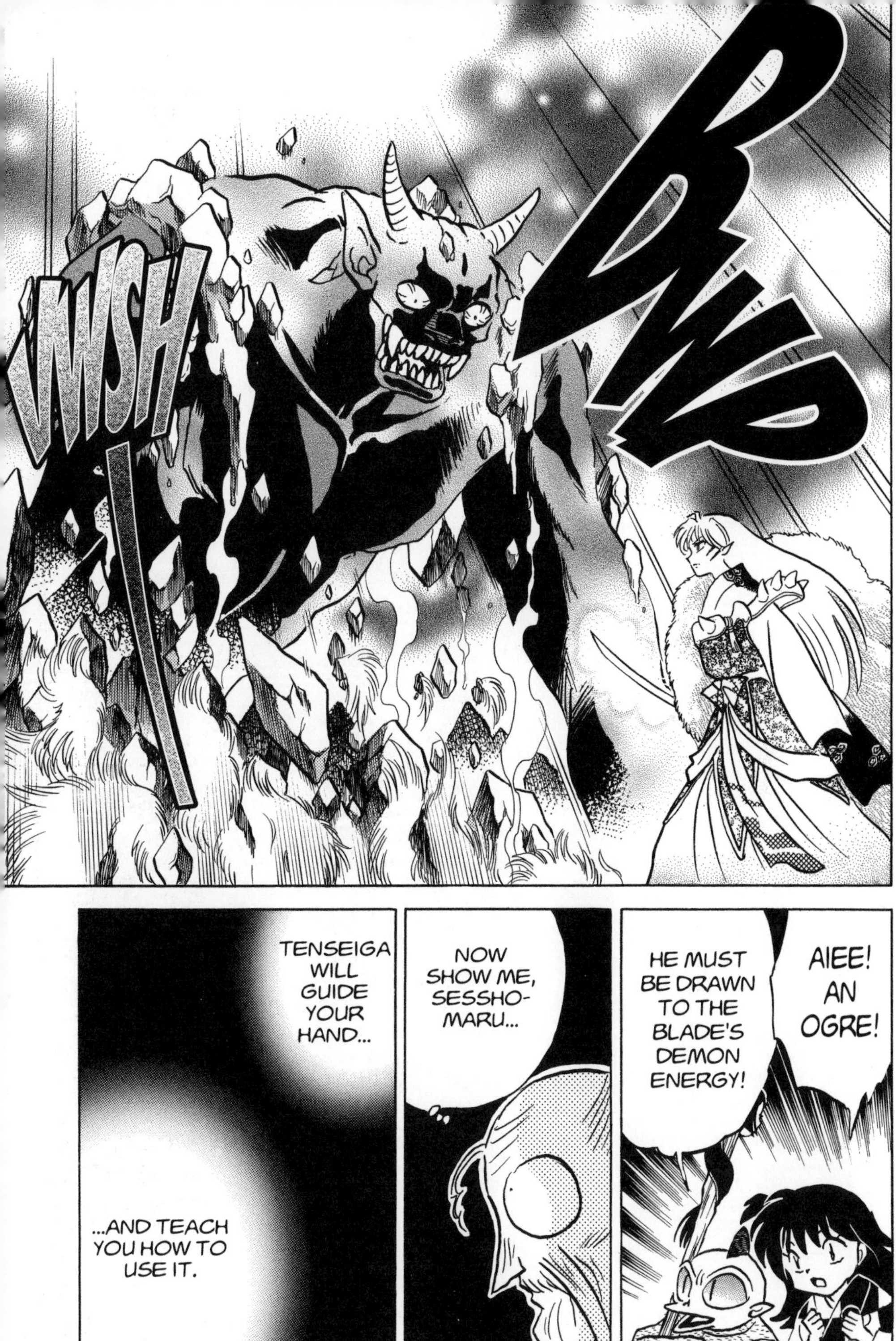
VWISH
AIEE! AN OGRE!
HE MUST BE DRAWN TO THE BLADE'S DEMON ENERGY!
NOW SHOW ME, SESSHO-MARU...
TENSEIGA WILL GUIDE YOUR HAND...
...AND TEACH YOU HOW TO USE IT.

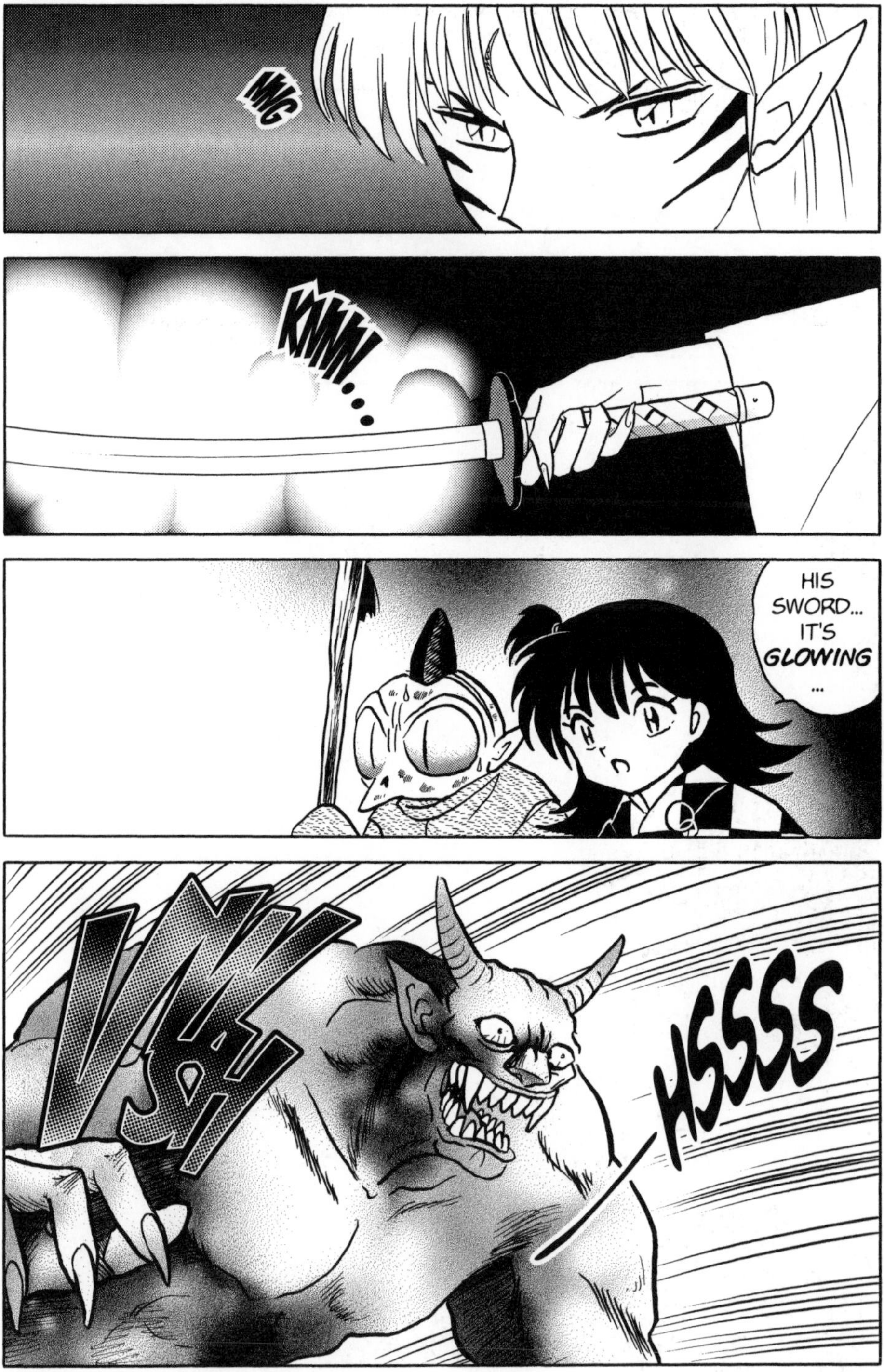
NNG
KNNN...
HIS SWORD... IT'S GLOWING ...
VSSH
HSSSS

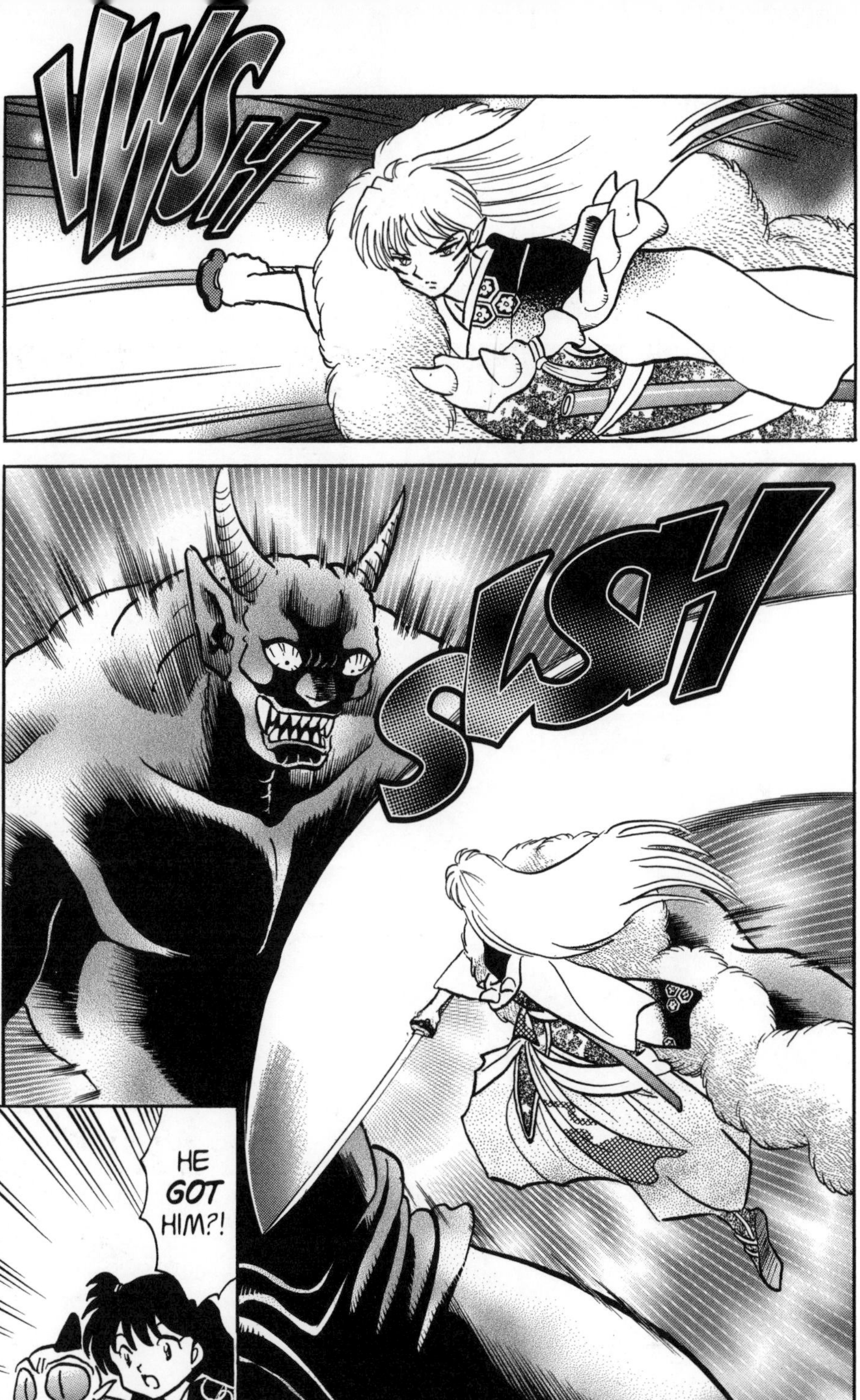
VWSH
SLSH
HE GOT HIM?!

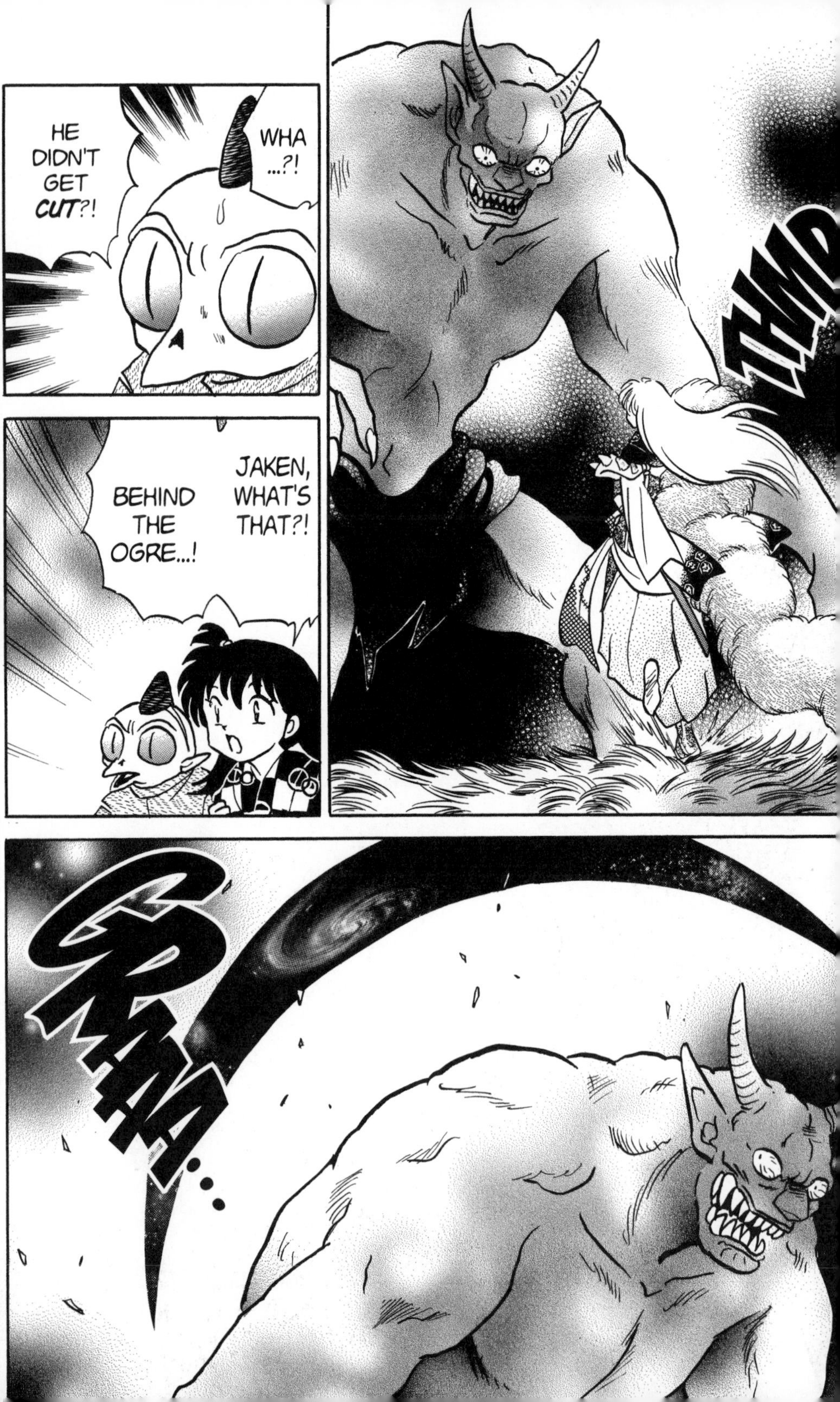
THMP
WHA ...?!
HE DIDN'T GET CUT?!
JAKEN, WHAT'S THAT?!
BEHIND THE OGRE...!

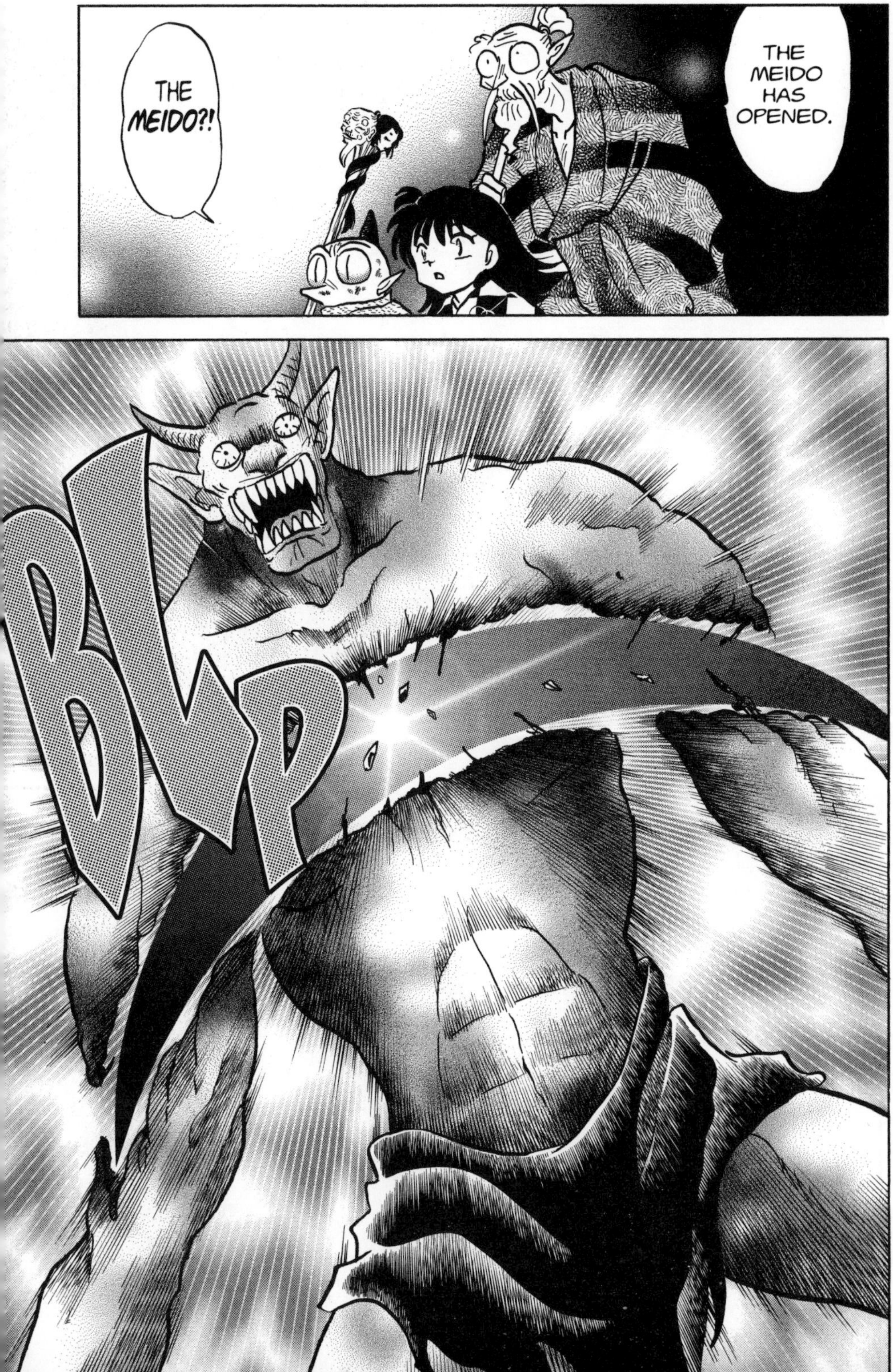
THE MEIDO HAS OPENED.
THE *MEIDO?!*
BLUP

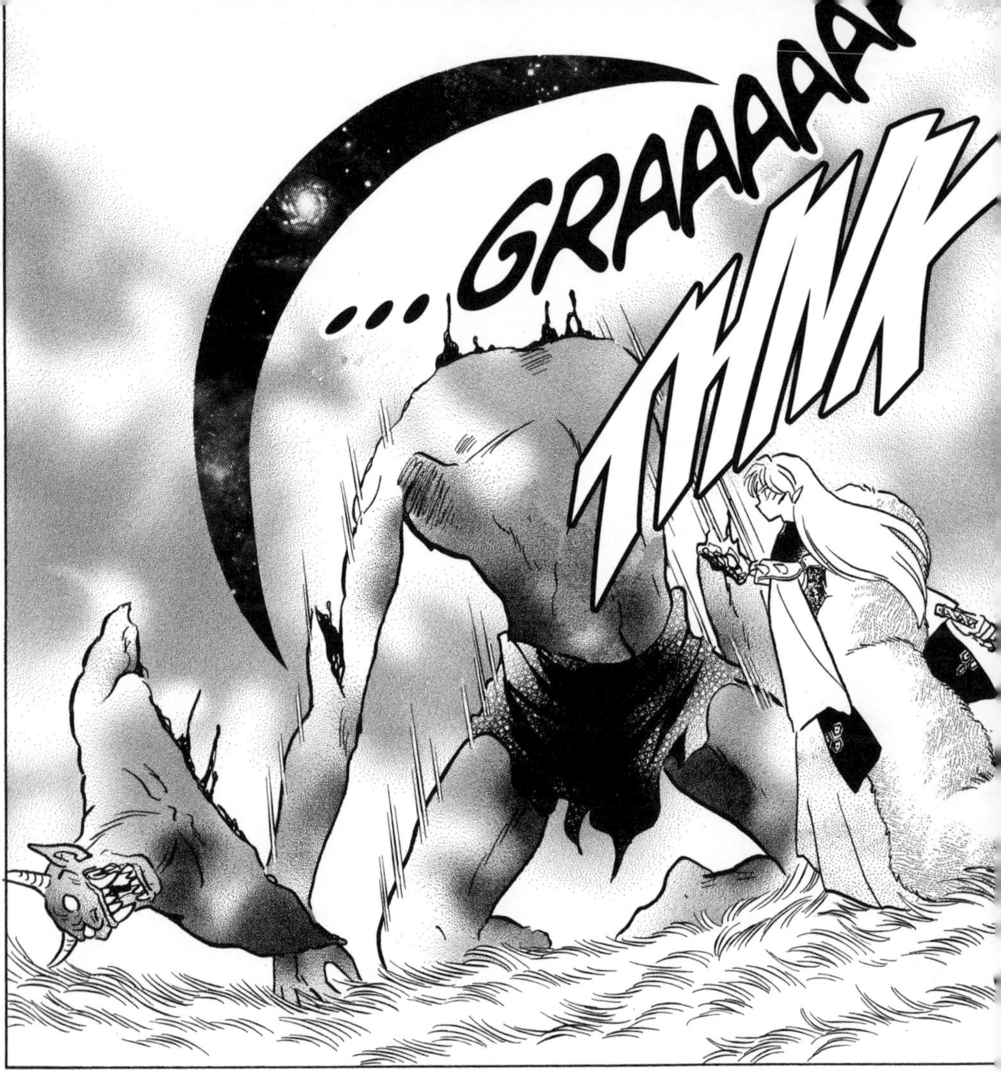
...GRAAAAA
THNK
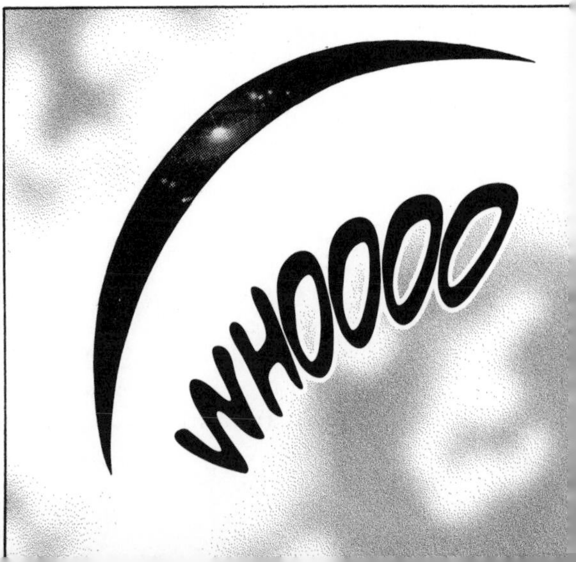
WHOOOO
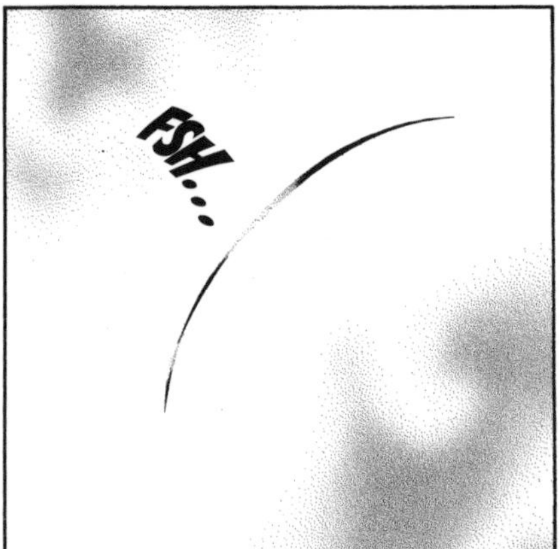
FSH...

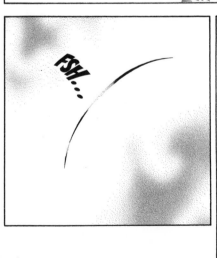

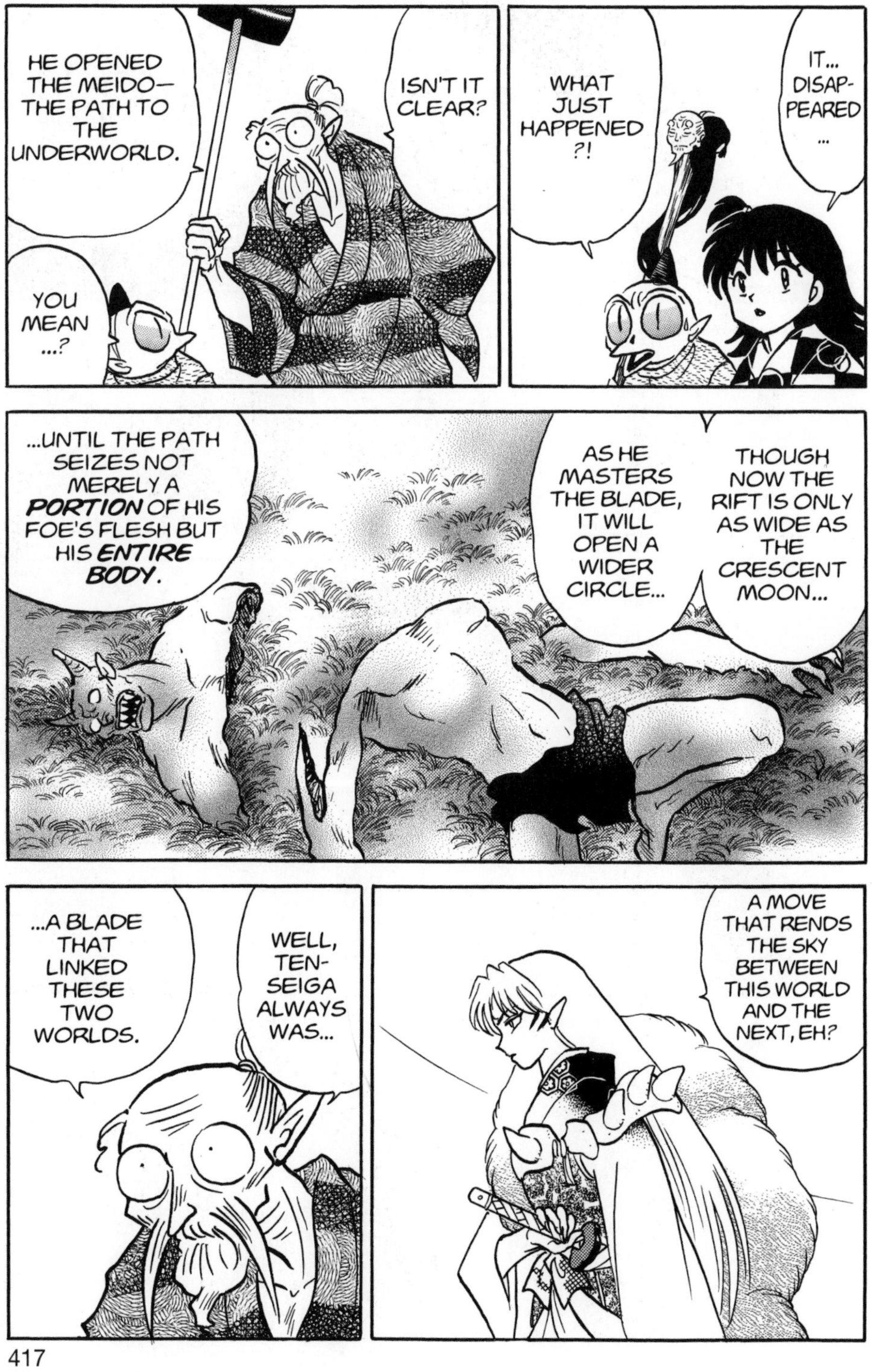
IT... DISAPPEARED...
WHAT JUST HAPPENED?!
ISN'T IT CLEAR?
HE OPENED THE MEIDO—THE PATH TO THE UNDERWORLD.
YOU MEAN...?
THOUGH NOW THE RIFT IS ONLY AS WIDE AS THE CRESCENT MOON...
AS HE MASTERS THE BLADE, IT WILL OPEN A WIDER CIRCLE...
...UNTIL THE PATH SEIZES NOT MERELY A PORTION OF HIS FOE'S FLESH BUT HIS ENTIRE BODY.
A MOVE THAT RENDS THE SKY BETWEEN THIS WORLD AND THE NEXT, EH?
WELL, TENSEIGA ALWAYS WAS...
...A BLADE THAT LINKED THESE TWO WORLDS.

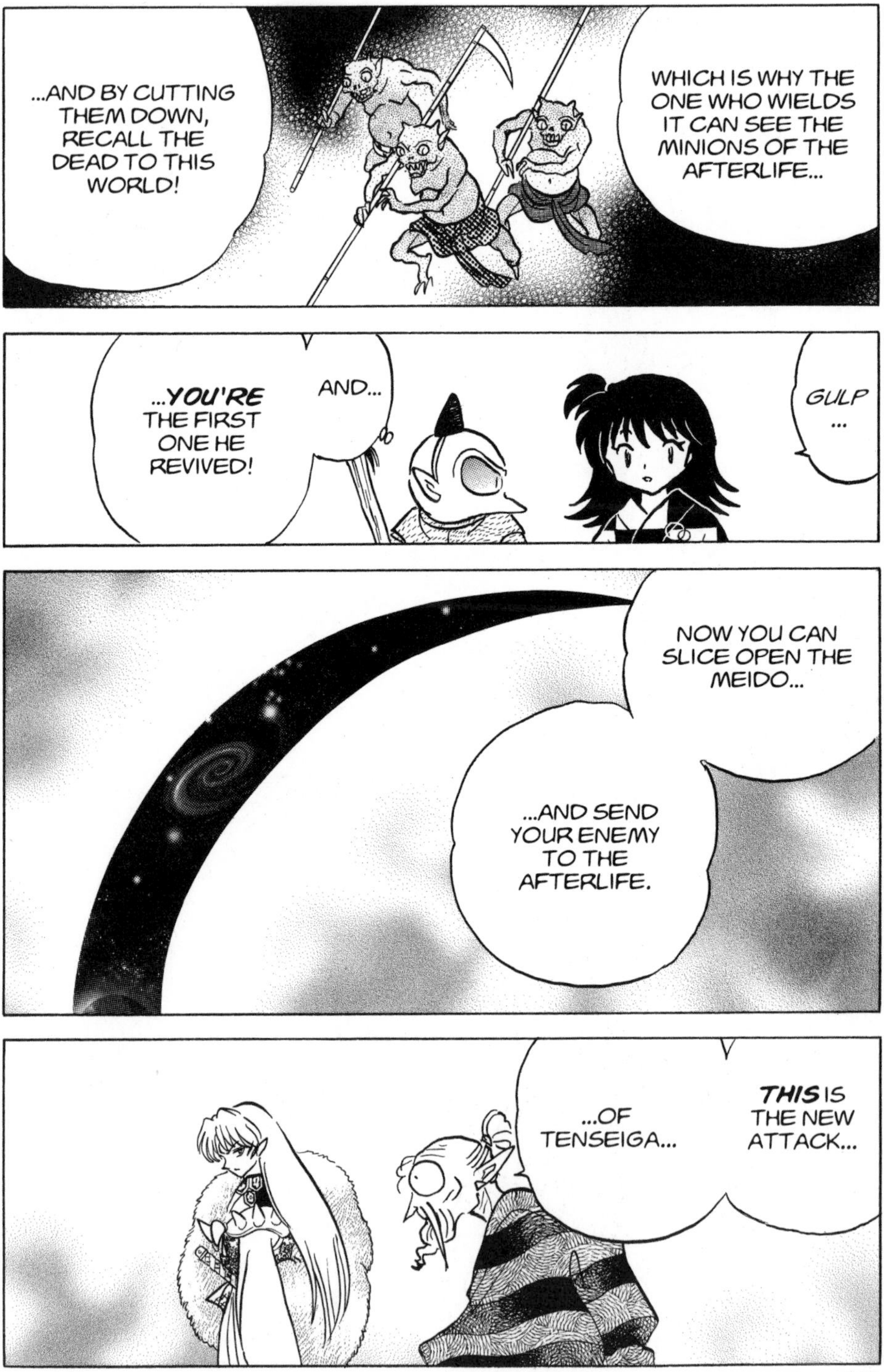
WHICH IS WHY THE ONE WHO WIELDS IT CAN SEE THE MINIONS OF THE AFTERLIFE...
...AND BY CUTTING THEM DOWN, RECALL THE DEAD TO THIS WORLD!
GULP ...
AND...
...*YOU'RE* THE FIRST ONE HE REVIVED!
NOW YOU CAN SLICE OPEN THE MEIDO...
...AND SEND YOUR ENEMY TO THE AFTERLIFE.
THIS IS THE NEW ATTACK...
...OF TENSEIGA...

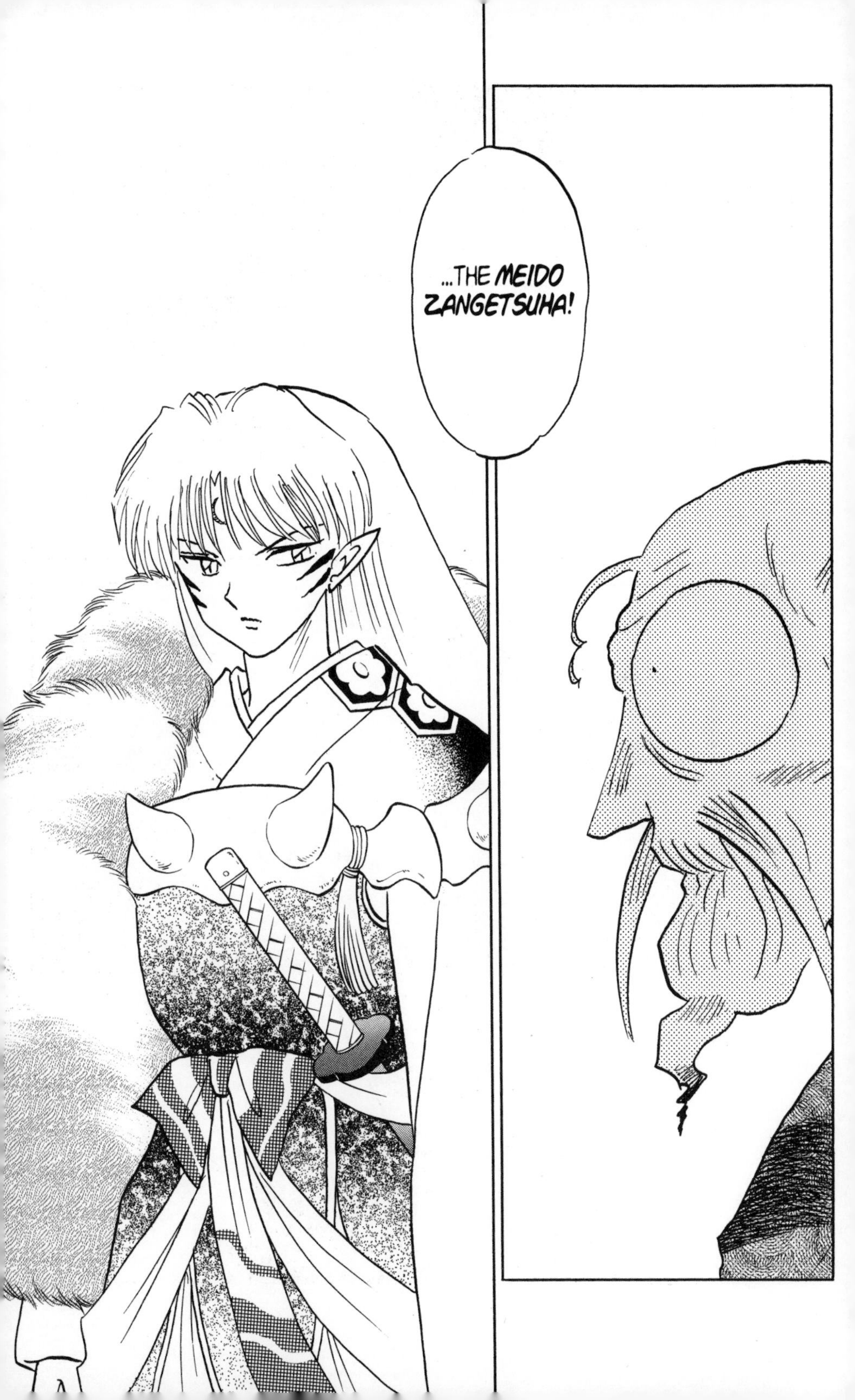
...THE *MEIDO ZANGETSUHA!*

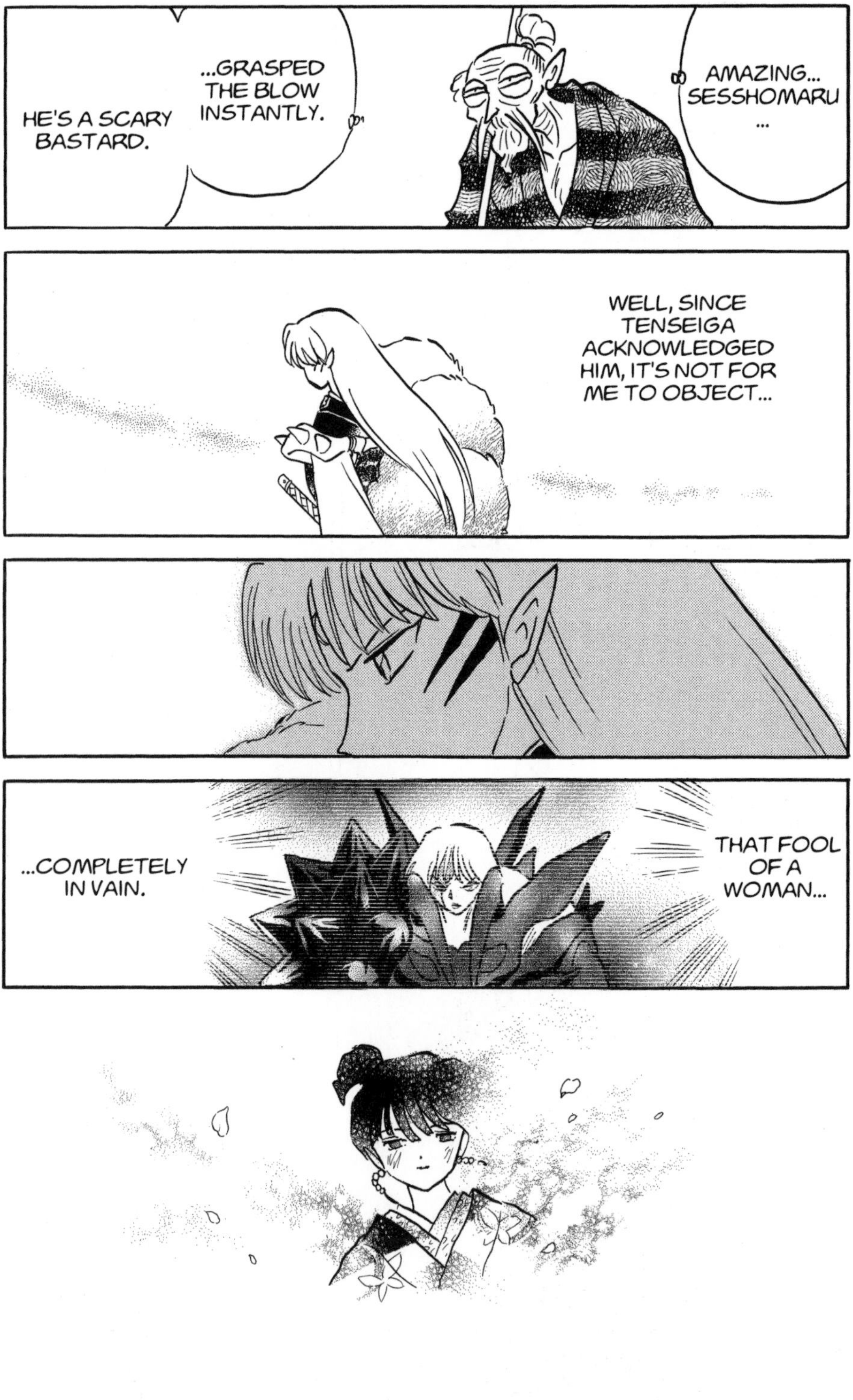
AMAZING... SESSHOMARU ...
...GRASPED THE BLOW INSTANTLY.
HE'S A SCARY BASTARD.
WELL, SINCE TENSEIGA ACKNOWLEDGED HIM, IT'S NOT FOR ME TO OBJECT...
THAT FOOL OF A WOMAN...
...COMPLETELY IN VAIN.

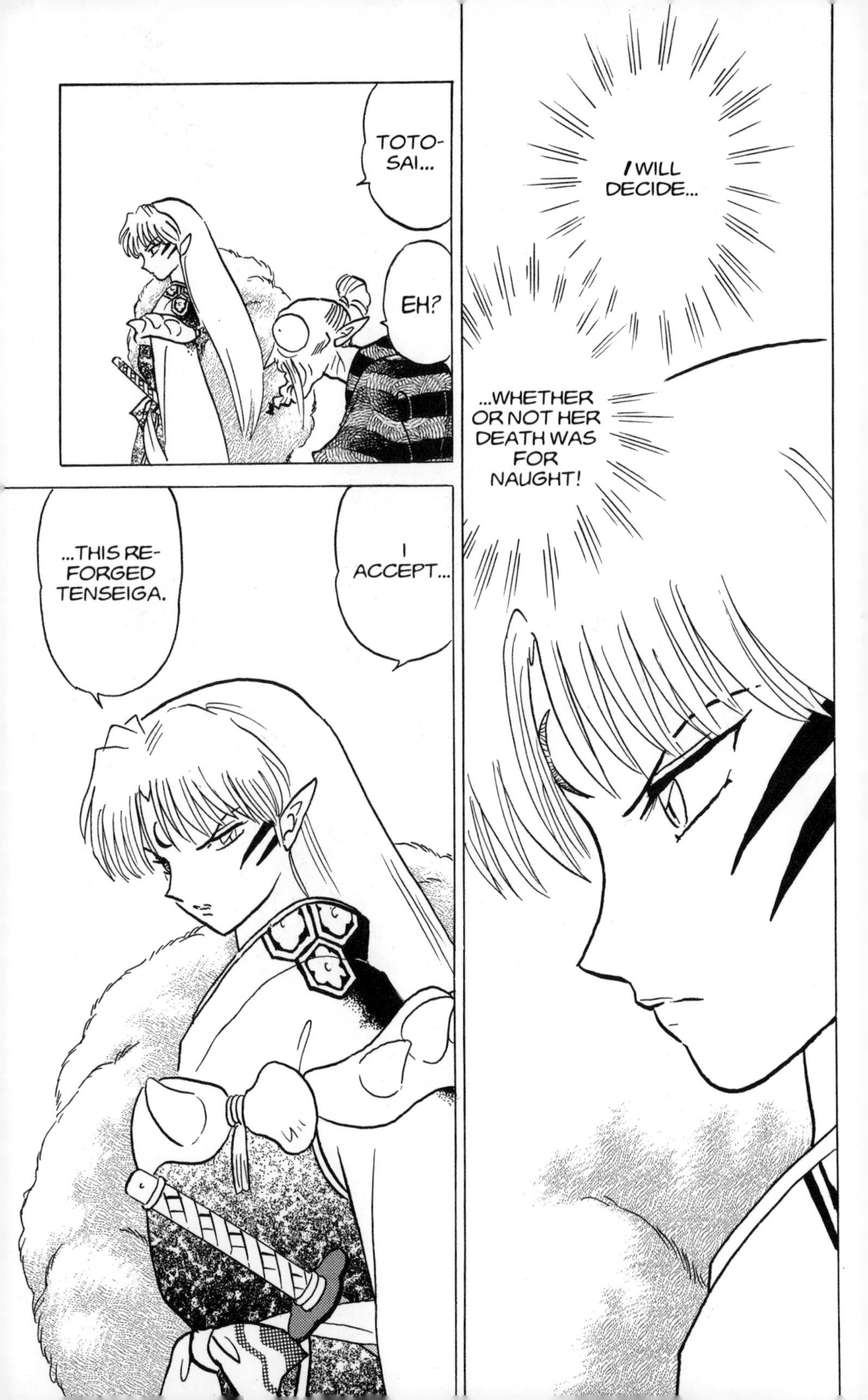

I WILL DECIDE...
...WHETHER OR NOT HER DEATH WAS FOR NAUGHT!
TOTO-SAI...
EH?
I ACCEPT...
...THIS RE-FORGED TENSEIGA.

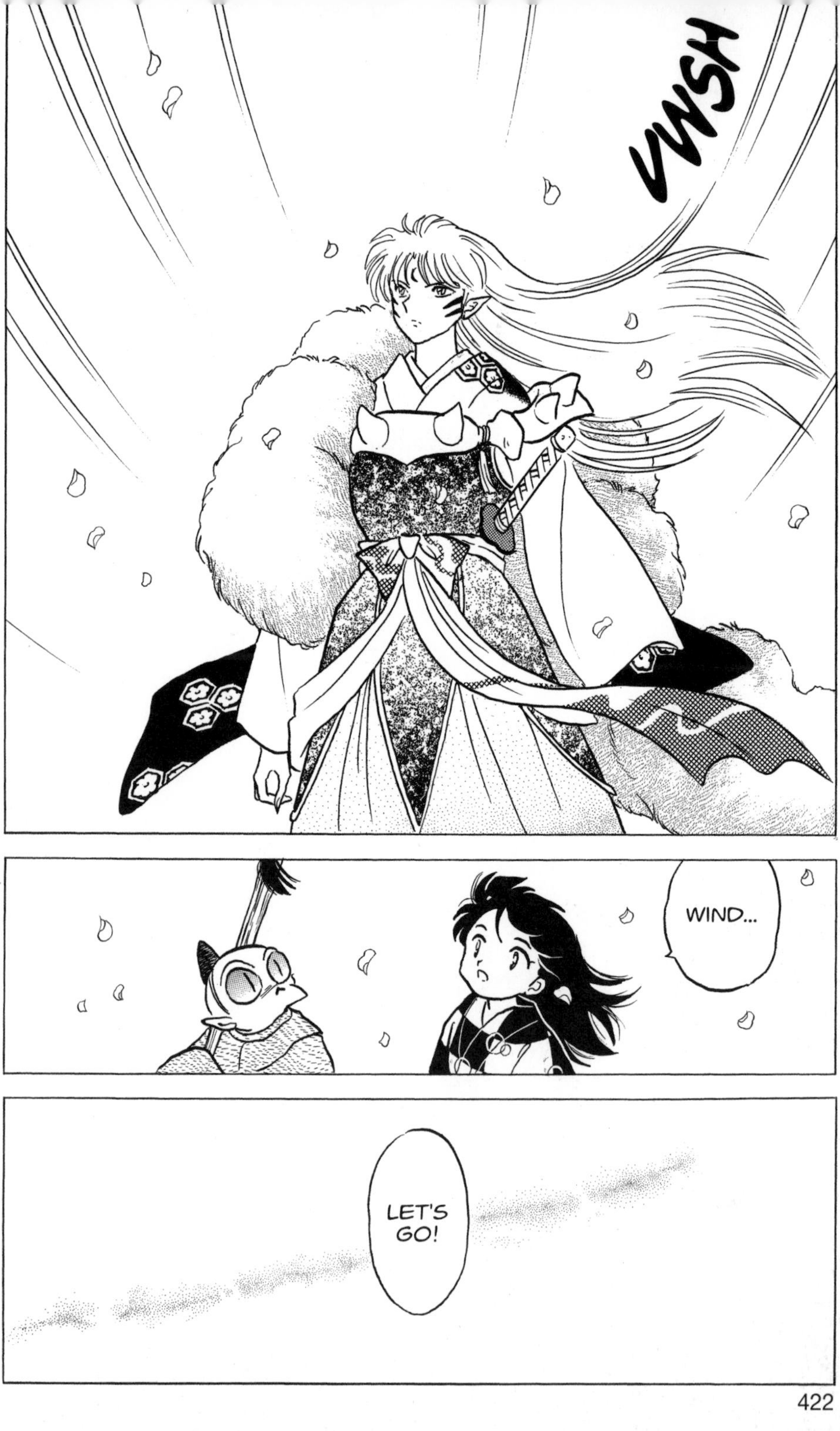
VWSH
WIND...
LET'S GO!

SCROLL THREE
THE KIND ONE

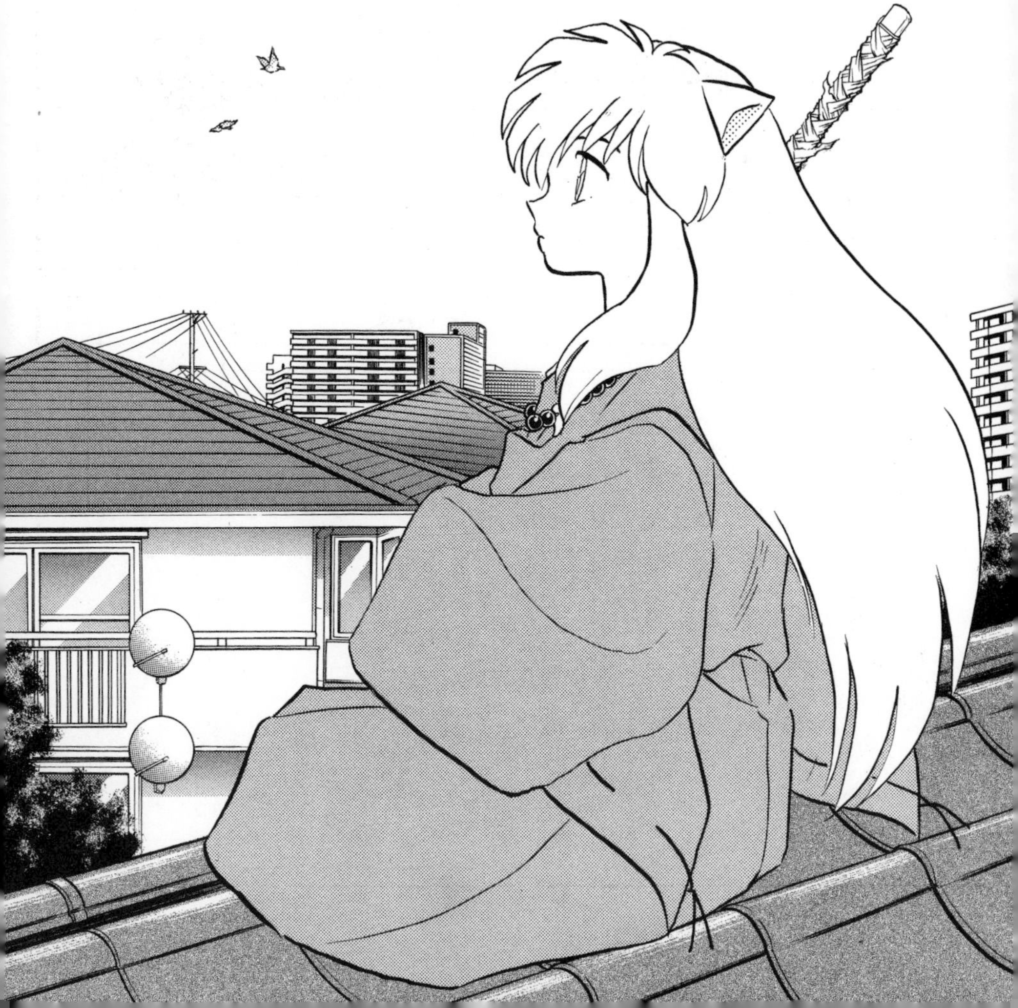

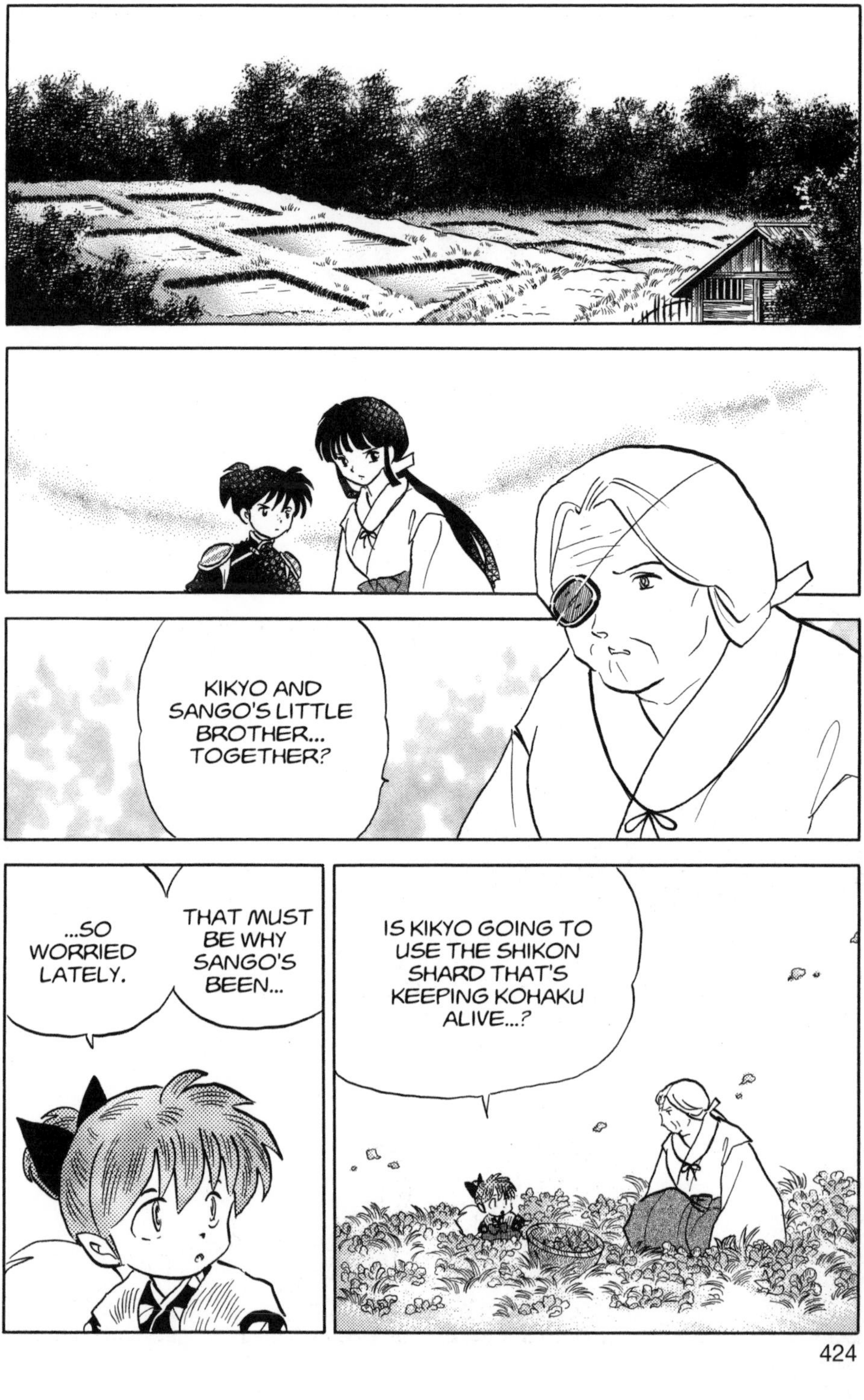
KIKYO AND SANGO'S LITTLE BROTHER... TOGETHER?
IS KIKYO GOING TO USE THE SHIKON SHARD THAT'S KEEPING KOHAKU ALIVE...?
THAT MUST BE WHY SANGO'S BEEN...
...SO WORRIED LATELY.

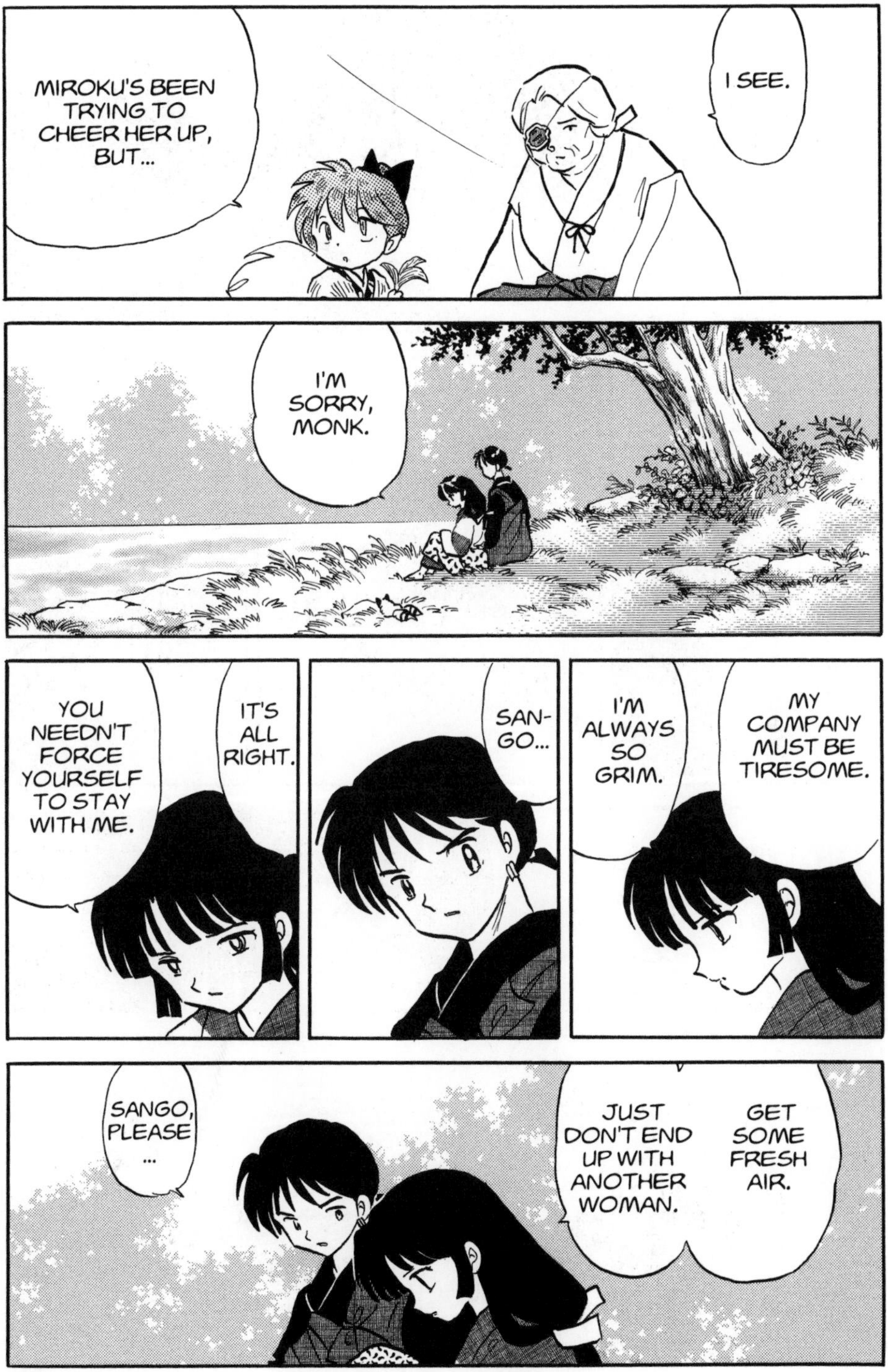
I SEE.
MIROKU'S BEEN TRYING TO CHEER HER UP, BUT...
I'M SORRY, MONK.
MY COMPANY MUST BE TIRESOME.
I'M ALWAYS SO GRIM.
SAN-GO...
IT'S ALL RIGHT.
YOU NEEDN'T FORCE YOURSELF TO STAY WITH ME.
GET SOME FRESH AIR.
JUST DON'T END UP WITH ANOTHER WOMAN.
SANGO, PLEASE ...

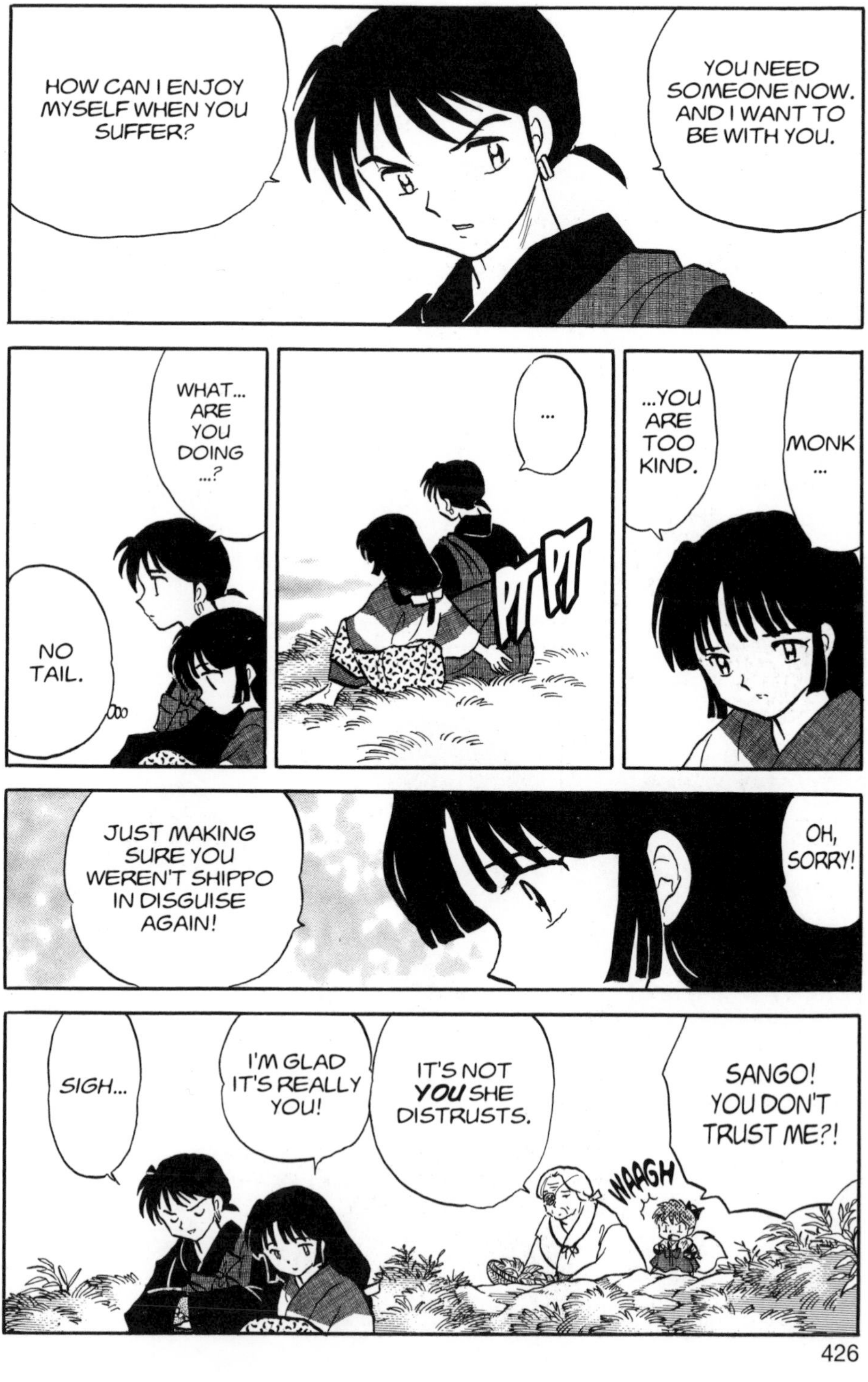
YOU NEED SOMEONE NOW. AND I WANT TO BE WITH YOU.
HOW CAN I ENJOY MYSELF WHEN YOU SUFFER?
MONK ...
...YOU ARE TOO KIND.
...
PT PT
WHAT... ARE YOU DOING ...?
NO TAIL.
OH, SORRY!
JUST MAKING SURE YOU WEREN'T SHIPPO IN DISGUISE AGAIN!
SANGO! YOU DON'T TRUST ME?!
WAAGH
IT'S NOT YOU SHE DISTRUSTS.
I'M GLAD IT'S REALLY YOU!
SIGH...

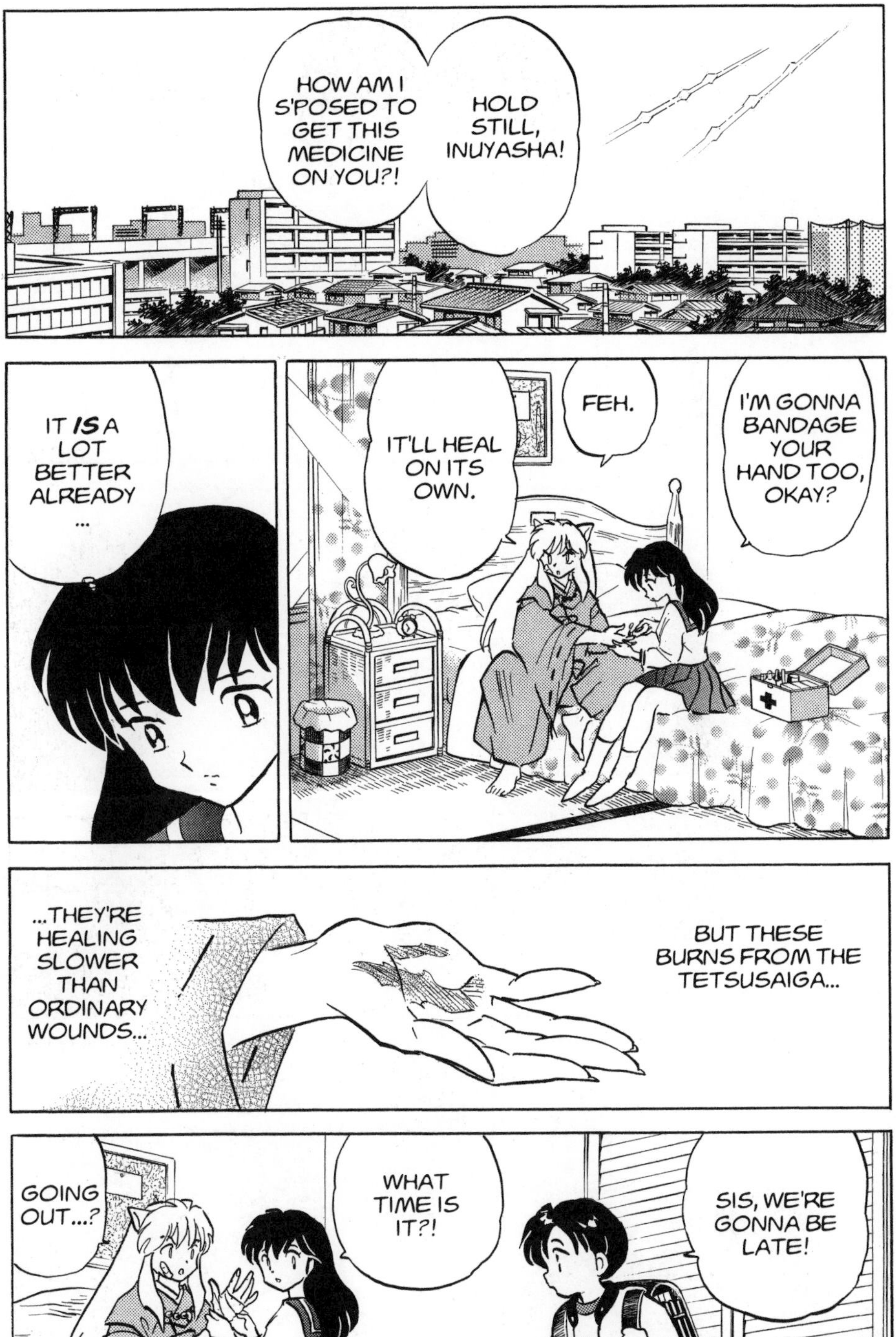
HOLD STILL, INUYASHA!
HOW AM I S'POSED TO GET THIS MEDICINE ON YOU?!
I'M GONNA BANDAGE YOUR HAND TOO, OKAY?
FEH.
IT'LL HEAL ON ITS OWN.
IT *IS* A LOT BETTER ALREADY ...
BUT THESE BURNS FROM THE TETSUSAIGA...
...THEY'RE HEALING SLOWER THAN ORDINARY WOUNDS...
SIS, WE'RE GONNA BE LATE!
WHAT TIME IS IT?!
GOING OUT...?

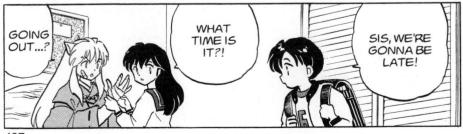

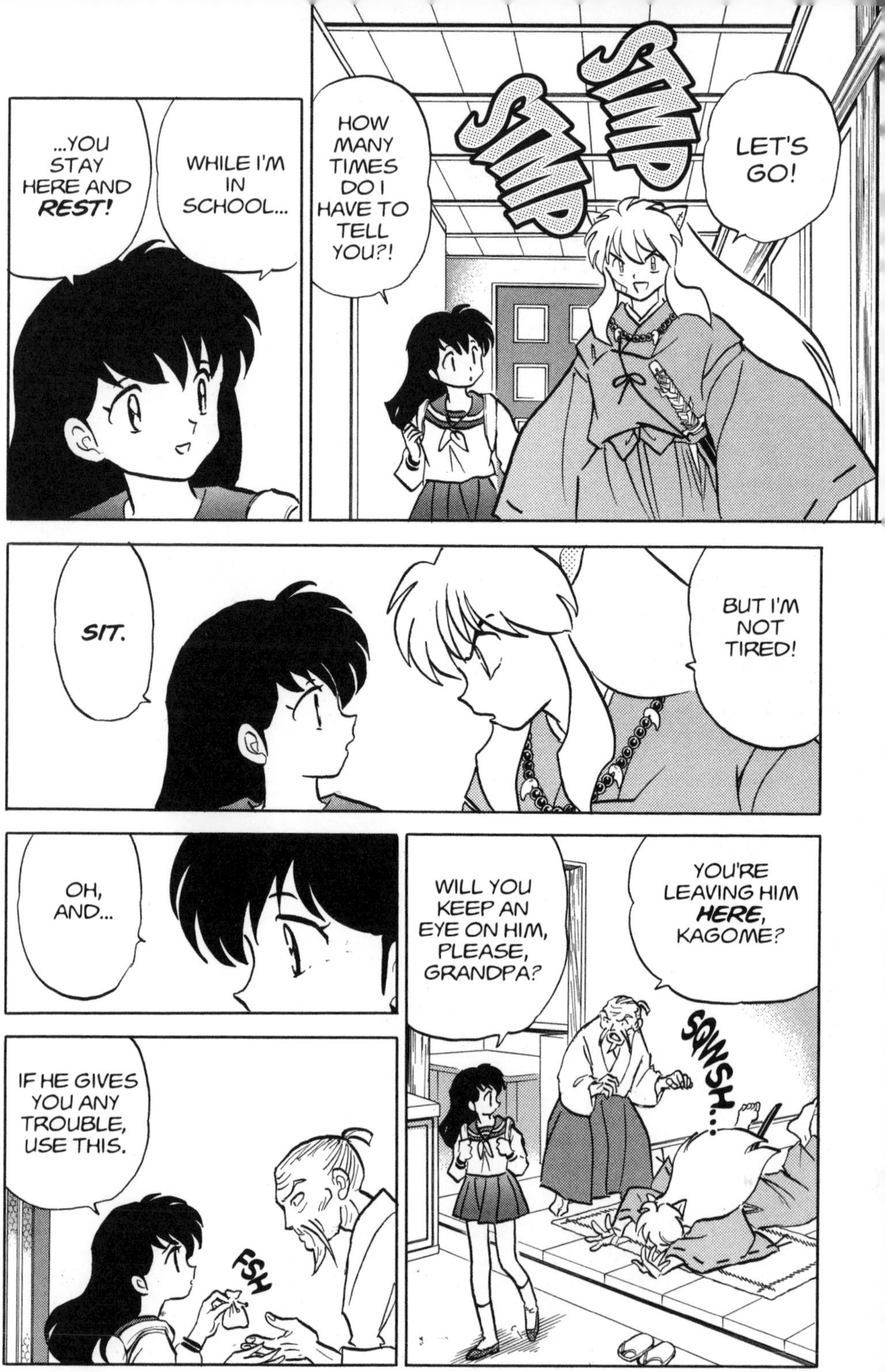
LET'S GO!
STMP
STMP
HOW MANY TIMES DO I HAVE TO TELL YOU?!
WHILE I'M IN SCHOOL...
...YOU STAY HERE AND **REST!**
BUT I'M NOT TIRED!
SIT.
YOU'RE LEAVING HIM ***HERE***, KAGOME?
WILL YOU KEEP AN EYE ON HIM, PLEASE, GRANDPA?
SQWSH...
OH, AND...
IF HE GIVES YOU ANY TROUBLE, USE THIS.
FSH

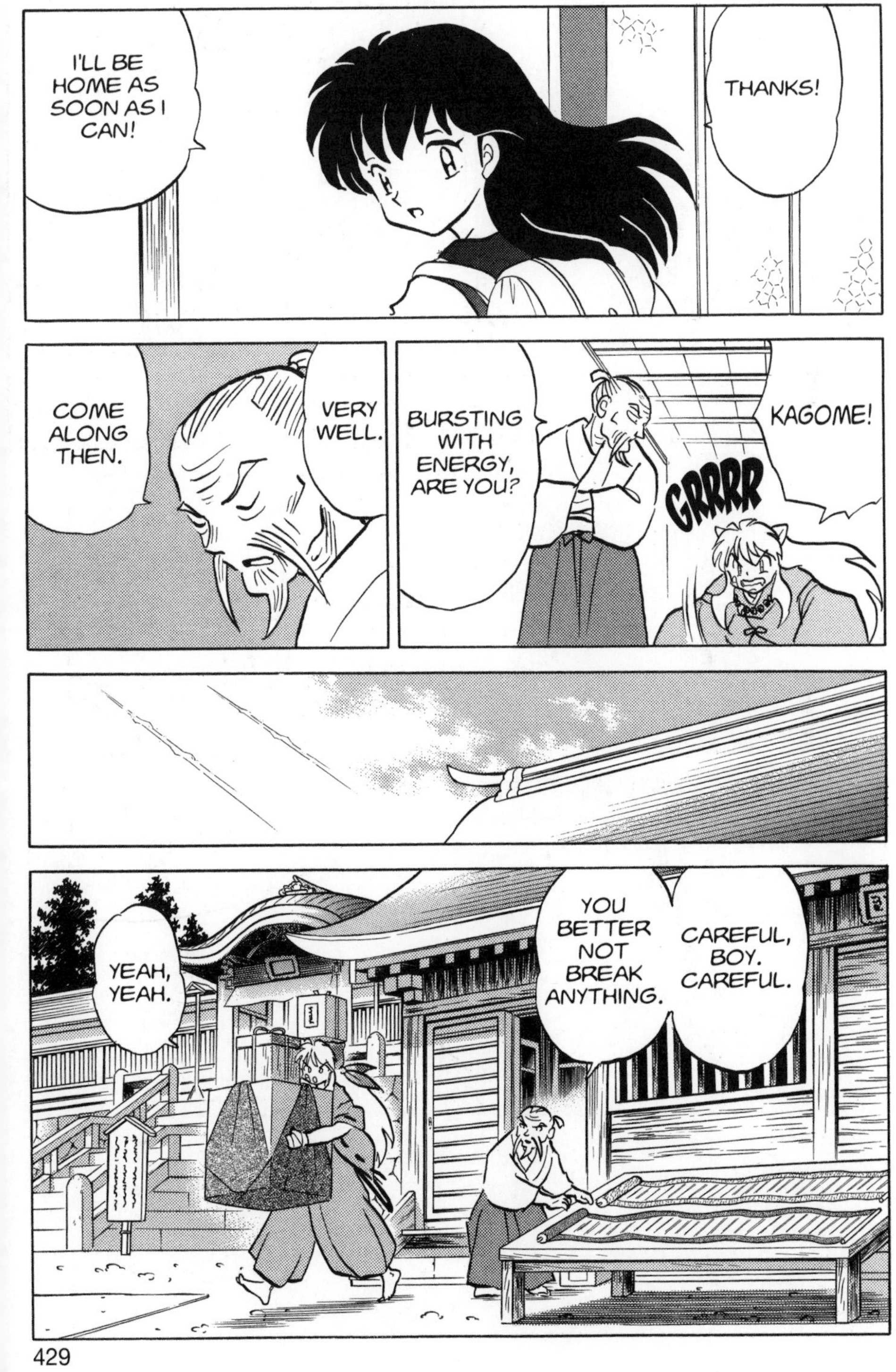
THANKS!
I'LL BE HOME AS SOON AS I CAN!
KAGOME!
GRRRR
BURSTING WITH ENERGY, ARE YOU?
VERY WELL.
COME ALONG THEN.
CAREFUL, BOY. CAREFUL.
YOU BETTER NOT BREAK ANYTHING.
YEAH, YEAH.

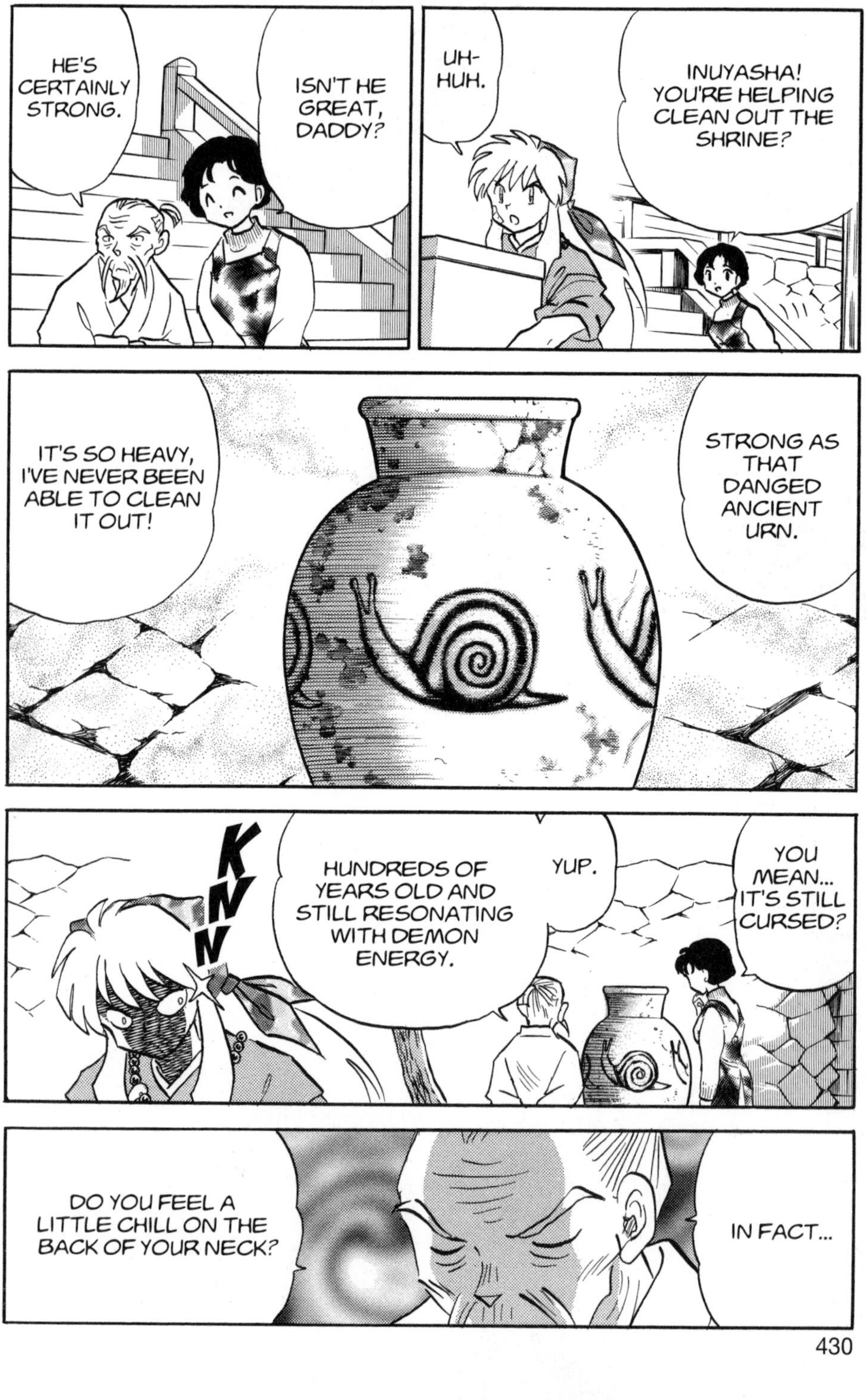
INUYASHA! YOU'RE HELPING CLEAN OUT THE SHRINE?
UH-HUH.
ISN'T HE GREAT, DADDY?
HE'S CERTAINLY STRONG.
STRONG AS THAT DANGED ANCIENT URN.
IT'S SO HEAVY, I'VE NEVER BEEN ABLE TO CLEAN IT OUT!
YOU MEAN... IT'S STILL CURSED?
YUP.
HUNDREDS OF YEARS OLD AND STILL RESONATING WITH DEMON ENERGY.
KNN
IN FACT...
DO YOU FEEL A LITTLE CHILL ON THE BACK OF YOUR NECK?

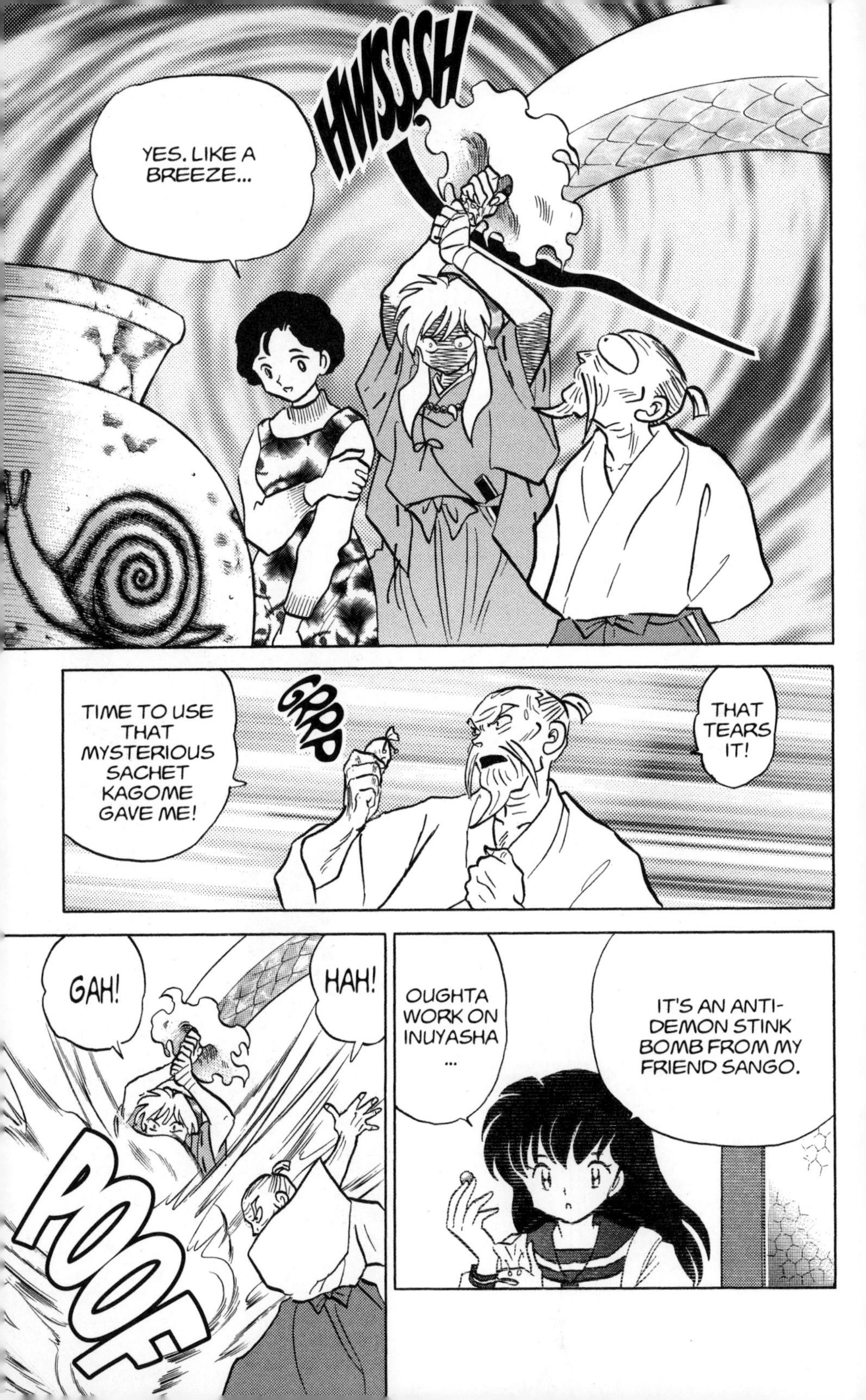
HWSSSH
YES. LIKE A BREEZE...
THAT TEARS IT!
GRRP
TIME TO USE THAT MYSTERIOUS SACHET KAGOME GAVE ME!
IT'S AN ANTI-DEMON STINK BOMB FROM MY FRIEND SANGO.
OUGHTA WORK ON INUYASHA ...
HAH!
GAH!
POOF

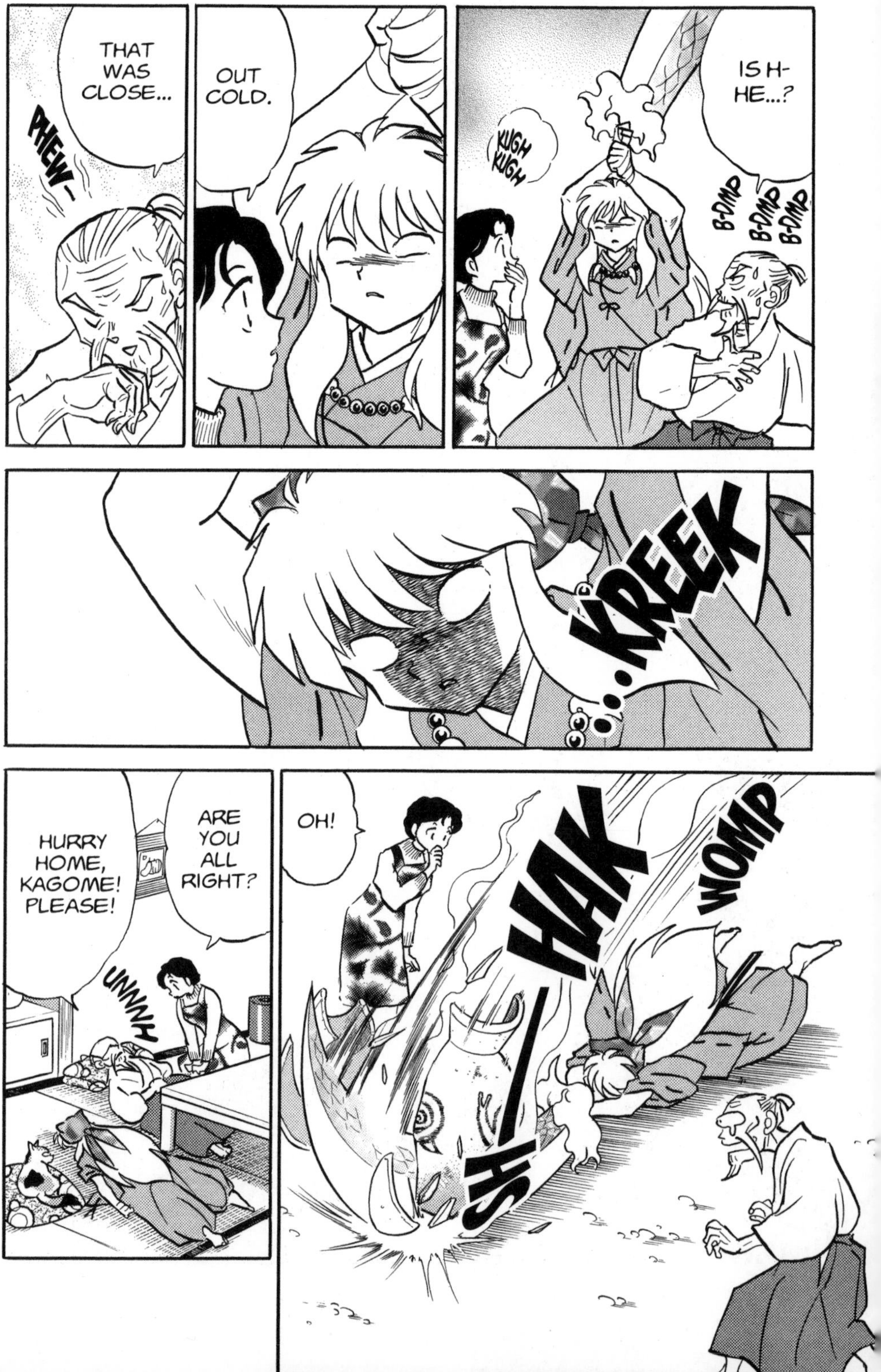
IS H- HE...?
B-DMP B-DMP B-DMP
KUGH KUGH
OUT COLD.
THAT WAS CLOSE...
PHEW-
...KREEK
WOMP
SH—HAK
OH!
ARE YOU ALL RIGHT?
HURRY HOME, KAGOME! PLEASE!
UNNNH

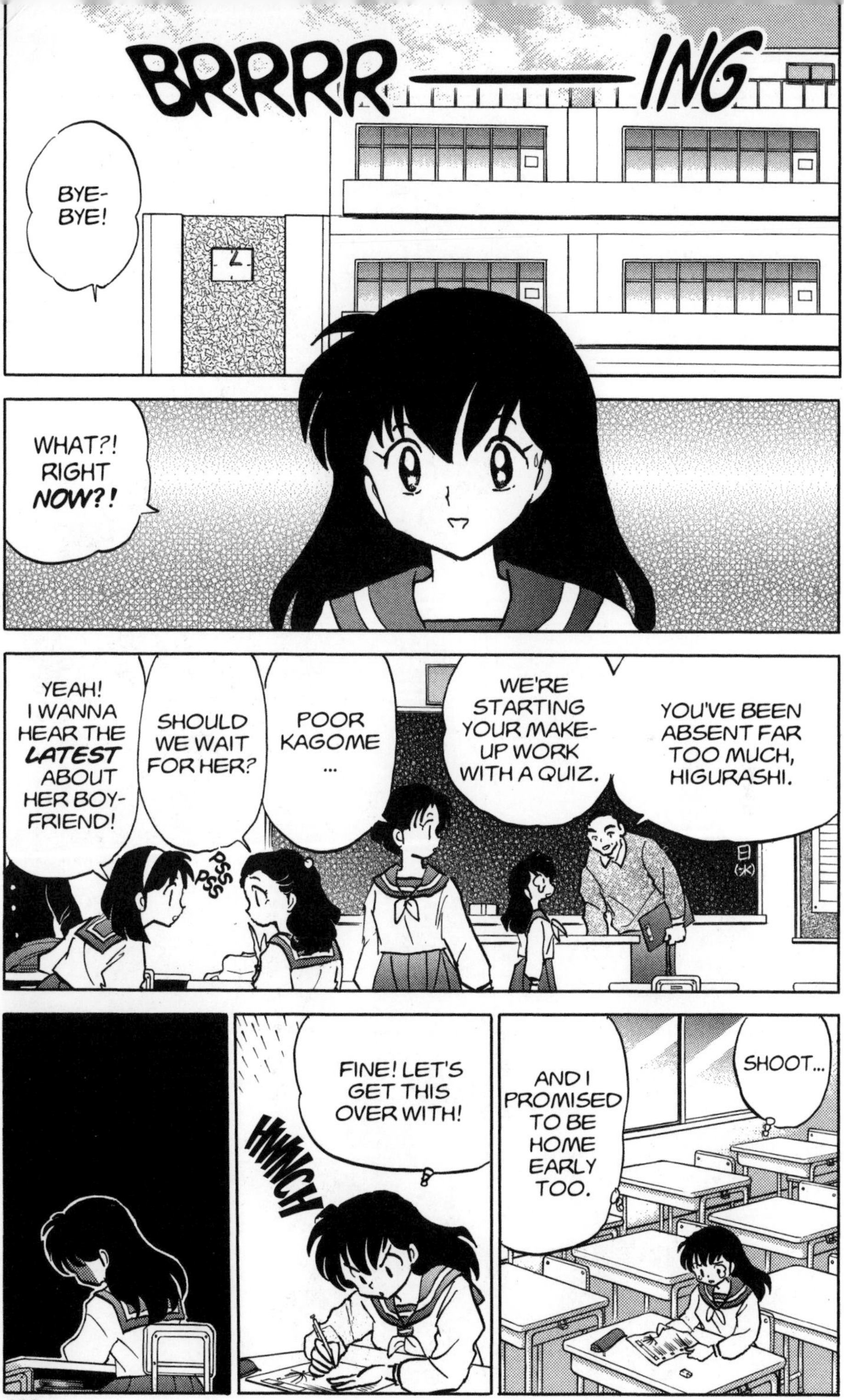
BRRRR——ING
BYE-BYE!
WHAT?! RIGHT NOW?!
YOU'VE BEEN ABSENT FAR TOO MUCH, HIGURASHI.
WE'RE STARTING YOUR MAKE-UP WORK WITH A QUIZ.
POOR KAGOME ...
SHOULD WE WAIT FOR HER?
PSS PSS
YEAH! I WANNA HEAR THE LATEST ABOUT HER BOY-FRIEND!
SHOOT...
AND I PROMISED TO BE HOME EARLY TOO.
FINE! LET'S GET THIS OVER WITH!
HWMCH

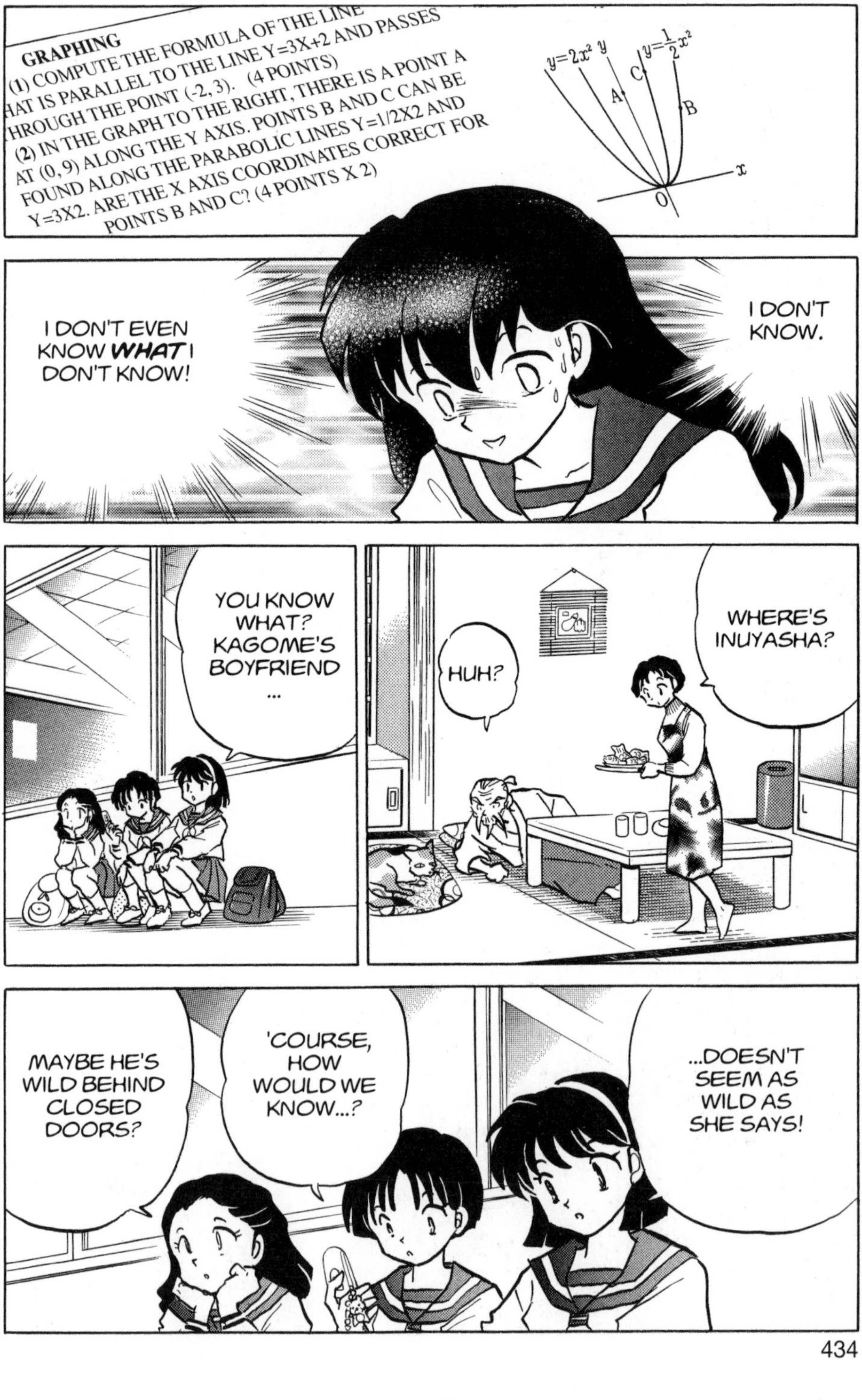
GRAPHING
(1) COMPUTE THE FORMULA OF THE LINE
HAT IS PARALLEL TO THE LINE Y=3X+2 AND PASSES
HROUGH THE POINT (-2, 3). (4 POINTS)
(2) IN THE GRAPH TO THE RIGHT, THERE IS A POINT A
AT (0, 9) ALONG THE Y AXIS. POINTS B AND C CAN BE
FOUND ALONG THE PARABOLIC LINES Y=1/2X2 AND
Y=3X2. ARE THE X AXIS COORDINATES CORRECT FOR
POINTS B AND C? (4 POINTS X 2)
$y=2x^2$
y
$y=\frac{1}{2}x^2$
C
A
B
x
O
I DON'T KNOW.
I DON'T EVEN KNOW ***WHAT*** I DON'T KNOW!
WHERE'S INUYASHA?
HUH?
YOU KNOW WHAT? KAGOME'S BOYFRIEND ...
...DOESN'T SEEM AS WILD AS SHE SAYS!
'COURSE, HOW WOULD WE KNOW...?
MAYBE HE'S WILD BEHIND CLOSED DOORS?

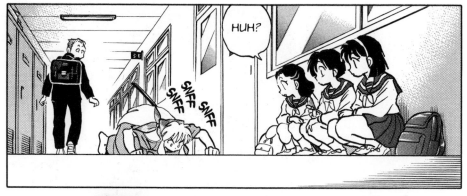

HUH?
SNIFF SNIFF SNIFF
UM... HI!
HUH?
STAY CALM! I REMEMBER THIS...
THESE QUESTIONS WERE IN THE TEXTBOOK...
!
THAT'S IT!!
PING
I'VE GOT IT!!
I CAN DO THIS!!
VISH
DID YOU COME TO WALK KAGOME HOME?!
THAT'S SO SWEET!
SORT OF...

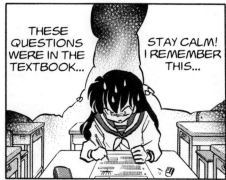

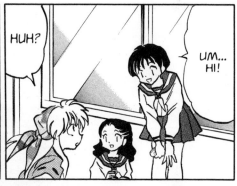

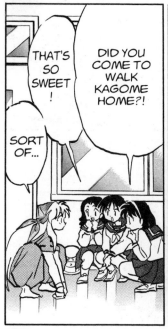

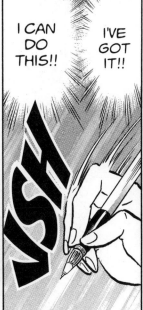

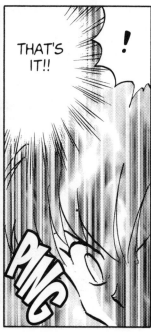

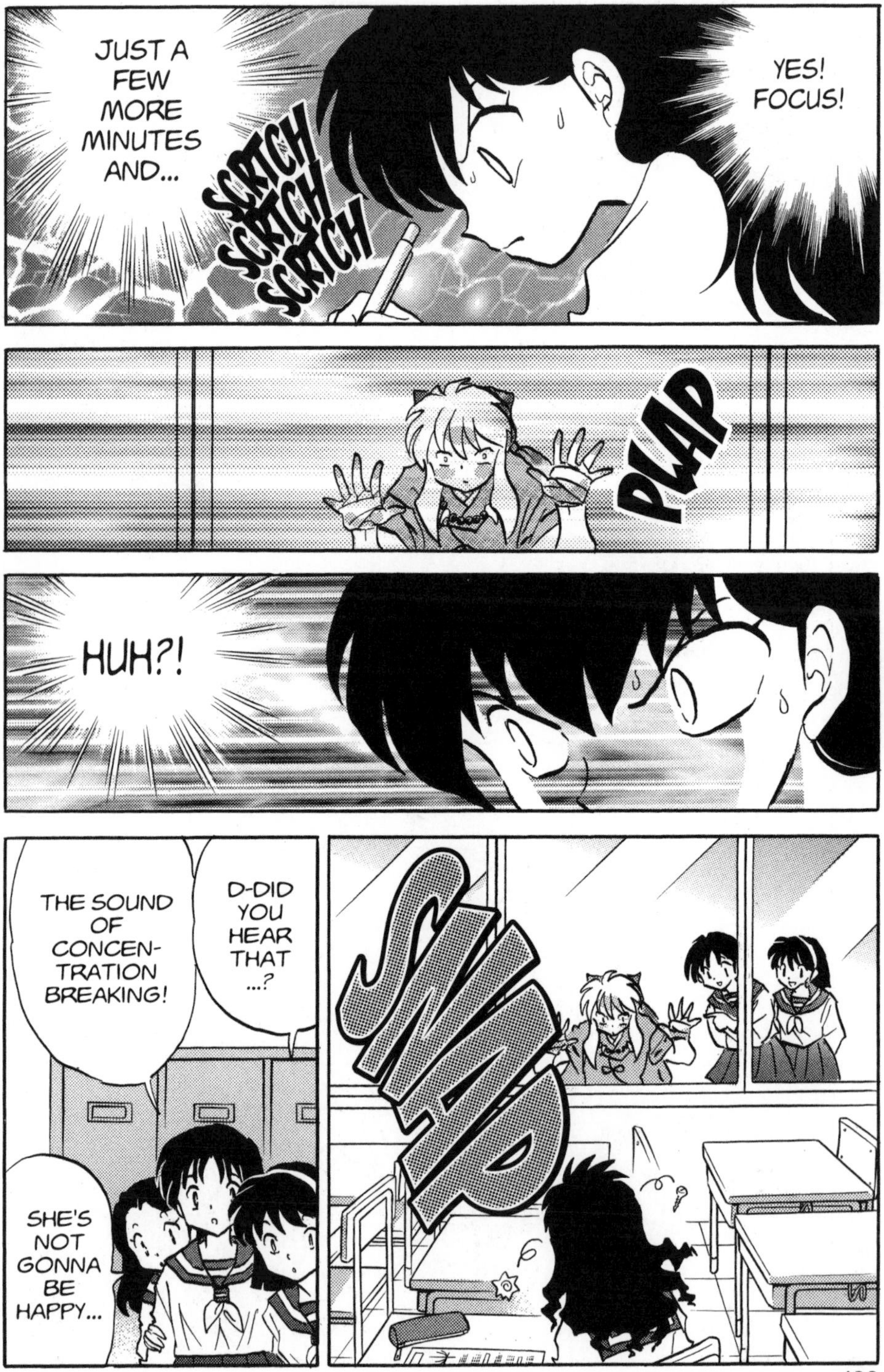
YES! FOCUS!
JUST A FEW MORE MINUTES AND...
SCRTCH SCRTCH SCRTCH
PWAP
HUH?!
SNAP
D-DID YOU HEAR THAT ...?
THE SOUND OF CONCEN-TRATION BREAKING!
SHE'S NOT GONNA BE HAPPY...

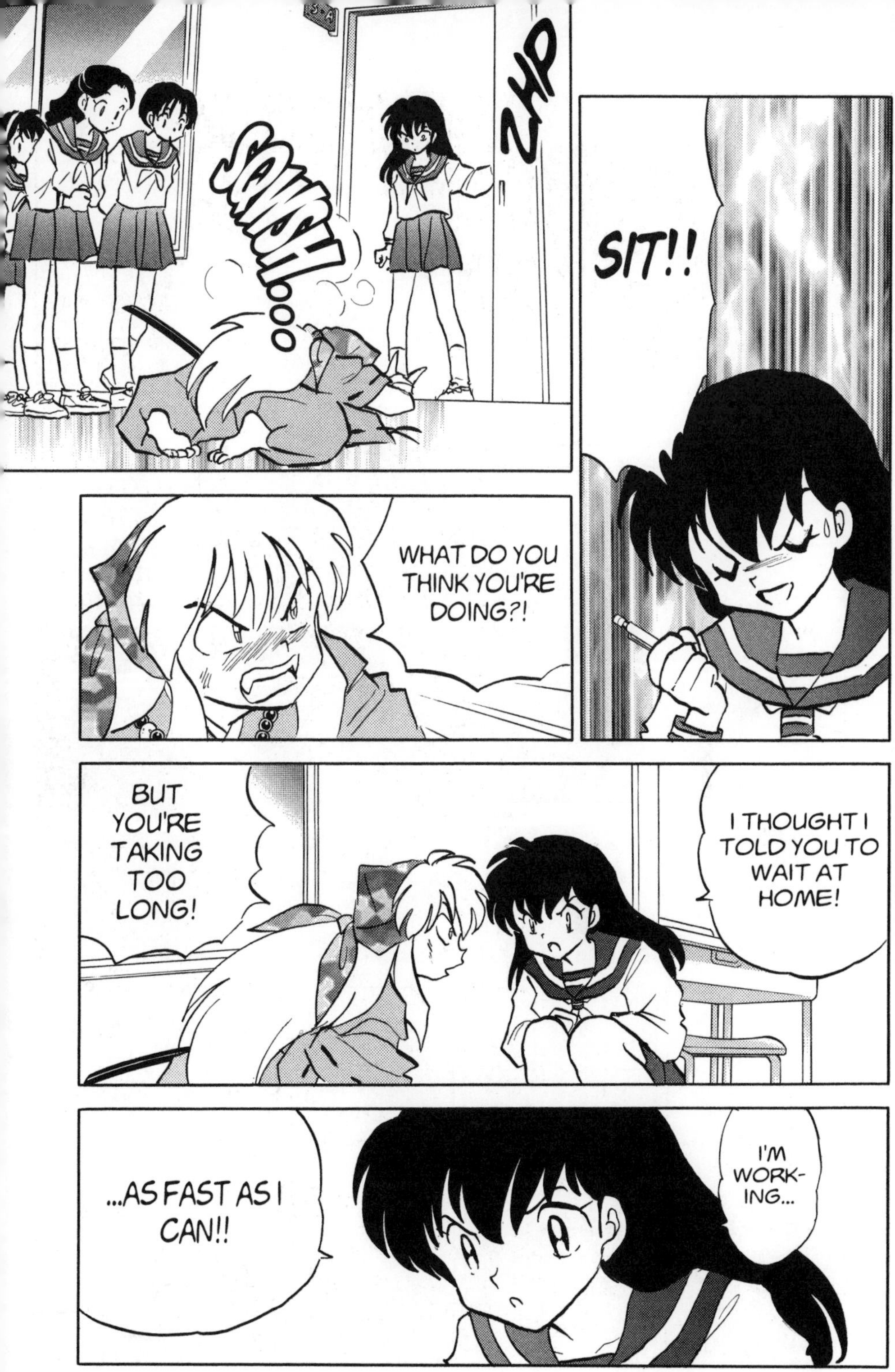
SIT!!
ZHP
SQUISHoooo
WHAT DO YOU THINK YOU'RE DOING?!
I THOUGHT I TOLD YOU TO WAIT AT HOME!
BUT YOU'RE TAKING TOO LONG!
I'M WORKING...
...AS FAST AS I CAN!!

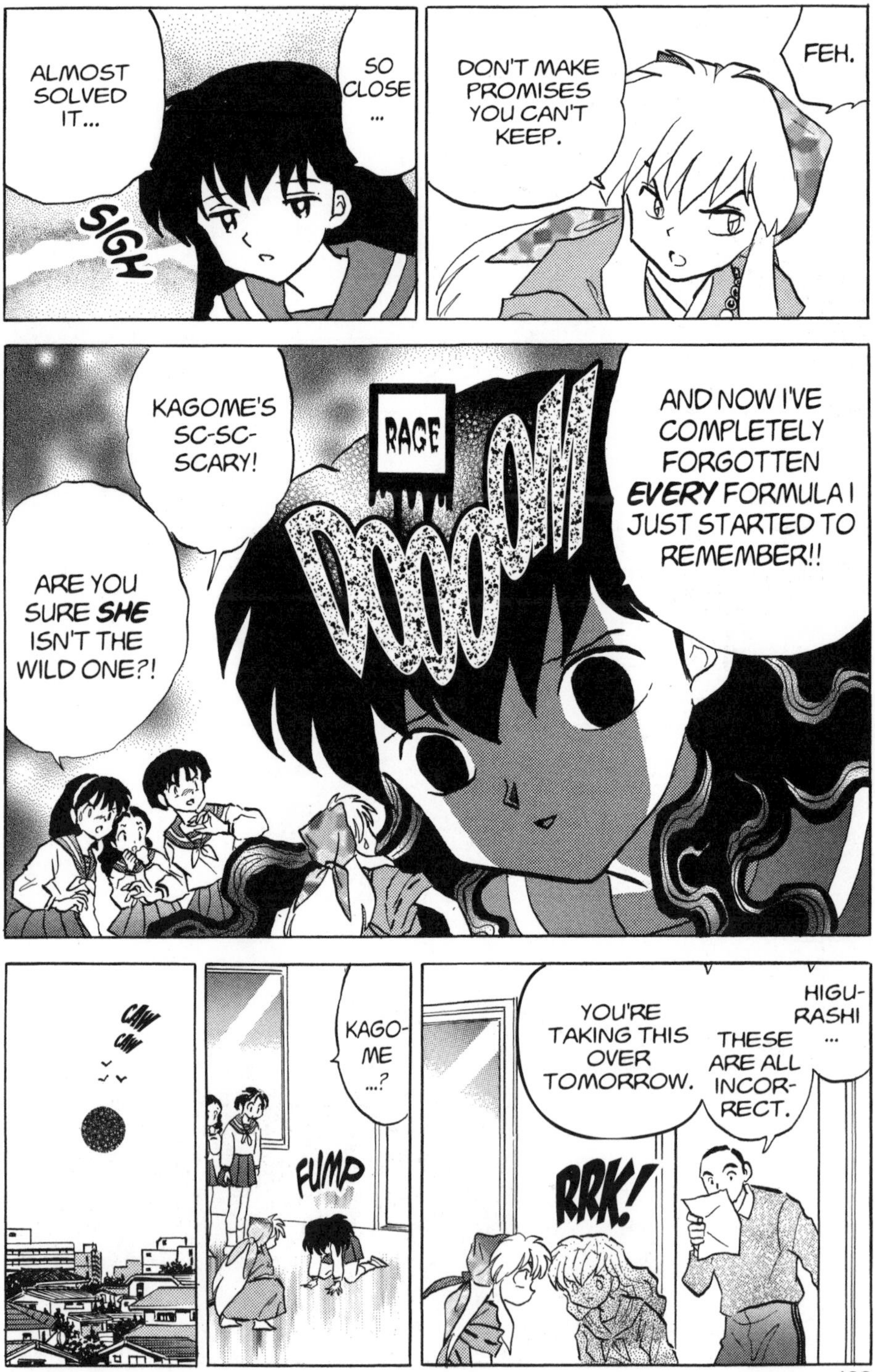
FEH.
DON'T MAKE PROMISES YOU CAN'T KEEP.
SO CLOSE ...
ALMOST SOLVED IT...
SIGH
AND NOW I'VE COMPLETELY FORGOTTEN **EVERY** FORMULA I JUST STARTED TO REMEMBER!!
DOOOOM
RAGE
KAGOME'S SC-SC-SCARY!
ARE YOU SURE **SHE** ISN'T THE WILD ONE?!
HIGU-RASHI ...
THESE ARE ALL INCOR-RECT.
YOU'RE TAKING THIS OVER TOMORROW.
RRK!
KAGO-ME ...?
FUMP
CAW CAW

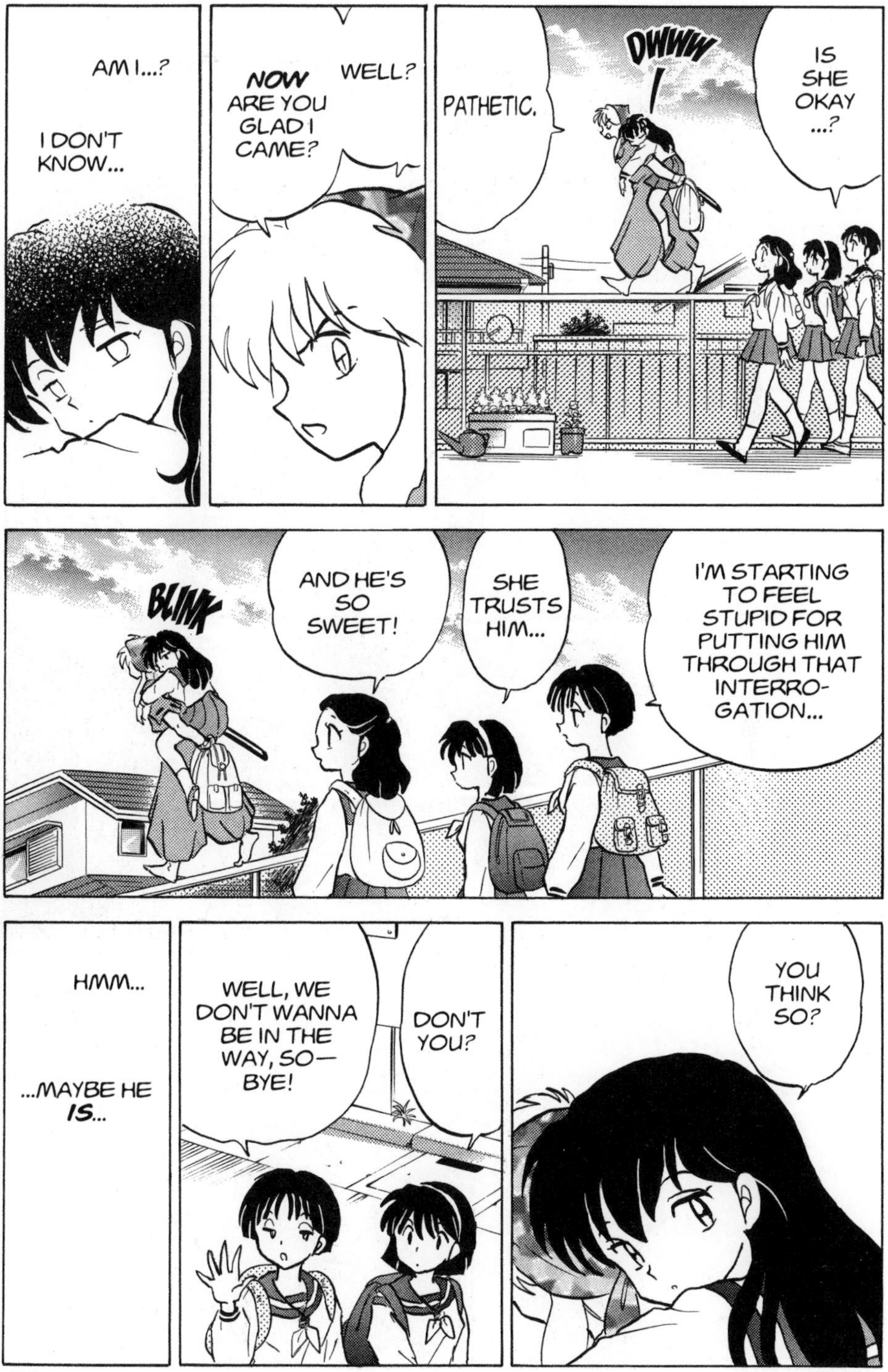
IS SHE OKAY ...?
DWWW
PATHETIC.
WELL?
NOW ARE YOU GLAD I CAME?
AM I...?
I DON'T KNOW...
I'M STARTING TO FEEL STUPID FOR PUTTING HIM THROUGH THAT INTERRO-GATION...
SHE TRUSTS HIM...
AND HE'S SO SWEET!
BLINK
YOU THINK SO?
DON'T YOU?
WELL, WE DON'T WANNA BE IN THE WAY, SO— BYE!
HMM...
...MAYBE HE *IS*...

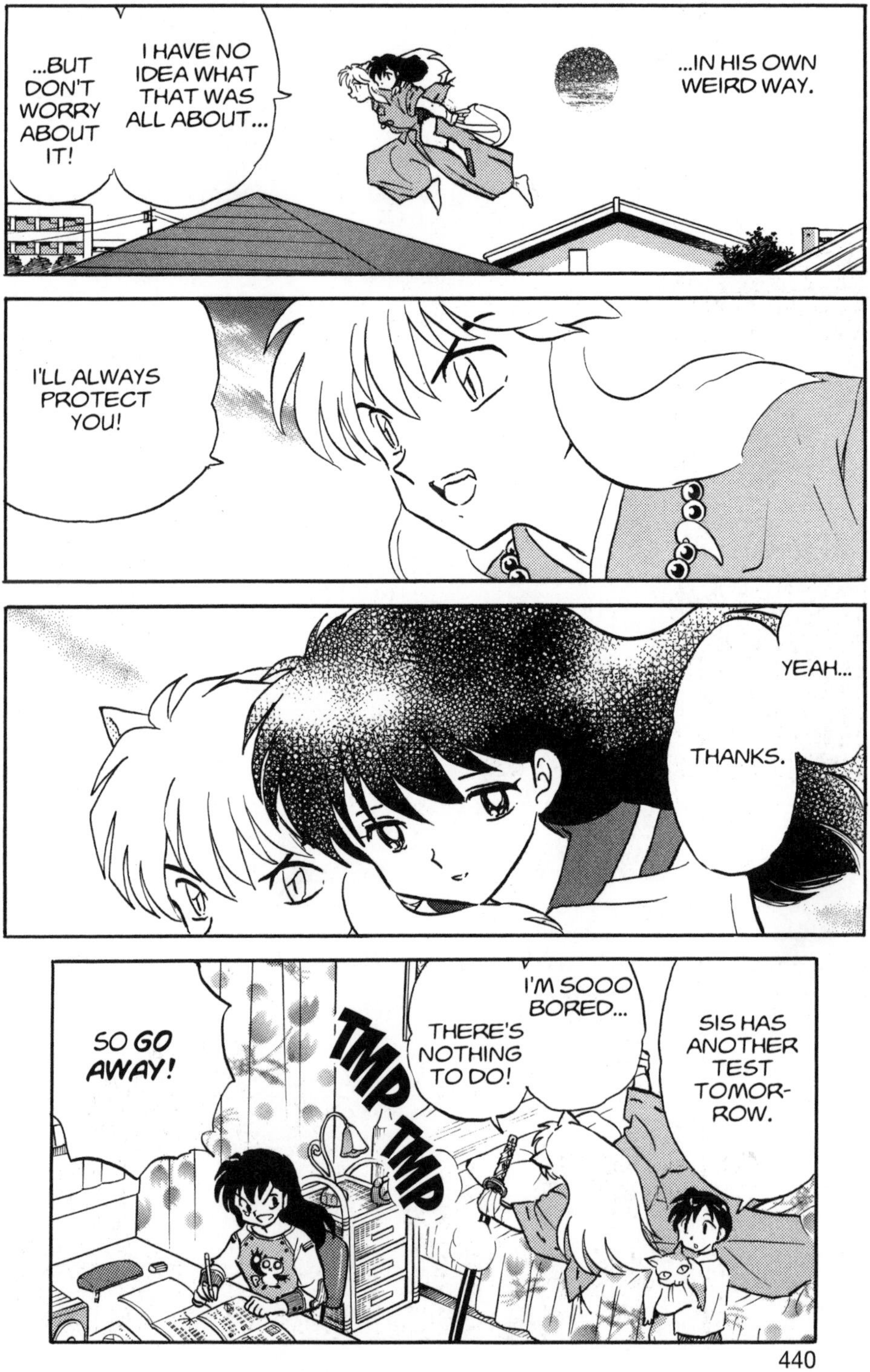
...IN HIS OWN WEIRD WAY.
I HAVE NO IDEA WHAT THAT WAS ALL ABOUT...
...BUT DON'T WORRY ABOUT IT!
I'LL ALWAYS PROTECT YOU!
YEAH...
THANKS.
SIS HAS ANOTHER TEST TOMOR-ROW.
I'M SOOO BORED...
THERE'S NOTHING TO DO!
TMP TMP
SO GO AWAY!

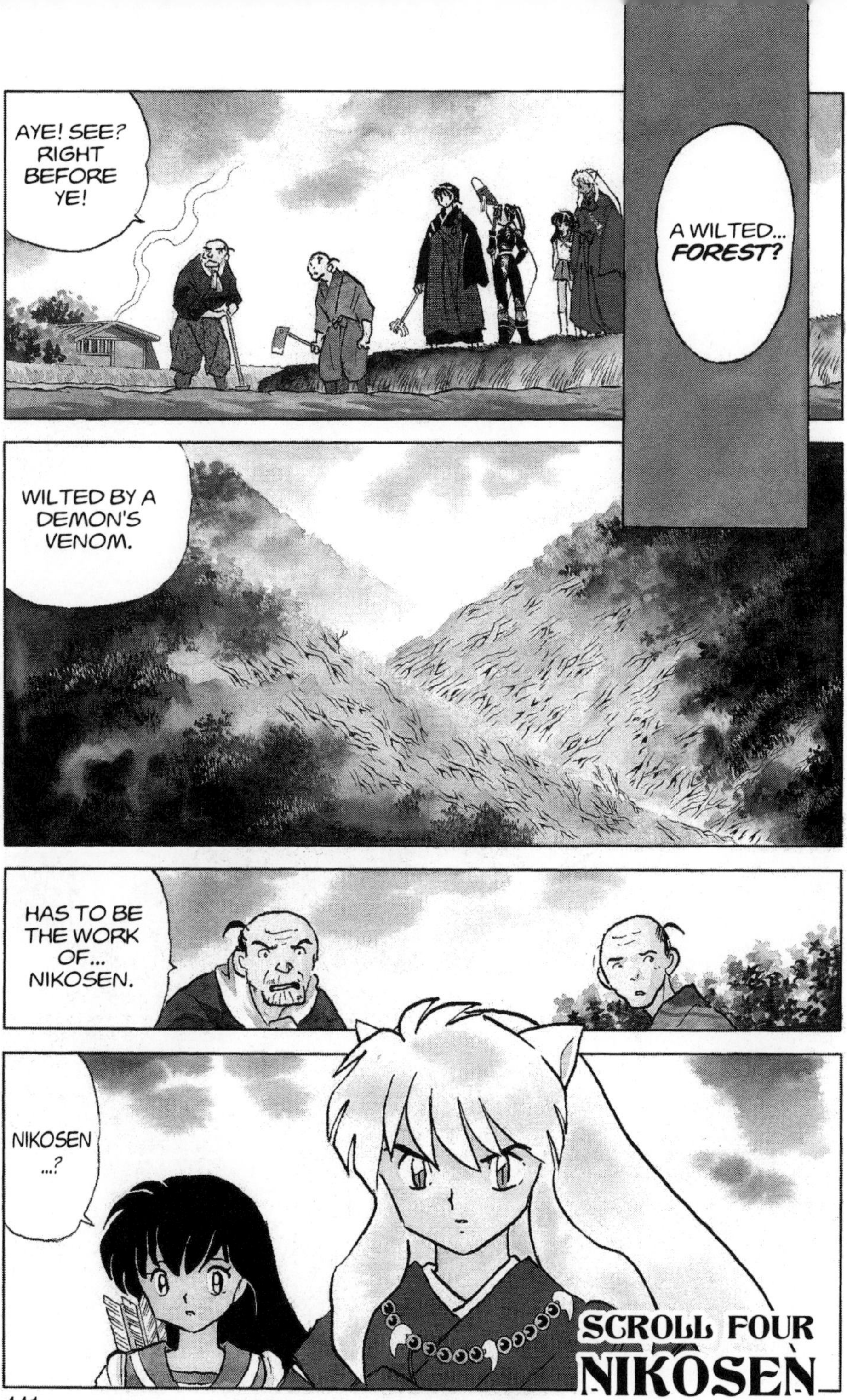
A WILTED... FOREST?
AYE! SEE? RIGHT BEFORE YE!
WILTED BY A DEMON'S VENOM.
HAS TO BE THE WORK OF... NIKOSEN.
NIKOSEN ...?
SCROLL FOUR NIKOSEǸ

SCROLL FOUR
NIKOSEN

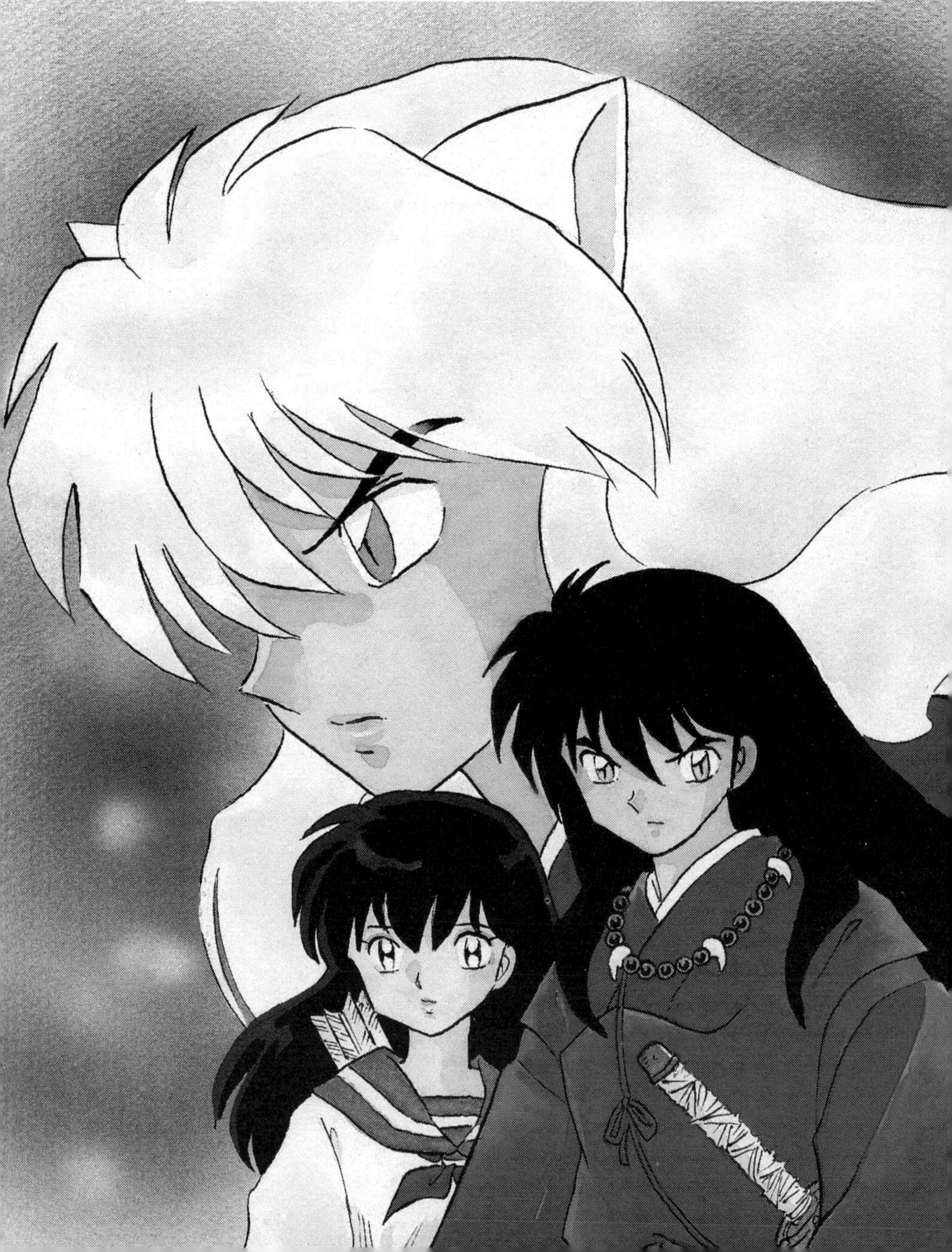

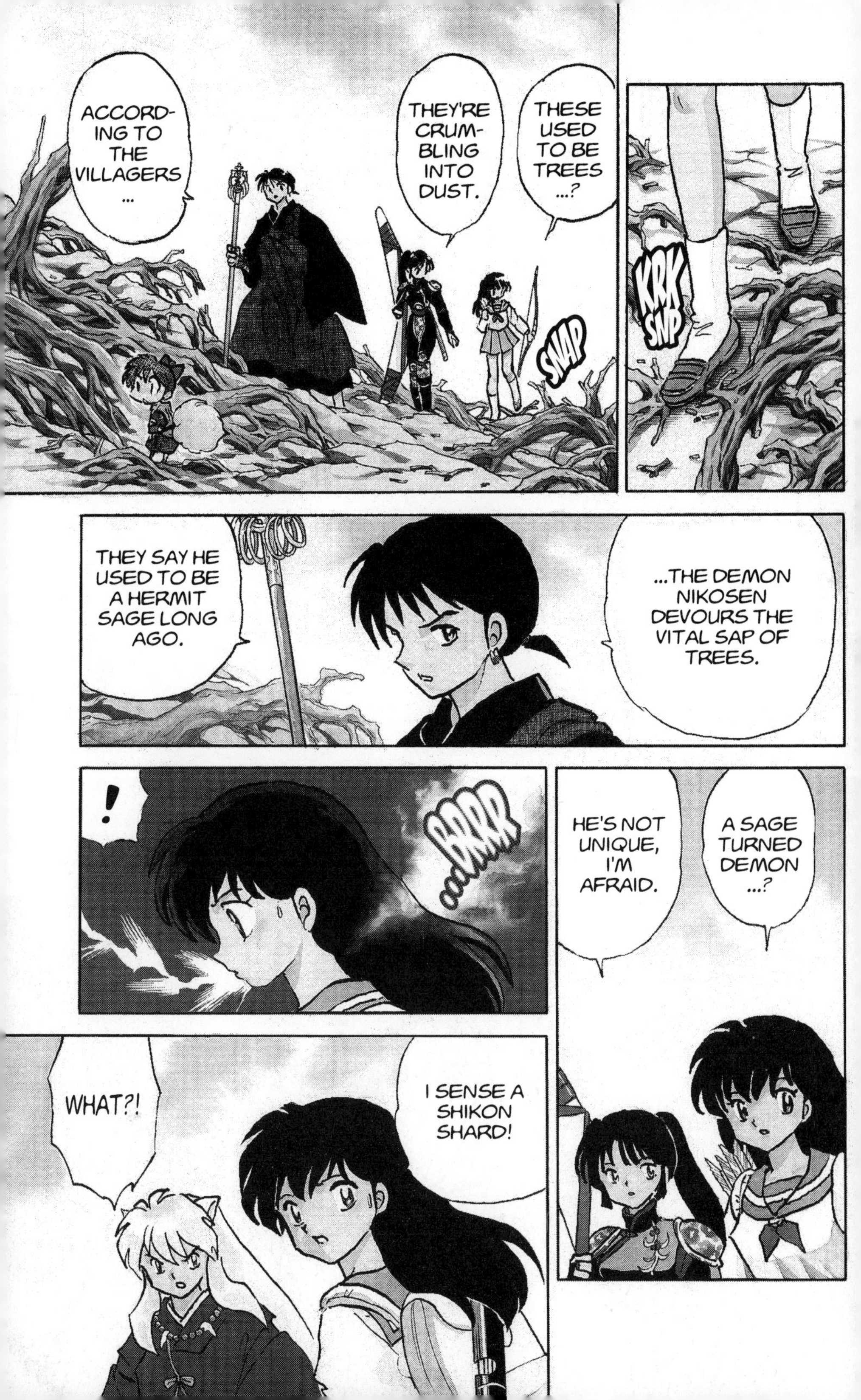
KRK SNP
THESE USED TO BE TREES ...?
THEY'RE CRUMBLING INTO DUST.
SNAP
ACCORDING TO THE VILLAGERS ...
...THE DEMON NIKOSEN DEVOURS THE VITAL SAP OF TREES.
THEY SAY HE USED TO BE A HERMIT SAGE LONG AGO.
A SAGE TURNED DEMON ...?
HE'S NOT UNIQUE, I'M AFRAID.
!
...BRRR
I SENSE A SHIKON SHARD!
WHAT?!

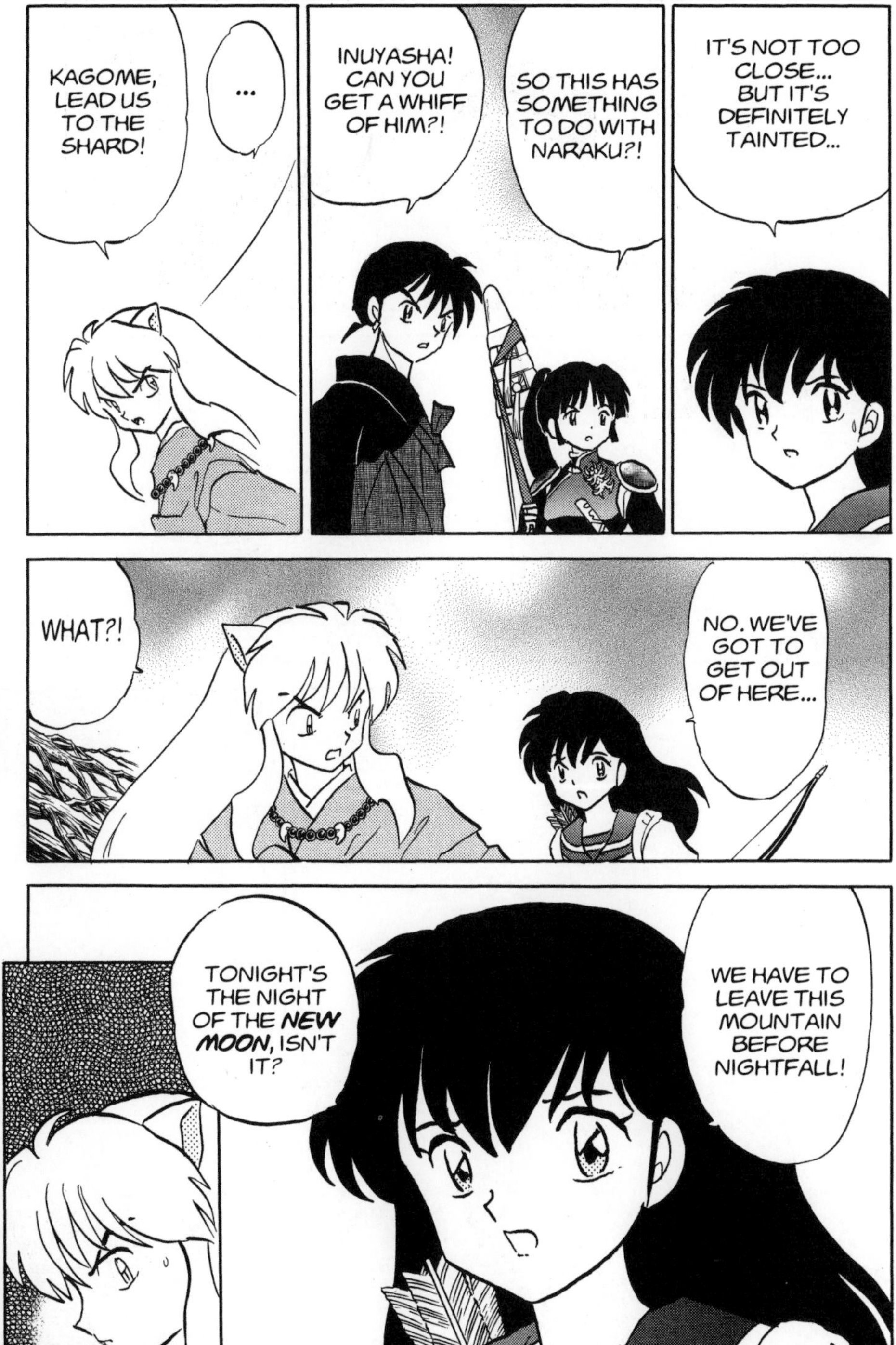
IT'S NOT TOO CLOSE... BUT IT'S DEFINITELY TAINTED...
SO THIS HAS SOMETHING TO DO WITH NARAKU?!
INUYASHA! CAN YOU GET A WHIFF OF HIM?!
...
KAGOME, LEAD US TO THE SHARD!
NO. WE'VE GOT TO GET OUT OF HERE...
WHAT?!
WE HAVE TO LEAVE THIS MOUNTAIN BEFORE NIGHTFALL!
TONIGHT'S THE NIGHT OF THE ***NEW MOON***, ISN'T IT?

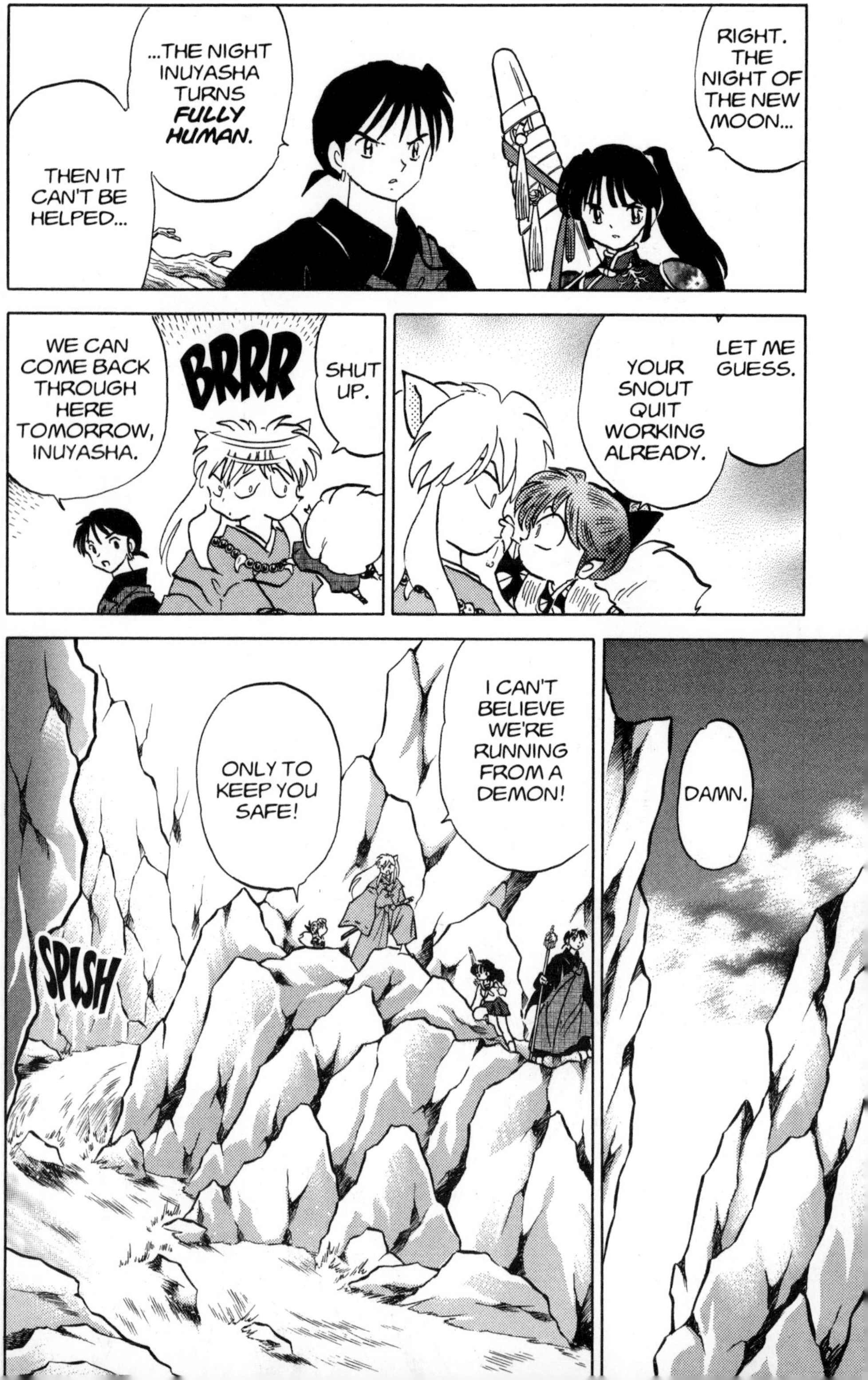
RIGHT. THE NIGHT OF THE NEW MOON...
...THE NIGHT INUYASHA TURNS FULLY HUMAN.
THEN IT CAN'T BE HELPED...
LET ME GUESS.
YOUR SNOUT QUIT WORKING ALREADY.
SHUT UP.
BRRR
WE CAN COME BACK THROUGH HERE TOMORROW, INUYASHA.
DAMN.
I CAN'T BELIEVE WE'RE RUNNING FROM A DEMON!
ONLY TO KEEP YOU SAFE!
SPLSH

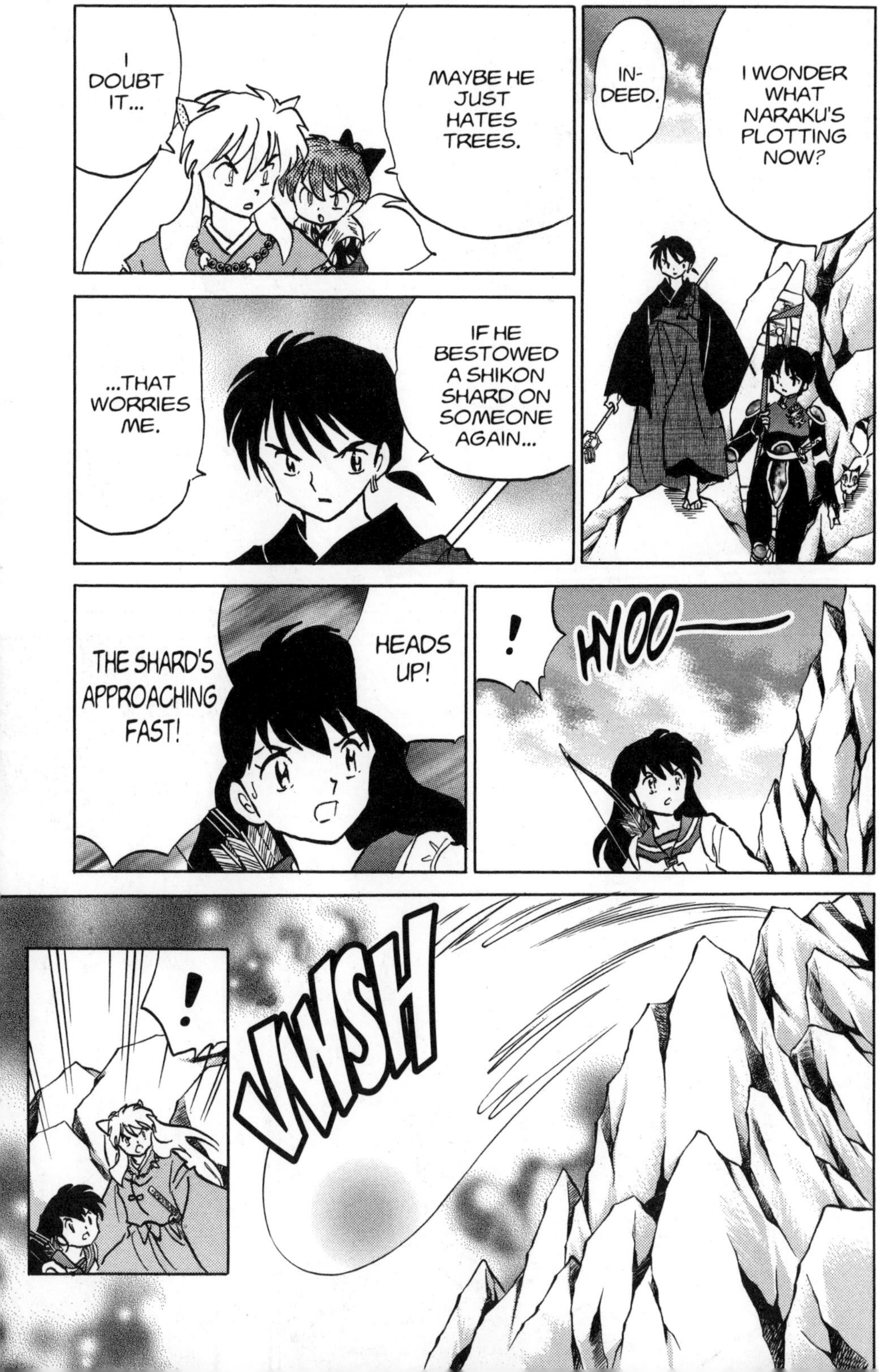
I WONDER WHAT NARAKU'S PLOTTING NOW?
IN-DEED.
MAYBE HE JUST HATES TREES.
I DOUBT IT...
IF HE BESTOWED A SHIKON SHARD ON SOMEONE AGAIN...
...THAT WORRIES ME.
HYOO—
!
HEADS UP!
THE SHARD'S APPROACHING FAST!
VWSH
!

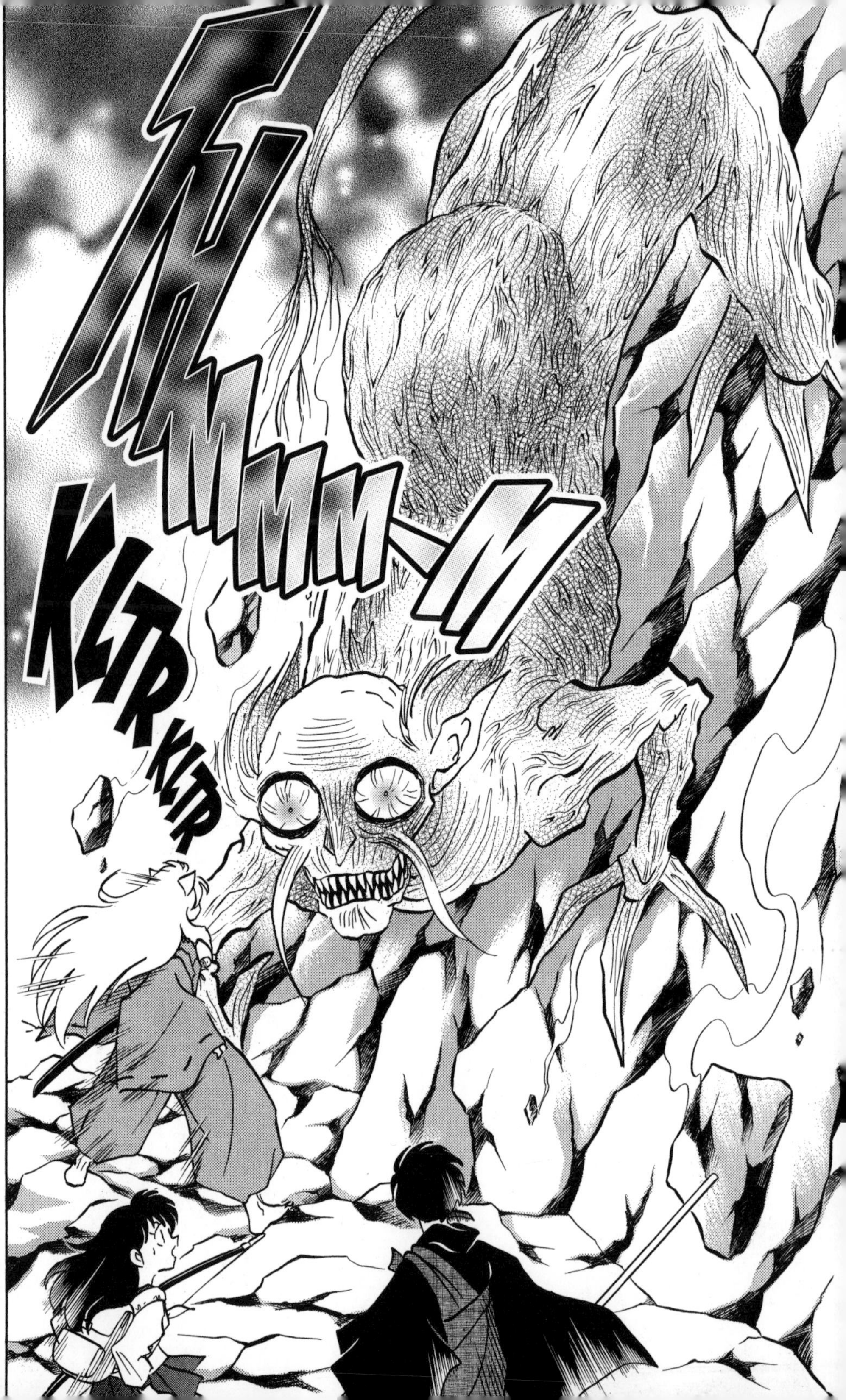

SHMMMM-M
KLTR KLTR KLTR

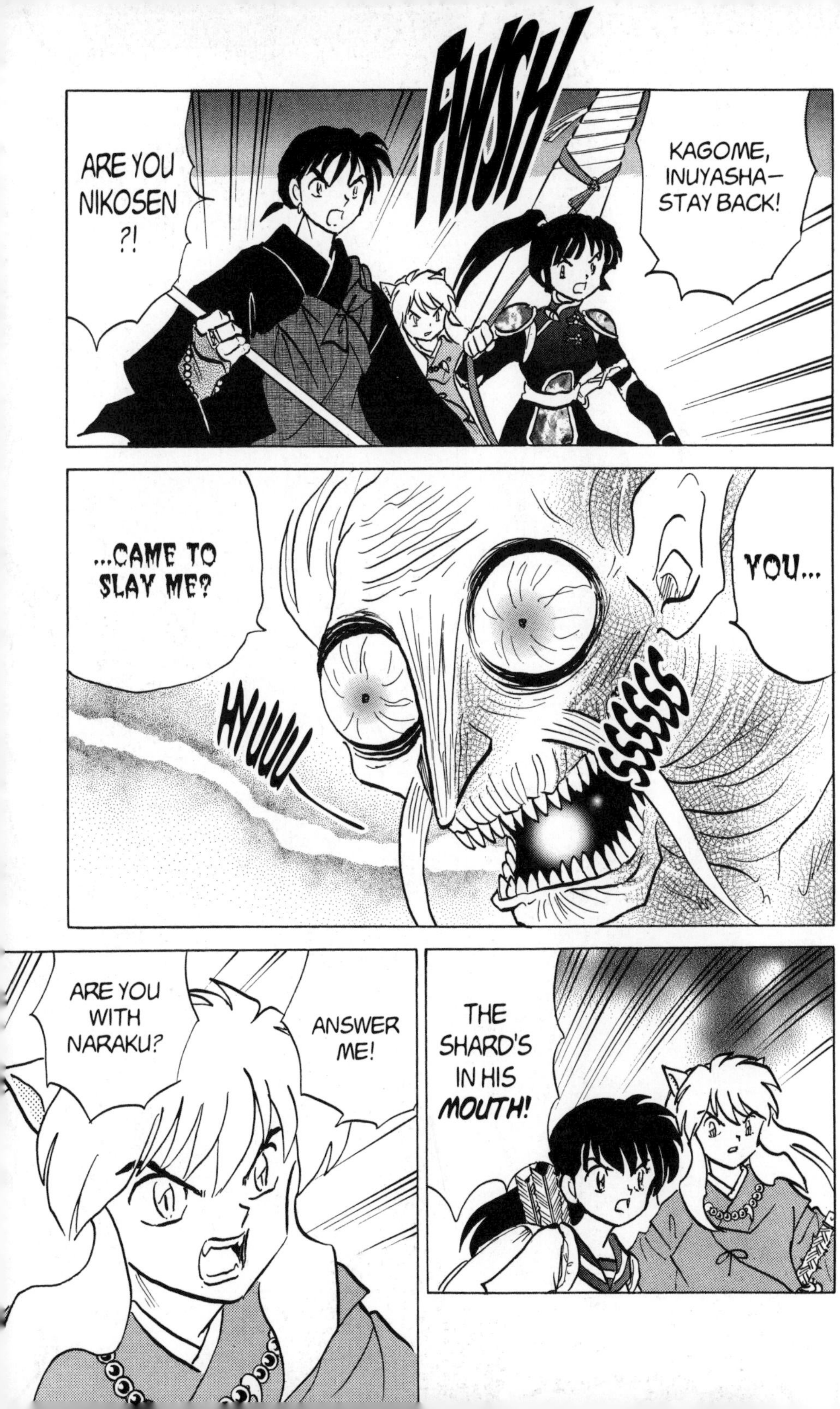
KAGOME, INUYASHA— STAY BACK!
FWSH
ARE YOU NIKOSEN ?!
YOU...
SSSSSS
HYUUUU
...CAME TO SLAY ME?
THE SHARD'S IN HIS *MOUTH!*
ARE YOU WITH NARAKU?
ANSWER ME!

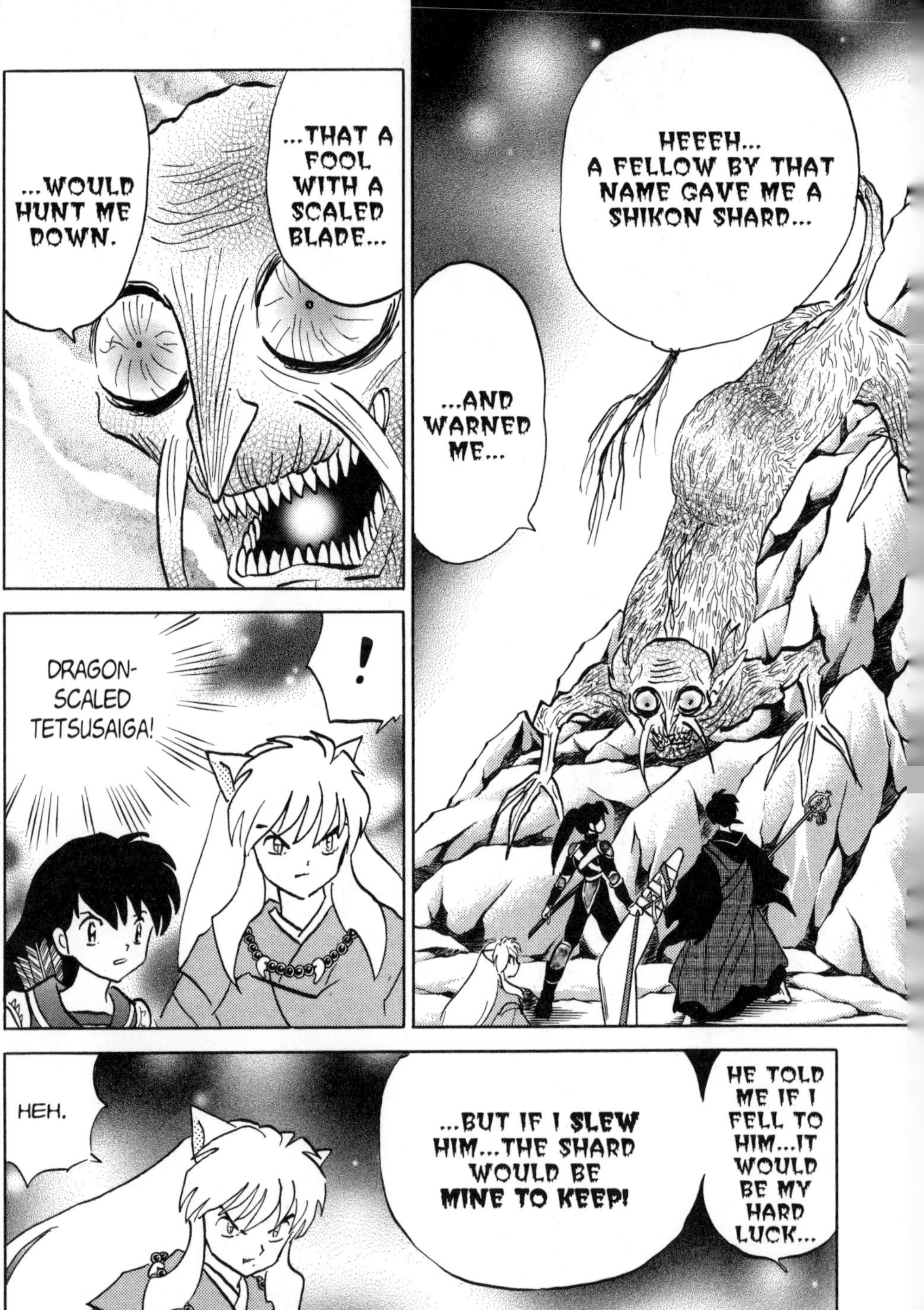
HEEEH... A FELLOW BY THAT NAME GAVE ME A SHIKON SHARD...
...AND WARNED ME...
...THAT A FOOL WITH A SCALED BLADE...
...WOULD HUNT ME DOWN.
!
DRAGON-SCALED TETSUSAIGA!
HE TOLD ME IF I FELL TO HIM...IT WOULD BE MY HARD LUCK...
...BUT IF I SLEW HIM...THE SHARD WOULD BE MINE TO KEEP!
HEH.

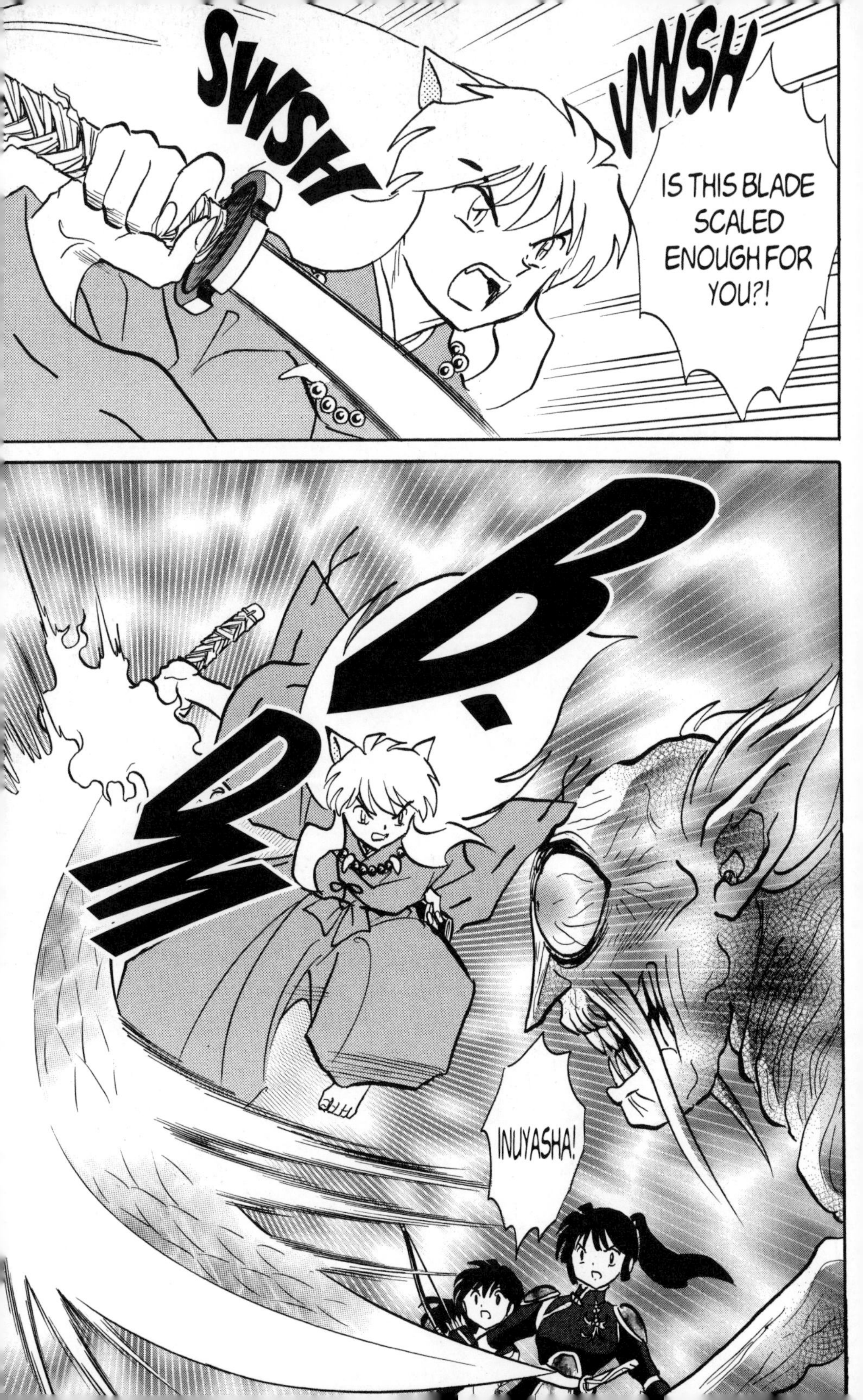
VWSH
IS THIS BLADE SCALED ENOUGH FOR YOU?!
SWSH
INUYASHA!

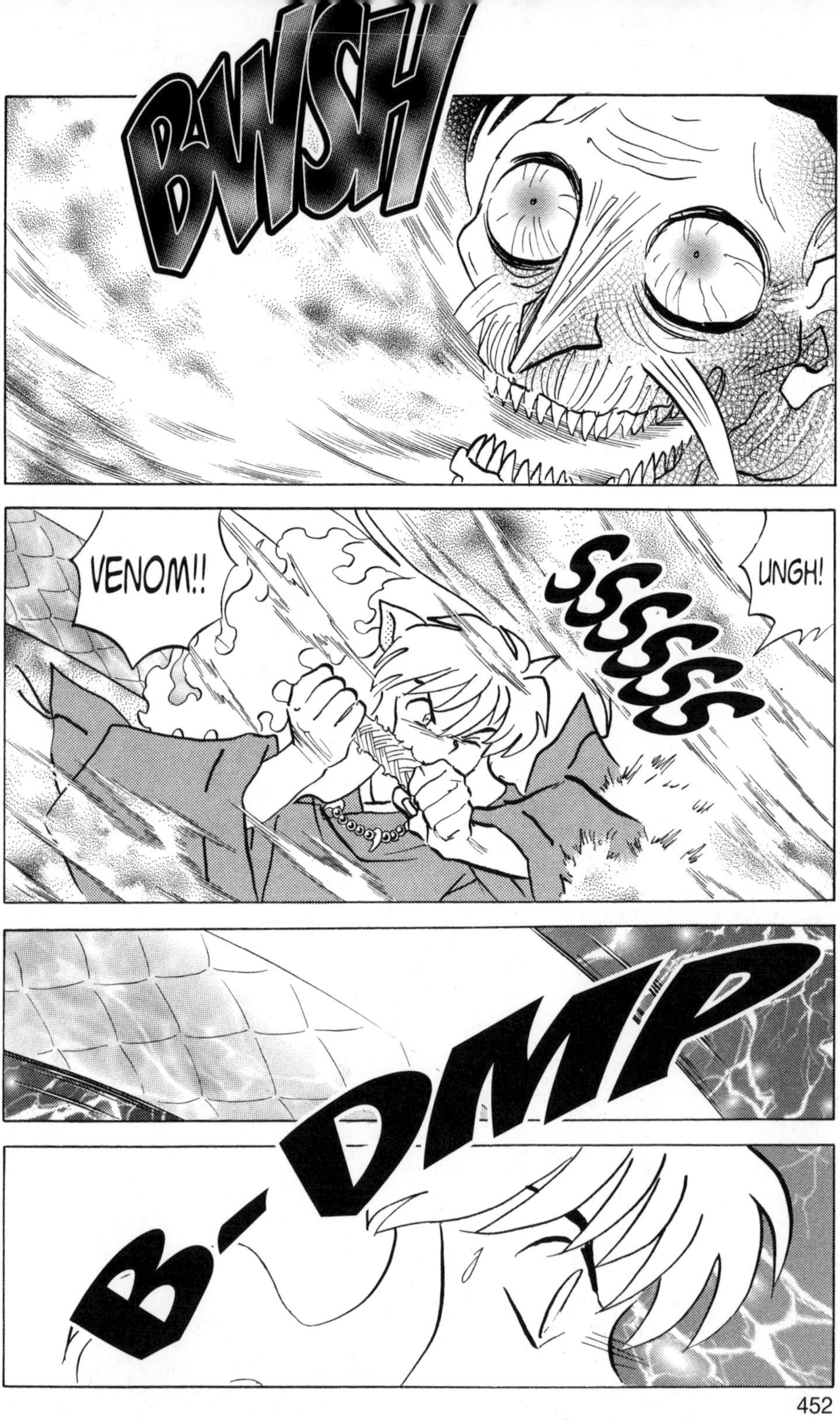
BWISH
UNGH!
SSSSSS
VENOM!!
B-DMP

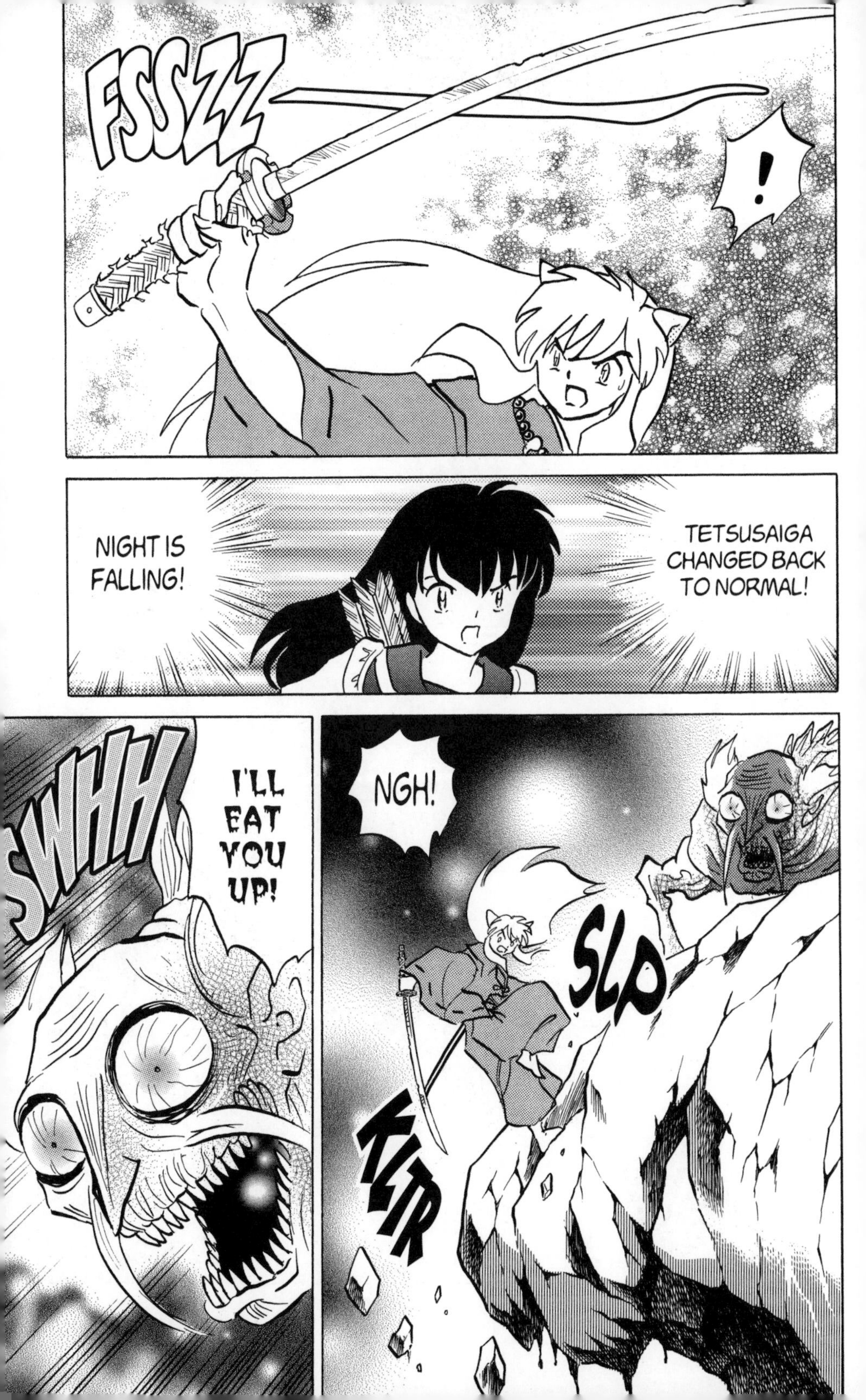
!
FSSZZ
TETSUSAIGA CHANGED BACK TO NORMAL!
NIGHT IS FALLING!
NGH!
SLP
KLTR
SWHH
I'LL EAT YOU UP!

BOOMER-
ANG
BONE!

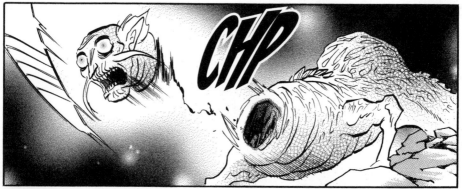

CHP

SPLSH

INU-
YASHA!

SLMM

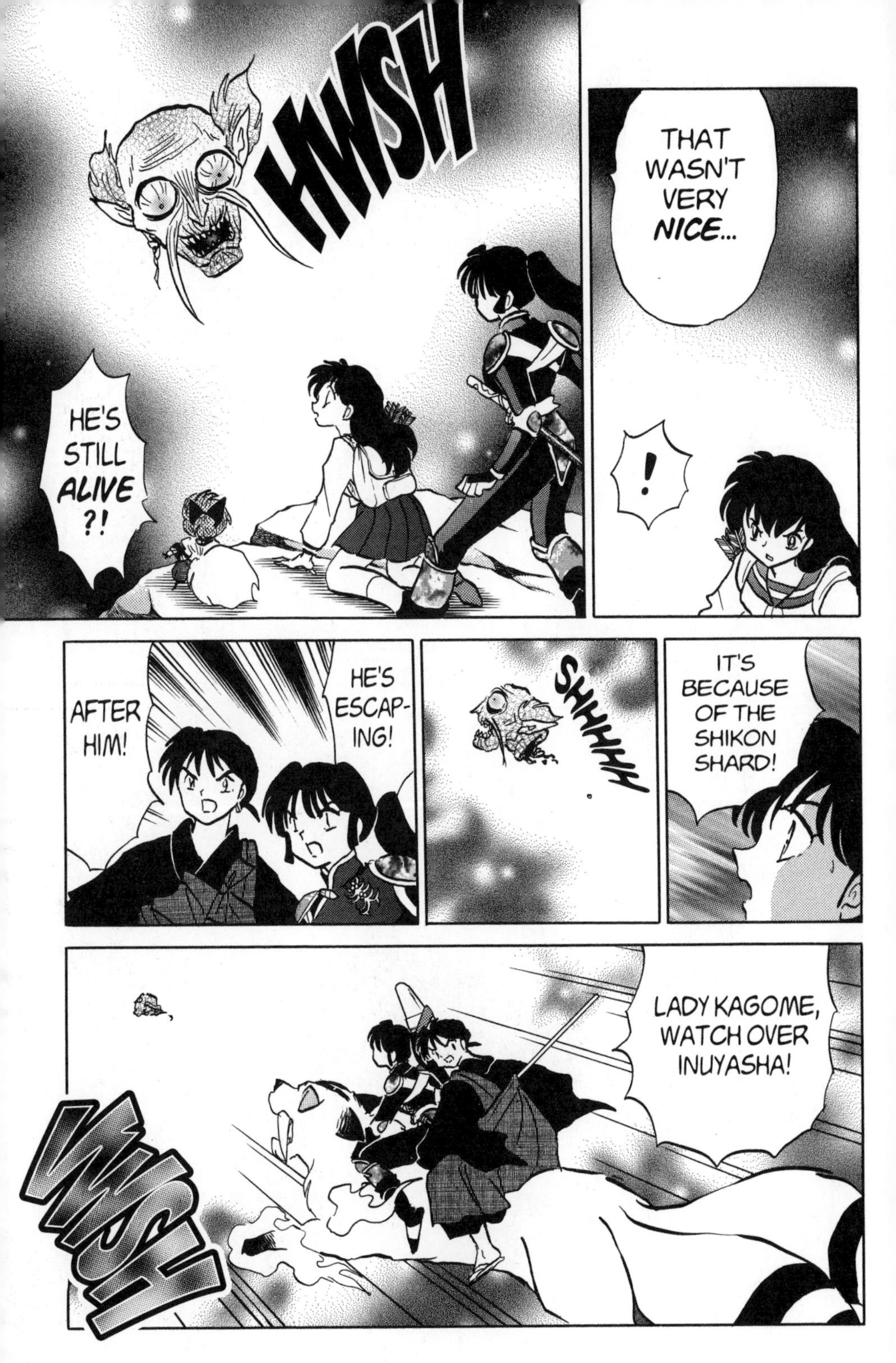
THAT WASN'T VERY NICE...
!
HWSH
HE'S STILL ALIVE ?!
IT'S BECAUSE OF THE SHIKON SHARD!
SHHHHHH
HE'S ESCAP-ING!
AFTER HIM!
LADY KAGOME, WATCH OVER INUYASHA!
WHSH

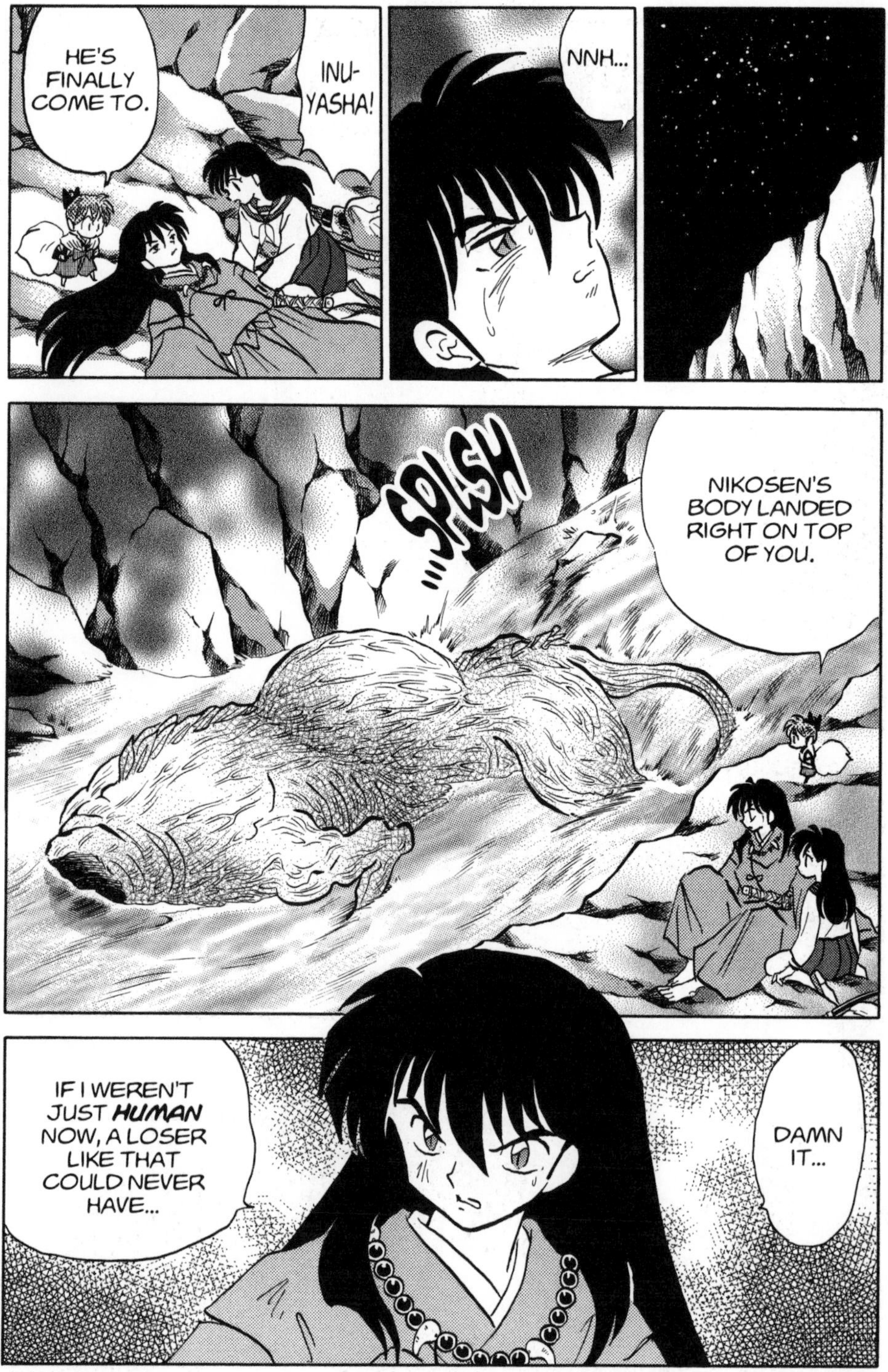
NNH...
INU-YASHA!
HE'S FINALLY COME TO.
NIKOSEN'S BODY LANDED RIGHT ON TOP OF YOU.
SPLSH
DAMN IT...
IF I WEREN'T JUST **HUMAN** NOW, A LOSER LIKE THAT COULD NEVER HAVE...

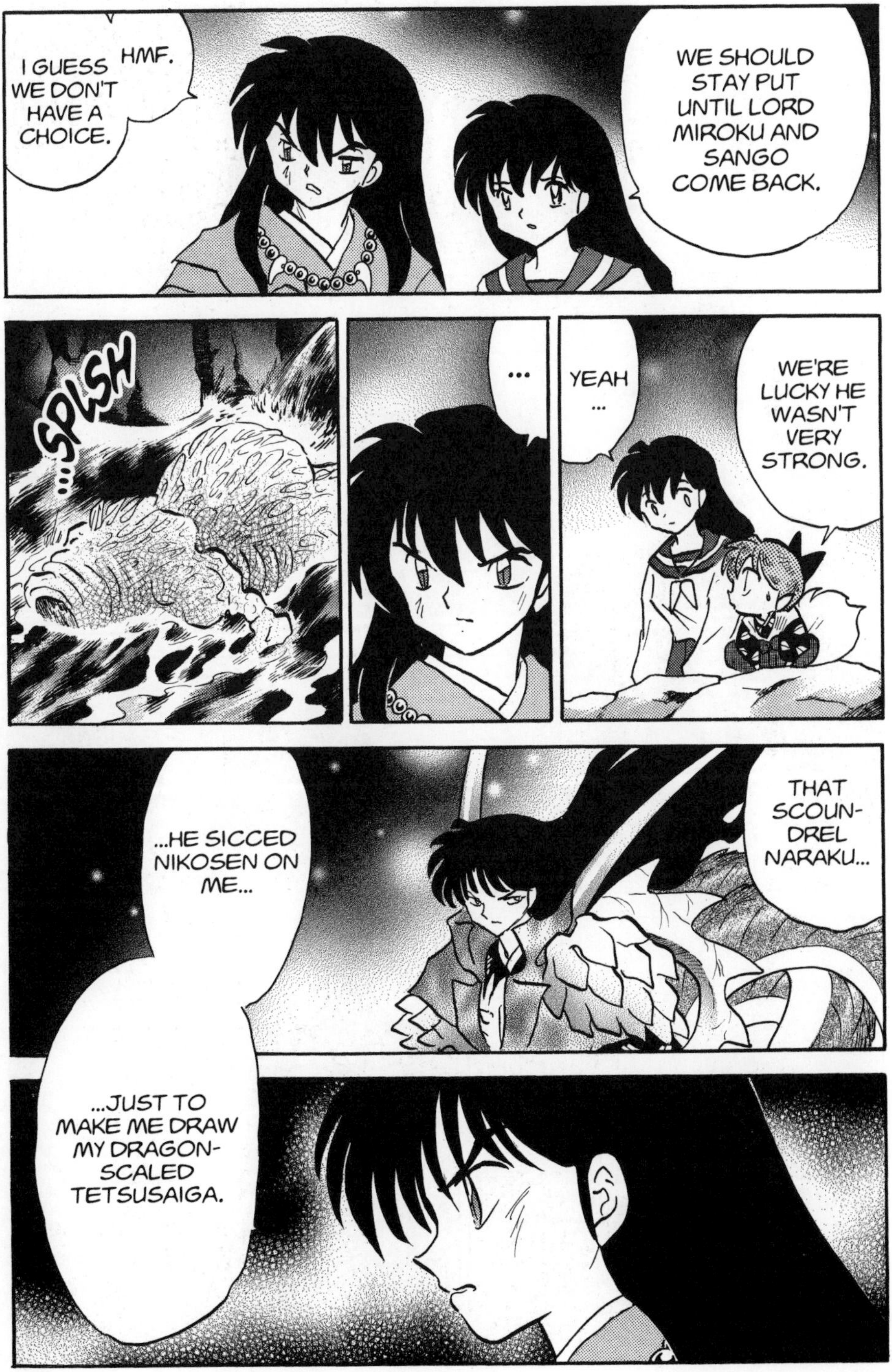
WE SHOULD STAY PUT UNTIL LORD MIROKU AND SANGO COME BACK.
HMF.
I GUESS WE DON'T HAVE A CHOICE.
WE'RE LUCKY HE WASN'T VERY STRONG.
YEAH ...
...
...SPLSH
THAT SCOUN-DREL NARAKU...
...HE SICCED NIKOSEN ON ME...
...JUST TO MAKE ME DRAW MY DRAGON-SCALED TETSUSAIGA.

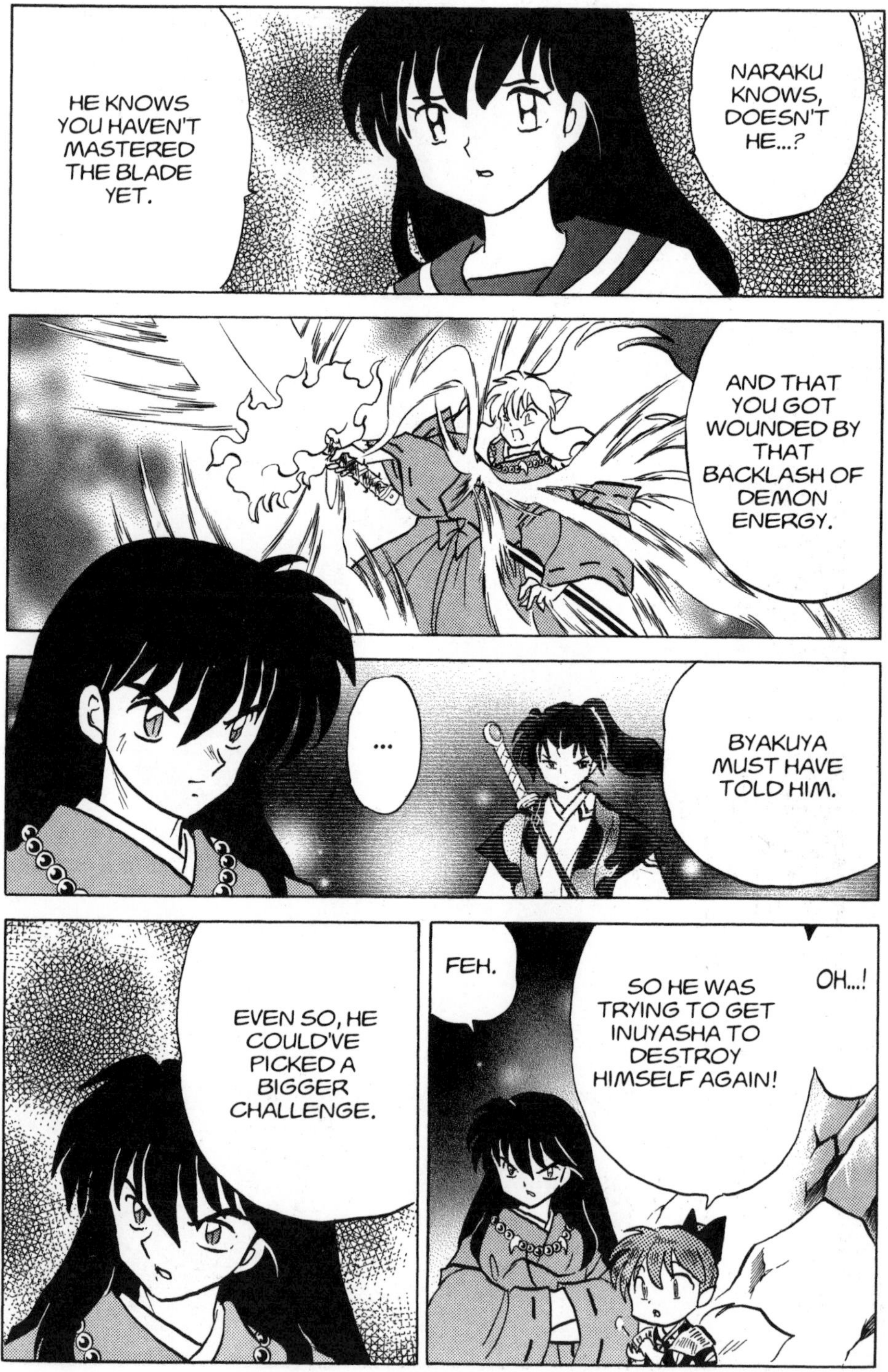
NARAKU KNOWS, DOESN'T HE...?
HE KNOWS YOU HAVEN'T MASTERED THE BLADE YET.
AND THAT YOU GOT WOUNDED BY THAT BACKLASH OF DEMON ENERGY.
BYAKUYA MUST HAVE TOLD HIM.
...
OH...!
SO HE WAS TRYING TO GET INUYASHA TO DESTROY HIMSELF AGAIN!
FEH.
EVEN SO, HE COULD'VE PICKED A BIGGER CHALLENGE.

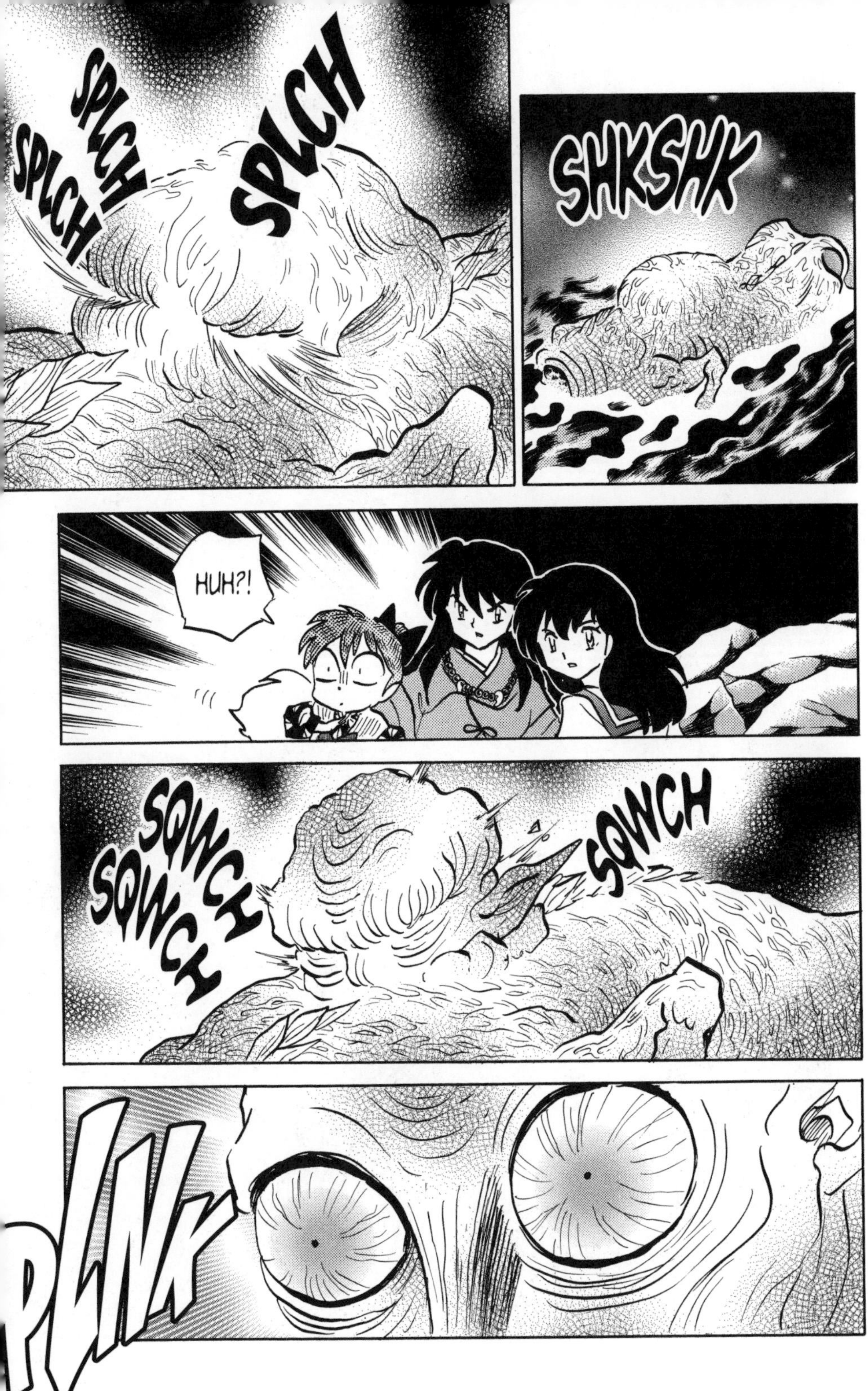
SHKSHK
SPLCH
SPLCH
SPLCH
HUH?!
SQWCH
SQWCH
SQWCH
PLINK

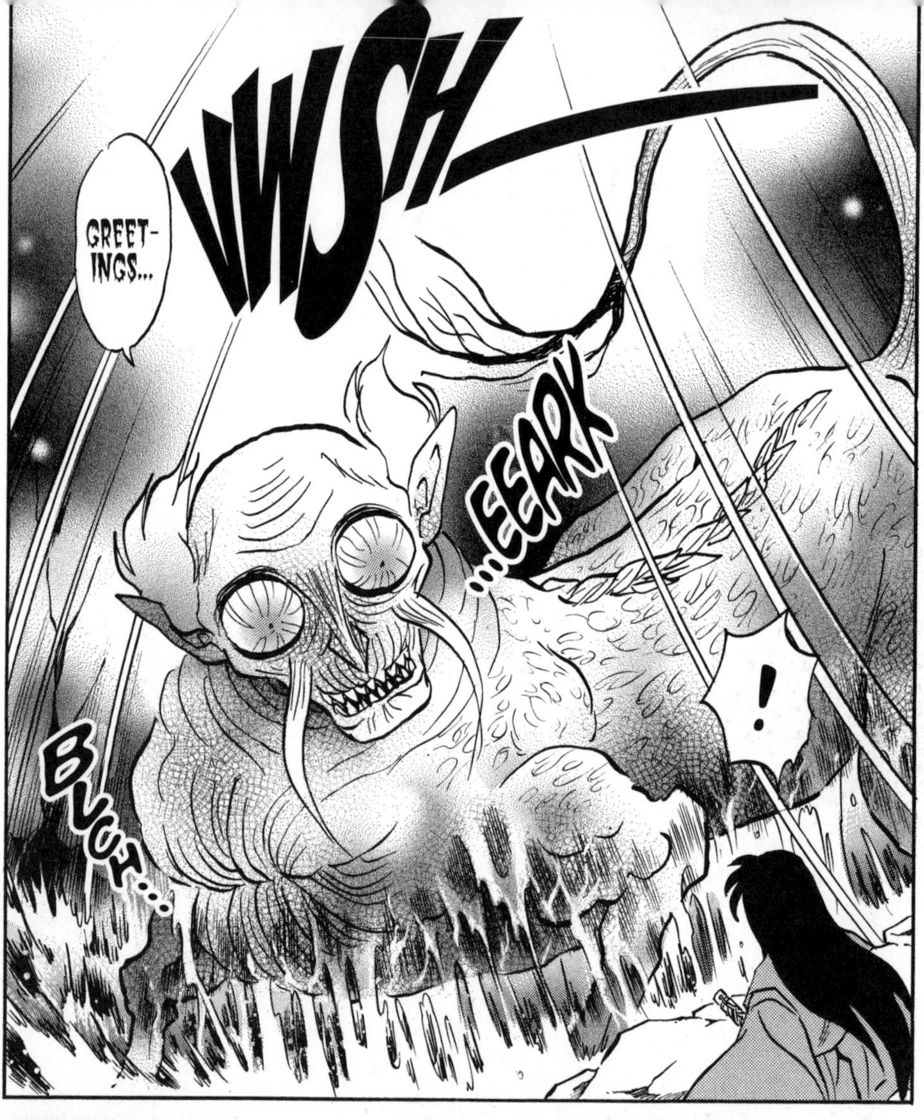
VWSH
GREET-
INGS...
...EEARK
!
BLUCH...

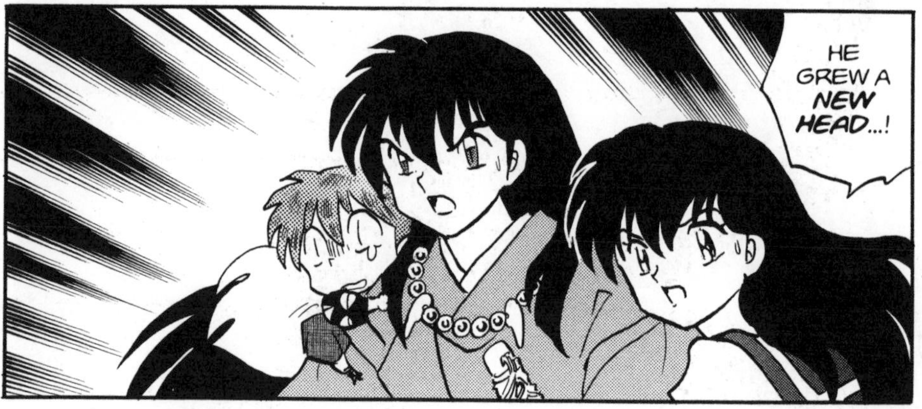
HE GREW A *NEW HEAD*...!

SCROLL FIVE
THE SECOND HEAD

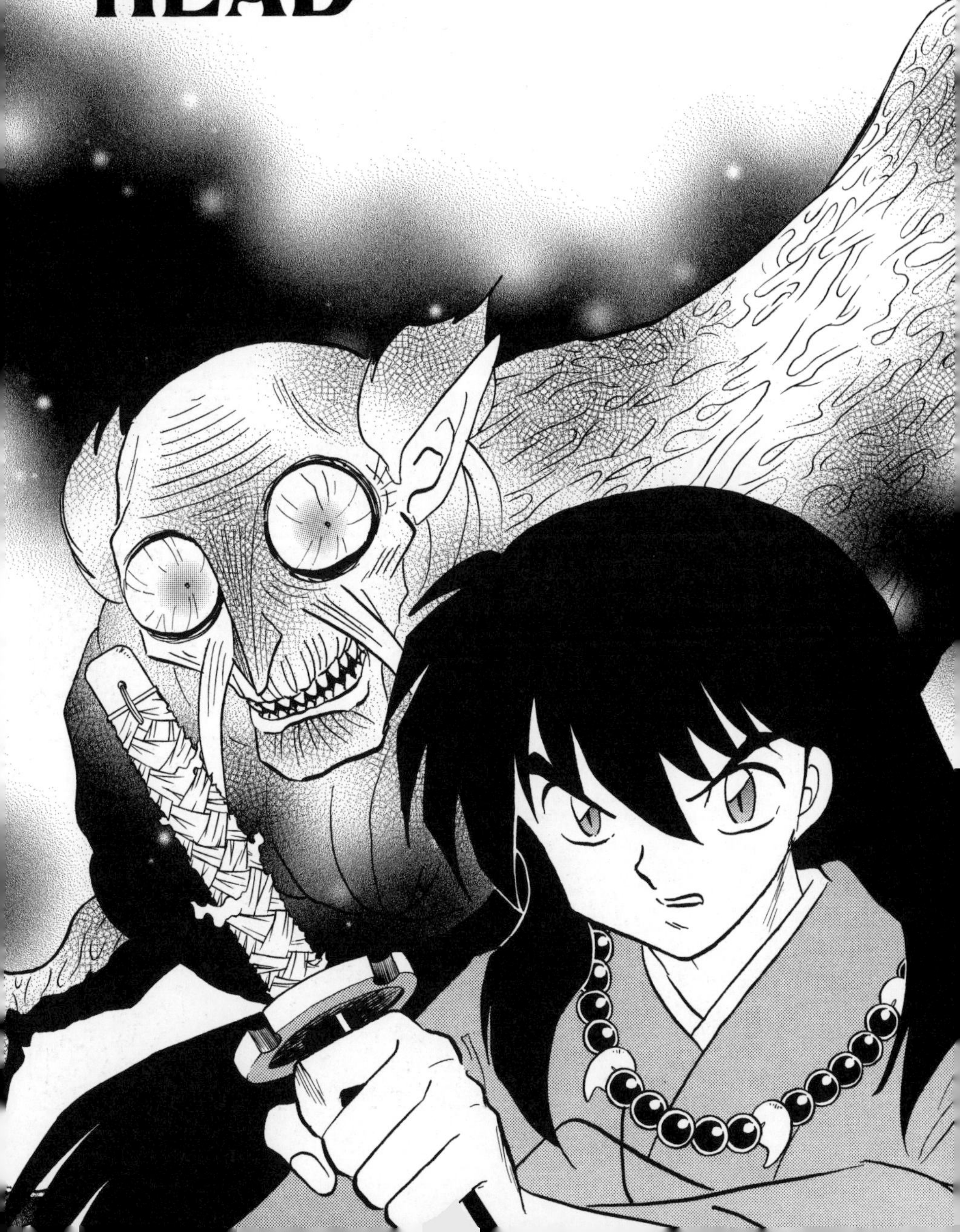

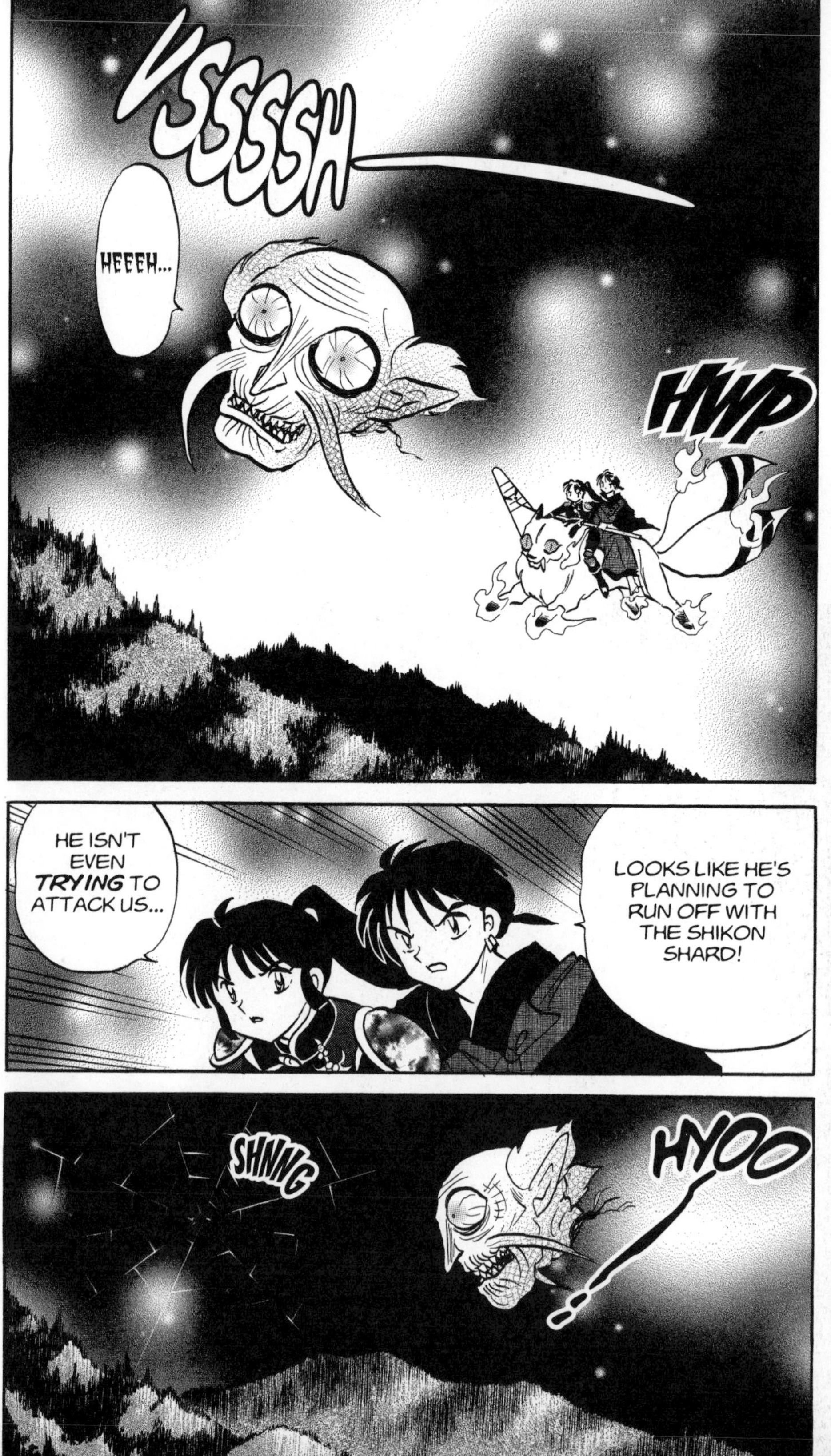
VSSSSH
HEEEH...
HWP
LOOKS LIKE HE'S PLANNING TO RUN OFF WITH THE SHIKON SHARD!
HE ISN'T EVEN *TRYING* TO ATTACK US...
HYOO
SHNNG

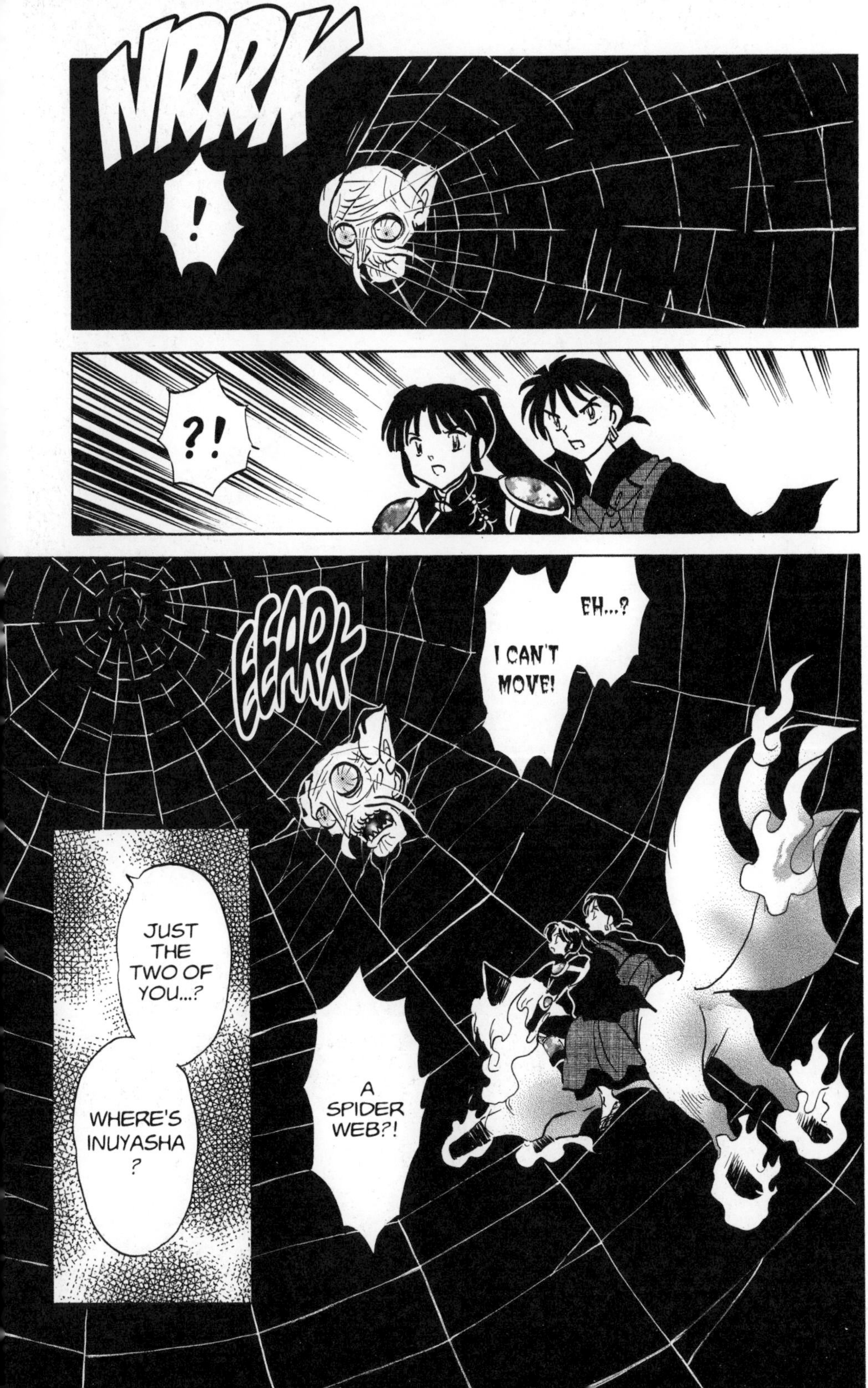
NRRK
!
?!
EH...?
I CAN'T MOVE!
EEARK
A SPIDER WEB?!
JUST THE TWO OF YOU...?
WHERE'S INUYASHA?

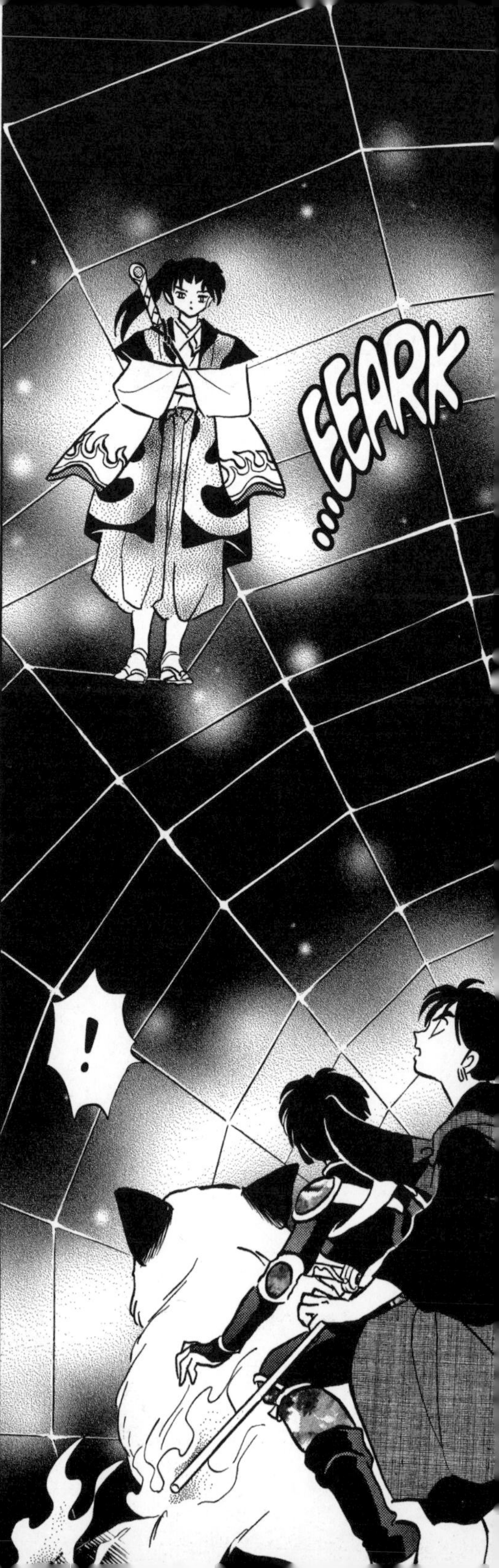
...EEARK
!

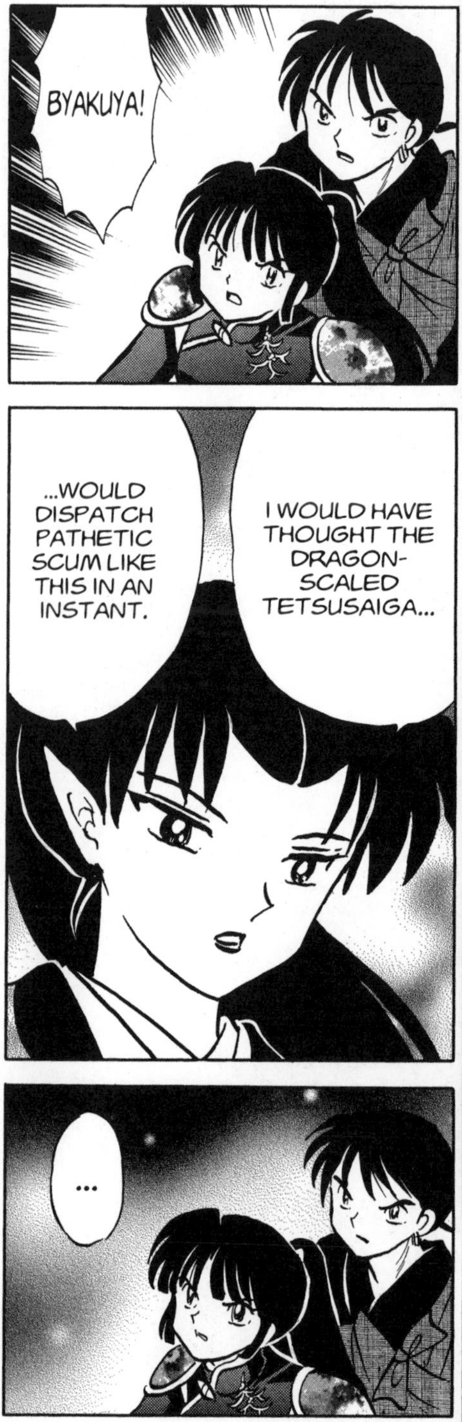
BYAKUYA!
I WOULD HAVE THOUGHT THE DRAGON-SCALED TETSUSAIGA...
...WOULD DISPATCH PATHETIC SCUM LIKE THIS IN AN INSTANT.
...

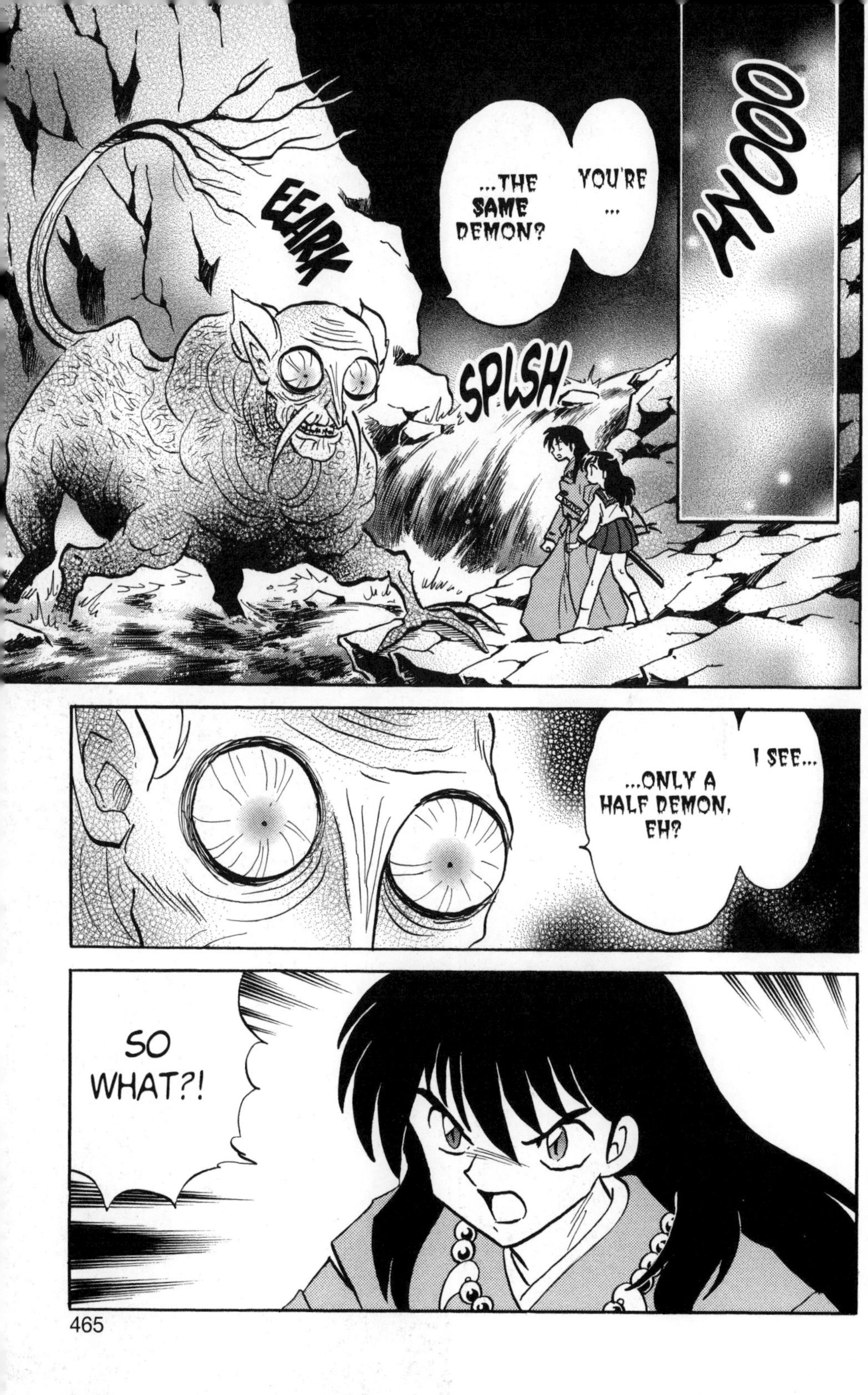
WOOO
YOU'RE ...
...THE SAME DEMON?
EEARK
SPLSH
I SEE...
...ONLY A HALF DEMON, EH?
SO WHAT?!

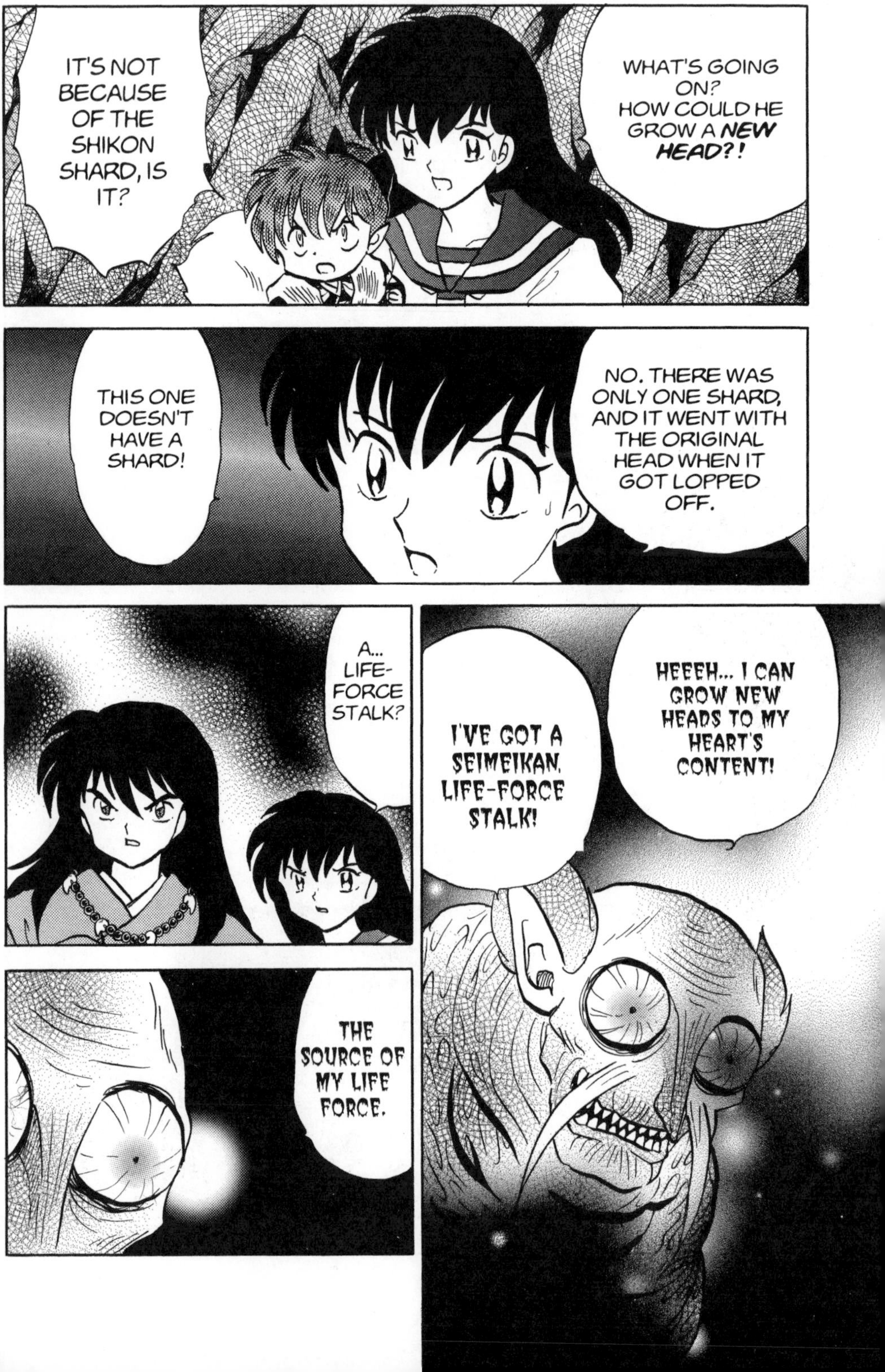
WHAT'S GOING ON? HOW COULD HE GROW A NEW HEAD?!
IT'S NOT BECAUSE OF THE SHIKON SHARD, IS IT?
NO. THERE WAS ONLY ONE SHARD, AND IT WENT WITH THE ORIGINAL HEAD WHEN IT GOT LOPPED OFF.
THIS ONE DOESN'T HAVE A SHARD!
HEEEH... I CAN GROW NEW HEADS TO MY HEART'S CONTENT!
I'VE GOT A SEIMEIKAN, LIFE-FORCE STALK!
A... LIFE-FORCE STALK?
THE SOURCE OF MY LIFE FORCE.

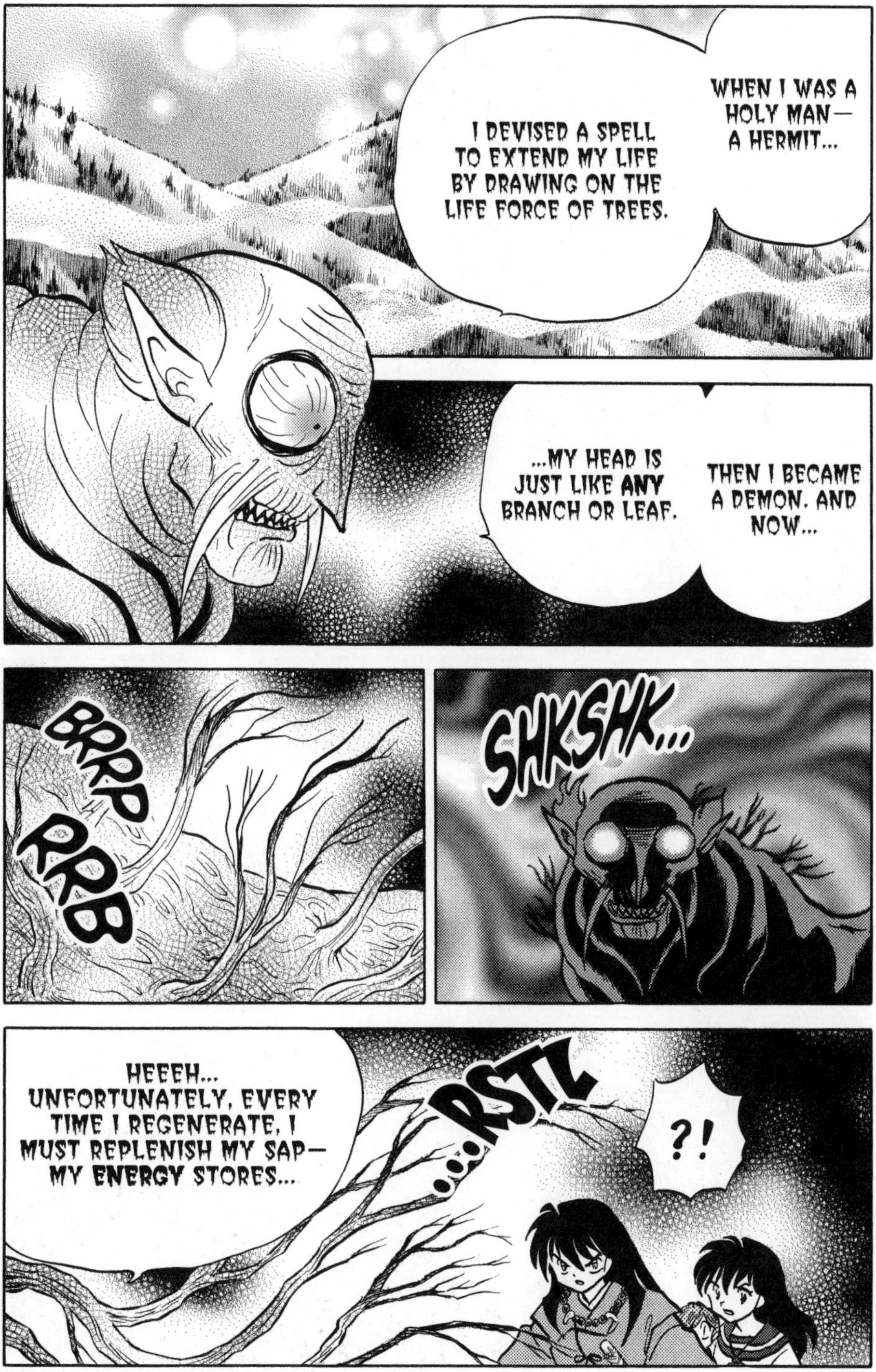
WHEN I WAS A HOLY MAN—A HERMIT...
I DEVISED A SPELL TO EXTEND MY LIFE BY DRAWING ON THE LIFE FORCE OF TREES.
THEN I BECAME A DEMON. AND NOW...
...MY HEAD IS JUST LIKE ANY BRANCH OR LEAF.
SHKSHK...
BRRP RRB
?!
...RSTZ
HEEEH... UNFORTUNATELY, EVERY TIME I REGENERATE, I MUST REPLENISH MY SAP—MY ENERGY STORES...

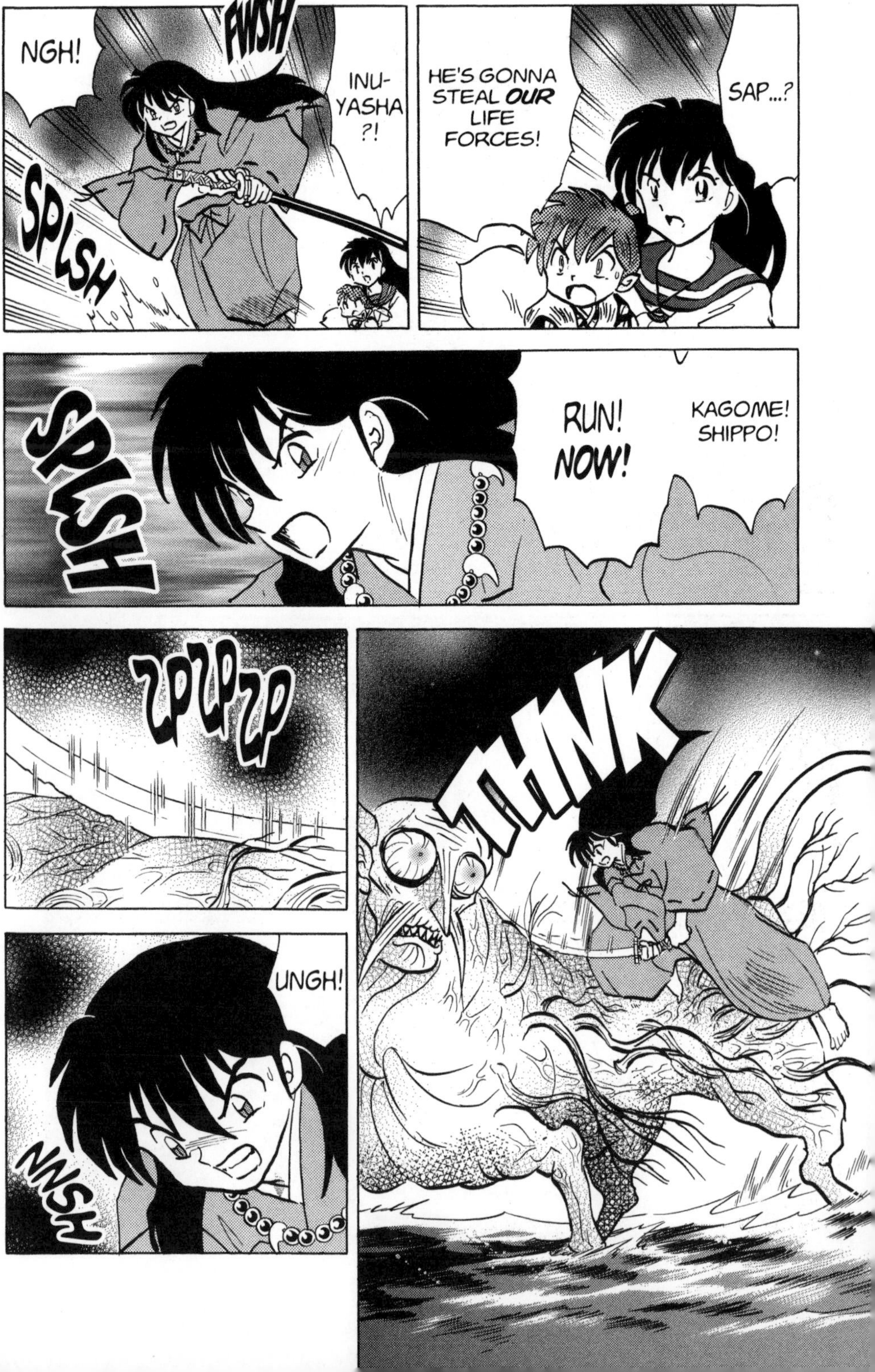
SAP...?
HE'S GONNA STEAL **OUR** LIFE FORCES!
INU-YASHA?!
FWSH
NGH!
SPLSH
KAGOME! SHIPPO!
RUN! **NOW!**
SPLSH
THINK
ZPZPZP
UNGH!
NNSH

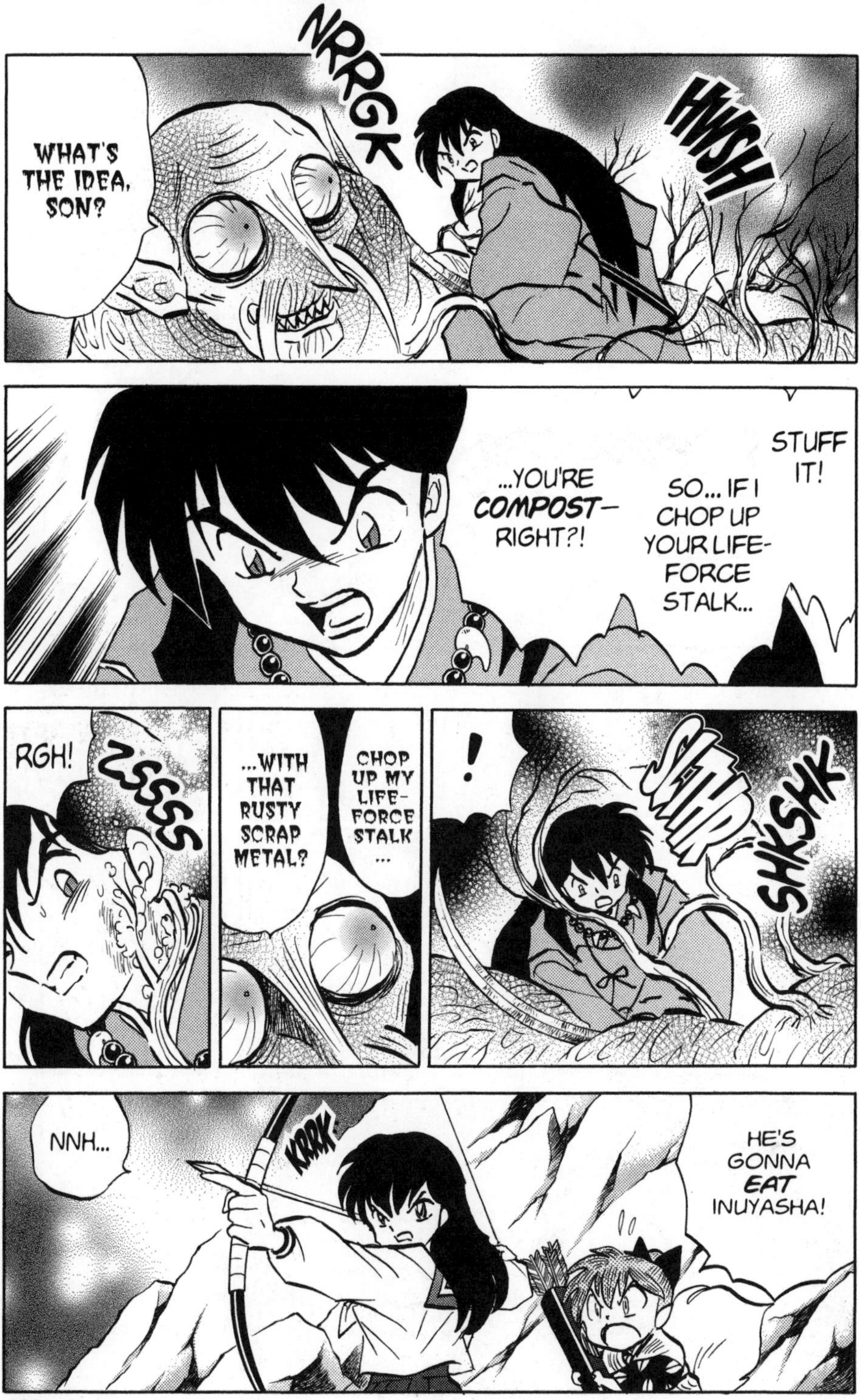
HWSH
NRRGK
WHAT'S THE IDEA, SON?
STUFF IT!
SO... IF I CHOP UP YOUR LIFE-FORCE STALK...
...YOU'RE **COMPOST**—RIGHT?!
!
SWHP
SHKSHK
CHOP UP MY LIFE-FORCE STALK...
...WITH THAT RUSTY SCRAP METAL?
ZSSSS
RGH!
HE'S GONNA **EAT** INUYASHA!
KRRK
NNH...

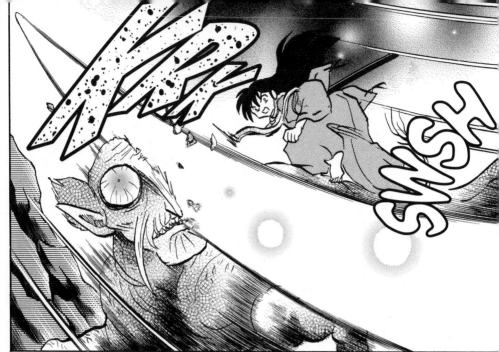

SILLY, SILLY...

ZSSSS

POISON SAP....?!

UNHHH...

ZSSSS

TMP

A TINY ARROW LIKE THAT CAN'T HARM ME!

ZWRL

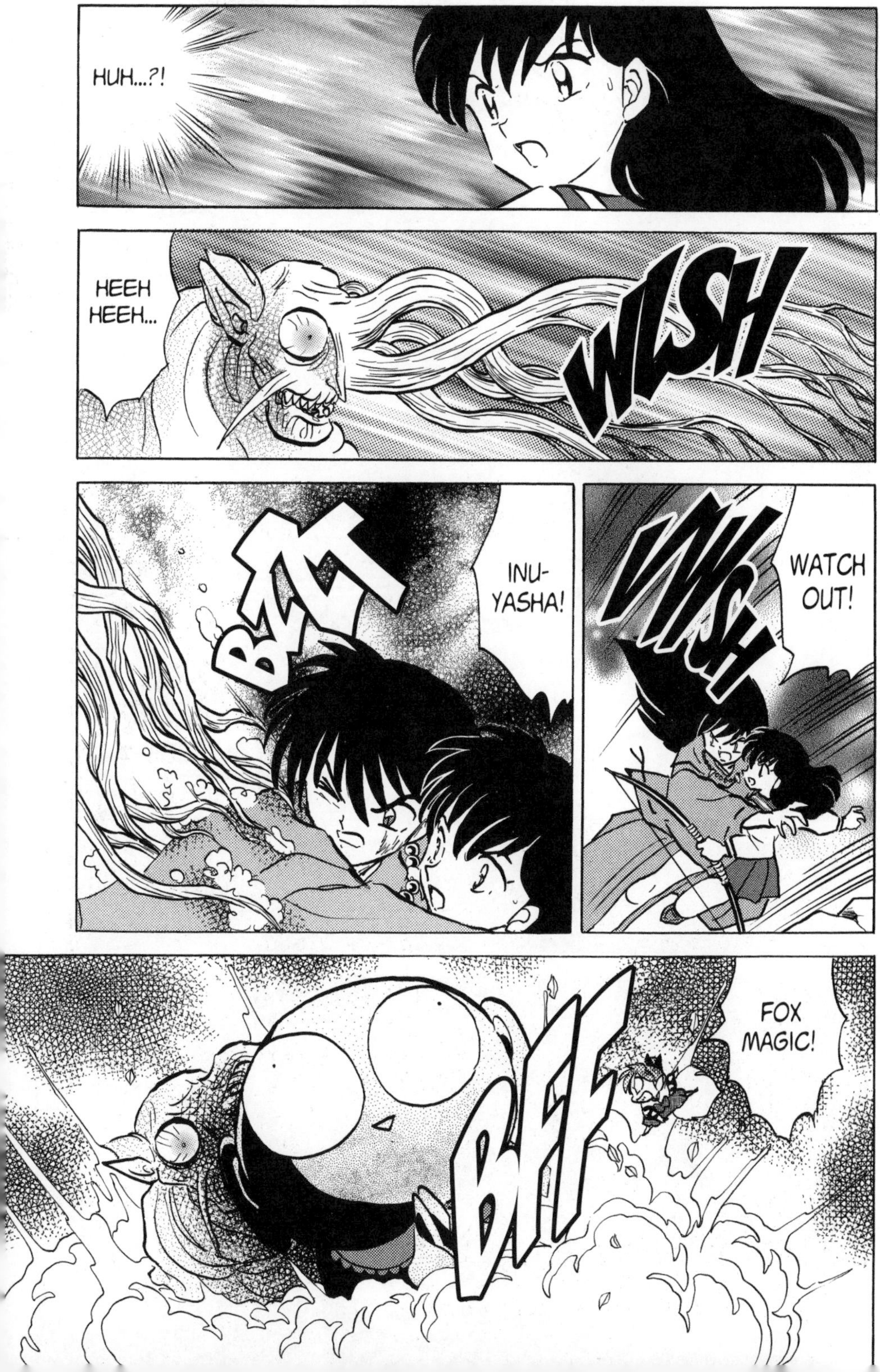
HUH...?!
HEEH HEEH...
WLSH
WATCH OUT!
VWSH
INU-YASHA!
BLST
FOX MAGIC!
BFF

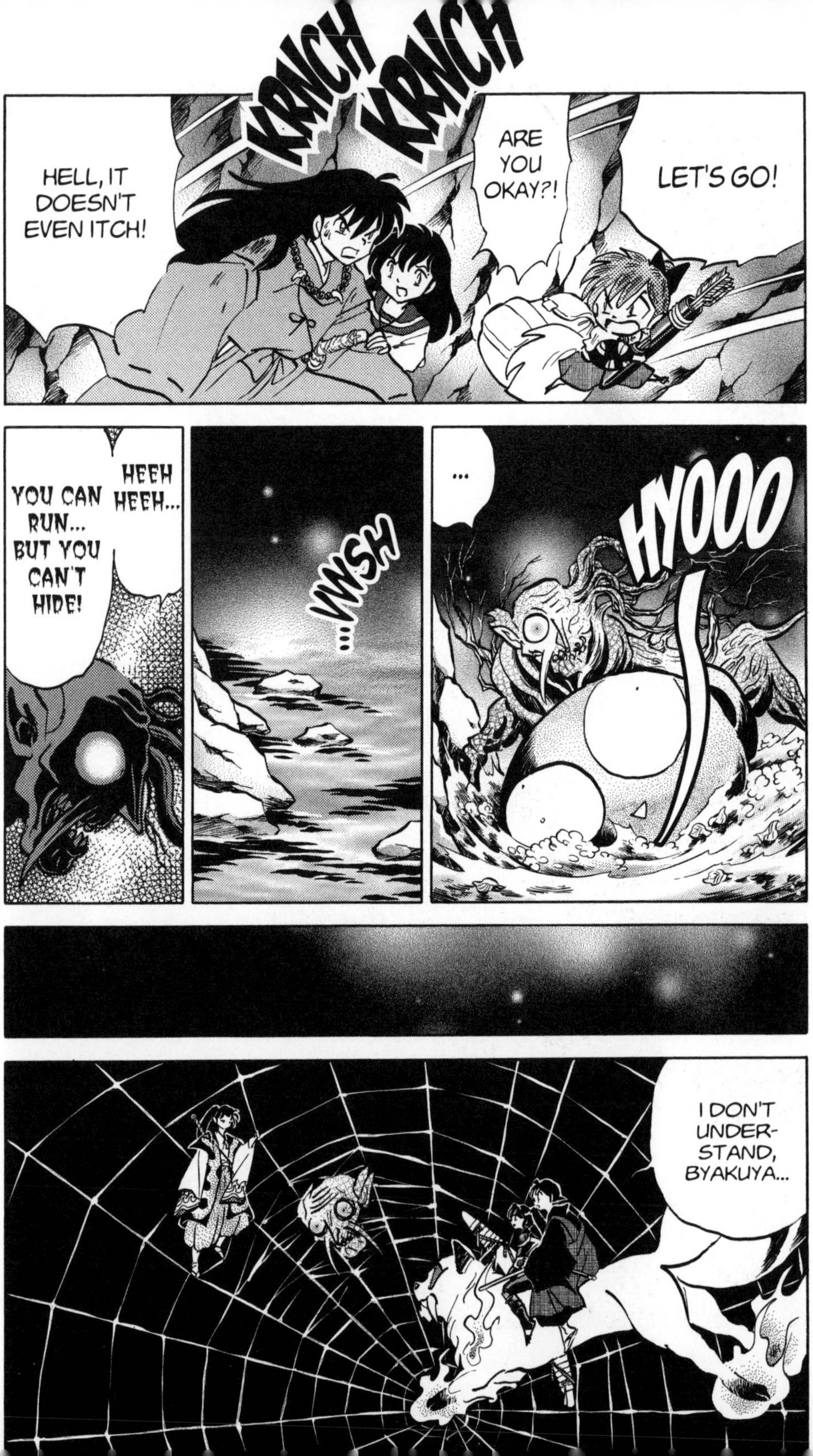
LET'S GO!
ARE YOU OKAY?!
KRNCH KRNCH
HELL, IT DOESN'T EVEN ITCH!
...
HYOOO
...VWSH
HEEH HEEH...
YOU CAN RUN... BUT YOU CAN'T HIDE!
I DON'T UNDER-STAND, BYAKUYA...

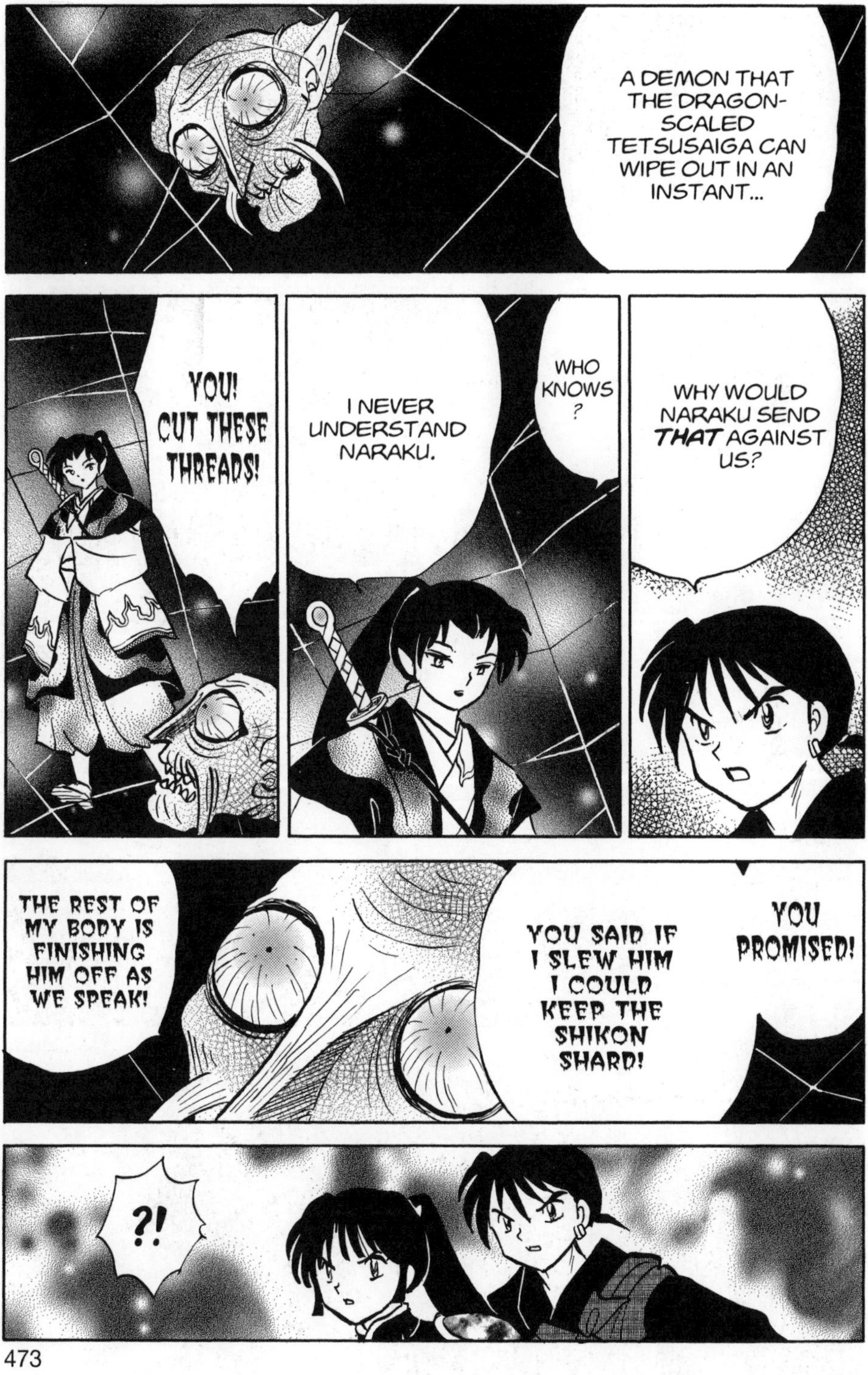
A DEMON THAT THE DRAGON-SCALED TETSUSAIGA CAN WIPE OUT IN AN INSTANT...
WHY WOULD NARAKU SEND THAT AGAINST US?
WHO KNOWS?
I NEVER UNDERSTAND NARAKU.
YOU! CUT THESE THREADS!
YOU PROMISED!
YOU SAID IF I SLEW HIM I COULD KEEP THE SHIKON SHARD!
THE REST OF MY BODY IS FINISHING HIM OFF AS WE SPEAK!
?!

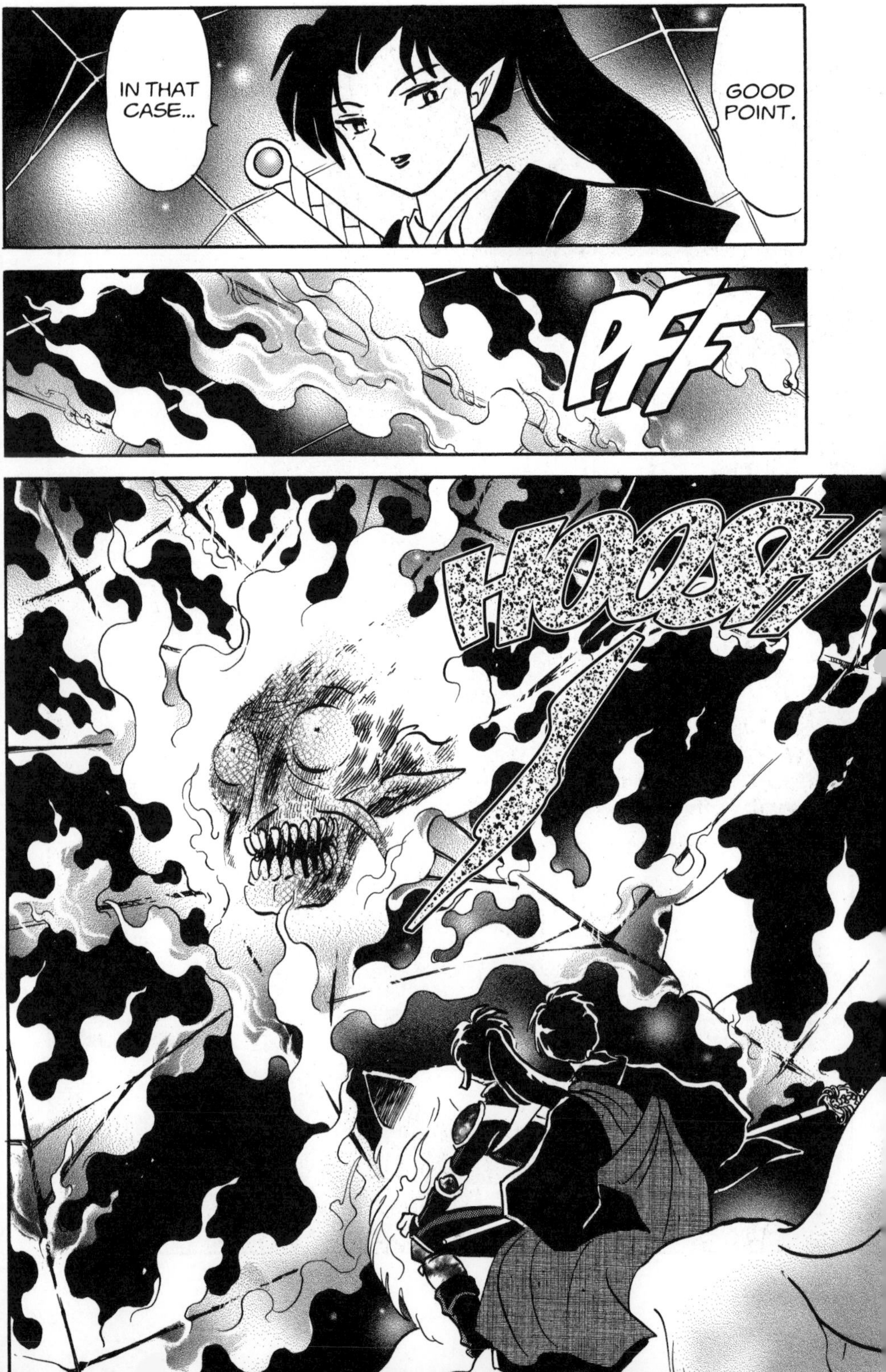
GOOD POINT.
IN THAT CASE...
PFF
HOOSH

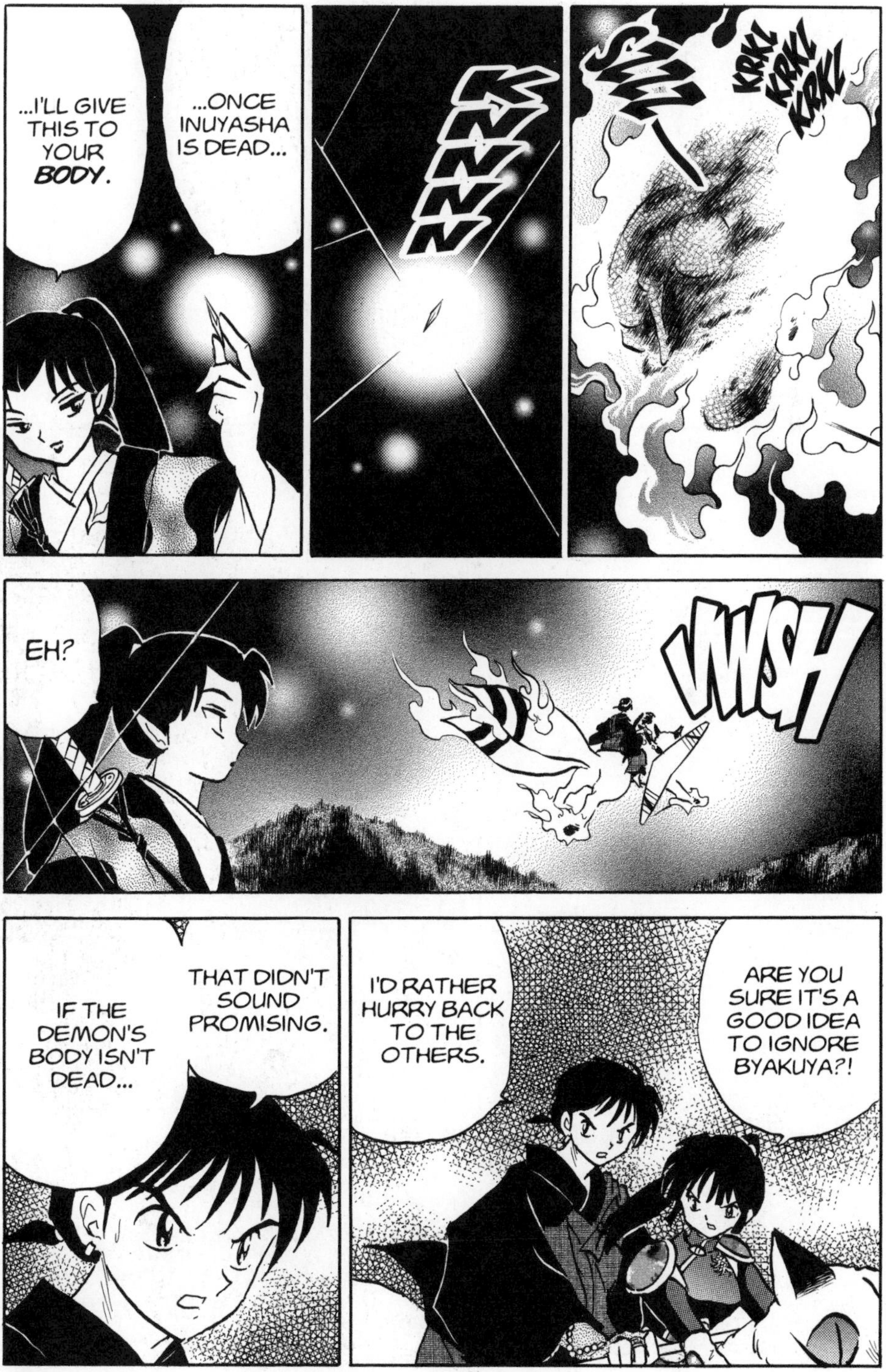
SWN
KRKL KRKL KRKL
KNNNN
...ONCE INUYASHA IS DEAD...
...I'LL GIVE THIS TO YOUR ***BODY***.
VWSH
EH?
ARE YOU SURE IT'S A GOOD IDEA TO IGNORE BYAKUYA?!
I'D RATHER HURRY BACK TO THE OTHERS.
THAT DIDN'T SOUND PROMISING.
IF THE DEMON'S BODY ISN'T DEAD...

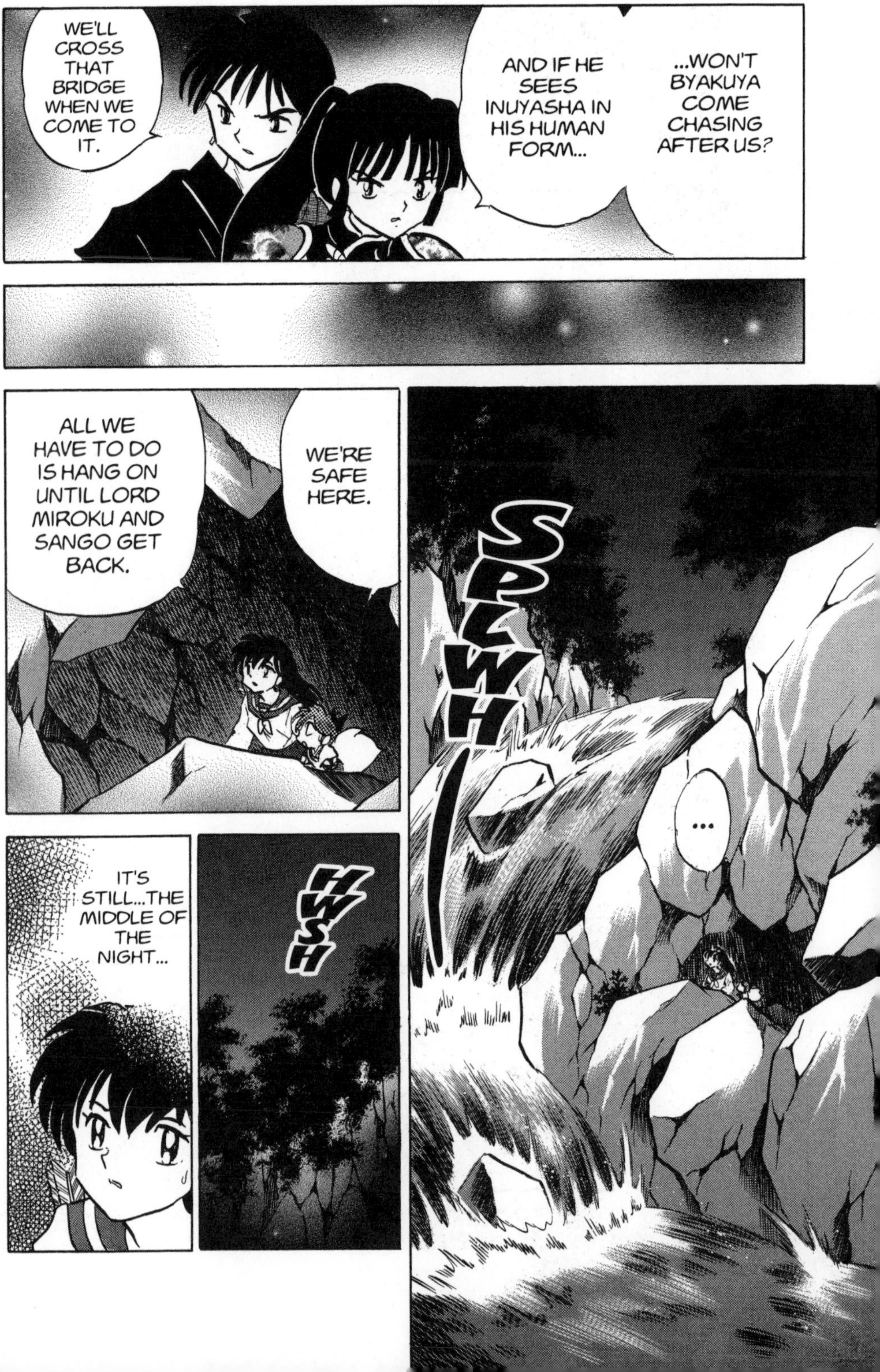
...WON'T BYAKUYA COME CHASING AFTER US?
AND IF HE SEES INUYASHA IN HIS HUMAN FORM...
WE'LL CROSS THAT BRIDGE WHEN WE COME TO IT.
SPLWH
...
WE'RE SAFE HERE.
ALL WE HAVE TO DO IS HANG ON UNTIL LORD MIROKU AND SANGO GET BACK.
HWSH
IT'S STILL...THE MIDDLE OF THE NIGHT...

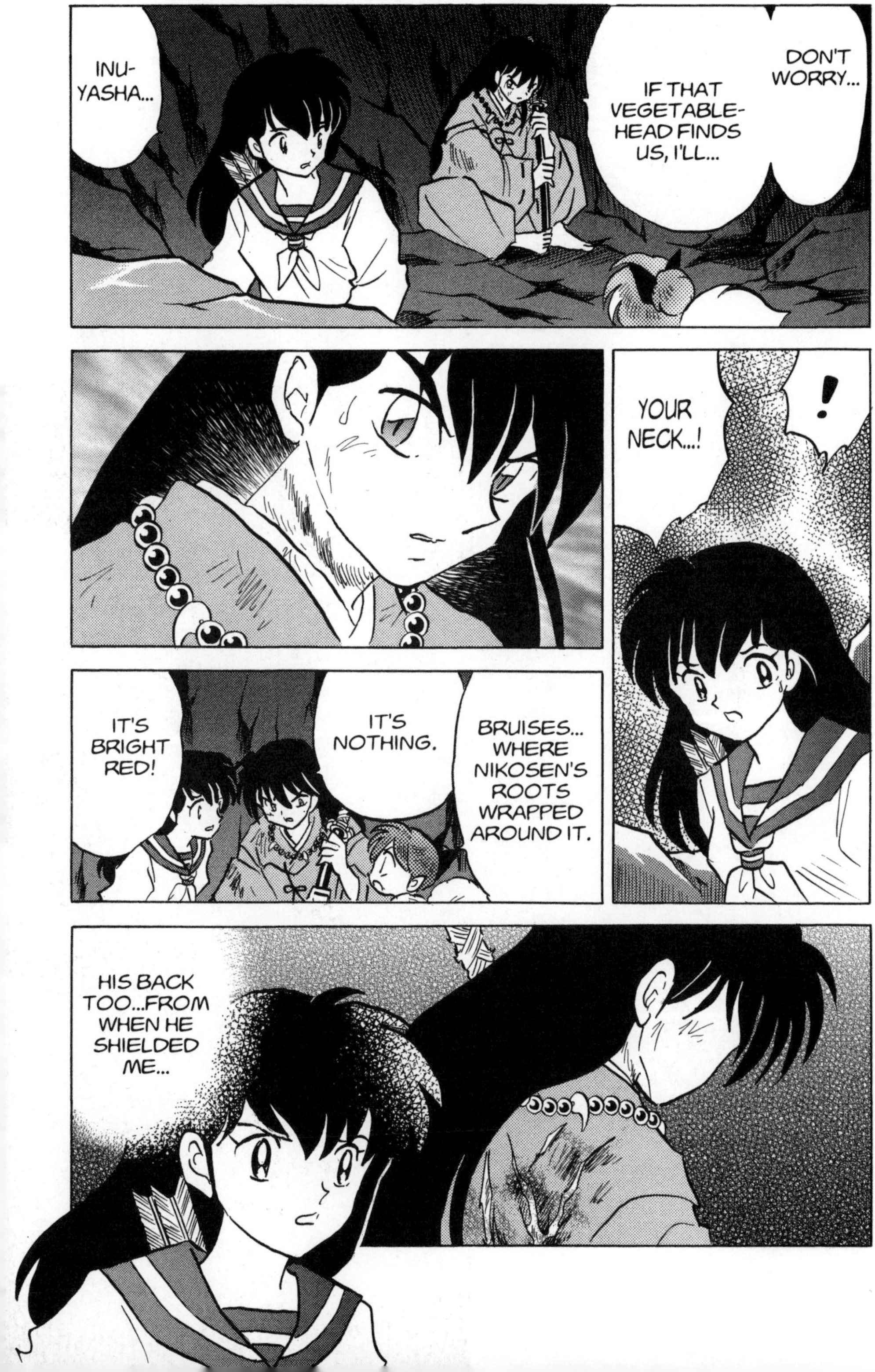
DON'T WORRY...
IF THAT VEGETABLE-HEAD FINDS US, I'LL...
INU-YASHA...
!
YOUR NECK...!
BRUISES... WHERE NIKOSEN'S ROOTS WRAPPED AROUND IT.
IT'S NOTHING.
IT'S BRIGHT RED!
HIS BACK TOO...FROM WHEN HE SHIELDED ME...

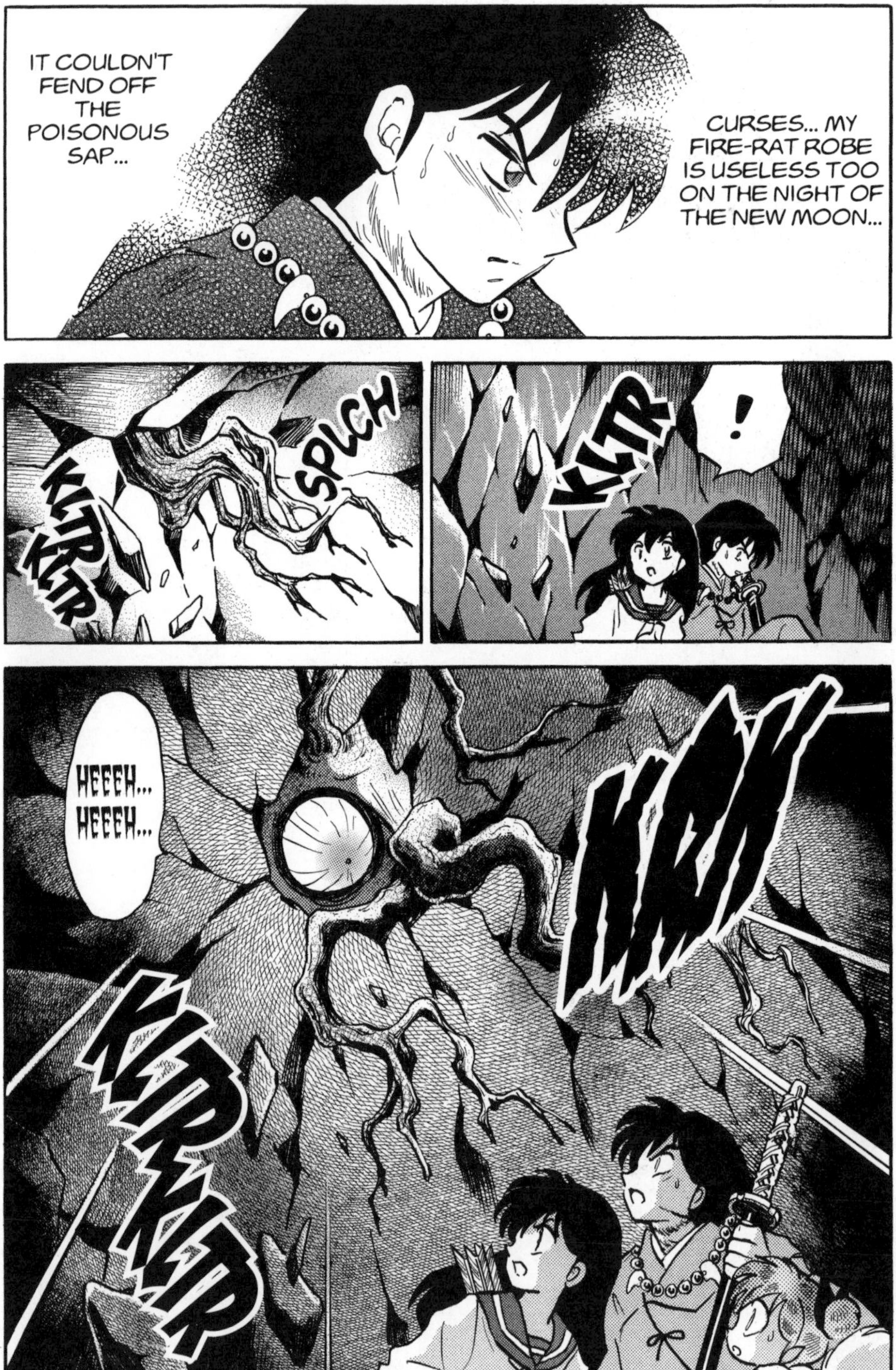
CURSES... MY FIRE-RAT ROBE IS USELESS TOO ON THE NIGHT OF THE NEW MOON...
IT COULDN'T FEND OFF THE POISONOUS SAP...
!
KLTR
SPLCH
KLTR KLTR
HEEEH... HEEEH...
KRTRKRTR

SCROLL SIX
SEIMEIKAN

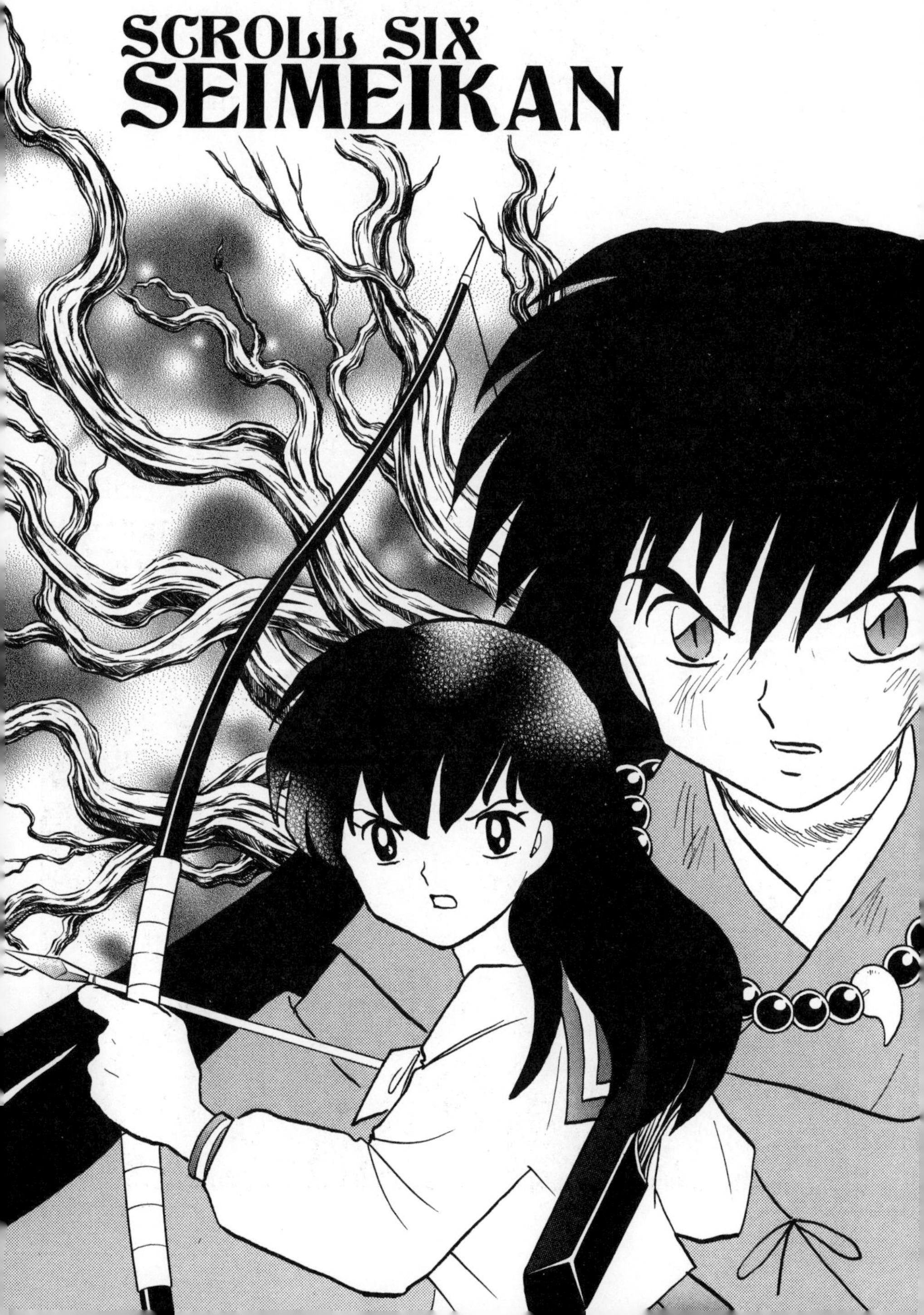

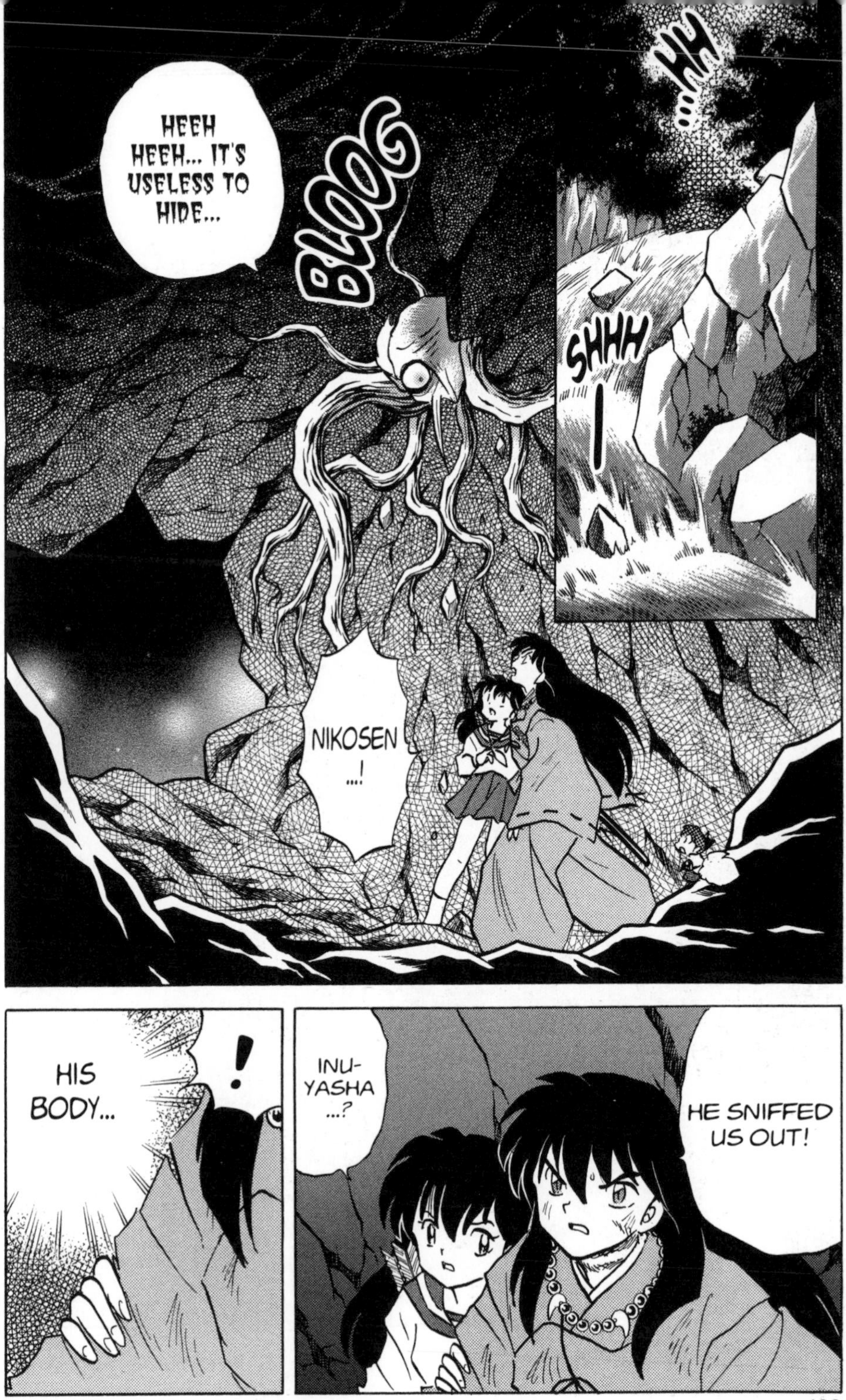
HH...
SHHH
BLOOG
HEEH HEEH... IT'S USELESS TO HIDE...
NIKOSEN ...!
HE SNIFFED US OUT!
INU-YASHA ...?
!
HIS BODY...

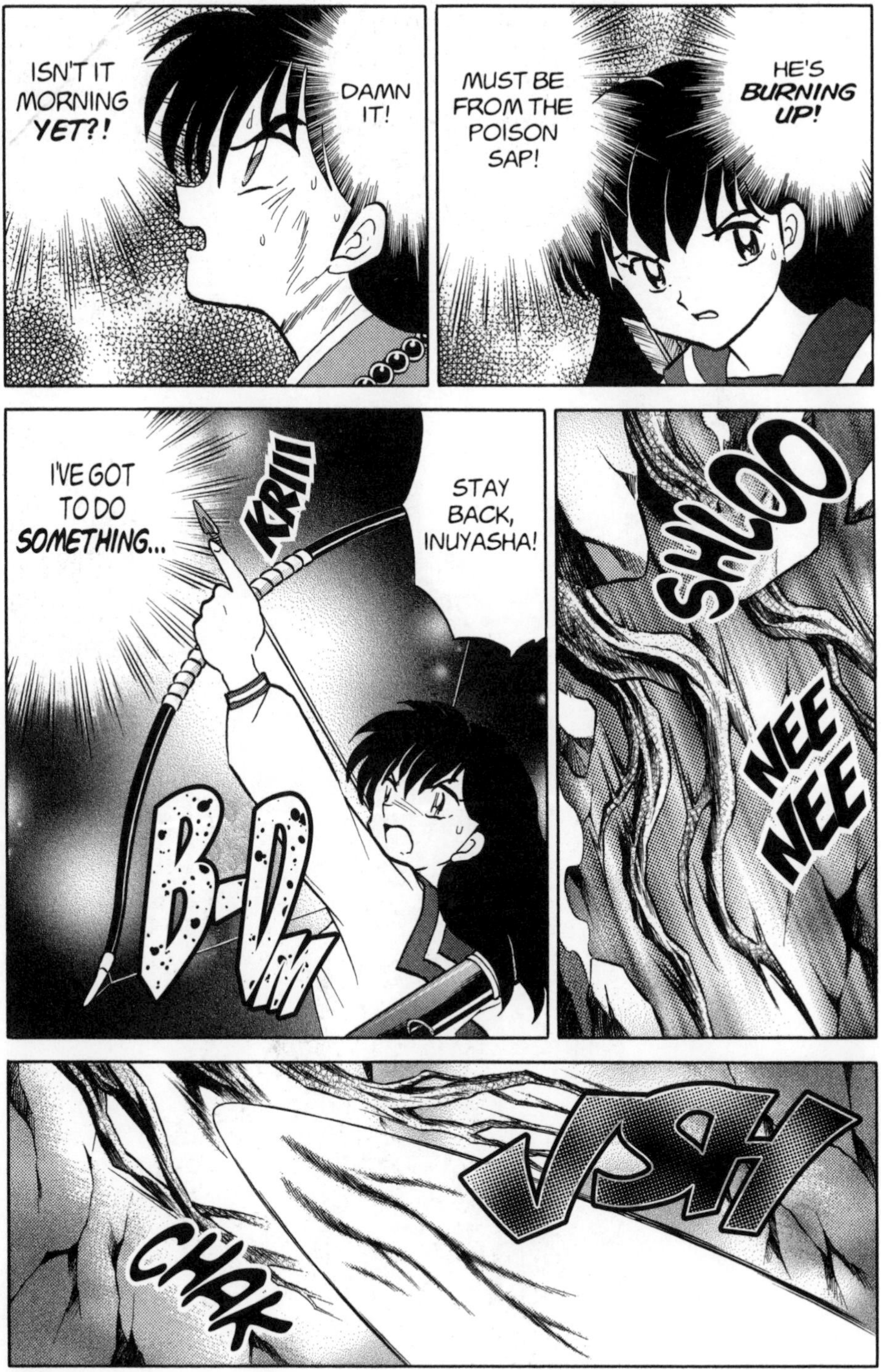
HE'S BURNING UP!
MUST BE FROM THE POISON SAP!
DAMN IT!
ISN'T IT MORNING YET?!
SHLOO
NEE NEE
STAY BACK, INUYASHA!
KRIII
I'VE GOT TO DO SOMETHING...
B-DM
JSH
CHAK

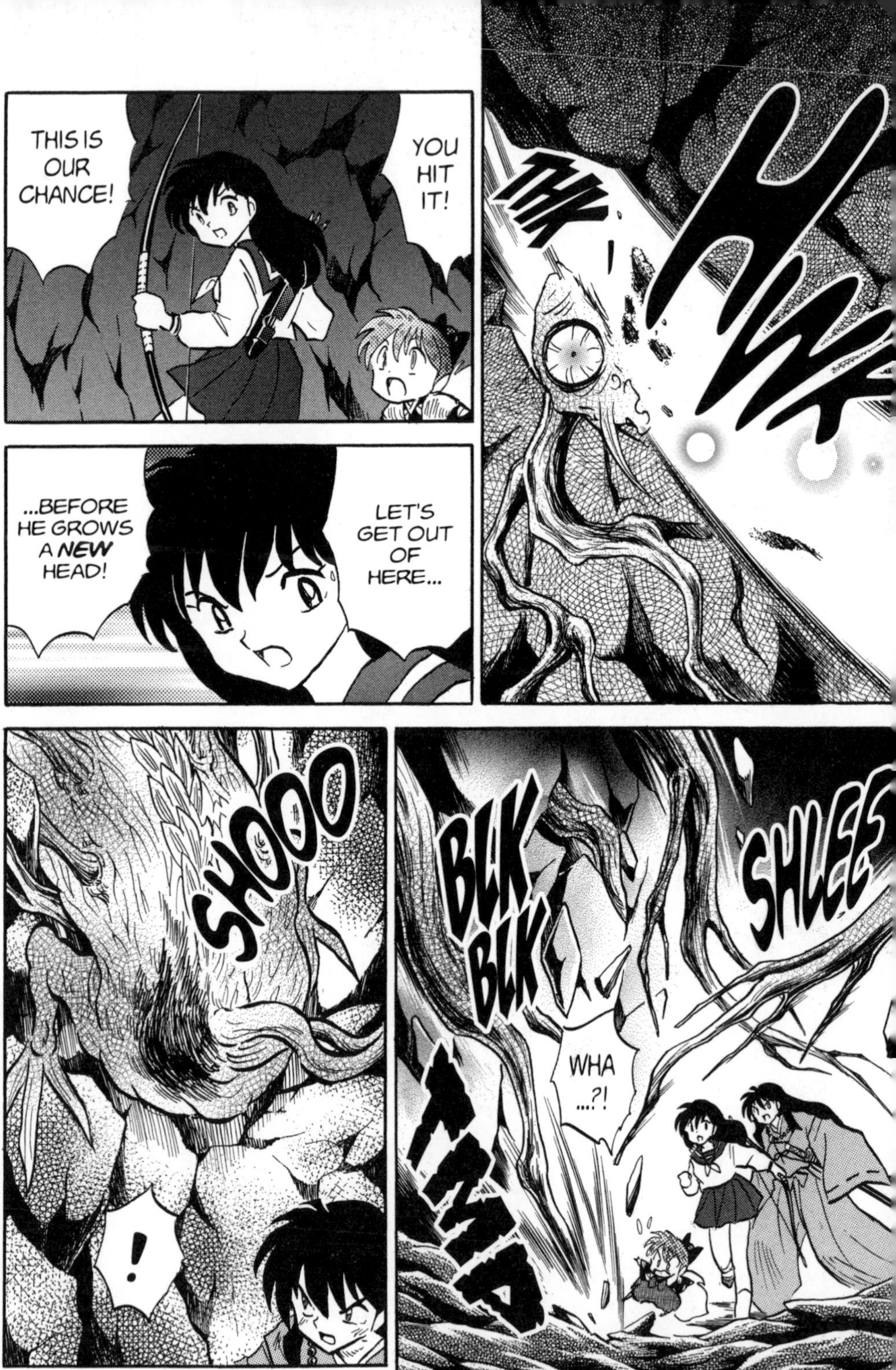
THK
YOU HIT IT!
THIS IS OUR CHANCE!
LET'S GET OUT OF HERE...
...BEFORE HE GROWS A **NEW** HEAD!
SHLEE
BLK BLK
WHA ...?!
THMP
SHOOO
!

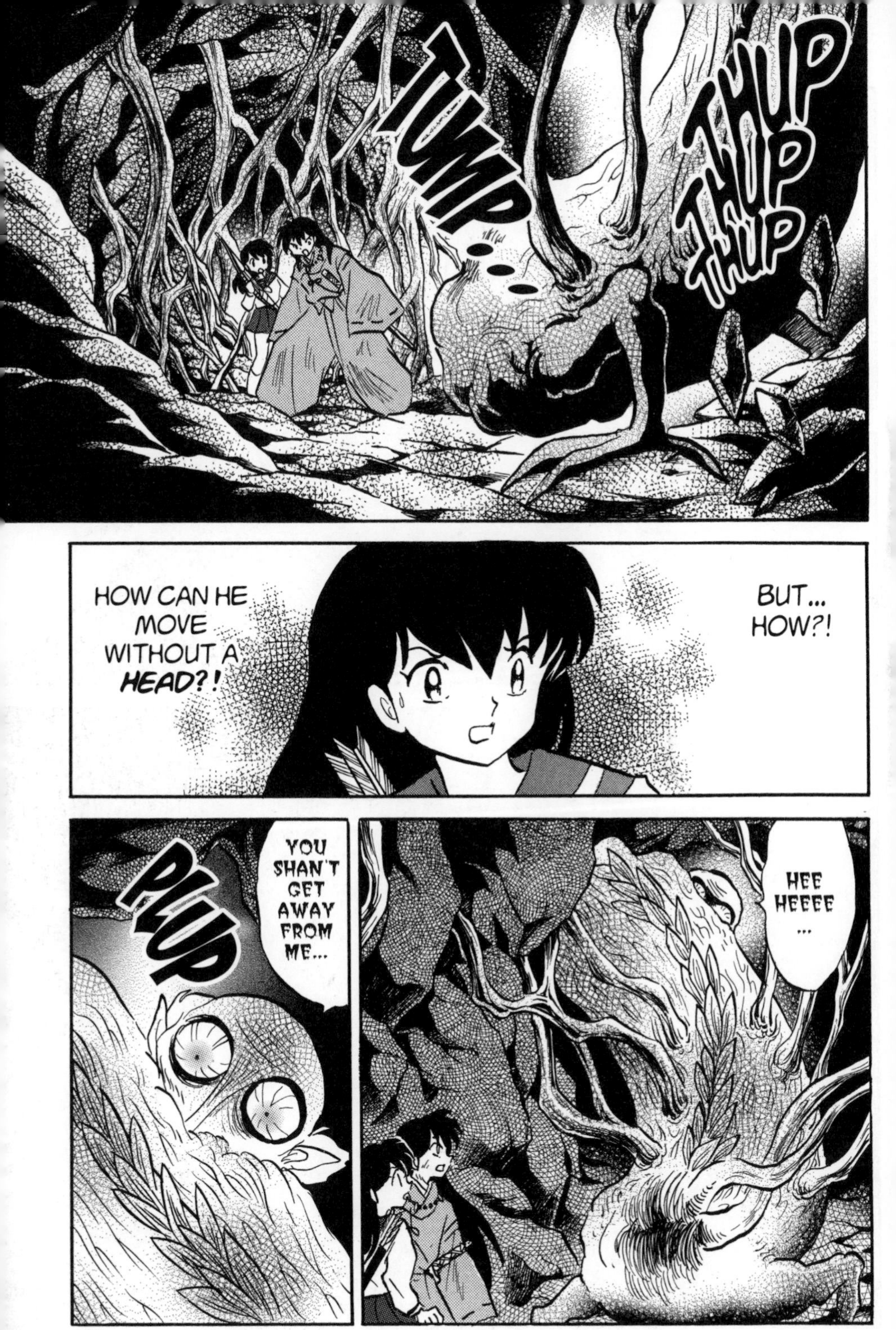
THUP THUP THUP
......
TUMP
BUT... HOW?!
HOW CAN HE MOVE WITHOUT A HEAD?!
HEE HEEEE ...
YOU SHAN'T GET AWAY FROM ME...
PLUP

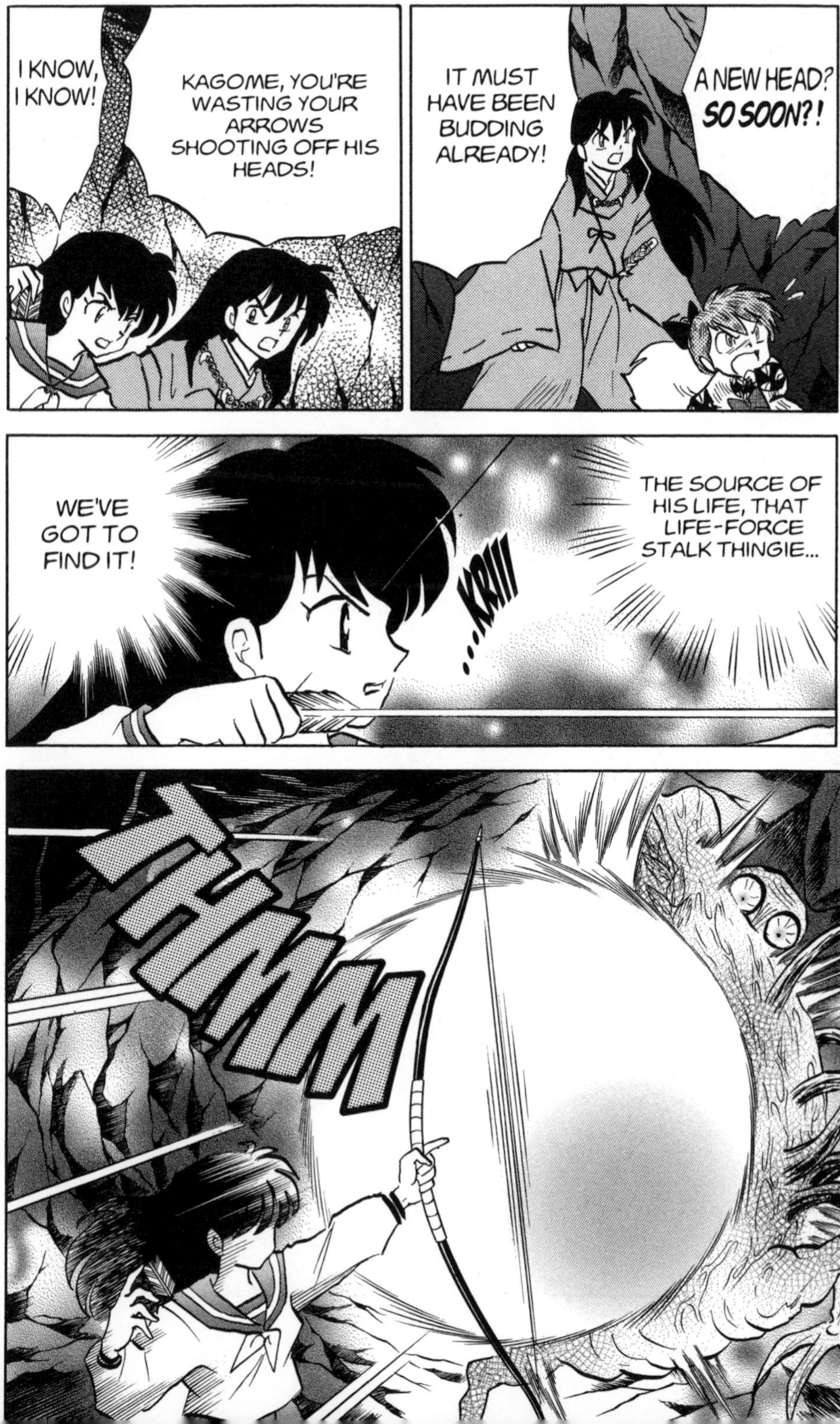

A NEW HEAD? SO SOON?!
IT MUST HAVE BEEN BUDDING ALREADY!
KAGOME, YOU'RE WASTING YOUR ARROWS SHOOTING OFF HIS HEADS!
I KNOW, I KNOW!
THE SOURCE OF HIS LIFE, THAT LIFE-FORCE STALK THINGIE...
WE'VE GOT TO FIND IT!
...KRIII
THMM

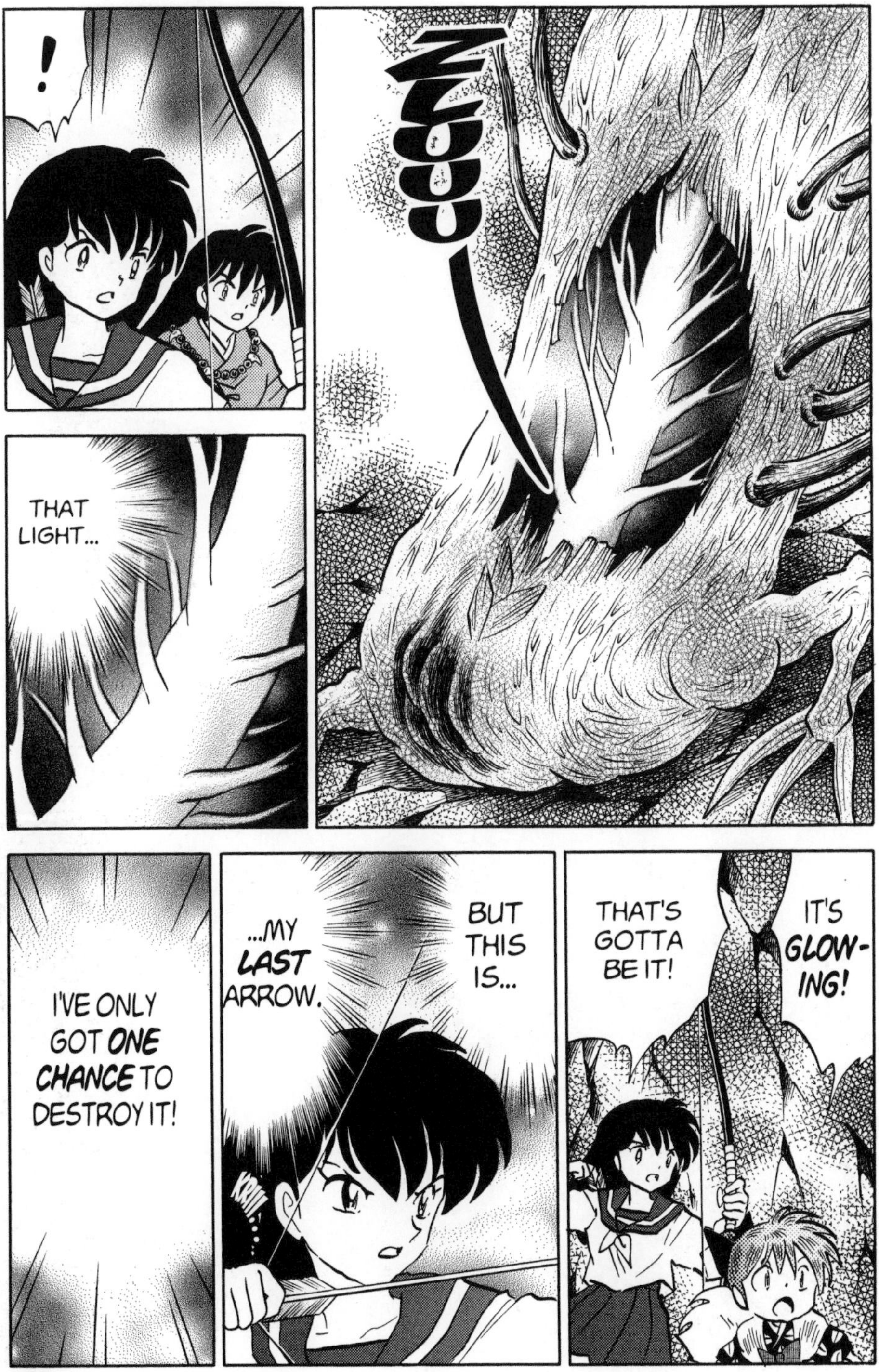
ZUUUU
!
THAT LIGHT...
IT'S GLOWING!
THAT'S GOTTA BE IT!
BUT THIS IS...
...MY LAST ARROW.
I'VE ONLY GOT ONE CHANCE TO DESTROY IT!

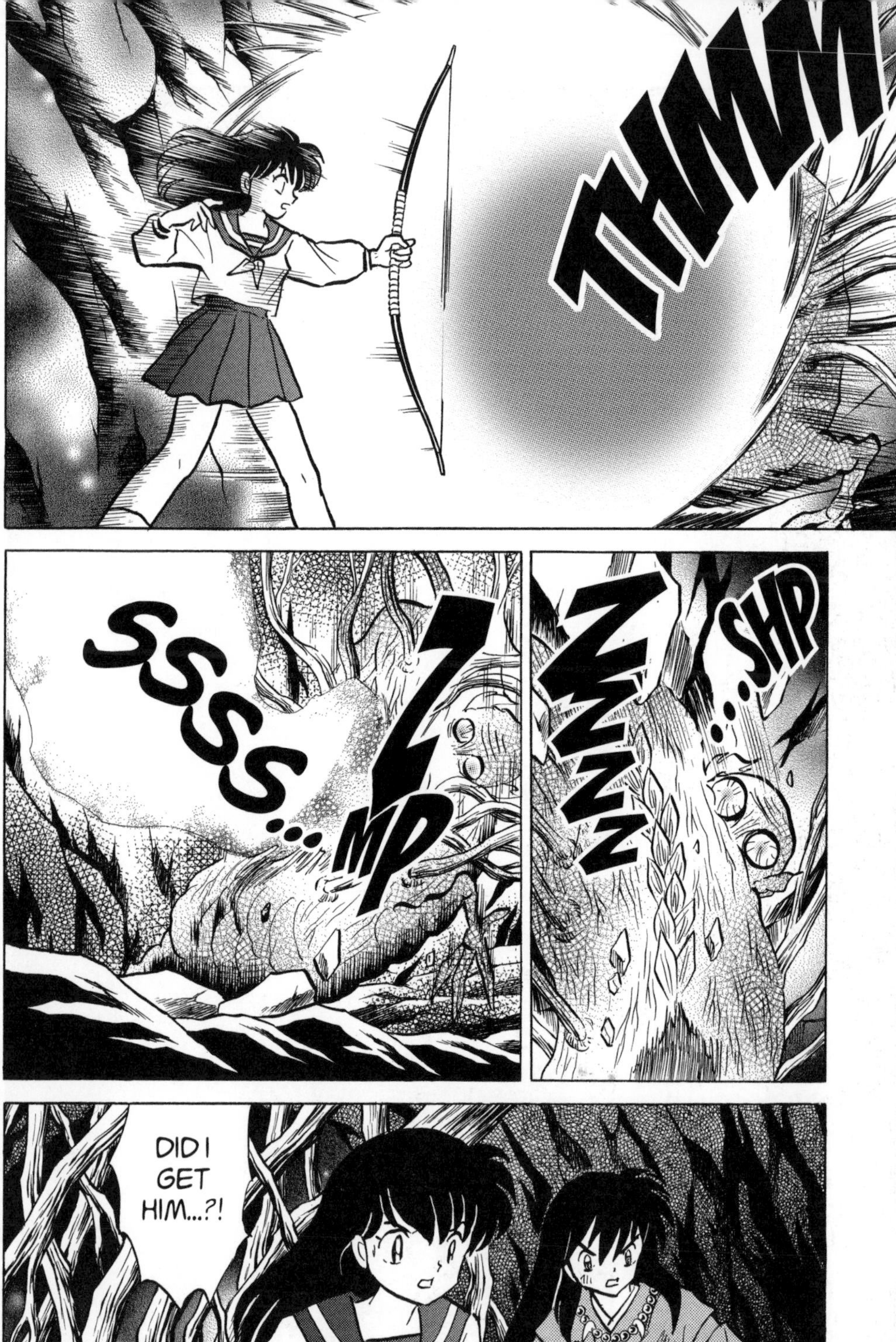
THMM
...SHP
SSSS...
DID I GET HIM...?!

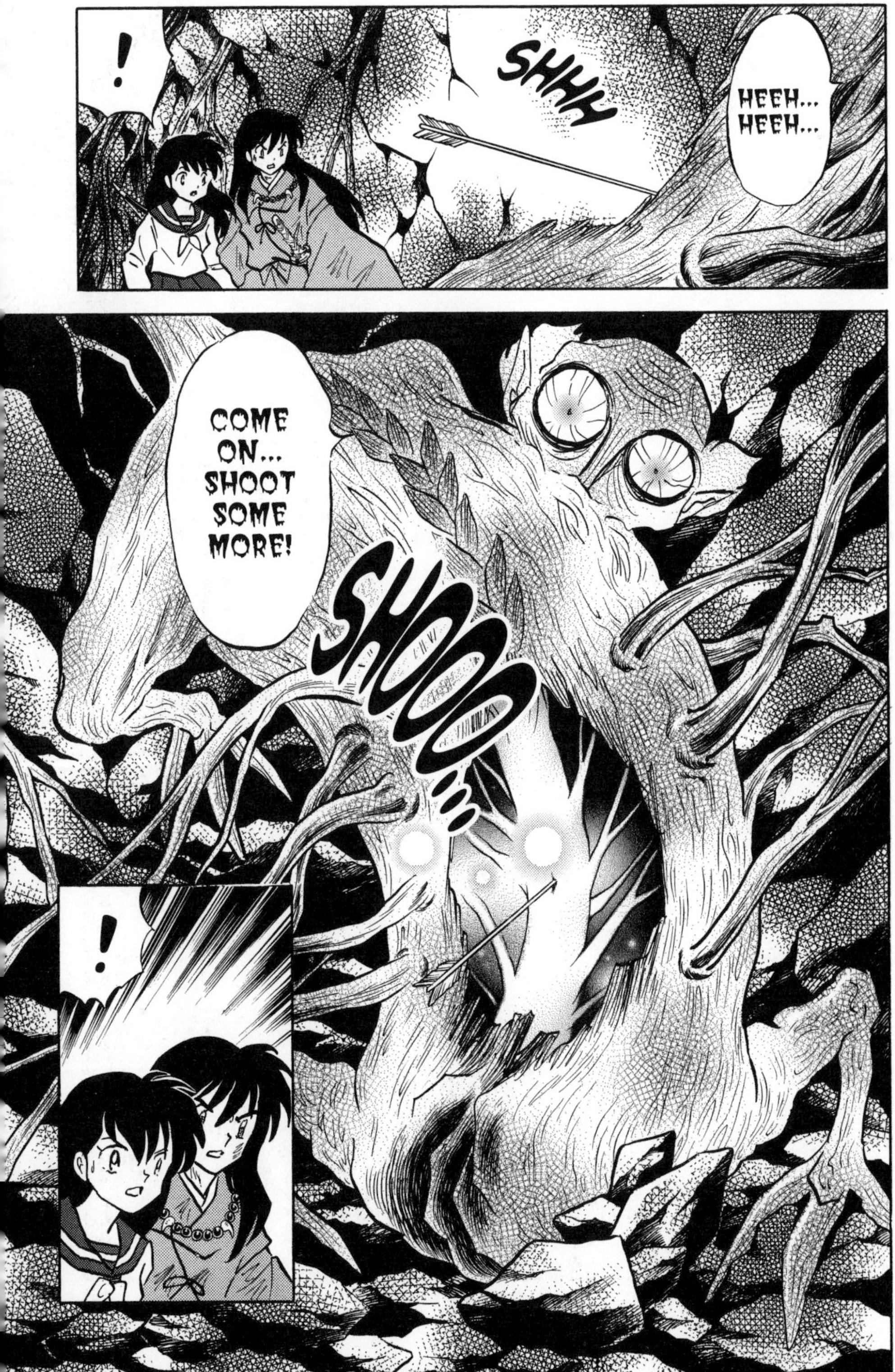
HEEH... HEEH...
SHHH
!
COME ON... SHOOT SOME MORE!
SHOOO...
!

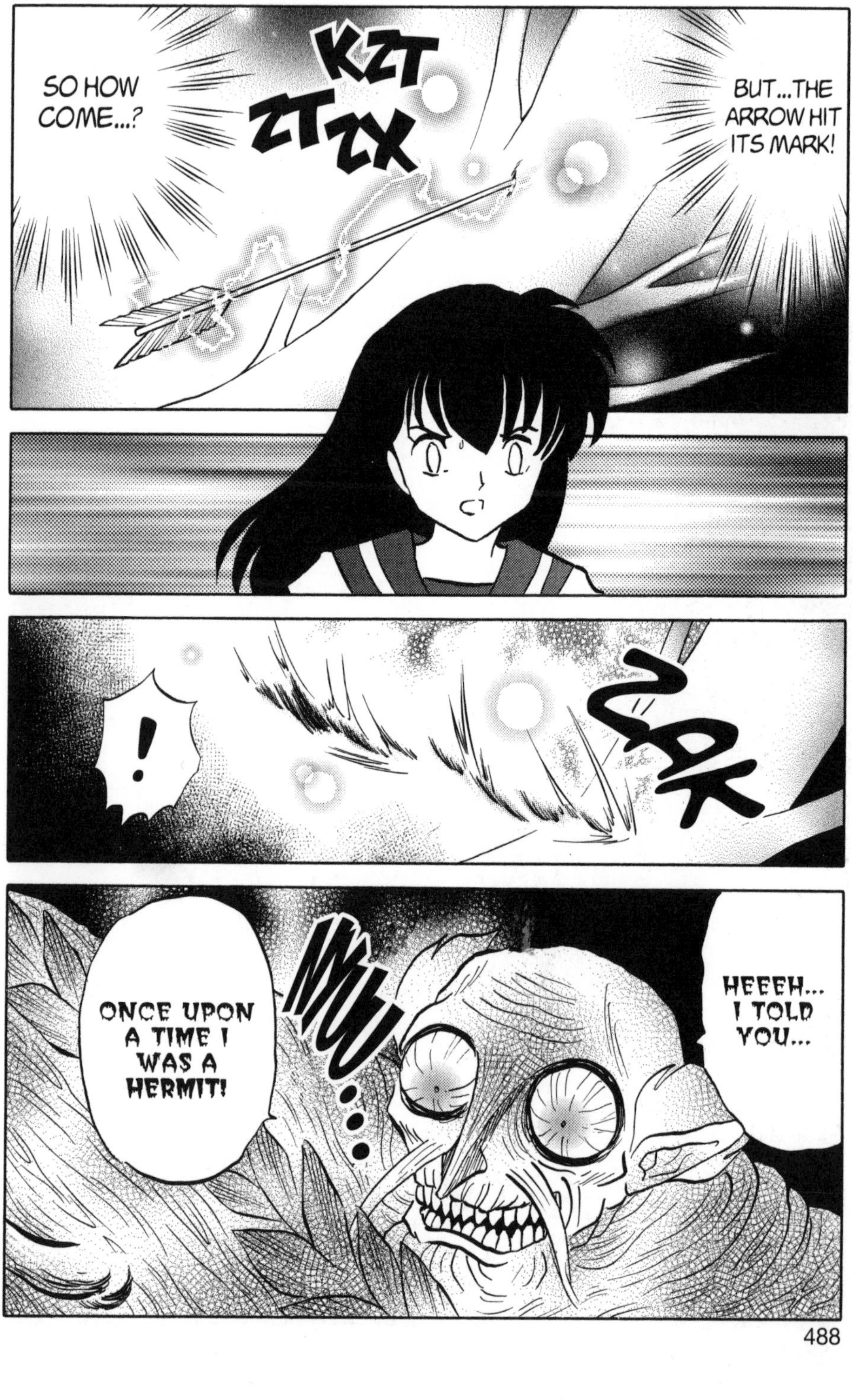
BUT...THE ARROW HIT ITS MARK!
KZT
ZT ZX
SO HOW COME...?
ZAK
!
HEEEH... I TOLD YOU...
ONCE UPON A TIME I WAS A HERMIT!

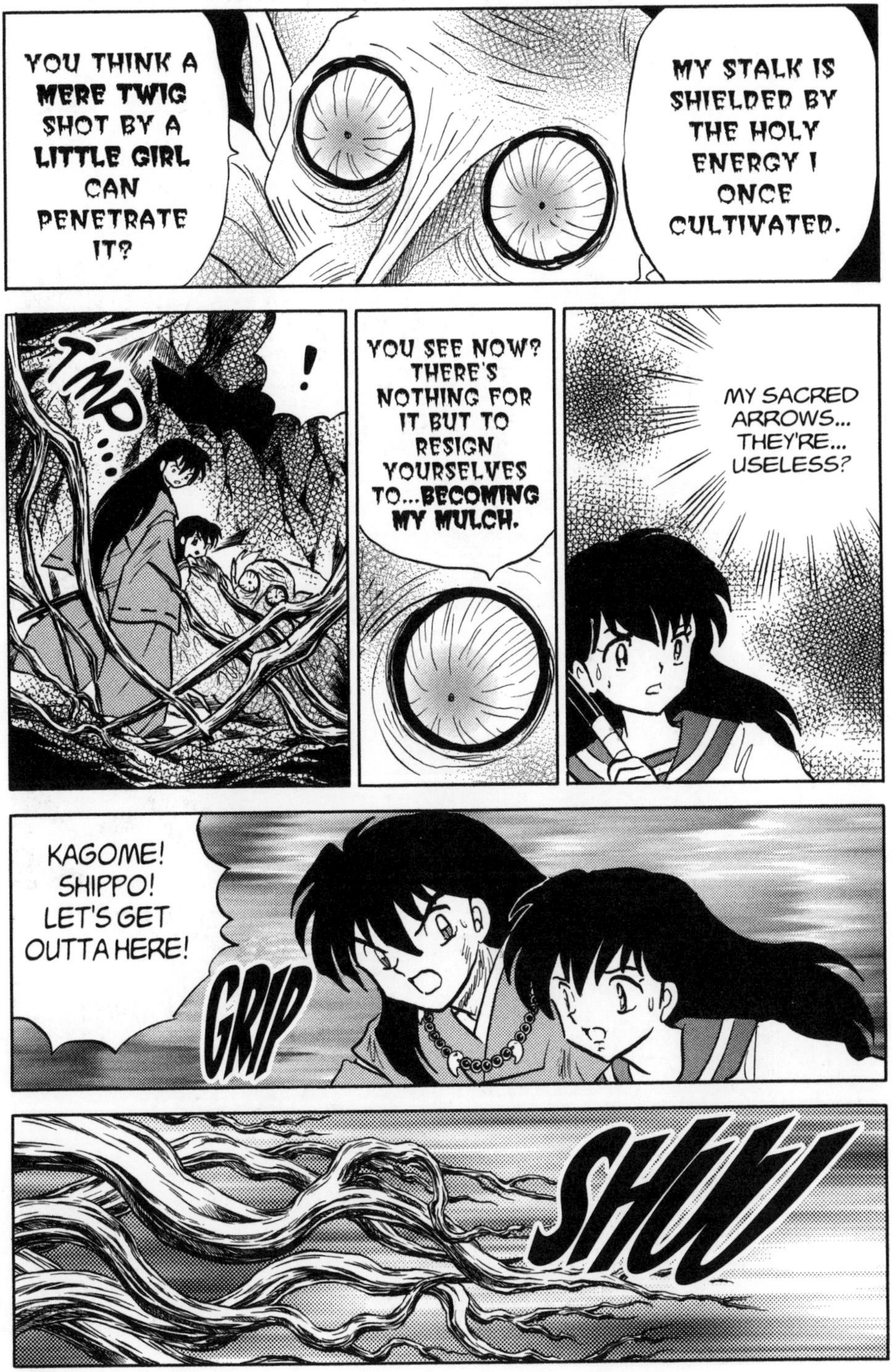
MY STALK IS SHIELDED BY THE HOLY ENERGY I ONCE CULTIVATED.
YOU THINK A MERE TWIG SHOT BY A LITTLE GIRL CAN PENETRATE IT?
MY SACRED ARROWS... THEY'RE... USELESS?
YOU SEE NOW? THERE'S NOTHING FOR IT BUT TO RESIGN YOURSELVES TO...BECOMING MY MULCH.
TMP...
!
KAGOME! SHIPPO! LET'S GET OUTTA HERE!
GRIP
SHW

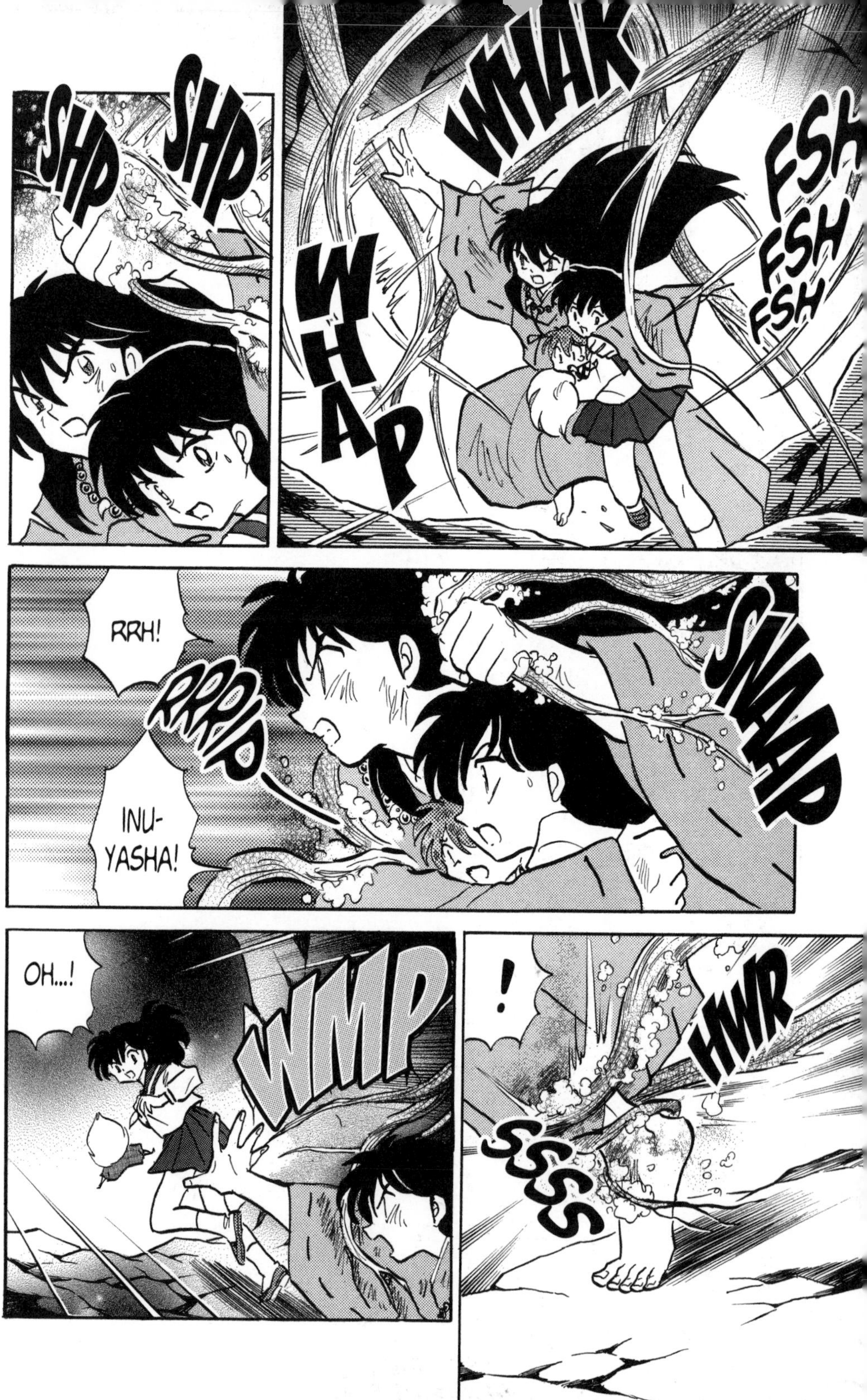
FSH
FSH
FSH
WHAK
WHAP
SHP
SHP
SNAAP
RRH!
RRRIP
INU-YASHA!
!
HWR
SSSS
OH...!
WMP

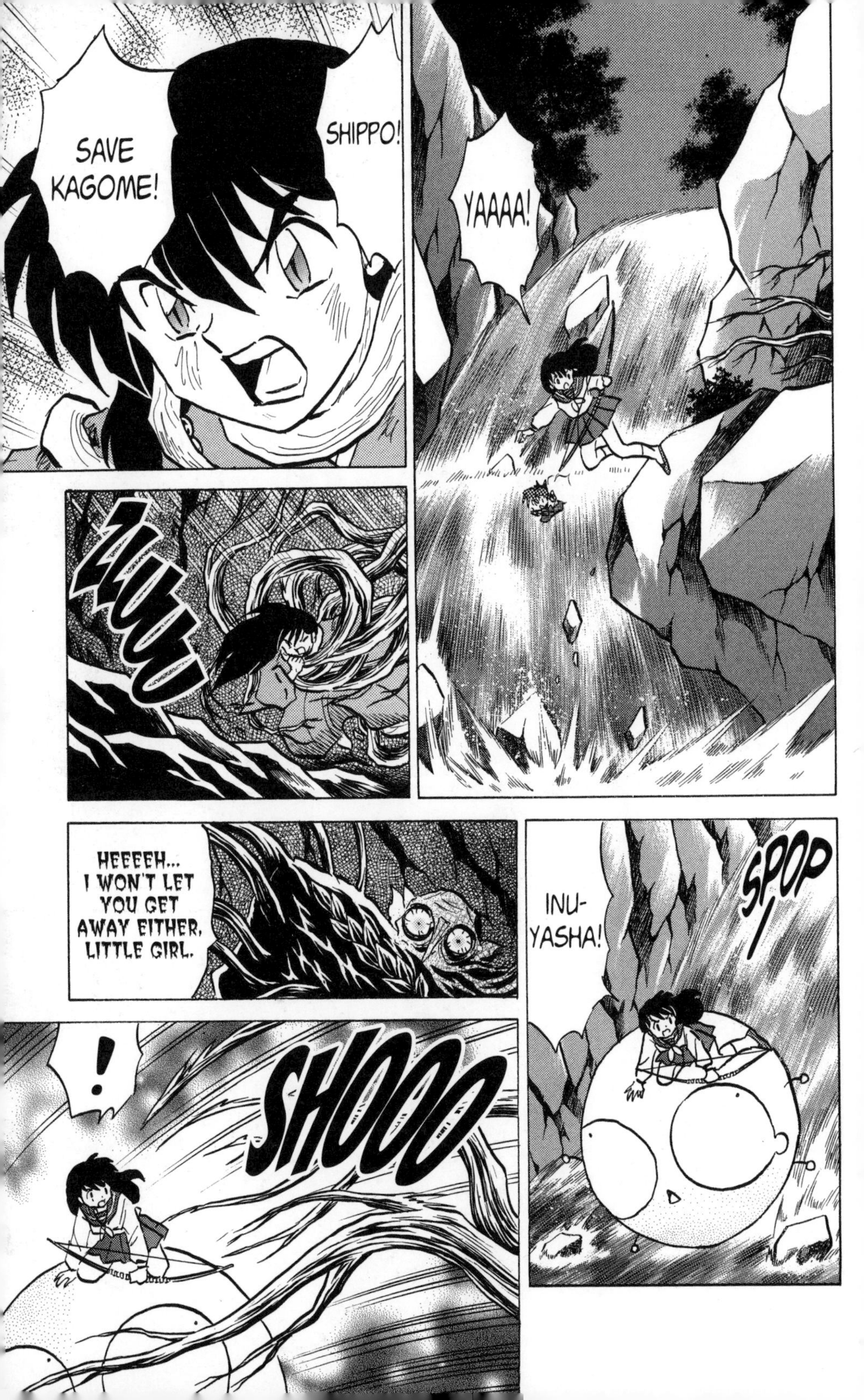
YAAAA!
SHIPPO!
SAVE KAGOME!
ZUUU
INU-YASHA!
SPOP
HEEEEH... I WON'T LET YOU GET AWAY EITHER, LITTLE GIRL.
!
SHOOO

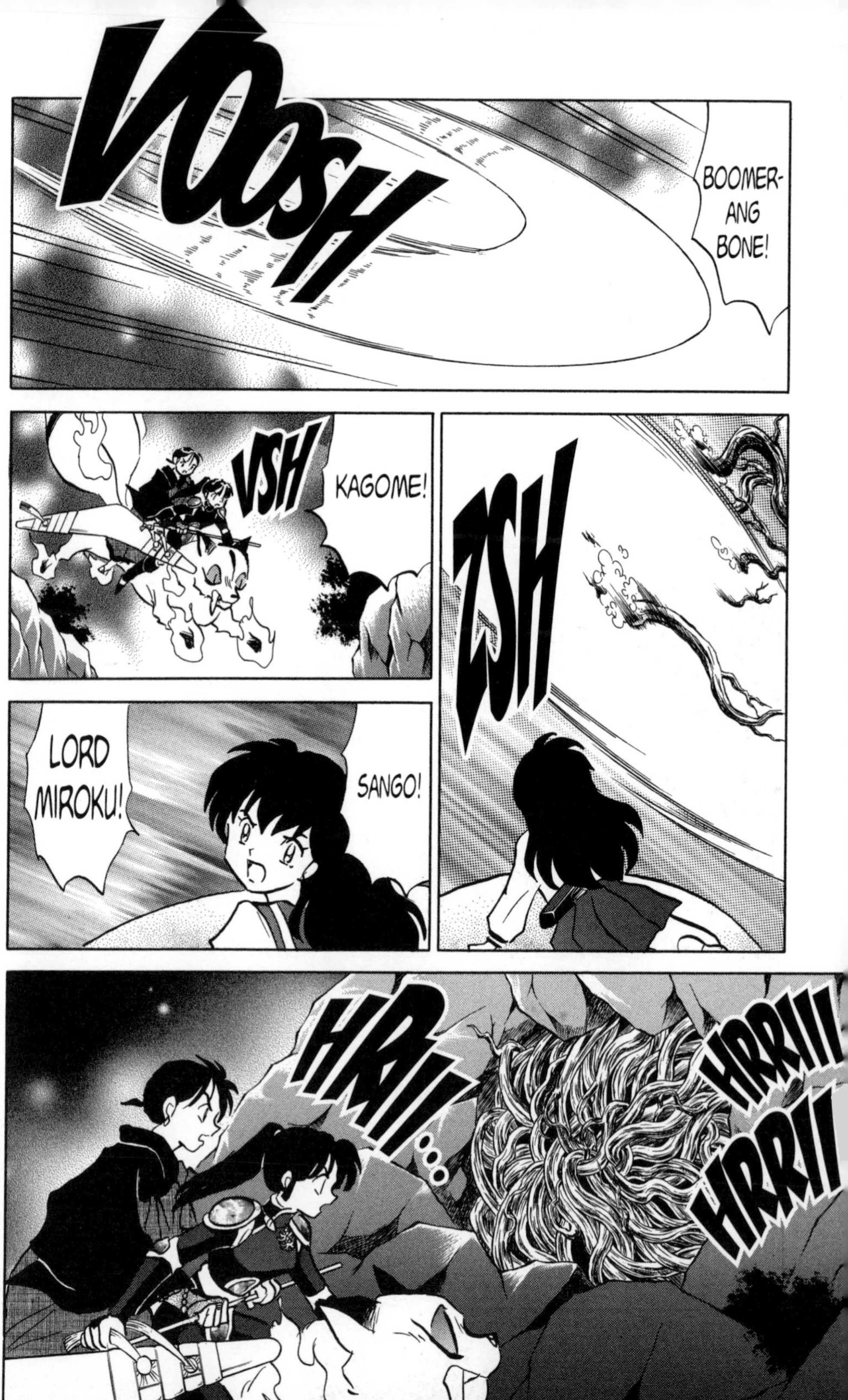
BOOMER-
ANG
BONE!
VOOSH
ZSH
KAGOME!
VSH
SANGO!
LORD
MIROKU!
HRRII
HRRII
HRR...

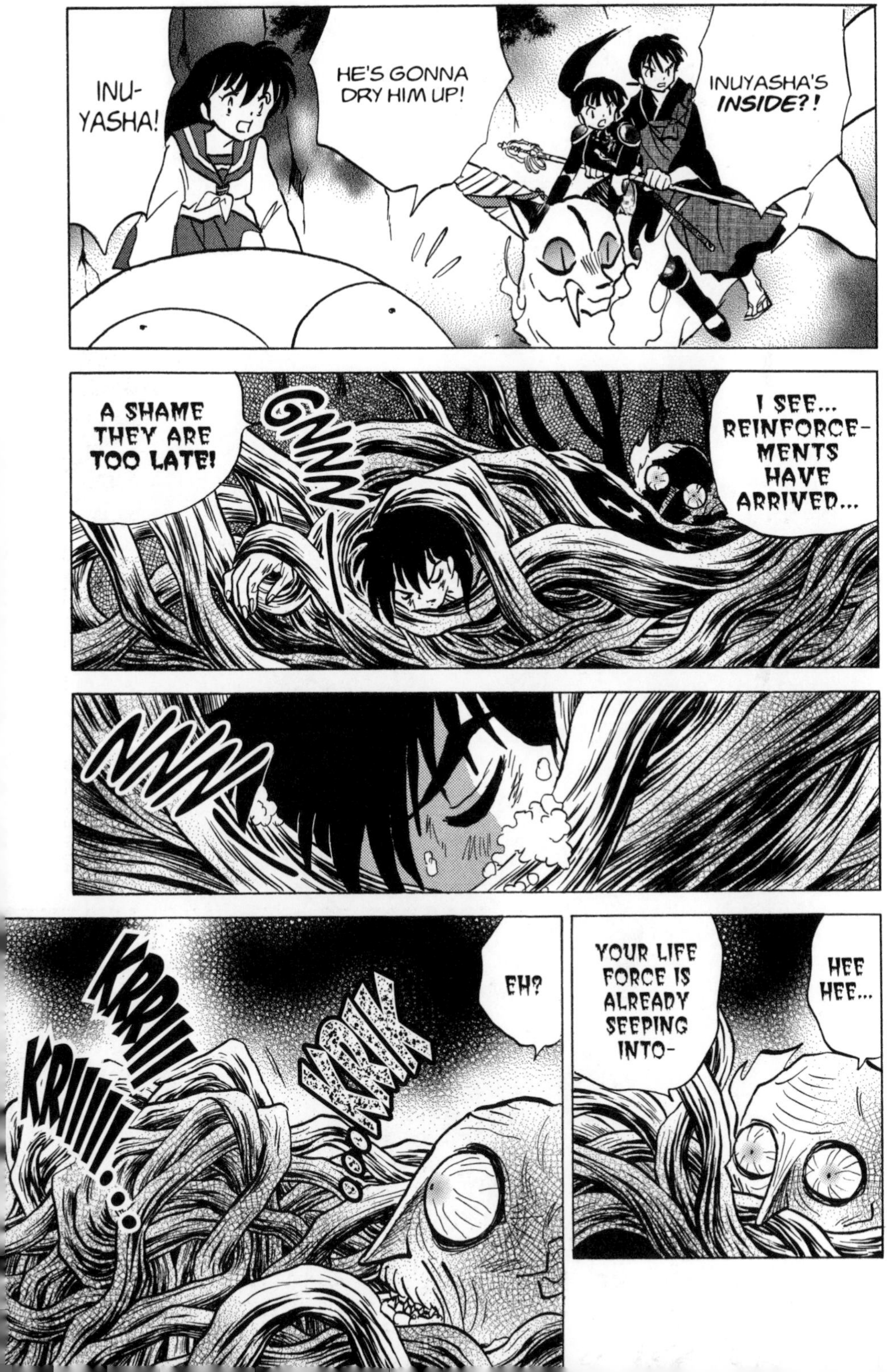
INUYASHA'S INSIDE?!
HE'S GONNA DRY HIM UP!
INU-YASHA!
I SEE... REINFORCE-MENTS HAVE ARRIVED...
GNNN
A SHAME THEY ARE TOO LATE!
NNNN
HEE HEE...
YOUR LIFE FORCE IS ALREADY SEEPING INTO-
EH?
KRIK...
KRRII
KRIIIII!!...

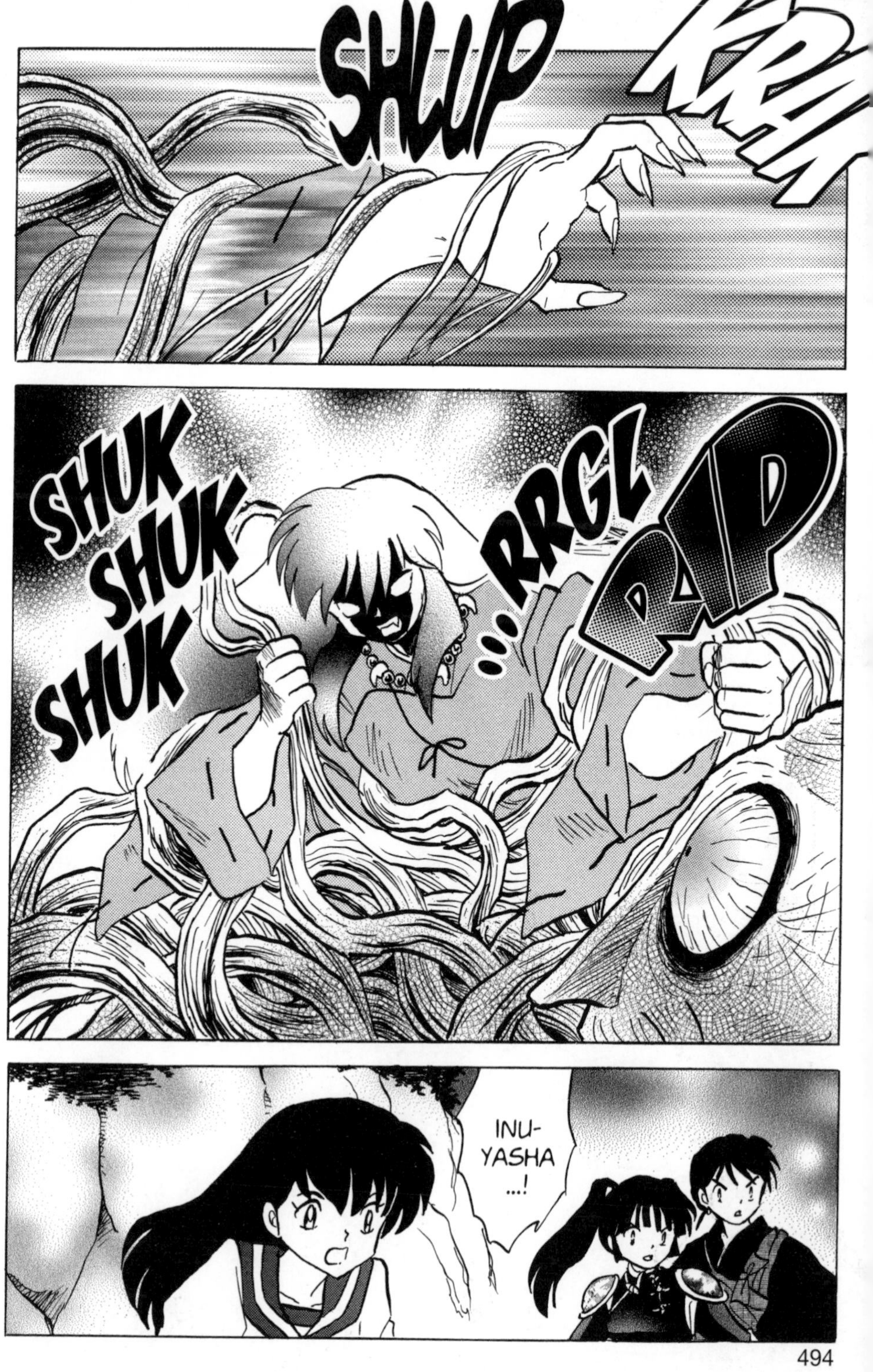
KRAK
SHLUP
RIP
...RRGL
SHUK SHUK SHUK
INU-YASHA ...!

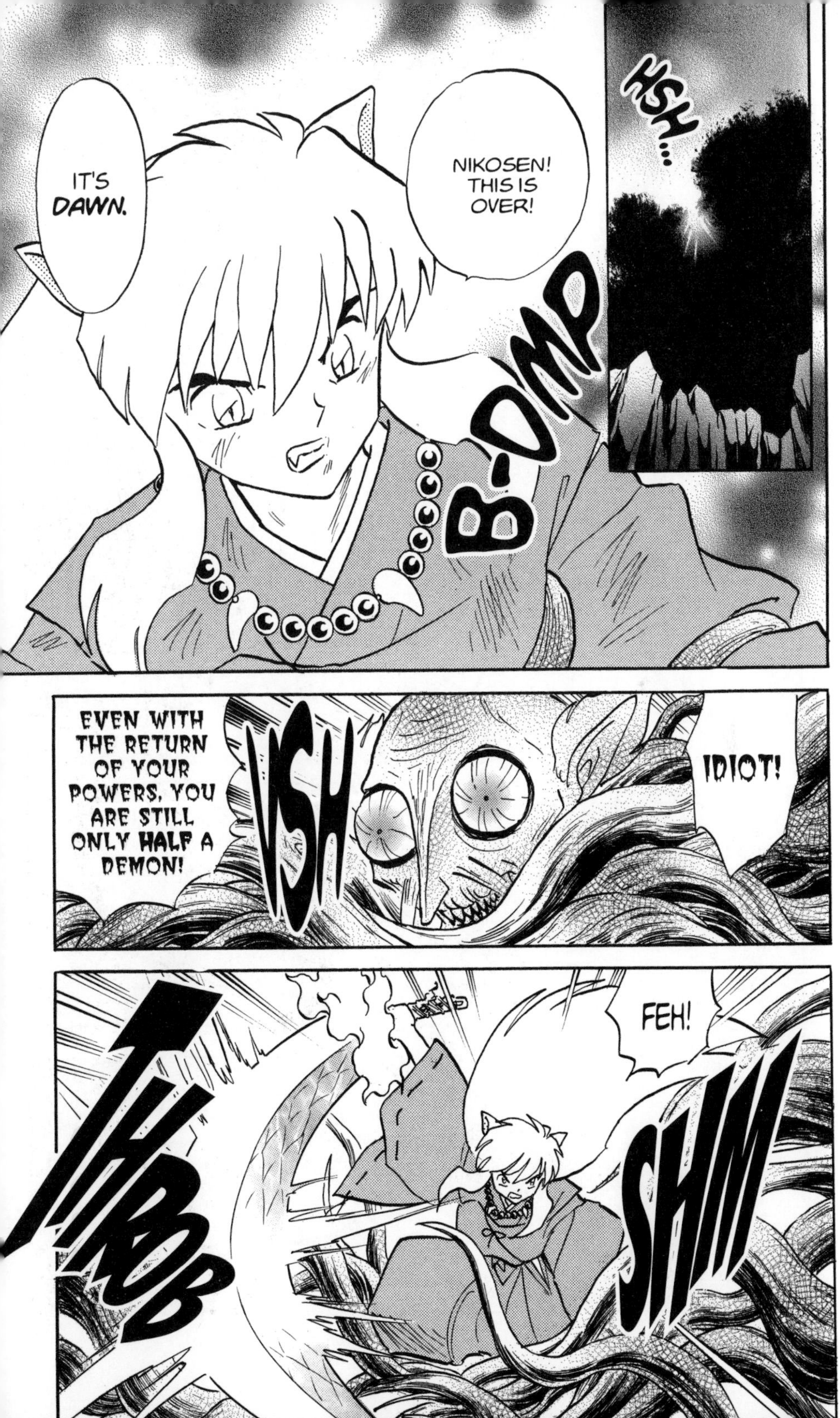

HSH...
NIKOSEN! THIS IS OVER!
IT'S DAWN.
B-DMP
IDIOT!
VSH
EVEN WITH THE RETURN OF YOUR POWERS, YOU ARE STILL ONLY HALF A DEMON!
FEH!
SHIN
THROB

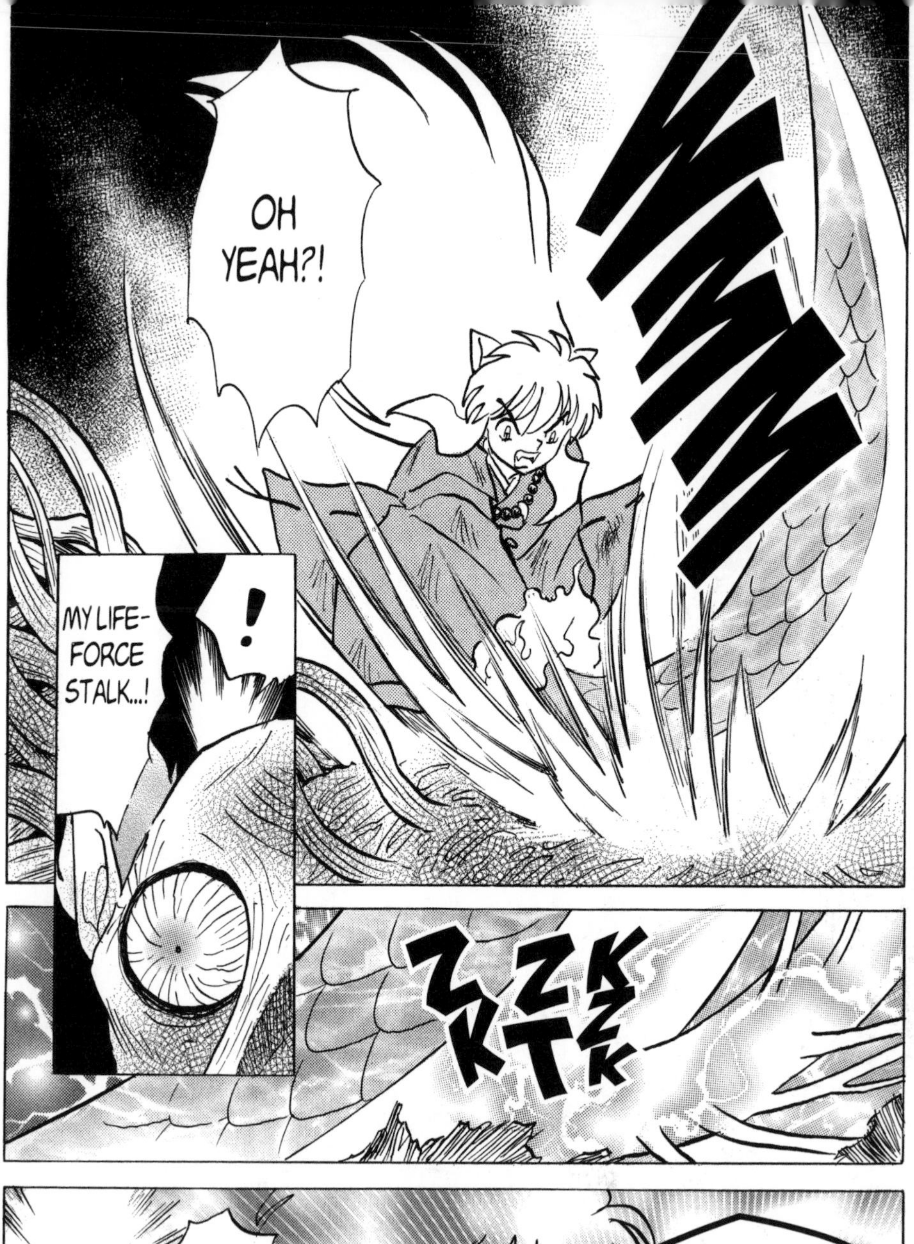
OH YEAH?!
!
MY LIFE-FORCE STALK...!
POF
?!
WHAT THE...?

SCROLL SEVEN
SENKI

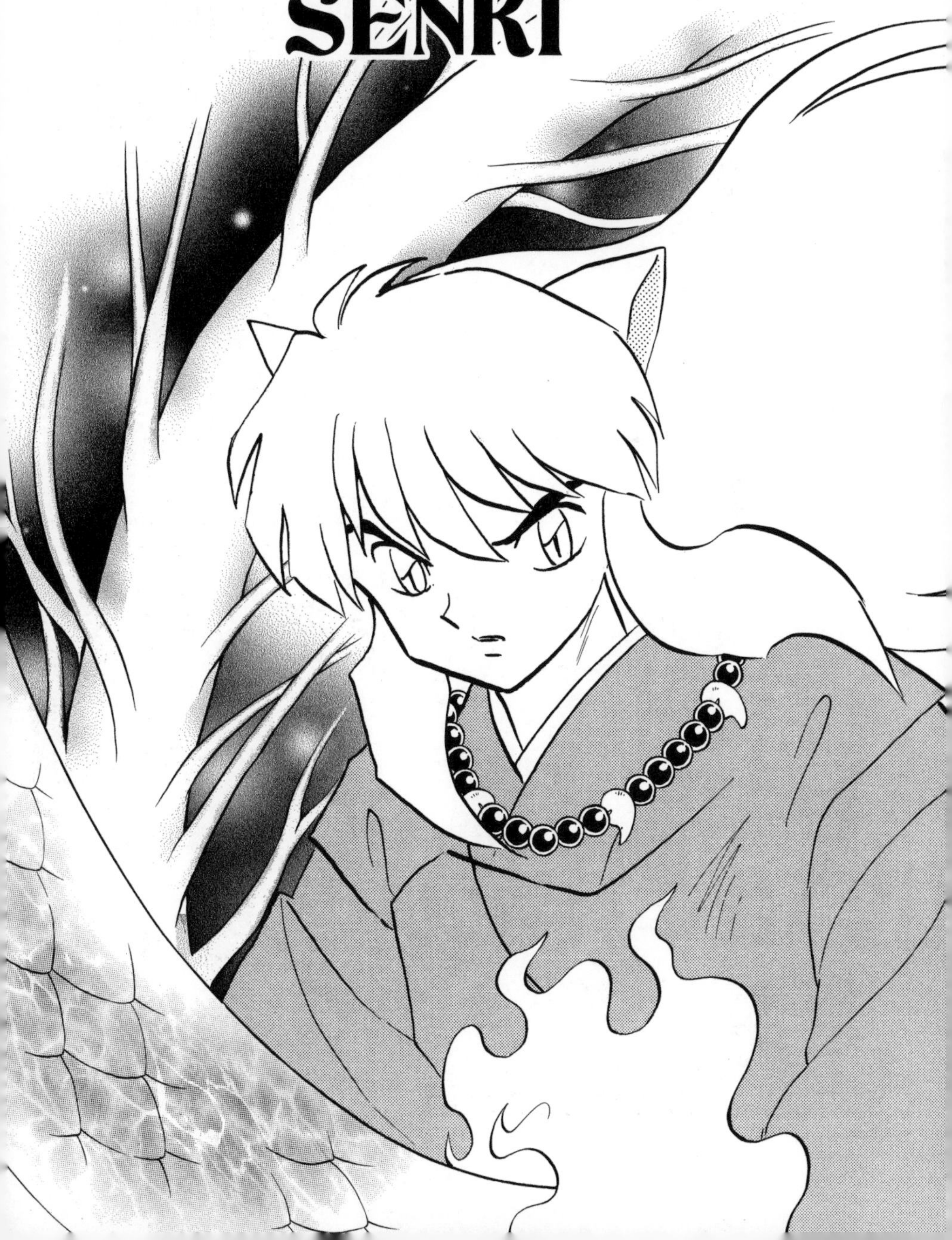

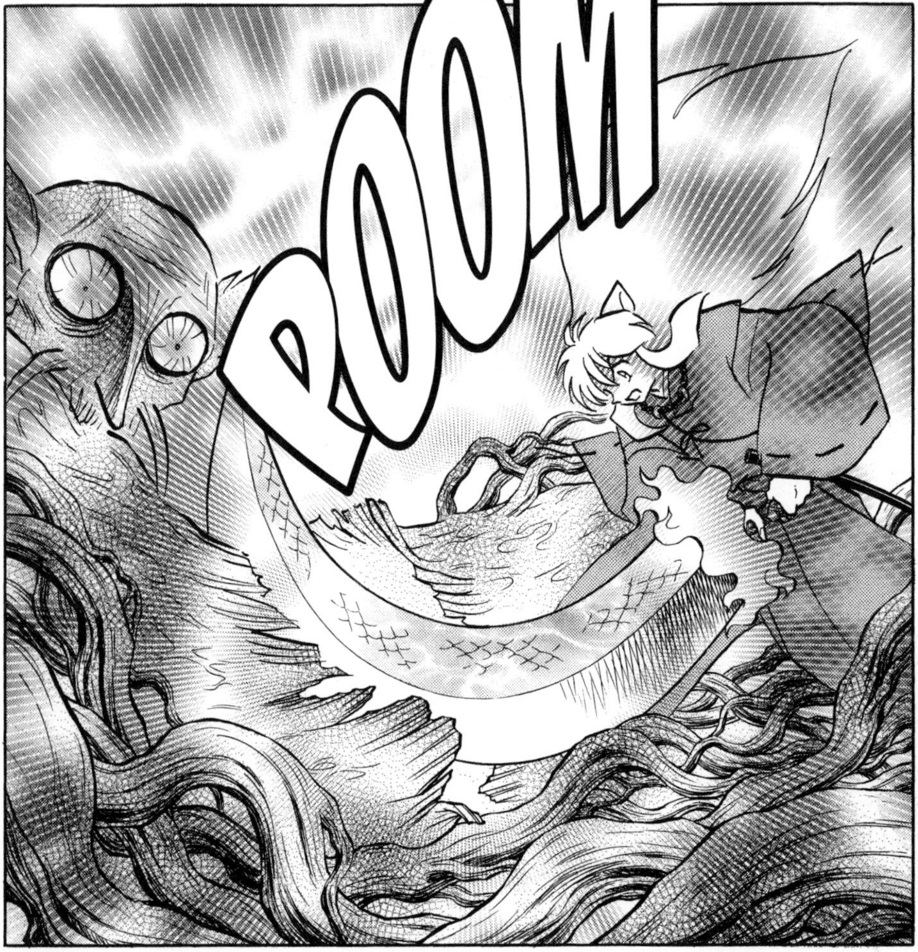
ROOOM

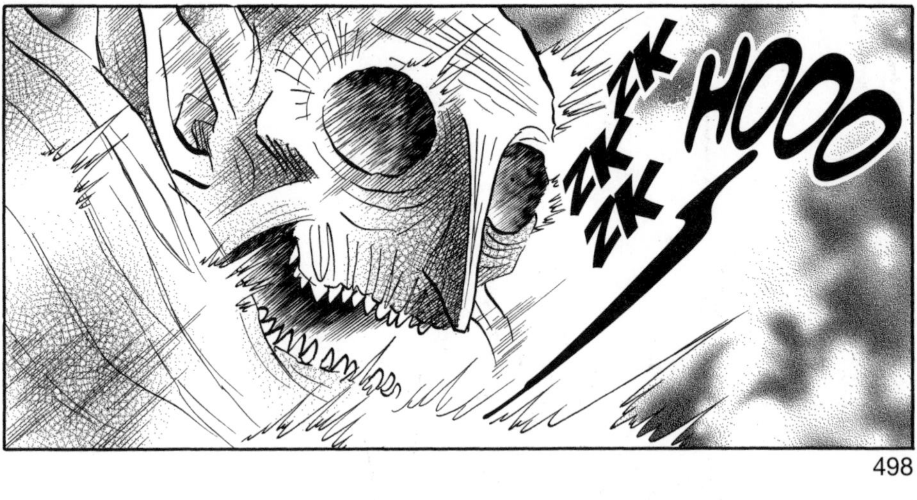
HOOO
ZK ZK ZK

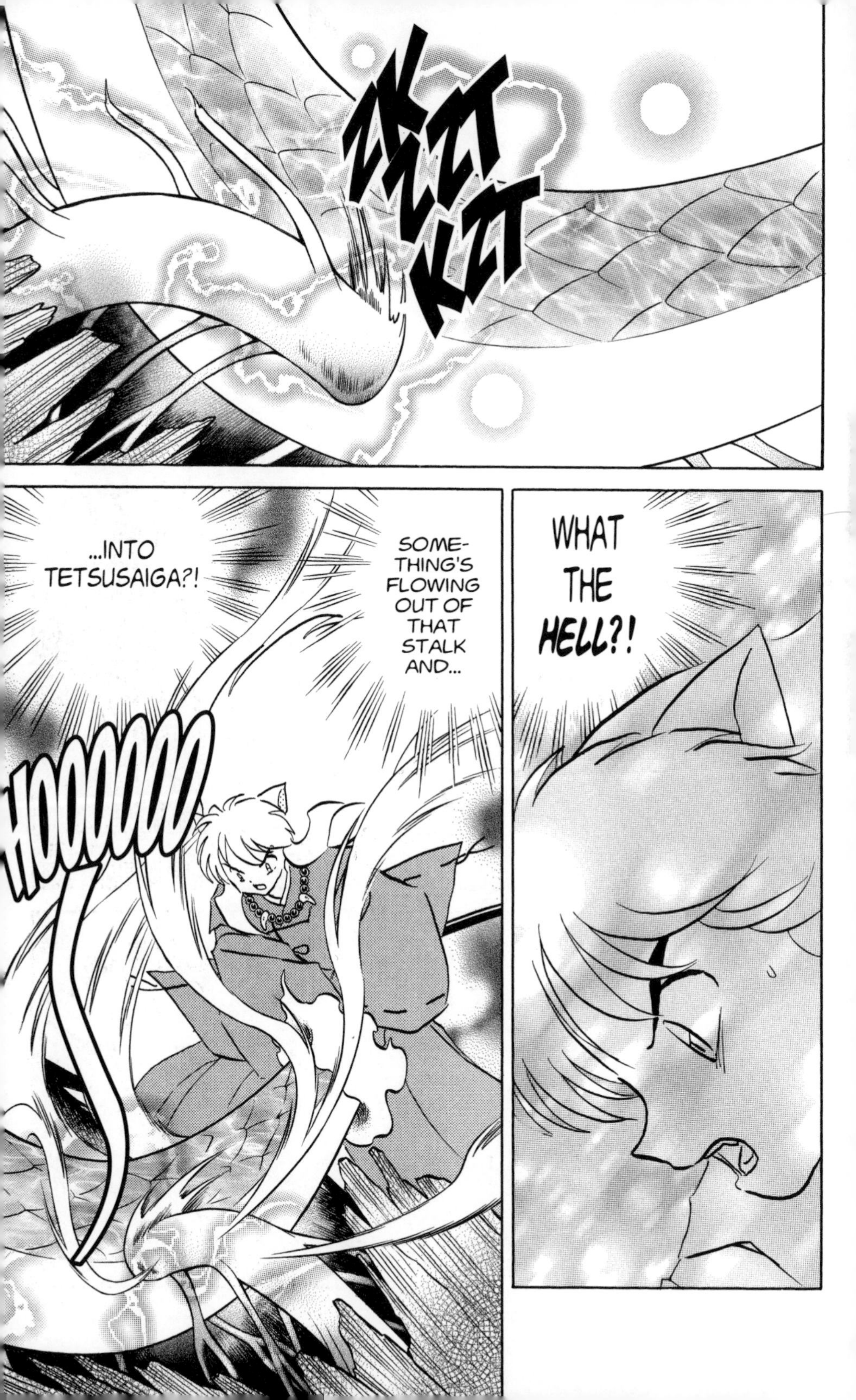
KZZT KZZT
WHAT THE HELL?!
SOME-THING'S FLOWING OUT OF THAT STALK AND...
...INTO TETSUSAIGA?!
HOOOOOO

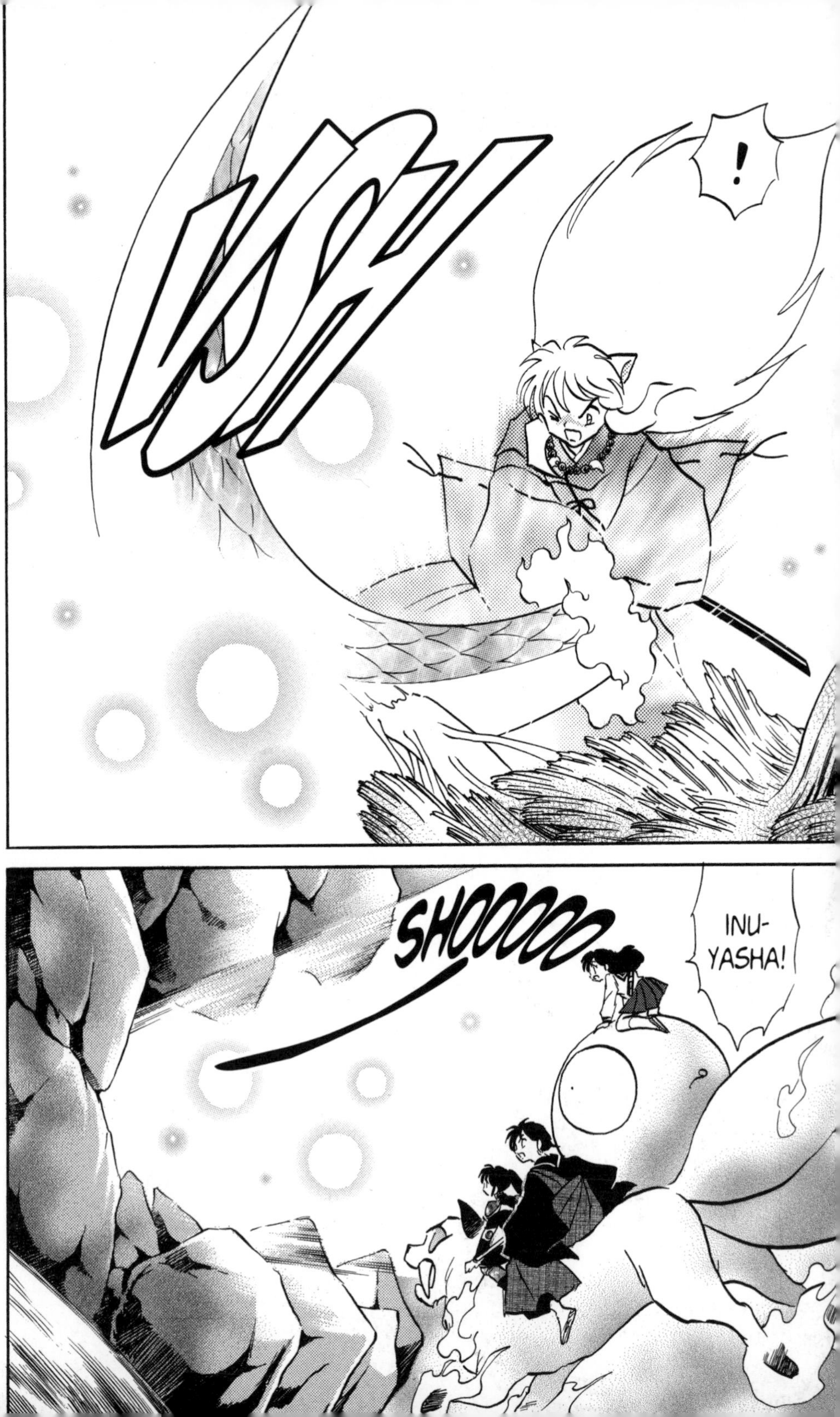
!
SHOOOOO
INU-
YASHA!

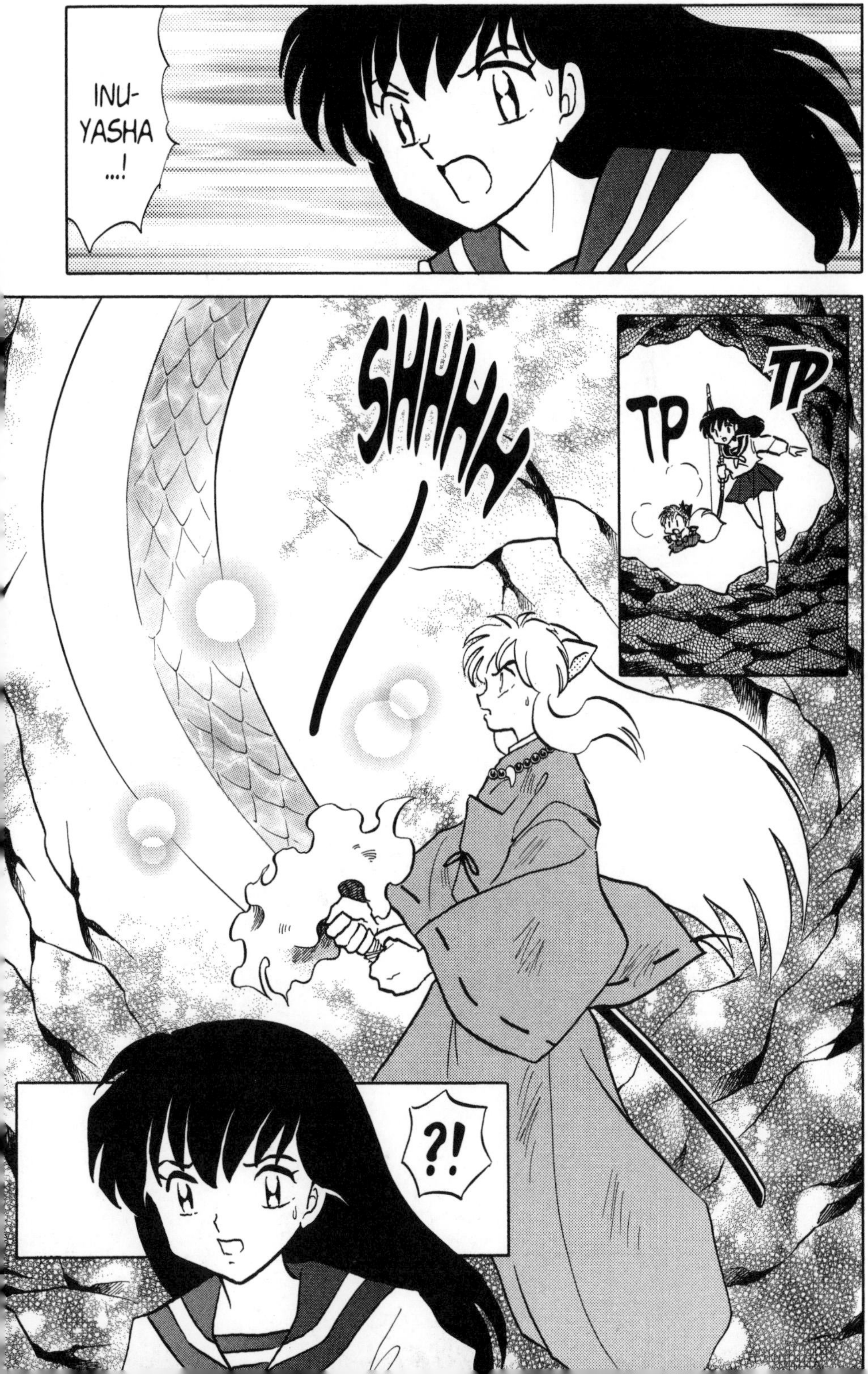
INU-YASHA ...!
TP
TP
SHHHH
?!

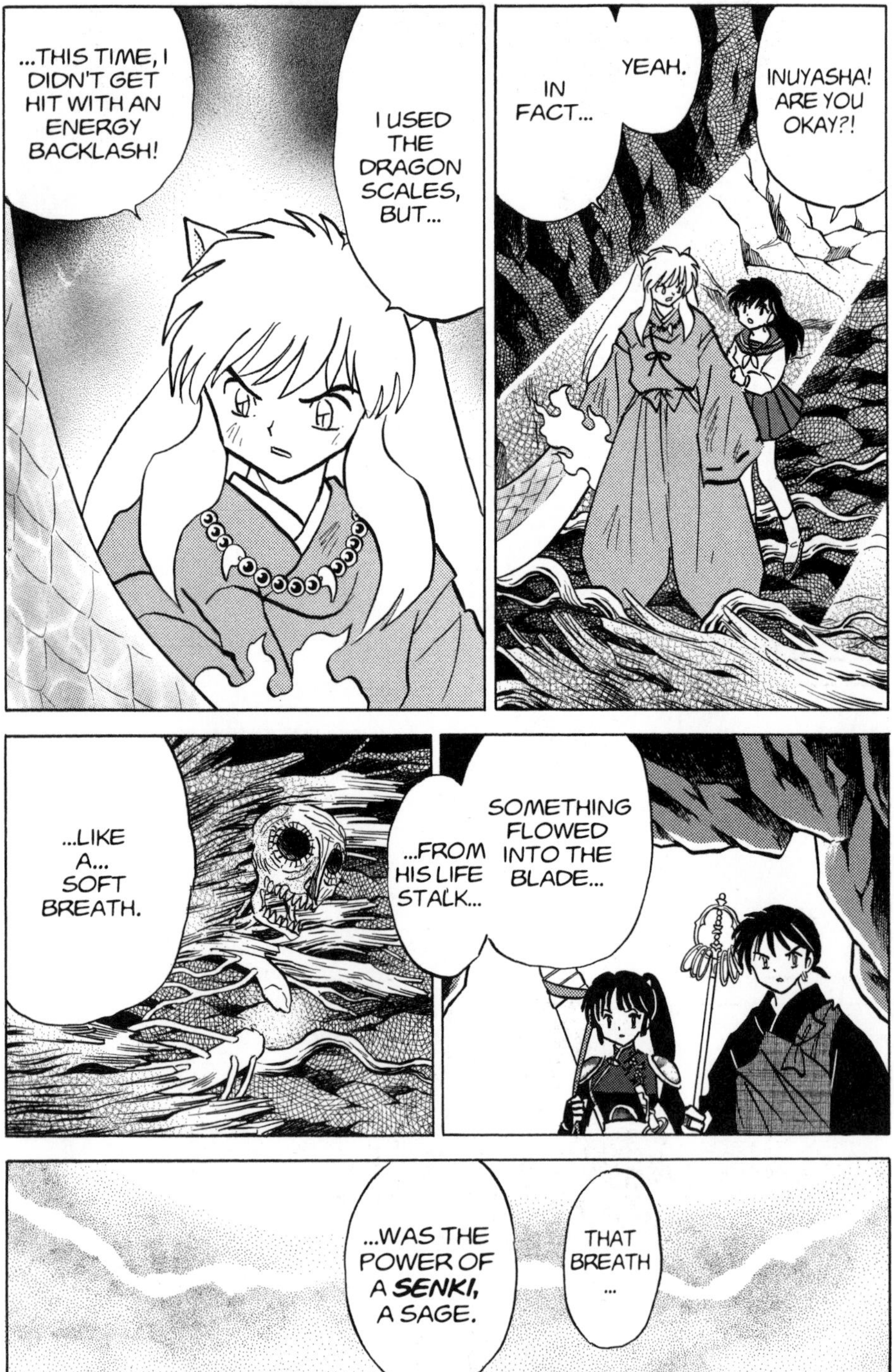
INUYASHA! ARE YOU OKAY?!
YEAH.
IN FACT...
I USED THE DRAGON SCALES, BUT...
...THIS TIME, I DIDN'T GET HIT WITH AN ENERGY BACKLASH!
SOMETHING FLOWED INTO THE BLADE...
...FROM HIS LIFE STALK...
...LIKE A... SOFT BREATH.
THAT BREATH ...
...WAS THE POWER OF A ***SENKI***, A SAGE.

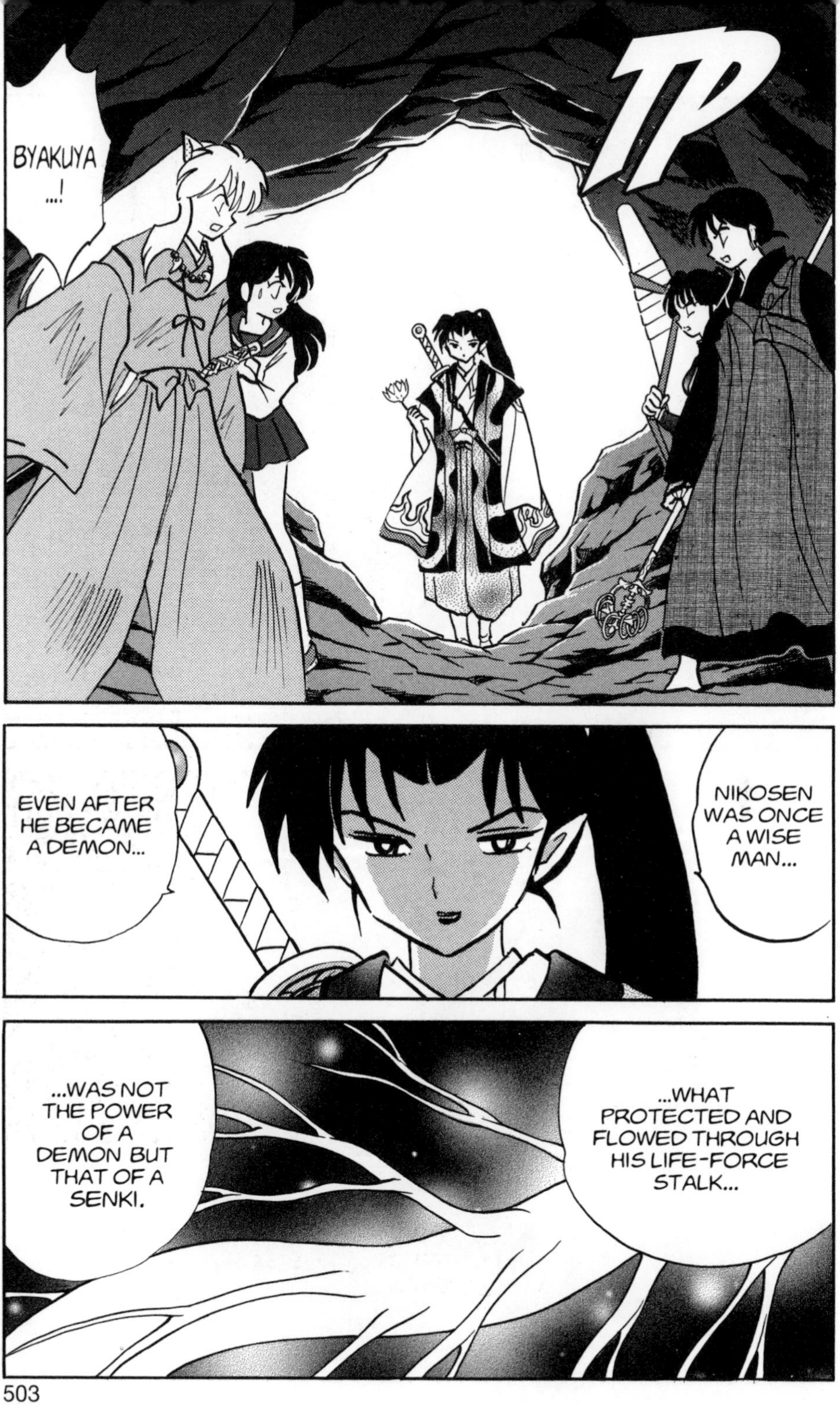
TP
BYAKUYA ...!
NIKOSEN WAS ONCE A WISE MAN...
EVEN AFTER HE BECAME A DEMON...
...WHAT PROTECTED AND FLOWED THROUGH HIS LIFE-FORCE STALK...
...WAS NOT THE POWER OF A DEMON BUT THAT OF A SENKI.

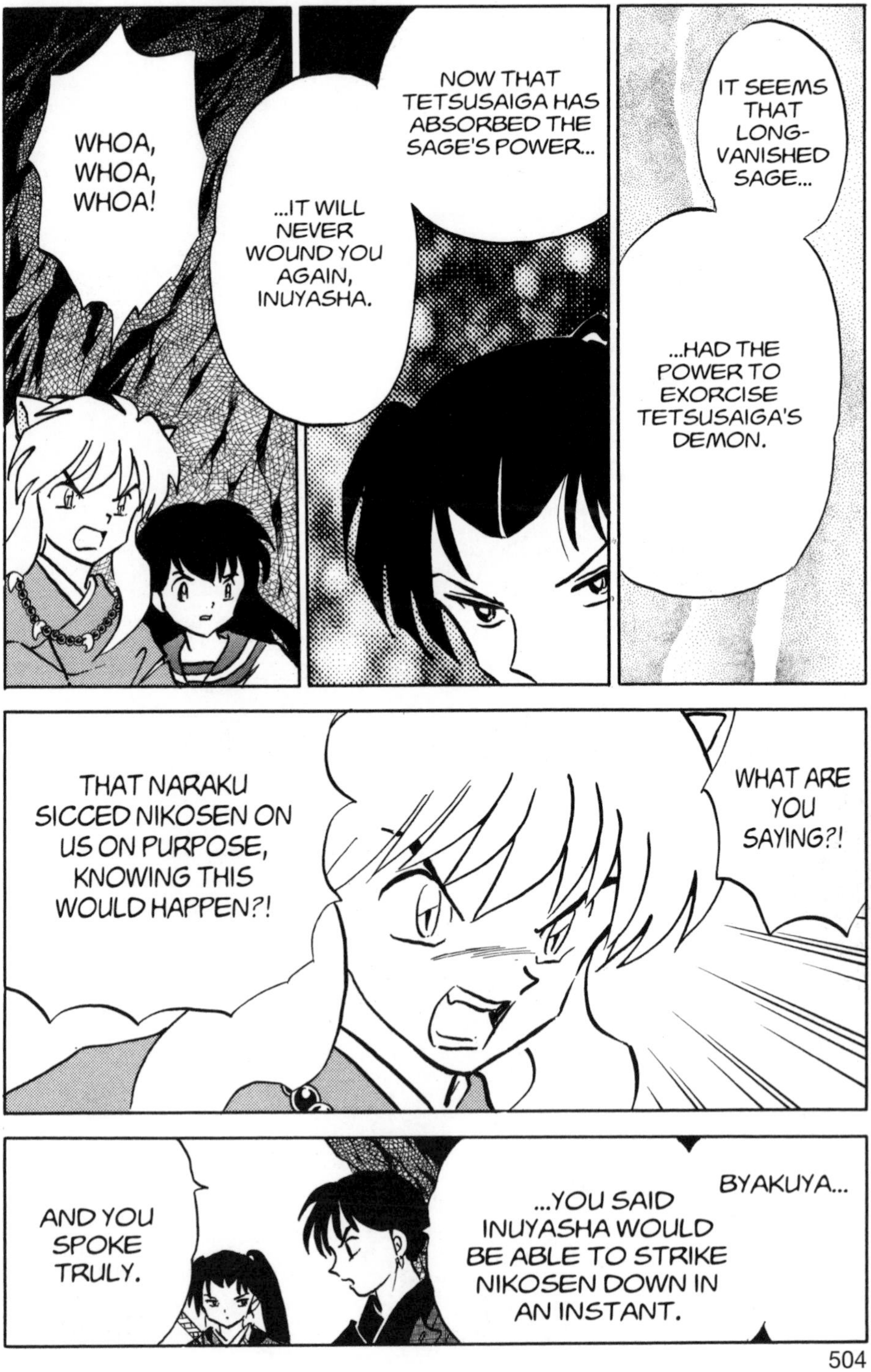
IT SEEMS THAT LONG-VANISHED SAGE...
...HAD THE POWER TO EXORCISE TETSUSAIGA'S DEMON.
NOW THAT TETSUSAIGA HAS ABSORBED THE SAGE'S POWER...
...IT WILL NEVER WOUND YOU AGAIN, INUYASHA.
WHOA, WHOA, WHOA!
WHAT ARE YOU SAYING?!
THAT NARAKU SICCED NIKOSEN ON US ON PURPOSE, KNOWING THIS WOULD HAPPEN?!
BYAKUYA...
...YOU SAID INUYASHA WOULD BE ABLE TO STRIKE NIKOSEN DOWN IN AN INSTANT.
AND YOU SPOKE TRULY.

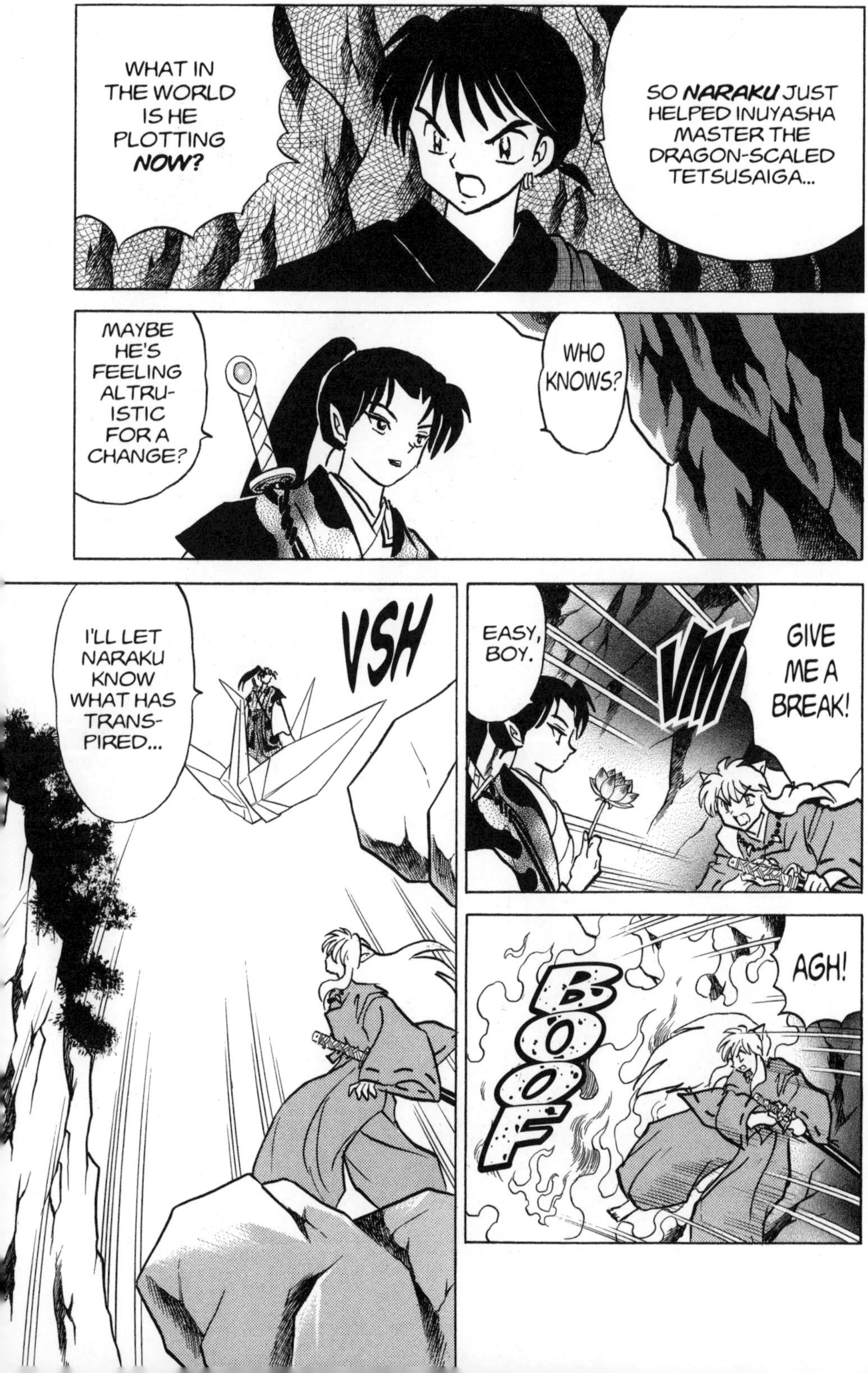
SO NARAKU JUST HELPED INUYASHA MASTER THE DRAGON-SCALED TETSUSAIGA...
WHAT IN THE WORLD IS HE PLOTTING NOW?
WHO KNOWS?
MAYBE HE'S FEELING ALTRU-ISTIC FOR A CHANGE?
GIVE ME A BREAK!
VM
EASY, BOY.
AGH!
BOOOF
VSH
I'LL LET NARAKU KNOW WHAT HAS TRANS-PIRED...

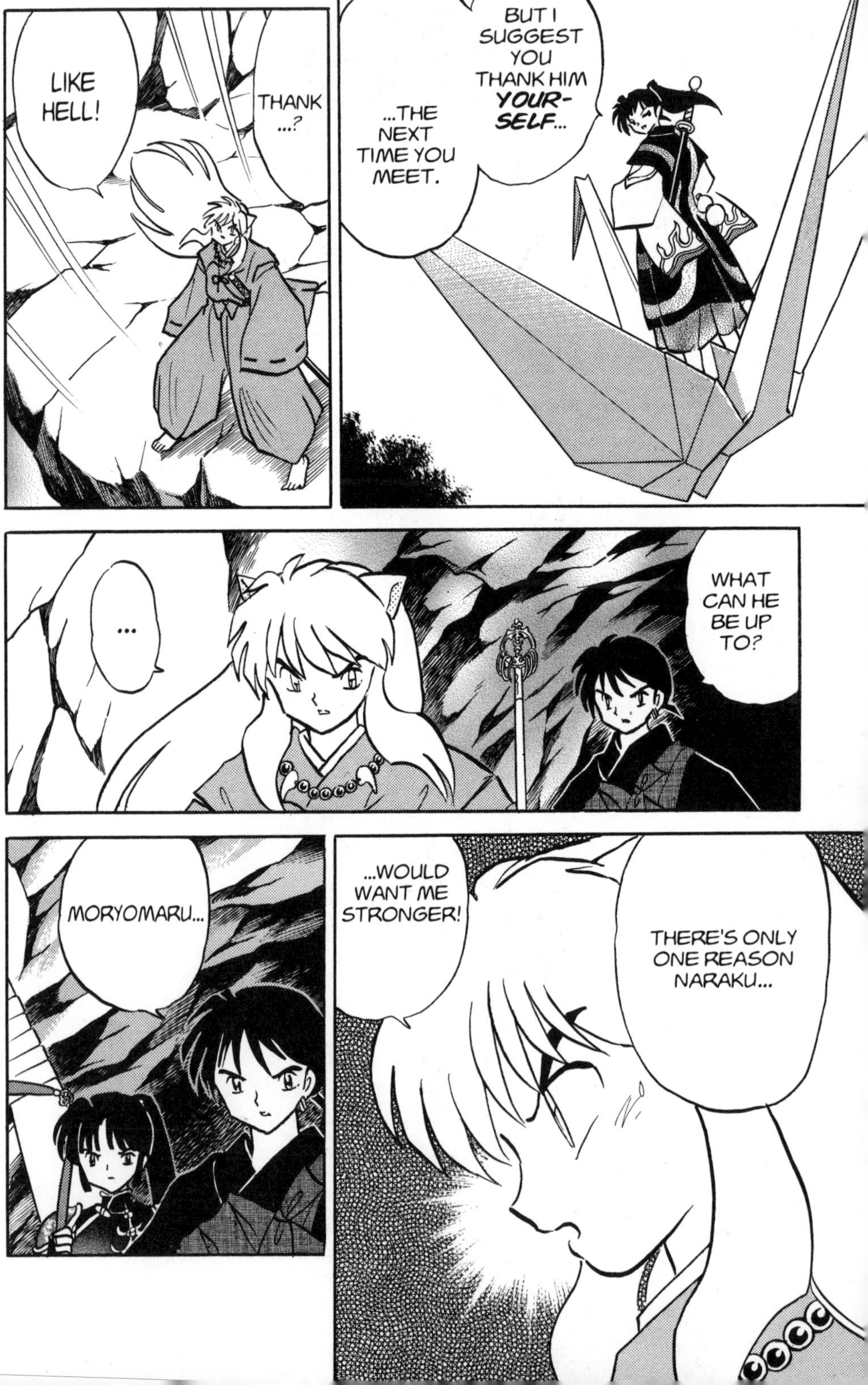
BUT I SUGGEST YOU THANK HIM YOURSELF...
...THE NEXT TIME YOU MEET.
THANK ...?
LIKE HELL!
WHAT CAN HE BE UP TO?
...
THERE'S ONLY ONE REASON NARAKU...
...WOULD WANT ME STRONGER!
MORYOMARU...

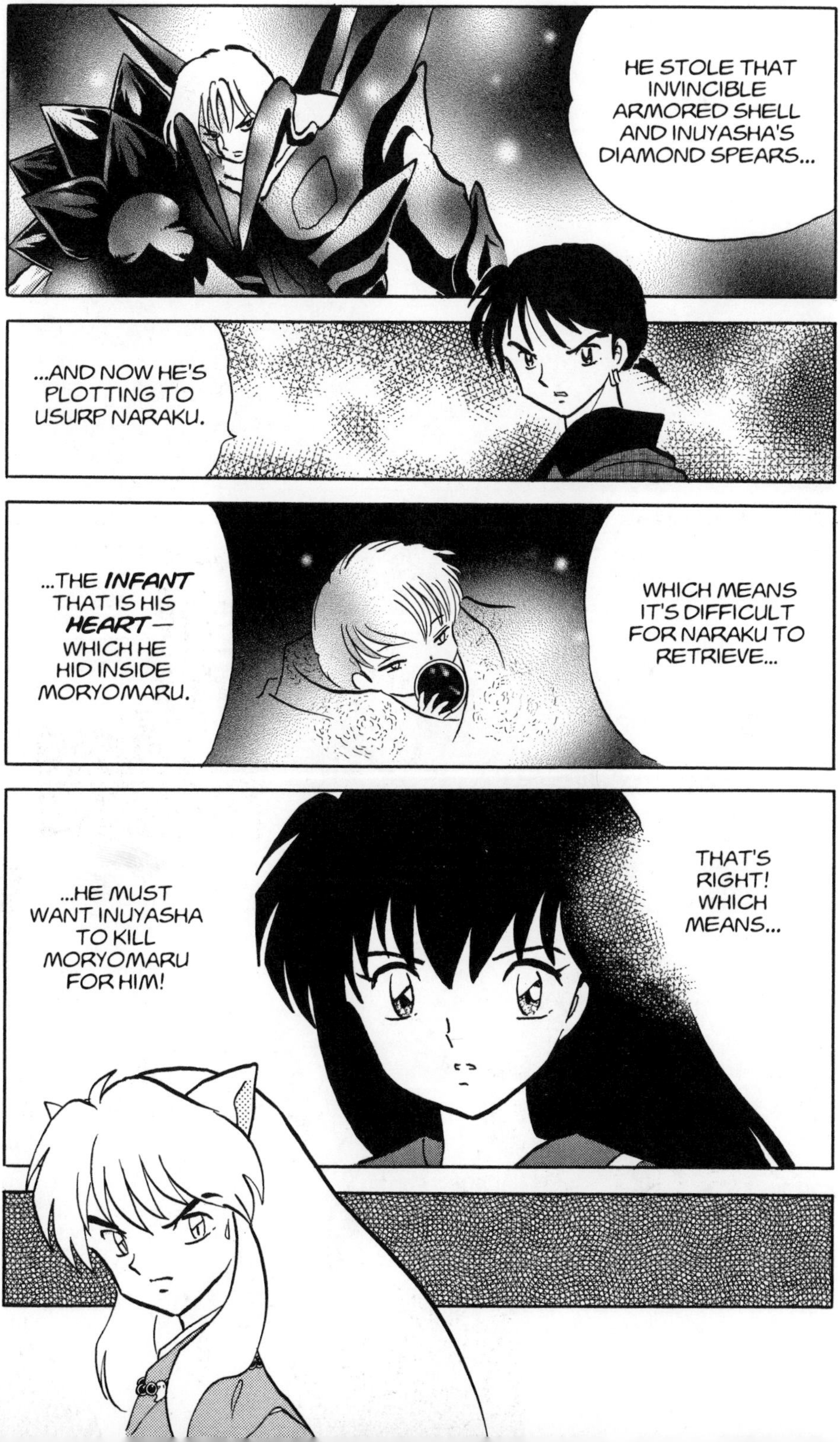
HE STOLE THAT INVINCIBLE ARMORED SHELL AND INUYASHA'S DIAMOND SPEARS...
...AND NOW HE'S PLOTTING TO USURP NARAKU.
WHICH MEANS IT'S DIFFICULT FOR NARAKU TO RETRIEVE...
...THE *INFANT* THAT IS HIS *HEART*—WHICH HE HID INSIDE MORYOMARU.
THAT'S RIGHT! WHICH MEANS...
...HE MUST WANT INUYASHA TO KILL MORYOMARU FOR HIM!

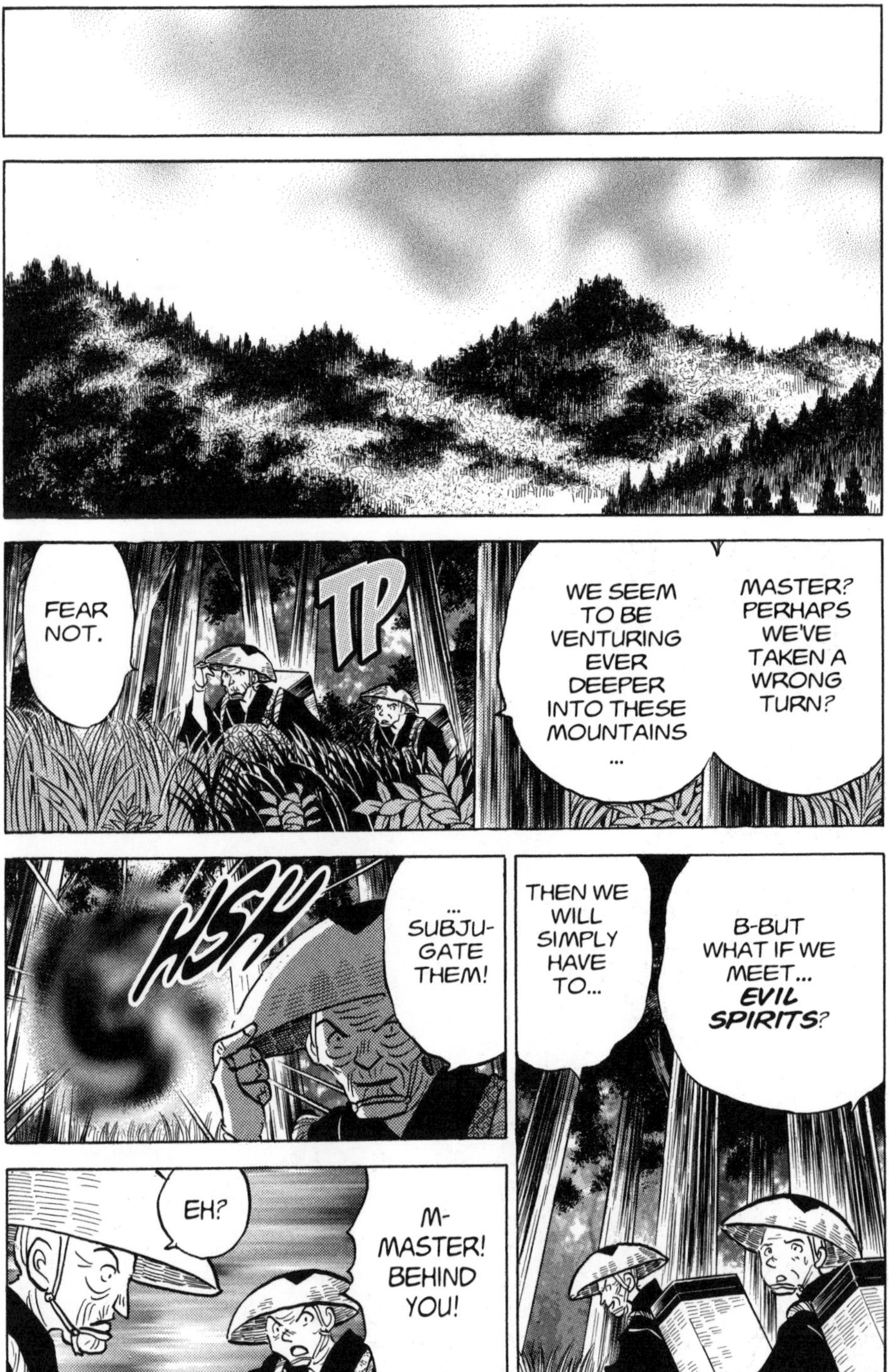
MASTER? PERHAPS WE'VE TAKEN A WRONG TURN?
WE SEEM TO BE VENTURING EVER DEEPER INTO THESE MOUNTAINS ...
TP
FEAR NOT.
B-BUT WHAT IF WE MEET... **EVIL SPIRITS**?
THEN WE WILL SIMPLY HAVE TO...
... SUBJU-GATE THEM!
HSH
M-MASTER! BEHIND YOU!
EH?

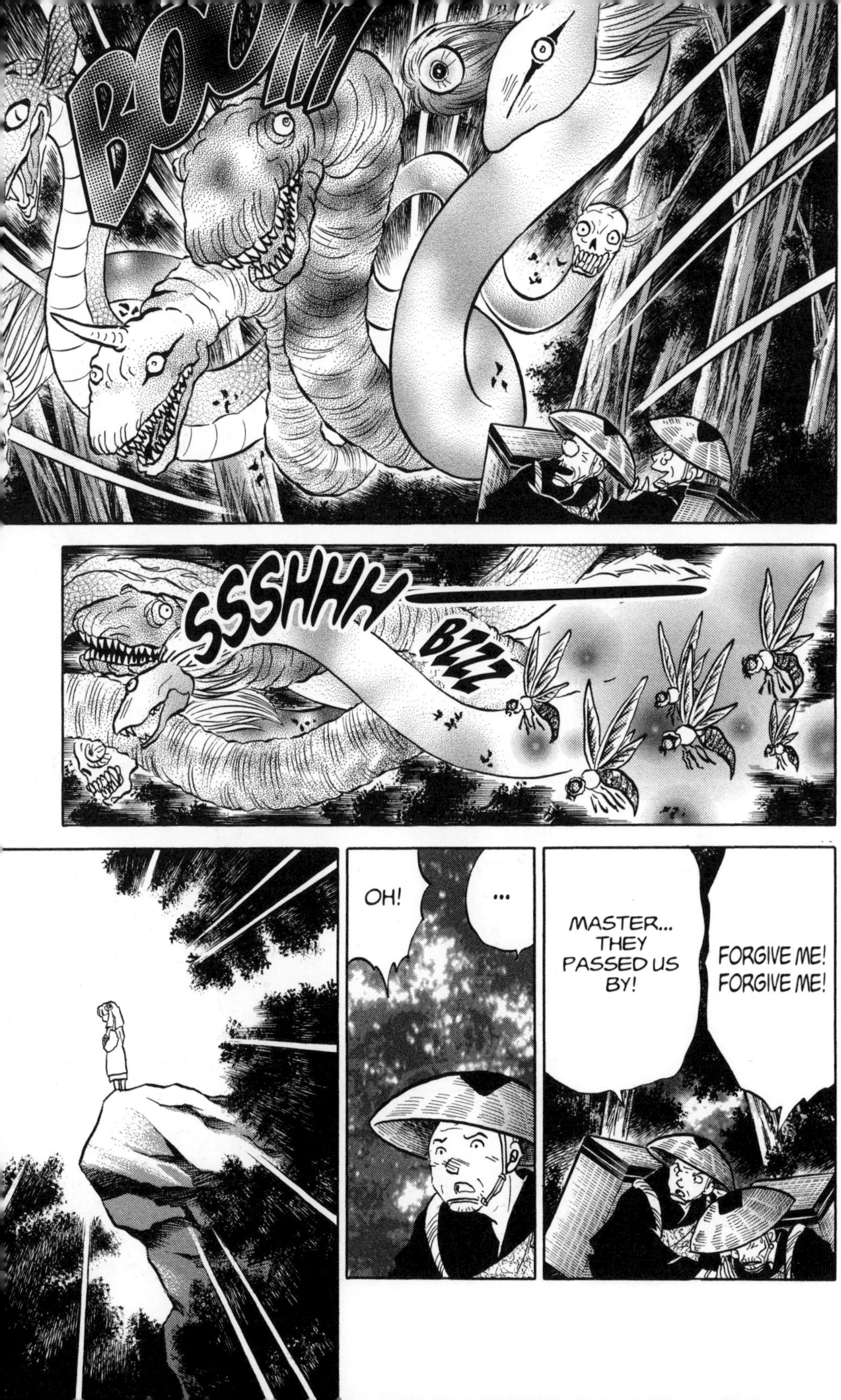
BOOM
SSSHHH
BZZZ
FORGIVE ME! FORGIVE ME!
MASTER... THEY PASSED US BY!
...
OH!

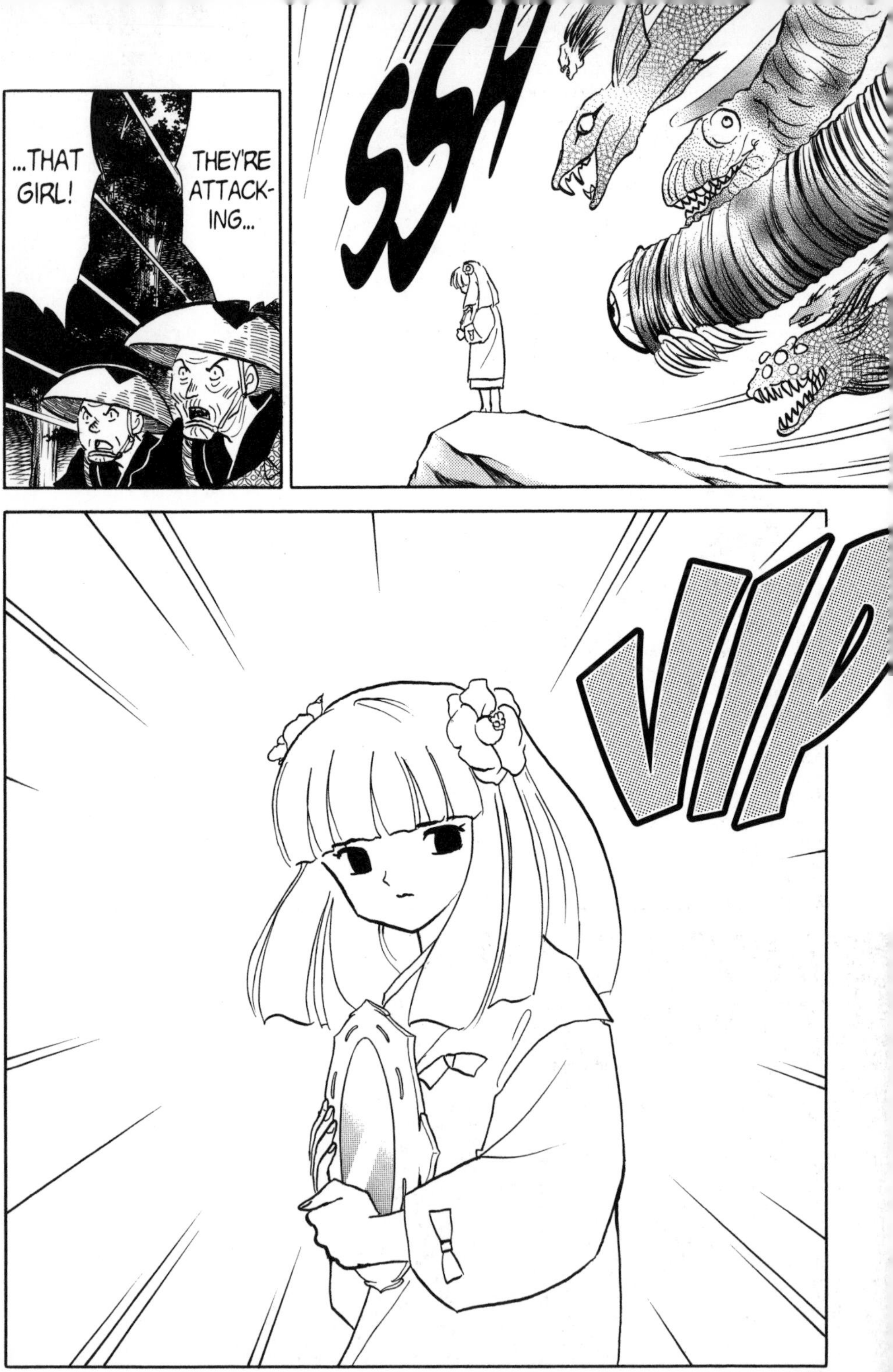
SSH
THEY'RE ATTACKING...
...THAT GIRL!
VIIP

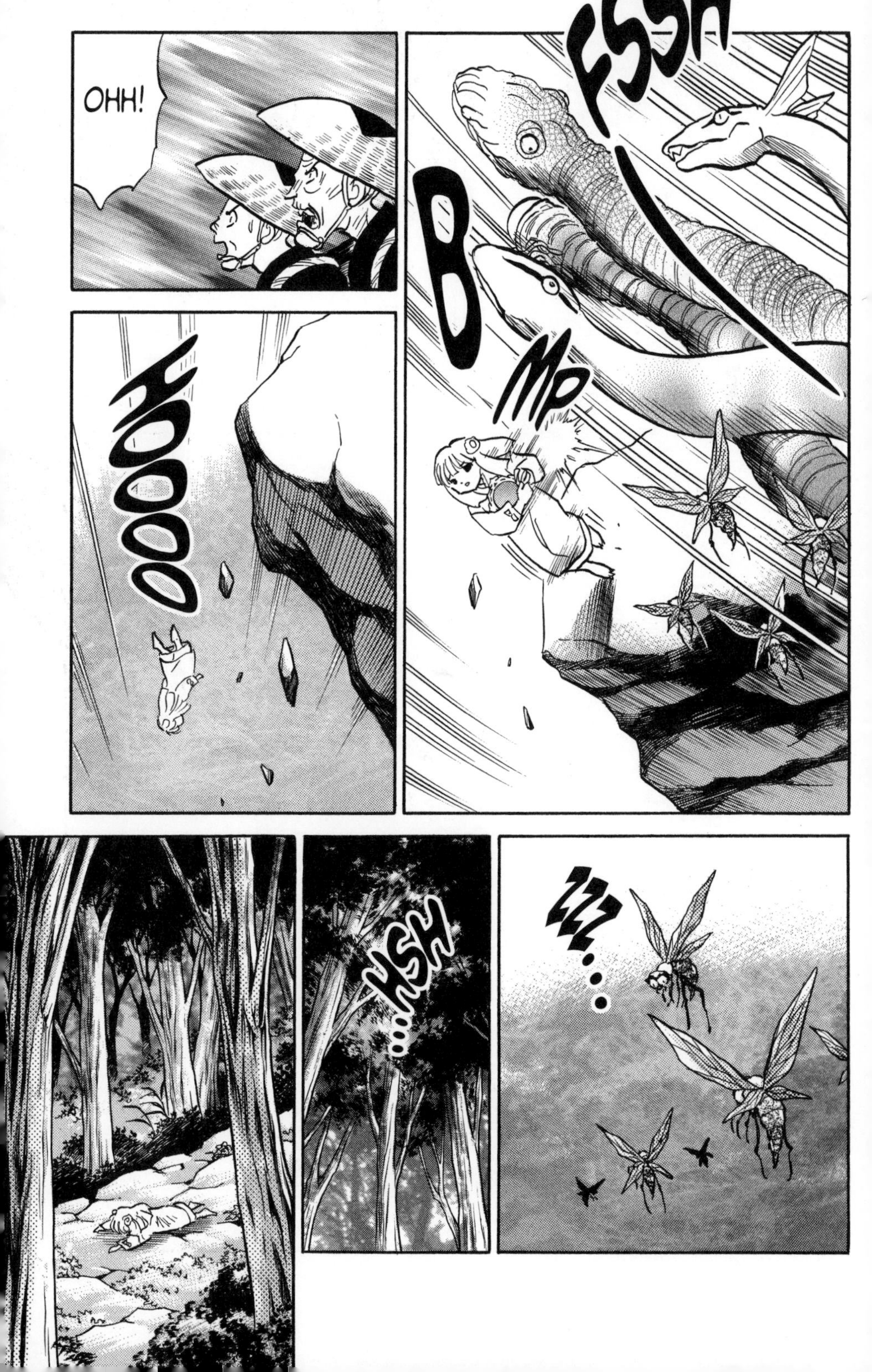
FSSH
BMP
OHH!
HOOOOO
ZZZ...
...HSH

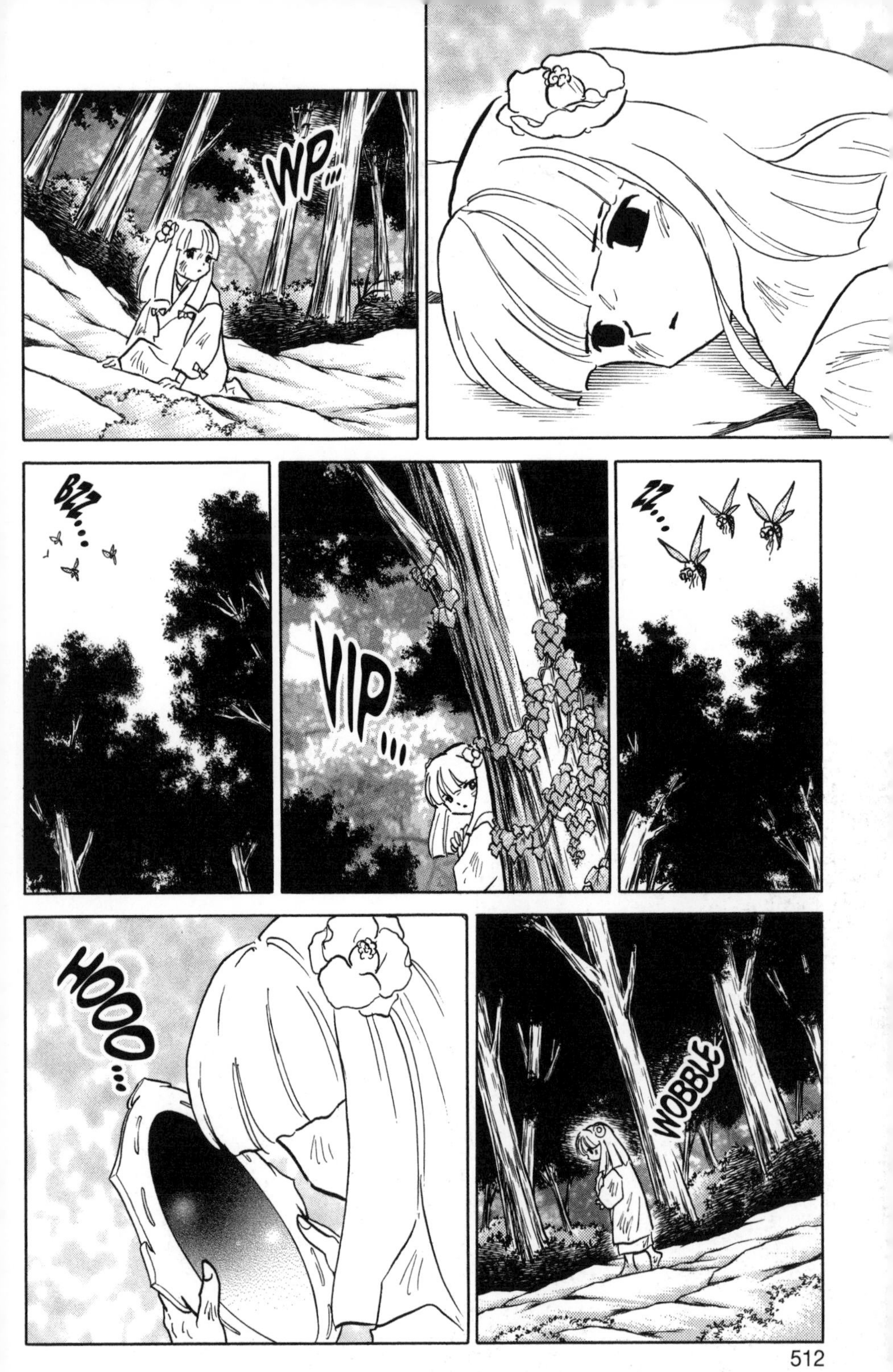
WP...
ZZ...
VIP...
BZZ...
WOBBLE
HOOO...

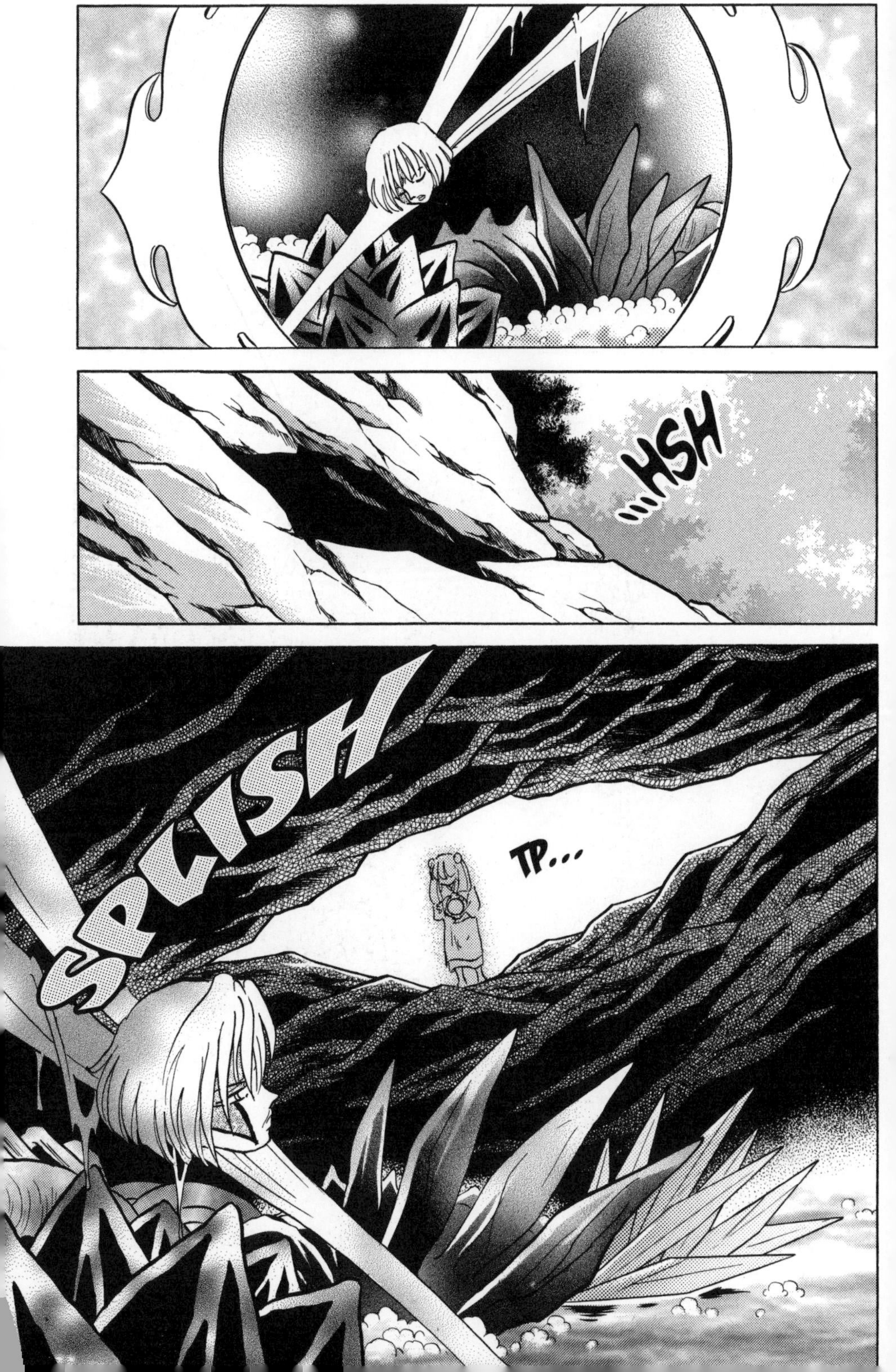
HSH...
SPLISH
TP...

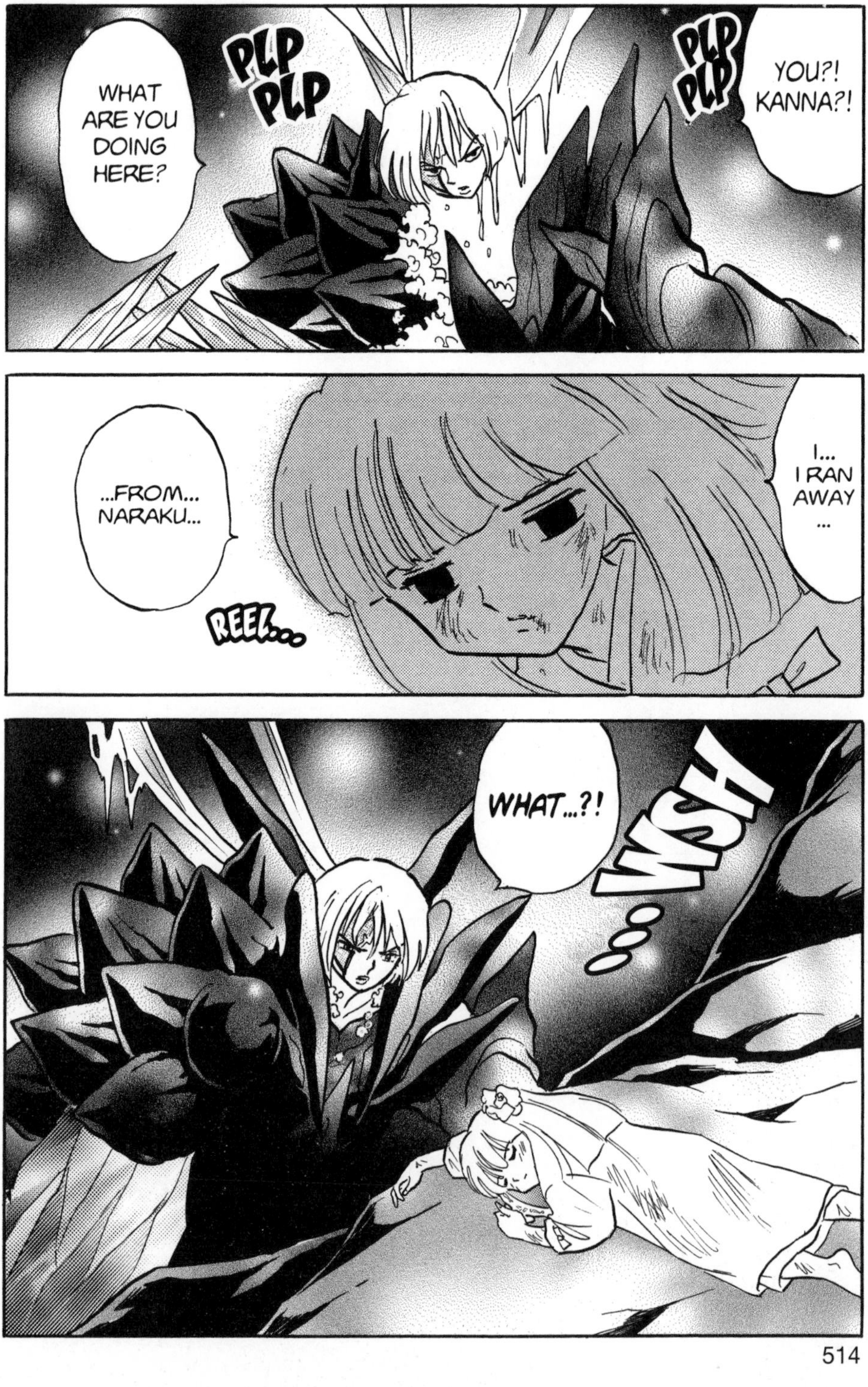
PLP PLP
YOU?! KANNA?!
PLP PLP
WHAT ARE YOU DOING HERE?
I... I RAN AWAY ...
...FROM... NARAKU...
REEL...
...WSH
WHAT...?!

SCROLL EIGHT
KINKA AND GINKA

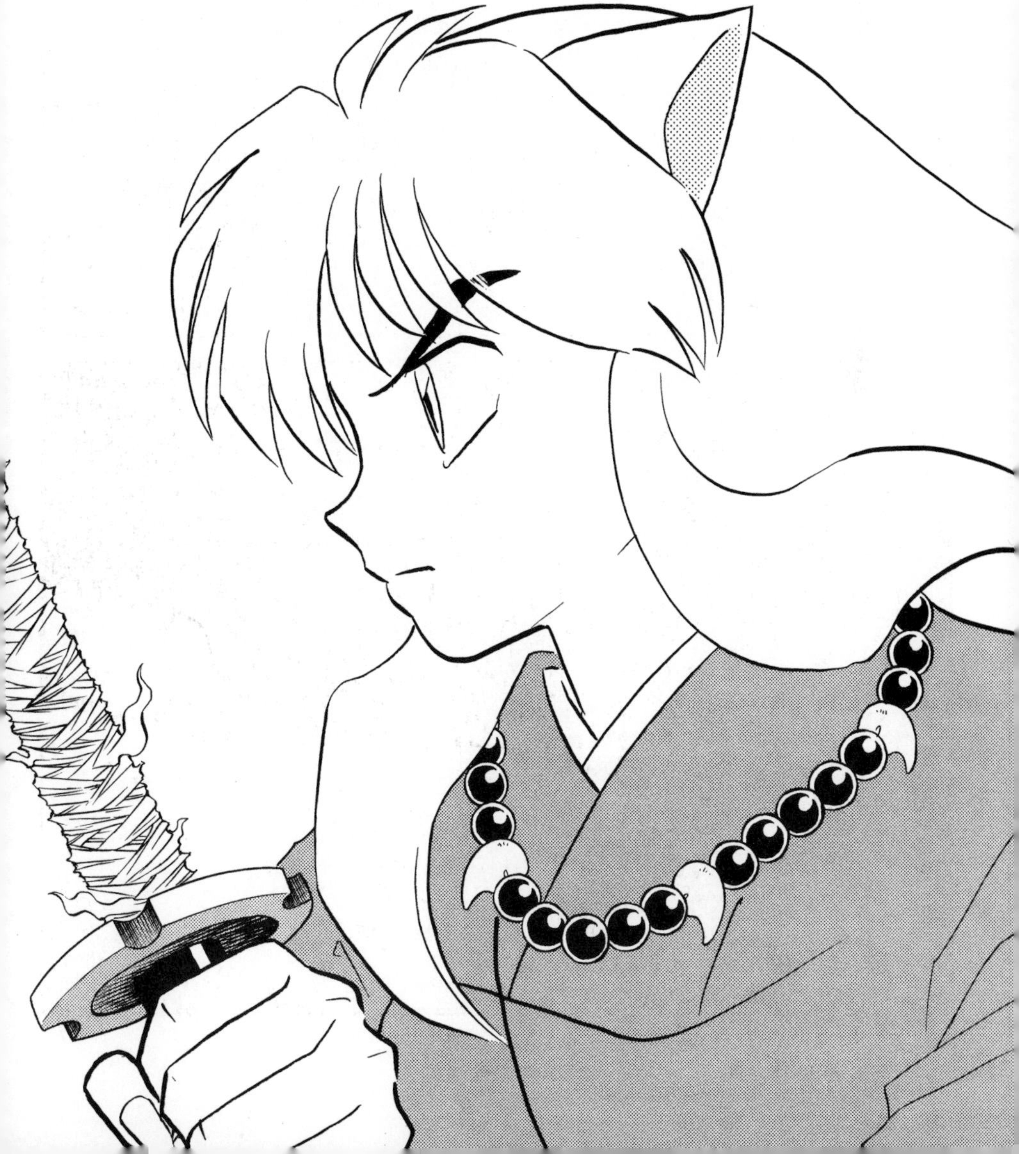

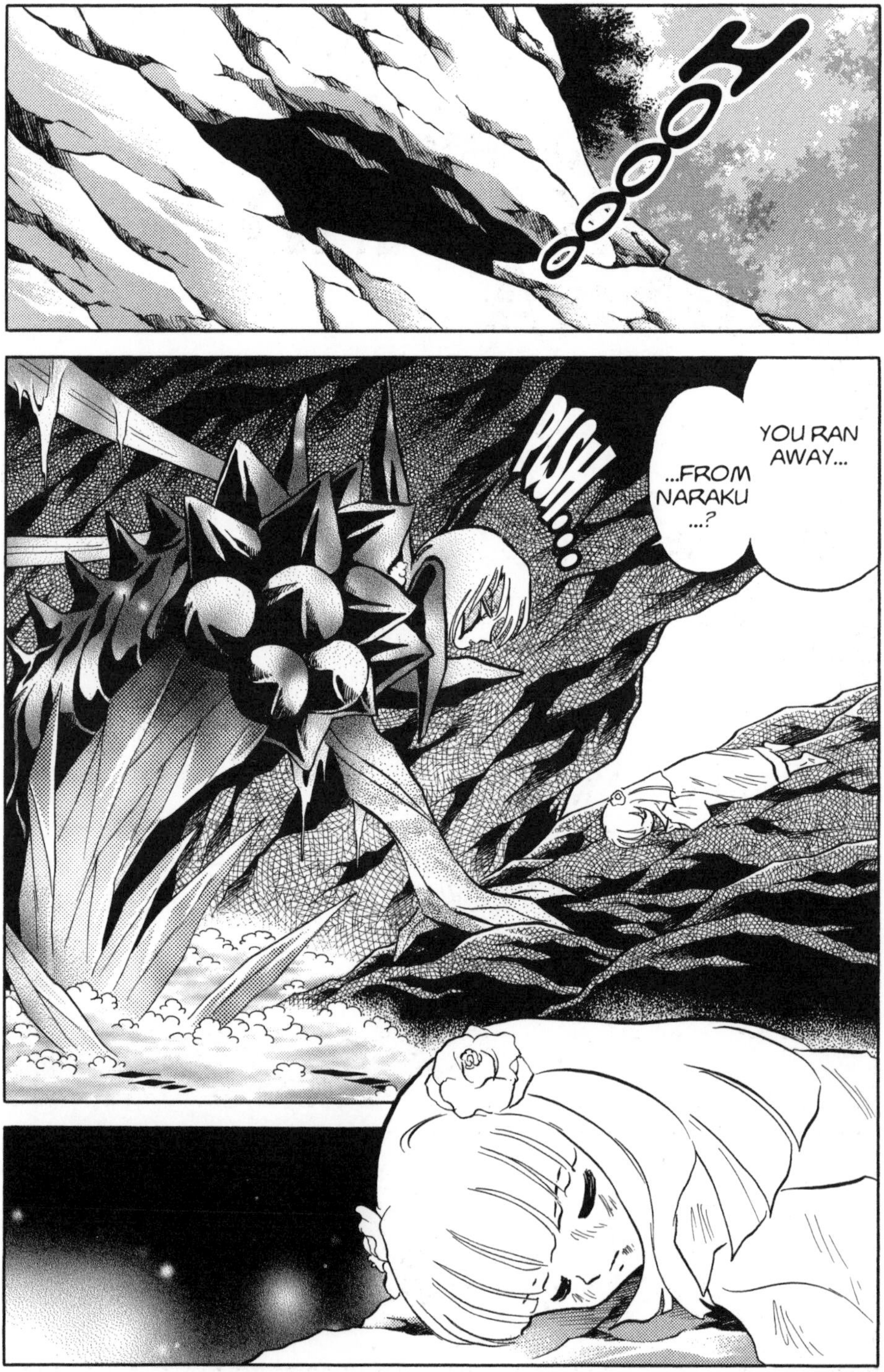
OOOOOH
YOU RAN AWAY...
...FROM NARAKU ...?
PLSH...

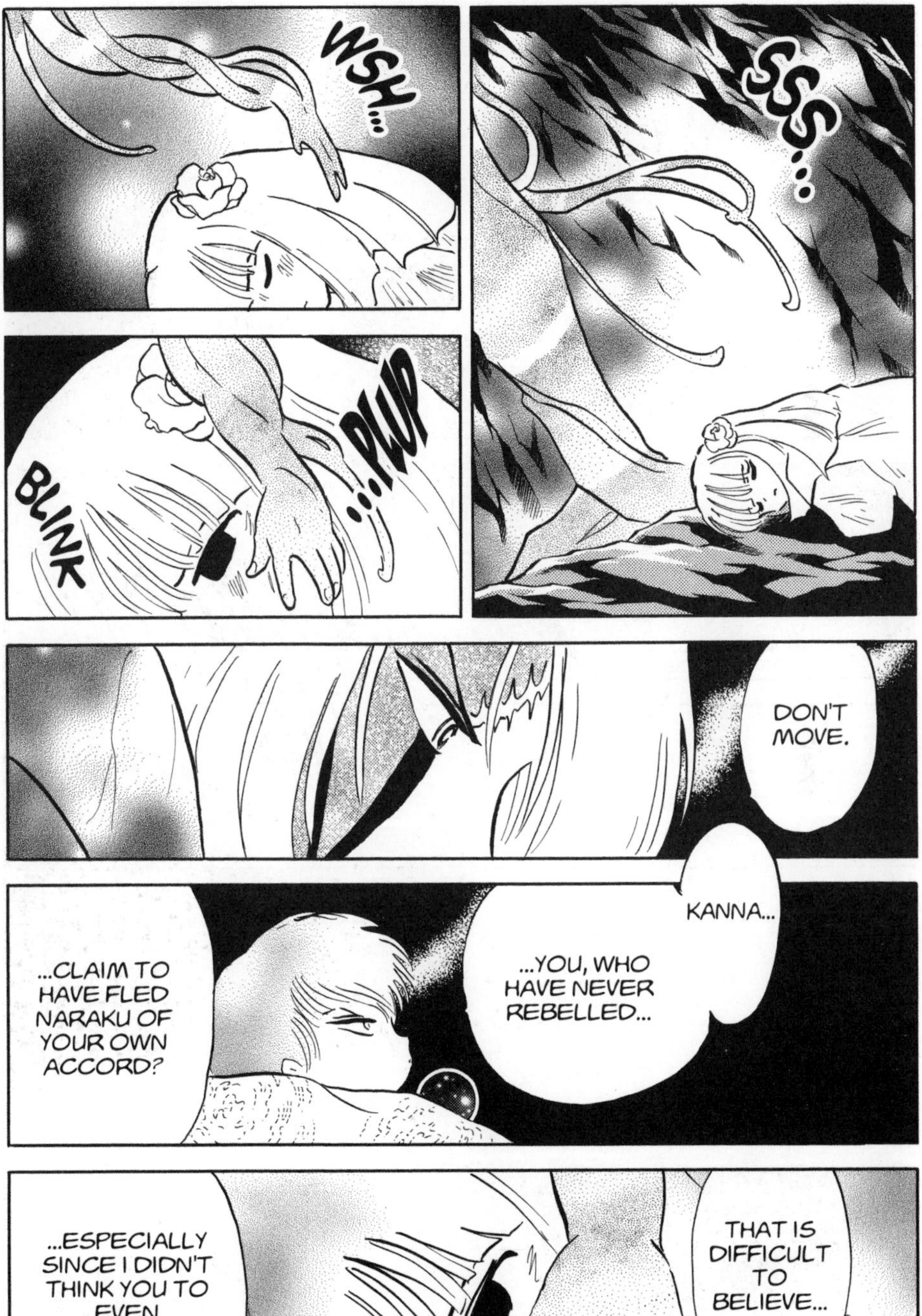
SSS...
WSH...
PLUP...
BLINK
DON'T MOVE.
KANNA...
...YOU, WHO HAVE NEVER REBELLED...
...CLAIM TO HAVE FLED NARAKU OF YOUR OWN ACCORD?
THAT IS DIFFICULT TO BELIEVE...
...ESPECIALLY SINCE I DIDN'T THINK YOU TO EVEN POSSESS A **SOUL**.

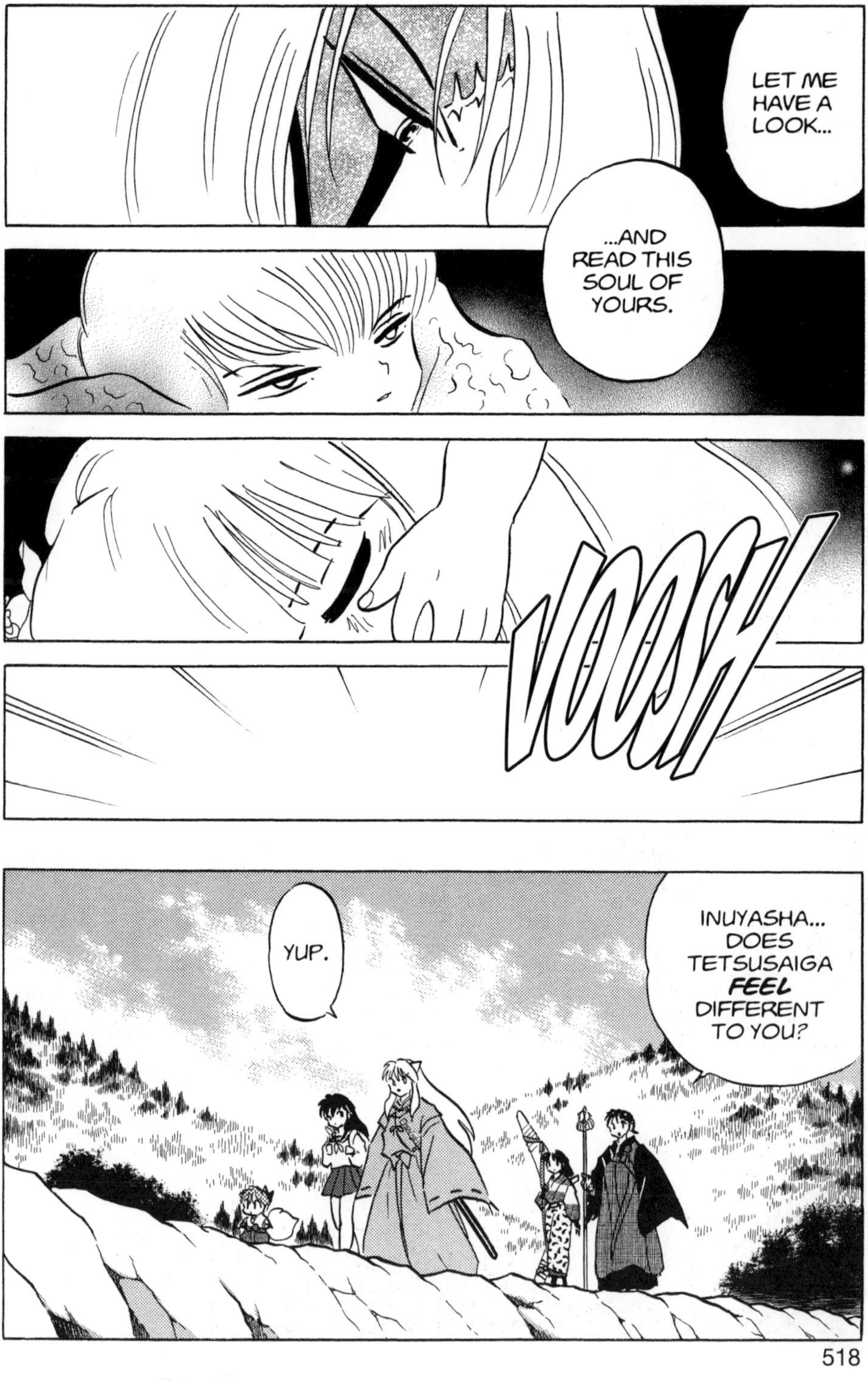
LET ME HAVE A LOOK...
...AND READ THIS SOUL OF YOURS.
VOOSH
INUYASHA... DOES TETSUSAIGA FEEL DIFFERENT TO YOU?
YUP.

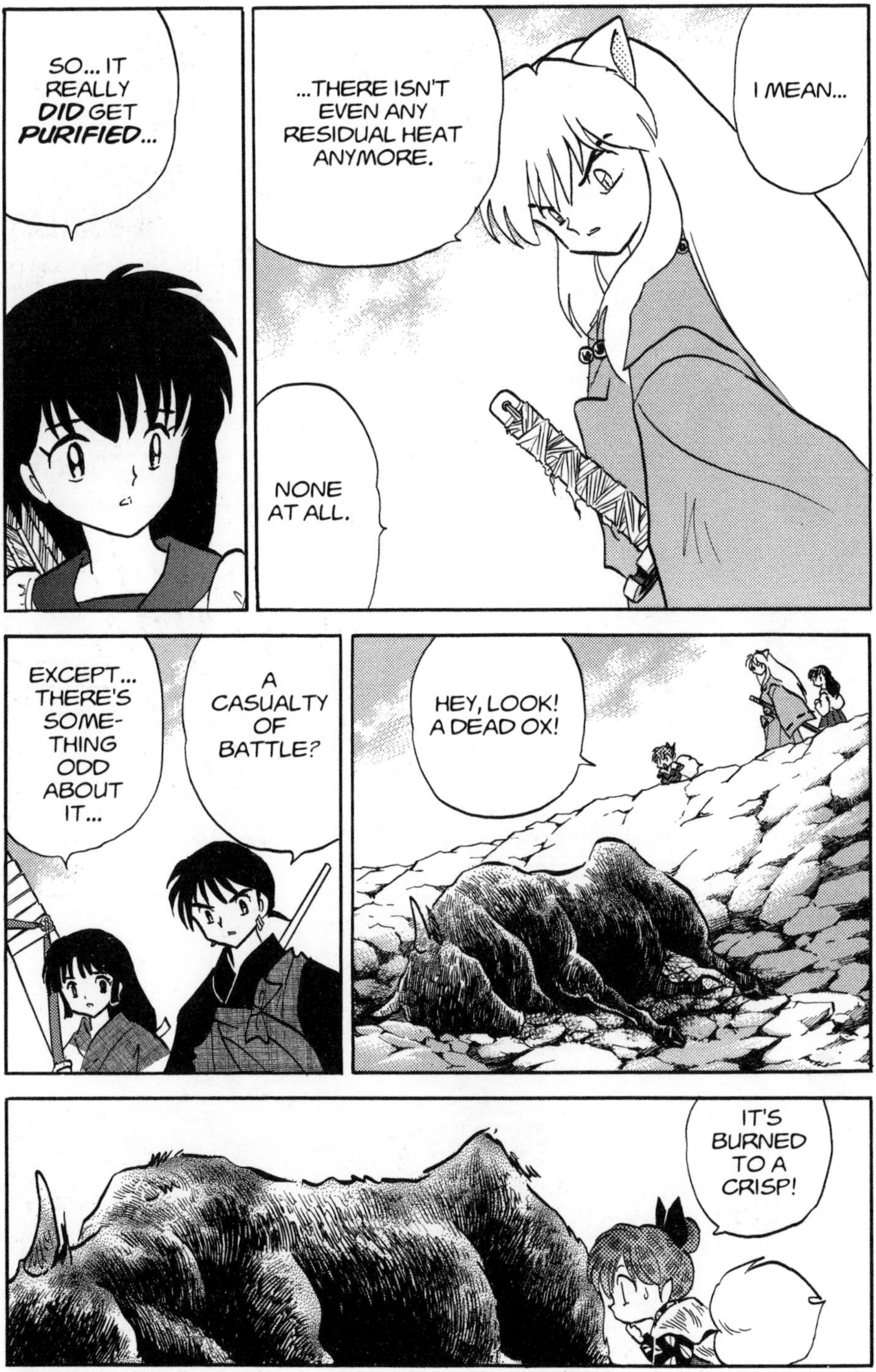
I MEAN...
...THERE ISN'T EVEN ANY RESIDUAL HEAT ANYMORE.
NONE AT ALL.
SO... IT REALLY **DID** GET ***PURIFIED***...
HEY, LOOK! A DEAD OX!
A CASUALTY OF BATTLE?
EXCEPT... THERE'S SOME-THING ODD ABOUT IT...
IT'S BURNED TO A CRISP!

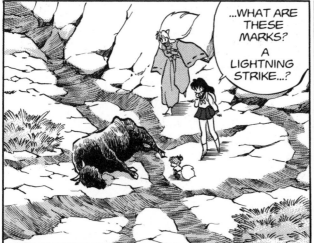

ALSO...
...WHAT ARE THESE MARKS?
A LIGHTNING STRIKE...?
HEY, YOU!
GET OUTTA THE WAY IF YOU DON'T WANNA GET CAUGHT IN THE LINE OF FIRE!
HUH?
AN ONGOING BATTLE... BETWEEN DEMONS?
YEAH. FOR DAYS ON END.
AND THANKS TO THEM, ALL THE VILLAGES 'ROUND HERE ARE IN RUINS!

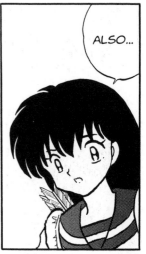

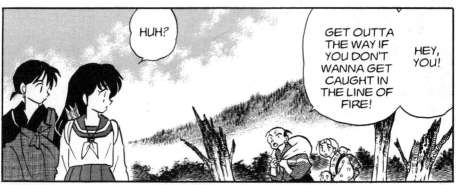

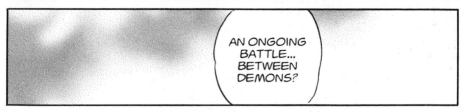

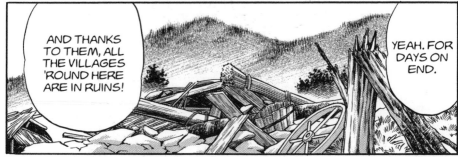

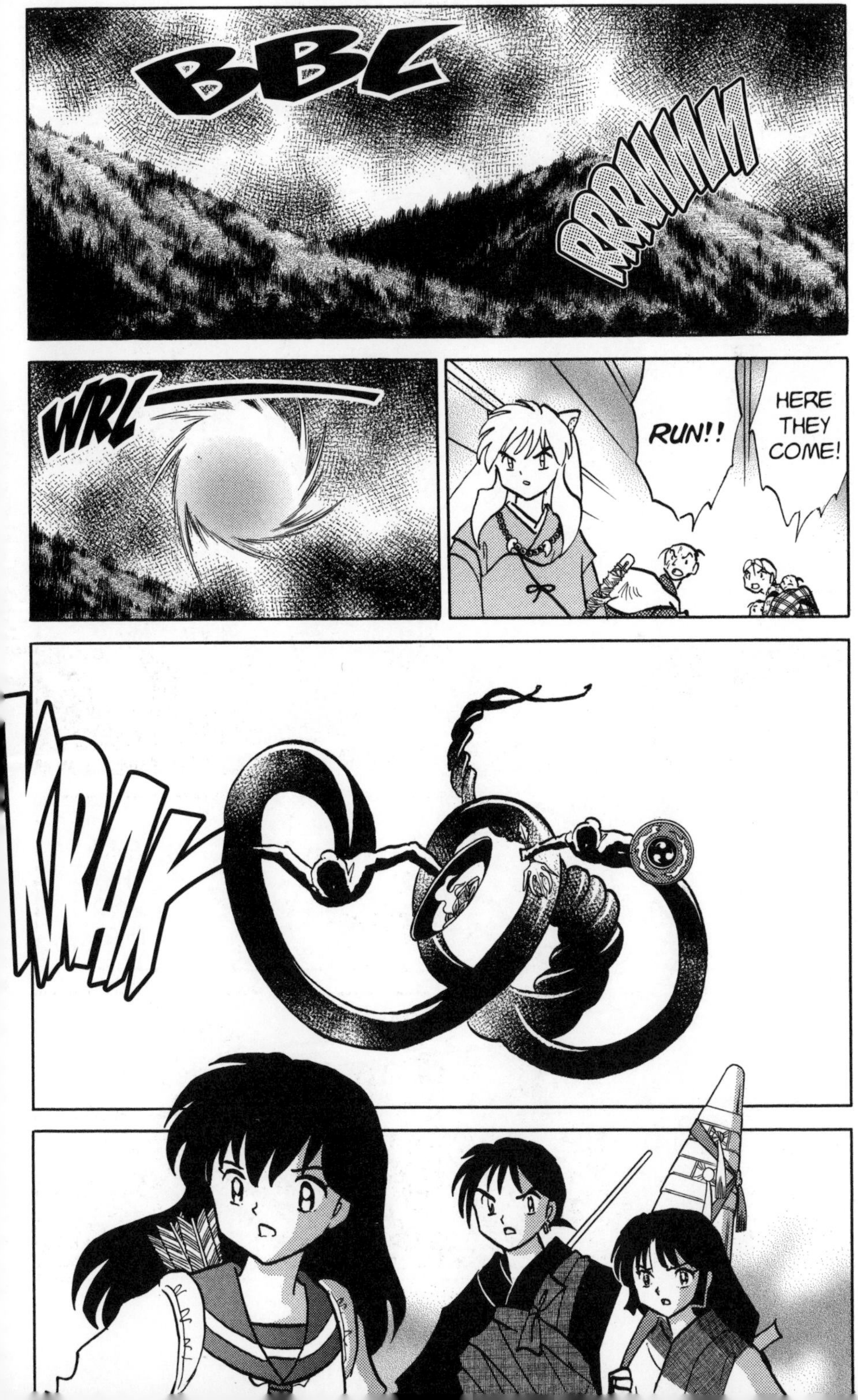
BBL
RRRMMMM
HERE THEY COME!
RUN!!
WRL
KRAK

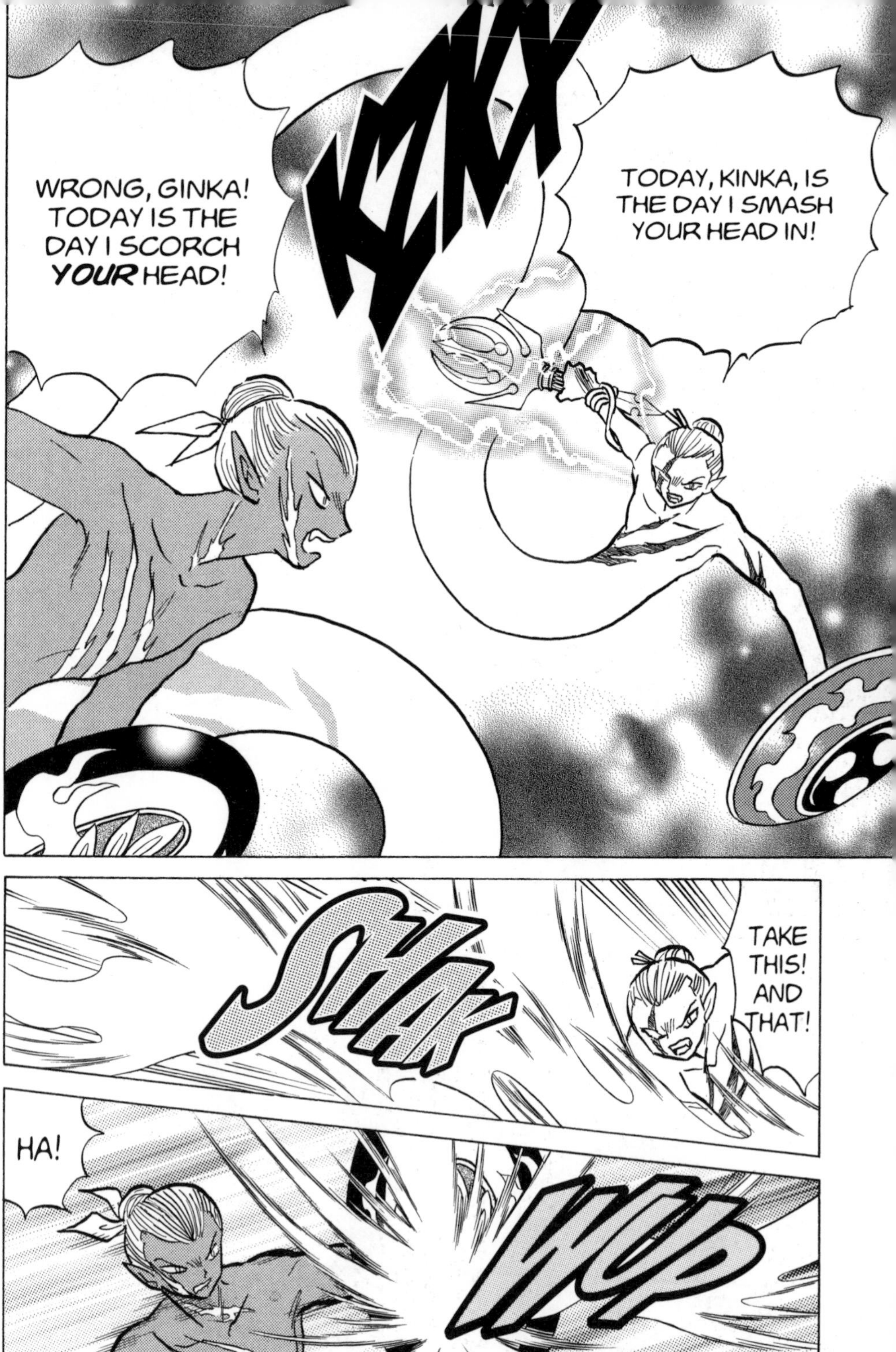
TODAY, KINKA, IS THE DAY I SMASH YOUR HEAD IN!
WRONG, GINKA! TODAY IS THE DAY I SCORCH **YOUR** HEAD!
TAKE THIS! AND THAT!
SHAK
HA!
WHUP

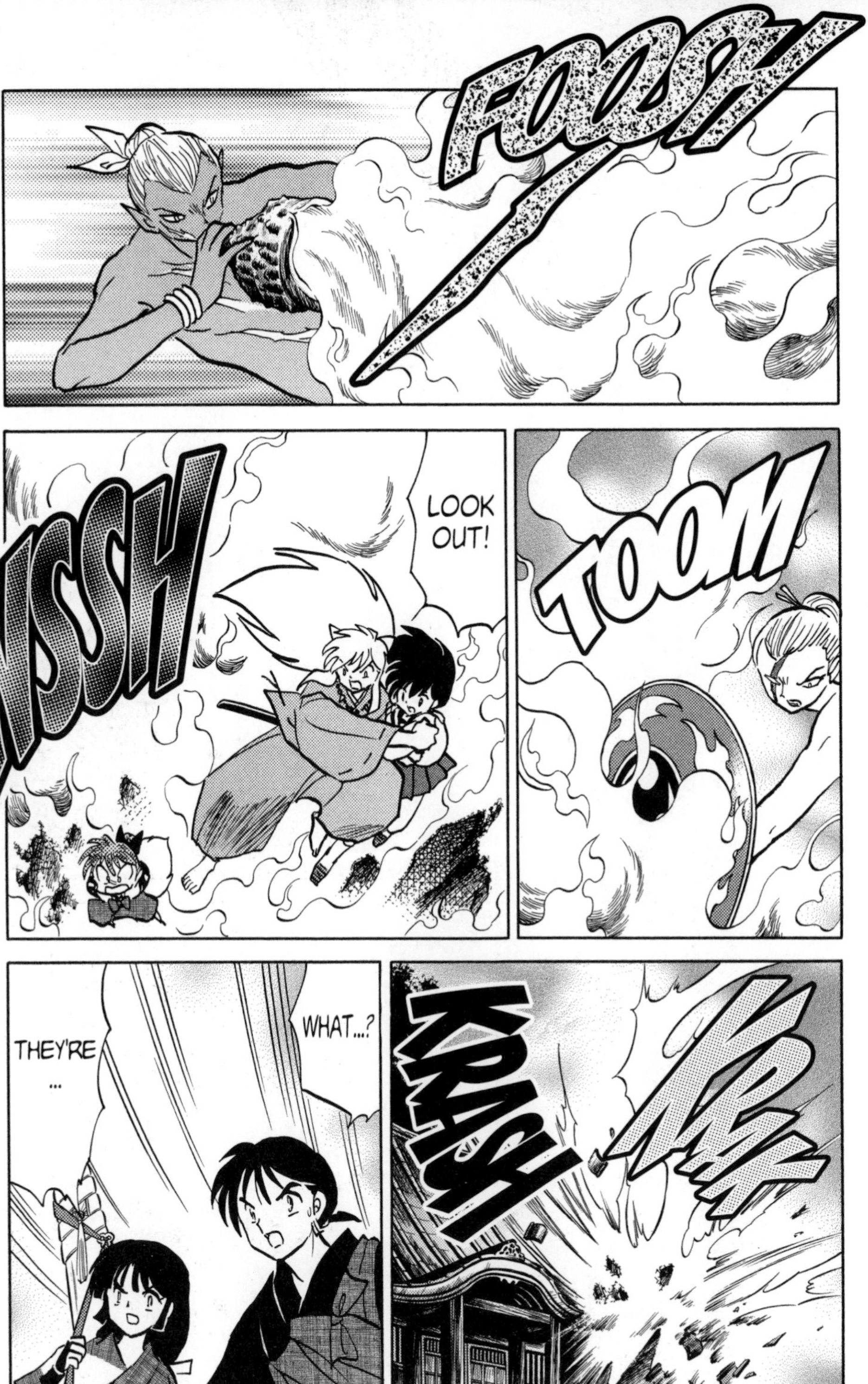
FOOOM
TOOM
LOOK OUT!
WSSH
KRASH
WHAT...?
THEY'RE ...

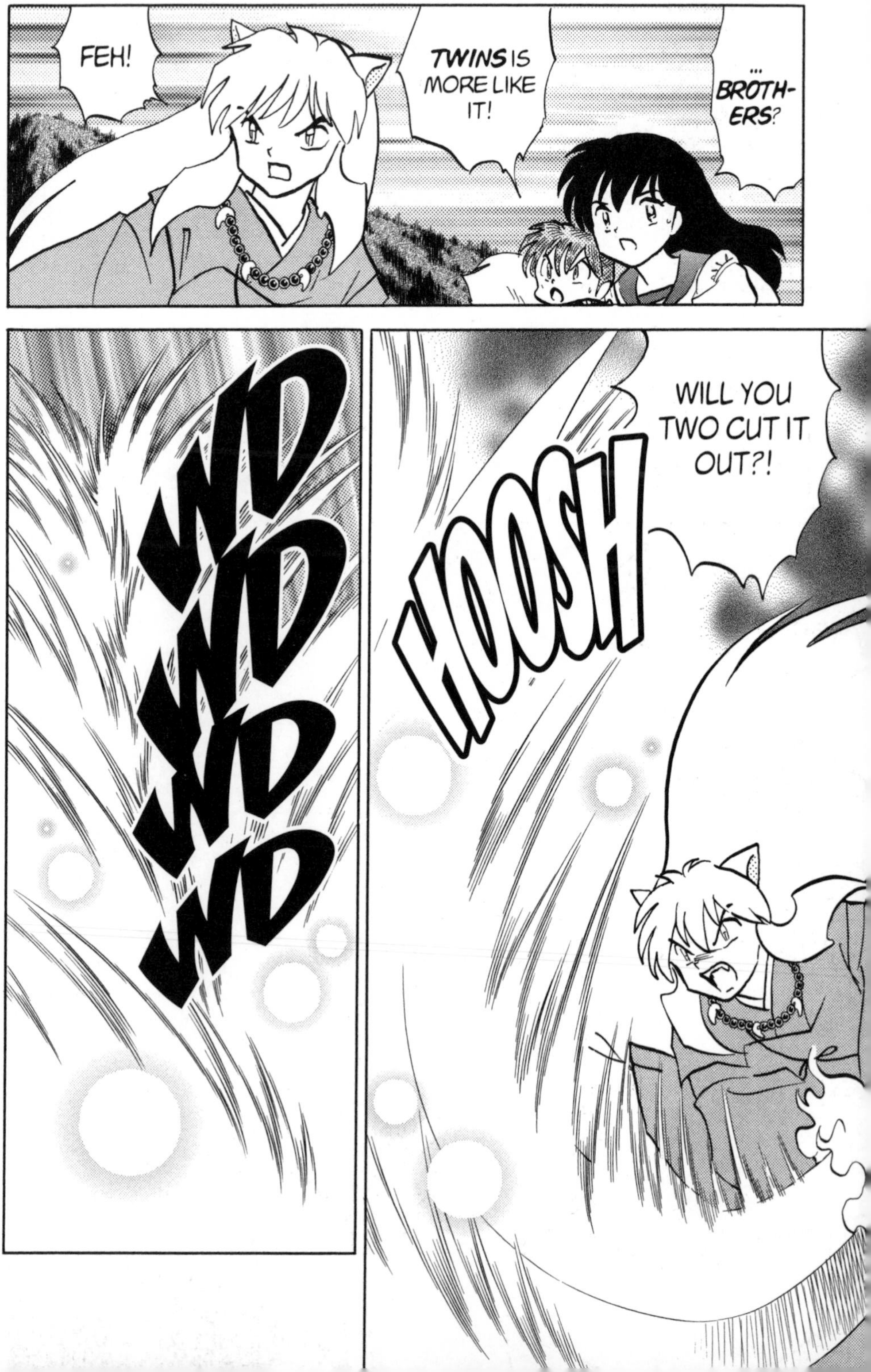
... BROTHERS?
TWINS IS MORE LIKE IT!
FEH!
WILL YOU TWO CUT IT OUT?!
HOOSH
WD WD WD WD WD

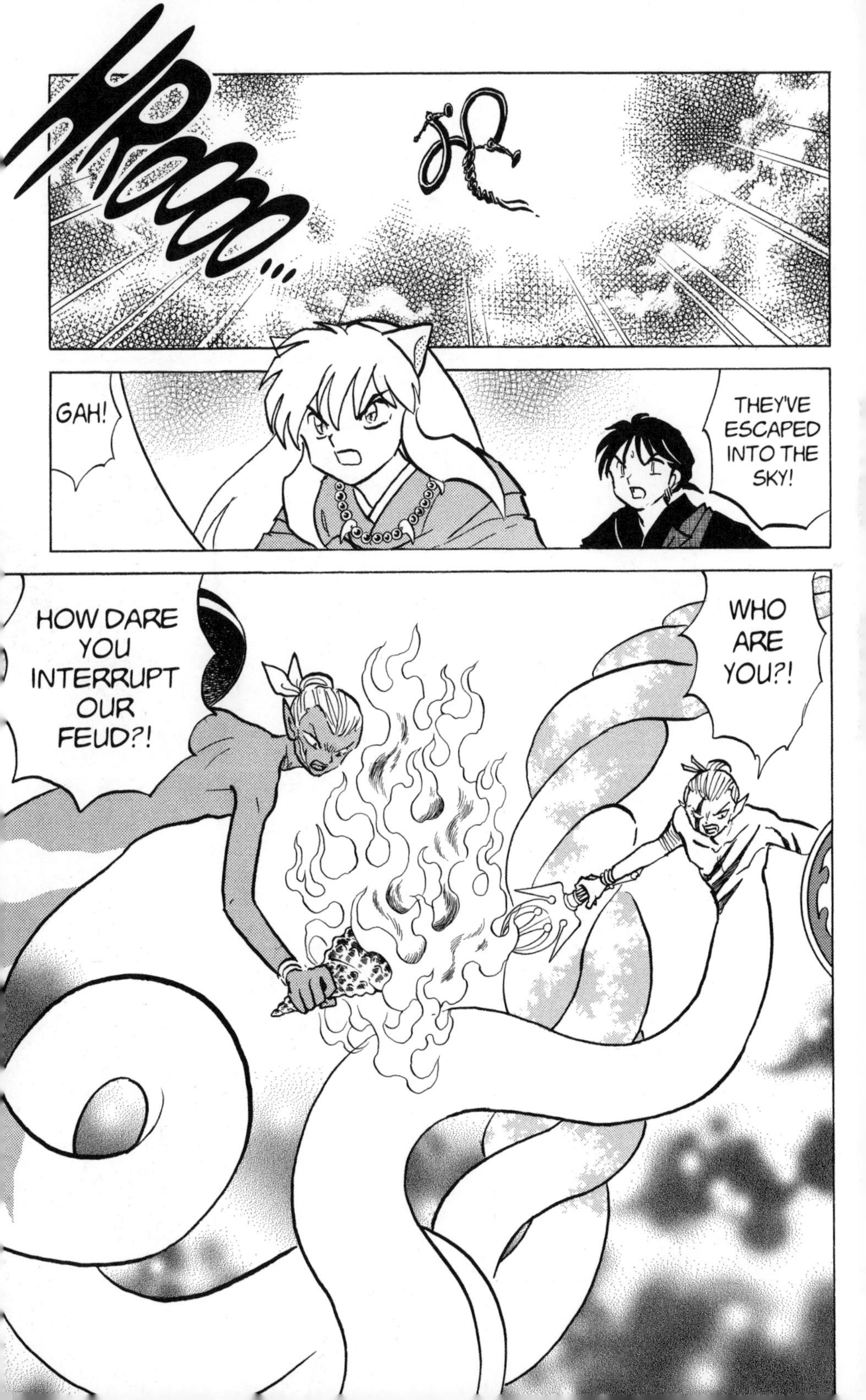
HROOO...
THEY'VE ESCAPED INTO THE SKY!
GAH!
WHO ARE YOU?!
HOW DARE YOU INTERRUPT OUR FEUD?!

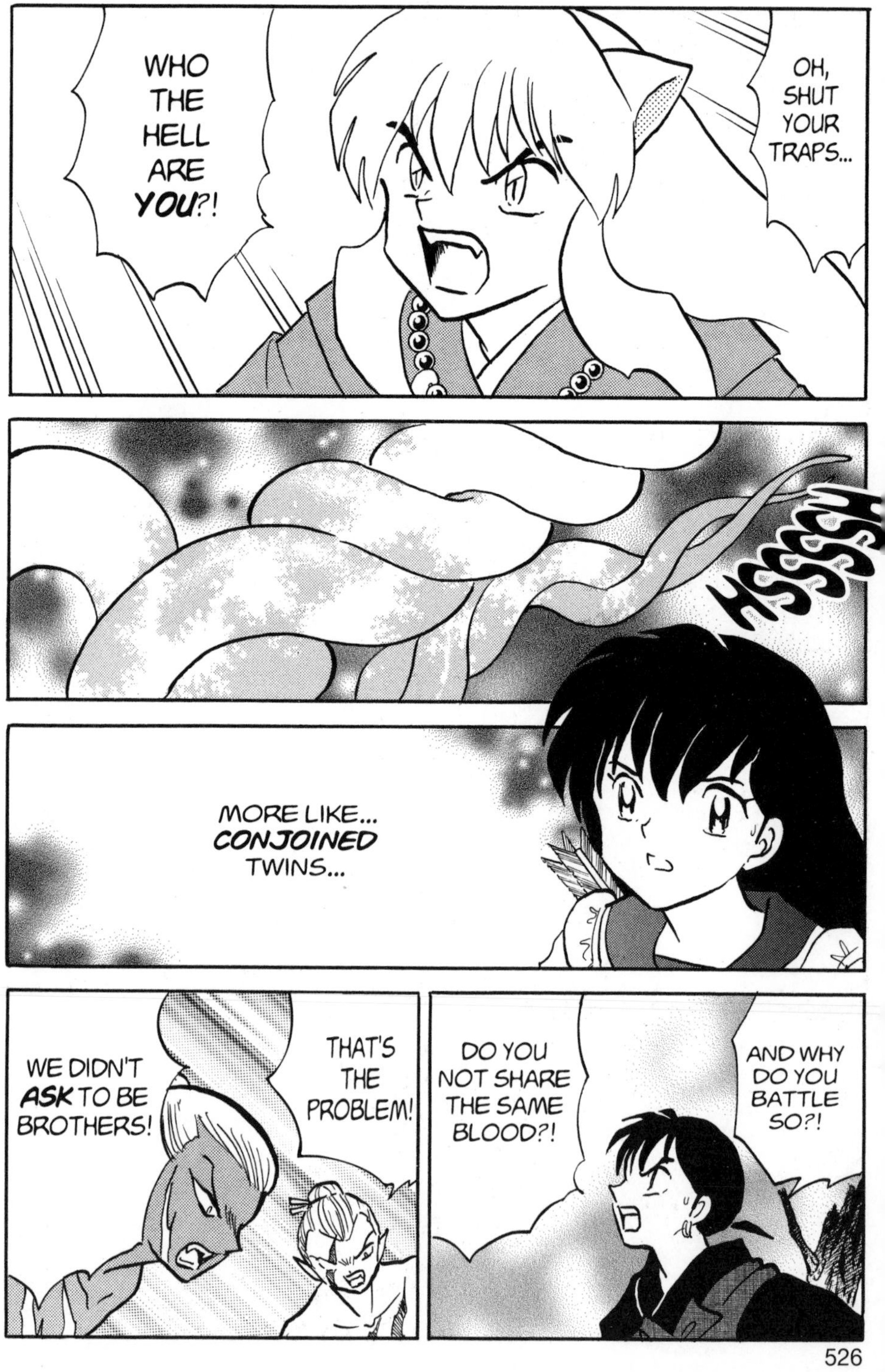
OH, SHUT YOUR TRAPS...
WHO THE HELL ARE YOU?!
HSSSSH
MORE LIKE... CONJOINED TWINS...
AND WHY DO YOU BATTLE SO?!
DO YOU NOT SHARE THE SAME BLOOD?!
THAT'S THE PROBLEM!
WE DIDN'T ASK TO BE BROTHERS!

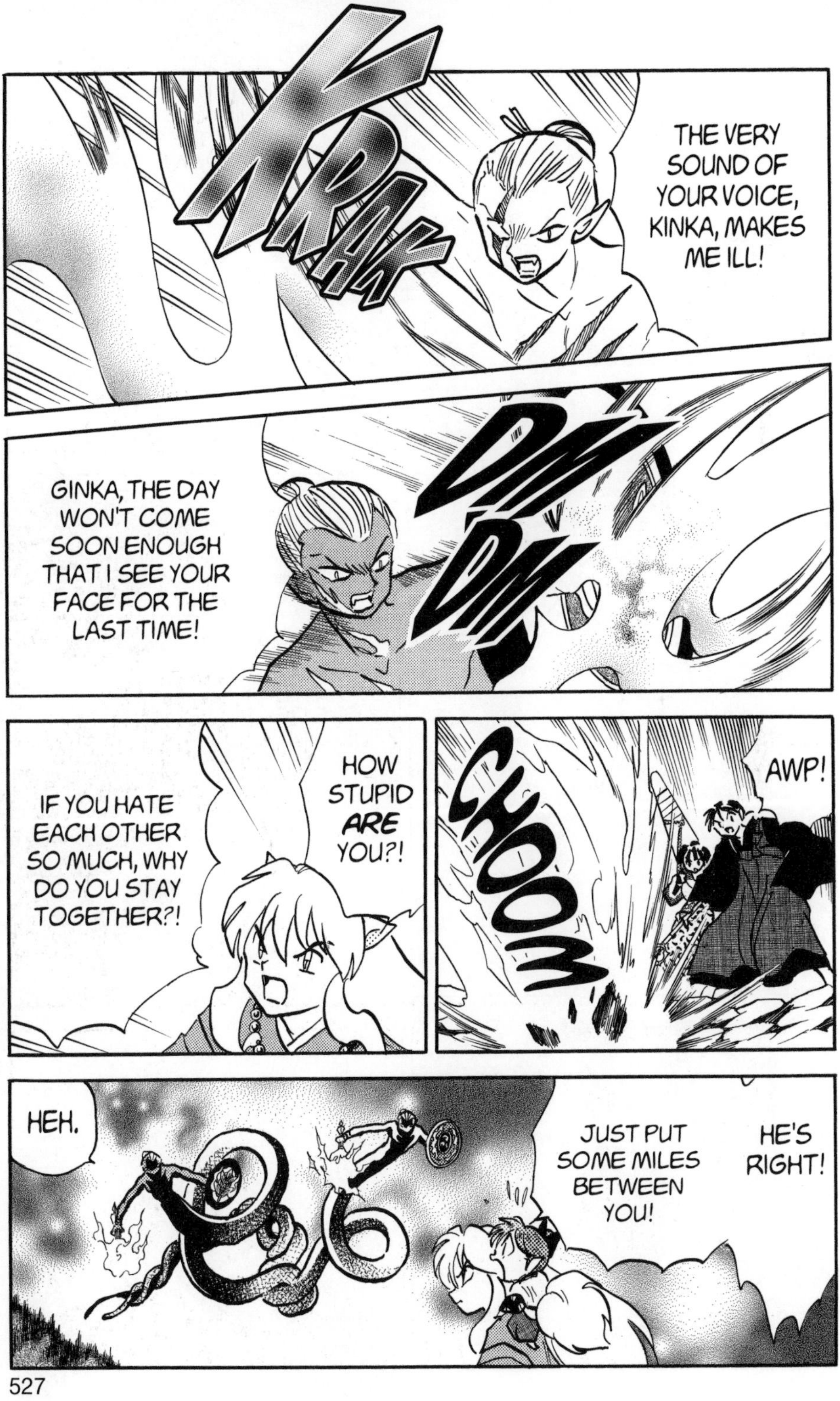
KRAK
THE VERY SOUND OF YOUR VOICE, KINKA, MAKES ME ILL!
DM DM
GINKA, THE DAY WON'T COME SOON ENOUGH THAT I SEE YOUR FACE FOR THE LAST TIME!
CHOOM
AWP!
HOW STUPID **ARE** YOU?!
IF YOU HATE EACH OTHER SO MUCH, WHY DO YOU STAY TOGETHER?!
HE'S RIGHT!
JUST PUT SOME MILES BETWEEN YOU!
HEH.

?!

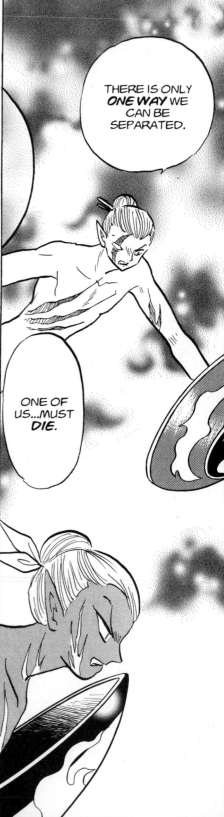

THERE IS ONLY **ONE WAY** WE CAN BE SEPARATED.

ONE OF US...MUST **DIE.**

THIS BODY...

...WAS ONLY MEANT TO BELONG TO ONE.

BUT SOON...

DEMONS OF OUR KIND ARE ALL BORN WITH TWO HEADS.

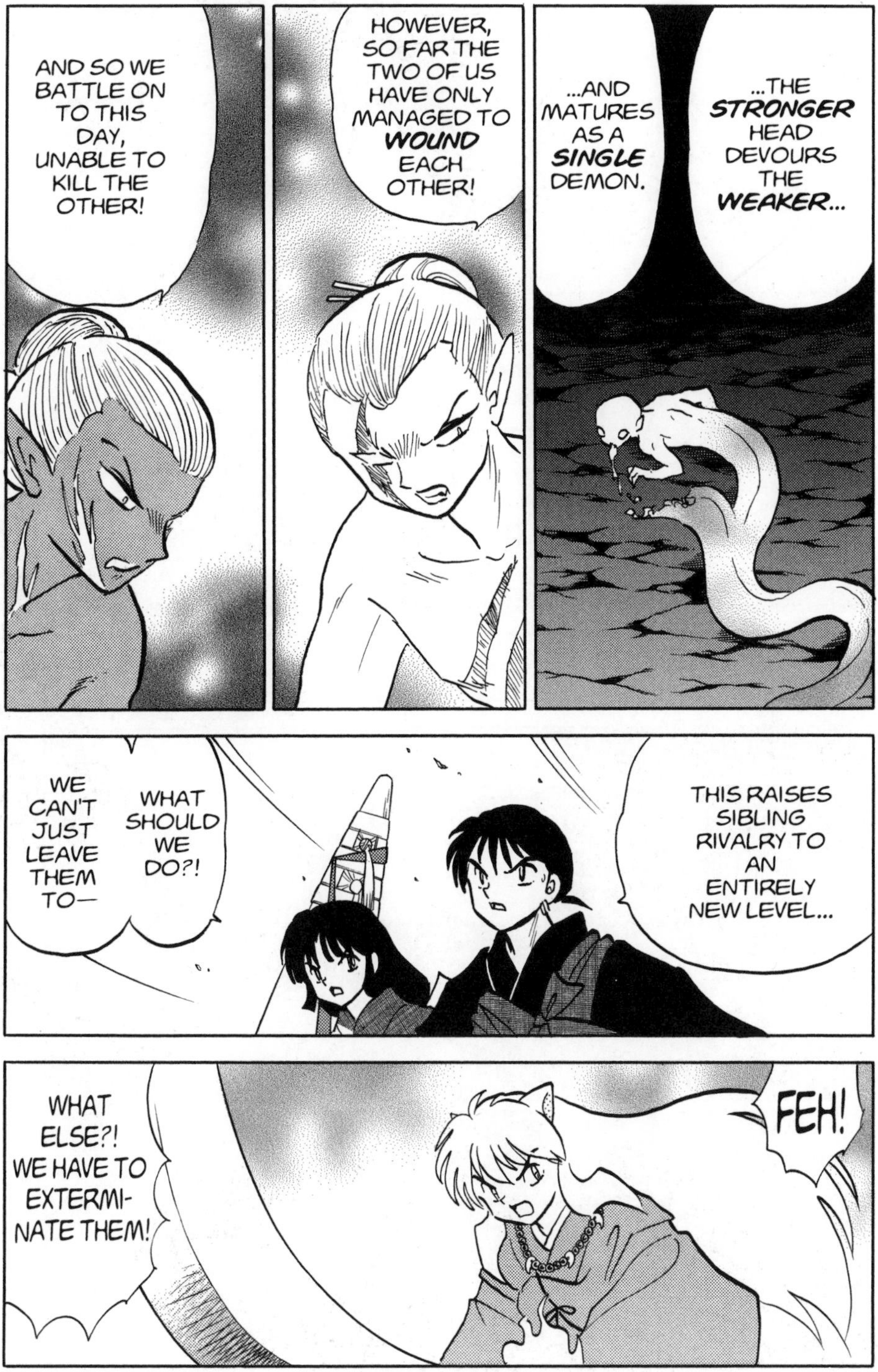
...THE STRONGER HEAD DEVOURS THE WEAKER...
...AND MATURES AS A SINGLE DEMON.
HOWEVER, SO FAR THE TWO OF US HAVE ONLY MANAGED TO WOUND EACH OTHER!
AND SO WE BATTLE ON TO THIS DAY, UNABLE TO KILL THE OTHER!
THIS RAISES SIBLING RIVALRY TO AN ENTIRELY NEW LEVEL...
WHAT SHOULD WE DO?!
WE CAN'T JUST LEAVE THEM TO—
FEH!
WHAT ELSE?! WE HAVE TO EXTERMI-NATE THEM!

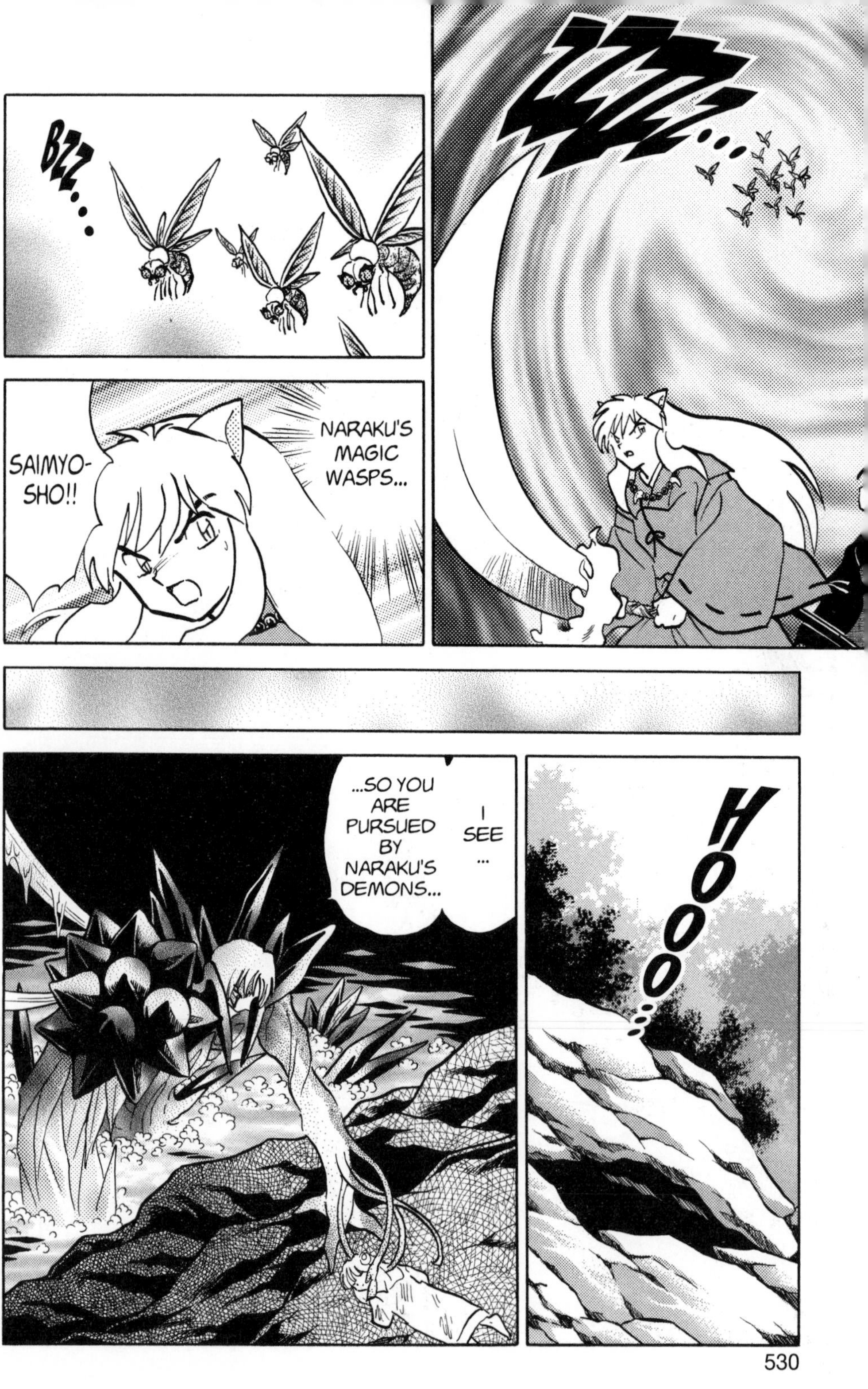
ZZZZ...
BZZ...
NARAKU'S MAGIC WASPS...
SAIMYO-SHO!!
HOOOO...
I SEE...
...SO YOU ARE PURSUED BY NARAKU'S DEMONS...

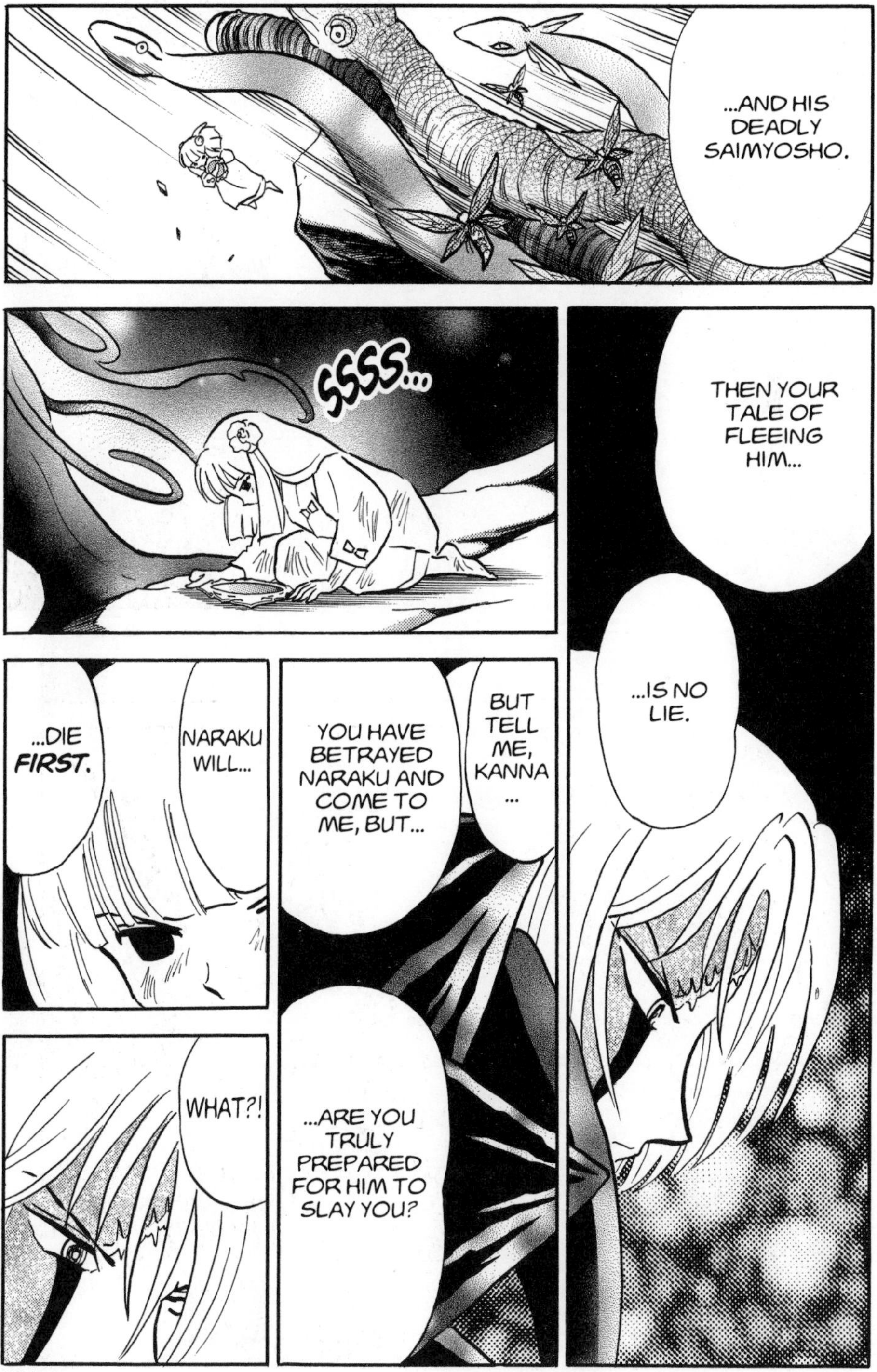
...AND HIS DEADLY SAIMYOSHO.
THEN YOUR TALE OF FLEEING HIM...
...IS NO LIE.
SSSS...
BUT TELL ME, KANNA...
YOU HAVE BETRAYED NARAKU AND COME TO ME, BUT...
...ARE YOU TRULY PREPARED FOR HIM TO SLAY YOU?
NARAKU WILL...
...DIE *FIRST*.
WHAT?!

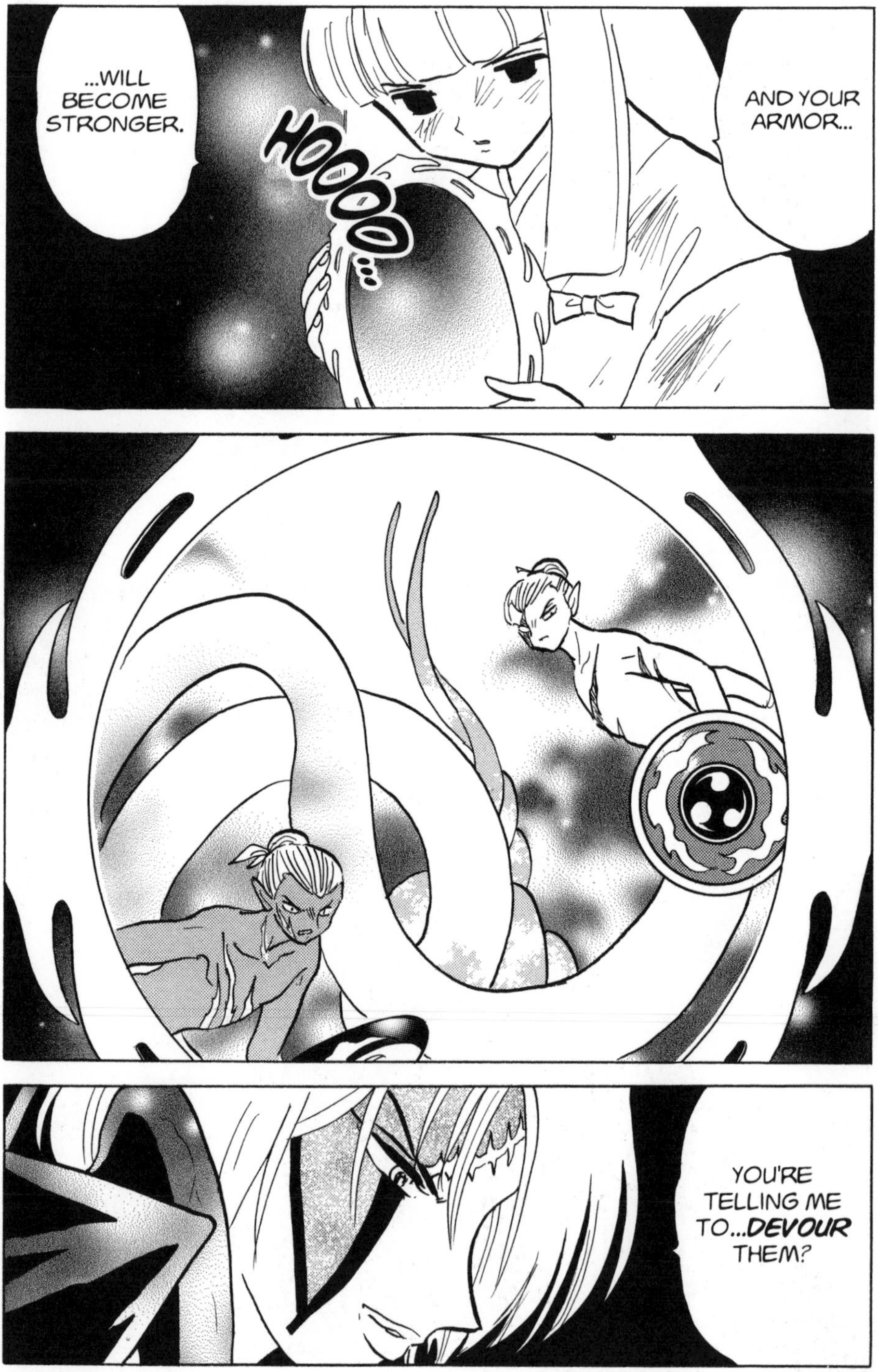
AND YOUR ARMOR...
HOOOO...
...WILL BECOME STRONGER.
YOU'RE TELLING ME TO...DEVOUR THEM?

SCROLL NINE
STRONG BONDS

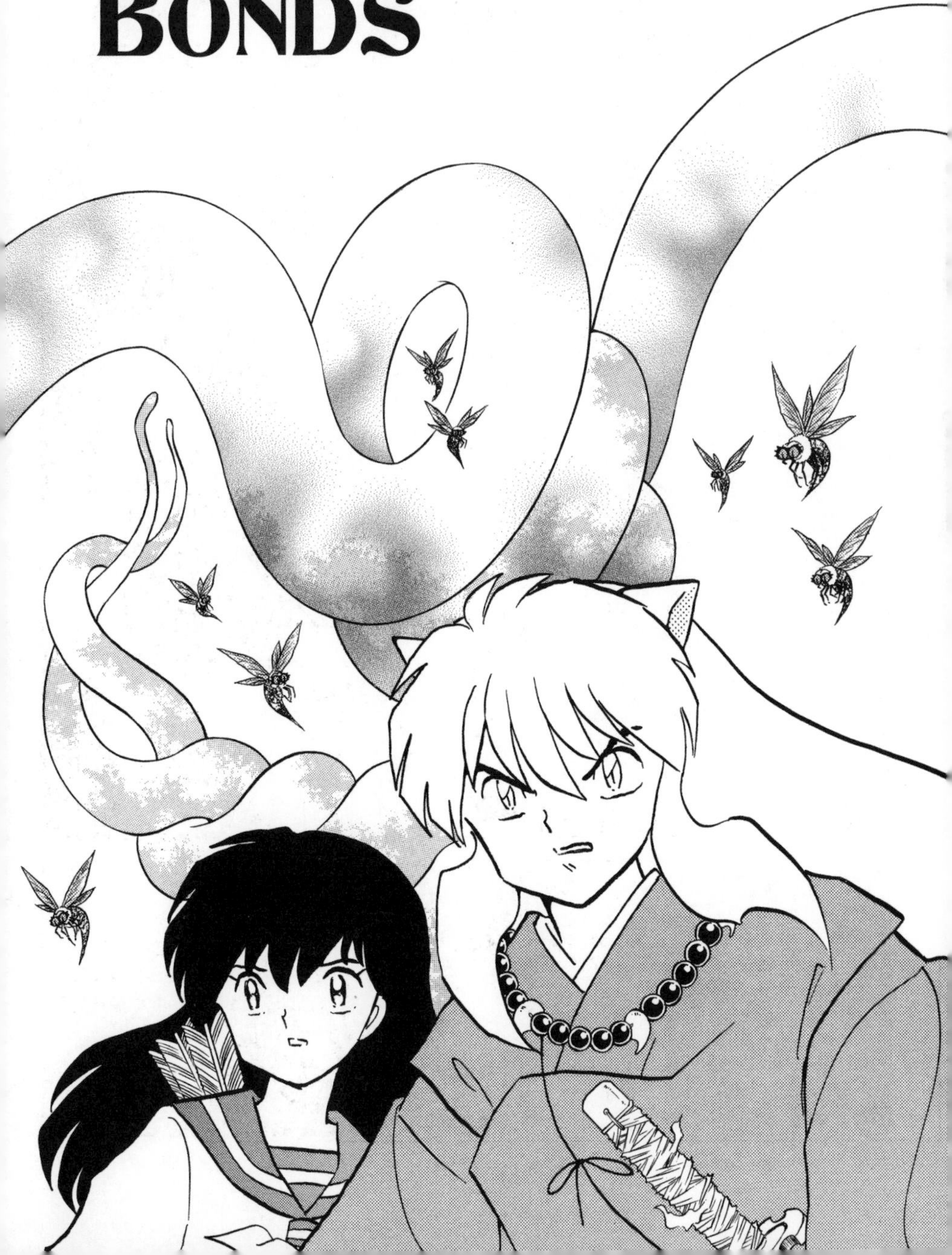

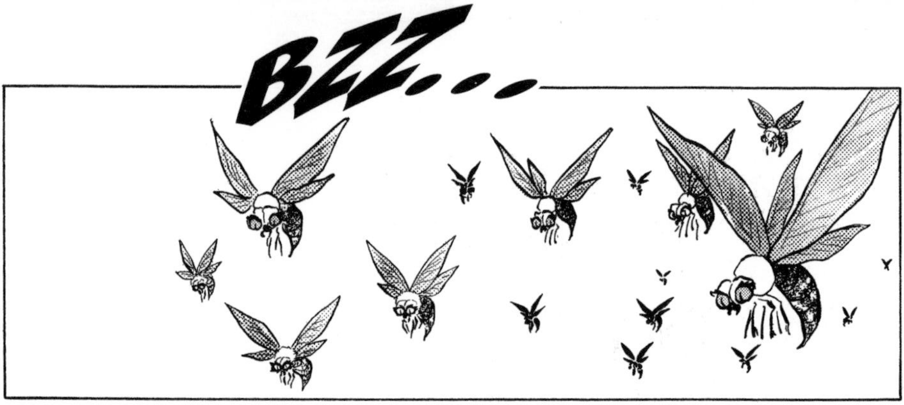
BZZ...

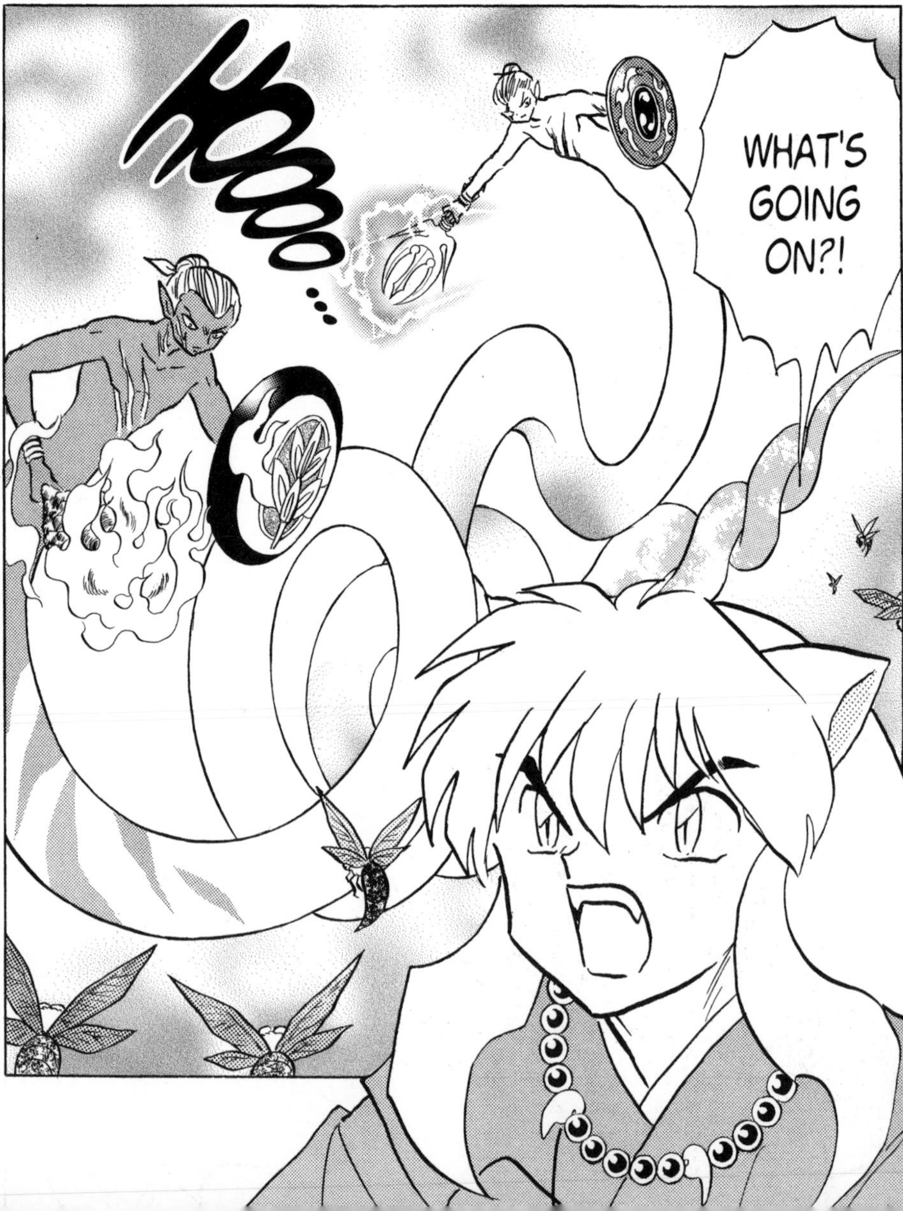
WHAT'S GOING ON?!
HOOOO...

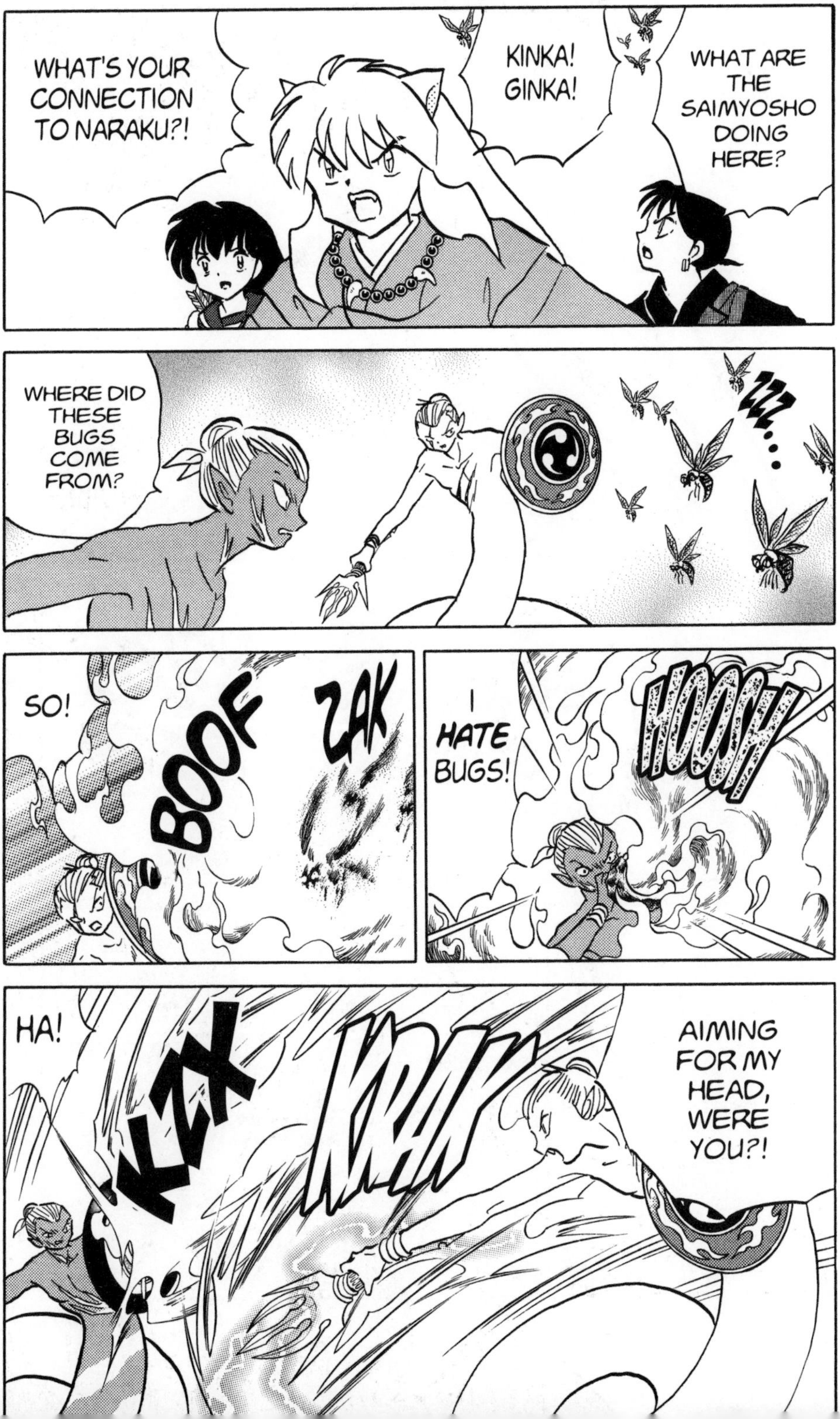
WHAT ARE THE SAIMYOSHO DOING HERE?
KINKA! GINKA!
WHAT'S YOUR CONNECTION TO NARAKU?!
ZZZ...
WHERE DID THESE BUGS COME FROM?
HOOSH
I HATE BUGS!
ZAK
BOOF
SO!
AIMING FOR MY HEAD, WERE YOU?!
KRAK
KZZK
HA!

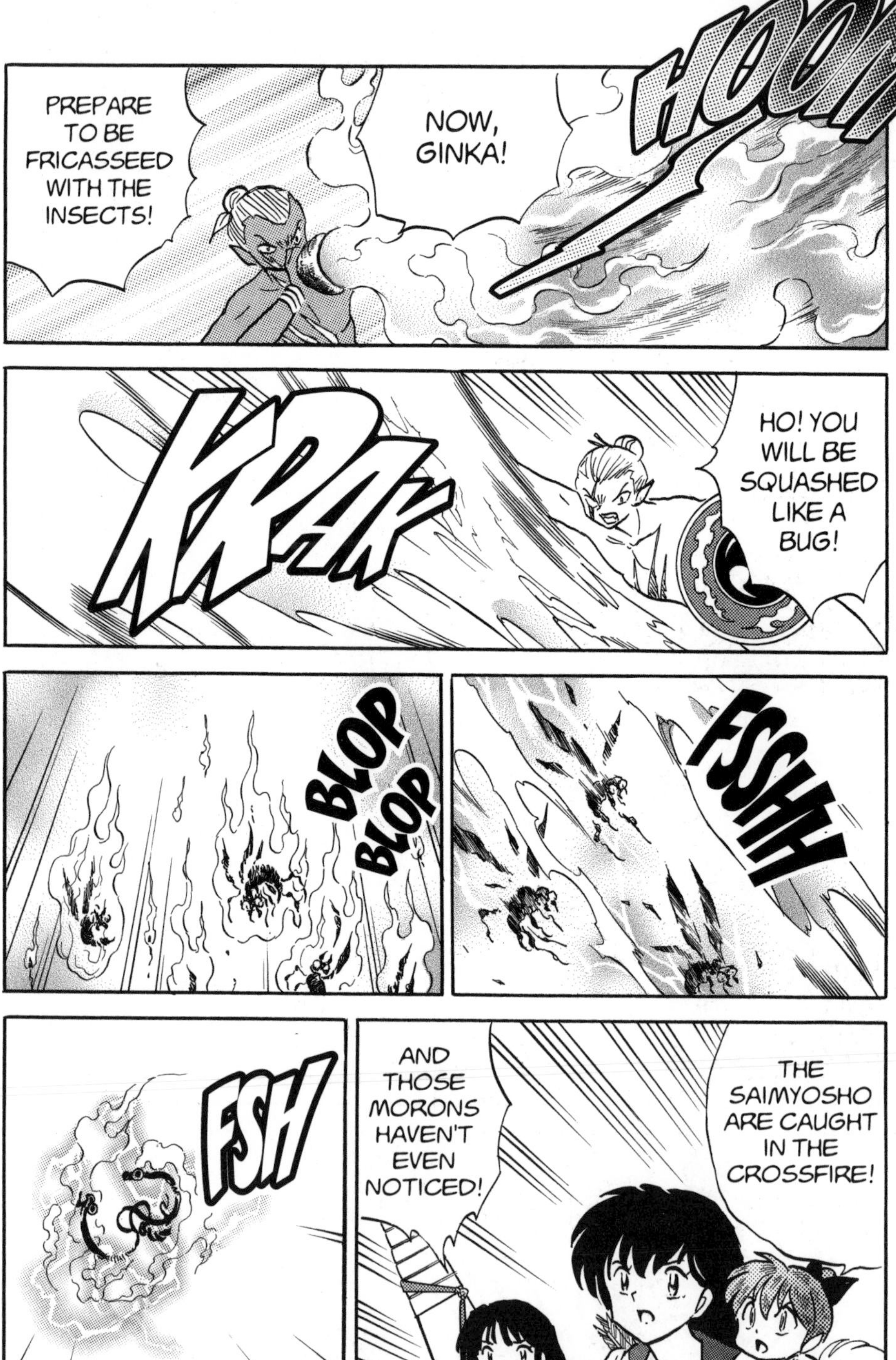
HOOM
NOW, GINKA!
PREPARE TO BE FRICASSEED WITH THE INSECTS!
HO! YOU WILL BE SQUASHED LIKE A BUG!
KRAK
FSHH
BLOP BLOP
THE SAIMYOSHO ARE CAUGHT IN THE CROSSFIRE!
AND THOSE MORONS HAVEN'T EVEN NOTICED!
FSH

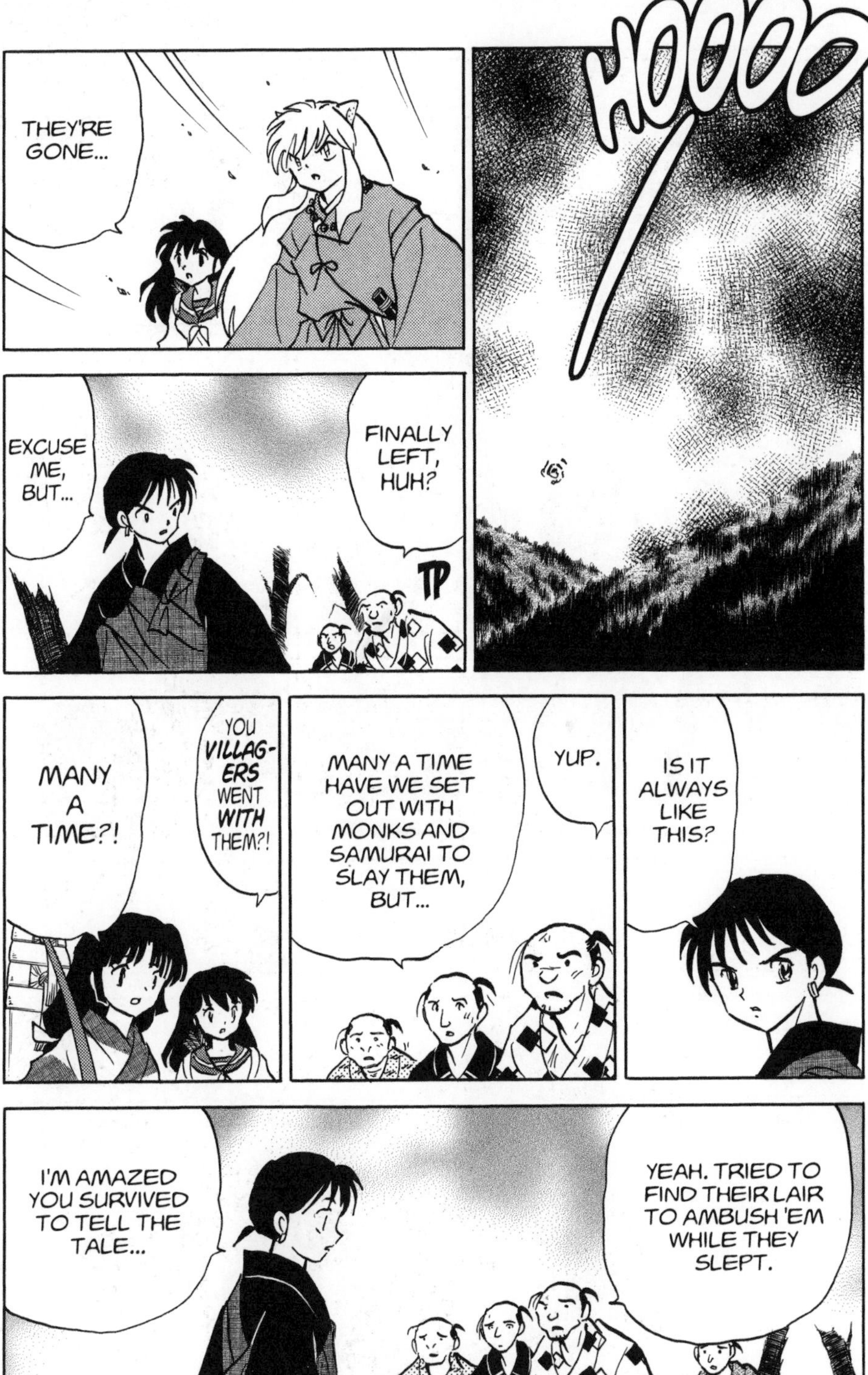
HOOOO
THEY'RE GONE...
FINALLY LEFT, HUH?
TP
EXCUSE ME, BUT...
IS IT ALWAYS LIKE THIS?
YUP.
MANY A TIME HAVE WE SET OUT WITH MONKS AND SAMURAI TO SLAY THEM, BUT...
YOU VILLAGERS WENT WITH THEM?!
MANY A TIME?!
YEAH. TRIED TO FIND THEIR LAIR TO AMBUSH 'EM WHILE THEY SLEPT.
I'M AMAZED YOU SURVIVED TO TELL THE TALE...

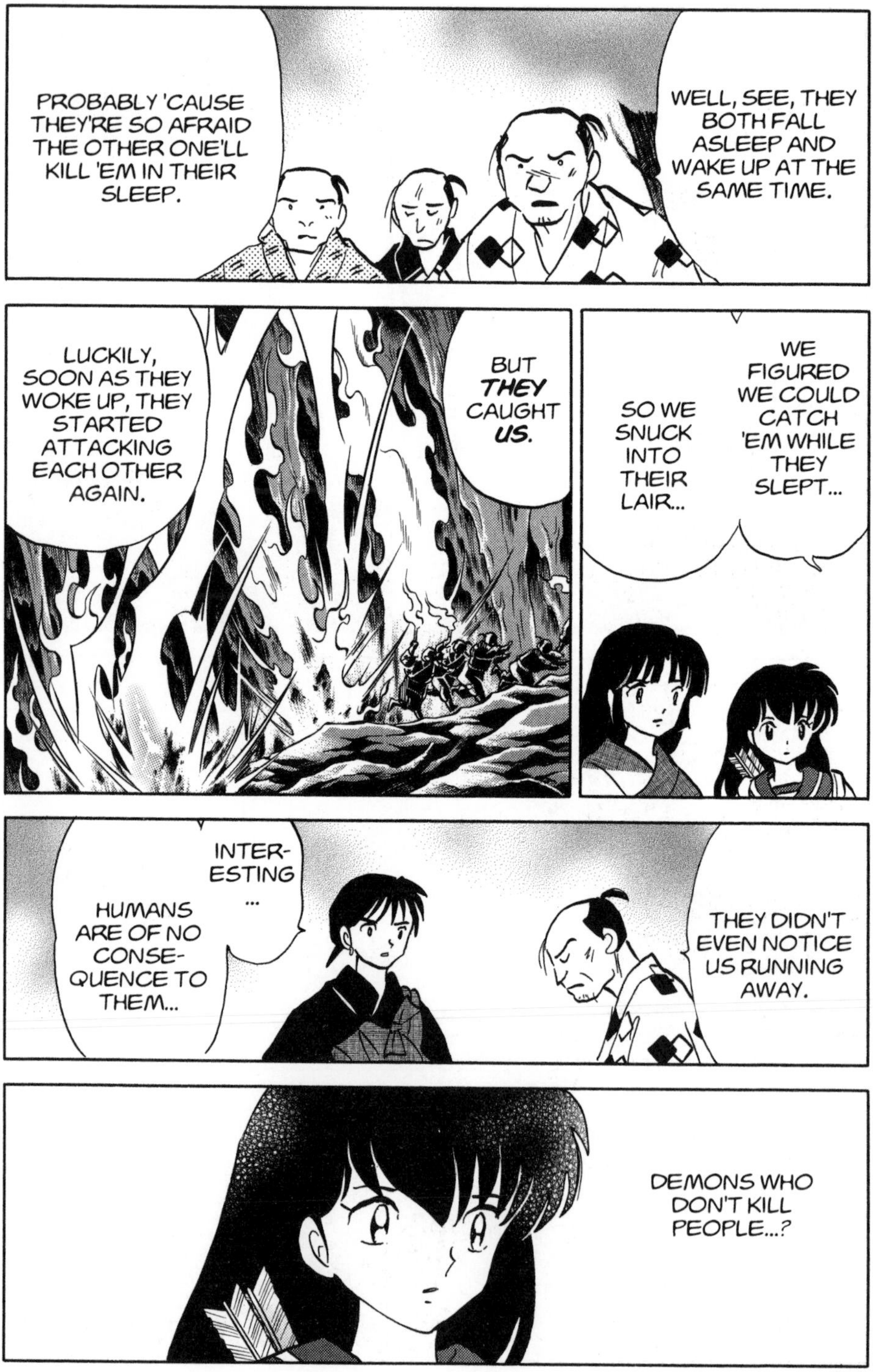
WELL, SEE, THEY BOTH FALL ASLEEP AND WAKE UP AT THE SAME TIME.
PROBABLY 'CAUSE THEY'RE SO AFRAID THE OTHER ONE'LL KILL 'EM IN THEIR SLEEP.
WE FIGURED WE COULD CATCH 'EM WHILE THEY SLEPT...
SO WE SNUCK INTO THEIR LAIR...
BUT THEY CAUGHT US.
LUCKILY, SOON AS THEY WOKE UP, THEY STARTED ATTACKING EACH OTHER AGAIN.
THEY DIDN'T EVEN NOTICE US RUNNING AWAY.
INTER-ESTING...
HUMANS ARE OF NO CONSE-QUENCE TO THEM...
DEMONS WHO DON'T KILL PEOPLE...?

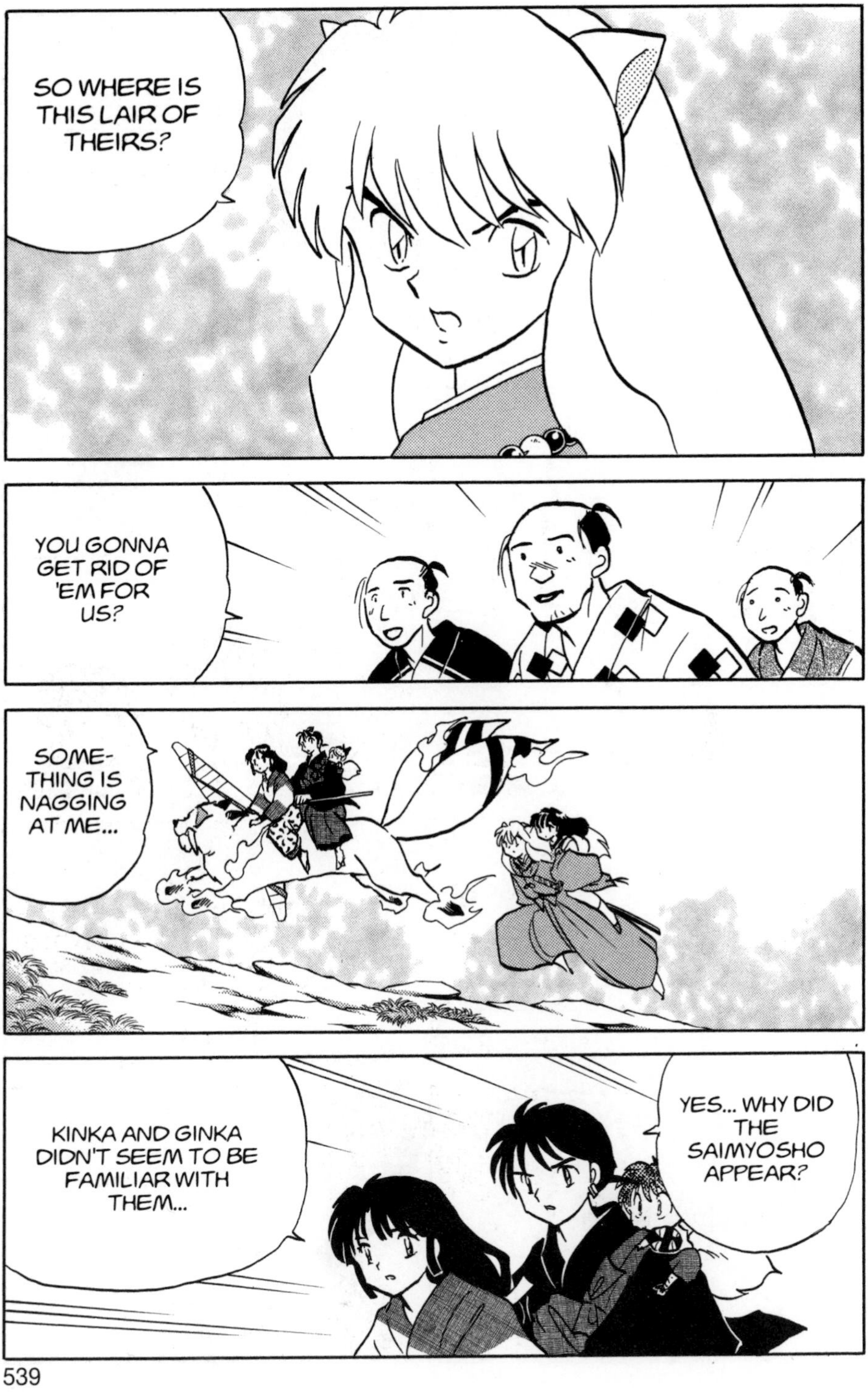
SO WHERE IS THIS LAIR OF THEIRS?
YOU GONNA GET RID OF 'EM FOR US?
SOME-THING IS NAGGING AT ME...
YES... WHY DID THE SAIMYOSHO APPEAR?
KINKA AND GINKA DIDN'T SEEM TO BE FAMILIAR WITH THEM...

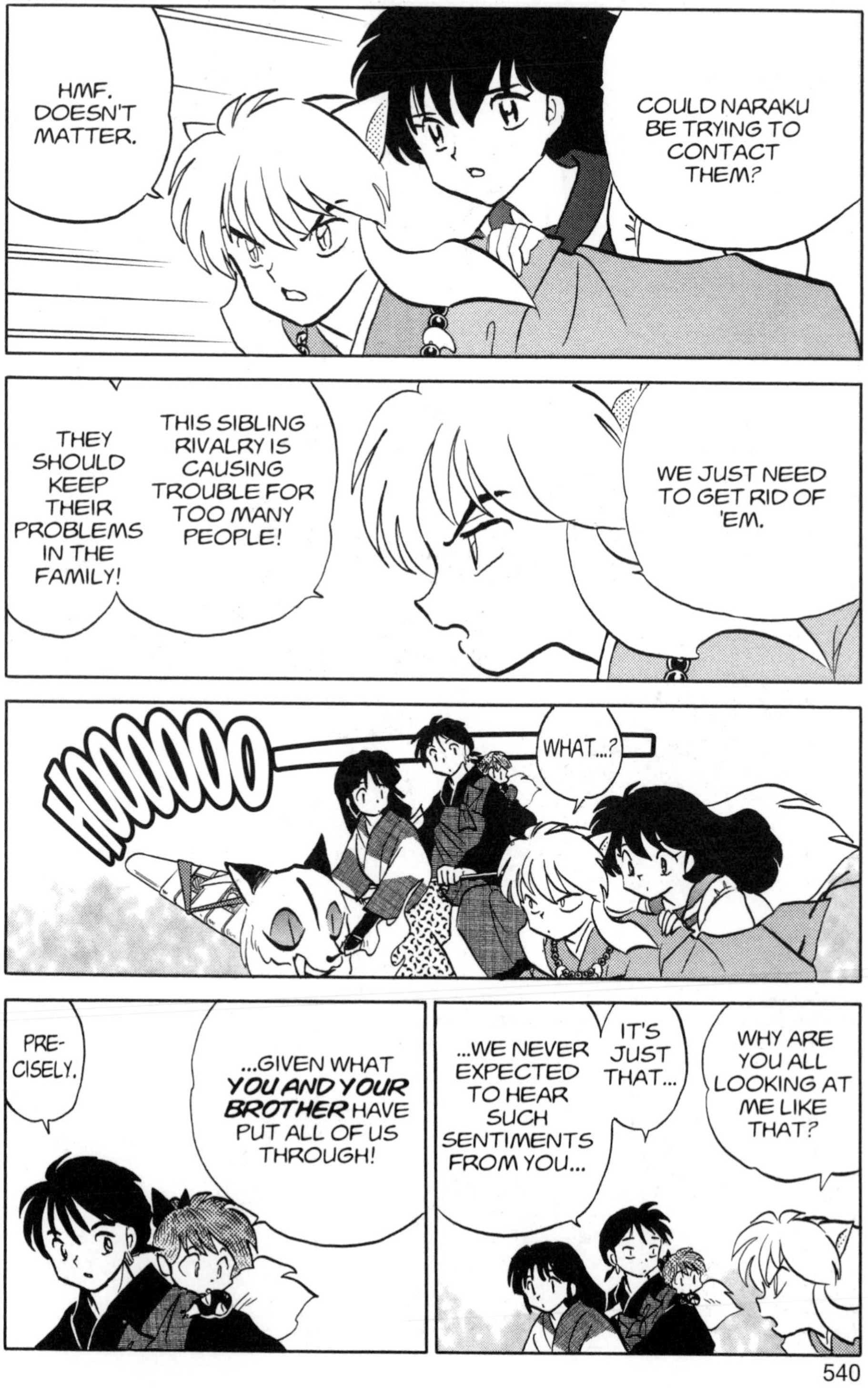
COULD NARAKU BE TRYING TO CONTACT THEM?
HMF. DOESN'T MATTER.
WE JUST NEED TO GET RID OF 'EM.
THIS SIBLING RIVALRY IS CAUSING TROUBLE FOR TOO MANY PEOPLE!
THEY SHOULD KEEP THEIR PROBLEMS IN THE FAMILY!
WHAT...?
HOOOOOO
WHY ARE YOU ALL LOOKING AT ME LIKE THAT?
IT'S JUST THAT...
...WE NEVER EXPECTED TO HEAR SUCH SENTIMENTS FROM YOU...
...GIVEN WHAT ***YOU AND YOUR BROTHER*** HAVE PUT ALL OF US THROUGH!
PRE-CISELY.

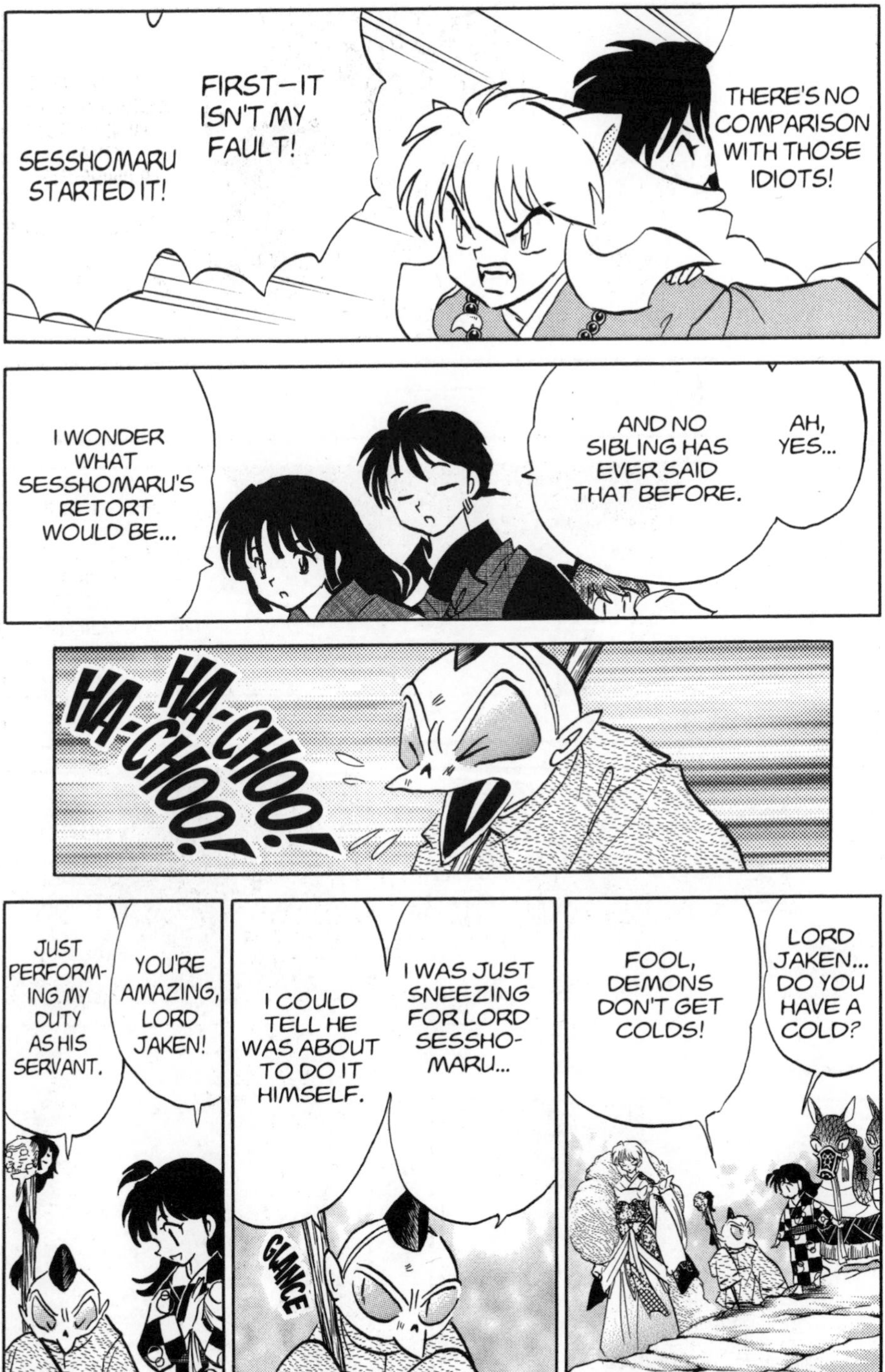
THERE'S NO COMPARISON WITH THOSE IDIOTS!
FIRST—IT ISN'T MY FAULT!
SESSHOMARU STARTED IT!
AH, YES...
AND NO SIBLING HAS EVER SAID THAT BEFORE.
I WONDER WHAT SESSHOMARU'S RETORT WOULD BE...
HA-CHOO! HA-CHOO!
LORD JAKEN... DO YOU HAVE A COLD?
FOOL, DEMONS DON'T GET COLDS!
I WAS JUST SNEEZING FOR LORD SESSHOMARU...
I COULD TELL HE WAS ABOUT TO DO IT HIMSELF.
GLANCE
YOU'RE AMAZING, LORD JAKEN!
JUST PERFORMING MY DUTY AS HIS SERVANT.

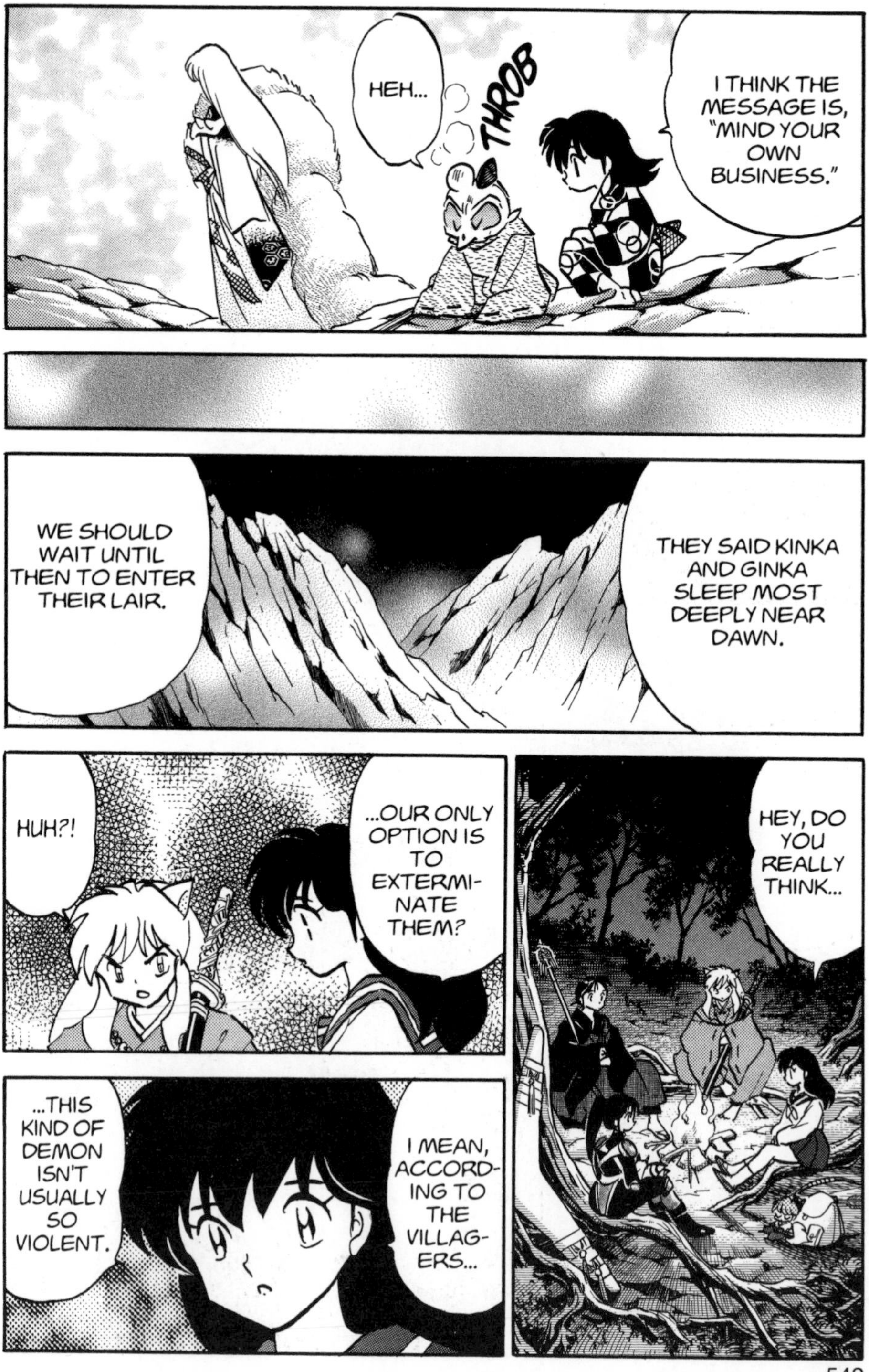
I THINK THE MESSAGE IS, "MIND YOUR OWN BUSINESS."
THROB
HEH...
THEY SAID KINKA AND GINKA SLEEP MOST DEEPLY NEAR DAWN.
WE SHOULD WAIT UNTIL THEN TO ENTER THEIR LAIR.
HEY, DO YOU REALLY THINK...
...OUR ONLY OPTION IS TO EXTERMINATE THEM?
HUH?!
I MEAN, ACCORDING TO THE VILLAGERS...
...THIS KIND OF DEMON ISN'T USUALLY SO VIOLENT.

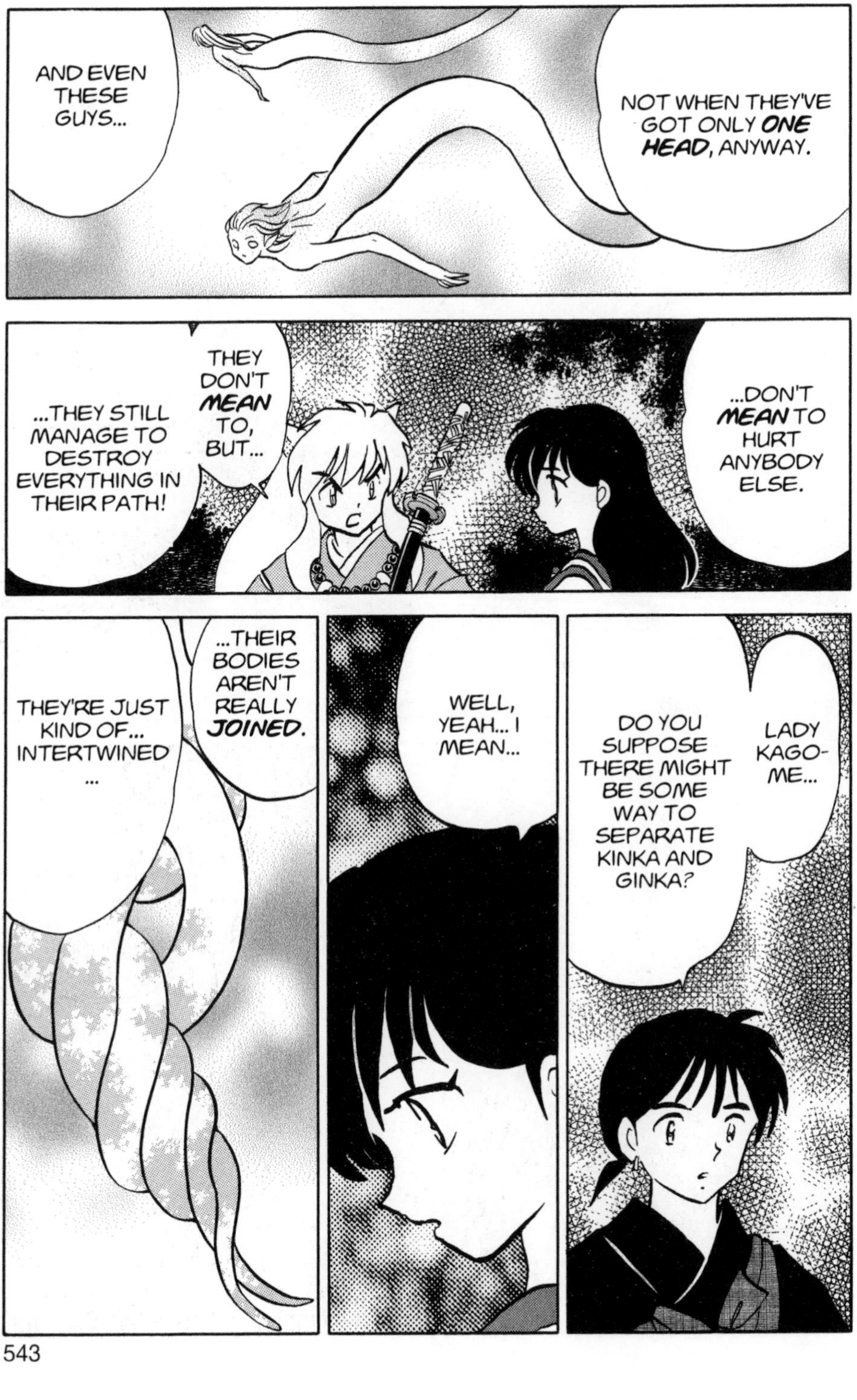
NOT WHEN THEY'VE GOT ONLY ONE HEAD, ANYWAY.
AND EVEN THESE GUYS...
...DON'T MEAN TO HURT ANYBODY ELSE.
THEY DON'T MEAN TO, BUT...
...THEY STILL MANAGE TO DESTROY EVERYTHING IN THEIR PATH!
LADY KAGOME...
DO YOU SUPPOSE THERE MIGHT BE SOME WAY TO SEPARATE KINKA AND GINKA?
WELL, YEAH... I MEAN...
...THEIR BODIES AREN'T REALLY JOINED.
THEY'RE JUST KIND OF... INTERTWINED ...

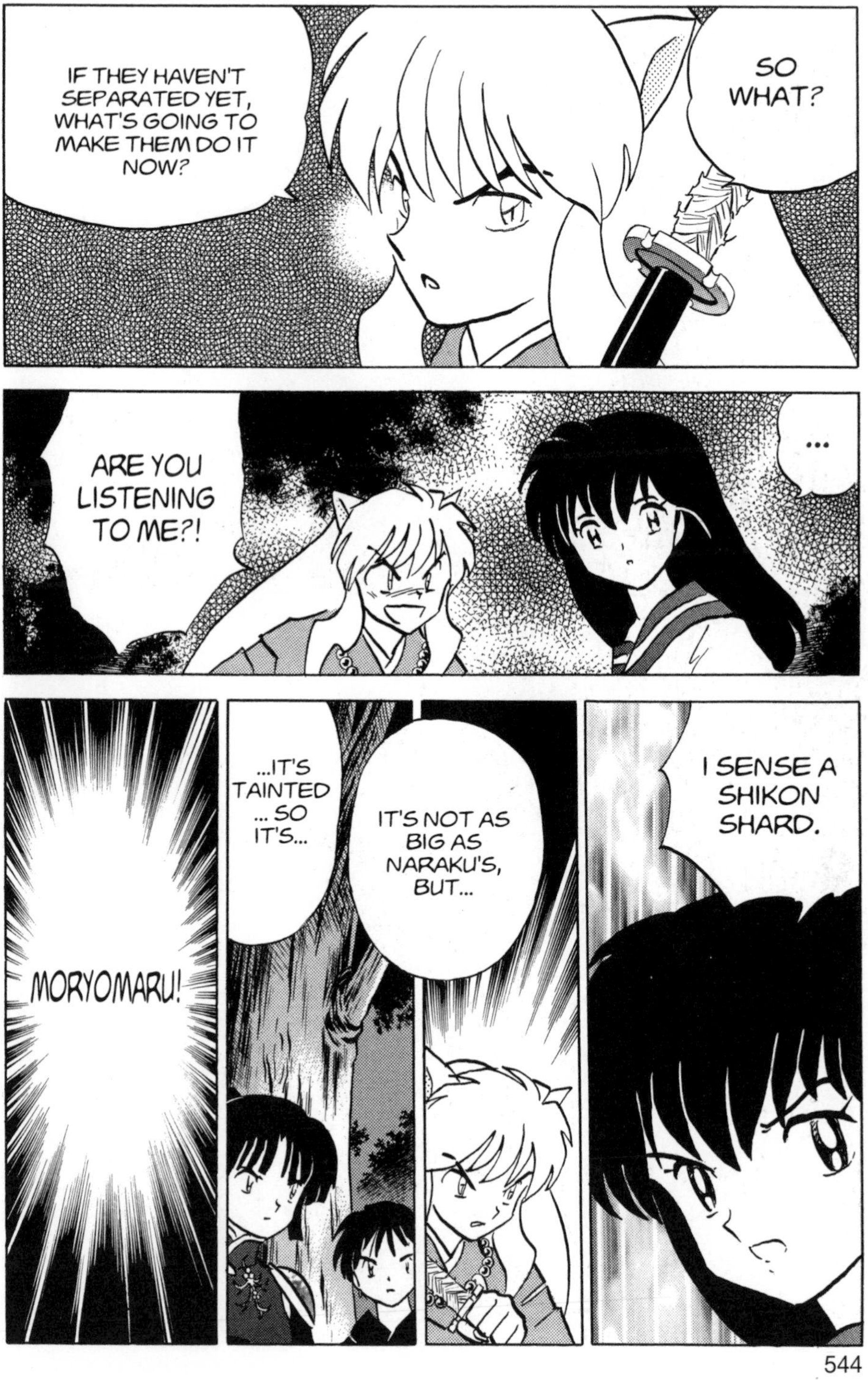
SO WHAT?
IF THEY HAVEN'T SEPARATED YET, WHAT'S GOING TO MAKE THEM DO IT NOW?
...
ARE YOU LISTENING TO ME?!
I SENSE A SHIKON SHARD.
IT'S NOT AS BIG AS NARAKU'S, BUT...
...IT'S TAINTED ... SO IT'S...
MORYOMARU!

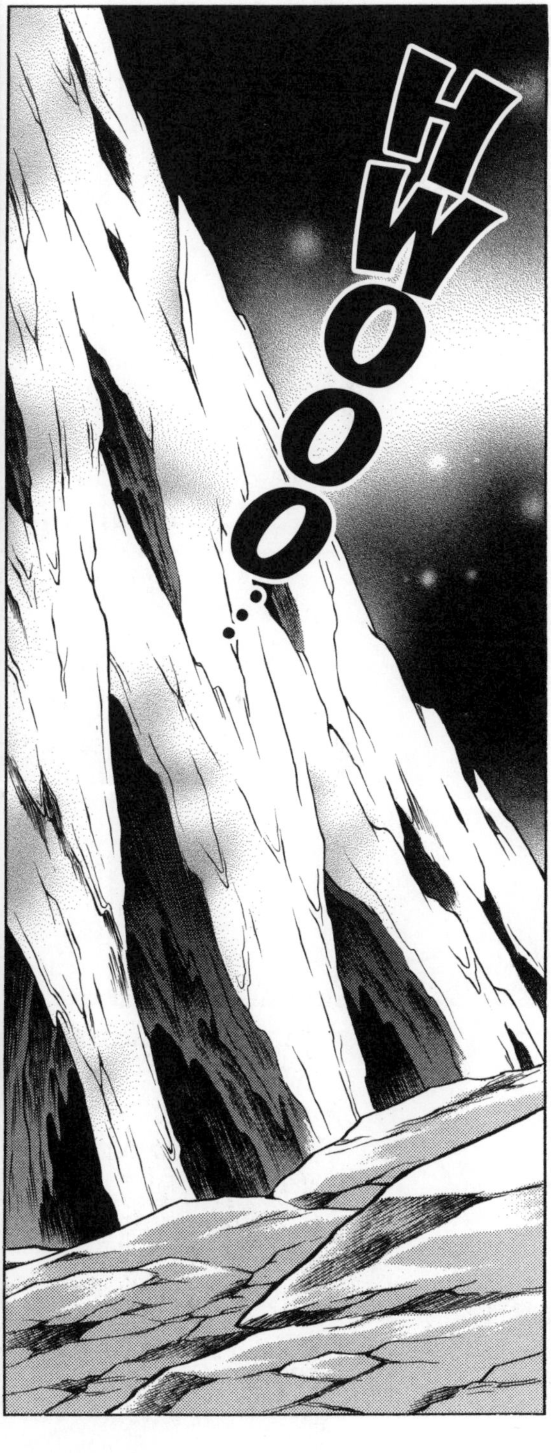
HWOOOO...
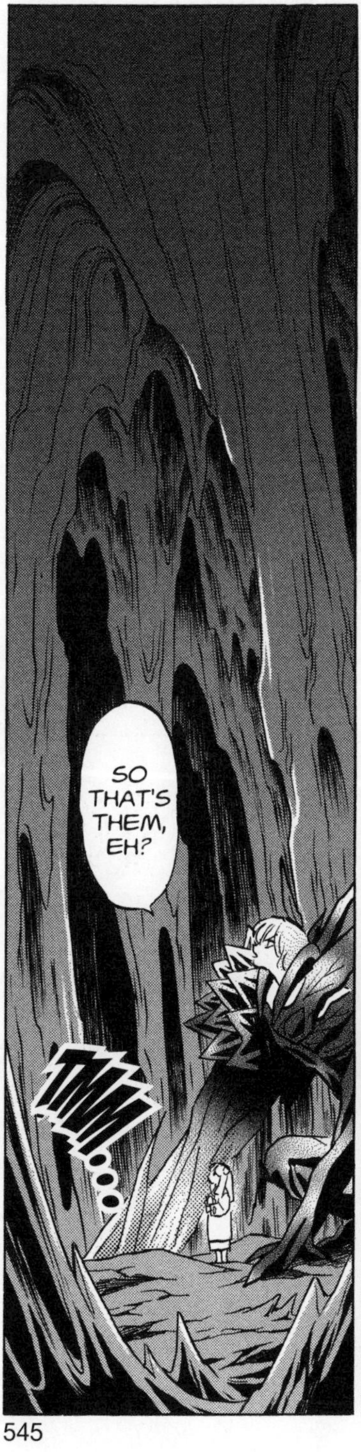
SO THAT'S THEM, EH?
TMM...

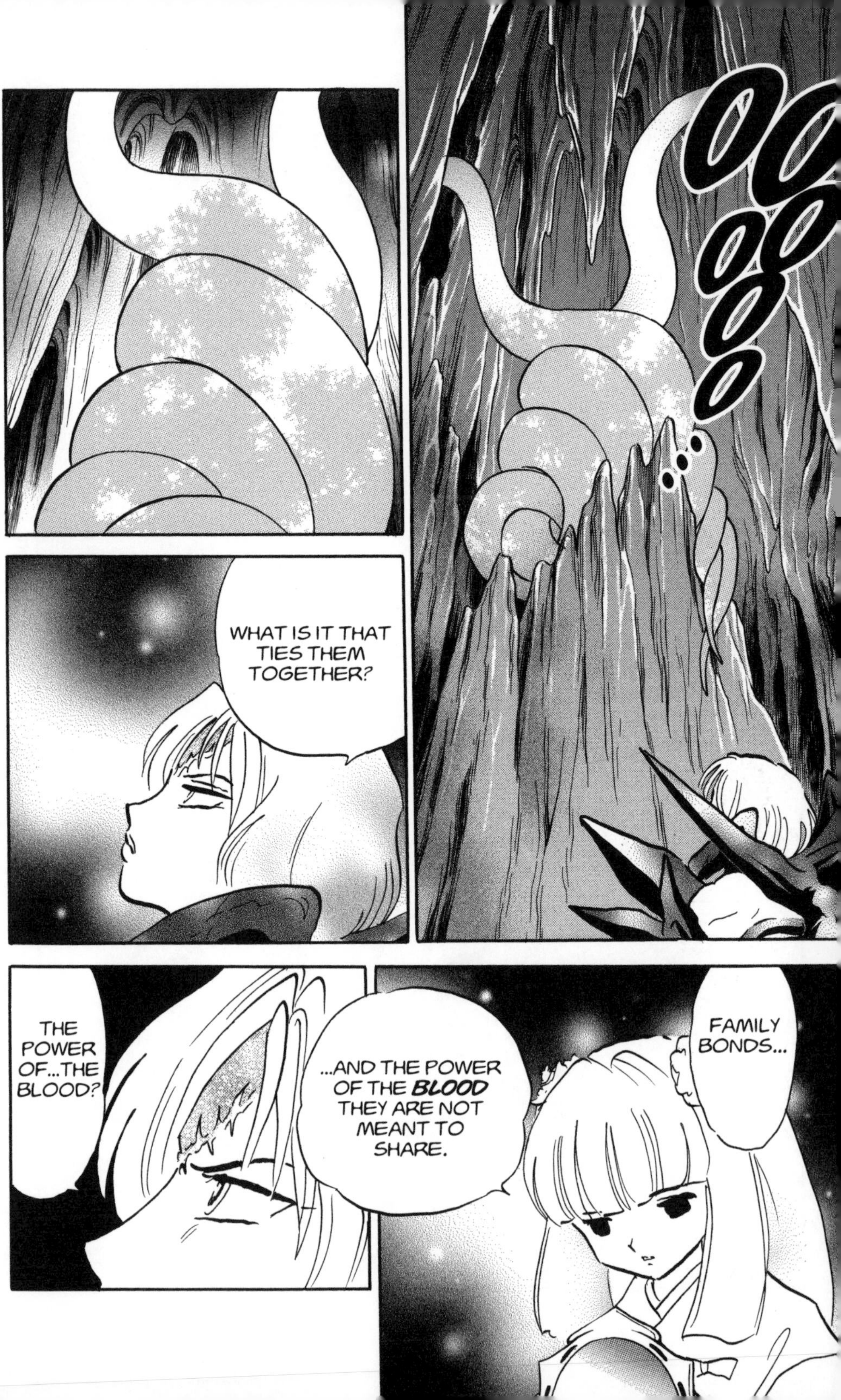
OOOOOOOO
WHAT IS IT THAT TIES THEM TOGETHER?
FAMILY BONDS...
...AND THE POWER OF THE *BLOOD* THEY ARE NOT MEANT TO SHARE.
THE POWER OF...THE BLOOD?

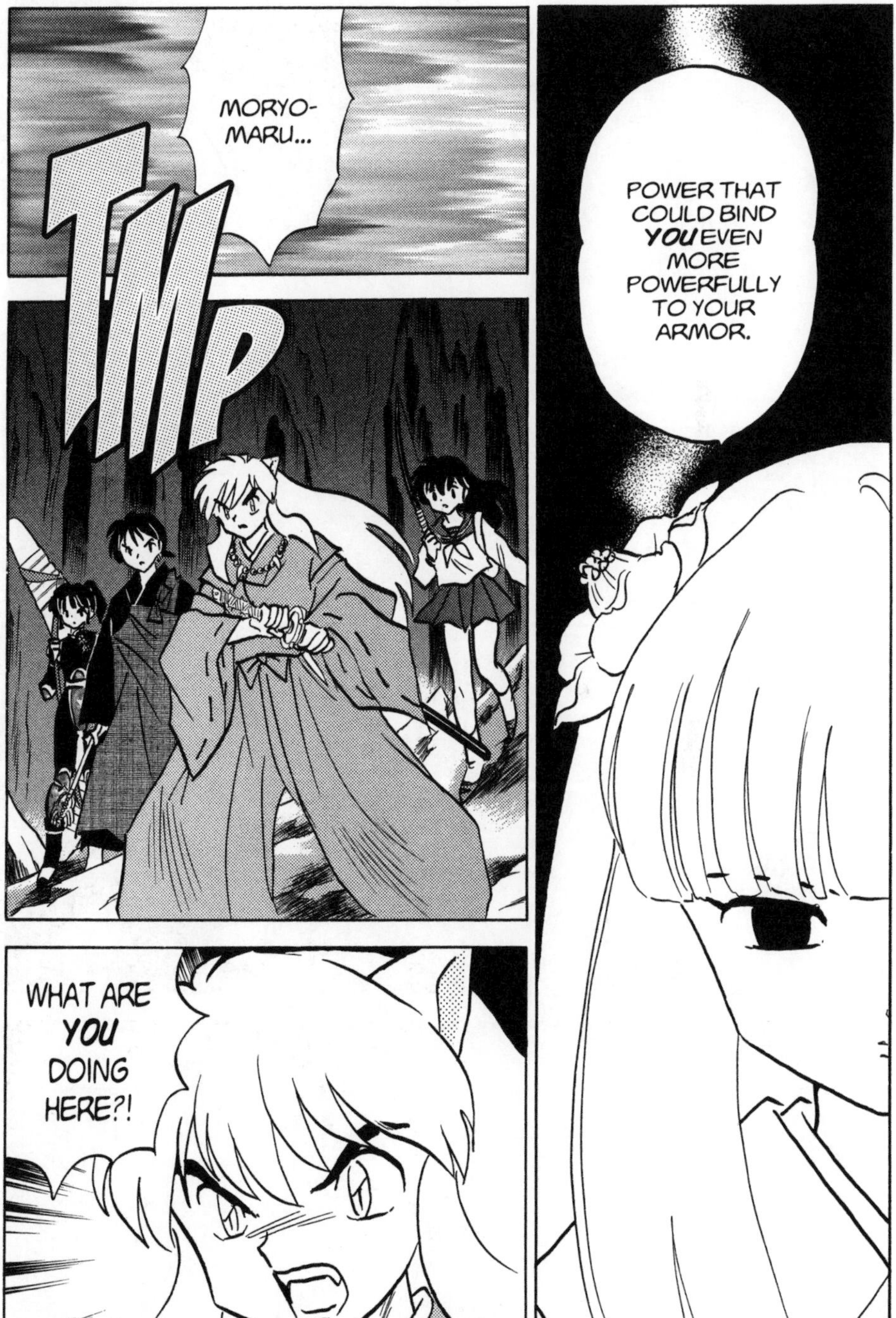
POWER THAT COULD BIND **YOU** EVEN MORE POWERFULLY TO YOUR ARMOR.
MORYO-MARU...
TMP
WHAT ARE **YOU** DOING HERE?!

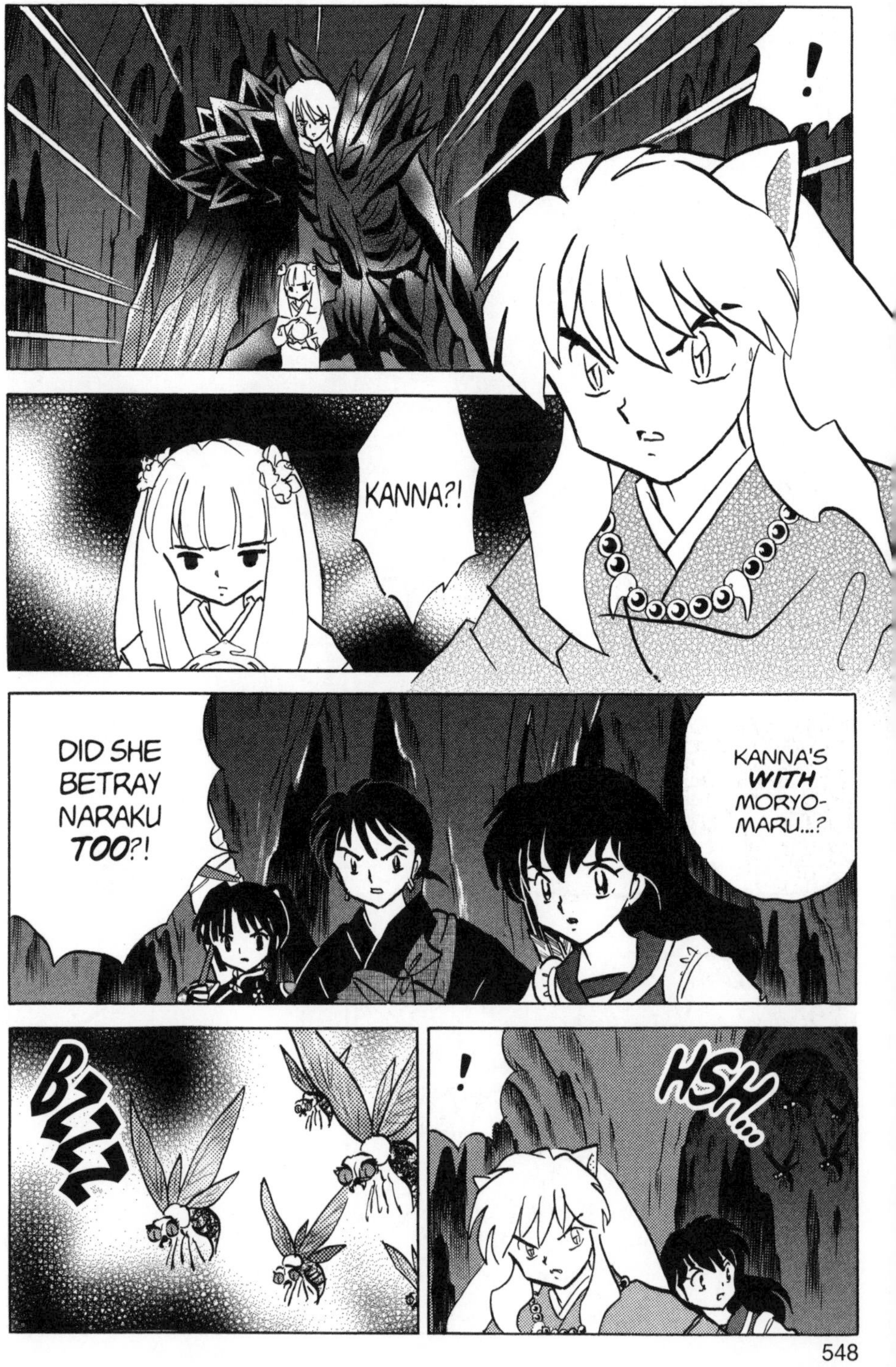
!
KANNA?!
KANNA'S **WITH** MORYO-MARU...?
DID SHE BETRAY NARAKU **TOO**?!
!
HSH...
BZZZ

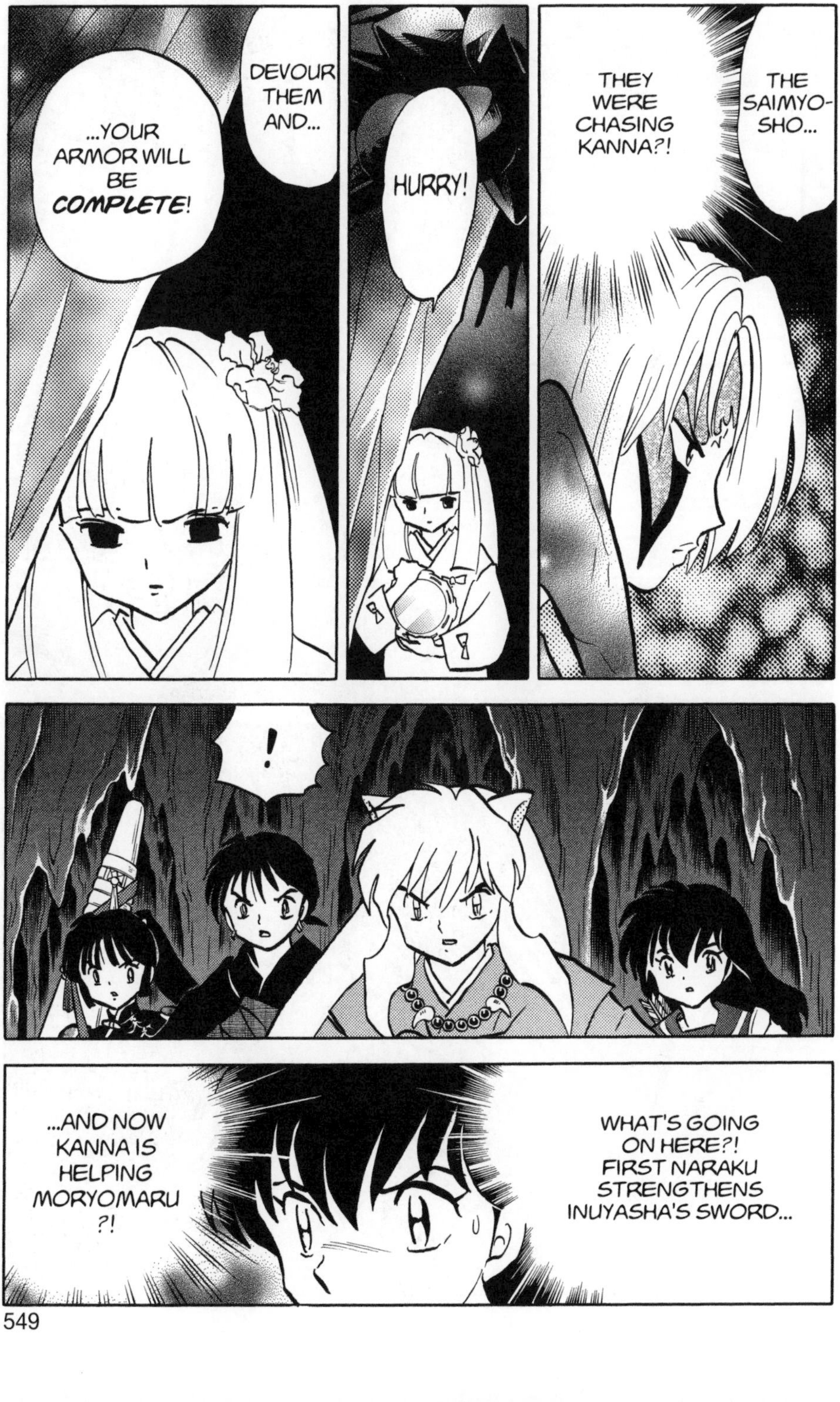
THE SAIMYO-SHO...
THEY WERE CHASING KANNA?!
HURRY!
DEVOUR THEM AND...
...YOUR ARMOR WILL BE **COMPLETE**!
!
WHAT'S GOING ON HERE?! FIRST NARAKU STRENGTHENS INUYASHA'S SWORD...
...AND NOW KANNA IS HELPING MORYOMARU ?!

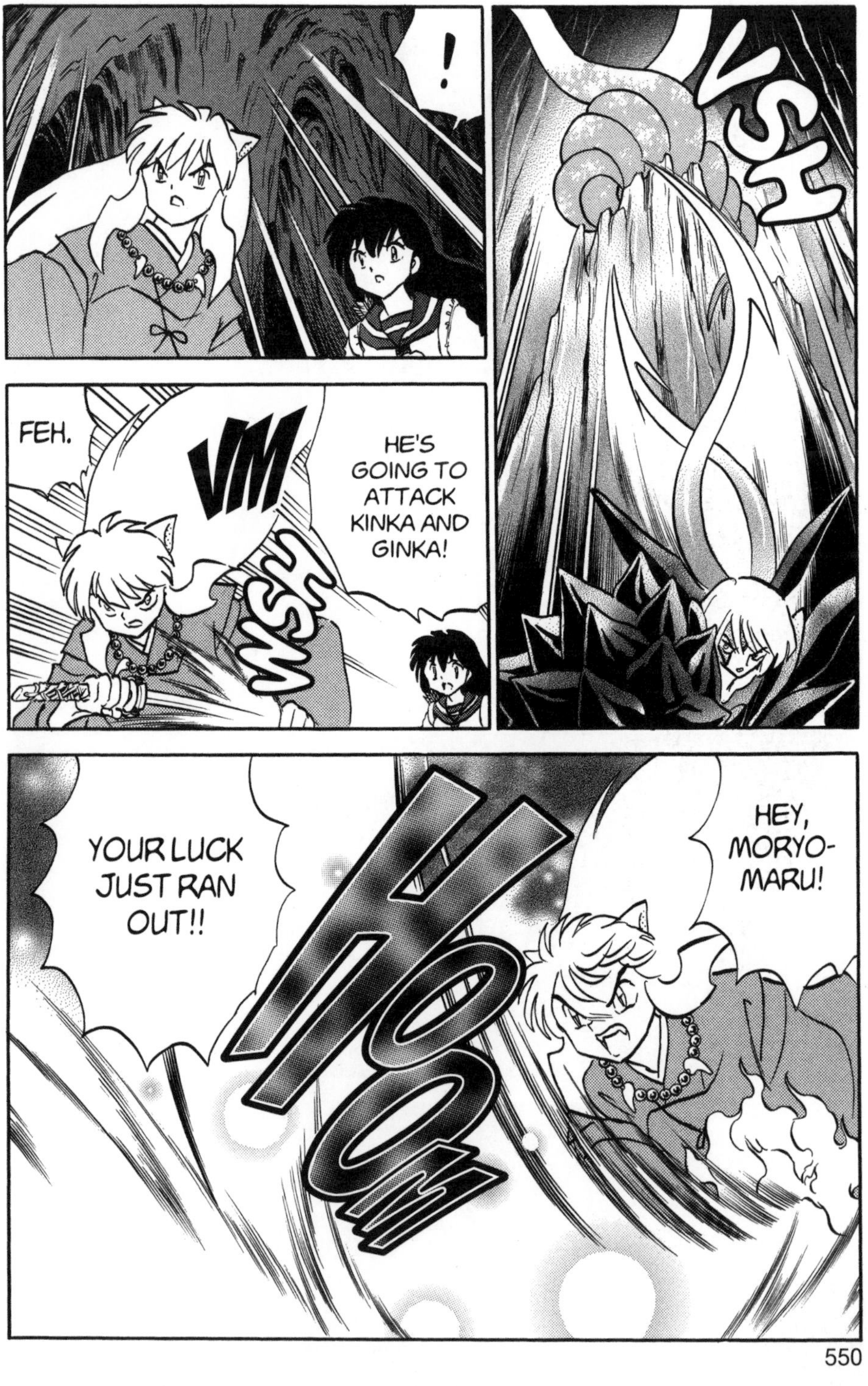
VSH
!
HE'S GOING TO ATTACK KINKA AND GINKA!
FEH.
VM
WSH
HEY, MORYOMARU!
YOUR LUCK JUST RAN OUT!!
VOOM

SCROLL TEN
THE BLOOD'S EFFECT

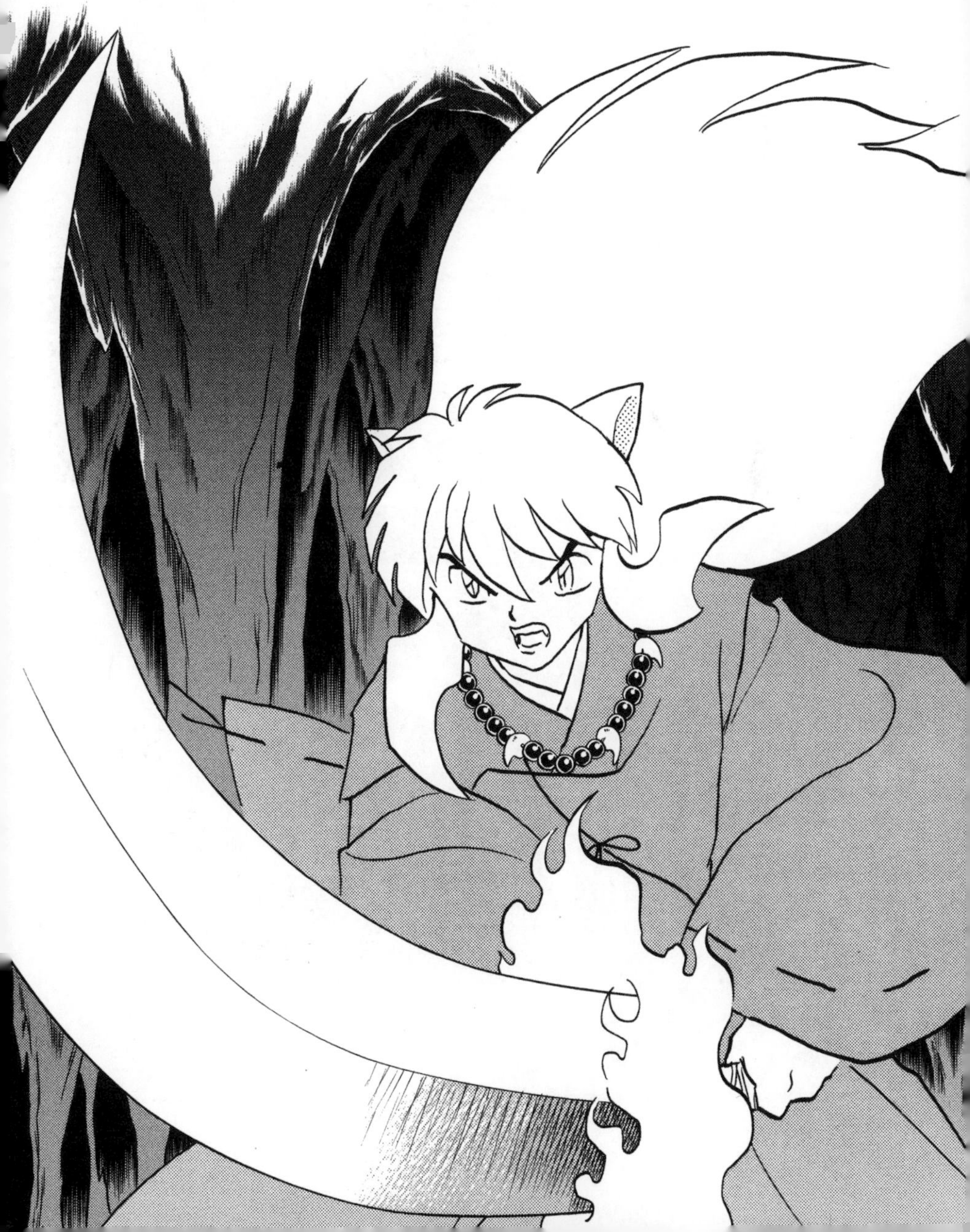

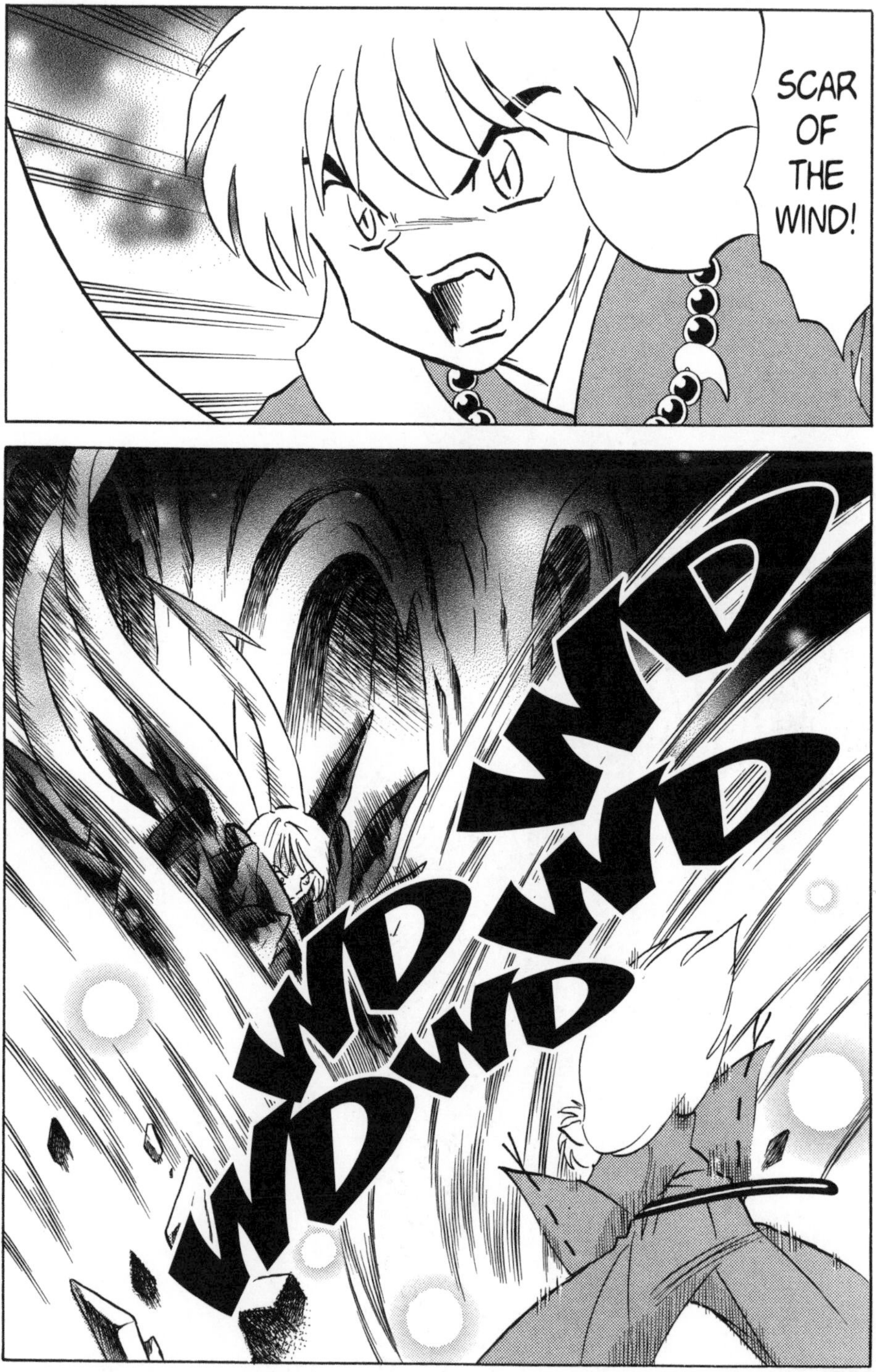
SCAR OF THE WIND!

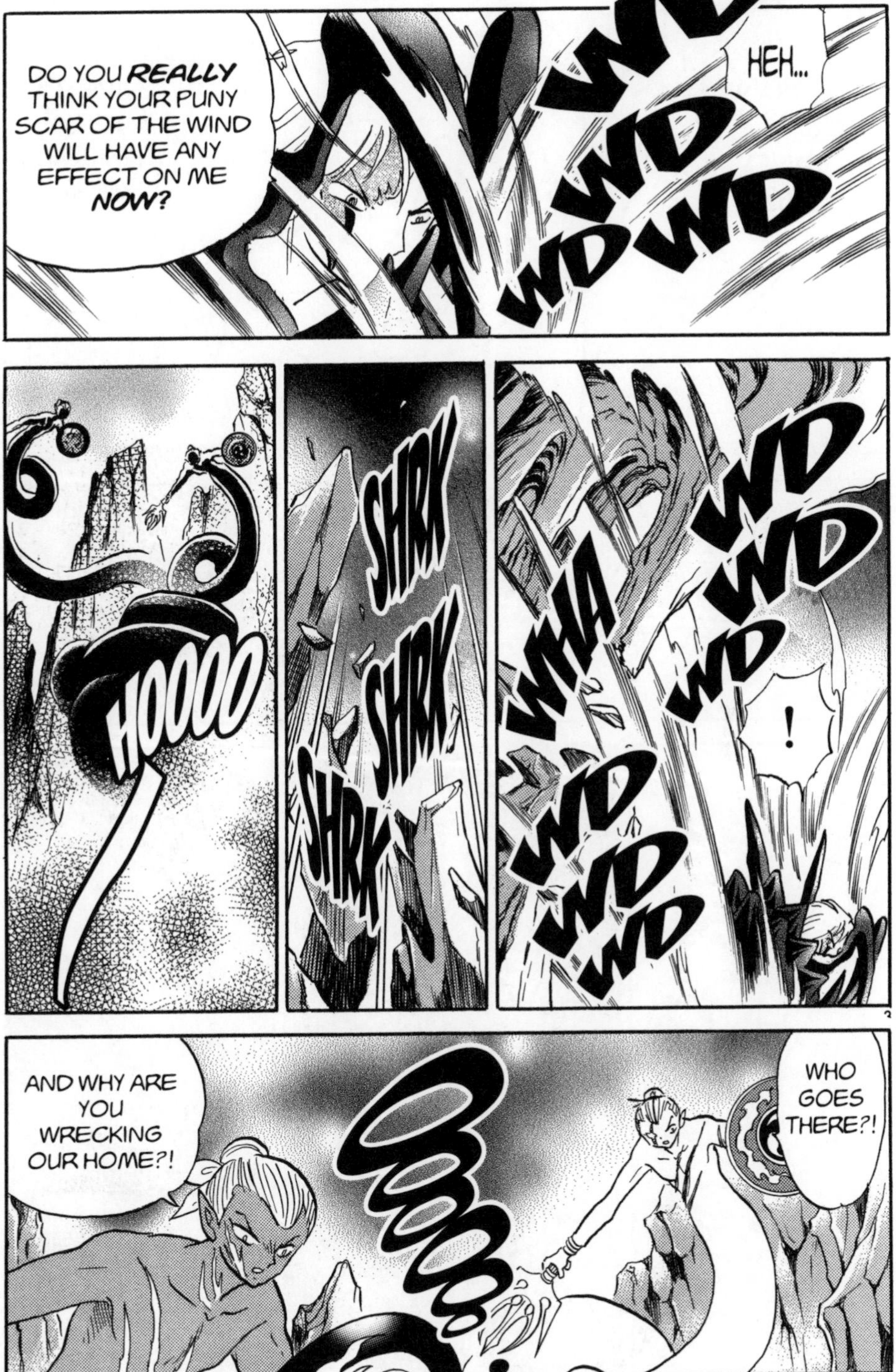
HEH...
DO YOU *REALLY* THINK YOUR PUNY SCAR OF THE WIND WILL HAVE ANY EFFECT ON ME *NOW?*
WD WD WD WD WD
WD WD WD
!
WHA
WD WD WD
SHRK SHRK SHRK
HOOOO
WHO GOES THERE?!
AND WHY ARE YOU WRECKING OUR HOME?!
OOOOO...

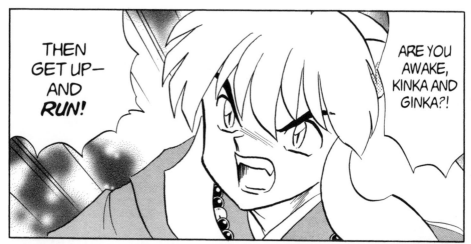

ARE YOU AWAKE, KINKA AND GINKA?!
THEN GET UP— AND *RUN!*
WHAT?!
DON'T LET THEM GET AWAY!
SSSS...
KRAK KRAK KRAK KRAK

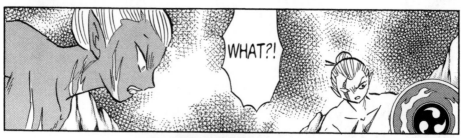

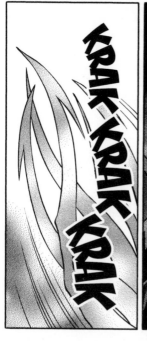

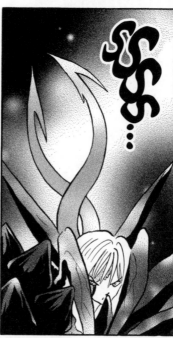

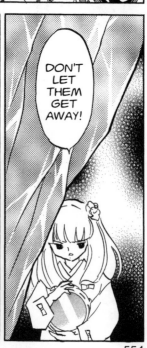

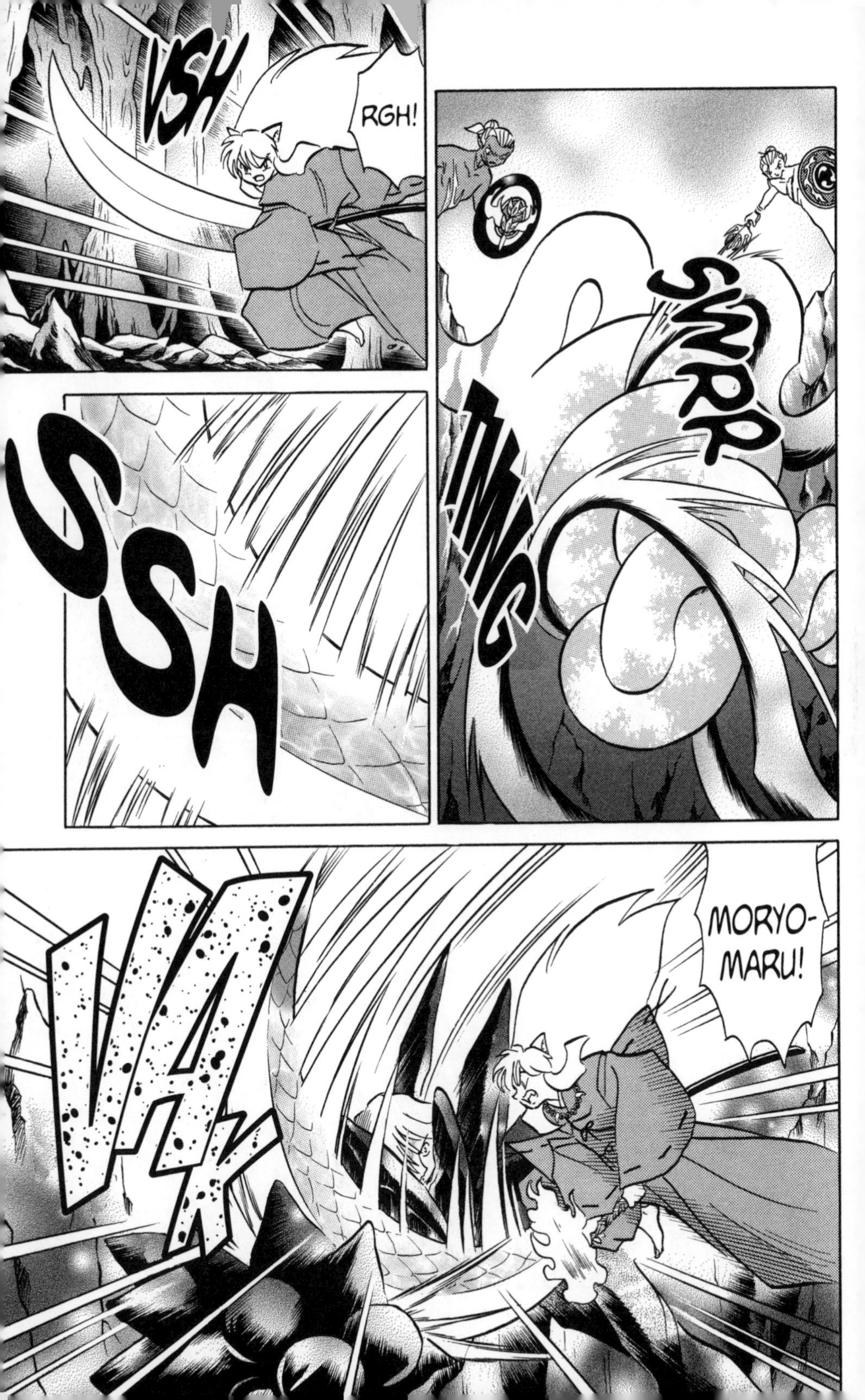
SWRR
TWNG
VSH
RGH!
SSH
MORYO-
MARU!

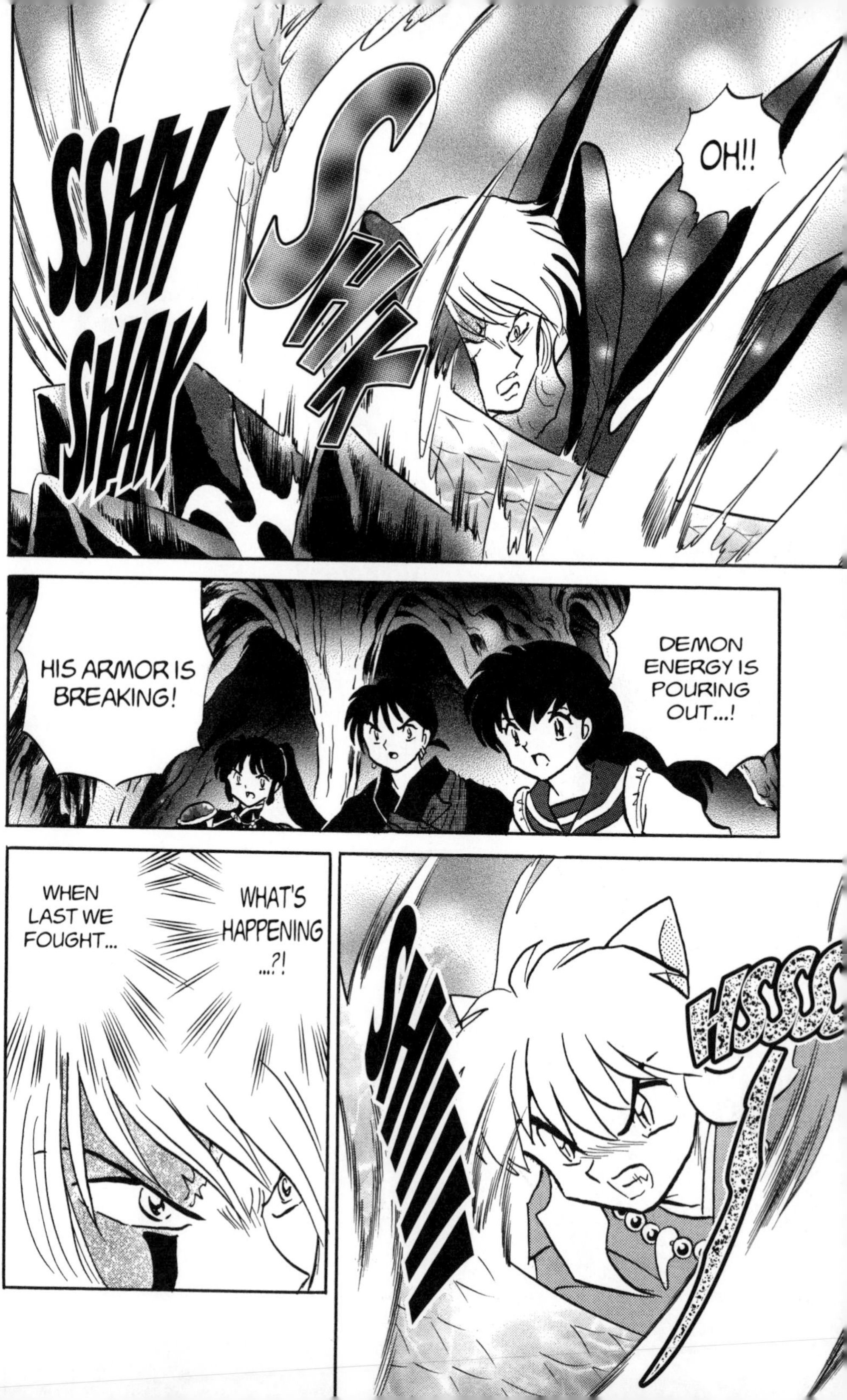
OH!!
SHAK
SSHH SHAK
DEMON ENERGY IS POURING OUT...!
HIS ARMOR IS BREAKING!
WHAT'S HAPPENING ...?!
WHEN LAST WE FOUGHT...

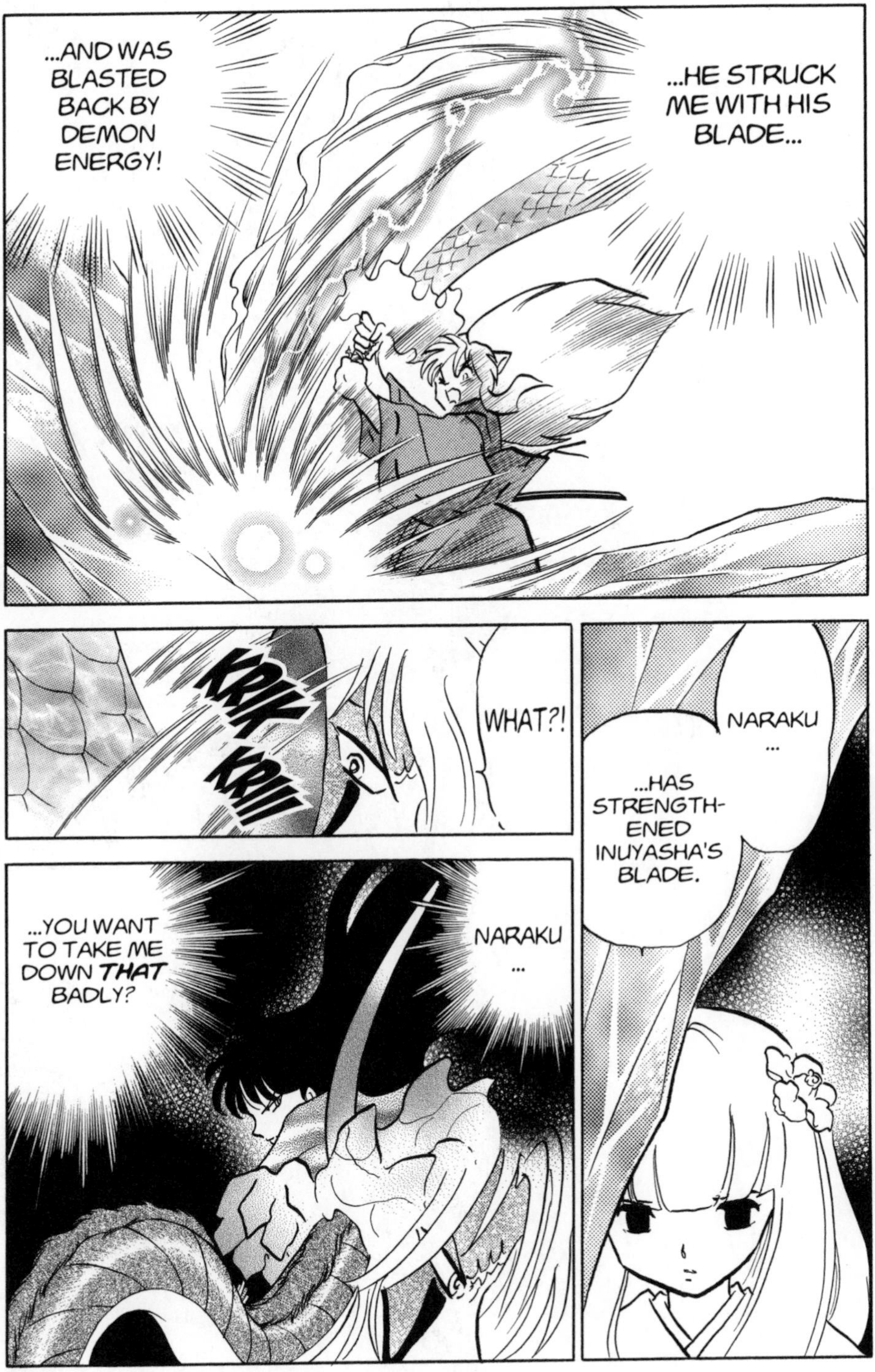
...HE STRUCK ME WITH HIS BLADE...
...AND WAS BLASTED BACK BY DEMON ENERGY!
NARAKU ...
...HAS STRENGTHENED INUYASHA'S BLADE.
WHAT?!
KRIK KRIII
NARAKU ...
...YOU WANT TO TAKE ME DOWN *THAT* BADLY?

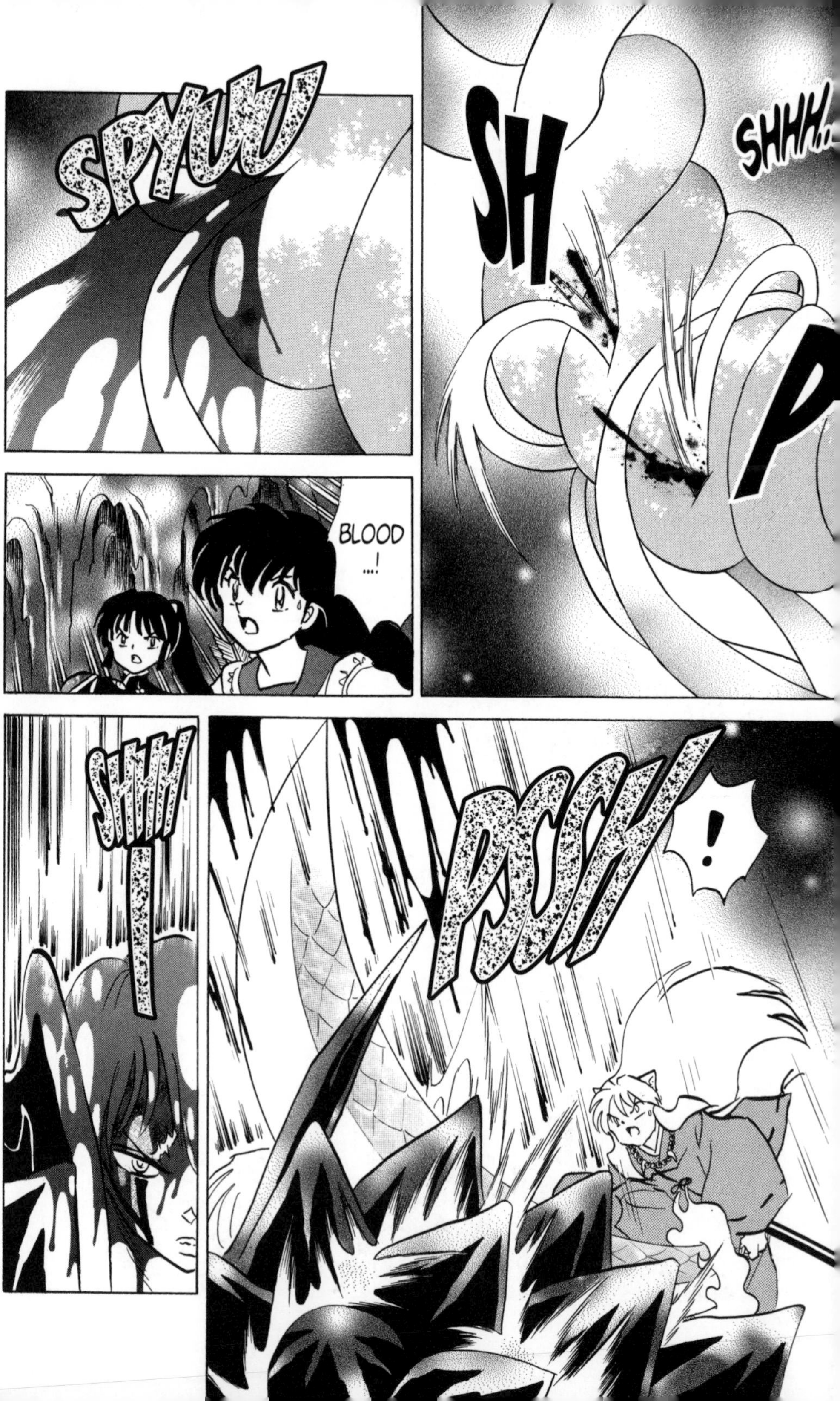
SHHH...
SH
P
SPYUUU
BLOOD
...!
PSSH
!
SHHH!

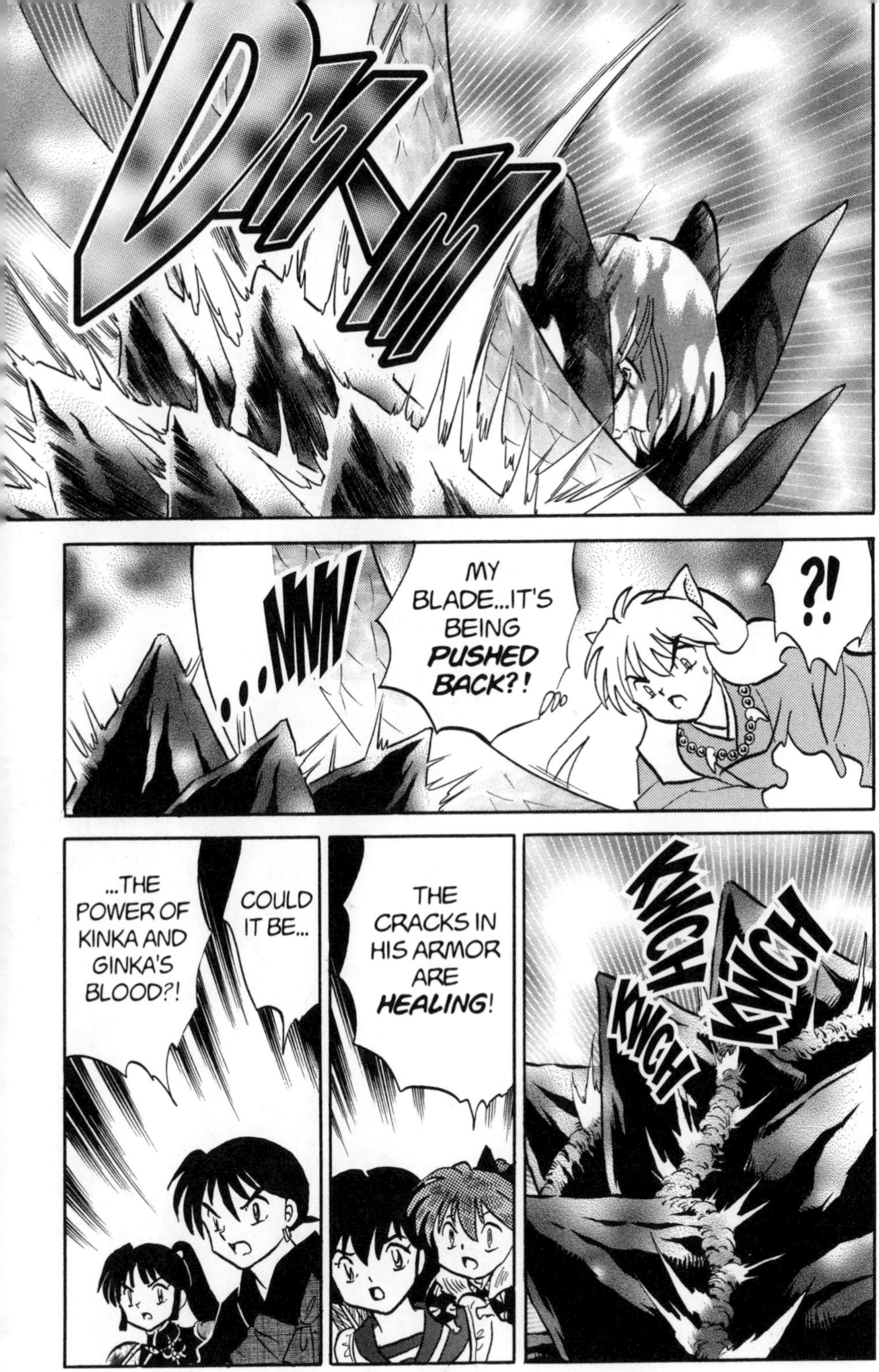
DHMM
?!
MY BLADE...IT'S BEING PUSHED BACK?!
...NNN
KWCH KWCH KWCH
THE CRACKS IN HIS ARMOR ARE HEALING!
COULD IT BE...
...THE POWER OF KINKA AND GINKA'S BLOOD?!

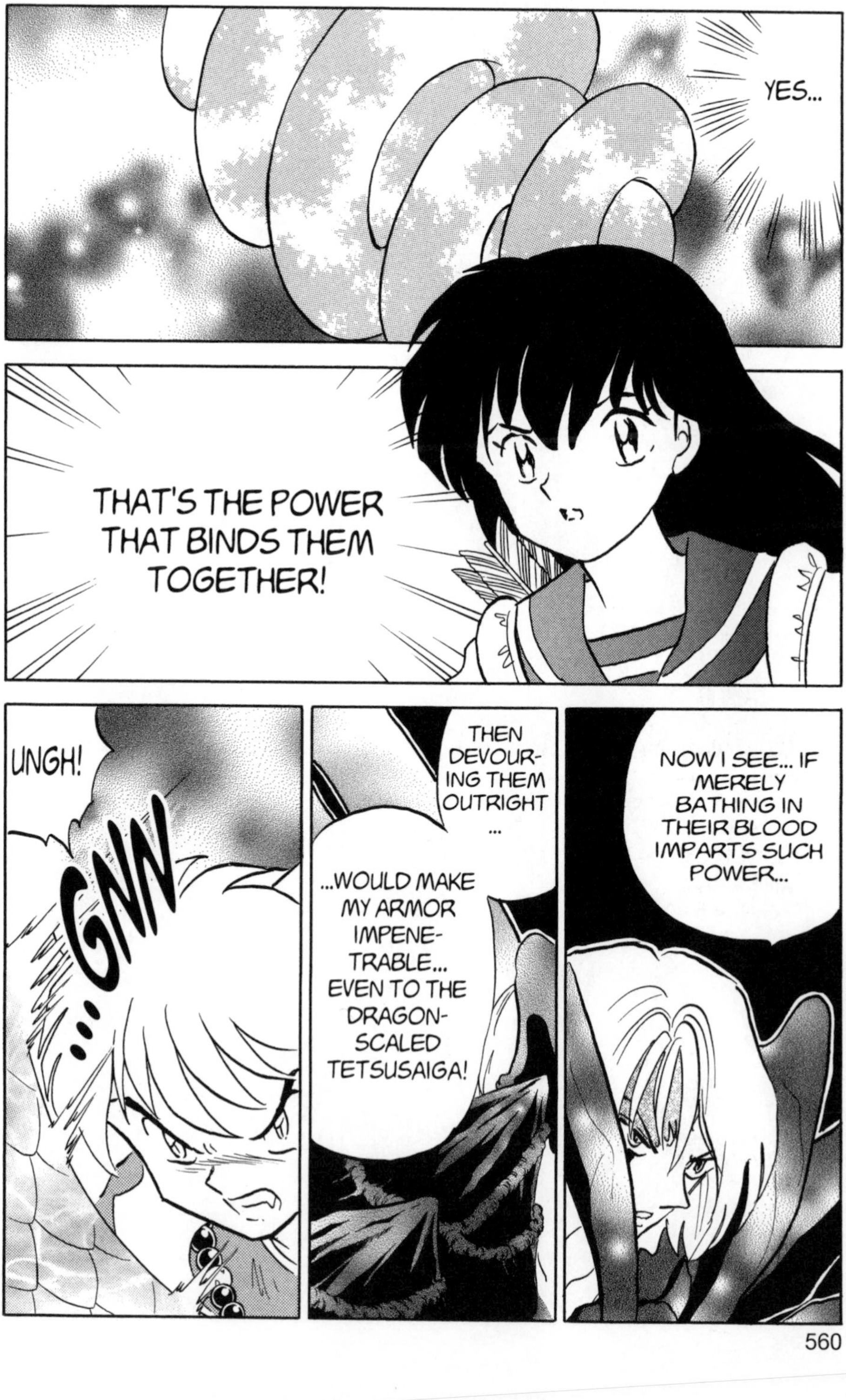
YES...
THAT'S THE POWER THAT BINDS THEM TOGETHER!
NOW I SEE... IF MERELY BATHING IN THEIR BLOOD IMPARTS SUCH POWER...
THEN DEVOURING THEM OUTRIGHT ...
...WOULD MAKE MY ARMOR IMPENETRABLE... EVEN TO THE DRAGON-SCALED TETSUSAIGA!
UNGH!
...GNN

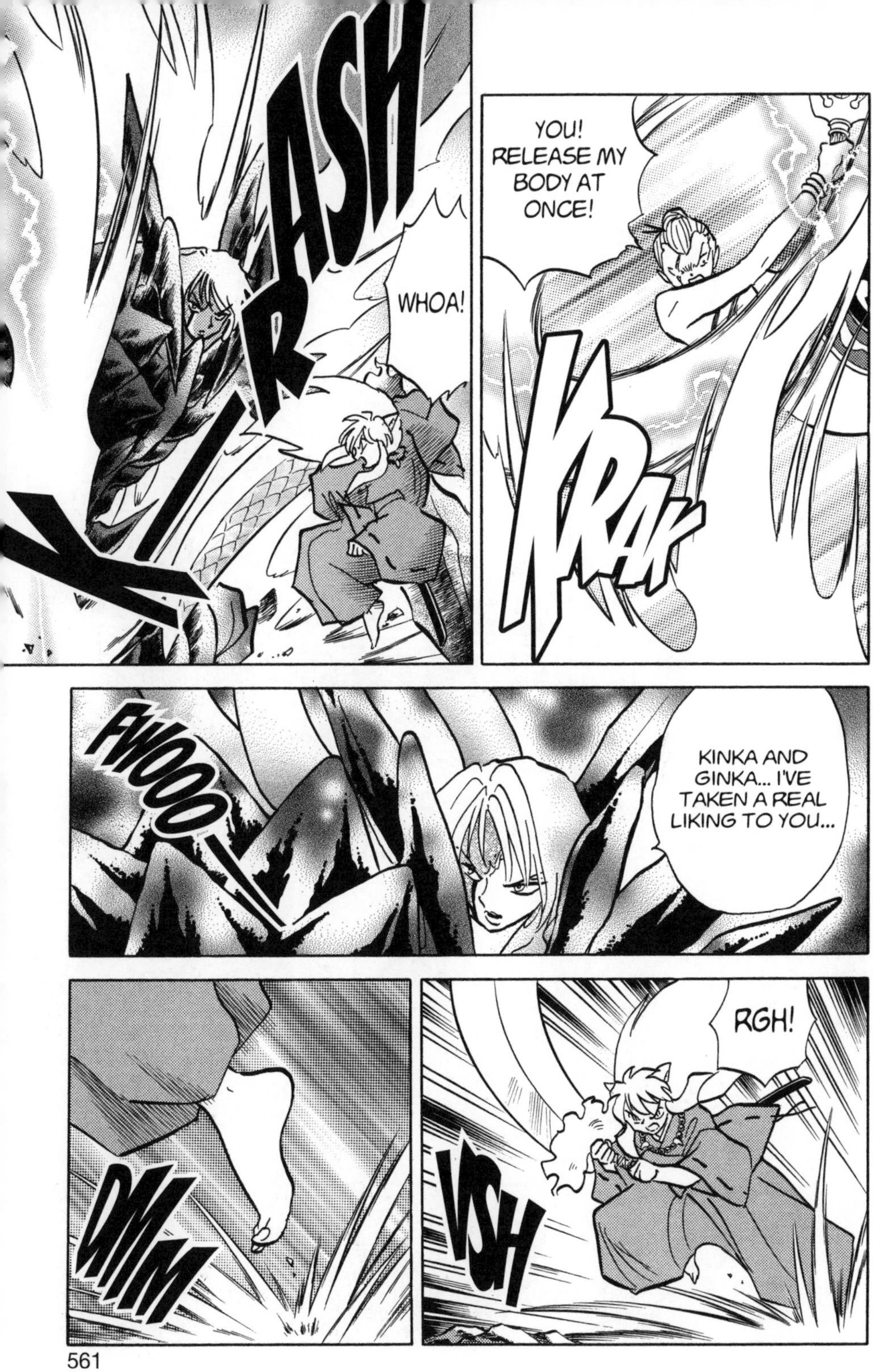
YOU! RELEASE MY BODY AT ONCE!
KRAK
WHOA!
KRASH
KINKA AND GINKA... I'VE TAKEN A REAL LIKING TO YOU...
FWOOO
RGH!
VSH
DMM

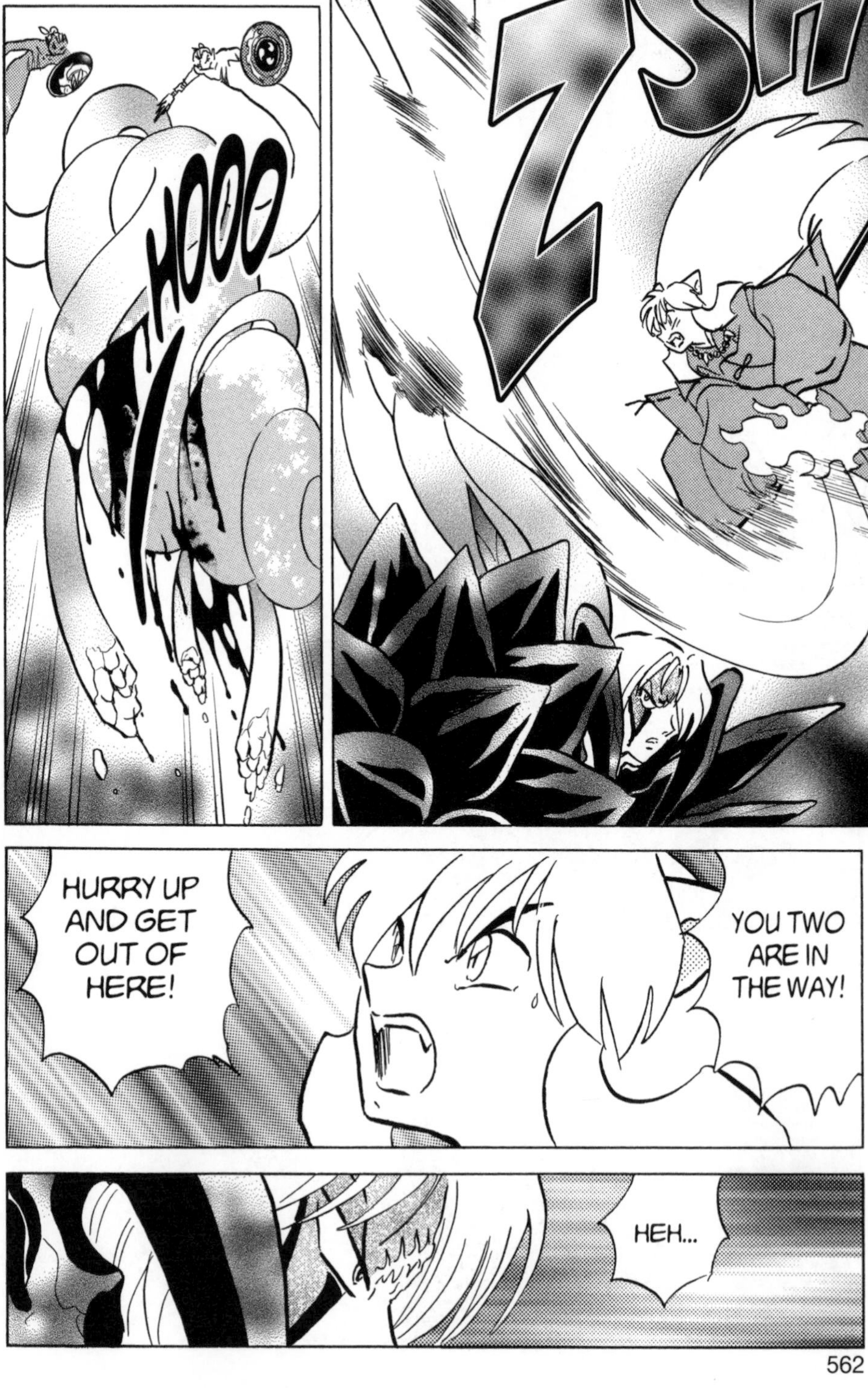
ZSH
HOOO
YOU TWO ARE IN THE WAY!
HURRY UP AND GET OUT OF HERE!
HEH...

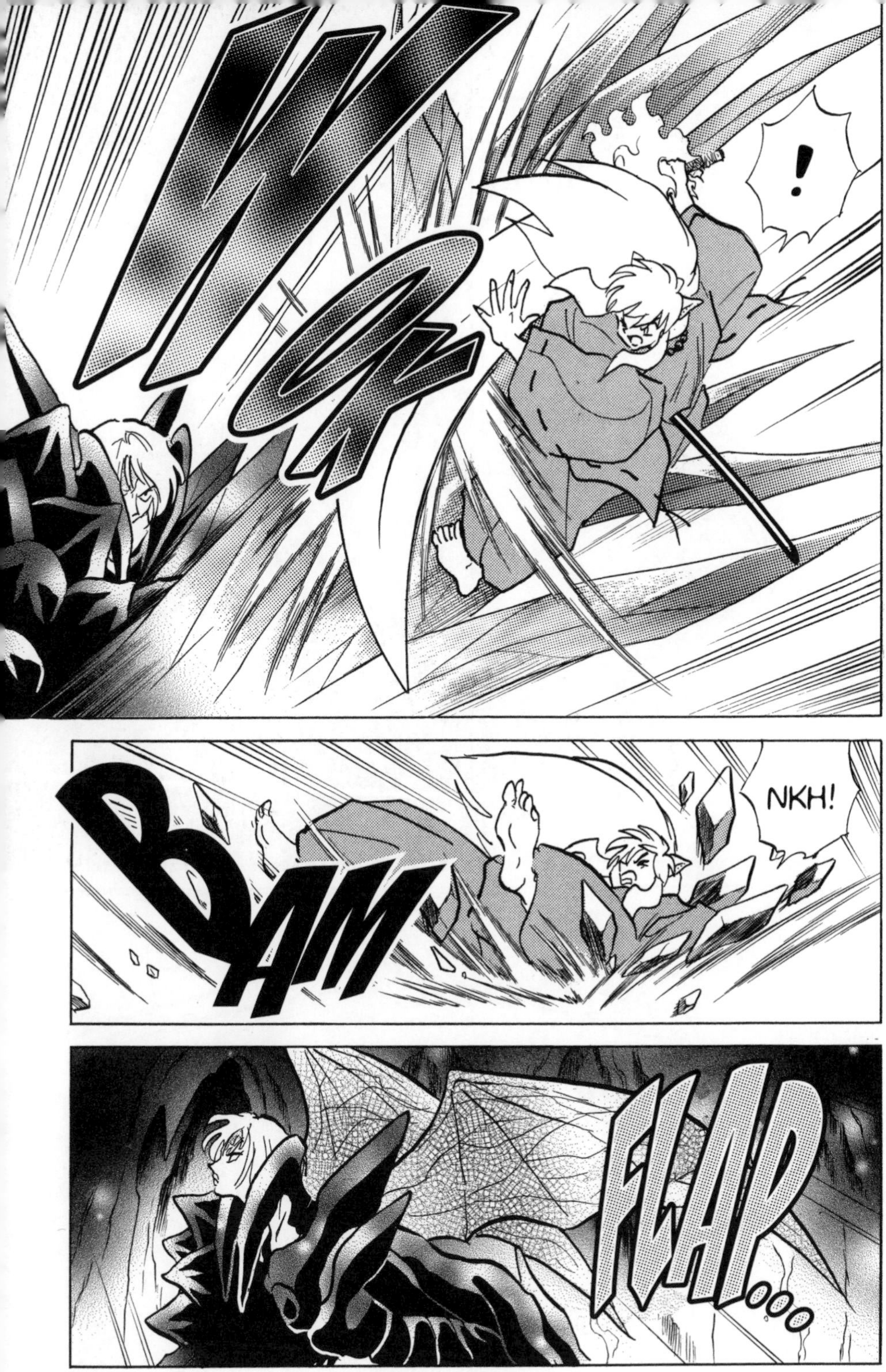
!
WHOA
NKH!
BAM
FLAP...

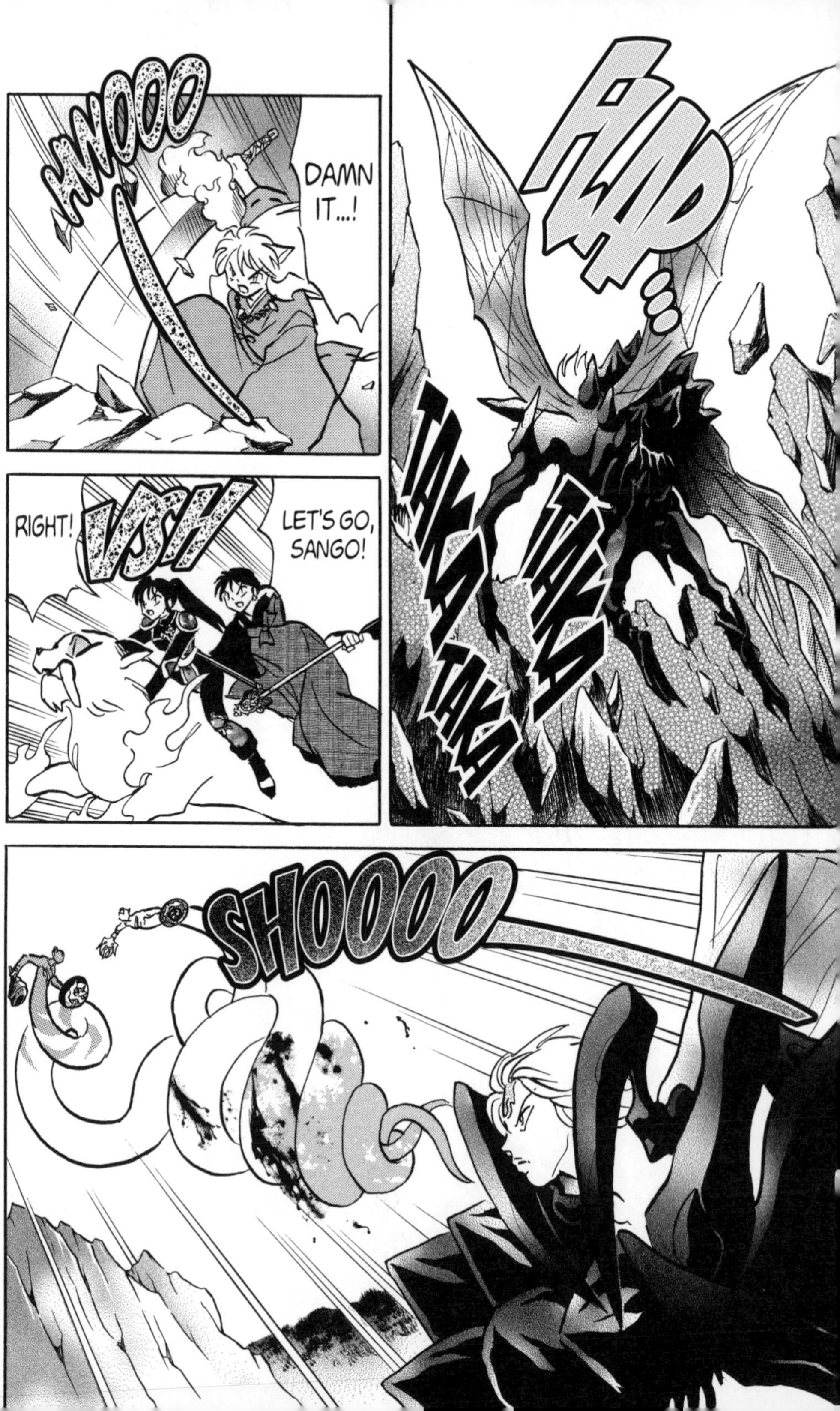
FLAP...
TAKA TAKA
TAKA TAKA
WHOOO
DAMN IT...!
LET'S GO, SANGO!
VSSH
RIGHT!
SHOOOO

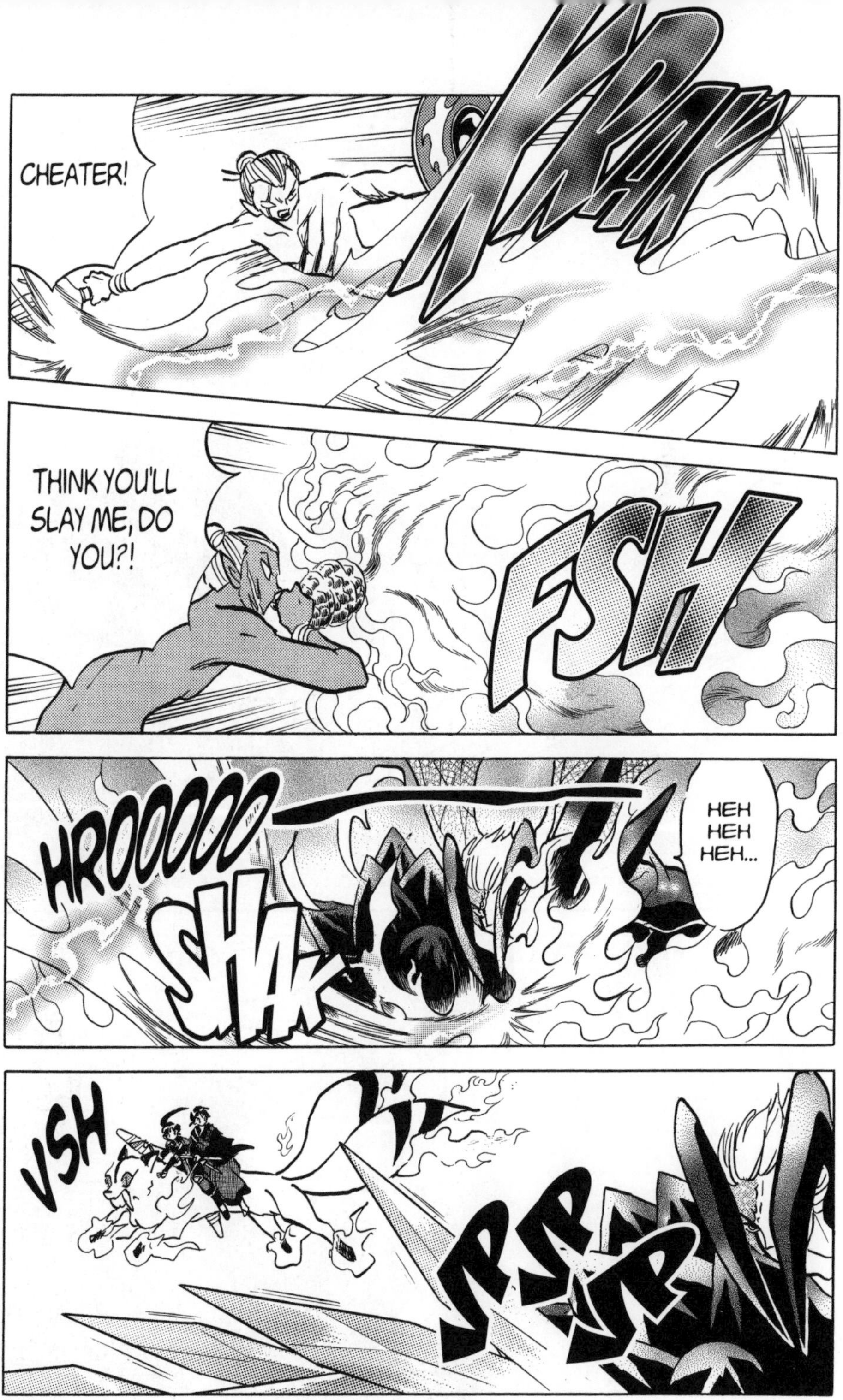
CHEATER!
THINK YOU'LL SLAY ME, DO YOU?!
FSH
HEH HEH HEH...
HROOOOOO
SHAK
VSH

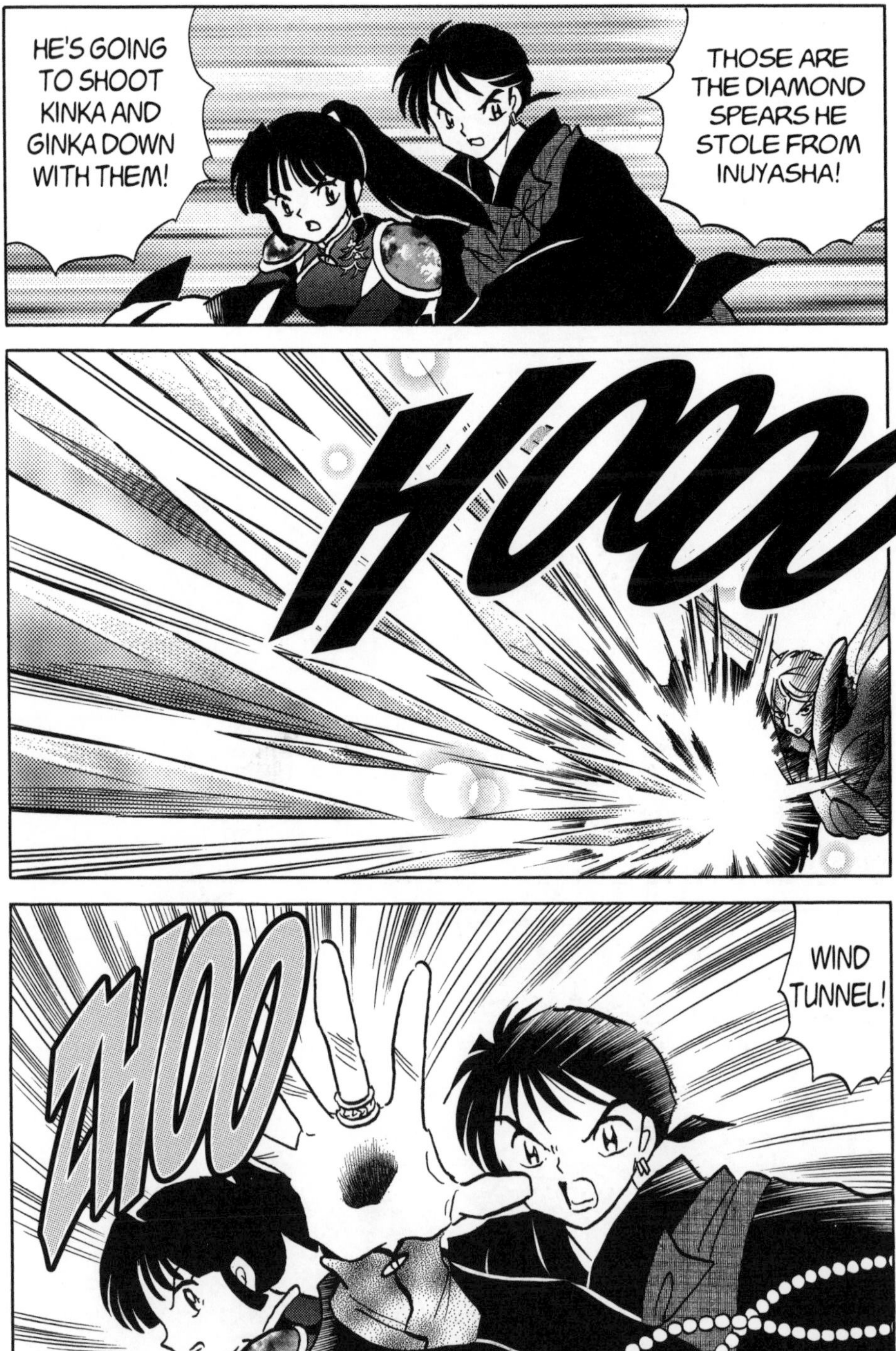
THOSE ARE THE DIAMOND SPEARS HE STOLE FROM INUYASHA!
HE'S GOING TO SHOOT KINKA AND GINKA DOWN WITH THEM!
WIND TUNNEL!
ZHOO

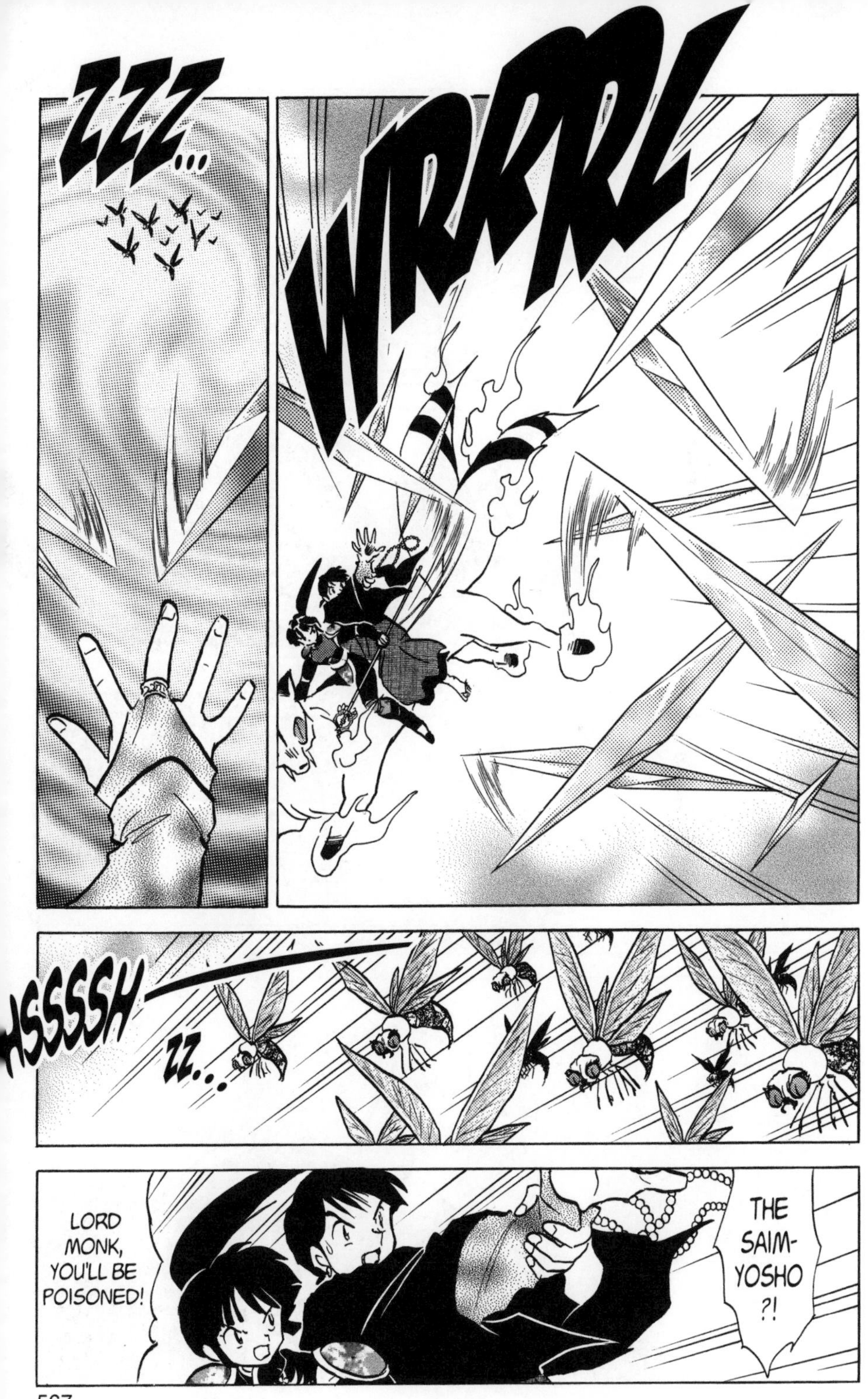
WRRRL!
ZZZ...
HSSSSH
ZZ...
THE SAIM-YOSHO?!
LORD MONK, YOU'LL BE POISONED!

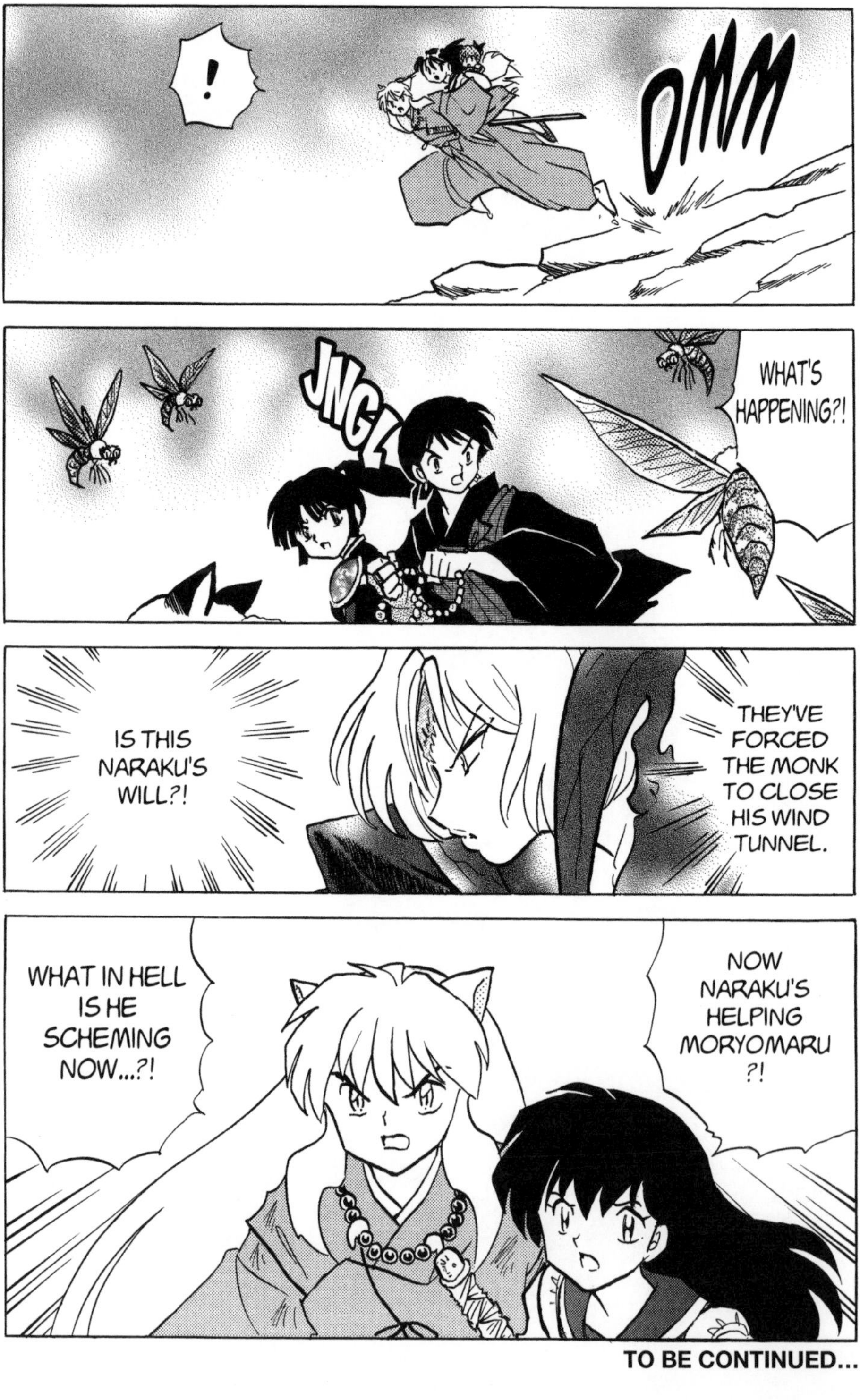
OMM
!
WHAT'S HAPPENING?!
JNGL
THEY'VE FORCED THE MONK TO CLOSE HIS WIND TUNNEL.
IS THIS NARAKU'S WILL?!
NOW NARAKU'S HELPING MORYOMARU ?!
WHAT IN HELL IS HE SCHEMING NOW...?!

TO BE CONTINUED...

Original Cover Art Gallery

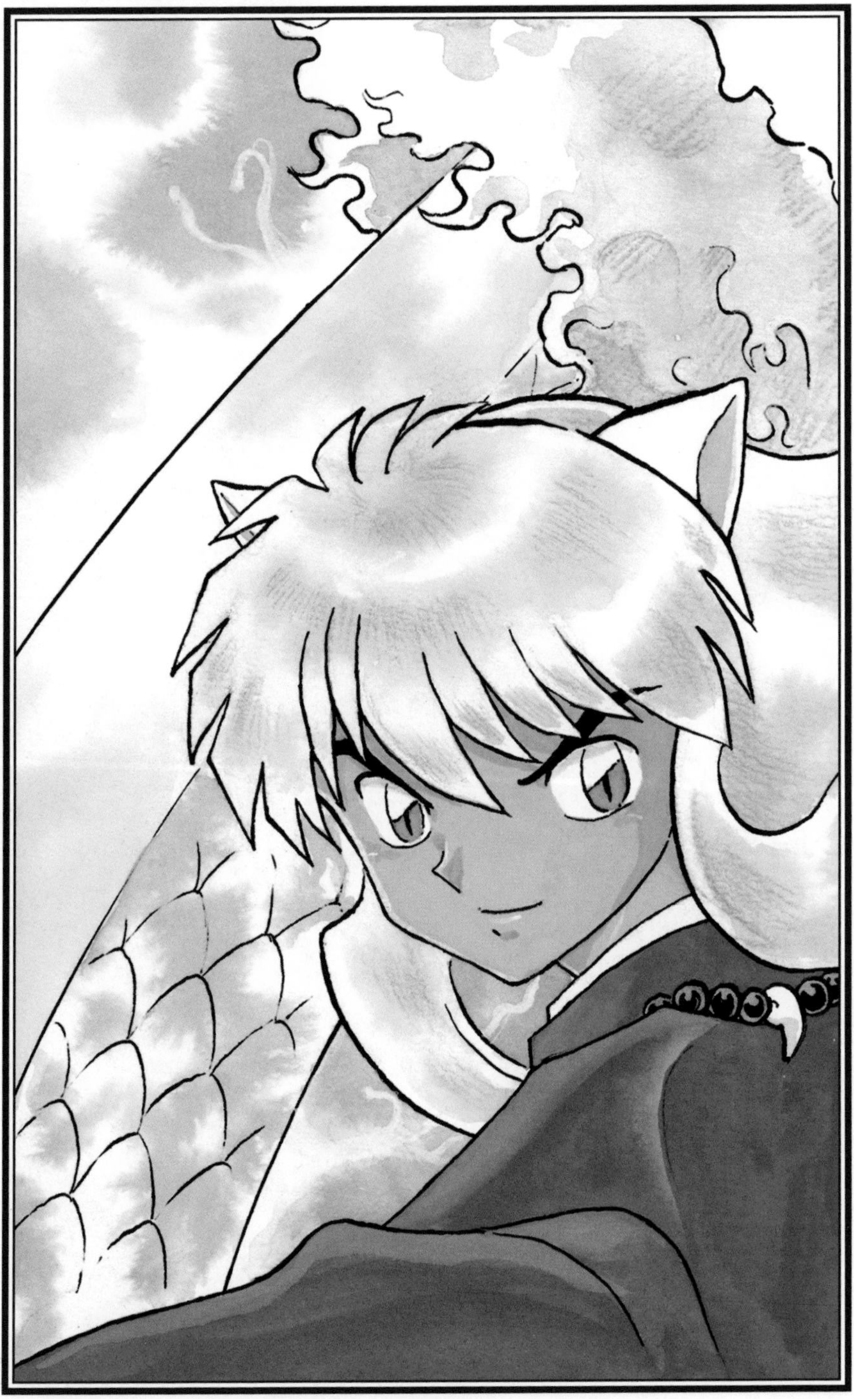

Original cover art from volume 40, published 2009

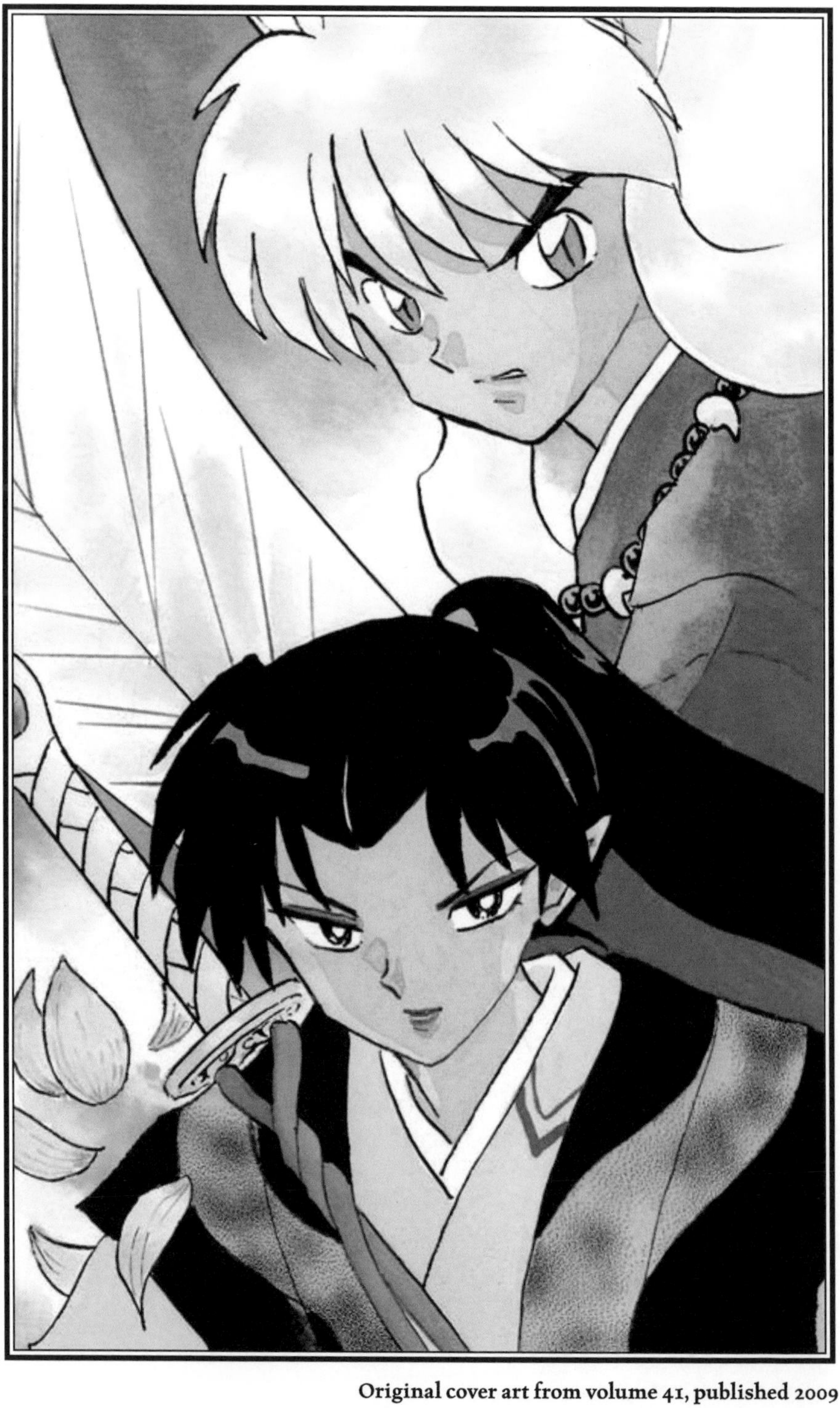

Original cover art from volume 41, published 2009

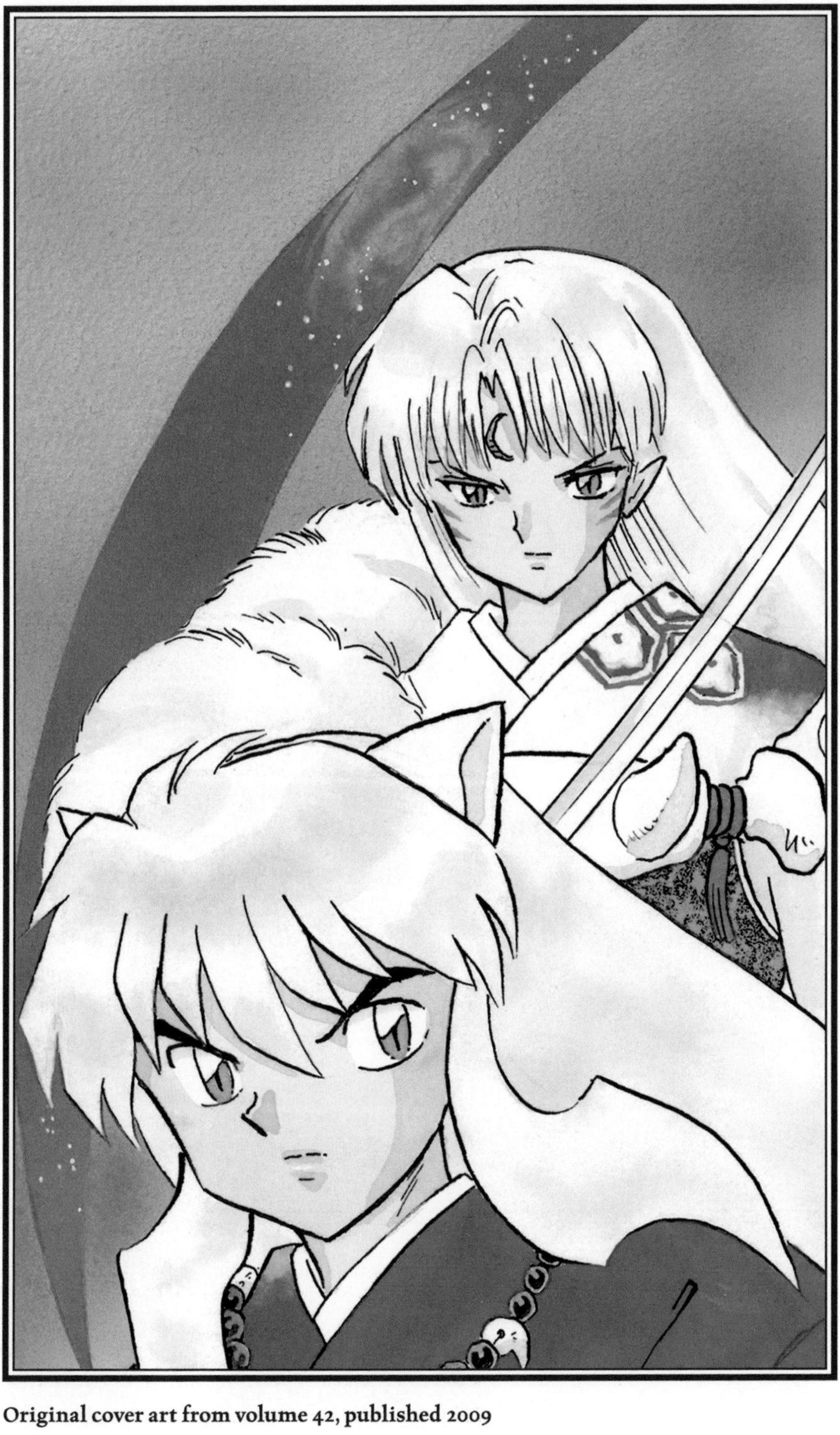

Original cover art from volume 42, published 2009

Bonus Art Gallery

Here we showcase some original color images by Rumiko Takahashi.

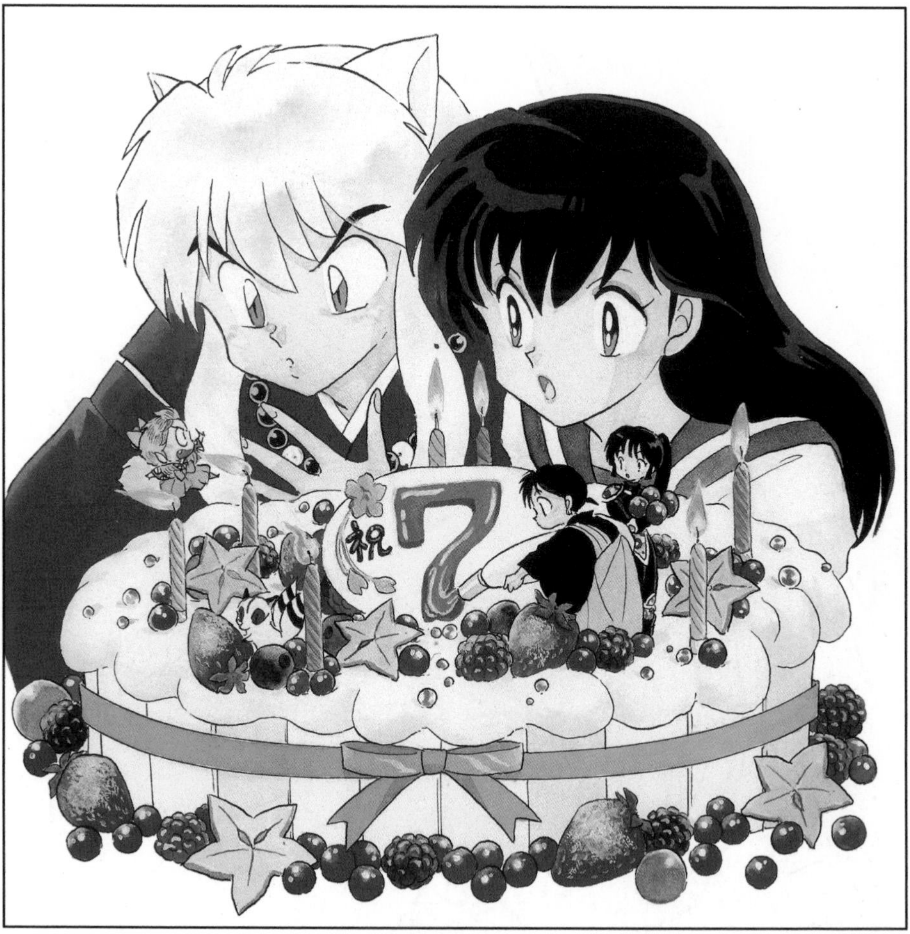
祝
7

Shonen Sunday vol. 51, 2003

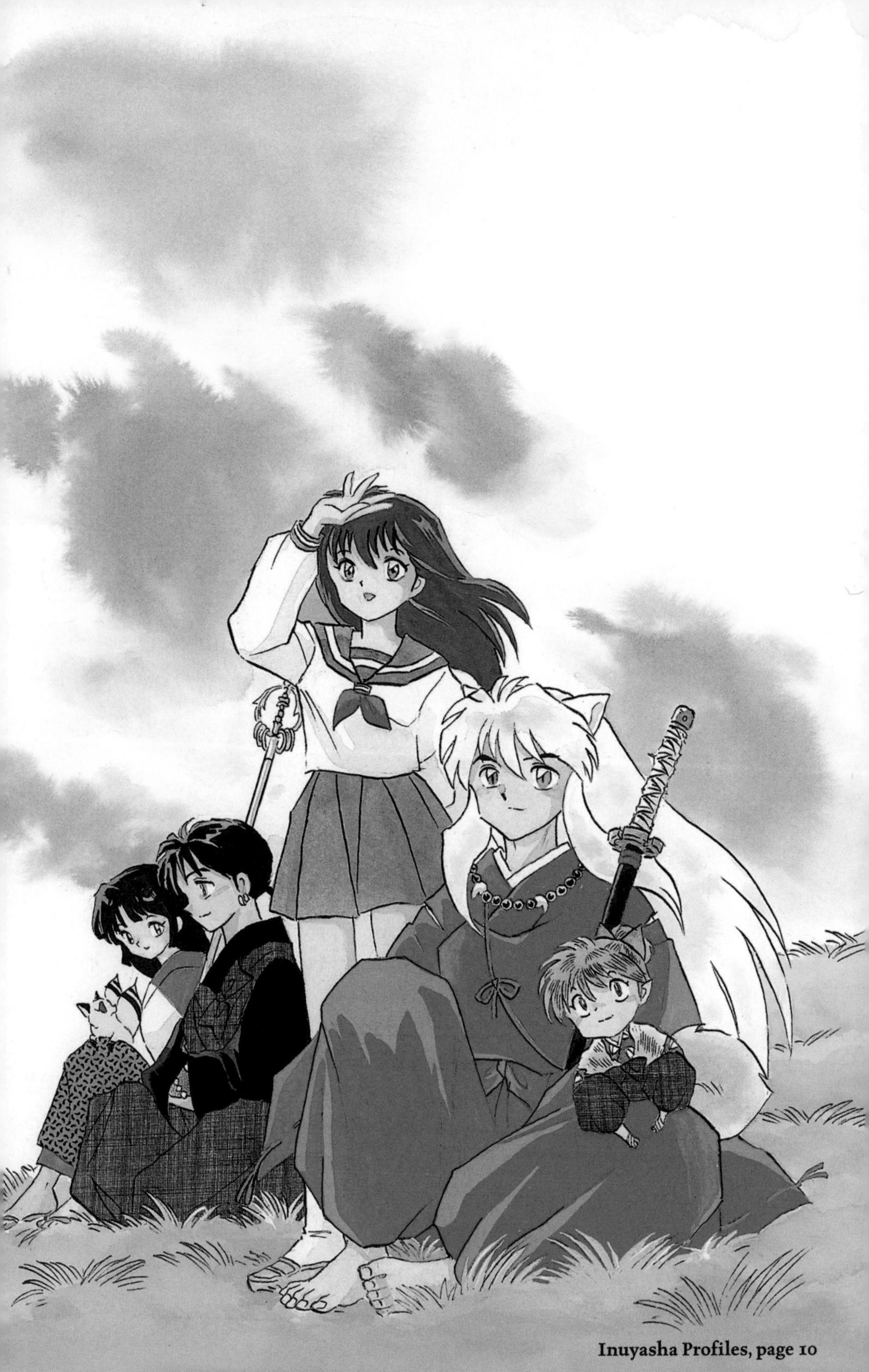

Inuyasha Profiles, page 10

Coming Next Volume

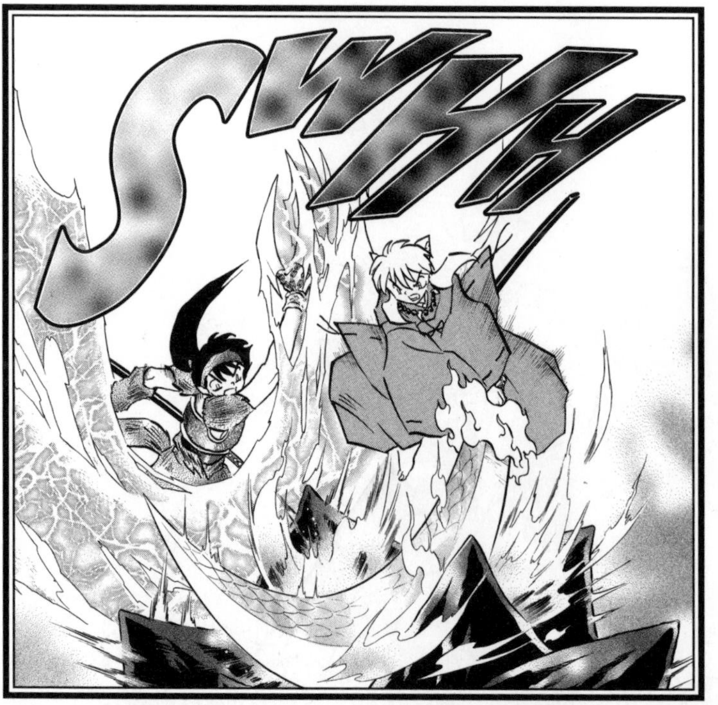
SWHH

Inuyasha embarks on a quest to learn how to properly handle his blade Tetsusaiga. Unfortunately, the master trainer he seeks has problems of his own. Can Inuyasha solve them without accidentally slaying innocent women, children, and even harmless demons? Then, Inuyasha must rescue wolf demon Koga, his rival for Kagome's affections—but at what terrible price?! When one of Naraku's plans backfires, the evil schemer must face an internal enemy as well as Moryomaru. Has Naraku finally met his match in the form of one of his own creations..?